## 11. Format for Bank Reconciliation:

| | | | |
|---|---|---|---|
| Cash balance according to bank statement ..................... | | | $xxx |
| Add: Additions by depositor not on bank statement ............................................... | $xx | | |
| Bank errors ................................................ | xx | xx | |
| | | | $xxx |
| Deduct: Deductions by depositor not on bank statement ........................................ | $xx | | |
| Bank errors ................................................ | xx | xx | |
| Adjusted balance.............................................. | | | $xxx |
| | | | |
| Cash balance according to depositor's records .............. | | | $xxx |
| Add: Additions by bank not recorded by depositor.. | $xx | | |
| Depositor errors......................................... | xx | xx | |
| | | | $xxx |
| Deduct: Deductions by bank not recorded by depositor .................................... | $xx | | |
| Depositor errors......................................... | xx | xx | |
| Adjusted balance.............................................. | | | $xxx |

## 12. Inventory Costing Methods:

1. First-in, First-out (fifo)
2. Last-in, First-out (lifo)
3. Average Cost

## 13. Interest Computations:

Interest = Face Amount (or Principal) × Rate × Time

## 14. Methods of Determining Annual Depreciation:

STRAIGHT-LINE: $\dfrac{\text{Cost} - \text{Estimated Residual Value}}{\text{Estimated Life}}$

DECLINING-BALANCE: Rate* × Book Value at Beginning of Period

*Rate is commonly twice the straight-line rate (1 ÷ Estimated Life).

## 15. Cash Provided by Operations on Statement of Cash Flows (indirect method):

| | | | |
|---|---|---|---|
| Net income, per income statement ................................. | | | $xx |
| Add: Depreciation of fixed assets ............................ | $xx | | |
| Amortization of bond payable discount and intangible assets.............................. | xx | | |
| Decreases in current assets (receivables, inventories, prepaid expenses)................. | xx | | |
| Increases in current liabilities (accounts and notes payable, accrued liabilities) .... | xx | | |
| Losses on disposal of assets and retirement of debt ........................................................ | xx | xx | |
| Deduct: Amortization of bond payable premium...... | $xx | | |
| Increases in current assets (receivables, inventories, prepaid expenses)................. | xx | | |
| Decreases in current liabilities (accounts and notes payable, accrued liabilities) .... | xx | | |
| Gains on disposal of assets and retirement of debt ........................................................ | xx | xx | |
| Net cash flow from operating activities.................... | | | $xx |

## 16. Contribution Margin Ratio = $\dfrac{\text{Sales} - \text{Variable Costs}}{\text{Sales}}$

## 17. Break-Even Sales (Units) = $\dfrac{\text{Fixed Costs}}{\text{Unit Contribution Margin}}$

## 18. Sales (Units) = $\dfrac{\text{Fixed Costs} + \text{Target Profit}}{\text{Unit Contribution Margin}}$

## 19. Margin of Safety = $\dfrac{\text{Sales} - \text{Sales at Break-Even Point}}{\text{Sales}}$

## 20. Operating Leverage = $\dfrac{\text{Contribution Margin}}{\text{Income from Operations}}$

## 21. Variances

$$\text{Direct Materials Price Variance} = \begin{pmatrix}\text{Actual Price per Unit} - \\ \text{Standard Price}\end{pmatrix} \times \begin{matrix}\text{Actual Quantity} \\ \text{Used}\end{matrix}$$

$$\text{Direct Materials Quantity Variance} = \begin{pmatrix}\text{Actual Quantity Used} - \\ \text{Standard Quantity}\end{pmatrix} \times \begin{matrix}\text{Standard Price} \\ \text{per Unit}\end{matrix}$$

$$\text{Direct Labor Rate Variance} = \begin{pmatrix}\text{Actual Rate per Hour} - \\ \text{Standard Rate}\end{pmatrix} \times \begin{matrix}\text{Actual Hours} \\ \text{Worked}\end{matrix}$$

$$\text{Direct Labor Time Variance} = \begin{pmatrix}\text{Actual Hours Worked} - \\ \text{Standard Hours}\end{pmatrix} \times \begin{matrix}\text{Standard Rate} \\ \text{per Hour}\end{matrix}$$

$$\begin{matrix}\text{Variable Factory} \\ \text{Overhead Controllable} \\ \text{Variance}\end{matrix} = \begin{matrix}\text{Actual} \\ \text{Factory} \\ \text{Overhead}\end{matrix} - \begin{matrix}\text{Budgeted Factory} \\ \text{Overhead for} \\ \text{Amount Produced}\end{matrix}$$

$$\begin{matrix}\text{Fixed Factory} \\ \text{Overhead Volume} \\ \text{Variance}\end{matrix} = \begin{matrix}\text{Budgeted Factory} \\ \text{Overhead for} \\ \text{Amount Produced}\end{matrix} - \begin{matrix}\text{Applied} \\ \text{Factory} \\ \text{Overhead}\end{matrix}$$

## 22. Rate of Return on Investment (ROI) = $\dfrac{\text{Income from Operations}}{\text{Invested Assets}}$

Alternative ROI Computation:

$$\text{ROI} = \dfrac{\text{Income from Operations}}{\text{Sales}} \times \dfrac{\text{Sales}}{\text{Invested Assets}}$$

## 23. Capital Investment Analysis Methods:

1. Methods That Ignore Present Values:
   A. Average Rate of Return Method
   B. Cash Payback Method
2. Methods That Use Present Values:
   A. Net Present Value Method
   B. Internal Rate of Return Method

## 24. Average Rate of Return = $\dfrac{\text{Estimated Average Annual Income}}{\text{Average Investment}}$

## 25. Present Value Index = $\dfrac{\text{Total Present Value of Net Cash Flow}}{\text{Amount to Be Invested}}$

## 26. Present Value Factor for an Annuity of $1 = $\dfrac{\text{Amount to Be Invested}}{\text{Equal Annual Net Cash Flows}}$

# FINANCIAL ACCOUNTING 9e

**CARL S. WARREN**
Professor Emeritus of Accounting
University of Georgia, Athens

**JAMES M. REEVE**
Professor of Accounting
University of Tennessee, Knoxville

**PHILIP E. FESS**
Professor Emeritus of Accounting
University of Illinois, Champaign-Urbana

THOMSON
SOUTH-WESTERN

Australia · Canada · Mexico · Singapore · Spain · United Kingdom · United States

THOMSON
———★———
SOUTH-WESTERN

**Financial Accounting 9e**

Carl S. Warren, James M. Reeve, Philip E. Fess

**VP/Editorial Director:**
Jack W. Calhoun

**VP/Editor-in-Chief:**
George Werthman

**Publisher:**
Rob Dewey

**Executive Editor:**
Sharon Oblinger

**Sr. Developmental Editor:**
Ken Martin

**Marketing Manager:**
Keith Chassé

**Sr. Production Editor:**
Deanna Quinn

**Media Technology Editor:**
Jim Rice

**Media Developmental Editor:**
Sally Nieman

**Media Production Editors:**
Robin Browning, Kelly Reid

**Manufacturing Coordinator:**
Doug Wilke

**Production House:**
Litten Editing and Production, Inc.

**Compositor:**
GGS Information Services, Inc.

**Printer:**
Quebecor World
Versailles, KY

**Sr. Design Project Manager:**
Michael H. Stratton

**Internal and Cover Designer:**
Michael H. Stratton

**Cover Illustration:**
Matsu

**Preface Designer:**
Kathy Heming

**Photography Manager:**
Deanna Ettinger

**Photo Researcher:**
Terri Miller

Library of Congress
Control Number:
2003114843

### Carl S. Warren

Dr. Carl S. Warren is Professor Emeritus of Accounting at the University of Georgia, Athens. He has also taught at the University of Iowa, Michigan State University, and the University of Chicago. He received his doctorate degree (Ph.D.) from Michigan State University and his undergraduate (B.B.A.) and masters (M.A.) degrees from the University of Iowa. Dr. Warren's primary teaching focus is on principles of accounting and auditing. He enjoys interacting and learning from colleagues on how to improve student learning and understanding of accounting. His outside interests include writing short stories, novels, oil painting, handball, golf, skiing, backpacking, and fly-fishing.

### James M. Reeve

Dr. James M. Reeve is the William and Sara Clark Professor of Accounting and Business at the University of Tennessee, Knoxville. He teaches and coordinates the Principles of Accounting course at the University of Tennessee. Dr. Reeve received his Ph.D. from Oklahoma State University in 1980. In addition to his teaching experience, he brings to this text a wealth of experience consulting on managerial accounting issues with numerous companies, including Procter & Gamble, Hershey Foods, Coca-Cola, Sony, and Boeing. Dr. Reeve's interests outside the classroom and business world revolve around reading and issues of faith.

## Philip E. Fess—40 Years Of Contributions

The 21st edition marks the 40th year of Phil Fess' contribution to this family of texts. Phil first co-authored the 9th edition of Accounting Principles with Rollie Niswonger, his mentor when he was a student at Miami University. Phil and Rollie worked closely together on six editions as they continued to improve accounting education through listening carefully to users of the texts and authoring thoughtfully. During his tenure as the Arthur Andersen & Co. Alumni Professor of Accountancy at the University of Illinois, Champaign-Urbana, Phil's creativity, innovative ideas, and clear, concise writing style enabled Accounting to retain its position as the leading accounting principles textbook of all time. This new edition still reflects Phil's attention to detail and his unique ability to make textbooks user-friendly. Phil's continuing legacy is the millions of students who, through using the texts, have gained a strong understanding of and appreciation for accounting and its usefulness.

# Warren
# Reeve
# Fess

## Prepare for Tomorrow Today

Even as the undisputed leaders in accounting textbook innovation, we faced a daunting challenge with the 9th edition. Yet once again, we are proud to present the world's best tool for teaching accounting, designed and engineered based on the solid foundation of our past success.

*Financial Accounting, 9e* presents, as always, the most comprehensive content in the market with strikingly clear organization and breakthrough pedagogy. Together with this solid textbook foundation, our leading-edge technology will guide your students toward success in the business world yet to unfold.

We invite you to experience this superior package of text and technology and see how well they perform together.

Warren
Reeve
Fess

# Tomorrow
## takes the WHEEL

Having reached more than 11.5 million students, it would be easy for the most widely used textbook for accounting principles, from which this text is derived, to coast on the momentum of its success. But being number one doesn't come from just coasting. It comes from continuing our long history of innovation with the 9th edition.

To our many colleagues who contributed their valuable assistance, we extend our gratitude. As users of the 8th edition, they shared their personal insights by providing classroom feedback, participating in focus groups, and filling out questionnaires. In addition, dozens of distinguished reviewers have kept us on track during the revision of this edition. We took all comments very seriously, and *Financial Accounting, 9e* is more robust than its predecessors because of the wide variety of advice we've incorporated.

*Financial Accounting, 9e* will remain the text of choice for other reasons as well. The companies we profile in the text have grown and changed over time, and so has our coverage of them. We've integrated our work with some of the most powerful and effective technology on the market today. A long list of distinguished authors, editors, and reviewers has guided *Financial Accounting* through the better part of the past quarter century. We are proud to take our part in the evolution of this great tradition.

Back in 1929, author James McKinsey could not have imagined the success and influence this family of texts has enjoyed or that his original vision would remain intact. As the current authors, we appreciate the responsibility of protecting this vision, while continuing to refine it to meet the changing needs of students and instructors. We sincerely thank our many colleagues who have helped to make it happen.

*[signature]*

*[signature]*

*[signature]*

> "**T**he teaching of accounting is no longer designed to train professional accountants only. With the growing complexity of business and the constantly increasing difficulty of the problems of management, it has become essential that everyone who aspires to a position of responsibility should have a knowledge of the fundamental principles of accounting."
>
> — James O. McKinsey, Author, first edition, 1929

# ACCOUNTING POWERED BY

Based squarely on the success of yesterday, *Financial Accounting, 9e* boldly leads the way into the accounting challenges of tomorrow with innovative learning systems that bring accounting principles and practices to life. Reflecting more realistically than ever the way business operates today, this edition integrates learning options designed to extend the classroom beyond its walls into the unlimited world of the Internet.

You are the best judge of which supplements will best suit your class. For this reason, we've engineered the following content-rich and pedagogically sound course-management technologies so that you can tailor them to meet the needs of your curriculum or a particular class.

These breakthrough technologies serve two important purposes: First, they help make sure your students receive the pedagogical benefits that come with completing homework assignments. Second, they give you more time to devote to other classroom activities.

## WebTutor™ Advantage on WebCT™ with Personal Trainer 3.0
## WebTutor™ Advantage on Blackboard™ with Personal Trainer 3.0

WebTutor Advantage provides you with the most robust and pedagogically advanced content for either the WebCT or Blackboard course management platform. Now you can enliven your course with interactive reinforcement for students as well as powerful instructor tools. With this newest version, the students' content comprehension is assessed after which they are referred to specific content features in WebTutor Advantage or the text to address areas in which they need additional help. Elements of WebTutor Advantage include:

### NEW Video Cases
Students get a taste of accounting in action by viewing these lively two- to five-minute segments. Each video covers a key accounting concept as it is played out in a real-world company or situation. Accompanying pedagogy includes a summary of each video, a short description about what the student should look for when watching, and some suggested critical-thinking questions for them to answer at the end.

### Chapter Introductory Videos
Students begin each chapter with a brief but engaging Flash introduction to the chapter objectives.

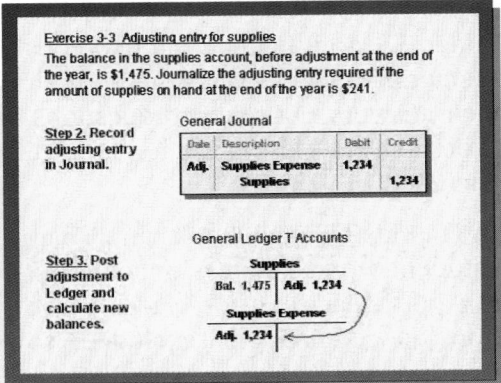

### e-Lectures
Because reinforcement is essential to concept retention, each chapter includes two or three Flash presentations that review the chapter's major topics. The presentations are in a visual lecture format with audio that covers one or two key chapter concepts.

### Illustrative Problems
These step-by-step Flash presentations review the Illustrative Problems and their solutions from each chapter.

### Accounting Cycle Review
With this tool, students get a firm grasp on the key concepts of the accounting cycle by applying what they've learned to realistic situations and problems. Found only in Chapter 4.

### NEW Exercise Demos
These demos allow students to review explanations of two to three representative exercises from each chapter in a step-by-step visual format with audio.

### Quizzes
Students make great strides with continuous reinforcement. Now they can select from a variety of intriguing options:

- **RE-ACT Quiz** Ten to fifteen multiple-choice and true-false questions cover key concepts in the chapter. Students are directed to specific resources for additional study related to their incorrect answers.

- **Achievement Tests** Similar to those found in the test bank, these tests provide additional opportunities for students to study and quiz themselves in multiple choice, true-false, and matching test formats.

- **Multiple-Choice, True-False, and Matching Quizzes** These quizzes are comprised of the questions provided in the study guide. Using WebTutor Advantage, students can answer them, have them graded, and submit the results directly to their instructor.

### QuizBowl
Popular with students, this engaging game allows them to review key accounting concepts.

### Crossword Puzzles
This captivating and rewarding option encourages students to go over key chapter terms.

### Spanish Dictionary
This timely resource defines common accounting terms in Spanish.

# ACCOUNTING POWERED BY

## Personal Trainer 3.0

Specifically designed to ease the time-consuming task of grading homework, Personal Trainer lets students complete their assigned homework from the text or practice on unassigned homework online. The results are instantaneously entered into a gradebook.

With annotated spreadsheets and full-blown gradebook functionality, the greatly enhanced Personal Trainer 3.0 provides an unprecedented real-time, guided, self-correcting, learning reinforcement system outside the classroom. Use this resource as an integrated solution for your distance learning or traditional course.

- **Enhanced Questions** Personal Trainer 3.0 now includes all exercises and problems. Students can get help entering their answers in the proper format and run a spell check on their answers. On selected questions, they can call up additional, similar questions for extra practice. Optional algorithmic questions will also be included.

- **Enhanced Instructor Capabilities** The flexible gradebook can display and download any combination of student work, chapters, or activities. Capture grades on demand or set a particular time for grades to be automatically captured. Tag questions as "required" or "excluded," so students can only access the questions you want them to complete.

- **Enhanced Hints** Students can get up to three hints per activity. These hints can be PowerPoint slides, video clips, images, and more. And instructors can add a hint of their own!

- **Enhanced Look-and-Feel** Fast, reliable, dependable, and even easier to use, Personal Trainer 3.0 sports a fresh, new graphic design.

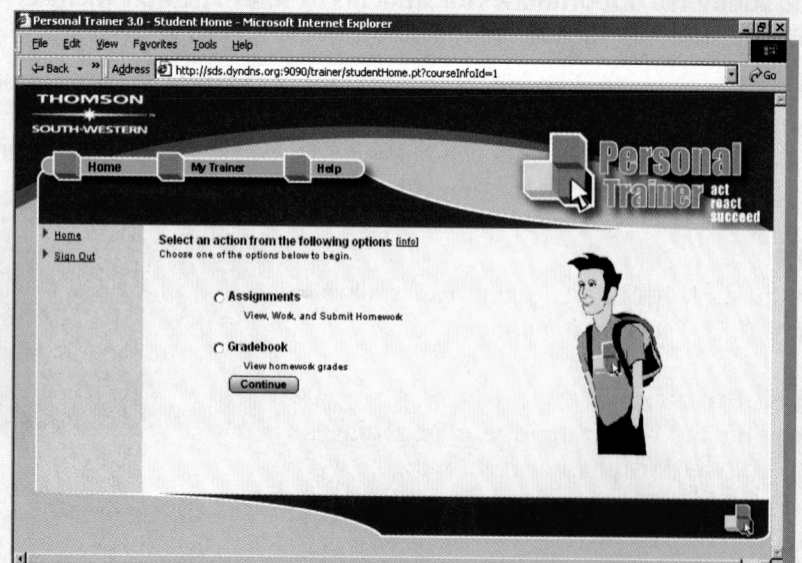

*Personal Trainer is included in WebTutor Advantage, or it can be purchased separately online.*

# TOMORROW'S TECHNOLOGY

## Xtra!

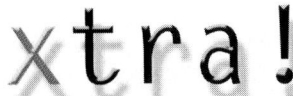

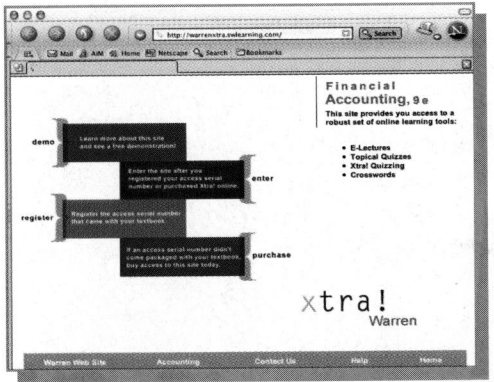

Available as an optional, free bundle with every new textbook, Xtra! gives students FREE access to the following online learning tools:

- **e-Lectures** Brief e-Lectures review more difficult concepts from the chapter.

- **Topical Quizzes** Quizzes measure a student's "test readiness" on the concepts in the chapter.

- **Multiple Choice Quizzes** Additional quizzes help students review chapter concepts and prepare for exams. Feedback on their answers gives page references so they know where to look up the questions they've missed!

- **Crosswords** The Crossword Puzzles are a fun way students can review their understanding of key terms and concepts.

## P.A.S.S.

Our best-selling computerized accounting software, by Dale Klooster and Warren Allen, **P**ower **A**ccounting **S**ystem **S**oftware *(formerly General Ledger Software)* shows students the effects that accounting entries have on financial statements. Solving end-of-chapter problems, the continuing problem, comprehensive problems, and practice sets with P.A.S.S. helps make learning relevant and interesting.

- **Problem Checker** This feature enables students to see if their entries are correct.

- **Real Business Forms** This feature provides students with experience creating invoices and doing payroll.

- **Charts, Graphs, and Ratios** Allows students to analyze financial data, including expense distribution, top customers, sales, budgets, most profitable items, and relevant ratios.

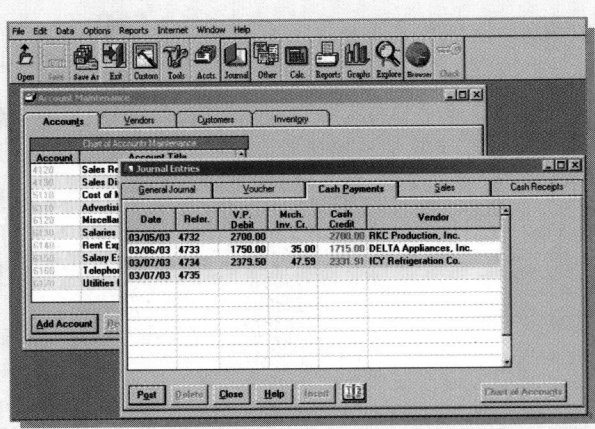

**P.A.S.S.**

*Each problem that can be completed with P.A.S.S. is marked with this icon in the text.*

# FREE WEB SITE

---

## Product Support Web Site — http://warren.swlearning.com

The Warren/Reeve/Fess Web site provides a variety of free instructor and student resources. There you'll find text-specific content and other related resources organized by chapter and topic.

The free Product Support Web site includes the highly stimulating Interactive Study Center, which provides students with a wide variety of materials for extra studying and review.

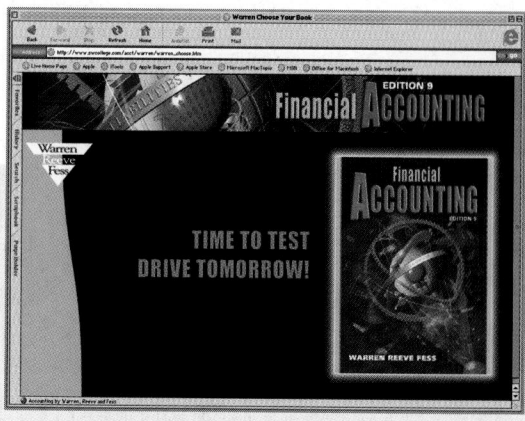

- **Key Points** All key points are pulled from the end of each chapter in the text so that students can review them online.

- **e-Lectures** Because reinforcement is essential to concept retention, each chapter includes a Flash presentation that reviews each chapter's major topics.

- **Review Problem** The Illustrative Problems found in each chapter are presented in a step-by-step fashion, helping students understand how the solutions to each were reached.

- **FAQs** Students can review these Frequently Asked Questions in accounting and learn more about many of the key topics in each chapter.

- **Internet Applications** These activities from the text allow students to apply chapter concepts and improve their online research skills.

- **Quizzes** Interactive quizzes in both True-False and Multiple Choice formats provide students with immediate feedback after they submit their answers.

**Instructor Resources** available to download from the secure instructor's area include the Instructor's Manual, Solutions Manual, PowerPoint Presentations, Spreadsheet Template Solutions, Instructor's Guide to Online Resources, and Technology Demos.

# UNIQUE CONTINUING PROBLEM

## Dancin Music Continuing Problem

Here's a great opportunity for students to practice what they've learned as they study each step of the accounting cycle. Dancin' Music, an imaginary and entrepreneurial company, provides a contemporary example of keen interest to students. As they follow Dancin' Music, they examine its transactions and see the effect of those transactions on its financial statements. They can use the P.A.S.S. software with this problem as well.

In **Chapter 1**, students **analyze the effects of Dancin Music's first month's transactions on the accounting equation.**

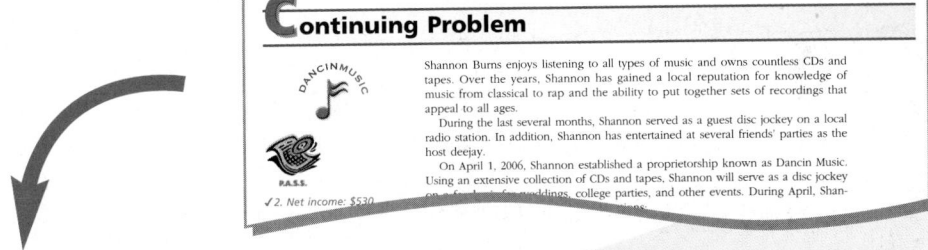

In **Chapter 2**, students **review debits and credits** by journalizing Dancin Music's second month's transactions.

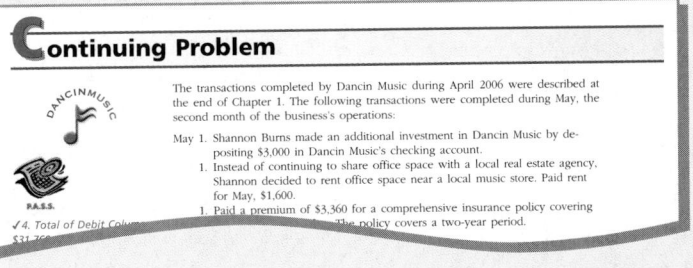

In **Chapter 3**, students **review the adjusting process** for Dancin Music.

In **Chapter 4**, building on what they've learned in Chapters 1, 2, and 3, students **complete the accounting cycle** for Dancin Music, including **preparing the financial statements**.

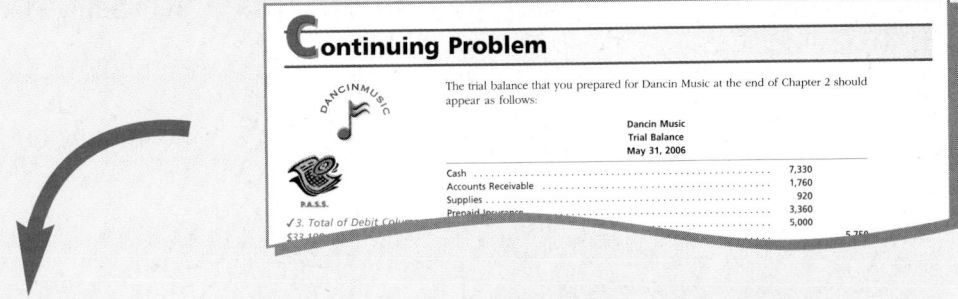

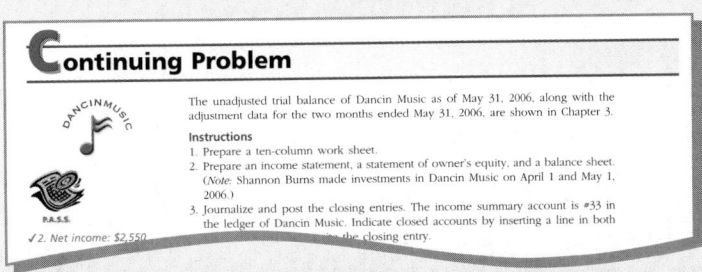

# ENHANCEMENTS TO

*Financial Accounting, 9e* speaks to anyone in an introductory financial accounting course, because 80% of those students will not be accounting majors. For this reason, *Financial Accounting, 9e* concentrates intentionally on the business of business—how accounting contributes to effective management while emphasizing the most important accounting procedures.

**Chapter 1** Opens with a section that defines "business" and describes common types of businesses and their strategies, value chains, and stakeholders. It also includes a section on business ethics.

**Chapter 4** Begins with a discussion of the accounting cycle. Then it introduces the worksheet as an optional tool for collecting accounting data from a company's records. Some of the end-of-chapter materials identify the worksheet as an optional requirement.

**Chapter 5** Includes an illustration of the revenue and collection cycle in a computerized accounting system using QuickBooks.

**Chapter 6** Introduces merchandising with an income statement that shows the effects of purchases on the cost of goods sold. Sales transactions are illustrated next, followed by purchases transactions and the special topics of transportation costs, sales taxes, and trade discounts.

**Chapter 9** Introduces the concept of inventory cost flows without reference to the perpetual or periodic systems. The journal entries in a perpetual system are presented alongside the inventory subsidiary ledger to illustrate the FIFO and LIFO flow of costs.

**Chapter 1 –** Introduction to Accounting and Business

**Chapter 2 –** Analyzing Transactions

**Chapter 3 –** The Matching Concept and the Adjusting Process

**Chapter 4 –** Completing the Accounting Cycle

**Chapter 5 –** Accounting Systems and Internal Controls

**Chapter 6 –** Accounting for Merchandising Businesses

**Chapter 7 –** Cash

**Chapter 8 –** Receivables

**Chapter 9 –** Inventories

# TIME-TESTED CONTENT

**Chapter 10** – Fixed Assets and Intangible Assets

**Chapter 11** – Current Liabilities

**Chapter 12** – Corporations: Organization, Capital Stock Transactions, and Dividends

**Chapter 13** – Accounting for Partnerships and Limited Liability Corporations

**Chapter 14** – Income Taxes, Unusual Income Items, and Investments in Stocks

**Chapter 15** – Bonds Payable and Investments in Bonds

**Chapter 16** – Statement of Cash Flows

**Chapter 17** – Financial Statement Analysis

**Chapter 10**
Includes a discussion of classifying the costs of fixed assets and accounting for donated assets. It continues with sections on stages of acquiring fixed assets and the impairment of goodwill.

**Chapter 11**
Includes a section on reporting the current portion of long-term debt and an expanded discussion of 401K plans.

**Chapter 12**
Discusses organization costs as expenses. The chapter also includes a comprehensive illustration of reporting stockholders' equity.

**Chapter 13**
Describes and illustrates the accounting treatment of equity transactions for partnerships and limited liability corporations. It includes a discussion of the lifecycle of a business.

**Chapter 14**
Includes the reporting of fixed asset impairments and restructuring charges. The section on comprehensive income examines a statement of comprehensive income and an illustration of reporting accumulated other comprehensive income in the stockholders' equity section of the balance sheet.

# FOCUS ON SKILLS

## Critical Thinking and Analysis

As you'd expect from the leader in pedagogical innovation, the colorful and dynamic *Financial Accounting, 9e* text visually highlights conceptual segments designed to help students make the connection between accounting and business. In addition, new box features found in each chapter make the content come to life.

- **Financial Analysis and Interpretation** To help students understand the information in financial statements and how that information is used, this feature describes an important element of financial analysis at the end of each chapter.

- **Special Activities** Students need to develop analytical abilities, not just memorize rules. These end-of-chapter activities focus on understanding and solving pertinent business and ethical issues. Some are presented as conversations in which students can "observe" and "participate" when they respond to the issue being discussed.

**WHAT DO YOU THINK?**

- **"What Do You Think?"** These exercises and activities encourage students to speculate about the real-world effects of newly learned material.

**WHAT'S WRONG WITH THIS?**

- **"What's Wrong With This?"** These innovative exercises challenge students to analyze and discover problems or errors in a financial statement, report, or management decision.

**INTERNET**

- **Technology-Assisted Learning System** Combined with WebTutor Advantage elements such as illustrative problems, quizzes, and Accounting Cycle Review, students continue to hone and reinforce their critical-thinking skills.

## Use of Technology

**Internet Activities**
These activities acquaint students with the ever-expanding accounting-related areas of the Web.

**Web References**
Real World Notes and end-of-chapter activities encourage students to engage in real business research.

**Technology-Assisted Learning**
Teaching and learning solutions are provided in an interactive learning environment. The learning system consists of three elements: WebTutor™ Advantage (on WebCT™ and Blackboard®), Personal Trainer 3.0, and the product Web site.

WebTUTOR™ Advantage

# FOR TOMORROW'S SUCCESS

## Real World Applications

### NEW Who Am I?
Presenting a set of intriguing clues about a real company, from The Motley Fool®, this intriguing feature challenges students to identify the company. They can check their decision against the answer provided later in the chapter.

I have 30,000 restaurants in 121 countries, with about 13,000 in the United States. I serve more than 45 million people each day and employ 1.5 million. Moscow's Pushkin Square sports one of my busiest stores. Fortune Magazine named me No. 1 for social responsibility. I'm busy cutting fat from my offerings. I use more than three million pounds of potatoes per day. My New Tastes Menu is Made for You. My spokesman's shoes are size 14½ and he helps sick kids. More

10  Chapter 1 • Introduction to Accounting and Business

### INTEGRITY IN BUSINESS

#### DOING THE RIGHT THING

*Time Magazine* named three women as "Persons of the Year 2002." Each of these not-so-ordinary women had the courage, determination, and integrity to do the right thing. Each risked their personal careers to expose shortcomings in their organizations. Sherron Watkins, an Enron vice-president, wrote a letter to Enron chairman, Kenneth Lay, — — countant, informed **WorldCom**'s Board of Directors of phony accounting that allowed WorldCom to cover up over $3 billion in losses and forced WorldCom into bankruptcy. Coleen Rowley, an FBI staff attorney, wrote a memo to FBI Director Robert Mueller, exposing how the Bureau brushed off her pleas to investigate Zacarias Moussaoui, who was indicted as a co-conspirator in the

### NEW Integrity in Business
Real-life, business situations provide students with an opportunity to consider ethical issues that they may encounter in the business world.

### NEW Spotlight on Strategy boxes
These stimulating, real-business scenarios introduce students to the effects and importance of strategic thinking and its impact on accounting.

### SPOTLIGHT ON STRATEGY

#### WHAT'S NEXT FOR AMAZON?

**A**mazon.com built its online business strategy on offering books at significant discounts that traditional chains couldn't match. Over the years, Amazon has expanded its online offerings to include DVDs, toys, electronics, and even kitchen appliances. But can its low-cost, discount strategy continue to work across a variety of products? Some have their doubts. The electronics business has lower margins and more competition than books. For example, **Dell Computers** is — — tive of their prices and have refused to make Amazon.com an authorized dealer. As Lauren Levitan, a noted financial analyst, recently said, "It's hard to be the low-cost retailer. You have to execute flawlessly on a very consistent basis. Most people who try a low-price strategy fail." This risk of failing at the low-cost strategy was validated by **Kmart**'s filing for bankruptcy protection in 2002 because of its inability to compete with **Wal-Mart**'s low prices.

Mercell, "A Profitable Amazon Looks to Do an Encore,"

### FINANCIAL REPORTING AND DISCLOSURE

#### UNEARNED REVENUE

**M**icrosoft Corporation develops, manufactures, licenses, and supports a wide range of computer software products, including Windows XP®, Windows NT®, Word®, Excel®, and the Xbox®. When Microsoft sells its products, it incurs an obligation to support its software with technical support and periodic updates. As a result, not all the revenue from selling software is earned on the date of sale. Instead, some of the revenue is unearned. That is, the portion — passes and the support services are provided to customers. Thus, it is necessary to make an adjusting entry each year to transfer unearned revenue to revenue.

The excerpts below from Microsoft's 2002 financial statements describe its accounting for unearned revenue. Microsoft further indicated that, of the $7,743 million of unearned revenue at June 30, 2002, it expected to recognize $5,917 million during the next year and $1,826 million in future years.

### NEW Financial Reporting and Disclosure
These boxes that feature actual companies take students through the rigors of the reporting and analysis skills they will need in business.

### Real World Notes
With these notes, students get a close-up look at how accounting operates in the marketplace. The following companies are among those highlighted in the margin of the text.

- AT&T
- Campbell Soup Co.
- Mercedes-Benz
- UPS
- Gillette
- Coca-Cola Enterprises Inc.
- J.C. Penney Co.
- Hewlett Packard
- Delta Air Lines
- General Electric
- Ford Motor Co.

**REAL WORLD**

**Sears, Roebuck and Co.** sells extended warranty contracts with terms between 12 and 36 months. The receipts from sales of these contracts are reported as unearned revenue (deferred revenue) on Sears' balance sheet. Revenue is recorded as the contracts expire.

# FOCUS ON SKILLS

## Points of Interest

These attention-getting margin notes offer insight into subjects of high interest to students, such as careers and current events, which helps keep accounting concepts relevant.

**POINT OF INTEREST**

The tuition you pay at the beginning of each term is an example of a deferred expense to you, as a student.

## Real World Exercises

Selected exercises and most special activities are based on real-world data to provide students with practice in working with real company data.

## Understand and Review

### Questions & Answers

Students check whether they understand what they've just read, using these activities in the margin of the text.

If NetSolutions' adjustment for unearned rent had incorrectly been made for $180 instead of $120, what would have been the effect on the financial statements?

--------------------------------------------

*Revenues would have been over-*

**A**ssume that you have been hired by a pizza restaurant to deliver pizzas, using your own car. You will be paid $6.00 per hour plus $0.30 per mile plus tips. What is the best way for you to determine how many miles you have driven each day in delivering pizzas?

One method would be to record the odometer mileage before work and then at quitting time. The difference would be the miles driven. For example, if the odometer read 56,743 at the start of work and 56,889 at the end of work, you would have driven 146 miles. This method is subject to error, however, if you copy down the wrong reading or make a math error.

In the sam_____ed information about the status of the busi_____seful for analyzing the

## Relevant Chapter Openers

The beginning of each chapter connects the student's own experiences to the chapter's topic. This tangible link is a great motivator.

## New Design

A lively, colorful, and interesting design invites students to read the text. Colorful, clear, and relevant infographics help clarify difficult concepts in a visual presentation.

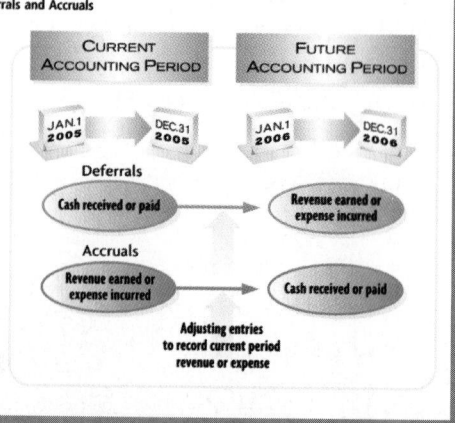

**•Exhibit 1**   Deferrals and Accruals

# FOR TOMORROW'S SUCCESS

## Continuing Case Study

A fictitious dot.com company, NetSolutions, is followed throughout Chapters 1–6 as the example company to demonstrate a variety of transactions.

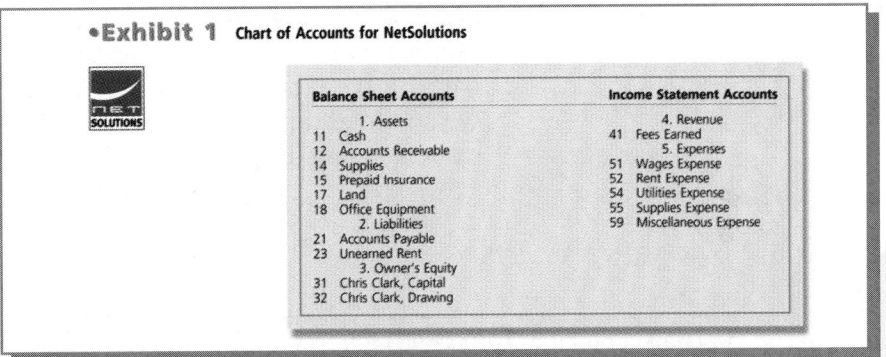

•**Exhibit 1**  Chart of Accounts for NetSolutions

| Balance Sheet Accounts | Income Statement Accounts |
|---|---|
| 1. Assets | 4. Revenue |
| 11 Cash | 41 Fees Earned |
| 12 Accounts Receivable | 5. Expenses |
| 14 Supplies | 51 Wages Expense |
| 15 Prepaid Insurance | 52 Rent Expense |
| 17 Land | 54 Utilities Expense |
| 18 Office Equipment | 55 Supplies Expense |
| 2. Liabilities | 59 Miscellaneous Expense |
| 21 Accounts Payable | |
| 23 Unearned Rent | |
| 3. Owner's Equity | |
| 31 Chris Clark, Capital | |
| 32 Chris Clark, Drawing | |

| | | | | | | | | |
|---|---|---|---|---|---|---|---|---|
| 20 | Miscellaneous Expense | 2 7 5 00 | | | 20 |
| 21 | Cash | | 3 6 5 0 00 | 21 |
| 22 | Paid expenses. | | | 22 |

> **The sum of the debits must always equal the sum of the credits.**

Regardless of the number of accounts, the sum of the debits is always equal to the sum of the credits in a journal entry. This equality of debits and credits for each transaction is built into the accounting equation: Assets = Liabilities + Owner's Equity. It is also because of this double equality that the system is known as ***double-entry accounting***.

On November 30, NetSolutions recorded the amount of supplies used in the operations during the month (transaction g). This transaction increases an

## Summaries

Within each chapter, these synopses draw special attention to important points and help clarify difficult concepts.

## Business Transactions

In Chapters 1 and 2, students are introduced to the dynamics of business transactions through non-business events to which they can easily relate.

**Transaction f**  When you pay your monthly credit card bill, you decrease the cash in your checking account and also decrease the amount you owe to the credit card company. Likewise, when NetSolutions pays $950 to creditors during the month, it reduces both assets and liabilities, as shown below.

Asse    Liabilities +    Owner's Equity

is Clark,

## Self-Examination Questions

Five multiple-choice questions, with answers at the end of the chapter, help students review and retain chapter concepts.

# Understand and Review (continued)

### Illustrative Problem and Solution
A solved problem models one or more of the chapter's assignment problems, so that students can apply the modeled procedures to end-of-chapter materials.

- **Illustrative Problem on WebTutor Advantage** The illustrative problem from the text is also available in a lively electronic version as part of WebTutor Advantage. In addition, several other features of WebTutor Advantage provide review and reinforce understanding: e-lectures, exercise demos, Accounting Cycle Review, games, quizzes, and more!

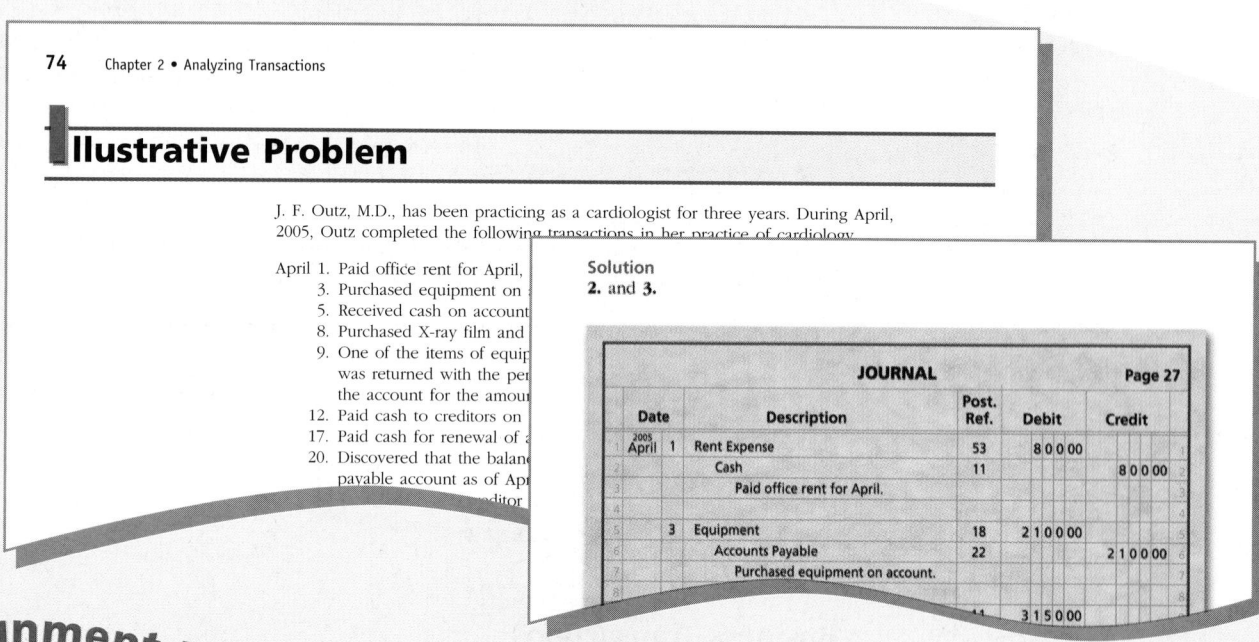

## Assignment Materials that Reinforce Learning and Thinking

Students need to practice accounting in order to understand and use it. To give your students the greatest possible advantages in the real world, *Financial Accounting, 9e* goes beyond presenting theory and procedure with the following end-of-chapter features.

- Discussion Questions
- Exercises
- Problems Series A
- Problems Series B
- Special Activities
- Continuing Problem, Chapters 1–4
- Comprehensive Problems

# FOR TOMORROW'S SUCCESS

Each chapter's Discussion Questions and Exercises can be assigned or used as examples in the classroom. An average of 25 exercises per chapter are included—more than any other text on the market! In addition, the two full sets of problems can be used as classroom illustrations, assignments, alternate assignments, or for independent study. And the Comprehensive Problems at the end of Chapters 4, 6, 11, and 15 integrate and summarize chapter concepts and test students' comprehension.

b. ▬▬▬ What conclusions concerning the company's ability to meets its financial obligations can you draw from these data?

- **Communication Items** These activities help students develop communication skills that will be essential on the job, regardless of the fields they pursue.

- **Team Building** Group Learning Activities let students learn accounting and business concepts while building teamwork skills.

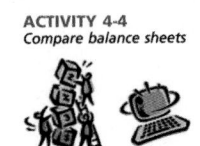

**ACTIVITY 4-4**
*Compare balance sheets*

GROUP ACTIVITY    INTERNET

In groups of three or four, compare the balance sheets of two different companies, and present to the class a summary of the similarities and differences of the two companies. You may obtain the balance sheets you need from one of the following sources:

1. Your school or local library.
2. The investor relations department of each company.
3. The company's Web site on the Internet.
4. EDGAR (Electronic Data Gathering, Analysis, and Retrieval), the electronic archives of financial statements filed with the Securities and Exchange Commission.

SEC documents can be retrieved using the EdgarScan™ service from Pricewaterhouse Coopers at **http://edgarscan.pwcglobal.com**. To obtain annual report information, key in a company name in the appropriate space. EdgarScan will list the ▬▬▬ company you've selected. Select the most recent an-▬▬▬ EdgarScan provid-

- **Complete homework online and receive immediate feedback!** Using Personal Trainer 3.0, students can complete all of the end-of-chapter assignment material, utilize hints and tips, and receive scoring feedback. These scores are then recorded into a gradebook for the instructor. Doing homework has never been so easy and fun!

- **Use P.A.S.S. to complete selected end-of-chapter problems** where several sequential activities need to be recorded and an understanding of their effects on the financial statements is required.

**P.A.S.S.**

# REINFORCEMENT TOOLS

*Financial Accounting, 9e* isn't the only "best in the business." Its supplements are top-notch too—a result of taking instructor and student comments to heart over the years and creating products based on those needs.

## Supplements for Students*

By offering a broad range of supplements—available both as print material and easy-to-use technologies—*Financial Accounting, 9e* not only helps students succeed in the course...but in the business world of tomorrow. Here's a look:

- **Personal Trainer** Specifically designed to ease the time-consuming task of grading homework, Personal Trainer 3.0 lets students complete online their assigned homework from the text or practice on unassigned homework. The results are instantaneously entered into a gradebook. With annotated spreadsheets and full-blown gradebook functionality, the greatly enhanced Personal Trainer 3.0 provides an unprecedented real-time, guided, self-correcting, learning reinforcement system outside the classroom. Use this resource as an integrated solution for your distance learning or traditional course.
*Personal Trainer* . . . . . . . . . . . . . . . . . . . . . . . . . . . . . . . . . . 0-324-20469-8

- **Xtra!** Available as an optional, free bundle with every new textbook, Xtra! gives students FREE access to the following online learning tools:

  — **e-Lectures** briefly review more difficult concepts from the chapter.

  — **Topical Quizzes** measure a student's "test readiness" on the concepts in the chapter.

  — **Multiple Choice Quizzes** help students review chapter concepts and prepare for exams. Feedback on their answers gives page references so they know where to look up the questions they've missed!

  — **Crossword Puzzles** are a fun way for students to review their understanding of key terms and concepts.
*Xtra!* . . . . . . . . . . . . . . . . . . . . . . . . . . . . . . . . . . . . . . . . . 0-324-20585-6

- **Product Support Web Site** at **http://warren.swlearning.com** This site provides students with a wealth of introductory financial accounting resources, including limited quizzing, Internet application questions, e-lectures, spreadsheet applications software, review problems, and more.

*Contact your local sales representative about package options.*

## • Study Guide

The Study Guide includes quiz and test tips, multiple choice, fill-in-the-blank, and true-false questions with solutions. It is designed to assist students in comprehending the concepts and principles presented in the text.

*Study Guide* . . . . . . . . . . . . . . . . . . . . . . . . . . . . . . . . . 0-324-20373-X

## • P.A.S.S. (Power Accounting System Software)
*(formerly General Ledger Software)*

Prepared by Dale Klooster and Warren Allen, this best-selling educational general ledger package makes solving end-of-chapter problems, the Continuing Problem, Comprehensive Problems, and practice sets as easy as clicking a mouse. It allows students to see the difference between manual and computerized accounting systems firsthand. It is enhanced with a problem checker that enables students to determine if their entries are correct and emulates commercial general ledger packages more closely than other educational packages. Problems that can be used with P.A.S.S. are highlighted by an icon. The benefits of using P.A.S.S. are that:

— Errors are more easily corrected than in commercial software.
— The Inspector Disk allows instructors to grade students' work.
— A free Network Version is available to schools whose students
   purchase P.A.S.S.

*P.A.S.S.* . . . . . . . . . . . . . . . . . . . . . . . . . . . . . . . . . . . . . . 0-324-20413-2
*P.A.S.S. Network Version* . . . . . . . . . . . . . . . . . . . . . . . . . 0-324-20412-4

## • Spreadsheet Applications Software

This set of electronic worksheets helps students solve selected exercises and problems that are identified in the text with an icon. These spreadsheets give students the opportunity to solve dozens of problems using Microsoft Excel®. The spreadsheets are available, free, for students to download from the Student Resources section of the product support site.

**SPREADSHEET**

## • Working Papers for Exercises and Problems

The traditional Working Papers include problem-specific forms for preparing solutions for Exercises, A and B Problems, the Continuing Problem, and the Comprehensive Problems from the text. These forms, with preprinted headings, provide a structure for the problems, which helps students get started and saves them time. Additional blank forms are included.

*Working Papers for Exercises and Problems* . . . . . . . . . . . . . 0-324-20375-6

# REINFORCEMENT TOOLS

- **Working Papers Plus for Selected Exercises and Problems**

  This alternative to traditional working papers integrates selected exercise and problem information into the forms needed to complete the activities. These working papers are invaluable homework aids, and they include learning objectives from the chapter and check figures for selected problems.

  *Working Papers Plus for Selected Exercises and Problems* .. 0-324-20377-2

- **Blank Working Papers**

  These Working Papers are available for completing exercises and problems from the text or instructor-prepared problems. They have no preprinted headings. A guide at the front of the Working Papers tells students which form they will need for each problem.

  *Blank Working Papers*. . . . . . . . . . . . . . . . . . . . . . . . . . . . . 0-324-20370-5

---

## Practice Sets

- **Tom's Asphalt** This set is a service business operated as a proprietorship. It includes a narrative of transactions and instructions for an optional solution with no debits and credits. This set can be solved manually or with the P.A.S.S. software in 5–7 hours.

  Tom's Asphalt with P.A.S.S. . . . . . . . . . . . . . . . . . . . . . . . . . . . . . 0-324-20520-1
  Tom's Asphalt Key with Inspector CD . . . . . . . . . . . . . . . . . . . 0-324-20522-8

- **Specialty Sports** Formerly published as "The Snow Shop," this set is a merchandising business operated as a proprietorship. It includes business documents, and it can be solved manually or with the P.A.S.S. software in 12–15 hours.

  Specialty Sports with P.A.S.S. . . . . . . . . . . . . . . . . . . . . . . . . . . 0-324-20525-2
  Specialty Sports Key with Inspector CD . . . . . . . . . . . . . . . . . 0-324-20526-0

- **Groom and Board** This completely revised set was formerly published as "The Coddled Canine" and includes payroll transactions for a merchandising business operated as a proprietorship. It includes business documents, and it can be solved manually or with the P.A.S.S. software in 12–15 hours.

  Groom and Board with P.A.S.S. . . . . . . . . . . . . . . . . . . . . . . . . . 0-324-20531-7
  Groom and Board Key with Inspector CD . . . . . . . . . . . . . . . . 0-324-20532-5

- **Coddled Canine with Peachtree® Accounting Software** Completely revised with current Peachtree software. New Instructor CD provides solutions to the Practice Set as well as helpful hints for incorporating the set into the classroom and tips on tailoring the set to fit the specific needs of each classroom. This set can be solved with the Peachtree software in 10–12 hours.

  Coddled Canine with Peachtree Software. . . . . . . . . . . . . . . . . 0-324-20588-0
  Coddled Canine Instructor CD . . . . . . . . . . . . . . . . . . . . . . . . . 0-324-23230-6

- **Nina's Decorating House** This set is a service and merchandising business operated as a corporation. It includes narrative for six months of transactions, which are to be recorded in a general journal. The set can be solved manually or with the P.A.S.S. software in 10–12 hours.

  Nina's Decorating House with P.A.S.S. . . . . . . . . . . . . . . . . . . . 0-324-20519-8
  Nina's Decorating House Key with Inspector CD . . . . . . . . . . . 0-324-20549-X

- **First Designs, Inc.** This set is a departmentalized merchandising business operated as a corporation. It includes a narrative of transactions, which are to be recorded in special journals. The set can be solved manually or with the P.A.S.S. software in 12–15 hours.

  First Designs with P.A.S.S. . . . . . . . . . . . . . . . . . . . . . . . . . . . . . 0-324-20528-7
  First Designs Key with Inspector CD . . . . . . . . . . . . . . . . . . . . 0-324-20530-9

# TEACHING RESOURCES

From traditional printed materials to the latest integrated classroom technology, the proven *Financial Accounting, 9e* is supported by the most extensive instructor resource package on the market. Just take a look.

## Supplements for Instructors

- **WebTutor™ Advantage on WebCT™ and WebTutor Advantage on Blackboard®** are platform-driven systems for complete Web-based course management and delivery. More than just an interactive study guide, WebTutor Advantage provides lecture replacement and concept review, in addition to reinforcement, in the forms of quizzing, video cases, and much more. Powerful instructor tools are also provided to assist communication and collaboration between students and faculty. When students purchase this product they also get automatic access to Personal Trainer.

  *Webtutor Advantage on WebCT* . . . . . . . . . . . . . . . . . . . . . 0-324-20477-9
  *Webtutor Advantage on Blackboard* . . . . . . . . . . . . . . . . . . . 0-324-20475-2

- **WebTutor™ Toolbox.**  WebTutor Toolbox on WebCT or Blackboard provides free limited content for your WebCT or Blackboard course.

  *Webtutor Toolbox on WebCT* . . . . . . . . . . . . . . . . . . . . . . . . 0-324-22358-7
  *Webtutor Toolbox on Blackboard* . . . . . . . . . . . . . . . . . . . . . 0-324-22357-9

- **An Instructor's Guide to Online Resources** This imaginative resource helps you connect your classroom with *Financial Accounting, 9e* and its dynamic spectrum of digital teaching and learning resources. This supplement is available not only in print form but also on the Instructor's Resource CD-ROM and for download from the Product Support Web site.

  *An Instructor's Guide to Online Resouces* . . . . . . . . . . . . . . . . 0-324-20459-1

- **Instructor's Resource CD-ROM** This convenient resource includes the PowerPoint® Presentations, Instructor's Manual, Solutions Manual, Test Bank, ExamView®, An Instructor's Guide to Online Resources, and Excel Application Solutions.  Lively demonstrations of support technology, including WebTutor Advantage, Personal Trainer 3.0, and P.A.S.S. are also included.  All the basic material an instructor would need is available in one place on this IRCD.

  *Instructor's Resource CD-ROM* . . . . . . . . . . . . . . . . . . . . . . . . 0-324-20416-7

- **Instructor's Manual**  This resource is organized around the chapter learning objectives and offer a comprehensive guide to teaching from the text. The teaching suggestions emulate many of the teaching initiatives being stressed in higher education today, including active learning, collaborative learning, critical thinking, and writing across the curriculum.

  — Demonstration problems can be used in the classroom to illustrate accounting practices. Working through an accounting problem gives the instructor an opportunity to point out pitfalls that students should avoid.

  — Group learning activities provide another opportunity to actively involve students in the learning process. These activities ask students to apply accounting topics by completing an assigned task in small groups of three to five students. Small group work is an excellent way to introduce variety into the accounting classroom and creates a more productive learning environment if top students are mixed with average and poor students.

  — Writing exercises provide an opportunity for students to develop good written communication skills essential to any business person. These exercises probe students' knowledge of conceptual issues related to accounting.

  — Three to five Accounting Scenarios can be used as handouts.

  — The Teaching Transparency Masters can be made into acetate transparencies or can be duplicated and used as handouts.

  *Instructor's Manual* . . . . . . . . . . . . . . . . . . . . . . . . . . . . . . . 0-324-20414-0

- **Solutions Manual**  The Solutions Manual provides the answers for all the end-of-chapter materials in the text. Solutions Transparencies are also available (see below.)

  *Solutions Manual* . . . . . . . . . . . . . . . . . . . . . . . . . . . . . . . 0-324-20420-5

- **Solutions Transparencies**  These acetate transparencies are available for all exercise and problem solutions.

  *Solutions Transparencies* A Problems and Exercises . . . . . . . . 0-324-20427-2
  *Solutions Transparencies* B Problems . . . . . . . . . . . . . . . . . . 0-324-20429-9

# TEACHING RESOURCES

- **Test Bank**  The Test Bank offers a variety of testing materials designed to test students' comprehension of the materials presented in the text. The relevant chapter learning objective and the level of difficulty of each question are included. Approximately 2,000 true-false questions, multiple choice questions, fill-in-the-blank questions, and problems are available. The Test Bank is available printed and bound as well as in a computerized version using the ExamView software found on the IRCD. Chapter and multi-chapter Achievement Tests assessing students' understanding of terms, calculations, and transaction recording are included in the printed Test Bank.

    *Test Bank* . . . . . . . . . . . . . . . . . . . . . . . . . . . . . . . . . . . . . . . . 0-324-20422-1

- **ExamView® Pro Testing Software** is easy-to-use software that allows you to customize exams, practice tests, and tutorials and deliver them over  a network, on the Web, or in printed form. The Test Bank can also easily be uploaded to your WebCT or Blackboard course. The ExamView software is included on the IRCD.

- **PowerPoint® Presentations.**  Each presentation, which is included on the IRCD and on the product support site, enhances lectures and simplifies class preparation. Using this popular software package, you can also add your own custom slides. The dynamic Flash version for students is available online.

- **Presentation Transparencies** are acetates of the PowerPoint presentation slides found on the IRCD.

    *Presentation Transparencies* . . . . . . . . . . . . . . . . . . . . . . . . . . . . 0-324-20418-3

- **Instructor Spreadsheet Templates** show the instructor the completed solutions for the exercises and problems marked with an icon in the text. These are available on the IRCD and for download at the product support site.

- **Tutorial Videos.** Completely revised and remastered, the tutorial videos provide seventeen hours of video instruction. Each chapter is presented in two half-hour, interactive, media-intensive segments that reinforce the concepts presented in the text. These videos are free to adopters and are now available in two formats, DVD and VHS.

  *Tutorial Videos on DVD* . . . . . . . . . . . . . . . . . . . . . . . . . . . . . 0-324-20431-0
  *Tutorial Videos on VHS* . . . . . . . . . . . . . . . . . . . . . . . . . . . . . 0-324-20742-5

- **Telecourse Videos.** These videos are designed for distributed learning courses and are based on the Tutorial Videos but are of high broadcast quality. The videos are made on demand, and orders must be placed directly with South-Western. Each license is sold for either a one-year or three-year time period.

  *Telecourse Videos* Three-Year License . . . . . . . . . . . . . . . . . 0-324-20409-4
  *Telecourse Videos* One-Year License . . . . . . . . . . . . . . . . . . . 0-324-20424-8

- **Product Support Web Site at** http://warren.swlearning.com
  A variety of instructor resources are available through South-Western's password-protected Web site. Downloadable instructor supplement files are available for the Instructor's Manual, Solutions Manual, Test Bank, ExamView, PowerPoint, and Spreadsheet Template Solutions, each organized by chapter. An Instructor's Guide to Online Resources can also be downloaded. Many of these resources are available on the Instructor's Resource CD-ROM.

# ACKNOWLEDGING THE

Because the textbook plays an important supporting role in the teaching/learning environment, our collaboration with instructors is invaluable. We thank them for their contribution to making *Financial Accounting, 9e* and its supplements unsurpassed in quality.

*The following instructors created content for the supplements that accompany the text:*

**Peggy Hussey**
*Colorado Technical College*
Spreadsheet Applications Software

**Gary Bower**
*Community College of Rhode Island*
Personal Trainer

**Deb Kiss**
*Davenport University*
WebTutor Advantage

**Terri Lukshaitis**
*Davenport University*
WebTutor Advantage

**Mike Gough**
*De Anza College*
Tutorial Videos

**John Wanlass**
*De Anza College*
Working Papers Plus for
Selected Exercises and Problems
Tutorial Videos
WebTutor Advantage

**Kevin McFarlane**
*Front Range Community College*
WebTutor Advantage

**Christine Jonick**
*Gainesville College*
Personal Trainer

**Cheryl Fries**
*Guilford Technical Community College*
Personal Trainer

**Leah O'Goley**
*Holyoke Community College*
WebTutor Advantage

**Don Lucy**
*Indian River Community College*
Groom and Board Practice Set
Dynamic Designs, Inc. Practice Set

**Ana Cruz**
*Miami-Dade Community College*
Nina's Decorating House Practice Set

**Edward Krohn**
*Miami-Dade Community College*
First Designs Practice Set

**Blanca Ortega**
*Miami-Dade Community College*
Nina's Decorating House Practice Set

**Janice Stoudemire**
*Midlands Technical College*
An Instructor's Guide to Online Resources

**L. L. Price**
*Pierce College*
Tom's Asphalt Practice Set
Test Banks

**Doug Cloud**
*Pepperdine University*
PowerPoint Presentations

**Robin Turner**
*Rowan-Cabarrus Community College*
Personal Trainer

**Donna Chadwick**
*Sinclair Community College*
Instructor's Manuals

**Jim Shimko**
*Sinclair Community College*
Personal Trainer

**John Godfrey**
*Springfield Tech Community College*
Test Banks

**Diane Glowacki**
*Tarrant County College – Northeast Campus*
Coddled Canine with Peachtree®
Software Practice Set

**Brenda Hester**
*Volunteer State Community College*
Specialty Sports Practice Set

*The instructors listed below, along with Fernando Rodriguez, a graduate of Miami-Dade Community College, provided invaluable verification of text and supplement content:*

**Gary Bower**
*Community College of Rhode Island*
Groom & Board Practice Set
Dynamic Designs Practice Set
Specialty Sports Practice Set
Coddled Canine with Peachtree Practice Set
Nina's Decorating House Practice Set

**Patty Holmes**
*Des Moines Area Community College*
Solutions Manuals

**Alice Sineath**
*Forsyth Technical Community College*
Solutions Manuals

**Jeff Ritter**
*St. Norbert College*
Test Banks

**James Emig**
*Villanova University*
Study Guides
Test Banks
WebTutor Advantage Quizzes

*The following instructors
participated in the reviewing process:*

Brenda Fowler
*Alamance Community College*

Tom Branton
*Alvin Community College*

Sanithia Boyd
*Arkansas State University*

Lenny Long
*Bay State Junior College*

Cathy Peck
*Belhaven College*

Stuart Brown
Carol Garand
*Bristol Community College*

Colin Battle
*Broward Community College*

Luther Ross
*Central Piedmont
Community College*

John Illig
Linda Mallory
*Central Virginia Community College*

Joan Ryan
*Clackamas Community College*

Lyle Hicks
*Danville Area Community College*

Deb Kiss
*Davenport University*

Bill Parrish
*Delgado Community College*

Cynthia McCall
Mike Prindle
Brad Smith
*Des Moines Area Community College*

Nino Gonzalez
*El Paso Community College*

William Hall
*Fayetteville Technical Community College*

Teresa Cook
*Ferris State University*

Alice Sineath
*Forsyth Technical Community College*

Karen Brayden
*Front Range Community
College – Fort Collins*

Joy Bruce
*Gaston College*

Cheryl Fries
*Guilford Technical Community College*

Linda Tarrago
*Hillsborough Community College*

Jack Klett
Don Lucy
*Indian River Community College*

Bob Urell
*Irvine Valley College*

Amy Haas
*Kingsborough Community College*

Tony Cioffi
*Lorain County Community College*

Paul Morgan
*Mississippi Gulf Coast Community College*

Gil Crain
*Montana State University*

Judy Parker
*North Idaho College*

Jim Weglin
*North Seattle Community College*

Karen Mozingo
*Pitt Community College*

Johnnie Atkins
*Rio Hondo College*

Fred Blake
Maria Davis
N. MaiLai Eng
*San Antonio College*

Margaret Black
*San Jacinto College – North*

Curt Gustafson
*South Dakota State University*

Bernie Hill
*Spokane Falls Community College*

Brian Nash
John Teter
*St. Petersburg College*

Ken O'Brien
*SUNY – Farmingdale*

Julie Dailey
*Tidewater Community College-Virginia Beach*

Paul Jensen
*University of Central Arkansas*

Connie Cooper
*University of Cincinnati*

Joanie Sompayrac
*University of Tennessee-Chattanooga*

Mark Henry
*Victoria College*

Brenda Hester
*Volunteer State Community College*

Dan Biagi
*Walla Walla Community College*

Lynette Teal
*Western Wisconsin Technical College*

Jean Meyer
*Xavier University*

# ACKNOWLEDGING THE

**The instructors listed below provided weekly feedback on their experience with the text:**

Mary Schaffler
*College of the Redwoods*

Karen Brayden
*Front Range Community College*

Joy Bruce
*Gaston College*

Cheryl Honore
*Riverside Community College*

Julie Billiris
*St. Petersburg Junior College*

Dawn Grimm
*William Rainey Harper College*

**The following instructors participated in focus groups:**

Julie Derrick
*Brevard Community College – Cocoa*

Pete Ciolfi
Margaret Cox
Randy Glover
*Brevard Community College – Melbourne*

Connie Culbreth
*Brevard Community College – Palm Bay*

J Pat Fuller
Bill Rushing
*Brevard Community College – Titusville*

Clarice McCoy
Camilla Richardson
*Brookhaven College*

Mark Fronke
*Cerritos College*

Elden Price
*Coastal Bend College*

Robert Carpenter
*Eastfield College*

Leah O'Goley
*Holyoke Community College*

Larry Allen
*Panola College*

Carol Wennagel
*San Jacinto College South*

Ann Gregory
*South Plains College*

Meg Bellucci
John Godfrey
William Herd
Pat McClure
Michael Tenerowicz
*Springfield Technical College*

George Katz
Wallace Satchell
*St. Philip's College*

Mark Henry
*Victoria College*

**The instructors listed below provided useful feedback by participating in a Web survey:**

Nick Lefakis
*Asnuntuck Community College*

Ronny Marchman
*Augusta Technical Institute*

Ann Henderson
*Austin Peay State University*

Rick Kwan
*Baker College*

William Parks
*Barber-Scotia College*

John Barden
*Binghamton University*

Bob Schweikle
*Blackburn College*

Michael Blue
Mike Shapeero
Anita Singer
*Bloomsburg University*

Roger Young
*Bluffton College*

Raymond Gaines
*Bossier Parish Community College*

Connie Culbreth
*Brevard Community College*

David Bland
Vickie Campbell
Robert Porter
*Cape Fear Community College*

Cynthia Thompson
*Carl Sandburg College*

Norma Montague
*Central Carolina Community College*

David Stone
*Central Carolina Technical College*

Michael Farina
*Cerritos Community College*

Janet Grange
*Chicago State University*

Nancy Burns
*Chipola Junior College*

Julie Miller
Brenda Thalacker
*Chippewa Valley Technical College*

Anthony Woods
*City College of San Francisco*

Cynthia Ewing
*Clarendon College*

Teri Zuccaro
*Clarke College*

Deborah Carter
*Coahoma Community College*

Jeanene Jones
*Coastal Bend College*

Mike Wirth
*College of Alameda*

Barry Stephens
*College of the Souhwest*

Karen Brayden
*Colorado Community College*

Stacey Stewart
*Colorado Northwestern Community College*

Joanne Green
Charles Miller
*Columbia State Community College*

Wanda Michaels
*Corinthian Colleges*

Evelyn Koonce
*Craven Community College*

Mike LaGrone
*Cumberland*

Dave Weaver
*Dallas County Community College*

Donna Larner
*Davenport University*

Mia Tipton
*De Anza College*

Patricia Holmes
Cynthia McCall
Mike Prindle
*Des Moines Area Community College*

Joan DiSalvio
*Drew University*

Terry Mullins
*Dyersburg State Community College*

Edwin Goldberg
*Florida Memorial College*

John Stancil
*Florida Southern College*

Alice Sineath
*Forsyth Technical Community College*

Jamie Payton
*Gadsden State Community College*

Mai-Ying Woo
*Golden West College*

Marlene Murphy
*Governors State University*

Sushila Kedia
*Grambling State University*

Lamar Creager
*Hagerstown Community College*

Susan Carbon
*Heritage College*

Jonathan Bradshaw
*Houghton College*

Joanne Avery
*Husson College*

John Eubanks
*Independence Community College*

Dale Fowler
*Indiana Wesleyan University*

Suzanne McKee
*Jackson Community College*

AJ Chase
Sabrina Segal
*Keiser College*

Joseph Kuvshinikov
*Kent State University*

Rose Garvey
Sueann Hely
*Kentucky Comm and Tech*

Carolyn Bottjer
*Lehigh Carbon Community College*

Kirk Canzano
*Long Beach City College*

Lou Wolff
*Los Angeles Harbor College*

Bradford Nash
*Los Medanos College*

Mary Dugan
*Mansfield University*

Ben Powell
*The Master's College*

Rod Boydstun
Sandra Lang
Kelly Witsberger
*McKendree College*

Martha Vidmar
*Mesabi Range Technical and Community College*

Peg Johnson
Idalene Williams
*Metropolitan Community College*

Jesse Calvin Nipper
*Middle Georgia College*

Karen McGuire
*Mid-Michigan Community College*

James Joyce
*Miles Community College*

Bob Mahan
*Milligan College*

Mary Holloway
*Mississippi Delta Community College*

Amy Chataginer
Paul Morgan
Terry Thompson
*Mississippi Gulf Coast Community College*

Judy Olsen
*Molloy College*

Carl Essig
Michael Lunday
*Montgomery County Community College*

Abby Fapetu
*Montreat College*

Ron Bowman
*Mt. San Jacinto College*

Tim Miller
*Murray State University*

Ruth Goran
Myung Yoon
*Northeastern Illinois College*

Dawn Stevens
*Northwest Mississippi Community College*

Von Plessner
*Northwest State Community College*

Jeff James
*Northwest Shoals Community College*

Dick Van Holland
*Northwestern College*

Larry Allen
*Panola College*

Nancy Schrumpf
Gregory Thom
*Parkland College*

Vaun Day
Thomas Joyce
Jeff Winter
*Pasadena City College*

Karen Barr
*Penn State University*

Clarence Duncan
Teresa Walker
*Piedmont College*

Peggy Newsome
Howard Roberts
*Pikeville College*

Mary Jo Mettler
*Pine Technical College*

John Daugherty
*Pitt Community College*

Linda Beuning
*Rasmussen Community College*

Larry Waugh
*Rio Hondo Community College*

Joe Reddick
Karen Williamson
*Rochester Community College*

Sue Cunningham
*Rowan-Cabarrus Community College*

Teri Bernstein
Pat Halliday
Ira Landis
*Santa Monica College*

Donna Chadwick
William Hoover
Robert Reas
*Sinclair Community College*

David Laurel
*South Texas Community College*

Daniel Holt
*Southeastern Illinois College*

J. Rendall Garrett
*Southern Nazarene University*

Glenn Brooks
*Southern Polytechnic State University*

Robert Consalvo
*Southern Vermont College*

Patricia McClure
*Springfield Tech Community College*

Kevin Leeds
*St. Peters College*

Joe Shambley
*Sullivan County Community College*

Philip Dunning
Cora Newcomb
*Technical College of the Lowcountry*

Mark Freeman
*Tuskegee University*

Rea Waldon
*Union Institute and University*

Larry Huus
*University of Minnesota*

Carol Collinsworth
Dennis Ortiz
Mary Sauceda
*University of Texas, Brownsville*

Mary Stevens
*University of Texas, El Paso*

Kathleen Fitzpatrick
*University of Toledo*

Henry Carbone
Richard Larson
Bernice Murphy
*University of Maine*

Pam Ondeck
*University of Pittsburg*

Ed Shannon
*Ursinus College*

Brenda Hester
*Volunteer State Community College*

John Haugen
*Wartburg College*

Clifford Bellers
*Washtenaw Community College*

Peggy Helms
*Wayne Community College*

Jeannette Eberle
John Logsdon
Robert Nagoda
*Webber International University*

Lynette Teal
*Western Wisconsin Technical College*

Rick Stevens
*Wheaton College*

Paul LoRusso
*Wilson Technical Community College*

Sharon Vetsch
*Wisconsin Indianhead Technical College*

Barbara Powers
*Wytheville Community College*

Annette Fisher
*Yavapai College*

# brief contents

# contents

**Practice Set: Tom's Asphalt**
This set is a service business operated as a proprietorship. It includes a narrative of transactions and instructions for an optional solution with no debits and credits. This set can be solved manually or with the P.A.S.S. software.

**Practice Set: Nina's Decorating House**
This set is a service and merchandising business operated as a corporation. It includes narrative for six months of transactions, which are to be recorded in a general journal. The set can be solved manually or with the P.A.S.S. software.

**Practice Set: First Designs, Inc.**
This set is a departmentalized merchandising business operated as a corporation. It includes a narrative of transactions, which are to be recorded in special journals. The set can be solved manually or with the P.A.S.S. software.

# FINANCIAL ACCOUNTING 9e

# INTRODUCTION TO ACCOUNTING AND BUSINESS

## objectives

*After studying this chapter, you should be able to:*

1  Describe the nature of a business.

2  Describe the role of accounting in business.

3  Describe the importance of business ethics and the basic principles of proper ethical conduct.

4  Describe the profession of accounting.

5  Summarize the development of accounting principles and relate them to practice.

6  State the accounting equation and define each element of the equation.

7  Explain how business transactions can be stated in terms of the resulting changes in the basic elements of the accounting equation.

8  Describe the financial statements of a proprietorship and explain how they interrelate.

9  Use the ratio of liabilities to owner's equity to analyze the ability of a business to withstand poor business conditions.

**D**o you use accounting? Yes, we all use accounting information in one form or another. For example, when you think about buying a car, you use accounting-type information to determine whether you can afford it and whether to lease or buy. Similarly, when you decided to attend college, you considered the costs (the tuition, textbooks, and so on). Most likely, you also considered the benefits (the ability to obtain a higher-paying job or a more desirable job).

Is accounting important to you? Yes, accounting is important in your personal life as well as your career, even though you may not become an accountant. For example, assume that you are the owner/manager of a small Mexican restaurant and are considering opening another restaurant in a neighboring town. Accounting information about the restaurant will be a major factor in your deciding whether to open the new restaurant and the bank's deciding whether to finance the expansion.

Our primary objective in this text is to illustrate basic accounting concepts that will help you to make good personal and business decisions. We begin by discussing what a business is, how it operates, and the role that accounting plays.

# Nature of a Business

**objective 1**

Describe the nature of a business.

You can probably list some examples of companies with which you have recently done business. Your examples might be large companies, such as **Coca-Cola**, **Dell Computer**, or **Amazon.com**. They might be local companies, such as gas stations or grocery stores, or perhaps employers. They might be restaurants, law firms, or medical offices. What do all these examples have in common that identify them as businesses?

In general, a ***business*** is an organization in which basic resources (inputs), such as materials and labor, are assembled and processed to provide goods or services (outputs) to customers.[1] Businesses come in all sizes, from a local coffee house to a **DaimlerChrysler**, which sells several billion dollars worth of cars and trucks each year. A business's customers are individuals or other businesses who purchase goods or services in exchange for money or other items of value. In contrast, a church is not a business because those who receive its services are not obligated to pay for them.

The objective of most businesses is to maximize profits. **Profit** is the difference between the amounts received from customers for goods or services provided and the amounts paid for the inputs used to provide the goods or services. Some businesses operate with an objective other than to maximize profits. The objective of such nonprofit businesses is to provide some benefit to society, such as medical research or conservation of natural resources. In other cases, governmental units such as cities operate water works or sewage treatment plants on a nonprofit basis. We will focus in this text on businesses operating to earn a profit. Keep in mind, though, that many of the same concepts and principles apply to nonprofit businesses as well.

## Types of Businesses

There are three different types of businesses that are operated for profit: manufacturing, merchandising, and service businesses. Each type of business has unique characteristics.

***Manufacturing businesses*** change basic inputs into products that are sold to individual customers. Examples of manufacturing businesses and some of their products are as follows.

---

[1]A complete glossary of terms appears at the end of the text.

| Manufacturing Business | Product |
|---|---|
| General Motors | Cars, trucks, vans |
| Intel | Computer chips |
| Boeing | Jet aircraft |
| Nike | Athletic shoes and apparel |
| Coca-Cola | Beverages |
| Sony | Stereos and televisions |

*Merchandising businesses* also sell products to customers. However, rather than making the products, they purchase them from other businesses (such as manufacturers). In this sense, merchandisers bring products and customers together. Examples of merchandising businesses and some of the products they sell are shown below.

| Merchandising Business | Product |
|---|---|
| Wal-Mart | General merchandise |
| Toys "R" Us | Toys |
| Circuit City | Consumer electronics |
| Lands' End | Apparel |
| Amazon.com | Internet books, music, video retailer |

*Service businesses* provide services rather than products to customers. Examples of service businesses and the types of services they offer are shown below.

| Service Business | Service |
|---|---|
| Disney | Entertainment |
| Delta Air Lines | Transportation |
| Marriott Hotels | Hospitality and lodging |
| Merrill Lynch | Financial advice |
| Sprint | Telecommunications |

**REAL WORLD**

Roughly eight out of every ten workers in the United States are service providers.

# Types of Business Organizations

The common forms of business organization are proprietorship, partnership, corporation, or limited liability corporation. In the following paragraphs, we briefly describe each form and discuss its advantages and disadvantages.

A *proprietorship* is owned by one individual. More than 70% of the businesses in the United States are organized as proprietorships. The popularity of this form is due to the ease and the low cost of organizing. The primary disadvantage of proprietorships is that the financial resources available to the business are limited to the individual owner's resources. Small local businesses such as hardware stores, repair shops, laundries, restaurants, and maid services are often organized as proprietorships.

As a business grows and more financial and managerial resources are needed, it may become a partnership. A *partnership* is owned by two or more individuals. Like proprietorships, small local businesses such as automotive repair shops, music stores, beauty salons, and clothing stores may be organized as partnerships. Currently, about 10% of the businesses in the United States are organized as partnerships.

A *corporation* is organized under state or federal statutes as a separate legal taxable entity. The ownership of a corporation is divided into shares of stock. A corporation issues the stock to individuals or other businesses, who then become owners or stockholders of the corporation.

A primary advantage of the corporate form is the ability to obtain large amounts of resources by issuing stock. For this reason, most companies that require large investments in equipment and facilities are organized as corporations. For example, **Toys "R" Us** has raised over $400 million by issuing shares of common stock to finance its operations. Other examples of corporations include **General Motors**, **Ford**, **International Business Machines (IBM)**, **Coca-Cola**, and **General Electric**.

About 20% of the businesses in the United States are organized as corporations. Given that most large companies are organized as corporations, over 90% of the total dollars of business receipts are received by corporations. Thus, corporations have a major influence on the economy.

> **Manufacturing, merchandising, and service businesses are commonly organized as either proprietorships, partnerships, corporations, or limited liability corporations.**

A *limited liability corporation* combines attributes of a partnership and a corporation in that it is organized as a corporation, but it can elect to be taxed as a partnership. Thus, its owners' (or members') liability is limited to their investment in the business, and its income is taxed when the owners report it on their individual tax returns.

The three types of businesses we discussed earlier—manufacturing, merchandising, and service—may be either proprietorships, partnerships, corporations, or limited liability corporations. However, because of the large amount of resources required to operate a manufacturing business, most manufacturing businesses are corporations. Likewise, most large retailers such as **Wal-Mart**, **Sears**, and **JCPenney** are corporations.

## Business Strategies

How does a business decide which products or services to offer its customers? For example, should **Best Buy** offer warranty and repair services to its customers? Many factors influence this decision, but ultimately the decision is made on the basis of whether it is consistent with the overall business strategy of the company.

A *business strategy* is an integrated set of plans and actions designed to enable the business to gain an advantage over its competitors, and in doing so, to maximize its profits. The two basic strategies a business may use are a low-cost strategy or a differentiation strategy.

Under a *low-cost strategy*, a business designs and produces products or services of acceptable quality at a cost lower than that of its competitors. **Wal-Mart** and **Southwest Airlines** are examples of businesses with a low-cost strategy. Such businesses often sell no-frills, standardized products to the most typical customer in the industry. Following this strategy, businesses must continually focus on lowering costs.

Businesses may try to achieve lower costs in a variety of ways. For example, a business may employ strict budgetary controls, use sophisticated training programs, implement simple manufacturing technologies, or enter into cost-saving supplier relationships. Such supplier relationships may involve linking the supplier's production process directly to the client's production processes to minimize inventory costs, variations in raw materials, and record keeping costs.

A primary concern of a business using a low-cost strategy is that a competitor may achieve even lower costs by replicating the low costs or developing technological advances. Another concern is that competitors may differentiate their products in such a way that customers no longer desire a standardized, no-frills product. For example, local pharmacies most often try to compete with **Wal-Mart** on the basis of personalized service rather than cost.

Under a *differentiation strategy*, a business designs and produces products or services that possess unique attributes or characteristics for which customers are willing to pay a premium price. For the differentiation strategy to be successful, a product or service must be truly unique or perceived as unique in quality, reliability, image, or design. To illustrate, **Maytag** attempts to differentiate its appliances on the basis of reliability, while **Tommy Hilfiger** differentiates its clothing on the basis of image.

Businesses using a differentiation strategy often use information systems to capture and analyze customer buying habits and preferences. For example, many grocery stores such as **Kroger** and **Safeway** issue magnetic cards to preferred customers that allow the consumer to receive special discounts on purchases. In addition to establishing brand loyalty, the cards allow the stores to track consumer preferences and buying habits for use in purchasing and advertising campaigns.

Companies may enhance differentiation by investing in manufacturing and service technologies, such as flexible manufacturing methods that allow timely product design and delivery. Some companies use marketing and sales efforts to promote product differences. Other companies use unique credit-granting arrangements, emphasize personal relationships with customers, or offer extensive training and after-sales service programs for customers.

A business using a differentiation strategy wants customers to pay a premium price for the differentiated features of its products. However, a business may provide features that exceed the customers' needs. In this case, competitors may be able to offer customers less differentiated products at lower costs. Also, customers' perceptions of the differentiated features may change. As a result, customers may not be willing to continue to pay a premium price for the products. For example, as **Tommy Hilfiger** clothing becomes more commonplace, customers may be unwilling to pay a premium price for Hilfiger clothing. Over time, customers may also become better educated about the products and the value of the differentiated features. For example, **IBM** personal computers were once viewed as being differentiated on quality. However, as consumers have become better educated and more experienced with personal computers, **Dell** computers have also become perceived as being of high quality.

A business may attempt to implement a ***combination strategy*** that includes elements of both the low-cost and differentiation strategies. That is, a business may attempt to develop a differentiated product at competitive, low-cost prices. For example, **Andersen Windows** allows customers to design their own windows through the use of its proprietary manufacturing software. By using flexible manufacturing, Andersen Windows can produce a variety of windows in small quantities with a low or moderate cost. Thus, Andersen windows sell at a higher price than standard low-cost windows but at a lower price than fully customized windows built on site.

Exhibit 1 summarizes the characteristics of the low-cost, differentiation, and combination strategies. In addition, some common examples of businesses that employ each strategy are also listed.

I have 30,000 restaurants in 121 countries, with about 13,000 in the United States. I serve more than 45 million people each day and employ 1.5 million. Moscow's Pushkin Square sports one of my busiest stores. Fortune Magazine named me No. 1 for social responsibility. I'm busy cutting fat from my offerings. I use more than three million pounds of potatoes per day. My New Tastes Menu is Made for You. My spokesman's shoes are size 14½ and he helps sick kids. More than 37 percent of my American owner/operators are women and minorities. Who am I? (Go to page 28 for answer.)

## •Exhibit 1   Business Strategies and Industries

| Business Strategy | Airline | Freight | Automotive | Retail | Financial Services | Hotel |
|---|---|---|---|---|---|---|
| Low cost | Southwest | Union Pacific | Saturn | Sam's Clubs | Schwab | Super 8 |
| Differentiated | Virgin Atlantic | Federal Express | BMW | Talbot's | Morgan Stanley | Four Seasons |
| Combination | Delta | United Postal Service | Ford | Target | Merrill Lynch | Marriott |

As you might expect, a danger of a business using a combination strategy is that its products might not adequately satisfy either end of the market. That is, because its products are differentiated, it cannot establish itself as the low-cost leader, and at the same time, its products may not be differentiated enough that customers are willing to pay a premium price. In other words, the business may become "stuck in the middle." For example, **J.C.Penney** has difficulty competing as a low-cost leader against **Wal-Mart**, **Kmart**, **Goody's Family Clothing**, **Fashion USA**, and **T.J. Maxx**. At the same time, J.C.Penney cannot adequately differentiate its stores and merchandise from such competitors as **The Gap**, **Old Navy**, **Eddie Bauer**, and **Talbot's** so that it can charge higher prices.

A business may also attempt to implement different strategies for different markets. For example, **Toyota** segments the market for automobiles by offering the Lexus to image- and quality-conscious buyers. To reinforce this image, Toyota developed a separate dealer network. At the same time, Toyota offers a low-cost automobile, the Echo, to price-sensitive buyers.

## Value Chain of a Business

Once a business has chosen a strategy, it must implement the strategy in its value chain. A *value chain* is the way a business adds value for its customers by processing inputs into a product or service, as shown in Exhibit 2.

### •Exhibit 2    The Value Chain

To illustrate, **Delta Air Lines**' value chain consists of taking inputs, such as people, aircraft, and equipment, and processing these inputs into a service of transporting goods and passengers throughout the world. The extent to which customers value Delta's passenger service is reflected by the air fares Delta is able to charge as well as passenger load factors (percentage of seats occupied). For example, the extent to which Delta can, on average, charge higher fares than discount airlines, such as **AirTran**, implies that passengers value Delta's services more than AirTran's. These services may include newer, more comfortable aircraft, the ability to earn frequent flyer miles, more convenient passenger schedules, passenger lounges for frequent flyers, and international connections.

A business's value chain can be divided into primary and supporting processes. Primary processes are those that are directly involved in creating value for customers. Examples of primary processes include manufacturing, selling, and customer service. Supporting processes are those that facilitate the primary processes. Examples of support processes include purchasing and personnel.[2] For Delta Air Lines, primary processes would include aircraft maintenance, baggage handling, ticketing, and flight operations. Secondary processes for Delta Air Lines would include the accounting and finance functions, contracting for fuel deliveries, and investor relations.

## Business Stakeholders

A *business stakeholder* is a person or entity having an interest in the economic performance of the business. These stakeholders normally include the owners, managers, employees, customers, creditors, and the government.

The **owners** who have invested resources in the business clearly have an interest in how well the business performs. Most owners want to get the most economic value for their investments. To the extent that the business is profitable, owners will expect to share in the business profits. Since owners may eventually decide to sell their business, they also have an interest in the total economic worth of the business. This economic worth may reflect results of past profits as well as prospects for future profits.

The **managers** are those individuals who the owners have authorized to operate the business. Managers are primarily evaluated on the economic performance of the business. The managers of poor-performing businesses are often fired by the owners. Thus, managers have an incentive to maximize the economic value of the

---

[2]The value chain is described and illustrated in most management textbooks.

business. Owners may offer managers salary contracts that are tied directly to how well the business performs. For example, a manager might receive a percent of the profits or a percent of the increase in profits. Such contracts are often referred to as profit-sharing plans.

The **employees** provide services to the business in exchange for a paycheck. The employees have an interest in the economic performance of the business because their jobs depend upon it. During business downturns, it is not unusual for a business to lay off workers for extended periods of time. Whenever a business fails, the employees lose their jobs permanently. Employee labor unions often use the good economic performance of a business to argue for wage increases. In contrast, businesses often cite poor economic performance as a reason for decreasing wages or denying raises.

The **customers** may also have an interest in the continued success of a business. For example, if **Apple Computer** were to fail, customers might not be able to get hardware and software for their computers. Likewise, customers who purchase advance tickets on **Southwest Airlines** have an interest in whether Southwest will continue in business. Frequent flyers on **Eastern Airlines** lost their accumulated frequent-flyer points when Eastern went out of business.

Like the owners, the **creditors** invest resources in the business by extending credit, such as a loan. They, too, have an interest in how well the business performs. In order for the creditors to recover their investment, the business must generate enough cash to pay them back. In addition, creditors view the business as their customer and thus have a stake in the continued success of the business.

Various **governments** have an interest in the economic performance of businesses. City, county, state, and federal governments collect taxes from businesses within their jurisdictions. The better a business does, the more taxes the government can collect. In addition, workers are taxed on their wages. In contrast, workers who are laid off and are unemployed can file claims for unemployment compensation, which results in a financial burden for the government. City and state governments often provide incentives for businesses to locate in their jurisdictions.

**REAL WORLD**

The state of Alabama offered **DaimlerChrysler** millions of dollars in incentives to locate a Mercedes plant in Alabama.

# SUCCESSFUL ENTREPRENEURS

What are the characteristics of entrepreneurs who successfully start and manage a new business?

It goes without saying that an entrepreneur must have a thorough technical knowledge of the business. For example, a successful computer consultant must have a thorough knowledge of computers. Entrepreneurs must also have basic management skills, such as the ability to organize and interact with others. Terms that are often used to describe entrepreneurs are listed below.

**Terms**

| | |
|---|---|
| Vision | Spirit of adventure |
| Perseverance | Need for achievement |
| Independent | Self-starter |
| Self-confident | Sense of commitment |
| Risk taker | Willingness to make |
| High energy level | personal sacrifices |
| Motivated | Communication skills |
| Personal drive | |

Examples of some well-known entrepreneurs and their companies are listed below.

| Entrepreneur | Company |
|---|---|
| Jeffrey Yang | Yahoo! |
| Henry Ford | Ford Motor Company |
| George Eastman | Kodak |
| King C. Gillette | Gillette Company |
| Steven Jobs | Apple Computer |
| Bill Gates | Microsoft |
| Frederick Smith | Federal Express |
| Sam Walton | Wal-Mart |

Examples of entrepreneurs also include the owners of many small businesses in your community, from local restaurants to video rental stores.

# The Role of Accounting in Business

objective **2**

Describe the role of accounting in business.

What is the role of accounting in business? The simplest answer to this question is that accounting provides information for managers to use in operating the business. In addition, accounting provides information to other stakeholders to use in assessing the economic performance and condition of the business.

In a general sense, ***accounting*** can be defined as an information system that provides reports to stakeholders about the economic activities and condition of a business. As we indicated earlier in this chapter, we will focus our discussions on accounting and its role in business. However, many of the concepts in this text apply also to individuals, governments, and other types of organizations. For example, individuals must account for activities such as hours worked, checks written, and bills due. Stakeholders for individuals include creditors, dependents, and the government. A main interest of the government is making sure that individuals pay the proper taxes.

> **Accounting is an information system that provides reports to stakeholders about the economic activities and condition of a business.**

You may think of accounting as the "language of business." This is because accounting is the means by which business information is communicated to the stakeholders. For example, accounting reports summarizing the profitability of a new product help **Coca-Cola**'s management decide whether to continue selling the product. Likewise, financial analysts use accounting reports in deciding whether to recommend the purchase of Coca-Cola's stock. Banks use accounting reports in determining the amount of credit to extend to Coca-Cola. Suppliers use accounting reports in deciding whether to offer credit for Coca-Cola's purchases of supplies and raw materials. State and federal governments use accounting reports as a basis for assessing taxes on Coca-Cola.

The process by which accounting provides information to business stakeholders is illustrated in Exhibit 3. A business must first identify its stakeholders. It must then assess the various informational needs of those stakeholders and design its accounting system to meet those needs. Finally, the accounting system records the economic data about business activities and events, which the business reports to the stakeholders according to their informational needs.

Stakeholders use accounting reports as a primary source of information on which they base their decisions. They use other information as well. For example, in deciding whether to extend credit to an appliance store, a banker might use economic forecasts to assess the future demand for the store's products. During periods of economic downturn, the demand for consumer appliances normally declines. The banker might inquire about the ability and reputation of the managers of the business. For small corporations, bankers may require major stockholders to personally guarantee the loans of the business. Finally, bankers might consult industry publications that rank similar businesses as to their quality of products, customer satisfaction, and future prospects for growth.

# Business Ethics

objective **3**

Describe the importance of business ethics and the basic principles of proper ethical conduct.

Individuals may have different views about what is "right" and "wrong" in a given situation. For example, you may believe it is wrong to copy another student's homework and hand it in as your own. Other students may feel that it is acceptable to copy homework if the instructor has no stated rule against it. Unfortunately, business managers sometimes find themselves in situations where they feel pressure to violate personal ethics. For example, managers of **Sears** automotive service departments were accused of recommending unnecessary repairs and overcharging customers for actual repairs in order to meet company goals and earn bonuses.

## •Exhibit 3   Accounting Information and the Stakeholders of a Business

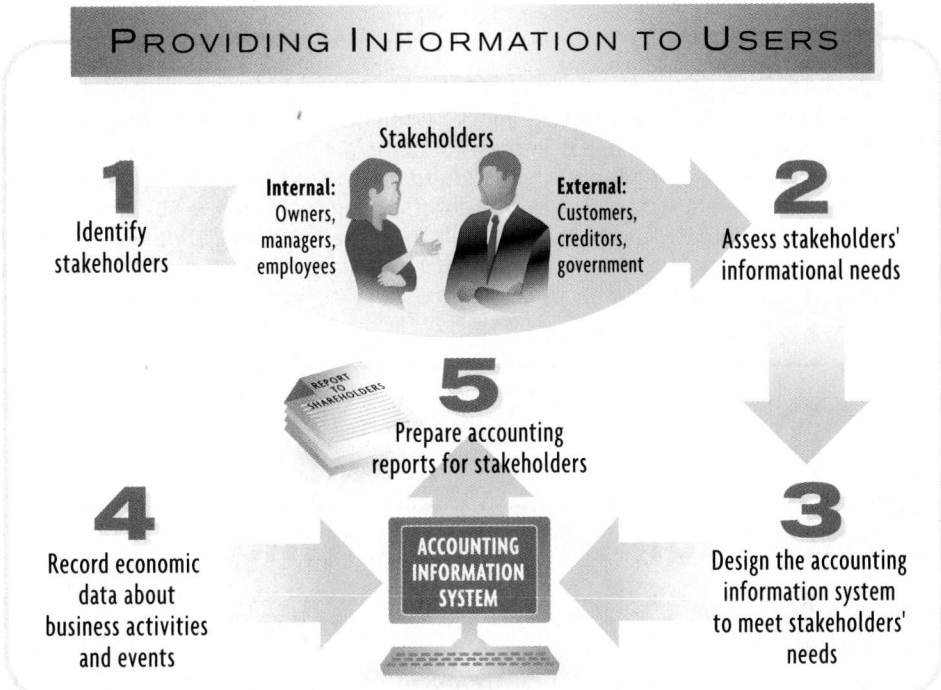

PROVIDING INFORMATION TO USERS

Stakeholders

**1** Identify stakeholders

**Internal:** Owners, managers, employees

**External:** Customers, creditors, government

**2** Assess stakeholders' informational needs

**5** Prepare accounting reports for stakeholders

REPORT TO SHAREHOLDERS

**4** Record economic data about business activities and events

ACCOUNTING INFORMATION SYSTEM

**3** Design the accounting information system to meet stakeholders' needs

**POINT OF INTEREST**

Most colleges and universities publish a Student Code of Conduct that sets forth the ethical conduct expected of students.

**REAL WORLD**

Stanley James Cardiges, the former top U.S. sales representative for **American Honda**, admitted to receiving $2 million to $5 million in illegal kickbacks from dealers. After being sentenced to five years in prison, he admitted to falling into a pattern of unethical behavior early in his career.

The moral principles that guide the conduct of individuals are called ***ethics***. Regardless of differences among individuals, proper ethical conduct implies a behavior that considers the impact of one's actions on society and others. In other words, proper ethical conduct implies that you not only consider what's in your best interest, but also what's in the best interests of others.

Ethical conduct is good business. For example, an automobile manufacturer that fails to correct a safety defect to save costs may later lose sales due to lack of consumer confidence. Likewise, a business that pollutes the environment may find itself the target of lawsuits and customer boycotts.

Businesspeople should work within an ethical framework.[3] Although an ethical framework is based on individual experiences and training, there are a number of sound principles that form the foundation for ethical behavior:

1. *Avoid small ethical lapses.* Small ethical lapses may appear harmless in and of themselves. Unfortunately, such lapses can compromise your work. Small ethical lapses can build up and lead to larger consequences later.
2. *Focus on your long-term reputation.* One characteristic of an ethical dilemma is that it places you under severe short-term pressure. The ethical dilemma is created by the stated or unstated threat that failure to "go along" may result in undesirable consequences. You should respond to ethical dilemmas by minimizing the short-term pressures and focusing on long-term reputation instead. Your reputation is very valuable. You will lose your effectiveness if your reputation becomes tarnished.
3. *You may suffer adverse personal consequences for holding to an ethical position.* In some unethical organizations, managers have endured career setbacks for not budging from their ethical positions. Some managers have resigned because they were unable to support management in what they perceived as unethical behavior. Thus, in the short term, ethical behavior can sometimes adversely affect your career.

---

[3]"Integrity in Business" items and end-of-chapter ethics discussion cases are provided throughout this text to focus attention on the importance of proper ethical conduct in business.

## INTEGRITY IN BUSINESS

### DOING THE RIGHT THING

*T*ime *Magazine* named three women as "Persons of the Year 2002." Each of these not-so-ordinary women had the courage, determination, and integrity to do the right thing. Each risked their personal careers to expose shortcomings in their organizations. Sherron Watkins, an Enron vice-president, wrote a letter to **Enron**'s chairman, Kenneth Lay, warning him of improper accounting that eventually led to Enron's collapse. Cynthia Cooper, an internal accountant, informed **WorldCom**'s Board of Directors of phony accounting that allowed WorldCom to cover up over $3 billion in losses and forced WorldCom into bankruptcy. Coleen Rowley, an **FBI** staff attorney, wrote a memo to FBI Director Robert Mueller, exposing how the Bureau brushed off her pleas to investigate Zacarias Moussaoui, who was indicted as a co-conspirator in the September 11 terrorist attacks.

# Profession of Accounting

objective **4**

Describe the profession of accounting.

Accountants engage in either private accounting or public accounting. Accountants employed by a business firm or a not-for-profit organization are said to be engaged in ***private accounting***. Accountants and their staff who provide services on a fee basis are said to be employed in ***public accounting***.

Because all functions within a business use accounting information, experience in private or public accounting provides a solid foundation for a career. Many positions in industry and in government agencies are held by individuals with accounting backgrounds. For example, in a Special Bonus Issue on "The Corporate Elite," *Business Week* reported the career paths for the chief executives of the 1,000 largest public corporations. These career paths are shown in Exhibit 4.

## •Exhibit 4

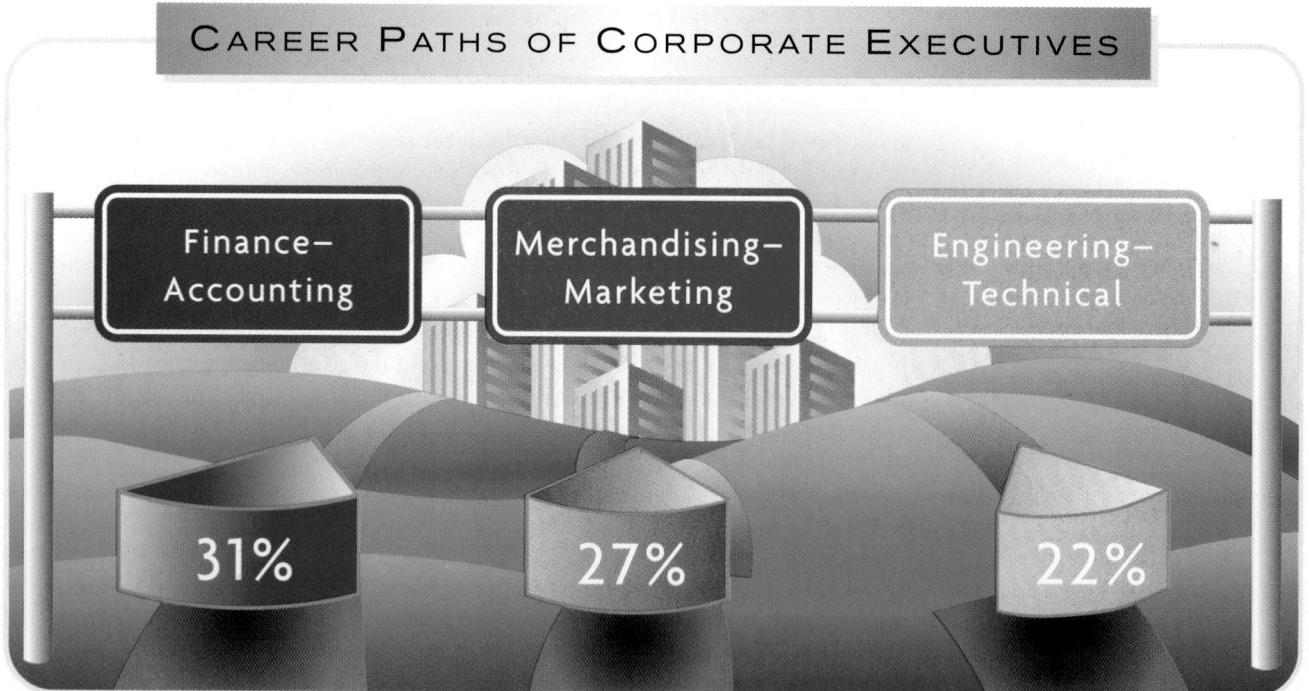

CAREER PATHS OF CORPORATE EXECUTIVES

Finance–Accounting    Merchandising–Marketing    Engineering–Technical

31%     27%     22%

**REAL WORLD**

A career in accounting can be financially rewarding. Warren Jensen, a Certified Public Accountant, accepted a position with **Amazon.com** as its Chief Financial Officer (CFO). Mr. Jensen, the former CFO of Delta Air Lines, received stock options in Amazon .com that are potentially worth over $100 million.

# Private Accounting

The scope of activities and duties of private accountants varies widely. Private accountants are frequently called management accountants. If they are employed by a manufacturer, they may be referred to as *industrial* or *cost accountants*. The chief accountant in a business may be called the **controller**. Various state and federal agencies and other not-for-profit agencies also employ accountants.

The Institute of Certified Management Accountants, an affiliate of the Institute of Management Accountants (IMA), sponsors the **Certified Management Accountant (CMA)** program. The CMA certificate is evidence of competence in management accounting. Becoming a CMA requires a college degree, two years of experience, and successful completion of a two-day examination. Continuing professional education is required for renewal of the CMA certificate. In addition, members of the IMA must adhere to standards of ethical conduct.

The Institute of Internal Auditors sponsors a similar program for internal auditors. Internal auditors are accountants who review the accounting and operating procedures prescribed by their firms. Accountants who specialize in internal auditing may be granted the **Certified Internal Auditor (CIA)** certificate.

# Public Accounting

In public accounting, an accountant may practice as an individual or as a member of a public accounting firm. Public accountants who have met a state's education, experience, and examination requirements may become *Certified Public Accountants (CPAs)*.

The requirements for obtaining a CPA certificate differ among the various states. All states require a college education in accounting, and most states require 150 semester hours of college credit. In addition, a candidate must pass an examination prepared by the American Institute of Certified Public Accountants (AICPA).

Most states do not permit individuals to practice as CPAs until they have had from one to three years' experience in public accounting. Some states, however, accept similar employment in private accounting as equivalent experience. All states require continuing professional education and adherence to standards of ethical conduct.[4]

## INTEGRITY IN BUSINESS

### ACCOUNTING REFORM

The financial accounting and reporting failures of **Enron**, **WorldCom**, **Tyco**, **Xerox**, and others shocked the investing public. The disclosure that some of the nation's largest and best-known corporations had overstated profits and misled investors raised the question: Where were the CPAs?

In response, Congress passed the Investor Protection, Auditor Reform, and Transparency Act of 2002, called the Sarbanes-Oxley Act. The Act establishes a Public Company Accounting Oversight Board to regulate the portion of the accounting profession that has public companies as clients. In addition, the Act prohibits auditors (CPAs) from providing certain types of nonaudit services, such as investment banking or legal services, to their clients, prohibits employment of auditors by clients for one year after they last audited the client, and increases penalties for the reporting of misleading financial statements.

# Specialized Accounting Fields

You may think that all accounting is the same. However, you will find several specialized fields of accounting in practice. The two most common are financial accounting and managerial accounting. Other fields include cost accounting, environmental

---

[4]The text of the *Code of Professional Conduct* of the American Institute of Certified Public Accountants is available on the AICPA Web site, which is linked to the text Web site at http://warren.swlearning.com.

accounting, tax accounting, accounting systems, international accounting, not-for-profit accounting, and social accounting.

*Financial accounting* is primarily concerned with the recording and reporting of economic data and activities for a business. Although such reports provide useful information for managers, they are the primary reports for owners, creditors, governmental agencies, and the public. For example, if you wanted to buy some stock in **PepsiCo**, **American Airlines**, or **McDonald's**, how would you know in which company to invest? One way is to review financial reports and compare the financial performance and condition of each company. The purpose of financial accounting is to provide such reports.

*Managerial accounting*, or **management accounting**, uses both financial accounting and estimated data to aid management in running day-to-day operations and in planning future operations. Management accountants gather and report information that is relevant and timely to the decision-making needs of management. For example, management might need information on alternative ways to finance the construction of a new building. Alternatively, management might need information on whether to expand its operations into a new product line. Thus, reports to management can differ widely in form and content.

# Generally Accepted Accounting Principles

objective **5**

Summarize the development of accounting principles and relate them to practice.

**REAL WORLD**

The FASB is also developing a broad conceptual framework for financial accounting. Seven Statements of *Financial Accounting Concepts* have been published to date.

If the management of a company could record and report financial data as it saw fit, comparisons among companies would be difficult, if not impossible. Thus, financial accountants follow *generally accepted accounting principles (GAAP)* in preparing reports. These reports allow investors and other stakeholders to compare one company to another.

To illustrate the importance of generally accepted accounting principles, assume that each sports conference in college football used different rules for counting touchdowns. For example, assume that the Pacific Athletic Conference (PAC 10) counted a touchdown as six points and the Atlantic Coast Conference (ACC) counted a touchdown as two points. It would be difficult to evaluate the teams under such different scoring systems. A standard set of rules and a standard scoring system help fans compare teams across conferences. Likewise, a standard set of generally accepted accounting principles allows for the comparison of financial performance and condition across companies.

Accounting principles and concepts develop from research, accepted accounting practices, and pronouncements of authoritative bodies. Currently, the *Financial Accounting Standards Board (FASB)* is the authoritative body having the primary responsibility for developing accounting principles. The FASB publishes *Statements of Financial Accounting Standards* and *Interpretations* to these Standards.

Because generally accepted accounting principles impact how companies report and what they report, all stakeholders are interested in the setting of these principles. For example, the setting of accounting standards for stock-based compensation or stock options has been especially controversial. Even the United States Senate has been involved in the debate. Many managers opposed an initial proposal by the FASB that would record the value of such options as a reduction of profits because doing so would negatively impact their financial results. The FASB issued a revised proposal, but investors, analysts, and other stakeholders criticized manager stock options in light of the poor financial performances of many companies and the financial failures of **Enron**, **Tyco**, and **WorldCom**. As the debate continues, some companies are voluntarily treating stock options as a reduction of profits.

In this chapter and throughout this text, we emphasize accounting principles and concepts. It is through this emphasis on the "why" of accounting as well as the "how" that you will gain an understanding of the full significance of accounting. In the following paragraphs, we discuss the business entity concept and the cost concept.

## Business Entity Concept

The individual business unit is the business entity for which economic data are needed. This entity could be an automobile dealer, a department store, or a grocery store. The business entity must be identified, so that the accountant can determine which economic data should be analyzed, recorded, and summarized in reports.

The ***business entity concept*** is important because it limits the economic data in the accounting system to data related directly to the activities of the business. In other words, the business is viewed as an entity separate from its owners, creditors, or other stakeholders. For example, the accountant for a business with one owner (a proprietorship) would record the activities of the business only, not the personal activities, property, or debts of the owner.

> Under the business entity concept, the activities of a business are recorded separately from the activities of the stakeholders.

## The Cost Concept

If a building is bought for $150,000, that amount should be entered into the buyer's accounting records. The seller may have been asking $170,000 for the building up to the time of the sale. The buyer may have initially offered $130,000 for the building. The building may have been assessed at $125,000 for property tax purposes. The buyer may have received an offer of $175,000 for the building the day after it was acquired. These latter amounts have no effect on the accounting records because they did not result in an exchange of the building from the seller to the buyer. The **cost concept** is the basis for entering the *exchange price, or cost, of $150,000* into the accounting records for the building.

Continuing the illustration, the $175,000 offer received by the buyer the day after the building was acquired indicates that it was a bargain purchase at $150,000. To use $175,000 in the accounting records, however, would record an illusory or unrealized profit. If, after buying the building, the buyer accepts the offer and sells the building for $175,000, a profit of $25,000 is then realized and recorded. The new owner would record $175,000 as the cost of the building.

Using the cost concept involves two other important accounting concepts— objectivity and the unit of measure. The **objectivity concept** requires that the accounting records and reports be based upon objective evidence. In exchanges between a buyer and a seller, both try to get the best price. Only the final agreed-upon amount is objective enough for accounting purposes. If the amounts at which properties were recorded were constantly being revised upward and downward based on offers, appraisals, and opinions, accounting reports could soon become unstable and unreliable.

The ***unit of measure concept*** requires that economic data be recorded in dollars. Money is a common unit of measurement for reporting uniform financial data and reports.

# Assets, Liabilities, and Owner's Equity

> **objective 6**
> State the accounting equation and define each element of the equation.

The resources owned by a business are its ***assets***. Examples of assets include cash, land, buildings, and equipment. The rights or claims to the properties are normally divided into two principal types: (1) the rights of creditors and (2) the rights of owners. The rights of creditors represent debts of the business and are called ***liabilities***. The rights of the owners are called ***owner's equity***. The relationship between the two may be stated in the form of an equation, as follows:

$$\text{Assets} = \text{Liabilities} + \text{Owner's Equity}$$

This equation is known as the ***accounting equation***. It is usual to place liabilities before owner's equity in the accounting equation because creditors have first

 If a company's assets increase by $20,000 and its liabilities decrease by $5,000, how much did the owner's equity increase or decrease?

| Change in Assets | = | Change in Liabilities | + | Change in Owner's Equity |
|---|---|---|---|---|
| +$20,000 | = | −$5,000 | + | X |
| +$25,000 | = | | | X |

rights to the assets. The claim of the owners is sometimes given greater emphasis by transposing liabilities to the other side of the equation, which yields:

$$\text{Assets} - \text{Liabilities} = \text{Owner's Equity}$$

To illustrate, if the assets owned by a business amount to $100,000 and the liabilities amount to $30,000, the owner's equity is equal to $70,000, as shown below.

| Assets | − | Liabilities | = | Owner's Equity |
|---|---|---|---|---|
| $100,000 | − | $30,000 | = | $70,000 |

---

## FINANCIAL REPORTING AND DISCLOSURE

### THE ACCOUNTING EQUATION

The accounting equation provides a basic framework for recording the effects of transactions on companies of all sizes and types. This basic framework serves as the foundation for accounting systems from the smallest business, such as a local convenience store, to the largest businesses. Some examples taken from recent financial reports of well-known companies are shown below.

| Company | Assets* | = | Liabilities | + | Owners' Equity |
|---|---|---|---|---|---|
| Coca-Cola | $22,417 | = | $11,051 | + | $11,366 |
| Circuit City | 3,815 | = | 1,436 | + | 2,379 |
| Dell Computer | 13,435 | = | 7,813 | + | 5,622 |
| eBay | 1,182 | = | 168 | + | 1,014 |
| Hilton Hotels | 9,140 | = | 7,498 | + | 1,642 |
| McDonald's | 22,535 | = | 13,047 | + | 9,488 |
| Microsoft | 59,257 | = | 11,968 | + | 47,289 |
| Southwest Airlines | 8,997 | = | 4,983 | + | 4,014 |
| Wal-Mart | 78,130 | = | 46,787 | + | 31,343 |

*Amounts are shown in millions of dollars.

---

# Business Transactions and the Accounting Equation

### objective 7

Explain how business transactions can be stated in terms of the resulting changes in the basic elements of the accounting equation.

Paying a monthly telephone bill of $168 affects a business's financial condition because it now has less cash on hand. Such an economic event or condition that directly changes an entity's financial condition or directly affects its results of operations is a *business transaction*. For example, purchasing land for $50,000 is a business transaction. In contrast, a change in a business's credit rating does not directly affect cash or any other element of its financial condition.

All business transactions can be stated in terms of changes in the elements of the accounting equation. You will see how business transactions affect the accounting equation by studying some typical transactions. As a basis for illustration, we will use a business organized by Chris Clark.

Assume that on November 1, 2005, Chris Clark begins a business that will be known as NetSolutions. The first phase of Chris's business plan is to operate Net-

> All business transactions can be stated in terms of changes in the elements of the accounting equation.

Solutions as a service business that provides assistance to individuals and small businesses in developing Web pages and in configuring and installing application software. Chris expects this initial phase of the business to last one to two years. During this period, Chris will gather information on the software and hardware needs of customers. During the second phase of the business plan, Chris plans to expand NetSolutions into a personalized retailer of software and hardware for individuals and small businesses.

Each transaction or group of similar transactions during NetSolutions' first month of operations is described in the following paragraphs. The effect of each transaction on the accounting equation is then shown.

**Transaction a**    Chris Clark deposits $25,000 in a bank account in the name of Net-Solutions. The effect of this transaction is to increase the asset cash (on the left side of the equation) by $25,000. To balance the equation, the owner's equity (on the right side of the equation) is increased by the same amount. The equity of the owner is referred to by using the owner's name and "Capital," such as "Chris Clark, Capital." The effect of this transaction on NetSolutions' accounting equation is shown below.

|    | Assets | = | Owner's Equity |
|----|--------|---|----------------|
|    | Cash   | = | Chris Clark, Capital |
| a. | 25,000 |   | 25,000   Investment by Chris Clark |

Note that since Chris Clark is the sole owner, NetSolutions is a proprietorship. Note, too, that the accounting equation shown above relates only to the business, NetSolutions. Under the business entity concept, Chris Clark's personal assets, such as a home or personal bank account, and personal liabilities are excluded from the equation.

**Transaction b**    If you purchased this textbook by paying cash, you entered into a transaction in which you exchanged one asset for another. That is, you exchanged cash for the textbook. Businesses often enter into similar transactions. NetSolutions, for example, exchanged $20,000 cash for land. The land is located in a new business park with convenient access to transportation facilities. Chris Clark plans to rent office space and equipment during the first phase of the business plan. During the second phase, Chris plans to build an office and warehouse on the land.

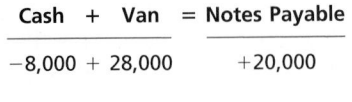

If NetSolutions had purchased a van for $28,000, paying $8,000 cash and signing a loan agreement (note payable) for $20,000, how would the transaction be recorded using the accounting equation?

| Cash | + | Van | = | Notes Payable |
|------|---|-----|---|---------------|
| −8,000 | + | 28,000 |  | +20,000 |

The purchase of the land changes the makeup of the assets but does not change the total assets. The items in the equation prior to this transaction and the effect of the transaction are shown next, as well as the new amounts, or *balances*, of the items.

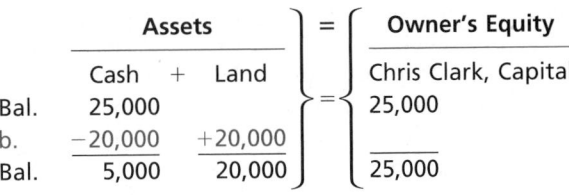

|      | Assets |   |       | = | Owner's Equity |
|------|--------|---|-------|---|----------------|
|      | Cash   | + | Land  | = | Chris Clark, Capital |
| Bal. | 25,000 |   |       |   | 25,000 |
| b.   | −20,000 | + | +20,000 |  |      |
| Bal. | 5,000  |   | 20,000 |  | 25,000 |

**Transaction c**    You have probably used a credit card at one time or another to buy clothing or other merchandise. In this type of transaction, you received clothing for a promise to pay your credit card bill in the future. That is, you received an asset and incurred a liability to pay a future bill. During the month, NetSolutions entered into a similar transaction, buying supplies for $1,350 and agreeing to pay the supplier in the near future. This type of transaction is called a purchase *on account*. The liability created is called an **account payable**. Items such as supplies that will be used in the business in the future are called **prepaid expenses**, which are assets. The effect of this transaction is to increase assets and liabilities by $1,350, as follows:

REAL WORLD

Other examples of common prepaid expenses include insurance and rent. Businesses usually report these assets together as a single item, prepaid expenses.

| | Assets | | | = | Liabilities + Owner's Equity | |
|---|---|---|---|---|---|---|
| | | | | | Accounts | Chris Clark, |
| | Cash | + Supplies | + Land | | Payable | + Capital |
| Bal. | 5,000 | | 20,000 | | | 25,000 |
| c. | | +1,350 | | | +1,350 | |
| Bal. | 5,000 | 1,350 | 20,000 | | 1,350 | 25,000 |

**Transaction d** You may have earned money by painting houses. If so, you received money for rendering services to a customer. Likewise, a business earns money by selling goods or services to its customers. This amount is called *revenue*.

During its first month of operations, NetSolutions provided services to customers, earning fees of $7,500 and receiving the amount in cash. The receipt of cash increases NetSolutions' assets and also increases Chris Clark's equity in the business. Thus, this transaction increased cash and the owner's equity by $7,500, as shown here.

| | Assets | | | = | Liabilities + | Owner's Equity | |
|---|---|---|---|---|---|---|---|
| | | | | | Accounts | Chris Clark, | |
| | Cash | + Supplies | + Land | | Payable | + Capital | |
| Bal. | 5,000 | 1,350 | 20,000 | | 1,350 | 25,000 | |
| d. | +7,500 | | | | | + 7,500 | Fees earned |
| Bal. | 12,500 | 1,350 | 20,000 | | 1,350 | 32,500 | |

Special terms may be used to describe certain kinds of revenue, such as **sales** for the sale of merchandise. Revenue from providing services is called **fees earned**. For example, a physician would record fees earned for services to patients. Other examples include **rent revenue** (money received for rent) and **interest revenue** (money received for interest).

Instead of requiring the payment of cash at the time services are provided or goods are sold, a business may accept payment at a later date. Such revenues are called *fees on account* or *sales on account*. In such cases, the firm has an *account receivable*, which is a claim against the customer. An account receivable is an asset, and the revenue is earned as if cash had been received. When customers pay their accounts, there is an exchange of one asset for another. Cash increases, while accounts receivable decreases.

**Transaction e** If you painted houses to earn money, you probably used your own ladders and brushes. NetSolutions also spent cash or used up other assets in earning revenue. The amounts used in this process of earning revenue are called *expenses*. Expenses include supplies used, wages of employees, and other assets and services used in operating the business.

For NetSolutions, the expenses paid during the month were as follows: wages, $2,125; rent, $800; utilities, $450; and miscellaneous, $275. Miscellaneous expenses include small amounts paid for such items as postage, coffee, and magazine subscriptions. The effect of this group of transactions is the opposite of the effect of revenues. These transactions reduce cash and owner's equity, as shown here.

| | Assets | | | = | Liabilities + | Owner's Equity | |
|---|---|---|---|---|---|---|---|
| | | | | | Accounts | Chris Clark, | |
| | Cash | + Supplies | + Land | | Payable | + Capital | |
| Bal. | 12,500 | 1,350 | 20,000 | | 1,350 | 32,500 | |
| e. | −3,650 | | | | | −2,125 | Wages expense |
| | | | | | | − 800 | Rent expense |
| | | | | | | − 450 | Utilities expense |
| | | | | | | − 275 | Misc. expense |
| | 8,850 | 1,350 | 20,000 | | 1,350 | 28,850 | |

Businesses usually record each revenue and expense transaction separately as it occurs. However, to simplify this illustration, we have summarized NetSolutions' revenues and expenses for the month in transactions (d) and (e).

**Transaction f**   When you pay your monthly credit card bill, you decrease the cash in your checking account and also decrease the amount you owe to the credit card company. Likewise, when NetSolutions pays $950 to creditors during the month, it reduces both assets and liabilities, as shown below.

|  | Assets | | | = | Liabilities + | Owner's Equity |
|---|---|---|---|---|---|---|
|  | Cash + | Supplies + | Land | = | Accounts Payable + | Chris Clark, Capital |
| Bal. | 8,850 | 1,350 | 20,000 | | 1,350 | 28,850 |
| f. | −950 | | | | −950 | |
| Bal. | 7,900 | 1,350 | 20,000 | | 400 | 28,850 |

You should note that paying an amount on account is different from paying an amount for an expense. The payment of an expense reduces owner's equity, as illustrated in transaction (e). Paying an amount on account reduces the amount owed on a liability.

If supplies of $2,500 were purchased during the month and supplies of $350 are on hand at the end of the month, how much is supplies expense for the month?

---

*$2,150 ($2,500 supplies purchased − $350 on hand)*

**Transaction g**   At the end of the month, the cost of the supplies on hand (not yet used) is $550. The remainder of the supplies ($1,350 − $550) was used in the operations of the business and is treated as an expense. This decrease of $800 in supplies and owner's equity is shown as follows:

|  | Assets | | | = | Liabilities + | Owner's Equity | |
|---|---|---|---|---|---|---|---|
|  | Cash + | Supplies + | Land | = | Accounts Payable + | Chris Clark, Capital | |
| Bal. | 7,900 | 1,350 | 20,000 | | 400 | 28,850 | |
| g. | | −800 | | | | − 800 | Supplies expense |
| Bal. | 7,900 | 550 | 20,000 | | 400 | 28,050 | |

**Transaction h**   At the end of the month, Chris Clark withdraws $2,000 in cash from the business for personal use. This transaction is the exact opposite of an investment in the business by the owner. Cash and owner's equity are decreased. The cash payment is not a business expense but a withdrawal of a part of the owner's equity. The effect of the $2,000 withdrawal is shown as follows:

|  | Assets | | | = | Liabilities + | Owner's Equity | |
|---|---|---|---|---|---|---|---|
|  | Cash + | Supplies + | Land | = | Accounts Payable + | Chris Clark, Capital | |
| Bal. | 7,900 | 550 | 20,000 | | 400 | 28,050 | |
| h. | −2,000 | | | | | −2,000 | Withdrawal |
| Bal. | 5,900 | 550 | 20,000 | | 400 | 26,050 | |

You should be careful not to confuse withdrawals by the owner with expenses. Withdrawals *do not* represent assets or services used in the process of earning revenues. The owner's equity decrease from the withdrawals is listed in the equation under Capital. This is because withdrawals are considered a distribution of capital to the owner.

**Summary**   The transactions of NetSolutions are summarized as follows. They are identified by letter, and the balance of each item is shown after each transaction.

| | Assets | | | = | Liabilities + | Owner's Equity | |
|---|---|---|---|---|---|---|---|
| | Cash | + Supplies + | Land | = | Accounts Payable + | Chris Clark, Capital | |
| a. | +25,000 | | | | | +25,000 | Investment by Chris Clark |
| b. | −20,000 | | +20,000 | | | | |
| Bal. | 5,000 | | 20,000 | | | 25,000 | |
| c. | | +1,350 | | | +1,350 | | |
| Bal. | 5,000 | 1,350 | 20,000 | | 1,350 | 25,000 | |
| d. | + 7,500 | | | | | + 7,500 | Fees earned |
| Bal. | 12,500 | 1,350 | 20,000 | | 1,350 | 32,500 | |
| e. | − 3,650 | | | | | − 2,125 | Wages expense |
| | | | | | | − 800 | Rent expense |
| | | | | | | − 450 | Utilities expense |
| | | | | | | − 275 | Misc. expense |
| Bal. | 8,850 | 1,350 | 20,000 | | 1,350 | 28,850 | |
| f. | − 950 | | | | − 950 | | |
| Bal. | 7,900 | 1,350 | 20,000 | | 400 | 28,850 | |
| g. | | − 800 | | | | − 800 | Supplies expense |
| Bal. | 7,900 | 550 | 20,000 | | 400 | 28,050 | |
| h. | − 2,000 | | | | | − 2,000 | Withdrawal |
| Bal. | 5,900 | 550 | 20,000 | | 400 | 26,050 | |

In reviewing the preceding summary, you should note the following, which apply to all types of businesses:

1. The effect of every transaction is *an increase or a decrease in one or more of the accounting equation elements.*
2. The two sides of the accounting equation are *always equal.*
3. The owner's equity is *increased by amounts invested by the owner* and is *decreased by withdrawals by the owner.* In addition, the owner's equity is *increased by revenues* and is *decreased by expenses.* The effects of these four types of transactions on owner's equity are illustrated in Exhibit 5.

## •Exhibit 5    Effects of Transactions on Owner's Equity

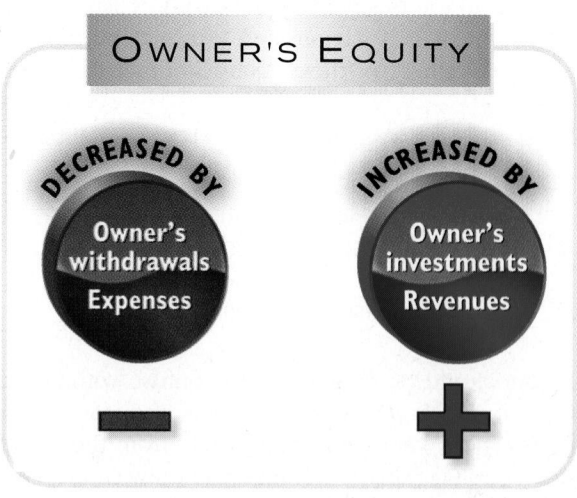

# Financial Statements

**Net income—the excess of revenue over expenses—increases owner's equity.**

After transactions have been recorded and summarized, reports are prepared for users. The accounting reports that provide this information are called ***financial statements***. The principal financial statements of a proprietorship are the income statement, the statement of owner's equity, the balance sheet, and the statement of cash flows. The order in which the statements are normally prepared and the nature of the data presented in each statement are as follows:

- ***Income statement***—A summary of the revenue and expenses *for a specific period of time*, such as a month or a year.
- ***Statement of owner's equity***—A summary of the changes in the owner's equity that have occurred *during a specific period of time*, such as a month or a year.
- ***Balance sheet***—A list of the assets, liabilities, and owner's equity *as of a specific date*, usually at the close of the last day of a month or a year.
- ***Statement of cash flows***—A summary of the cash receipts and cash payments *for a specific period of time*, such as a month or a year.

The basic features of the four statements and their interrelationships are illustrated in Exhibit 6. The data for the statements were taken from the summary of transactions of NetSolutions.

All financial statements should be identified by the name of the business, the title of the statement, and the *date* or *period of time*. The data presented in the income statement, the statement of owner's equity, and the statement of cash flows are for a period of time. The data presented in the balance sheet are for a specific date.

You should note the use of indents, captions, dollar signs, and rulings in the financial statements. They aid the reader by emphasizing the sections of the statements.

## Income Statement

The income statement reports the revenues and expenses for a period of time, based on the ***matching concept***. This concept is applied by *matching* the expenses with the revenue generated during a period by those expenses. The income statement also reports the excess of the revenue over the expenses incurred. This excess of the revenue over the expenses is called ***net income*** or **net profit**. If the expenses exceed the revenue, the excess is a ***net loss***.

The effects of revenue earned and expenses incurred during the month for NetSolutions were shown in the equation as increases and decreases in owner's equity (capital). Net income for a period has the effect of increasing owner's equity (capital) for the period, whereas a net loss has the effect of decreasing owner's equity (capital) for the period.

The revenue, expenses, and the net income of $3,050 for NetSolutions are reported in the income statement in Exhibit 6. The order in which the expenses are listed in the income statement varies among businesses. One method is to list them in order of size, beginning with the larger items. Miscellaneous expense is usually shown as the last item, regardless of the amount.

## Statement of Owner's Equity

The statement of owner's equity reports the changes in the owner's equity for a period of time. It is prepared *after* the income statement because the net income or net loss for the period must be reported in this statement. Similarly, it is prepared *before* the balance sheet, since the amount of owner's equity at the end of the period must be reported on the balance sheet. Because of this, the statement of owner's equity is often viewed as the connecting link between the income statement and balance sheet.

## •Exhibit 6

**Financial Statements**

### NetSolutions
### Income Statement
### For the Month Ended November 30, 2005

| | | | |
|---|---:|---:|---:|
| Fees earned | | | $7 5 0 0 00 |
| Operating expenses: | | | |
| Wages expense | $2 1 2 5 00 | | |
| Rent expense | 8 0 0 00 | | |
| Supplies expense | 8 0 0 00 | | |
| Utilities expense | 4 5 0 00 | | |
| Miscellaneous expense | 2 7 5 00 | | |
| Total operating expenses | | 4 4 5 0 00 | |
| Net income | | | $3 0 5 0 00 |

### NetSolutions
### Statement of Owner's Equity
### For the Month Ended November 30, 2005

| | | | |
|---|---:|---:|---:|
| Chris Clark, capital, November 1, 2005 | | | $ 0 |
| Investment on November 1, 2005 | $25 0 0 0 00 | | |
| Net income for November | 3 0 5 0 00 | | |
| | $28 0 5 0 00 | | |
| Less withdrawals | 2 0 0 0 00 | | |
| Increase in owner's equity | | 26 0 5 0 00 | |
| Chris Clark, capital, November 30, 2005 | | $26 0 5 0 00 | |

### NetSolutions
### Balance Sheet
### November 30, 2005

| Assets | | Liabilities | |
|---|---:|---|---:|
| Cash | $ 5 9 0 0 00 | Accounts payable | $ 4 0 0 00 |
| Supplies | 5 5 0 00 | **Owner's Equity** | |
| Land | 20 0 0 0 00 | Chris Clark, capital | 26 0 5 0 00 |
| | | Total liabilities and | |
| Total assets | $26 4 5 0 00 | owner's equity | $26 4 5 0 00 |

### NetSolutions
### Statement of Cash Flows
### For the Month Ended November 30, 2005

| | | | |
|---|---:|---:|---:|
| Cash flows from operating activities: | | | |
| Cash received from customers | $ 7 5 0 0 00 | | |
| Deduct cash payments for expenses and | | | |
| payments to creditors | 4 6 0 0 00 | | |
| Net cash flow from operating activities | | | $ 2 9 0 0 00 |
| Cash flows from investing activities: | | | |
| Cash payments for acquisition of land | | | |
| Cash flows from financing activities: | | | (20 0 0 0 00) |
| Cash received as owner's investment | $25 0 0 0 00 | | |
| Deduct cash withdrawal by owner | 2 0 0 0 00 | | |
| Net cash flow from financing activities | | | 23 0 0 0 00 |
| Net cash flow and November 30, 2005 cash balance | | | $ 5 9 0 0 00 |

Financial statements are used to evaluate the current financial condition of a business and to predict its future operating results and cash flows. For example, bank loan officers use a business's financial statements in deciding whether to grant a loan to the business. Once the loan is granted, the borrower may be required to maintain a certain level of assets in excess of liabilities. The business's financial statements are used to monitor this level.

Three types of transactions affected owner's equity for NetSolutions during November: (1) the original investment of $25,000, (2) the revenue and expenses that resulted in net income of $3,050 for the month, and (3) a withdrawal of $2,000 by the owner. This information is summarized in the statement of owner's equity in Exhibit 6.

# Balance Sheet

The balance sheet in Exhibit 6 reports the amounts of NetSolutions' assets, liabilities, and owner's equity at the end of November. These amounts are taken from the last line of the summary of transactions presented earlier. The form of balance sheet shown in Exhibit 6 is called the ***account form*** because it resembles the basic format of the accounting equation, with assets on the left side and the liabilities and owner's equity sections on the right side. We illustrate an alternative form of balance sheet called the ***report form*** in a later chapter. It presents the liabilities and owner's equity sections below the assets section.

The assets section of the balance sheet normally presents assets in the order that they will be converted into cash or used in operations. Cash is presented first, followed by receivables, supplies, prepaid insurance, and other assets. The assets of a more permanent nature are shown next, such as land, buildings, and equipment.

In the liabilities section of the balance sheet in Exhibit 6, accounts payable is the only liability. When there are two or more categories of liabilities, each should be listed and the total amount of liabilities presented as follows.

| Liabilities | | |
|---|---|---|
| Accounts payable | $12,900 | |
| Wages payable | 2,570 | |
| Total liabilities | | $15,470 |

# Statement of Cash Flows

The statement of cash flows consists of three sections, as we see in Exhibit 6: (1) operating activities, (2) investing activities, and (3) financing activities. Each of these sections is briefly described below.

## Cash Flows from Operating Activities

This section reports a summary of cash receipts and cash payments from operations. The net cash flow from operating activities ($2,900 in Exhibit 6) will normally differ from the amount of net income for the period ($3,050 in Exhibit 6). This difference occurs because revenues and expenses may not be recorded at the same time that cash is received from customers or paid to creditors.

## Cash Flows from Investing Activities

This section reports the cash transactions for the acquisition and sale of relatively permanent assets.

## Cash Flows from Financing Activities

This section reports the cash transactions related to cash investments by the owner, borrowings, and cash withdrawals by the owner.

Preparing the statement of cash flows requires an understanding of concepts that we have not discussed in this chapter. Therefore, we will illustrate the preparation of the statement of cash flows in a later chapter.

# Financial Analysis and Interpretation

As we discussed earlier in this chapter, financial statements are useful to bankers, creditors, owners, and other stakeholders in analyzing and interpreting the financial performance and condition of a business. Throughout this text, we will discuss various tools that are often used in practice to analyze and interpret the financial performance and condition of a business. The first such tool we will introduce is especially useful in analyzing the ability of a business to pay its creditors.

The relationship between liabilities and owner's equity, expressed as a ratio, is calculated as follows:

$$\text{Ratio of liabilities to owner's equity} = \frac{\text{Total liabilities}}{\text{Total owner's equity (or Total stockholders' equity)}}$$

To illustrate, NetSolutions' ratio of liabilities to owner's equity at the end of November is 0.015, as calculated below.

$$\text{Ratio of liabilities to owner's equity} = \frac{\$400}{\$26,050} = 0.015$$

Corporations normally refer to total owner's equity as total stockholders' equity. Thus, you should substitute total stockholders' equity for total owner's equity when computing this ratio for a corporation.

The rights of creditors to a business's assets take precedence over the rights of the owners or stockholders. Thus, the lower the ratio of liabilities to owner's equity, the better able the business is to withstand poor business conditions and still fully meet its obligations to creditors.

To illustrate, a ratio of 1 indicates that the liabilities and owner's equity are equal. In other words, if the business suffers a loss equal to the total liabilities, the amount of total assets available to creditors will not drop below their claims on the assets. If this were to happen, the creditors could collect their claims and the owner would be left with nothing.

## SPOTLIGHT ON STRATEGY

### IT'S ALL IN THE NAME

Intel develops and produces microprocessors for use in electronic equipment, including personal computers and organizers. Beginning with the 8086 processor and continuing with the 286, 386, and 486 processors, Intel's processors were widely used in personal computers during the 1980s and 1990s. Intel's competitors, however, also developed and sold 386 and 486 processors. In doing so, its competitors were able to erode Intel's market share. In responding, Intel named its next microprocessor the "Pentium," rather than the 586, and registered "Pentium" as a trademark. By doing so, Intel prevented its competitors from selling their products as "Pentiums." Thus, Intel developed a "differentiated" brand name that its competitors were unable to duplicate. Intel's newest processor is called the "Pentium M."

# Key Points

## 1 Describe the nature of a business.

A business is an organization in which basic resources (inputs), such as materials and labor, are assembled and processed to provide goods or services (outputs) to customers. The objective of most businesses is to maximize profits.

There are three different types of businesses that are operated for profit: manufacturing, merchandising, and service businesses. A business is normally organized in one of the following forms: proprietorship, partnership, corporation, or limited liability corporation. A business stakeholder is a person or entity (such as an owner, manager, employee, customer, creditor, or the government) who has an interest in the economic performance of the business.

## 2 Describe the role of accounting in business.

Accounting is an information system that provides reports to stakeholders about the economic activities and condition of a business. Accounting is the "language of business."

## 3 Describe the importance of business ethics and the basic principles of proper ethical conduct.

Ethics are moral principles that guide the conduct of individuals. Proper ethical conduct implies a behavior that considers the impact of one's actions on society and others. Sound ethical principles include (1) avoiding small ethical lapses, (2) focusing on your long-term reputation, and (3) being willing to suffer adverse personal consequences for holding to an ethical position.

## 4 Describe the profession of accounting.

Accountants are engaged in either private accounting or public accounting. The two most common specialized fields of accounting are financial accounting and managerial accounting. Other fields include cost accounting, environmental accounting, tax accounting, accounting systems, international accounting, not-for-profit accounting, and social accounting.

## 5 Summarize the development of accounting principles and relate them to practice.

Financial accountants follow generally accepted accounting principles (GAAP) in preparing reports so that stakeholders can compare one company to another. Accounting principles and concepts develop from research, accepted accounting practices, and pronouncements of authoritative bodies. Currently, the Financial Accounting Standards Board (FASB) is the authoritative body having the primary responsibility for developing accounting principles.

The business entity concept views the business as an entity separate from its owners, creditors, or other stakeholders. The business entity limits the economic data in the accounting system to that related directly to the activities of the business. The cost concept requires that properties and services bought by a business be recorded in terms of actual cost. The objectivity concept requires that the accounting records and reports be based upon objective evidence. The unit of measure concept requires that economic data be recorded in dollars.

## 6 State the accounting equation and define each element of the equation.

The resources owned by a business and the rights or claims to these resources may be stated in the form of an equation, as follows:

Assets = Liabilities + Owner's Equity

## 7 Explain how business transactions can be stated in terms of the resulting changes in the basic elements of the accounting equation.

All business transactions can be stated in terms of the change in one or more of the three elements of the accounting equation. That is, the effect of every transaction can be stated in terms of increases or decreases in one or more of these elements, while maintaining the equality between the two sides of the equation.

## 8 Describe the financial statements of a proprietorship and explain how they interrelate.

The principal financial statements of a proprietorship are the income statement, the statement of owner's equity, the balance sheet, and the statement of cash flows. The income statement reports a period's net income or net loss, which also appears on the statement of owner's equity. The ending owner's capital reported on the statement of owner's equity is also reported on the balance sheet. The ending cash balance is reported on the balance sheet and the statement of cash flows.

## 9 Use the ratio of liabilities to owner's equity to analyze the ability of a business to withstand poor business conditions.

The ratio of liabilities to owner's equity is useful in analyzing the ability of a business to pay its creditors. The lower the ratio, the better able the business is to withstand poor business conditions and still fully meet its obligations to creditors.

# Key Terms

account form (21)
account payable (15)
account receivable (16)
accounting (8)
accounting equation (13)
assets (13)
balance sheet (19)
business (2)
business entity concept (13)
business stakeholder (6)
business strategy (4)
business transaction (14)
Certified Public Accountant (CPA) (11)
combination strategy (5)
corporation (3)

differentiation strategy (4)
ethics (9)
expenses (16)
financial accounting (12)
Financial Accounting Standards Board (FASB) (12)
financial statements (19)
generally accepted accounting principles (GAAP) (12)
income statement (19)
liabilities (13)
limited liability corporation (4)
low-cost strategy (4)
managerial accounting (12)
manufacturing business (2)
matching concept (19)

merchandising business (3)
net income (19)
net loss (19)
owner's equity (13)
partnership (3)
prepaid expenses (15)
private accounting (10)
proprietorship (3)
public accounting (10)
report form (21)
revenue (16)
service business (3)
statement of cash flows (19)
statement of owner's equity (19)
unit of measure concept (13)
value chain (6)

# Illustrative Problem

Cecil Jameson, Attorney-at-Law, is a proprietorship owned and operated by Cecil Jameson. On July 1, 2005, Cecil Jameson, Attorney-at-Law, has the following assets and liabilities: cash, $1,000; accounts receivable, $3,200; supplies, $850; land, $10,000; accounts payable, $1,530. Office space and office equipment are currently being rented, pending the construction of an office complex on land purchased last year. Business transactions during July are summarized as follows:

a. Received cash from clients for services, $3,928.
b. Paid creditors on account, $1,055.
c. Received cash from Cecil Jameson as an additional investment, $3,700.
d. Paid office rent for the month, $1,200.
e. Charged clients for legal services on account, $2,025.
f. Purchased office supplies on account, $245.
g. Received cash from clients on account, $3,000.
h. Received invoice for paralegal services from Legal Aid Inc. for July (to be paid on August 10), $1,635.
i. Paid the following: wages expense, $850; answering service expense, $250; utilities expense, $325; and miscellaneous expense, $75.
j. Determined that the cost of office supplies on hand was $980; therefore, the cost of supplies used during the month was $115.
k. Jameson withdrew $1,000 in cash from the business for personal use.

### Instructions

1. Determine the amount of owner's equity (Cecil Jameson's capital) as of July 1, 2005.
2. State the assets, liabilities, and owner's equity as of July 1 in equation form similar to that shown in this chapter. In tabular form below the equation, indicate the increases and decreases resulting from each transaction and the new balances after each transaction. Explain the nature of each increase and decrease in owner's equity by an appropriate notation at the right of the amount.

3. Prepare an income statement for July, a statement of owner's equity for July, and a balance sheet as of July 31, 2005.

## Solution

**1.** Assets − Liabilities = Owner's Equity (Cecil Jameson, capital)

$15,050 − $1,530 = Owner's Equity (Cecil Jameson, capital)

$13,520 = Owner's Equity (Cecil Jameson, capital)

**2.**

| | Cash | + Receivable | + Supplies | + Land | = Payable | + Cecil Jameson, Capital | |
|---|---|---|---|---|---|---|---|
| | | Accounts | | | Accounts | | |
| Bal. | 1,000 | 3,200 | 850 | 10,000 | 1,530 | 13,520 | |
| a. | +3,928 | | | | | + 3,928 | Fees earned |
| Bal. | 4,928 | 3,200 | 850 | 10,000 | 1,530 | 17,448 | |
| b. | −1,055 | | | | −1,055 | | |
| Bal. | 3,873 | 3,200 | 850 | 10,000 | 475 | 17,448 | |
| c. | +3,700 | | | | | + 3,700 | Investment |
| Bal. | 7,573 | 3,200 | 850 | 10,000 | 475 | 21,148 | |
| d. | −1,200 | | | | | − 1,200 | Rent expense |
| Bal. | 6,373 | 3,200 | 850 | 10,000 | 475 | 19,948 | |
| e. | | +2,025 | | | | + 2,025 | Fees earned |
| Bal. | 6,373 | 5,225 | 850 | 10,000 | 475 | 21,973 | |
| f. | | | + 245 | | + 245 | | |
| Bal. | 6,373 | 5,225 | 1,095 | 10,000 | 720 | 21,973 | |
| g. | +3,000 | −3,000 | | | | | |
| Bal. | 9,373 | 2,225 | 1,095 | 10,000 | 720 | 21,973 | |
| h. | | | | | +1,635 | − 1,635 | Paralegal exp. |
| Bal. | 9,373 | 2,225 | 1,095 | 10,000 | 2,355 | 20,338 | |
| i. | −1,500 | | | | | − 850 | Wages exp. |
| | | | | | | − 250 | Answ. svc. exp. |
| | | | | | | − 325 | Utilities exp. |
| | | | | | | − 75 | Misc. exp. |
| Bal. | 7,873 | 2,225 | 1,095 | 10,000 | 2,355 | 18,838 | |
| j. | | | − 115 | | | − 115 | Supplies exp. |
| Bal. | 7,873 | 2,225 | 980 | 10,000 | 2,355 | 18,723 | |
| k. | −1,000 | | | | | − 1,000 | Withdrawal |
| | 6,873 | 2,225 | 980 | 10,000 | 2,355 | 17,723 | |

Column group headers: **Assets** = **Liabilities** + **Owner's Equity**

**3.**

### Cecil Jameson, Attorney-at-Law
### Income Statement
### For the Month Ended July 31, 2005

| | | |
|---|---:|---:|
| Fees earned | | $5 9 5 3 00 |
| Operating expenses: | | |
| Paralegal expense | $1 6 3 5 00 | |
| Rent expense | 1 2 0 0 00 | |
| Wages expense | 8 5 0 00 | |
| Utilities expense | 3 2 5 00 | |
| Answering service expense | 2 5 0 00 | |
| Supplies expense | 1 1 5 00 | |
| Miscellaneous expense | 7 5 00 | |
| Total operating expenses | | 4 4 5 0 00 |
| Net income | | $1 5 0 3 00 |

*(continued)*

**Cecil Jameson, Attorney-at-Law**
**Statement of Owner's Equity**
**For the Month Ended July 31, 2005**

| | | |
|---|---|---|
| Cecil Jameson, capital, July 1, 2005 | | $13 5 2 0 00 |
| Additional investment by owner | $3 7 0 0 00 | |
| Net income for the month | 1 5 0 3 00 | |
| | $5 2 0 3 00 | |
| Less withdrawals | 1 0 0 0 00 | |
| Increase in owner's equity | | 4 2 0 3 00 |
| Cecil Jameson, capital, July 31, 2005 | | $17 7 2 3 00 |

**Cecil Jameson, Attorney-at-Law**
**Balance Sheet**
**July 31, 2005**

| Assets | | Liabilities | |
|---|---|---|---|
| Cash | $ 6 8 7 3 00 | Accounts payable | $ 2 3 5 5 00 |
| Accounts receivable | 2 2 2 5 00 | **Owner's Equity** | |
| Supplies | 9 8 0 00 | Cecil Jameson, capital | 17 7 2 3 00 |
| Land | 10 0 0 0 00 | Total liabilities and | |
| Total assets | $20 0 7 8 00 | owner's equity | $20 0 7 8 00 |

# Self-Examination Questions (Answers at End of Chapter)

1. A profit-making business operating as a separate legal entity and in which ownership is divided into shares of stock is known as a:
   A. proprietorship.   C. partnership.
   B. service business.   D. corporation.

2. The resources owned by a business are called:
   A. assets.
   B. liabilities.
   C. the accounting equation.
   D. owner's equity.

3. A listing of a business entity's assets, liabilities, and owner's equity as of a specific date is:
   A. a balance sheet.
   B. an income statement.
   C. a statement of owner's equity.
   D. a statement of cash flows.

4. If total assets increased $20,000 during a period and total liabilities increased $12,000 during the same period, the amount and direction (increase or decrease) of the change in owner's equity for that period is:
   A. a $32,000 increase.   C. an $8,000 increase.
   B. a $32,000 decrease.   D. an $8,000 decrease.

5. If revenue was $45,000, expenses were $37,500, and the owner's withdrawals were $10,000, the amount of net income or net loss would be:
   A. $45,000 net income.   C. $37,500 net loss.
   B. $7,500 net income.   D. $2,500 net loss.

# Class Discussion Questions

1. What is the objective of most businesses?
2. What is the difference between a manufacturing business and a service business? Is a restaurant a manufacturing business, a service business, or both?
3. Why are most large companies like **Microsoft, Pepsi, Caterpillar**, and **AutoZone** organized as corporations?
4. Both **KIA** and **Porche** produce and sell automobiles. Describe and contrast the business strategies of KIA and Porche.
5. Assume that a friend of yours operates a family-owned pharmacy. A **Super Wal-Mart** is scheduled to open in the next several months that will also offer pharmacy services. What business strategy would your friend use to compete with the Super Wal-Mart pharmacy?
6. How does **eBay** offer value to its customers?
7. Who are normally included as the stakeholders of a business?
8. What is the role of accounting in business?
9. Deana Moran is the owner of First Delivery Service. Recently, Deana paid interest of $3,600 on a personal loan of $60,000 that she used to begin the business. Should First Delivery Service record the interest payment? Explain.
10. On July 10, Elrod Repair Service extended an offer of $100,000 for land that had been priced for sale at $120,000. On July 25, Elrod Repair Service accepted the seller's counteroffer of $112,000. Describe how Elrod Repair Service should record the land.
11. a. Land with an assessed value of $300,000 for property tax purposes is acquired by a business for $500,000. Seven years later, the plot of land has an assessed value of $400,000 and the business receives an offer of $600,000 for it. Should the monetary amount assigned to the land in the business records now be increased?
    b. Assuming that the land acquired in (a) was sold for $600,000, how would the various elements of the accounting equation be affected?
12. Describe the difference between an account receivable and an account payable.
13. A business had revenues of $280,000 and operating expenses of $315,000. Did the business (a) incur a net loss or (b) realize net income?
14. A business had revenues of $750,000 and operating expenses of $670,000. Did the business (a) incur a net loss or (b) realize net income?
15. What particular item of financial or operating data appears on both the income statement and the statement of owner's equity? What item appears on both the balance sheet and the statement of owner's equity? What item appears on both the balance sheet and statement of cash flows?

## PREPARE FOR TOMORROW TODAY!

Thank you for following in the tradition of 11 million students who have achieved outstanding results using this very text. To help you even further, we have developed incredible resources to make learning accounting even easier. Shop online today by visiting

### http://warren.swlearning.com

 **Answer:** McDonald's

**WebTutor Advantage on WebCT or Blackboard with Personal Trainer 3.0**

Get the most robust interactive study materials available on the Web! Includes:

- Automatic and immediate feedback from Pre-Tests, Achievement Tests, Multiple-Choice and True-False Quizzes, and Quiz Bowl.
- Exercise Demos and Illustrative Problems in Flash presentations that review and reinforce what you've learned.
- Video cases that cover key concepts in the context of a real company.
- A Flash introduction with audio for each chapter.
- E-lectures that provide Flash lecture presentations with audio to help you review one or two key concepts in each chapter.
- Crossword Puzzles to test your knowledge of the glossary.

**Xtreme!**
0-324-20436-1

This hybrid CD-ROM and Internet-based product provides you with the same media-rich content from WebTutor Advantage, but without the WebCT or Blackboard platforms.

**Xtra!**
0-324-20379-9

This CD-ROM provides lecture replacement resources and access to interactive quizzes to test your understanding of the content of the text.

**Personal Trainer**
0-324-20372-1

This product helps you complete the end-of-chapter exercises and problems from the text using:

- Concept warm-ups.
- Helpful hints.
- Immediate feedback.
- A personal gradebook.

**P.A.S.S. Software (formerly General Ledger Software)**
0-324-20413-2

- This software package teaches you the basics of a computerized accounting system in an easy-to-use environment.
- You will get hints and tips for completing end-of-chapter problems.
- You will get immediate feedback to determine if you have done the problems correctly.

**Study Guide**
Chapters 1-17    0-324-20373-X
Chapters 12-25    0-324-20374-8

- This guide will give you quiz and test hints.
- You can practice chapter concepts, learn through numerous multiple choice, fill-in-the-blank, true-false questions, and exercises, and check your answers against the provided solutions.

**Working Papers for Exercises and Problems**
Chapters 1-17    0-324-20375-6
Chapters 12-25    0-324-20376-4

This supplement contains forms that help you organize your solutions.

**Working Papers Plus for Selected Exercises and Problems**
Chapters 1-17    0-324-23077-2
Chapters 12-25    0-324-20378-0

This supplement includes selected exercises and problems from the text, along with the forms for your use in solving them.

# Exercises

**EXERCISE 1-1**
*Types of businesses*
**Objective 1**

Indicate whether each of the following companies is primarily a service, merchandise, or manufacturing business. If you are unfamiliar with the company, you may use the Internet to locate the company's home page or use the finance Web site of **Yahoo.com.**

1. **Ford Motor**
2. **Citigroup**
3. **Sears Roebuck**
4. **AT&T**
5. **H&R Block Inc.**
6. **Boeing**
7. **First Union Corporation**
8. **Alcoa**
9. **CVS**
10. **Caterpillar**
11. **FedEx**
12. **Dow Chemical**
13. **Gap**
14. **Hilton Hotels**
15. **Procter & Gamble**

**EXERCISE 1-2**
*Business strategy*
**Objective 1**

Identify the primary business strategy of each of the following companies as (a) a low-cost strategy, (b) a differentiation strategy, or (c) a combination strategy. If you are unfamiliar with the company, you may use the Internet to locate the company's home page or use the finance Web site of **Yahoo.com.**

1. **Southwest Airlines**
2. **Home Depot**
3. **BMW**
4. **Coca-Cola**
5. **Target**
6. **Goldman Sachs Group**
7. **Sara Lee**
8. **Delta Air Lines**
9. **Circuit City Stores**
10. **Maytag**
11. **Office Depot**
12. **Nike**
13. **Charles Schwab**
14. **Dollar General**
15. **General Motors**

**EXERCISE 1-3**
*Professional ethics*
**Objective 3**

ETHICS

A fertilizer manufacturing company wants to relocate to Collier County. A 13-year-old report from a fired researcher at the company says the company's product is releasing toxic by-products. The company has suppressed that report. A second report commissioned by the company shows there is no problem with the fertilizer.

➤ Should the company's chief executive officer reveal the context of the unfavorable report in discussions with Collier County representatives? Discuss.

**EXERCISE 1-4**
*Business entity concept*
**Objective 5**

Bechler Sports sells hunting and fishing equipment and provides guided hunting and fishing trips. Bechler Sports is owned and operated by Lefty Wisman, a well-known sports enthusiast and hunter. Lefty's wife, Betsy, owns and operates Eagle Boutique, a women's clothing store. Lefty and Betsy have established a trust fund to finance their children's college education. The trust fund is maintained by First Montana Bank in the name of the children, Jeff and Steph.

For each of the following transactions, identify which of the entities listed should record the transaction in its records.

| Entities | |
| --- | --- |
| B | Bechler Sports |
| F | First Montana Bank |
| E | Eagle Boutique |
| X | None of the above |

1. Lefty paid a local doctor for his annual physical, which was required by the workmen's compensation insurance policy carried by Bechler Sports.

*(continued)*

2. Lefty received a cash advance from customers for a guided hunting trip.
3. Betsy purchased two dozen spring dresses from a Billings (MT) designer for a special spring sale.
4. Betsy deposited a $2,000 personal check in the trust fund at First Montana Bank.
5. Lefty paid for an advertisement in a hunters' magazine.
6. Betsy purchased mutual fund shares as an investment for the children's trust.
7. Lefty paid for dinner and a movie to celebrate their twentieth wedding anniversary.
8. Betsy donated several dresses from inventory for a local charity auction for the benefit of a women's abuse shelter.
9. Betsy paid her dues to the YWCA.
10. Lefty paid a breeder's fee for an English springer spaniel to be used as a hunting guide dog.

**EXERCISE 1-5**
*Accounting equation*
**Objective 6**

**REAL WORLD**

✓ *Coca-Cola, $11,800*

The total assets and total liabilities of **Coca-Cola** and **PepsiCo** are shown below.

|  | Coca-Cola (in millions) | PepsiCo (in millions) |
|---|---|---|
| Assets | $24,501 | $23,474 |
| Liabilities | 12,701 | 14,183 |

Determine the owners' equity of each company.

**EXERCISE 1-6**
*Accounting equation*
**Objective 6**

✓ *Toys "R" Us, $4,030*

The total assets and total liabilities of **Toys "R" Us Inc.** and **Estée Lauder Companies Inc.** are shown below.

|  | Toys "R" Us (in millions) | Estée Lauder Companies (in millions) |
|---|---|---|
| Assets | $9,397 | $3,417 |
| Liabilities | 5,367 | 1,955 |

Determine the owners' equity of each company.

**EXERCISE 1-7**
*Accounting equation*
**Objective 6**

✓ *a. $96,500*

Determine the missing amount for each of the following:

| | Assets | = Liabilities | + Owner's Equity |
|---|---|---|---|
| a. | X | = $25,000 + | $71,500 |
| b. | $82,750 | = X + | 15,000 |
| c. | 37,000 | = 17,500 + | X |

**EXERCISE 1-8**
*Accounting equation*
**Objectives 6, 8**

✓ *b. $310,000*

Chris Lund is the owner and operator of Saluki, a motivational consulting business. At the end of its accounting period, December 31, 2005, Saluki has assets of $475,000 and liabilities of $200,000. Using the accounting equation and considering each case independently, determine the following amounts:

a. Chris Lund, capital, as of December 31, 2005.
b. Chris Lund, capital, as of December 31, 2006, assuming that assets increased by $75,000 and liabilities increased by $40,000 during 2006.
c. Chris Lund, capital, as of December 31, 2006, assuming that assets decreased by $15,000 and liabilities increased by $27,000 during 2006.
d. Chris Lund, capital, as of December 31, 2006, assuming that assets increased by $125,000 and liabilities decreased by $65,000 during 2006.
e. Net income (or net loss) during 2006, assuming that as of December 31, 2006, assets were $425,000, liabilities were $105,000, and there were no additional investments or withdrawals.

**EXERCISE 1-9**
*Asset, liability, owner's equity items*

**Objective 7**

Indicate whether each of the following is identified with (1) an asset, (2) a liability, or (3) owner's equity:

a. wages expense

b. accounts payable

c. cash

d. land

e. fees earned

f. supplies

**EXERCISE 1-10**
*Effect of transactions on accounting equation*

**Objective 7**

Describe how the following business transactions affect the three elements of the accounting equation.

a. Received cash for services performed.

b. Invested cash in business.

c. Paid for utilities used in the business.

d. Purchased supplies on account.

e. Purchased supplies for cash.

**EXERCISE 1-11**
*Effect of transactions on accounting equation*

**Objective 7**

✓ *(a)(1) increase $80,000*

a. A vacant lot acquired for $50,000 is sold for $130,000 in cash. What is the effect of the sale on the total amount of the seller's (1) assets, (2) liabilities, and (3) owner's equity?

b. Assume that the seller owes $30,000 on a loan for the land. After receiving the $130,000 cash in (a), the seller pays the $30,000 owed. What is the effect of the payment on the total amount of the seller's (1) assets, (2) liabilities, and (3) owner's equity?

**EXERCISE 1-12**
*Effect of transactions on owner's equity*

**Objective 7**

Indicate whether each of the following types of transactions will (a) increase owner's equity or (b) decrease owner's equity:

1. revenues

2. expenses

3. owner's investments

4. owner's withdrawals

**EXERCISE 1-13**
*Transactions*

**Objective 7**

The following selected transactions were completed by Salvo Delivery Service during February:

1. Received cash from owner as additional investment, $35,000.

2. Received cash for providing delivery services, $15,000.

3. Paid creditors on account, $1,800.

4. Billed customers for delivery services on account, $11,250.

5. Paid advertising expense, $750.

6. Purchased supplies for cash, $800.

7. Paid rent for February, $2,000.

8. Received cash from customers on account, $6,740.

9. Determined that the cost of supplies on hand was $135; therefore, $665 of supplies had been used during the month.

10. Paid cash to owner for personal use, $1,000.

Indicate the effect of each transaction on the accounting equation by listing the numbers identifying the transactions, (1) through (10), in a vertical column, and inserting at the right of each number the appropriate letter from the following list:

a. Increase in an asset, decrease in another asset.

b. Increase in an asset, increase in a liability.

c. Increase in an asset, increase in owner's equity.

d. Decrease in an asset, decrease in a liability.

e. Decrease in an asset, decrease in owner's equity.

**EXERCISE 1-14**
*Nature of transactions*

**Objective 7**

✓ *d. $7,600*

Mike Renner operates his own catering service. Summary financial data for March are presented in equation form as follows. Each line designated by a number indicates the effect of a transaction on the equation. Each increase and decrease in owner's equity, except transaction (5), affects net income.

| | Cash | + Supplies + | Land | = Liabilities + | Owner's Equity |
|---|---|---|---|---|---|
| Bal. | 18,000 | 1,500 | 54,000 | 15,000 | 58,500 |
| 1. | +25,000 | | | | +25,000 |
| 2. | −10,000 | | +10,000 | | |
| 3. | −16,000 | | | | −16,000 |
| 4. | | + 800 | | + 800 | |
| 5. | − 2,000 | | | | − 2,000 |
| 6. | −10,600 | | | −10,600 | |
| 7. | | −1,400 | | | − 1,400 |
| Bal. | 4,400 | 900 | 64,000 | 5,200 | 64,100 |

a. Describe each transaction.
b. What is the amount of net decrease in cash during the month?
c. What is the amount of net increase in owner's equity during the month?
d. What is the amount of the net income for the month?
e. How much of the net income for the month was retained in the business?

**EXERCISE 1-15**
*Net income and owner's withdrawals*
**Objective 8**

The income statement of a proprietorship for the month of October indicates a net income of $158,250. During the same period, the owner withdrew $180,000 in cash from the business for personal use.

Would it be correct to say that the business incurred a net loss of $21,750 during the month? Discuss.

**EXERCISE 1-16**
*Net income and owner's equity for four businesses*
**Objective 8**

✓ *Company O: Net loss, ($50,000)*

Four different proprietorships, M, N, O, and P, show the same balance sheet data at the beginning and end of a year. These data, exclusive of the amount of owner's equity, are summarized as follows:

| | Total Assets | Total Liabilities |
|---|---|---|
| Beginning of the year | $750,000 | $300,000 |
| End of the year | $1,200,000 | $650,000 |

On the basis of the above data and the following additional information for the year, determine the net income (or loss) of each company for the year. (*Hint:* First determine the amount of increase or decrease in owner's equity during the year.)

**Company M:** The owner had made no additional investments in the business and had made no withdrawals from the business.
**Company N:** The owner had made no additional investments in the business but had withdrawn $60,000.
**Company O:** The owner had made an additional investment of $150,000 but had made no withdrawals.
**Company P:** The owner had made an additional investment of $150,000 and had withdrawn $60,000.

**EXERCISE 1-17**
*Balance sheet items*
**Objective 8**

From the following list of selected items taken from the records of Ishmael Appliance Service as of a specific date, identify those that would appear on the balance sheet:

1. Supplies
2. Wages Expense
3. Cash
4. Land
5. Utilities Expense
6. Fees Earned
7. Supplies Expense
8. Accounts Payable
9. Melinda Elder, Capital
10. Wages Payable

**EXERCISE 1-18**
*Income statement items*
**Objective 8**

Based on the data presented in Exercise 1-17, identify those items that would appear on the income statement.

**EXERCISE 1-19**
*Statement of owner's equity*
**Objective 8**

SPREADSHEET

✓ *Leo Perkins, capital April 30, 2006: $358,200*

Financial information related to Madras Company, a proprietorship, for the month ended April 30, 2006, is as follows:

| | |
|---|---|
| Net income for April | $ 73,000 |
| Leo Perkins's withdrawals during April | 12,000 |
| Leo Perkins, capital, April 1, 2006 | 297,200 |

Prepare a statement of owner's equity for the month ended April 30, 2006.

**EXERCISE 1-20**
*Income statement*
**Objective 8**

SPREADSHEET

✓ *Net income: $89,320*

Hercules Services was organized on November 1, 2006. A summary of the revenue and expense transactions for November follows:

| | |
|---|---|
| Fees earned | $232,120 |
| Wages expense | 100,100 |
| Miscellaneous expense | 3,150 |
| Rent expense | 35,000 |
| Supplies expense | 4,550 |

Prepare an income statement for the month ended November 30.

**EXERCISE 1-21**
*Missing amounts from balance sheet and income statement data*
**Objective 8**

✓ *(a) $156,300*

One item is omitted in each of the following summaries of balance sheet and income statement data for four different proprietorships, A, B, C, and D.

| | A | B | C | D |
|---|---|---|---|---|
| Beginning of the year: | | | | |
| Assets | $720,000 | $125,000 | $160,000 | (d) |
| Liabilities | 432,000 | 65,000 | 121,600 | $150,000 |
| End of the year: | | | | |
| Assets | 894,000 | 175,000 | 144,000 | 310,000 |
| Liabilities | 390,000 | 55,000 | 128,000 | 170,000 |
| During the year: | | | | |
| Additional investment in the business | (a) | 25,000 | 16,000 | 50,000 |
| Withdrawals from the business | 48,000 | 8,000 | (c) | 75,000 |
| Revenue | 237,300 | (b) | 184,000 | 140,000 |
| Expenses | 129,600 | 32,000 | 196,000 | 160,000 |

Determine the missing amounts, identifying them by letter. (*Hint:* First determine the amount of increase or decrease in owner's equity during the year.)

**EXERCISE 1-22**
*Balance sheets, net income*
**Objective 8**

SPREADSHEET

✓ *b. $36,340*

Financial information related to the proprietorship of Derby Interiors for October and November 2006 is as follows:

| | October 31, 2006 | November 30, 2006 |
|---|---|---|
| Accounts payable | $12,320 | $13,280 |
| Accounts receivable | 27,200 | 31,300 |
| Mary Lou Reily, capital | ? | ? |
| Cash | 48,000 | 81,600 |
| Supplies | 2,400 | 2,000 |

a. Prepare balance sheets for Derby Interiors as of October 31 and as of November 30, 2006.
b. Determine the amount of net income for November, assuming that the owner made no additional investments or withdrawals during the month.
c. Determine the amount of net income for November, assuming that the owner made no additional investments but withdrew $10,000 during the month.

**EXERCISE 1-23**
*Financial statements*
Objective 8

REAL WORLD

Each of the following items is shown in the financial statements of **Exxon Mobil Corporation**. Identify the financial statement (balance sheet or income statement) in which each item would appear.

a. Operating expenses
b. Crude oil inventory
c. Income taxes payable
d. Sales
e. Investments
f. Marketable securities
g. Exploration expenses
h. Notes and loans payable

i. Cash equivalents
j. Long-term debt
k. Selling expenses
l. Notes receivable
m. Equipment
n. Accounts payable
o. Prepaid taxes

**EXERCISE 1-24**
*Statement of cash flows*
Objective 8

Indicate whether each of the following activities would be reported on the statement of cash flows as (a) an operating activity, (b) an investing activity, or (c) a financing activity:

1. Cash paid for land
2. Cash received from fees earned
3. Cash received as owner's investment
4. Cash paid for expenses

**EXERCISE 1-25**
*Financial statements*
Objective 8

WHAT'S WRONG
WITH THIS?

✓ *Correct Amount of Total Assets is $19,600*

Caddis Realty, organized June 1, 2006, is owned and operated by Jerry Maris. How many errors can you find in the following financial statements for Caddis Realty, prepared after its second month of operations?

**Caddis Realty**
**Income Statement**
**July 31, 2006**

| | | |
|---|---:|---:|
| Sales commissions | | $51,900 |
| Operating expenses: | | |
| Office salaries expense | $32,400 | |
| Rent expense | 11,000 | |
| Automobile expense | 2,500 | |
| Miscellaneous expense | 800 | |
| Supplies expense | 300 | |
| Total operating expenses | | 47,000 |
| Net income | | $14,900 |

**Jerry Maris**
**Statement of Owner's Equity**
**July 31, 2005**

| | |
|---|---:|
| Jerry Maris, capital, July 1, 2006 | $10,400 |
| Less withdrawals during July | 2,000 |
| | $ 8,400 |
| Additional investment during July | 2,500 |
| | $10,900 |
| Net income for the month | 14,900 |
| Jerry Maris, capital, July 31, 2006 | $25,800 |

**Balance Sheet**
**For the Month Ended July 31, 2006**

| Assets | | Liabilities | |
|---|---:|---|---:|
| Cash | $3,300 | Accounts receivable | $14,300 |
| Accounts payable | 3,800 | Supplies | 2,000 |
| | | **Owner's Equity** | |
| | | Jerry Maris, capital | 25,800 |
| Total assets | $7,100 | Total liabilities and owner's equity | $42,100 |

**EXERCISE 1-26**
*Ratio of liabilities to stockholders' equity*

Objective 9

REAL WORLD

The **Home Depot, Inc.**, is the world's largest home improvement retailer and one of the largest retailers in the United States based on net sales volume. The Home Depot operates over 1,100 Home Depot® stores that sell a wide assortment of building materials and home improvement and lawn and garden products. The Home Depot also operates over 25 EXPO Design Center stores that offer interior design products, such as kitchen and bathroom cabinetry, tiles, flooring, and lighting fixtures, and installation services.

For the years ending February 2, 2003, and February 3, 2002, The Home Depot reported the following balance sheet data (in millions):

|  | 2003 | 2002 |
|---|---|---|
| Total assets | $30,011 | $26,394 |
| Total stockholders' equity | 19,802 | 18,082 |

a. Determine the total liabilities as of February 2, 2003, and February 3, 2002.
b. Determine the ratio of liabilities to stockholders' equity for 2003 and 2002. Round to two decimal places.
c. What conclusions regarding the margin of protection to the creditors can you draw from (b)?

**EXERCISE 1-27**
*Ratio of liabilities to stockholders' equity*

Objective 9

REAL WORLD

**Lowe's**, a major competitor of The Home Depot in the home improvement business, operates over 700 stores. For the years ending January 31, 2003, and February 1, 2002, Lowe's reported the following balance sheet data (in millions):

|  | 2003 | 2002 |
|---|---|---|
| Total assets | $16,109 | $13,736 |
| Total liabilities | 8,302 | 7,062 |

a. Determine the total stockholders' equity as of January 31, 2003, and February 1, 2002.
b. Determine the ratio of liabilities to stockholders' equity for 2003 and 2002. Round to two decimal places.
c. What conclusions regarding the margin of protection to the creditors can you draw from (b)?
d. How does the ratio of liabilities to stockholders' equity of Lowe's compare to that of The Home Depot?

# Problems Series A

**PROBLEM 1-1A**
*Transactions*

Objective 7

✓ Cash bal. at end of July: $16,000

Duane Mays established an insurance agency on July 1 of the current year and completed the following transactions during July:

a. Opened a business bank account with a deposit of $18,000 from personal funds.
b. Purchased supplies on account, $950.
c. Paid creditors on account, $575.
d. Received cash from fees earned on insurance commissions, $4,250.
e. Paid rent on office and equipment for the month, $1,200.
f. Paid automobile expenses for month, $600, and miscellaneous expenses, $375.
g. Paid office salaries, $1,500.
h. Determined that the cost of supplies on hand was $225; therefore, the cost of supplies used was $725.
i. Billed insurance companies for sales commissions earned, $6,350.
j. Withdrew cash for personal use, $2,000.

**Instructions**

1. Indicate the effect of each transaction and the balances after each transaction, using the following tabular headings:

| Assets | = | Liabilities | + | Owner's Equity |
|---|---|---|---|---|

Cash + Accounts Receivable + Supplies = Accounts Payable + Duane Mays, Capital

Explain the nature of each increase and decrease in owner's equity by an appropriate notation at the right of the amount.

2. ▭▶ Briefly explain why the owner's investment and revenues increased owner's equity, while withdrawals and expenses decreased owner's equity.

---

**PROBLEM 1-2A**
*Financial statements*

**Objective 8**

SPREADSHEET

✓ *Net income: $55,550*

The amounts of the assets and liabilities of Chickadee Travel Service at April 30, 2006, the end of the current year, and its revenue and expenses for the year are listed below. The capital of Adam Cellini, owner, was $50,000 at May 1, 2005, the beginning of the current year, and the owner withdrew $30,000 during the current year.

| | | | |
|---|---|---|---|
| Accounts payable | $ 12,200 | Supplies | $ 3,350 |
| Accounts receivable | 31,350 | Supplies expense | 7,100 |
| Cash | 53,050 | Taxes expense | 5,600 |
| Fees earned | 263,200 | Utilities expense | 22,500 |
| Miscellaneous expense | 2,950 | Wages expense | 131,700 |
| Rent expense | 37,800 | | |

**Instructions**

1. Prepare an income statement for the current year ended April 30, 2006.
2. Prepare a statement of owner's equity for the current year ended April 30, 2006.
3. Prepare a balance sheet as of April 30, 2006.

---

**PROBLEM 1-3A**
*Financial statements*

**Objective 8**

SPREADSHEET

✓ *Net income: $5,950*

Jeanine Sykes established Linchpin Computer Services on August 1, 2006. The effect of each transaction and the balances after each transaction for August are as follows:

| | Assets | | | = Liabilities + | Owner's Equity | |
|---|---|---|---|---|---|---|
| | Cash | + Accounts Receivable | + Supplies = | Accounts Payable | + Jeanine Sykes, Capital | |
| a. | +10,000 | | | | +10,000 | Investment |
| b. | | | +1,440 | +1,440 | | |
| Bal. | 10,000 | | 1,440 | 1,440 | 10,000 | |
| c. | + 9,000 | | | | + 9,000 | Fees earned |
| Bal. | 19,000 | | 1,440 | 1,440 | 19,000 | |
| d. | − 3,600 | | | | − 3,600 | Rent expense |
| Bal. | 15,400 | | 1,440 | 1,440 | 15,400 | |
| e. | − 500 | | | − 500 | | |
| Bal. | 14,900 | | 1,440 | 940 | 15,400 | |
| f. | | +7,500 | | | + 7,500 | Fees earned |
| Bal. | 14,900 | 7,500 | 1,440 | 940 | 22,900 | |
| g. | − 2,300 | | | | − 1,550 | Auto expense |
| | | | | | − 750 | Misc. expense |
| Bal. | 12,600 | 7,500 | 1,440 | 940 | 20,600 | |
| h. | − 4,000 | | | | − 4,000 | Salaries expense |
| Bal. | 8,600 | 7,500 | 1,440 | 940 | 16,600 | |
| i. | | | − 650 | | − 650 | Supplies expense |
| Bal. | 8,600 | 7,500 | 790 | 940 | 15,950 | |
| j. | − 2,000 | | | | − 2,000 | Withdrawal |
| Bal. | 6,600 | 7,500 | 790 | 940 | 13,950 | |

**Instructions**

1. Prepare an income statement for the month ended August 31, 2006.
2. Prepare a statement of owner's equity for the month ended August 31, 2006.
3. Prepare a balance sheet as of August 31, 2006.

**PROBLEM 1-4A**
*Transactions; financial statements*
Objectives 7, 8

SPREADSHEET

✓ *Net income: $9,545*

On August 1, 2006, Shad Menard established Centillion Realty. Shad completed the following transactions during the month of August:

a. Opened a business bank account with a deposit of $15,000 from personal funds.
b. Paid rent on office and equipment for the month, $2,400.
c. Paid automobile expenses (including rental charge) for month, $750, and miscellaneous expenses, $380.
d. Purchased supplies (pens, file folders, and copy paper) on account, $950.
e. Earned sales commissions, receiving cash, $17,350.
f. Paid creditor on account, $580.
g. Paid office salaries, $3,600.
h. Withdrew cash for personal use, $1,500.
i. Determined that the cost of supplies on hand was $275; therefore, the cost of supplies used was $675.

**Instructions**
1. Indicate the effect of each transaction and the balances after each transaction, using the following tabular headings:

| Assets | = | Liabilities | + | Owner's Equity |
|---|---|---|---|---|
| Cash + Supplies | = | Accounts Payable | + | Shad Menard, Capital |

Explain the nature of each increase and decrease in owner's equity by an appropriate notation at the right of the amount.
2. Prepare an income statement for August, a statement of owner's equity for August, and a balance sheet as of August 31.

**PROBLEM 1-5A**
*Transactions; financial statements*
Objectives 7, 8

SPREADSHEET
P.A.S.S.

✓ *Net income: $7,850*

Eureka Dry Cleaners is owned and operated by Vince Fry. A building and equipment are currently being rented, pending expansion to new facilities. The actual work of dry cleaning is done by another company at wholesale rates. The assets and the liabilities of the business on June 1, 2006, are as follows: Cash, $8,600; Accounts Receivable, $9,500; Supplies, $1,875; Land, $15,000; Accounts Payable, $4,100. Business transactions during June are summarized as follows:

a. Paid rent for the month, $4,000.
b. Charged customers for dry cleaning sales on account, $8,150.
c. Paid creditors on account, $2,680.
d. Purchased supplies on account, $1,500.
e. Received cash from cash customers for dry cleaning sales, $17,600.
f. Received cash from customers on account, $8,450.
g. Received monthly invoice for dry cleaning expense for June (to be paid on July 10), $7,400.
h. Paid the following: wages expense, $2,800; truck expense, $825; utilities expense, $710; miscellaneous expense, $390.
i. Determined that the cost of supplies on hand was $1,600; therefore, the cost of supplies used during the month was $1,775.
j. Withdrew $3,500 for personal use.

**Instructions**
1. Determine the amount of Vince Fry's capital as of June 1.
2. State the assets, liabilities, and owner's equity as of June 1 in equation form similar to that shown in this chapter. In tabular form below the equation, indicate increases and decreases resulting from each transaction and the new balances after each transaction. Explain the nature of each increase and decrease in owner's equity by an appropriate notation at the right of the amount.
3. Prepare an income statement for June, a statement of owner's equity for June, and a balance sheet as of June 30.

**PROBLEM 1-6A**
*Missing amounts from financial statements*

The financial statements at the end of Ameba Realty's first month of operations are shown on the next page.

**Objective 8**

SPREADSHEET

✓ i. $40,440

## Ameba Realty
### Income Statement
### For the Month Ended June 30, 2006

| | | | |
|---|---:|---:|---:|
| Fees earned | | | $18 8 0 0 00 |
| Operating expenses: | | | |
|     Wages expense | $ (a) | | |
|     Rent expense | 1 9 2 0 00 | | |
|     Supplies expense | 1 6 0 0 00 | | |
|     Utilities expense | 1 0 8 0 00 | | |
|     Miscellaneous expense | 6 6 0 00 | | |
|       Total operating expenses | | 9 5 6 0 00 | |
| Net income | | | (b) |

## Ameba Realty
### Statement of Owner's Equity
### For the Month Ended June 30, 2006

| | | |
|---|---:|---:|
| Terry Garcia, capital, June 1, 2006 | | $ (c) |
| Investment on June 1, 2006 | $ (d) | |
| Net income for June | (e) | |
| | (f) | |
| Less withdrawals | (g) | |
| Increase in owner's equity | | (h) |
| Terry Garcia, capital, June 30, 2006 | | (i) |

## Ameba Realty
### Balance Sheet
### June 30, 2006

| Assets | | Liabilities | |
|---|---:|---|---:|
| Cash | $11 8 0 0 00 | Accounts payable | $ 9 6 0 00 |
| Supplies | 8 0 0 00 | **Owner's Equity** | |
| Land | (j) | Terry Garcia, capital | (l) |
| | | Total liabilities and | |
| Total assets | (k) |   owner's equity | (m) |

## Ameba Realty
### Statement of Cash Flows
### For the Month Ended June 30, 2006

| | | |
|---|---:|---:|
| Cash flows from operating activities: | | |
|   Cash received from customers | $ (n) | |
|   Deduct cash payments for expenses and | | |
|     payments to creditors | 9 4 0 0 00 | |
|   Net cash flow from operating activities | | $ (o) |
| Cash flows from investing activities: | | |
|   Cash payments for acquisition of land | | 28 8 0 0 00 |
| Cash flows from financing activities: | | |
|   Cash received as owner's investment | $ 36 0 0 0 00 | |
|   Deduct cash withdrawal by owner | 4 8 0 0 00 | |
|   Net cash flow from financing activities | | (p) |
| Net cash flow and June 30, 2006 cash balance | | (q) |

**Instructions**

By analyzing the interrelationships among the four financial statements, determine the proper amounts for (a) through (q).

 **roblems Series B**

**PROBLEM 1-1B**
*Transactions*
**Objective 7**

✓ *Cash bal. at end of Sept.:*
*$13,775*

On September 1 of the current year, Pamela Larsen established a business to manage rental property. She completed the following transactions during September:

a. Opened a business bank account with a deposit of $15,000 from personal funds.
b. Purchased supplies (pens, file folders, and copy paper) on account, $1,350.
c. Received cash from fees earned for managing rental property, $6,500.
d. Paid rent on office and equipment for the month, $2,500.
e. Paid creditors on account, $700.
f. Billed customers for fees earned for managing rental property, $1,250.
g. Paid automobile expenses (including rental charges) for month, $550, and miscellaneous expenses, $675.
h. Paid office salaries, $1,800.
i. Determined that the cost of supplies on hand was $380; therefore, the cost of supplies used was $970.
j. Withdrew cash for personal use, $1,500.

**Instructions**

1. Indicate the effect of each transaction and the balances after each transaction, using the following tabular headings:

| Assets | = | Liabilities | + | Owner's Equity |
|---|---|---|---|---|

Cash + Accounts Receivable + Supplies = Accounts Payable + Pamela Larsen, Capital

Explain the nature of each increase and decrease in owner's equity by an appropriate notation at the right of the amount.

2. ▉▉▉▶ Briefly explain why the owner's investment and revenues increased owner's equity, while withdrawals and expenses decreased owner's equity.

**PROBLEM 1-2B**
*Financial statements*
**Objective 8**

**SPREADSHEET**

✓ *Net income: $71,400*

Following are the amounts of the assets and liabilities of Greco Travel Agency at December 31, 2006, the end of the current year, and its revenue and expenses for the year. The capital of Petrea Kraft, owner, was $16,200 on January 1, 2006, the beginning of the current year. During the current year, Kraft withdrew $47,000.

| | | | |
|---|---|---|---|
| Accounts payable | $ 5,120 | Rent expense | $36,000 |
| Accounts receivable | 31,200 | Supplies | 3,000 |
| Cash | 11,520 | Supplies expense | 4,500 |
| Fees earned | 188,000 | Utilities expense | 16,500 |
| Miscellaneous expense | 2,800 | Wages expense | 56,800 |

**Instructions**

1. Prepare an income statement for the current year ended December 31, 2006.
2. Prepare a statement of owner's equity for the current year ended December 31, 2006.
3. Prepare a balance sheet as of December 31, 2006.

**PROBLEM 1-3B**
*Financial statements*
**Objective 8**

Lynn Rosberg established Jack-in-the-Pulpit Financial Services on January 1, 2006. Jack-in-the-Pulpit Financial Services offers financial planning advice to its clients. The effect of each transaction and the balances after each transaction for January are as follows:

✓ *Net income: $14,080*

| | Assets | | | = Liabilities + | Owner's Equity |
|---|---|---|---|---|---|
| | | Accounts | | Accounts | |
| | Cash | + Receivable | + Supplies = | Payable | + Lynn Rosberg, Capital |
| a. | +30,000 | | | | +30,000 Investment |
| b. | | | +3,180 | +3,180 | |
| Bal. | 30,000 | | 3,180 | 3,180 | 30,000 |
| c. | − 2,000 | | | −2,000 | |
| Bal. | 28,000 | | 3,180 | 1,180 | 30,000 |
| d. | +21,000 | | | | +21,000 Fees earned |
| Bal. | 49,000 | | 3,180 | 1,180 | 51,000 |
| e. | − 6,000 | | | | − 6,000 Rent expense |
| Bal. | 43,000 | | 3,180 | 1,180 | 45,000 |
| f. | − 3,800 | | | | − 3,000 Auto expense |
| | | | | | − 800 Misc. expense |
| Bal. | 39,200 | | 3,180 | 1,180 | 41,200 |
| g. | − 5,000 | | | | − 5,000 Salaries expense |
| Bal. | 34,200 | | 3,180 | 1,180 | 36,200 |
| h. | | | −2,520 | | − 2,520 Supplies expense |
| Bal. | 34,200 | | 660 | 1,180 | 33,680 |
| i. | | +10,400 | | | +10,400 Fees earned |
| Bal. | 34,200 | 10,400 | 660 | 1,180 | 44,080 |
| j. | − 7,000 | | | | − 7,000 Withdrawal |
| Bal. | 27,200 | 10,400 | 660 | 1,180 | 37,080 |

**Instructions**

1. Prepare an income statement for the month ended January 31, 2006.
2. Prepare a statement of owner's equity for the month ended January 31, 2006.
3. Prepare a balance sheet as of January 31, 2006.

**PROBLEM 1-4B**

*Transactions; financial statements*

**Objectives 7, 8**

✓ *Net income: $6,700*

On July 1, 2006, Beth Nesbit established Patriotic Realty. Nesbit completed the following transactions during the month of July:

a. Opened a business bank account with a deposit of $18,000 from personal funds.
b. Purchased supplies (pens, file folders, fax paper, etc.) on account, $1,650.
c. Paid creditor on account, $1,100.
d. Earned sales commissions, receiving cash, $25,200.
e. Paid rent on office and equipment for the month, $7,200.
f. Withdrew cash for personal use, $10,000.
g. Paid automobile expenses (including rental charge) for month, $1,500, and miscellaneous expenses, $750.
h. Paid office salaries, $8,000.
i. Determined that the cost of supplies on hand was $600; therefore, the cost of supplies used was $1,050.

**Instructions**

1. Indicate the effect of each transaction and the balances after each transaction, using the following tabular headings:

| Assets | = | Liabilities | + | Owner's Equity |
|---|---|---|---|---|
| Cash + Supplies | = | Accounts Payable | + | Beth Nesbit, Capital |

Explain the nature of each increase and decrease in owner's equity by an appropriate notation at the right of the amount.

2. Prepare an income statement for July, a statement of owner's equity for July, and a balance sheet as of July 31.

**PROBLEM 1-5B**

*Transactions; financial statements*

**Objectives 7, 8**

Daisy Dry Cleaners is owned and operated by Gloria Carson. A building and equipment are currently being rented, pending expansion to new facilities. The actual work of dry cleaning is done by another company at wholesale rates. The assets and the liabilities of the business on March 1, 2006, are as follows: Cash, $7,150;

SPREADSHEET
P.A.S.S.

✓ Net income: $12,330

Accounts Receivable, $12,880; Supplies, $3,400; Land, $20,000; Accounts Payable, $6,360. Business transactions during March are summarized as follows:

a. Received cash from cash customers for dry cleaning sales, $22,000.
b. Paid rent for the month, $3,500.
c. Purchased supplies on account, $2,100.
d. Paid creditors on account, $4,800.
e. Charged customers for dry cleaning sales on account, $11,700.
f. Received monthly invoice for dry cleaning expense for March (to be paid on April 10), $8,400.
g. Paid the following: wages expense, $3,400; truck expense, $1,580; utilities expense, $960; miscellaneous expense, $630.
h. Received cash from customers on account, $10,100.
i. Determined that the cost of supplies on hand was $2,600; therefore, the cost of supplies used during the month was $2,900.
j. Withdrew $6,000 cash for personal use.

**Instructions**
1. Determine the amount of Gloria Carson's capital as of March 1 of the current year.
2. State the assets, liabilities, and owner's equity as of March 1 in equation form similar to that shown in this chapter. In tabular form below the equation, indicate increases and decreases resulting from each transaction and the new balances after each transaction. Explain the nature of each increase and decrease in owner's equity by an appropriate notation at the right of the amount.
3. Prepare an income statement for March, a statement of owner's equity for March, and a balance sheet as of March 31.

**PROBLEM 1-6B**
*Missing amounts from financial statements*

**Objective 8**

SPREADSHEET

✓ k. $30,000

The financial statements at the end of Zeppelin Realty's first month of operations are shown below and on the next page.

### Zeppelin Realty
### Income Statement
### For the Month Ended November 30, 2006

| | | | |
|---|---|---|---|
| Fees earned | | $ | (a) |
| Operating expenses: | | | |
| Wages expense | $8 5 0 0 00 | | |
| Rent expense | 3 2 0 0 00 | | |
| Supplies expense | (b) | | |
| Utilities expense | 1 8 0 0 00 | | |
| Miscellaneous expense | 1 1 0 0 00 | | |
| Total operating expenses | | 17 6 0 0 00 | |
| Net income | | $12 4 0 0 00 | |

### Zeppelin Realty
### Statement of Owner's Equity
### For the Month Ended November 30, 2006

| | | | |
|---|---|---|---|
| Craig Haas, capital, November 1, 2006 | | $ | (c) |
| Investment on November 1, 2006 | $40 0 0 0 00 | | |
| Net income for November | (d) | | |
| | (e) | | |
| Less withdrawals | 6 0 0 0 00 | | |
| Increase in owner's equity | | (f) | |
| Craig Haas, capital, November 30, 2006 | | (g) | |

**Zeppelin Realty**
**Balance Sheet**
**November 30, 2006**

| Assets | | | Liabilities | | |
|---|---|---|---|---|---|
| Cash | $ 5 8 0 0 00 | | Accounts payable | $ 1 6 0 0 00 | |
| Supplies | 2 2 0 0 00 | | **Owner's Equity** | | |
| Land | 40 0 0 0 00 | | Craig Haas, capital | | (i) |
| | | | Total liabilities and | | |
| Total assets | | (h) | owner's equity | | (j) |

**Zeppelin Realty**
**Statement of Cash Flows**
**For the Month Ended November 30, 2006**

| | | | | |
|---|---|---|---|---|
| Cash flows from operating activities: | | | | |
| Cash received from customers | $ | (k) | | |
| Deduct cash payments for expenses and | | | | |
| payments to creditors | 18 2 0 0 00 | | | |
| Net cash flow from operating activities | | | $ | (l) |
| Cash flows from investing activities: | | | | |
| Cash payments for acquisition of land | | | | (m) |
| Cash flows from financing activities: | | | | |
| Cash received as owner's investment | | (n) | | |
| Deduct cash withdrawal by owner | | (o) | | |
| Net cash flow from financing activities | | | | (p) |
| Net cash flow and November 30, 2006 cash balance | | | | (q) |

**Instructions**

By analyzing the interrelationships among the four financial statements, determine the proper amounts for (a) through (q).

# Continuing Problem

**P.A.S.S.**

✔ 2. Net income: $530

Shannon Burns enjoys listening to all types of music and owns countless CDs and tapes. Over the years, Shannon has gained a local reputation for knowledge of music from classical to rap and the ability to put together sets of recordings that appeal to all ages.

During the last several months, Shannon served as a guest disc jockey on a local radio station. In addition, Shannon has entertained at several friends' parties as the host deejay.

On April 1, 2006, Shannon established a proprietorship known as Dancin Music. Using an extensive collection of CDs and tapes, Shannon will serve as a disc jockey on a fee basis for weddings, college parties, and other events. During April, Shannon entered into the following transactions:

April 1. Deposited $7,000 in a checking account in the name of Dancin Music.
    2. Received $2,000 from a local radio station for serving as the guest disc jockey for April.

April 2. Agreed to share office space with a local real estate agency, Folsom Realty. Dancin Music will pay one-fourth of the rent. In addition, Dancin Music agreed to pay a portion of the salary of the receptionist and to pay one-fourth of the utilities. Paid $1,000 for the rent of the office.

4. Purchased supplies (blank cassette tapes, poster board, extension cords, etc.) from Rockne Office Supply Co. for $350. Agreed to pay $100 within 10 days and the remainder by May 3, 2006.

6. Paid $600 to a local radio station to advertise the services of Dancin Music twice daily for two weeks.

8. Paid $650 to a local electronics store for renting digital recording equipment.

12. Paid $200 (music expense) to Rocket Music for the use of its current music demos to make various music sets.

13. Paid Rockne Office Supply Co. $100 on account.

16. Received $150 from a dentist for providing two music sets for the dentist to play for her patients.

22. Served as disc jockey for a wedding party. The father of the bride agreed to pay $1,200 the 1st of May.

25. Received $500 from a friend for serving as the disc jockey for a cancer charity ball hosted by the local hospital.

29. Paid $240 (music expense) to Score Music for the use of its library of music demos.

30. Received $900 for serving as disc jockey for a local club's monthly dance.

30. Paid Folsom Realty $400 for Dancin Music's share of the receptionist's salary for April.

30. Paid Folsom Realty $300 for Dancin Music's share of the utilities for April.

30. Determined that the cost of supplies on hand is $170. Therefore, the cost of supplies used during the month was $180.

30. Paid for miscellaneous expenses, $150.

30. Paid $500 royalties (music expense) to Federated Clearing for use of various artists' music during the month.

30. Withdrew $250 of cash from Dancin Music for personal use.

**Instructions**

1. Indicate the effect of each transaction and the balances after each transaction, using the following tabular headings:

| Assets | = | Liabilities | + | Owner's Equity |
|---|---|---|---|---|
| Cash + Accounts Receivable + Supplies | = | Accounts Payable | + | Shannon Burns, Capital |

Explain the nature of each increase and decrease in owner's equity by an appropriate notation at the right of the amount.

2. Prepare an income statement for Dancin Music for the month ended April 30, 2006.

3. Prepare a statement of owner's equity for Dancin Music for the month ended April 30, 2006.

4. Prepare a balance sheet for Dancin Music as of April 30, 2006.

# Special Activities

**ACTIVITY 1-1**
*Ethics and professional conduct in business*

Sue Alejandro, president of Tobago Enterprises, applied for a $300,000 loan from First National Bank. The bank requested financial statements from Tobago Enterprises as a basis for granting the loan. Sue has told her accountant to provide the bank with a balance sheet. Sue has decided to omit the other financial statements because there was a net loss during the past year.

GROUP ACTIVITY   ETHICS

In groups of three or four, discuss the following questions:

1. Is Sue behaving in a professional manner by omitting some of the financial statements?
2. a. What types of information about their businesses would owners be willing to provide bankers? What types of information would owners not be willing to provide?
   b. What types of information about a business would bankers want before extending a loan?
   c. What common interests are shared by bankers and business owners?

**ACTIVITY 1-2**
*Business strategy*

GROUP ACTIVITY

Assume that you are the chief executive officer for Gold Kist Inc., a national poultry producer. The company's operations include hatching chickens through the use of breeder stock and feeding, raising, and processing the mature chicks into finished products. The finished products include breaded chicken nuggets and patties and deboned, skinless, and marinated chicken. Gold Kist sells its products to schools, military services, fast food chains, and grocery stores.

In groups of four or five, discuss the following business strategy and risk issues:

1. In a commodity business like poultry production, what do you think is the dominant business strategy? What are the implications in this dominant strategy for how you would run Gold Kist?
2. Identify at least two major business risks for operating Gold Kist.
3. How could Gold Kist try to differentiate its products?

**ACTIVITY 1-3**
*Net income*

On January 3, 2005, Dr. Rosa Smith established First Opinion, a medical practice organized as a proprietorship. The following conversation occurred the following August between Dr. Smith and a former medical school classmate, Dr. Brett Wommack, at an American Medical Association convention in Nassau.

*Dr. Wommack:* Rosa, good to see you again. Why didn't you call when you were in Las Vegas? We could have had dinner together.
*Dr. Smith:* Actually, I never made it to Las Vegas this year. My husband and kids went up to our Lake Tahoe condo twice, but I got stuck in New York. I opened a new consulting practice this January and haven't had any time for myself since.
*Dr. Wommack:* I heard about it . . . First . . . something . . . right?
*Dr. Smith:* Yes, First Opinion. My husband chose the name.
*Dr. Wommack:* I've thought about doing something like that. Are you making any money? I mean, is it worth your time?
*Dr. Smith:* You wouldn't believe it. I started by opening a bank account with $60,000, and my July bank statement has a balance of $240,000. Not bad for seven months—all pure profit.
*Dr. Wommack:* Maybe I'll try it in Las Vegas. Let's have breakfast together tomorrow and you can fill me in on the details.

➤ Comment on Dr. Smith's statement that the difference between the opening bank balance ($60,000) and the July statement balance ($240,000) is pure profit.

**ACTIVITY 1-4**
*Transactions and financial statements*

Dawn Ivy, a junior in college, has been seeking ways to earn extra spending money. As an active sports enthusiast, Dawn plays tennis regularly at the Racquet Club, where her family has a membership. The president of the club recently approached Dawn with the proposal that she manage the club's tennis courts. Dawn's primary duty would be to supervise the operation of the club's four indoor and six outdoor courts, including court reservations.

In return for her services, the club would pay Dawn $150 per week, plus Dawn could keep whatever she earned from lessons and the fees from the use of the ball machine. The club and Dawn agreed to a one-month trial, after which both would consider an arrangement for the remaining two years of Dawn's college career. On this basis, Dawn organized Deuce. During June 2005, Dawn managed the tennis courts and entered into the following transactions:

a. Opened a business account by depositing $1,000.
b. Paid $320 for tennis supplies (practice tennis balls, etc.).
c. Paid $160 for the rental of videotape equipment to be used in offering lessons during June.
d. Arranged for the rental of two ball machines during September for $200. Paid $140 in advance, with the remaining $60 due July 1.
e. Received $1,600 for lessons given during June.
f. Received $300 in fees from the use of the ball machines during June.
g. Paid $600 for salaries of part-time employees who answered the telephone and took reservations while Dawn was giving lessons.
h. Paid $150 for miscellaneous expenses.
i. Received $600 from the club for managing the tennis courts during June.
j. Determined that the cost of supplies on hand at the end of the month totaled $150; therefore, the cost of supplies used was $170.
k. Withdrew $800 for personal use on June 30.

As a friend and accounting student, you have been asked by Dawn to aid her in assessing the venture.

1. Indicate the effect of each transaction and the balances after each transaction, using the following tabular headings:

| Assets | = | Liabilities | + | Owner's Equity |
|---|---|---|---|---|
| Cash + Supplies | = | Accounts Payable | + | Dawn Ivy, Capital |

Explain the nature of each increase and decrease in owner's equity by an appropriate notation at the right of the amount.
2. Prepare an income statement for June.
3. Prepare a statement of owner's equity for June.
4. Prepare a balance sheet as of June 30.
5. a. Assume that Dawn Ivy could earn $8 per hour working 30 hours as a waitress. Evaluate which of the two alternatives, working as a waitress or operating Deuce, would provide Dawn with the most income per month.
   b. ▰▰▰➤ Discuss any other factors that you believe Dawn should consider before discussing a long-term arrangement with the Racquet Club.

**ACTIVITY 1-5**
*Certification requirements for accountants*

INTERNET

By satisfying certain specific requirements, accountants may become certified as public accountants (CPAs), management accountants (CMAs), or internal auditors (CIAs). Find the certification requirements for one of these accounting groups by accessing the appropriate Internet site listed below.

| Site | Description |
|---|---|
| http://www.ais-cpa.com | This site lists the address and/or Internet link for each state's board of accountancy. Find your state's requirements. |
| http://www.imanet.org | This site lists the requirements for becoming a CMA. |
| http://www.theiia.org | This site lists the requirements for becoming a CIA. |

**ACTIVITY 1-6**
*Cash flows*

REAL WORLD

**Amazon.com**, an Internet retailer, was incorporated in July 1994, and opened its virtual doors on the Web in July 1995. On the statement of cash flows, would you expect Amazon.com's net cash flows from operating, investing, and financing activities to be positive or negative for each year, 1996, 1997, and 1998? Use the following format for your answers, and briefly explain your logic.

| | 1998 | 1997 | 1996 |
|---|---|---|---|
| Net cash flows from operating activities | positive | | |
| Net cash flows from investing activities | | | |
| Net cash flows from financing activities | | | |

**ACTIVITY 1-7**
*Financial analysis of Enron Corporation*

REAL WORLD          INTERNET

The now defunct **Enron Corporation**, headquartered in Houston, Texas, provided products and services for natural gas, electricity, and communications to wholesale and retail customers. Enron's operations were conducted through a variety of subsidiaries and affiliates that involved transporting gas through pipelines, transmitting electricity, and managing energy commodities. The following data were taken from Enron's December 31, 2000 financial statements.

|  | In millions |
|---|---|
| Total revenues | $100,789 |
| Total costs and expenses | 98,836 |
| Operating income | 1,953 |
| Net income | 979 |
| Total assets | 65,503 |
| Total liabilities | 54,033 |
| Total stockholders' equity | 11,470 |
| Net cash flows from operating activities | 4,779 |
| Net cash flows from investing activities | (4,264) |
| Net cash flows from financing activities | 571 |
| Net increase in cash | 1,086 |

At the end of 2000, the market price of Enron's stock was approximately $83 per share. By March 15, 2002, Enron's stock was selling for $0.22 per share.

 Review the preceding financial statement data and search the Internet for articles on Enron Corporation. Briefly explain why Enron's stock dropped so dramatically in such a short time.

# Answers to Self-Examination Questions

1. **D**  A corporation, organized in accordance with state or federal statutes, is a separate legal entity in which ownership is divided into shares of stock (answer D). A proprietorship (answer A) is an unincorporated business owned by one individual. A service business (answer B) provides services to its customers. It can be organized as a proprietorship, partnership, corporation, or limited liability corporation. A partnership (answer C) is an unincorporated business owned by two or more individuals.

2. **A**  The resources owned by a business are called assets (answer A). The debts of the business are called liabilities (answer B), and the equity of the owners is called owner's equity (answer D). The relationship between assets, liabilities, and owner's equity is expressed as the accounting equation (answer C).

3. **A**  The balance sheet is a listing of the assets, liabilities, and owner's equity of a business at a specific date (answer A). The income statement (answer B) is a summary of the revenue and expenses of a business for a specific period of time. The statement of owner's equity (answer C) summarizes the changes in owner's equity for a pro-

prietorship or partnership during a specific period of time. The statement of cash flows (answer D) summarizes the cash receipts and cash payments for a specific period of time.

4. **C**  The accounting equation is:

Assets = Liabilities + Owner's Equity

Therefore, if assets increased by $20,000 and liabilities increased by $12,000, owner's equity must have increased by $8,000 (answer C), as indicated in the following computation:

| Assets | = Liabilities + Owner's Equity |
|---|---|
| +$20,000 | = +$12,000 + Owner's Equity |
| +$20,000 − $12,000 = | Owner's Equity |
| +$8,000 | = Owner's Equity |

5. **B**  Net income is the excess of revenue over expenses, or $7,500 (answer B). If expenses exceed revenue, the difference is a net loss. Withdrawals by the owner are the opposite of the owner's investing in the business and do not affect the amount of net income or net loss.

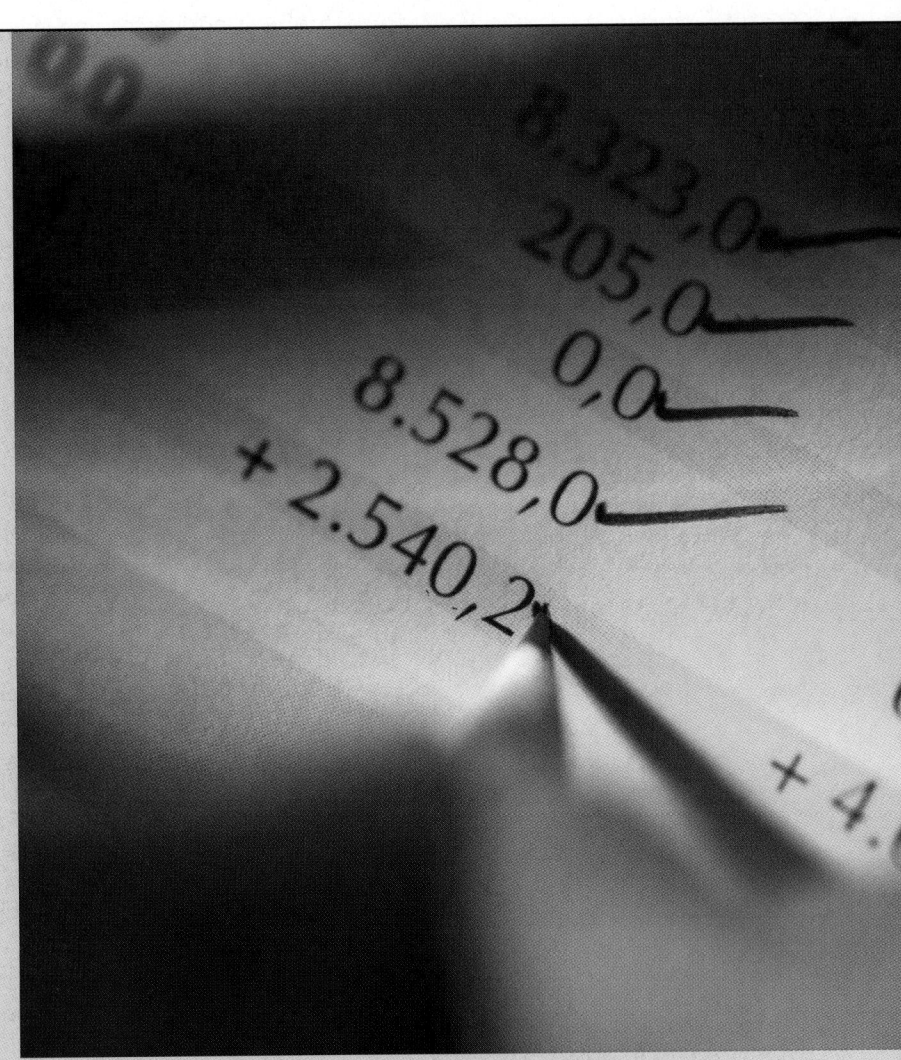

# 2

# ANALYZING TRANSACTIONS

## objectives

*After studying this chapter, you should be able to:*

**1** Explain why accounts are used to record and summarize the effects of transactions on financial statements.

**2** Describe the characteristics of an account.

**3** List the rules of debit and credit and the normal balances of accounts.

**4** Analyze and summarize the financial statement effects of transactions.

**5** Prepare a trial balance and explain how it can be used to discover errors.

**6** Discover errors in recording transactions and correct them.

**7** Use horizontal analysis to compare financial statements from different periods.

$\textbf{A}$ssume that you have been hired by a pizza restaurant to deliver pizzas, using your own car. You will be paid $6.00 per hour plus $0.30 per mile plus tips. What is the best way for you to determine how many miles you have driven each day in delivering pizzas?

One method would be to record the odometer mileage before work and then at quitting time. The difference would be the miles driven. For example, if the odometer read 56,743 at the start of work and 56,889 at the end of work, you would have driven 146 miles. This method is subject to error, however, if you copy down the wrong reading or make a math error.

In the same way, business managers need information about the status of the business at different points in time. Such information is useful for analyzing the effects of transactions on the business and for making decisions. For example, the manager of your neighborhood dry cleaners needs to know how much cash is available, how much has been spent, and what services have been provided.

In Chapter 1, we analyzed and recorded this kind of information by using the accounting equation, Assets = Liabilities + Owner's Equity. Since such a format is not practical for most businesses, in Chapter 2 we will study more efficient methods of recording transactions. We will conclude this chapter by discussing how accounting errors may occur and how they may be detected by the accounting process.

# Usefulness of an Account

objective   1

Explain why accounts are used to record and summarize the effects of transactions on financial statements.

Before making a major cash purchase, such as buying a digital camera, you need to know the balance of your bank account. Likewise, managers need timely, useful information in order to make good decisions about their businesses.

How are accounting systems designed to provide this information? We illustrated a very simple design in Chapter 1, where transactions were recorded and summarized in the accounting equation format. However, this format is difficult to use when thousands of transactions must be recorded daily. Thus, accounting systems are designed to show the increases and decreases in each financial statement item in a separate record. This record is called an $\textbf{\textit{account}}$. For example, since cash appears on the balance sheet, a separate record is kept of the increases and decreases in cash. Likewise, a separate record is kept of the increases and decreases for supplies, land, accounts payable, and the other balance sheet items. Similar records would be kept for income statement items, such as fees earned, wages expense, and rent expense.

A group of accounts for a business entity is called a $\textbf{\textit{ledger}}$. A list of the accounts in the ledger is called a $\textbf{\textit{chart of accounts}}$. The accounts are normally listed in the order in which they appear in the financial statements. The balance sheet accounts are usually listed first, in the order of assets, liabilities, and owner's equity. The income statement accounts are then listed in the order of revenues and expenses. Each of these major account classifications is briefly described below.

$\textbf{\textit{Assets}}$ are resources owned by the business entity. These resources can be physical items, such as cash and supplies, or intangibles that have value, such as patent rights. Some other examples of assets include accounts receivable, prepaid expenses (such as insurance), buildings, equipment, and land.

$\textbf{\textit{Liabilities}}$ are debts owed to outsiders (creditors). Liabilities are often identified on the balance sheet by titles that include the word $payable$. Examples of liabilities include accounts payable, notes payable, and wages payable. Cash received before services are delivered creates a liability to perform the services. These future service commitments are often called $unearned\ revenues$. Examples of unearned revenues are magazine subscriptions received by a publisher and tuition received by a college at the beginning of a term.

$\textbf{\textit{Owner's equity}}$ is the owner's right to the assets of the business. For a proprietorship, the owner's equity on the balance sheet is represented by the balance of

The increases and decreases in each financial statement item are shown in an account.

the owner's *capital* account. A ***drawing*** account represents the amount of withdrawals made by the owner.

***Revenues*** are increases in owner's equity as a result of selling services or products to customers. Examples of revenues include fees earned, fares earned, commissions revenue, and rent revenue.

The using up of assets or consuming services in the process of generating revenues results in ***expenses***. Examples of typical expenses include wages expense, rent expense, utilities expense, supplies expense, and miscellaneous expense.

A chart of accounts is designed to meet the information needs of a company's managers and other users of its financial statements. The accounts within the chart of accounts are numbered for use as references. A flexible numbering system is normally used, so that new accounts can be added without affecting other account numbers.

Exhibit 1 is NetSolutions' chart of accounts that we will be using in this chapter. Additional accounts will be introduced in later chapters. In Exhibit 1, each account number has two digits. The first digit indicates the major classification of the ledger in which the account is located. Accounts beginning with 1 represent assets; 2, liabilities; 3, owner's equity; 4, revenue; and 5, expenses. The second digit indicates the location of the account within its class.

**Procter & Gamble**'s account numbers have over 30 digits to reflect P&G's many different operations and regions.

## •Exhibit 1    Chart of Accounts for NetSolutions

| Balance Sheet Accounts | Income Statement Accounts |
|---|---|
| **1. Assets** | **4. Revenue** |
| 11 Cash | 41 Fees Earned |
| 12 Accounts Receivable | **5. Expenses** |
| 14 Supplies | 51 Wages Expense |
| 15 Prepaid Insurance | 52 Rent Expense |
| 17 Land | 54 Utilities Expense |
| 18 Office Equipment | 55 Supplies Expense |
| **2. Liabilities** | 59 Miscellaneous Expense |
| 21 Accounts Payable | |
| 23 Unearned Rent | |
| **3. Owner's Equity** | |
| 31 Chris Clark, Capital | |
| 32 Chris Clark, Drawing | |

# Characteristics of an Account

**objective 2**

Describe the characteristics of an account.

An account, in its simplest form, has three parts. First, each account has a title, which is the name of the item recorded in the account. Second, each account has a space for recording increases in the amount of the item. Third, each account has a space for recording decreases in the amount of the item. The account form presented below is called a ***T account*** because it resembles the letter T. The left side of the account is called the *debit* side, and the right side is called the *credit* side.[1]

**Title**

| Left side | Right side |
|---|---|
| *debit* | *credit* |

Amounts entered on the left side of an account, regardless of the account title, are called ***debits*** to the account. When debits are entered in an account, the account

---
[1]The terms *debit* and *credit* are derived from the Latin *debere* and *credere*.

is said to be *debited* (or charged). Amounts entered on the right side of an account are called **credits**, and the account is said to be *credited*. Debits and credits are sometimes abbreviated as *Dr.* and *Cr.*

In the cash account that follows, transactions involving receipts of cash are listed on the debit side of the account. The transactions involving cash payments are listed on the credit side. If at any time the total of the cash receipts is needed, the entries on the debit side of the account may be added and the total ($10,950) inserted below the last debit.[2] The total of the cash payments, $6,850 in the example, may be inserted on the credit side in a similar manner. Subtracting the smaller sum from the larger, $10,950 − $6,850, identifies the amount of cash on hand, $4,100. This amount is called the **balance of the account**. It may be inserted in the account, next to the total of the debit column. In this way, the balance is identified as a **debit balance**. If a balance sheet were to be prepared at this time, cash of $4,100 would be reported.

> **Amounts entered on the left side of an account are debits, and amounts entered on the right side of an account are credits.**

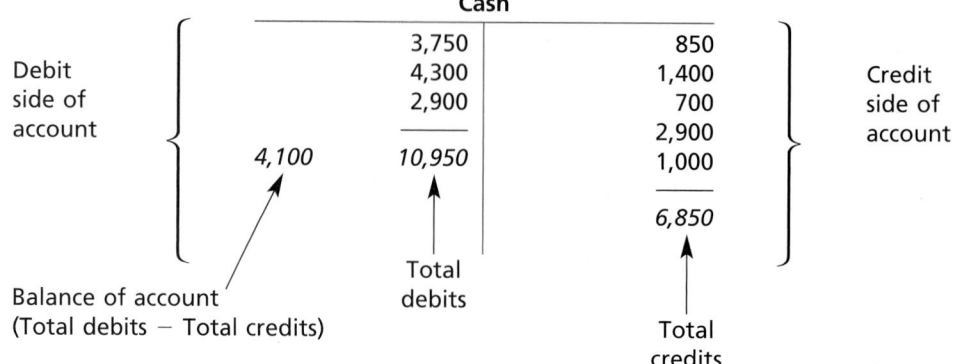

# Analyzing and Summarizing Transactions in Accounts

Every business transaction affects at least two accounts. To illustrate how transactions are analyzed and summarized in accounts, we will use the NetSolutions transactions from Chapter 1, with dates added. First, we illustrate how transactions (a), (b), (c), and (f) are analyzed and summarized in balance sheet accounts (assets, liabilities, and owner's equity). Next, we illustrate how transactions (d), (e), and (g) are analyzed and summarized in income statement accounts (revenues and expenses). Finally, we illustrate how the withdrawal of cash by Chris Clark, transaction (h), is analyzed and summarized in the accounts.

## Transactions and Balance Sheet Accounts

> **Every transaction affects at least two accounts.**

Chris Clark's first transaction, (a), was to deposit $25,000 in a bank account in the name of NetSolutions. The effect of this November 1 transaction on the balance sheet is to increase assets and owner's equity, as shown below.

| NetSolutions Balance Sheet November 1, 2005 | | | | | | | | | | |
|---|---|---|---|---|---|---|---|---|---|---|
| **Assets** | | | | | | **Owner's Equity** | | | | |
| Cash | $25 | 0 | 0 | 0 | 00 | Chris Clark, capital | $25 | 0 | 0 | 0 | 00 |

---

[2]This amount, called a *memorandum balance*, should be written in small figures or identified in some other way to avoid mistaking the amount for an additional debit.

This transaction is initially entered in a record called a *journal*. The title of the account to be debited is listed first, followed by the amount to be debited. The title of the account to be credited is listed below and to the right of the debit, followed by the amount to be credited. This process of recording a transaction in the journal is called *journalizing*. This form of recording a transaction is called a *journal entry*. The journal entry for transaction (a) is shown below.

**Entry A**

| | JOURNAL | | | | Page 1 |
|---|---|---|---|---|---|
| Date | Description | Post. Ref. | Debit | Credit | |
| 2005 Nov. 1 | Cash | | 25 000 00 | | 1 |
| | Chris Clark, Capital | | | 25 000 00 | 2 |
| | Invested cash in NetSolutions. | | | | 3 |

The increase in the asset (Cash), which is reported on the left side of the balance sheet, is debited to the cash account. The increase in owner's equity, which is reported on the right side of the balance sheet, is credited to the Chris Clark, capital account. As other assets are acquired, the increases are also recorded as debits to asset accounts. Likewise, other increases in owner's equity will be recorded as credits to owner's equity accounts.

The effects of this transaction are shown in the accounts by transferring the amount and date of the journal entry to the left (debit) side of Cash and to the right (credit) side of Chris Clark, Capital, as follows:

| Cash | | Chris Clark, Capital | |
|---|---|---|---|
| Nov. 1    25,000 | | | Nov. 1    25,000 |

On November 5 (transaction b), NetSolutions bought land for $20,000, paying cash. This transaction increases one asset account and decreases another. It is entered in the journal as a $20,000 increase (debit) to Land and a $20,000 decrease (credit) to Cash, as shown below.

**Entry B**

| | | | | | | |
|---|---|---|---|---|---|---|
| | | | | | | 4 |
| | 5 | Land | | 20 000 00 | | 5 |
| | | Cash | | | 20 000 00 | 6 |
| | | Purchased land for building site. | | | | 7 |

The effect of this entry is shown in the accounts of NetSolutions as follows:

| Cash | | Land | | Chris Clark, Capital | |
|---|---|---|---|---|---|
| Nov. 1 25,000 | Nov. 5 20,000 | Nov. 5 20,000 | | | Nov. 1 25,000 |

On November 10 (transaction c), NetSolutions purchased supplies on account for $1,350. This transaction increases an asset account and increases a liability account. It is entered in the journal as a $1,350 increase (debit) to Supplies and a $1,350 increase (credit) to Accounts Payable, as shown below. To simplify the illustration, the effect of entry (c) and the remaining journal entries for NetSolutions will be shown in the accounts later.

**Entry C**

| | | | | | | |
|---|---|---|---|---|---|---|
| | | | | | | 8 |
| | 10 | Supplies | | 1 350 00 | | 9 |
| | | Accounts Payable | | | 1 350 00 | 10 |
| | | Purchased supplies on account. | | | | 11 |

On November 30 (transaction f), NetSolutions paid creditors on account, $950. This transaction decreases a liability account and decreases an asset account. It is entered in the journal as a $950 decrease (debit) to Accounts Payable and a $950 decrease (credit) to Cash, as shown below.

**Entry F**

| 23 | | | | | | | 23 |
|----|----|-------------------------|----------|----------|----|
| 24 | 30 | Accounts Payable | 9 5 0 00 | | 24 |
| 25 | | Cash | | 9 5 0 00 | 25 |
| 26 | | Paid creditors on account. | | | 26 |

> The left side of all accounts is the debit side, and the right side is the credit side.

In the preceding examples, you should observe that the left side of asset accounts is used for recording increases and the right side is used for recording decreases. Also, the right side of liability and owner's equity accounts is used to record increases, and the left side of such accounts is used to record decreases. The left side of all accounts, whether asset, liability, or owner's equity, is the debit side, and the right side is the credit side. Thus, a debit may be either an increase or a decrease, depending on the account affected. Likewise, a credit may be either an increase or a decrease, depending on the account. The general rules of debit and credit for balance sheet accounts may be thus stated as follows:

| | Debit | Credit |
|---|---|---|
| Asset accounts ...................... | Increase (+) | Decrease (−) |
| Liability accounts .................... | Decrease (−) | Increase (+) |
| Owner's equity (capital) accounts ......... | Decrease (−) | Increase (+) |

The rules of debit and credit may also be stated in relationship to the accounting equation, as shown below.

### Balance Sheet Accounts

| ASSETS | LIABILITIES |
|---|---|
| Asset Accounts | Liability Accounts |

| Debit for increases (+) | Credit for decreases (−) | Debit for decreases (−) | Credit for increases (+) |
|---|---|---|---|

**OWNER'S EQUITY**
**Owner's Equity Accounts**

| Debit for decreases (−) | Credit for increases (+) |
|---|---|

## Income Statement Accounts

The analysis of revenue and expense transactions focuses on how each transaction affects owner's equity. Transactions that increase revenue will increase owner's equity. Just as increases in owner's equity are recorded as credits, so, too, are increases in revenue accounts. Transactions that increase expense will decrease owner's equity. Just as decreases in owner's equity are recorded as debits, increases in expense accounts are recorded as debits.

We will use NetSolutions' transactions (d), (e), and (g) to illustrate the analysis of transactions and the rules of debit and credit for revenue and expense accounts. On November 18 (transaction d), NetSolutions received fees of $7,500 from customers for services provided. This transaction increases an asset account and in-

# FINANCIAL REPORTING AND DISCLOSURE

## THE HIJACKING RECEIVABLE

**A** company's chart of accounts should reflect the basic nature of its operations. Occasionally, however, transactions take place that give rise to unusual accounts. The following is a story of one such account.

During the early 1970s, before strict airport security was implemented across the United States, several airlines experienced hijacking incidents. One such incident occurred on November 10, 1972, when a Southern Airways DC-9 en route from Memphis to Miami was hijacked during a stopover in Birmingham, Alabama. The three hijackers boarded the plane in Birmingham armed with handguns and hand grenades. At gunpoint, the hijackers took the plane, the plane's crew of four, and 27 passengers to nine American cities, Toronto, and eventually to Havana, Cuba.

During the long flight, the hijackers threatened to crash the plane into the Oak Ridge, Tennessee, nuclear facilities, insisted on talking with President Nixon, and demanded a ransom of $10 million. **Southern Airways**, however, was only able to come up with $2 million. Eventually, the pilot

talked the hijackers into settling for the $2 million when the plane landed in Chattanooga for refueling.

Upon landing in Havana, the Cuban authorities arrested the hijackers and, after a brief delay, sent the plane, passengers, and crew back to the United States. The hijackers and $2 million stayed in Cuba.

How did Southern Airways account for and report the hijacking payment in its subsequent financial statements? As you might have analyzed, the initial entry credited Cash for $2 million. The debit was to an account entitled "Hijacking Payment." This account was reported as a type of receivable under "other assets" on Southern's balance sheet. The company maintained that it would be able to collect the cash from the Cuban government and that, therefore, a receivable existed. In fact, in August 1975, Southern Airways was repaid $2 million by the Cuban government, which was, at that time, attempting to improve relations with the United States.

creases a revenue account. It is entered in the journal as a $7,500 increase (debit) to Cash and a $7,500 increase (credit) to Fees Earned, as shown below.

**Entry D**

| 12 | | | | | 12 |
|----|----|------------------------|----------|----------|----|
| 13 | 18 | Cash | 7 5 0 0 00 | | 13 |
| 14 | | Fees Earned | | 7 5 0 0 00 | 14 |
| 15 | | Received fees from customers. | | | 15 |

Throughout the month, NetSolutions incurred the following expenses: wages, $2,125; rent, $800; utilities, $450; and miscellaneous, $275. To simplify the illustration, the entry to journalize the payment of these expenses is recorded on November 30 (transaction e), as shown below. This transaction increases various expense accounts and decreases an asset account.

**Entry E**

| 17 | 30 | Wages Expense | 2 1 2 5 00 | | 17 |
|----|----|------------------------|----------|----------|----|
| 18 | | Rent Expense | 8 0 0 00 | | 18 |
| 19 | | Utilities Expense | 4 5 0 00 | | 19 |
| 20 | | Miscellaneous Expense | 2 7 5 00 | | 20 |
| 21 | | Cash | | 3 6 5 0 00 | 21 |
| 22 | | Paid expenses. | | | 22 |

**The sum of the debits must always equal the sum of the credits.**

Regardless of the number of accounts, the sum of the debits is always equal to the sum of the credits in a journal entry. This equality of debits and credits for each transaction is built into the accounting equation: Assets = Liabilities + Owner's Equity. It is also because of this double equality that the system is known as ***double-entry accounting***.

On November 30, NetSolutions recorded the amount of supplies used in the operations during the month (transaction g). This transaction increases an expense account and decreases an asset account. The journal entry for transaction (g) is shown below.

**Entry G**

| 28 | | 30 | Supplies Expense | | 8 0 0 00 | | 28 |
| 29 | | | Supplies | | | 8 0 0 00 | 29 |
| 30 | | | Supplies used during November. | | | | 30 |

The general rules of debit and credit for analyzing transactions affecting income statement accounts are stated as follows:

**POINT OF INTEREST**

In 1494, Luca Pacioli, a Franciscan monk, invented the double-entry accounting system that is still used today.

| | Debit | Credit |
|---|---|---|
| Revenue accounts | Decrease (−) | Increase (+) |
| Expense accounts | Increase (+) | Decrease (−) |

The rules of debit and credit for income statement accounts may also be summarized in relationship to the owner's equity in the accounting equation, as shown below.

**Income Statement Accounts**

| Expense Accounts | | Revenue Accounts | |
|---|---|---|---|
| Debit for increases (+) | Credit for decreases (−) | Debit for decreases (−) | Credit for increases (+) |

# Withdrawals by the Owner

The owner of a proprietorship may withdraw cash from the business for personal use. This is common practice for owners devoting full time to the business, since the business may be the owner's main source of income. Such withdrawals have the effect of decreasing owner's equity. Just as decreases in owner's equity are recorded as debits, increases in withdrawals are recorded as debits. Withdrawals are debited to an account with the owner's name followed by *Drawing* or *Personal*.

In transaction (h), Chris Clark withdrew $2,000 in cash from NetSolutions for personal use. The effect of this transaction is to increase the drawing account and decrease the cash account. The journal entry for transaction (h) is shown below.

**Entry H**

| 1 | 2005 Nov. | 30 | Chris Clark, Drawing | | 2 0 0 0 00 | | 1 |
| 2 | | | Cash | | | 2 0 0 0 00 | 2 |
| 3 | | | Chris Clark withdrew cash for | | | | 3 |
| 4 | | | personal use. | | | | 4 |

## INTEGRITY IN BUSINESS

### WILL JOURNALIZING PREVENT FRAUD?

While journalizing transactions reduces the possibility of fraud, it by no means eliminates it. For example, embezzlement can be hidden within the double-entry bookkeeping system by creating fictitious suppliers to whom checks are issued.

# Normal Balances of Accounts

The sum of the increases recorded in an account is usually equal to or greater than the sum of the decreases recorded in the account. For this reason, the normal balances of all accounts are positive rather than negative. For example, the total debits (increases) in an asset account will ordinarily be greater than the total credits (decreases). Thus, asset accounts normally have debit balances.

The rules of debit and credit and the normal balances of the various types of accounts are summarized as follows:

A debit balance in which of the following accounts—Cash, Drawing, Wages Expense, Supplies, Fees Earned—would indicate that an error has occurred?

---------------------------------

*Fees Earned*

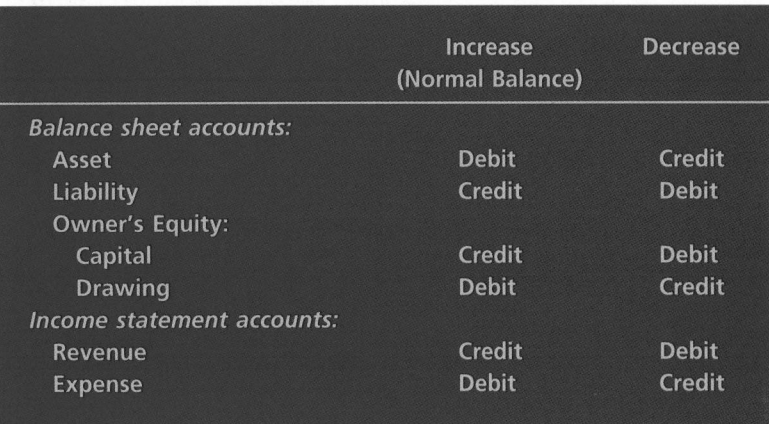

|  | Increase (Normal Balance) | Decrease |
|---|---|---|
| *Balance sheet accounts:* |  |  |
| Asset | Debit | Credit |
| Liability | Credit | Debit |
| Owner's Equity: |  |  |
| Capital | Credit | Debit |
| Drawing | Debit | Credit |
| *Income statement accounts:* |  |  |
| Revenue | Credit | Debit |
| Expense | Debit | Credit |

When an account normally having a debit balance actually has a credit balance, or vice versa, an error may have occurred or an unusual situation may exist. For example, a credit balance in the office equipment account could result only from an error. On the other hand, a debit balance in an accounts payable account could result from an overpayment.

# Illustration of Analyzing and Summarizing Transactions

**objective 4**

Analyze and summarize the financial statement effects of transactions.

**POINT OF INTEREST**

In computerized accounting systems, some transactions may be automatically authorized and recorded when certain events occur. For example, the salaries of managers may be paid automatically at the end of each pay period.

How does a transaction take place in a business? First, a manager or other employee authorizes the transaction. The transaction then takes place. The businesses involved in the transaction usually prepare documents that give details of the transaction. These documents then become the basis for analyzing and recording the transaction. For example, Chris  Clark might authorize the purchase of supplies for NetSolutions by telling an employee to buy computer paper at the local office supply store. The employee purchases the supplies for cash and receives a sales slip from the office supply store listing the supplies bought. The employee then gives the sales slip to Chris Clark, who verifies and records the transaction.

As we discussed in the preceding section, a transaction is first recorded in a journal. Thus, the journal is a history of transactions by date. Periodically, the journal entries are transferred to the accounts in the ledger. The ledger is a history of transactions by account. The process of transferring the debits and credits from the journal entries to the accounts is called **posting**. The flow of a transaction from its authorization to its posting in the accounts is shown in Exhibit 2.

In practice, businesses use a variety of formats for recording journal entries. A business may use one all-purpose journal, sometimes called a **two-column journal**, or it may use several journals. In the latter case, each journal is used to record different types of transactions, such as cash receipts or cash payments. The journals may be part of either a manual accounting system or a computerized accounting system.[3]

---

[3]The use of special journals and computerized accounting systems is discussed in later chapters, after the basics of accounting systems have been covered.

**•Exhibit 2**

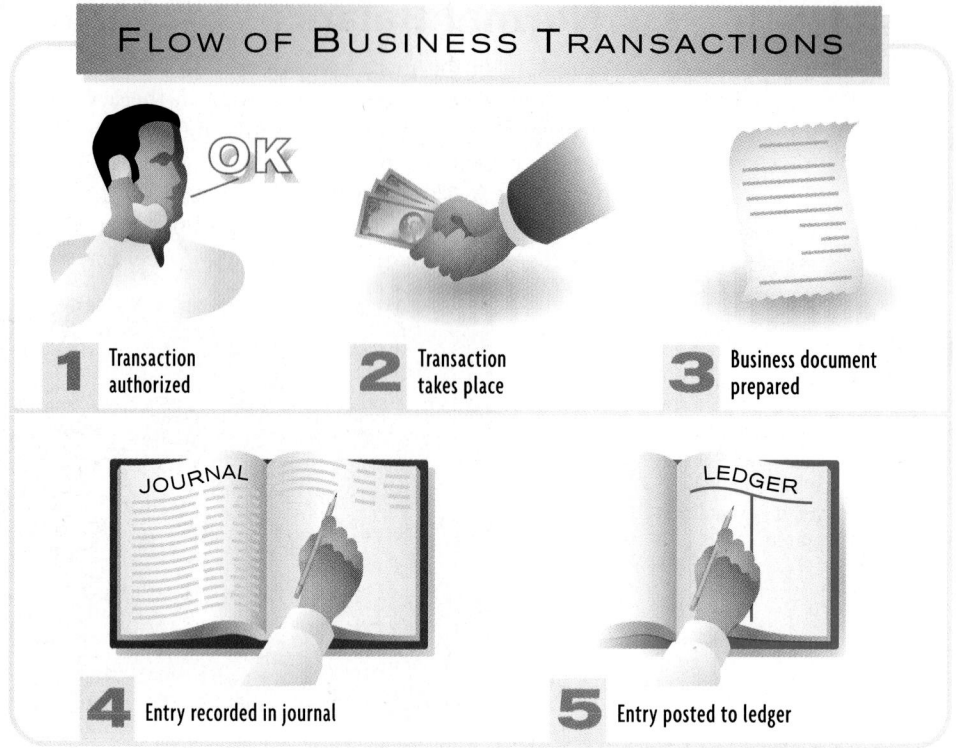

# FLOW OF BUSINESS TRANSACTIONS

**1** Transaction authorized

**2** Transaction takes place

**3** Business document prepared

**4** Entry recorded in journal

**5** Entry posted to ledger

I was founded in 1866, when a pharmacist tried to develop an economical alternative to breast milk for mothers who couldn't nurse their babies. Today I'm Switzerland's largest industrial company and the world's largest food company, employing nearly a quarter of a million people. My brands are available in almost every nation, and include Taster's Choice, Carnation, Libby's, PowerBar, Maggi, Buitoni, Stouffer's, KitKat, Smarties, After Eight, Baby Ruth, Butterfinger, Friskies, Fancy Feast, Alpo, and Mighty Dog. I also hold a major interest in L'Oréal. Sales of my instant coffee more than doubled during World War II. Who am I? (Go to page 81 for answer.)

The double-entry accounting system is a very powerful tool in analyzing the effects of transactions. Using this system to analyze transactions is summarized as follows:

1. Determine whether an asset, a liability, owner's equity, revenue, or expense account is affected by the transaction.
2. For each account affected by the transaction, determine whether the account increases or decreases.
3. Determine whether each increase or decrease should be recorded as a debit or a credit.

To illustrate recording a transaction in an all-purpose journal and posting in a manual accounting system, we will use the December transactions of NetSolutions. The first transaction in December occurred on December 1.

Dec. 1.   NetSolutions paid a premium of $2,400 for a comprehensive insurance policy covering liability, theft, and fire. The policy covers a two-year period.

**Analysis**   When you purchased insurance for your automobile, you may have been required to pay the insurance premium in advance. In this case, your transaction was similar to NetSolutions. Advance payments of expenses such as insurance are prepaid expenses, which are assets. For NetSolutions, the asset acquired for the cash payment is insurance protection for 24 months. The asset Prepaid Insurance increases and is debited for $2,400. The asset Cash decreases and is credited for $2,400. The recording and posting of this transaction is shown in Exhibit 3.

Note where the date of the transaction is recorded in the journal. Also note that the entry is explained as the payment of an insurance premium. Such explanations should be brief. For unusual and complex transactions, such as a long-term rental arrangement, the journal entry explanation may include a reference to the rental agreement or other business document.

**•Exhibit 3**    **Diagram of the Recording and Posting of a Debit and a Credit**

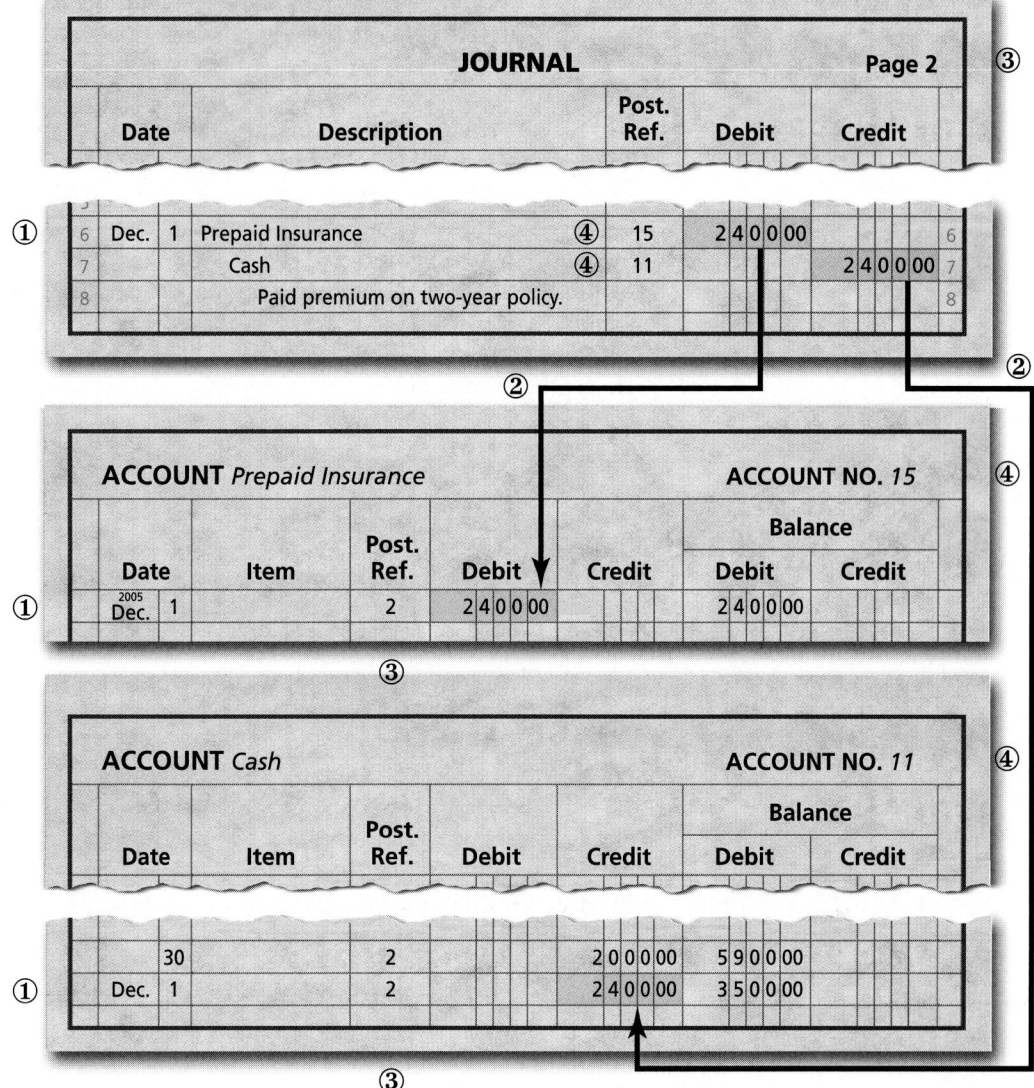

You will note that the T account form is not used in this illustration. Although the T account clearly separates debit and credit entries, it is inefficient for summarizing a large quantity of transactions. In practice, the T account is usually replaced with the standard form shown in Exhibit 3.

The debits and credits for each journal entry are posted to the accounts in the order in which they occur in the journal. In posting to the standard account, (1) the date is entered, and (2) the amount of the entry is entered. For future reference, (3) the journal page number is inserted in the Posting Reference column of the account, and (4) the account number is inserted in the Posting Reference column of the journal.

The remaining December transactions for NetSolutions are analyzed in the following paragraphs. These transactions are posted to the ledger in Exhibit 4, shown later. To simplify and reduce repetition, some of the December transactions are stated in summary form. For example, cash received for services is normally recorded on a daily basis. In this example, however, only summary totals are recorded at the middle and end of the month. Likewise, all fees earned on account during December are recorded at the middle and end of the month. In practice, each fee earned is recorded separately.

Dec. 1. NetSolutions paid rent for December, $800. The company from which NetSolutions is renting its store space now requires the payment of rent on the 1st of each month, rather than at the end of the month.

**Analysis**    You may pay monthly rent on an apartment on the first of each month. Your rent transaction is similar to NetSolutions. The advance payment of rent is an asset, much like the advance payment of the insurance premium in the preceding transaction. However, unlike the insurance premium, this prepaid rent will expire in one month. When an asset that is purchased will be used up in a short period of time, such as a month, it is normal to debit an expense account initially. This avoids having to transfer the balance from an asset account (Prepaid Rent) to an expense account (Rent Expense) at the end of the month. Thus, when the rent for December is prepaid at the beginning of the month, Rent Expense is debited for $800 and Cash is credited for $800.

| 10 | 1 | Rent Expense | 52 | 8 0 0 00 | | 10 |
|---|---|---|---|---|---|---|
| 11 | | Cash | 11 | | 8 0 0 00 | 11 |
| 12 | | Paid rent for December. | | | | 12 |

What would likely cause the cash account to have a credit balance?

*An error or an overdrawn cash account.*

Dec. 1. NetSolutions received an offer from a local retailer to rent the land purchased on November 5. The retailer plans to use the land as a parking lot for its employees and customers. NetSolutions agreed to rent the land to the retailer for three months, with the rent payable in advance. NetSolutions received $360 for three months' rent beginning December 1.

**Analysis**    By agreeing to rent the land and accepting the $360, NetSolutions has incurred an obligation (liability) to the retailer. This obligation is to make the land available for use for three months and not to interfere with its use. The liability created by receiving the cash in advance of providing the service is called ***unearned revenue***. Thus, the $360 received is an increase in an asset and is debited to Cash. The liability account Unearned Rent increases and is credited for $360. As time passes, the unearned rent liability will decrease and will become revenue.

| 14 | 1 | Cash | 11 | 3 6 0 00 | | 14 |
|---|---|---|---|---|---|---|
| 15 | | Unearned Rent | 23 | | 3 6 0 00 | 15 |
| 16 | | Received advance payment for | | | | 16 |
| 17 | | three months' rent on land. | | | | 17 |

Dec. 4. NetSolutions purchased office equipment on account from Executive Supply Co. for $1,800.

**Analysis**    The asset account Office Equipment increases and is therefore debited for $1,800. The liability account Accounts Payable increases and is credited for $1,800.

| 19 | 4 | Office Equipment | 18 | 1 8 0 0 00 | | 19 |
|---|---|---|---|---|---|---|
| 20 | | Accounts Payable | 21 | | 1 8 0 0 00 | 20 |
| 21 | | Purchased office equipment | | | | 21 |
| 22 | | on account. | | | | 22 |

**REAL WORLD**

Magazines that receive subscriptions in advance must record the receipts as unearned revenues. Likewise, airlines that receive ticket payments in advance must record the receipts as unearned revenues until the passengers use the tickets.

Dec. 6. NetSolutions paid $180 for a newspaper advertisement.

**Analysis**   An expense increases and is debited for $180. The asset Cash decreases and is credited for $180. Expense items that are expected to be minor in amount are normally included as part of the miscellaneous expense. Thus, Miscellaneous Expense is debited for $180.

| | | | | | | |
|---|---|---|---|---|---|---|
| 24 | 6 | Miscellaneous Expense | 59 | 1 8 0 00 | | 24 |
| 25 | | Cash | 11 | | 1 8 0 00 | 25 |
| 26 | | Paid for newspaper ad. | | | | 26 |

Dec. 11.  NetSolutions paid creditors $400.

**Analysis**   This payment decreases the liability account Accounts Payable, which is debited for $400. Cash also decreases and is credited for $400.

| | | | | | | |
|---|---|---|---|---|---|---|
| 28 | 11 | Accounts Payable | 21 | 4 0 0 00 | | 28 |
| 29 | | Cash | 11 | | 4 0 0 00 | 29 |
| 30 | | Paid creditors on account. | | | | 30 |

Dec. 13.  NetSolutions paid a receptionist and a part-time assistant $950 for two weeks' wages.

**Analysis**   This transaction is similar to the December 6 transaction, where an expense account is increased and Cash is decreased. Thus, Wages Expense is debited for $950, and Cash is credited for $950.

| | | | | | | | |
|---|---|---|---|---|---|---|---|
| | | | **JOURNAL** | | | | **Page 3** |
| | **Date** | | **Description** | **Post. Ref.** | **Debit** | **Credit** | |
| 1 | 2005 Dec. | 13 | Wages Expense | 51 | 9 5 0 00 | | 1 |
| 2 | | | Cash | 11 | | 9 5 0 00 | 2 |
| 3 | | | Paid two weeks' wages. | | | | 3 |

Dec. 16.  NetSolutions received $3,100 from fees earned for the first half of December.

**Analysis**   Cash increases and is debited for $3,100. The revenue account Fees Earned increases and is credited for $3,100.

| | | | | | | |
|---|---|---|---|---|---|---|
| 5 | 16 | Cash | 11 | 3 1 0 0 00 | | 5 |
| 6 | | Fees Earned | 41 | | 3 1 0 0 00 | 6 |
| 7 | | Received fees from customers. | | | | 7 |

Dec. 16.  Fees earned on account totaled $1,750 for the first half of December.

**Analysis**   Assume that you have agreed to take care of a neighbor's dog for a week for $100. At the end of the week, you agree to wait until the first of the next month to receive the $100. Like NetSolutions, you have provided services on account and thus have a right to receive the payment from your neighbor. When a business agrees that payment for services provided or goods sold can be accepted at a later date, the firm has an **account receivable**, which is a claim against the customer. The account receivable is an asset, and the revenue is earned even though no cash has been received. Thus, Accounts Receivable increases and is debited for $1,750. The revenue account Fees Earned increases and is credited for $1,750.

| | | | | | | | |
|---|---|---|---|---|---|---|---|
| 9 | 16 | Accounts Receivable | 12 | 1 7 5 0 00 | | | 9 |
| 10 | | Fees Earned | 41 | | 1 7 5 0 00 | | 10 |
| 11 | | Recorded fees earned on account. | | | | | 11 |

Dec. 20. NetSolutions paid $900 to Executive Supply Co. on the $1,800 debt owed from the December 4 transaction.

**Analysis**   This is similar to the transaction of December 11.

| | | | | | | | |
|---|---|---|---|---|---|---|---|
| 13 | 20 | Accounts Payable | 21 | 9 0 0 00 | | | 13 |
| 14 | | Cash | 11 | | 9 0 0 00 | | 14 |
| 15 | | Paid part of amount owed to | | | | | 15 |
| 16 | | Executive Supply Co. | | | | | 16 |

Dec. 21. NetSolutions received $650 from customers in payment of their accounts.

**Analysis**   When customers pay amounts owed for services they have previously received, one asset increases and another asset decreases. Thus, Cash is debited for $650, and Accounts Receivable is credited for $650.

| | | | | | | | |
|---|---|---|---|---|---|---|---|
| 18 | 21 | Cash | 11 | 6 5 0 00 | | | 18 |
| 19 | | Accounts Receivable | 12 | | 6 5 0 00 | | 19 |
| 20 | | Received cash from customers | | | | | 20 |
| 21 | | on account. | | | | | 21 |

Dec. 23. NetSolutions paid $1,450 for supplies.

**Analysis**   The asset account Supplies increases and is debited for $1,450. The asset account Cash decreases and is credited for $1,450.

| | | | | | | | |
|---|---|---|---|---|---|---|---|
| 23 | 23 | Supplies | 14 | 1 4 5 0 00 | | | 23 |
| 24 | | Cash | 11 | | 1 4 5 0 00 | | 24 |
| 25 | | Purchased supplies. | | | | | 25 |

Dec. 27. NetSolutions paid the receptionist and the part-time assistant $1,200 for two weeks' wages.

**Analysis**   This is similar to the transaction of December 13.

| | | | | | | | |
|---|---|---|---|---|---|---|---|
| 27 | 27 | Wages Expense | 51 | 1 2 0 0 00 | | | 27 |
| 28 | | Cash | 11 | | 1 2 0 0 00 | | 28 |
| 29 | | Paid two weeks' wages. | | | | | 29 |

Dec. 31. NetSolutions paid its $310 telephone bill for the month.

**Analysis**   You pay a telephone bill each month. Businesses, such as NetSolutions, also must pay monthly utility bills. Such transactions are similar to the transaction of December 6. The expense account Utilities Expense is debited for $310, and Cash is credited for $310.

| 31 | | 31 | Utilities Expense | 54 | 3 1 0 00 | | 31 |
| 32 | | | Cash | 11 | | 3 1 0 00 | 32 |
| 33 | | | Paid telephone bill. | | | | 33 |

Dec. 31. NetSolutions paid its $225 electric bill for the month.

**Analysis**   This is similar to the preceding transaction.

| | | **JOURNAL** | | | | **Page 4** |
| --- | --- | --- | --- | --- | --- | --- |
| | **Date** | **Description** | **Post. Ref.** | **Debit** | **Credit** | |
| 1 | 2005 Dec. 31 | Utilities Expense | 54 | 2 2 5 00 | | 1 |
| 2 | | Cash | 11 | | 2 2 5 00 | 2 |
| 3 | | Paid electric bill. | | | | 3 |

Dec. 31. NetSolutions received $2,870 from fees earned for the second half of December.

**Analysis**   This is similar to the transaction of December 16.

| 5 | | 31 | Cash | 11 | 2 8 7 0 00 | | 5 |
| 6 | | | Fees Earned | 41 | | 2 8 7 0 00 | 6 |
| 7 | | | Received fees from customers. | | | | 7 |

Dec. 31. Fees earned on account totaled $1,120 for the second half of December.

**Analysis**   This is similar to the transaction of December 16.

| 9 | | 31 | Accounts Receivable | 12 | 1 1 2 0 00 | | 9 |
| 10 | | | Fees Earned | 41 | | 1 1 2 0 00 | 10 |
| 11 | | | Recorded fees earned on account. | | | | 11 |

Dec. 31. Chris Clark withdrew $2,000 for personal use.

**Analysis**   This transaction resulted in an increase in the amount of withdrawals and is recorded by a $2,000 debit to Chris Clark, Drawing. The decrease in business cash is recorded by a $2,000 credit to Cash.

| 13 | | 31 | Chris Clark, Drawing | 32 | 2 0 0 0 00 | | 13 |
| 14 | | | Cash | 11 | | 2 0 0 0 00 | 14 |
| 15 | | | Chris Clark withdrew cash for | | | | 15 |
| 16 | | | personal use. | | | | 16 |

The journal for NetSolutions since it was organized on November 1 is shown in Exhibit 4. Exhibit 4 also shows the ledger after the transactions for both November and December have been posted.

•**Exhibit 4**   Journal and Ledger—NetSolutions

| | JOURNAL | | | | | | Page 1 |
|---|---|---|---|---|---|---|---|
| | **Date** | **Description** | **Post. Ref.** | **Debit** | **Credit** | |
| 1 | 2005 Nov. 1 | Cash | 11 | 25 000 00 | | 1 |
| 2 | | Chris Clark, Capital | 31 | | 25 000 00 | 2 |
| 3 | | Invested cash in NetSolutions. | | | | 3 |
| 4 | | | | | | 4 |
| 5 | 5 | Land | 17 | 20 000 00 | | 5 |
| 6 | | Cash | 11 | | 20 000 00 | 6 |
| 7 | | Purchased land for building site. | | | | 7 |
| 8 | | | | | | 8 |
| 9 | 10 | Supplies | 14 | 1 350 00 | | 9 |
| 10 | | Accounts Payable | 21 | | 1 350 00 | 10 |
| 11 | | Purchased supplies on account. | | | | 11 |
| 12 | | | | | | 12 |
| 13 | 18 | Cash | 11 | 7 500 00 | | 13 |
| 14 | | Fees Earned | 41 | | 7 500 00 | 14 |
| 15 | | Received fees from customers. | | | | 15 |
| 16 | | | | | | 16 |
| 17 | 30 | Wages Expense | 51 | 2 125 00 | | 17 |
| 18 | | Rent Expense | 52 | 800 00 | | 18 |
| 19 | | Utilities Expense | 54 | 450 00 | | 19 |
| 20 | | Miscellaneous Expense | 59 | 275 00 | | 20 |
| 21 | | Cash | 11 | | 3 650 00 | 21 |
| 22 | | Paid expenses. | | | | 22 |
| 23 | | | | | | 23 |
| 24 | 30 | Accounts Payable | 21 | 950 00 | | 24 |
| 25 | | Cash | 11 | | 950 00 | 25 |
| 26 | | Paid creditors on account. | | | | 26 |
| 27 | | | | | | 27 |
| 28 | 30 | Supplies Expense | 55 | 800 00 | | 28 |
| 29 | | Supplies | 14 | | 800 00 | 29 |
| 30 | | Supplies used during November. | | | | 30 |

| | JOURNAL | | | | | | Page 2 |
|---|---|---|---|---|---|---|---|
| | **Date** | **Description** | **Post. Ref.** | **Debit** | **Credit** | |
| 1 | 2005 Nov. 30 | Chris Clark, Drawing | 32 | 2 000 00 | | 1 |
| 2 | | Cash | 11 | | 2 000 00 | 2 |
| 3 | | Chris Clark withdrew cash for | | | | 3 |
| 4 | | personal use. | | | | 4 |

**•Exhibit 4**
(continued)

## JOURNAL — Page 2

| | Date | | Description | Post. Ref. | Debit | Credit | |
|---|---|---|---|---|---|---|---|
| 6 | 2005 Dec. | 1 | Prepaid Insurance | 15 | 2 4 0 0 00 | | 6 |
| 7 | | | Cash | 11 | | 2 4 0 0 00 | 7 |
| 8 | | | Paid premium on two-year policy. | | | | 8 |
| 9 | | | | | | | 9 |
| 10 | | 1 | Rent Expense | 52 | 8 0 0 00 | | 10 |
| 11 | | | Cash | 11 | | 8 0 0 00 | 11 |
| 12 | | | Paid rent for December. | | | | 12 |
| 13 | | | | | | | 13 |
| 14 | | 1 | Cash | 11 | 3 6 0 00 | | 14 |
| 15 | | | Unearned Rent | 23 | | 3 6 0 00 | 15 |
| 16 | | | Received advance payment for | | | | 16 |
| 17 | | | three months' rent on land. | | | | 17 |
| 18 | | | | | | | 18 |
| 19 | | 4 | Office Equipment | 18 | 1 8 0 0 00 | | 19 |
| 20 | | | Accounts Payable | 21 | | 1 8 0 0 00 | 20 |
| 21 | | | Purchased office equipment | | | | 21 |
| 22 | | | on account. | | | | 22 |
| 23 | | | | | | | 23 |
| 24 | | 6 | Miscellaneous Expense | 59 | 1 8 0 00 | | 24 |
| 25 | | | Cash | 11 | | 1 8 0 00 | 25 |
| 26 | | | Paid for newspaper ad. | | | | 26 |
| 27 | | | | | | | 27 |
| 28 | | 11 | Accounts Payable | 21 | 4 0 0 00 | | 28 |
| 29 | | | Cash | 11 | | 4 0 0 00 | 29 |
| 30 | | | Paid creditors on account. | | | | 30 |

## JOURNAL — Page 3

| | Date | | Description | Post. Ref. | Debit | Credit | |
|---|---|---|---|---|---|---|---|
| 1 | 2005 Dec. | 13 | Wages Expense | 51 | 9 5 0 00 | | 1 |
| 2 | | | Cash | 11 | | 9 5 0 00 | 2 |
| 3 | | | Paid two weeks' wages. | | | | 3 |
| 4 | | | | | | | 4 |
| 5 | | 16 | Cash | 11 | 3 1 0 0 00 | | 5 |
| 6 | | | Fees Earned | 41 | | 3 1 0 0 00 | 6 |
| 7 | | | Received fees from customers. | | | | 7 |
| 8 | | | | | | | 8 |
| 9 | | 16 | Accounts Receivable | 12 | 1 7 5 0 00 | | 9 |
| 10 | | | Fees Earned | 41 | | 1 7 5 0 00 | 10 |
| 11 | | | Recorded fees earned on account. | | | | 11 |
| 12 | | | | | | | 12 |
| 13 | | 20 | Accounts Payable | 21 | 9 0 0 00 | | 13 |
| 14 | | | Cash | 11 | | 9 0 0 00 | 14 |
| 15 | | | Paid part of amount owed to | | | | 15 |
| 16 | | | Executive Supply Co. | | | | 16 |

•**Exhibit 4**
(continued)

| | Date | | Description | Post. Ref. | Debit | Credit | |
|---|---|---|---|---|---|---|---|
| 18 | 2005 Dec. | 21 | Cash | 11 | 6 5 0 00 | | 18 |
| 19 | | | Accounts Receivable | 12 | | 6 5 0 00 | 19 |
| 20 | | | Received cash from customers | | | | 20 |
| 21 | | | on account. | | | | 21 |
| 22 | | | | | | | 22 |
| 23 | | 23 | Supplies | 14 | 1 4 5 0 00 | | 23 |
| 24 | | | Cash | 11 | | 1 4 5 0 00 | 24 |
| 25 | | | Purchased supplies. | | | | 25 |
| 26 | | | | | | | 26 |
| 27 | | 27 | Wages Expense | 51 | 1 2 0 0 00 | | 27 |
| 28 | | | Cash | 11 | | 1 2 0 0 00 | 28 |
| 29 | | | Paid two weeks' wages. | | | | 29 |
| 30 | | | | | | | 30 |
| 31 | | 31 | Utilities Expense | 54 | 3 1 0 00 | | 31 |
| 32 | | | Cash | 11 | | 3 1 0 00 | 32 |
| 33 | | | Paid telephone bill. | | | | 33 |

**JOURNAL** — Page 3

| | Date | | Description | Post. Ref. | Debit | Credit | |
|---|---|---|---|---|---|---|---|
| 1 | 2005 Dec. | 31 | Utilities Expense | 54 | 2 2 5 00 | | 1 |
| 2 | | | Cash | 11 | | 2 2 5 00 | 2 |
| 3 | | | Paid electric bill. | | | | 3 |
| 4 | | | | | | | 4 |
| 5 | | 31 | Cash | 11 | 2 8 7 0 00 | | 5 |
| 6 | | | Fees Earned | 41 | | 2 8 7 0 00 | 6 |
| 7 | | | Received fees from customers. | | | | 7 |
| 8 | | | | | | | 8 |
| 9 | | 31 | Accounts Receivable | 12 | 1 1 2 0 00 | | 9 |
| 10 | | | Fees Earned | 41 | | 1 1 2 0 00 | 10 |
| 11 | | | Recorded fees earned on account. | | | | 11 |
| 12 | | | | | | | 12 |
| 13 | | 31 | Chris Clark, Drawing | 32 | 2 0 0 0 00 | | 13 |
| 14 | | | Cash | 11 | | 2 0 0 0 00 | 14 |
| 15 | | | Chris Clark withdrew cash for | | | | 15 |
| 16 | | | personal use. | | | | 16 |

**JOURNAL** — Page 4

**•Exhibit 4**
(continued)

# LEDGER

**ACCOUNT** *Cash*  **ACCOUNT NO.** *11*

| Date | Item | Post. Ref. | Debit | Credit | Balance Debit | Balance Credit |
|------|------|-----------|-------|--------|---------------|----------------|
| 2005 Nov. 1 | | 1 | 25 0 0 0 00 | | 25 0 0 0 00 | |
| 5 | | 1 | | 20 0 0 0 00 | 5 0 0 0 00 | |
| 18 | | 1 | 7 5 0 0 00 | | 12 5 0 0 00 | |
| 30 | | 1 | | 3 6 5 0 00 | 8 8 5 0 00 | |
| 30 | | 1 | | 9 5 0 00 | 7 9 0 0 00 | |
| 30 | | 2 | | 2 0 0 0 00 | 5 9 0 0 00 | |
| Dec. 1 | | 2 | | 2 4 0 0 00 | 3 5 0 0 00 | |
| 1 | | 2 | | 8 0 0 00 | 2 7 0 0 00 | |
| 1 | | 2 | 3 6 0 00 | | 3 0 6 0 00 | |
| 6 | | 2 | | 1 8 0 00 | 2 8 8 0 00 | |
| 11 | | 2 | | 4 0 0 00 | 2 4 8 0 00 | |
| 13 | | 3 | | 9 5 0 00 | 1 5 3 0 00 | |
| 16 | | 3 | 3 1 0 0 00 | | 4 6 3 0 00 | |
| 20 | | 3 | | 9 0 0 00 | 3 7 3 0 00 | |
| 21 | | 3 | 6 5 0 00 | | 4 3 8 0 00 | |
| 23 | | 3 | | 1 4 5 0 00 | 2 9 3 0 00 | |
| 27 | | 3 | | 1 2 0 0 00 | 1 7 3 0 00 | |
| 31 | | 3 | | 3 1 0 00 | 1 4 2 0 00 | |
| 31 | | 4 | | 2 2 5 00 | 1 1 9 5 00 | |
| 31 | | 4 | 2 8 7 0 00 | | 4 0 6 5 00 | |
| 31 | | 4 | | 2 0 0 0 00 | 2 0 6 5 00 | |

**ACCOUNT** *Accounts Receivable*  **ACCOUNT NO.** *12*

| Date | Item | Post. Ref. | Debit | Credit | Balance Debit | Balance Credit |
|------|------|-----------|-------|--------|---------------|----------------|
| 2005 Dec. 16 | | 3 | 1 7 5 0 00 | | 1 7 5 0 00 | |
| 21 | | 3 | | 6 5 0 00 | 1 1 0 0 00 | |
| 31 | | 4 | 1 1 2 0 00 | | 2 2 2 0 00 | |

**ACCOUNT** *Supplies*  **ACCOUNT NO.** *14*

| Date | Item | Post. Ref. | Debit | Credit | Balance Debit | Balance Credit |
|------|------|-----------|-------|--------|---------------|----------------|
| 2005 Nov. 10 | | 1 | 1 3 5 0 00 | | 1 3 5 0 00 | |
| 30 | | 1 | | 8 0 0 00 | 5 5 0 00 | |
| Dec. 23 | | 3 | 1 4 5 0 00 | | 2 0 0 0 00 | |

**•Exhibit 4**
(continued)

**ACCOUNT** *Prepaid Insurance*          **ACCOUNT NO. 15**

| Date | Item | Post. Ref. | Debit | Credit | Balance Debit | Balance Credit |
|------|------|-----------|-------|--------|-------|--------|
| 2005 Dec. 1 | | 2 | 2 4 0 0 00 | | 2 4 0 0 00 | |

**ACCOUNT** *Land*          **ACCOUNT NO. 17**

| Date | Item | Post. Ref. | Debit | Credit | Balance Debit | Balance Credit |
|------|------|-----------|-------|--------|-------|--------|
| 2005 Nov. 5 | | 1 | 20 0 0 0 00 | | 20 0 0 0 00 | |

**ACCOUNT** *Office Equipment*          **ACCOUNT NO. 18**

| Date | Item | Post. Ref. | Debit | Credit | Balance Debit | Balance Credit |
|------|------|-----------|-------|--------|-------|--------|
| 2005 Dec. 4 | | 2 | 1 8 0 0 00 | | 1 8 0 0 00 | |

**ACCOUNT** *Accounts Payable*          **ACCOUNT NO. 21**

| Date | Item | Post. Ref. | Debit | Credit | Balance Debit | Balance Credit |
|------|------|-----------|-------|--------|-------|--------|
| 2005 Nov. 10 | | 1 | | 1 3 5 0 00 | | 1 3 5 0 00 |
| 30 | | 1 | 9 5 0 00 | | | 4 0 0 00 |
| Dec. 4 | | 2 | | 1 8 0 0 00 | | 2 2 0 0 00 |
| 11 | | 2 | 4 0 0 00 | | | 1 8 0 0 00 |
| 20 | | 3 | 9 0 0 00 | | | 9 0 0 00 |

**ACCOUNT** *Unearned Rent*          **ACCOUNT NO. 23**

| Date | Item | Post. Ref. | Debit | Credit | Balance Debit | Balance Credit |
|------|------|-----------|-------|--------|-------|--------|
| 2005 Dec. 1 | | 2 | | 3 6 0 00 | | 3 6 0 00 |

**•Exhibit 4**
(continued)

**ACCOUNT** *Chris Clark, Capital*     **ACCOUNT NO.** *31*

| Date | Item | Post. Ref. | Debit | Credit | Balance Debit | Balance Credit |
|---|---|---|---|---|---|---|
| 2005 Nov. 1 | | 1 | | 25 000 00 | | 25 000 00 |

**ACCOUNT** *Chris Clark, Drawing*     **ACCOUNT NO.** *32*

| Date | Item | Post. Ref. | Debit | Credit | Balance Debit | Balance Credit |
|---|---|---|---|---|---|---|
| 2005 Nov. 30 | | 2 | 2 000 00 | | 2 000 00 | |
| Dec. 31 | | 4 | 2 000 00 | | 4 000 00 | |

**ACCOUNT** *Fees Earned*     **ACCOUNT NO.** *41*

| Date | Item | Post. Ref. | Debit | Credit | Balance Debit | Balance Credit |
|---|---|---|---|---|---|---|
| 2005 Nov. 18 | | 1 | | 7 500 00 | | 7 500 00 |
| Dec. 16 | | 3 | | 3 100 00 | | 10 600 00 |
| 16 | | 3 | | 1 750 00 | | 12 350 00 |
| 31 | | 4 | | 2 870 00 | | 15 220 00 |
| 31 | | 4 | | 1 120 00 | | 16 340 00 |

**ACCOUNT** *Wages Expense*     **ACCOUNT NO.** *51*

| Date | Item | Post. Ref. | Debit | Credit | Balance Debit | Balance Credit |
|---|---|---|---|---|---|---|
| 2005 Nov. 30 | | 1 | 2 125 00 | | 2 125 00 | |
| Dec. 13 | | 3 | 950 00 | | 3 075 00 | |
| 27 | | 3 | 1 200 00 | | 4 275 00 | |

**ACCOUNT** *Rent Expense*     **ACCOUNT NO.** *52*

| Date | Item | Post. Ref. | Debit | Credit | Balance Debit | Balance Credit |
|---|---|---|---|---|---|---|
| 2005 Nov. 30 | | 1 | 800 00 | | 800 00 | |
| Dec. 1 | | 2 | 800 00 | | 1 600 00 | |

•**Exhibit 4**
(concluded)

| ACCOUNT *Utilities Expense* | | | | | ACCOUNT NO. *54* | |
|---|---|---|---|---|---|---|
| | | Post. | | | Balance | |
| Date | Item | Ref. | Debit | Credit | Debit | Credit |
| 2005 Nov. 30 | | 1 | 4 5 0 00 | | 4 5 0 00 | |
| Dec. 31 | | 3 | 3 1 0 00 | | 7 6 0 00 | |
| 31 | | 4 | 2 2 5 00 | | 9 8 5 00 | |

| ACCOUNT *Supplies Expense* | | | | | ACCOUNT NO. *55* | |
|---|---|---|---|---|---|---|
| | | Post. | | | Balance | |
| Date | Item | Ref. | Debit | Credit | Debit | Credit |
| 2005 Nov. 30 | | 1 | 8 0 0 00 | | 8 0 0 00 | |

| ACCOUNT *Miscellaneous Expense* | | | | | ACCOUNT NO. *59* | |
|---|---|---|---|---|---|---|
| | | Post. | | | Balance | |
| Date | Item | Ref. | Debit | Credit | Debit | Credit |
| 2005 Nov. 30 | | 1 | 2 7 5 00 | | 2 7 5 00 | |
| Dec. 6 | | 2 | 1 8 0 00 | | 4 5 5 00 | |

# Trial Balance

objective **5**

Prepare a trial balance and explain how it can be used to discover errors.

How can you be sure that you have not made an error in posting the debits and credits to the ledger? One way is to determine the equality of the debits and credits in the ledger. This equal-

POINT OF INTEREST

The proof of the equality of the debit and credit balances is called a trial balance because a "trial" is a process of proving or testing.

ity should be proved at the end of each accounting period, if not more often. Such a proof, called a *trial balance*, may be in the form of a computer printout or in the form shown in Exhibit 5.

The first step in preparing the trial balance is to determine the balance of each account in the ledger. When the standard account form is used, the balance of each account appears in the balance column on the same line as the last posting to the account.

The trial balance does not provide complete proof of the accuracy of the ledger. It indicates only that the debits and the credits are equal. This proof is of value, however, because errors often affect the equality of debits and credits. If the two totals of a trial balance are not equal, an error has occurred. In the next section of this chapter, we will discuss procedures for discovering and correcting errors.

If you incorrectly record $1,000 received on account as a debit to Cash and a credit to Accounts Payable, will the trial balance totals be equal?

--------------------------------------------------

*Yes.*

## •Exhibit 5  Trial Balance

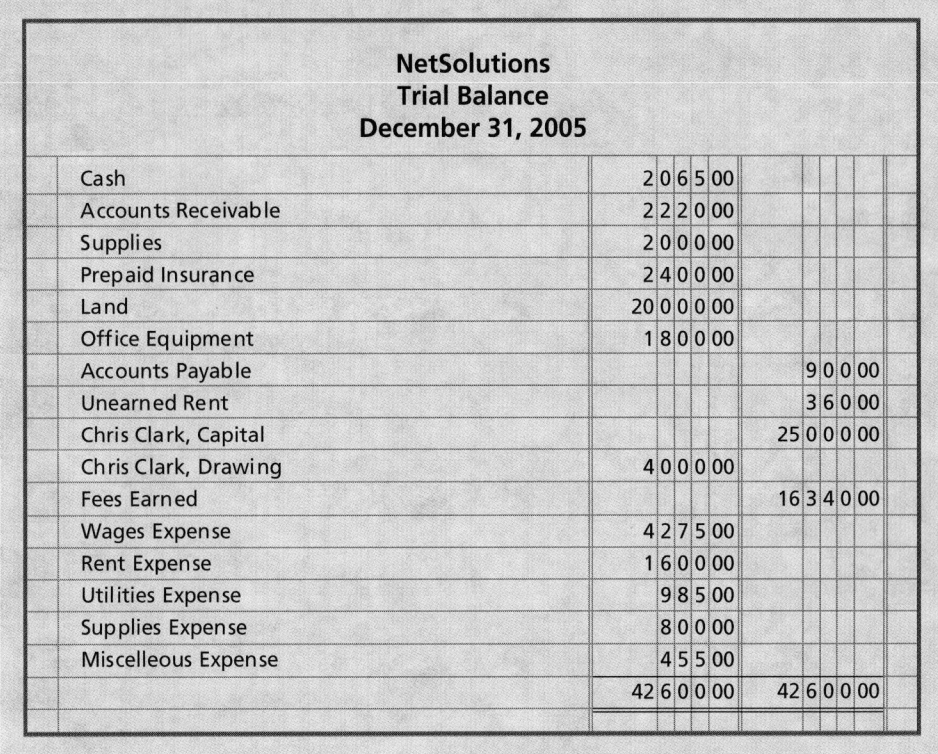

| | | | | |
|---|---|---|---|---|
| **NetSolutions** | | | | |
| **Trial Balance** | | | | |
| **December 31, 2005** | | | | |
| Cash | 2 0 6 5 00 | | | |
| Accounts Receivable | 2 2 2 0 00 | | | |
| Supplies | 2 0 0 0 00 | | | |
| Prepaid Insurance | 2 4 0 0 00 | | | |
| Land | 20 0 0 0 00 | | | |
| Office Equipment | 1 8 0 0 00 | | | |
| Accounts Payable | | | 9 0 0 00 | |
| Unearned Rent | | | 3 6 0 00 | |
| Chris Clark, Capital | | | 25 0 0 0 00 | |
| Chris Clark, Drawing | 4 0 0 0 00 | | | |
| Fees Earned | | | 16 3 4 0 00 | |
| Wages Expense | 4 2 7 5 00 | | | |
| Rent Expense | 1 6 0 0 00 | | | |
| Utilities Expense | 9 8 5 00 | | | |
| Supplies Expense | 8 0 0 00 | | | |
| Miscelleous Expense | 4 5 5 00 | | | |
| | 42 6 0 0 00 | | 42 6 0 0 00 | |

# Discovery and Correction of Errors

**objective  6**

Discover errors in recording transactions and correct them.

**REAL WORLD**

Many large corporations such as **Microsoft** and **Quaker Oats** round the figures in their financial statements to millions of dollars.

Errors will sometimes occur in journalizing and posting transactions. In some cases, however, an error might not be significant enough to affect the decisions of management or others. In such cases, the ***materiality concept*** implies that the error may be treated in the easiest possible way. For example, an error of a few dollars in recording an asset as an expense for a business with millions of dollars in assets would be considered immaterial, and a correction would not be necessary. In the remaining paragraphs, we assume that errors discovered are material and should be corrected.

## Discovery of Errors

As mentioned previously, preparing the trial balance is one of the primary ways to discover errors in the ledger. However, it indicates only that the debits and credits are equal. If the two totals of the trial balance are not equal, it is probably due to one or more of the errors described in Exhibit 6.

Among the types of errors that will *not* cause the trial balance totals to be unequal are the following:

1. Failure to record a transaction or to post a transaction.
2. Recording the same erroneous amount for both the debit and the credit parts of a transaction.
3. Recording the same transaction more than once.
4. Posting a part of a transaction correctly as a debit or credit but to the wrong account.

## •Exhibit 6 Errors Causing Unequal Trial Balance

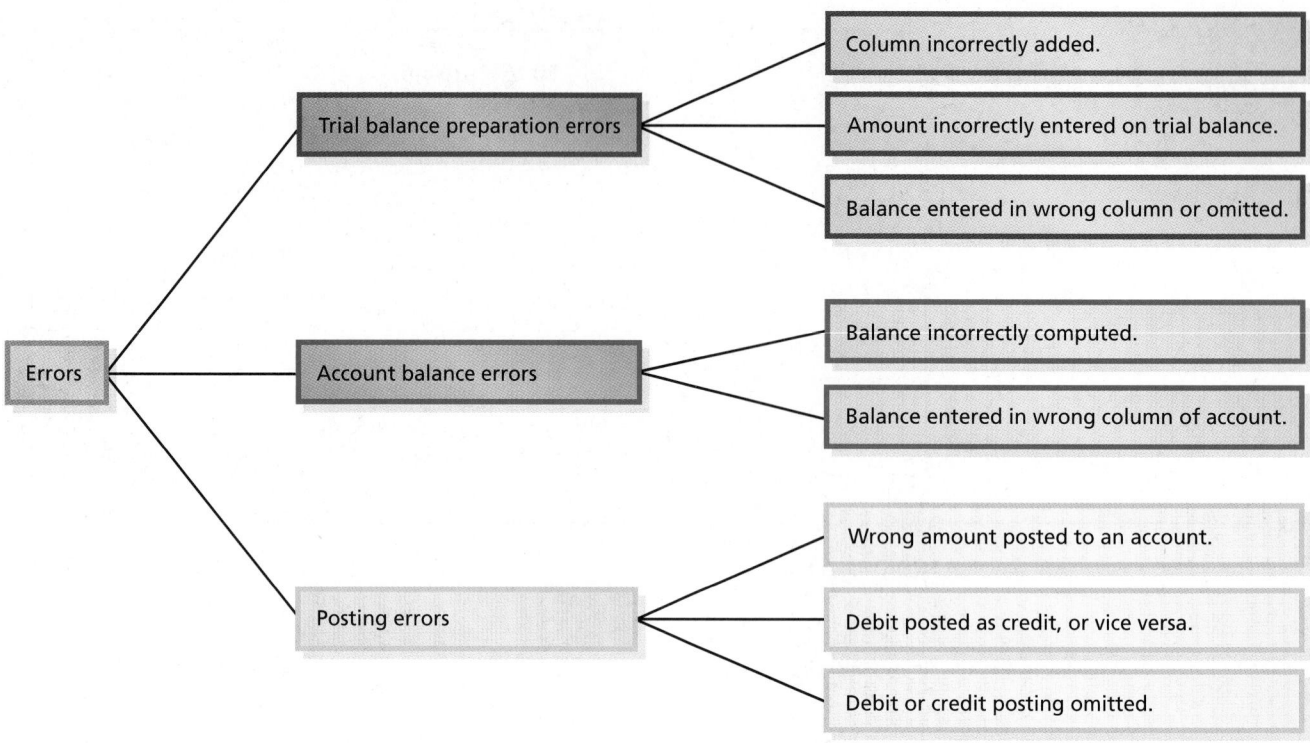

It is obvious that care should be used in recording transactions in the journal and in posting to the accounts. The need for accuracy in determining account balances and reporting them on the trial balance is also evident.

Errors in the accounts may be discovered in various ways: (1) through audit procedures, (2) by looking at the trial balance or (3) by chance. If the two trial balance totals are not equal, the amount of the difference between the totals should be determined before searching for the error.

The amount of the difference between the two totals of a trial balance sometimes gives a clue as to the nature of the error or where it occurred. For example, a difference of 10, 100, or 1,000 between two totals is often the result of an error in addition. A difference between totals can also be due to omitting a debit or a credit posting. If the difference can be evenly divided by 2, the error may be due to the posting of a debit as a credit, or vice versa. For example, if the debit total is $20,640 and the credit total is $20,236, the difference of $404 may indicate that a credit posting of $404 was omitted or that a credit of $202 was incorrectly posted as a debit.

Two other common types of errors are known as transpositions and slides. A *transposition* occurs when the order of the digits is changed mistakenly, such as writing $542 as $452 or $524. In a *slide*, the entire number is mistakenly moved one or more spaces to the right or the left, such as writing $542.00 as $54.20 or $5,420.00. If an error of either type has occurred and there are no other errors, the difference between the two trial balance totals can be evenly divided by 9.

If an error is not revealed by the trial balance, the steps in the accounting process must be retraced, beginning with the last step and working back to the entries in the journal. Usually, errors causing the trial balance totals to be unequal will be discovered before all of the steps are retraced.

What type of error occurs when $14,500 is recorded as $15,400?

--------------------------------------------

*A transposition.*

## Correction of Errors

The procedures used to correct an error in journalizing or posting vary according to the nature of the error and when the error is discovered. These procedures are summarized in Exhibit 7.

## •Exhibit 7    Procedures for Correcting Errors

| Error | Correction Procedure |
|---|---|
| 1. Journal entry is incorrect but not posted. | Draw a line through the error and insert correct title or amount. |
| 2. Journal entry is correct but posted incorrectly. | Draw a line through the error and post correctly. |
| 3. Journal entry is incorrect and posted. | Journalize and post a correcting entry. |

Correcting the first two types of errors shown in Exhibit 7 involves simply drawing a line through the error and inserting the correct title or amount. Usually, the person making corrections initials the correction in case questions arise later.

Correcting the third type of error in Exhibit 7 is more complex. To illustrate, assume that on May 5 a $12,500 purchase of office equipment on account was incorrectly journalized and posted as a debit to Supplies and a credit to Accounts Payable for $12,500. This posting of the incorrect entry is shown in the following T accounts.

|  | Supplies |  | Accounts Payable |  |
|---|---|---|---|---|
| *Incorrect:* | 12,500 | | | 12,500 |

Before making a correcting entry, it is best to determine the debit(s) and credit(s) that should have been recorded. These are shown in the following T accounts.

|  | Office Equipment |  | Accounts Payable |  |
|---|---|---|---|---|
| *Correct:* | 12,500 | | | 12,500 |

Comparing the two sets of T accounts shows that the incorrect debit to Supplies may be corrected by debiting Office Equipment for $12,500 and crediting Supplies for $12,500. The following correcting entry is then journalized and posted:

*Entry to Correct Error:*

| 18 | May | 31 | Office Equipment | 18 | 12 5 0 0 00 |  | 18 |
| 19 | | | Supplies | 14 | | 12 5 0 0 00 | 19 |
| 20 | | | To correct erroneous debit | | | | 20 |
| 21 | | | to Supplies on May 5. See invoice | | | | 21 |
| 22 | | | from Bell Office Equipment Co. | | | | 22 |

# Financial Analysis and Interpretation

objective    7

Use horizontal analysis to compare financial statements from different periods.

A single item appearing in a financial statement is often useful in interpreting the financial results of a business. However, comparing this item in a current statement with the same item in prior statements often makes the financial information more useful. **Horizontal analysis** is the term used to describe such comparisons.

In horizontal analysis, the amount of each item on the current financial statements is compared with the same item on one or more earlier statements. The increase or decrease in the *amount* of the item is computed, together with the *percent* of increase or decrease. When two statements are being compared, the earlier statement is used as the base for computing the amount and the percent of change.

To illustrate, the horizontal analysis of two income statements for J. Holmes, Attorney-at-Law, is shown in Exhibit 8. Exhibit 8 indicates both favorable and unfavorable trends affecting the income statement of J. Holmes, Attorney-at-Law. The increase in fees earned is a favorable trend, as is the decrease in supplies expense. Unfavorable trends include the increase in wages expense, utilities expense, and miscellaneous expense. These expenses increased faster than the increase in revenues, with total operating expenses increasing by 30.6%. Overall, net income increased by $15,800, or 19.9%, a favorable trend.

The significance of the various increases and decreases in the revenue and expense items in Exhibit 8 should be investigated to see if operations could be further improved. For example, the increase in utilities expense of 38.9% was the result of renting additional office space for use by a part-time law student in performing paralegal services. This explains the increase in rent expense of 25% and the increase in wages expense of 33.3%. The increase in revenues of 25% reflects the fees generated by the new paralegal.

The preceding example illustrates how horizontal analysis can be useful in interpreting and analyzing financial statements. Horizontal analyses similar to that shown in Exhibit 8 can also be performed for the balance sheet, the statement of owner's equity, and the statement of cash flows.

## •Exhibit 8    Horizontal Analysis of Income Statement

### J. Holmes, Attorney-at-Law
### Income Statement
### For the Years Ended December 31, 2005 and 2006

|  | 2006 | 2005 | Increase (Decrease) Amount | Increase (Decrease) Percent |
|---|---|---|---|---|
| Fees earned | $187,500 | $150,000 | $37,500 | 25.0%* |
| Operating expenses: | | | | |
| Wages expense | $ 60,000 | $ 45,000 | $15,000 | 33.3% |
| Rent expense | 15,000 | 12,000 | 3,000 | 25.0% |
| Utilities expense | 12,500 | 9,000 | 3,500 | 38.9% |
| Supplies expense | 2,700 | 3,000 | (300) | (10.0)% |
| Miscellaneous expense | 2,300 | 1,800 | 500 | 27.8% |
| Total operating expenses | $ 92,500 | $ 70,800 | $21,700 | 30.6% |
| Net income | $ 95,000 | $ 79,200 | $15,800 | 19.9% |

*$37,500 ÷ $150,000

## SPOTLIGHT ON STRATEGY

### GOT THE FLU? WHY NOT CHEW SOME GUM?

Facing a slumping market for sugared chewing gum, such as Juicy Fruit and Doublemint, **Wm. J. Wrigley Jr. Company** is reinventing itself with a strategy to expand its product lines and introduce new chewing gum applications. Wrigley's new products include sugarless breath mints and more powerful flavored mint chewing gum, like Extra Polar Ice. In addition, Wrigley is experimenting with health-care applications of chewing gum. Wrigley's Health Care Division has already developed Surpass, an antacid chewing gum to compete with Rolaids and Mylanta. In addition, Wrigley is experimenting with a cold-relief chewing gum and a gum that would provide dental benefits, such as whitening teeth and reducing plaque. Given that the U.S. population is aging, the company figures that people might prefer chewing gum to taking pills for sore throats, colds, or the flu. The effects of these new strategic initiatives will ultimately be reflected in Wrigley's financial statements.

**Source:** Adapted from "A Young Heir Has New Plans at Old Company," by David Barboza, *The New York Times*, August 28, 2001.

# Key Points

**1 Explain why accounts are used to record and summarize the effects of transactions on financial statements.**

The record used for recording individual transactions is an account. A group of accounts is called a ledger. The system of accounts that make up a ledger is called a chart of accounts. The accounts are numbered and listed in the order in which they appear in the balance sheet and the income statement.

**2 Describe the characteristics of an account.**

The simplest form of an account, a T account, has three parts: (1) a title, which is the name of the item recorded in the account; (2) a left side, called the debit side; (3) a right side, called the credit side. Amounts entered on the left side of an account, regardless of the account title, are called debits to the account. Amounts entered on the right side of an account are called credits. Periodically, the debits in an account are added, the credits in the account are added, and the balance of the account is determined.

**3 List the rules of debit and credit and the normal balances of accounts.**

General rules of debit and credit have been established for recording increases or decreases in asset, liability, owner's equity, revenue, expense, and drawing accounts. Each transaction is recorded so that the sum of the debits is always equal to the sum of the credits. Transactions are initially entered in a record called a journal.

The sum of the increases recorded in an account is usually equal to or greater than the sum of the decreases recorded in the account. For this reason, the normal balance of an account is indicated by the side of the account (debit or credit) that receives the increases.

The rules of debit and credit and normal account balances are summarized in the following table:

|  | Increase (Normal Balance) | Decrease |
|---|---|---|
| *Balance sheet accounts:* | | |
| Asset | Debit | Credit |
| Liability | Credit | Debit |
| Owner's Equity: | | |
| Capital | Credit | Debit |
| Drawing | Debit | Credit |
| *Income statement accounts:* | | |
| Revenue | Credit | Debit |
| Expense | Debit | Credit |

**4 Analyze and summarize the financial statement effects of transactions.**

Transactions are analyzed by determining whether: (1) an asset, liability, owner's equity, revenue, or expense account is affected, (2) each account affected increases or decreases, and (3) each increase or decrease is recorded as a debit or a credit. A journal is used for recording the transaction initially. The journal entries are periodically posted to the accounts.

**5 Prepare a trial balance and explain how it can be used to discover errors.**

A trial balance is prepared by listing the accounts from the ledger and their balances. If the two totals of the trial balance are not equal, an error has occurred.

**6 Discover errors in recording transactions and correct them.**

Errors may be discovered (1) by audit procedures, (2) by looking at the trial balance or (3) by chance. The procedures for correcting errors are summarized in Exhibit 7.

**7 Use horizontal analysis to compare financial statements from different periods.**

In horizontal analysis, the amount of each item on the current financial statements is compared with the same item on one or more earlier statements. The increase or decrease in the *amount* of the item is computed, together with the *percent* of increase or decrease.

# Key Terms

# Illustrative Problem

J. F. Outz, M.D., has been practicing as a cardiologist for three years. During April, 2005, Outz completed the following transactions in her practice of cardiology.

April 1. Paid office rent for April, $800.
  3. Purchased equipment on account, $2,100.
  5. Received cash on account from patients, $3,150.
  8. Purchased X-ray film and other supplies on account, $245.
  9. One of the items of equipment purchased on April 3 was defective. It was returned with the permission of the supplier, who agreed to reduce the account for the amount charged for the item, $325.
  12. Paid cash to creditors on account, $1,250.
  17. Paid cash for renewal of a six-month property insurance policy, $370.
  20. Discovered that the balances of the cash account and the accounts payable account as of April 1 were overstated by $200. A payment of that amount to a creditor in March had not been recorded. Journalize the $200 payment as of April 20.
  24. Paid cash for laboratory analysis, $545.
  27. Paid cash from business bank account for personal and family expenses, $1,250.
  30. Recorded the cash received in payment of services (on a cash basis) to patients during April, $1,720.
  30. Paid salaries of receptionist and nurses, $1,725.
  30. Paid various utility expenses, $360.
  30. Recorded fees charged to patients on account for services performed in April, $5,145.
  30. Paid miscellaneous expenses, $132.

Outz's account titles, numbers, and balances as of April 1 (all normal balances) are listed as follows: Cash, 11, $4,123; Accounts Receivable, 12, $6,725; Supplies, 13, $290; Prepaid Insurance, 14, $465; Equipment, 18, $19,745; Accounts Payable, 22, $765; J. F. Outz, Capital, 31, $30,583; J. F. Outz, Drawing, 32; Professional Fees, 41; Salary Expense, 51; Rent Expense, 53; Laboratory Expense, 55; Utilities Expense, 56; Miscellaneous Expense, 59.

## Instructions

1. Open a ledger of standard four-column accounts for Dr. Outz as of April 1. Enter the balances in the appropriate balance columns and place a check mark (✓) in the posting reference column. (*Hint:* Verify the equality of the debit and credit balances in the ledger before proceeding with the next instruction.)
2. Journalize each transaction in a two-column journal.
3. Post the journal to the ledger, extending the month-end balances to the appropriate balance columns after each posting.
4. Prepare a trial balance as of April 30.

**Solution**

**2.** and **3.**

| | | | JOURNAL | | | Page 27 | |
|---|---|---|---|---|---|---|---|
| | **Date** | | **Description** | **Post. Ref.** | **Debit** | **Credit** | |
| 1 | 2005 April | 1 | Rent Expense | 53 | 8 0 0 00 | | 1 |
| 2 | | | Cash | 11 | | 8 0 0 00 | 2 |
| 3 | | | Paid office rent for April. | | | | 3 |
| 4 | | | | | | | 4 |
| 5 | | 3 | Equipment | 18 | 2 1 0 0 00 | | 5 |
| 6 | | | Accounts Payable | 22 | | 2 1 0 0 00 | 6 |
| 7 | | | Purchased equipment on account. | | | | 7 |
| 8 | | | | | | | 8 |
| 9 | | 5 | Cash | 11 | 3 1 5 0 00 | | 9 |
| 10 | | | Accounts Receivable | 12 | | 3 1 5 0 00 | 10 |
| 11 | | | Received cash on account. | | | | 11 |
| 12 | | | | | | | 12 |
| 13 | | 8 | Supplies | 13 | 2 4 5 00 | | 13 |
| 14 | | | Accounts Payable | 22 | | 2 4 5 00 | 14 |
| 15 | | | Purchased supplies. | | | | 15 |
| 16 | | | | | | | 16 |
| 17 | | 9 | Accounts Payable | 22 | 3 2 5 00 | | 17 |
| 18 | | | Equipment | 18 | | 3 2 5 00 | 18 |
| 19 | | | Returned defective equipment. | | | | 19 |
| 20 | | | | | | | 20 |
| 21 | | 12 | Accounts Payable | 22 | 1 2 5 0 00 | | 21 |
| 22 | | | Cash | 11 | | 1 2 5 0 00 | 22 |
| 23 | | | Paid creditors on account. | | | | 23 |
| 24 | | | | | | | 24 |
| 25 | | 17 | Prepaid Insurance | 14 | 3 7 0 00 | | 25 |
| 26 | | | Cash | 11 | | 3 7 0 00 | 26 |
| 27 | | | Renewed 6-month property policy. | | | | 27 |
| 28 | | | | | | | 28 |
| 29 | | 20 | Accounts Payable | 22 | 2 0 0 00 | | 29 |
| 30 | | | Cash | 11 | | 2 0 0 00 | 30 |
| 31 | | | Recorded March payment | | | | 31 |
| 32 | | | to creditor. | | | | 32 |
| 33 | | | | | | | 33 |

| | | | JOURNAL | | | Page 28 | |
|---|---|---|---|---|---|---|---|
| | **Date** | | **Description** | **Post. Ref.** | **Debit** | **Credit** | |
| 1 | 2005 April | 24 | Laboratory Expense | 55 | 5 4 5 00 | | 1 |
| 2 | | | Cash | 11 | | 5 4 5 00 | 2 |
| 3 | | | Paid for laboratory analysis. | | | | 3 |
| 4 | | | | | | | 4 |

**JOURNAL**          Page 28

| | Date | | Description | Post. Ref. | Debit | Credit | |
|---|---|---|---|---|---|---|---|
| 5 | 2005 April | 27 | J. F. Outz, Drawing | 32 | 1 2 5 0 00 | | 5 |
| 6 | | | Cash | 11 | | 1 2 5 0 00 | 6 |
| 7 | | | J. F. Outz withdrew cash for | | | | 7 |
| 8 | | | personal use. | | | | 8 |
| 9 | | | | | | | 9 |
| 10 | | 30 | Cash | 11 | 1 7 2 0 00 | | 10 |
| 11 | | | Professional Fees | 41 | | 1 7 2 0 00 | 11 |
| 12 | | | Received fees from patients. | | | | 12 |
| 13 | | | | | | | 13 |
| 14 | | 30 | Salary Expense | 51 | 1 7 2 5 00 | | 14 |
| 15 | | | Cash | 11 | | 1 7 2 5 00 | 15 |
| 16 | | | Paid salaries. | | | | 16 |
| 17 | | | | | | | 17 |
| 18 | | 30 | Utilities Expense | 56 | 3 6 0 00 | | 18 |
| 19 | | | Cash | 11 | | 3 6 0 00 | 19 |
| 20 | | | Paid utilities. | | | | 20 |
| 21 | | | | | | | 21 |
| 22 | | 30 | Accounts Receivable | 12 | 5 1 4 5 00 | | 22 |
| 23 | | | Professional Fees | 41 | | 5 1 4 5 00 | 23 |
| 24 | | | Recorded fees earned on account. | | | | 24 |
| 25 | | | | | | | 25 |
| 26 | | 30 | Miscellaneous Expense | 59 | 1 3 2 00 | | 26 |
| 27 | | | Cash | 11 | | 1 3 2 00 | 27 |
| 28 | | | Paid expenses. | | | | 28 |

**1.** and **3.**

**ACCOUNT** *Cash*          **ACCOUNT NO.** *11*

| Date | | Item | Post. Ref. | Debit | Credit | Balance Debit | Balance Credit |
|---|---|---|---|---|---|---|---|
| 2005 April | 1 | Balance | ✓ | | | 4 1 2 3 00 | |
| | 1 | | 27 | | 8 0 0 00 | 3 3 2 3 00 | |
| | 5 | | 27 | 3 1 5 0 00 | | 6 4 7 3 00 | |
| | 12 | | 27 | | 1 2 5 0 00 | 5 2 2 3 00 | |
| | 17 | | 27 | | 3 7 0 00 | 4 8 5 3 00 | |
| | 20 | | 27 | | 2 0 0 00 | 4 6 5 3 00 | |
| | 24 | | 28 | | 5 4 5 00 | 4 1 0 8 00 | |
| | 27 | | 28 | | 1 2 5 0 00 | 2 8 5 8 00 | |
| | 30 | | 28 | 1 7 2 0 00 | | 4 5 7 8 00 | |
| | 30 | | 28 | | 1 7 2 5 00 | 2 8 5 3 00 | |
| | 30 | | 28 | | 3 6 0 00 | 2 4 9 3 00 | |
| | 30 | | 28 | | 1 3 2 00 | 2 3 6 1 00 | |

**ACCOUNT** *Accounts Receivable*        **ACCOUNT NO.** *12*

| Date | | Item | Post. Ref. | Debit | Credit | Balance Debit | Balance Credit |
|---|---|---|---|---|---|---|---|
| 2005 April | 1 | Balance | ✓ | | | 6 7 2 5 00 | |
| | 5 | | 27 | | 3 1 5 0 00 | 3 5 7 5 00 | |
| | 30 | | 28 | 5 1 4 5 00 | | 8 7 2 0 00 | |

**ACCOUNT** *Supplies*        **ACCOUNT NO.** *13*

| Date | | Item | Post. Ref. | Debit | Credit | Balance Debit | Balance Credit |
|---|---|---|---|---|---|---|---|
| 2005 April | 1 | Balance | ✓ | | | 2 9 0 00 | |
| | 8 | | 27 | 2 4 5 00 | | 5 3 5 00 | |

**ACCOUNT** *Prepaid Insurance*        **ACCOUNT NO.** *14*

| Date | | Item | Post. Ref. | Debit | Credit | Balance Debit | Balance Credit |
|---|---|---|---|---|---|---|---|
| 2005 April | 1 | Balance | ✓ | | | 4 6 5 00 | |
| | 17 | | 27 | 3 7 0 00 | | 8 3 5 00 | |

**ACCOUNT** *Equipment*        **ACCOUNT NO.** *18*

| Date | | Item | Post. Ref. | Debit | Credit | Balance Debit | Balance Credit |
|---|---|---|---|---|---|---|---|
| 2005 April | 1 | Balance | ✓ | | | 19 7 4 5 00 | |
| | 3 | | 27 | 2 1 0 0 00 | | 21 8 4 5 00 | |
| | 9 | | 27 | | 3 2 5 00 | 21 5 2 0 00 | |

**ACCOUNT** *Accounts Payable*        **ACCOUNT NO.** *22*

| Date | | Item | Post. Ref. | Debit | Credit | Balance Debit | Balance Credit |
|---|---|---|---|---|---|---|---|
| 2005 April | 1 | Balance | ✓ | | | | 7 6 5 00 |
| | 3 | | 27 | | 2 1 0 0 00 | | 2 8 6 5 00 |
| | 8 | | 27 | | 2 4 5 00 | | 3 1 1 0 00 |
| | 9 | | 27 | 3 2 5 00 | | | 2 7 8 5 00 |
| | 12 | | 27 | 1 2 5 0 00 | | | 1 5 3 5 00 |
| | 20 | | 27 | 2 0 0 00 | | | 1 3 3 5 00 |

**ACCOUNT** *J. F. Outz, Capital*                          **ACCOUNT NO.** *31*

| Date | Item | Post. Ref. | Debit | Credit | Balance Debit | Balance Credit |
|------|------|-----------|-------|--------|-------|--------|
| 2005 April 1 | Balance | ✓ | | | | 3 0 5 8 3 00 |

**ACCOUNT** *J. F. Outz, Drawing*                          **ACCOUNT NO.** *32*

| Date | Item | Post. Ref. | Debit | Credit | Balance Debit | Balance Credit |
|------|------|-----------|-------|--------|-------|--------|
| 2005 April 27 | | 28 | 1 2 5 0 00 | | 1 2 5 0 00 | |

**ACCOUNT** *Professional Fees*                          **ACCOUNT NO.** *41*

| Date | Item | Post. Ref. | Debit | Credit | Balance Debit | Balance Credit |
|------|------|-----------|-------|--------|-------|--------|
| 2005 April 30 | | 28 | | 1 7 2 0 00 | | 1 7 2 0 00 |
| 30 | | 28 | | 5 1 4 5 00 | | 6 8 6 5 00 |

**ACCOUNT** *Salary Expense*                          **ACCOUNT NO.** *51*

| Date | Item | Post. Ref. | Debit | Credit | Balance Debit | Balance Credit |
|------|------|-----------|-------|--------|-------|--------|
| 2005 April 30 | | 28 | 1 7 2 5 00 | | 1 7 2 5 00 | |

**ACCOUNT** *Rent Expense*                          **ACCOUNT NO.** *53*

| Date | Item | Post. Ref. | Debit | Credit | Balance Debit | Balance Credit |
|------|------|-----------|-------|--------|-------|--------|
| 2005 April 1 | | 27 | 8 0 0 00 | | 8 0 0 00 | |

**ACCOUNT** *Laboratory Expense*                          **ACCOUNT NO.** *55*

| Date | Item | Post. Ref. | Debit | Credit | Balance Debit | Balance Credit |
|------|------|-----------|-------|--------|-------|--------|
| 2005 April 24 | | 28 | 5 4 5 00 | | 5 4 5 00 | |

| ACCOUNT Utilities Expense | | | | | | ACCOUNT NO. 56 |
|---|---|---|---|---|---|---|
| Date | Item | Post. Ref. | Debit | Credit | Balance Debit | Balance Credit |
| 2005 April 30 | | 28 | 3 6 0 00 | | 3 6 0 00 | |

| ACCOUNT Miscellaneous Expense | | | | | | ACCOUNT NO. 59 |
|---|---|---|---|---|---|---|
| Date | Item | Post. Ref. | Debit | Credit | Balance Debit | Balance Credit |
| 2005 April 30 | | 28 | 1 3 2 00 | | 1 3 2 00 | |

4.

### J. F. Outz, M.D.
### Trial Balance
### April 30, 2005

| | Debit | Credit |
|---|---|---|
| Cash | 2 3 6 1 00 | |
| Accounts Receivable | 8 7 2 0 00 | |
| Supplies | 5 3 5 00 | |
| Prepaid Insurance | 8 3 5 00 | |
| Equipment | 21 5 2 0 00 | |
| Accounts Payable | | 1 3 3 5 00 |
| J. F. Outz, Capital | | 30 5 8 3 00 |
| J. F. Outz, Drawing | 1 2 5 0 00 | |
| Professional Fees | | 6 8 6 5 00 |
| Salary Expense | 1 7 2 5 00 | |
| Rent Expense | 8 0 0 00 | |
| Laboratory Expense | 5 4 5 00 | |
| Utilities Expense | 3 6 0 00 | |
| Miscellaneous Expense | 1 3 2 00 | |
| | 38 7 8 3 00 | 38 7 8 3 00 |

# Self-Examination Questions (Answers at End of Chapter)

1. A debit may signify:
   A. an increase in an asset account.
   B. a decrease in an asset account.
   C. an increase in a liability account.
   D. an increase in the owner's capital account.

2. The type of account with a normal credit balance is:
   A. an asset.
   B. drawing.
   C. a revenue.
   D. an expense.

3. A debit balance in which of the following accounts would indicate a likely error?
   A. Accounts Receivable
   B. Cash
   C. Fees Earned
   D. Miscellaneous Expense

4. The receipt of cash from customers in payment of their accounts would be recorded by a:
   A. debit to Cash; credit to Accounts Receivable.
   B. debit to Accounts Receivable; credit to Cash.
   C. debit to Cash; credit to Accounts Payable.
   D. debit to Accounts Payable; credit to Cash.

5. The form listing the titles and balances of the accounts in the ledger on a given date is the:
   A. income statement.
   B. balance sheet.
   C. statement of owner's equity.
   D. trial balance.

# Class Discussion Questions

1. What is the difference between an account and a ledger?
2. Do the terms *debit* and *credit* signify increase or decrease or can they signify either? Explain.
3. Explain why the rules of debit and credit are the same for liability accounts and owner's equity accounts.
4. What is the effect (increase or decrease) of a debit to an expense account (a) in terms of owner's equity and (b) in terms of expense?
5. What is the effect (increase or decrease) of a credit to a revenue account (a) in terms of owner's equity and (b) in terms of revenue?
6. Kemp Company adheres to a policy of depositing all cash receipts in a bank account and making all payments by check. The cash account as of August 31 has a credit balance of $3,000, and there is no undeposited cash on hand. (a) Assuming no errors occurred during journalizing or posting, what caused this unusual balance? (b) Is the $3,000 credit balance in the cash account an asset, a liability, owner's equity, a revenue, or an expense?
7. McElwee Company performed services in May for a specific customer, for a fee of $7,500. Payment was received the following June. (a) Was the revenue earned in May or June? (b) What accounts should be debited and credited in (1) May and (2) June?
8. What proof is provided by a trial balance?
9. If the two totals of a trial balance are equal, does it mean that there are no errors in the accounting records? Explain.
10. Assume that a trial balance is prepared with an account balance of $18,950 listed as $18,590 and an account balance of $7,200 listed as $720. Identify the transposition and the slide.
11. Assume that when a purchase of supplies of $1,250 for cash was recorded, both the debit and the credit were journalized and posted as $1,520. (a) Would this error cause the trial balance to be out of balance? (b) Would the trial balance be out of balance if the $1,250 entry had been journalized correctly but the credit to Cash had been posted as $1,520?
12. Assume that Margarita Consulting erroneously recorded the payment of $7,500 of owner withdrawals as a debit to salary expense. (a) How would this error affect the equality of the trial balance? (b) How would this error affect the income statement, statement of owner's equity, and balance sheet?
13. Assume that Blitzkrieg Realty Co. borrowed $25,000 from First Union Bank and Trust. In recording the transaction, Blitzkrieg erroneously recorded the receipt of $25,000 as a debit to cash, $25,000, and a credit to fees earned, $25,000. (a) How would this error affect the equality of the trial balance? (b) How would this error affect the income statement, statement of owner's equity, and balance sheet?

14. In journalizing and posting the entry to record the purchase of supplies on account, the accounts receivable account was credited in error. What is the preferred procedure to correct this error?

15. Banks rely heavily upon customers' deposits as a source of funds. Demand deposits normally pay interest to the customer, who is entitled to withdraw at any time without prior notice to the bank. Checking and NOW (negotiable order of withdrawal) accounts are the most common form of demand deposits for banks. Assume that Kennon Storage has a checking account at Livingston Savings Bank. What type of account (asset, liability, owner's equity, revenue, expense, drawing) does the account balance of $15,600 represent from the viewpoint of (a) Kennon Storage and (b) Livingston Savings Bank?

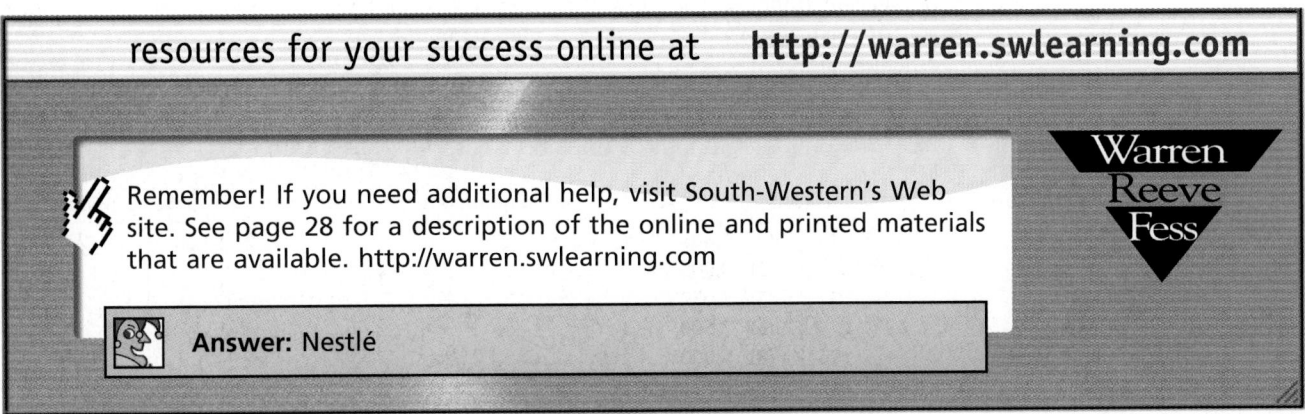

# Exercises

**EXERCISE 2-1**
*Chart of accounts*
**Objective 1**

The following accounts appeared in recent financial statements of **Continental Airlines**:

| | |
|---|---|
| Accounts Payable | Flight Equipment |
| Aircraft Fuel Expense | Landing Fees |
| Air Traffic Liability | Passenger Revenue |
| Cargo and Mail Revenue | Purchase Deposits for Flight Equipment |
| Commissions | Spare Parts and Supplies |

Identify each account as either a balance sheet account or an income statement account. For each balance sheet account, identify it as an asset, a liability, or owner's equity. For each income statement account, identify it as a revenue or an expense.

**EXERCISE 2-2**
*Chart of accounts*
**Objective 1**

Clarendon Interiors is owned and operated by Corey Krum, an interior decorator. In the ledger of Clarendon Interiors, the first digit of the account number indicates its major account classification (1—assets, 2—liabilities, 3—owner's equity, 4—revenues, 5—expenses). The second digit of the account number indicates the specific account within each of the preceding major account classifications.

Match each account number with its most likely account in the list below. The account numbers are 11, 12, 13, 21, 31, 32, 41, 51, 52, and 53.

Accounts:
| | |
|---|---|
| Accounts Payable | Fees Earned |
| Accounts Receivable | Land |
| Cash | Miscellaneous Expense |
| Corey Krum, Capital | Supplies Expense |
| Corey Krum, Drawing | Wages Expense |

**EXERCISE 2-3**
*Chart of accounts*

**Objective 1**

The Inflorescence School is a newly organized business that teaches people how to inspire and influence others. The list of accounts to be opened in the general ledger is as follows:

| | | |
|---|---|---|
| Accounts Payable | Millard Fillmore, Capital | Supplies |
| Accounts Receivable | Millard Fillmore, Drawing | Supplies Expense |
| Cash | Miscellaneous Expense | Unearned Rent |
| Equipment | Prepaid Insurance | Wages Expense |
| Fees Earned | Rent Expense | |

List the accounts in the order in which they should appear in the ledger of The Inflorescence School and assign account numbers. Each account number is to have two digits: the first digit is to indicate the major classification (*1* for assets, etc.), and the second digit is to identify the specific account within each major classification (*11* for Cash, etc.).

**EXERCISE 2-4**
*Identifying transactions*

**Objectives 2, 3**

Malta Co. is a travel agency. The nine transactions recorded by Malta during February 2006, its first month of operations, are indicated in the following T accounts:

| Cash | | |
|---|---|---|
| (1) 40,000 | (2) | 1,800 |
| (7)  9,500 | (3) | 9,000 |
| | (4) | 3,050 |
| | (6) | 7,500 |
| | (8) | 5,000 |

| Equipment | |
|---|---|
| (3) 24,000 | |

| Ira Janke, Drawing | |
|---|---|
| (8)  5,000 | |

| Accounts Receivable | |
|---|---|
| (5) 12,000 | (7)  9,500 |

| Accounts Payable | |
|---|---|
| (6)  7,500 | (3) 15,000 |

| Service Revenue | |
|---|---|
| | (5) 12,000 |

| Supplies | |
|---|---|
| (2)  1,800 | (9)  1,050 |

| Ira Janke, Capital | |
|---|---|
| | (1) 40,000 |

| Operating Expenses | |
|---|---|
| (4)  3,050 | |
| (9)  1,050 | |

Indicate for each debit and each credit: (a) whether an asset, liability, owner's equity, drawing, revenue, or expense account was affected and (b) whether the account was increased (+) or decreased (−). Present your answers in the following form, with transaction (1) given as an example:

| | Account Debited | | Account Credited | |
|---|---|---|---|---|
| Transaction | Type | Effect | Type | Effect |
| (1) | asset | + | owner's equity | + |

**EXERCISE 2-5**
*Journal entries*

**Objectives 3, 4**

Based upon the T accounts in Exercise 2-4, prepare the nine journal entries from which the postings were made. Journal entry explanations may be omitted.

**EXERCISE 2-6**
*Trial balance*

**Objective 5**

SPREADSHEET

✓*Total Debit Column:*
*$59,500*

Based upon the data presented in Exercise 2-4, prepare a trial balance, listing the accounts in their proper order.

**EXERCISE 2-7**
*Normal entries for accounts*
**Objective 3**

During the month, Orion Labs Co. has a substantial number of transactions affecting each of the following accounts. State for each account whether it is likely to have (a) debit entries only, (b) credit entries only, or (c) both debit and credit entries.

1. Accounts Payable
2. Accounts Receivable
3. Cash
4. Fees Earned

5. Heidi Ibach, Drawing
6. Insurance Expense
7. Supplies Expense

**EXERCISE 2-8**
*Normal balances of accounts*
**Objective 3**

Identify each of the following accounts of Universal Services Co. as asset, liability, owner's equity, revenue, or expense, and state in each case whether the normal balance is a debit or a credit.

a. Accounts Payable
b. Accounts Receivable
c. Cash
d. Cindy Yost, Capital
e. Cindy Yost, Drawing

f. Fees Earned
g. Office Equipment
h. Rent Expense
i. Supplies
j. Wages Expense

**EXERCISE 2-9**
*Rules of debit and credit*
**Objective 3**

The following table summarizes the rules of debit and credit. For each of the items (a) through (l), indicate whether the proper answer is a debit or a credit.

| | Increase | Decrease | Normal Balance |
|---|---|---|---|
| Balance sheet accounts: | | | |
| Asset | Debit | (a) | Debit |
| Liability | (b) | (c) | (d) |
| Owner's Equity: | | | |
| Capital | Credit | (e) | (f) |
| Drawing | (g) | Credit | (h) |
| Income statement accounts: | | | |
| Revenue | Credit | (i) | (j) |
| Expense | (k) | (l) | Debit |

**EXERCISE 2-10**
*Capital account balance*
**Objectives 2, 3**

As of January 1, Seth Fite, Capital, had a credit balance of $10,500. During the year, withdrawals totaled $4,000 and the business incurred a net loss of $8,000.

a. Calculate the balance of Seth Fite, Capital, as of the end of the year.
b. Assuming that there have been no recording errors, will the balance sheet prepared at December 31 balance? Explain.

**EXERCISE 2-11**
*Cash account balance*
**Objectives 2, 3**

During the month, Wembley Co. received $212,500 in cash and paid out $183,750 in cash.

a. Do the data indicate that Wembley Co. earned $28,750 during the month? Explain.
b. If the balance of the cash account is $36,300 at the end of the month, what was the cash balance at the beginning of the month?

**EXERCISE 2-12**
*Account balances*
**Objectives 2, 3**
✓c. $20,800

a. On April 1, the cash account balance was $7,850. During April, cash receipts totaled $41,850 and the April 30 balance was $9,150. Determine the cash payments made during April.
b. On July 1, the accounts receivable account balance was $15,500. During July, $61,000 was collected from customers on account. Assuming the July 31 balance was $17,500, determine the fees billed to customers on account during July.
c. During January, $40,500 was paid to creditors on account and purchases on account were $57,700. Assuming the January 31 balance of Accounts Payable was $38,000, determine the account balance on January 1.

**EXERCISE 2-13**
*Transactions*
**Objectives 3, 4**

The Zuni Co. has the following accounts in its ledger: Cash; Accounts Receivable; Supplies; Office Equipment; Accounts Payable; Gayle McCall, Capital; Gayle McCall, Drawing; Fees Earned; Rent Expense; Advertising Expense; Utilities Expense; Miscellaneous Expense.

Journalize the following selected transactions for August 2005 in a two-column journal. Journal entry explanations may be omitted.

August 1. Paid rent for the month, $1,500.
　　　 2. Paid advertising expense, $700.
　　　 4. Paid cash for supplies, $1,050.
　　　 6. Purchased office equipment on account, $7,500.
　　　 8. Received cash from customers on account, $3,600.
　　　 12. Paid creditor on account, $1,150.
　　　 20. Withdrew cash for personal use, $1,000.
　　　 25. Paid cash for repairs to office equipment, $500.
　　　 30. Paid telephone bill for the month, $195.
　　　 31. Fees earned and billed to customers for the month, $10,150.
　　　 31. Paid electricity bill for the month, $380.

**EXERCISE 2-14**
*Journalizing and posting*
**Objectives 3, 4**

On October 27, 2006, Lintel Co. purchased $1,320 of supplies on account. In Lintel Co.'s chart of accounts, the supplies account is No. 15 and the accounts payable account is No. 21.

a. Journalize the October 27, 2006 transaction on page 43 of Lintel Co.'s two-column journal. Include an explanation of the entry.
b. Prepare a four-column account for Supplies. Enter a debit balance of $585 as of October 1, 2006. Place a check mark (✓) in the posting reference column.
c. Prepare a four-column account for Accounts Payable. Enter a credit balance of $6,150 as of October 1, 2006. Place a check mark (✓) in the posting reference column.
d. Post the October 27, 2006 transaction to the accounts.

**EXERCISE 2-15**
*Transactions and T accounts*
**Objectives 2, 3, 4**

SPREADSHEET

The following selected transactions were completed during May of the current year:

1. Billed customers for fees earned, $12,190.
2. Purchased supplies on account, $1,250.
3. Received cash from customers on account, $9,150.
4. Paid creditors on account, $750.

a. Journalize the above transactions in a two-column journal, using the appropriate number to identify the transactions. Journal entry explanations may be omitted.
b. Post the entries prepared in (a) to the following T accounts: Cash, Supplies, Accounts Receivable, Accounts Payable, Fees Earned. To the left of each amount posted in the accounts, place the appropriate number to identify the transactions.

**EXERCISE 2-16**
*Trial balance*
**Objective 5**

SPREADSHEET

✓*Total Credit Column:*
*$464,350*

The accounts in the ledger of Haleakala Park Co. as of March 31, 2006, are listed in alphabetical order as follows. All accounts have normal balances. The balance of the cash account has been intentionally omitted.

| Accounts Payable | $ 18,710 | Notes Payable | $ 40,000 |
|---|---|---|---|
| Accounts Receivable | 37,500 | Prepaid Insurance | 3,000 |
| Cash | ? | Rent Expense | 60,000 |
| Fees Earned | 310,000 | Supplies | 2,100 |
| Insurance Expense | 6,000 | Supplies Expense | 7,900 |
| Land | 85,000 | Unearned Rent | 9,000 |
| Miscellaneous Expense | 8,900 | Utilities Expense | 41,500 |
| Neil Orzeck, Capital | 86,640 | Wages Expense | 175,000 |
| Neil Orzeck, Drawing | 20,000 | | |

Prepare a trial balance, listing the accounts in their proper order and inserting the missing figure for cash.

**EXERCISE 2-17**
*Effect of errors on trial balance*

**Objective 5**

Indicate which of the following errors, each considered individually, would cause the trial balance totals to be unequal:

a. A payment of $7,000 for equipment purchased was posted as a debit of $700 to Equipment and a credit of $700 to Cash.

b. Payment of a cash withdrawal of $12,000 was journalized and posted as a debit of $21,000 to Salary Expense and a credit of $12,000 to Cash.

c. A fee of $1,850 earned and due from a client was not debited to Accounts Receivable or credited to a revenue account, because the cash had not been received.

d. A payment of $1,475 to a creditor was posted as a debit of $1,475 to Accounts Payable and a debit of $1,475 to Cash.

e. A receipt of $325 from an account receivable was journalized and posted as a debit of $325 to Cash and a credit of $325 to Fees Earned.

**EXERCISE 2-18**
*Errors in trial balance*

**Objective 5**

✓ *Total of Credit Column: $181,600*

The following preliminary trial balance of Escalade Co., a sports ticket agency, does not balance:

**Escalade Co.**
**Trial Balance**
**December 31, 2006**

| | | |
|---|---:|---:|
| Cash | 47,350 | |
| Accounts Receivable | 22,100 | |
| Prepaid Insurance | | 8,000 |
| Equipment | 57,000 | |
| Accounts Payable | | 12,980 |
| Unearned Rent | | 4,520 |
| Erin Capelli, Capital | 82,420 | |
| Erin Capelli, Drawing | 10,000 | |
| Service Revenue | | 83,750 |
| Wages Expense | | 42,000 |
| Advertising Expense | 7,200 | |
| Miscellaneous Expense | | 1,425 |
| | 226,070 | 152,675 |

When the ledger and other records are reviewed, you discover the following: (1) the debits and credits in the cash account total $47,350 and $33,975, respectively; (2) a billing of $2,500 to a customer on account was not posted to the accounts receivable account; (3) a payment of $1,800 made to a creditor on account was not posted to the accounts payable account; (4) the balance of the unearned rent account is $4,250; (5) the correct balance of the equipment account is $75,000; and (6) each account has a normal balance.

Prepare a corrected trial balance.

**EXERCISE 2-19**
*Effect of errors on trial balance*

**Objective 5**

The following errors occurred in posting from a two-column journal:

1. A debit of $1,250 to Supplies was posted twice.
2. A debit of $3,575 to Wages Expense was posted as $3,557.
3. A credit of $4,175 to Accounts Payable was not posted.
4. A debit of $400 to Accounts Payable was posted as a credit.
5. An entry debiting Accounts Receivable and crediting Fees Earned for $6,000 was not posted.
6. A credit of $350 to Cash was posted as $530.
7. A debit of $1,000 to Cash was posted to Miscellaneous Expense.

Considering each case individually (i.e., assuming that no other errors had occurred), indicate: (a) by "yes" or "no" whether the trial balance would be out of balance; (b) if answer to (a) is "yes," the amount by which the trial balance totals would differ; and (c) whether the debit or credit column of the trial balance would have the larger total. Answers should be presented in the following form, with error (1) given as an example:

*(continued)*

| Error | (a) Out of Balance | (b) Difference | (c) Larger Total |
|---|---|---|---|
| 1. | yes | $1,250 | debit |

**EXERCISE 2-20**
*Errors in trial balance*
**Objective 5**

**WHAT'S WRONG WITH THIS?**

✓ *Total of Credit Column:*
*$125,000*

Identify the errors in the following trial balance. All accounts have normal balances.

**Dinero Co.**
**Trial Balance**
**For the Month Ending January 31, 2006**

| | | |
|---|---|---|
| Cash ....................................................... | 7,500 | |
| Accounts Receivable .................................. | | 16,400 |
| Prepaid Insurance ..................................... | 3,600 | |
| Equipment ............................................... | 50,000 | |
| Accounts Payable ...................................... | 1,850 | |
| Salaries Payable ....................................... | | 1,250 |
| Susan Appleby, Capital .............................. | | 43,200 |
| Susan Appleby, Drawing ............................ | | 6,000 |
| Service Revenue ....................................... | | 78,700 |
| Salary Expense ......................................... | 32,810 | |
| Advertising Expense .................................. | | 7,200 |
| Miscellaneous Expense .............................. | 1,490 | |
| | 152,750 | 152,750 |

**EXERCISE 2-21**
*Entries to correct errors*
**Objective 6**

The following errors took place in journalizing and posting transactions:

a. A withdrawal of $15,000 by Gerald Owen, owner of the business, was recorded as a debit to Wages Expense and a credit to Cash.
b. Rent of $4,500 paid for the current month was recorded as a debit to Rent Expense and a credit to Prepaid Rent.

Journalize the entries to correct the errors. Omit explanations.

**EXERCISE 2-22**
*Entries to correct errors*
**Objective 6**

The following errors took place in journalizing and posting transactions:

a. A $550 purchase of supplies on account was recorded as a debit to Miscellaneous Expense and a credit to Prepaid Rent.
b. Cash of $3,750 received on account was recorded as a debit to Accounts Payable and a credit to Cash.

Journalize the entries to correct the errors. Omit explanations.

**EXERCISE 2-23**
*Horizontal analysis of income statement*
**Objective 7**

**REAL WORLD**

The financial statements for **The Home Depot** are presented in Appendix E at the end of the text.

a. For Home Depot, comparing 2003 with 2002, determine the amount of change in millions and the percent of change for
   1. net sales (revenues) and
   2. total operating expenses.
b. ▬▬▶ What conclusions can you draw from your analysis of the net sales and the total operating expenses?

**EXERCISE 2-24**
*Horizontal analysis of income statement*
**Objective 7**

**REAL WORLD**

The following data were adapted from the financial statements of **Kmart Corporation**, prior to its filing for bankruptcy:

| | In millions | |
|---|---|---|
| **For years ending January 31** | **2000** | **1999** |
| Sales | $37,028 | $35,925 |
| Cost of sales (expense) | (29,658) | (28,111) |
| Selling, general, and administrative expenses | (7,415) | (6,514) |
| Operating income (loss) | (45) | 1,300 |

a. Prepare a horizontal analysis for the income statement showing the amount and percent of change in each of the following:
1. Sales
2. Cost of sales
3. Selling, general, and administative expenses
4. Operating income (loss)
b. Comment on the results of your horizontal analysis in (a).

# Problems Series A

**PROBLEM 2-1A**
*Entries into T accounts and trial balance*

**Objectives 2, 3, 4, 5**

✓ *3. Total of Debit Column: $39,875*

Shaun Wilcox, an architect, opened an office on April 1, 2006. During the month, he completed the following transactions connected with his professional practice:

a. Transferred cash from a personal bank account to an account to be used for the business, $17,500.
b. Purchased used automobile for $15,300, paying $4,000 cash and giving a note payable for the remainder.
c. Paid April rent for office and workroom, $2,200.
d. Paid cash for supplies, $660.
e. Purchased office and computer equipment on account, $5,200.
f. Paid cash for annual insurance policies on automobile and equipment, $1,200.
g. Received cash from a client for plans delivered, $3,725.
h. Paid cash to creditors on account, $1,800.
i. Paid cash for miscellaneous expenses, $235.
j. Received invoice for blueprint service, due in May, $650.
k. Recorded fee earned on plans delivered, payment to be received in May, $3,500.
l. Paid salary of assistant, $1,300.
m. Paid cash for miscellaneous expenses, $105.
n. Paid installment due on note payable, $200.
o. Paid gas, oil, and repairs on automobile for April, $115.

**Instructions**
1. Record the foregoing transactions directly in the following T accounts, without journalizing: Cash; Accounts Receivable; Supplies; Prepaid Insurance; Automobiles; Equipment; Notes Payable; Accounts Payable; Shaun Wilcox, Capital; Professional Fees; Rent Expense; Salary Expense; Blueprint Expense; Automobile Expense; Miscellaneous Expense. To the left of each amount entered in the accounts, place the appropriate letter to identify the transaction.
2. Determine the balances of the T accounts having two or more debits or credits. A memorandum balance should be inserted in accounts having both debits and credits, in the manner illustrated in the chapter. For accounts with entries on one side only (such as Professional Fees), there is no need to insert the memorandum balance in the item column. For accounts containing only a single debit and a single credit (such as Notes Payable), the memorandum balance should be inserted in the appropriate item column. Accounts containing a single entry only (such as Prepaid Insurance) do not need a memorandum balance.
3. Prepare a trial balance for Shaun Wilcox, Architect, as of April 30, 2006.

**PROBLEM 2-2A**
*Journal entries and trial balance*

**Objectives 2, 3, 4, 5**

On March 1, 2006, Tim Cochran established Star Realty, which completed the following transactions during the month:

a. Tim Cochran transferred cash from a personal bank account to an account to be used for the business, $12,000.
b. Purchased supplies on account, $850.
c. Earned sales commissions, receiving cash, $12,600.

✓ 4. c. $4,920

d. Paid rent on office and equipment for the month, $2,000.
e. Paid creditor on account, $450.
f. Withdrew cash for personal use, $1,500.
g. Paid automobile expenses (including rental charge) for month, $1,700, and miscellaneous expenses, $375.
h. Paid office salaries, $3,000.
i. Determined that the cost of supplies used was $605.

**Instructions**

1. Journalize entries for transactions (a) through (i), using the following account titles: Cash; Supplies; Accounts Payable; Tim Cochran, Capital; Tim Cochran, Drawing; Sales Commissions; Rent Expense; Office Salaries Expense; Automobile Expense; Supplies Expense; Miscellaneous Expense. Journal entry explanations may be omitted.

2. Prepare T accounts, using the account titles in (1). Post the journal entries to these accounts, placing the appropriate letter to the left of each amount to identify the transactions. Determine the account balances, after all posting is complete, for all accounts having two or more debits or credits. A memorandum balance should be inserted in accounts having both debits and credits, in the manner illustrated in the chapter. For accounts with entries on one side only, there is no need to insert a memorandum balance in the item column. For accounts containing only a single debit and a single credit, the memorandum balance should be inserted in the appropriate item column.

3. Prepare a trial balance as of March 31, 2006.

4. Determine the following:
   a. Amount of total revenue recorded in the ledger.
   b. Amount of total expenses recorded in the ledger.
   c. Amount of net income for March.

**PROBLEM 2-3A**
*Journal entries and trial balance*

**Objectives 2, 3, 4, 5**

✓ 3. Total of Credit Column: $40,880

On July 1, 2006, Leon Cruz established an interior decorating business, Ingres Designs. During the remainder of the month, Leon Cruz completed the following transactions related to the business:

July 1. Leon transferred cash from a personal bank account to an account to be used for the business, $18,000.
    5. Paid rent for period of July 5 to end of month, $1,500.
    10. Purchased a truck for $15,000, paying $5,000 cash and giving a note payable for the remainder.
    13. Purchased equipment on account, $4,500.
    14. Purchased supplies for cash, $975.
    15. Paid annual premiums on property and casualty insurance, $3,000.
    15. Received cash for job completed, $4,100.
    21. Paid creditor a portion of the amount owed for equipment purchased on July 13, $2,400.
    24. Recorded jobs completed on account and sent invoices to customers, $6,100.
    26. Received an invoice for truck expenses, to be paid in August, $580.
    27. Paid utilities expense, $950.
    27. Paid miscellaneous expenses, $315.
    29. Received cash from customers on account, $3,420.
    30. Paid wages of employees, $2,500.
    31. Withdrew cash for personal use, $2,000.

**Instructions**

1. Journalize each transaction in a two-column journal, referring to the following chart of accounts in selecting the accounts to be debited and credited. (Do not insert the account numbers in the journal at this time.) Journal entry explanations may be omitted.

| | | |
|---|---|---|
| 11 | Cash | 31 Leon Cruz, Capital |
| 12 | Accounts Receivable | 32 Leon Cruz, Drawing |
| 13 | Supplies | 41 Fees Earned |
| 14 | Prepaid Insurance | 51 Wages Expense |
| 16 | Equipment | 53 Rent Expense |
| 18 | Truck | 54 Utilities Expense |
| 21 | Notes Payable | 55 Truck Expense |
| 22 | Accounts Payable | 59 Miscellaneous Expense |

2. Post the journal to a ledger of four-column accounts, inserting appropriate posting references as each item is posted. Extend the balances to the appropriate balance columns after each transaction is posted.
3. Prepare a trial balance for Ingres Designs as of July 31, 2006.

**PROBLEM 2-4A**
*Journal entries and trial balance*

**Objectives 2, 3, 4, 5**

SPREADSHEET
P.A.S.S.

✓ 4. Total of Debit Column: $374,650

Fickle Realty acts as an agent in buying, selling, renting, and managing real estate. The account balances at the end of July 2006 are as follows:

| | | | |
|---|---|---|---|
| 11 | Cash | 31,200 | |
| 12 | Accounts Receivable | 45,750 | |
| 13 | Prepaid Insurance | 2,800 | |
| 14 | Office Supplies | 1,000 | |
| 16 | Land | 0 | |
| 21 | Accounts Payable | | 5,200 |
| 22 | Unearned Rent | | 0 |
| 23 | Notes Payable | | 0 |
| 31 | Larissa Sanchez, Capital | | 39,700 |
| 32 | Larissa Sanchez, Drawing | 16,000 | |
| 41 | Fees Earned | | 224,000 |
| 51 | Salary and Commission Expense | 133,000 | |
| 52 | Rent Expense | 17,500 | |
| 53 | Advertising Expense | 14,300 | |
| 54 | Automobile Expense | 6,400 | |
| 59 | Miscellaneous Expense | 950 | |
| | | 268,900 | 268,900 |

The following business transactions were completed by Fickle Realty during August 2006:

Aug. 1. Purchased office supplies on account, $1,760.
2. Paid rent on office for month, $2,500.
3. Received cash from clients on account, $38,720.
5. Paid annual insurance premiums, $3,600.
9. Returned a portion of the office supplies purchased on August 1, receiving full credit for their cost, $240.
17. Paid advertising expense, $3,450.
23. Paid creditors on account, $2,670.
29. Paid miscellaneous expenses, $350.
30. Paid automobile expense (including rental charges for an automobile), $1,360.
31. Discovered an error in computing a commission; received cash from the salesperson for the overpayment, $800.
31. Paid salaries and commissions for the month, $17,400.
31. Recorded revenue earned and billed to clients during the month, $41,900.
31. Purchased land for a future building site for $75,000, paying $10,000 in cash and giving a note payable for the remainder.
31. Withdrew cash for personal use, $2,500.
31. Rented land purchased on August 31 to local university for use as a parking lot during football season (September, October, and November), received advance payment of $1,500.

**Instructions**
1. Record the August 1 balance of each account in the appropriate balance column of a four-column account, write *Balance* in the item section, and place a check mark (✓) in the posting reference column. *(continued)*

2. Journalize the transactions for August in a two-column journal. Journal entry explanations may be omitted.
3. Post to the ledger, extending the account balance to the appropriate balance column after each posting.
4. Prepare a trial balance of the ledger as of August 31, 2006.

*If the working papers correlating with this textbook are not used, omit Problem 2-5A.*

**PROBLEM 2-5A**
*Errors in trial balance*
**Objectives 5, 6**

**WHAT'S WRONG WITH THIS?**

✓ *7. Total of Credit Column: $43,338.10*

The following records of Cypress TV Repair are presented in the working papers:

• Journal containing entries for the period July 1–31.
• Ledger to which the July entries have been posted.
• Preliminary trial balance as of July 31, which does not balance.

Locate the errors, supply the information requested, and prepare a corrected trial balance according to the following instructions. The balances recorded in the accounts as of July 1 and the entries in the journal are correctly stated. If it is necessary to correct any posted amounts in the ledger, a line should be drawn through the erroneous figure and the correct amount inserted above. Corrections or notations may be inserted on the preliminary trial balance in any manner desired. It is not necessary to complete all of the instructions if equal trial balance totals can be obtained earlier. However, the requirements of instructions (6) and (7) should be completed in any event.

**Instructions**
1. Verify the totals of the preliminary trial balance, inserting the correct amounts in the schedule provided in the working papers.
2. Compute the difference between the trial balance totals.
3. Compare the listings in the trial balance with the balances appearing in the ledger, and list the errors in the space provided in the working papers.
4. Verify the accuracy of the balance of each account in the ledger, and list the errors in the space provided in the working papers.
5. Trace the postings in the ledger back to the journal, using small check marks to identify items traced. Correct any amounts in the ledger that may be necessitated by errors in posting, and list the errors in the space provided in the working papers.
6. Journalize as of July 31 the payment of $210.00 for gas and electricity. The bill had been paid on July 31 but was inadvertently omitted from the journal. Post to the ledger. (Revise any amounts necessitated by posting this entry.)
7. Prepare a new trial balance.

**PROBLEM 2-6A**
*Corrected trial balance*
**Objectives 5, 6**

**SPREADSHEET**

✓ *1. Total of Debit Column: $156,000*

Onyx Videography has the following trial balance as of August 31, 2006:

| | | |
|---|---:|---:|
| Cash | 4,700 | |
| Accounts Receivable | 8,450 | |
| Supplies | 1,464 | |
| Prepaid Insurance | 140 | |
| Equipment | 36,000 | |
| Notes Payable | | 16,500 |
| Accounts Payable | | 3,470 |
| Jerri Orr, Capital | | 19,800 |
| Jerri Orr, Drawing | 7,200 | |
| Fees Earned | | 118,680 |
| Wages Expense | 68,000 | |
| Rent Expense | 13,900 | |
| Advertising Expense | 630 | |
| Gas, Electricity, and Water Expense | 3,780 | |
| | 144,264 | 158,450 |

The debit and credit totals are not equal as a result of the following errors:

a. The balance of cash was overstated by $3,500.

b. A cash receipt of $2,100 was posted as a credit to Cash of $1,200.

c. A debit of $1,750 to Accounts Receivable was not posted.

d. A return of $115 of defective supplies was erroneously posted as a $151 credit to Supplies.

e. An insurance policy acquired at a cost of $500 was posted as a credit to Prepaid Insurance.

f. The balance of Notes Payable was overstated by $4,500.

g. A credit of $250 in Accounts Payable was overlooked when the balance of the account was determined.

h. A debit of $1,800 for a withdrawal by the owner was posted as a debit to Jerri Orr, Capital.

i. The balance of $6,300 in Advertising Expense was entered as $630 in the trial balance.

j. Miscellaneous Expense, with a balance of $1,680, was omitted from the trial balance.

**Instructions**

1. Prepare a corrected trial balance as of August 31 of the current year.

2. ▭▭▭▶ Does the fact that the trial balance in (1) is balanced mean that there are no errors in the accounts? Explain.

# Problems Series B

**PROBLEM 2-1B**
*Entries into T accounts and trial balance*

**Objectives 2, 3, 4, 5**

✓ *3. Total of Debit Column: $43,475*

Christina Kiff, an architect, opened an office on July 1, 2006. During the month, she completed the following transactions connected with her professional practice:

a. Transferred cash from a personal bank account to an account to be used for the business, $18,000.

b. Paid July rent for office and workroom, $1,500.

c. Purchased used automobile for $16,500, paying $1,500 cash and giving a note payable for the remainder.

d. Purchased office and computer equipment on account, $6,500.

e. Paid cash for supplies, $1,050.

f. Paid cash for annual insurance policies, $1,200.

g. Received cash from client for plans delivered, $2,750.

h. Paid cash for miscellaneous expenses, $140.

i. Paid cash to creditors on account, $3,000.

j. Paid installment due on note payable, $450.

k. Received invoice for blueprint service, due in August, $525.

l. Recorded fee earned on plans delivered, payment to be received in August, $4,150.

m. Paid salary of assistant, $1,000.

n. Paid gas, oil, and repairs on automobile for July, $130.

**Instructions**

1. Record the foregoing transactions directly in the following T accounts, without journalizing: Cash; Accounts Receivable; Supplies; Prepaid Insurance; Automobiles; Equipment; Notes Payable; Accounts Payable; Christina Kiff, Capital; Professional Fees; Rent Expense; Salary Expense; Automobile Expense; Blueprint Expense; Miscellaneous Expense. To the left of the amount entered in the accounts, place the appropriate letter to identify the transaction.

2. Determine the balances of the T accounts having two or more debits or credits. A memorandum balance should be inserted in accounts having both debits and credits, in the manner illustrated in the chapter. For accounts with entries on one side only (such as Professional Fees), there is no need to insert the memorandum balance in the item column. For accounts containing only a single debit and

a single credit (such as Notes Payable), the memorandum balance should be inserted in the appropriate item column. Accounts containing a single entry only (such as Prepaid Insurance) do not need a memorandum balance.

3. Prepare a trial balance for Christina Kiff, Architect, as of July 31, 2006.

**PROBLEM 2-2B**
*Journal entries and trial balance*

**Objectives 2, 3, 4, 5**

SPREADSHEET
P.A.S.S.

✓ *4. c. $3,795*

On January 2, 2006, Lela Peterson established Acadia Realty, which completed the following transactions during the month:

a. Lela Peterson transferred cash from a personal bank account to an account to be used for the business, $9,000.
b. Paid rent on office and equipment for the month, $2,000.
c. Purchased supplies on account, $700.
d. Paid creditor on account, $290.
e. Earned sales commissions, receiving cash, $10,750.
f. Paid automobile expenses (including rental charge) for month, $1,400, and miscellaneous expenses, $480.
g. Paid office salaries, $2,500.
h. Determined that the cost of supplies used was $575.
i. Withdrew cash for personal use, $1,000.

**Instructions**

1. Journalize entries for transactions (a) through (i), using the following account titles: Cash; Supplies; Accounts Payable; Lela Peterson, Capital; Lela Peterson, Drawing; Sales Commissions; Office Salaries Expense; Rent Expense; Automobile Expense; Supplies Expense; Miscellaneous Expense. Explanations may be omitted.
2. Prepare T accounts, using the account titles in (1). Post the journal entries to these accounts, placing the appropriate letter to the left of each amount to identify the transactions. Determine the account balances, after all posting is complete, for all accounts having two or more debits or credits. A memorandum balance should also be inserted in accounts having both debits and credits, in the manner illustrated in the chapter. For accounts with entries on one side only, there is no need to insert a memorandum balance in the item column. For accounts containing only a single debit and a single credit, the memorandum balance should be inserted in the appropriate item column.
3. Prepare a trial balance as of January 31, 2006.
4. Determine the following:
   a. Amount of total revenue recorded in the ledger.
   b. Amount of total expenses recorded in the ledger.
   c. Amount of net income for January.

**PROBLEM 2-3B**
*Journal entries and trial balance*

**Objectives 2, 3, 4, 5**

SPREADSHEET
P.A.S.S.

✓ *3. Total of Credit Column: $41,425*

On November 2, 2006, Nicole Oliver established an interior decorating business, Devon Designs. During the remainder of the month, Nicole completed the following transactions related to the business:

Nov. 2. Nicole transferred cash from a personal bank account to an account to be used for the business, $15,000.
  5. Paid rent for period of November 5 to end of month, $1,750.
  6. Purchased office equipment on account, $8,500.
  8. Purchased a used truck for $18,000, paying $10,000 cash and giving a note payable for the remainder.
  10. Purchased supplies for cash, $1,115.
  12. Received cash for job completed, $7,500.
  15. Paid annual premiums on property and casualty insurance, $2,400.
  23. Recorded jobs completed on account and sent invoices to customers, $3,950.
  24. Received an invoice for truck expenses, to be paid in December, $600.
  29. Paid utilities expense, $750.
  29. Paid miscellaneous expenses, $310.
  30. Received cash from customers on account, $2,200.
  30. Paid wages of employees, $2,700.

Nov. 30. Paid creditor a portion of the amount owed for equipment purchased on November 6, $2,125.

30. Withdrew cash for personal use, $1,400.

**Instructions**

1. Journalize each transaction in a two-column journal, referring to the following chart of accounts in selecting the accounts to be debited and credited. (Do not insert the account numbers in the journal at this time.) Explanations may be omitted.

| | | | |
|---|---|---|---|
| 11 | Cash | 31 | Nicole Oliver, Capital |
| 12 | Accounts Receivable | 32 | Nicole Oliver, Drawing |
| 13 | Supplies | 41 | Fees Earned |
| 14 | Prepaid Insurance | 51 | Wages Expense |
| 16 | Equipment | 53 | Rent Expense |
| 18 | Truck | 54 | Utilities Expense |
| 21 | Notes Payable | 55 | Truck Expense |
| 22 | Accounts Payable | 59 | Miscellaneous Expense |

2. Post the journal to a ledger of four-column accounts, inserting appropriate posting references as each item is posted. Extend the balances to the appropriate balance columns after each transaction is posted.

3. Prepare a trial balance for Devon Designs as of November 30, 2006.

**PROBLEM 2-4B**
*Journal entries and trial balance*

**Objectives 2, 3, 4, 5**

SPREADSHEET
P.A.S.S.

✓ *4. Total of Debit Column: $465,275*

Boomerang Realty acts as an agent in buying, selling, renting, and managing real estate. The account balances at the end of October 2006 are as follows:

| | | | |
|---|---|---|---|
| 11 | Cash | 36,300 | |
| 12 | Accounts Receivable | 97,500 | |
| 13 | Prepaid Insurance | 2,200 | |
| 14 | Office Supplies | 2,100 | |
| 16 | Land | 0 | |
| 21 | Accounts Payable | | 23,020 |
| 22 | Unearned Rent | | 0 |
| 23 | Notes Payable | | 0 |
| 31 | Drew Felkel, Capital | | 68,680 |
| 32 | Drew Felkel, Drawing | 2,000 | |
| 41 | Fees Earned | | 253,000 |
| 51 | Salary and Commission Expense | 148,200 | |
| 52 | Rent Expense | 30,000 | |
| 53 | Advertising Expense | 17,800 | |
| 54 | Automobile Expense | 5,500 | |
| 59 | Miscellaneous Expense | 3,100 | |
| | | 344,700 | 344,700 |

The following business transactions were completed by Boomerang Realty during November 2006:

Nov. 1. Paid rent on office for month, $7,000.

2. Purchased office supplies on account, $1,675.

5. Paid annual insurance premiums, $4,800.

10. Received cash from clients on account, $52,000.

15. Purchased land for a future building site for $90,000, paying $10,000 in cash and giving a note payable for the remainder.

17. Paid creditors on account, $9,100.

20. Returned a portion of the office supplies purchased on November 2, receiving full credit for their cost, $400.

23. Paid advertising expense, $2,050.

27. Discovered an error in computing a commission; received cash from the salesperson for the overpayment, $700.

28. Paid automobile expense (including rental charges for an automobile), $1,100.

29. Paid miscellaneous expenses, $390.

30. Recorded revenue earned and billed to clients during the month, $48,400.

Nov. 30. Paid salaries and commissions for the month, $24,000.

30. Withdrew cash for personal use, $7,500.

30. Rented land purchased on November 15 to local merchants association for use as a parking lot in December and January, during a street rebuilding program, received advance payment of $2,000.

**Instructions**

1. Record the November 1, 2006 balance of each account in the appropriate balance column of a four-column account, write *Balance* in the item section, and place a check mark (✔) in the posting reference column.
2. Journalize the transactions for November in a two-column journal. Journal entry explanations may be omitted.
3. Post to the ledger, extending the account balance to the appropriate balance column after each posting.
4. Prepare a trial balance of the ledger as of November 30, 2006.

*If the working papers correlating with this textbook are not used, omit Problem 2-5B.*

**PROBLEM 2-5B**
*Errors in trial balance*

**Objectives 5, 6**

**WHAT'S WRONG WITH THIS?**

✔ *7. Total of Debit Column: $43,338.10*

The following records of Cypress TV Repair are presented in the working papers:

- Journal containing entries for the period July 1–31.
- Ledger to which the July entries have been posted.
- Preliminary trial balance as of July 31, which does not balance.

Locate the errors, supply the information requested, and prepare a corrected trial balance according to the following instructions. The balances recorded in the accounts as of July 1 and the entries in the journal are correctly stated. If it is necessary to correct any posted amounts in the ledger, a line should be drawn through the erroneous figure and the correct amount inserted above. Corrections or notations may be inserted on the preliminary trial balance in any manner desired. It is not necessary to complete all of the instructions if equal trial balance totals can be obtained earlier. However, the requirements of instructions (6) and (7) should be completed in any event.

**Instructions**

1. Verify the totals of the preliminary trial balance, inserting the correct amounts in the schedule provided in the working papers.
2. Compute the difference between the trial balance totals.
3. Compare the listings in the trial balance with the balances appearing in the ledger, and list the errors in the space provided in the working papers.
4. Verify the accuracy of the balance of each account in the ledger, and list the errors in the space provided in the working papers.
5. Trace the postings in the ledger back to the journal, using small check marks to identify items traced. Correct any amounts in the ledger that may be necessitated by errors in posting, and list the errors in the space provided in the working papers.
6. Journalize as of July 31 the payment of $175 for advertising expense. The bill had been paid on July 31 but was inadvertently omitted from the journal. Post to the ledger. (Revise any amounts necessitated by posting this entry.)
7. Prepare a new trial balance.

**PROBLEM 2-6B**
*Corrected trial balance*

**Objectives 5, 6**

**SPREADSHEET**

✔ *1. Total of Debit Column: $125,000*

Montero Carpet has the trial balance at the top of the following page as of October 31, 2006. The debit and credit totals are not equal as a result of the following errors:

a. The balance of cash was understated by $1,500.
b. A cash receipt of $2,500 was posted as a debit to Cash of $5,200.
c. A debit of $2,000 for a withdrawal by the owner was posted as a credit to Tyca Seagle, Capital.
d. The balance of $4,480 in Advertising Expense was entered as $448 in the trial balance.
e. A debit of $750 to Accounts Receivable was not posted.

f. A return of $125 of defective supplies was erroneously posted as a $215 credit to Supplies.

g. The balance of Notes Payable was overstated by $5,000.

h. An insurance policy acquired at a cost of $200 was posted as a credit to Prepaid Insurance.

i. Gas, Electricity, and Water Expense, with a balance of $4,400, was omitted from the trial balance.

j. A credit of $625 in Accounts Payable was overlooked when determining the balance of the account.

| | | |
|---|---:|---:|
| Cash | 5,200 | |
| Accounts Receivable | 7,825 | |
| Supplies | 1,450 | |
| Prepaid Insurance | 370 | |
| Equipment | 35,000 | |
| Notes Payable | | 26,000 |
| Accounts Payable | | 4,850 |
| Tyca Seagle, Capital | | 23,825 |
| Tyca Seagle, Drawing | 9,200 | |
| Fees Earned | | 76,700 |
| Wages Expense | 43,540 | |
| Rent Expense | 10,400 | |
| Advertising Expense | 448 | |
| Miscellaneous Expense | 1,095 | |
| | 114,528 | 131,375 |

### Instructions

1. Prepare a corrected trial balance as of October 31, 2006.
2. ▭▭▭▶ Does the fact that the trial balance in (1) is balanced mean that there are no errors in the accounts? Explain.

# Continuing Problem

**P.A.S.S.**

✓ 4. Total of Debit Column: $31,760

The transactions completed by Dancin Music during April 2006 were described at the end of Chapter 1. The following transactions were completed during May, the second month of the business's operations:

May 1. Shannon Burns made an additional investment in Dancin Music by depositing $3,000 in Dancin Music's checking account.

    1. Instead of continuing to share office space with a local real estate agency, Shannon decided to rent office space near a local music store. Paid rent for May, $1,600.

    1. Paid a premium of $3,360 for a comprehensive insurance policy covering liability, theft, and fire. The policy covers a two-year period.

    2. Received $1,200 on account.

    3. On behalf of Dancin Music, Shannon signed a contract with a local radio station, KPRG, to provide guest spots for the next three months. The contract requires Dancin Music to provide a guest disc jockey for 80 hours per month for a monthly fee of $2,400. Any additional hours beyond 80 will be billed to KPRG at $40 per hour. In accordance with the contract, Shannon received $4,800 from KPRG as an advance payment for the first two months.

    3. Paid $250 on account.

    4. Paid an attorney $150 for reviewing the May 3rd contract with KPRG. (Record as Miscellaneous Expense.)

    5. Purchased office equipment on account from One-Stop Office Mart, $5,000.

    8. Paid for a newspaper advertisement, $200.

May 11. Received $600 for serving as a disc jockey for a college fraternity party.

13. Paid $500 to a local audio electronics store for rental of digital recording equipment.

14. Paid wages of $1,200 to receptionist and part-time assistant.

16. Received $1,100 for serving as a disc jockey for a wedding reception.

18. Purchased supplies on account, $750.

21. Paid $240 to Rocket Music for use of its current music demos in making various music sets.

22. Paid $500 to a local radio station to advertise the services of Dancin Music twice daily for the remainder of May.

23. Served as disc jockey for a party for $1,560. Received $400, with the remainder due June 4, 2006.

27. Paid electric bill, $560.

28. Paid wages of $1,200 to receptionist and part-time assistant.

29. Paid miscellaneous expenses, $170.

30. Served as a disc jockey for a charity ball for $1,200. Received $600, with the remainder due on June 9, 2006.

31. Received $2,000 for serving as a disc jockey for a party.

31. Paid $600 royalties (music expense) to Federated Clearing for use of various artists' music during May.

31. Withdrew $2,000 cash from Dancin Music for personal use.

Dancin Music's chart of accounts and the balance of accounts as of May 1, 2006 (all normal balances), are as follows:

| 11 | Cash | $6,160 | 41 | Fees Earned | $4,750 |
|----|------|--------|----|-------------|--------|
| 12 | Accounts Receivable | 1,200 | 50 | Wages Expense | 400 |
| 14 | Supplies | 170 | 51 | Office Rent Expense | 1,000 |
| 15 | Prepaid Insurance | — | 52 | Equipment Rent Expense | 650 |
| 17 | Office Equipment | — | 53 | Utilities Expense | 300 |
| 21 | Accounts Payable | 250 | 54 | Music Expense | 940 |
| 23 | Unearned Revenue | — | 55 | Advertising Expense | 600 |
| 31 | Shannon Burns, Capital | 7,000 | 56 | Supplies Expense | 180 |
| 32 | Shannon Burns, Drawing | 250 | 59 | Miscellaneous Expense | 150 |

### Instructions

1. Enter the May 1, 2006 account balances in the appropriate balance column of a four-column account. Write *Balance* in the Item column, and place a check mark (✔) in the Posting Reference column. (*Hint:* Verify the equality of the debit and credit balances in the ledger before proceeding with the next instruction.)

2. Analyze and journalize each transaction in a two-column journal, omitting journal entry explanations.

3. Post the journal to the ledger, extending the account balance to the appropriate balance column after each posting.

4. Prepare a trial balance as of May 31, 2006.

# Special Activities

**ACTIVITY 2-1**
*Ethics and professional conduct in business*

ETHICS

At the end of the current month, Ross Heimlich prepared a trial balance for Main Street Motor Co. The credit side of the trial balance exceeds the debit side by a significant amount. Ross has decided to add the difference to the balance of the miscellaneous expense account in order to complete the preparation of the current month's financial statements by a 5 o'clock deadline. Ross will look for the difference next week when he has more time.

➤ Discuss whether Ross is behaving in a professional manner.

**ACTIVITY 2-2**
*Account for revenue*

**WHAT DO YOU THINK?**

Krypton College requires students to pay tuition each term before classes begin. Students who have not paid their tuition are not allowed to enroll or to attend classes.

What journal entry do you think Krypton College would use to record the receipt of the students' tuition payments? Describe the nature of each account in the entry.

**ACTIVITY 2-3**
*Record transactions*

The following discussion took place between Heather Sims, the office manager of Sedgemoor Data Company, and a new accountant, Ed Hahn.

*Ed:* I've been thinking about our method of recording entries. It seems that it's inefficient.

*Heather:* In what way?

*Ed:* Well—correct me if I'm wrong—it seems like we have unnecessary steps in the process. We could easily develop a trial balance by posting our transactions directly into the ledger and bypassing the journal altogether. In this way we could combine the recording and posting process into one step and save ourselves a lot of time. What do you think?

*Heather:* We need to have a talk.

➡ What should Heather say to Ed?

**ACTIVITY 2-4**
*Debits and credits*

**GROUP ACTIVITY**

The following excerpt is from a conversation between Peter Kaiser, the president and chief operating officer of Sprocket Construction Co., and his neighbor, Doris Nesmith.

*Doris:* Peter, I'm taking a course in night school, "Intro to Accounting." I was wondering—could you answer a couple of questions for me?

*Peter:* Well, I will if I can.

*Doris:* Okay, our instructor says that it's critical we understand the basic concepts of accounting, or we'll never get beyond the first test. My problem is with those rules of debit and credit . . . you know, assets increase with debits, decrease with credits, etc.

*Peter:* Yes, pretty basic stuff. You just have to memorize the rules. It shouldn't be too difficult.

*Doris:* Sure, I can memorize the rules, but my problem is I want to be sure I understand the basic concepts behind the rules.

For example, why can't assets be increased with credits and decreased with debits like revenue? As long as everyone did it that way, why not? It would seem easier if we had the same rules for all increases and decreases in accounts.

Also, why is the left side of an account called the debit side? Why couldn't it be called something simple . . . like the "LE" for Left Entry? The right side could be called just "RE" for Right Entry.

Finally, why are there just two sides to an entry? Why can't there be three or four sides to an entry?

In a group of four or five, select one person to play the role of Peter and one person to play the role of Doris.

1. After listening to the conversation between Peter and Doris, help Peter answer Doris's questions.
2. What information (other than just debit and credit journal entries) could the accounting system gather that might be useful to Peter in managing Sprocket Construction Co.?

**ACTIVITY 2-5**
*Transactions and income statement*

Kercy Hepner is planning to manage and operate Eagle Caddy Service at Helena Golf and Country Club during June through August 2006. Kercy will rent a small maintenance building from the country club for $300 per month and will offer caddy services, including cart rentals, to golfers. Kercy has had no formal training in record keeping.

Kercy keeps notes of all receipts and expenses in a shoe box. An examination of Kercy's shoe box records for June revealed the following:

June 1. Withdrew $2,250 from personal bank account to be used to operate the caddy service.
   1. Paid rent to Helena Golf and Country Club, $300.
   2. Paid for golf supplies (practice balls, etc.), $225.
   3. Arranged for the rental of forty regular (pulling) golf carts and ten gasoline-driven carts for $1,500 per month. Paid $1,125 in advance, with the remaining $375 due June 20.
   7. Purchased supplies, including gasoline, for the golf carts on account, $270. Helena Golf and Country Club has agreed to allow Kercy to store the gasoline in one of its fuel tanks at no cost.
   15. Received cash for services from June 1–15, $1,680.
   17. Paid cash to creditors on account, $270.
   20. Paid remaining rental on golf carts, $375.
   22. Purchased supplies, including gasoline, on account, $255.
   25. Accepted IOUs from customers on account, $570.
   28. Paid miscellaneous expenses, $180.
   30. Received cash for services from June 16-30, $2,200.
   30. Paid telephone and electricity (utilities) expenses, $160.
   30. Paid wages of part-time employees, $390.
   30. Received cash in payment of IOUs on account, $270.
   30. Determined the amount of supplies on hand at the end of June, $140.

Kercy has asked you several questions concerning her financial affairs to date, and she has asked you to assist with her record keeping and reporting of financial data.

a. To assist Kercy with her record keeping, prepare a chart of accounts that would be appropriate for Eagle Caddy Service.
b. Prepare an income statement for June in order to help Kercy assess the profitability of Eagle Caddy Service. For this purpose, the use of T accounts may be helpful in analyzing the effects of each June transaction.
c. Based on Kercy's records of receipts and payments, calculate the amount of cash on hand on June 30. For this purpose, a T account for cash may be useful.
d. ⟹ A count of the cash on hand on June 30 totaled $3,180. Briefly discuss the possible causes of the difference between the amount of cash computed in (c) and the actual amount of cash on hand.

**ACTIVITY 2-6**
*Business strategy*

GROUP ACTIVITY

Assume that you are considering developing a nationwide chain of women's clothing stores. You have contacted a Houston-based firm that specializes in financing new business ventures and enterprises. Such firms, called venture capital firms, finance new businesses in exchange for a percentage of the ownership.

1. In groups of four or five, discuss the different business strategies that you might use in your venture.
2. For each strategy you listed in (1), provide an example of a real world business using the same strategy.
3. What percentage of the ownership would you be willing to give the venture capital firm in exchange for its financing?

**ACTIVITY 2-7**
*Opportunities for accountants*

The increasing complexity of the current business and regulatory environment has created an increased demand for accountants who can analyze business transactions and interpret their effects on the financial statements. In addition, a basic ability to analyze the effects of transactions is necessary to be successful in all fields of business as well as in other disciplines, such as law. To better understand the

importance of accounting in today's environment, search the Internet or your local newspaper for job opportunities. One possible Internet site is **http://www.jobweb .com**. Then do one of the following:

1. Print a listing of at least two ads for accounting jobs. Alternatively, bring to class at least two newspaper ads for accounting jobs.
2. Print a listing of at least two ads for nonaccounting jobs for which some knowledge of accounting is preferred or necessary. Alternatively, bring to class at least two newspaper ads for such jobs.

# Answers to Self-Examination Questions

1. **A**   A debit may signify an increase in an asset account (answer A) or a decrease in a liability or owner's capital account. A credit may signify a decrease in an asset account (answer B) or an increase in a liability or owner's capital account (answers C and D).

2. **C**   Liability, capital, and revenue (answer C) accounts have normal credit balances. Asset (answer A), drawing (answer B), and expense (answer D) accounts have normal debit balances.

3. **C**   Accounts Receivable (answer A), Cash (answer B), and Miscellaneous Expense (answer D) would all normally have debit balances. Fees Earned should normally have a credit balance. Hence, a debit balance in Fees Earned (answer C) would indicate a likely error in the recording process.

4. **A**   The receipt of cash from customers on account increases the asset Cash and decreases the asset Accounts Receivable, as indicated by answer A. Answer B has the debit and credit reversed, and answers C and D involve transactions with creditors (accounts payable) and not customers (accounts receivable).

5. **D**   The trial balance (answer D) is a listing of the balances and the titles of the accounts in the ledger on a given date, so that the equality of the debits and credits in the ledger can be verified. The income statement (answer A) is a summary of revenue and expenses for a period of time. The balance sheet (answer B) is a presentation of the assets, liabilities, and owner's equity on a given date. The statement of owner's equity (answer C) is a summary of the changes in owner's equity for a period of time.

# THE MATCHING CONCEPT AND THE ADJUSTING PROCESS

## objectives

*After studying this chapter, you should be able to:*

**1** Explain how the matching concept relates to the accrual basis of accounting.

**2** Explain why adjustments are necessary and list the characteristics of adjusting entries.

**3** Journalize entries for accounts requiring adjustment.

**4** Summarize the adjustment process and prepare an adjusted trial balance.

**5** Use vertical analysis to compare financial statement items with each other and with industry averages.

**A**ssume that you rented an apartment last month and signed a nine-month lease. When you signed the lease agreement, you were required to pay the final month's rent of $500. This amount is not returnable to you.

You are now applying for a student loan at a local bank. The loan application requires a listing of all your assets. Should you list the $500 deposit as an asset?

The answer to this question is "yes." The deposit is an asset to you until you receive the use of the apartment in the ninth month.

A business faces similar accounting problems at the end of a period. A business must determine what assets, liabilities, and owner's equity should be reported on its balance sheet. It must also determine what revenues and expenses should be reported on its income statement.

As we illustrated in previous chapters, transactions are normally recorded as they take place. Periodically, financial statements are prepared, summarizing the effects of the transactions on the financial position and operations of the business.

At any one point in time, however, the accounting records may not reflect all transactions. For example, most businesses do not record the daily use of supplies. Likewise, revenue may have been earned from providing services to customers, yet the customers have not been billed by the time the accounting period ends. Thus, at the end of the period, the revenue and receivable accounts must be updated.

In this chapter, we describe and illustrate this updating process. We will focus on accounts that normally require updating and the journal entries that update them.

# The Matching Concept

**objective** 1

Explain how the matching concept relates to the accrual basis of accounting.

When accountants prepare financial statements, they assume that the economic life of the business can be divided into time periods. Using this *accounting period concept*, accountants must determine in which period the revenues and expenses of the business should be reported. To determine the appropriate period, accountants will use either (1) the cash basis of accounting or (2) the accrual basis of accounting.

Under the *cash basis*, revenues and expenses are reported in the income statement in the period in which cash is received or paid. For example, fees are recorded when cash is received from clients, and wages are recorded when cash is paid to employees. The net income (or net loss) is the difference between the cash receipts (revenues) and the cash payments (expenses).

Under the *accrual basis*, revenues are reported in the income statement in the period in which they are earned. For example, revenue is reported when the services are provided to customers. Cash may or may not be received from customers during this period. The concept that supports this reporting of revenues is called the *revenue recognition concept*.

Under the accrual basis, expenses are reported in the same period as the revenues to which they relate. For example, employee wages are reported as an expense in the period in which the employees provided services to customers, and not necessarily when the wages are paid.

The accounting concept that supports reporting revenues and related expenses in the same period is called the *matching concept*, or **matching principle**. Under this concept, an income statement will report the resulting income or loss for the period.

> **The matching concept supports reporting revenues and related expenses in the same period.**

Generally accepted accounting principles require the use of the accrual basis. However, small service businesses may use the cash basis because they have few receivables and payables. For example, attorneys, physicians, and real estate agents often use the cash basis. For them, the cash basis will yield financial statements similar to those prepared under the accrual basis.

For most large businesses, the cash basis will not provide accurate financial statements for user needs. For this reason, we will emphasize the accrual basis in this text. The accrual basis and its related matching concept require an analysis and updating of some accounts when financial statements are prepared. In the following paragraphs, we will describe and illustrate this process, called the ***adjusting process***.

# Nature of the Adjusting Process

> objective **2**
>
> Explain why adjustments are necessary and list the characteristics of adjusting entries.

At the end of an accounting period, many of the balances of accounts in the ledger can be reported, without change, in the financial statements. For example, the balance of the cash account is normally the amount reported on the balance sheet.

Some accounts in the ledger, however, require updating. For example, the balances listed for prepaid expenses are normally overstated because the use of these assets is not recorded on a day-to-day basis. The balance of the supplies account usually represents the cost of supplies at the beginning of the period plus the cost of supplies acquired during the period. To record the daily use of supplies would require many entries with small amounts. In addition, the total amount of supplies is small relative to other assets, and managers usually do not require day-to-day information about supplies.

> **All adjusting entries affect at least one income statement account and one balance sheet account.**

The journal entries that bring the accounts up to date at the end of the accounting period are called ***adjusting entries***. All adjusting entries affect at least one income statement account and one balance sheet account. Thus, an adjusting entry will *always* involve a revenue or an expense account *and* an asset or a liability account.

Is there an easy way to know when an adjusting entry is needed? Yes, four basic items require adjusting entries. The first two items are ***deferrals***. Deferrals are created by recording a transaction in a way that *delays* or *defers* the recognition of an expense or a revenue, as described below.

- ***Deferred expenses***, or ***prepaid expenses***, are items that have been initially recorded as assets but are expected to become expenses over time or through the normal operations of the business. Supplies and prepaid insurance are two examples of prepaid expenses that may require adjustment at the end of an accounting period. Other examples include prepaid advertising and prepaid interest.

- ***Deferred revenues***, or ***unearned revenues***, are items that have been initially recorded as liabilities but are expected to become revenues over time or through the normal operations of the business. An example of deferred revenue is unearned rent. Other examples include tuition received in advance by a school, an annual retainer fee received by an attorney, premiums received in advance by an insurance company, and magazine subscriptions received in advance by a publisher.

The second two items that require adjusting entries are accruals. ***Accruals*** are created by an unrecorded expense that has been incurred or an unrecorded revenue that has been earned, as described below.

- ***Accrued expenses***, or ***accrued liabilities***, are expenses that have been incurred *but have not been recorded* in the accounts. An example of an accrued expense is accrued wages owed to employees at the end of a period. Other examples include accrued interest on notes payable and accrued taxes.

- *Accrued revenues*, or *accrued assets*, are revenues that have been earned *but have not been recorded* in the accounts. An example of an accrued revenue is fees for services that an attorney has provided but hasn't billed to the client at the end of the period. Other examples include unbilled commissions by a travel agent, accrued interest on notes receivable, and accrued rent on property rented to others.

How do you tell the difference between deferrals and accruals? Determine when cash is received or paid, as shown in Exhibit 1. If cash is received (for revenue) or paid (for expense) in the *current* period, but the revenue or expense relates to a future period, the revenue or expense is a deferred item. If cash will not be received or paid until a *future* period, but the revenue or expense relates to the current period, the revenue or expense is an accrued item.

## •Exhibit 1   Deferrals and Accruals

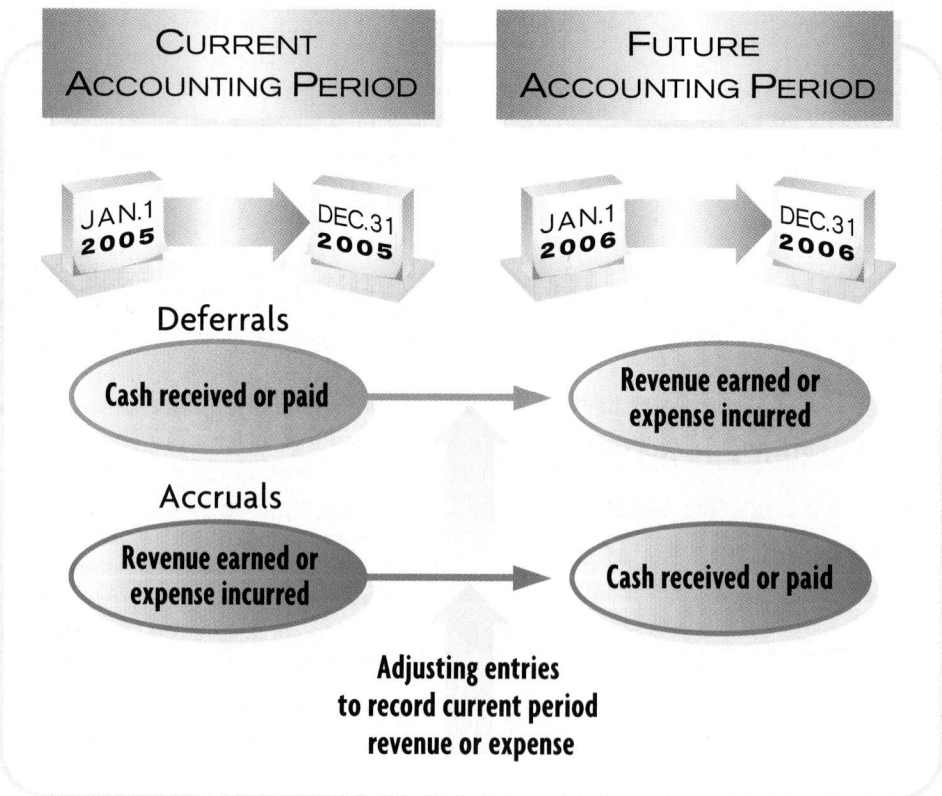

# Recording Adjusting Entries

**objective   3**

Journalize entries for accounts requiring adjustment.

The examples of adjusting entries in the following paragraphs are based on the ledger of NetSolutions as reported in the December 31, 2005 trial balance in Exhibit 2. The adjusting entries are shown in color in T accounts to separate them from other transactions. An expanded chart of accounts for NetSolutions is shown in Exhibit 3. The additional accounts that will be used in this chapter are shown in color.

## •Exhibit 2   Unadjusted Trial Balance for NetSolutions

**NetSolutions**
**Trial Balance**
**December 31, 2005**

| | | |
|---|---:|---:|
| Cash | 2 0 6 5 00 | |
| Accounts Receivable | 2 2 2 0 00 | |
| Supplies | 2 0 0 0 00 | |
| Prepaid Insurance | 2 4 0 0 00 | |
| Land | 20 0 0 0 00 | |
| Office Equipment | 1 8 0 0 00 | |
| Accounts Payable | | 9 0 0 00 |
| Unearned Rent | | 3 6 0 00 |
| Chris Clark, Capital | | 25 0 0 0 00 |
| Chris Clark, Drawing | 4 0 0 0 00 | |
| Fees Earned | | 16 3 4 0 00 |
| Wages Expense | 4 2 7 5 00 | |
| Rent Expense | 1 6 0 0 00 | |
| Utilities Expense | 9 8 5 00 | |
| Supplies Expense | 8 0 0 00 | |
| Miscelleous Expense | 4 5 5 00 | |
| | 42 6 0 0 00 | 42 6 0 0 00 |

## •Exhibit 3   Expanded Chart of Accounts for NetSolutions

| Balance Sheet Accounts | Income Statement Accounts |
|---|---|
| 1. Assets | 4. Revenue |
| 11  Cash | 41  Fees Earned |
| 12  Accounts Receivable | 42  Rent Revenue |
| 14  Supplies | 5. Expenses |
| 15  Prepaid Insurance | 51  Wages Expense |
| 17  Land | 52  Rent Expense |
| 18  Office Equipment | 53  Depreciation Expense |
| 19  Accumulated Depreciation | 54  Utilities Expense |
| 2. Liabilities | 55  Supplies Expense |
| 21  Accounts Payable | 56  Insurance Expense |
| 22  Wages Payable | 59  Miscellaneous Expense |
| 23  Unearned Rent | |
| 3. Owner's Equity | |
| 31  Chris Clark, Capital | |
| 32  Chris Clark, Drawing | |

# Deferred Expenses (Prepaid Expenses)

The concept of adjusting the accounting records was introduced in Chapters 1 and 2 in the illustration for NetSolutions. In that illustration, supplies were purchased on November 10 (transaction c). The supplies used during November were recorded on November 30 (transaction g).

The balance in NetSolutions' **supplies** account on December 31 is $2,000. Some of these supplies (computer diskettes, paper, envelopes, etc.) were used during December, and some are still on hand (not used). If either amount is known, the other can be determined. It is normally easier to determine the cost of the supplies on hand at the end of the month than it is to keep a daily record of those used. Assuming that on December 31 the amount of supplies on hand is $760, the amount to be transferred from the asset account to the expense account is $1,240, computed as follows:

| | |
|---|---|
| Supplies available during December (balance of account) | $2,000 |
| Supplies on hand, December 31 | 760 |
| Supplies used (amount of adjustment) | $1,240 |

As we discussed in Chapter 2, increases in expense accounts are recorded as debits and decreases in asset accounts are recorded as credits. Hence, at the end of December, the supplies expense account should be debited for $1,240, and the supplies account should be credited for $1,240 to record the supplies used during December. The adjusting journal entry and T accounts for Supplies and Supplies Expense are as follows:

| | 2005 | | | | | | |
|---|---|---|---|---|---|---|---|
| 2 | Dec. | 31 | Supplies Expense | 55 | 1 2 4 0 00 | | 2 |
| 3 | | | Supplies | 14 | | 1 2 4 0 00 | 3 |

| **Supplies** | | | | **Supplies Expense** | |
|---|---|---|---|---|---|
| Bal. | 2,000 | Dec. 31 | 1,240 | Bal. | 800 |
| *760* | | | | Dec. 31 | 1,240 |
| | | | | | *2,040* |

After the adjustment has been recorded and posted, the supplies account has a debit balance of $760. This balance represents an asset that will become an expense in a future period.

The debit balance of $2,400 in NetSolutions' **prepaid insurance** account represents a December 1 prepayment of insurance for 24 months. At the end of December, the insurance expense account should be increased (debited), and the prepaid insurance account should be decreased (credited) by $100, the insurance for one month. The adjusting journal entry and T accounts for Prepaid Insurance and Insurance Expense are as follows:

> **The balance of a prepaid (deferred) expense is an asset that will become an expense in a future period.**

| | | | | | | | |
|---|---|---|---|---|---|---|---|
| 5 | | 31 | Insurance Expense | 56 | 1 0 0 00 | | 5 |
| 6 | | | Prepaid Insurance | 15 | | 1 0 0 00 | 6 |

| **Prepaid Insurance** | | | | **Insurance Expense** | |
|---|---|---|---|---|---|
| Bal. | 2,400 | Dec. 31 | 100 | Dec. 31 | 100 |
| *2,300* | | | | | |

**POINT OF INTEREST**

The tuition you pay at the beginning of each term is an example of a deferred expense to you, as a student.

After the adjustment has been recorded and posted, the prepaid insurance account has a debit balance of $2,300. This balance represents an asset that will become an expense in future periods. The insurance expense account has a debit balance of $100, which is an expense of the current period.

What is the effect of omitting adjusting entries? If the preceding adjustments for supplies ($1,240) and insurance ($100) are not recorded, the financial statements prepared as of December 31 will be misstated. On the income statement, Supplies Expense and Insurance Expense will be understated by a total of $1,340, and net income will be overstated by $1,340. On the balance sheet, Supplies and Prepaid Insurance will be overstated by a total of $1,340. Since net income increases owner's equity, Chris Clark, Capital will also be overstated by $1,340 on the balance sheet. The effects of omitting these adjusting entries on the income statement and balance sheet are shown below.

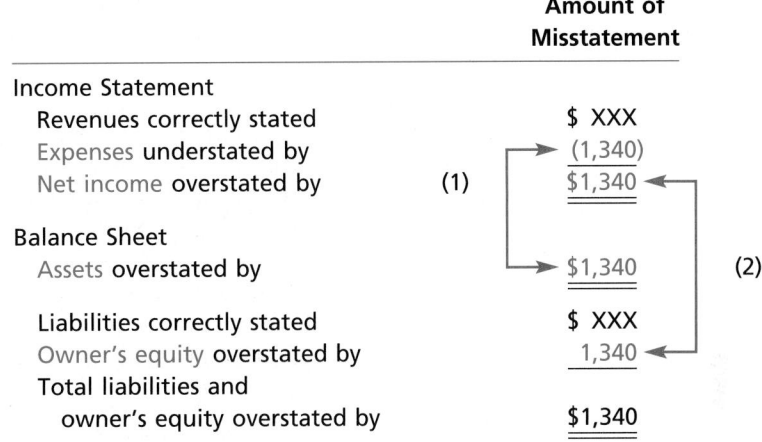

| | Amount of Misstatement |
|---|---|
| Income Statement | |
| Revenues correctly stated | $ XXX |
| Expenses understated by | (1,340) |
| Net income overstated by (1) | $1,340 |
| Balance Sheet | |
| Assets overstated by | $1,340   (2) |
| Liabilities correctly stated | $ XXX |
| Owner's equity overstated by | 1,340 |
| Total liabilities and owner's equity overstated by | $1,340 |

Arrow (1) indicates the effect of the understated expenses on assets. Arrow (2) indicates the effect of the overstated net income on owner's equity.

Prepayments of expenses are sometimes made at the beginning of the period in which they will be *entirely consumed*. On December 1, for example, NetSolutions paid rent of $800 for the month. On December 1, the rent payment represents the asset prepaid rent. The prepaid rent expires daily, and at the end of December, the entire amount has become an expense (rent expense). In cases such as this, the initial payment is recorded as an expense rather than as an asset. Thus, if the payment is recorded as a debit to Rent Expense, no adjusting entry is needed at the end of the period.[1]

Supplies of $1,250 were on hand at the beginning of the period, supplies of $3,800 were purchased during the period, and supplies of $1,000 were on hand at the end of the period. What is the supplies expense for the period?

----------

*$4,050 ($1,250 + $3,800 − $1,000)*

---

## INTEGRITY IN BUSINESS

### FREE ISSUE

Office supplies are often available to employees on a "free issue" basis. This means employees do not have to "sign" for the release of office supplies but merely obtain the necessary supplies from a local storage area as needed.

Just because supplies are easily available, however, doesn't mean they can be taken for personal use. There are many instances when employees have been terminated for taking supplies home for personal use.

## Deferred Revenue (Unearned Revenue)

According to NetSolutions' trial balance on December 31, the balance in the **unearned rent** account is $360. This balance represents the receipt of three months' rent on December 1 for December, January, and February. At the end of December, the unearned rent account should be decreased (debited) by $120, and the rent

----------

[1]This alternative treatment of recording the cost of supplies, rent, and other prepayments of expenses is discussed in Appendix B.

revenue account should be increased (credited) by $120. The $120 represents the rental revenue for one month ($360/3). The adjusting journal entry and T accounts are shown below.

| 8 | | 31 | Unearned Rent | 23 | 1 2 0 00 | | 8 |
| 9 | | | Rent Revenue | 42 | | 1 2 0 00 | 9 |

| Unearned Rent | | | | Rent Revenue | |
|---|---|---|---|---|---|
| Dec. 31 | 120 | Bal. | 360 | | |
| | | *240* | | Dec. 31 | 120 |

After the adjustment has been recorded and posted, the unearned rent account, which is a liability, has a credit balance of $240. This amount represents a deferral that will become revenue in a future period. The rent revenue account has a balance of $120, which is revenue of the current period.[2]

If the preceding adjustment of unearned rent and rent revenue is not recorded, the financial statements prepared on December 31 will be misstated. On the income statement, Rent Revenue and the net income will be understated by $120. On the balance sheet, Unearned Rent will be overstated by $120, and Chris Clark, Capital will be understated by $120. The effects of omitting this adjusting entry are shown below.

**REAL WORLD**

**Sears, Roebuck and Co.** sells extended warranty contracts with terms between 12 and 36 months. The receipts from sales of these contracts are reported as unearned revenue (deferred revenue) on Sears' balance sheet. Revenue is recorded as the contracts expire.

If NetSolutions' adjustment for unearned rent had incorrectly been made for $180 instead of $120, what would have been the effect on the financial statements?

*Revenues would have been overstated by $60; net income would have been overstated by $60; liabilities would have been understated by $60; and owner's equity would have been overstated by $60.*

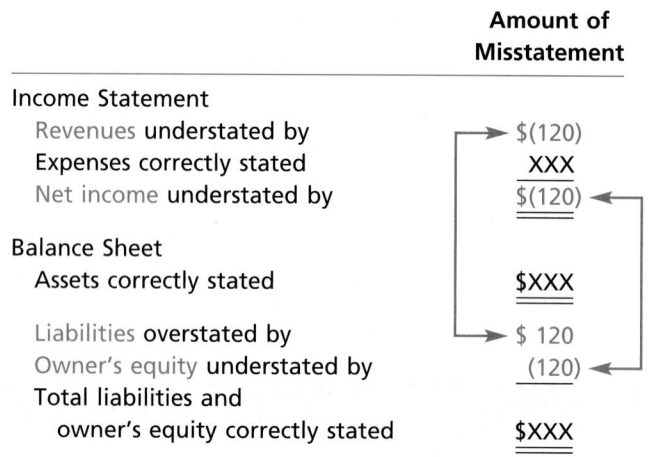

|  | Amount of Misstatement |
|---|---|
| **Income Statement** | |
| Revenues **understated by** | $(120) |
| Expenses **correctly stated** | XXX |
| Net income **understated by** | $(120) |
| | |
| **Balance Sheet** | |
| Assets **correctly stated** | $XXX |
| | |
| Liabilities **overstated by** | $ 120 |
| Owner's equity **understated by** | (120) |
| Total liabilities and | |
| owner's equity **correctly stated** | $XXX |

# Accrued Expenses (Accrued Liabilities)

Some types of services, such as insurance, are normally paid for *before* they are used. These prepayments are deferrals. Other types of services are paid for *after* the service has been performed. For example, wages expense accumulates or *accrues* hour by hour and day by day, but payment may be made only weekly, biweekly, or monthly. The amount of such an accrued but unpaid item at the end of the accounting period is both an expense and a liability. In the case of wages expense, if the last day of a pay period is not the last day of the accounting period, the accrued wages expense and the related liability must be recorded in the accounts by an adjusting entry. This adjusting entry is necessary so that expenses are properly matched to the period in which they were incurred.

At the end of December, accrued wages for NetSolutions were $250. This amount is an additional expense of December and is debited to the **wages expense** account. It is also a liability as of December 31 and is credited to Wages Payable. The adjusting journal entry and T accounts are as follows.

**REAL WORLD**

**Callaway Golf Company,** a manufacturer of such innovative golf clubs as the "Big Bertha" driver, reports accrued warranty expense on its balance sheet.

---

[2]An alternative treatment of recording revenues received in advance of their being earned is discussed in Appendix B.

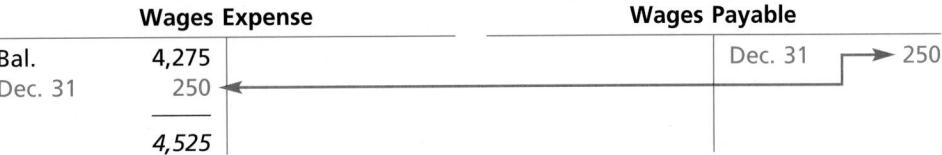

# FINANCIAL REPORTING AND DISCLOSURE

## UNEARNED REVENUE

**M**icrosoft Corporation develops, manufactures, licenses, and supports a wide range of computer software products, including Windows XP®, Windows NT®, Word®, Excel®, and the Xbox®. When Microsoft sells its products, it incurs an obligation to support its software with technical support and periodic updates. As a result, not all the revenue from selling software is earned on the date of sale. Instead, some of the revenue is unearned. That is, the portion of revenue related to support services, such as updates and technical support, is earned only as time

passes and the support services are provided to customers. Thus, it is necessary to make an adjusting entry each year to transfer unearned revenue to revenue.

The excerpts below from Microsoft's 2002 financial statements describe its accounting for unearned revenue. Microsoft further indicated that, of the $7,743 million of unearned revenue at June 30, 2002, it expected to recognize $5,917 million during the next year and $1,826 million in future years.

---

UNEARNED REVENUE

. . . Revenue attributable [to] technical support and Internet browser technologies . . . is recognized ratably . . . over the product's life cycle. The percentage of revenue recognized ratably . . . ranges from approximately 20% to 25% for Windows XP Home, approximately 10% to 15% for Windows XP Professional, and approximately 10% to 15% for desktop applications . . . Product life cycles are currently estimated at three years for Windows operating systems and 18 months for desktop applications. The unearned revenue as of June 30, 2002, was as follows:

|  | In Millions | |
| --- | --- | --- |
| **June 30** | **2001** | **2002** |
| Unearned revenue | $5,614 | $7,743 |

Unearned revenue by product was as follows:

|  | In Millions | |
| --- | --- | --- |
| **June 30** | **2001** | **2002** |
| Desktop applications | $2,189 | $3,489 |
| Desktop platforms | 2,586 | 3,198 |
| Enterprise software and services | 391 | 791 |
| Desktop and enterprise software and services | 5,166 | 7,478 |
| Consumer software, services, and devices, and other | 448 | 265 |
| Unearned revenue | $5,614 | $7,743 |

I'm 165 years old and came to life as a small family-run soap and candle company in Cincinnati. My celestial logo dates back to the 1850s. I recorded $1 million in annual sales in 1859 and take in around $40 billion annually now. I sell more than 250 items in 130 nations to more than five billion consumers. My Cheer-y and Joyous customers shout Olay! They've a Zest for my Bounty, which Cascades over their Head and Shoulders and Pampers them. It's no Secret that they Sure have a Gleam in their eyes and a Bounce in their step, Always. Who am I? (Go to page 123 for answer.)

After the adjustment has been recorded and posted, the debit balance of the wages expense account is $4,525, which is the wages expense for the two months, November and December. The credit balance of $250 in Wages Payable is the amount of the liability for wages owed as of December 31.

The accrual of the wages expense for NetSolutions is summarized in Exhibit 4. Note that NetSolutions paid wages of $950 on December 13 and $1,200 on December 27. These payments covered the biweekly pay periods that ended on those days. The wages of $250 incurred for Monday and Tuesday, December 30 and 31, are accrued at December 31. The wages paid on January 10 totaled $1,275, which included the $250 accrued wages of December 31.

## •Exhibit 4   Accrued Wages

1. Wages are paid on the second and fourth Fridays for the two-week periods ending on those Fridays. The payments were $950 on December 13 and $1,200 on December 27.

2. The wages accrued for Monday and Tuesday, December 30 and 31, are $250.

3. Wages paid on Friday, January 10, total $1,275.

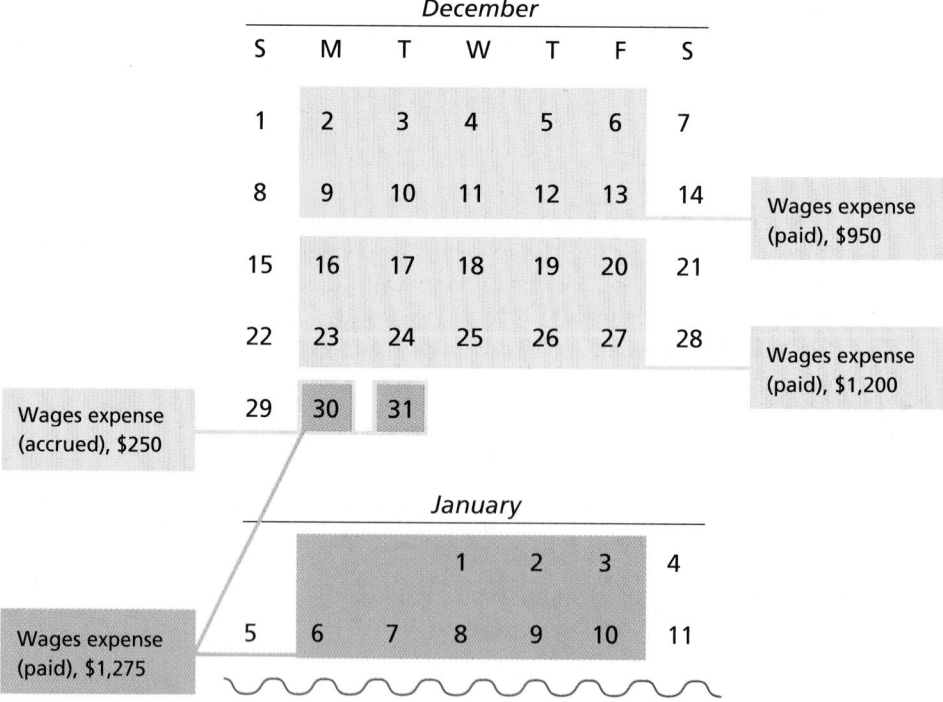

What would be the effect on the financial statements if the adjustment for wages ($250) is not recorded? On the income statement, Wages Expense will be understated by $250, and the net income will be overstated by $250. On the balance sheet, Wages Payable will be understated by $250, and Chris Clark, Capital will be overstated by $250. The effects of omitting this adjusting entry are shown as follows.

Assume that weekly wages of $1,500 are paid on Fridays. If wages are incurred evenly throughout the week, what is the accrued wages payable if the accounting period ends on a Tuesday?

----------------------------------------

*$600 ($1,500/5 × 2 days)*

**REAL WORLD**

**Radio Shack Corporation** is engaged in consumer electronics retailing. Radio Shack accrues revenue (accrued receivables) for finance charges, late charges, and returned check fees related to its credit operations.

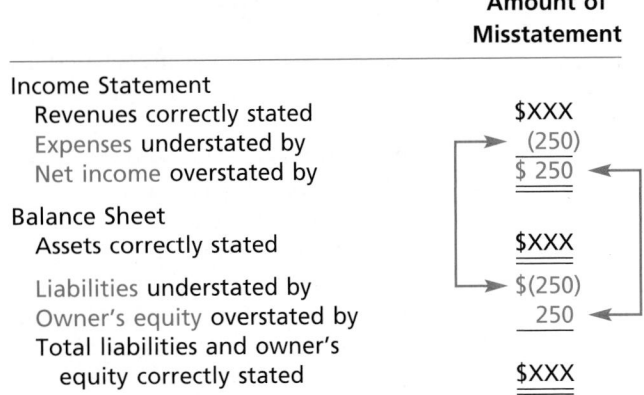

| | Amount of Misstatement |
|---|---|
| **Income Statement** | |
| Revenues correctly stated | $XXX |
| Expenses understated by | (250) |
| Net income overstated by | $ 250 |
| **Balance Sheet** | |
| Assets correctly stated | $XXX |
| Liabilities understated by | $(250) |
| Owner's equity overstated by | 250 |
| Total liabilities and owner's equity correctly stated | $XXX |

# Accrued Revenues (Accrued Assets)

During an accounting period, some revenues are recorded only when cash is received. Thus, at the end of an accounting period, there may be items of revenue that have been earned *but have not been recorded*. In such cases, the amount of the revenue should be recorded by debiting an asset account and crediting a revenue account.

To illustrate, assume that NetSolutions signed an agreement with Dankner Co. on December 15. The agreement provides that NetSolutions will be on call to answer computer questions and render assistance to Dankner Co.'s employees. The services provided will be billed to Dankner Co. on the fifteenth of each month at a rate of $20 per hour. As of December 31, NetSolutions had provided 25 hours of assistance to Dankner Co. Although the revenue of $500 (25 hours × $20) will be billed and collected in January, NetSolutions earned the revenue in December. The adjusting journal entry and T accounts to record the claim against the customer (an account receivable) and the **fees earned** in December are shown below.

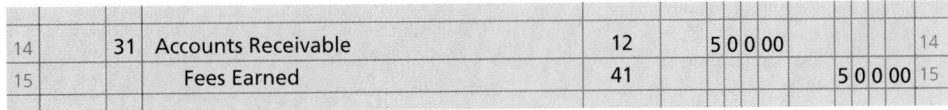

| | | | | | | |
|---|---|---|---|---|---|---|
| 14 | 31 | Accounts Receivable | 12 | 5 0 0 00 | | 14 |
| 15 | | Fees Earned | 41 | | 5 0 0 00 | 15 |

| **Accounts Receivable** | | | **Fees Earned** | |
|---|---|---|---|---|
| Bal. | 2,220 | | Bal. | 16,340 |
| Dec. 31 | 500 | | Dec. 31 | 500 |
| | 2,720 | | | 16,840 |

If the adjustment for the accrued asset ($500) is not recorded, Fees Earned and the net income will be understated by $500 on the income statement. On the balance sheet, Accounts Receivable and Chris Clark, Capital will be understated by $500. The effects of omitting this adjusting entry are shown below.

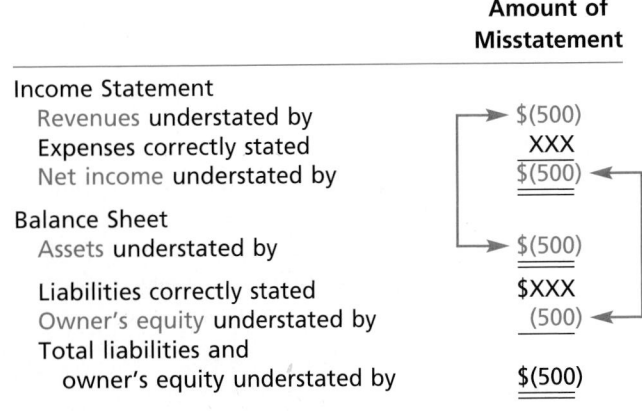

| | Amount of Misstatement |
|---|---|
| **Income Statement** | |
| Revenues understated by | $(500) |
| Expenses correctly stated | XXX |
| Net income understated by | $(500) |
| **Balance Sheet** | |
| Assets understated by | $(500) |
| Liabilities correctly stated | $XXX |
| Owner's equity understated by | (500) |
| Total liabilities and owner's equity understated by | $(500) |

# Fixed Assets

Physical resources that are owned and used by a business and are permanent or have a long life are called *fixed assets*, or **plant assets**. In a sense, fixed assets are a type of long-term deferred expense. However, because of their nature and long life, they are discussed separately from other deferred expenses, such as supplies and prepaid insurance.

NetSolutions' fixed assets include office equipment that is used much like supplies are used to generate revenue. Unlike supplies, however, there is no visible reduction in the quantity of the equipment. Instead, as time passes, the equipment loses its ability to provide useful services. This decrease in usefulness is called *depreciation*.

All fixed assets, except land, lose their usefulness. Decreases in the usefulness of assets that are used in generating revenue are recorded as expenses. However, such decreases for fixed assets are difficult to measure. For this reason, a portion of the cost of a fixed asset is recorded as an expense each year of its useful life. This periodic expense is called *depreciation expense*. Methods of computing depreciation expense are discussed and illustrated in a later chapter.

The adjusting entry to record depreciation is similar to the adjusting entry for supplies used. The account debited is a depreciation expense account. However, the asset account Office Equipment is not credited because both the original cost of a fixed asset and the amount of depreciation recorded since its purchase are normally reported on the balance sheet. The account credited is an *accumulated depreciation* account. Accumulated depreciation accounts are called *contra accounts*, or **contra asset accounts** because they are deducted from the related asset accounts on the balance sheet.

Normal titles for fixed asset accounts and their related contra asset accounts are as follows:

| Fixed Asset | Contra Asset |
| --- | --- |
| Land | None—Land is not depreciated. |
| Buildings | Accumulated Depreciation—Buildings |
| Store Equipment | Accumulated Depreciation—Store Equipment |
| Office Equipment | Accumulated Depreciation—Office Equipment |

The adjusting entry to record depreciation for December for NetSolutions is illustrated in the following journal entry and T accounts. The estimated amount of depreciation for the month is assumed to be $50.

| | 31 | Depreciation Expense | 53 | 50 00 | | 17 |
| --- | --- | --- | --- | --- | --- | --- |
| 18 | | Accumulated Depreciation— | | | | 18 |
| 19 | | Office Equipment | 19 | | 50 00 | 19 |

| Office Equipment | | Accumulated Depreciation | |
| --- | --- | --- | --- |
| Bal. 1,800 | | Dec. 31 | 50 |

| Depreciation Expense | |
| --- | --- |
| Dec. 31 | 50 |

The $50 increase in the accumulated depreciation account is subtracted from the $1,800 cost recorded in the related fixed asset account. The difference between the two balances is the $1,750 cost that has not yet been depreciated. This amount ($1,750) is called the *book value of the asset* (or **net book value**), which may be presented on the balance sheet in the following manner:

| Office equipment | $1,800 | |
| Less accumulated depreciation | 50 | $1,750 |

You should note that the market value of a fixed asset usually differs from its book value. This is because depreciation is an *allocation* method, not a *valuation* method. That is, depreciation allocates the cost of a fixed asset to expense over its estimated life. Depreciation does not attempt to measure changes in market values, which may vary significantly from year to year.

If the previous adjustment for depreciation ($50) is not recorded, Depreciation Expense on the income statement will be understated by $50, and the net income will be overstated by $50. On the balance sheet, the book value of Office Equipment and Chris Clark, Capital will be overstated by $50. The effects of omitting the adjustment for depreciation are shown below.

|  | Amount of Misstatement |
| --- | --- |
| **Income Statement** | |
| Revenues correctly stated | $XX |
| Expenses understated by | (50) |
| Net income overstated by | $ 50 |
| **Balance Sheet** | |
| Assets overstated by | $ 50 |
| Liabilities correctly stated | $XX |
| Owner's equity overstated by | 50 |
| Total liabilities and owner's equity overstated by | $ 50 |

# Summary of Adjustment Process

We have described and illustrated the basic types of adjusting entries in the preceding section. A summary of these basic adjustments, including the type of adjustment, the adjusting entry, and the effect of omitting an adjustment on the financial statements, is shown in Exhibit 5.

The adjusting entries for NetSolutions that we illustrated in this chapter are shown in Exhibit 6. The adjusting entries are dated as of the last day of the period. However, because some time may be needed for collecting the adjustment information, the entries are usually recorded at a later date. Each entry may be supported by an explanation, but a caption above the first adjusting entry is acceptable.

These adjusting entries have been posted to the ledger for Net-Solutions, and are shown in color in Exhibit 7 on pages 115–116. You should note that in the posting process the Post. Ref. column of the journal indicates the account number to which the entry was posted. The corresponding Post. Ref. column of the account indicates the journal page from which the entry was posted.

After all the adjusting entries have been posted, another trial balance, called the **adjusted trial balance**, is prepared. The purpose of the adjusted trial balance is to verify the equality of the total debit balances and total credit balances before we prepare the financial statements. If the adjusted trial balance does not balance, an error has occurred. However, as we discussed in Chapter 2, errors may have occurred even though the adjusted trial balance totals agree. For example, the adjusted trial balance totals would agree if an adjusting entry has been omitted.

## •Exhibit 5   Summary of Basic Adjustments

| Type of Adjustment | Adjusting Entry | Effect of Omitting Adjusting Entry on the Balance Sheet and Income Statement |
|---|---|---|
| Deferred expense | Dr. Expense | Expenses Understated and Net Income Overstated |
| | Cr. Asset | Assets Overstated and Owner's Equity Overstated |
| Deferred revenue | Dr. Liability | Liabilities Overstated and Owner's Equity Understated |
| | Cr. Revenue | Revenues Understated and Net Income Understated |
| Accrued expense | Dr. Expense | Expenses Understated and Net Income Overstated |
| | Cr. Liability | Liabilities Understated and Owner's Equity Overstated |
| Accrued revenue | Dr. Asset | Assets Understated and Owner's Equity Understated |
| | Cr. Revenue | Revenues Understated and Net Income Understated |
| Fixed assets | Dr. Expense | Expenses Understated and Net Income Overstated |
| | Cr. Contra Asset | Assets Overstated and Owner's Equity Overstated |

## •Exhibit 6   Adjusting Entries—NetSolutions

| | Date | Description | Post. Ref. | Debit | Credit |
|---|---|---|---|---|---|
| | | **JOURNAL** | | | Page 5 |
| 1 | | Adjusting Entries | | | |
| 2 | 2005 Dec. 31 | Supplies Expense | 55 | 1 240 00 | |
| 3 | | Supplies | 14 | | 1 240 00 |
| 5 | 31 | Insurance Expense | 56 | 100 00 | |
| 6 | | Prepaid Insurance | 15 | | 100 00 |
| 8 | 31 | Unearned Rent | 23 | 120 00 | |
| 9 | | Rent Revenue | 42 | | 120 00 |
| 11 | 31 | Wages Expense | 51 | 250 00 | |
| 12 | | Wages Payable | 22 | | 250 00 |
| 14 | 31 | Accounts Receivable | 12 | 500 00 | |
| 15 | | Fees Earned | 41 | | 500 00 |
| 17 | 31 | Depreciation Expense | 53 | 50 00 | |
| 18 | | Accumulated Depreciation— | | | |
| 19 | | Office Equipment | 19 | | 50 00 |

## •Exhibit 7    Ledger with Adjusting Entries—NetSolutions

**ACCOUNT** *Cash*  ACCOUNT NO. 11

| Date | Item | Post. Ref. | Debit | Credit | Balance Debit | Balance Credit |
|------|------|-----------|-------|--------|-------|--------|
| 2005 Nov. 1 | | 1 | 25,000 | | 25,000 | |
| 5 | | 1 | | 20,000 | 5,000 | |
| 18 | | 1 | 7,500 | | 12,500 | |
| 30 | | 1 | | 3,650 | 8,850 | |
| 30 | | 1 | | 950 | 7,900 | |
| 30 | | 2 | | 2,000 | 5,900 | |
| Dec. 1 | | 2 | | 2,400 | 3,500 | |
| 1 | | 2 | | 800 | 2,700 | |
| 1 | | 2 | 360 | | 3,060 | |
| 6 | | 2 | | 180 | 2,880 | |
| 11 | | 2 | | 400 | 2,480 | |
| 13 | | 3 | | 950 | 1,530 | |
| 16 | | 3 | 3,100 | | 4,630 | |
| 20 | | 3 | | 900 | 3,730 | |
| 21 | | 3 | 650 | | 4,380 | |
| 23 | | 3 | | 1,450 | 2,930 | |
| 27 | | 3 | | 1,200 | 1,730 | |
| 31 | | 3 | | 310 | 1,420 | |
| 31 | | 4 | | 225 | 1,195 | |
| 31 | | 4 | 2,870 | | 4,065 | |
| 31 | | 4 | | 2,000 | 2,065 | |

**ACCOUNT** *Accounts Receivable*  ACCOUNT NO. 12

| Date | Item | Post. Ref. | Debit | Credit | Balance Debit | Balance Credit |
|------|------|-----------|-------|--------|-------|--------|
| 2005 Dec. 16 | | 3 | 1,750 | | 1,750 | |
| 21 | | 3 | | 650 | 1,100 | |
| 31 | | 4 | 1,120 | | 2,220 | |
| 31 | Adjusting | 5 | 500 | | 2,720 | |

**ACCOUNT** *Supplies*  ACCOUNT NO. 14

| Date | Item | Post. Ref. | Debit | Credit | Balance Debit | Balance Credit |
|------|------|-----------|-------|--------|-------|--------|
| 2005 Nov. 10 | | 1 | 1,350 | | 1,350 | |
| 30 | | 1 | | 800 | 550 | |
| Dec. 23 | | 3 | 1,450 | | 2,000 | |
| 31 | Adjusting | 5 | | 1,240 | 760 | |

**ACCOUNT** *Prepaid Insurance*  ACCOUNT NO. 15

| Date | Item | Post. Ref. | Debit | Credit | Balance Debit | Balance Credit |
|------|------|-----------|-------|--------|-------|--------|
| 2005 Dec. 1 | | 2 | 2,400 | | 2,400 | |
| 31 | Adjusting | 5 | | 100 | 2,300 | |

**ACCOUNT** *Land*  ACCOUNT NO. 17

| Date | Item | Post. Ref. | Debit | Credit | Balance Debit | Balance Credit |
|------|------|-----------|-------|--------|-------|--------|
| 2005 Nov. 5 | | 1 | 20,000 | | 20,000 | |

**ACCOUNT** *Office Equipment*  ACCOUNT NO. 18

| Date | Item | Post. Ref. | Debit | Credit | Balance Debit | Balance Credit |
|------|------|-----------|-------|--------|-------|--------|
| 2005 Dec. 4 | | 2 | 1,800 | | 1,800 | |

**ACCOUNT** *Accumulated Depreciation*  ACCOUNT NO. 19

| Date | Item | Post. Ref. | Debit | Credit | Balance Debit | Balance Credit |
|------|------|-----------|-------|--------|-------|--------|
| 2005 Dec. 31 | Adjusting | 5 | | 50 | | 50 |

**ACCOUNT** *Accounts Payable*  ACCOUNT NO. 21

| Date | Item | Post. Ref. | Debit | Credit | Balance Debit | Balance Credit |
|------|------|-----------|-------|--------|-------|--------|
| 2005 Nov. 10 | | 1 | | 1,350 | | 1,350 |
| 30 | | 1 | 950 | | | 400 |
| Dec. 4 | | 2 | | 1,800 | | 2,200 |
| 11 | | 2 | 400 | | | 1,800 |
| 20 | | 3 | 900 | | | 900 |

**ACCOUNT** *Wages Payable*  ACCOUNT NO. 22

| Date | Item | Post. Ref. | Debit | Credit | Balance Debit | Balance Credit |
|------|------|-----------|-------|--------|-------|--------|
| 2005 Dec. 31 | Adjusting | 5 | | 250 | | 250 |

**ACCOUNT** *Unearned Rent*  ACCOUNT NO. 23

| Date | Item | Post. Ref. | Debit | Credit | Balance Debit | Balance Credit |
|------|------|-----------|-------|--------|-------|--------|
| 2005 Dec. 1 | | 2 | | 360 | | 360 |
| 31 | Adjusting | 5 | 120 | | | 240 |

**ACCOUNT** *Chris Clark, Capital*  ACCOUNT NO. 31

| Date | Item | Post. Ref. | Debit | Credit | Balance Debit | Balance Credit |
|------|------|-----------|-------|--------|-------|--------|
| 2005 Nov. 1 | | 1 | | 25,000 | | 25,000 |

**ACCOUNT** *Chris Clark, Drawing*  ACCOUNT NO. 32

| Date | Item | Post. Ref. | Debit | Credit | Balance Debit | Balance Credit |
|------|------|-----------|-------|--------|-------|--------|
| 2005 Nov. 30 | | 2 | 2,000 | | 2,000 | |
| Dec. 31 | | 4 | 2,000 | | 4,000 | |

•**Exhibit 7**   (concluded)

**ACCOUNT** *Fees Earned*      **ACCOUNT NO.** *41*

| Date | Item | Post. Ref. | Debit | Credit | Balance Debit | Balance Credit |
|---|---|---|---|---|---|---|
| 2005 Nov. 18 | | 1 | | 7,500 | | 7,500 |
| Dec. 16 | | 3 | | 3,100 | | 10,600 |
| 16 | | 3 | | 1,750 | | 12,350 |
| 31 | | 4 | | 2,870 | | 15,220 |
| 31 | | 4 | | 1,120 | | 16,340 |
| 31 | Adjusting | 5 | | 500 | | 16,840 |

**ACCOUNT** *Rent Revenue*      **ACCOUNT NO.** *42*

| Date | Item | Post. Ref. | Debit | Credit | Balance Debit | Balance Credit |
|---|---|---|---|---|---|---|
| 2005 Dec. 31 | Adjusting | 5 | | 120 | | 120 |

**ACCOUNT** *Wages Expense*      **ACCOUNT NO.** *51*

| Date | Item | Post. Ref. | Debit | Credit | Balance Debit | Balance Credit |
|---|---|---|---|---|---|---|
| 2005 Nov. 30 | | 1 | 2,125 | | 2,125 | |
| Dec. 13 | | 3 | 950 | | 3,075 | |
| 27 | | 3 | 1,200 | | 4,275 | |
| 31 | Adjusting | 5 | 250 | | 4,525 | |

**ACCOUNT** *Rent Expense*      **ACCOUNT NO.** *52*

| Date | Item | Post. Ref. | Debit | Credit | Balance Debit | Balance Credit |
|---|---|---|---|---|---|---|
| 2005 Nov. 30 | | 1 | 800 | | 800 | |
| Dec. 1 | | 2 | 800 | | 1,600 | |

**ACCOUNT** *Depreciation Expense*      **ACCOUNT NO.** *53*

| Date | Item | Post. Ref. | Debit | Credit | Balance Debit | Balance Credit |
|---|---|---|---|---|---|---|
| 2005 Dec. 31 | Adjusting | 5 | 50 | | 50 | |

**ACCOUNT** *Utilities Expense*      **ACCOUNT NO.** *54*

| Date | Item | Post. Ref. | Debit | Credit | Balance Debit | Balance Credit |
|---|---|---|---|---|---|---|
| 2005 Nov. 30 | | 1 | 450 | | 450 | |
| Dec. 31 | | 3 | 310 | | 760 | |
| 31 | | 4 | 225 | | 985 | |

**ACCOUNT** *Supplies Expense*      **ACCOUNT NO.** *55*

| Date | Item | Post. Ref. | Debit | Credit | Balance Debit | Balance Credit |
|---|---|---|---|---|---|---|
| 2005 Nov. 30 | | 1 | 800 | | 800 | |
| Dec. 31 | Adjusting | 5 | 1,240 | | 2,040 | |

**ACCOUNT** *Insurance Expense*      **ACCOUNT NO.** *56*

| Date | Item | Post. Ref. | Debit | Credit | Balance Debit | Balance Credit |
|---|---|---|---|---|---|---|
| 2005 Dec. 31 | Adjusting | 5 | 100 | | 100 | |

**ACCOUNT** *Miscellaneous Expense*      **ACCOUNT NO.** *59*

| Date | Item | Post. Ref. | Debit | Credit | Balance Debit | Balance Credit |
|---|---|---|---|---|---|---|
| 2005 Nov. 30 | | 1 | 275 | | 275 | |
| Dec. 6 | | 2 | 180 | | 455 | |

To highlight the effect of the adjustments on the accounts, Exhibit 8 shows the unadjusted trial balance, the accounts affected by the adjustments, and the adjusted trial balance. In Chapter 4, we discuss how financial statements, including a classified balance sheet, can be prepared from an adjusted trial balance. We also discuss the use of a work sheet as an aid to summarize the data for preparing adjusting entries and financial statements.

## •Exhibit 8   Trial Balances

| | NetSolutions Unadjusted Trial Balance December 31, 2005 | | | | Effect of Adjusting Entry | | | NetSolutions Adjusted Trial Balance December 31, 2005 | | |
|---|---|---|---|---|---|---|---|---|---|---|
| 1 | Cash | 2,065 | | 1 | | 1 | Cash | 2,065 | | 1 |
| 2 | Accounts Receivable | 2,220 | | 2 | + 500 | 2 | Accounts Receivable | 2,720 | | 2 |
| 3 | Supplies | 2,000 | | 3 | −1,240 | 3 | Supplies | 760 | | 3 |
| 4 | Prepaid Insurance | 2,400 | | 4 | − 100 | 4 | Prepaid Insurance | 2,300 | | 4 |
| 5 | Land | 20,000 | | 5 | | 5 | Land | 20,000 | | 5 |
| 6 | Office Equipment | 1,800 | | 6 | | 6 | Office Equipment | 1,800 | | 6 |
| 7 | Accumulated Depreciation | | | 7 | + 50 | 7 | Accumulated Depreciation | | 50 | 7 |
| 8 | Accounts Payable | | 900 | 8 | | 8 | Accounts Payable | | 900 | 8 |
| 9 | Wages Payable | | | 9 | + 250 | 9 | Wages Payable | | 250 | 9 |
| 10 | Unearned Rent | | 360 | 10 | − 120 | 10 | Unearned Rent | | 240 | 10 |
| 11 | Chris Clark, Capital | | 25,000 | 11 | | 11 | Chris Clark, Capital | | 25,000 | 11 |
| 12 | Chris Clark, Drawing | 4,000 | | 12 | | 12 | Chris Clark, Drawing | 4,000 | | 12 |
| 13 | Fees Earned | | 16,340 | 13 | + 500 | 13 | Fees Earned | | 16,840 | 13 |
| 14 | Rent Revenue | | | 14 | + 120 | 14 | Rent Revenue | | 120 | 14 |
| 15 | Wages Expense | 4,275 | | 15 | + 250 | 15 | Wages Expense | 4,525 | | 15 |
| 16 | Rent Expense | 1,600 | | 16 | | 16 | Rent Expense | 1,600 | | 16 |
| 17 | Depreciation Expense | | | 17 | + 50 | 17 | Depreciation Expense | 50 | | 17 |
| 18 | Utilities Expense | 985 | | 18 | | 18 | Utilities Expense | 985 | | 18 |
| 19 | Supplies Expense | 800 | | 19 | +1,240 | 19 | Supplies Expense | 2,040 | | 19 |
| 20 | Insurance Expense | | | 20 | + 100 | 20 | Insurance Expense | 100 | | 20 |
| 21 | Miscellaneous Expense | 455 | | 21 | | 21 | Miscellaneous Expense | 455 | | 21 |
| 22 | | 42,600 | 42,600 | 22 | | 22 | | 43,400 | 43,400 | 22 |

# Financial Analysis and Interpretation

**objective 5**

Use vertical analysis to compare financial statement items with each other and with industry averages.

Comparing each item in a current statement with a total amount within that same statement can be useful in highlighting significant relationships within a financial statement. ***Vertical analysis*** is the term used to describe such comparisons.

In vertical analysis of a balance sheet, each asset item is stated as a percent of the total assets. Each liability and owner's equity item is stated as a percent of the total liabilities and owner's equity. In vertical analysis of an income statement, each item is stated as a percent of revenues or fees earned.

Vertical analysis may also be prepared for several periods to highlight changes in relationships over time. Vertical analysis of two years of income statements for J. Holmes, Attorney-at-Law, is shown in Exhibit 9. This exhibit indicates both favorable and unfavorable trends affecting the income statement of J. Holmes, Attorney-at-Law. The increase in wages expense of 2% (32% − 30%) is an unfavorable trend, as is the increase in utilities expense of 0.7% (6.7% − 6.0%). A favorable trend is the decrease in supplies expense of 0.6% (2.0% − 1.4%). Rent expense and miscellaneous expense as a percent of fees earned were constant. The net result of these trends was that net income decreased as a percent of fees earned from 52.8% to 50.7%.

The analysis of the various percentages shown for J. Holmes, Attorney-at-Law, can be enhanced by comparisons with industry averages published by trade associations and financial information services. Any major differences between industry averages should be investigated.

## •Exhibit 9    Vertical Analysis of Income Statements

**J. Holmes, Attorney-at-Law**
**Income Statements**
**For the Years Ended December 31, 2005 and 2006**

|  | 2006 | | 2005 | |
|---|---|---|---|---|
|  | Amount | Percent | Amount | Percent |
| Fees earned . . . . . . . . . . . . . | $187,500 | 100.0% | $150,000 | 100.0% |
| Operating expenses: |  |  |  |  |
| Wages expense . . . . . . . . . . | $ 60,000 | 32.0% | $ 45,000 | 30.0%* |
| Rent expense . . . . . . . . . . . . | 15,000 | 8.0% | 12,000 | 8.0% |
| Utilities expense . . . . . . . . . . | 12,500 | 6.7% | 9,000 | 6.0% |
| Supplies expense . . . . . . . . . | 2,700 | 1.4% | 3,000 | 2.0% |
| Miscellaneous expense . . . . . | 2,300 | 1.2% | 1,800 | 1.2% |
| Total operating expenses . . | $ 92,500 | 49.3% | $ 70,800 | 47.2% |
| Net income . . . . . . . . . . . . . | $ 95,000 | 50.7% | $ 79,200 | 52.8% |

*$45,000 ÷ $150,000

---

## SPOTLIGHT ON STRATEGY

### NOT CUTTING CORNERS

**H**ave you ever ordered a hamburger from **Wendy's** and noticed that the meat patty is square? The square meat patty reflects a business strategy instilled in Wendy's by its founder, Dave Thomas. Mr. Thomas's strategy was to offer high-quality products at a fair price in a friendly atmosphere, without "cutting corners"; hence, the square meat patty. In the highly competitive fast-food industry,

Dave Thomas's strategy enabled Wendy's to grow to be the third largest fast-food restaurant in the world, with annual sales of over $7 billion.

**Source:** "Dave Thomas, 69, Wendy's Founder, Dies," by Douglas Martin, *The New York Times*, January 9, 2002.

---

# **K**ey Points

**1 Explain how the matching concept relates to the accrual basis of accounting.**

The accrual basis of accounting requires the use of an adjusting process at the end of the accounting period to match revenues and expenses properly. Revenues are reported in the period in which they are earned, and expenses are matched with the revenues they generate.

**2 Explain why adjustments are necessary and list the characteristics of adjusting entries.**

At the end of an accounting period, some of the amounts listed on the trial balance are not necessarily current balances. For example, amounts listed for prepaid expenses are normally overstated because the use of these assets has not been recorded on a daily basis. A delay in recog-

nizing an expense already paid or a revenue already received is called a deferral.

Some revenues and expenses related to a period may not be recorded at the end of the period, since these items are normally recorded only when cash has been received or paid. A revenue or expense that has not been paid or recorded is called an accrual.

The entries required at the end of an accounting period to bring accounts up to date and to ensure the proper matching of revenues and expenses are called adjusting entries. Adjusting entries require a debit or a credit to a revenue or an expense account and an offsetting debit or credit to an asset or a liability account.

Adjusting entries affect amounts reported in the income statement and the balance sheet. Thus, if an adjusting entry is not recorded, these financial statements will be incorrect (misstated).

## 3 Journalize entries for accounts requiring adjustment.

Adjusting entries illustrated in this chapter include deferred (prepaid) expenses, deferred (unearned) revenues, accrued expenses (accrued liabilities), and accrued revenues (accrued assets). In addition, the adjusting entry necessary to record depreciation on fixed assets was illustrated.

## 4 Summarize the adjustment process and prepare an adjusted trial balance.

A summary of adjustments, including the type of adjustment, the adjusting entry, and the effect of omitting an adjustment on the financial statements, is shown in Exhibit 5. After all the adjusting entries have been posted, the equality of the total debit balances and total credit balances is verified by an adjusted trial balance.

## 5 Use vertical analysis to compare financial statement items with each other and with industry averages.

Comparing each item in a current statement with a total amount within the same statement is called vertical analysis. In vertical analysis of a balance sheet, each asset item is stated as a percent of the total assets. Each liability and owner's equity item is stated as a percent of the total liabilities and owner's equity. In vertical analysis of an income statement, each item is stated as a percent of revenues or fees earned.

# Key Terms

accounting period concept (102)
accrual basis (102)
accruals (103)
accrued assets (104)
accrued expenses (103)
accrued liabilities (103)
accrued revenues (104)
accumulated depreciation (112)
adjusted trial balance (113)

adjusting entries (103)
adjusting process (103)
book value of the asset (112)
cash basis (102)
contra account (112)
deferrals (103)
deferred expenses (103)
deferred revenues (103)
depreciation (112)

depreciation expense (112)
fixed assets (112)
matching concept (102)
prepaid expenses (103)
revenue recognition concept (102)
unearned revenues (103)
vertical analysis (116)

# Illustrative Problem

Three years ago, T. Roderick organized Harbor Realty. At July 31, 2006, the end of the current year, the unadjusted trial balance of Harbor Realty appears as shown at the top of the following page. The data needed to determine year-end adjustments are as follows:

a. Supplies on hand at July 31, 2006, 380.
b. Insurance premiums expired during the year, $315.
c. Depreciation of equipment during the year, $4,950.
d. Wages accrued but not paid at July 31, 2006, $440.
e. Accrued fees earned but not recorded at July 31, 2006, $1,000.
f. Unearned fees on July 31, 2006, $750.

## Instructions

1. Prepare the necessary adjusting journal entries.
2. Determine the balance of the accounts affected by the adjusting entries and prepare an adjusted trial balance.

**Harbor Realty**
**Trial Balance**
**July 31, 2006**

| | Debit | Credit |
|---|---|---|
| Cash | 3 4 2 5 00 | |
| Accounts Receivable | 7 0 0 0 00 | |
| Supplies | 1 2 7 0 00 | |
| Prepaid Insurance | 6 2 0 00 | |
| Office Equipment | 51 6 5 0 00 | |
| Accumulated Depreciation | | 9 7 0 0 00 |
| Accounts Payable | | 9 2 5 00 |
| Wages Payable | | 0 00 |
| Unearned Fees | | 1 2 5 0 00 |
| T. Roderick, Capital | | 29 0 0 0 00 |
| T. Roderick, Drawing | 5 2 0 0 00 | |
| Fees Earned | | 59 1 2 5 00 |
| Wages Expense | 22 4 1 5 00 | |
| Depreciation Expense | 0 00 | |
| Rent Expense | 4 2 0 0 00 | |
| Utilities Expense | 2 7 1 5 00 | |
| Supplies Expense | 0 00 | |
| Insurance Expense | 0 00 | |
| Miscellaneous Expense | 1 5 0 5 00 | |
| | 100 0 0 0 00 | 100 0 0 0 00 |

## Solution

1.

**JOURNAL**

| | Date | | Description | Post. Ref. | Debit | Credit | |
|---|---|---|---|---|---|---|---|
| 1 | 2006 July | 31 | Supplies Expense | | 8 9 0 00 | | 1 |
| 2 | | | Supplies | | | 8 9 0 00 | 2 |
| 3 | | | | | | | 3 |
| 4 | | 31 | Insurance Expense | | 3 1 5 00 | | 4 |
| 5 | | | Prepaid Insurance | | | 3 1 5 00 | 5 |
| 6 | | | | | | | 6 |
| 7 | | 31 | Depreciation Expense | | 4 9 5 0 00 | | 7 |
| 8 | | | Accumulated Depreciation | | | 4 9 5 0 00 | 8 |
| 9 | | | | | | | 9 |
| 10 | | 31 | Wages Expense | | 4 4 0 00 | | 10 |
| 11 | | | Wages Payable | | | 4 4 0 00 | 11 |
| 12 | | | | | | | 12 |
| 13 | | 31 | Accounts Receivable | | 1 0 0 0 00 | | 13 |
| 14 | | | Fees Earned | | | 1 0 0 0 00 | 14 |
| 15 | | | | | | | 15 |
| 16 | | 31 | Unearned Fees | | 5 0 0 00 | | 16 |
| 17 | | | Fees Earned | | | 5 0 0 00 | 17 |

2.

| Harbor Realty<br>Adjusted Trial Balance<br>July 31, 2006 | | |
|---|---|---|
| Cash | 3 4 2 5 00 | |
| Accounts Receivable | 8 0 0 0 00 | |
| Supplies | 3 8 0 00 | |
| Prepaid Insurance | 3 0 5 00 | |
| Office Equipment | 51 6 5 0 00 | |
| Accumulated Depreciation | | 14 6 5 0 00 |
| Accounts Payable | | 9 2 5 00 |
| Wages Payable | | 4 4 0 00 |
| Unearned Fees | | 7 5 0 00 |
| T. Roderick, Capital | | 29 0 0 0 00 |
| T. Roderick, Drawing | 5 2 0 0 00 | |
| Fees Earned | | 60 6 2 5 00 |
| Wages Expense | 22 8 5 5 00 | |
| Depreciation Expense | 4 9 5 0 00 | |
| Rent Expense | 4 2 0 0 00 | |
| Utilities Expense | 2 7 1 5 00 | |
| Supplies Expense | 8 9 0 00 | |
| Insurance Expense | 3 1 5 00 | |
| Miscellaneous Expense | 1 5 0 5 00 | |
| | 106 3 9 0 00 | 106 3 9 0 00 |

# Self-Examination Questions (Answers at End of Chapter)

1. Which of the following items represents a deferral?
   A. Prepaid insurance
   B. Wages payable
   C. Fees earned
   D. Accumulated depreciation

2. If the supplies account, before adjustment on May 31, indicated a balance of $2,250, and supplies on hand at May 31 totaled $950, the adjusting entry would be:
   A. debit Supplies, $950; credit Supplies Expense, $950.
   B. debit Supplies, $1,300; credit Supplies Expense, $1,300.
   C. debit Supplies Expense, $950; credit Supplies, $950.
   D. debit Supplies Expense, $1,300; credit Supplies, $1,300.

3. The balance in the unearned rent account for Jones Co. as of December 31 is $1,200. If Jones Co. failed to record the adjusting entry for $600 of rent earned during December, the effect on the balance sheet and income statement for December is:
   A. assets understated $600; net income overstated $600.
   B. liabilities understated $600; net income understated $600.
   C. liabilities overstated $600; net income understated $600.
   D. liabilities overstated $600; net income overstated $600.

4. If the estimated amount of depreciation on equipment for a period is $2,000, the adjusting entry to record depreciation would be:
   A. debit Depreciation Expense, $2,000; credit Equipment, $2,000.
   B. debit Equipment, $2,000; credit Depreciation Expense, $2,000.
   C. debit Depreciation Expense, $2,000; credit Accumulated Depreciation, $2,000.
   D. debit Accumulated Depreciation, $2,000; credit Depreciation Expense, $2,000.

5. If the equipment account has a balance of $22,500 and its accumulated depreciation account has a balance of $14,000, the book value of the equipment is:

A. $36,500.    C. $14,000.
B. $22,500.    D. $8,500.

# Class Discussion Questions

1. How are revenues and expenses reported on the income statement under (a) the cash basis of accounting and (b) the accrual basis of accounting?
2. Fees for services provided are billed to a customer during 2005. The customer remits the amount owed in 2006. During which year would the revenues be reported on the income statement under (a) the cash basis? (b) the accrual basis?
3. Employees performed services in 2005, but the wages were not paid until 2006. During which year would the wages expense be reported on the income statement under (a) the cash basis? (b) the accrual basis?
4. Is the matching concept related to (a) the cash basis of accounting or (b) the accrual basis of accounting?
5. Is the balance listed for cash on the trial balance, before the accounts have been adjusted, the amount that should normally be reported on the balance sheet? Explain.
6. Is the balance listed for supplies on the trial balance, before the accounts have been adjusted, the amount that should normally be reported on the balance sheet? Explain.
7. Why are adjusting entries needed at the end of an accounting period?
8. What is the difference between *adjusting entries* and *correcting entries*?
9. Identify the five different categories of adjusting entries frequently required at the end of an accounting period.
10. If the effect of the credit portion of an adjusting entry is to increase the balance of a liability account, which of the following statements describes the effect of the debit portion of the entry?
   a. Increases the balance of a revenue account.
   b. Increases the balance of an expense account.
   c. Increases the balance of an asset account.
11. If the effect of the debit portion of an adjusting entry is to increase the balance of an asset account, which of the following statements describes the effect of the credit portion of the entry?
   a. Increases the balance of a revenue account.
   b. Increases the balance of an expense account.
   c. Increases the balance of a liability account.
12. Does every adjusting entry have an effect on determining the amount of net income for a period? Explain.
13. What is the nature of the balance in the prepaid insurance account at the end of the accounting period (a) before adjustment? (b) after adjustment?
14. On August 1 of the current year, a business paid the August rent on the building that it occupies. (a) Do the rights acquired at August 1 represent an asset or an expense? (b) What is the justification for debiting Rent Expense at the time of payment?
15. (a) Explain the purpose of the two accounts: Depreciation Expense and Accumulated Depreciation. (b) What is the normal balance of each account? (c) Is it customary for the balances of the two accounts to be equal in amount? (d) In what financial statements, if any, will each account appear?

Remember! If you need additional help, visit South-Western's Web site. See page 28 for a description of the online and printed materials that are available. http://warren.swlearning.com

**Answer:** Procter & Gamble

# Exercises

**EXERCISE 3-1**
*Classify accruals and deferrals*

**Objectives 2, 3**

Classify the following items as (a) deferred expense (prepaid expense), (b) deferred revenue (unearned revenue), (c) accrued expense (accrued liability), or (d) accrued revenue (accrued asset).

1. Salary owed but not yet paid.
2. Supplies on hand.
3. Fees received but not yet earned.
4. Fees earned but not yet received.
5. Taxes owed but payable in the following period.
6. Utilities owed but not yet paid.
7. A two-year premium paid on a fire insurance policy.
8. Subscriptions received in advance by a magazine publisher.

**EXERCISE 3-2**
*Classify adjusting entries*

**Objectives 2, 3**

The following accounts were taken from the unadjusted trial balance of Dobro Co., a congressional lobbying firm. Indicate whether or not each account would normally require an adjusting entry. If the account normally requires an adjusting entry, use the following notation to indicate the type of adjustment:

AE—Accrued Expense
AR—Accrued Revenue
DR—Deferred Revenue
DE—Deferred Expense

To illustrate, the answers for the first two accounts are shown below.

| Account | Answer |
| --- | --- |
| Aaron Piper, Drawing . . . . . . . . . . | Does not normally require adjustment. |
| Accounts Receivable . . . . . . . . . . | Normally requires adjustment (AR). |
| Accumulated Depreciation . . . . . . . | |
| Cash . . . . . . . . . . . . . . . . . . . | |
| Interest Payable . . . . . . . . . . . . . | |
| Interest Receivable . . . . . . . . . . . | |
| Land . . . . . . . . . . . . . . . . . . . | |
| Office Equipment . . . . . . . . . . . . | |
| Prepaid Rent . . . . . . . . . . . . . . . | |
| Supplies Expense . . . . . . . . . . . . | |
| Unearned Fees . . . . . . . . . . . . . | |
| Wages Expense . . . . . . . . . . . . . | |

**EXERCISE 3-3**
*Adjusting entry for supplies*
Objective 3

The balance in the supplies account, before adjustment at the end of the year, is $1,175. Journalize the adjusting entry required if the amount of supplies on hand at the end of the year is $374.

**EXERCISE 3-4**
*Determine supplies purchased*
Objective 3

The supplies and supplies expense accounts at December 31, after adjusting entries have been posted at the end of the first year of operations, are shown in the following T accounts:

| Supplies | | Supplies Expense | |
|---|---|---|---|
| Bal. | 118 | Bal. | 949 |

Determine the amount of supplies purchased during the year.

**EXERCISE 3-5**
*Effect of omitting adjusting entry*
Objective 3

At December 31, the end of the first month of operations, the usual adjusting entry transferring prepaid insurance expired to an expense account is omitted. Which items will be incorrectly stated, because of the error, on (a) the income statement for December and (b) the balance sheet as of December 31? Also indicate whether the items in error will be overstated or understated.

**EXERCISE 3-6**
*Adjusting entries for prepaid insurance*
Objective 3

The balance in the prepaid insurance account, before adjustment at the end of the year, is $2,475. Journalize the adjusting entry required under each of the following *alternatives* for determining the amount of the adjustment: (a) the amount of insurance expired during the year is $1,215; (b) the amount of unexpired insurance applicable to future periods is $1,260.

**EXERCISE 3-7**
*Adjusting entries for prepaid insurance*
Objective 3

The prepaid insurance account had a balance of $5,600 at the beginning of the year. The account was debited for $1,800 for premiums on policies purchased during the year. Journalize the adjusting entry required at the end of the year for each of the following situations: (a) the amount of unexpired insurance applicable to future periods is $3,680; (b) the amount of insurance expired during the year is $3,720.

**EXERCISE 3-8**
*Adjusting entries for unearned fees*
Objective 3
✓ *Amount of entry: $9,570*

The balance in the unearned fees account, before adjustment at the end of the year, is $21,880. Journalize the adjusting entry required if the amount of unearned fees at the end of the year is $12,310.

**EXERCISE 3-9**
*Effect of omitting adjusting entry*
Objective 3

At the end of July, the first month of the business year, the usual adjusting entry transferring rent earned to a revenue account from the unearned rent account was omitted. Indicate which items will be incorrectly stated, because of the error, on (a) the income statement for July and (b) the balance sheet as of July 31. Also indicate whether the items in error will be overstated or understated.

**EXERCISE 3-10**
*Adjusting entries for accrued salaries*
Objective 3
✓ *a. Amount of entry: $9,360*

Xenon Realty Co. pays weekly salaries of $15,600 on Friday for a five-day week ending on that day. Journalize the necessary adjusting entry at the end of the accounting period, assuming that the period ends (a) on Wednesday, (b) on Thursday.

**EXERCISE 3-11**
*Determine wages paid*
Objective 3

The wages payable and wages expense accounts at August 31, after adjusting entries have been posted at the end of the first month of operations, are shown in the following T accounts:

| Wages Payable | | Wages Expense | |
|---|---|---|---|
| Bal. | 3,150 | Bal. | 63,000 |

Determine the amount of wages paid during the month.

**EXERCISE 3-12**
*Effect of omitting adjusting entry*
**Objective 3**

Accrued salaries of $1,590 owed to employees for December 30 and 31 are not considered in preparing the financial statements for the year ended December 31. Indicate which items will be erroneously stated, because of the error, on (a) the income statement for the year and (b) the balance sheet as of December 31. Also indicate whether the items in error will be overstated or understated.

**EXERCISE 3-13**
*Effect of omitting adjusting entry*
**Objective 3**

Assume that the error in Exercise 3-12 was not corrected and that the $1,590 of accrued salaries was included in the first salary payment in January. Indicate which items will be erroneously stated, because of failure to correct the initial error, on (a) the income statement for the month of January and (b) the balance sheet as of January 31.

**EXERCISE 3-14**
*Adjusting entries for prepaid and accrued taxes*
**Objective 3**
✓ b. $9,695

Titanium Financial Services was organized on April 1 of the current year. On April 2, Titanium prepaid $1,260 to the city for taxes (license fees) for the *next* 12 months and debited the prepaid taxes account. Titanium is also required to pay in January an annual tax (on property) for the *previous* calendar year. The estimated amount of the property tax for the current year (April 1 to December 31) is $8,750. (a) Journalize the two adjusting entries required to bring the accounts affected by the two taxes up to date as of December 31, the end of the current year. (b) What is the amount of tax expense for the current year?

**EXERCISE 3-15**
*Effects of errors on financial statements*
**Objective 3**

For a recent period, **Circuit City Stores** reported accrued expenses and other current liabilities of $128,776,000. For the same period, Circuit City reported earnings of $67,040,000 before income taxes. If accrued expenses and other current liabilities had not been recorded, what would have been the earnings (loss) before income taxes?

**EXERCISE 3-16**
*Effects of errors on financial statements*
**Objective 3**

The balance sheet for **The Campbell Soup Co.** as of July 31, 2002, includes accrued liabilities of $503,000,000. The income before taxes for The Campbell Soup Co. for the year ended July 28, 2002, was $798,000,000. (a) If the accruals had not been recorded at July 28, 2002, by how much would income before taxes have been misstated for the fiscal year ended July 28, 2002? (b) What is the percentage of the misstatement in (a) to the reported income of $798,000,000?

**EXERCISE 3-17**
*Effects of errors on financial statements*
**Objective 3**
✓ 1. a. Revenue understated, $6,900

The accountant for Glacier Medical Co., a medical services consulting firm, mistakenly omitted adjusting entries for (a) unearned revenue earned during the year ($6,900) and (b) accrued wages ($3,740). Indicate the effect of each error, considered individually, on the income statement for the current year ended December 31. Also indicate the effect of each error on the December 31 balance sheet. Set up a table similar to the following, and record your answers by inserting the dollar amount in the appropriate spaces. Insert a zero if the error does not affect the item.

|  | Error (a) | | Error (b) | |
|---|---|---|---|---|
|  | Over-stated | Under-stated | Over-stated | Under-stated |
| 1. Revenue for the year would be | $ | $ | $ | $ |
| 2. Expenses for the year would be | $ | $ | $ | $ |
| 3. Net income for the year would be | $ | $ | $ | $ |

*(continued)*

| | Error (a) | | Error (b) | |
|---|---|---|---|---|
| | Over-stated | Under-stated | Over-stated | Under-stated |
| 4. Assets at December 31 would be | $ | $ | $ | $ |
| 5. Liabilities at December 31 would be | $ | $ | $ | $ |
| 6. Owner's equity at December 31 would be | $ | $ | $ | $ |

**EXERCISE 3-18**
*Effects of errors on financial statements*
**Objective 3**

If the net income for the current year had been $172,680 in Exercise 3-17, what would be the correct net income if the proper adjusting entries had been made?

**EXERCISE 3-19**
*Adjusting entry for accrued fees*
**Objective 3**

At the end of the current year, $11,500 of fees have been earned but have not been billed to clients.

a. Journalize the adjusting entry to record the accrued fees.
b. If the cash basis rather than the accrual basis had been used, would an adjusting entry have been necessary? Explain.

**EXERCISE 3-20**
*Adjusting entries for unearned and accrued fees*
**Objective 3**

The balance in the unearned fees account, before adjustment at the end of the year, is $27,600. Of these fees, $8,100 have been earned. In addition, $6,450 of fees have been earned but have not been billed. Journalize the adjusting entries (a) to adjust the unearned fees account and (b) to record the accrued fees.

**EXERCISE 3-21**
*Effect on financial statements of omitting adjusting entry*
**Objective 3**

The adjusting entry for accrued fees was omitted at December 31, the end of the current year. Indicate which items will be in error, because of the omission, on (a) the income statement for the current year and (b) the balance sheet as of December 31. Also indicate whether the items in error will be overstated or understated.

**EXERCISE 3-22**
*Adjustment for depreciation*
**Objective 3**

The estimated amount of depreciation on equipment for the current year is $5,200. Journalize the adjusting entry to record the depreciation.

**EXERCISE 3-23**
*Determine fixed asset's book value*
**Objective 3**

The balance in the equipment account is $318,500, and the balance in the accumulated depreciation—equipment account is $113,900.

a. What is the book value of the equipment?
b. Does the balance in the accumulated depreciation account mean that the equipment's loss of value is $113,900? Explain.

**EXERCISE 3-24**
*Book value of fixed assets*
**Objective 3**

**REAL WORLD**

**Microsoft Corporation** reported *Property, Plant, and Equipment* of $5,891 million and *Accumulated Depreciation* of $3,623 million at June 30, 2002.

a. What was the book value of the fixed assets at June 30, 2002?
b. Would the book value of Microsoft Corporation's fixed assets normally approximate their fair market values?

**EXERCISE 3-25**
*Adjusting entries for depreciation; effect of error*
**Objective 3**

On December 31, a business estimates depreciation on equipment used during the first year of operations to be $7,500. (a) Journalize the adjusting entry required as of December 31. (b) If the adjusting entry in (a) were omitted, which items would be erroneously stated on (1) the income statement for the year and (2) the balance sheet as of December 31?

**EXERCISE 3-26**
*Adjusting entries from trial balances*
**Objectives 3, 4**

The unadjusted and adjusted trial balances for Aleutian Services Co. on December 31, 2006, are shown below.

**Aleutian Services Co.**
**Trial Balance**
**December 31, 2006**

| | Unadjusted | | Adjusted | |
|---|---|---|---|---|
| Cash | 16 | | 16 | |
| Accounts Receivable | 38 | | 42 | |
| Supplies | 12 | | 9 | |
| Prepaid Insurance | 20 | | 12 | |
| Land | 26 | | 26 | |
| Equipment | 40 | | 40 | |
| Accumulated Depreciation—Equipment | | 8 | | 13 |
| Accounts Payable | | 26 | | 26 |
| Wages Payable | | 0 | | 1 |
| Brian Stuart, Capital | | 92 | | 92 |
| Brian Stuart, Drawing | 8 | | 8 | |
| Fees Earned | | 74 | | 78 |
| Wages Expense | 24 | | 25 | |
| Rent Expense | 8 | | 8 | |
| Insurance Expense | 0 | | 8 | |
| Utilities Expense | 4 | | 4 | |
| Depreciation Expense | 0 | | 5 | |
| Supplies Expense | 0 | | 3 | |
| Miscellaneous Expense | 4 | | 4 | |
| Totals | 200 | 200 | 210 | 210 |

Journalize the five entries that adjusted the accounts at December 31, 2006. None of the accounts were affected by more than one adjusting entry.

**EXERCISE 3-27**
*Adjusting entries from trial balances*
**Objectives 3, 4**

**WHAT'S WRONG WITH THIS?**

✓ *Corrected trial balance totals, $168,450*

The accountant for Minaret Laundry prepared the following unadjusted and adjusted trial balances. Assume that all balances in the unadjusted trial balance and the amounts of the adjustments are correct. Identify the errors in the accountant's adjusting entries.

**Minaret Laundry**
**Trial Balance**
**May 31, 2006**

| | Unadjusted | | Adjusted | |
|---|---|---|---|---|
| Cash | 2,500 | | 2,500 | |
| Accounts Receivable | 7,500 | | 9,500 | |
| Laundry Supplies | 1,750 | | 2,850 | |
| Prepaid Insurance* | 2,825 | | 1,125 | |
| Laundry Equipment | 85,600 | | 80,000 | |
| Accumulated Depreciation | | 55,700 | | 55,700 |
| Accounts Payable | | 4,950 | | 4,950 |
| Wages Payable | | | | 850 |
| Troy Jobe, Capital | | 32,450 | | 32,450 |
| Troy Jobe, Drawing | 10,000 | | 10,000 | |
| Laundry Revenue | | 66,900 | | 66,900 |
| Wages Expense | 24,500 | | 24,500 | |
| Rent Expense | 15,575 | | 15,575 | |
| Utilities Expense | 8,500 | | 8,500 | |
| Depreciation Expense | | | 5,600 | |
| Laundry Supplies Expense | | | 1,100 | |
| Insurance Expense | | | 700 | |
| Miscellaneous Expense | 1,250 | | 1,250 | |
| | 160,000 | 160,000 | 163,200 | 160,850 |

*$1,700 of insurance expired during the year.

**EXERCISE 3-28**
*Vertical analysis of income statement*
**Objective 5**

REAL WORLD

The financial statements for **The Home Depot** are presented in Appendix E at the end of the text.

a. Determine for Home Depot:
   1. The amount of the change (in millions) and percent of change in net earnings (net income) for the year ended February 2, 2003.
   2. The percentage relationship between net earnings (net income) and net sales (net earnings divided by net sales) for the years ended February 2, 2003 and February 3, 2002.

b. What conclusions can you draw from your analysis?

**EXERCISE 3-29**
*Vertical analysis of income statement*
**Objective 5**

REAL WORLD

The following income statement data (in thousands) for **Dell Computer Corporation** and **Gateway Inc.** were taken from their recent annual reports:

|  | Dell | Gateway |
|---|---|---|
| Net sales | $35,404,000 | $ 4,171,325 |
| Cost of goods sold (expense) | (29,055,000) | (3,605,120) |
| Operating expenses | (3,505,000) | (1,077,447) |
| Operating income (loss) | $ 2,844,000 | $ (511,242) |

a. Prepare a vertical analysis of the income statement for Dell.
b. Prepare a vertical analysis of the income statement for Gateway.
c. Based upon (a) and (b), how does Dell compare to Gateway?

# Problems Series A

**PROBLEM 3-1A**
*Adjusting entries*
**Objective 3**

On August 31, 2006, the following data were accumulated to assist the accountant in preparing the adjusting entries for Osage Realty:

a. Fees accrued but unbilled at August 31 are $7,100.
b. The supplies account balance on August 31 is $3,010. The supplies on hand at August 31 are $1,150.
c. Wages accrued but not paid at August 31 are $1,380.
d. The unearned rent account balance at August 31 is $4,950, representing the receipt of an advance payment on August 1 of three months' rent from tenants.
e. Depreciation of office equipment is $1,120.

**Instructions**
1. Journalize the adjusting entries required at August 31, 2006.
2. Briefly explain the difference between adjusting entries and entries that would be made to correct errors.

**PROBLEM 3-2A**
*Adjusting entries*
**Objective 3**

Selected account balances before adjustment for Flanders Realty at March 31, 2006, the end of the current year, are as follows:

|  | Debits | Credits |  | Debits | Credits |
|---|---|---|---|---|---|
| Accounts Receivable | $28,250 |  | Unearned Fees |  | $ 4,800 |
| Supplies | 1,770 |  | Fees Earned |  | 170,850 |
| Prepaid Rent | 15,500 |  | Wages Expense | $69,750 |  |
| Equipment | 80,500 |  | Rent Expense | — |  |
| Accumulated Depreciation |  | $16,900 | Depreciation Expense | — |  |
| Wages Payable |  | — | Supplies Expense | — |  |

Data needed for year-end adjustments are as follows:

a. Supplies on hand at March 31, $350.
b. Depreciation of equipment during year, $1,450.
c. Rent expired during year, $9,500.
d. Wages accrued but not paid at March 31, $1,050.
e. Unearned fees at March 31, $1,200.
f. Unbilled fees at March 31, $7,100.

**Instructions**
Journalize the six adjusting entries required at March 31, based upon the data presented.

**PROBLEM 3-3A**
*Adjusting entries*
**Objective 3**

P.A.S.S.

Wild Trout Co., an outfitter store for fishing treks, prepared the following trial balance at the end of its first year of operations:

**Wild Trout Co.**
**Trial Balance**
**November 30, 2006**

| | | |
|---|---:|---:|
| Cash . . . . . . . . . . . . . . . . . . . . . . . . . . . . . . . . . . . . . . . | 1,610 | |
| Accounts Receivable . . . . . . . . . . . . . . . . . . . . . . . . . . | 11,900 | |
| Supplies . . . . . . . . . . . . . . . . . . . . . . . . . . . . . . . . . . . . . | 1,820 | |
| Equipment . . . . . . . . . . . . . . . . . . . . . . . . . . . . . . . . . . . | 27,860 | |
| Accounts Payable . . . . . . . . . . . . . . . . . . . . . . . . . . . . . | | 1,050 |
| Unearned Fees . . . . . . . . . . . . . . . . . . . . . . . . . . . . . . . . | | 2,800 |
| Angie Sanders, Capital . . . . . . . . . . . . . . . . . . . . . . . . . | | 37,800 |
| Angie Sanders, Drawing . . . . . . . . . . . . . . . . . . . . . . . . | 1,400 | |
| Fees Earned . . . . . . . . . . . . . . . . . . . . . . . . . . . . . . . . . . | | 51,450 |
| Wages Expense . . . . . . . . . . . . . . . . . . . . . . . . . . . . . . . | 28,210 | |
| Rent Expense . . . . . . . . . . . . . . . . . . . . . . . . . . . . . . . . . | 13,790 | |
| Utilities Expense . . . . . . . . . . . . . . . . . . . . . . . . . . . . . . | 5,250 | |
| Miscellaneous Expense . . . . . . . . . . . . . . . . . . . . . . . . . | 1,260 | |
| | 93,100 | 93,100 |

For preparing the adjusting entries, the following data were assembled:

a. Supplies on hand on November 30 were $315.
b. Fees earned but unbilled on November 30 were $1,750.
c. Depreciation of equipment was estimated to be $1,600 for the year.
d. Unpaid wages accrued on November 30 were $380.
e. The balance in unearned fees represented the November 1 receipt in advance for services to be provided. Only $700 of the services were provided between November 1 and November 30.

**Instructions**
Journalize the adjusting entries necessary on November 30.

**PROBLEM 3-4A**
*Adjusting entries*
**Objectives 3, 4**

P.A.S.S.

Dynamo Company specializes in the maintenance and repair of signs, such as billboards. On March 31, 2006, the accountant for Dynamo Company prepared the trial balances shown at the top of the next page.

**Instructions**
Journalize the seven entries that adjusted the accounts at March 31. None of the accounts were affected by more than one adjusting entry.

*(continued)*

**Dynamo Company**
**Trial Balance**
**March 31, 2006**

| | Unadjusted | | Adjusted | |
|---|---:|---:|---:|---:|
| Cash | 4,750 | | 4,750 | |
| Accounts Receivable | 17,400 | | 17,400 | |
| Supplies | 3,880 | | 1,175 | |
| Prepaid Insurance | 4,800 | | 3,200 | |
| Land | 47,500 | | 47,500 | |
| Buildings | 111,590 | | 111,590 | |
| Accumulated Depreciation—Buildings | | 56,600 | | 60,700 |
| Trucks | 73,000 | | 73,000 | |
| Accumulated Depreciation—Trucks | | 11,800 | | 20,300 |
| Accounts Payable | | 6,920 | | 7,435 |
| Salaries Payable | | — | | 1,080 |
| Unearned Service Fees | | 6,400 | | 4,750 |
| Joy Autry, Capital | | 125,600 | | 125,600 |
| Joy Autry, Drawing | 5,000 | | 5,000 | |
| Service Fees Earned | | 152,680 | | 154,330 |
| Salary Expense | 73,600 | | 74,680 | |
| Depreciation Expense—Trucks | — | | 8,500 | |
| Rent Expense | 9,600 | | 9,600 | |
| Supplies Expense | — | | 2,705 | |
| Utilities Expense | 6,200 | | 6,715 | |
| Depreciation Expense—Buildings | — | | 4,100 | |
| Taxes Expense | 1,720 | | 1,720 | |
| Insurance Expense | — | | 1,600 | |
| Miscellaneous Expense | 960 | | 960 | |
| | 360,000 | 360,000 | 374,195 | 374,195 |

**PROBLEM 3-5A**
*Adjusting entries and adjusted trial balances*

**Objectives 3, 4**

**SPREADSHEET**
**P.A.S.S.**

✓ *2. Total of Debit Column:*
*$552,520*

Greco Service Co., which specializes in appliance repair services, is owned and operated by Curtis Loomis. Greco Service Co.'s accounting clerk prepared the following trial balance at December 31, 2006:

**Greco Service Co.**
**Trial Balance**
**December 31, 2006**

| | | |
|---|---:|---:|
| Cash | 4,200 | |
| Accounts Receivable | 20,600 | |
| Prepaid Insurance | 6,000 | |
| Supplies | 1,450 | |
| Land | 100,000 | |
| Building | 161,500 | |
| Accumulated Depreciation—Building | | 75,700 |
| Equipment | 80,100 | |
| Accumulated Depreciation—Equipment | | 35,300 |
| Accounts Payable | | 7,500 |
| Unearned Rent | | 7,200 |
| Curtis Loomis, Capital | | 157,100 |
| Curtis Loomis, Drawing | 5,000 | |
| Fees Earned | | 257,200 |
| Salaries and Wages Expense | 101,800 | |
| Utilities Expense | 28,200 | |
| Advertising Expense | 15,000 | |
| Repairs Expense | 12,100 | |
| Miscellaneous Expense | 4,050 | |
| | 540,000 | 540,000 |

The data needed to determine year-end adjustments are as follows:

a. Depreciation of building for the year, $3,600.
b. Depreciation of equipment for the year, $2,400.
c. Accrued salaries and wages at December 31, $2,170.

d. Unexpired insurance at December 31, $3,500.
e. Fees earned but unbilled on December 31, $4,350.
f. Supplies on hand at December 31, $375.
g. Rent unearned at December 31, $2,800.

**Instructions**
1. Journalize the adjusting entries. Add additional accounts as needed.
2. Determine the balances of the accounts affected by the adjusting entries and prepare an adjusted trial balance.

**PROBLEM 3-6A**
*Adjusting entries and errors*
Objective 3

SPREADSHEET

✓ *Corrected Net Income:*
*$127,900*

At the end of July, the first month of operations, the following selected data were taken from the financial statements of Kay Lopez, an attorney:

| | |
|---|---|
| Net income for July | $124,350 |
| Total assets at July 31 | 500,000 |
| Total liabilities at July 31 | 125,000 |
| Total owner's equity at July 31 | 375,000 |

In preparing the financial statements, adjustments for the following data were overlooked:

a. Unbilled fees earned at July 31, $9,600.
b. Depreciation of equipment for July, $3,500.
c. Accrued wages at July 31, $1,450.
d. Supplies used during July, $1,100.

**Instructions**
1. Journalize the entries to record the omitted adjustments.
2. Determine the correct amount of net income for July and the total assets, liabilities, and owner's equity at July 31. In addition to indicating the corrected amounts, indicate the effect of each omitted adjustment by setting up and completing a columnar table similar to the following. Adjustment (a) is presented as an example.

| | Net Income | Total Assets | Total Liabilities | Total Owner's Equity |
|---|---|---|---|---|
| Reported amounts | $124,350 | $500,000 | $125,000 | $375,000 |
| Corrections: | | | | |
| Adjustment (a) | +9,600 | +9,600 | 0 | +9,600 |
| Adjustment (b) | _____ | _____ | _____ | _____ |
| Adjustment (c) | _____ | _____ | _____ | _____ |
| Adjustment (d) | _____ | _____ | _____ | _____ |
| Corrected amounts | _____ | _____ | _____ | _____ |

# Problems Series B

**PROBLEM 3-1B**
*Adjusting entries*
Objective 3

On October 31, 2006, the following data were accumulated to assist the accountant in preparing the adjusting entries for Melville Realty:

a. The supplies account balance on October 31 is $1,875. The supplies on hand on October 31 are $310.
b. The unearned rent account balance on October 31 is $4,020, representing the receipt of an advance payment on October 1 of three months' rent from tenants.
c. Wages accrued but not paid at October 31 are $2,150.
d. Fees accrued but unbilled at October 31 are $11,278.
e. Depreciation of office equipment is $1,000.

**Instructions**

1. Journalize the adjusting entries required at October 31, 2006.
2. Briefly explain the difference between adjusting entries and entries that would be made to correct errors.

**PROBLEM 3-2B**
*Adjusting entries*
**Objective 3**

Selected account balances before adjustment for Maltese Realty at May 31, 2006, the end of the current year, are as follows:

| | Debits | Credits | | Debits | Credits |
|---|---|---|---|---|---|
| Accounts Receivable | $11,250 | | Unearned Fees | | $ 6,500 |
| Supplies | 1,750 | | Fees Earned | | 117,950 |
| Prepaid Rent | 7,500 | | Wages Expense | $59,400 | |
| Equipment | 52,500 | | Rent Expense | — | |
| Accumulated Depreciation | | $8,900 | Depreciation Expense | — | |
| Wages Payable | | — | Supplies Expense | — | |

Data needed for year-end adjustments are as follows:

a. Unbilled fees at May 31, $1,150.
b. Supplies on hand at May 31, $360.
c. Rent expired $6,000.
d. Depreciation of equipment during year, $1,650.
e. Unearned fees at May 31, $1,775.
f. Wages accrued but not paid at May 31, $2,180.

**Instructions**
Journalize the six adjusting entries required at May 31, based upon the data presented.

**PROBLEM 3-3B**
*Adjusting entries*
**Objective 3**

P.A.S.S.

Anguilla Company, an electronics repair store, prepared the following trial balance at the end of its first year of operations:

**Anguilla Company**
**Trial Balance**
**April 30, 2006**

| | | |
|---|---|---|
| Cash | 2,300 | |
| Accounts Receivable | 15,000 | |
| Supplies | 3,600 | |
| Equipment | 75,800 | |
| Accounts Payable | | 3,500 |
| Unearned Fees | | 4,000 |
| Oscar Daly, Capital | | 52,000 |
| Oscar Daly, Drawing | 3,000 | |
| Fees Earned | | 90,500 |
| Wages Expense | 21,000 | |
| Rent Expense | 16,000 | |
| Utilities Expense | 11,500 | |
| Miscellaneous Expense | 1,800 | |
| | 150,000 | 150,000 |

For preparing the adjusting entries, the following data were assembled:

a. Fees earned but unbilled on April 30 were $3,200.
b. Supplies on hand on April 30 were $1,010.
c. Depreciation of equipment was estimated to be $3,850 for the year.
d. The balance in unearned fees represented the April 1 receipt in advance for services to be provided. Only $1,000 of the services was provided between April 1 and April 30.
e. Unpaid wages accrued on April 30 were $820.

**Instructions**
Journalize the adjusting entries necessary on April 30, 2006.

**PROBLEM 3-4B**
*Adjusting entries*
Objectives 3, 4

P.A.S.S.

Expose' Company specializes in the repair of music equipment and is owned and operated by Gavin Staub. On June 30, 2006, the end of the current year, the accountant for Expose' Company prepared the following trial balances:

**Expose' Company**
**Trial Balance**
**June 30, 2006**

| | Unadjusted | | Adjusted | |
|---|---|---|---|---|
| Cash | 8,315 | | 8,315 | |
| Accounts Receivable | 30,500 | | 30,500 | |
| Supplies | 3,750 | | 1,080 | |
| Prepaid Insurance | 4,750 | | 2,200 | |
| Equipment | 92,150 | | 92,150 | |
| Accumulated Depreciation—Equipment | | 33,480 | | 40,500 |
| Automobiles | 36,500 | | 36,500 | |
| Accumulated Depreciation—Automobiles | | 18,250 | | 21,900 |
| Accounts Payable | | 8,310 | | 8,730 |
| Salaries Payable | | — | | 1,560 |
| Unearned Service Fees | | 6,000 | | 4,000 |
| Gavin Staub, Capital | | 69,360 | | 69,360 |
| Gavin Staub, Drawing | 5,000 | | 5,000 | |
| Service Fees Earned | | 244,600 | | 246,600 |
| Salary Expense | 172,300 | | 173,860 | |
| Rent Expense | 18,000 | | 18,000 | |
| Supplies Expense | — | | 2,670 | |
| Depreciation Expense—Equipment | — | | 7,020 | |
| Depreciation Expense—Automobiles | — | | 3,650 | |
| Utilities Expense | 4,300 | | 4,720 | |
| Taxes Expense | 2,725 | | 2,725 | |
| Insurance Expense | — | | 2,550 | |
| Miscellaneous Expense | 1,710 | | 1,710 | |
| | 380,000 | 380,000 | 392,650 | 392,650 |

**Instructions**
Journalize the seven entries that adjusted the accounts at June 30. None of the accounts were affected by more than one adjusting entry.

**PROBLEM 3-5B**
*Adjusting entries and adjusted trial balances*
Objectives 3, 4

SPREADSHEET
P.A.S.S.

✓ *2. Total of Debit Column: $510,380*

Berserk Company is a small editorial services company owned and operated by Ethel Pringle. On December 31, 2006, the end of the current year, Berserk Company's accounting clerk prepared the trial balance shown at the top of the next page.

The data needed to determine year-end adjustments are as follows:

a. Unexpired insurance at December 31, $1,600.
b. Supplies on hand at December 31, $280.
c. Depreciation of building for the year, $1,320.
d. Depreciation of equipment for the year, $4,100.
e. Rent unearned at December 31, $1,500.
f. Accrued salaries and wages at December 31, $1,760.
g. Fees earned but unbilled on December 31, $3,200.

**Instructions**
1. Journalize the adjusting entries. Add additional accounts as needed.
2. Determine the balances of the accounts affected by the adjusting entries and prepare an adjusted trial balance.

*(continued)*

**Berserk Company**
**Trial Balance**
**December 31, 2006**

| | | |
|---|---:|---:|
| Cash | 3,700 | |
| Accounts Receivable | 18,900 | |
| Prepaid Insurance | 4,800 | |
| Supplies | 1,320 | |
| Land | 75,000 | |
| Building | 141,500 | |
| Accumulated Depreciation—Building | | 91,700 |
| Equipment | 90,200 | |
| Accumulated Depreciation—Equipment | | 65,300 |
| Accounts Payable | | 8,100 |
| Unearned Rent | | 4,500 |
| Ethel Pringle, Capital | | 134,000 |
| Ethel Pringle, Drawing | 10,000 | |
| Fees Earned | | 196,400 |
| Salaries and Wages Expense | 95,580 | |
| Utilities Expense | 28,250 | |
| Advertising Expense | 15,200 | |
| Repairs Expense | 11,500 | |
| Miscellaneous Expense | 4,050 | |
| | 500,000 | 500,000 |

**PROBLEM 3-6B**
*Adjusting entries and errors*
Objective 3

SPREADSHEET

✓ *Corrected Net Income:*
*$209,745*

At the end of November, the first month of operations, the following selected data were taken from the financial statements of Jaime McCune, an attorney:

| | |
|---|---:|
| Net income for November | $207,320 |
| Total assets at November 30 | 440,960 |
| Total liabilities at November 30 | 29,720 |
| Total owner's equity at November 30 | 411,240 |

In preparing the financial statements, adjustments for the following data were overlooked:

a. Supplies used during November, $1,025.
b. Unbilled fees earned at November 30, $7,650.
c. Depreciation of equipment for November, $3,100.
d. Accrued wages at November 30, $1,100.

**Instructions**

1. Journalize the entries to record the omitted adjustments.
2. Determine the correct amount of net income for November and the total assets, liabilities, and owner's equity at November 30. In addition to indicating the corrected amounts, indicate the effect of each omitted adjustment by setting up and completing a columnar table similar to the following. Adjustment (a) is presented as an example.

| | Net Income | Total Assets | Total Liabilities | Total Owner's Equity |
|---|---:|---:|---:|---:|
| Reported amounts | $207,320 | $440,960 | $29,720 | $411,240 |
| Corrections: | | | | |
| Adjustment (a) | −1,025 | −1,025 | 0 | −1,025 |
| Adjustment (b) | | | | |
| Adjustment (c) | | | | |
| Adjustment (d) | | | | |
| Corrected amounts | | | | |

# Continuing Problem

✓ *3. Total of Debit Column:*
*$33,190*

The trial balance that you prepared for Dancin Music at the end of Chapter 2 should appear as follows:

**Dancin Music**
**Trial Balance**
**May 31, 2006**

| | | |
|---|---:|---:|
| Cash | 7,330 | |
| Accounts Receivable | 1,760 | |
| Supplies | 920 | |
| Prepaid Insurance | 3,360 | |
| Office Equipment | 5,000 | |
| Accounts Payable | | 5,750 |
| Unearned Revenue | | 4,800 |
| Shannon Burns, Capital | | 10,000 |
| Shannon Burns, Drawing | 2,250 | |
| Fees Earned | | 11,210 |
| Wages Expense | 2,800 | |
| Office Rent Expense | 2,600 | |
| Equipment Rent Expense | 1,150 | |
| Utilities Expense | 860 | |
| Music Expense | 1,780 | |
| Advertising Expense | 1,300 | |
| Supplies Expense | 180 | |
| Miscellaneous Expense | 470 | |
| | 31,760 | 31,760 |

The data needed to determine adjustments for the two-month period ending May 31, 2006, are as follows:

a. During May, Dancin Music provided guest disc jockeys for KPRG for a total of 110 hours. For information on the amount of the accrued revenue to be billed to KPRG, see the contract described in the May 3, 2006 transaction at the end of Chapter 2.
b. Supplies on hand at May 31, $170.
c. The balance of the prepaid insurance account relates to the May 1, 2006 transaction at the end of Chapter 2.
d. Depreciation of the office equipment is $100.
e. The balance of the unearned revenue account relates to the contract between Dancin Music and KPRG, described in the May 3, 2006 transaction at the end of Chapter 2.
f. Accrued wages as of May 31, 2006, were $130.

## Instructions

1. Prepare adjusting journal entries. You will need the following additional accounts:

    18 Accumulated Depreciation—Office Equipment
    22 Wages Payable
    57 Insurance Expense
    58 Depreciation Expense

2. Post the adjusting entries, inserting balances in the accounts affected.
3. Prepare an adjusted trial balance.

# Special Activities

**ACTIVITY 3-1**
*Ethics and professional conduct in business*

ETHICS

Ruth Harbin opened Macaw Real Estate Co. on January 1, 2005. At the end of the first year, the business needed additional capital. On behalf of Macaw Real Estate, Ruth applied to First City Bank for a loan of $120,000. Based on Macaw Real Estate's financial statements, which had been prepared on a cash basis, the First City Bank loan officer rejected the loan as too risky.

After receiving the rejection notice, Ruth instructed her accountant to prepare the financial statements on an accrual basis. These statements included $41,500 in accounts receivable and $13,200 in accounts payable. Ruth then instructed her accountant to record an additional $12,500 of accounts receivable for commissions on property for which a contract had been signed on December 28, 2005, but which would not be formally "closed" and the title transferred until January 20, 2006.

Ruth then applied for a $120,000 loan from Second National Bank, using the revised financial statements. On this application, Ruth indicated that she had not previously been rejected for credit.

Discuss the ethical and professional conduct of Ruth Harbin in applying for the loan from Second National Bank.

**ACTIVITY 3-2**
*Accrued expense*

REAL WORLD

On December 30, 2006, you buy a Ford Expedition. It comes with a three-year, 36,000-mile warranty. On January 18, 2007, you return the Expedition to the dealership for some basic repairs covered under the warranty. The cost of the repairs to the dealership is $725. In what year, 2006 or 2007, should **Ford Motor Co.** recognize the cost of the warranty repairs as an expense?

**ACTIVITY 3-3**
*Accrued revenue*

REAL WORLD     WHAT DO YOU THINK?

The following is an excerpt from a conversation between Nathan Cisneros and Sonya Lucas just before they boarded a flight to Paris on **American Airlines**. They are going to Paris to attend their company's annual sales conference.

*Nathan:* Sonya, aren't you taking an introductory accounting course at college?
*Sonya:* Yes, I decided it's about time I learned something about accounting. You know, our annual bonuses are based upon the sales figures that come from the accounting department.
*Nathan:* I guess I never really thought about it.
*Sonya:* You should think about it! Last year, I placed a $300,000 order on December 27. But when I got my bonus, the $300,000 sale wasn't included. They said it hadn't been shipped until January 5, so it would have to count in next year's bonus.
*Nathan:* A real bummer!
*Sonya:* Right! I was counting on that bonus including the $300,000 sale.
*Nathan:* Did you complain?
*Sonya:* Yes, but it didn't do any good. Beth, the head accountant, said something about matching revenues and expenses. Also, something about not recording revenues until the sale is final. I figure I'd take the accounting course and find out whether she's just jerking me around.
*Nathan:* I never really thought about it. When do you think American Airlines will record its revenues from this flight?
*Sonya:* Mmm . . . I guess it could record the revenue when it sells the ticket . . . or . . . when the boarding passes are taken at the door . . . or . . . when we get off the plane . . . or when our company pays for the tickets . . . or . . . I don't know. I'll ask my accounting instructor.

Discuss when American Airlines should recognize the revenue from ticket sales to properly match revenues and expenses.

**ACTIVITY 3-4**
*Adjustments and financial statements*

Several years ago, your brother opened Chestnut Television Repair. He made a small initial investment and added money from his personal bank account as needed. He withdrew money for living expenses at irregular intervals. As the business grew, he hired an assistant. He is now considering adding more employees, purchasing additional service trucks, and purchasing the building he now rents. To secure funds for the expansion, your brother submitted a loan application to the bank and included the most recent financial statements (shown below) prepared from accounts maintained by a part-time bookkeeper.

**Chestnut Television Repair**
**Income Statement**
**For the Year Ended August 31, 2006**

| | | |
|---|---:|---:|
| Service revenue | | $83,280 |
| Less: Rent paid | $20,000 | |
| Wages paid | 18,500 | |
| Supplies paid | 5,100 | |
| Utilities paid | 3,175 | |
| Insurance paid | 2,400 | |
| Miscellaneous payments | 2,150 | 51,325 |
| Net income | | $31,955 |

**Chestnut Television Repair**
**Balance Sheet**
**August 31, 2006**

**Assets**

| | |
|---|---:|
| Cash | $11,150 |
| Amounts due from customers | 6,100 |
| Truck | 30,000 |
| Total assets | $47,250 |

**Equities**

| | |
|---|---:|
| Owner's capital | $47,250 |

After reviewing the financial statements, the loan officer at the bank asked your brother if he used the accrual basis of accounting for revenues and expenses. Your brother responded that he did and that is why he included an account for "Amounts Due from Customers." The loan officer then asked whether or not the accounts were adjusted prior to the preparation of the statements. Your brother answered that they had not been adjusted.

a. Why do you think the loan officer suspected that the accounts had not been adjusted prior to the preparation of the statements?
b. Indicate possible accounts that might need to be adjusted before an accurate set of financial statements could be prepared.

**ACTIVITY 3-5**
*Codes of ethics*

GROUP ACTIVITY    ETHICS

Obtain a copy of your college or university's student code of conduct. In groups of three or four, answer the following question.

1. Compare this code of conduct with the accountant's Codes of Professional Conduct, which is linked to the text Web site at http://warren.swlearning.com.
2. One of your classmates asks you for permission to copy your homework, which your instructor will be collecting and grading for part of your overall term grade. Although your instructor has not stated whether one student may or may not copy another student's homework, is it ethical for you to allow your classmate to copy your homework? Is it ethical for your classmate to copy your homework?

**ACTIVITY 3-6**
*Business strategy*

GROUP ACTIVITY

Assume that you and two friends are debating whether to open an automotive and service retail chain that will be called Auto-Mart. Initially, Auto-Mart will open three stores locally, but the business plan anticipates going nationwide within five years.

Currently, you and your future business partners are debating whether to focus Auto-Mart on a "do-it-yourself" or "do-it-for-me" business strategy. A "do-it-yourself" business strategy emphasizes the sale of retail auto parts that customers will use themselves to repair and service their cars. A "do-it-for-me" business strategy emphasizes the offering of maintenance and service for customers.

1. In groups of three or four, discuss whether to implement a "do-it-yourself" or "do-it-for-me" business strategy. List the advantages of each strategy and arrive at a conclusion as to which strategy to implement.
2. Provide examples of real world businesses that use "do-it-yourself" or "do-it-for-me" business strategies.

# Answers to Self-Examination Questions

1. **A**   A deferral is the delay in recording an expense already paid, such as prepaid insurance (answer A). Wages payable (answer B) is considered an accrued expense or accrued liability. Fees earned (answer C) is a revenue item. Accumulated depreciation (answer D) is a contra account to a fixed asset.
2. **D**   The balance in the supplies account, before adjustment, represents the amount of supplies available. From this amount ($2,250) is subtracted the amount of supplies on hand ($950) to determine the supplies used ($1,300). Since increases in expense accounts are recorded by debits and decreases in asset accounts are recorded by credits, answer D is the correct entry.
3. **C**   The failure to record the adjusting entry debiting unearned rent, $600, and crediting rent revenue,

$600, would have the effect of overstating liabilities by $600 and understating net income by $600 (answer C).
4. **C**   Since increases in expense accounts (such as depreciation expense) are recorded by debits and it is customary to record the decreases in usefulness of fixed assets as credits to accumulated depreciation accounts, answer C is the correct entry.
5. **D**   The book value of a fixed asset is the difference between the balance in the asset account and the balance in the related accumulated depreciation account, or $22,500 − $14,000, as indicated by answer D ($8,500).

# COMPLETING THE ACCOUNTING CYCLE

## objectives

*After studying this chapter, you should be able to:*

1 Review the seven basic steps of the accounting cycle.

2 Prepare a work sheet.

3 Prepare financial statements from a work sheet.

4 Prepare the adjusting and closing entries from a work sheet.

5 Explain what is meant by the fiscal year and the natural business year.

6 Analyze and interpret the financial solvency of a business by computing working capital and the current ratio.

**M**ost of us have had to file a personal tax return. At the beginning of the year, you estimate your upcoming income and decide whether you need to increase your payroll tax withholdings or perhaps pay estimated taxes. During the year, you earn income, make investments, and enter into other tax-related transactions, such as making charitable contributions. At the end of the year, your employer sends you a tax withholding information form (W-2 form), and you collect the tax records needed for completing your yearly tax forms. If any tax is owed, you pay it; if you overpaid your taxes, you file for a refund. As the next year begins, you start the cycle all over again.

Businesses also go through a cycle of activities. At the beginning of the cycle, management plans where it wants the business to go and begins the necessary actions to achieve its operating goals. Throughout the cycle, which is normally one year, the accountant records the operating activities (transactions) of the business. At the end of the cycle, the accountant prepares financial statements that summarize the operating activities for the year. The accountant then prepares the accounts for recording the operating activities in the next cycle.

As we saw in Chapter 1, the initial cycle for NetSolutions began with Chris Clark's investment in the business on November 1, 2005. The cycle continued with recording NetSolutions' transactions for November and December, as we discussed in Chapters 1 and 2. In Chapter 3, the cycle continued and we recorded the adjusting entries for the two months ending December 31, 2005. Now, in this chapter, we discuss the flow of the adjustment data into the accounts and into the financial statements.

# **A**ccounting Cycle

<table>
<tr><td>objective 1</td></tr>
<tr><td>Review the seven basic steps of the accounting cycle.</td></tr>
</table>

In a computerized accounting system, the software automatically records and posts transactions. The ledger and supporting records are maintained in computerized master files. In addition, a work sheet is normally not prepared.

REAL WORLD

The accounting process that begins with analyzing and journalizing transactions and ends with summarizing and reporting these transactions is called the ***accounting cycle***. The most important output of this cycle is the financial statements.

The basic steps of the accounting cycle are shown, by number, in the flowchart in Exhibit 1.

In earlier chapters, we described and illustrated the analysis and recording of transactions, posting to the ledger, preparing a trial balance, analyzing adjustment data, preparing adjusting entries, and preparing financial statements. In this chapter, we complete our discussion of the accounting cycle by describing how work sheets may be used as an aid in preparing the financial statements. We also describe and illustrate how closing entries and a post-closing trial balance are used in preparing the accounting records for the next period.

# **W**ork Sheet

<table>
<tr><td>objective 2</td></tr>
<tr><td>Prepare a work sheet.</td></tr>
</table>

Common spreadsheet programs used in business include Microsoft Excel® and Lotus 1-2-3®.

REAL WORLD

Accountants often use **working papers** for collecting and summarizing data they need for preparing various analyses and reports. Such working papers are useful tools, but they are not considered a part of the formal accounting records. This is in contrast to the chart of accounts, the journal, and the ledger, which are essential parts of the accounting system. Working papers are usually prepared by using a spreadsheet program on a computer.

The ***work sheet*** is a working paper that accountants can use to summarize adjusting entries and the account balances for the financial statements. In small companies with few accounts and adjustments, a work sheet may not be necessary. For example, the financial statements for NetSolutions can be prepared directly from the adjusted trial balance illustrated in Chapter 3. In a computerized accounting system,

## •Exhibit 1   Accounting Cycle

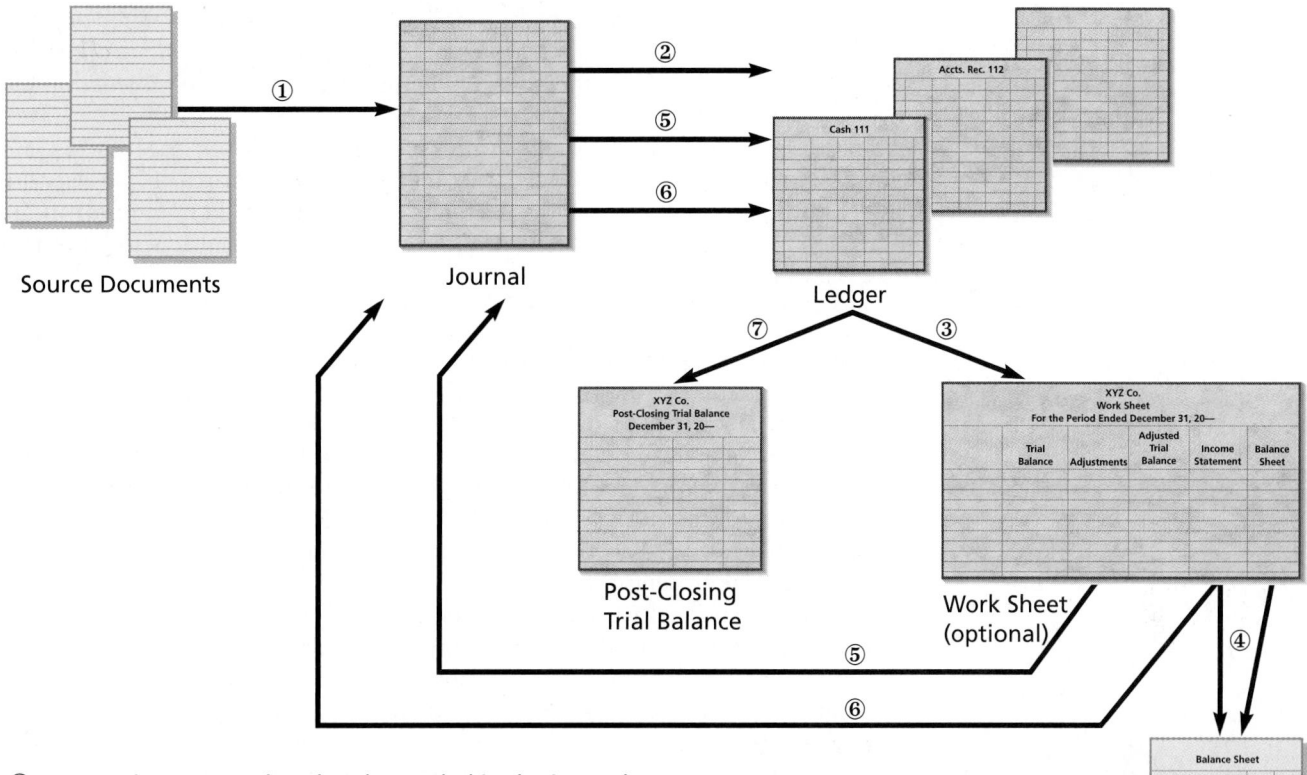

Source Documents          Journal          Ledger

Post-Closing Trial Balance

Work Sheet (optional)

Financial Statements

① Transactions are analyzed and recorded in the journal.
② Transactions are posted to the ledger.
③ A trial balance is prepared, adjustment data are assembled, and an optional work sheet is completed.
④ Financial statements are prepared.
⑤ Adjusting entries are journalized and posted to the ledger.
⑥ Closing entries are journalized and posted to the ledger.
⑦ A post-closing trial balance is prepared.

a work sheet may not be necessary because the software program automatically posts entries to the accounts and prepares financial statements.

The work sheet (Exhibits 2 through 5 on pages 144B–144C) is a useful device for understanding the flow of the accounting data from the unadjusted trial balance to the financial statements (Exhibit 6). This flow of data is the same in either a manual or a computerized accounting system.

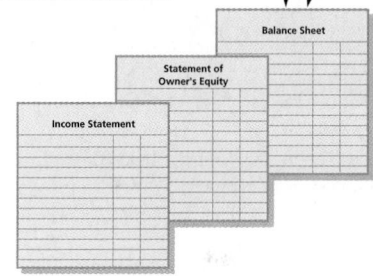

**The work sheet is a useful device for understanding the flow of the accounting data from the unadjusted trial balance to the financial statements.**

## Unadjusted Trial Balance Columns

To begin the work sheet, list at the top the name of the business, the type of working paper (work sheet), and the period of time, as shown in Exhibit 2. Next, enter the unadjusted trial balance directly on the work sheet. The work sheet in Exhibit 2 shows the unadjusted trial balance for NetSolutions at December 31, 2005.

# Adjustments Columns

The adjustments that we explained and illustrated for NetSolutions in Chapter 3 are entered in the Adjustments columns, as shown in Exhibit 3. Cross-referencing (by letters) the debit and credit of each adjustment is useful in reviewing the work sheet. It is also helpful for identifying the adjusting entries that need to be recorded in the journal.

The order in which the adjustments are entered on the work sheet is not important. Most accountants enter the adjustments in the order in which the data are assembled. If the titles of some of the accounts to be adjusted do not appear in the trial balance, they should be inserted in the Account Title column, below the trial balance totals, as needed.

To review, the entries in the Adjustments columns of the work sheet are:

(a) **Supplies.** The supplies account has a debit balance of $2,000. The cost of the supplies on hand at the end of the period is $760. Therefore, the supplies expense for December is the difference between the two amounts, or $1,240. Enter the adjustment by writing (1) $1,240 in the Adjustments Debit column on the same line as Supplies Expense and (2) $1,240 in the Adjustments Credit column on the same line as Supplies.

(b) **Prepaid Insurance.** The prepaid insurance account has a debit balance of $2,400, which represents the prepayment of insurance for 24 months beginning December 1. Thus, the insurance expense for December is $100 ($2,400/24). Enter the adjustment by writing (1) $100 in the Adjustments Debit column on the same line as Insurance Expense and (2) $100 in the Adjustments Credit column on the same line as Prepaid Insurance.

(c) **Unearned Rent.** The unearned rent account has a credit balance of $360, which represents the receipt of three months' rent, beginning with December. Thus, the rent revenue for December is $120. Enter the adjustment by writing (1) $120 in the Adjustments Debit column on the same line as Unearned Rent and (2) $120 in the Adjustments Credit column on the same line as Rent Revenue.

(d) **Wages.** Wages accrued but not paid at the end of December total $250. This amount is an increase in expenses and an increase in liabilities. Enter the adjustment by writing (1) $250 in the Adjustments Debit column on the same line as Wages Expense and (2) $250 in the Adjustments Credit column on the same line as Wages Payable.

(e) **Accrued Fees.** Fees accrued at the end of December but not recorded total $500. This amount is an increase in an asset and an increase in revenue. Enter the adjustment by writing (1) $500 in the Adjustments Debit column on the same line as Accounts Receivable and (2) $500 in the Adjustments Credit column on the same line as Fees Earned.

(f) **Depreciation.** Depreciation of the office equipment is $50 for December. Enter the adjustment by writing (1) $50 in the Adjustments Debit column on the same line as Depreciation Expense and (2) $50 in the Adjustments Credit column on the same line as Accumulated Depreciation.

Total the Adjustments columns to verify the mathematical accuracy of the adjustment data. The total of the Debit column must equal the total of the Credit column.

# Adjusted Trial Balance Columns

The adjustment data are added to or subtracted from the amounts in the unadjusted Trial Balance columns. The adjusted amounts are then extended to (placed in) the Adjusted Trial Balance columns, as shown in Exhibit 3. For example, the cash amount of $2,065 is extended to the Adjusted Trial Balance Debit column, since no adjustments affected Cash. Accounts Receivable has an initial balance of $2,220 and a debit adjustment (increase) of $500. The amount to write in the Adjusted Trial Balance Debit column is the debit balance of $2,720. The same procedure continues until all account balances are extended to the Adjusted Trial Balance columns. Total the columns of the Adjusted Trial Balance to verify the equality of debits and credits.

## Income Statement and Balance Sheet Columns

The work sheet is completed by extending the adjusted trial balance amounts to the Income Statement and Balance Sheet columns. The amounts for revenues and expenses are extended to the Income Statement columns. The amounts for assets, liabilities, owner's capital, and drawing are extended to the Balance Sheet columns.[1]

In the NetSolutions work sheet, the first account listed is Cash, and the balance appearing in the Adjusted Trial Balance Debit column is $2,065. Cash is an asset, is listed on the balance sheet, and has a debit balance. Therefore, $2,065 is extended to the Balance Sheet Debit column. The Fees Earned balance of $16,840 is extended to the Income Statement Credit column. The same procedure continues until all account balances have been extended to the proper columns, as shown in Exhibit 4.

After all of the balances have been extended to the four statement columns, total each of these columns, as shown in Exhibit 5. The difference between the two Income Statement column totals is the amount of the net income or the net loss for the period. Likewise, the difference between the two Balance Sheet column totals is also the amount of the net income or net loss for the period.

If the Income Statement Credit column total (representing total revenue) is greater than the Income Statement Debit column total (representing total expenses), the difference is the net income. If the Income Statement Debit column total is greater than the Income Statement Credit column total, the difference is a net loss. For Net-Solutions, the computation of net income is as follows:

| | |
|---|---:|
| Total of Credit column (revenues) | $16,960 |
| Total of Debit column (expenses) | 9,755 |
| Net income (excess of revenues over expenses) | $ 7,205 |

If the total of the Balance Sheet Debit column of the work sheet is $350,000 and the total of the Balance Sheet Credit column is $400,000, what is the net income or net loss?

---

*$50,000 net loss ($350,000 − $400,000)*

As shown in Exhibit 5, write the amount of the net income, $7,205, in the Income Statement Debit column and the Balance Sheet Credit column. Write the term *Net income* in the Account Title column. If there was a net loss instead of net income, you would write the amount in the Income Statement Credit column and the Balance Sheet Debit column and the term *Net loss* in the Account Title column. Inserting the net income or net loss in the statement columns on the work sheet shows the effect of transferring the net balance of the revenue and expense accounts to the owner's capital account. Later in this chapter, we explain how to journalize this transfer.

After the net income or net loss has been entered on the work sheet, again total each of the four statement columns. The totals of the two Income Statement columns must now be equal. The totals of the two Balance Sheet columns must also be equal.

# Financial Statements

objective 3

Prepare financial statements from a work sheet.

The work sheet is an aid in preparing the income statement, the statement of owner's equity, and the balance sheet, which are presented in Exhibit 6. In the following paragraphs, we discuss these financial statements for NetSolutions, prepared from the completed work sheet in Exhibit 5. The statements are similar in form to those presented in Chapter 1.

---

[1]The balances of the capital and drawing accounts are also extended to the Balance Sheet columns because this work sheet does not provide for separate Statement of Owner's Equity columns.

# Income Statement

The income statement is normally prepared directly from the work sheet. However, the order of the expenses may be changed. As we did in Chapter 1, we list the expenses in the income statement in Exhibit 6 in order of size, beginning with the larger items. Miscellaneous expense is the last item, regardless of its amount.

---

## INTEGRITY IN BUSINESS

### THE ROUND TRIP

**A** common type of fraud involves artificially inflating revenue. One fraudulent method of inflating revenue is called "round tripping." Under this scheme, a selling company (S) "lends" money to a customer company (C). The money is then used by C to purchase a product from S. Thus, S sells product to C and is paid with the money just loaned to C! This looks like a sale in the accounting records, but in reality, S is shipping free product. The fraud is exposed when it is determined that there was no intent to repay the original loan.

---

I'm one of the world's largest hotel operating companies, with names such as these under my roof: Sheraton, Westin, St. Regis, W, Ciga, Luxury Collection and Four Points. Some of my better known units include the St. Regis in New York; the Phoenician in Scottsdale, Ariz.; the Hotel Danieli in Venice; and the Palace Hotel in Madrid. My Westin division recently bought nine legendary luxury hotels in Europe. I own, lease, manage or franchise more than 700 hotels with more than 217,000 rooms in some 80 countries. I aim to increase earnings per share by 15 percent annually. Who am I? (Go to page 163 for answer.)

# Statement of Owner's Equity

The first item normally presented on the statement of owner's equity is the balance of the proprietor's capital account at the beginning of the period. On the work sheet, however, the amount listed as capital is not always the account balance at the beginning of the period. The proprietor may have invested additional assets in the business during the period. Hence, for the beginning balance and any additional investments, it is necessary to refer to the capital account in the ledger. These amounts, along with the net income (or net loss) and the drawing amount shown in the work sheet, are used to determine the ending capital account balance.

The basic form of the statement of owner's equity is shown in Exhibit 6. For Net-Solutions, the amount of drawings by the owner was less than the net income. If the owner's withdrawals had exceeded the net income, the order of the net income and the withdrawals would have been reversed. The difference between the two items would then be deducted from the beginning capital account balance. Other factors, such as additional investments or a net loss, also require some change in the form, as shown in the following example:

| | | |
|---|---:|---:|
| Allan Johnson, capital, January 1, 2005 | $39,000 | |
| Additional investment during the year | 6,000 | |
|   Total | | $45,000 |
| Net loss for the year | $ 5,600 | |
| Withdrawals | 9,500 | |
| Decrease in owner's equity | | 15,100 |
| Allan Johnson, capital, December 31, 2005 | | $29,900 |

# Balance Sheet

The balance sheet in Exhibit 6 was expanded by adding subsections for current assets; property, plant, and equipment; and current liabilities. Such a balance sheet is a *classified* balance sheet. In the following paragraphs, we describe some of the sections and subsections that may be used in a balance sheet. We will introduce additional sections in later chapters.

## Assets

Assets are commonly divided into classes for presentation on the balance sheet. Two of these classes are (1) current assets and (2) property, plant, and equipment.

> Two common classes of assets are current assets and property, plant, and equipment.

**Current Assets**  Cash and other assets that are expected to be converted to cash or sold or used up usually within one year or less, through the normal operations of the business, are called *current assets*. In addition to cash, the current assets usually owned by a service business are notes receivable, accounts receivable, supplies, and other prepaid expenses.

*Notes receivable* are amounts customers owe. They are written promises to pay the amount of the note and possibly interest at an agreed rate. Accounts receivable are also amounts customers owe, but they are less formal than notes and do not provide for interest. Accounts receivable normally result from providing services or selling merchandise on account. Notes receivable and accounts receivable are current assets because they will usually be converted to cash within one year or less.

**Property, Plant, and Equipment**  The property, plant, and equipment section may also be described as *fixed assets* or *plant assets*. These assets include equipment, machinery, buildings, and land. With the exception of land, as we discussed in Chapter 3, fixed assets depreciate over a period of time. The cost, accumulated depreciation, and book value of each major type of fixed asset is normally reported on the balance sheet or in accompanying notes.

## Liabilities

Liabilities are the amounts the business owes to creditors. The two most common classes of liabilities are (1) current liabilities and (2) long-term liabilities.

> Two common classes of liabilities are current liabilities and long-term liabilities.

**Current Liabilities**  Liabilities that will be due within a short time (usually one year or less) and that are to be paid out of current assets are called *current liabilities*. The most common liabilities in this group are notes payable and accounts payable. Other current liability accounts commonly found in the ledger are Wages Payable, Interest Payable, Taxes Payable, and Unearned Fees.

**Long-Term Liabilities**  Liabilities that will not be due for a long time (usually more than one year) are called *long-term liabilities*. If NetSolutions had long-term liabilities, they would be reported below the current liabilities. As long-term liabilities come due and are to be paid within one year, they are classified as current liabilities. If they are to be renewed rather than paid, they would continue to be classified as long-term. When an asset is pledged as security for a liability, the obligation may be called a *mortgage note payable* or a *mortgage payable*.

## Owner's Equity

The owner's right to the assets of the business is presented on the balance sheet below the liabilities section. The owner's equity is added to the total liabilities, and this total must be equal to the total assets.

# •Exhibit 2    Work Sheet with Unadjusted Trial Balance Entered

NetSolutions
Work Sheet
For the Two Months Ended December 31, 2005

| | Account Title | Trial Balance Dr. | Trial Balance Cr. | Adjustments Dr. | Adjustments Cr. | Adjusted Trial Balance Dr. | Adjusted Trial Balance Cr. | Income Statement Dr. | Income Statement Cr. | Balance Sheet Dr. | Balance Sheet Cr. | |
|---|---|---|---|---|---|---|---|---|---|---|---|---|
| 1 | Cash | 2,065 | | | | | | | | | | 1 |
| 2 | Accounts Receivable | 2,220 | | | | | | | | | | 2 |
| 3 | Supplies | 2,000 | | | | | | | | | | 3 |
| 4 | Prepaid Insurance | 2,400 | | | | | | | | | | 4 |
| 5 | Land | 20,000 | | | | | | | | | | 5 |
| 6 | Office Equipment | 1,800 | | | | | | | | | | 6 |
| 7 | Accounts Payable | | 900 | | | | | | | | | 7 |
| 8 | Unearned Rent | | 360 | | | | | | | | | 8 |
| 9 | Chris Clark, Capital | | 25,000 | | | | | | | | | 9 |
| 10 | Chris Clark, Drawing | 4,000 | | | | | | | | | | 10 |
| 11 | Fees Earned | | 16,340 | | | | | | | | | 11 |
| 12 | Wages Expense | 4,275 | | | | | | | | | | 12 |
| 13 | Rent Expense | 1,600 | | | | | | | | | | 13 |
| 14 | Utilities Expense | 985 | | | | | | | | | | 14 |
| 15 | Supplies Expense | 800 | | | | | | | | | | 15 |
| 16 | Miscellaneous Expense | 455 | | | | | | | | | | 16 |
| 17 | | 42,600 | 42,600 | | | | | | | | | 17 |
| 18 | | | | | | | | | | | | 18 |
| 19 | | | | | | | | | | | | 19 |
| 20 | | | | | | | | | | | | 20 |
| 21 | | | | | | | | | | | | 21 |
| 22 | | | | | | | | | | | | 22 |
| 23 | | | | | | | | | | | | 23 |
| 24 | | | | | | | | | | | | 24 |
| 25 | | | | | | | | | | | | 25 |

The work sheet is used for summarizing the effects of adjusting entries. It also aids in preparing financial statements.

**•Exhibit 6** Financial Statements Prepared from Work Sheet

## NetSolutions
## Income Statement
## For the Two Months Ended December 31, 2005

| | | |
|---|---:|---:|
| Fees earned | $16 8 4 0 00 | |
| Rent revenue | 1 2 0 00 | |
| Total revenues | | $16 9 6 0 00 |
| Expenses: | | |
| Wages expense | $ 4 5 2 5 00 | |
| Supplies expense | 2 0 4 0 00 | |
| Rent expense | 1 6 0 0 00 | |
| Utilities expense | 9 8 5 00 | |
| Insurance expense | 1 0 0 00 | |
| Depreciation expense | 5 0 00 | |
| Miscellaneous expense | 4 5 5 00 | |
| Total expenses | | 9 7 5 5 00 |
| Net income | | $ 7 2 0 5 00 |

## NetSolutions
## Statement of Owner's Equity
## For the Two Months Ended December 31, 2005

| | | |
|---|---:|---:|
| Chris Clark, capital, November 1, 2005 | | $ 0 |
| Investment on November 1, 2005 | $25 0 0 0 00 | |
| Net income for November and December | 7 2 0 5 00 | |
| | $32 2 0 5 00 | |
| Less withdrawals | 4 0 0 0 00 | |
| Increase in owner's equity | | 28 2 0 5 00 |
| Chris Clark, capital, December 31, 2005 | | $28 2 0 5 00 |

## NetSolutions
## Balance Sheet
## December 31, 2005

| Assets | | | Liabilities | | |
|---|---:|---:|---|---:|---:|
| Current assets: | | | Current liabilities: | | |
| Cash | $ 2 0 6 5 00 | | Accounts payable | $ 9 0 0 00 | |
| Accounts receivable | 2 7 2 0 00 | | Wages payable | 2 5 0 00 | |
| Supplies | 7 6 0 00 | | Unearned rent | 2 4 0 00 | |
| Prepaid insurance | 2 3 0 0 00 | | Total liabilities | | $ 1 3 9 0 00 |
| Total current assets | | $ 7 8 4 5 00 | | | |
| Property, plant, and equipment: | | | | | |
| Land | $20 0 0 0 00 | | | | |
| Office equipment $1,800 | | | | | |
| Less accum. depr. 50 | 1 7 5 0 00 | | **Owner's Equity** | | |
| Total property, plant, | | | Chris Clark, capital | | 28 2 0 5 00 |
| and equipment | | 21 7 5 0 00 | Total liabilities and | | |
| Total assets | | $29 5 9 5 00 | owner's equity | | $29 5 9 5 00 |

# Adjusting and Closing Entries

objective 4

Prepare the adjusting and closing entries from a work sheet.

As we discussed in Chapter 3, the adjusting entries are recorded in the journal at the end of the accounting period. If a work sheet has been prepared, the data for these entries are in the Adjustments columns. For NetSolutions, the adjusting entries prepared from the work sheet are shown in Exhibit 7.

After the adjusting entries have been posted to NetSolutions' ledger, shown in Exhibit 11 (on pages 147–151), the ledger is in agreement with the data reported on the financial statements. The balances of the accounts reported on the balance sheet are carried forward from year to year. Because they are relatively permanent, these accounts are called *real accounts*. The balances of the accounts reported on the income statement are *not* carried forward from year to year. Likewise, the balance of the owner's withdrawal account, which is reported on the statement of owner's equity, is not carried forward. Because these accounts report amounts for only one period, they are called *temporary accounts* or *nominal accounts*.

## •Exhibit 7

**Adjusting Entries for NetSolutions**

| | JOURNAL | | | Page 5 | |
|---|---|---|---|---|---|
| Date | Description | Post. Ref. | Debit | Credit | |
| | Adjusting Entries | | | | 1 |
| 2005 Dec. 31 | Supplies Expense | 55 | 1 2 4 0 00 | | 2 |
| | Supplies | 14 | | 1 2 4 0 00 | 3 |
| | | | | | 4 |
| 31 | Insurance Expense | 56 | 1 0 0 00 | | 5 |
| | Prepaid Insurance | 15 | | 1 0 0 00 | 6 |
| | | | | | 7 |
| 31 | Unearned Rent | 23 | 1 2 0 00 | | 8 |
| | Rent Revenue | 42 | | 1 2 0 00 | 9 |
| | | | | | 10 |
| 31 | Wages Expense | 51 | 2 5 0 00 | | 11 |
| | Wages Payable | 22 | | 2 5 0 00 | 12 |
| | | | | | 13 |
| 31 | Accounts Receivable | 12 | 5 0 0 00 | | 14 |
| | Fees Earned | 41 | | 5 0 0 00 | 15 |
| | | | | | 16 |
| 31 | Depreciation Expense | 53 | 5 0 00 | | 17 |
| | Accumulated Depreciation— | | | | 18 |
| | Office Equipment | 19 | | 5 0 00 | 19 |

---

**Closing entries transfer the balances of temporary accounts to the owner's capital account.**

To report amounts for only one period, temporary accounts should have zero balances at the beginning of a period. How are these balances converted to zero? The revenue and expense account balances are transferred to an account called *Income Summary*. The balance of Income Summary is then transferred to the owner's capital account. The balance of the owner's drawing account is also transferred to the owner's capital account. The entries that transfer these balances are called *closing entries*. The transfer process is called the *closing process*. Exhibit 8 is a diagram of this process.

•Exhibit 8

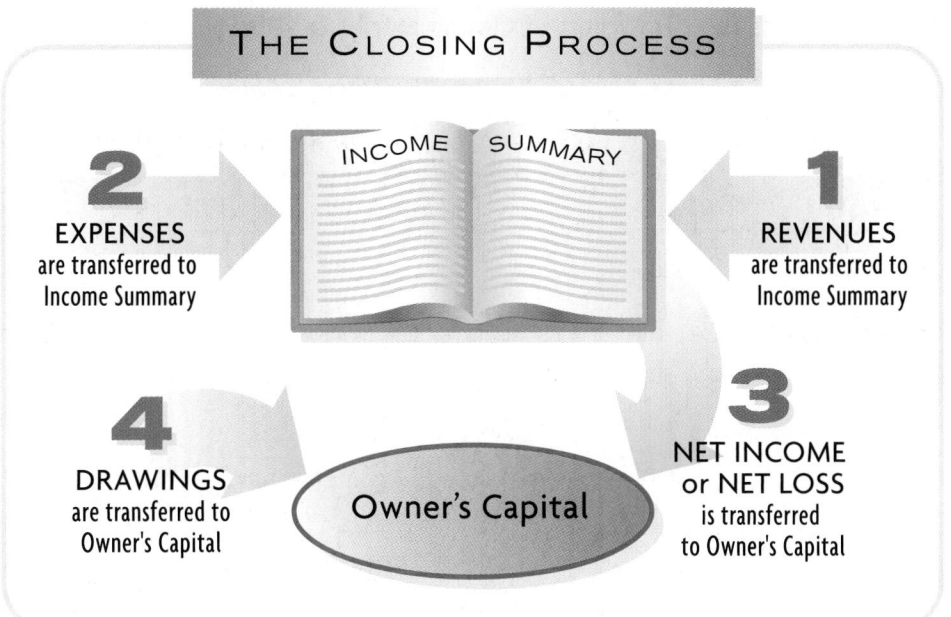

**THE CLOSING PROCESS**

**2** EXPENSES are transferred to Income Summary

INCOME SUMMARY

**1** REVENUES are transferred to Income Summary

**4** DRAWINGS are transferred to Owner's Capital

Owner's Capital

**3** NET INCOME or NET LOSS is transferred to Owner's Capital

**The income summary account does not appear on the financial statements.**

You should note that Income Summary is used only at the end of the period. At the beginning of the closing process, Income Summary has no balance. During the closing process, Income Summary will be debited and credited for various amounts. At the end of the closing process, Income Summary will again have no balance. Because Income Summary has the effect of clearing the revenue and expense accounts of their balances, it is sometimes called a *clearing account*.

Other titles used for this account include Revenue and Expense Summary, Profit and Loss Summary, and Income and Expense Summary.

It is possible to close the temporary revenue and expense accounts without using a clearing account such as Income Summary. In this case, the balances of the revenue and expense accounts are closed directly to the owner's capital account. This process is automatic in a computerized accounting system. In a manual system, the use of an income summary account aids in detecting and correcting errors.

## Journalizing and Posting Closing Entries

Four closing entries are required at the end of an accounting period, as outlined in Exhibit 8. The account titles and balances needed in preparing these entries may be obtained from the work sheet, the income statement and the statement of owner's equity, or the ledger. If a work sheet is used, the data for the first two entries appear in the Income Statement columns. The amount for the third entry is the net income or net loss appearing at the bottom of the work sheet. The amount for the fourth entry is the drawing account balance that appears in the Balance Sheet Debit column of the work sheet.

A flowchart of the closing entries for NetSolutions is shown in Exhibit 9. The balances in the accounts are those shown in the Adjusted Trial Balance columns of the work sheet in Exhibit 3.

The closing entries for NetSolutions are shown in Exhibit 10. After the closing entries have been posted to the ledger, as shown in Exhibit 11 (on pages 147–151), the balance in the capital account will agree with the amount reported on the statement of owner's equity and the balance sheet. In addition, the revenue, expense, and drawing accounts will have zero balances.

After the entry to close an account has been posted, a line should be inserted in both balance columns opposite the final entry. The next period's transactions for the revenue, expense, and drawing accounts will be posted directly below the closing entry.

If total revenues are $600,000, total expenses are $525,000, and drawing is $50,000, what is the balance of the income summary account that is closed to the owner's capital?

----

*$75,000 ($600,000 − $525,000). The drawing account balance is closed directly to the owner's capital, rather than to Income Summary.*

## •Exhibit 9   Flowchart of Closing Entries for NetSolutions

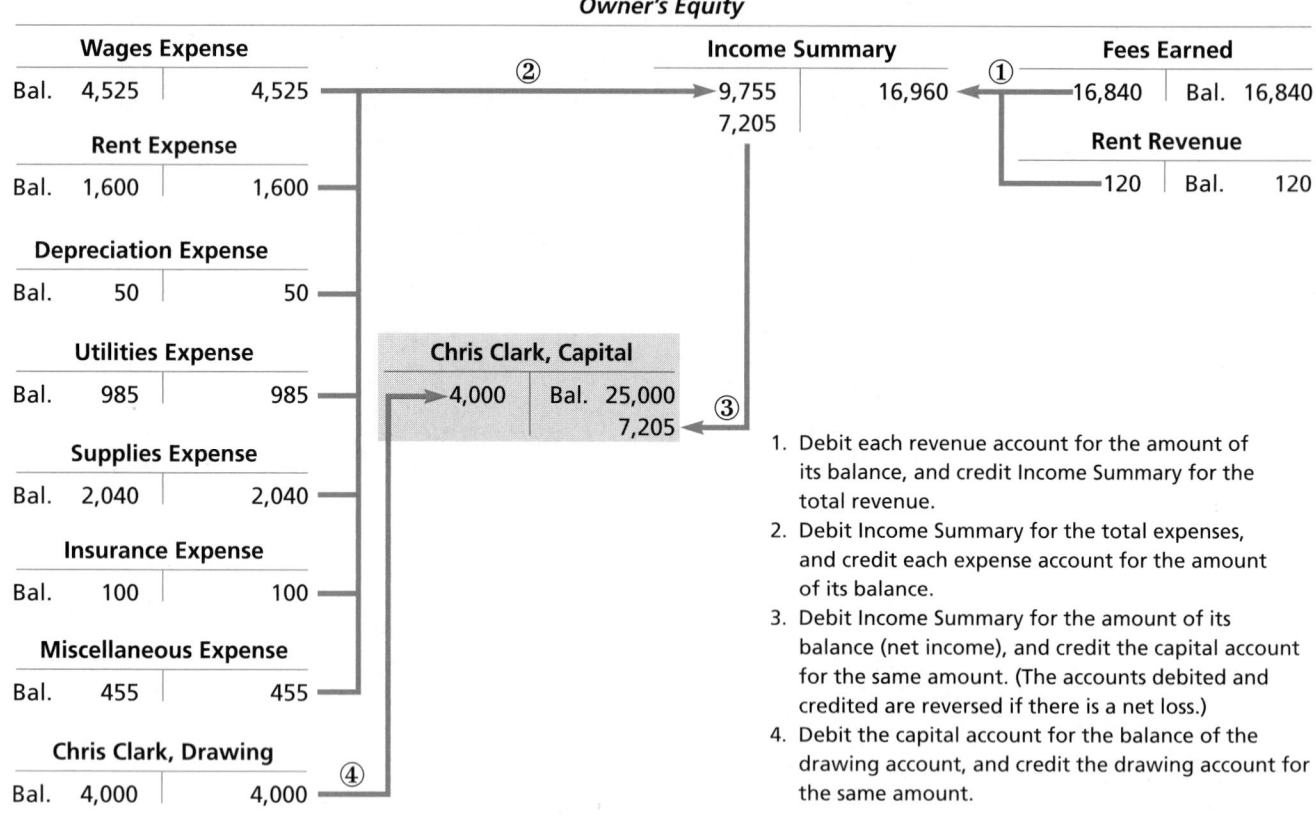

1. Debit each revenue account for the amount of its balance, and credit Income Summary for the total revenue.
2. Debit Income Summary for the total expenses, and credit each expense account for the amount of its balance.
3. Debit Income Summary for the amount of its balance (net income), and credit the capital account for the same amount. (The accounts debited and credited are reversed if there is a net loss.)
4. Debit the capital account for the balance of the drawing account, and credit the drawing account for the same amount.

## •Exhibit 10   Closing Entries for NetSolutions

| | | | | | | |
|---|---|---|---|---|---|---|
| **JOURNAL** | | | | | | **Page 6** |
| Date | | Description | Post. Ref. | Debit | Credit | |
| 1 | | Closing Entries | | | | 1 |
| 2 | 2005 Dec. 31 | Fees Earned | 41 | 16 8 4 0 00 | | 2 |
| 3 | | Rent Revenue | 42 | 1 2 0 00 | | 3 |
| 4 | | Income Summary | 33 | | 16 9 6 0 00 | 4 |
| 5 | | | | | | 5 |
| 6 | 31 | Income Summary | 33 | 9 7 5 5 00 | | 6 |
| 7 | | Wages Expense | 51 | | 4 5 2 5 00 | 7 |
| 8 | | Rent Expense | 52 | | 1 6 0 0 00 | 8 |
| 9 | | Depreciation Expense | 53 | | 5 0 00 | 9 |
| 10 | | Utilities Expense | 54 | | 9 8 5 00 | 10 |
| 11 | | Supplies Expense | 55 | | 2 0 4 0 00 | 11 |
| 12 | | Insurance Expense | 56 | | 1 0 0 00 | 12 |
| 13 | | Miscellaneous Expense | 59 | | 4 5 5 00 | 13 |
| 14 | | | | | | 14 |
| 15 | 31 | Income Summary | 33 | 7 2 0 5 00 | | 15 |
| 16 | | Chris Clark, Capital | 31 | | 7 2 0 5 00 | 16 |
| 17 | | | | | | 17 |
| 18 | 31 | Chris Clark, Capital | 31 | 4 0 0 0 00 | | 18 |
| 19 | | Chris Clark, Drawing | 32 | | 4 0 0 0 00 | 19 |

•**Exhibit 11**   **Ledger for NetSolutions**

**LEDGER**

**ACCOUNT** *Cash*                                                              **ACCOUNT NO.** *11*

| Date | | Item | Post. Ref. | Debit | Credit | Balance | |
|---|---|---|---|---|---|---|---|
| | | | | | | Debit | Credit |
| 2005 Nov. | 1 | | 1 | 25 0 0 0 00 | | 25 0 0 0 00 | |
| | 5 | | 1 | | 20 0 0 0 00 | 5 0 0 0 00 | |
| | 18 | | 1 | 7 5 0 0 00 | | 12 5 0 0 00 | |
| | 30 | | 1 | | 3 6 5 0 00 | 8 8 5 0 00 | |
| | 30 | | 1 | | 9 5 0 00 | 7 9 0 0 00 | |
| | 30 | | 2 | | 2 0 0 0 00 | 5 9 0 0 00 | |
| Dec. | 1 | | 2 | | 2 4 0 0 00 | 3 5 0 0 00 | |
| | 1 | | 2 | | 8 0 0 00 | 2 7 0 0 00 | |
| | 1 | | 2 | 3 6 0 00 | | 3 0 6 0 00 | |
| | 6 | | 2 | | 1 8 0 00 | 2 8 8 0 00 | |
| | 11 | | 2 | | 4 0 0 00 | 2 4 8 0 00 | |
| | 13 | | 3 | | 9 5 0 00 | 1 5 3 0 00 | |
| | 16 | | 3 | 3 1 0 0 00 | | 4 6 3 0 00 | |
| | 20 | | 3 | | 9 0 0 00 | 3 7 3 0 00 | |
| | 21 | | 3 | 6 5 0 00 | | 4 3 8 0 00 | |
| | 23 | | 3 | | 1 4 5 0 00 | 2 9 3 0 00 | |
| | 27 | | 3 | | 1 2 0 0 00 | 1 7 3 0 00 | |
| | 31 | | 3 | | 3 1 0 00 | 1 4 2 0 00 | |
| | 31 | | 4 | | 2 2 5 00 | 1 1 9 5 00 | |
| | 31 | | 4 | 2 8 7 0 00 | | 4 0 6 5 00 | |
| | 31 | | 4 | | 2 0 0 0 00 | 2 0 6 5 00 | |

**ACCOUNT** *Accounts Receivable*                                             **ACCOUNT NO.** *12*

| Date | | Item | Post. Ref. | Debit | Credit | Balance | |
|---|---|---|---|---|---|---|---|
| | | | | | | Debit | Credit |
| 2005 Dec. | 16 | | 3 | 1 7 5 0 00 | | 1 7 5 0 00 | |
| | 21 | | 3 | | 6 5 0 00 | 1 1 0 0 00 | |
| | 31 | | 4 | 1 1 2 0 00 | | 2 2 2 0 00 | |
| | 31 | Adjusting | 5 | 5 0 0 00 | | 2 7 2 0 00 | |

**ACCOUNT** *Supplies*                                                         **ACCOUNT NO.** *14*

| Date | | Item | Post. Ref. | Debit | Credit | Balance | |
|---|---|---|---|---|---|---|---|
| | | | | | | Debit | Credit |
| 2005 Nov. | 10 | | 1 | 1 3 5 0 00 | | 1 3 5 0 00 | |
| | 30 | | 1 | | 8 0 0 00 | 5 5 0 00 | |
| | 23 | | 3 | 1 4 5 0 00 | | 2 0 0 0 00 | |
| Dec. | 31 | Adjusting | 5 | | 1 2 4 0 00 | 7 6 0 00 | |

•**Exhibit 11**
(continued)

**ACCOUNT** *Prepaid Insurance*                                        **ACCOUNT NO.** *15*

| Date | | Item | Post. Ref. | Debit | Credit | Balance | |
|---|---|---|---|---|---|---|---|
| | | | | | | Debit | Credit |
| 2005 Dec. | 1 | | 2 | 2 4 0 0 00 | | 2 4 0 0 00 | |
| | 31 | Adjusting | 5 | | 1 0 0 00 | 2 3 0 0 00 | |

**ACCOUNT** *Land*                                        **ACCOUNT NO.** *17*

| Date | | Item | Post. Ref. | Debit | Credit | Balance | |
|---|---|---|---|---|---|---|---|
| | | | | | | Debit | Credit |
| 2005 Nov. | 5 | | 1 | 20 0 0 0 00 | | 20 0 0 0 00 | |

**ACCOUNT** *Office Equipment*                                        **ACCOUNT NO.** *18*

| Date | | Item | Post. Ref. | Debit | Credit | Balance | |
|---|---|---|---|---|---|---|---|
| | | | | | | Debit | Credit |
| 2005 Dec. | 4 | | 2 | 1 8 0 0 00 | | 1 8 0 0 00 | |

**ACCOUNT** *Accumulated Depreciation*                                        **ACCOUNT NO.** *19*

| Date | | Item | Post. Ref. | Debit | Credit | Balance | |
|---|---|---|---|---|---|---|---|
| | | | | | | Debit | Credit |
| 2005 Dec. | 31 | Adjusting | 5 | | 5 0 00 | | 5 0 00 |

**ACCOUNT** *Accounts Payable*                                        **ACCOUNT NO.** *21*

| Date | | Item | Post. Ref. | Debit | Credit | Balance | |
|---|---|---|---|---|---|---|---|
| | | | | | | Debit | Credit |
| 2005 Nov. | 10 | | 1 | | 1 3 5 0 00 | | 1 3 5 0 00 |
| | 30 | | 1 | 9 5 0 00 | | | 4 0 0 00 |
| Dec. | 4 | | 2 | | 1 8 0 0 00 | | 2 2 0 0 00 |
| | 11 | | 2 | 4 0 0 00 | | | 1 8 0 0 00 |
| | 20 | | 3 | 9 0 0 00 | | | 9 0 0 00 |

•**Exhibit 11**
(continued)

**ACCOUNT** *Wages Payable*  **ACCOUNT NO.** *22*

| Date | Item | Post. Ref. | Debit | Credit | Balance Debit | Balance Credit |
|---|---|---|---|---|---|---|
| 2005 Dec. 31 | Adjusting | 5 | | 2 5 0 00 | | 2 5 0 00 |

**ACCOUNT** *Unearned Rent*  **ACCOUNT NO.** *23*

| Date | Item | Post. Ref. | Debit | Credit | Balance Debit | Balance Credit |
|---|---|---|---|---|---|---|
| 2005 Dec. 1 | | 2 | | 3 6 0 00 | | 3 6 0 00 |
| 31 | Adjusting | 5 | 1 2 0 00 | | | 2 4 0 00 |

**ACCOUNT** *Chris Clark, Capital*  **ACCOUNT NO.** *31*

| Date | Item | Post. Ref. | Debit | Credit | Balance Debit | Balance Credit |
|---|---|---|---|---|---|---|
| 2005 Nov. 1 | | 1 | | 25 0 0 0 00 | | 25 0 0 0 00 |
| Dec. 31 | Closing | 6 | | 7 2 0 5 00 | | 32 2 0 5 00 |
| 31 | Closing | 6 | 4 0 0 0 00 | | | 28 2 0 5 00 |

**ACCOUNT** *Chris Clark, Drawing*  **ACCOUNT NO.** *32*

| Date | Item | Post. Ref. | Debit | Credit | Balance Debit | Balance Credit |
|---|---|---|---|---|---|---|
| 2005 Nov. 30 | | 2 | 2 0 0 0 00 | | 2 0 0 0 00 | |
| Dec. 31 | | 4 | 2 0 0 0 00 | | 4 0 0 0 00 | |
| 31 | Closing | 6 | | 4 0 0 0 00 | — | — |

**ACCOUNT** *Income Summary*  **ACCOUNT NO.** *33*

| Date | Item | Post. Ref. | Debit | Credit | Balance Debit | Balance Credit |
|---|---|---|---|---|---|---|
| 2005 Dec. 31 | Closing | 6 | | 16 9 6 0 00 | | 16 9 6 0 00 |
| 31 | Closing | 6 | 9 7 5 5 00 | | | 7 2 0 5 00 |
| 31 | Closing | 6 | 7 2 0 5 00 | | — | — |

•**Exhibit 11**
(continued)

**ACCOUNT** *Fees Earned*      **ACCOUNT NO.** *41*

| Date | | Item | Post. Ref. | Debit | Credit | Balance Debit | Balance Credit |
|---|---|---|---|---|---|---|---|
| 2005 Nov. | 18 | | 1 | | 7 5 0 0 00 | | 7 5 0 0 00 |
| Dec. | 16 | | 3 | | 3 1 0 0 00 | | 10 6 0 0 00 |
| | 16 | | 3 | | 1 7 5 0 00 | | 12 3 5 0 00 |
| | 31 | | 4 | | 2 8 7 0 00 | | 15 2 2 0 00 |
| | 31 | | 4 | | 1 1 2 0 00 | | 16 3 4 0 00 |
| | 31 | Adjusting | 5 | | 5 0 0 00 | | 16 8 4 0 00 |
| | 31 | Closing | 6 | 16 8 4 0 00 | | — | — |

**ACCOUNT** *Rent Revenue*      **ACCOUNT NO.** *42*

| Date | | Item | Post. Ref. | Debit | Credit | Balance Debit | Balance Credit |
|---|---|---|---|---|---|---|---|
| 2005 Dec. | 31 | Adjusting | 5 | | 1 2 0 00 | | 1 2 0 00 |
| | 31 | Closing | 6 | 1 2 0 00 | | — | — |

**ACCOUNT** *Wages Expense*      **ACCOUNT NO.** *51*

| Date | | Item | Post. Ref. | Debit | Credit | Balance Debit | Balance Credit |
|---|---|---|---|---|---|---|---|
| 2005 Nov. | 30 | | 1 | 2 1 2 5 00 | | 2 1 2 5 00 | |
| Dec. | 13 | | 3 | 9 5 0 00 | | 3 0 7 5 00 | |
| | 27 | | 3 | 1 2 0 0 00 | | 4 2 7 5 00 | |
| | 31 | Adjusting | 5 | 2 5 0 00 | | 4 5 2 5 00 | |
| | 31 | Closing | 6 | | 4 5 2 5 00 | — | — |

**ACCOUNT** *Rent Expense*      **ACCOUNT NO.** *52*

| Date | | Item | Post. Ref. | Debit | Credit | Balance Debit | Balance Credit |
|---|---|---|---|---|---|---|---|
| 2005 Nov. | 30 | | 1 | 8 0 0 00 | | 8 0 0 00 | |
| Dec. | 1 | | 2 | 8 0 0 00 | | 1 6 0 0 00 | |
| | 31 | Closing | 6 | | 1 6 0 0 00 | — | — |

•**Exhibit 11**
(concluded)

**ACCOUNT** *Depreciation Expense*                                            **ACCOUNT NO.** *53*

| Date | | Item | Post. Ref. | Debit | Credit | Balance | |
|---|---|---|---|---|---|---|---|
| | | | | | | Debit | Credit |
| 2005 Dec. | 31 | Adjusting | 5 | 5 0 00 | | 5 0 00 | |
| | 31 | Closing | 6 | | 5 0 00 | — | — |

**ACCOUNT** *Utilities Expense*                                              **ACCOUNT NO.** *54*

| Date | | Item | Post. Ref. | Debit | Credit | Balance | |
|---|---|---|---|---|---|---|---|
| | | | | | | Debit | Credit |
| 2005 Nov. | 30 | | 1 | 4 5 0 00 | | 4 5 0 00 | |
| Dec. | 31 | | 3 | 3 1 0 00 | | 7 6 0 00 | |
| | 31 | | 4 | 2 2 5 00 | | 9 8 5 00 | |
| | 31 | Closing | 6 | | 9 8 5 00 | — | — |

**ACCOUNT** *Supplies Expense*                                              **ACCOUNT NO.** *55*

| Date | | Item | Post. Ref. | Debit | Credit | Balance | |
|---|---|---|---|---|---|---|---|
| | | | | | | Debit | Credit |
| 2005 Nov. | 30 | | 1 | 8 0 0 00 | | 8 0 0 00 | |
| Dec. | 31 | Adjusting | 5 | 1 2 4 0 00 | | 2 0 4 0 00 | |
| | 31 | Closing | 6 | | 2 0 4 0 00 | — | — |

**ACCOUNT** *Insurance Expense*                                             **ACCOUNT NO.** *56*

| Date | | Item | Post. Ref. | Debit | Credit | Balance | |
|---|---|---|---|---|---|---|---|
| | | | | | | Debit | Credit |
| 2005 Dec. | 31 | Adjusting | 5 | 1 0 0 00 | | 1 0 0 00 | |
| | 31 | Closing | 6 | | 1 0 0 00 | — | — |

**ACCOUNT** *Miscellaneous Expense*                                         **ACCOUNT NO.** *59*

| Date | | Item | Post. Ref. | Debit | Credit | Balance | |
|---|---|---|---|---|---|---|---|
| | | | | | | Debit | Credit |
| 2005 Nov. | 30 | | 1 | 2 7 5 00 | | 2 7 5 00 | |
| Dec. | 6 | | 2 | 1 8 0 00 | | 4 5 5 00 | |
| | 31 | Closing | 6 | | 4 5 5 00 | — | — |

# Post-Closing Trial Balance

The last accounting procedure for a period is to prepare a trial balance after the closing entries have been posted. The purpose of the **post-closing** (after closing) **trial balance** is to make sure that the ledger is in balance at the beginning of the next period. The accounts and amounts should agree exactly with the accounts and amounts listed on the balance sheet at the end of the period. The post-closing trial balance for NetSolutions is shown in Exhibit 12.

**•Exhibit 12**   Post-Closing Trial Balance

**NetSolutions**
**Post-Closing Trial Balance**
**December 31, 2005**

| Account | Debit | Credit |
|---|---:|---:|
| Cash | 2 0 6 5 00 | |
| Accounts Receivable | 2 7 2 0 00 | |
| Supplies | 7 6 0 00 | |
| Prepaid Insurance | 2 3 0 0 00 | |
| Land | 20 0 0 0 00 | |
| Office Equipment | 1 8 0 0 00 | |
| Accumulated Depreciation | | 5 0 00 |
| Accounts Payable | | 9 0 0 00 |
| Wages Payable | | 2 5 0 00 |
| Unearned Rent | | 2 4 0 00 |
| Chris Clark, Capital | | 28 2 0 5 00 |
| | 29 6 4 5 00 | 29 6 4 5 00 |

Instead of preparing a formal post-closing trial balance, it is possible to list the accounts directly from the ledger, using a computer. The computer printout, in effect, becomes the post-closing trial balance. Without such a printout, there is no efficient means of determining the cause of unequal trial balance totals.

## FINANCIAL REPORTING AND DISCLOSURE

### INTERNATIONAL DIFFERENCES

Financial statements prepared under accounting practices in other countries often differ from those prepared under generally accepted accounting principles found in the United States. This is to be expected, since cultures and market structures differ from country to country.

To illustrate, **BMW Group** prepares its financial statements under German law and German accounting principles. In doing so, BMW's balance sheet reports fixed assets first, followed by current assets. It also reports owner's equity before the liabilities. In contrast, balance sheets prepared under U.S. accounting principles report current assets followed by fixed assets and current liabilities followed by long-term liabilities and owner's equity. The U.S. form

of balance sheet is organized to emphasize creditor interpretation and analysis. For example, current assets and current liabilities are presented first, so that working capital (current assets − current liabilities) and the current ratio (current assets ÷ current liabilities) can be easily computed. Likewise, to emphasize their importance, liabilities are reported before owner's equity.

Regardless of these differences, the basic principles underlying the accounting equation and the double-entry accounting system are the same in Germany and the United States. Even though differences in recording and reporting exist, the accounting equation holds true: the total assets still equal the total liabilities and owner's equity.

# Fiscal Year

| objective | 5 |
|-----------|---|

Explain what is meant by the fiscal year and the natural business year.

In the NetSolutions illustration, operations began on November 1 and the accounting period was for two months, November and December. A proprietorship is required by the federal income tax law, except in rare cases, to maintain the same accounting period as its owner. Since Chris Clark maintains a calendar-year accounting period for tax purposes, NetSolutions must also close its accounts on December 31, 2005. In future years, the financial statements for NetSolutions will be prepared for twelve months ending on December 31 each year.

The annual accounting period adopted by a business is known as its *fiscal year*. Fiscal years begin with the first day of the month selected and end on the last day of the following twelfth month. The period most commonly used is the calendar year. Other periods are not unusual, especially for businesses organized as corporations. For example, a corporation may adopt a fiscal year that ends when business activities have reached the lowest point in its annual operating cycle. Such a fiscal year is called the *natural business year*. At the low point in its operating cycle, a business has more time to analyze the results of operations and to prepare financial statements.

Because companies with fiscal years often have highly seasonal operations, investors and others should be careful in interpreting partial-year reports for such companies. That is, you should expect the results of operations for these companies to vary significantly throughout the fiscal year.

The financial history of a business may be shown by a series of balance sheets and income statements for several fiscal years. If the life of a business is expressed by a line moving from left to right, the series of balance sheets and income statements may be graphed as follows:

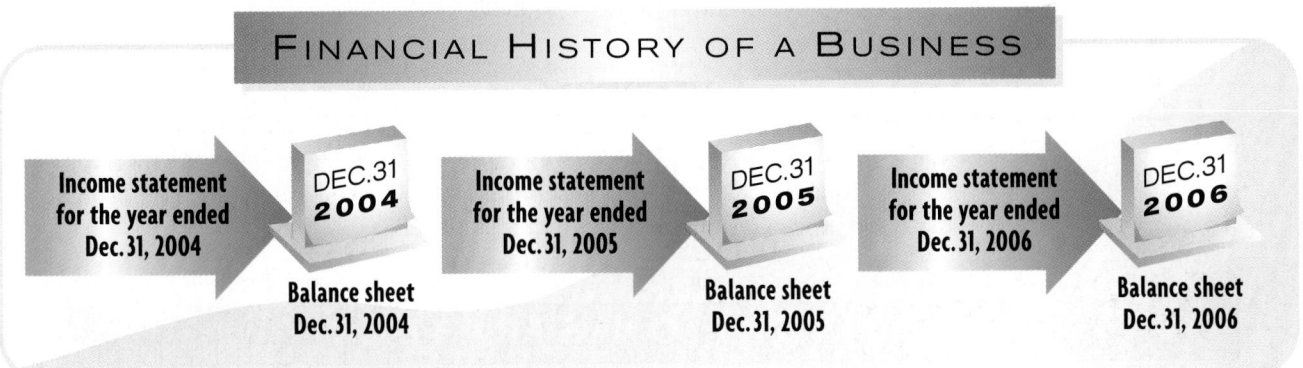

FINANCIAL HISTORY OF A BUSINESS

| Percentage of Companies with Fiscal Years Ending in: | | | |
|---|---|---|---|
| January | 5% | July | 1% |
| February | 2 | August | 3 |
| March | 3 | September | 6 |
| April | 1 | October | 3 |
| May | 3 | November | 3 |
| June | 8 | December | 62 |

**Source:** *Accounting Trends & Techniques,* 56th edition, 2002 (New York: American Institute of Certified Public Accountants).

You may think of the income statements, balance sheets, and financial history of a business as similar to the record of a college football team. The final score of each football game is similar to the net income reported on the income statement of a business. The team's season record after each game is similar to the balance sheet. At the end of the season, the final record of the team measures its success or failure. Likewise, at the end of a life of a business, its final balance sheet is a measure of its financial success or failure.

# Financial Analysis and Interpretation

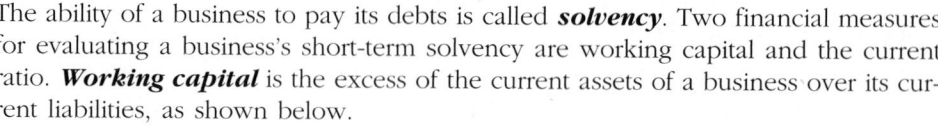

objective **6**

Analyze and interpret the financial solvency of a business by computing working capital and the current ratio.

The ability of a business to pay its debts is called **solvency**. Two financial measures for evaluating a business's short-term solvency are working capital and the current ratio. **Working capital** is the excess of the current assets of a business over its current liabilities, as shown below.

Working capital = Current assets − Current liabilities

An excess of the current assets over the current liabilities implies that the business is able to pay its current liabilities. If the current liabilities are greater than the current assets, the business may not be able to pay its debts and continue in business.

To illustrate, NetSolutions' working capital at the end of 2005 is $6,455, as computed below. This amount of working capital implies that NetSolutions can pay its current liabilities.

Working capital = Current assets − Current liabilities<br>Working capital = $7,845 − $1,390<br>Working capital = $6,455

The **current ratio** is another means of expressing the relationship between current assets and current liabilities. The current ratio is computed by dividing current assets by current liabilities, as shown below.

Current ratio = Current assets/Current liabilities

To illustrate, the current ratio for NetSolutions at the end of 2005 is 5.6, computed as follows:

Current ratio = Current assets/Current liabilities<br>Current ratio = $7,845/$1,390 = 5.6

The current ratio is useful in making comparisons across companies and with industry averages. To illustrate, assume that as of December 31, 2005, the working capital of a company that competes with NetSolutions is much greater than $6,455, but its current ratio is only 1.3. Considering these facts alone, NetSolutions is in a more favorable position to obtain short-term credit, even though the competing company has a greater amount of working capital.

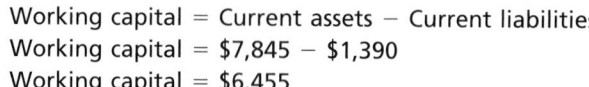

## SPOTLIGHT ON STRATEGY

### WHAT'S NEXT FOR AMAZON?

**A**mazon.com built its online business strategy on offering books at significant discounts that traditional chains couldn't match. Over the years, Amazon has expanded its online offerings to include DVDs, toys, electronics, and even kitchen appliances. But can its low-cost, discount strategy continue to work across a variety of products? Some have their doubts. The electronics business has lower margins and more competition than books. For example, **Dell Computers** is already an established low-cost provider of personal computers and software. In addition, some electronic manufacturers such as **Sony** are protec-

tive of their prices and have refused to make Amazon.com an authorized dealer. As Lauren Levitan, a noted financial analyst, recently said, "It's hard to be the low-cost retailer. You have to execute flawlessly on a very consistent basis. Most people who try a low-price strategy fail." This risk of failing at the low-cost strategy was validated by **Kmart**'s filing for bankruptcy protection in 2002 because of its inability to compete with **Wal-Mart**'s low prices.

**Source:** Saul Hansell, "A Profitable Amazon Looks to Do an Encore," *The New York Times*, January 26, 2002.

# **A**ppendix   Reversing Entries

Some of the adjusting entries recorded at the end of an accounting period have an important effect on otherwise routine transactions that occur in the following period. A typical example is accrued wages owed to employees at the end of a period. If there has been an adjusting entry for accrued wages expense, the first payment of wages in the following period will include the accrual. In the absence of some special provision, Wages Payable must be debited for the amount owed for the earlier period, and Wages Expense must be debited for the portion of the payroll that represents expense for the later period. However, an *optional* entry—the reversing entry—may be used to simplify the analysis and recording of this first payroll entry in a period. As the term implies, a **reversing entry** is the exact opposite of the adjusting entry to which it relates. The amounts and accounts are the same as the adjusting entry; the debits and credits are reversed.

We will illustrate the use of reversing entries by using the data for NetSolutions' accrued wages, which were presented in Chapter 3. These data are summarized in Exhibit 13.

## •**Exhibit 13**   Accrued Wages

1. Wages are paid on the second and fourth Fridays for the two-week periods ending on those Fridays.

2. The wages accrued for Monday and Tuesday, December 30 and 31, are $250.

3. Wages paid on Friday, January 10, total $1,275.

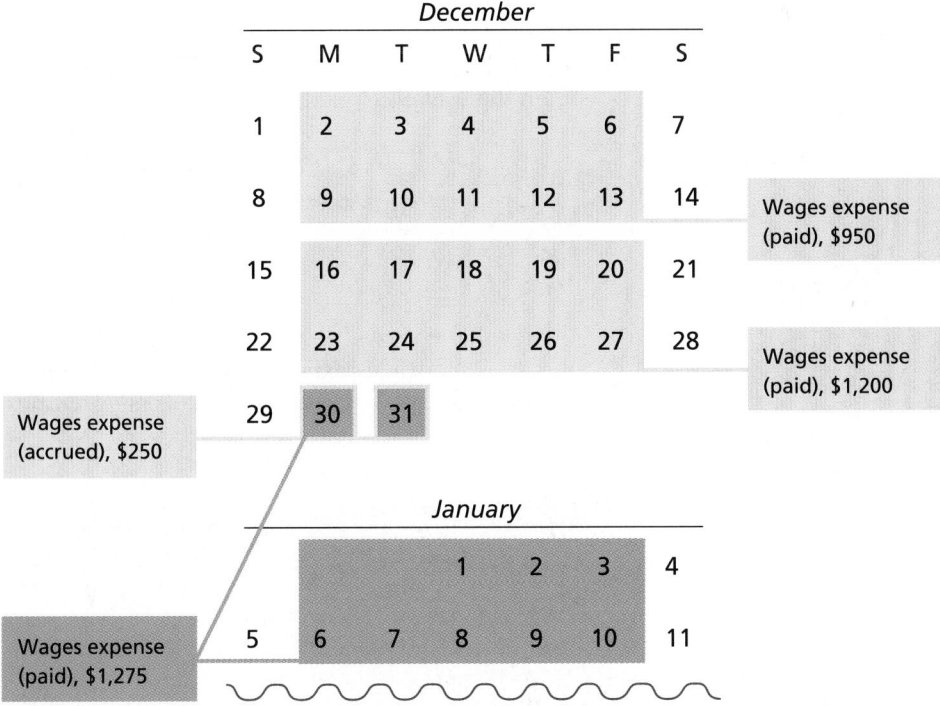

The adjusting entry for the accrued wages of December 30 and 31 is as follows:

| Dec. | 31 | Wages Expense | 51 | 2 5 0 00 | |
|------|----|---------------|----|----------|--|
| | | Wages Payable | 22 | | 2 5 0 00 |

After the adjusting entry has been posted, Wages Expense will have a debit balance of $4,525 ($4,275 + $250), and Wages Payable will have a credit balance of $250. After the closing process is completed, Wages Expense will have a zero balance and will be ready for entries in the next period. Wages Payable, on the other hand, has a balance of $250. Without a reversing entry, it is necessary to record the $1,275 payroll on January 10 as follows:

| 2006 Jan. | 10 | Wages Payable | 22 | 2 5 0 00 | |
|-----------|----|---------------|----|----------|--|
| | | Wages Expense | 51 | 1 0 2 5 00 | |
| | | Cash | 11 | | 1 2 7 5 00 |

The employee who records the January 10th entry must refer to the prior period's adjusting entry to determine the amount of the debits to Wages Payable and Wages Expense. Because the January 10th payroll is not recorded in the usual manner, there is a greater chance that an error may occur. This chance of error is reduced by recording a reversing entry as of the first day of the fiscal period. For example, the reversing entry for the accrued wages expense is as follows:

| 2006 Jan. | 1 | Wages Payable | 22 | 2 5 0 00 | |
|-----------|---|---------------|----|----------|--|
| | | Wages Expense | 51 | | 2 5 0 00 |

The reversing entry transfers the $250 liability from Wages Payable to the credit side of Wages Expense. The nature of the $250 is unchanged—it is still a liability. When the payroll is paid on January 10, the following entry is recorded:

| Jan. | 10 | Wages Expense | 51 | 1 2 7 5 00 | |
|------|----|---------------|----|------------|--|
| | | Cash | 11 | | 1 2 7 5 00 |

After this entry is posted, Wages Expense has a debit balance of $1,025. This amount is the wages expense for the period January 1–10. The sequence of entries, including adjusting, closing, and reversing entries, is illustrated in the following accounts:

**ACCOUNT** *Wages Payable*  **ACCOUNT NO.** *22*

| Date | | Item | Post. Ref. | Debit | Credit | Balance Debit | Balance Credit |
|------|--|------|-----------|-------|--------|-------|--------|
| 2005 Dec. | 31 | Adjusting | 5 | | 2 5 0 00 | | 2 5 0 00 |
| 2006 Jan. | 1 | Reversing | 7 | 2 5 0 00 | | — | — |

| ACCOUNT *Wages Expense* | | | | | | | ACCOUNT NO. *51* |
|---|---|---|---|---|---|---|---|
| | | **Post. Ref.** | **Debit** | **Credit** | **Balance** | | |
| **Date** | **Item** | | | | **Debit** | **Credit** | |
| 2005 Nov. 30 | | 1 | 2 1 2 5 00 | | 2 1 2 5 00 | | |
| Dec. 13 | | 3 | 9 5 0 00 | | 3 0 7 5 00 | | |
| 27 | | 3 | 1 2 0 0 00 | | 4 2 7 5 00 | | |
| 31 | Adjusting | 5 | 2 5 0 00 | | 4 5 2 5 00 | | |
| 31 | Closing | 6 | | 4 5 2 5 00 | — | — | |
| 2006 Jan. 1 | Reversing | 7 | | 2 5 0 00 | | 2 5 0 00 | |
| 10 | | 7 | 1 2 7 5 00 | | 1 0 2 5 00 | | |

In addition to accrued expenses (accrued liabilities), reversing entries may be journalized for accrued revenues (accrued assets). For example, the following reversing entry could be recorded for NetSolutions' accrued fees earned:

| | | | | | |
|---|---|---|---|---|---|
| Jan. | 1 | Fees Earned | 41 | 5 0 0 00 | |
| | | Accounts Receivable | 12 | | 5 0 0 00 |

Reversing entries may also be journalized for prepaid expenses that are initially recorded as expenses and unearned revenues that are initially recorded as revenues. These situations are described and illustrated in Appendix C.

As we mentioned, the use of reversing entries is optional. However, with the increased use of computerized accounting systems, data entry personnel may be inputting routine accounting entries. In such an environment, reversing entries may be useful, since these individuals may not recognize the impact of adjusting entries on the related transactions in the following period.

# Key Points

## 1 Review the seven basic steps of the accounting cycle.

The basic steps of the accounting cycle are:

1. Transactions are analyzed and recorded in a journal.
2. Transactions are posted to the ledger.
3. A trial balance is prepared, adjustment data are assembled, and an optional work sheet is completed.
4. Financial statements are prepared.
5. Adjusting entries are journalized and posted to the ledger.
6. Closing entries are journalized and posted to the ledger.

7. A post-closing trial balance is prepared.

## 2 Prepare a work sheet.

The work sheet is prepared by first entering a trial balance in the Trial Balance columns. The adjustments are then entered in the Adjustments Debit and Credit columns. The Trial Balance amounts plus or minus the adjustments are extended to the Adjusted Trial Balance columns. The work sheet is completed by extending the Adjusted Trial Balance amounts of assets, liabilities, owner's capital, and drawing to the Balance

Sheet columns. The Adjusted Trial Balance amounts of revenues and expenses are extended to the Income Statement columns. The net income (or net loss) for the period is entered on the work sheet in the Income Statement Debit (or Credit) column and the Balance Sheet Credit (or Debit) column. Each of the four statement columns is then totaled.

## 3 Prepare financial statements from a work sheet.

The income statement is normally prepared directly from the work sheet. On the income statement, the expenses are normally presented in the order of size, from largest to smallest.

The basic form of the statement of owner's equity is prepared by listing the beginning balance of owner's equity, adding investments in the business and net income during the period, and deducting the owner's withdrawals. The amount listed on the work sheet as capital does not always represent the account balance at the beginning of the accounting period. The proprietor may have invested additional assets in the business during the period. Hence, for the beginning balance and any additional investments, it is necessary to refer to the capital account.

Various sections and subsections are often used in preparing a balance sheet. Two common classes of assets are current assets and fixed assets. Cash and other assets that are normally expected to be converted to cash or sold or used up within one year or less are called current assets. Property, plant, and equipment may also be called fixed assets or plant assets. The cost, accumulated depreciation, and book value of each major type of fixed asset are normally reported on the balance sheet.

Two common classes of liabilities are current liabilities and long-term liabilities. Liabilities that will be due within a short time (usually one year or less) and that are to be paid out of current assets are called current liabilities. Liabilities that will not be due for a long time (usually more than one year) are called long-term liabilities.

The owner's claim against the assets is presented below the liabilities section and added to the total liabilities. The total liabilities and total owner's equity must equal the total assets.

**4 Prepare the adjusting and closing entries from a work sheet.**

The data for journalizing the adjusting entries are in the Adjustments columns of the work sheet. The four entries required in closing the temporary accounts are:

1. Debit each revenue account for the amount of its balance, and credit Income Summary for the total revenue.
2. Debit Income Summary for the total expenses, and credit each expense account for the amount of its balance.
3. Debit Income Summary for the amount of its balance (net income), and credit the capital account for the same amount. (Debit and credit are reversed if there is a net loss.)
4. Debit the capital account for the balance of the drawing account, and credit the drawing account for the same amount.

After the closing entries have been posted to the ledger, the balance in the capital account will agree with the amount reported on the statement of owner's equity and balance sheet. In addition, the revenue, expense, and drawing accounts will have zero balances.

The last step of the accounting cycle is to prepare a post-closing trial balance. The purpose of the post-closing trial balance is to make sure that the ledger is in balance at the beginning of the next period.

**5 Explain what is meant by the fiscal year and the natural business year.**

The annual accounting period adopted by a business is known as its fiscal year. A corporation may adopt a fiscal year that ends when business activities have reached the lowest point in its annual operating cycle. Such a fiscal year is called the natural business year.

**6 Analyze and interpret the financial solvency of a business by computing working capital and the current ratio.**

The ability of a business to pay its debts is called solvency. Two financial measures for evaluating a business's short-term solvency are working capital and the current ratio. Working capital is the excess of the current assets of a business over its current liabilities. The current ratio is computed by dividing current assets by current liabilities.

# Key Terms

accounting cycle (140)
clearing account (145)
closing entries (144D)
closing process (144D)
current assets (144A)
current liabilities (144A)
current ratio (154)
fiscal year (153)

fixed (plant) assets (144A)
Income Summary (144D)
long-term liabilities (144A)
natural business year (153)
note receivable (144A)
post-closing trial balance (152)
property, plant, and equipment (144A)

real accounts (144D)
reversing entry (155)
solvency (154)
temporary (nominal) accounts (144D)
work sheet (140)
working capital (154)

# Illustrative Problem

Three years ago, T. Roderick organized Harbor Realty. At July 31, 2006, the end of the current fiscal year, the trial balance of Harbor Realty is as follows:

**Harbor Realty**
**Trial Balance**
**July 31, 2006**

| | Debit | Credit |
|---|---|---|
| Cash | 3 4 2 5 00 | |
| Accounts Receivable | 7 0 0 0 00 | |
| Supplies | 1 2 7 0 00 | |
| Prepaid Insurance | 6 2 0 00 | |
| Office Equipment | 51 6 5 0 00 | |
| Accumulated Depreciation | | 9 7 0 0 00 |
| Accounts Payable | | 9 2 5 00 |
| Unearned Fees | | 1 2 5 0 00 |
| T. Roderick, Capital | | 29 0 0 0 00 |
| T. Roderick, Drawing | 5 2 0 0 00 | |
| Fees Earned | | 59 1 2 5 00 |
| Wages Expense | 22 4 1 5 00 | |
| Rent Expense | 4 2 0 0 00 | |
| Utilities Expense | 2 7 1 5 00 | |
| Miscellaneous Expense | 1 5 0 5 00 | |
| | 100 0 0 0 00 | 100 0 0 0 00 |

The data needed to determine year-end adjustments are as follows:

a. Supplies on hand at July 31, 2006, are $380.
b. Insurance premiums expired during the year are $315.
c. Depreciation of equipment during the year is $4,950.
d. Wages accrued but not paid at July 31, 2006, are $440.
e. Accrued fees earned but not recorded at July 31, 2006, are $1,000.
f. Unearned fees on July 31, 2006, are $750.

## Instructions

1. Enter the trial balance on a ten-column work sheet and complete the work sheet.
2. Prepare an income statement, a statement of owner's equity (no additional investments were made during the year), and a balance sheet.
3. On the basis of the data in the work sheet, journalize the closing entries.

Solution

**1.**

**Harbor Realty**
**Work Sheet**
**For the Year Ended July 31, 2006**

| | Account Title | Trial Balance Dr. | Trial Balance Cr. | Adjustments Dr. | Adjustments Cr. | Adjusted Trial Balance Dr. | Adjusted Trial Balance Cr. | Income Statement Dr. | Income Statement Cr. | Balance Sheet Dr. | Balance Sheet Cr. | |
|---|---|---|---|---|---|---|---|---|---|---|---|---|
| 1 | Cash | 3 4 2 5 | | | | 3 4 2 5 | | | | 3 4 2 5 | | 1 |
| 2 | Accounts Receivable | 7 0 0 0 | | (e)1 0 0 0 | | 8 0 0 0 | | | | 8 0 0 0 | | 2 |
| 3 | Supplies | 1 2 7 0 | | | (a) 8 9 0 | 3 8 0 | | | | 3 8 0 | | 3 |
| 4 | Prepaid Insurance | 6 2 0 | | | (b) 3 1 5 | 3 0 5 | | | | 3 0 5 | | 4 |
| 5 | Office Equipment | 51 6 5 0 | | | | 51 6 5 0 | | | | 51 6 5 0 | | 5 |
| 6 | Accum. Depreciation | | 9 7 0 0 | | (c)4 9 5 0 | | 14 6 5 0 | | | | 14 6 5 0 | 6 |
| 7 | Accounts Payable | | 9 2 5 | | | | 9 2 5 | | | | 9 2 5 | 7 |
| 8 | Unearned Fees | | 1 2 5 0 | (f) 5 0 0 | | | 7 5 0 | | | | 7 5 0 | 8 |
| 9 | T. Roderick, Capital | | 29 0 0 0 | | | | 29 0 0 0 | | | | 29 0 0 0 | 9 |
| 10 | T. Roderick, Drawing | 5 2 0 0 | | | | 5 2 0 0 | | | | 5 2 0 0 | | 10 |
| 11 | Fees Earned | | 59 1 2 5 | | (e)1 0 0 0 | | 60 6 2 5 | | 60 6 2 5 | | | 11 |
| 12 | | | | | (f) 5 0 0 | | | | | | | 12 |
| 13 | Wages Expense | 22 4 1 5 | | (d) 4 4 0 | | 22 8 5 5 | | 22 8 5 5 | | | | 13 |
| 14 | Rent Expense | 4 2 0 0 | | | | 4 2 0 0 | | 4 2 0 0 | | | | 14 |
| 15 | Utilities Expense | 2 7 1 5 | | | | 2 7 1 5 | | 2 7 1 5 | | | | 15 |
| 16 | Miscellaneous Expense | 1 5 0 5 | | | | 1 5 0 5 | | 1 5 0 5 | | | | 16 |
| 17 | | 100 0 0 0 | 100 0 0 0 | | | | | | | | | 17 |
| 18 | Supplies Expense | | | (a) 8 9 0 | | 8 9 0 | | 8 9 0 | | | | 18 |
| 19 | Insurance Expense | | | (b) 3 1 5 | | 3 1 5 | | 3 1 5 | | | | 19 |
| 20 | Depreciation Expense | | | (c)4 9 5 0 | | 4 9 5 0 | | 4 9 5 0 | | | | 20 |
| 21 | Wages Payable | | | | (d) 4 4 0 | | 4 4 0 | | | | 4 4 0 | 21 |
| 22 | | | | 8 0 9 5 | 8 0 9 5 | 106 3 9 0 | 106 3 9 0 | 37 4 3 0 | 60 6 2 5 | 68 9 6 0 | 45 7 6 5 | 22 |
| 23 | Net Income | | | | | | | 23 1 9 5 | | | 23 1 9 5 | 23 |
| 24 | | | | | | | | 60 6 2 5 | 60 6 2 5 | 68 9 6 0 | 68 9 6 0 | 24 |

**2.**

**Harbor Realty Inc.**
**Income Statement**
**For the Year Ended July 31, 2006**

| | | |
|---|---|---|
| Fees earned | | $60 6 2 5 00 |
| Operating expenses: | | |
| Wages expense | $22 8 5 5 00 | |
| Depreciation expense | 4 9 5 0 00 | |
| Rent expense | 4 2 0 0 00 | |
| Utilities expense | 2 7 1 5 00 | |
| Supplies expense | 8 9 0 00 | |
| Insurance expense | 3 1 5 00 | |
| Miscellaneous expense | 1 5 0 5 00 | |
| Total operating expenses | | 37 4 3 0 00 |
| Net income | | $23 1 9 5 00 |

**Harbor Realty**
**Statement of Owner's Equity**
**For the Year Ended July 31, 2006**

| | | |
|---|---|---|
| T. Roderick, capital, August 1, 2005 | | $29 0 0 0 00 |
| Net income for the year | $23 1 9 5 00 | |
| Less withdrawals | 5 2 0 0 00 | |
| Increase in owner's equity | | 17 9 9 5 00 |
| T. Roderick, capital, July 31, 2006 | | $46 9 9 5 00 |

**Harbor Realty**
**Balance Sheet**
**July 31, 2006**

| Assets | | | Liabilities | | |
|---|---|---|---|---|---|
| Current assets: | | | Current liabilities: | | |
| Cash | $ 3 4 2 5 00 | | Accounts payable | $ 9 2 5 00 | |
| Accounts receivable | 8 0 0 0 00 | | Unearned fees | 7 5 0 00 | |
| Supplies | 3 8 0 00 | | Wages payable | 4 4 0 00 | |
| Prepaid insurance | 3 0 5 00 | | Total liabilities | | $ 2 1 1 5 00 |
| Total current assets | | $12 1 1 0 00 | | | |
| Property, plant, and equipment: | | | **Owner's Equity** | | |
| Office equipment | $51 6 5 0 00 | | T. Roderick, capital | | 46 9 9 5 00 |
| Less accumulated depr. | 14 6 5 0 00 | 37 0 0 0 00 | Total liabilities and | | |
| Total assets | | $49 1 1 0 00 | owner's equity | | $49 1 1 0 00 |

3.

| | | | JOURNAL | | | | Page | |
|---|---|---|---|---|---|---|---|---|
| | Date | | Description | Post. Ref. | Debit | Credit | | |
| 1 | | | Closing Entries | | | | | 1 |
| 2 | 2006 July | 31 | Fees Earned | | 60 6 2 5 00 | | | 2 |
| 3 | | | Income Summary | | | 60 6 2 5 00 | | 3 |
| 4 | | | | | | | | 4 |
| 5 | | 31 | Income Summary | | 37 4 3 0 00 | | | 5 |
| 6 | | | Wages Expense | | | 22 8 5 5 00 | | 6 |
| 7 | | | Rent Expense | | | 4 2 0 0 00 | | 7 |
| 8 | | | Utilities Expense | | | 2 7 1 5 00 | | 8 |
| 9 | | | Miscellaneous Expense | | | 1 5 0 5 00 | | 9 |
| 10 | | | Supplies Expense | | | 8 9 0 00 | | 10 |
| 11 | | | Insurance Expense | | | 3 1 5 00 | | 11 |
| 12 | | | Depreciation Expense | | | 4 9 5 0 00 | | 12 |
| 13 | | | | | | | | 13 |
| 14 | | 31 | Income Summary | | 23 1 9 5 00 | | | 14 |
| 15 | | | T. Roderick, Capital | | | 23 1 9 5 00 | | 15 |
| 16 | | | | | | | | 16 |
| 17 | | 31 | T. Roderick, Capital | | 5 2 0 0 00 | | | 17 |
| 18 | | | T. Roderick, Drawing | | | 5 2 0 0 00 | | 18 |

# Self-Examination Questions (Answers at End of Chapter)

1. Which of the following accounts in the Adjusted Trial Balance columns of the work sheet would be extended to the Balance Sheet columns?
   A. Utilities Expense
   B. Rent Revenue
   C. M. E. Jones, Drawing
   D. Miscellaneous Expense

2. Which of the following accounts would be classified as a current asset on the balance sheet?
   A. Office Equipment
   B. Land
   C. Accumulated Depreciation
   D. Accounts Receivable

3. Which of the following entries closes the owner's drawing account at the end of the period?
   A. Debit the drawing account, credit the income summary account.
   B. Debit the owner's capital account, credit the drawing account.
   C. Debit the income summary account, credit the drawing account.
   D. Debit the drawing account, credit the owner's capital account.

4. Which of the following accounts would not be closed to the income summary account at the end of a period?
   A. Fees Earned
   B. Wages Expense
   C. Rent Expense
   D. Accumulated Depreciation

5. Which of the following accounts would not be included in a post-closing trial balance?
   A. Cash
   B. Fees Earned
   C. Accumulated Depreciation
   D. J. C. Smith, Capital

# Class Discussion Questions

1. (a) What is the most important output of the accounting cycle? (b) Do all companies have an accounting cycle? Explain.
2. Is the work sheet a substitute for the financial statements? Discuss.
3. In the Income Statement columns of the work sheet, the Debit column total is greater than the Credit column total before the amount for the net income or net loss has been included. Would the income statement report a net income or a net loss? Explain.
4. In the Balance Sheet columns of the work sheet for Teton Co. for the current year, the Debit column total is $68,500 greater than the Credit column total before the amount for net income or net loss has been included. Would the income statement report a net income or a net loss? Explain.
5. Describe the nature of the assets that compose the following sections of a balance sheet: (a) current assets, (b) property, plant, and equipment.
6. What is the difference between a current liability and a long-term liability?
7. What types of accounts are referred to as temporary accounts?
8. Why are closing entries required at the end of an accounting period?
9. What is the difference between adjusting entries and closing entries?
10. Describe the four entries that close the temporary accounts.
11. What is the purpose of the post-closing trial balance?
12. What is the natural business year?
13. Why might a department store select a fiscal year ending January 31, rather than a fiscal year ending December 31?
14. The fiscal years for several well-known companies were as follows:

| Company | Fiscal Year Ending | Company | Fiscal Year Ending |
| --- | --- | --- | --- |
| Kmart | January 30 | Toys "R" Us, Inc. | February 3 |
| JCPenney | January 26 | Federated Department Stores | February 3 |
| Zayre Corp. | January 26 | The Limited, Inc. | February 2 |

REAL WORLD

What general characteristic shared by these companies explains why they do not have fiscal years ending December 31?

15. If a company has positive working capital, will its current ratio always be greater than 1? Explain.

# Exercises

**EXERCISE 4-1**
*Steps in the accounting cycle*
**Objective 1**

Rearrange the following steps in the accounting cycle in proper sequence:

a. Closing entries are journalized and posted to the ledger.
b. Adjusting entries are journalized and posted to the ledger.
c. Transactions are posted to the ledger.
d. A post-closing trial balance is prepared.
e. Transactions are analyzed and recorded in the journal.
f. Financial statements are prepared.
g. A trial balance is prepared, adjustment data are assembled, and an optional work sheet is completed.

**EXERCISE 4-2**
*Place account balances in a work sheet*
**Objective 2**

The balances for the accounts listed below appear in the Adjusted Trial Balance columns of the work sheet. Indicate whether each balance should be extended to (a) an Income Statement column or (b) a Balance Sheet column.

1. Accounts Payable
2. Accounts Receivable
3. Fees Earned
4. Kathy Chang, Drawing
5. Kathy Chang, Capital
6. Supplies
7. Unearned Fees
8. Utilities Expense
9. Wages Expense
10. Wages Payable

**EXERCISE 4-3**
*Classify accounts*
**Objective 2**

Balances for each of the following accounts appear in an adjusted trial balance. Identify each as (a) asset, (b) liability, (c) revenue, or (d) expense.

1. Accounts Receivable
2. Fees Earned
3. Insurance Expense
4. Land
5. Prepaid Advertising
6. Prepaid Insurance
7. Rent Revenue
8. Salary Expense
9. Salary Payable
10. Supplies
11. Supplies Expense
12. Unearned Rent

**EXERCISE 4-4**
*Steps in completing a work sheet*
**Objective 2**

The steps performed in completing a work sheet are listed below in random order.

a. Extend the adjusted trial balance amounts to the Income Statement columns and the Balance Sheet columns.

*(continued)*

b. Enter the adjusting entries into the work sheet, based upon the adjustment data.

c. Add the Debit and Credit columns of the unadjusted Trial Balance columns of the work sheet to verify that the totals are equal.

d. Enter the amount of net income or net loss for the period in the proper Income Statement column and Balance Sheet column.

e. Add the Debit and Credit columns of the Balance Sheet and Income Statement columns of the work sheet to verify that the totals are equal.

f. Enter the unadjusted account balances from the general ledger into the unadjusted Trial Balance columns of the work sheet.

g. Add or deduct adjusting entry data to trial balance amounts and extend amounts to the Adjusted Trial Balance columns.

h. Add the Debit and Credit columns of the Adjustments columns of the work sheet to verify that the totals are equal.

i. Add the Debit and Credit columns of the Balance Sheet and Income Statement columns of the work sheet to determine the amount of net income or net loss for the period.

j. Add the Debit and Credit columns of the Adjusted Trial Balance columns of the work sheet to verify that the totals are equal.

Indicate the order in which the preceding steps would be performed in preparing and completing a work sheet.

**EXERCISE 4-5**
*Adjustment data on work sheet*
**Objective 2**

**SPREADSHEET**

✓ *Total debits of Adjustments column: $24*

Ithaca Services Co. offers cleaning services to business clients. The trial balance for Ithaca Services Co. has been prepared on the work sheet for the year ended January 31, 2006, shown below.

**Ithaca Services Co.**
**Work Sheet**
**For the Year Ended January 31, 2006**

| Account Title | Trial Balance Dr. | Trial Balance Cr. | Adjustments Dr. | Adjustments Cr. | Adjusted Trial Balance Dr. | Adjusted Trial Balance Cr. |
|---|---|---|---|---|---|---|
| Cash | 8 | | | | | |
| Accounts Receivable | 50 | | | | | |
| Supplies | 8 | | | | | |
| Prepaid Insurance | 12 | | | | | |
| Land | 50 | | | | | |
| Equipment | 32 | | | | | |
| Accumulated Depr.—Equip. | | 2 | | | | |
| Accounts Payable | | 26 | | | | |
| Wages Payable | | 0 | | | | |
| Terry Dagley, Capital | | 112 | | | | |
| Terry Dagley, Drawing | 8 | | | | | |
| Fees Earned | | 60 | | | | |
| Wages Expense | 16 | | | | | |
| Rent Expense | 8 | | | | | |
| Insurance Expense | 0 | | | | | |
| Utilities Expense | 6 | | | | | |
| Depreciation Expense | 0 | | | | | |
| Supplies Expense | 0 | | | | | |
| Miscellaneous Expense | 2 | | | | | |
| Totals | 200 | 200 | | | | |

The data for year-end adjustments are as follows:

a. Fees earned, but not yet billed, $7.

b. Supplies on hand, $3.

c. Insurance premiums expired, $6.

d. Depreciation expense, $5.

e. Wages accrued, but not paid, $1.

Enter the adjustment data, and place the balances in the Adjusted Trial Balance columns.

**EXERCISE 4-6**
*Complete a work sheet*
**Objective 2**

SPREADSHEET

✓ *Net income: $18*

Ithaca Services Co. offers cleaning services to business clients. Complete the following work sheet for Ithaca Services Co.

**Ithaca Services Co.**
**Work Sheet**
**For the Year Ended January 31, 2006**

| Account Title | Adjusted Trial Balance | | Income Statement | | Balance Sheet | |
|---|---|---|---|---|---|---|
| | Dr. | Cr. | Dr. | Cr. | Dr. | Cr. |
| Cash | 8 | | | | | |
| Accounts Receivable | 57 | | | | | |
| Supplies | 3 | | | | | |
| Prepaid Insurance | 6 | | | | | |
| Land | 50 | | | | | |
| Equipment | 32 | | | | | |
| Accumulated Depr.—Equip. | | 7 | | | | |
| Accounts Payable | | 26 | | | | |
| Wages Payable | | 1 | | | | |
| Terry Dagley, Capital | | 112 | | | | |
| Terry Dagley, Drawing | 8 | | | | | |
| Fees Earned | | 67 | | | | |
| Wages Expense | 17 | | | | | |
| Rent Expense | 8 | | | | | |
| Insurance Expense | 6 | | | | | |
| Utilities Expense | 6 | | | | | |
| Depreciation Expense | 5 | | | | | |
| Supplies Expense | 5 | | | | | |
| Miscellaneous Expense | 2 | | | | | |
| Totals | 213 | 213 | | | | |
| Net income (loss) | | | | | | |

**EXERCISE 4-7**
*Financial statements*
**Objective 3**

SPREADSHEET

✓ *Terry Dagley, capital, Jan. 31, 2006: $122*

Based upon the data in Exercise 4-6, prepare an income statement, statement of owner's equity, and balance sheet for Ithaca Services Co.

**EXERCISE 4-8**
*Adjusting entries*
**Objective 4**

Based upon the data in Exercise 4-5, prepare the adjusting entries for Ithaca Services Co.

**EXERCISE 4-9**
*Closing entries*
**Objective 4**

Based upon the data in Exercise 4-6, prepare the closing entries for Ithaca Services Co.

**EXERCISE 4-10**
*Income statement*
**Objective 3**

The following account balances were taken from the Adjusted Trial Balance columns of the work sheet for Larynx Messenger Service, a delivery service firm, for the current fiscal year ended June 30, 2006:

SPREADSHEET

| | | | |
|---|---|---|---|
| Fees Earned | $273,700 | Supplies Expense | $2,750 |
| Salaries Expense | 77,100 | Miscellaneous Expense | 1,350 |
| Rent Expense | 22,500 | Insurance Expense | 1,500 |
| Utilities Expense | 6,500 | Depreciation Expense | 5,200 |

Prepare an income statement.

**EXERCISE 4-11**
*Income statement; net loss*

**Objective 3**

SPREADSHEET

The following revenue and expense account balances were taken from the ledger of Sirocco Services Co. after the accounts had been adjusted on March 31, 2006, the end of the current fiscal year:

| | | | |
|---|---|---|---|
| Depreciation Expense | $ 8,000 | Service Revenue | $103,850 |
| Insurance Expense | 4,100 | Supplies Expense | 3,100 |
| Miscellaneous Expense | 2,250 | Utilities Expense | 11,500 |
| Rent Expense | 21,270 | Wages Expense | 56,800 |

Prepare an income statement.

**EXERCISE 4-12**
*Income statement*

**Objective 3**

REAL WORLD

INTERNET

SPREADSHEET

✓ *a. Net income: $443*

**FedEx Corporation** had the following revenue and expense account balances (in millions) at its fiscal year-end of May 31, 2002:

| | | | |
|---|---|---|---|
| Rentals and Landing Fees | $1,524 | Depreciation and Amortization | $ 806 |
| Maintenance and Repairs | 980 | Interest Expense | 56 |
| Purchased Transportation | 562 | Revenues | 15,327 |
| Fuel | 1,009 | Provision for Income Taxes | 260 |
| Salaries and Employee Benefits | 6,467 | Other Expenses | 52 |
| Other Operating Expenses | 3,168 | | |

a. Prepare an income statement.

b. ⬛▬▶ Compare your income statement with the 2002 income statement that is available at the FedEx Corporation Web site, which is linked to the text's Web site at **http://warren.swlearning.com**. What similarities and differences do you see?

**EXERCISE 4-13**
*Statement of owner's equity*

**Objective 3**

SPREADSHEET

✓ *Suzanne Jacob, capital, Oct. 31, 2006: $206,000*

Synthesis Systems Co. offers its services to residents in the Dillon City area. Selected accounts from the ledger of Synthesis Systems Co. for the current fiscal year ended October 31, 2006, are as follows:

**Suzanne Jacob, Capital**

| | | | |
|---|---|---|---|
| Oct. 31 | 12,000 | Nov. 1 (2005) | 173,750 |
| | | Oct. 31 | 44,250 |

**Suzanne Jacob, Drawing**

| | | | |
|---|---|---|---|
| Jan. 31 | 3,000 | Oct. 31 | 12,000 |
| Apr. 30 | 3,000 | | |
| July 31 | 3,000 | | |
| Oct. 31 | 3,000 | | |

**Income Summary**

| | | | |
|---|---|---|---|
| Oct. 31 | 277,150 | Oct. 31 | 321,400 |
| 31 | 44,250 | | |

Prepare a statement of owner's equity for the year.

**EXERCISE 4-14**
*Statement of owner's equity; net loss*

**Objective 3**

SPREADSHEET

Selected accounts from the ledger of Bobcat Sports for the current fiscal year ended August 31, 2006, are as follows:

**John Kramer, Capital**

| | | | |
|---|---|---|---|
| Aug. 31 | 16,000 | Sep. 1 (2005) | 210,300 |
| 31 | 49,650 | | |

**John Kramer, Drawing**

| | | | |
|---|---|---|---|
| Nov. 30 | 4,000 | Aug. 31 | 16,000 |
| Feb. 28 | 4,000 | | |
| May 31 | 4,000 | | |
| Aug. 31 | 4,000 | | |

✓ *John Kramer, capital,*
*Aug. 31, 2006: $144,650*

**Income Summary**

| | | | | |
|---|---|---|---|---|
| Aug. 31 | 224,900 | Aug. 31 | 175,250 |
| | | 31 | 49,650 |

Prepare a statement of owner's equity for the year.

**EXERCISE 4-15**
*Classify assets*
**Objective 3**

Identify each of the following as (a) a current asset or (b) property, plant, and equipment:

1. Cash
2. Equipment
3. Accounts receivable
4. Building
5. Prepaid insurance
6. Supplies

**EXERCISE 4-16**
*Balance sheet classification*
**Objective 3**

At the balance sheet date, a business owes a mortgage note payable of $500,000, the terms of which provide for monthly payments of $13,750.

➡ Explain how the liability should be classified on the balance sheet.

**EXERCISE 4-17**
*Balance sheet*
**Objective 3**

**SPREADSHEET**

✓ *Total assets: $126,650*

Tudor Co. offers personal weight reduction consulting services to individuals. After all the accounts have been closed on April 30, 2006, the end of the current fiscal year, the balances of selected accounts from the ledger of Tudor Co. are as follows:

| | | | |
|---|---|---|---|
| Accounts Payable | $ 9,500 | Vernon Posey, Capital | $114,200 |
| Accounts Receivable | 21,850 | Prepaid Insurance | 7,200 |
| Accumulated Depreciation— | | Prepaid Rent | 4,800 |
| Equipment | 21,100 | Salaries Payable | 1,750 |
| Cash | ? | Supplies | 1,800 |
| Equipment | 80,600 | Unearned Fees | 1,200 |

Prepare a classified balance sheet that includes the correct balance for Cash.

**EXERCISE 4-18**
*Balance sheet*
**Objective 3**

**SPREADSHEET    WHAT'S WRONG WITH THIS?**

✓ *Corrected balance sheet, total assets: $140,500*

List the errors you find in the following balance sheet. Prepare a corrected balance sheet.

**Warburg Services Co.**
**Balance Sheet**
**For the Year Ended May 31, 2006**

| Assets | | | Liabilities | |
|---|---|---|---|---|
| Current assets: | | | Current liabilities: | |
| Cash | $ 4,170 | | Accounts receivable | $ 12,500 |
| Accounts payable | 7,250 | | Accum. depr.—building | 23,000 |
| Supplies | 1,650 | | Accum. depr.—equipment | 16,000 |
| Prepaid insurance | 2,400 | | Net loss | 10,000 |
| Land | 75,000 | | Total liabilities | $ 61,500 |
| Total current assets | | $ 90,470 | | |
| Property, plant, | | | | |
| and equipment: | | | **Owner's Equity** | |
| Building | $ 55,500 | | Wages payable | $ 1,500 |
| Equipment | 28,280 | | Erin Gentry, capital | 131,750 |
| Total property, plant, | | | Total owner's equity | $133,250 |
| and equipment | | $104,280 | Total liabilities and | |
| Total assets | | $194,750 | owner's equity | $194,750 |

**EXERCISE 4-19**
*Adjusting entries from work sheet*
**Objective 4**

Green Earth Co. is a consulting firm specializing in pollution control. The entries in the Adjustments columns of the work sheet for Green Earth Co. are as follows.

| | Adjustments | |
|---|---|---|
| | Dr. | Cr. |
| Accounts Receivable | 4,100 | |
| Supplies | | 1,300 |
| Prepaid Insurance | | 2,000 |
| Accumulated Depreciation—Equipment | | 2,800 |
| Wages Payable | | 1,000 |
| Unearned Rent | 2,500 | |
| Fees Earned | | 4,100 |
| Wages Expense | 1,000 | |
| Supplies Expense | 1,300 | |
| Rent Revenue | | 2,500 |
| Insurance Expense | 2,000 | |
| Depreciation Expense | 2,800 | |

Prepare the adjusting journal entries.

**EXERCISE 4-20**
*Identify accounts to be closed*
**Objective 4**

From the following list, identify the accounts that should be closed to Income Summary at the end of the fiscal year:

a. Accounts Payable
b. Accumulated Depreciation— Equipment
c. Depreciation Expense—Equipment
d. Doyle Bradford, Capital
e. Doyle Bradford, Drawing
f. Equipment
g. Fees Earned
h. Land
i. Salaries Expense
j. Salaries Payable
k. Supplies
l. Supplies Expense

**EXERCISE 4-21**
*Closing entries*
**Objective 4**

Prior to its closing, Income Summary had total debits of $450,750 and total credits of $712,500.

Briefly explain the purpose served by the income summary account and the nature of the entries that resulted in the $450,750 and the $712,500.

**EXERCISE 4-22**
*Closing entries with net income*
**Objective 4**
✓ b. $284,900

After all revenue and expense accounts have been closed at the end of the fiscal year, Income Summary has a debit of $312,600 and a credit of $480,150. At the same date, Sue Alewine, Capital has a credit balance of $142,350, and Sue Alewine, Drawing has a balance of $25,000. (a) Journalize the entries required to complete the closing of the accounts. (b) Determine the amount of Sue Alewine, Capital at the end of the period.

**EXERCISE 4-23**
*Closing entries with net loss*
**Objective 4**

Edessa Services Co. offers its services to individuals desiring to improve their personal images. After the accounts have been adjusted at March 31, the end of the fiscal year, the following balances were taken from the ledger of Edessa Services Co.

| | |
|---|---|
| Emil Carr, Capital | $225,750 |
| Emil Carr, Drawing | 50,000 |
| Fees Earned | 180,700 |
| Wages Expense | 180,000 |
| Rent Expense | 75,000 |
| Supplies Expense | 24,000 |
| Miscellaneous Expense | 6,200 |

Journalize the four entries required to close the accounts.

**EXERCISE 4-24**
*Identify permanent accounts*
**Objective 4**

Which of the following accounts will usually appear in the post-closing trial balance?

a. Accounts Receivable
b. Accumulated Depreciation
c. Cash
d. Depreciation Expense
e. Equipment
f. Estella Hall, Capital
g. Estella Hall, Drawing
h. Fees Earned
i. Supplies
j. Wages Expense
k. Wages Payable

**EXERCISE 4-25**
*Post-closing trial balance*

**Objective 4**

SPREADSHEET    WHAT'S WRONG
               WITH THIS?

✓ *Correct column totals,*
*$107,505*

An accountant prepared the following post-closing trial balance:

**Rhombic Repairs Co.**
**Post-Closing Trial Balance**
**March 31, 2006**

| | | |
|---|---:|---:|
| Cash | 9,225 | |
| Accounts Receivable | 33,300 | |
| Supplies | | 1,980 |
| Equipment | | 63,000 |
| Accumulated Depreciation—Equipment | 19,980 | |
| Accounts Payable | 11,250 | |
| Salaries Payable | | 2,700 |
| Unearned Rent | 5,400 | |
| Angie Hammill, Capital | 68,175 | |
| | 147,330 | 67,680 |

Prepare a corrected post-closing trial balance. Assume that all accounts have normal balances and that the amounts shown are correct.

**EXERCISE 4-26**
*Working capital and current ratio*

**Objective 6**

REAL WORLD

The financial statements for **The Home Depot** are presented in Appendix E at the end of the text.

a. Determine the working capital (in millions) and the current ratio for Home Depot as of February 2, 2003 and February 3, 2002.
b. ▭▭▶ What conclusions concerning the company's ability to meets its financial obligations can you draw from these data?

**EXERCISE 4-27**
*Working capital and current ratio*

**Objective 6**

The following data (in thousands) were taken from recent financial statements of **7 Eleven, Inc.**, a convenience store chain:

| | December 31 | |
|---|---|---|
| | **2002** | **2001** |
| Current assets | $624,176 | $632,247 |
| Current liabilities | 767,210 | 791,700 |

a. Compute the working capital and the current ratio as of December 31, 2002 and 2001. Round to two decimal places.
b. What conclusions concerning the company's ability to meet its financial obligations can you draw from (a)?

**APPENDIX**
**EXERCISE 4-28**
*Adjusting and reversing entries*

On the basis of the following data, (a) journalize the adjusting entries at December 31, the end of the current fiscal year, and (b) journalize the reversing entries on January 1, the first day of the following year.

1. Sales salaries are uniformly $16,200 for a five-day workweek, ending on Friday. The last payday of the year was Friday, December 27.
2. Accrued fees earned but not recorded at December 31, $10,250.

**APPENDIX**
**EXERCISE 4-29**
*Entries posted to the wages expense account*

Portions of the wages expense account of a business are shown at the top of the following page.

a. Indicate the nature of the entry (payment, adjusting, closing, reversing) from which each numbered posting was made.
b. Journalize the complete entry from which each numbered posting was made.

| ACCOUNT | Wages Expense | | | | | | ACCOUNT NO. 53 |
|---|---|---|---|---|---|---|---|
| | | | | | | Balance | |
| Date | Item | Post. Ref. | Dr. | Cr. | | Dr. | Cr. |
| 2006 | | | | | | | |
| Dec. 26 | (1) | 91 | 45,000 | | | 1,102,800 | |
| 31 | (2) | 92 | 18,000 | | | 1,120,800 | |
| 31 | (3) | 93 | | 1,120,800 | | — | — |
| 2007 | | | | | | | |
| Jan. 1 | (4) | 94 | | 18,000 | | | 18,000 |
| 2 | (5) | 95 | 43,000 | | | 25,000 | |

# Problems Series A

**PROBLEM 4-1A**
*Work sheet and related items*

**Objectives 2, 3, 4**

**SPREADSHEET**
**P.A.S.S.**

✓ 2. Net income: $25,100

The trial balance of Dynamite Laundry at July 31, 2006, the end of the current fiscal year, and the data needed to determine year-end adjustments are as follows:

**Dynamite Laundry**
**Trial Balance**
**July 31, 2006**

| | | |
|---|---|---|
| Cash | 2,900 | |
| Laundry Supplies | 7,500 | |
| Prepaid Insurance | 4,800 | |
| Laundry Equipment | 109,050 | |
| Accumulated Depreciation | | 41,100 |
| Accounts Payable | | 6,100 |
| David Duffy, Capital | | 37,800 |
| David Duffy, Drawing | 2,000 | |
| Laundry Revenue | | 165,000 |
| Wages Expense | 71,400 | |
| Rent Expense | 36,000 | |
| Utilities Expense | 13,650 | |
| Miscellaneous Expense | 2,700 | |
| | 250,000 | 250,000 |

a. Wages accrued but not paid at July 31 are $1,200.
b. Depreciation of equipment during the year is $6,800.
c. Laundry supplies on hand at July 31 are $1,750.
d. Insurance premiums expired during the year are $2,400.

**Instructions**
1. Enter the trial balance on a ten-column work sheet and complete the work sheet. Add accounts as needed.
2. Prepare an income statement, a statement of owner's equity (no additional investments were made during the year), and a balance sheet.
3. On the basis of the adjustment data in the work sheet, journalize the adjusting entries.
4. On the basis of the data in the work sheet, journalize the closing entries.

**PROBLEM 4-2A**
*Adjusting and closing entries; statement of owner's equity*

**Objectives 3, 4**

The Xavier Company is a financial planning services firm owned and operated by Kim Bosworth. As of August 31, 2006, the end of the current fiscal year, the accountant for The Xavier Company prepared a work sheet, part of which is shown on the following page.

✓ 2. Kim Bosworth, capital,
Aug. 31: $164,000

**The Xavier Company**
**Work Sheet (Partial)**
**August 31, 2006**

| | Income Statement | | Balance Sheet | |
|---|---|---|---|---|
| Cash ............................... | | | 4,650 | |
| Accounts Receivable ................. | | | 13,960 | |
| Supplies .......................... | | | 2,800 | |
| Prepaid Insurance ................... | | | 2,500 | |
| Land ............................... | | | 60,000 | |
| Buildings ......................... | | | 120,000 | |
| Accumulated Depreciation—Buildings ..... | | | | 72,400 |
| Equipment ......................... | | | 86,090 | |
| Accumulated Depreciation—Equipment .... | | | | 40,900 |
| Accounts Payable ................... | | | | 7,100 |
| Salaries Payable ................... | | | | 1,100 |
| Taxes Payable ...................... | | | | 4,000 |
| Unearned Rent ..................... | | | | 500 |
| Kim Bosworth, Capital ............... | | | | 113,500 |
| Kim Bosworth, Drawing .............. | | | 10,000 | |
| Service Fees Earned .................. | 175,000 | | | |
| Rent Revenue ...................... | 1,500 | | | |
| Salary Expense .................... | 73,000 | | | |
| Depreciation Expense—Equipment ....... | 9,500 | | | |
| Rent Expense ...................... | 8,500 | | | |
| Supplies Expense ................... | 7,650 | | | |
| Utilities Expense ................... | 5,300 | | | |
| Depreciation Expense—Buildings ........ | 5,200 | | | |
| Taxes Expense ...................... | 4,150 | | | |
| Insurance Expense ................... | 1,000 | | | |
| Miscellaneous Expense ............... | 1,700 | | | |
| | 116,000 | 176,500 | 300,000 | 239,500 |
| Net income ....................... | 60,500 | | | 60,500 |
| | 176,500 | 176,500 | 300,000 | 300,000 |

**Instructions**

1. Journalize the entries that were required to close the accounts at August 31.
2. Prepare a statement of owner's equity for the fiscal year ended August 31. There were no additional investments during the year.
3. If the balance of Kim Bosworth, Capital decreased $15,000 after the closing entries were posted, and the withdrawals remained the same, what was the amount of net income or net loss?

*If the working papers correlating with this textbook are not used, omit Problem 4-3A.*

**PROBLEM 4-3A**
*Ledger accounts and work sheet, and related items*

**Objectives 2, 3, 4**

✓ 2. Net income: $18,017

The ledger and trial balance of Lithium Services Co. as of March 31, 2006, the end of the first month of its current fiscal year, are presented in the working papers.

**Instructions**

1. Complete the ten-column work sheet. Data needed to determine the necessary adjusting entries are as follows:
   a. Service revenue accrued at March 31 is $1,500.
   b. Supplies on hand at March 31 are $300.
   c. Insurance premiums expired during March are $150.
   d. Depreciation of the building during March is $625.
   e. Depreciation of equipment during March is $200.
   f. Unearned rent at March 31 is $2,100.
   g. Wages accrued but not paid at March 31 are $501.
2. Prepare an income statement, a statement of owner's equity, and a balance sheet. (*Note:* The owner made an additional investment during the period.)
3. Journalize and post the adjusting entries, inserting balances in the accounts affected.

*(continued)*

4. Journalize and post the closing entries. Indicate closed accounts by inserting a line in both Balance columns opposite the closing entry. Insert the new balance of the capital account.

5. Prepare a post-closing trial balance.

**PROBLEM 4-4A**
*Optional work sheet and financial statements*

Objectives 2, 3, 4

SPREADSHEET
P.A.S.S.

✓ *4. Net loss: $6,720*

Heritage Company offers legal consulting advice to death-row inmates. Heritage Company prepared the following trial balance at April 30, 2006, the end of the current fiscal year:

**Heritage Company**
**Trial Balance**
**April 30, 2006**

| | | |
|---|---:|---:|
| Cash | 3,200 | |
| Accounts Receivable | 10,500 | |
| Prepaid Insurance | 1,800 | |
| Supplies | 1,350 | |
| Land | 50,000 | |
| Building | 136,500 | |
| Accumulated Depreciation—Building | | 50,700 |
| Equipment | 92,700 | |
| Accumulated Depreciation—Equipment | | 36,300 |
| Accounts Payable | | 6,500 |
| Unearned Rent | | 3,000 |
| Shelby Powers, Capital | | 212,500 |
| Shelby Powers, Drawing | 10,000 | |
| Fees Revenue | | 191,000 |
| Salaries and Wages Expense | 96,200 | |
| Advertising Expense | 63,200 | |
| Utilities Expense | 18,000 | |
| Repairs Expense | 12,500 | |
| Miscellaneous Expense | 4,050 | |
| | 500,000 | 500,000 |

The data needed to determine year-end adjustments are as follows:

a. Accrued fees revenue at April 30 are $2,800.
b. Insurance expired during the year is $450.
c. Supplies on hand at April 30 are $650.
d. Depreciation of building for the year is $1,620.
e. Depreciation of equipment for the year is $3,500.
f. Accrued salaries and wages at April 30 are $1,800.
g. Unearned rent at April 30 is $1,500.

**Instructions**
1. **Optional:** Enter the trial balance on a ten-column work sheet and complete the work sheet. Add accounts as needed.
2. Journalize the adjusting entires, adding accounts as needed.
3. Prepare an adjusted trial balance of April 30, 2006.
4. Prepare an income statement for the year ended April 30.
5. Prepare a statement of owner's equity for the year ended April 30. No additional investments were made during the year.
6. Prepare a balance sheet as of April 30.
7. Compute the percent of total revenue to total assets for the year.

**PROBLEM 4-5A**
*Ledger accounts, optional work sheet, and related items*

Objectives 2, 3, 4

The trial balance of Pablo Repairs at December 31, 2006, the end of the current year, is shown at the top of the following page.

4. Prepare an adjusted trial balance.
5. Prepare an income statement, a statement of owner's equity (no additional investments were made during the year), and a balance sheet.
6. Journalize and post the closing entries. (Income Summary is account #33 in the chart of accounts.) Indicate closed accounts by inserting a line in both Balance columns opposite the closing entry.
7. Prepare a post-closing trial balance.

# Continuing Problem

P.A.S.S.

✓ *2. Net income: $2,550*

The unadjusted trial balance of Dancin Music as of May 31, 2006, along with the adjustment data for the two months ended May 31, 2006, are shown in Chapter 3.

**Instructions**
1. Prepare a ten-column work sheet.
2. Prepare an income statement, a statement of owner's equity, and a balance sheet. (*Note:* Shannon Burns made investments in Dancin Music on April 1 and May 1, 2006.)
3. Journalize and post the closing entries. The income summary account is #33 in the ledger of Dancin Music. Indicate closed accounts by inserting a line in both Balance columns opposite the closing entry.
4. Prepare a post-closing trial balance.

# Comprehensive Problem 1

P.A.S.S.

✓ *4. Net income: $17,930*

For the past several years, Kelly Pitney has operated a part-time consulting business from her home. As of April 1, 2006, Kelly decided to move to rented quarters and to operate the business, which was to be known as Hippocrates Consulting, on a full-time basis. Hippocrates Consulting entered into the following transactions during April:

April 1. The following assets were received from Kelly Pitney: cash, $13,100; accounts receivable, $3,000; supplies, $1,400; and office equipment, $12,500. There were no liabilities received.
1. Paid three months' rent on a lease rental contract, $4,800.
2. Paid the premiums on property and casualty insurance policies, $1,800.
4. Received cash from clients as an advance payment for services to be provided and recorded it as unearned fees, $5,000.
5. Purchased additional office equipment on account from Office Station Co., $2,000.
6. Received cash from clients on account, $1,800.
10. Paid cash for a newspaper advertisement, $120.
12. Paid Office Station Co. for part of the debt incurred on April 5, $1,200.
12. Recorded services provided on account for the period April 1–12, $4,200.
14. Paid part-time receptionist for two weeks' salary, $750.
17. Recorded cash from cash clients for fees earned during the period April 1–16, $6,250.
18. Paid cash for supplies, $800.
20. Recorded services provided on account for the period April 13–20, $2,100.
24. Recorded cash from cash clients for fees earned for the period April 17–24, $3,850.
26. Received cash from clients on account, $5,600.
27. Paid part-time receptionist for two weeks' salary, $750.
29. Paid telephone bill for April, $130.

April 30. Paid electricity bill for April, $200.
    30. Recorded cash from cash clients for fees earned for the period April 25–30, $3,050.
    30. Recorded services provided on account for the remainder of April, $1,500.
    30. Kelly withdrew $6,000 for personal use.

### Instructions

1. Journalize each transaction in a two-column journal, referring to the following chart of accounts in selecting the accounts to be debited and credited. (Do not insert the account numbers in the journal at this time.)

| | |
|---|---|
| 11 Cash | 31 Kelly Pitney, Capital |
| 12 Accounts Receivable | 32 Kelly Pitney, Drawing |
| 14 Supplies | 41 Fees Earned |
| 15 Prepaid Rent | 51 Salary Expense |
| 16 Prepaid Insurance | 52 Rent Expense |
| 18 Office Equipment | 53 Supplies Expense |
| 19 Accumulated Depreciation | 54 Depreciation Expense |
| 21 Accounts Payable | 55 Insurance Expense |
| 22 Salaries Payable | 59 Miscellaneous Expense |
| 23 Unearned Fees | |

2. Post the journal to a ledger of four-column accounts.
3. Prepare a trial balance as of April 30, 2006, on a ten-column work sheet, listing all the accounts in the order given in the ledger. Complete the work sheet, using the following adjustment data:
   a. Insurance expired during April is $300.
   b. Supplies on hand on April 30 are $1,350.
   c. Depreciation of office equipment for April is $700.
   d. Accrued receptionist salary on April 30 is $120.
   e. Rent expired during April is $1,600.
   f. Unearned fees on April 30 are $2,500.
4. Prepare an income statement, a statement of owner's equity, and a balance sheet.
5. Journalize and post the adjusting entries.
6. Journalize and post the closing entries. (Income Summary is account #33 in the chart of accounts.) Indicate closed accounts by inserting a line in both Balance columns opposite the closing entry.
7. Prepare a post-closing trial balance.

### Alternative Instructions for P.A.S.S.

Complete the above instructions in the following order: 1, 2, 5 (using the adjustment data in 3), and 4.

# Special Activities

**ACTIVITY 4-1**
*Ethics and professional conduct in business*

Lighthouse Co. is a graphics arts design consulting firm. Robin Dover, its treasurer and vice president of finance, has prepared a classified balance sheet as of July 31, 2006, the end of its fiscal year. This balance sheet will be submitted with Lighthouse's loan application to Central Trust & Savings Bank.

In the Current Assets section of the balance sheet, Robin reported an $80,000 receivable from Ron Knoll, the president of Lighthouse, as a trade account receivable. Ron borrowed the money from Lighthouse in February 2005 for a down payment on a new home. He has orally assured Robin that he will pay off the account receivable within the next year. Robin reported the $80,000 in the same manner on the preceding year's balance sheet.

➤ Evaluate whether it is acceptable for Robin Dover to prepare the July 31, 2006 balance sheet in the manner indicated above.

**ACTIVITY 4-2**
*Financial statements*

The following is an excerpt from a telephone conversation between Pedro Mendoza, president of Goliath Supplies Co., and Natalie Welch, owner of Flint Employment Co.

*Pedro:* Natalie, you're going to have to do a better job of finding me a new computer programmer. That last guy was great at programming, but he didn't have any common sense.

*Natalie:* What do you mean? The guy had a master's degree with straight A's.

*Pedro:* Yes, well, last month he developed a new financial reporting system. He said we could do away with manually preparing a work sheet and financial statements. The computer would automatically generate our financial statements with "a push of a button."

*Natalie:* So what's the big deal? Sounds to me like it would save you time and effort.

*Pedro:* Right! The balance sheet showed a minus for supplies!

*Natalie:* Minus supplies? How can that be?

*Pedro:* That's what I asked.

*Natalie:* So, what did he say?

*Pedro:* Well, after he checked the program, he said that it must be right. The minuses were greater than the pluses . . .

*Natalie:* Didn't he know that supplies can't have a credit balance—it must have a debit balance?

*Pedro:* He asked me what a debit and credit were.

*Natalie:* I see your point.

1. ▭▭▸ Comment on (a) the desirability of computerizing Goliath Supplies Co.'s financial reporting system, (b) the elimination of the work sheet in a computerized accounting system, and (c) the computer programmer's lack of accounting knowledge.

2. ▭▭▸ Explain to the programmer why supplies could not have a credit balance.

**ACTIVITY 4-3**
*Financial statements*

Assume that you recently accepted a position with the Bozeman National Bank as an assistant loan officer. As one of your first duties, you have been assigned the responsibility of evaluating a loan request for $150,000 from Sasquatch.com, a small proprietorship. In support of the loan application, Samantha Joyner, owner, submitted a "Statement of Accounts" (trial balance) for the first year of operations ended December 31, 2006.

1. ▭▭▸ Explain to Samantha Joyner why a set of financial statements (income statement, statement of owner's equity, and balance sheet) would be useful to you in evaluating the loan request.

2. In discussing the "Statement of Accounts" with Samantha Joyner, you discovered that the accounts had not been adjusted at December 31. Analyze the "Statement of Accounts" (shown below) and indicate possible adjusting entries that might be necessary before an accurate set of financial statements could be prepared.

**Sasquatch.com**
**Statement of Accounts**
**December 31, 2006**

| | | |
|---|---:|---:|
| Cash | 4,100 | |
| Billings Due from Others | 30,150 | |
| Supplies (chemicals, etc.) | 14,950 | |
| Trucks | 52,750 | |
| Equipment | 16,150 | |
| Amounts Owed to Others | | 5,700 |
| Investment in Business | | 47,000 |
| Service Revenue | | 147,300 |
| Wages Expense | 60,100 | |
| Utilities Expense | 14,660 | |
| Rent Expense | 4,800 | |
| Insurance Expense | 1,400 | |
| Other Expenses | 940 | |
| | 200,000 | 200,000 |

*(continued)*

3. ▭▬▶ Assuming that an accurate set of financial statements will be submitted by Samantha Joyner in a few days, what other considerations or information would you require before making a decision on the loan request?

**ACTIVITY 4-4**
*Compare balance sheets*

GROUP ACTIVITY    INTERNET

In groups of three or four, compare the balance sheets of two different companies, and present to the class a summary of the similarities and differences of the two companies. You may obtain the balance sheets you need from one of the following sources:

1. Your school or local library.
2. The investor relations department of each company.
3. The company's Web site on the Internet.
4. EDGAR (Electronic Data Gathering, Analysis, and Retrieval), the electronic archives of financial statements filed with the Securities and Exchange Commission.

SEC documents can be retrieved using the EdgarScan™ service from **Pricewater-houseCoopers** at **http://edgarscan.pwcglobal.com**. To obtain annual report information, key in a company name in the appropriate space. EdgarScan will list the reports available to you for the company you've selected. Select the most recent annual report filing, identified as a 10-K or 10-K405. EdgarScan provides an outline of the report, including the separate financial statements, which can also be selected in an Excel® spreadsheet.

**ACTIVITY 4-5**
*Business strategy*

REAL WORLD    INTERNET

**Mohawk Industries** is a leading distributor of carpets and rugs in the United States. The company sells its carpets and rugs to locally-owned, independent carpet retailers, home centers such as **Home Depot** and **Lowe's**, and department stores such as **Sears**. Mohawk's carpets are marked under the brand names that include "Aladdin, Mohawk Home, Bigelow, Custom Weave, Durkan, Karastan, and Townhouse."

1. ▭▬▶ List some factors that increase the demand for carpet.
2. ▭▬▶ From a strategic viewpoint, do you think Mohawk should view itself as a carpet or floorcovering manufacturer? Discuss the advantages and disadvantages of Mohawk viewing itself as a floorcovering manufacturer rather than just a carpet manufacturer.
3. ▭▬▶ Read Mohawk's latest 10-K filing with the **Securities and Exchange Commission** by using EdgarScan (**http://edgarscan.pwcglobal.com**). Does Mohawk view itself as a carpet manufacturer or as a floorcovering manufacturer? Explain.

# Answers to Self-Examination Questions

1. **C** The drawing account, M. E. Jones, Drawing (answer C), would be extended to the Balance Sheet columns of the work sheet. Utilities Expense (answer A), Rent Revenue (answer B), and Miscellaneous Expense (answer D) would all be extended to the Income Statement columns of the work sheet.

2. **D** Cash or other assets that are expected to be converted to cash or sold or used up within one year or less, through the normal operations of the business, are classified as current assets on the balance sheet. Accounts Receivable (answer D) is a current asset, since it will normally be converted to cash within one year. Office Equipment (answer A),

Land (answer B), and Accumulated Depreciation (answer C) are all reported in the property, plant, and equipment section of the balance sheet.

3. **B** The entry to close the owner's drawing account is to debit the owner's capital account and credit the drawing account (answer B).

4. **D** Since all revenue and expense accounts are closed at the end of the period, Fees Earned (answer A), Wages Expense (answer B), and Rent Expense (answer C) would all be closed to Income Summary. Accumulated Depreciation (answer D) is a contra asset account that is not closed.

5. **B**  Since the post-closing trial balance includes only balance sheet accounts (all of the revenue, expense, and drawing accounts are closed), Cash (answer A), Accumulated Depreciation (answer C), and J. C. Smith, Capital (answer D) would appear on the post-closing trial balance. Fees Earned (answer B) is a temporary account that is closed prior to preparing the post-closing trial balance.

# 5

# ACCOUNTING SYSTEMS AND INTERNAL CONTROLS

## objectives

*After studying this chapter, you should be able to:*

1    Define an accounting system and describe its implementation.

2    List the three objectives of internal control, and define and give examples of the five elements of internal control.

3    Journalize and post transactions in a manual accounting system that uses subsidiary ledgers and special journals.

4    Describe and give examples of additional subsidiary ledgers and modified special journals.

5    Apply computerized accounting to the revenue and collection cycle.

6    Describe the basic features of e-commerce.

**C**ontrols are a part of your everyday life. At one extreme, laws are used to govern your behavior. For example, the speed limit is a control on your driving, designed for traffic safety. In addition, you are also affected by many nonlegal controls. For example, you can keep credit card receipts in order to compare your transactions to the monthly credit card statement. Comparing receipts to the monthly statement is a control designed to catch mistakes made by the credit card company. Likewise, recording checks in your checkbook is a control that you can use at the end of the month to verify the accuracy of your bank statement. In addition, banks give you a personal identification number (PIN) as a control against unauthorized access to your cash if you lose your automated teller machine (ATM) card. Dairies use freshness dating on their milk containers as a control to prevent the purchase or sale of soured milk. As you can see, you use and encounter controls every day.

Just as there are many examples of controls throughout society, businesses must also implement controls to help guide the behavior of their employees toward business objectives. For example, some businesses require you to punch a time card when you enter and leave the workplace. This is a control used to verify that you get paid for the actual hours you worked.

In this chapter, we will discuss controls that can be included in accounting systems to provide reasonable assurance that the financial statements are reliable. We will apply the principles of accounting systems design to manual systems as well as computerized accounting systems.

# **B**asic Accounting Systems

**objective  1**

Define an accounting system and describe its implementation.

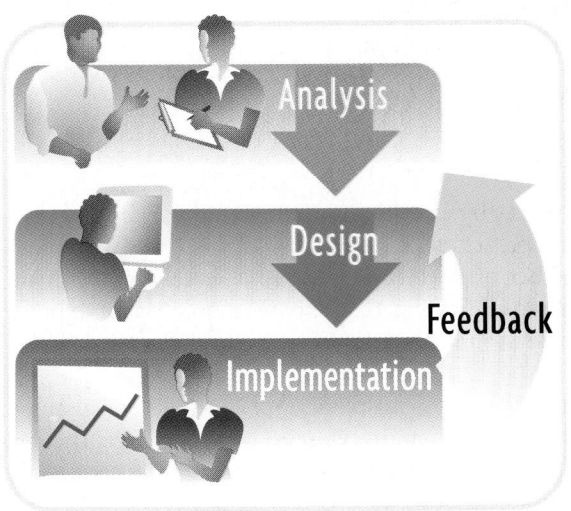

In the four previous chapters, we developed an accounting system for NetSolutions. An **accounting system** is the methods and procedures for collecting, classifying, summarizing, and reporting a business's financial and operating information. The accounting system for most businesses, however, is more complex than NetSolutions'. Accounting systems for large businesses must be able to collect, accumulate, and report many types of transactions. For example, **American Airlines**' accounting system collects and maintains information on ticket reservations, credit card collections, aircraft maintenance, employee hours, frequent-flier mileage balances, fuel consumption, and travel agent commissions, just to name a few. As you might expect, American Airlines' accounting system has evolved as the company has grown.

Accounting systems evolve through a three-step process as a business grows and changes. The first step in this process is **analysis**, which consists of (1) identifying the needs of those who use the business's financial information and (2) determining how the system should provide this information. For NetSolutions, we determined that Chris Clark would need financial statements for the new business. In the second step, the system is **designed** so that it will meet the users' needs. For NetSolutions, a very basic manual system was designed. This system included a chart of accounts, a two-column journal, and a general ledger. Finally, the system is **implemented** and used. For NetSolutions, the system was used to record transactions and prepare financial statements.

Once a system has been implemented, **feedback**, or input, from the users of the information can be used to analyze and improve the system. For example, in later chapters we will see that NetSolutions will expand its chart of accounts as it becomes a more complex business.

Internal controls and information processing methods are essential in an accounting system. **Internal controls** are the

**Hershey Foods** learned the hard way about the importance of careful analysis and design prior to implementing a complex information system. Hershey implemented a $112 million computer system by using a "big-bang" start-up, rather than using a gradual implementation strategy. When the switch was thrown, the company ran into immediate problems shipping orders to customers. As a result, profits were cut by 20%, and product shipments during the all-important Halloween selling season were delayed.

policies and procedures that protect assets from misuse, ensure that business information is accurate, and ensure that laws and regulations are being followed. **Processing methods** are the means by which the system collects, summarizes, and reports accounting information. These methods may be either *manual* or *computerized*. In the following sections, we will discuss internal controls, manual accounting systems that use special journals, and computerized accounting systems.

# Internal Control

List the three objectives of internal control, and define and give examples of the five elements of internal control.

Businesses use internal controls to guide their operations, safeguard assets, and prevent abuses of their systems. For example, assume that you own and manage a lawn care service. Your business uses several employee teams, and you provide each team with a vehicle and lawn equipment. What are some of the issues you would face as a manager in controlling the operations of this business? Below are some examples.

- Lawn care must be provided on time.
- The quality of lawn care services must meet customer expectations.
- Employees must provide work for the hours they are paid.
- Lawn care equipment should be used for business purposes only.
- Vehicles should be used for business purposes only.
- Customers must be billed and bills collected for services rendered.

How would you address these issues? You could, for example, develop a schedule at the beginning of each day and then inspect the work at the end of the day to verify that it was completed according to quality standards. You could have "surprise" inspections by arriving on site at random times to verify that the teams are working according to schedule. You could require employees to "clock in" at the beginning of the day and "clock out" at the end of the day to make sure that they are paid for hours worked. You could require the work teams to return the vehicles and equipment to a central location to prevent unauthorized use. You could keep a log of odometer readings at the end of each day to verify that the vehicle has not been used for "joy riding." You could bill customers after you have inspected the work and then monitor the collection of all receivables. All of these are examples of internal control.

## Objectives of Internal Control

The objectives of internal control are to provide reasonable assurance that:

1. assets are safeguarded and used for business purposes.
2. business information is accurate.
3. employees comply with laws and regulations.

The Association of Certified Fraud Examiners has estimated that businesses will lose over $600 billion, or around 6% of revenue, to employee fraud. The study also showed that falsifying financial statements is the costliest form of fraud, with a median loss of $4.25 million per event.

**Source:** *2002 Report to the Nation: Occupational Fraud and Abuse,* Association of Certified Fraud Examiners.

Internal control can safeguard assets by preventing theft, fraud, misuse, or misplacement. One of the most serious breaches of internal control is employee fraud. ***Employee fraud*** is the intentional act of deceiving an employer for personal gain. Such deception may range from purposely overstating expenses on a travel expense report in order to receive a higher reimbursement to embezzling millions of dollars through complex schemes.

Accurate business information is necessary for operating a business successfully. The safeguarding of assets and accurate information often go hand-in-hand. The reason is that employees attempting to defraud a business will also need to adjust the accounting records in order to hide the fraud.

Businesses must comply with applicable laws, regulations, and financial reporting standards. Examples of such standards and laws include environmental regulations, contract terms, safety regulations, and generally accepted accounting principles (GAAP).

# Elements of Internal Control

How does management achieve its internal control objectives? Management is responsible for designing and applying five *elements of internal control* to meet the three internal control objectives. These elements are:[1]

1. the control environment
2. risk assessment
3. control procedures
4. monitoring
5. information and communication

The elements of internal control are illustrated in Exhibit 1. In this exhibit, the elements of internal control form an umbrella over the business to protect it from control threats. The business's control environment is represented by the size of the umbrella. Risk assessment, control procedures, and monitoring are the fabric that keeps the umbrella from leaking. Information and communication links the umbrella to management. In the following paragraphs, we discuss each of these elements.

•Exhibit 1

ELEMENTS OF INTERNAL CONTROL

CONTROL THREATS

Control Environment
Risk Assessment
Control Procedures
Monitoring

Information and Communication

Management

## Control Environment

A business's control environment is the overall attitude of management and employees about the importance of controls. One of the factors that influences the control environment is *management's philosophy and operating style*. A management that overemphasizes operating goals and deviates from control policies may indirectly encourage employees to ignore controls. For example, the pressure to achieve revenue targets may encourage employees to fraudulently record sham sales. On

---

[1]*Internal Control—Integrated Framework by the Committee of Sponsoring Organizations* of the Treadway Commission (COSO), pp. 12–14. This document provides a professionally sponsored framework for internal control.

How do companies discover fraud? Most fraud is discovered from tips by employees, customers, suppliers, or anonymous sources. Coming in second place is fraud discovered by accident.

**Source:** *2002 Report to the Nation: Occupational Fraud and Abuse,* Association of Certified Fraud Examiners.

the other hand, a management that emphasizes the importance of controls and encourages adherence to control policies will create an effective control environment.

The business's *organizational structure*, which is the framework for planning and controlling operations, also influences the control environment. For example, a department store chain might organize each of its stores as separate business units. Each store manager has full authority over pricing and other operating activities. In such a structure, each store manager has the responsibility for establishing an effective control environment.

*Personnel policies* also affect the control environment. Personnel policies involve the hiring, training, evaluation, compensation, and promotion of employees. In addition, job descriptions, employee codes of ethics, and conflict-of-interest policies are part of the personnel policies. Such policies and procedures can enhance the internal control environment if they provide reasonable assurance that only competent, honest employees are hired and retained.

### Risk Assessment

All organizations face risks. Examples of risk include changes in customer requirements, competitive threats, regulatory changes, changes in economic factors such as interest rates, and employee violations of company policies and procedures. Management should assess these risks and take necessary actions to control them, so that the objectives of internal control can be achieved.

Once risks are identified, they can be analyzed to estimate their significance, to assess their likelihood of occurring, and to determine actions that will minimize them. For example, the manager of a warehouse operation may analyze the risk of employee back injuries, which might give rise to lawsuits. If the manager determines that the risk is significant, the company may take action by purchasing back support braces for its warehouse employees and requiring them to wear the braces.

### Control Procedures

Control procedures are established to provide reasonable assurance that business goals will be achieved, including the prevention of fraud. In the following paragraphs, we will briefly discuss control procedures that can be integrated throughout the accounting system. These procedures are listed in Exhibit 2.

### •Exhibit 2

An accounting clerk for the Grant County (Washington) Alcoholism Program was in charge of collecting money, making deposits, and keeping the records. While the clerk was away on maternity leave, the replacement clerk discovered a fraud: $17,800 in fees had been collected but had been hidden for personal gain.

**Competent Personnel, Rotating Duties, and Mandatory Vacations**    The successful operation of an accounting system requires procedures to ensure that people are able to perform the duties to which they are assigned. Hence, it is necessary that all accounting employees be adequately trained and supervised in performing their jobs. It may also be advisable to rotate duties of clerical personnel and mandate vacations for nonclerical personnel. These policies encourage employees to adhere to prescribed procedures. In addition, existing errors or fraud may be detected.

**Separating Responsibilities for Related Operations**    To decrease the possibility of inefficiency, errors, and fraud, the responsibility for related operations should be divided among two or more persons. For example, the responsibilities for purchasing, receiving, and paying for computer supplies should be divided among three persons or departments. If the same person orders supplies, verifies the receipt of the supplies, and pays the supplier, the following abuses are possible:

1. Orders may be placed on the basis of friendship with a supplier, rather than on price, quality, and other objective factors.
2. The quantity and quality of supplies received may not be verified, thus causing payment for supplies not received or poor-quality supplies.
3. Supplies may be stolen by the employee.
4. The validity and accuracy of invoices may be verified carelessly, thus causing the payment of false or inaccurate invoices.

The "checks and balances" provided by dividing responsibilities among various departments requires no duplication of effort. The business documents prepared by one department are designed to coordinate with and support those prepared by other departments.

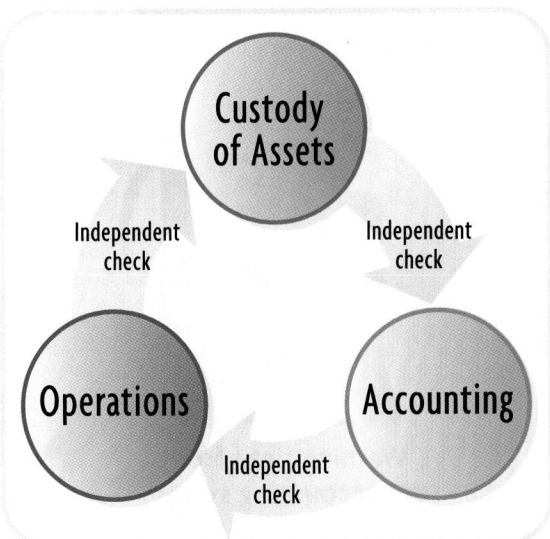

**Separating Operations, Custody of Assets, and Accounting**    Control policies should establish the responsibilities for various business activities. To reduce the possibility of errors and fraud, the responsibilities for operations, custody of assets, and accounting should be separated. The accounting records then serve as an independent check on the individuals who have custody of the assets and who engage in the business operations. For example, the employees entrusted with handling cash receipts from credit customers should not record cash receipts in the accounting records. To do so would allow employees to borrow or steal cash and hide the theft in the records. Likewise, if those engaged in operating activities also record the results of operations, they could distort the accounting reports to show favorable results. For example, a store manager whose year-end bonus is based upon operating profits might be tempted to record fictitious sales in order to receive a larger bonus.

Why is separation of duties considered a control procedure?

------------------------------------

*Internal control is enhanced by separating the control of a transaction from the record-keeping function. Fraud is more easily committed when a single individual controls both the transaction and the accounting for the transaction.*

**Proofs and Security Measures**    Proofs and security measures should be used to safeguard assets and ensure reliable accounting data. This control procedure applies to many different techniques, such as authorization, approval, and reconciliation procedures. For example, employees who travel on company business may be required to obtain a department manager's approval on a travel request form.

Other examples of control procedures include the use of bank accounts and other measures to ensure the safety of cash and valuable documents. A cash register that displays the amount recorded for each sale and provides the customer a printed receipt can be an effective part of the internal control structure. An all-night convenience store could use the following security measures to deter robberies:

1. Locate the cash register near the door, so that it is fully visible from outside the store; have two employees work late hours; employ a security guard.
2. Deposit cash in the bank daily, before 5 p.m.

3. Keep only small amounts of cash on hand after 5 p.m. by depositing excess cash in a store safe that can't be opened by employees on duty.
4. Install cameras and alarm systems.

---

## INTEGRITY IN BUSINESS

### FRAUDULENT AID

In one of the largest frauds ever committed against a university, a former financial aid officer for **New York University** was charged with stealing $4.1 million from the state of New York. The aid officer allegedly falsified over a thousand tuition assistance checks to students who were not entitled to receive aid and who did not know about the checks. The aid officer deposited the bogus checks for personal use. The initial evidence of the fraud was the officer's spending of $785,000 on expensive jewelry.

---

## Monitoring

Monitoring the internal control system locates weaknesses and improves control effectiveness. The internal control system can be monitored through either ongoing efforts by management or by separate evaluations. Ongoing monitoring efforts may include observing both employee behavior and warning signs from the accounting system. The indicators shown in Exhibit 3 may be clues to internal control problems.[2]

•**Exhibit 3**

### CLUES TO POTENTIAL PROBLEMS

**Warning signs with regard to people**

1. Abrupt change in lifestyle (without winning the lottery).
2. Close social relationships with suppliers.
3. Refusing to take a vacation.
4. Frequent borrowing from other employees.
5. Excessive use of alcohol or drugs.

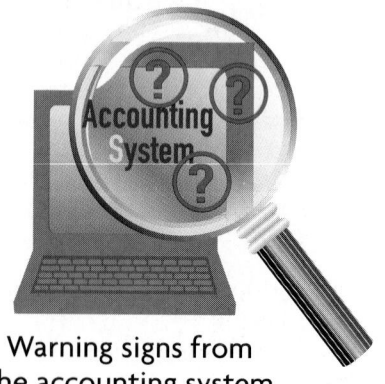

**Warning signs from the accounting system**

1. Missing documents or gaps in transaction numbers (could mean documents are being used for fraudulent transactions).
2. An unusual increase in customer refunds (refunds may be phony).
3. Differences between daily cash receipts and bank deposits (could mean receipts are being pocketed before being deposited).
4. Sudden increase in slow payments (employee may be pocketing the payment).
5. Backlog in recording transactions (possibly an attempt to delay detection of fraud).

---

[2]Edwin C. Bliss, "Employee Theft," *Boardroom Reports*, July 15, 1994, pp. 5–6.

Over $700,000 of child support money disappeared over seven years due to the alleged falsification of checks by an accountant in Indiana's Family and Social Services Administration. The fraud could have been discovered, according to the State Examiner, if the agency reconciled its books, controlled access to blank checks, and used receipts.

Separate monitoring evaluations are generally performed when there are major changes in strategy, senior management, business structure, or operations. In large businesses, internal auditors who are independent of operations normally are responsible for monitoring the internal control system. Internal auditors can report issues and concerns to an audit committee of the board of directors, who are independent of management. In addition, external auditors also evaluate internal control as a normal part of their annual financial statement audit.

## Information and Communication

Information and communication are essential elements of internal control. Information about the control environment, risk assessment, control procedures, and monitoring are needed by management to guide operations and ensure compliance with reporting, legal, and regulatory requirements.

Management can also use external information to assess events and conditions that impact decision making and external reporting. For example, management uses information from the Financial Accounting Standards Board (FASB) to assess the impact of possible changes in reporting standards.

---

## FINANCIAL REPORTING AND DISCLOSURE

### INTERNAL CONTROL REPORT OF MANAGEMENT

The financial statements of public companies are required, under the recently legislated Sarbanes-Oxley Act, to report on management's conclusions about the effectiveness of the company's internal controls and procedures, including any material weaknesses in internal controls. An example of such a report for **Bank of America** follows:

*Report of Management*

*. . . The Corporation maintains a system of internal accounting controls to provide reasonable assurance that assets are safeguarded and that transactions are executed in accordance with management's authorization and recorded properly to permit the preparation of consolidated financial statements in accordance with accounting principles generally accepted in the United States of America. Management recognizes that even a highly effective internal control system has inherent risks, including the possibility of human error and the circumvention or overriding of controls, and that the effectiveness of an internal control system can change with circumstances. However, management believes that the internal control system provides reasonable assurance that errors or irregularities that could be material to the consolidated financial statements are prevented or would be detected on a timely basis and corrected through the normal course of business. As of December 31, 2001, management believes that the internal controls are in place and operating effectively.*

*The **Internal Audit Division** of the Corporation reviews, evaluates, monitors and makes recommendations on both administrative and accounting control and acts as an integral, but independent, part of the system of internal controls.*

*The **independent accountants** were engaged to perform an independent audit of the consolidated financial statements. In determining the nature and extent of their auditing procedures, they have evaluated the Corporation's accounting policies and procedures and the effectiveness of the related internal control system. . . .*

*The Board of Directors discharges its responsibility for the Corporation's . . . financial statements through its **Audit Committee**. The Audit Committee meets periodically with the independent accountants, internal auditors and management. Both the independent accountants and internal auditors have direct access to the Audit Committee to discuss the scope and results of their work, the adequacy of internal accounting controls and the quality of financial reporting. . . .*

As can be seen, internal auditors, independent accountants, and the Audit Committee of the Board of Directors oversee Bank of America's internal control system. Even so, management recognizes these will not guarantee the elimination of fraud.

# Manual Accounting Systems

After the internal control procedures have been developed, the basic processing method must be selected. Accounting systems may be either manual or computerized. Since an understanding of manual accounting systems assists managers in recognizing the relationships that exist between accounting data and accounting reports, we illustrate manual systems first.

In preceding chapters, all transactions for NetSolutions were manually recorded in an all-purpose (two-column) journal. The journal entries were then posted individually to the accounts in the ledger. Such manual accounting systems are simple to use and easy to understand. Manually kept records may serve a business reasonably well when the amount of data collected, stored, and used is relatively small. For a large business with a large database, however, such manual processing is too costly and time-consuming. For example, a large company such as **AT&T** has millions of long-distance telephone fees earned on account with millions of customers daily. Each telephone fee on account requires an entry debiting Accounts Receivable and crediting Fees Earned. In addition, a record of each customer's receivable must be kept. Clearly, a simple manual system would not serve the business needs of AT&T.

When a business has a large number of similar transactions, using an all-purpose journal is inefficient and impractical. In such cases, subsidiary ledgers and special journals are useful. In addition, the manual system can be supplemented or replaced by a computerized system. Although we will illustrate the manual use of subsidiary ledgers and special journals, the basic principles described in the following paragraphs also apply to a computerized accounting system.

## Subsidiary Ledgers

An accounting system should be designed to provide information on the amounts due from various customers (accounts receivable) and amounts owed to various creditors (accounts payable). A separate account for each customer and creditor could be added to the ledger. However, as the number of customers and creditors increases, the ledger becomes awkward to use when it includes many customers and creditors.

A large number of individual accounts with a common characteristic can be grouped together in a separate ledger called a **subsidiary ledger**. The primary ledger, which contains all of the balance sheet and income statement accounts, is then called the **general ledger**. Each subsidiary ledger is represented in the general ledger by a summarizing account, called a **controlling account**. The sum of the balances of the accounts in a subsidiary ledger must equal the balance of the related controlling account. Thus, you may think of a subsidiary ledger as a secondary ledger that supports a controlling account in the general ledger.

> **The sum of the balances of the subsidiary ledger accounts must equal the balance of the related controlling account.**

The individual accounts with customers are arranged in alphabetical order in a subsidiary ledger called the **accounts receivable subsidiary ledger**, or **customers ledger**. The controlling account in the general ledger that summarizes the debits and credits to the individual customer accounts is *Accounts Receivable*. The individual accounts with creditors are arranged in alphabetical order in a subsidiary ledger called the **accounts payable subsidiary ledger**, or **creditors ledger**. The related controlling account in the general ledger is *Accounts Payable*. The relationship between the general ledger and these subsidiary ledgers is illustrated in Exhibit 4.

## Special Journals

One method of processing data more efficiently in a manual accounting system is to expand the all-purpose two-column journal to a multicolumn journal. Each col-

## •Exhibit 4    General Ledger and Subsidiary Ledgers

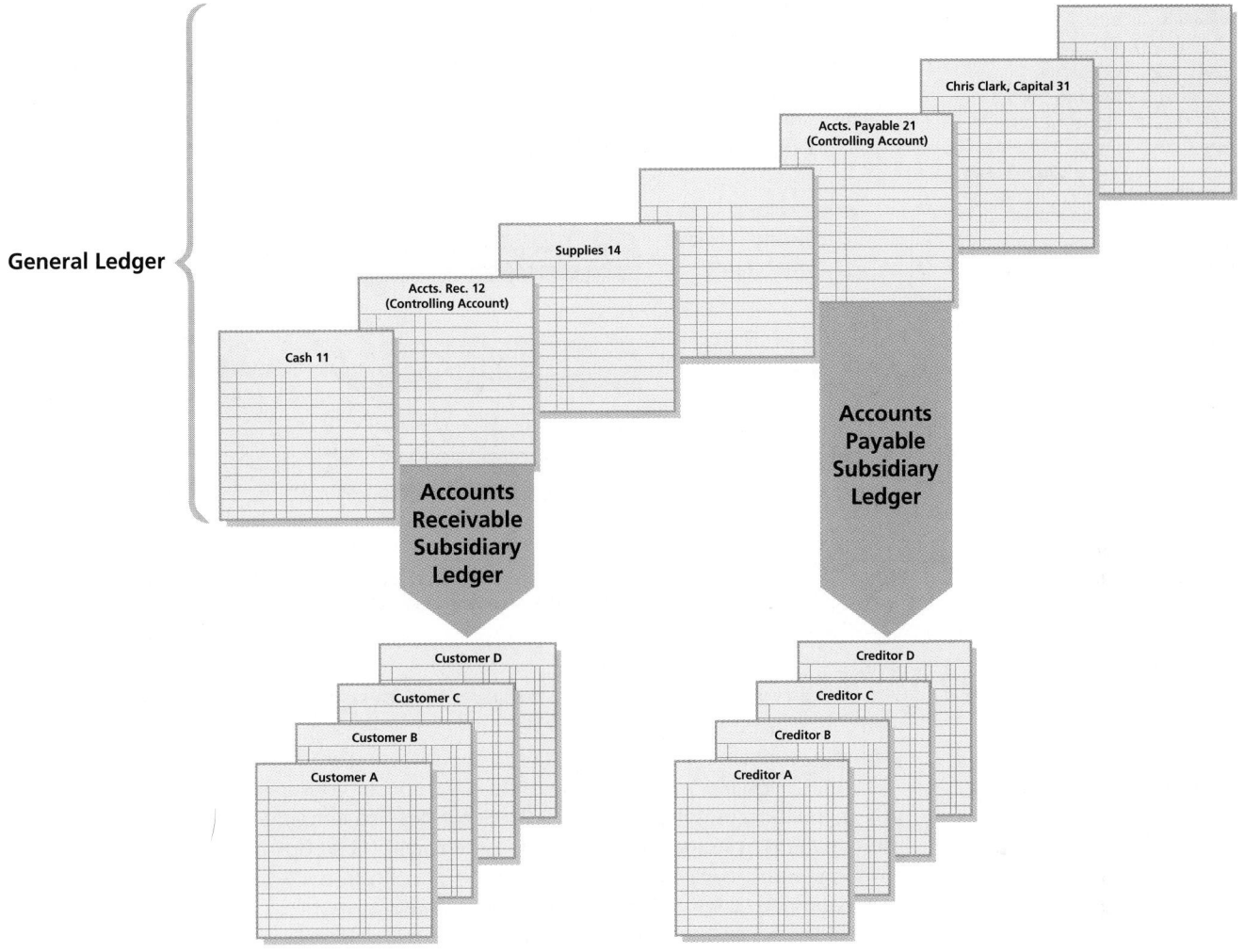

umn in a multicolumn journal is used only for recording transactions that affect a certain account. For example, a special column could be used only for recording debits to the cash account, and another special column could be used only for recording credits to the cash account. The addition of the two special columns would eliminate the writing of *Cash* in the journal for every receipt and every payment of cash. Also, there would be no need to post each individual debit and credit to the cash account. Instead, the *Cash Dr.* and *Cash Cr.* columns could be totaled periodically and only the totals posted. In a similar way, special columns could be added for recording credits to Fees Earned, debits and credits to Accounts Receivable and Accounts Payable, and for other entries that are often repeated.

An all-purpose multicolumn journal may be adequate for a small business that has many transactions of a similar nature. However, a journal that has many columns for recording many different types of transactions is impractical for larger businesses.

> **Special journals are a method of summarizing transactions.**

The next logical extension of the accounting system is to replace the single multicolumn journal with several ***special journals***. Each special journal is designed to be used for recording a single kind of transaction that occurs frequently. For example, since most businesses have many transactions in which cash is paid out, they will likely use a special journal for recording cash payments. Likewise, they will use another special journal for recording cash receipts. Special journals are a method of summarizing transactions, which is a basic feature of any accounting system.

My $35 billion business stems from the mammal *mus musculus*, cousin of Speedy, Mighty, Jerry, Danger, Fievel, Itchy, and Motor. My founder once tried to build an ideal city, an "Experimental Prototype Community of Tomorrow." Near it today is my current version of an ideal city, Celebration, Florida. Many people, especially small ones, think I'm supercalifragilisticexpialidocious. I have a big park scheduled to open in Hong Kong by 2006. My first one opened in 1955. I'm the second-biggest media conglomerate in the world and my TV network is easy as 1-2-3. Who am I? (Go to page 210 for answer.)

The format and number of special journals that a business uses depends upon the nature of the business. A business that gives credit might use a special journal designed for recording only revenue from services provided on credit. On the other hand, a business that does not give credit would have no need for such a journal. In other cases, record-keeping costs may be reduced by using supporting documents as special journals.

The transactions that occur most often in a small- to medium-size service business and the special journals in which they are recorded are as follows:

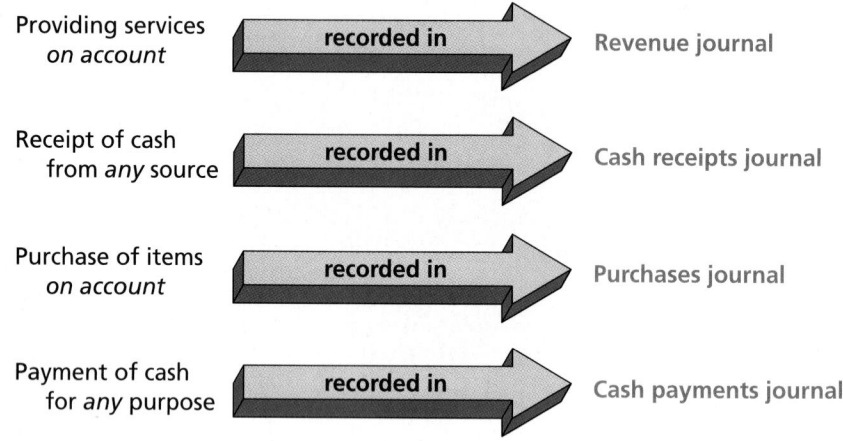

The all-purpose two-column journal, called the **general journal** or simply the **journal**, can be used for entries that do not fit into any of the special journals. For example, adjusting and closing entries are recorded in the general journal.

In the following paragraphs, we illustrate special journals and subsidiary ledgers in a manual accounting system for NetSolutions. To simplify the illustration, we will use a minimum number of transactions. We will focus our discussion on two common operating cycles: (1) the revenue and collection cycle and (2) the purchase and payment cycle. We will assume that NetSolutions had the following selected general ledger balances on March 1, 2006:

| Account Number | Account | Balance |
|---|---|---|
| 11 | Cash | $6,200 |
| 12 | Accounts Receivable | 3,400 |
| 14 | Supplies | 2,500 |
| 18 | Office Equipment | 2,500 |
| 21 | Accounts Payable | 1,230 |

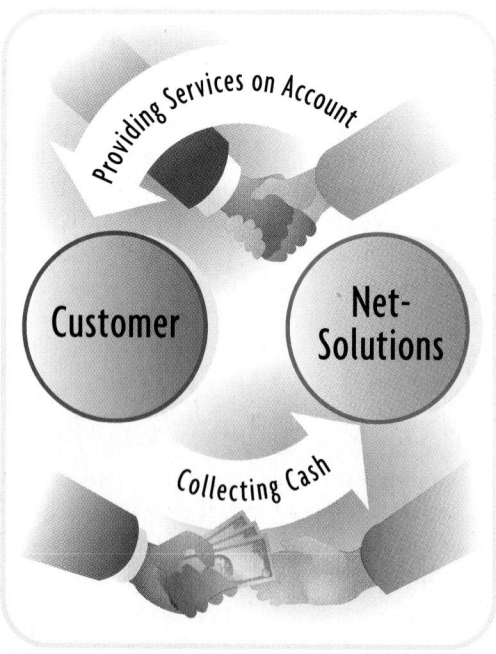

# Manual Accounting System: The Revenue and Collection Cycle

The **revenue and collection cycle** for NetSolutions consists of providing services on account and collecting cash from customers. Revenues earned on account create a customer receivable and will be recorded in a revenue journal. Customers' accounts receivable are collected and will be recorded in a cash receipts journal.

Internal control is enhanced by separating the function of recording revenue transactions in the revenue journal from recording cash collections in the cash receipts journal. For example, if these duties are separated, it is more difficult for one person to embezzle cash collections and manipulate the accounting records.

## Revenue Journal

The *revenue journal* is used only for recording **fees earned on account**. *Cash fees earned would be recorded in the cash receipts journal.* The sale of products is recorded in a **sales journal**, which is similar to the revenue journal. We will compare the efficiency of using a revenue journal with a general journal by assuming that NetSolutions recorded the following revenue transactions in a general journal:

| 2006 | | | | | | |
|---|---|---|---|---|---|---|
| Mar. | 2 | Accounts Receivable—MyMusicClub.com | 12/✔ | 2 2 0 0 00 | |
| | | Fees Earned | 41 | | 2 2 0 0 00 |
| | 6 | Accounts Receivable—RapZone.com | 12/✔ | 1 7 5 0 00 | |
| | | Fees Earned | 41 | | 1 7 5 0 00 |
| | 18 | Accounts Receivable—Web Cantina | 12/✔ | 2 6 5 0 00 | |
| | | Fees Earned | 41 | | 2 6 5 0 00 |
| | 27 | Accounts Receivable—MyMusicClub.com | 12/✔ | 3 0 0 0 00 | |
| | | Fees Earned | 41 | | 3 0 0 0 00 |

> The general journal entry on March 2 is posted as a $2,200 debit to Accounts Receivable in the general ledger, a $2,200 debit to MyMusicClub.com in the accounts receivable subsidiary ledger, and a $2,200 credit to Fees Earned in the general ledger.

For these four transactions, NetSolutions recorded eight account titles and eight amounts. In addition, NetSolutions made 12 postings to the ledgers—four to Accounts Receivable in the general ledger, four to the accounts receivable subsidiary ledger (indicated by each check mark), and four to Fees Earned in the general ledger. These transactions could be recorded more efficiently in a revenue journal, as shown in Exhibit 5. In each revenue transaction, the amount of the debit to Accounts Receivable is the same as the amount of the credit to Fees Earned. Therefore, only a single amount column is necessary. The date, invoice number, customer name, and amount are entered separately for each transaction.

## •Exhibit 5    Revenue Journal

| | | | REVENUE JOURNAL | | | Page 35 | |
|---|---|---|---|---|---|---|---|
| | Date | Invoice No. | Account Debited | Post. Ref. | Accts. Rec. Dr. Fees Earned Cr. | |
| 1 | 2006 Mar. 2 | 615 | MyMusicClub.com | | 2 2 0 0 00 | 1 |
| 2 | 6 | 616 | RapZone.com | | 1 7 5 0 00 | 2 |
| 3 | 18 | 617 | Web Cantina | | 2 6 5 0 00 | 3 |
| 4 | 27 | 618 | MyMusicClub.com | | 3 0 0 0 00 | 4 |
| 5 | 31 | | | | 9 6 0 0 00 | 5 |

The basic procedure of posting from a revenue journal is shown in Exhibit 6. A single monthly total is posted to Accounts Receivable and Fees Earned in the general ledger. Each transaction, such as the $2,200 debit to MyMusicClub.com, must also be posted individually to a customer account in the accounts receivable subsidiary ledger. These postings to customer accounts should be made frequently. In

What is the relationship between the revenue journal and the ledger accounts?

--------------------------------------------

*Revenue transactions are recorded and summarized in the revenue journal. Thus, the revenue journal is the source of postings to the subsidiary and general ledger accounts. The fees earned from services provided on account to individual customers are posted from the revenue journal to the customer subsidiary ledger accounts. At the end of the period, the total of the revenue journal column is then posted as a debit to the accounts receivable controlling account and a credit to the revenue account.*

this way, management has information on the current balance of each customer's account. Since the balances in the customer accounts are usually debit balances, the three-column account form shown in the exhibit is often used.

To provide a trail of the entries posted to the subsidiary ledger, the source of these entries is indicated in the *Posting Reference* column of each account by inserting the letter *R* (for revenue journal) and the page number of the revenue journal. A check mark (✔) instead of a number is then inserted in the *Posting Reference* column of the revenue journal, as shown in Exhibit 6.

If a customer's account has a credit balance, that fact should be indicated by an asterisk or parentheses in the *Balance* column. When an account's balance is zero, a line may be drawn in the *Balance* column.

At the end of each month, the amount column of the revenue journal is totaled. This total is equal to the sum of the month's debits to the individual accounts in the subsidiary ledger. It is posted in the general ledger as a debit to Accounts Receivable

## •Exhibit 6    Revenue Journal Postings to Ledgers

**REVENUE JOURNAL**    Page 35

| | Date | Invoice No. | Account Debited | Post. Ref. | Accts. Rec. Dr. Fees Earned Cr. | |
|---|---|---|---|---|---|---|
| | 2006 | | | | | |
| 1 | Mar. 2 | 615 | MyMusicClub.com | ✔ | 2,200 | 1 |
| 2 | 6 | 616 | RapZone.com | ✔ | 1,750 | 2 |
| 3 | 18 | 617 | Web Cantina | ✔ | 2,650 | 3 |
| 4 | 27 | 618 | MyMusicClub.com | ✔ | 3,000 | 4 |
| 5 | 31 | | | | 9,600 | 5 |
| 6 | | | | | (12) (41) | 6 |

### GENERAL LEDGER

**ACCOUNT**   Accounts Receivable    Account No. 12

| Date | Item | Post. Ref. | Dr. | Cr. | Balance Dr. | Balance Cr. |
|---|---|---|---|---|---|---|
| 2006 | | | | | | |
| Mar. 1 | Balance | ✔ | | | 3,400 | |
| 31 | | R35 | 9,600 | | 13,000 | |

**ACCOUNT**   Fees Earned    Account No. 41

| Date | Item | Post. Ref. | Dr. | Cr. | Balance Dr. | Balance Cr. |
|---|---|---|---|---|---|---|
| 2006 | | | | | | |
| Mar. 31 | | R35 | | 9,600 | | 9,600 |

### ACCOUNTS RECEIVABLE SUBSIDIARY LEDGER

**NAME: MyMusicClub.com**

| Date | Item | Post. Ref. | Dr. | Cr. | Balance |
|---|---|---|---|---|---|
| 2006 | | | | | |
| Mar. 2 | | R35 | 2,200 | | 2,200 |
| 27 | | R35 | 3,000 | | 5,200 |

**NAME: RapZone.com**

| Date | Item | Post. Ref. | Dr. | Cr. | Balance |
|---|---|---|---|---|---|
| 2006 | | | | | |
| Mar. 6 | | R35 | 1,750 | | 1,750 |

**NAME: Web Cantina**

| Date | Item | Post. Ref. | Dr. | Cr. | Balance |
|---|---|---|---|---|---|
| 2006 | | | | | |
| Mar. 1 | Balance | ✔ | | | 3,400 |
| 18 | | R35 | 2,650 | | 6,050 |

and a credit to Fees Earned, as shown in Exhibit 6. The respective account numbers (12 and 41) are then inserted below the total in the revenue journal to indicate that the posting is completed, as shown in Exhibit 6. In this way, all of the transactions for fees earned during the month are posted to the general ledger only once—at the end of the month—greatly simplifying the posting process.

## Cash Receipts Journal

All transactions that involve the receipt of cash are recorded in a **cash receipts journal**. Thus, the cash receipts journal has a column entitled *Cash Dr.*, as shown in Exhibit 7. All transactions recorded in the cash receipts journal will involve an entry in the *Cash Dr.* column. For example, on March 28 NetSolutions received cash of $2,200 from MyMusicClub.com and entered that amount in the *Cash Dr.* column.

## •Exhibit 7  Cash Receipts Journal and Postings

### CASH RECEIPTS JOURNAL — Page 14

| | Date | Account Credited | Post. Ref. | Other Accounts Cr. | Accounts Receivable Cr. | Cash Dr. | |
|---|---|---|---|---|---|---|---|
| 1 | 2006 Mar. 1 | Rent Revenue | 42 | 400 | | 400 | 1 |
| 2 | 19 | Web Cantina | ✔ | | 3,400 | 3,400 | 2 |
| 3 | 28 | MyMusicClub.com | ✔ | | 2,200 | 2,200 | 3 |
| 4 | 30 | RapZone.com | ✔ | | 1,750 | 1,750 | 4 |
| 5 | 31 | | | 400 | 7,350 | 7,750 | 5 |
| 6 | | | | (✔) | (12) | (11) | 6 |

### GENERAL LEDGER

**ACCOUNT  Rent Revenue** — Account No. 42

| Date | Item | Post. Ref. | Dr. | Cr. | Balance Dr. | Balance Cr. |
|---|---|---|---|---|---|---|
| 2006 Mar. 1 | | CR14 | | 400 | | 400 |

**ACCOUNT  Accounts Receivable** — Account No. 12

| Date | Item | Post. Ref. | Dr. | Cr. | Balance Dr. | Balance Cr. |
|---|---|---|---|---|---|---|
| 2006 Mar. 1 | Balance | ✔ | | | 3,400 | |
| 31 | | R35 | 9,600 | | 13,000 | |
| 31 | | CR14 | | 7,350 | 5,650 | |

**ACCOUNT  Cash** — Account No. 11

| Date | Item | Post. Ref. | Dr. | Cr. | Balance Dr. | Balance Cr. |
|---|---|---|---|---|---|---|
| 2006 Mar. 1 | Balance | ✔ | | | 6,200 | |
| 31 | | CR14 | 7,750 | | 13,950 | |

### ACCOUNTS RECEIVABLE SUBSIDIARY LEDGER

**NAME: MyMusicClub.com**

| Date | Item | Post. Ref. | Dr. | Cr. | Balance |
|---|---|---|---|---|---|
| 2006 Mar. 2 | | R35 | 2,200 | | 2,200 |
| 27 | | R35 | 3,000 | | 5,200 |
| 28 | | CR14 | | 2,200 | 3,000 |

**NAME: RapZone.com**

| Date | Item | Post. Ref. | Dr. | Cr. | Balance |
|---|---|---|---|---|---|
| 2006 Mar. 6 | | R35 | 1,750 | | 1,750 |
| 30 | | CR14 | | 1,750 | — |

**NAME: Web Cantina**

| Date | Item | Post. Ref. | Dr. | Cr. | Balance |
|---|---|---|---|---|---|
| 2006 Mar. 1 | Balance | ✔ | | | 3,400 |
| 18 | | R35 | 2,650 | | 6,050 |
| 19 | | CR14 | | 3,400 | 2,650 |

The kinds of transactions in which cash is received and how often they occur determine the titles of the other columns. For NetSolutions, the most frequent source of cash is collections from customers. Thus, the cash receipts journal in Exhibit 7 has an *Accounts Receivable Cr.* column. On March 28, when MyMusicClub.com made a payment on its account, NetSolutions entered *MyMusicClub.com* in the *Account Credited* column and entered *2,200* in the *Accounts Receivable Cr.* column.

The *Other Accounts Cr.* column in Exhibit 7 is used for recording credits to any account for which there is no special credit column. For example, NetSolutions received cash on March 1 for rent. Since no special column exists for Rent Revenue, NetSolutions entered *Rent Revenue* in the *Account Credited* column and entered *400* in the *Other Accounts Cr.* column.

Postings from the cash receipts journal to the ledgers of NetSolutions are also shown in Exhibit 7. This posting process is similar to that of the revenue journal. At regular intervals, each amount in the *Other Accounts Cr.* column is posted to the proper account in the general ledger. The posting is indicated by inserting the account number in the *Posting Reference* column of the cash receipts journal. The posting reference *CR* (for cash receipts journal) and the proper page number are inserted in the *Posting Reference* columns of the accounts.

The amounts in the *Accounts Receivable Cr.* column are posted individually to the customer accounts in the accounts receivable subsidiary ledger. These postings should be made frequently. The posting reference *CR* and the proper page number are inserted in the *Posting Reference* column of each customer's account. A check mark is placed in the *Posting Reference* column of the cash receipts journal to show that each amount has been posted. None of the individual amounts in the *Cash Dr.* column is posted separately.

At the end of the month, all of the amount columns are totaled. The debits should equal the credits. Because each amount in the *Other Accounts Cr.* column has been posted individually to a general ledger account, a check mark is inserted below the column total to indicate that no further action is needed. The totals of the *Accounts Receivable Cr.* and *Cash Dr.* columns are posted to the proper accounts in the general ledger, and their account numbers are inserted below the totals to show that the postings have been completed.

### Accounts Receivable Control and Subsidiary Ledger

After all posting has been completed for the month, the sum of the balances in the accounts receivable subsidiary ledger should be compared with the balance of the accounts receivable controlling account in the general ledger. If the controlling account and the subsidiary ledger do not agree, the error or errors must be located and corrected. The balances of the individual customer accounts may be summarized in a schedule of accounts receivable. The total of NetSolutions' schedule of accounts receivable, $5,650, agrees with the balance of its accounts receivable controlling account on March 31, 2006, as shown below.

| Accounts Receivable— (Controlling) | | NetSolutions Schedule of Accounts Receivable March 31, 2006 | |
|---|---|---|---|
| Balance, March 1, 2006 | $3,400 | MyMusicClub.com | $3,000 |
| Total debits (from revenue journal) | 9,600 | RapZone.com | 0 |
| Total credits (from cash receipts journal) | (7,350) | Web Cantina | 2,650 |
| Balance, March 31, 2006 | $5,650 | Total accounts receivable | $5,650 |

# Manual Accounting System: The Purchase and Payment Cycle

The **purchase and payment cycle** for NetSolutions consists of purchases on account and payments of cash to suppliers. To make purchases of supplies and other

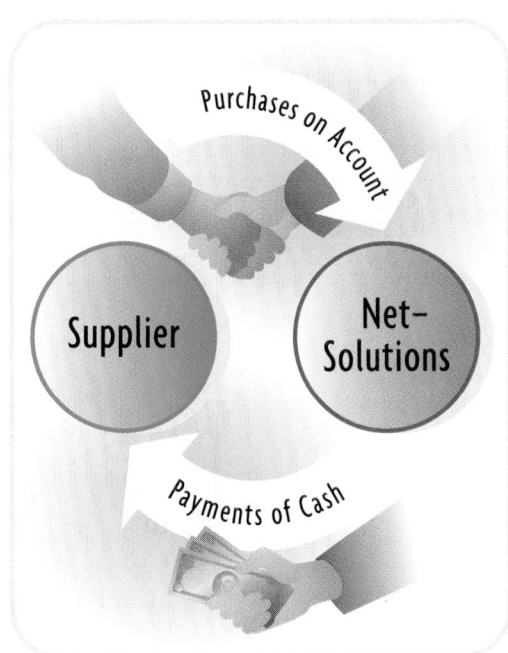

items on account requires establishing a supplier account payable. These transactions will be recorded in a purchases journal. The payments of suppliers' accounts payable will be recorded in the cash payments journal.

Internal control is enhanced by separating the function of recording purchases in the purchases journal from recording cash payments in the cash payments journal. Separating duties in this way prevents an individual from establishing a fictitious supplier and then collecting payments for fictitious purchases from this supplier.

## Purchases Journal

The *purchases journal* is designed for recording all **purchases on account**. *Cash purchases would be recorded in the cash payments journal*. The purchases journal has a column entitled *Accounts Payable Cr.* The purchases journal also has special columns for recording debits to the accounts most often affected. Since Net-Solutions makes frequent debits to its supplies account, a *Supplies Dr.* column is included for these transactions. For example, as shown in Exhibit 8, NetSolutions recorded the purchase of supplies on March 3 by entering *600* in the *Supplies Dr.* column, *600* in the *Accounts Payable Cr.* column, and *Howard Supplies* in the *Account Credited* column.

The *Other Accounts Dr.* column in Exhibit 8 is used to record purchases, on account, of any item for which there is no special debit column. The title of the account to be debited is entered in the *Other Accounts* column, and the amount is entered in the *Amount* column. For example, NetSolutions recorded the purchase of office equipment on account on March 12 by entering *Office Equipment* in the *Other Accounts Dr.* column, *2,800* in the *Amount* column, *2,800* in the *Accounts Payable Cr.* column, and *Jewett Business Systems* in the *Account Credited* column.

Postings from the purchases journal to the ledgers of NetSolutions are also shown in Exhibit 8. The principles used in posting the purchases journal are similar to those used in posting the revenue and cash receipts journals. The source of the entries posted to the subsidiary and general ledgers is indicated in the *Posting Reference* column of each account by inserting the letter *P* (for purchases journal) and the page number of the purchases journal. A check mark (✓) is inserted in the *Posting Reference* column of the purchases journal after each credit is posted to a creditor's account in the accounts payable subsidiary ledger.

At regular intervals, the amounts in the *Other Accounts Dr.* column are posted to the accounts in the general ledger. As each amount is posted, the related general ledger account number is inserted in the *Posting Reference* column of the *Other Accounts* section.

At the end of each month, the amount columns in the purchases journal are totaled. The sum of the two debit column totals should equal the sum of the credit column.

The totals of the *Accounts Payable Cr.* and *Supplies Dr.* columns are posted to the appropriate general ledger accounts in the usual manner, with the related account numbers inserted below the column totals. Because each amount in the *Other Accounts Dr.* column was posted individually, a check mark is placed below the $2,800 total to show that no further action is needed.

## Cash Payments Journal

The special columns for the *cash payments journal* are determined in the same manner as for the revenue, cash receipts, and purchases journals. The determining factors are the kinds of transactions to be recorded and how often they occur.

The cash payments journal has a *Cash Cr.* column, as shown in Exhibit 9 on page 199. All transactions recorded in the cash payments journal will involve an entry in this column. Payments to creditors on account happen often enough to require an *Accounts Payable Dr.* column. Debits to creditor accounts for invoices paid are recorded in the *Accounts Payable Dr.* column. For example, on March 15

# •Exhibit 8  Purchases Journal and Postings

| | | PURCHASES JOURNAL | | | | | | Page 11 |
|---|---|---|---|---|---|---|---|---|
| Date | Account Credited | Post. Ref. | Accounts Payable Cr. | Supplies Dr. | Other Accounts Dr. | Post. Ref. | Amount | |
| 2006 | | | | | | | | |
| 1 | Mar. 3 | Howard Supplies | ✔ | 600 | 600 | | | | 1 |
| 2 | 7 | Donnelly Supplies | ✔ | 420 | 420 | | | | 2 |
| 3 | 12 | Jewett Business Systems | ✔ | 2,800 | | Office Equipment | 18 | 2,800 | 3 |
| 4 | 19 | Donnelly Supplies | ✔ | 1,450 | 1,450 | | | | 4 |
| 5 | 27 | Howard Supplies | ✔ | 960 | 960 | | | | 5 |
| 6 | 31 | | | 6,230 | 3,430 | | | 2,800 | 6 |
| 7 | | | | (21) | (14) | | | (✔) | 7 |

## GENERAL LEDGER

**ACCOUNT  Accounts Payable**  Account No. 21

| Date | Item | Post. Ref. | Dr. | Cr. | Balance |
|---|---|---|---|---|---|
| 2006 | | | | | |
| Mar. 1 | Balance | ✔ | | | 1,230 |
| 31 | | P11 | | 6,230 | 7,460 |

**ACCOUNT  Supplies**  Account No. 14

| Date | Item | Post. Ref. | Dr. | Cr. | Balance |
|---|---|---|---|---|---|
| 2006 | | | | | |
| Mar. 1 | Balance | ✔ | | | 2,500 |
| 31 | | P11 | 3,430 | | 5,930 |

**ACCOUNT  Office Equipment**  Account No. 18

| Date | Item | Post. Ref. | Dr. | Cr. | Balance |
|---|---|---|---|---|---|
| 2006 | | | | | |
| Mar. 1 | Balance | ✔ | | | 2,500 |
| 12 | | P11 | 2,800 | | 5,300 |

## ACCOUNTS PAYABLE SUBSIDIARY LEDGER

**NAME: Donnelly Supplies**

| Date | Item | Post. Ref. | Dr. | Cr. | Balance |
|---|---|---|---|---|---|
| 2006 | | | | | |
| Mar. 7 | | P11 | | 420 | 420 |
| 19 | | P11 | | 1,450 | 1,870 |

**NAME: Grayco Supplies**

| Date | Item | Post. Ref. | Dr. | Cr. | Balance |
|---|---|---|---|---|---|
| 2006 | | | | | |
| Mar. 1 | Balance | ✔ | | | 1,230 |

**NAME: Howard Supplies**

| Date | Item | Post. Ref. | Dr. | Cr. | Balance |
|---|---|---|---|---|---|
| 2006 | | | | | |
| Mar. 3 | | P11 | | 600 | 600 |
| 27 | | P11 | | 960 | 1,560 |

**NAME: Jewett Business Systems**

| Date | Item | Post. Ref. | Dr. | Cr. | Balance |
|---|---|---|---|---|---|
| 2006 | | | | | |
| Mar. 12 | | P11 | | 2,800 | 2,800 |

NetSolutions paid $1,230 on its account with Grayco Supplies. NetSolutions recorded this transaction by entering *1,230* in the *Accounts Payable Dr.* column, *1,230* in the *Cash Cr.* column, and *Grayco Supplies* in the *Account Debited* column.

NetSolutions makes all payments by check. As each transaction is recorded in the cash payments journal, the related check number is entered in the column at the right of the *Date* column. The check numbers are helpful in controlling cash payments, and they provide a useful cross-reference.

**•Exhibit 9**    **Cash Payments Journal and Postings**

## CASH PAYMENTS JOURNAL                                                  Page 7

| | Date | Ck. No. | Account Debited | Post. Ref. | Other Accounts Dr. | Accounts Payable Dr. | Cash Cr. | |
|---|---|---|---|---|---|---|---|---|
| | 2006 | | | | | | | |
| 1 | Mar. 2 | 150 | Rent Expense | 52 | 1,600 | | 1,600 | 1 |
| 2 | 15 | 151 | Grayco Supplies | ✔ | | 1,230 | 1,230 | 2 |
| 3 | 21 | 152 | Jewett Business Systems | ✔ | | 2,800 | 2,800 | 3 |
| 4 | 22 | 153 | Donnelly Supplies | ✔ | | 420 | 420 | 4 |
| 5 | 30 | 154 | Utilities Expense | 54 | 1,050 | | 1,050 | 5 |
| 6 | 31 | 155 | Howard Supplies | ✔ | | 600 | 600 | 6 |
| 7 | 31 | | | | 2,650 | 5,050 | 7,700 | 7 |
| 8 | | | | | (✔) | (21) | (11) | 8 |

### GENERAL LEDGER

**ACCOUNT**  Accounts Payable                **Account No. 21**

| Date | Item | Post. Ref. | Dr. | Cr. | Balance |
|---|---|---|---|---|---|
| 2006 | | | | | |
| Mar. 1 | Balance | ✔ | | | 1,230 |
| 31 | | P11 | | 6,230 | 7,460 |
| 31 | | CP7 | 5,050 | | 2,410 |

**ACCOUNT**  Cash                          **Account No. 11**

| Date | Item | Post. Ref. | Dr. | Cr. | Balance |
|---|---|---|---|---|---|
| 2006 | | | | | |
| Mar. 1 | Balance | ✔ | | | 6,200 |
| 31 | | CR14 | 7,750 | | 13,950 |
| 31 | | CP7 | | 7,700 | 6,250 |

**ACCOUNT**  Rent Expense                   **Account No. 52**

| Date | Item | Post. Ref. | Dr. | Cr. | Balance |
|---|---|---|---|---|---|
| 2006 | | | | | |
| Mar. 2 | | CP7 | 1,600 | | 1,600 |

**ACCOUNT**  Utilities Expense              **Account No. 54**

| Date | Item | Post. Ref. | Dr. | Cr. | Balance |
|---|---|---|---|---|---|
| 2006 | | | | | |
| Mar. 30 | | CP7 | 1,050 | | 1,050 |

### ACCOUNTS PAYABLE SUBSIDIARY LEDGER

**NAME: Donnelly Supplies**

| Date | Item | Post. Ref. | Dr. | Cr. | Balance |
|---|---|---|---|---|---|
| 2006 | | | | | |
| Mar. 7 | | P11 | | 420 | 420 |
| 19 | | P11 | | 1,450 | 1,870 |
| 22 | | CP7 | 420 | | 1,450 |

**NAME: Grayco Supplies**

| Date | Item | Post. Ref. | Dr. | Cr. | Balance |
|---|---|---|---|---|---|
| 2006 | | | | | |
| Mar. 1 | Balance | ✔ | | | 1,230 |
| 15 | | CP7 | 1,230 | | — |

**NAME: Howard Supplies**

| Date | Item | Post. Ref. | Dr. | Cr. | Balance |
|---|---|---|---|---|---|
| 2006 | | | | | |
| Mar. 3 | | P11 | | 600 | 600 |
| 27 | | P11 | | 960 | 1,560 |
| 31 | | CP7 | 600 | | 960 |

**NAME: Jewett Business Systems**

| Date | Item | Post. Ref. | Dr. | Cr. | Balance |
|---|---|---|---|---|---|
| 2006 | | | | | |
| Mar. 12 | | P11 | | 2,800 | 2,800 |
| 21 | | CP7 | 2,800 | | — |

The *Other Accounts Dr.* column is used for recording debits to any account for which there is no special column. For example, NetSolutions paid $1,600 on March 2 for rent. The transaction was recorded by entering *Rent Expense* in the space provided and *1,600* in the *Other Accounts Dr.* and *Cash Cr.* columns.

Postings from the cash payments journal to the ledgers of NetSolutions are also shown in Exhibit 9. The amounts entered in the *Accounts Payable Dr.* column are posted to the individual creditor accounts in the accounts payable subsidiary ledger. These postings should be made frequently. After each posting, *CP* (for cash payments journal) and the page number of the journal are inserted in the *Posting Reference* column of the account. A check mark is placed in the *Posting Reference* column of the cash payments journal to indicate that each amount has been posted.

At regular intervals, each item in the *Other Accounts Dr.* column is also posted individually to an account in the general ledger. The posting is indicated by writing the account number in the *Posting Reference* column of the cash payments journal.

At the end of the month, each of the amount columns in the cash payments journal is totaled. The sum of the two debit totals is compared with the credit total to determine their equality. A check mark is placed below the total of the *Other Accounts Dr.* column to indicate that no further action is needed. When each of the totals of the other two columns is posted to the general ledger, an account number is inserted below each column total.

## Accounts Payable Control and Subsidiary Ledger

After all posting has been completed for the month, the sum of the balances in the accounts payable subsidiary ledger should be compared with the balance of the accounts payable controlling account in the general ledger. If the controlling account and the subsidiary ledger do not agree, the error or errors must be located and corrected. The balances of the individual supplier accounts may be summarized in a schedule of accounts payable. The total of NetSolutions' schedule of accounts payable, $2,410, agrees with the balance of the accounts payable controlling account on March 31, 2006, as shown below.

| Accounts Payable—(Controlling) | | NetSolutions Schedule of Accounts Payable March 31, 2006 | |
| --- | --- | --- | --- |
| Balance, March 1, 2006 | $1,230 | Donnelly Supplies | $1,450 |
| Total credits (from purchases journal) | 6,230 | Grayco Supplies | 0 |
| Total debits | | Howard Supplies | 960 |
| (from cash payments journal) | (5,050) | Jewett Business Systems | 0 |
| Balance, March 31, 2006 | $2,410 | Total | $2,410 |

# Adapting Manual Accounting Systems

**objective 4**

Describe and give examples of additional subsidiary ledgers and modified special journals.

The preceding sections of this chapter illustrate subsidiary ledgers and special journals that are common for a medium-size business. Many businesses use subsidiary ledgers for other accounts, in addition to Accounts Receivable and Accounts Payable. Also, special journals are often adapted or modified in practice to meet the specific needs of a business. In the following paragraphs, we describe other subsidiary ledgers and modified special journals.

## Additional Subsidiary Ledgers

Generally, subsidiary ledgers are used for accounts that consist of a large number of individual items, each of which has unique characteristics. For example, businesses may use a subsidiary equipment ledger to keep track of each item of equipment purchased, its cost, location, and other data. Such ledgers are similar to the accounts receivable and accounts payable subsidiary ledgers that we illustrated in this chapter.

# Modified Special Journals

A business may modify its special journals by adding one or more columns for recording transactions that occur frequently. For example, a business may collect sales taxes that must be remitted periodically to the taxing authorities. Thus, the business may add a special column for *Sales Taxes Payable* in its revenue journal, as shown below.

| | Date | Invoice No. | Account Debited | Post. Ref. | Accts. Rec. Dr. | Fees Earned Cr. | Sales Taxes Payable Cr. | |
|---|---|---|---|---|---|---|---|---|
| | | | **REVENUE JOURNAL** | | | | Page 40 | |
| 1 | 2006 Nov. 2 | 842 | Litten Co. | ✔ | 4 7 7 0 00 | 4 5 0 0 00 | 2 7 0 00 | 1 |
| 2 | 3 | 843 | Kauffman Supply Co. | ✔ | 1 1 6 6 00 | 1 1 0 0 00 | 6 6 00 | 2 |

Some other examples of how special journals may be modified for a variety of different types of businesses are:

- **Farm**—The purchases journal may be modified to include columns for various types of seeds (corn, wheat), livestock (cows, hogs, sheep), fertilizer, and fuel.
- **Automobile Repair Shop**—The revenue journal may be modified to include columns for each major type of repair service. In addition, columns for warranty repairs, credit card charges, and sales taxes may be added.
- **Hospital**—The cash receipts journal may be modified to include columns for receipts from patients on account, from Blue Cross/Blue Shield or other major insurance reimbursers, and Medicare.
- **Movie Theater**—The cash receipts journal may be modified to include columns for revenues from admissions, gift certificates, and concession sales.
- **Restaurant**—The purchases journal may be modified to include columns for food, linen, silverware and glassware, and kitchen supplies.

Regardless of how a special journal is modified, the basic principles and procedures discussed in this chapter apply. For example, the columns in special journals are normally totaled at periodic intervals. The totals of the debit and credit columns are then compared to verify their equality before the totals are posted to the general ledger accounts.

---

## ACCOUNTING SYSTEMS AND PROFIT MEASUREMENT

**A** Greek restaurant owner in Canada had his own system of accounting. He kept his accounts payable in a cigar box on the left-hand side of his cash register, his daily cash returns in the cash register, and his receipts for paid bills in another cigar box on the right. A truly "manual" system.

When his youngest son graduated as an accountant, he was appalled by his father's primitive methods. "I don't know how you can run a business that way," he said. "How do you know what your profits are?"

"Well, son," the father replied, "when I got off the boat from Greece, I had nothing but the pants I was wearing. Today, your brother is a doctor. You are an accountant. Your sister is a speech therapist. Your mother and I have a nice car, a city house, and a country home. We have a good business, and everything is paid for. . . ."

"So, you add all that together, subtract the pants, and there's your profit!"

# Computerized Accounting Systems

Computerized accounting systems have become more widely used as the cost of hardware and software has declined. In addition, computerized accounting systems have three main advantages over manual systems. First, computerized systems simplify the record-keeping process. Transactions are recorded in electronic forms and, at the same time, posted electronically to general and subsidiary ledger accounts. Second, computerized systems are generally more accurate than manual systems. Third, computerized systems provide management current account balance information to support decision making, since account balances are posted as the transactions occur.

How do computerized accounting systems work? We will illustrate the revenue and collection cycle of NetSolutions by using a popular accounting application called QuickBooks®.

As shown in Exhibit 10, the first step is to enter information onto an electronic invoice form, as illustrated for the March 2 MyMusicClub.com invoice (No. 615). An electronic form is a window that appears like a paper form. The form has spaces, or fields, in which to input information about a particular type of transaction. Many of the information spaces have pull-down lists for easy data entry. When the form is completed, it may be printed out and mailed to the customer. In addition, upon completing the invoice form, the software automatically posts the $2,200 debit to the MyMusicClub.com account receivable and the credit to fees earned.

In step two, the collection from the customer is received. Upon collection, the "receive payment" electronic form is opened and completed. In Exhibit 10, this form indicates that a $2,200 payment was collected from MyMusicClub.com on March 28. This amount was applied to invoice 615, as shown by the check mark next to the March 2 date at the bottom of the form. The March 27 invoice of $3,000 remains uncollected, as shown at the bottom of the form. When this screen is completed, a debit of $2,200 is automatically posted to the cash account, and a credit for the same amount is posted to the MyMusicClub.com accounts, causing the balance to be reduced from $5,200 to $3,000.

At any time, managers may request reports from the software. In step three, three such reports are illustrated in Exhibit 10: (1) the customer balance summary, (2) the fees earned by customer summary, and (3) the cash receipts. The reports are shown for March 31, 2006. Notice that the customer balance summary lists the outstanding accounts receivable balances by customer. This is essentially a report providing the details of the accounts receivable subsidiary ledger. It shows essentially the same information as NetSolutions' Schedule of Accounts Receivable on p. 196. The fees earned by customer summary provides a listing of revenue by customer, which is similar to information provided by the revenue journal in a manual system. This listing is created from the electronic invoice form used in the first step of the cycle. The cash receipts report provides a listing of NetSolution's cash receipts during the month. This report is similar to the cash receipts journal in Exhibit 7.

At the end of the month, the manual system posted revenue journal and cash collection totals to the accounts receivable controlling account. In a computerized system, special journals typically are not used. Instead, transactions are recorded in electronic forms, which are automatically posted to affected accounts at the time the form is completed. In a manual system, the controlling account balance can be reconciled to the sum of the individual customer account balances to identify any posting and mathematical errors. The computer, however, does not make posting and mathematical errors. Thus, there are no month-end postings to controlling accounts. Controlling accounts are simply the sum of the balances of any individual subsidiary account balances.

We have illustrated the revenue and collection cycle to help you understand how a portion of a computerized accounting system works. A similar description could

## •Exhibit 10    The Revenue and Collection Cycle in QuickBooks®

1. Record fee by filling out an electronic invoice form.

**Automatic Postings**

Dr. Accounts Receivable—
MyMusicClub.com
   Cr. Revenue

Mail invoice
to customer.

Receive payment

2. Record collection of payment by filling out "receive payment" form.

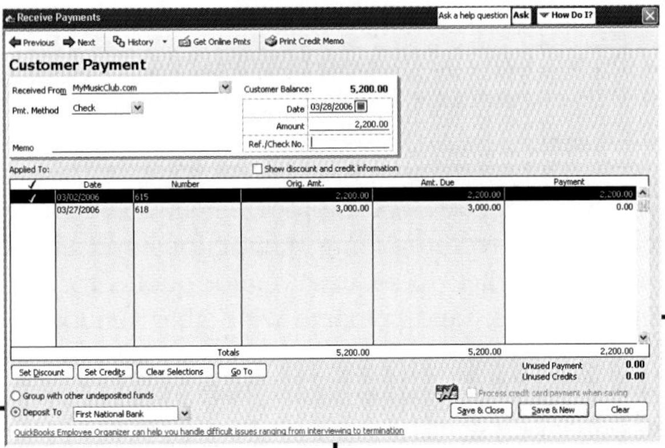

Dr. Cash
   Cr. Accounts Receivable—
       MyMusicClub.com

3. Prepare reports.

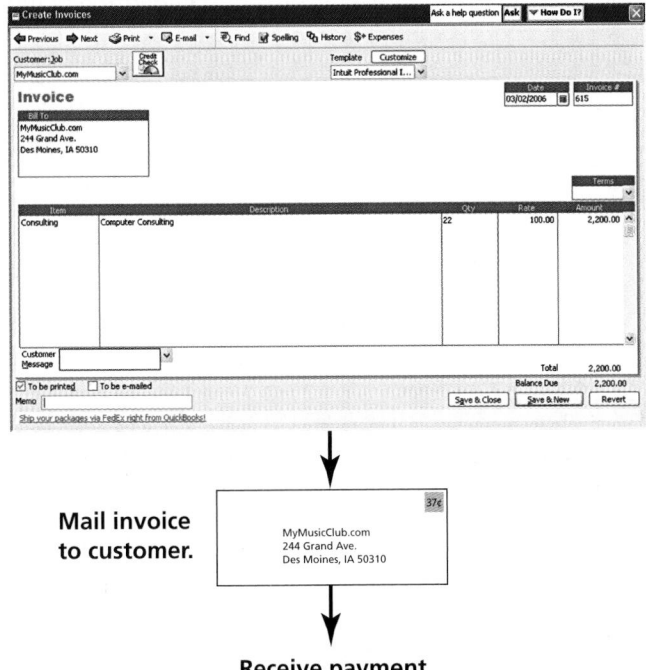

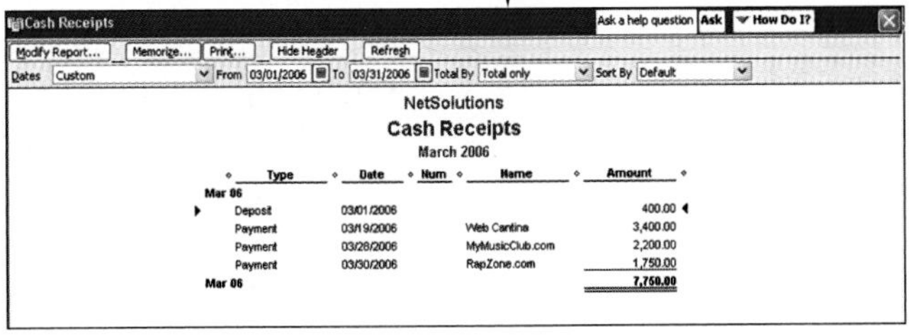

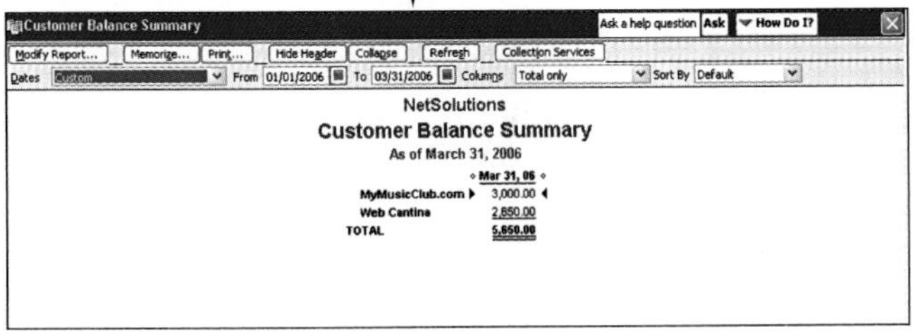

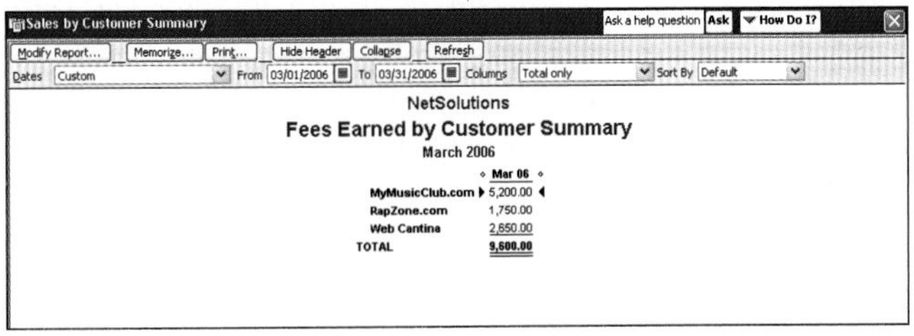

be provided for the purchases and payments cycle. A description of a complete computerized accounting system is beyond our scope. However, a thorough understanding of this chapter provides a solid foundation for applying the accounting system concepts in either a manual or a computerized system.

# E-Commerce

One survey has indicated that over 60% of businesses are embracing e-commerce in some form. Using the Internet to perform business transactions is termed *e-commerce*. When transactions are between a company and a consumer, it is termed B2C (business-to-consumer) e-commerce. Examples of companies engaged in B2C e-commerce include **Amazon.com, Inc.**, **Priceline.com, Inc.**, and **Dell Computer Corp.** The B2C business adds value by allowing the consumer to shop and receive goods at home, rather than going to the store for an item. For example, **Whirlpool Corp.** created its "e-Partners" program so consumers could shop for appliances online. Consumers use the site to order appliances, selecting color and other features. After paying for the appliance online with a credit card, customers can then receive direct delivery from the Whirlpool factory. Thus, the revenue and collection cycle illustrated earlier in the text under the manual system is shortened under e-commerce. For example, Whirlpool receives cash from an Internet transaction *before* the goods are actually shipped.

When transactions are conducted between a company and another company, it is termed B2B (business-to-business) e-commerce. Examples of companies engaged in B2B e-commerce include **Cisco Systems, Inc.**, an Internet equipment manufacturer, and **Bristol-Myers Squibb (BMS)**, a pharmaceutical company. BMS, for example, launched an e-procurement solution for purchasing supplies and equipment from its suppliers. The e-procurement solution streamlines the purchase and payment cycle by automating transactions and eliminating paperwork. BMS uses an Internet "market" to request vendor quotes for supplies. Vendors place bids on the Internet market and compete with other vendors for BMS's business. Using an Internet market in this way, called a *reverse auction*, is fast becoming a popular method for purchasing common items. BMS claims over $90 million in savings by placing its purchase/payment cycle on the Internet.

The Internet creates opportunities for improving the speed and efficiency in conducting transactions. Many companies are realizing these benefits of using e-commerce in their revenue/collection and purchase/payment cycles, as illustrated above. In addition, three more advanced areas where the Internet is being used for business purposes are:

1. **Supply chain management (SCM):** Internet applications to plan and coordinate suppliers.
2. **Customer relationship management (CRM):** Internet applications to plan and coordinate marketing and sales effort.
3. **Product life-cycle management (PLM):** Internet applications to plan and coordinate the product development and design process.

E-commerce also provides opportunities for faster business processes that operate at lower costs. New Internet applications are being introduced continuously as the Internet matures into a preferred method of conducting business.

## SPOTLIGHT ON STRATEGY

### PRODUCT LIFE-CYCLE MANAGEMENT

**W**e have all heard the expression "time is money." One area where this expression is especially true is in reducing the *time to market*, or the time it takes to move from product concept to final production. The shorter this time frame, the faster a company is able to implement strategies, earn profits from an idea, and match the product designs with customer tastes and preferences. New information technology, termed **product life-cycle management (PLM)** software, can help companies reduce the time to market. **Lockheed Martin**, the United States' largest defense contractor, replaced fax machines, clipboards, and spreadsheets with an integrated system for designing the new Joint Strike Fighter, the world's first "paperless plane." Currently, the system puts engineering drawings, manufacturing guidelines, and parts simulations online, so that nearly 3,000 engineers across 80 different companies are able to collaborate on the design. **Procter & Gamble**, the largest consumer packaged goods manufacturer in the United States, created a database of over 250,000 approved product formulas, chemicals, and packaging materials. As a result, P&G chemists were able to find an approved orange dye needed for the new Citrus Breeze® dishwashing liquid, thus saving two months of safety testing. In the past, "only if someone in beauty care talked to someone in fabric-and-home care would that information have been shared." The power behind speed to market is causing product life-cycle management software to be the fastest growing business application segment in North America.

**Source:** Andrew Raskin, "A Faster Ride to Market," *Business 2.0*, October 2002.

# Key Points

**1 Define an accounting system and describe its implementation.**

An accounting system is the methods and procedures for collecting, classifying, summarizing, and reporting a business's financial information. The three steps through which an accounting system evolves are (1) analysis of information needs, (2) design of the system, and (3) implementation of the system's design.

**2 List the three objectives of internal control, and define and give examples of the five elements of internal control.**

Internal control provides reasonable assurance that (1) assets are safeguarded and used for business purposes, (2) business information is accurate, and (3) laws and regulations are complied with. The five elements of internal control are the control environment, risk assessment, control procedures, monitoring, and information and communication.

**3 Journalize and post transactions in a manual accounting system that uses subsidiary ledgers and special journals.**

Subsidiary ledgers may be used to maintain separate records for each customer (the accounts receivable subsidiary ledger) and creditor (the accounts payable subsidiary ledger). Each subsidiary ledger is represented in the general ledger by a summarizing account, called a controlling account. The sum of the balances of the accounts in a subsidiary ledger must agree with the balance of the related controlling account.

Special journals may be used to reduce the processing time and expense of recording a large number of similar transactions. The revenue journal is used to record the sale of services on account. The cash receipts journal is used to record all receipts of cash. The purchases journal is used to record purchases on account. The cash payments journal is used to record all payments of cash. The general journal is used for recording transactions that do not fit in any of the special journals. The use of each special journal and the accounts receivable and accounts payable subsidiary ledgers is illustrated in the chapter.

**4 Describe and give examples of additional subsidiary ledgers and modified special journals.**

Subsidiary ledgers may be maintained for a variety of accounts, such as fixed assets, as well as accounts receivable and accounts payable. Special journals may be modified by adding columns in which to record frequently occurring transactions. For example, an additional column is often added to the revenue journal for recording the collection of sales taxes payable.

**5 Apply computerized accounting to the revenue and collection cycle.**

Computerized accounting systems are similar to manual accounting systems. The main advantages of a computerized accounting system are the simultaneous recording and posting of transactions, the high degree of accuracy, and the timeliness of reporting. An example of the revenue and collection cycle using QuickBooks® is provided in the chapter.

## 6 Describe the basic features of e-commerce.

Using the Internet to perform business transactions is termed e-commerce. B2C e-commerce involves Internet transactions between a business and consumer, while B2B e-commerce involves Internet transactions between a business and another busi-

ness. E-commerce can be used to improve the speed and efficiency of the revenue/collection and purchase/payment cycles. More elaborate e-commerce applications involve planning and coordinating suppliers, customers, and the product design process.

# Key Terms

accounting system (183)
accounts payable subsidiary ledger (190)
accounts receivable subsidiary ledger (190)
cash payments journal (197)

cash receipts journal (195)
controlling account (190)
e-commerce (204)
elements of internal control (185)
employee fraud (184)
general journal (192)

general ledger (190)
internal controls (183)
purchases journal (197)
revenue journal (193)
special journals (191)
subsidiary ledger (190)

# Illustrative Problem

Selected transactions of O'Malley Co. for the month of May are as follows:

a. May 1 Issued Check No. 1001 in payment of rent for May, $1,200.
b. 2 Purchased office supplies on account from McMillan Co., $3,600.
c. 4 Issued Check No. 1003 in payment of freight charges on the supplies purchased on May 2, $320.
d. 8 Provided services on account to Waller Co., Invoice No. 51, $4,500.
e. 9 Issued Check No. 1005 for office supplies purchased, $450.
f. 10 Received cash for office supplies sold to employees at cost, $120.
g. 11 Purchased office equipment on account from Fender Office Products, $15,000.
h. 12 Issued Check No. 1010 in payment of the supplies purchased from McMillan Co. on May 2, $3,600.
i. 16 Provided services on account to Riese Co., Invoice No. 58, $8,000.
j. 18 Received $4,500 from Waller Co. in payment of May 8 invoice.
k. 20 Invested additional cash in the business, $10,000.
l. 25 Provided services for cash, $15,900.
m. 30 Issued Check No. 1040 for withdrawal of cash for personal use, $1,000.
n. 30 Issued Check No. 1041 in payment of electricity and water bills, $690.
o. 30 Issued Check No. 1042 in payment of office and sales salaries for May, $15,800.
p. 31 Journalized adjusting entries from the work sheet prepared for the fiscal year ended May 31.

O'Malley Co. maintains a revenue journal, a cash receipts journal, a purchases journal, a cash payments journal, and a general journal. In addition, accounts receivable and accounts payable subsidiary ledgers are used.

**Instructions**
1. Indicate the journal in which each of the preceding transactions, (a) through (p), would be recorded.

2. Indicate whether an account in the accounts receivable or accounts payable subsidiary ledgers would be affected for each of the preceding transactions.
3. Journalize transactions (b), (c), (d), (h), and (j) in the appropriate journals.

## Solution

| **1.** | Journal | **2.** | Subsidiary Ledger |
|---|---|---|---|
| a. | Cash payments journal | | |
| b. | Purchases journal | | Accounts payable ledger |
| c. | Cash payments journal | | |
| d. | Revenue journal | | Accounts receivable ledger |
| e. | Cash payments journal | | |
| f. | Cash receipts journal | | |
| g. | Purchases journal | | Accounts payable ledger |
| h. | Cash payments journal | | Accounts payable ledger |
| i. | Revenue journal | | Accounts receivable ledger |
| j. | Cash receipts journal | | Accounts receivable ledger |
| k. | Cash receipts journal | | |
| l. | Cash receipts journal | | |
| m. | Cash payments journal | | |
| n. | Cash payments journal | | |
| o. | Cash payments journal | | |
| p. | General journal | | |

**3.**

**Transaction (b):**

### PURCHASES JOURNAL

| Date | Account Credited | Post. Ref. | Accounts Payable Cr. | Office Supplies Dr. | Other Accounts Dr. | Post. Ref. | Amount |
|---|---|---|---|---|---|---|---|
| May 2 | McMillan Co. | | 3 600 00 | 3 600 00 | | | |

**Transactions (c) and (h):**

### CASH PAYMENTS JOURNAL

| Date | Ck. No. | Account Debited | Post. Ref. | Other Accounts Dr. | Accounts Payable Dr. | Cash Cr. |
|---|---|---|---|---|---|---|
| May 4 | 1003 | Freight Expense | | 3 20 00 | | 3 20 00 |
| 12 | 1010 | McMillan Co. | | | 3 600 00 | 3 600 00 |

Transaction (d):

| REVENUE JOURNAL | | | | | |
|---|---|---|---|---|---|
| Date | Invoice No. | Account Debited | Post. Ref. | Accts. Rec. Dr. Fees Earned Cr. | |
| May 8 | 51 | Waller Co. | | 4 5 0 0 00 | |

Transaction (j):

| CASH RECEIPTS JOURNAL | | | | | |
|---|---|---|---|---|---|
| Date | Account Credited | Post. Ref. | Other Accounts Cr. | Accounts Receivable Cr. | Cash Dr. |
| May 18 | Waller Co. | | | 4 5 0 0 00 | 4 5 0 0 00 |

# Self-Examination Questions (Answers at End of Chapter)

1. The initial step in the process of developing an accounting system is called:
   A. analysis
   B. design
   C. implementation
   D. feedback

2. The policies and procedures used by management to protect assets from misuse, ensure accurate business information, and ensure compliance with laws and regulations are called:
   A. internal controls
   B. systems analysis
   C. systems design
   D. systems implementation

3. A payment of cash for the purchase of services should be recorded in the:
   A. purchases journal
   B. cash payments journal
   C. revenue journal
   D. cash receipts journal

4. When there are a large number of individual accounts with a common characteristic, it is common to place them in a separate ledger called:
   A. a subsidiary ledger
   B. a creditors ledger
   C. an accounts payable ledger
   D. an accounts receivable ledger

5. Which of the following would be used in a computerized accounting system?
   A. Revenue journal
   B. Cash receipts journal
   C. Electronic invoice form
   D. Month-end postings to the general ledger

# Class Discussion Questions

1. How does a policy of rotating clerical employees from job to job aid in strengthening the control procedures within the control environment?
2. Why should the responsibility for a sequence of related operations be divided among different persons?
3. Why should the employee who handles cash receipts not have the responsibility for maintaining the accounts receivable records?
4. In an attempt to improve operating efficiency, one employee was made responsible for all purchasing, receiving, and storing of supplies. Is this organizational change wise from an internal control standpoint? Explain.
5. The ticket seller at a movie theater doubles as a ticket taker for a few minutes each day while the ticket taker is on a break. Which control procedure of a business's system of internal control is violated in this situation?
6. Why should the responsibility for maintaining the accounting records be separated from the responsibility for operations?
7. Why would a company maintain separate accounts receivable ledgers for each customer, as opposed to maintaining a single accounts receivable ledger for all customers?
8. What are the major advantages of the use of special journals?
9. In recording 250 fees earned on account during a single month, how many times will it be necessary to write Fees Earned (a) if each transaction, including fees earned, is recorded individually in a two-column general journal; (b) if each transaction for fees earned is recorded in a revenue journal?
10. How many postings to Fees Earned for the month would be needed in Question 9 if the procedure described in (a) had been used; if the procedure described in (b) had been used?
11. During the current month, the following errors occurred in recording transactions in the purchases journal or in posting from it.
    a. An invoice for $900 of supplies from Hoffman Co. was recorded as having been received from Hoffer Co., another supplier.
    b. A credit of $840 to JPC Company was posted as $480 in the subsidiary ledger.
    c. An invoice for equipment of $6,500 was recorded as $5,500.
    d. The Accounts Payable column of the purchases journal was overstated by $2,000.
    How will each error come to the bookkeeper's attention, other than by chance discovery?
12. The Accounts Payable and Cash columns in the cash payments journal were unknowingly overstated by $100 at the end of the month. (a) Assuming no other errors in recording or posting, will the error cause the trial balance totals to be unequal? (b) Will the creditors ledger agree with the accounts payable controlling account?
13. Assuming the use of a two-column general journal, a purchases journal, and a cash payments journal as illustrated in this chapter, indicate the journal in which each of the following transactions should be recorded:
    a. Purchase of supplies for cash.
    b. Purchase of office supplies on account.
    c. Payment of cash on account to creditor.
    d. Purchase of store equipment on account.
    e. Payment of cash for office supplies.
14. What is an electronic form and how is it used in a computerized accounting system?
15. Do computerized systems use controlling accounts to verify the accuracy of the subsidiary accounts?

16. What happens to the special journal in a computerized accounting system that uses electronic forms?

17. How would e-commerce improve the revenue/collection cycle?

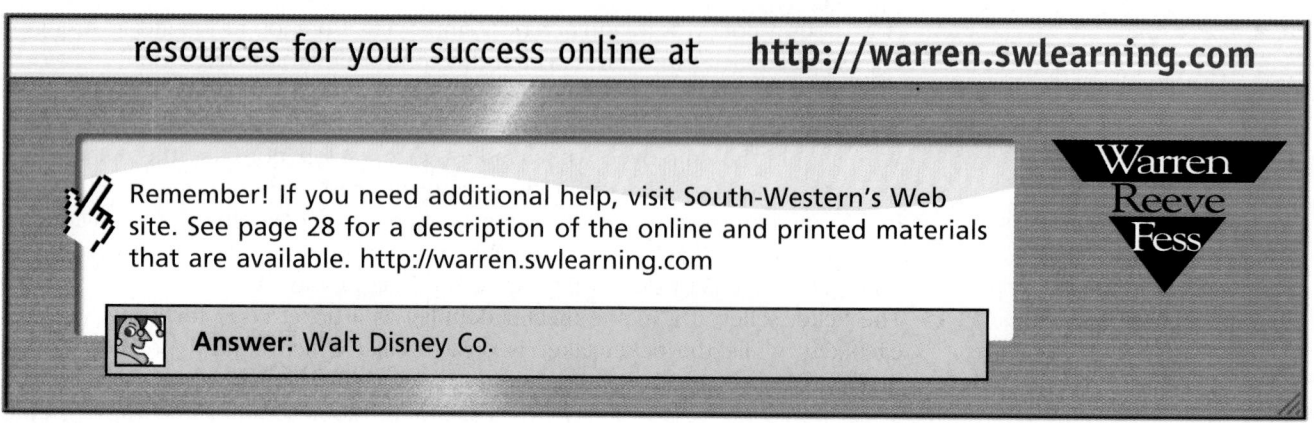

resources for your success online at **http://warren.swlearning.com**

Remember! If you need additional help, visit South-Western's Web site. See page 28 for a description of the online and printed materials that are available. http://warren.swlearning.com

Warren
Reeve
Fess

**Answer:** Walt Disney Co.

# Exercises

**EXERCISE 5-1**
*Internal controls*
**Objective 2**

Barbara Holmes has recently been hired as the manager of Fresh Start Coffee. Fresh Start Coffee is a national chain of franchised coffee shops. During her first month as store manager, Barbara encountered the following internal control situations:

a. Fresh Start Coffee has one cash register. Prior to Barbara's joining the coffee shop, each employee working on a shift would take a customer order, accept payment, and then prepare the order. Barbara made one employee on each shift responsible for taking orders and accepting the customer's payment. Other employees prepare the orders.

b. Since only one employee uses the cash register, that employee is responsible for counting the cash at the end of the shift and verifying that the cash in the drawer matches the amount of cash sales recorded by the cash register. Barbara expects each cashier to balance the drawer to the penny *every* time—no exceptions.

c. Barbara caught an employee putting a box of 100 single-serving tea bags in his car. Not wanting to create a scene, Barbara smiled and said, "I don't think you're putting those tea bags on the right shelf. Don't they belong inside the coffee shop?" The employee returned the tea bags to the stockroom.

State whether you agree or disagree with Barbara's method of handling each situation and explain your answer.

**EXERCISE 5-2**
*Internal controls*
**Objective 2**

Elegance by Elaine is a retail store specializing in women's clothing. The store has established a liberal return policy for the holiday season in order to encourage gift purchases. Any item purchased during November and December may be returned through January 31, with a receipt, for cash or exchange. If the customer does not have a receipt, cash will still be refunded for any item under $50. If the item is more than $50, a check is mailed to the customer.

Whenever an item is returned, a store clerk completes a return slip, which the customer signs. The return slip is placed in a special box. The store manager visits the return counter approximately once every two hours to authorize the return slips. Clerks are instructed to place the returned merchandise on the proper rack on the selling floor as soon as possible.

This year, returns at Elegance by Elaine have reached an all-time high. There are a large number of returns under $50 without receipts.

a. ▭▬▶ How can sales clerks employed at Elegance by Elaine use the store's return policy to steal money from the cash register?

b. 1. ▭▬▶ What internal control weaknesses do you see in the return policy that make cash thefts easier?

   2. Would issuing a store credit in place of a cash refund for all merchandise returned without a receipt reduce the possibility of theft? List some advantages and disadvantages of issuing a store credit in place of a cash refund.

   3. Assume that Elegance by Elaine is committed to the current policy of issuing cash refunds without a receipt. What changes could be made in the store's procedures regarding customer refunds in order to improve internal control?

**EXERCISE 5-3**
*Internal controls for bank lending*
**Objective 2**

First Charter Bank provides loans to businesses in the community through its Commercial Lending Department. Small loans (less than $100,000) may be approved by an individual loan officer, while larger loans (greater than $100,000) must be approved by a board of loan officers. Once a loan is approved, the funds are made available to the loan applicant under agreed-upon terms. The president of First Charter Bank has instituted a policy whereby she has the individual authority to approve loans up to $5,000,000. The president believes that this policy will allow flexibility to approve loans to valued clients much quicker than under the previous policy.

▭▬▶ As an internal auditor of First Charter Bank, how would you respond to this change in policy?

**EXERCISE 5-4**
*Internal controls*
**Objective 2**

REAL WORLD

One of the largest fraud losses in history involved a securities trader for the Singapore office of **Barings Bank**, a British merchant bank. The trader established an unauthorized account number that was used to hide $1.4 billion in losses. Even after Barings' internal auditors noted that the trader both executed trades and recorded them, management did not take action. As a result, a lone individual in a remote office bankrupted an internationally recognized firm overnight.

▭▬▶ What general weaknesses in Barings' internal controls contributed to the occurrence and size of the fraud?

**EXERCISE 5-5**
*Internal controls*
**Objective 2**

REAL WORLD

An employee of **JHT Holdings Inc.**, a trucking company, was responsible for resolving roadway accident claims under $25,000. The employee created fake accident claims and wrote settlement checks of between $5,000 and $25,000 to friends or acquaintances acting as phony "victims." One friend recruited subordinates at his place of work to cash some of the checks. Beyond this, the JHT employee also recruited lawyers, who he paid to represent both the trucking company and the fake victims in the bogus accident settlements. When the lawyers cashed the checks, they allegedly split the money with the corrupt JHT employee. This fraud went undetected for two years.

▭▬▶ Why would it take so long to discover such a fraud?

**EXERCISE 5-6**
*Internal controls*
**Objective 2**

Event Sound Co. discovered a fraud whereby one of its front office administrative employees used company funds to purchase goods, such as computers, digital cameras, compact disk players, and other electronic items for her own use. The fraud was discovered when employees noticed an increase in delivery frequency from vendors and the use of unusual vendors. After some investigation, it was discovered that the employee would alter the description or change the quantity on an invoice in order to explain the cost on the bill.

▭▬▶ What general internal control weaknesses contributed to this fraud?

**EXERCISE 5-7**
*Financial statement fraud*
**Objective 2**

The former chairman, the CFO, and the controller of **Donnkenny**, an apparel company that makes sportswear for Pierre Cardin and Victoria Jones, pleaded guilty to financial statement fraud. These managers used false journal entries to record fictitious sales, hid inventory in public warehouses so that it could be recorded as "sold,"

REAL WORLD

and required sales orders to be backdated so that the sale could be moved back to an earlier period. The combined effect of these actions caused $25 million out of $40 million in quarterly sales to be phony.

a. ▭▶ Why might control procedures listed in this chapter be insufficient in stopping this type of fraud?

b. ▭▶ How could this type of fraud be stopped?

**EXERCISE 5-8**
*Identify postings from revenue journal*
**Objective 3**

Using the following revenue journal for Delta Consulting Co., identify each of the posting references, indicated by a letter, as representing (1) posting to general ledger accounts, or (2) posting to subsidiary ledger accounts.

REVENUE JOURNAL

| Date | Invoice No. | Account Debited | Post. Ref. | Accounts Receivable Dr. Fees Earned Cr. |
|------|------|------|------|------|
| 2006 | | | | |
| Nov. 1 | 772 | Environmental Safety Co. | (a) | $2,625 |
| 10 | 773 | Greenberg Co. | (b) | 1,050 |
| 20 | 774 | Smith and Smith | (c) | 1,600 |
| 27 | 775 | Envirolab | (d) | 965 |
| 30 | | | | $6,240 |
| | | | | (e) |

**EXERCISE 5-9**
*Accounts receivable ledger*
**Objective 3**

SPREADSHEET

✓d. Total accounts
receivable, $6,720

Based upon the data presented in Exercise 5-8, assume that the beginning balances for the customer accounts were zero, except for Envirolab, which had a $480 beginning balance. In addition, there were no collections during the period.

a. Set up a T account for Accounts Receivable and T accounts for the four accounts needed in the customer ledger.
b. Post to the T accounts.
c. Determine the balance in the accounts.
d. Prepare a schedule of accounts receivable at November 30, 2006.

**EXERCISE 5-10**
*Identify journals*
**Objective 3**

Assuming the use of a two-column (all-purpose) general journal, a revenue journal, and a cash receipts journal as illustrated in this chapter, indicate the journal in which each of the following transactions should be recorded:

a. Providing services for cash.
b. Receipt of cash from sale of office equipment.
c. Sale of office supplies on account, at cost, to a neighboring business.
d. Closing of drawing account at the end of the year.
e. Receipt of cash refund from overpayment of taxes.
f. Receipt of cash for rent.
g. Investment of additional cash in the business by the owner.
h. Providing services on account.
i. Receipt of cash on account from a customer.
j. Adjustment to record accrued salaries at the end of the year.

**EXERCISE 5-11**
*Identify journals*
**Objective 3**

Assuming the use of a two-column (all-purpose) general journal, a purchases journal, and a cash payments journal as illustrated in this chapter, indicate the journal in which each of the following transactions should be recorded:

a. Payment of six months' rent in advance.
b. Purchase of office supplies on account.
c. Purchase of office supplies for cash.
d. Adjustment to prepaid rent at the end of the month.
e. Adjustment to prepaid insurance at the end of the month.

f. Purchase of office equipment for cash.
g. Purchase of an office computer on account.
h. Advance payment of a one-year fire insurance policy on the office.
i. Adjustment to record accrued salaries at the end of the period.
j. Adjustment to record depreciation at the end of the month.
k. Purchase of services on account.

**EXERCISE 5-12**
*Identify transactions in accounts receivable ledger*
**Objective 3**

The debits and credits from three related transactions are presented in the following customer's account taken from the accounts receivable subsidiary ledger.

NAME   *Good Times Catering*
ADDRESS   *1319 Elm Street*

| Date | Item | Post. Ref. | Debit | Credit | Balance |
|------|------|------------|-------|--------|---------|
| 2006 | | | | | |
| Nov.  3 | | R50 | 570 | | 570 |
| 9 | | J9 | | 80 | 490 |
| 13 | | CR38 | | 490 | — |

Describe each transaction, and identify the source of each posting.

**EXERCISE 5-13**
*Schedule of accounts receivable*
**Objective 3**

SPREADSHEET

✓ *Accounts Receivable balance, April 30, $6,865*

The revenue and cash receipts journals for Gold Coast Production Co. are shown below. The accounts receivable control account has an April 1, 2006 balance of $4,670, consisting of an amount due from Trask Co.

| | | **REVENUE JOURNAL** | | **Page 16** |
|---|---|---|---|---|
| Date | Invoice No. | Account Debited | Post. Ref. | Accounts Rec. Dr. Fees Earned Cr. |
| 2006 | | | | |
| April  6 | 1 | Central States Broadcasting Co. . . . . . . . . . . . | ✓ | 1,800 |
| 14 | 2 | Star Media Inc. . . . . . . . . . . . . . . . . . . . . . . | ✓ | 7,500 |
| 22 | 3 | Central States Broadcasting Co. . . . . . . . . . . . | ✓ | 2,450 |
| 27 | 4 | Korvette Co. . . . . . . . . . . . . . . . . . . . . . . . . | ✓ | 975 |
| 28 | 5 | Trask Co. . . . . . . . . . . . . . . . . . . . . . . . . . | ✓ | 3,440 |
| 30 | | | | 16,165 |
| | | | | (12) (41) |

| | | **CASH RECEIPTS JOURNAL** | | | **Page 36** | |
|---|---|---|---|---|---|---|
| Date | Account Credited | | Post. Ref. | Fees Earned Cr. | Accts. Rec. Cr. | Cash Dr. |
| 2006 | | | | | | |
| April  6 | Trask Co. . . . . . . . . . . . . . . . . . . . . . . . . | | ✓ | — | 4,670 | 4,670 |
| 11 | Fees Earned . . . . . . . . . . . . . . . . . . . . . . | | | 3,400 | | 3,400 |
| 18 | Central States Broadcasting Co. . . . . . . . . . . . | | ✓ | — | 1,800 | 1,800 |
| 28 | Star Media Inc. . . . . . . . . . . . . . . . . . . . . | | ✓ | — | 7,500 | 7,500 |
| 30 | | | | 3,400 | 13,970 | 17,370 |
| | | | | (41) | (12) | (11) |

Prepare the schedule of accounts receivable and determine that the total agrees with the ending balance of the Accounts Receivable controlling account.

**EXERCISE 5-14**
*Revenue and cash receipts journals*
**Objective 3**

Transactions related to revenue and cash receipts completed by Starcom Inc. during the month of March 2006 are as follows:

Mar. 2. Issued Invoice No. 512 to Conrad Co., $790.
    4. Received cash from CMI, Inc., on account, for $240.
    8. Issued Invoice No. 513 to Orlando Co., $310.

Mar. 12. Issued Invoice No. 514 to Drake Inc., $580.
   19. Received cash from Drake Inc., on account, $530.
   22. Issued Invoice No. 515 to Electronic Central, Inc., $250.
   27. Received cash from Higgins, Inc. for services provided, $70.
   29. Received cash from Conrad Co. for invoice of March 2.
   31. Received cash from McCleary Co. for services provided, $40.

Prepare a single-column revenue journal and a cash receipts journal to record these transactions. Use the following column headings for the cash receipts journal: Fees Earned, Accounts Receivable, and Cash. Place a check mark (✓) in the Post. Ref. Column, as appropriate.

**EXERCISE 5-15**
*Identify postings from purchases journal*
Objective 3

Using the following purchases journal, identify each of the posting references, indicated by a letter, as representing (1) a posting to a general ledger account, (2) a posting to a subsidiary ledger account, or (3) that no posting is required.

**PURCHASES JOURNAL**                                                                Page 49

| | | | | | | Other Accounts Dr. | | |
| Date | Account Credited | Post. Ref. | Accounts Payable Cr. | Store Supplies Dr. | Office Supplies Dr. | Account | Post. Ref. | Amount |
|---|---|---|---|---|---|---|---|---|
| 2006 | | | | | | | | |
| April 4 | Corter Supply Co. | (a) | 4,200 | | 4,200 | | | |
| 6 | Coastal Insurance Co. | (b) | 5,325 | | | Prepaid Insurance | (c) | 5,325 |
| 11 | Keller Bros. | (d) | 2,000 | | | Office Equipment | (e) | 2,000 |
| 13 | Taylor Products | (f) | 1,675 | 1,400 | 275 | | | |
| 20 | Keller Bros. | (g) | 5,500 | | | Store Equipment | (h) | 5,500 |
| 27 | Miller Supply Co. | (i) | 2,740 | 2,740 | | | | |
| 30 | | | 21,440 | 4,140 | 4,475 | | | 12,825 |
| | | | (j) | (k) | (l) | | | (m) |

**EXERCISE 5-16**
*Identify postings from cash payments journal*
Objective 3

Using the following cash payments journal, identify each of the posting references, indicated by a letter, as representing (1) a posting to a general ledger account, (2) a posting to a subsidiary ledger account, or (3) that no posting is required.

**CASH PAYMENTS JOURNAL**                                                          Page 46

| Date | Ck. No. | Account Debited | Post. Ref. | Other Accounts Dr. | Accounts Payable Dr. | Cash Cr. |
|---|---|---|---|---|---|---|
| 2006 | | | | | | |
| Aug. 3 | 611 | Aquatic Systems Co. | (a) | | 4,000 | 4,000 |
| 5 | 612 | Utilities Expense | (b) | 325 | | 325 |
| 10 | 613 | Prepaid Rent | (c) | 3,200 | | 3,200 |
| 17 | 614 | Advertising Expense | (d) | 640 | | 640 |
| 20 | 615 | Derby Co. | (e) | | 1,450 | 1,450 |
| 22 | 616 | Office Equipment | (f) | 3,900 | | 3,900 |
| 25 | 617 | Office Supplies | (g) | 250 | | 250 |
| 27 | 618 | Evans Co. | (h) | | 5,500 | 5,500 |
| 31 | 619 | Salaries Expense | (i) | 1,750 | | 1,750 |
| 31 | | | | 10,065 | 10,950 | 21,015 |
| | | | | (j) | (k) | (l) |

**EXERCISE 5-17**
*Identify transactions in accounts payable ledger account*
Objective 3

The debits and credits from three related transactions are presented in the following creditor's account taken from the accounts payable ledger.

NAME   *Echo Co.*
ADDRESS   *1717 Kirby Street*

| Date | Item | Post. Ref. | Debit | Credit | Balance |
|------|------|------------|-------|--------|---------|
| 2006 | | | | | |
| Feb.  6 | | P34 | | 12,200 | 12,200 |
| 10 | | J10 | 400 | | 11,800 |
| 16 | | CP37 | 11,800 | | — |

Describe each transaction, and identify the source of each posting.

**EXERCISE 5-18**
*Schedule of accounts payable*
**Objective 3**

SPREADSHEET

✓ *Accts. Pay., June 30, $11,580*

The cash payment and purchases journals for Lasting Spring Landscaping Co. are shown below. The accounts payable control account has a June 1, 2007 balance of $1,620, consisting of an amount owed to Augusta Sod Co.

**CASH PAYMENTS JOURNAL**                                                                      Page 31

| Date | Ck. No. | Account Debited | Post. Ref. | Other Accounts Dr. | Accounts Payable Dr. | Cash Cr. |
|------|---------|-----------------|------------|--------------------|--------------------|----------|
| 2007 | | | | | | |
| June  4 | 203 | Augusta Sod Co. | ✓ | | 1,620 | 1,620 |
| 5 | 204 | Utilities Expense | 54 | 325 | | 325 |
| 15 | 205 | Mayfield Lumber Co. | ✓ | | 3,850 | 3,850 |
| 27 | 206 | Owens Fertilizer | ✓ | | 970 | 970 |
| 30 | | | | 325 | 6,440 | 6,765 |
| | | | | (✓) | (21) | (11) |

**PURCHASES JOURNAL**                                                                      Page 22

| Date | Account Credited | Post. Ref. | Accounts Payable Cr. | Landscaping Supplies Dr. | Other Accounts Dr. Account | Post Ref. | Amount |
|------|------------------|------------|--------------------|------------------------|--------------------------|-----------|--------|
| 2007 | | | | | | | |
| June  3 | Mayfield Lumber Co. | ✓ | 3,850 | 3,850 | | | |
| 7 | Gibraltar Insurance Co. | ✓ | 1,100 | | Prepaid Insurance | 17 | 1,100 |
| 14 | Owens Fertilizer | ✓ | 970 | 970 | | | |
| 24 | Augusta Sod Co. | ✓ | 7,340 | 7,340 | | | |
| 29 | Mayfield Lumber Co. | ✓ | 3,140 | 3,140 | | | |
| 30 | | | 16,400 | 15,300 | | | 1,100 |
| | | | (21) | (14) | | | (✓) |

Prepare the schedule of accounts payable and determine that the total agrees with the ending balance of the Accounts Payable controlling account.

**EXERCISE 5-19**
*Purchases and cash payments journals*
**Objective 3**

Transactions related to purchases and cash payments completed by Safety Clean Inc. during the month of May 2007 are as follows:

May 1. Issued Check No. 57 to Liquid Klean Supplies, Inc., in payment of account, $145.
3. Purchased cleaning supplies on account from Industrial Products, Inc., $85.
8. Issued Check No. 58 to purchase equipment from Hamilton Equipment Sales, $450.
12. Purchased cleaning supplies on account from Carver Paper Products, Inc., $205.
15. Issued Check No. 59 to Fountain Laundry Service in payment of account, $115.
17. Purchased supplies on account from Liquid Klean Supplies, $170.
20. Purchased laundry services from Fountain Laundry Service on account, $70.

*(continued)*

May 25. Issued Check No. 60 to Industrial Products, Inc. in payment of May 3rd invoice.

31. Issued Check No. 61 in payment of salaries, $2,900.

Prepare a purchases journal and a cash payments journal to record these transactions. The forms of the journals are similar to those illustrated in the text. Place a check mark (✓) in the Post. Ref. Column, as appropriate. Safety Clean uses the following accounts:

| | |
|---|---|
| Equipment | 18 |
| Salary Expense | 51 |
| Laundry Service Expense | 53 |

**EXERCISE 5-20**
*Error in accounts payable ledger and schedule of accounts payable*

**Objective 3**

**WHAT'S WRONG WITH THIS?**

✓ b. Total accounts payable, $36,650

After Mineral Assay Services Inc. had completed all postings for October in the current year (2006), the sum of the balances in the following accounts payable ledger did not agree with the $36,650 balance of the controlling account in the general ledger.

NAME  *Martinez Mining Co.*
ADDRESS  *1240 W. Main Street*

| Date | Item | Post. Ref. | Debit | Credit | Balance |
|---|---|---|---|---|---|
| 2006 | | | | | |
| Oct.  1 | Balance | ✓ | | | 4,750 |
| 10 | | CP22 | 4,750 | | — |
| 17 | | P30 | | 3,900 | 3,900 |
| 25 | | J7 | 650 | | 2,250 |

NAME  *Cutler and Powell*
ADDRESS  *717 Elm Street*

| Date | Item | Post. Ref. | Debit | Credit | Balance |
|---|---|---|---|---|---|
| 2006 | | | | | |
| Oct.  1 | Balance | ✓ | | | 6,100 |
| 18 | | CP23 | 6,100 | | — |
| 29 | | P31 | | 9,100 | 9,100 |

NAME  *C. D. Greer and Son*
ADDRESS  *972 S. Tenth Street*

| Date | Item | Post. Ref. | Debit | Credit | Balance |
|---|---|---|---|---|---|
| 2006 | | | | | |
| Oct. 17 | | P30 | | 3,750 | 3,750 |
| 27 | | P31 | | 10,000 | 13,750 |

NAME  *Donnelly Minerals Inc.*
ADDRESS  *1170 Mattis Avenue*

| Date | Item | Post. Ref. | Debit | Credit | Balance |
|---|---|---|---|---|---|
| 2006 | | | | | |
| Oct.  1 | Balance | ✓ | | | 8,300 |
| 7 | | P30 | | 4,900 | 13,300 |
| 12 | | J7 | 300 | | 13,000 |
| 20 | | CP23 | 5,500 | | 7,500 |

NAME  *Valley Power*
ADDRESS  *915 E. Walnut Street*

| Date | Item | Post. Ref. | Debit | Credit | Balance |
|---|---|---|---|---|---|
| 2006 | | | | | |
| Oct.  5 | | P30 | | 3,150 | 3,150 |

Assuming that the controlling account balance of $36,650 has been verified as correct, (a) determine the error(s) in the preceding accounts and (b) prepare a schedule of accounts payable from the corrected accounts payable subsidiary ledger.

**EXERCISE 5-21**
*Identify postings from special journals*
**Objective 3**

TechSolve Consulting Company makes most of its sales and purchases on credit. It uses the five journals described in this chapter (revenue, cash receipts, purchases, cash payments, and general journals). Identify the journal most likely used in recording the postings for selected transactions indicated by letter in the following T accounts:

| Cash | | | | Prepaid Rent | | |
|---|---|---|---|---|---|---|
| a. | 11,190 | b. | 9,280 | | c. | 400 |

| Accounts Receivable | | | | Accounts Payable | | |
|---|---|---|---|---|---|---|
| d. | 12,410 | e. | 10,500 | f. | 7,600 g. | 6,500 |

| Office Supplies | | | | Fees Earned | | |
|---|---|---|---|---|---|---|
| h. | 6,500 | | | | i. | 12,410 |

| Rent Expense | |
|---|---|
| j. | 400 |

**EXERCISE 5-22**
*Cash receipts journal*
**Objective 3**

**WHAT'S WRONG WITH THIS?**

The following cash receipts journal headings have been suggested for a small service firm. List the errors you find in the headings.

| | | | CASH RECEIPTS JOURNAL | | | Page 12 |
|---|---|---|---|---|---|---|
| Date | Account Credited | Post. Ref. | Fees Earned Cr. | Accounts Rec. Cr. | Cash Cr. | Other Accounts Dr. |

**EXERCISE 5-23**
*Modified special journals*
**Objectives 3, 4**
✓ c. 2. $987

Chen Consulting Services, Inc. was established on June 15, 2006. The clients for whom Chen provided consulting services during the remainder of June are listed below. These clients pay Chen the amount indicated plus a 5% sales tax.

June 16. A. Sommerfeld on account, Invoice No. 1, $300 plus tax.
    19. K. Lee, Invoice No. 2, $120 plus tax.
    21. J. Koss, Invoice No. 3, $80 plus tax.
    22. D. Jeffries, Invoice No. 4, $120 plus tax.
    24. K. Sallinger, in exchange for office supplies having a value of $160, plus tax.
    26. J. Koss, Invoice No. 5, $260 plus tax.
    28. K. Lee, Invoice No. 6, $60 plus tax.

a. Journalize the transactions for June, using a three-column revenue journal and a two-column general journal. Post the customer accounts in the accounts receivable subsidiary ledger and insert the balance immediately after recording each entry.
b. Post the general journal and the revenue journal to the following general ledger accounts, inserting account balances only after the last postings:

    12   Accounts Receivable
    14   Office Supplies
    22   Sales Tax Payable
    41   Fees Earned

c. 1. What is the sum of the balances in the accounts receivable subsidiary ledger at June 30?
   2. What is the balance of the controlling account at June 30?

**EXERCISE 5-24**
*Computerized accounting systems*

**Objective 5**

Most computerized accounting systems use electronic forms to record transaction information, such as the invoice form illustrated in Exhibit 10.

a. Identify the key input fields (spaces) in an electronic invoice form.
b. What accounts are posted from an electronic invoice form?
c. Why aren't special journal totals posted to control accounts at the end of the month in an electronic accounting system?

# Problems Series A

**PROBLEM 5-1A**
*Revenue journal; accounts receivable and general ledgers*

**Objective 3**

SPREADSHEET

✓1. Revenue journal, total fees earned, $10,715

SafeGuard Security Services was established on August 15, 2006, to provide security services. The services provided during the remainder of the month are listed below.

Aug. 18. Jacob Co., Invoice No. 1, $920 on account.
      20. Ro-Gain Co., Invoice No. 2, $650 on account.
      22. Great Northern Co., Invoice No. 3, $2,480 on account.
      27. Carson Co., Invoice No. 4, $1,870 on account.
      28. Bower Co., Invoice No. 5, $950 on account.
      28. Ro-Gain Co., $575 in exchange for supplies.
      30. Ro-Gain Co., Invoice No. 6, $2,860 on account.
      31. Great Northern Co., Invoice No. 7, $985 on account.

**Instructions**

1. Journalize the transactions for August, using a single-column revenue journal and a two-column general journal. Post to the following customer accounts in the accounts receivable ledger, and insert the balance immediately after recording each entry: Bower Co.; Carson Co.; Great Northern Co.; Jacob Co.; Ro-Gain Co.
2. Post the revenue journal to the following accounts in the general ledger, inserting the account balances only after the last postings:

| 12 | Accounts Receivable |
|----|---------------------|
| 14 | Supplies |
| 41 | Fees Earned |

3. a. What is the sum of the balances of the accounts in the subsidiary ledger at August 31?
   b. What is the balance of the controlling account at August 31?
4. Assume that on September 1, the state in which SafeGuard operates begins requiring that sales tax be collected on accounting services. Briefly explain how the revenue journal may be modified to accommodate sales of services on account requiring the collection of a state sales tax.

**PROBLEM 5-2A**
*Revenue and cash receipts journals; accounts receivable and general ledgers*

**Objective 3**

P.A.S.S.

✓3. Total cash receipts, $30,410

Transactions related to revenue and cash receipts completed by Broadway Engineering Services during the period November 2–30, 2006, are as follows:

Nov. 2. Issued Invoice No. 717 to Yamura Co., $6,420.
      3. Received cash from AGI Co. for the balance owed on its account.
      7. Issued Invoice No. 718 to Dover Co., $4,120.
     10. Issued Invoice No. 719 to Ross and Son, $10,140.
         *Post revenue and collections to the accounts receivable subsidiary ledger.*
     14. Received cash from Dover Co. for the balance owed on November 1.
     16. Issued Invoice No. 720 to Dover Co., $8,320.
         *Post revenue and collections to the accounts receivable subsidiary ledger.*
     19. Received cash from Yamura Co. for the balance due on invoice of November 2.
     20. Received cash from Dover Co. for invoice of November 7.
     23. Issued Invoice No. 721 to AGI Co., $8,950.

Nov. 30. Recorded cash fees earned, $4,550.

30. Received office equipment of $9,000 in partial settlement of balance due on the Ross and Son account.

*Post revenue and collections to the accounts receivable subsidiary ledger.*

## Instructions

1. Insert the following balances in the general ledger as of November 1:

| 11 | Cash | $18,940 |
|----|------|---------|
| 12 | Accounts Receivable | 15,320 |
| 18 | Office Equipment | 32,600 |
| 41 | Fees Earned | — |

2. Insert the following balances in the accounts receivable subsidiary ledger as of November 1:

| AGI Co. | $12,340 |
|---------|---------|
| Dover Co. | 2,980 |
| Ross and Son | — |
| Yamura Co. | — |

3. Prepare a single-column revenue journal and a cash receipts journal. Use the following column headings for the cash receipts journal: Fees Earned, Accounts Receivable, and Cash. The Fees Earned column is used to record cash fees. Insert a check mark (✔) in the Post. Ref. Column.

4. Using the two special journals and the two-column general journal, journalize the transactions for November. Post to the accounts receivable subsidiary ledger, and insert the balances at the points indicated in the narrative of transactions. Determine the balance in the customer's account before recording a cash receipt.

5. Total each of the columns of the special journals, and post the individual entries and totals to the general ledger. Insert account balances after the last posting.

6. Determine that the subsidiary ledger agrees with the controlling account in the general ledger.

**PROBLEM 5-3A**
*Purchases, accounts payable account, and accounts payable ledger*

**Objective 3**

**P.A.S.S.**

✔ *3. Total accounts payable credit, $23,660*

Arc-Tangent Surveyors provides survey work for construction projects. The office staff use office supplies, while surveying crews use field supplies. Purchases on account completed by Arc-Tangent Surveyors during May 2006 are as follows:

May 1. Purchased field supplies on account from Wendell Co., $3,720.

3. Purchased office supplies on account from Lassiter Co., $320.

8. Purchased field supplies on account from Timberland Supply, $2,010.

12. Purchased field supplies on account from Wendell Co., $2,000.

15. Purchased office supplies on account from J-Mart Co., $485.

19. Purchased office equipment on account from Eskew Co., $6,500.

23. Purchased field supplies on account from Timberland Supply, $2,450.

26. Purchased office supplies on account from J-Mart Co., $575.

30. Purchased field supplies on account from Timberland Supply, $5,600.

## Instructions

1. Insert the following balances in the general ledger as of May 1:

| 14 | Field Supplies | $ 5,300 |
|----|----------------|---------|
| 15 | Office Supplies | 1,230 |
| 18 | Office Equipment | 18,400 |
| 21 | Accounts Payable | 3,240 |

2. Insert the following balances in the accounts payable subsidiary ledger as of May 1:

| Eskew Co. | $2,200 |
|-----------|--------|
| J-Mart Co. | 620 |
| Lassiter Co. | 420 |
| Timberland Supply | — |
| Wendell Co. | — |

3. Journalize the transactions for May, using a purchases journal similar to the one illustrated in this chapter. Prepare the purchases journal with columns for Accounts Payable, Field Supplies, Office Supplies, and Other Accounts. Post to the creditor accounts in the accounts payable ledger immediately after each entry.
4. Post the purchases journal to the accounts in the general ledger.
5. a. What is the sum of the balances in the subsidiary ledger at May 31?
   b. What is the balance of the controlling account at May 31?

**PROBLEM 5-4A**
*Purchases and cash payments journals; accounts payable and general ledgers*

**Objective 3**

**P.A.S.S.**

✓ *1. Total cash payments, $111,400*

Black Gold Exploration Co. was established on March 15, 2006, to provide oil-drilling services. Black Gold uses field equipment (rigs and pipe) and field supplies (drill bits and lubricants) in its operations. Transactions related to purchases and cash payments during the remainder of March are as follows:

Mar. 16. Issued Check No. 1 in payment of rent for the remainder of March, $2,400.
   16. Purchased field equipment on account from PMI Sales, Inc., $32,400.
   17. Purchased field supplies on account from Culver Supply Co., $12,300.
   18. Issued Check No. 2 in payment of field supplies, $1,400, and office supplies, $440.
   20. Purchased office supplies on account from Castle Office Supply Co., $3,060.
      *Post the journals to the accounts payable subsidiary ledger.*
   24. Issued Check No. 3 to PMI Sales, Inc., in payment of March 16 invoice.
   26. Issued Check No. 4 to Culver Supply Co. in payment of March 17 invoice.
   28. Issued Check No. 5 to purchase land from the owner, $38,000.
   28. Purchased office supplies on account from Castle Office Supply Co., $3,600.
      *Post the journals to the accounts payable subsidiary ledger.*
   30. Purchased the following from PMI Sales, Inc. on account: field supplies, $18,500, and office equipment, $16,400.
   30. Issued Check No. 6 to Castle Office Supply Co. in payment of March 20 invoice.
   30. Purchased field supplies on account from Culver Supply Co., $9,200.
   31. Issued Check No. 7 in payment of salaries, $21,400.
   31. Acquired land in exchange for field equipment having a cost of $13,100.
      *Post the journals to the accounts payable subsidiary ledger.*

**Instructions**

1. Journalize the transactions for March. Use a purchases journal and a cash payments journal, similar to those illustrated in this chapter, and a two-column general journal. Set debit columns for Field Supplies, Office Supplies, and Other Accounts in the purchases journal. Refer to the following partial chart of accounts:

| | | | |
|---|---|---|---|
| 11 | Cash | 19 | Land |
| 14 | Field Supplies | 21 | Accounts Payable |
| 15 | Office Supplies | 61 | Salary Expense |
| 17 | Field Equipment | 71 | Rent Expense |
| 18 | Office Equipment | | |

At the points indicated in the narrative of transactions, post to the following accounts in the accounts payable ledger:

Castle Office Supply Co.
Culver Supply Co.
PMI Sales, Inc.

2. Post the individual entries (Other Accounts columns of the purchases journal and the cash payments journal; both columns of the general journal) to the appropriate general ledger accounts.

3. Total each of the columns of the purchases journal and the cash payments journal, and post the appropriate totals to the general ledger. (Because the problem does not include transactions related to cash receipts, the cash account in the ledger will have a credit balance.)
4. Prepare a schedule of accounts payable.

**PROBLEM 5-5A**
*All journals and general ledger; trial balance*

**Objective 3**

**P.A.S.S.**

✓ *2. Total cash receipts, $75,095*

The transactions completed by Paul Revere Courier Company during May 2006, the first month of the fiscal year, were as follows:

May 1. Issued Check No. 205 for May rent, $900.
2. Purchased a vehicle on account from McIntyre Sales Co., $26,800.
3. Purchased office equipment on account from Office Mate, Inc., $4,500.
5. Issued Invoice No. 91 to Martin Co., $7,230.
6. Received check for $6,245 from Baker Co. in payment of invoice.
7. Issued Invoice No. 92 to Trent Co., $4,340.
9. Issued Check No. 206 for fuel expense, $680.
10. Received check for $10,890 from Sing Co. in payment of invoice.
10. Issued Check No. 207 to Office City in payment of $510 invoice.
10. Issued Check No. 208 to Bastille Co. in payment of $2,010 invoice.
11. Issued Invoice No. 93 to Joy Co., $5,200.
11. Issued Check No. 209 to Porter Co. in payment of $270 invoice.
12. Received check for $7,230 from Martin Co. in payment of invoice.
13. Issued Check No. 210 to McIntyre Sales Co. in payment of $26,800 invoice.
16. Cash fees earned for May 1–16, $14,450.
16. Issued Check No. 211 for purchase of a vehicle, $31,400.
17. Issued Check No. 212 for miscellaneous administrative expenses, $280.
18. Purchased maintenance supplies on account from Bastille Co., $1,480.
18. Received check for rent revenue on office space, $1,400.
19. Purchased the following on account from Master Supply Co.: maintenance supplies, $1,950, and office supplies, $550.
20. Issued Check No. 213 in payment of advertising expense, $6,800.
20. Used maintenance supplies with a cost of $3,000 to repair vehicles.
21. Purchased office supplies on account from Office City, $610.
24. Issued Invoice No. 94 to Sing Co., $11,530.
25. Received check for $15,680 from Baker Co. in payment of invoice.
25. Issued Invoice No. 95 to Trent Co., $5,900.
26. Issued Check No. 214 to Office Mate, Inc. in payment of $4,500 invoice.
27. Issued Check No. 215 to F. Melendez as a personal withdrawal, $4,000.
30. Issued Check No. 216 in payment of driver salaries, $23,500.
31. Issued Check No. 217 in payment of office salaries, $16,750.
31. Issued Check No. 218 for office supplies, $230.
31. Cash fees earned for May 17–31, $19,200.

**Instructions**
1. Enter the following account balances in the general ledger as of May 1:

| | | | | | |
|---|---|---|---|---|---|
| 11 | Cash | $ 57,900 | 32 | F. Melendez, Drawing | — |
| 12 | Accounts Receivable | 32,815 | 41 | Fees Earned | — |
| 14 | Maintenance Supplies | 6,150 | 42 | Rent Revenue | — |
| 15 | Office Supplies | 2,580 | 51 | Driver Salaries Expense | — |
| 16 | Office Equipment | 14,370 | 52 | Maintenance Supplies | |
| 17 | Accumulated Depreciation | | | Expense | — |
| | —Office Equipment | 3,000 | 53 | Fuel Expense | — |
| 18 | Vehicles | 48,000 | 61 | Office Salaries Expense | — |
| 19 | Accumulated Depreciation | | 62 | Rent Expense | — |
| | —Vehicles | 13,590 | 63 | Advertising Expense | — |
| 21 | Accounts Payable | 2,790 | 64 | Miscellaneous Adminis- | |
| 31 | F. Melendez, Capital | 142,435 | | trative Expense | — |

*(continued)*

2. Journalize the transactions for May 2006, using the following journals similar to those illustrated in this chapter: single-column revenue journal, cash receipts journal, purchases journal (with columns for Accounts Payable, Maintenance Supplies, Office Supplies, and Other Accounts), cash payments journal, and two-column general journal. Assume that the daily postings to the individual accounts in the accounts payable ledger and the accounts receivable ledger have been made.
3. Post the appropriate individual entries to the general ledger.
4. Total each of the columns of the special journals, and post the appropriate totals to the general ledger; insert the account balances.
5. Prepare a trial balance.
6. Verify the agreement of each subsidiary ledger with its controlling account. The sum of the balances of the accounts in the subsidiary ledgers as of May 31 are as follows:

| | |
|---|---|
| Accounts receivable | $26,970 |
| Accounts payable | 4,590 |

# Problems Series B

## PROBLEM 5-1B
*Revenue journal; accounts receivable and general ledgers*

**Objective 3**

SPREADSHEET

✓ *1. Revenue journal, total fees earned, $930*

Stillman Learning Centers was established on January 20, 2006, to provide educational services. The services provided during the remainder of the month are as follows:

Jan. 21. J. Dunlop, Invoice No. 1, $70 on account.
    22. L. Summers, Invoice No. 2, $225 on account.
    24. T. Morris, Invoice No. 3, $65 on account.
    25. L. Summers, $115 in exchange for educational supplies.
    27. F. Mintz, Invoice No. 4, $190 on account.
    28. D. Bennett, Invoice No. 5, $145 on account.
    30. L. Summers, Invoice No. 6, $105 on account.
    31. T. Morris, Invoice No. 7, $130 on account.

### Instructions

1. Journalize the transactions for January, using a single-column revenue journal and a two-column general journal. Post to the following customer accounts in the accounts receivable ledger, and insert the balance immediately after recording each entry: D. Bennett; J. Dunlop; F. Mintz; T. Morris; L. Summers.
2. Post the revenue journal and the general journal to the following accounts in the general ledger, inserting the account balances only after the last postings:

| | |
|---|---|
| 12 | Accounts Receivable |
| 13 | Supplies |
| 41 | Fees Earned |

3. a. What is the sum of the balances of the accounts in the subsidiary ledger at January 31?
   b. What is the balance of the controlling account at January 31?
4. Assume that on February 1, the state in which Stillman operates begins requiring that sales tax be collected on educational services. Briefly explain how the revenue journal may be modified to accommodate sales of services on account that require the collection of a state sales tax.

## PROBLEM 5-2B
*Revenue and cash receipts journals; accounts receivable and general ledgers*

**Objective 3**

Transactions related to revenue and cash receipts completed by Newport Architects Co. during the period June 2–30, 2006, are as follows:

✓ *3. Total cash receipts,*
*$39,040*

June 2. Issued Invoice No. 793 to Morton Co., $7,300.
   5. Received cash from Mendez Co. for the balance owed on its account.
   6. Issued Invoice No. 794 to Quest Co., $1,980.
  13. Issued Invoice No. 795 to Ping Co., $5,050.
     *Post revenue and collections to the accounts receivable subsidiary ledger.*
  15. Received cash from Quest Co. for the balance owed on June 1.
  16. Issued Invoice No. 796 to Quest Co., $4,600.
     *Post revenue and collections to the accounts receivable subsidiary ledger.*
  19. Received cash from Morton Co. for the balance due on invoice of June 2.
  20. Received cash from Quest Co. for invoice of June 6.
  22. Issued Invoice No. 797 to Mendez Co., $7,150.
  25. Received $4,400 note receivable in partial settlement of the balance due on the Ping Co. account.
  30. Recorded cash fees earned, $10,880.
     *Post revenue and collections to the accounts receivable subsidiary ledger.*

**Instructions**

1. Insert the following balances in the general ledger as of June 1:

| | | |
|---|---|---|
| 11 | Cash | $12,150 |
| 12 | Accounts Receivable | 18,880 |
| 14 | Notes Receivable | 5,000 |
| 41 | Fees Earned | — |

2. Insert the following balances in the accounts receivable subsidiary ledger as of June 1:

| | |
|---|---|
| Mendez Co. | $10,670 |
| Morton Co. | — |
| Ping Co. | — |
| Quest Co. | 8,210 |

3. Prepare a single-column revenue journal and a cash receipts journal. Use the following column headings for the cash receipts journal: Fees Earned, Accounts Receivable, and Cash. The Fees Earned column is used to record cash fees. Insert a check mark (✔) in the Post. Ref. Column.
4. Using the two special journals and the two-column general journal, journalize the transactions for June. Post to the accounts receivable subsidiary ledger, and insert the balances at the points indicated in the narrative of transactions. Determine the balance in the customer's account before recording a cash receipt.
5. Total each of the columns of the special journals, and post the individual entries and totals to the general ledger. Insert account balances after the last posting.
6. Determine that the subsidiary ledger agrees with the controlling account in the general ledger.

**PROBLEM 5-3B**
*Purchases, accounts payable account, and accounts payable ledger*
**Objective 3**

✓ *3. Total accounts payable credit, $16,025*

Natural Beauty Landscaping designs and installs landscaping. The landscape designers and office staff use office supplies, while field supplies (rock, bark, etc.) are used in the actual landscaping. Purchases on account completed by Natural Beauty Landscaping during July 2006 are as follows:

July 2. Purchased office supplies on account from Lapp Co., $1,050.
   5. Purchased office equipment on account from Peach Computers Co., $4,500.
   9. Purchased office supplies on account from Executive Office Supply Co., $265.
  13. Purchased field supplies on account from Yin Co., $980.
  14. Purchased field supplies on account from Nelson Co., $3,610.
  17. Purchased field supplies on account from Yin Co., $1,345.
  24. Purchased field supplies on account from Nelson Co., $2,975.
  29. Purchased office supplies on account from Executive Office Supply Co., $295.
  31. Purchased field supplies on account from Nelson Co., $1,005.

## Instructions

1. Insert the following balances in the general ledger as of July 1:

| 14 | Field Supplies | $ 5,820 |
|----|----------------|---------|
| 15 | Office Supplies | 830 |
| 18 | Office Equipment | 14,300 |
| 21 | Accounts Payable | 1,055 |

2. Insert the following balances in the accounts payable subsidiary ledger as of July 1:

| Executive Office Supply | $365 |
|-------------------------|------|
| Lapp Co. | 690 |
| Nelson Co. | — |
| Peach Computers Co. | — |
| Yin Co. | — |

3. Journalize the transactions for July, using a purchases journal similar to the one illustrated in this chapter. Prepare the purchases journal with columns for Accounts Payable, Field Supplies, Office Supplies, and Other Accounts. Post to the creditor accounts in the accounts payable subsidiary ledger immediately after each entry.
4. Post the purchases journal to the accounts in the general ledger.
5. a. What is the sum of the balances in the subsidiary ledger at July 31?
   b. What is the balance of the controlling account at July 31?

**PROBLEM 5-4B**
*Purchases and cash payments journals; accounts payable and general ledgers*

**Objective 3**

P.A.S.S.

✓ *1. Total cash payments, $71,935*

Arctic Springs Water Testing Service was established on June 16, 2006. Arctic uses field equipment and field supplies (chemicals and other supplies) to analyze water for unsafe contaminants in streams, lakes, and ponds. Transactions related to purchases and cash payments during the remainder of June are as follows:

June 16. Issued Check No. 1 in payment of rent for the remainder of June, $1,200.
   16. Purchased field supplies on account from Heath Supply Co., $3,920.
   16. Purchased field equipment on account from Test-Rite Equipment Co., $12,200.
   17. Purchased office supplies on account from Aztec Supply Co., $415.
   19. Issued Check No. 2 in payment of field supplies, $2,050, and office supplies, $250.
      *Post the journals to the accounts payable subsidiary ledger.*
   23. Purchased office supplies on account from Aztec Supply Co., $545.
   23. Issued Check No. 3 to purchase land from the owner, $35,000.
   24. Issued Check No. 4 to Heath Supply Co. in payment of invoice, $3,920.
   26. Issued Check No. 5 to Test-Rite Equipment Co. in payment of invoice, $12,200.
      *Post the journals to the accounts payable subsidiary ledger.*
   30. Acquired land in exchange for field equipment having a cost of $7,500.
   30. Purchased field supplies on account from Heath Supply Co., $5,300.
   30. Issued Check No. 6 to Aztec Supply Co. in payment of invoice, $415.
   30. Purchased the following from Test-Rite Equipment Co. on account: field supplies, $900, and field equipment, $3,200.
   30. Issued Check No. 7 in payment of salaries, $16,900.
      *Post the journals to the accounts payable subsidiary ledger.*

## Instructions

1. Journalize the transactions for June. Use a purchases journal and a cash payments journal, similar to those illustrated in this chapter, and a two-column general journal. Set debit columns for Field Supplies, Office Supplies, and Other Accounts in the purchases journal. Refer to the following partial chart of accounts:

| 11 | Cash | 19 | Land |
|----|------|----|------|
| 14 | Field Supplies | 21 | Accounts Payable |
| 15 | Office Supplies | 61 | Salary Expense |
| 17 | Field Equipment | 71 | Rent Expense |

At the points indicated in the narrative of transactions, post to the following accounts in the accounts payable subsidiary ledger:

Aztec Supply Co.
Heath Supply Co.
Test-Rite Equipment Co.

2. Post the individual entries (Other Accounts columns of the purchases journal and the cash payments journal and both columns of the general journal) to the appropriate general ledger accounts.
3. Total each of the columns of the purchases journal and the cash payments journal and post the appropriate totals to the general ledger. (Because the problem does not include transactions related to cash receipts, the cash account in the ledger will have a credit balance.)
4. Prepare a schedule of accounts payable.

**PROBLEM 5-5B**
*All journals and general ledger; trial balance*

**Objective 3**

**P.A.S.S.**

✓ *2. Total cash receipts,*
*$51,390*

The transactions completed by Next Day Delivery Company during July 2006, the first month of the fiscal year, were as follows:

July 1. Issued Check No. 610 for July rent, $5,500.
    2. Issued Invoice No. 940 to Capps Co., $2,980.
    3. Received check for $5,400 from Pease Co. in payment of account.
    5. Purchased a vehicle on account from Browning Transportation, $31,600.
    6. Purchased office equipment on account from Bell Computer Co., $4,200.
    6. Issued Invoice No. 941 to Collins Co., $6,210.
    9. Issued Check No. 611 for fuel expense, $850.
   10. Received check from Sokol Co. in payment of $5,980 invoice.
   10. Issued Check No. 612 for $1,140 to Office To Go, Inc., in payment of invoice.
   10. Issued Invoice No. 942 to Joy Co., $2,470.
   11. Issued Check No. 613 for $2,980 to Crowne Supply Co. in payment of account.
   11. Issued Check No. 614 for $960 to Porter Co. in payment of account.
   12. Received check from Capps Co. in payment of $2,980 invoice.
   13. Issued Check No. 615 to Browning Transportation in payment of $31,600 balance.
   16. Issued Check No. 616 for $27,900 for cash purchase of a vehicle.
   16. Cash fees earned for July 1–16, $15,900.
   17. Issued Check No. 617 for miscellaneous administrative expense, $430.
   18. Purchased maintenance supplies on account from Crowne Supply Co., $2,445.
   19. Purchased the following on account from McClain Co.: maintenance supplies, $1,915; office supplies, $545.
   20. Issued Check No. 618 in payment of advertising expense, $1,500.
   20. Used $3,800 maintenance supplies to repair delivery vehicles.
   23. Purchased office supplies on account from Office To Go, Inc., $700.
   24. Issued Invoice No. 943 to Sokol Co., $4,090.
   24. Issued Check No. 619 to K. Huss as a personal withdrawal, $2,000.
   25. Issued Invoice No. 944 to Collins Co., $4,670.
   25. Received check for $3,950 from Pease Co. in payment of balance.
   26. Issued Check No. 620 to Bell Computer Co. in payment of $4,200 invoice of July 6.
   30. Issued Check No. 621 for monthly salaries as follows: driver salaries, $15,400; office salaries, $7,500.
   31. Cash fees earned for July 17–31, $17,180.
   31. Issued Check No. 622 in payment for office supplies, $900.

**Instructions**
1. Enter the following account balances in the general ledger as of July 1:

| | | | | | | |
|---|---|---|---|---|---|---|
| 11 | Cash | $ 56,800 | | 32 | K. Huss, Drawing | — |
| 12 | Accounts Receivable | 15,330 | | 41 | Fees Earned | — |
| 14 | Maintenance Supplies | 9,300 | | 51 | Driver Salaries Expense | — |
| 15 | Office Supplies | 4,500 | | 52 | Maintenance Supplies | |
| 16 | Office Equipment | 24,300 | | | Expense | — |
| 17 | Accumulated Depreciation | | | 53 | Fuel Expense | — |
| | —Office Equipment | 4,500 | | 61 | Office Salaries Expense | — |
| 18 | Vehicles | 84,600 | | 62 | Rent Expense | — |
| 19 | Accumulated Depreciation | | | 63 | Advertising Expense | — |
| | —Vehicles | 12,300 | | 64 | Miscellaneous Adminis- | |
| 21 | Accounts Payable | 5,080 | | | trative Expense | — |
| 31 | K. Huss, Capital | 172,950 | | | | |

2. Journalize the transactions for July 2006, using the following journals similar to those illustrated in this chapter: cash receipts journal, purchases journal (with columns for Accounts Payable, Maintenance Supplies, Office Supplies, and Other Accounts), single-column revenue journal, cash payments journal, and two-column general journal. Assume that the daily postings to the individual accounts in the accounts payable ledger and the accounts receivable ledger have been made.
3. Post the appropriate individual entries to the general ledger.
4. Total each of the columns of the special journals and post the appropriate totals to the general ledger; insert the account balances.
5. Prepare a trial balance.
6. Verify the agreement of each subsidiary ledger with its controlling account. The sum of the balances of the accounts in the subsidiary ledgers as of July 31 are:

| | |
|---|---|
| Accounts receivable | $17,440 |
| Accounts payable | 5,605 |

# Special Activities

**ACTIVITY 5-1**
*Ethics and professional conduct in business*

ETHICS

Lee Garrett sells security systems for Guardsman Security Co. Garrett has a monthly sales quota of $40,000. If Garrett exceeds this quota, he is awarded a bonus. In measuring the quota, a sale is credited to the salesperson when a customer signs a contract for installation of a security system. Through the 25th of the current month, Garrett has sold $30,000 in security systems.

Vortex Co., a business rumored to be on the verge of bankruptcy, contacted Garrett on the 26th of the month about having a security system installed. Garrett estimates that the contract would yield about $14,000 worth of business for Guardsman Security Co. In addition, this contract would be large enough to put Garrett "over the top" for a bonus in the current month. However, Garrett is concerned that Vortex Co. will not be able to make the contract payment after the security system is installed. In fact, Garrett has heard rumors that a competing security services company refused to install a system for Vortex Co. because of these concerns.

Upon further consideration, Garrett concluded that his job is to sell security systems and that it's someone else's problem to collect the resulting accounts receivable. Thus, Garrett wrote the contract with Vortex Co. and received a bonus for the month.

a. Discuss whether Lee Garrett was acting in an ethical manner.
b. How might Guardsman Security Co. use internal controls to prevent this scenario from occurring?

**ACTIVITY 5-2**
*Ethics and financial
statement fraud*

REAL WORLD          ETHICS

**Worldcom Corporation,** the second largest telecommunications company in the United States, became the largest bankruptcy in history due to financial reporting irregularities and misstatements of nearly $7 billion. Worldcom's controller, director of general accounting, and director of management reporting all pleaded guilty to financial reporting fraud. These employees all stated that they were ordered by superiors to adjust the records to artificially boost the company's profits. Under protest, these employees made the adjustments.

a. ▭➤ Should these employees be held responsible for their actions, since they were "following orders"?
b. ▭➤ How should an employee respond to questionable or unethical requests from superiors?

**ACTIVITY 5-3**
*Manual vs. computerized
accounting systems*

The following conversation took place between Empire Paving Co.'s bookkeeper, Kelly Monroe, and the accounting supervisor, Jan Hargrove.

*Jan:* Kelly, I'm thinking about bringing in a new computerized accounting system to replace our manual system. I guess this will mean that you will need to learn how to do computerized accounting.
*Kelly:* What does computerized accounting mean?
*Jan:* I'm not sure, but you'll need to prepare for this new way of doing business.
*Kelly:* I'm not so sure we need a computerized system. I've been looking at some of the sample reports from the software vendor. It looks to me as if the computer will not add much to what we are already doing.
*Jan:* What do you mean?
*Kelly:* Well, look at these reports. This Sales by Customer Report looks like our revenue journal, and the Deposit Detail Report looks like our cash receipts journal. Granted, the computer types them, so they look much neater than my special journals, but I don't see that we're gaining much from this change.
*Jan:* Well, surely there's more to it than nice-looking reports. I've got to believe that a computerized system will save us time and effort someplace.
*Kelly:* I don't see how. We still need to key in transactions into the computer. If anything, there may be more work when it's all said and done.

▭➤ Do you agree with Kelly? Why might a computerized environment be preferred over the manual system?

**ACTIVITY 5-4**
*Internal controls*

WHAT DO YOU THINK?

Like most businesses, when Falcon Company renders services to another business, it is typical that the service is rendered "on account," rather than as a cash transaction. As a result, Falcon Company has an account receivable for the service provided. Likewise, the company receiving the service has an account payable for the amount owed for services received. At a later date, Falcon Company will receive cash from the customer to satisfy the accounts receivable balance. However, when individuals conduct transactions with each other, it is common for the transaction to be for cash. For example, when you buy a pizza, you often pay with cash.
▭➤ Why is it unusual for businesses such as Falcon Company to engage in cash transactions, while for individuals it is more common?

**ACTIVITY 5-5**
*The virtual close*

REAL WORLD          INTERNET

**Cisco Systems, Inc.** pioneered the concept of a "virtual close" of the financial records. A virtual close is described as follows:

*The traditional practice of closing a company's books on a monthly, quarterly, or annual basis is out of sync with the dynamics of the new economy. In the past, the financial close and subsequent report generation was a static, scheduled event. It consumed days, weeks, and months and was based on a "thick black book." The new paradigm is driven by dynamic information accessible anytime and anywhere. Web-based reporting tools allow for real-time access to the very latest data and make interaction, summary to detail drill downs, and various data views possible. The result is fast, intuitive, on-the-fly creation of information views targeted for a specific analytical need to answer a specific question.*

**Source:** *Virtual Close—A Financial Management Solution*, Cisco Systems, Inc., and Bearingpoint Consulting Solutions Brief, 2001.

Additional information about the virtual close can be found at Cisco's Web site, which is linked to the text's Web site at **http://warren.swlearning.com**.

a. ▮▮▮▮▶ How is a virtual close different from traditional practice?
b. ▮▮▮▮▶ How does the virtual close impact the decision-making ability of Cisco's management.

**ACTIVITY 5-6**
*Design of accounting systems*

For the past few years, your client, Chow Medical Group (CMG), has operated a small medical practice. CMG's current annual revenues are $420,000. Because the accountant has been spending more and more time each month recording all transactions in a two-column journal and preparing the financial statements, CMG is considering improving the accounting system by adding special journals and subsidiary ledgers. CMG has asked you to help with this project and has compiled the following information:

| Type of Transaction | Estimated Frequency per Month |
|---|---|
| Fees earned on account | 240 |
| Purchase of medical supplies on account | 190 |
| Cash receipts from patients on account | 175 |
| Cash payments on account | 160 |
| Cash receipts from patients at time services provided | 120 |
| Purchase of office supplies on account | 35 |
| Purchase of magazine subscriptions on account | 5 |
| Purchase of medical equipment on account | 4 |
| Cash payments for office salaries | 3 |
| Cash payments for utilities expense | 3 |

A local sales tax is collected on all patient bills, and monthly financial statements are prepared.

1. ▮▮▮▮▶ Briefly discuss the circumstances under which special journals would be used in place of a two-column (all-purpose) journal. Include in your answer your recommendations for CMG's medical practice.
2. Assume that CMG has decided to use a revenue journal and a purchases journal. Design the format for each journal, giving special consideration to the needs of the medical practice.
3. Which subsidiary ledgers would you recommend for the medical practice?

**ACTIVITY 5-7**
*Web-based accounting systems*

**INTERNET**

Web-based application software is a recent trend in business computing. Major software firms such as **Oracle**, **SAP**, and **Seibel Systems** are running their core products on the Web. **NetLedger**, from Oracle, is one of the first small business Web-based accounting systems.

▮▮▮▮▶ Go to the text's Web site at **http://warren.swlearning.com** and click on the link to the NetLedger site. Read about the product from the site, and prepare a memo to management, defining Web-based accounting. Also, outline the advantages and disadvantages of Web-based accounting compared to running software on a company's internal computer network.

**ACTIVITY 5-8**
*SCM and CRM*

**GROUP ACTIVITY    INTERNET**

The two leading software application providers for supply chain management (SCM) and customer relationship management (CRM) software are **Manugistics** and **Siebel Systems**, respectively. In groups of two or three, go to the Web site for each company (linked to the text's Web site at **http://warren.swlearning.com**) and list the functions provided by each company's application.

# Answers to Self-Examination Questions

1. **A**  Analysis (answer A) is the initial step of determining the informational needs and how the system provides this information. Design (answer B) is the step in which proposals for changes are developed. Implementation (answer C) is the final step involving carrying out or implementing the proposals for changes. Feedback (answer D) is not a separate step but is considered part of the systems implementation.

2. **A**  The policies and procedures that are established to safeguard assets, ensure accurate business information, and ensure compliance with laws and regulations are called internal controls (answer A). The three steps in setting up an accounting system are (1) analysis (answer B), (2) design (answer C), and (3) implementation (answer D).

3. **B**  All payments of cash for any purpose are recorded in the cash payments journal (answer B). Only purchases of services or other items on account are recorded in the purchases journal (answer A). All sales of services on account are recorded in the revenue journal (answer C), and all receipts of cash are recorded in the cash receipts journal (answer D).

4. **A**  The general term used to describe the type of separate ledger that contains a large number of individual accounts with a common characteristic is a subsidiary ledger (answer A). The creditors ledger (answer B), sometimes called the accounts payable ledger (answer C), is a specific subsidiary ledger containing only individual accounts with creditors. Likewise, the accounts receivable ledger (answer D), also called the customers ledger, is a specific subsidiary ledger containing only individual accounts with customers.

5. **C**  Both the revenue journal (answer A) and the cash receipts journal (answer B) are generally not used in a computerized accounting system. Rather, electronic forms, such as an electronic invoice form (answer C), are used to record original transactions. The computer automatically posts transactions from electronic forms to the general ledger and individual accounts at the time the transactions are recorded. Therefore, month-end postings to the general ledger (answer D) are not necessary in a computerized accounting system.

# 6

# ACCOUNTING FOR MERCHANDISING BUSINESSES

## objectives

*After studying this chapter, you should be able to:*

1  Distinguish the activities of a service business from those of a merchandising business.

2  Describe and illustrate the financial statements of a merchandising business.

3  Describe the accounting for the sale of merchandise.

4  Describe the accounting for the purchase of merchandise.

5  Describe the accounting for transportation costs, sales taxes, and trade discounts.

6  Illustrate the dual nature of merchandising transactions.

7  Prepare a chart of accounts for a merchandising business.

8  Describe the accounting cycle for a merchandising business.

9  Compute the ratio of net sales to assets as a measure of how effectively a business is using its assets.

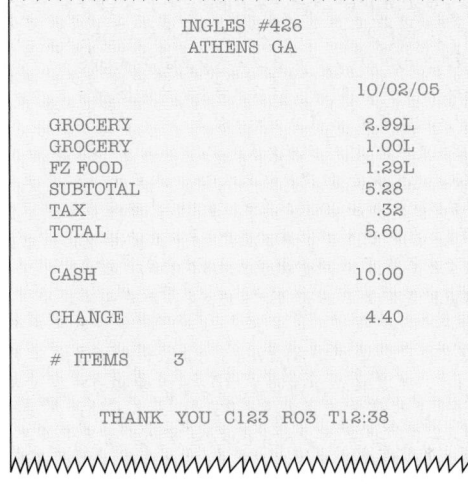

```
       INGLES #426
       ATHENS GA

                        10/02/05

GROCERY                 2.99L
GROCERY                 1.00L
FZ FOOD                 1.29L
SUBTOTAL                5.28
TAX                      .32
TOTAL                   5.60

CASH                   10.00

CHANGE                  4.40

# ITEMS    3

     THANK YOU C123 R03 T12:38
```

ssume that you bought groceries at a store and received the receipt shown here. This receipt indicates that you purchased three items totaling $5.28, the sales tax was $0.32 (6%), the total due was $5.60, you gave the clerk $10.00, and you received change of $4.40. The receipt also indicates that the sale was made by Store #426 of the Ingles chain, located in Athens, Georgia. The date and time of the sale and other data used internally by the store are also indicated.

When you buy groceries, textbooks, school supplies, or an automobile, you are doing business with a retail or merchandising business. The accounting for a merchandising business is more complex than for a service business. For example, the accounting system for a merchandiser must be designed to record the receipt of goods for resale, keep track of the goods available for sale, and record the sale and cost of the merchandise sold.

In this chapter, we will focus on the accounting principles and concepts for merchandising businesses. We begin our discussion by highlighting the basic differences between the activities of merchandise and service businesses. We then describe and illustrate financial statements for merchandising businesses and purchases and sales transactions.

# Nature of Merchandising Businesses

objective 1

Distinguish the activities of a service business from those of a merchandising business.

**REAL WORLD**

For many merchandising businesses, the cost of merchandise sold is usually the largest expense. For example, the approximate percentage of cost of merchandise sold to sales is 70% for **J.C.Penney Company** and 72% for **The Home Depot**.

How do the activities of NetSolutions, an attorney, and an architect, which are service businesses, differ from those of **Wal-Mart** or **Best Buy**, which are merchandising businesses? These differences are best illustrated by focusing on the revenues and expenses in the following condensed income statements:

| Service Business | | Merchandising Business | |
|---|---|---|---|
| Fees earned | $XXX | Sales | $XXX |
| Operating expenses | −XXX | Cost of merchandise sold | −XXX |
| Net income | $XXX | Gross profit | $XXX |
| | | Operating expenses | −XXX |
| | | Net income | $XXX |

The revenue activities of a service business involve providing services to customers. On the income statement for a service business, the revenues from services are reported as *fees earned*. The operating expenses incurred in providing the services are subtracted from the fees earned to arrive at *net income*.

In contrast, the revenue activities of a merchandising business involve the buying and selling of merchandise. A merchandising business must first purchase merchandise to sell to its customers. When this merchandise is sold, the revenue is reported as sales, and its cost is recognized as an expense called the **cost of merchandise sold**. The cost of merchandise sold is subtracted from sales to arrive at gross profit. This amount is called **gross profit** because it is the profit *before* deducting operating expenses.

Merchandise on hand (not sold) at the end of an accounting period is called **merchandise inventory**. Merchandise inventory is reported as a current asset on the balance sheet.

In the remainder of this chapter, we illustrate merchandiser financial statements and transactions that affect the income statement (sales, cost of merchandise sold, and gross profit) and the balance sheet (merchandise inventory).

| Sales − | Cost of Merchandise Sold | = | Gross Profit |
|---|---|---|---|
| Gross Profit | − Operating Expenses | = | Net Income |

# THE OPERATING CYCLE

The operations of a manufacturing business involve the purchase of raw materials (purchasing activity), the conversion of the raw materials into a product through the use of labor and machinery (production activity), the sale and distribution of the products to customers (sales activity), and the receipt of cash from customers (collection activity). This overall process is referred to as the *operating cycle*. Thus, the operating cycle begins with spending cash and it ends with receiving cash from customers. The operating cycle for a manufacturing business is shown below.

Operating cycles differ, depending upon the nature of the business and its operations. For example, the operating cycles for tobacco, distillery, and lumber industries are much longer than the operating cycles of the automobile, consumer electronics, and home furnishings industries. Likewise, the operating cycles for retailers are usually shorter than for manufacturers because retailers purchase goods in a form ready for sale to the customer. Of course, some retailers will have shorter operating cycles than others because of the nature of their products. For example, a jewelry store or an automobile dealer normally has a longer operating cycle than a consumer electronics store or a grocery store.

Businesses with longer operating cycles normally have higher profit margins on their products than businesses with shorter operating cycles. For example, it is not unusual for jewelry stores to price their jewelry at 30%–50% above cost. In contrast, grocery stores operate on very small profit margins, often below 5%. Grocery stores make up the difference by selling their products more quickly.

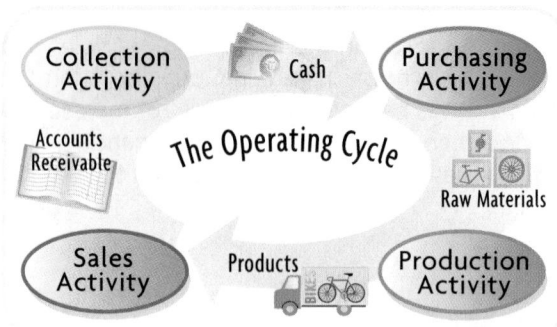

# Financial Statements for a Merchandising Business

**objective 2**

Describe and illustrate the financial statements of a merchandising business.

In this section, we illustrate the financial statements for NetSolutions after it becomes a retailer of computer hardware and software. During 2005, we assume that Chris Clark implemented the second phase of NetSolutions' business plan. Accordingly, Chris notified clients that beginning July 1, 2006, NetSolutions would be terminating its consulting services. Instead, it would become a personalized retailer.

NetSolutions' business strategy is to focus on offering personalized service to individuals and small businesses who are upgrading or purchasing new computer systems. NetSolutions' personal service before the sale will include a no-obligation, on-site assessment of the customer's computer needs. By providing tailor-made solutions, personalized service, and follow-up, Chris feels that NetSolutions can compete effectively against larger retailers, such as **Best Buy** or **Office Depot**.

## Multiple-Step Income Statement

The 2007 income statement for NetSolutions is shown in Exhibit 1.[1] This form of income statement, called a **multiple-step income statement**, contains several sections, subsections, and subtotals.

**Sales** is the total amount charged customers for merchandise sold, including cash sales and sales on account. Both sales returns and allowances and sales discounts are subtracted in arriving at net sales.

[1]We use the NetSolutions income statement for 2007 as a basis for illustration because, as will be shown, it allows us to better illustrate the computation of the cost of merchandise sold.

## •Exhibit 1    Multiple-Step Income Statement

| NetSolutions<br>Income Statement<br>For the Year Ended December 31, 2007 | | | | |
|---|---:|---:|---:|---:|
| Revenue from sales: | | | | |
| Sales | | $720 1 8 5 00 | | |
| Less: Sales returns and allowances | $ 6 1 4 0 00 | | | |
| Sales discounts | 5 7 9 0 00 | 11 9 3 0 00 | | |
| Net sales | | | $708 2 5 5 00 | |
| Cost of merchandise sold | | | 525 3 0 5 00 | |
| Gross profit | | | $182 9 5 0 00 | |
| Operating expenses: | | | | |
| Selling expenses: | | | | |
| Sales salaries expense | $56 2 3 0 00 | | | |
| Advertising expense | 10 8 6 0 00 | | | |
| Depr. expense—store equipment | 3 1 0 0 00 | | | |
| Miscellaneous selling expense | 6 3 0 00 | | | |
| Total selling expenses | | $ 70 8 2 0 00 | | |
| Administrative expenses: | | | | |
| Office salaries expense | $21 0 2 0 00 | | | |
| Rent expense | 8 1 0 0 00 | | | |
| Depr. expense—office equipment | 2 4 9 0 00 | | | |
| Insurance expense | 1 9 1 0 00 | | | |
| Office supplies expense | 6 1 0 00 | | | |
| Misc. administrative expense | 7 6 0 00 | | | |
| Total administrative expenses | | 34 8 9 0 00 | | |
| Total operating expenses | | | 105 7 1 0 00 | |
| Income from operations | | | $ 77 2 4 0 00 | |
| Other income and expense: | | | | |
| Rent revenue | | | $ 6 0 0 00 | |
| Interest expense | | | (2 4 4 0 00) | (1 8 4 0 00) |
| Net income | | | | $ 75 4 0 0 00 |

***Sales returns and allowances*** are granted by the seller to customers for damaged or defective merchandise. For example, rather than have a buyer return merchandise, a seller may offer a $500 allowance to the customer as compensation for damaged merchandise. Sales returns and allowances are recorded when the merchandise is returned or when the allowance is granted by the seller.

***Sales discounts*** are granted by the seller to customers for early payment of amounts owed. For example, a seller may offer a customer a 2% discount on a sale of $10,000 if the customer pays within ten days. If the customer pays within the ten-day period, the seller receives cash of $9,800 and the buyer receives a discount of $200 ($10,000 × 2%). Sales discounts are recorded when the customer pays the bill.

**Net sales** is determined by subtracting sales returns and allowances and sales discounts from sales. Rather than reporting sales, sales returns and allowances, and sales discounts as shown in Exhibit 1, many companies report only net sales.

**Cost of merchandise sold** is the cost of the merchandise sold to customers. To illustrate the determination of the cost of merchandise sold, assume that NetSolutions purchased $340,000 of merchandise during the last half of 2006. If the inventory at December 31, 2006, the end of the year, is $59,700, the cost of the merchandise sold during 2006 is $280,300, as shown on the top of the next page.

Assume that sales are $790,000, sales discounts are $35,000, and net sales are $680,000. What are the sales returns and allowances?

-----------------------------------------------

$75,000 ($790,000 − $35,000 − $680,000)

| | |
|---|---|
| Purchases | $340,000 |
| Less merchandise inventory, December 31, 2006 | 59,700 |
| Cost of merchandise sold | $280,300 |

As we discussed in the preceding paragraphs, sellers may offer customers sales discounts for early payment of their bills. Such discounts are referred to as *purchases discounts* by the buyer. Purchase discounts reduce the cost of merchandise. A buyer may return merchandise to the seller (a *purchase return*), or the buyer may receive a reduction in the initial price at which the merchandise was purchased (a *purchase allowance*). Like purchase discounts, purchases returns and allowances reduce the cost of merchandise purchased during a period. In addition, transportation costs paid by the buyer for merchandise also increase the cost of merchandise purchased.

To continue the illustration, assume that during 2007 NetSolutions purchased additional merchandise of $521,980. It received credit for purchases returns and allowances of $9,100, took purchases discounts of $2,525, and paid transportation costs of $17,400. The purchases returns and allowances and the purchases discounts are deducted from the total purchases to yield the *net purchases*. The transportation costs, termed **transportation in**, are added to the net purchases to yield the *cost of merchandise purchased* of $527,755, as shown below.

| | | |
|---|---|---|
| Purchases | | $521,980 |
| Less: Purchases returns and allowances | $9,100 | |
| Purchases discounts | 2,525 | 11,625 |
| Net purchases | | $510,355 |
| Add transportation in | | 17,400 |
| Cost of merchandise purchased | | $527,755 |

Assume that purchases are $480,000, purchases returns and allowances are $25,000, and purchases discounts are $60,000. What are the net purchases?

----------------------------------------

$395,000 ($480,000 − $25,000 − $60,000)

The ending inventory of NetSolutions on December 31, 2006, $59,700, becomes the beginning inventory for 2007. This beginning inventory is added to the cost of merchandise purchased to yield **merchandise available for sale**. The ending inventory, which is assumed to be $62,150, is then subtracted from the merchandise available for sale to yield the cost of merchandise sold of $525,305, as shown in Exhibit 2.

## •Exhibit 2   Cost of Merchandise Sold

| | | | |
|---|---|---|---|
| Merchandise inventory, January 1, 2007 . . . . . . . . | | | $ 59,700 |
| Purchases . . . . . . . . . . . . . . . . . . . . . . . . . . . . | | $521,980 | |
| Less: Purchases returns and allowances . . . . . . . . | $9,100 | | |
| Purchases discounts . . . . . . . . . . . . . . . . . | 2,525 | 11,625 | |
| Net purchases . . . . . . . . . . . . . . . . . . . . . . . | | $510,355 | |
| Add transportation in . . . . . . . . . . . . . . . . . . | | 17,400 | |
| Cost of merchandise purchased . . . . . . . . . . . . | | | 527,755 |
| Merchandise available for sale . . . . . . . . . . . . . . | | | $587,455 |
| Less merchandise inventory, December 31, 2007 . . | | | 62,150 |
| Cost of merchandise sold . . . . . . . . . . . . . . . . . | | | $525,305 |

The cost of merchandise sold was determined by deducting the merchandise on hand at the end of the period from the merchandise available for sale during the period. The merchandise on hand at the end of the period is determined by taking a physical count of inventory on hand. This method of determining the cost of merchandise sold and the amount of merchandise on hand is called the ***periodic***

If merchandise available for sale is $1,375,000 and the cost of merchandise sold is $950,000, what is the ending merchandise inventory?

*$425,000 ($1,375,000 − $950,000)*

**REAL WORLD**

Retailers, such as **Best Buy**, **Sears**, and **Wal-Mart**, and grocery store chains, such as **Winn-Dixie** and **Kroger**, use bar codes and optical scanners as part of their computerized inventory systems.

*method* of accounting for merchandise inventory. Under the periodic method, the inventory records do not show the amount available for sale or the amount sold during the period. In contrast, under the ***perpetual method*** of accounting for merchandise inventory, each purchase and sale of merchandise is recorded in the inventory and the cost of merchandise sold accounts. As a result, the amount of merchandise available for sale and the amount sold are continuously (perpetually) disclosed in the inventory records.

Most large retailers and many small merchandising businesses use computerized perpetual inventory systems. Such systems normally use bar codes, such as the one on the back of this textbook. An optical scanner reads the bar code to record merchandise purchased and sold. Merchandise businesses using a perpetual inventory system report the cost of merchandise sold as a single line on the income statement, as shown in Exhibit 1 for NetSolutions. Merchandise businesses using the periodic inventory method report the cost of merchandise sold by using the format shown in Exhibit 2. Because of its wide use, we will use the perpetual inventory method throughout the remainder of this chapter.

**Gross profit** is determined by subtracting the cost of merchandise sold from net sales. Exhibit 1 shows that NetSolutions reported gross profit of $182,950 in 2007. *Operating income*, sometimes called ***income from operations***, is determined by subtracting operating expenses from gross profit. Most merchandising businesses classify operating expenses as either selling expenses or administrative expenses. Expenses that are incurred directly in the selling of merchandise are ***selling expenses***. They include such expenses as salespersons' salaries, store supplies used, depreciation of store equipment, and advertising. Expenses incurred in the administration or general operations of the business are ***administrative expenses*** or *general expenses*. Examples of these expenses are office salaries, depreciation of office equipment, and office supplies used. Credit card expense is also normally classified as an administrative expense. Although selling and administrative expenses may be reported separately, many companies report operating expenses as a single item.

## FINANCIAL REPORTING AND DISCLOSURE

### H&R BLOCK VERSUS HOME DEPOT

**H**&R Block is a service business that primarily offers tax planning and preparation to its customers. **Home Depot** is the world's largest home improvement retailer and the second largest merchandise business in the United States. The differences in the operations of a service and merchandise business are illustrated in their income statements, as shown below.

As will be discussed in a later chapter, corporations are subject to income taxes. Thus, the income statements of H&R Block and Home Depot report "income taxes" as a deduction from "income before income taxes" in arriving at net income. This is in contrast to a proprietorship such as NetSolutions, which is not subject to income taxes.

**H&R Block Inc.**
**Condensed Income Statement**
**For the Year Ending April 30, 2002**
**(in millions)**

| | |
|---|---:|
| Revenue . . . . . . . . . . . . . . . . . . . . . . . . . . | $3,318 |
| Operating expenses . . . . . . . . . . . . . . . . . . . . | 2,602 |
| Operating income . . . . . . . . . . . . . . . . . . . . | $ 716 |
| Other income . . . . . . . . . . . . . . . . . . . . . . | 1 |
| Income before taxes . . . . . . . . . . . . . . . . . . | $ 717 |
| Income taxes . . . . . . . . . . . . . . . . . . . . . . | 283 |
| Net income . . . . . . . . . . . . . . . . . . . . . . . | $ 434 |

**Home Depot Inc.**
**Condensed Income Statement**
**For the Year Ending February 2, 2003**
**(in millions)**

| | |
|---|---:|
| Net sales . . . . . . . . . . . . . . . . . . . . . . . . . | $58,247 |
| Cost of merchandise sold . . . . . . . . . . . . . . . . . | 40,139 |
| Gross profit . . . . . . . . . . . . . . . . . . . . . . . | $18,108 |
| Operating expenses . . . . . . . . . . . . . . . . . . . . | 12,278 |
| Operating income . . . . . . . . . . . . . . . . . . . . | $ 5,830 |
| Other income . . . . . . . . . . . . . . . . . . . . . . | 42 |
| Income before taxes . . . . . . . . . . . . . . . . . . | $ 5,872 |
| Income taxes . . . . . . . . . . . . . . . . . . . . . . | 2,208 |
| Net income . . . . . . . . . . . . . . . . . . . . . . . | $ 3,664 |

**Other income and expense** is reported on NetSolutions' income statement in Exhibit 1. Revenue from sources other than the primary operating activity of a business is classified as *other income*. In a merchandising business, these items include income from interest, rent, and gains resulting from the sale of fixed assets.

Expenses that cannot be traced directly to operations are identified as *other expense*. Interest expense that results from financing activities and losses incurred in the disposal of fixed assets are examples of these items.

Other income and other expense are offset against each other on the income statement, as shown in Exhibit 1. If the total of other income exceeds the total of other expense, the difference is added to income from operations to determine net income. If the reverse is true, the difference is subtracted from income from operations.

## Single-Step Income Statement

An alternate form of income statement is the *single-step income statement*. As shown in Exhibit 3, the income statement for NetSolutions deducts the total of all expenses *in one step* from the total of all revenues.

The single-step form emphasizes total revenues and total expenses as the factors that determine net income. A criticism of the single-step form is that such amounts as gross profit and income from operations are not readily available for analysis.

**•Exhibit 3**    Single-Step Income Statement

**NetSolutions**
**Income Statement**
**For the Year Ended December 31, 2007**

| | | |
|---|---|---|
| Revenues: | | |
| Net sales | | $708 255 00 |
| Rent revenue | | 6 00 00 |
| Total revenues | | $708 855 00 |
| Expenses: | | |
| Cost of merchandise sold | $525 305 00 | |
| Selling expenses | 70 820 00 | |
| Administrative expenses | 34 890 00 | |
| Interest expense | 2 440 00 | |
| Total expenses | | 633 455 00 |
| Net income | | $ 75 400 00 |

## Statement of Owner's Equity

The statement of owner's equity for NetSolutions is shown in Exhibit 4. This statement is prepared in the same manner that we described previously for a service business.

## Balance Sheet

As we discussed and illustrated in previous chapters, the balance sheet may be presented with assets on the left-hand side and the liabilities and owner's equity on the right-hand side. This form of the balance sheet is called the *account form*. The balance sheet may also be presented in a downward sequence in three sections. This form of balance sheet is called the *report form*. The report form of balance sheet for NetSolutions is shown in Exhibit 5. In this balance sheet, note that merchandise inventory at the end of the period is reported as a current asset and that the current portion of the note payable is $5,000.

## •Exhibit 4   Statement of Owner's Equity for Merchandising Business

| NetSolutions<br>Statement of Owner's Equity<br>For the Year Ended December 31, 2007 | | |
|---|---|---|
| Chris Clark, capital, January 1, 2007 | | $153 8 0 0 00 |
| Net income for year | $75 4 0 0 00 | |
| Less withdrawals | 18 0 0 0 00 | |
| Increase in owner's equity | | 57 4 0 0 00 |
| Chris Clark, capital, December 31, 2007 | | $211 2 0 0 00 |

## •Exhibit 5   Report Form of Balance Sheet

| NetSolutions<br>Balance Sheet<br>December 31, 2007 | | | |
|---|---|---|---|
| **Assets** | | | |
| Current assets: | | | |
| Cash | | $52 9 5 0 00 | |
| Accounts receivable | | 91 0 8 0 00 | |
| Merchandise inventory | | 62 1 5 0 00 | |
| Office supplies | | 4 8 0 00 | |
| Prepaid insurance | | 2 6 5 0 00 | |
| Total current assets | | | $209 3 1 0 00 |
| Property, plant, and equipment: | | | |
| Land | | $20 0 0 0 00 | |
| Store equipment | $27 1 0 0 00 | | |
| Less accumulated depreciation | 5 7 0 0 00 | 21 4 0 0 00 | |
| Office equipment | $15 5 7 0 00 | | |
| Less accumulated depreciation | 4 7 2 0 00 | 10 8 5 0 00 | |
| Total property, plant, and equipment | | | 52 2 5 0 00 |
| Total assets | | | $261 5 6 0 00 |
| **Liabilities** | | | |
| Current liabilities: | | | |
| Accounts payable | | $22 4 2 0 00 | |
| Note payable (current portion) | | 5 0 0 0 00 | |
| Salaries payable | | 1 1 4 0 00 | |
| Unearned rent | | 1 8 0 0 00 | |
| Total current liabilities | | | $ 30 3 6 0 00 |
| Long-term liabilities: | | | |
| Note payable (final payment due 2017) | | | 20 0 0 0 00 |
| Total liabilities | | | $ 50 3 6 0 00 |
| **Owner's Equity** | | | |
| Chris Clark, capital | | | 211 2 0 0 00 |
| Total liabilities and owner's equity | | | $261 5 6 0 00 |

# Sales Transactions

objective **3**

Describe the accounting for the sale of merchandise.

In the remainder of this chapter, we illustrate transactions that affect the financial statements of a merchandising business. These transactions affect the reporting of net sales, cost of merchandise sold, gross profit, and merchandise inventory.

Merchandise transactions are recorded in the accounts, using the rules of debit and credit that we described and illustrated in earlier chapters. Special journals may be used, or transactions may be entered, recorded, and posted to the accounts electronically. Although journal entries may not be manually prepared, we will use a two-column general journal format in this chapter in order to simplify the discussion.[2]

## Cash Sales

A business may sell merchandise for cash. Cash sales are normally rung up (entered) on a cash register and recorded in the accounts. To illustrate, assume that on January 3, NetSolutions sells merchandise for $1,800. These cash sales can be recorded as follows:

| | | | **JOURNAL** | | | **Page 25** |
|---|---|---|---|---|---|---|
| **Date** | | **Description** | **Post. Ref.** | **Debit** | | **Credit** |
| 2007 Jan. | 3 | Cash | | 1 8 0 0 00 | | |
| | | Sales | | | | 1 8 0 0 00 |
| | | To record cash sales. | | | | |

Under the perpetual inventory system, the cost of merchandise sold and the reduction in merchandise inventory should also be recorded. In this way, the merchandise inventory account will indicate the amount of merchandise on hand (not sold). To illustrate, assume that the cost of merchandise sold on January 3 was $1,200. The entry to record the cost of merchandise sold and the reduction in the merchandise inventory is as follows:

| | | | | | |
|---|---|---|---|---|---|
| Jan. | 3 | Cost of Merchandise Sold | 1 2 0 0 00 | | |
| | | Merchandise Inventory | | 1 2 0 0 00 | |
| | | To record the cost of merchandise | | | |
| | | sold. | | | |

How do retailers record sales made with the use of credit cards? Sales made to customers using credit cards issued by banks, such as **MasterCard** or **VISA**, are recorded as *cash sales*. The seller deposits the credit card receipts for these sales directly into its bank account.

Normally, banks charge service fees for handling credit card sales. The seller debits these service fees to an expense account. An entry at the end of a month to record the payment of service charges on bank credit card sales is shown below.

| | | | | | |
|---|---|---|---|---|---|
| Jan. | 31 | Credit Card Expense | 4 8 00 | | |
| | | Cash | | 4 8 00 | |
| | | To record service charges on credit | | | |
| | | card sales for the month. | | | |

---

[2]Special journals and computerized accounting systems for merchandising businesses are described in Appendix 1 at the end of this chapter.

# Sales on Account

A business may sell merchandise on account. The seller records such sales as a debit to Accounts Receivable and a credit to Sales. An example of an entry for a NetSolutions sale on account of $510 follows. The cost of merchandise sold was $280.

| | | | | | |
|---|---|---|---|---|---|
| Jan. | 12 | Accounts Receivable—Sims Co. | 5 1 0 00 | | |
| | | Sales | | 5 1 0 00 | |
| | | Invoice No. 7172. | | | |
| | | | | | |
| | 12 | Cost of Merchandise Sold | 2 8 0 00 | | |
| | | Merchandise Inventory | | 2 8 0 00 | |
| | | Cost of merchandise sold on Invoice | | | |
| | | No. 7172. | | | |

**REAL WORLD**

A retailer may accept **MasterCard** or **VISA** but not **American Express**. Why? The service fees that credit card companies charge retailers are the primary reason that some businesses do not accept all credit cards. For example, American Express Co.'s service fees are normally higher than MasterCard's or VISA's. As a result, some retailers choose not to accept American Express cards. The disadvantage of this practice is that the retailer may lose customers to competitors who do accept American Express cards.

Sales may also be made to customers using nonbank credit cards. An example of a nonbank credit card is the **American Express** card. Nonbank credit card sales may first be reported to the card company before cash is received. Therefore, such sales create a *receivable* with the card company. Before the card company pays cash, it normally deducts a service fee. For example, assume that American Express card sales of $1,000 are made by NetSolutions and reported to the card company on January 20. The cost of the merchandise sold was $550. On January 27, the card company deducts a service fee of $50 and sends $950 to NetSolutions. These transactions are recorded by NetSolutions as follows:

| | | | | | |
|---|---|---|---|---|---|
| Jan. | 20 | Accounts Receivable—American Express | 1 0 0 0 00 | | |
| | | Sales | | 1 0 0 0 00 | |
| | | American Express (nonbank) credit | | | |
| | | card sales. | | | |
| | | | | | |
| | 20 | Cost of Merchandise Sold | 5 5 0 00 | | |
| | | Merchandise Inventory | | 5 5 0 00 | |
| | | Cost of merchandise sold on | | | |
| | | American Express credit card sales. | | | |
| | | | | | |
| | 27 | Cash | 9 5 0 00 | | |
| | | Credit Card Expense | 5 0 00 | | |
| | | Accounts Receivable—American Express | | 1 0 0 0 00 | |
| | | Received cash from American Express | | | |
| | | for sales reported on January 20. | | | |

# Sales Discounts

If an invoice dated August 13 has terms n/30, what is the due date of the invoice?

-------------------------------------

*September 12 [30 days = 18 days in August (31 days − 13 days) + 12 days in September]*

The terms of a sale are normally indicated on the ***invoice*** or bill that the seller sends to the buyer. An example of a sales invoice for NetSolutions is shown in Exhibit 6.

The terms for when payments for merchandise are to be made, agreed on by the buyer and the seller, are called the **credit terms**. If payment is required on delivery, the terms are *cash* or *net cash*. Otherwise, the buyer is allowed an amount of time, known as the **credit period**, in which to pay.

The credit period usually begins with the date of the sale as shown on the invoice. If payment is due within a stated number of days after the date of the invoice,

## •Exhibit 6  Invoice

| | | 106-8 |
|---|---|---|
| **net SOLUTIONS** Invoice | **5101 Washington Ave. Cincinnati, OH 45227-5101** | Made in U.S.A. |

| **SOLD TO** Omega Technologies 1000 Matrix Blvd. San Jose, CA. 95116–1000 | | **CUSTOMER'S ORDER NO. & DATE** 412 Jan. 10, 2007 | |
|---|---|---|---|
| **DATE SHIPPED** Jan. 12, 2007 | **HOW SHIPPED AND ROUTE** US Express Trucking Co. | **TERMS** 2/10, n/30 | **INVOICE DATE** Jan. 12, 2007 |
| **FROM** Cincinnati | **F.O.B.** Cincinnati | | |
| **QUANTITY** 10 | **DESCRIPTION** 3COM Megahertz 10/100 Lan PC Card | **UNIT PRICE** 150.00 | **AMOUNT** 1,500.00 |

such as 30 days, the terms are *net 30 days*. These terms may be written as *n/30*.[3] If payment is due by the end of the month in which the sale was made, the terms are written as *n/eom*.

As a means of encouraging the buyer to pay before the end of the credit period, the seller may offer a discount. For example, a seller may offer a 2% discount if the buyer pays within 10 days of the invoice date. If the buyer does not take the discount, the total amount is due within 30 days. These terms are expressed as *2/10, n/30* and are read as *2% discount if paid within 10 days, net amount due within 30 days*. The credit terms of 2/10, n/30 are summarized in Exhibit 7, using the information from the invoice in Exhibit 6.

## •Exhibit 7  Credit Terms

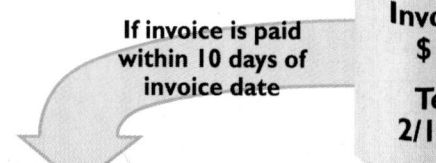

If an invoice dated November 22 has credit terms 2/10, n/30, what is (a) the last day the invoice may be paid within the discount period and (b) the last day of the credit period if the discount is not taken?

--------------------------------------------

*(a) December 2 [10 days = 8 days in November (30 days − 22 days) + 2 days in December]; (b) December 22 [30 days = 8 days in November (30 days − 22 days) + 22 days in December]*

Discounts taken by the buyer for early payment are recorded as sales discounts by the seller. Since managers may want to know the amount of the sales discounts for a period, the seller normally records the sales discounts in a separate account. The sales discounts account is a *contra* (or *offsetting*) account to Sales. To illustrate, assume that cash is received within the discount period (10 days) from the credit sale of $1,500, shown on the invoice in Exhibit 6. NetSolutions would record the receipt of the cash as follows:

---

[3]The word *net* as used here does not have the usual meaning of a number after deductions have been subtracted, as in *net income*.

| | | | | | | | |
|---|---|---|---|---|---|---|---|
| Jan. | 22 | Cash | | 1 4 7 0 00 | | | |
| | | Sales Discounts | | 3 0 00 | | | |
| | | Accounts Receivable—Omega | | | | 1 5 0 0 00 | |
| | | Technologies | | | | | |
| | | Collection on Invoice No. 106-8, less | | | | | |
| | | 2% discount. | | | | | |

# Sales Returns and Allowances

Merchandise sold may be returned to the seller (**sales return**). In addition, because of defects or for other reasons, the seller may reduce the initial price at which the goods were sold (**sales allowance**). If the return or allowance is for a sale on account, the seller usually issues the buyer a ***credit memorandum***. This memorandum shows the amount of and the reason for the seller's credit to an account receivable. A credit memorandum issued by NetSolutions is illustrated in Exhibit 8.

**•Exhibit 8**    Credit Memorandum

Like sales discounts, sales returns and allowances reduce sales revenue. They also result in additional shipping and other expenses. Since managers often want to know the amount of returns and allowances for a period, the seller records sales returns and allowances in a separate account. Sales Returns and Allowances is a *contra* (or *offsetting*) account to Sales.

The seller debits Sales Returns and Allowances for the amount of the return or allowance. If the original sale was on account, the seller credits Accounts Receivable. Since the merchandise inventory is kept up to date in a perpetual system, the seller adds the cost of the returned merchandise to the merchandise inventory account. The seller must also credit the cost of returned merchandise to the cost of merchandise sold account, since this account was debited when the original sale was recorded. To illustrate, assume that the cost of the merchandise returned in Exhibit 8 was $140. NetSolutions records the credit memo in Exhibit 8 as follows:

**REAL WORLD**

Book publishers often experience large returns if a book is not immediately successful. For example, 35% of adult hardcover books shipped to retailers are returned to publishers, according to the Association of American Publishers.

| | | | | | | |
|---|---|---|---|---|---|---|
| Jan. | 13 | Sales Returns and Allowances | | 2 2 5 00 | | |
| | | Accounts Receivable—Krier Company | | | | 2 2 5 00 |
| | | Credit Memo No. 32. | | | | |

| Jan. | 13 | Merchandise Inventory | | 1 4 0 00 | |
| | | Cost of Merchandise Sold | | | 1 4 0 00 |
| | | Cost of merchandise returned, Credit | | | |
| | | Memo No. 32. | | | |

What if the buyer pays for the merchandise and the merchandise is later returned? In this case, the seller may issue a credit and apply it against other accounts receivable owed by the buyer, or the cash may be refunded. If the credit is applied against the buyer's other receivables, the seller records entries similar to those preceding. If cash is refunded for merchandise returned or for an allowance, the seller debits Sales Returns and Allowances and credits Cash.

## INTEGRITY IN BUSINESS

### THE CASE OF THE FRAUDULENT PRICE TAGS

One of the challenges for a retailer is policing its sales return policy. There are many ways in which customers can unethically or illegally abuse such policies. In one case, a couple was accused of attaching **Marshall's** store price tags to cheaper merchandise bought or obtained elsewhere. The couple then returned the cheaper goods and received the substantially higher refund amount. Company security officials discovered the fraud and had the couple arrested after they had allegedly bilked the company for over $1 million.

# Purchase Transactions

**objective 4**

Describe the accounting for the purchase of merchandise.

As we indicated earlier in this chapter, most large retailers and many small merchandising businesses use computerized perpetual inventory systems. Under the perpetual inventory system, cash purchases of merchandise are recorded as follows:

| | | JOURNAL | | | Page 24 |
| Date | | Description | Post. Ref. | Debit | Credit |
| 2007 Jan. | 3 | Merchandise Inventory | | 2 5 1 0 00 | |
| | | Cash | | | 2 5 1 0 00 |
| | | Purchased inventory from Bowen Co. | | | |

Purchases of merchandise on account are recorded as follows:

| Jan. | 4 | Merchandise Inventory | | 9 2 5 0 00 | |
| | | Accounts Payable—Thomas Corporation | | | 9 2 5 0 00 |
| | | Purchased inventory on account. | | | |

## Purchases Discounts

Purchases discounts taken by the buyer for early payment of an invoice reduce the cost of the merchandise purchased. Most businesses design their accounting systems

so that all available discounts are taken. Even if the buyer has to borrow to make the payment within a discount period, it is normally to the buyer's advantage to do so. To illustrate, assume that Alpha Technologies issues an invoice for $3,000 to Net-Solutions, dated March 12, with terms 2/10, n/30. The last day of the discount period in which the $60 discount can be taken is March 22. Assume that in order to pay the invoice on March 22, NetSolutions borrows the money for the remaining 20 days of the credit period. If we assume an annual interest rate of 6% and a 360-day year, the interest on the loan of $2,940 ($3,000 − $60) is $9.80 ($2,940 × 6% × 20/360). The net savings to NetSolutions is $50.20, computed as follows:

| | |
|---|---:|
| Discount of 2% on $3,000 | $60.00 |
| Interest for 20 days at rate of 6% on $2,940 | −9.80 |
| Savings from borrowing | $50.20 |

The savings can also be seen by comparing the interest rate on the money *saved* by taking the discount and the interest rate on the money *borrowed* to take the discount. For NetSolutions, the interest rate on the money saved in this example is estimated by converting 2% for 20 days to a yearly rate, as follows:

$$2\% \times \frac{360 \text{ days}}{20 \text{ days}} = 2\% \times 18 = 36\%$$

If NetSolutions borrows the money to take the discount, it *pays* interest of 6%. If NetSolutions does not take the discount, it *pays* estimated interest of 36% for using the $60 for an additional 20 days.

Under the perpetual inventory system, the buyer initially debits the merchandise inventory account for the amount of the invoice. When paying the invoice, the buyer credits the merchandise inventory account for the amount of the discount. In this way, the merchandise inventory shows the *net* cost to the buyer. For example, Net-Solutions would record the Alpha Technologies invoice and its payment at the end of the discount period as follows:

| | | | | | |
|---|---|---|---:|---:|---:|
| Mar. | 12 | Merchandise Inventory | 3 0 0 0 00 | | |
| | | Accounts Payable—Alpha Technologies | | 3 0 0 0 00 | |
| | | | | | |
| | 22 | Accounts Payable—Alpha Technologies | 3 0 0 0 00 | | |
| | | Cash | | 2 9 4 0 00 | |
| | | Merchandise Inventory | | 6 0 00 | |

If NetSolutions does not take the discount because it does not pay the invoice until April 11, it would record the payment as follows:

| | | | | |
|---|---|---|---:|---:|
| Apr. | 11 | Accounts Payable—Alpha Technologies | 3 0 0 0 00 | |
| | | Cash | | 3 0 0 0 00 |

## Purchases Returns and Allowances

When merchandise is returned (**purchases return**) or a price adjustment is requested (**purchases allowance**), the buyer (debtor) usually sends the seller a letter or a debit memorandum. A ***debit memorandum***, shown in Exhibit 9, informs the seller of the amount the buyer proposes to *debit* to the account payable due the seller. It also states the reasons for the return or the request for a price reduction.

## •Exhibit 9  Debit Memorandum

The buyer may use a copy of the debit memorandum as the basis for recording the return or allowance or wait for approval from the seller (creditor). In either case, the buyer must debit Accounts Payable and credit Merchandise Inventory. To illustrate, NetSolutions records the return of the merchandise indicated in the debit memo in Exhibit 9 as follows:

| | | | | |
|---|---|---|---|---|
| Mar. | 7 | Accounts Payable—Maxim Systems | 900 00 | |
| | | Merchandise Inventory | | 900 00 |
| | | Debit Memo No. 18. | | |

Ennis Co. purchases merchandise of $8,000 on terms 2/10, n/30. Ennis pays the original invoice, less a return of $2,500, within the discount period. How much did Ennis Co. pay?

---------------------------------------

$5,390 [($8,000 − $2,500) × 2% = $110 discount; $8,000 − $2,500 − $110 = $5,390]

When a buyer returns merchandise or has been granted an allowance prior to paying the invoice, the amount of the debit memorandum is deducted from the invoice amount. The amount is deducted before the purchase discount is computed. For example, assume that on May 2, NetSolutions purchases $5,000 of merchandise from Delta Data Link, subject to terms 2/10, n/30. On May 4, NetSolutions returns $3,000 of the merchandise, and on May 12, NetSolutions pays the original invoice less the return. NetSolutions would record these transactions as follows:

| | | | | |
|---|---|---|---|---|
| May | 2 | Merchandise Inventory | 5000 00 | |
| | | Accounts Payable—Delta Data Link | | 5000 00 |
| | | Purchased merchandise. | | |
| | | | | |
| | 4 | Accounts Payable—Delta Data Link | 3000 00 | |
| | | Merchandise Inventory | | 3000 00 |
| | | Returned portion of merchandise | | |
| | | purchased. | | |
| | | | | |
| | 12 | Accounts Payable—Delta Data Link | 2000 00 | |
| | | Cash | | 1960 00 |
| | | Merchandise Inventory | | 40 00 |
| | | Paid invoice [($5,000 − $3,000) × 2% | | |
| | | = $40; $2,000 − $40 = $1,960]. | | |

# Transportation Costs, Sales Taxes, and Trade Discounts

In the preceding two sections, we described and illustrated merchandise transactions involving sales and purchases. In this section, we discuss merchandise transactions involving transportation costs, sales taxes, and trade discounts.

## Transportation Costs

The terms of a sale should indicate when the ownership (title) of the merchandise passes to the buyer. This point determines which party, the buyer or the seller, must pay the transportation costs.[4]

The ownership of the merchandise may pass to the buyer when the seller delivers the merchandise to the transportation company or freight carrier. For example, **DaimlerChrysler** records the sale and the transfer of ownership of its vehicles to dealers when the vehicles are shipped from the factory. In this case, the terms are said to be *FOB (free on board) shipping point*. This term means that the dealer pays the transportation costs from the shipping point (factory) to the final destination. Such costs are part of the dealer's total cost of purchasing inventory and should be added to the cost of the inventory by debiting Merchandise Inventory.

To illustrate, assume that on June 10, NetSolutions buys merchandise from Magna Data on account, $900, terms FOB shipping point, and pays the transportation cost of $50. NetSolutions records these two transactions as follows:

> **The buyer bears the transportation costs if the shipping terms are FOB shipping point.**

| | | | | | |
|---|---|---|---|---|---|
| June | 10 | Merchandise Inventory | | 900 00 | |
| | | Accounts Payable—Magna Data | | | 900 00 |
| | | Purchased merchandise, terms FOB | | | |
| | | shipping point. | | | |
| | 10 | Merchandise Inventory | | 50 00 | |
| | | Cash | | | 50 00 |
| | | Paid shipping cost on merchandise | | | |
| | | purchased. | | | |

**REAL WORLD**

Sometimes FOB shipping point and FOB destination are expressed in terms of the location at which the title to the merchandise passes to the buyer. For example, if **Toyota Motor Co.**'s assembly plant in Osaka, Japan, sells automobiles to a dealer in Chicago, FOB shipping point could be expressed as FOB Osaka. Likewise, FOB destination could be expressed as FOB Chicago.

The ownership of the merchandise may pass to the buyer when the buyer receives the merchandise. In this case, the terms are said to be *FOB (free on board) destination*. This term means that the seller delivers the merchandise to the buyer's final destination, free of transportation charges to the buyer. The seller thus pays the transportation costs to the final destination. The seller debits Transportation Out or Delivery Expense, which is reported on the seller's income statement as an expense.

> **The seller bears the transportation costs if the shipping terms are FOB destination.**

To illustrate, assume that on June 15, NetSolutions sells merchandise to Kranz Company on account, $700, terms FOB destination. The cost of the merchandise sold is $480, and NetSolutions pays the transportation cost of $40. NetSolutions records the sale, the cost of the sale, and the transportation cost as follows:

[4]The passage of title also determines whether the buyer or seller must pay other costs, such as the cost of insurance, while the merchandise is in transit.

| | | | | | | |
|---|---|---|---|---|---|---|
| June | 15 | Accounts Receivable—Kranz Company | | 7 0 0 00 | | |
| | | Sales | | | | 7 0 0 00 |
| | |     Sold merchandise, terms FOB | | | | |
| | |     destination. | | | | |
| | | | | | | |
| | 15 | Cost of Merchandise Sold | | 4 8 0 00 | | |
| | | Merchandise Inventory | | | | 4 8 0 00 |
| | |     Recorded cost of merchandise sold to | | | | |
| | |     Kranz Company. | | | | |
| | | | | | | |
| | 15 | Transportation Out | | 4 0 00 | | |
| | | Cash | | | | 4 0 00 |
| | |     Paid shipping cost on merchandise | | | | |
| | |     sold. | | | | |

Martin Co. sells $4,000 of merchandise to Oblinger Co. on account on terms 2/10, n/30, FOB shipping point. As a convenience to Oblinger, Martin Co. pays transportation costs of $250 and adds those costs to the invoice. (a) How much will Martin Co. bill Oblinger? (b) If Oblinger Co. pays within the discount period, what amount will Oblinger pay Martin?

------------------------------------

*(a) $4,250 ($4,000 + $250); (b) $4,170 [$4,000 − ($4,000 × 2%) + $250]*

As a convenience to the buyer, the seller may prepay the transportation costs, even though the terms are FOB shipping point. The seller will then add the transportation costs to the invoice. The buyer will debit Merchandise Inventory for the total amount of the invoice, including the transportation costs. Any discount terms would not apply to the prepaid transportation costs.

To illustrate, assume that on June 20, NetSolutions sells merchandise to Planter Company on account, $800, terms FOB shipping point. NetSolutions pays the transportation cost of $45 and adds it to the invoice. The cost of the merchandise sold is $360. NetSolutions records these transactions as follows:

| | | | | | | |
|---|---|---|---|---|---|---|
| June | 20 | Accounts Receivable—Planter Company | | 8 0 0 00 | | |
| | | Sales | | | | 8 0 0 00 |
| | |     Sold merchandise, terms FOB shipping | | | | |
| | |     point. | | | | |
| | | | | | | |
| | 20 | Cost of Merchandise Sold | | 3 6 0 00 | | |
| | | Merchandise Inventory | | | | 3 6 0 00 |
| | |     Recorded cost of merchandise sold to | | | | |
| | |     Planter Company. | | | | |
| | | | | | | |
| | 20 | Accounts Receivable—Planter Company | | 4 5 00 | | |
| | | Cash | | | | 4 5 00 |
| | |     Prepaid shipping cost on merchandise | | | | |
| | |     sold. | | | | |

Shipping terms, the passage of title, and whether the buyer or seller is to pay the transportation costs are summarized in Exhibit 10.

## Sales Taxes

Almost all states and many other taxing units levy a tax on sales of merchandise.[5] The liability for the sales tax is incurred when the sale is made.

At the time of a cash sale, the seller collects the sales tax. When a sale is made on account, the seller charges the tax to the buyer by debiting Accounts Receivable.

**REAL WORLD**

The five states with the highest sales tax are Illinois, Minnesota, Nevada, Texas, and Washington. Some states have no sales tax, including Alaska, Delaware, Montana, New Hampshire, and Oregon.

---

[5]Businesses that purchase merchandise for resale to others are normally exempt from paying sales taxes on their purchases. Only final buyers of merchandise normally pay sales taxes.

## •Exhibit 10    Transportation Terms

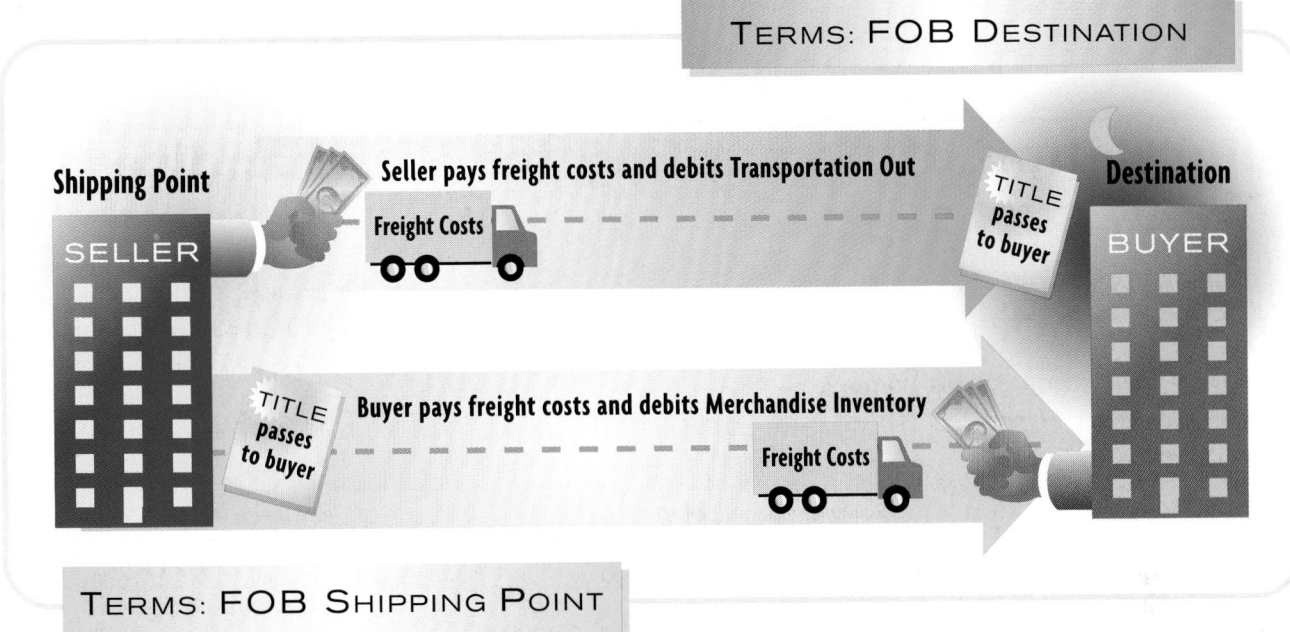

The seller credits the sales account for the amount of the sale and credits the tax to Sales Tax Payable. For example, the seller would record a sale of $100 on account, subject to a tax of 6%, as follows:

| | | | | |
|---|---|---|---|---|
| Aug. | 12 | Accounts Receivable—Lemon Co. | 1 0 6 00 | |
| | | Sales | | 1 0 0 00 |
| | | Sales Tax Payable | | 6 00 |
| | | Invoice No. 339. | | |

Normally on a regular basis, the seller pays to the taxing unit the amount of the sales tax collected. The seller records such a payment as follows:

| | | | | |
|---|---|---|---|---|
| Sept. | 15 | Sales Tax Payable | 2 9 0 0 00 | |
| | | Cash | | 2 9 0 0 00 |
| | | Payment for sales taxes collected | | |
| | | during August. | | |

A seller offered a 30% trade discount on an item listed in its catalog for $2,400. At what amount would the seller record the sale?

---

*$1,680 [$2,400 − ($2,400 × 30%), or $2,400 × 70%]*

## Trade Discounts

Wholesalers are businesses that sell merchandise to other businesses rather than to the general public. Many wholesalers publish catalogs. Rather than updating their catalogs frequently, wholesalers often publish price updates, which may involve large discounts from the list prices in their catalogs. In addition, wholesalers may offer special discounts to certain classes of buyers, such as government agencies or businesses that order large quantities. Such discounts are called **trade discounts**.

Sellers and buyers do not normally record the list prices of merchandise and the related trade discounts in their accounts. For example, assume that an item has a list price of $1,000 and a 40% trade discount. The seller records the sale of the item at $600 [$1,000 less the trade discount of $400 ($1,000 × 40%)]. Likewise, the buyer records the purchase at $600.

# Illustration of Accounting for Merchandise Transactions

objective **6**

Illustrate the dual nature of merchandising transactions.

Each merchandising transaction affects a buyer and a seller. In the following illustration, we show how the same transactions would be recorded by both the seller and the buyer. In this example, the seller is Scully Company and the buyer is Burton Co.

| Transaction | Scully Company (Seller) | | Burton Co. (Buyer) | |
|---|---|---|---|---|
| July 1. Scully Company sold merchandise on account to Burton Co., $7,500, terms FOB shipping point, n/45. The cost of the merchandise sold was $4,500. | Accounts Receivable—Burton Co.     Sales | 7,500         7,500 | Merchandise Inventory     Accounts Payable—Scully Co. | 7,500         7,500 |
| | Cost of Merchandise Sold     Merchandise Inventory | 4,500         4,500 | | |
| July 2. Burton Co. paid transportation charges of $150 on July 1 purchase from Scully Company. | No entry. | | Merchandise Inventory     Cash | 150         150 |
| July 5. Scully Company sold merchandise on account to Burton Co., $5,000, terms FOB destination, n/30. The cost of the merchandise sold was $3,500. | Accounts Receivable—Burton Co.     Sales | 5,000         5,000 | Merchandise Inventory     Accounts Payable—Scully Co. | 5,000         5,000 |
| | Cost of Merchandise Sold     Merchandise Inventory | 3,500         3,500 | | |
| July 7. Scully Company paid transportation costs of $250 for delivery of merchandise sold to Burton Co. on July 5. | Transportation Out     Cash | 250         250 | No entry. | |
| July 13. Scully Company issued Burton Co. a credit memorandum for merchandise returned, $1,000. The merchandise had been purchased by Burton Co. on account on July 5. The cost of the merchandise returned was $700. | Sales Returns & Allowances     Accounts Receivable—Burton Co. | 1,000         1,000 | Accounts Payable—Scully Co.     Merchandise Inventory | 1,000         1,000 |
| | Merchandise Inventory     Cost of Merchandise Sold | 700         700 | | |
| July 15. Scully Company received payment from Burton Co. for purchase of July 5. | Cash     Accounts Receivable—Burton Co. | 4,000         4,000 | Accounts Payable—Scully Co.     Cash | 4,000         4,000 |

| Transaction | Scully Company (Seller) | | | Burton Co. (Buyer) | | |
|---|---|---|---|---|---|---|
| July 18. Scully Company sold merchandise on account to Burton Co., $12,000, terms FOB shipping point, 2/10, n/eom. Scully Company prepaid transportation costs of $500, which were added to the invoice. The cost of the merchandise sold was $7,200. | Accounts Receivable—Burton Co. | 12,000 | | Merchandise Inventory | 12,500 | |
| | Sales | | 12,000 | Accounts Payable—Scully Co. | | 12,500 |
| | | | | | | |
| | Accounts Receivable—Burton Co. | 500 | | | | |
| | Cash | | 500 | | | |
| | | | | | | |
| | Cost of Merchandise Sold | 7,200 | | | | |
| | Merchandise Inventory | | 7,200 | | | |
| July 28. Scully Company received payment from Burton Co. for purchase of July 18, less discount (2% × $12,000). | Cash | 12,260 | | Accounts Payable—Scully Co. | 12,500 | |
| | Sales Discounts | 240 | | Merchandise Inventory | | 240 |
| | Accounts Receivable—Burton Co. | | 12,500 | Cash | | 12,260 |

# Chart of Accounts for a Merchandising Business

**objective 7**

Prepare a chart of accounts for a merchandising business.

The chart of accounts for a merchandising business should reflect the types of merchandising transactions we have described in this chapter. As a basis for illustration, we use NetSolutions.

On July 1, 2006, when NetSolutions began its operations as a personalized retailer of software and hardware, its chart of accounts changed from that of a service business to that of a merchandiser. The new chart of accounts is shown in Exhibit 11. The accounts related to merchandising transactions are shown in color.

**•Exhibit 11**

**Chart of Accounts for NetSolutions, Merchandising Business**

| Balance Sheet Accounts | | Income Statement Accounts | |
|---|---|---|---|
| | **100 Assets** | | **400 Revenues** |
| 110 | Cash | 410 | Sales |
| 112 | Accounts Receivable | 411 | Sales Returns and Allowances |
| 115 | Merchandise Inventory | 412 | Sales Discounts |
| 116 | Office Supplies | | |
| 117 | Prepaid Insurance | | **500 Costs and Expenses** |
| 120 | Land | 510 | Cost of Merchandise Sold |
| 123 | Store Equipment | 520 | Sales Salaries Expense |
| 124 | Accumulated Depreciation— Store Equipment | 521 | Advertising Expense |
| | | 522 | Depreciation Expense—Store Equipment |
| 125 | Office Equipment | 523 | Transportation Out |
| 126 | Accumulated Depreciation— Office Equipment | 529 | Miscellaneous Selling Expense |
| | | 530 | Office Salaries Expense |
| | **200 Liabilities** | 531 | Rent Expense |
| 210 | Accounts Payable | 532 | Depreciation Expense—Office Equipment |
| 211 | Salaries Payable | | |
| 212 | Unearned Rent | 533 | Insurance Expense |
| 215 | Notes Payable | 534 | Office Supplies Expense |
| | | 539 | Misc. Administrative Expense |
| | **300 Owner's Equity** | | |
| 310 | Chris Clark, Capital | | **600 Other Income** |
| 311 | Chris Clark, Drawing | 610 | Rent Revenue |
| 312 | Income Summary | | |
| | | | **700 Other Expense** |
| | | 710 | Interest Expense |

NetSolutions is now using three-digit account numbers, which permits it to add new accounts as they are needed. The first digit indicates the major financial statement classification (1 for assets, 2 for liabilities, and so on). The second digit indicates the subclassification (e.g., 11 for current assets, 12 for noncurrent assets). The third digit identifies the specific account (e.g., 110 for Cash, 123 for Store Equipment).

NetSolutions is using a more complex numbering system because it has a greater variety of transactions. In addition, its growth creates a need for more detailed information for use in managing it. For example, a wages expense account was adequate for NetSolutions when it was a small service business with few employees. However, as a merchandising business, NetSolutions now uses two payroll accounts, one for Sales Salaries Expense and one for Office Salaries Expense.

# The Accounting Cycle for a Merchandising Business

**objective 8**

Describe the accounting cycle for a merchandising business.

We have described and illustrated the chart of accounts and the analysis and recording of transactions for a merchandising business. We have also illustrated the preparation of financial statements for a merchandiser, NetSolutions, at the end of an accounting cycle. In the remainder of this chapter, we describe the other elements of the accounting cycle for a merchandising business. In this discussion, we will focus primarily on the elements of this cycle that are likely to differ from those of a service business.

## Merchandise Inventory Shrinkage

$62,150 Actual Inventory Per Physical Count

$1,800 Shrinkage

$63,950 Available For Sale Per Records

Under the perpetual inventory system, a separate merchandise inventory account is maintained in the ledger. During the accounting period, this account shows the amount of merchandise for sale at any time. However, merchandising businesses may experience some loss of inventory due to shoplifting, employee theft, or errors in recording or counting inventory. As a result, the physical inventory taken at the end of the accounting period may differ from the amount of inventory shown in the inventory records. Normally, the amount of merchandise for sale, as indicated by the balance of the merchandise inventory account, is larger than the total amount of merchandise counted during the physical inventory. For this reason, the difference is often called ***inventory shrinkage*** or **inventory shortage**.

To illustrate, NetSolutions' inventory records indicate that $63,950 of merchandise should be available for sale on December 31, 2007. The physical inventory taken on December 31, 2007, however, indicates that only $62,150 of merchandise is actually available. Thus, the inventory shrinkage for the year ending December 31, 2007, is $1,800 ($63,950 − $62,150), as shown at the left. This amount is recorded by the following adjusting entry:

| | | | | | | |
|---|---|---|---|---|---|---|
| | | Adjusting Entry | | | | |
| Dec. | 31 | Cost of Merchandise Sold | | 1 8 0 0 00 | | |
| | | Merchandise Inventory | | | | 1 8 0 0 00 |

**REAL WORLD**

Retailers lose an estimated $30 billion to inventory shrinkage. The primary causes of the shrinkage are employee theft and shoplifting.

If the inventory account has a balance of $280,000 and the physical inventory indicates merchandise on hand of $265,000, what is the amount of inventory shrinkage?

--------------------------------------------------

*$15,000 ($280,000 − $265,000)*

After this entry has been recorded, the accounting records agree with the actual physical inventory at the end of the period. Since no system of procedures and safeguards can totally eliminate it, inventory shrinkage is often considered a normal cost of operations. If the amount of the shrinkage is abnormally large, it may be disclosed separately on the income statement. In such cases, the shrinkage may be recorded in a separate account, such as Loss from Merchandise Inventory Shrinkage.

## Work Sheet

Merchandising businesses that use a perpetual inventory system are also likely to use a computerized accounting system. In a computerized system, the adjusting entries are recorded and financial statements prepared without using a work sheet. For this reason, we illustrate the work sheet and the adjusting entries for NetSolutions in the appendix at the end of this chapter.

## Closing Entries

The closing entries for a merchandising business are similar to those for a service business. The first entry closes the temporary accounts with credit balances, such as Sales, to the income summary account. The second entry closes the temporary accounts with debit balances, including Sales Returns and Allowances, Sales Discounts, and Cost of Merchandise Sold, to the income summary account. The third entry closes the balance of the income summary account to the owner's capital account. The fourth entry closes the owner's drawing account to the owner's capital account.

In a computerized accounting system, the closing entries are prepared automatically. For this reason, we illustrate the closing entries for NetSolutions in the appendix at the end of this chapter.

---

## INTEGRITY IN BUSINESS

### THE COST OF EMPLOYEE THEFT

**O**ne survey reported that the 30 largest retail store chains have lost over $5 billion to shoplifting and employee theft. Of this amount only 3.45% of the losses resulted in any recovery. The stores apprehended over 600,000 shoplifters and 78,000 dishonest employees. Approximately one out of every 27 employees was apprehended for theft from his or her employer. Each dishonest employee stole approximately 8 times the amount stolen by shoplifters ($900 vs. $114).

**Source:** Jack L. Hayes International, *Fourteenth Annual Retail Theft Survey*, 2001.

---

# Financial Analysis and Interpretation

The ratio of net sales to assets measures how effectively a business is using its assets to generate sales. A high ratio indicates an effective use of assets. The assets used in computing the ratio may be the total assets at the end of the year, the average of the total assets at the beginning and end of the year, or the average of the monthly assets. For our purposes, we will use the average of the total assets at the beginning and end of the year. The ratio is computed as follows:

$$\text{Ratio of net sales to assets} = \frac{\text{Net sales}}{\text{Average total assets}}$$

To illustrate the use of this ratio, the following data are taken from annual reports of **Sears** and **J.C.Penney**:

|  | Sears | J.C.Penney |
|---|---|---|
| Net sales (in millions) | $41,366 | $31,846 |
| Total assets (in millions): |  |  |
| Beginning of year | 50,409 | 19,742 |
| End of year | 44,317 | 20,908 |

The ratio of net sales to assets for each company is as follows:

|  | Sears | J.C.Penney |
|---|---|---|
| Ratio of net sales to assets | 0.87* | 1.57** |

*$41,366/[($50,409 + $44,317)/2]
**$31,846/[($19,742 + $20,908)/2]

Based on these ratios, J.C.Penney appears better than Sears in utilizing its assets to generate sales. Comparing this ratio over time for both Sears and J.C.Penney, as well as comparing it with industry averages, would provide a better basis for interpreting the financial performance of each company.

## SPOTLIGHT ON STRATEGY

### UNDER ONE ROOF AT J.C.PENNEY

**M**ost businesses cannot be all things to all people. Businesses must seek a position in the marketplace to serve a unique customer need. Companies that are unable to do this can be squeezed out of the marketplace. The mall-based department store has been under pressure from both ends of the retail spectrum. At the discount store end of the market, **Wal-Mart** has been a formidable competitor. At the high end, specialty retailers have established strong presence in identifiable niches, such as electronics and apparel. Over a decade ago, **J.C.Penney** abandoned its "hard goods," such as electronics and sporting goods, in favor of providing "soft goods" because of the emerg-ing strength of specialty retailers in the hard goods segments. J.C.Penney is positioning itself against these forces by "exceeding the fashion, quality, selection, and service components of the discounter, equaling the merchandise intensity of the specialty store, and providing the selection and 'under one roof' shopping convenience of the department store." J.C.Penney merchandise strategy is focused toward customers it terms the "modern spender" and "starting outs." It views these segments as most likely to value its higher-end merchandise offered under the convenience of "one roof."

# Appendix 1   Accounting Systems for Merchandisers

Merchandising companies may use either manual or computerized accounting systems, similar to those used by service businesses. In this appendix, we describe and illustrate special journals and electronic forms that merchandise businesses may use in these systems.

## Manual Accounting System

In a manual accounting system, a merchandise business normally uses four special journals: sales journal (for sales on account), purchases journal (for purchases on account), cash receipts journal, and cash payments journal. These journals can be adapted from the special journals that we illustrated earlier for a service business.

Exhibit 12 illustrates NetSolutions' sales journal, which is modified from a revenue journal. In a sales journal, each transaction is recorded by entering the sales amount in the *Accounts Receivable Dr./Sales Cr.* column and entering the cost of the merchandise sold amount in the *Cost of Merchandise Sold Dr./Merchandise Inventory Cr.* column. The totals of the two columns would be posted to the four general ledger accounts. The inventory and accounts receivable subsidiary ledgers would be updated when each transaction is recorded.

# •Exhibit 12   Sales Journal for a Merchandising Business

| | Date | Invoice No. | Account Debited | Post. Ref. | Accts. Rec. Dr. Sales Cr. | Cost of Merchandise Sold Dr. Merchandise Inventory Cr. | |
|---|---|---|---|---|---|---|---|
| | **SALES JOURNAL** | | | | | Page 35 | |
| 1 | 2007 Mar. 2 | 810 | Berry Co. | ✔ | 2 7 5 0 00 | 2 0 0 0 00 | 1 |
| 2 | 14 | 811 | Handler Co. | ✔ | 4 2 6 0 00 | 3 4 7 0 00 | 2 |
| 3 | 19 | 812 | Jordan Co. | ✔ | 5 8 0 0 00 | 4 6 5 0 00 | 3 |
| 4 | 26 | 813 | Kenner Co. | ✔ | 4 5 0 0 00 | 3 8 4 0 00 | 4 |
| 5 | | | | | 17 3 1 0 00 | 13 9 6 0 00 | 5 |
| 6 | | | | | (112) (410) | (510) (115) | 6 |

Exhibit 13 illustrates a purchases journal for NetSolutions' merchandising business. This journal is similar to the purchases journal for NetSolutions' service business that we illustrated previously. It includes an *Accounts Payable Cr.* column and a *Merchandise Inventory Dr.* column, rather than a *Supplies Dr.* column. At the end of the month, these two column totals would be posted to the general ledger controlling accounts, Accounts Payable and Merchandise Inventory. The amounts in *Other Accounts Dr.* would be posted individually. The inventory and accounts payable subsidiary ledgers would be updated when each transaction is recorded.

Exhibit 14 illustrates a portion of NetSolutions' cash receipts journal. In this journal, cash sales are recorded in a *Sales Cr.* column rather than a *Fees Earned Cr.* column. In addition, the cost of merchandise sold for cash is recorded in a *Cost of*

# •Exhibit 13   Purchases Journal for a Merchandising Business

| | Date | Account Credited | Post. Ref. | Accounts Payable Cr. | Merchandise Inventory Dr. | Other Accounts Dr. | Post. Ref. | Amount | |
|---|---|---|---|---|---|---|---|---|---|
| | **PURCHASES JOURNAL** | | | | | | | Page 11 | |
| 1 | 2007 Mar. 4 | Compu-Tek | ✔ | 13 8 8 0 00 | 13 8 8 0 00 | | | | 1 |
| 2 | 7 | Omega Technologies | ✔ | 4 6 5 0 00 | 4 6 5 0 00 | | | | 2 |
| 3 | 15 | Dale Furniture Co. | ✔ | 5 7 0 0 00 | | Store Equipment | 123 | 5 7 0 0 00 | 3 |
| 4 | 22 | Delta Data Link | ✔ | 3 8 4 0 00 | 3 8 4 0 00 | | | | 4 |
| 5 | 29 | Power Electronics | ✔ | 3 2 0 0 00 | 3 2 0 0 00 | | | | 5 |
| 6 | | | | 31 2 7 0 00 | 25 5 7 0 00 | | | 5 7 0 0 00 | 6 |
| 7 | | | | (210) | (115) | | | (✔) | 7 |

## •Exhibit 14  Cash Receipts Journal for Merchandising Business

| | Date | | Account Credited | Post. Ref. | Other Accounts Cr. | Cost of Merchandise Sold Dr. Merchandise Inventory Cr. | Sales Cr. | Accounts Receivable Cr. | Sales Discounts Dr. | Cash Dr. | |
|---|---|---|---|---|---|---|---|---|---|---|---|
| | **CASH RECEIPTS JOURNAL** | | | | | | | | | Page 14 | |
| 1 | 2007 Mar. | 3 | Sales | ✔ | | 4 0 0 00 | 6 0 0 00 | | | 6 0 0 00 | 1 |
| 2 | | 12 | Berry Co. | ✔ | | | | 2 7 5 0 00 | 5 5 00 | 2 6 9 5 00 | 2 |

*Merchandise Sold Dr./Merchandise Inventory Cr.* column. Each entry in this column is posted to the inventory subsidiary ledger at the time the transaction is recorded. Sales discounts are recorded in a *Sales Discounts Dr.* column. At the end of the month, all the column totals except for *Other Accounts Cr.* are posted to the general ledger.

Exhibit 15 illustrates a portion of the cash payments journal for NetSolutions. This journal is modified for a merchandising business by adding a *Merchandise Inventory Cr.* column for recording discounts on purchases paid within the discount period. Each entry in this column is posted to the inventory subsidiary ledger at the time the transaction is recorded. At the end of the month, all the column totals except for *Other Accounts Dr.* are posted to the general ledger.

## •Exhibit 15  Cash Payments Journal for Merchandising Business

| | Date | Ck. No. | Account Debited | Post. Ref. | Other Accounts Dr. | Accounts Payable Dr. | Merchandise Inventory Cr. | Cash Cr. | |
|---|---|---|---|---|---|---|---|---|---|
| | **CASH PAYMENTS JOURNAL** | | | | | | | Page 7 | |
| 1 | 2007 Mar. 14 | 210 | Compu-Tek | ✔ | | 13 8 8 0 00 | | 13 8 8 0 00 | 1 |
| 2 | 17 | 211 | Omega Technologies | ✔ | | 4 6 5 0 00 | 9 3 00 | 4 5 5 7 00 | 2 |

# Computerized Accounting Systems

In computerized accounting systems, special journals may be replaced by electronic forms that capture the necessary information. The software then uses this information as the basis for making entries automatically. In QuickBooks, for example, the inventory items to be purchased and sold must first be identified, using an "Edit Item" form. The software will later record each item's purchase or sale, using information from this form. The Edit Item form in Exhibit 16 shows this information for NetSolutions' purchase of LT-1000 network servers from Compu-Tek. Each server cost $3,470 per unit and will be sold for $4,260 per unit.

After inventory items have been described inside QuickBooks, transaction data can be entered. We will begin with NetSolutions' March 4, 2007 purchase from Compu-Tek, which we illustrated previously in the purchases journal in Exhibit 13. We will use the "Enter Bills" form, shown in Exhibit 17, to record the purchase of four LT-1000s from Compu-Tek.

## •Exhibit 16 Edit Item Form

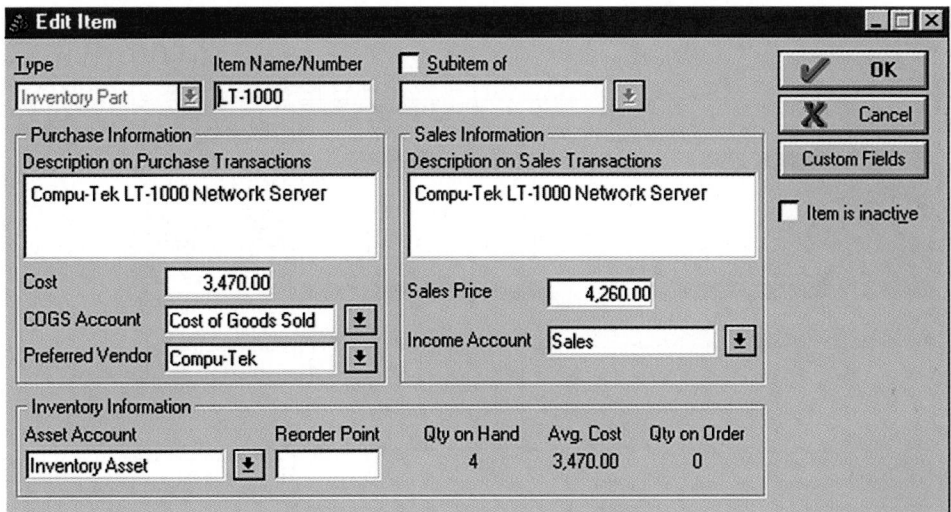

## •Exhibit 17 Enter Bills Form

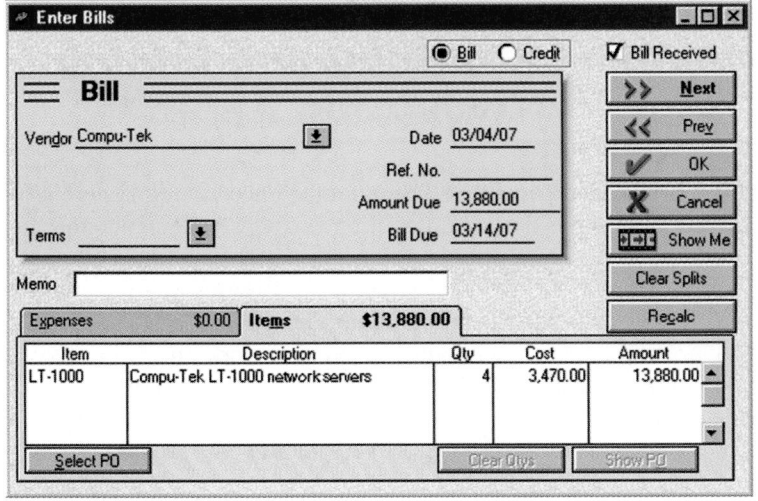

**Automatic Postings**

| | | |
|---|---|---|
| Dr. Merch. Inv.—LT-1000 | 13,880 | |
| Cr. Accounts Payable—Compu-Tek | | 13,880 |

After the Enter Bills form has been completed, the software adds the cost of four LT-1000s to NetSolutions' inventory. At the same time, it establishes an account payable to Compu-Tek for $13,880.

Now, assume that on March 14 NetSolutions invoices Handler Co. for one of these network servers, as illustrated in the sales journal in Exhibit 12. Using the "Create Invoices" form in QuickBooks, as shown in Exhibit 18, we enter the sale and the software establishes an account receivable for Handler Co. In addition, the software reduces the inventory stock level of the LT-1000 by $3,470 and records the cost of goods sold. This latter transaction is recorded automatically and is not shown on the Create Invoices form.

An income statement prepared after these forms have been completed would show sales of $4,260, cost of goods sold of $3,470, and gross profit of $790. A balance sheet would show accounts receivable of $4,260, inventory of $10,410 (3 × $3,470), and accounts payable of $13,880.

## •Exhibit 18   Create Invoices Form

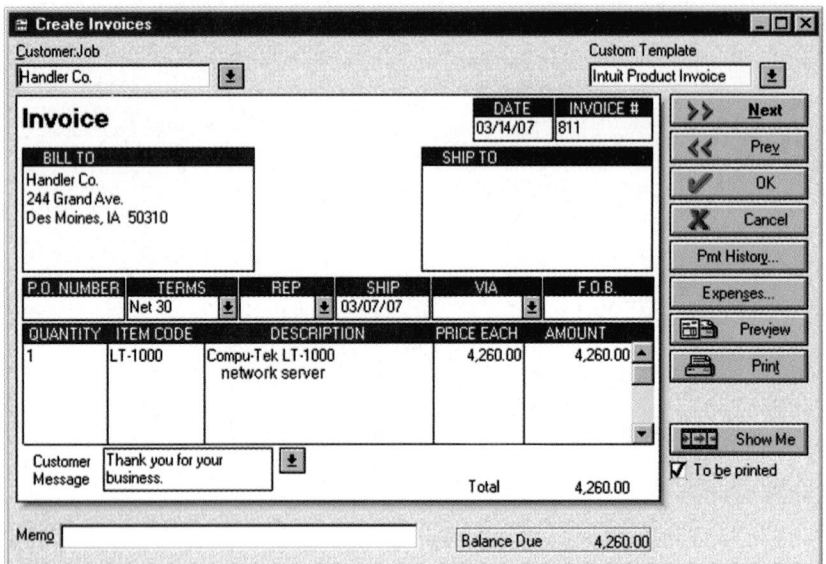

**Automatic Postings**

| | | |
|---|---|---|
| Dr. Accts. Rec.—Handler Co. | 4,260 | |
| Cr. Sales | | 4,260 |
| | | |
| Dr. Cost of Merch. Sold | 3,470 | |
| Cr. Merch. Inv.—LT-1000 | | 3,470 |

# Appendix 2   Work Sheet and Adjusting and Closing Entries for a Merchandising Business

A merchandising business that does not use a computerized accounting system may use a work sheet in assembling the data for preparing financial statements and adjusting and closing entries. In this appendix, we illustrate such a work sheet, along with the adjusting and closing entries for a merchandising business.

The work sheet in Exhibit 19 is for NetSolutions on December 31, 2007, the end of its second year of operations as a merchandiser. In this work sheet, we list all of the accounts, including the accounts that have no balances, in the order that they appear in NetSolutions' ledger.

The data needed for adjusting the accounts of NetSolutions are as follows:

| | | |
|---|---|---:|
| Physical merchandise inventory on December 31, 2007 . . . . . . . . | | $62,150 |
| Office supplies on hand on December 31, 2007 . . . . . . . . . . . . | | 480 |
| Insurance expired during 2007 . . . . . . . . . . . . . . . . . . . . . . . . | | 1,910 |
| Depreciation during 2007 on: Store equipment . . . . . . . . . . . . . | | 3,100 |
| Office equipment . . . . . . . . . . . . . . | | 2,490 |
| Salaries accrued on December 31, 2007: Sales salaries . . . . . . . . . | $780 | |
| Office salaries . . . . . . . . | 360 | 1,140 |
| Rent earned during 2007 . . . . . . . . . . . . . . . . . . . . . . . . . . . . . | | 600 |

There is no specific order in which to analyze the accounts in the work sheet, assemble the adjustment data, and make the adjusting entries. However, you can normally save time by selecting the accounts in the order in which they appear on the trial balance. Using this approach, the adjustment for merchandise inventory shrinkage is listed first {entry (a) on the work sheet}, followed by the adjustment for office supplies used {entry (b) on the work sheet}, and so on.

After all the adjustments have been entered on the work sheet, the Adjustments columns are totaled to prove the equality of debits and credits. As we illustrated in a previous chapter, the adjusted amounts of the balances in the Trial Balance columns

# •Exhibit 19   Work Sheet for Merchandising Business

**NetSolutions**
**Work Sheet**
**For the Year Ended December 31, 2007**

| | Account Title | Trial Balance | | Adjustments | | Adjusted Trial Balance | | Income Statement | | Balance Sheet | | |
|---|---|---|---|---|---|---|---|---|---|---|---|---|
| | | Dr. | Cr. | Dr. | Cr. | Dr. | Cr. | Dr. | Cr. | Dr. | Cr. | |
| 1 | Cash | 52,950 | | | | 52,950 | | | | 52,950 | | 1 |
| 2 | Accounts Receivable | 91,080 | | | | 91,080 | | | | 91,080 | | 2 |
| 3 | Merchandise Inventory | 63,950 | | | (a)1,800 | 62,150 | | | | 62,150 | | 3 |
| 4 | Office Supplies | 1,090 | | | (b) 610 | 480 | | | | 480 | | 4 |
| 5 | Prepaid Insurance | 4,560 | | | (c)1,910 | 2,650 | | | | 2,650 | | 5 |
| 6 | Land | 20,000 | | | | 20,000 | | | | 20,000 | | 6 |
| 7 | Store Equipment | 27,100 | | | | 27,100 | | | | 27,100 | | 7 |
| 8 | Accum. Depr.—Store Equipment | | 2,600 | | (d)3,100 | | 5,700 | | | | 5,700 | 8 |
| 9 | Office Equipment | 15,570 | | | | 15,570 | | | | 15,570 | | 9 |
| 10 | Accum. Depr.—Office Equipment | | 2,230 | | (e)2,490 | | 4,720 | | | | 4,720 | 10 |
| 11 | Accounts Payable | | 22,420 | | | | 22,420 | | | | 22,420 | 11 |
| 12 | Salaries Payable | | | | (f)1,140 | | 1,140 | | | | 1,140 | 12 |
| 13 | Unearned Rent | | 2,400 | (g) 600 | | | 1,800 | | | | 1,800 | 13 |
| 14 | Notes Payable | | | | | | | | | | | 14 |
| 15 |    (final payment due 2017) | | 25,000 | | | | 25,000 | | | | 25,000 | 15 |
| 16 | Chris Clark, Capital | | 153,800 | | | | 153,800 | | | | 153,800 | 16 |
| 17 | Chris Clark, Drawing | 18,000 | | | | 18,000 | | | | 18,000 | | 17 |
| 18 | Sales | | 720,185 | | | | 720,185 | | 720,185 | | | 18 |
| 19 | Sales Returns and Allowances | 6,140 | | | | 6,140 | | 6,140 | | | | 19 |
| 20 | Sales Discounts | 5,790 | | | | 5,790 | | 5,790 | | | | 20 |
| 21 | Cost of Merchandise Sold | 523,505 | | (a)1,800 | | 525,305 | | 525,305 | | | | 21 |
| 22 | Sales Salaries Expense | 55,450 | | (f) 780 | | 56,230 | | 56,230 | | | | 22 |
| 23 | Advertising Expense | 10,860 | | | | 10,860 | | 10,860 | | | | 23 |
| 24 | Depr. Exp.—Store Equipment | | | (d)3,100 | | 3,100 | | 3,100 | | | | 24 |
| 25 | Miscellaneous Selling Expense | 630 | | | | 630 | | 630 | | | | 25 |
| 26 | Office Salaries Expense | 20,660 | | (f) 360 | | 21,020 | | 21,020 | | | | 26 |
| 27 | Rent Expense | 8,100 | | | | 8,100 | | 8,100 | | | | 27 |
| 28 | Depr. Exp.—Office Equipment | | | (e)2,490 | | 2,490 | | 2,490 | | | | 28 |
| 29 | Insurance Expense | | | (c)1,910 | | 1,910 | | 1,910 | | | | 29 |
| 30 | Office Supplies Expense | | | (b) 610 | | 610 | | 610 | | | | 30 |
| 31 | Misc. Administrative Expense | 760 | | | | 760 | | 760 | | | | 31 |
| 32 | Rent Revenue | | | | (g) 600 | | 600 | | 600 | | | 32 |
| 33 | Interest Expense | 2,440 | | | | 2,440 | | 2,440 | | | | 33 |
| 34 | | 928,635 | 928,635 | 11,650 | 11,650 | 935,365 | 935,365 | 645,385 | 720,785 | 289,980 | 214,580 | 34 |
| 35 | Net income | | | | | | | 75,400 | | | 75,400 | 35 |
| 36 | | | | | | | | 720,785 | 720,785 | 289,980 | 289,980 | 36 |

(a) Merchandise inventory shrinkage for period, $1,800 ($63,950 − $62,150).

(b) Office supplies used, $610 ($1,090 − $480).

(c) Insurance expired, $1,910.

(d) Depreciation of store equipment, $3,100.

(e) Depreciation of office equipment, $2,490.

(f) Salaries accrued but not paid (sales salaries, $780; office salaries, $360), $1,140.

(g) Rent earned from amount received in advance, $600.

are extended to the Adjusted Trial Balance columns.[6] The Adjusted Trial Balance columns are then totaled to prove the equality of debits and credits.

The balances, as adjusted, are then extended to the statement columns. The four statement columns are totaled, and the net income or net loss is determined. For NetSolutions, the difference between the credit and debit columns of the Income Statement section is $75,400, the amount of the net income. The difference between the debit and credit columns of the Balance Sheet section is also $75,400, which is the increase in owner's equity as a result of the net income. Agreement between the two balancing amounts is evidence of debit-credit equality and mathematical accuracy.

The income statement, statement of owner's equity, and balance sheet are prepared from the work sheet in a manner similar to that of a service business. These financial statements are shown in Exhibits 3, 4, and 5. The Adjustments columns in the work sheet provide the data for journalizing the adjusting entries. NetSolutions' adjusting entries at the end of 2007 are as follows:

| | | | JOURNAL | | | Page 28 |
|---|---|---|---|---|---|---|
| | Date | | Description | Post. Ref. | Debit | Credit |
| 1 | 2007 | | Adjusting Entries | | | |
| 2 | Dec. | 31 | Cost of Merchandise Sold | 510 | 1 8 0 0 00 | |
| 3 | | | Merchandise Inventory | 115 | | 1 8 0 0 00 |
| 4 | | | | | | |
| 5 | | 31 | Office Supplies Expense | 534 | 6 1 0 00 | |
| 6 | | | Office Supplies | 116 | | 6 1 0 00 |
| 7 | | | | | | |
| 8 | | 31 | Insurance Expense | 533 | 1 9 1 0 00 | |
| 9 | | | Prepaid Insurance | 117 | | 1 9 1 0 00 |
| 10 | | | | | | |
| 11 | | 31 | Depreciation Expense— | | | |
| 12 | | | Store Equipment | 522 | 3 1 0 0 00 | |
| 13 | | | Accumulated Depreciation— | | | |
| 14 | | | Store Equipment | 124 | | 3 1 0 0 00 |
| 15 | | | | | | |
| 16 | | 31 | Depreciation Expense— | | | |
| 17 | | | Office Equipment | 532 | 2 4 9 0 00 | |
| 18 | | | Accumulated Depreciation— | | | |
| 19 | | | Office Equipment | 126 | | 2 4 9 0 00 |
| 20 | | | | | | |
| 21 | | 31 | Sales Salaries Expense | 520 | 7 8 0 00 | |
| 22 | | | Office Salaries Expense | 530 | 3 6 0 00 | |
| 23 | | | Salaries Payable | 211 | | 1 1 4 0 00 |
| 24 | | | | | | |
| 25 | | 31 | Unearned Rent | 212 | 6 0 0 00 | |
| 26 | | | Rent Revenue | 610 | | 6 0 0 00 |

The Income Statement columns of the work sheet provide the data for preparing the closing entries. The closing entries for NetSolutions at the end of 2007 are as follows:

---

[6]Some accountants prefer to eliminate the Adjusted Trial Balance columns and to extend the adjusted balances directly to the statement columns. Such a work sheet is often used if there are only a few adjustment items.

| | Date | Item | Post. Ref. | Debit | Credit | |
|---|---|---|---|---|---|---|
| | | JOURNAL | | | Page 29 | |
| 1 | 2007 | Closing Entries | | | | 1 |
| 2 | Dec. 31 | Sales | 410 | 720 185 00 | | 2 |
| 3 | | Rent Revenue | 610 | 6 00 00 | | 3 |
| 4 | | Income Summary | 312 | | 720 785 00 | 4 |
| 5 | | | | | | 5 |
| 6 | 31 | Income Summary | 312 | 645 385 00 | | 6 |
| 7 | | Sales Returns and Allowances | 411 | | 6 140 00 | 7 |
| 8 | | Sales Discounts | 412 | | 5 790 00 | 8 |
| 9 | | Cost of Merchandise Sold | 510 | | 525 305 00 | 9 |
| 10 | | Sales Salaries Expense | 520 | | 56 230 00 | 10 |
| 11 | | Advertising Expense | 521 | | 10 860 00 | 11 |
| 12 | | Depr. Expense—Store Equipment | 522 | | 3 100 00 | 12 |
| 13 | | Miscellaneous Selling Expense | 529 | | 630 00 | 13 |
| 14 | | Office Salaries Expense | 530 | | 21 020 00 | 14 |
| 15 | | Rent Expense | 531 | | 8 100 00 | 15 |
| 16 | | Depr. Expense—Office Equipment | 532 | | 2 490 00 | 16 |
| 17 | | Insurance Expense | 533 | | 1 910 00 | 17 |
| 18 | | Office Supplies Expense | 534 | | 610 00 | 18 |
| 19 | | Misc. Administrative Expense | 539 | | 760 00 | 19 |
| 20 | | Interest Expense | 710 | | 2 440 00 | 20 |
| 21 | | | | | | 21 |
| 22 | 31 | Income Summary | 312 | 75 400 00 | | 22 |
| 23 | | Chris Clark, Capital | 310 | | 75 400 00 | 23 |
| 24 | | | | | | 24 |
| 25 | 31 | Chris Clark, Capital | 310 | 18 000 00 | | 25 |
| 26 | | Chris Clark, Drawing | 311 | | 18 000 00 | 26 |

The balance of Income Summary, after the first two closing entries have been posted, is the net income or net loss for the period. The third closing entry transfers this balance to the owner's capital account. NetSolutions' income summary account after the closing entries have been posted is as follows:

**ACCOUNT** *Income Summary*    **ACCOUNT NO. 312**

| Date | Item | Post. Ref. | Debit | Credit | Balance Debit | Balance Credit |
|---|---|---|---|---|---|---|
| 2007 Dec. 31 | Revenues | 29 | | 720 785 00 | | 720 785 00 |
| 31 | Expenses | 29 | 645 385 00 | | | 75 400 00 |
| 31 | Net income | 29 | 75 400 00 | | — | — |

After the closing entries have been prepared and posted to the accounts, a post-closing trial balance may be prepared to verify the debit-credit equality. The only accounts that should appear on the post-closing trial balance are the asset, contra asset, liability, and owner's capital accounts with balances. These are the same accounts that appear on the end-of-period balance sheet.

# Key Points

## 1 Distinguish the activities of a service business from those of a merchandising business.

The primary differences between a service business and a merchandising business relate to revenue activities. Merchandising businesses purchase merchandise for selling to customers.

On a merchandising business's income statement, revenue from selling merchandise is reported as sales. The cost of the merchandise sold is subtracted from sales to arrive at gross profit. The operating expenses are subtracted from gross profit to arrive at net income.

Merchandise inventory, which is merchandise not sold, is reported as a current asset on the balance sheet.

## 2 Describe and illustrate the financial statements of a merchandising business.

The multiple-step income statement of a merchandiser reports sales, sales returns and allowances, sales discounts, and net sales. The cost of the merchandise sold is subtracted from net sales to determine the gross profit. The cost of merchandise sold is determined by using either the periodic or perpetual method. Operating income is determined by subtracting operating expenses from gross profit. Operating expenses are normally classified as selling or administrative expenses. Net income is determined by adding or subtracting the net of other income and expense. The income statement may also be reported in a single-step form. The statement of owner's equity is similar to that for a service business. The balance sheet reports merchandise inventory at the end of the period as a current asset.

## 3 Describe the accounting for the sale of merchandise.

Sales of merchandise for cash or on account are recorded by crediting Sales. The cost of merchandise sold and the reduction in merchandise inventory are also recorded for the sale. For sales of merchandise on ac-count, the credit terms may allow discounts for early payment. Such discounts are recorded by the seller as a debit to Sales Discounts. Sales discounts are reported as a deduction from the amount initially recorded in Sales. Likewise, when merchandise is returned or a price adjustment is granted, the seller debits Sales Returns and Allowances. For sales on account, a subsidiary ledger is maintained for individual customer accounts receivable.

Under the perpetual inventory system, the cost of merchandise sold and the reduction of merchandise inventory on hand are recorded at the time of sale. In this way, the merchandise inventory account indicates the amount of merchandise on hand at all times. Likewise, any returned merchandise is recorded in the merchandise inventory account, with a related reduction in the cost of merchandise sold.

## 4 Describe the accounting for the purchase of merchandise.

Purchases of merchandise for cash or on account are recorded by debiting Merchandise Inventory. For purchases of merchandise on account, the credit terms may allow cash discounts for early payment. Such purchases discounts are viewed as a reduction in the cost of the merchandise purchased. When merchandise is returned or a price adjustment is granted, the buyer credits Merchandise Inventory.

## 5 Describe the accounting for transportation costs, sales taxes, and trade discounts.

When merchandise is shipped FOB shipping point, the buyer pays the transportation costs and debits Merchandise Inventory. When merchandise is shipped FOB destination, the seller pays the transportation costs and debits Transportation Out or Delivery Expense. If the seller prepays transportation costs as a convenience to the buyer, the seller debits Accounts Receivable for the costs.

The liability for sales tax is incurred when the sale is made and is recorded by the seller as a credit to the sales tax payable account. When the amount of the sales tax is paid to the taxing unit, Sales Tax Payable is debited and Cash is credited.

Many wholesalers offer trade discounts, which are discounts off the list prices of merchandise. Normally, neither the seller or the buyer records the list price and the related trade discount in the accounts.

## 6 Illustrate the dual nature of merchandising transactions.

Each merchandising transaction affects a buyer and a seller. The illustration in this chapter shows how the same transactions would be recorded by both.

## 7 Prepare a chart of accounts for a merchandising business.

The chart of accounts for a merchandising business is more complex than that for a service business and normally includes accounts such as Sales, Sales Discounts, Sales Returns and Allowances, Cost of Merchandise Sold, and Merchandise Inventory.

## 8 Describe the accounting cycle for a merchandising business.

The accounting cycle for a merchandising business is similar to that of a service business. However, a merchandiser is likely to experience inventory shrinkage, which must be recorded. The normal adjusting entry is to debit Cost of Merchandise Sold and credit Merchandise Inventory for the amount of the shrinkage.

## 9 Compute the ratio of net sales to assets as a measure of how effectively a business is using its assets.

The assets used in computing the ratio of net sales to assets may be total assets at the end of the year, the average of the total assets at the beginning and end of the year, or the average of the monthly assets. A high ratio of net sales to assets indicates an effective use of assets.

# Key Terms

account form (236)

administrative expenses (general expenses) (235)

cost of merchandise sold (231)

credit memorandum (241)

debit memorandum (243)

FOB (free on board) destination (245)

FOB (free on board) shipping point (245)

gross profit (231)

income from operations (operating income) (235)

inventory shrinkage (250)

invoice (239)

merchandise inventory (231)

multiple-step income statement (232)

other expense (236)

other income (236)

periodic method (234)

perpetual method (235)

purchase return or allowance (234)

purchases discounts (234)

report form (236)

sales (232)

sales discounts (233)

sales returns and allowances (233)

selling expenses (235)

single-step income statement (236)

trade discounts (247)

# Illustrative Problem

The following transactions were completed by Montrose Company during May of the current year. Montrose Company uses a perpetual inventory system.

May 3. Purchased merchandise on account from Floyd Co., $4,000, terms FOB shipping point, 2/10, n/30, with prepaid transportation costs of $120 added to the invoice.

5. Purchased merchandise on account from Kramer Co., $8,500, terms FOB destination, 1/10, n/30.

6. Sold merchandise on account to C. F. Howell Co., list price $4,000, trade discount 30%, terms 2/10, n/30. The cost of the merchandise sold was $1,125.

8. Purchased office supplies for cash, $150.

10. Returned merchandise purchased on May 5 from Kramer Co., $1,300.

13. Paid Floyd Co. on account for purchase of May 3, less discount.

14. Purchased merchandise for cash, $10,500.

15. Paid Kramer Co. on account for purchase of May 5, less return of May 10 and discount.

16. Received cash on account from sale of May 6 to C. F. Howell Co., less discount.

19. Sold merchandise on nonbank credit cards and reported accounts to the card company, American Express, $2,450. The cost of the merchandise sold was $980.

22. Sold merchandise on account to Comer Co., $3,480, terms 2/10, n/30. The cost of the merchandise sold was $1,400.

24. Sold merchandise for cash, $4,350. The cost of the merchandise sold was $1,750.

25. Received merchandise returned by Comer Co. from sale on May 22, $1,480. The cost of the returned merchandise was $600.

31. Received cash from card company for nonbank credit card sales of May 19, less $140 service fee.

## Instructions

1. Journalize the preceding transactions.
2. Journalize the adjusting entry for merchandise inventory shrinkage, $3,750.

### Solution

**1.**

| Date | | Account | Debit | Credit |
|---|---|---|---|---|
| May | 3 | Merchandise Inventory | 4,120 | |
| | | Accounts Payable—Floyd Co. | | 4,120 |
| | 5 | Merchandise Inventory | 8,500 | |
| | | Accounts Payable—Kramer Co. | | 8,500 |
| | 6 | Accounts Receivable—C. F. Howell Co. | 2,800 | |
| | | Sales | | 2,800 |
| | | [$4,000 − (30% × $4,000)] | | |
| | 6 | Cost of Merchandise Sold | 1,125 | |
| | | Merchandise Inventory | | 1,125 |
| | 8 | Office Supplies | 150 | |
| | | Cash | | 150 |
| | 10 | Accounts Payable—Kramer Co. | 1,300 | |
| | | Merchandise Inventory | | 1,300 |
| | 13 | Accounts Payable—Floyd Co. | 4,120 | |
| | | Merchandise Inventory | | 80 |
| | | Cash | | 4,040 |
| | | [$4,000 − (2% × $4,000) + $120] | | |
| | 14 | Merchandise Inventory | 10,500 | |
| | | Cash | | 10,500 |
| | 15 | Accounts Payable—Kramer Co. | 7,200 | |
| | | Merchandise Inventory | | 72 |
| | | Cash | | 7,128 |
| | | [($8,500 − $1,300) × 1% = $72; | | |
| | | $8,500 − $1,300 − $72 = $7,128] | | |
| | 16 | Cash | 2,744 | |
| | | Sales Discounts | 56 | |
| | | Accounts Receivable—C. F. Howell Co. | | 2,800 |
| | 19 | Accounts Receivable—American Express | 2,450 | |
| | | Sales | | 2,450 |
| | 19 | Cost of Merchandise Sold | 980 | |
| | | Merchandise Inventory | | 980 |
| | 22 | Accounts Receivable—Comer Co. | 3,480 | |
| | | Sales | | 3,480 |
| | 22 | Cost of Merchandise Sold | 1,400 | |
| | | Merchandise Inventory | | 1,400 |
| | 24 | Cash | 4,350 | |
| | | Sales | | 4,350 |
| | 24 | Cost of Merchandise Sold | 1,750 | |
| | | Merchandise Inventory | | 1,750 |
| | 25 | Sales Returns and Allowances | 1,480 | |
| | | Accounts Receivable—Comer Co. | | 1,480 |
| | 25 | Merchandise Inventory | 600 | |
| | | Cost of Merchandise Sold | | 600 |
| | 31 | Cash | 2,310 | |
| | | Credit Card Expense | 140 | |
| | | Accounts Receivable—American Express | | 2,450 |
| **2.** | May 31 | Cost of Merchandise Sold | 3,750 | |
| | | Merchandise Inventory | | 3,750 |

# Self-Examination Questions (Answers at End of Chapter)

1. If merchandise purchased on account is returned, the buyer may inform the seller of the details by issuing:

A. a debit memorandum
B. a credit memorandum
C. an invoice
D. a bill

2. If merchandise is sold on account to a customer for $1,000, terms FOB shipping point, 1/10, n/30, and the seller prepays $50 in transportation costs, the amount of the discount for early payment would be:

A. $0        C. $10.00
B. $5.00     D. $10.50

3. The income statement in which the total of all expenses is deducted from the total of all revenues is termed:

A. multiple-step form    C. account form
B. single-step form      D. report form

4. On a multiple-step income statement, the excess of net sales over the cost of merchandise sold is called:

A. operating income
B. income from operations
C. gross profit
D. net income

5. Which of the following expenses would normally be classified as Other expense on a multiple-step income statement?

A. Depreciation expense—office equipment
B. Sales salaries expense
C. Insurance expense
D. Interest expense

# Class Discussion Questions

1. What distinguishes a merchandising business from a service business?
2. Can a business earn a gross profit but incur a net loss? Explain.
3. In computing the cost of merchandise sold, does each of the following items increase or decrease that cost? (a) transportation costs, (b) beginning merchandise inventory, (c) purchase discounts, (d) ending merchandise inventory.
4. Describe how the periodic method differs from the perpetual method of accounting for merchandise inventory.
5. Differentiate between the multiple-step and the single-step forms of the income statement.
6. What are the major advantages and disadvantages of the single-step form of income statement compared to the multiple-step statement?
7. What type of revenue is reported in the Other income section of the multiple-step income statement?
8. How does the accounting for sales to customers using bank credit cards, such as MasterCard and VISA, differ from accounting for sales to customers using non-bank credit cards, such as American Express?
9. The credit period during which the buyer of merchandise is allowed to pay usually begins with what date?
10. What is the meaning of (a) 2/10, n/60; (b) n/30; (c) n/eom?
11. What is the nature of (a) a credit memorandum issued by the seller of merchandise, (b) a debit memorandum issued by the buyer of merchandise?
12. Who bears the transportation costs when the terms of sale are (a) FOB shipping point, (b) FOB destination?
13. Name at least three accounts that would normally appear in the chart of accounts of a merchandising business but would not appear in the chart of accounts of a service business.
14. Rogers Office Equipment, which uses a perpetual inventory system, experienced a normal inventory shrinkage of $17,352. What accounts would be debited and credited to record the adjustment for the inventory shrinkage at the end of the accounting period?
15. Assume that Rogers Office Equipment in Question 14 experienced an abnormal inventory shrinkage of $185,750. Rogers Office Equipment has decided to record the abnormal inventory shrinkage so that it would be separately disclosed on the income statement. What account would be debited for the abnormal inventory shrinkage?

# Exercises

**EXERCISE 6-1**
*Determining gross profit*
**Objective 1**

During the current year, merchandise is sold for $250,000 cash and for $975,000 on account. The cost of the merchandise sold is $735,000.

a. What is the amount of the gross profit?
b. Compute the gross profit percentage (gross profit divided by sales).
c. ➤ Will the income statement necessarily report a net income? Explain.

**EXERCISE 6-2**
*Determining cost of merchandise sold*
**Objective 1**

REAL WORLD

In 2003, **Best Buy Co.** reported net sales of $20,946 million. Its gross profit was $5,236 million. What was the amount of Best Buy's cost of merchandise sold?

**EXERCISE 6-3**
*Identify items missing in determining cost of merchandise sold*
**Objective 2**

For (a) through (d), identify the items designated by "X" and "Y."

a. Purchases − (X + Y) = Net purchases.
b. Net purchases + X = Cost of merchandise purchased.
c. Merchandise inventory (beginning) + Cost of merchandise purchased = X.
d. Merchandise available for sale − X = Cost of merchandise sold.

**EXERCISE 6-4**
*Cost of merchandise sold and related items*
**Objective 2**

SPREADSHEET

✓ a. Cost of merchandise sold, $931,000

The following data were extracted from the accounting records of Meniscus Company for the year ended April 30, 2006:

| | |
|---|---:|
| Merchandise Inventory, May 1, 2005 | $ 121,200 |
| Merchandise Inventory, April 30, 2006 | 142,000 |
| Purchases | 985,000 |
| Purchases Returns and Allowances | 23,500 |
| Purchases Discounts | 21,000 |
| Sales | 1,420,000 |
| Transportation In | 11,300 |

a. Prepare the cost of merchandise sold section of the income statement for the year ended April 30, 2006, using the periodic inventory method.
b. Determine the gross profit to be reported on the income statement for the year ended April 30, 2006.

**EXERCISE 6-5**
*Cost of merchandise sold*
**Objective 2**

WHAT'S WRONG
WITH THIS?

✓ *Correct cost of
merchandise sold, $599,500*

Identify the errors in the following schedule of cost of merchandise sold for the current year ended December 31, 2006:

| Cost of merchandise sold: | | | |
|---|---|---|---|
| Merchandise inventory, December 31, 2006 . . . . . . . | | | $120,000 |
| Purchases . . . . . . . . . . . . . . . . . . . . . . . . . . . . . . . . . . | | $600,000 | |
| Plus: Purchases returns and allowances . . . . . . . . . . | $14,000 | | |
| Purchases discounts . . . . . . . . . . . . . . . . . . . | 6,000 | 20,000 | |
| Gross purchases . . . . . . . . . . . . . . . . . . . . . . . . . . . . | | $620,000 | |
| Less transportation in . . . . . . . . . . . . . . . . . . . . . . . | | 7,500 | |
| Cost of merchandise purchased . . . . . . . . . . . . . . | | | 612,500 |
| Merchandise available for sale . . . . . . . . . . . . . . . | | | $732,500 |
| Less merchandise inventory, January 1, 2006 . . . . . . . | | | 132,000 |
| Cost of merchandise sold . . . . . . . . . . . . . . . . . | | | $600,500 |

**EXERCISE 6-6**
*Income statement for
merchandiser*
**Objective 2**

For the fiscal year, sales were $3,570,000, sales discounts were $320,000, sales returns and allowances were $240,000, and the cost of merchandise sold was $2,142,000. What was the amount of net sales and gross profit?

**EXERCISE 6-7**
*Income statement for
merchandiser*
**Objective 2**

The following expenses were incurred by a merchandising business during the year. In which expense section of the income statement should each be reported: (a) selling, (b) administrative, or (c) other?

1. Advertising expense.
2. Depreciation expense on office equipment.
3. Insurance expense on store equipment.
4. Interest expense on notes payable.
5. Office supplies used.
6. Rent expense on office building.
7. Salaries of office personnel.
8. Salary of sales manager.

**EXERCISE 6-8**
*Single-step income
statement*
**Objective 2**
✓ *Net income: $1,362,500*

Summary operating data for The Meriden Company during the current year ended June 30, 2006, are as follows: cost of merchandise sold, $3,240,000; administrative expenses, $300,000; interest expense, $47,500; rent revenue, $30,000; net sales, $5,400,000; and selling expenses, $480,000. Prepare a single-step income statement.

**EXERCISE 6-9**
*Multiple-step income
statement*
**Objective 2**

WHAT'S WRONG
WITH THIS?

Identify the errors in the following income statement:

**The Plautus Company**
**Income Statement**
**For the Year Ended October 31, 2006**

| Revenue from sales: | | | |
|---|---|---|---|
| Sales . . . . . . . . . . . . . . . . . . . . . . . . . . . . . . . | | $4,200,000 | |
| Add: Sales returns and allowances . . . . . . . . . . | $81,200 | | |
| Sales discounts . . . . . . . . . . . . . . . . . . . . . . . . | 20,300 | 101,500 | |
| Gross sales . . . . . . . . . . . . . . . . . . . . . . . . . . . . | | | $4,301,500 |
| Cost of merchandise sold . . . . . . . . . . . . . . . . | | | 2,093,000 |
| Income from operations . . . . . . . . . . . . . . . . . . . | | | $2,208,500 |
| Operating expenses: | | | |
| Selling expenses . . . . . . . . . . . . . . . . . . . . . . . . | | $ 203,000 | |
| Transportation out . . . . . . . . . . . . . . . . . . . . . . | | 7,500 | |
| Administrative expenses . . . . . . . . . . . . . . . . . . | | 122,000 | |
| Total operating expenses . . . . . . . . . . . . . . . | | | 332,500 |
| | | | $1,876,000 |
| Other expense: | | | |
| Interest revenue . . . . . . . . . . . . . . . . . . . . . . . . | | | 66,500 |
| Gross profit . . . . . . . . . . . . . . . . . . . . . . . . . . . . | | | $1,809,500 |

**EXERCISE 6-10**
*Determining amounts for items omitted from income statement*

**Objective 2**

✓ a. $25,000

✓ h. $690,000

Two items are omitted in each of the following four lists of income statement data. Determine the amounts of the missing items, identifying them by letter.

| | | | | |
|---|---|---|---|---|
| Sales | $393,000 | $500,000 | $930,000 | $ (g) |
| Sales returns and allowances | (a) | 15,000 | (e) | 30,500 |
| Sales discounts | 18,000 | 8,000 | 30,000 | 37,000 |
| Net sales | 350,000 | (c) | 860,000 | (h) |
| Cost of merchandise sold | (b) | 285,000 | (f) | 540,000 |
| Gross profit | 140,000 | (d) | 340,000 | 150,000 |

**EXERCISE 6-11**
*Multiple-step income statement*

**Objective 2**

SPREADSHEET

✓ Net income: $77,500

On January 31, 2006, the balances of the accounts appearing in the ledger of Calloway Company, a furniture wholesaler, are as follows:

| | | | |
|---|---|---|---|
| Administrative Expenses | $ 80,000 | Notes Payable | $ 25,000 |
| Building | 512,500 | Office Supplies | 10,600 |
| Cash | 48,500 | Salaries Payable | 3,220 |
| Cost of Merchandise Sold | 560,000 | Sales | 925,000 |
| Interest Expense | 7,500 | Sales Discounts | 20,000 |
| Mark Donovan, Capital | 628,580 | Sales Returns and Allowances | 60,000 |
| Mark Donovan, Drawing | 25,000 | Selling Expenses | 120,000 |
| Merchandise Inventory | 130,000 | Store Supplies | 7,700 |

a. Prepare a multiple-step income statement for the year ended January 31, 2006.
b. Compare the major advantages and disadvantages of the multiple-step and single-step forms of income statements.

**EXERCISE 6-12**
*Sales-related transactions, including the use of credit cards*

**Objective 3**

Journalize the entries for the following transactions:

a. Sold merchandise for cash, $6,900. The cost of the merchandise sold was $4,830.
b. Sold merchandise on account, $7,500. The cost of the merchandise sold was $5,625.
c. Sold merchandise to customers who used MasterCard and VISA, $10,200. The cost of the merchandise sold was $6,630.
d. Sold merchandise to customers who used American Express, $7,200. The cost of the merchandise sold was $5,040.
e. Paid an invoice from City National Bank for $675, representing a service fee for processing MasterCard and VISA sales.
f. Received $6,875 from American Express Company after a $325 collection fee had been deducted.

**EXERCISE 6-13**
*Sales returns and allowances*

**Objective 3**

WHAT'S WRONG
WITH THIS?

During the year, sales returns and allowances totaled $235,750. The cost of the merchandise returned was $141,450. The accountant recorded all the returns and allowances by debiting the sales account and crediting Cost of Merchandise Sold for $235,750.
➤ Was the accountant's method of recording returns acceptable? Explain. In your explanation, include the advantages of using a sales returns and allowances account.

**EXERCISE 6-14**
*Sales-related transactions*

**Objective 3**

After the amount due on a sale of $7,500, terms 2/10, n/eom, is received from a customer within the discount period, the seller consents to the return of the entire shipment. The cost of the merchandise returned was $4,500. (a) What is the amount of the refund owed to the customer? (b) Journalize the entries made by the seller to record the return and the refund.

**EXERCISE 6-15**
*Sales-related transactions*

**Objective 3**

The debits and credits for three related transactions are presented in the following T accounts. Describe each transaction.

| Cash | | | | Sales | | |
|---|---|---|---|---|---|---|
| (5) | 9,405 | | | | (1) | 12,000 |

| Accounts Receivable | | | | Sales Discounts | | |
|---|---|---|---|---|---|---|
| (1) | 12,000 | (3) | 2,500 | (5) | 95 | |
| | | (5) | 9,500 | | | |

| Merchandise Inventory | | | | Sales Returns and Allowances | | |
|---|---|---|---|---|---|---|
| (4) | 1,625 | (2) | 7,800 | (3) | 2,500 | |

| Cost of Merchandise Sold | | |
|---|---|---|
| (2) | 7,800 | (4) | 1,625 |

**EXERCISE 6-16**
*Sales-related transactions*
**Objective 3**
✓ *d. $17,835*

Merchandise is sold on account to a customer for $18,000, terms FOB shipping point, 3/10, n/30. The seller paid the transportation costs of $375. Determine the following: (a) amount of the sale, (b) amount debited to Accounts Receivable, (c) amount of the discount for early payment, and (d) amount due within the discount period.

**EXERCISE 6-17**
*Purchase-related transaction*
**Objective 4**

Cheddar Company purchased merchandise on account from a supplier for $8,500, terms 2/10, n/30. Cheddar Company returned $800 of the merchandise and received full credit.

a. If Cheddar Company pays the invoice within the discount period, what is the amount of cash required for the payment?
b. Under a perpetual inventory system, what account is credited by Cheddar Company to record the return?

**EXERCISE 6-18**
*Purchase-related transactions*
**Objective 4**
✓ *A: $39,825*

A retailer is considering the purchase of one hundred units of a specific item from either of two suppliers. Their offers are as follows:

A: $400 a unit, total of $40,000, 2/10, n/30, plus transportation costs of $625.
B: $403 a unit, total of $40,300, 1/10, n/30, no charge for transportation.

Which of the two offers, A or B, yields the lower price?

**EXERCISE 6-19**
*Purchase-related transactions*
**Objective 4**

The debits and credits from four related transactions are presented in the following T accounts. Describe each transaction.

| Cash | | | | Accounts Payable | | |
|---|---|---|---|---|---|---|
| | | (2) | 175 | (3) | 1,000 | (1) | 8,000 |
| | | (4) | 6,860 | (4) | 7,000 | | |

| Merchandise Inventory | | | |
|---|---|---|---|
| (1) | 8,000 | (3) | 1,000 |
| (2) | 175 | (4) | 140 |

**EXERCISE 6-20**
*Purchase-related transactions*
**Objective 4**
✓ *(c) Cash, cr. $6,174*

Enid Co., a women's clothing store, purchased $7,500 of merchandise from a supplier on account, terms FOB destination, 2/10, n/30. Enid Co. returned $1,200 of the merchandise, receiving a credit memorandum, and then paid the amount due within the discount period. Journalize Enid Co.'s entries to record (a) the purchase, (b) the merchandise return, and (c) the payment.

**EXERCISE 6-21**
*Purchase-related transactions*
**Objective 4**
✓ *(e) Cash, dr. $940*

Journalize entries for the following related transactions of Regius Company:

a. Purchased $12,000 of merchandise from Loew Co. on account, terms 2/10, n/30.
b. Paid the amount owed on the invoice within the discount period.
c. Discovered that $3,000 of the merchandise was defective and returned items, receiving credit.

*(continued)*

    d. Purchased $2,000 of merchandise from Loew Co. on account, terms n/30.

    e. Received a check for the balance owed from the return in (c), after deducting for the purchase in (d).

---

**EXERCISE 6-22**
*Determining amounts to be paid on invoices*
Objective 5
✓a. $10,500

Determine the amount to be paid in full settlement of each of the following invoices, assuming that credit for returns and allowances was received prior to payment and that all invoices were paid within the discount period.

| | Merchandise | Transportation Paid by Seller | | Returns and Allowances |
|---|---|---|---|---|
| a. | $12,000 | — | FOB destination, n/30 | $1,500 |
| b. | 4,500 | $200 | FOB shipping point, 1/10, n/30 | 500 |
| c. | 5,000 | — | FOB destination, 2/10, n/30 | — |
| d. | 5,000 | — | FOB shipping point, 1/10, n/30 | 1,000 |
| e. | 1,500 | 50 | FOB shipping point, 2/10, n/30 | 700 |

---

**EXERCISE 6-23**
*Sales tax*
Objective 5
✓c. $4,280

A sale of merchandise on account for $4,000 is subject to a 7% sales tax. (a) Should the sales tax be recorded at the time of sale or when payment is received? (b) What is the amount of the sale? (c) What is the amount debited to Accounts Receivable? (d) What is the title of the account to which the $280 is credited?

---

**EXERCISE 6-24**
*Sales tax transactions*
Objective 5

Journalize the entries to record the following selected transactions:

a. Sold $9,000 of merchandise on account, subject to a sales tax of 8%. The cost of the merchandise sold was $6,300.

b. Paid $9,175 to the state sales tax department for taxes collected.

---

**EXERCISE 6-25**
*Sales-related transactions*
Objectives 3, 6

Superior Co., a furniture wholesaler, sells merchandise to Beta Co. on account, $11,500, terms 2/15, n/30. The cost of the merchandise sold is $6,900. Superior Co. issues a credit memorandum for $900 for merchandise returned and subsequently receives the amount due within the discount period. The cost of the merchandise returned is $540. Journalize Superior Co.'s entries for (a) the sale, including the cost of the merchandise sold, (b) the credit memorandum, including the cost of the returned merchandise, and (c) the receipt of the check for the amount due from Beta Co.

---

**EXERCISE 6-26**
*Purchase-related transactions*
Objectives 4, 6

Based on the data presented in Exercise 6-25, journalize Beta Co.'s entries for (a) the purchase, (b) the return of the merchandise for credit, and (c) the payment of the invoice within the discount period.

---

**EXERCISE 6-27**
*Normal balances of merchandise accounts*
Objectives 3, 4, 5

What is the normal balance of the following accounts: (a) Cost of Merchandise Sold, (b) Merchandise Inventory, (c) Sales, (d) Sales Discounts, (e) Sales Returns and Allowances, (f) Transportation Out?

---

**EXERCISE 6-28**
*Chart of accounts*
Objective 7

Igloo Co. is a newly organized business with a list of accounts at the top of the next page, arranged in alphabetical order.

    Construct a chart of accounts, assigning account numbers and arranging the accounts in balance sheet and income statement order, as illustrated in Exhibit 11. Each account number is three digits: the first digit is to indicate the major classification ("1" for assets, and so on); the second digit is to indicate the subclassification ("11" for current assets, and so on); and the third digit is to identify the specific account ("110" for Cash, and so on).

| | |
|---|---|
| Accounts Payable | Miscellaneous Selling Expense |
| Accounts Receivable | Notes Payable (short-term) |
| Accumulated Depreciation—Office Equipment | Office Equipment |
| Accumulated Depreciation—Store Equipment | Office Salaries Expense |
| Advertising Expense | Office Supplies |
| Cash | Office Supplies Expense |
| Cost of Merchandise Sold | Prepaid Insurance |
| Depreciation Expense—Office Equipment | Rent Expense |
| Depreciation Expense—Store Equipment | Salaries Payable |
| Income Summary | Sales |
| Insurance Expense | Sales Discounts |
| Interest Expense | Sales Returns and Allowances |
| Kimberly Skilling, Capital | Sales Salaries Expense |
| Kimberly Skilling, Drawing | Store Equipment |
| Land | Store Supplies |
| Merchandise Inventory | Store Supplies Expense |
| Miscellaneous Administrative Expense | Transportation Out |

**EXERCISE 6-29**
*Adjusting entry for merchandise inventory shrinkage*
Objective 8

Pulmonary Inc.'s perpetual inventory records indicate that $382,800 of merchandise should be on hand on March 31, 2006. The physical inventory indicates that $371,250 of merchandise is actually on hand. Journalize the adjusting entry for the inventory shrinkage for Pulmonary Inc. for the year ended March 31, 2006.

**EXERCISE 6-30**
*Closing the accounts of a merchandiser*
Objective 8

From the following list, identify the accounts that should be closed to Income Summary at the end of the fiscal year: (a) Accounts Receivable, (b) Cost of Merchandise Sold, (c) Merchandise Inventory, (d) Sales, (e) Sales Discounts, (f) Sales Returns and Allowances, (g) Salaries Expense, (h) Salaries Payable, (i) Supplies, (j) Supplies Expense.

**EXERCISE 6-31**
*Ratio of net sales to total assets*
Objective 9

REAL WORLD

The financial statements for **Home Depot** are presented in Appendix E at the end of the text.

a. Determine the ratio of net sales to average total assets for Home Depot for the years ended February 2, 2003, and February 3, 2002.
b. What conclusions can be drawn from these ratios concerning the trend in the ability of Home Depot to effectively use its assets to generate sales?

*Note:* Home Depot's total assets on January 28, 2001, were $21,385,000,000.

**EXERCISE 6-32**
*Ratio of net sales to total assets*
Objective 9

REAL WORLD

**Winn-Dixie Stores** reported the following data in its financial statements for 2002:

| | |
|---|---|
| Net sales and revenues | $12,334,353,000 |
| Total assets at end of 2002 | 2,937,578,000 |
| Total assets at end of 2001 | 3,041,670,000 |

a. Compute the ratio of net sales to assets for 2002. Round to two decimal places.
b. Would you expect the ratio of net sales to assets for Winn-Dixie to be similar to or different from that of **Zales Corp.**? Zales is the largest North American retailer of jewelry, with a ratio of net sales to assets of 1.53.

**APPENDIX 1**
**EXERCISE 6-33**
*Merchandising special journals*

✓ d. $30,000

Myrina Rug Company had the following credit sales transactions during August 2006:

| Date | Customer | Quantity | Rug Style | Sales |
|------|----------|----------|-----------|-------|
| Aug. 3 | Adrienne Richt | 1 | 10 by 6 Chinese | $12,000 |
| 8 | K. Smith | 1 | 8 by 10 Persian | 10,000 |
| 19 | L. Lao | 1 | 8 by 10 Indian | 9,000 |
| 26 | Cheryl Pugh | 1 | 10 by 12 Persian | 14,000 |

The August 1 inventory was $19,000, consisting of:

| Quantity | Style | Cost per Rug | Total Cost |
|----------|-------|--------------|------------|
| 2 | 10 by 6 Chinese | $4,000 | $ 8,000 |
| 2 | 8 by 10 Persian | 5,500 | 11,000 |

During August, Myrina Rug Company purchased the following rugs from Draco Rug Importers:

| Date | Quantity | Rug Style | Cost per Rug | Amount |
|------|----------|-----------|--------------|--------|
| Aug. 10 | 2 | 8 by 10 Indian | $4,000 | $ 8,000 |
| 12 | 1 | 10 by 6 Chinese | 3,500 | 3,500 |
| 21 | 3 | 10 by 12 Persian | 6,500 | 19,500 |

The general ledger includes the following accounts:

| Account Number | Account |
|----------------|---------|
| 11 | Accounts Receivable |
| 12 | Merchandise Inventory |
| 21 | Accounts Payable |
| 41 | Sales |
| 51 | Cost of Merchandise Sold |

a. Record the sales in a two-column sales journal. Use the sales journal form shown in the appendix at the end of this chapter. Begin with Invoice Number 80.
b. Record the purchases in a purchases journal. Use the purchases journal form shown in the appendix at the end of this chapter.
c. Assume that you have posted the journal entries to the appropriate ledgers. Insert the correct posting references in the sales and purchases journals.
d. Determine the August 31 balance of Merchandise Inventory.

**APPENDIX 2**
**EXERCISE 6-34**
*Closing entries*

Based on the data presented in Exercise 6-11, journalize the closing entries.

# Problems Series A

**PROBLEM 6-1A**
*Multiple-step income statement and report form of balance sheet*

**Objective 2**

SPREADSHEET
P.A.S.S.

✓ 1. Net income: $81,600

The following selected accounts and their current balances appear in the ledger of Sombrero Co. for the fiscal year ended November 30, 2006:

| | | | |
|---|---|---|---|
| Cash | $ 91,800 | Accumulated Depreciation— | |
| Accounts Receivable | 74,400 | Store Equipment | $ 58,320 |
| Merchandise Inventory | 120,000 | Accounts Payable | 32,400 |
| Office Supplies | 3,120 | Salaries Payable | 2,400 |
| Prepaid Insurance | 8,160 | Note Payable | |
| Office Equipment | 76,800 | (final payment due 2016) | 36,000 |
| Accumulated Depreciation— | | Hector Rodrique, Capital | 321,600 |
| Office Equipment | 12,960 | Hector Rodrique, Drawing | 30,000 |
| Store Equipment | 141,000 | Sales | 1,802,400 |

(continued)

| | | | |
|---|---|---|---|
| Sales Returns and Allowances | $ 25,200 | Rent Expense | $26,580 |
| Sales Discounts | 13,200 | Insurance Expense | 15,300 |
| Cost of Merchandise Sold | 1,284,000 | Depreciation Expense— | |
| Sales Salaries Expense | 252,000 | Office Equipment | 10,800 |
| Advertising Expense | 33,960 | Office Supplies Expense | 1,080 |
| Depreciation Expense— | | Miscellaneous Administrative | |
| Store Equipment | 5,520 | Expense | 1,440 |
| Miscellaneous Selling Expense | 1,320 | Interest Expense | 1,200 |
| Office Salaries Expense | 49,200 | | |

## Instructions

1. Prepare a multiple-step income statement.
2. Prepare a statement of owner's equity.
3. Prepare a report form of balance sheet, assuming that the current portion of the note payable is $3,000.
4. Briefly explain (a) how multiple-step and single-step income statements differ and (b) how report-form and account-form balance sheets differ.

**PROBLEM 6-2A**
*Single-step income statement and account form of balance sheet*

**Objective 2**

SPREADSHEET

✓ 3. Total assets: $444,000

Selected accounts and related amounts for Sombrero Co. for the fiscal year ended November 30, 2006, are presented in Problem 6-1A.

## Instructions

1. Prepare a single-step income statement in the format shown in Exhibit 3.
2. Prepare a statement of owner's equity.
3. Prepare an account form of balance sheet, assuming that the current portion of the note payable is $3,000.

**PROBLEM 6-3A**
*Sales-related transactions*

**Objectives 3, 5**

P.A.S.S.

The following selected transactions were completed by Interstate Supplies Co., which sells irrigation supplies primarily to wholesalers and occasionally to retail customers.

Mar. 1. Sold merchandise on account to Babcock Co., $7,500, terms FOB shipping point, n/eom. The cost of merchandise sold was $4,500.
2. Sold merchandise for $8,000 plus 6% sales tax to cash customers. The cost of merchandise sold was $4,750.
5. Sold merchandise on account to North Star Company, $16,000, terms FOB destination, 1/10, n/30. The cost of merchandise sold was $10,500.
8. Sold merchandise for $6,150 plus 6% sales tax to customers who used VISA cards. Deposited credit card receipts into the bank. The cost of merchandise sold was $3,700.
13. Sold merchandise to customers who used American Express cards, $6,500. The cost of merchandise sold was $3,600.
14. Sold merchandise on account to Blech Co., $7,500, terms FOB shipping point, 1/10, n/30. The cost of merchandise sold was $4,000.
15. Received check for amount due from North Star Company for sale on March 5.
16. Issued credit memorandum for $800 to Blech Co. for merchandise returned from sale on March 14. The cost of the merchandise returned was $360.
18. Sold merchandise on account to Westech Company, $6,850, terms FOB shipping point, 2/10, n/30. Paid $210 for transportation costs and added them to the invoice. The cost of merchandise sold was $4,100.
24. Received check for amount due from Blech Co. for sale on March 14 less credit memorandum of May 16 and discount.
27. Received $7,680 from American Express for $8,000 of sales reported during the week of May 1–12.
28. Received check for amount due from Westech Company for sale of March 18.

Mar. 31. Paid Downtown Delivery Service $1,275 for merchandise delivered during March to customers under shipping terms of FOB destination.

31. Received check for amount due from Babcock Co. for sale of March 1.

April 3. Paid First National Bank $725 for service fees for handling MasterCard sales during March.

10. Paid $2,800 to state sales tax division for taxes owed on March sales.

### Instructions
Journalize the entries to record the transactions of Interstate Supplies Co.

**PROBLEM 6-4A**
*Purchase-related transactions*

**Objectives 4, 5**

P.A.S.S.

The following selected transactions were completed by Petunia Co. during August of the current year:

Aug. 1. Purchased merchandise from Fisher Co., $8,500, terms FOB shipping point, 2/10, n/eom. Prepaid transportation costs of $250 were added to the invoice.

5. Purchased merchandise from Byrd Co., $10,400, terms FOB destination, n/30.

10. Paid Fisher Co. for invoice of August 1, less discount.

13. Purchased merchandise from Mickle Co., $7,500, terms FOB destination, 1/10, n/30.

14. Issued debit memorandum to Mickle Co. for $2,500 of merchandise returned from purchase on August 13.

18. Purchased merchandise from Lanning Company, $10,000, terms FOB shipping point, n/eom.

18. Paid transportation charges of $150 on August 18 purchase from Lanning Company.

19. Purchased merchandise from Hatcher Co., $7,500, terms FOB destination, 2/10, n/30.

23. Paid Mickle Co. for invoice of August 13, less debit memorandum of August 14 and discount.

29. Paid Hatcher Co. for invoice of August 19, less discount.

31. Paid Lanning Company for invoice of August 18.

31. Paid Byrd Co. for invoice of August 5.

### Instructions
Journalize the entries to record the transactions of Petunia Co. for August.

**PROBLEM 6-5A**
*Sales-related and purchase-related transactions*

**Objectives 3, 4, 5**

P.A.S.S.

The following were selected from among the transactions completed by Ingress Company during January of the current year:

Jan. 3. Purchased merchandise on account from Pynn Co., list price $16,000, trade discount 35%, terms FOB shipping point, 2/10, n/30, with prepaid transportation costs of $320 added to the invoice.

5. Purchased merchandise on account from Wilhelm Co., $8,000, terms FOB destination, 1/10, n/30.

6. Sold merchandise on account to Sievert Co., list price $12,500, trade discount 40%, terms 2/10, n/30. The cost of the merchandise sold was $4,500.

7. Returned $1,800 of merchandise purchased on January 5 from Wilhelm Co.

13. Paid Pynn Co. on account for purchase of January 3, less discount.

15. Paid Wilhelm Co. on account for purchase of January 5, less return of January 7 and discount.

16. Received cash on account from sale of January 6 to Sievert Co., less discount.

19. Sold merchandise on nonbank credit cards and reported accounts to the card company, American Express, $6,450. The cost of the merchandise sold was $3,950.

22. Sold merchandise on account to Elk River Co., $3,480, terms 2/10, n/30. The cost of the merchandise sold was $1,400.

23. Sold merchandise for cash, $9,350. The cost of the merchandise sold was $5,750.

Jan. 25. Received merchandise returned by Elk River Co. from sale on January 22, $1,480. The cost of the returned merchandise was $600.

31. Received cash from American Express for nonbank credit card sales of January 19, less $225 service fee.

**Instructions**

Journalize the transactions.

**PROBLEM 6-6A**
*Sales-related and purchase-related transactions for seller and buyer*

**Objective 6**

The following selected transactions were completed during June between Schnaps Company and Brandy Company:

June 2. Schnaps Company sold merchandise on account to Brandy Company, $14,000, terms FOB shipping point, 2/10, n/30. Schnaps Company paid transportation costs of $350, which were added to the invoice. The cost of the merchandise sold was $8,000.

8. Schnaps Company sold merchandise on account to Brandy Company, $12,500, terms FOB destination, 1/15, n/eom. The cost of the merchandise sold was $7,500.

8. Schnaps Company paid transportation costs of $550 for delivery of merchandise sold to Brandy Company on June 8.

12. Brandy Company returned $3,000 of merchandise purchased on account on June 8 from Schnaps Company. The cost of the merchandise returned was $1,800.

12. Brandy Company paid Schnaps Company for purchase of June 2, less discount.

23. Brandy Company paid Schnaps Company for purchase of June 8, less discount and less return of June 12.

24. Schnaps Company sold merchandise on account to Brandy Company, $10,000, terms FOB shipping point, n/eom. The cost of the merchandise sold was $6,000.

26. Brandy Company paid transportation charges of $310 on June 24 purchase from Schnaps Company.

30. Brandy Company paid Schnaps Company on account for purchase of June 24.

**Instructions**

Journalize the June transactions for (1) Schnaps Company and (2) Brandy Company.

**APPENDIX 2**
**PROBLEM 6-7A**
*Work sheet, financial statements, and adjusting and closing entries*

**SPREADSHEET**

✓ *2. Net income: $73,665*

The accounts and their balances in the ledger of Glycol Co. on December 31, 2006, are as follows:

| | | | |
|---|---|---|---|
| Cash | $ 11,165 | Sales | $847,500 |
| Accounts Receivable | 86,100 | Sales Returns and Allowances | 15,500 |
| Merchandise Inventory | 235,000 | Sales Discounts | 6,000 |
| Prepaid Insurance | 10,600 | Cost of Merchandise Sold | 501,200 |
| Store Supplies | 3,750 | Sales Salaries Expense | 86,400 |
| Office Supplies | 1,700 | Advertising Expense | 29,450 |
| Store Equipment | 225,000 | Depreciation Expense— | |
| Accumulated Depreciation— | | Store Equipment | — |
| Store Equipment | 40,300 | Store Supplies Expense | — |
| Office Equipment | 72,000 | Miscellaneous Selling Expense | 1,885 |
| Accumulated Depreciation— | | Office Salaries Expense | 60,000 |
| Office Equipment | 17,200 | Rent Expense | 30,000 |
| Accounts Payable | 56,700 | Insurance Expense | — |
| Salaries Payable | — | Depreciation Expense— | |
| Unearned Rent | 1,200 | Office Equipment | — |
| Note Payable | | Office Supplies Expense | — |
| (final payment due 2016) | 185,000 | Miscellaneous Administrative | |
| Doug Easterly, Capital | 282,100 | Expense | 1,650 |
| Doug Easterly, Drawing | 40,000 | Rent Revenue | — |
| Income Summary | — | Interest Expense | 12,600 |

The data needed for year-end adjustments on December 31 are as follows:

| | | |
|---|---:|---:|
| Physical merchandise inventory on December 31 | | $228,600 |
| Insurance expired during the year | | 5,000 |
| Supplies on hand on December 31: | | |
|   Store supplies | | 1,200 |
|   Office supplies | | 900 |
| Depreciation for the year: | | |
|   Store equipment | | 8,500 |
|   Office equipment | | 4,500 |
| Salaries payable on December 31: | | |
|   Sales salaries | $1,450 | |
|   Office salaries | 750 | 2,200 |
| Unearned rent on December 31 | | 400 |

### Instructions

1. Prepare a work sheet for the fiscal year ended December 31, 2006. List all accounts in the order given.
2. Prepare a multiple-step income statement.
3. Prepare a statement of owner's equity.
4. Prepare a report form of balance sheet, assuming that the current portion of the note payable is $25,000.
5. Journalize the adjusting entries.
6. Journalize the closing entries.

# Problems Series B

**PROBLEM 6-1B**
*Multiple-step income statement and report form of balance sheet*

**Objective 2**

SPREADSHEET
P.A.S.S.

✓ 1. Net income: $80,000

The following selected accounts and their current balances appear in the ledger of Sciatic Co. for the fiscal year ended July 31, 2006:

| | | | | |
|---|---:|---|---|---:|
| Cash | $ 123,000 | | Sales Returns and Allowances | $ 18,480 |
| Accounts Receivable | 96,800 | | Sales Discounts | 17,520 |
| Merchandise Inventory | 140,000 | | Cost of Merchandise Sold | 620,000 |
| Office Supplies | 4,480 | | Sales Salaries Expense | 138,560 |
| Prepaid Insurance | 2,720 | | Advertising Expense | 35,040 |
| Office Equipment | 68,000 | | Depreciation Expense— | |
| Accumulated Depreciation— | | |   Store Equipment | 5,120 |
|   Office Equipment | 10,240 | | Miscellaneous Selling Expense | 1,280 |
| Store Equipment | 122,400 | | Office Salaries Expense | 67,320 |
| Accumulated Depreciation— | | | Rent Expense | 25,080 |
|   Store Equipment | 27,360 | | Depreciation Expense— | |
| Accounts Payable | 44,480 | |   Office Equipment | 10,160 |
| Salaries Payable | 1,920 | | Insurance Expense | 3,120 |
| Note Payable | | | Office Supplies Expense | 1,040 |
|   (final payment due 2016) | 44,800 | | Miscellaneous Administrative | |
| Gary McNiven, Capital | 376,600 | |   Expense | 1,280 |
| Gary McNiven, Drawing | 28,000 | | Interest Expense | 4,000 |
| Sales | 1,028,000 | | | |

### Instructions

1. Prepare a multiple-step income statement.
2. Prepare a statement of owner's equity.
3. Prepare a report form of balance sheet, assuming that the current portion of the note payable is $6,000.
4. Briefly explain (a) how multiple-step and single-step income statements differ and (b) how report-form and account-form balance sheets differ.

**PROBLEM 6-2B**
*Single-step income statement and account form of balance sheet*

**Objective 2**

SPREADSHEET

✓ 3. *Total assets: $519,800*

Selected accounts and related amounts for Sciatic Co. for the fiscal year ended July 31, 2006, are presented in Problem 6-1B.

**Instructions**

1. Prepare a single-step income statement in the format shown in Exhibit 3.
2. Prepare a statement of owner's equity.
3. Prepare an account form of balance sheet, assuming that the current portion of the note payable is $6,000.

**PROBLEM 6-3B**
*Sales-related transactions*

**Objectives 3, 5**

P.A.S.S.

The following selected transactions were completed by Holistic Supply Co., which sells office supplies primarily to wholesalers and occasionally to retail customers.

Aug. 2. Sold merchandise on account to Runyan Co., $12,800, terms FOB destination, 2/10, n/30. The cost of the merchandise sold was $7,600.
   3. Sold merchandise for $5,000 plus 7% sales tax to cash customers. The cost of merchandise sold was $3,000.
   4. Sold merchandise on account to McNutt Co., $2,800, terms FOB shipping point, n/eom. The cost of merchandise sold was $1,800.
   5. Sold merchandise for $4,400 plus 7% sales tax to customers who used MasterCard. Deposited credit card receipts into the bank. The cost of merchandise sold was $2,500.
   12. Received check for amount due from Runyan Co. for sale on August 2.
   14. Sold merchandise to customers who used American Express cards, $15,000. The cost of merchandise sold was $9,200.
   16. Sold merchandise on account to Westpark Co., $12,000, terms FOB shipping point, 1/10, n/30. The cost of merchandise sold was $7,200.
   18. Issued credit memorandum for $3,000 to Westpark Co. for merchandise returned from sale on August 16. The cost of the merchandise returned was $1,800.
   19. Sold merchandise on account to DeGroot Co., $9,500, terms FOB shipping point, 1/10, n/30. Added $200 to the invoice for transportation costs prepaid. The cost of merchandise sold was $5,700.
   26. Received check for amount due from Westpark Co. for sale on August 16 less credit memorandum of August 18 and discount.
   27. Received $7,680 from American Express for $8,000 of sales reported August 1–12.
   28. Received check for amount due from DeGroot Co. for sale of August 19.
   31. Received check for amount due from McNutt Co. for sale of August 4.
   31. Paid Fast Delivery Service $1,050 for merchandise delivered during August to customers under shipping terms of FOB destination.
Sept. 3. Paid First City Bank $850 for service fees for handling MasterCard sales during August.
   15. Paid $4,100 to state sales tax division for taxes owed on August sales.

**Instructions**
Journalize the entries to record the transactions of Holistic Supply Co.

**PROBLEM 6-4B**
*Purchase-related transactions*

**Objectives 4, 5**

P.A.S.S.

The following selected transactions were completed by Daffodil Company during March of the current year:

Mar. 1. Purchased merchandise from Fastow Co., $16,000, terms FOB destination, n/30.
   3. Purchased merchandise from Moss Co., $9,000, terms FOB shipping point, 2/10, n/eom. Prepaid transportation costs of $150 were added to the invoice.

*(continued)*

Mar. 4. Purchased merchandise from Picadilly Co., $7,500, terms FOB destination, 2/10, n/30.

6. Issued debit memorandum to Picadilly Co. for $1,000 of merchandise returned from purchase on March 4.

13. Paid Moss Co. for invoice of March 3, less discount.

14. Paid Picadilly Co. for invoice of March 4, less debit memorandum of March 6 and discount.

19. Purchased merchandise from Reardon Co., $12,000, terms FOB shipping point, n/eom.

19. Paid transportation charges of $500 on March 19 purchase from Reardon Co.

20. Purchased merchandise from Hatcher Co., $8,000, terms FOB destination, 1/10, n/30.

30. Paid Hatcher Co. for invoice of March 20, less discount.

31. Paid Fastow Co. for invoice of March 1.

31. Paid Reardon Co. for invoice of March 19.

**Instructions**

Journalize the entries to record the transactions of Daffodil Company for March.

**PROBLEM 6-5B**
*Sales-related and purchase-related transactions*

**Objectives 3, 4, 5**

P.A.S.S.

The following were selected from among the transactions completed by Girder Company during November of the current year:

Nov. 3. Purchased merchandise on account from Whiting Co., list price $25,000, trade discount 20%, terms FOB destination, 2/10, n/30.

4. Sold merchandise for cash, $7,100. The cost of the merchandise sold was $4,150.

5. Purchased merchandise on account from Alamosa Co., $10,500, terms FOB shipping point, 2/10, n/30, with prepaid transportation costs of $300 added to the invoice.

6. Returned $5,000 of merchandise purchased on November 3 from Whiting Co.

11. Sold merchandise on account to Bowles Co., list price $2,250, trade discount 20%, terms 1/10, n/30. The cost of the merchandise sold was $1,050.

13. Paid Whiting Co. on account for purchase of November 3, less return of November 6 and discount.

14. Sold merchandise on nonbank credit cards and reported accounts to the card company, American Express, $9,850. The cost of the merchandise sold was $5,900.

15. Paid Alamosa Co. on account for purchase of November 5, less discount.

21. Received cash on account from sale of November 11 to Bowles Co., less discount.

24. Sold merchandise on account to Kapinos Co., $4,200, terms 1/10, n/30. The cost of the merchandise sold was $1,850.

28. Received cash from American Express for nonbank credit card sales of November 14, less $440 service fee.

30. Received merchandise returned by Kapinos Co. from sale on November 24, $1,100. The cost of the returned merchandise was $600.

**Instructions**

Journalize the transactions.

**PROBLEM 6-6B**
*Sales-related and purchase-related transactions for seller and buyer*

**Objective 6**

The following selected transactions were completed during March between Snyder Company and Brooks Co.:

Mar. 1. Snyder Company sold merchandise on account to Brooks Co., $12,750, terms FOB destination, 2/15, n/eom. The cost of the merchandise sold was $6,000.

Mar. 2. Snyder Company paid transportation costs of $150 for delivery of merchandise sold to Brooks Co. on March 1.

5. Snyder Company sold merchandise on account to Brooks Co., $18,500, terms FOB shipping point, n/eom. The cost of the merchandise sold was $11,000.

6. Brooks Co. returned $2,000 of merchandise purchased on account on March 1 from Snyder Company. The cost of the merchandise returned was $1,200.

9. Brooks Co. paid transportation charges of $180 on March 5 purchase from Snyder Company.

15. Snyder Company sold merchandise on account to Brooks Co., $20,000, terms FOB shipping point, 1/10, n/30. Snyder Company paid transportation costs of $1,750, which were added to the invoice. The cost of the merchandise sold was $12,000.

16. Brooks Co. paid Snyder Company for purchase of March 1, less discount and less return of March 6.

25. Brooks Co. paid Snyder Company on account for purchase of March 15, less discount.

31. Brooks Co. paid Snyder Company on account for purchase of March 5.

## Instructions

Journalize the March transactions for (1) Snyder Company and (2) Brooks Co.

**APPENDIX 2
PROBLEM 6-7B**
*Work sheet, financial statements, and adjusting and closing entries*

SPREADSHEET

✓ 2. Net income: $127,250

The accounts and their balances in the ledger of Viaduct Co. on December 31, 2006, are as follows:

| | | | |
|---|---|---|---|
| Cash | $ 18,000 | Sales | $815,000 |
| Accounts Receivable | 82,500 | Sales Returns and Allowances | 11,900 |
| Merchandise Inventory | 165,000 | Sales Discounts | 7,100 |
| Prepaid Insurance | 9,700 | Cost of Merchandise Sold | 476,200 |
| Store Supplies | 4,250 | Sales Salaries Expense | 76,400 |
| Office Supplies | 2,100 | Advertising Expense | 25,000 |
| Store Equipment | 157,000 | Depreciation Expense— | |
| Accumulated Depreciation— | | Store Equipment | — |
| Store Equipment | 40,300 | Store Supplies Expense | — |
| Office Equipment | 50,000 | Miscellaneous Selling Expense | 1,600 |
| Accumulated Depreciation— | | Office Salaries Expense | 34,000 |
| Office Equipment | 17,200 | Rent Expense | 16,000 |
| Accounts Payable | 66,700 | Insurance Expense | — |
| Salaries Payable | — | Depreciation Expense— | |
| Unearned Rent | 1,200 | Office Equipment | — |
| Note Payable | | Office Supplies Expense — | |
| (final payment due 2016) | 105,000 | Miscellaneous Administrative | |
| Robbin Jaeger, Capital | 134,600 | Expense | 1,650 |
| Robbin Jaeger, Drawing | 30,000 | Rent Revenue | — |
| Income Summary | — | Interest Expense | 11,600 |

The data needed for year-end adjustments on December 31 are as follows:

| | | |
|---|---|---|
| Physical merchandise inventory on December 31 . . . . . . . . . . . . . . . . . . | | $157,500 |
| Insurance expired during the year . . . . . . . . . . . . . . . . . . . . . . . . . . | | 4,000 |
| Supplies on hand on December 31: | | |
| Store supplies . . . . . . . . . . . . . . . . . . . . . . . . . . . . . . . . . . . . . . | | 1,100 |
| Office supplies . . . . . . . . . . . . . . . . . . . . . . . . . . . . . . . . . . . . . | | 600 |
| Depreciation for the year: | | |
| Store equipment . . . . . . . . . . . . . . . . . . . . . . . . . . . . . . . . . . . . | | 4,500 |
| Office equipment . . . . . . . . . . . . . . . . . . . . . . . . . . . . . . . . . . . . | | 2,800 |
| Salaries payable on December 31: | | |
| Sales salaries . . . . . . . . . . . . . . . . . . . . . . . . . . . . . . . . . . . . . . | $2,850 | |
| Office salaries . . . . . . . . . . . . . . . . . . . . . . . . . . . . . . . . . . . . . | 800 | 3,650 |
| Unearned rent on December 31 . . . . . . . . . . . . . . . . . . . . . . . . . . . . | | 400 |

**Instructions**

1. Prepare a work sheet for the fiscal year ended December 31, 2006. List all accounts in the order given.
2. Prepare a multiple-step income statement.
3. Prepare a statement of owner's equity.
4. Prepare a report form of balance sheet, assuming that the current portion of the note payable is $15,000.
5. Journalize the adjusting entries.
6. Journalize the closing entries.

# Comprehensive Problem 2

**P.A.S.S.**

✓ 5. Net income: $163,105

Lyre Co. is a merchandising business. The account balances for Lyre Co. as of August 1, 2006 (unless otherwise indicated), are as follows:

| | | |
|---|---|---:|
| 110 | Cash | $ 14,160 |
| 112 | Accounts Receivable | 34,220 |
| 115 | Merchandise Inventory | 133,900 |
| 116 | Prepaid Insurance | 3,750 |
| 117 | Store Supplies | 2,550 |
| 123 | Store Equipment | 104,300 |
| 124 | Accumulated Depreciation—Store Equipment | 12,600 |
| 210 | Accounts Payable | 21,450 |
| 211 | Salaries Payable | — |
| 310 | Kevin Wilcox, Capital, September 1, 2005 | 103,280 |
| 311 | Kevin Wilcox, Drawing | 10,000 |
| 312 | Income Summary | — |
| 410 | Sales | 715,800 |
| 411 | Sales Returns and Allowances | 20,600 |
| 412 | Sales Discounts | 13,200 |
| 510 | Cost of Merchandise Sold | 360,500 |
| 520 | Sales Salaries Expense | 74,400 |
| 521 | Advertising Expense | 18,000 |
| 522 | Depreciation Expense | — |
| 523 | Store Supplies Expense | — |
| 529 | Miscellaneous Selling Expense | 2,800 |
| 530 | Office Salaries Expense | 40,500 |
| 531 | Rent Expense | 18,600 |
| 532 | Insurance Expense | — |
| 539 | Miscellaneous Administrative Expense | 1,650 |

During August, the last month of the fiscal year, the following transactions were completed:

Aug. 1. Paid rent for August, $1,600.
3. Purchased merchandise on account from Biathlon Co., terms 2/10, n/30, FOB shipping point, $15,000.
4. Paid transportation charges on purchase of August 3, $400.
6. Sold merchandise on account to Hillcrest Co., terms 2/10, n/30, FOB shipping point, $8,500. The cost of the merchandise sold was $5,000.
7. Received $7,500 cash from Aaberg Co. on account, no discount.
10. Sold merchandise for cash, $18,300. The cost of the merchandise sold was $11,000.
13. Paid for merchandise purchased on August 3, less discount.
14. Received merchandise returned on sale of August 6, $1,500. The cost of the merchandise returned was $900.
15. Paid advertising expense for last half of August, $1,500.

Aug. 16. Received cash from sale of August 6, less return of August 14 and discount.

19. Purchased merchandise for cash, $8,100.

19. Paid $6,100 to Ramler Co. on account, no discount.

20. Sold merchandise on account to Petroski Co., terms 1/10, n/30, FOB shipping point, $16,000. The cost of the merchandise sold was $9,600.

21. For the convenience of the customer, paid shipping charges on sale of August 20, $600.

21. Received $11,750 cash from Phillips Co. on account, no discount.

21. Purchased merchandise on account from Walden Co., terms 1/10, n/30, FOB destination, $15,000.

24. Returned $3,500 of damaged merchandise purchased on August 21, receiving credit from the seller.

26. Refunded cash on sales made for cash, $720. The cost of the merchandise returned was $380.

28. Paid sales salaries of $1,750 and office salaries of $950.

29. Purchased store supplies for cash, $550.

30. Sold merchandise on account to Whitetail Co., terms 2/10, n/30, FOB shipping point, $18,750. The cost of the merchandise sold was $11,250.

30. Received cash from sale of August 20, less discount, plus transportation paid on August 21.

31. Paid for purchase of August 21, less return of August 24 and discount.

## Instructions

(*Note:* If the work sheet described in the appendix is used, follow the alternative instructions.)

1. Enter the balances of each of the accounts in the appropriate balance column of a four-column account. Write *Balance* in the item section, and place a check mark (✔) in the Posting Reference column.

2. Journalize the transactions for August.

3. Post the journal to the general ledger, extending the month-end balances to the appropriate balance columns after all posting is completed. In this problem, you are not required to update or post to the accounts receivable and accounts payable subsidiary ledgers.

4. Journalize and post the adjusting entries, using the following adjustment data:

| | | | |
|---|---|---|---|
| a. | Merchandise inventory on August 31 | | $124,115 |
| b. | Insurance expired during the year | | 1,250 |
| c. | Store supplies on hand on August 31 | | 975 |
| d. | Depreciation for the current year | | 7,400 |
| e. | Accrued salaries on August 31: | | |
| | Sales salaries | $350 | |
| | Office salaries | 180 | 530 |

5. Prepare a multiple-step income statement, a statement of owner's equity, and a report form of balance sheet.

6. Journalize and post the closing entries. Indicate closed accounts by inserting a line in both balance columns opposite the closing entry. Insert the new balance in the owner's capital account.

7. Prepare a post-closing trial balance.

## Alternative Instructions

1. Enter the balances of each of the accounts in the appropriate balance column of a four-column account. Write *Balance* in the item section, and place a check mark (✔) in the Posting Reference column.

2. Journalize the transactions for August.

3. Post the journal to the general ledger, extending the month-end balances to the appropriate balance columns after all posting is completed. In this problem, you are not required to update or post to the accounts receivable and accounts payable subsidiary ledgers.

*(continued)*

4. Prepare a trial balance as of August 31 on a ten-column work sheet, listing all accounts in the order given in the ledger. Complete the work sheet for the fiscal year ended August 31, using the following adjustment data:

| | | |
|---|---|---:|
| a. | Merchandise inventory on August 31 | $124,115 |
| b. | Insurance expired during the year | 1,250 |
| c. | Store supplies on hand on August 31 | 975 |
| d. | Depreciation for the current year | 7,400 |
| e. | Accrued salaries on August 31: | |

| | | |
|---|---:|---:|
| Sales salaries | $350 | |
| Office salaries | 180 | 530 |

5. Prepare a multiple-step income statement, a statement of owner's equity, and a report form of balance sheet.
6. Journalize and post the adjusting entries.
7. Journalize and post the closing entries. Indicate closed accounts by inserting a line in both balance columns opposite the closing entry. Insert the new balance in the owner's capital account.
8. Prepare a post-closing trial balance.

# Special Activities

**ACTIVITY 6-1**
*Ethics and professional conduct in business*

ETHICS

On December 1, 2006, Cardinal Company, a garden retailer, purchased $20,000 of corn seed, terms 2/10, n/30, from Iowa Farm Co. Even though the discount period had expired, Sandi Kurtz subtracted the discount of $400 when she processed the documents for payment on December 15, 2006.

Discuss whether Sandi Kurtz behaved in a professional manner by subtracting the discount, even though the discount period had expired.

**ACTIVITY 6-2**
*Purchases discounts and accounts payable*

The Video Store Co. is owned and operated by Todd Shovic. The following is an excerpt from a conversation between Todd Shovic and Susan Mastin, the chief accountant for The Video Store.

*Todd:* Susan, I've got a question about this recent balance sheet.
*Susan:* Sure, what's your question?
*Todd:* Well, as you know, I'm applying for a bank loan to finance our new store in Three Forks, and I noticed that the accounts payable are listed as $110,000.
*Susan:* That's right. Approximately $90,000 of that represents amounts due our suppliers, and the remainder is miscellaneous payables to creditors for utilities, office equipment, supplies, etc.
*Todd:* That's what I thought. But as you know, we normally receive a 2% discount from our suppliers for earlier payment, and we always try to take the discount.
*Susan:* That's right. I can't remember the last time we missed a discount.
*Todd:* Well, in that case, it seems to me the accounts payable should be listed minus the 2% discount. Let's list the accounts payable due suppliers as $88,200, rather than $90,000. Every little bit helps. You never know. It might make the difference between getting the loan and not.

How would you respond to Todd Shovic's request?

**ACTIVITY 6-3**
*Determining cost of purchase*

The following is an excerpt from a conversation between Brad Hass and Terry Fauck. Brad is debating whether to buy a stereo system from Radiant Sound, a locally owned electronics store, or Audio Pro Electronics, a mail-order electronics company.

*Brad:* Terry, I don't know what to do about buying my new stereo.

*Terry:* What's the problem?

*Brad:* Well, I can buy it locally at Radiant Sound for $395.00. However, Audio Pro Electronics has the same system listed for $399.99.

*Terry:* So what's the big deal? Buy it from Radiant Sound.

*Brad:* It's not quite that simple. Audio Pro said something about not having to pay sales tax, since I was out-of-state.

*Terry:* Yes, that's a good point. If you buy it at Radiant Sound, they'll charge you 6% sales tax.

*Brad:* But Audio Pro Electronics charges $12.50 for shipping and handling. If I have them send it next-day air, it'll cost $25 for shipping and handling.

*Terry:* I guess it is a little confusing.

*Brad:* That's not all. Radiant Sound will give an additional 1% discount if I pay cash. Otherwise, they will let me use my MasterCard, or I can pay it off in three monthly installments.

*Terry:* Anything else???

*Brad:* Well . . . Audio Pro says I have to charge it on my MasterCard. They don't accept checks.

*Terry:* I am not surprised. Many mail-order houses don't accept checks.

*Brad:* I give up. What would you do?

1. Assuming that Audio Pro Electronics doesn't charge sales tax on the sale to Brad, which company is offering the best buy?
2. ▰▰▰► What might be some considerations other than price that might influence Brad's decision on where to buy the stereo system?

**ACTIVITY 6-4**
*Sales discounts*

Your sister operates Callender Parts Company, a mail-order boat parts distributorship that is in its third year of operation. The following income statement was recently prepared for the year ended March 31, 2006:

**Callender Parts Company**
**Income Statement**
**For the Year Ended March 31, 2006**

| | | |
|---|---:|---:|
| Revenues: | | |
| Net sales ........................................ | | $960,000 |
| Interest revenue ................................ | | 8,000 |
| Total revenues ............................... | | $968,000 |
| Expenses: | | |
| Cost of merchandise sold ....................... | $672,000 | |
| Selling expenses ............................... | 105,600 | |
| Administrative expenses ........................ | 54,400 | |
| Interest expense .............................. | 16,000 | |
| Total expenses ............................... | | 848,000 |
| Net income ..................................... | | $120,000 |

Your sister is considering a proposal to increase net income by offering sales discounts of 2/15, n/30, and by shipping all merchandise FOB shipping point. Currently, no sales discounts are allowed and merchandise is shipped FOB destination. It is estimated that these credit terms will increase net sales by 10%. The ratio of the cost of merchandise sold to net sales is expected to be 70%. All selling and administrative expenses are expected to remain unchanged, except for store supplies, miscellaneous selling, office supplies, and miscellaneous administrative expenses, which are expected to increase proportionately with increased net sales. The amounts of these preceding items for the year ended March 31, 2006, were as follows:

| | |
|---|---:|
| Store supplies expense | $8,000 |
| Miscellaneous selling expense | 3,200 |
| Office supplies expense | 1,600 |
| Miscellaneous administrative expense | 2,880 |

The other income and other expense items will remain unchanged. The shipment of all merchandise FOB shipping point will eliminate all transportation-out expenses, which for the year ended March 31, 2006, were $32,240.

1. Prepare a projected single-step income statement for the year ending March 31, 2007, based on the proposal. Assume all sales are collected within the discount period.
2. a. ➤ Based on the projected income statement in (1), would you recommend the implementation of the proposed changes?
   b. Describe any possible concerns you may have related to the proposed changes described in (1).

**ACTIVITY 6-5**
*Shopping for a television*

REAL WORLD

Assume that you are planning to purchase a 50-inch Plasma television. In groups of three or four, determine the lowest cost for the television, considering the available alternatives and the advantages and disadvantages of each alternative. For example, you could purchase locally, through mail order, or through an Internet shopping service. Consider such factors as delivery charges, interest-free financing, discounts, coupons, and availability of warranty services. Prepare a report for presentation to the class.

# Answers to Self-Examination Questions

1. **A**  A debit memorandum (answer A), issued by the buyer, indicates the amount the buyer proposes to debit to the accounts payable account. A credit memorandum (answer B), issued by the seller, indicates the amount the seller proposes to credit to the accounts receivable account. An invoice (answer C) or a bill (answer D), issued by the seller, indicates the amount and terms of the sale.
2. **C**  The amount of discount for early payment is $10 (answer C), or 1% of $1,000. Although the $50 of transportation costs paid by the seller is debited to the customer's account, the customer is not entitled to a discount on that amount.
3. **B**  The single-step form of income statement (answer B) is so named because the total of all expenses is deducted in one step from the total of all revenues. The multiple-step form (answer A) includes numerous sections and subsections with several subtotals. The account form (answer C) and

the report form (answer D) are two common forms of the balance sheet.
4. **C**  Gross profit (answer C) is the excess of net sales over the cost of merchandise sold. Operating income (answer A) or income from operations (answer B) is the excess of gross profit over operating expenses. Net income (answer D) is the final figure on the income statement after all revenues and expenses have been reported.
5. **D**  Expenses such as interest expense (answer D) that cannot be associated directly with operations are identified as *Other expense* or *Nonoperating expense*. Depreciation expense—office equipment (answer A) is an administrative expense. Sales salaries expense (answer B) is a selling expense. Insurance expense (answer C) is a mixed expense with elements of both selling expense and administrative expense. For small businesses, insurance expense is usually reported as an administrative expense.

# 7

# CASH

## objectives

*After studying this chapter, you should be able to:*

1 Describe the nature of cash and the importance of internal control over cash.

2 Summarize basic procedures for achieving internal control over cash receipts.

3 Summarize basic procedures for achieving internal control over cash payments, including the use of a voucher system.

4 Describe the nature of a bank account and its use in controlling cash.

5 Prepare a bank reconciliation and journalize any necessary entries.

6 Account for small cash transactions using a petty cash fund.

7 Summarize how cash is presented on the balance sheet.

8 Compute and interpret the ratio of cash to current liabilities.

If your bank returns checks it has paid from your account, along with your monthly bank statement, you may have noticed a magnetic coding in the bottom right-hand corner of each check. This coding indicates the amount of the check. In the past, you may have accepted this coding, as well as the bank statement, as correct. However, a clerk may have entered the magnetic coding incorrectly, which causes the check to be processed for the wrong amount. For example, the following check written for $25 was incorrectly processed as $250:

| | | |
|---|---|---|
| **Ed Smith** | | 7406 |
| 1026 3rd Ave., So. | 7/23/20 06 | |
| Lansing, Wisconsin 58241 | | 64-7088/2611 |

PAY TO THE ORDER OF _Jones Co._ _____ $ *25* 00/100

*Twenty-Five Dollars and* no/100 _____ DOLLARS

FIRST FEDERAL
SAVINGS BANK
OF WISCONSIN
LANSING, WISCONSIN

FOR _____ *Ed Smith*

⑆261170889⑆ 04 33 503662⑉ 7406 ⑈000002 5000⑈

We are all concerned about our cash. Likewise, businesses are concerned about safeguarding and controlling cash. Inadequate controls can and often do lead to theft, misuse of funds, or otherwise embarrassing situations. For example, in one of the biggest errors in banking history, **Chemical Bank** incorrectly deducted customer automated teller machine (ATM) withdrawals twice from each customer's account. For instance, if a customer withdrew $100 from an account, the customer actually had $200 deducted from the account balance. Before the error was discovered, Chemical Bank mistakenly deducted about $15 million from more than 100,000 customer accounts.

To detect errors, control procedures should be used by both you and the bank. In this chapter, we will apply basic internal control concepts and procedures to the control of cash.

# Nature of Cash and the Importance of Controls Over Cash

objective   1

Describe the nature of cash and the importance of internal control over cash.

**POINT OF INTEREST**

The Internet has given rise to a form of cash called "cybercash."

*Cash* includes coins, currency (paper money), checks, money orders, and money on deposit that is available for unrestricted withdrawal from banks and other financial institutions. Normally, you can think of cash as anything that a bank would accept for deposit in your account. For example, a check made payable to you could normally be deposited in a bank and thus is considered cash.

We will assume in this chapter that a business maintains only *one* bank account, represented in the ledger as *Cash*. In practice, however, a business may have several bank accounts, such as one for general cash payments and another for payroll. For each of its bank accounts, the business will maintain a ledger account, one of which may be called *Cash in Bank—First Bank*, for example. It will also maintain separate ledger accounts for cash that it does not keep in the bank, such as cash for small payments, and cash used for special purposes, such as travel reimbursements. We will introduce some of these other cash accounts in the chapter.

Because of the ease with which money can be transferred, cash is the asset most likely to be diverted and used improperly by employees. In addition, many transactions either directly or indirectly affect the receipt or the payment of cash. Businesses must therefore design and use controls that safeguard cash and control the authorization of cash transactions. In the following paragraphs, we will discuss these controls.

# Control of Cash Receipts

To protect cash from theft and misuse, a business must control cash from the time it is received until it is deposited in a bank. Such procedures are called **preventive controls**. Procedures that are designed to detect theft or misuse of cash are called **detective controls**. In a sense, detective controls are also preventive in nature, since employees are less likely to steal or misuse cash if they know there is a good chance they will be discovered.

Retail businesses normally receive cash from two main sources: (1) cash receipts from customers and (2) mail receipts from customers making payments on account. These two sources of cash are shown in Exhibit 1.

## •Exhibit 1

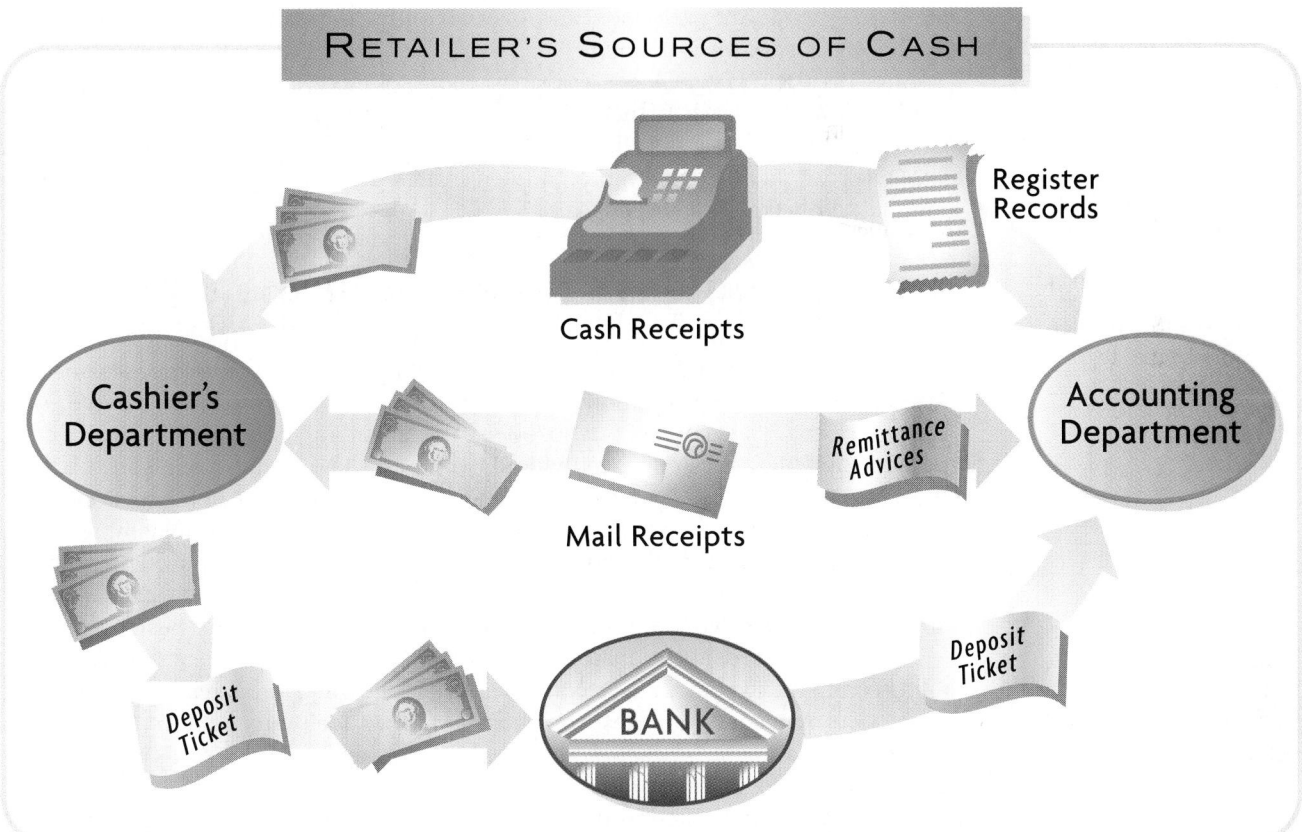

RETAILER'S SOURCES OF CASH

Cash Receipts

Register Records

Cashier's Department

Mail Receipts

Remittance Advices

Accounting Department

Deposit Ticket

BANK

Deposit Ticket

## Controlling Cash Received from Cash Sales

Regardless of the source of cash receipts, every business must properly safeguard and record its cash receipts. One of the most important controls to protect cash received in over-the-counter sales is a cash register. You may have noticed that when a clerk (cashier) enters the amount of a sale, the cash register normally displays the amount. This is a control to ensure that the clerk has charged you the correct amount. You also receive a receipt to verify the accuracy of the amount.

Fast-food restaurants, such as **McDonald's**, **Wendy's**, and **Burger King**, receive cash primarily from over-the-counter sales to customers. Mail-order and Internet retailers, such as **Lands' End, Orvis, L.L. Bean,** and **Amazon.com**, receive cash primarily through the mail and from credit card companies.

I rake in more than $4 billion per year as the world's largest athletic footwear and apparel retailer, with more than 5,900 stores around the globe. I think I've "turned the sport of sneaker shopping into a theatrical and entertainment experience." My brand names include Champs Sports, direct marketer Eastbay, and San Francisco Music Box gift stores. Online I offer 10,000 footwear and apparel products and 150 brands. I serve ladies and kids, too, and have the ultimate ticker symbol. I used to be Venator Group, and before that, Woolworth. Who am I? (Go to page 302 for answer.)

Some retail companies use debit card systems to transfer and record the receipt of cash. In a debit card system, a customer pays for goods at the time of purchase by presenting a plastic card. The card authorizes the electronic transfer of cash from the customer's checking account to the retailer's bank account at the time of the sale.

At the beginning of a work shift, each cash register clerk is given a cash drawer that contains a predetermined amount of cash for making change for customers. The amount in each drawer is sometimes called a **change fund**. At the end of the work shift, each clerk and the supervisor count the cash in the clerk's cash drawer. The amount of cash in each drawer should equal the beginning amount of cash plus the cash sales for the day. However, errors in recording cash sales or errors in making change cause the amount of actual cash on hand to differ from this amount. Such differences are recorded in a ***cash short and over account***. For example, the following entry records a clerk's cash sales of $3,150 when the actual cash on hand is $3,142:

| | | | | | |
|---|---|---|---|---|---|
| Cash | | 3 1 4 2 00 | | | |
| Cash Short and Over | | 8 00 | | | |
| Sales | | | | 3 1 5 0 00 | |
| To record cash sales and actual cash | | | | | |
| on hand. | | | | | |

At the end of the accounting period, a debit balance in the cash short and over account is included in Miscellaneous Administrative Expense in the income statement. A credit balance is included in the Other Income section. If a clerk consistently has significant cash short and over amounts, the supervisor may require the clerk to take additional training.

After a cash register clerk's cash has been counted and recorded on a memorandum form, the cash is then placed in a store safe in the Cashier's Department until it can be deposited in the bank. The supervisor forwards the clerk's cash register records to the Accounting Department, where they become the basis for recording the transactions for the day.

## Controlling Cash Received in the Mail

Cash is received in the mail when customers pay their bills. This cash is usually in the form of checks and money orders. Most companies' invoices are designed so that customers return a portion of the invoice, called a **remittance advice**, with their payment. The employee who opens the incoming mail should initially compare the amount of cash received with the amount shown on the remittance advice. If a customer does not return a remittance advice, an employee prepares one. Like the cash register, the remittance advice serves as a record of cash initially received. It also helps ensure that the posting to the customer's account is accurate. Finally, as a preventive control, the employee opening the mail normally also stamps checks and money orders "For Deposit Only" in the bank account of the business.

All cash received in the mail is sent to the Cashier's Department. An employee there combines it with the receipts from cash sales and prepares a bank deposit ticket. The remittance advices and their summary totals are delivered to the Accounting Department. An accounting clerk then prepares the records of the transactions and posts them to the customer accounts.

When cash is deposited in the bank, the bank normally stamps a duplicate copy of the deposit ticket with the amount received. This bank receipt is returned to the Accounting Department, where a clerk then compares the receipt with the total amount that should have been deposited. This control helps ensure that all the cash is deposited and that no cash is lost or stolen on the way to the bank. Any shortages are thus promptly detected.

The separation of the duties of the Cashier's Department, which handles cash, and the Accounting Department, which records cash, is a preventive control. If Accounting Department employees both handled and recorded cash, an employee could steal cash and change the accounting records to hide the theft.

# Internal Control of Cash Payments

**objective 3**

Summarize basic procedures for achieving internal control over cash payments, including the use of a voucher system.

Internal control of cash payments should provide reasonable assurance that payments are made for only authorized transactions. In addition, controls should ensure that cash is used efficiently. For example, controls should ensure that all available discounts, such as purchase and trade discounts, are taken.

In a small business, an owner/manager may sign all checks, based upon personal knowledge of goods and services purchased. In a large business, however, checks are often prepared by employees who do not have such a complete knowledge of the transactions. In a large business, for example, the duties of purchasing goods, inspecting the goods received, and verifying the invoices are usually performed by different employees. These duties must be coordinated to ensure that checks for proper amounts are issued to creditors. One system used for this purpose is the voucher system.

**Howard Schultz & Associates (HS&A)** specializes in reviewing cash payments for its clients. HS&A searches for errors, such as duplicate payments, failures to take discounts, and inaccurate computations. Amounts recovered for clients ranged from thousands to millions of dollars.

REAL WORLD

## INTEGRITY IN BUSINESS

### THE THEFT AT PERINI CORPORATION

The financial vice president of **Perini Corporation** received a disturbing call from one of the company's banks. The bank reported that Perini's bank account was substantially overdrawn. Perini, a large construction company based near Boston, had never overdrawn any of its bank accounts in over twenty-five years. Shortly thereafter, another of Perini's banks called and reported that its Perini account was also overdrawn. A review of the recent bank statements, which had been lying around unreconciled for two weeks, revealed canceled checks of more than $1.1 million that had not been recorded.

Perini kept its unused checks in an unlocked room. Perini also kept its supply of coffee cups in the same room, where every clerk and secretary had access to them. A quick review revealed two missing boxes of checks.

Perini used a checkwriting machine that automatically signed the vice president's name. Unfortunately, Perini didn't implement the controls suggested by its accountant. Instead, the machine-processed checks were placed in an unlocked box, there was no reconciliation of the counter on the machine with the number of checks that should have been written, and the keys to lock the machine were not carefully safeguarded. The vice president said that such controls were "too much trouble," even though one purpose of controls is to help insure integrity in business.

## Basic Features of the Voucher System

A *voucher system* is a set of procedures for authorizing and recording liabilities and cash payments. A voucher system normally uses (1) vouchers, (2) a file for unpaid vouchers, and (3) a file for paid vouchers. Generally, a voucher is any document that serves as proof of authority to pay cash. For example, an invoice properly approved for payment could be considered a voucher. In many businesses, however, a *voucher* is a special form for recording relevant data about a liability and the details of its payment. An example of such a form is shown in Exhibit 2.

Each voucher includes the creditor's invoice number and the amount and terms of the invoice. The accounts used in recording the purchase (or transaction) are listed in the *account distribution*.

A voucher is normally prepared in the Accounting Department, after all necessary supporting documents have been received. For example, when a voucher is prepared for the purchase of goods, the voucher should be supported by the supplier's invoice, a purchase order, and a receiving report. In preparing the voucher, an accounts payable clerk verifies the quantity, price, and mathematical accuracy of

## •Exhibit 2   Voucher

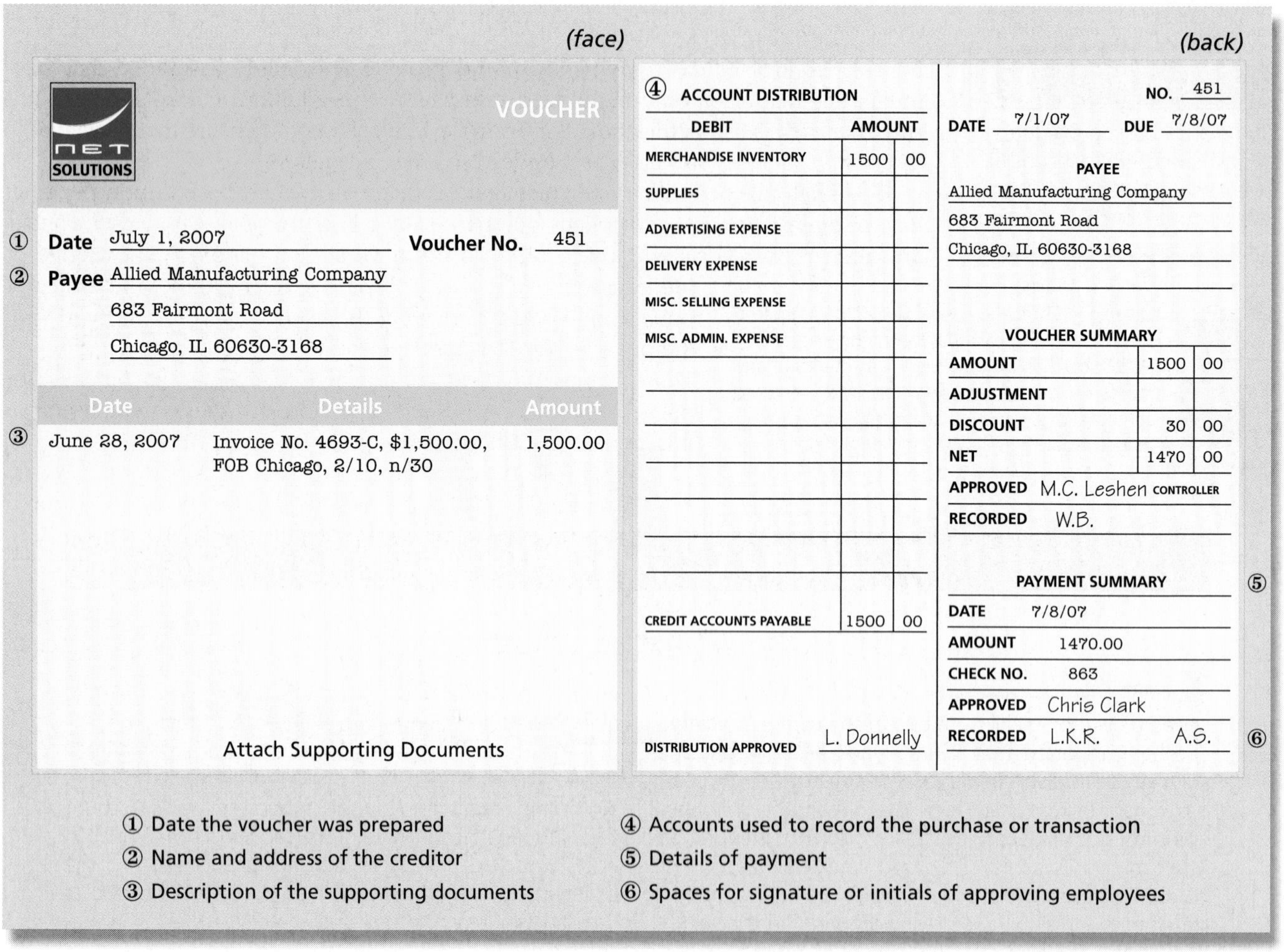

*(face)*                                                           *(back)*

**VOUCHER**

④ **ACCOUNT DISTRIBUTION**

| DEBIT | AMOUNT | |
|---|---|---|
| MERCHANDISE INVENTORY | 1500 | 00 |
| SUPPLIES | | |
| ADVERTISING EXPENSE | | |
| DELIVERY EXPENSE | | |
| MISC. SELLING EXPENSE | | |
| MISC. ADMIN. EXPENSE | | |
| | | |
| | | |
| | | |
| | | |
| | | |
| | | |
| | | |
| | | |
| CREDIT ACCOUNTS PAYABLE | 1500 | 00 |

① **Date** July 1, 2007          **Voucher No.** 451

② **Payee** Allied Manufacturing Company

683 Fairmont Road

Chicago, IL 60630-3168

| Date | Details | Amount |
|---|---|---|
| ③ June 28, 2007 | Invoice No. 4693-C, $1,500.00, FOB Chicago, 2/10, n/30 | 1,500.00 |

**Attach Supporting Documents**

DISTRIBUTION APPROVED   *L. Donnelly*

NO. 451

DATE 7/1/07      DUE 7/8/07

**PAYEE**

Allied Manufacturing Company

683 Fairmont Road

Chicago, IL 60630-3168

**VOUCHER SUMMARY**

| AMOUNT | 1500 | 00 |
|---|---|---|
| ADJUSTMENT | | |
| DISCOUNT | 30 | 00 |
| NET | 1470 | 00 |

APPROVED  *M.C. Leshen* CONTROLLER

RECORDED  *W.B.*

**PAYMENT SUMMARY**   ⑤

| DATE | 7/8/07 |
|---|---|
| AMOUNT | 1470.00 |
| CHECK NO. | 863 |
| APPROVED | *Chris Clark* |
| RECORDED | *L.K.R.*   *A.S.* ⑥ |

① Date the voucher was prepared
② Name and address of the creditor
③ Description of the supporting documents

④ Accounts used to record the purchase or transaction
⑤ Details of payment
⑥ Spaces for signature or initials of approving employees

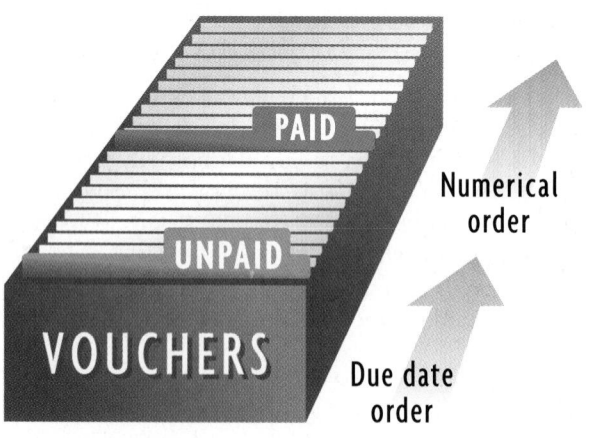

the supporting documents. This provides assurance that the payment is for goods that were properly ordered and received.

After a voucher is prepared, the voucher and its supporting documents are given to the proper official for approval. After it has been approved, the voucher is returned to the Accounting Department, where it is recorded in the accounts. It is then filed in an unpaid voucher file by its due date so that all available purchase discounts are taken.[1]

On its due date, the voucher is removed from the unpaid voucher file. The date, the number, and the amount of the check written in payment are listed on the back of the voucher. The payment of the voucher is recorded in the same manner as the payment of an account payable.

After payment, vouchers are marked "Paid" and are usually filed in numerical order in a paid voucher file. They are then readily available for examination by employees needing information about past payments.

A voucher system may be either manual or computerized. In a computerized system, properly approved supporting documents (such as purchase orders and receiving reports)

---

[1]Occasionally, a purchase discount is missed. Some companies record the amounts of missed discounts in an account titled *Discounts Lost*. Doing so allows managers to monitor the significance of discounts lost. Since most companies design controls to take all purchase discounts, we do not illustrate the use of a discounts lost account.

would be entered directly into computer files. At the due date, the checks would be automatically generated and mailed to creditors. At that time, the voucher would be automatically transferred to a paid voucher file. In some cases, payments may be made electronically rather than by check.

## Electronic Funds Transfer

With rapidly changing technology, new systems are being devised to more efficiently record and transfer cash among companies. Such systems often use *electronic funds transfer (EFT)*. In an EFT system, computers rather than paper (money, checks, etc.) are used to effect cash transactions. For example, a business may pay its employees by means of EFT. Under such a system, employees may authorize the deposit of their payroll checks directly into checking accounts. Each pay period, the business electronically transfers the employees' net pay to their checking accounts through the use of computer systems and telephone lines. Likewise, many companies are using EFT systems to pay their suppliers and other vendors.

# Bank Accounts: Their Nature and Use as a Control Over Cash

**objective 4**

Describe the nature of a bank account and its use in controlling cash.

**REAL WORLD**

Many businesses and individuals are now using Internet banking services, which provide for the payment of funds electronically. Also, **TeleCheck Services, Inc.**, the world's leading check acceptance company, offers an online real-time check payment option for purchases made over the Internet. "It is apparent from the rapid growth of online sales that many consumers are as comfortable writing checks for Internet purchases as they are at their local brick-and-mortar store," explains Steve Shaper, chief executive officer of TeleCheck.

Most of you are already familiar with bank accounts. You have a checking account at a local bank, credit union, savings and loan association, or other financial institution. In this section, we discuss the nature of a bank account used by a business. The features of such accounts will be similar to your own bank account. We then discuss the use of bank accounts as an additional control over cash.

## Business Bank Accounts

A business often maintains several bank accounts. The forms used with each bank account are a signature card, deposit ticket, check, and record of checks drawn.

When you open a checking account, you sign a **signature card**. This card is used by the bank to verify the signature on checks that are submitted for payment. Also, when you open an account, the bank assigns an identifying number to the account.

The details of a deposit are listed by the depositor on a printed **deposit ticket** supplied by the bank. These forms are often prepared in duplicate. The bank teller stamps or initials a copy of the deposit ticket and gives it to the depositor as a receipt. Other types of receipts may also be used to give the depositor written proof of the date and the total amount of the deposit.

A **check** is a written document signed by the depositor, ordering the bank to pay a sum of money to an individual or entity. There are three parties to a check—the drawer, the drawee, and the payee. The **drawer** is the one who signs the check, ordering payment by the bank. The **drawee** is the bank on which the check is drawn. The **payee** is the party to whom payment is to be made.

Drawer          Payee          Drawee

The name and address of the depositor are usually printed on each check. In addition, checks are prenumbered, so that they can easily be kept track of by both the issuer and the bank. Banks encode their identification number and the depositor's account number in magnetic ink on each check. These numbers make it possible for the bank to sort and post checks automatically. When a check is presented for payment, the amount for which it is drawn is inserted, next to the account number, in magnetic ink. The processed check shown at the beginning of this chapter illustrated these features.

A record of each check should be prepared at the time a check is written. A small booklet called a **transactions register** is often used by both businesses and individuals for this purpose.

The purpose of a check may be written in space provided on the check or on an attachment to the check. Normally, checks issued to a creditor on account are sent with a form that identifies the specific invoice that is being paid. The purpose of this **remittance advice** is to make sure that proper credit is recorded in the accounts of the creditor. In this way, mistakes are less likely to occur. A check and remittance advice is shown in Exhibit 3.

## •Exhibit 3

**Check and Remittance Advice**

| POWER NETWORKING | | | | 363 |
|---|---|---|---|---|
| 1000 Belkin  Los Angeles, CA 90014-1000 | | | July 07  20 06 | 9-42/720 |

Pay to the Order of _____ Interface Data Systems _____ $ 921.20

Nine hundred twenty-one 20/100 ----------------------------- **Dollars**

**VALLEY NATIONAL BANK OF LOS ANGELES**

_K.R. Simons_ **Treasurer**

_Earl M. Hartman_ **Vice President**

LOS ANGELES, CA 90020-4283    (310) 851-5151    MEMBER FDIC

⑆072000423⑆    162702    363⑈

**DETACH THIS PORTION BEFORE CASHING**

| Date | Description | Gross Amount | Deductions | Net Amount |
|---|---|---|---|---|
| 07/07/06 | Invoice No. 529482 | 940.00 | 18.80 | 921.20 |

**POWER NETWORKING**

Before depositing the check, the payee removes the remittance advice. The payee may then use the remittance advice as written proof of the details of the cash receipt.

# Bank Statement

Banks usually maintain a record of all checking account transactions. A summary of all transactions, called a **statement of account**, is mailed to the depositor, usually each month. Like any account with a customer or a creditor, the bank statement shows the beginning balance, additions, deductions, and the balance at the end of the period. A typical bank statement is shown in Exhibit 4.

•**Exhibit 4**

**Bank Statement**

```
                                MEMBER FDIC                         PAGE   1

VALLEY NATIONAL BANK                        ACCOUNT NUMBER   1627042
OF LOS ANGELES
                                            FROM  6/30/06   TO  7/31/06
LOS ANGELES, CA 90020-4253    (310)851-5151
                                            BALANCE              4,218.60

                                          22 DEPOSITS           13,749.75

       POWER NETWORKING                    52 WITHDRAWALS        14,698.57
       1000 Belkin Street
       Los Angeles, CA 90014-1000           3 OTHER DEBITS
                                              AND CREDITS          90.00CR

                                            NEW BALANCE          3,359.78
```

| * – CHECKS AND OTHER DEBITS – – | | | * – – DEPOSITS – – | * – DATE – – | * – – BALANCE – * |
|---|---|---|---|---|---|
| 819.40 | 122.54 | | 585.75 | 07/01 | 3,862.41 |
| 369.50 | 732.26 | 20.15 | 421.53 | 07/02 | 3,162.03 |
| 600.00 | 190.70 | 52.50 | 781.30 | 07/03 | 3,100.13 |
| 25.93 | 160.00 | | 662.50 | 07/05 | 3,576.70 |
| 921.20 | NSF 300.00 | | 503.18 | 07/07 | 2,858.68 |
| 32.26 | 535.09 | | 932.00 | 07/29 | 3,404.40 |
| 21.10 | 126.20 | | 705.21 | 07/30 | 3,962.31 |
| | SC 18.00 | | MS 408.00 | 07/30 | 4,352.31 |
| 26.12 | 1,615.13 | | 648.72 | 07/31 | 3,359.78 |

```
       EC—ERROR CORRECTION              OD—OVERDRAFT
       MS—MISCELLANEOUS                 PS—PAYMENT STOPPED
       NSF—NOT SUFFICENT FUNDS          SC—SERVICE CHARGE

 * * *                      * * *                          * * *
       THE RECONCILEMENT OF THIS STATEMENT WITH YOUR RECORDS IS ESSENTIAL.
       ANY ERROR OR EXCEPTION SHOULD BE REPORTED IMMEDIATELY.
```

The depositor's checks received by the bank during the period may accompany the bank statement, arranged in the order of payment. The paid checks are stamped "Paid," together with the date of payment. Other entries that the bank has made in the depositor's account may be described in debit or credit memorandums enclosed with the statement.

## INTEGRITY IN BUSINESS

### CHECK FRAUD

Check fraud involves counterfeiting, altering, or otherwise manipulating the information on checks in order to fraudulently cash a check. According to the **National Check Fraud Center**, check fraud and counterfeiting are among the fastest growing problems affecting the financial system, generating over $10 billion in losses annually.

Criminals perpetrate the fraud by taking blank checks from your checkbook, finding a canceled check in the garbage, or removing a check you have mailed to pay bills. Consumers can prevent check fraud by carefully storing blank checks, placing outgoing mail in postal mailboxes, and shredding canceled checks.

You should note that a depositor's checking account balance *in the bank's records* is a liability with a credit balance. Debit memorandums issued by the bank on a depositor's account therefore decrease the depositor's balance. Likewise, credit memorandums increase the depositor's balance. A bank issues a debit memorandum to charge (decrease) a depositor's account for service charges or for deposited checks returned because of insufficient funds. Likewise, a bank issues a credit memorandum when it increases the depositor's account for collecting a note receivable for the depositor, making a loan to the depositor, receiving a wire deposit, or adding interest to the depositor's account.[2]

> A bank account and a business's records provide a double record of cash transactions.

# Bank Accounts as a Control Over Cash

A bank account is one of the primary tools a business uses to control cash. For example, businesses often require that all cash receipts be initially deposited in a bank account. Likewise, businesses usually use checks to make all cash payments, except for very small amounts. When such a system is used, there is a double record of cash transactions—one by the business and the other by the bank.

A business can use a bank statement to compare the cash transactions recorded in its accounting records to those recorded by the bank. The cash balance shown by a bank statement is usually different from the cash balance shown in the accounting records of the business, as shown in Exhibit 5.

**•Exhibit 5**   **Power Networking's Records and Bank Statement**

| Bank Statement | | | Power Networking Records | |
|---|---|---|---|---|
| Beginning Balance . . . . . . . . | | $ 4,218.60 | Beginning Balance . . . . . . . . | $ 4,227.60 |
| Additions: | | | | |
|    Deposits . . . . . . . . . . . . . | | 13,749.75 | Deposits . . . . . . . . . . . . . . . | 14,565.95 |
|    Miscellaneous . . . . . . . . . | | 408.00 | | |
| Deductions: | | | | |
|    Checks . . . . . . . . . . . . . . | | 14,698.57 | Checks . . . . . . . . . . . . . . . . | 16,243.56 |
|    NSF Check . . . . . . . . . . . . | $300 | | | |
|    Service Charge . . . . . . . . | 18 | 318.00 | | |
| Ending Balance . . . . . . . . . . | | $ 3,359.78 | Ending Balance . . . . . . . . . . | $ 2,549.99 |

Power Networking should determine the reason for the difference in these two amounts.

This difference may be the result of a delay by either party in recording transactions. For example, there is a time lag of one day or more between the date a check is written and the date that it is presented to the bank for payment. If the depositor mails deposits to the bank or uses the night depository, a time lag between the date of the deposit and the date that it is recorded by the bank is also probable. The bank may also debit or credit the depositor's account for transactions about which the depositor will not be informed until later.

The difference may be the result of errors made by either the business or the bank in recording transactions. For example, the business may incorrectly post to Cash a check written for $4,500 as $450. Likewise, a bank may incorrectly record the amount of a check, as we illustrated at the beginning of this chapter.

---

[2]Although interest-bearing checking accounts are common for individuals, Federal Reserve Regulation Q prohibits the paying of interest on corporate checking accounts.

# Bank Reconciliation

objective    5

Prepare a bank reconciliation
and journalize any necessary
entries.

For effective control, the reasons for the difference between the cash balance on
the bank statement and the cash balance in the accounting records should be determined by preparing a bank reconciliation. A **bank reconciliation** is a listing of
the items and amounts that cause the cash balance reported in the bank statement
to differ from the balance of the cash account in the ledger.

A bank reconciliation is usually divided into two sections. The first section begins with the cash balance according to the bank statement and ends with the adjusted balance. The second section begins with the cash balance according to the
depositor's records and ends with the adjusted balance. The two amounts designated as the adjusted balance must be equal. The content of the bank reconciliation is shown below.

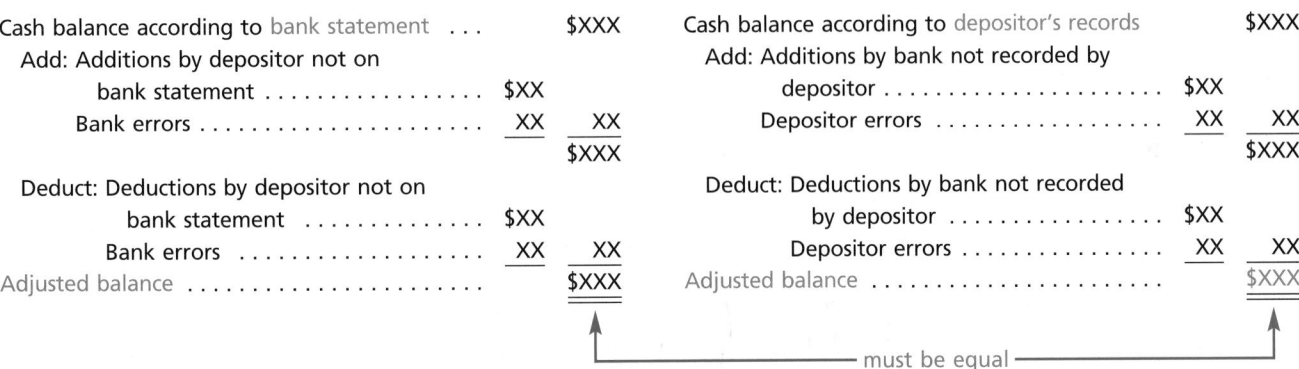

The following steps are useful in finding the reconciling items and determining
the adjusted balance of Cash:

1. Compare each deposit listed on the bank statement with unrecorded deposits appearing in the preceding period's reconciliation and with deposit receipts or other
records of deposits. *Add deposits not recorded by the bank to the balance according to the bank statement.*
2. Compare paid checks with outstanding checks appearing on the preceding
period's reconciliation and with recorded checks. *Deduct checks outstanding
that have not been paid by the bank from the balance according to the bank
statement.*
3. Compare bank credit memorandums to entries in the journal. For example, a bank
would issue a credit memorandum for a note receivable and interest that it collected for a depositor. *Add credit memorandums that have not been recorded to
the balance according to the depositor's records.*
4. Compare bank debit memorandums to entries recording cash payments. For example, a bank normally issues debit memorandums for service charges and check
printing charges. A bank also issues debit memorandums for not-sufficient-funds
checks. A *not-sufficient-funds (NSF) check* is a customer's check that was recorded
and deposited but was not paid when it was presented to the customer's bank
for payment. NSF checks are normally charged back to the customer as an account receivable. *Deduct debit memorandums that have not been recorded from
the balance according to the depositor's records.*
5. List any errors discovered during the preceding steps. For example, if an amount
has been recorded incorrectly by the depositor, the amount of the error should
be added to or deducted from the cash balance according to the depositor's
records. Similarly, errors by the bank should be added to or deducted from the
cash balance according to the bank statement.

To illustrate a bank reconciliation, we will use the bank statement for Power Networking in Exhibit 4. This bank statement shows a balance of $3,359.78 as of July 31. The cash balance in Power Networking's ledger as of the same date is $2,549.99. The following reconciling items are revealed by using the steps outlined above:

Deposit of July 31, not recorded on bank statement . . . . . . . . . . . . . . . . . . . .    $  816.20
Checks outstanding: No. 812, $1,061.00; No. 878, $435.39; No. 883, $48.60 . . .    1,544.99
Note plus interest of $8 collected by bank (credit memorandum), not
    recorded in the journal . . . . . . . . . . . . . . . . . . . . . . . . . . . . . . . . . . . . . . . . . . .    408.00
Check from customer (Thomas Ivey) returned by bank because of
    insufficient funds (NSF) . . . . . . . . . . . . . . . . . . . . . . . . . . . . . . . . . . . . . . . . . .    300.00
Bank service charges (debit memorandum), not recorded in the journal . . . . .    18.00
Check No. 879 for $732.26 to Taylor Co. on account, recorded in the
    journal as $723.26  . . . . . . . . . . . . . . . . . . . . . . . . . . . . . . . . . . . . . . . . . . . . .    9.00

The bank reconciliation based on the bank statement and the reconciling items is shown in Exhibit 6.

## •Exhibit 6    Bank Reconciliation for Power Networking

**Power Networking**
**Bank Reconciliation**
**July 31, 2006**

| | | | | | | |
|---|---|---|---|---|---|---|
| Cash balance according to | | | Cash balance according to | | | |
| bank statement | | $3 3 5 9 78 | depositor's records | | | $2 5 4 9 99 |
| Add deposit of July 31, not | | | Add note and interest | | | |
| recorded by bank | | 8 1 6 20 | collected by bank | | | 4 0 8 00 |
| | | $4 1 7 5 98 | | | | $2 9 5 7 99 |
| | | | Deduct: Check returned because | | | |
| Deduct outstanding checks: | | | of insufficient funds | $ 3 0 0 00 | | |
| No. 812 | $1 0 6 1 00 | | Bank service charges | 1 8 00 | | |
| No. 878 | 4 3 5 39 | | Error in recording | | | |
| No. 883 | 4 8 60 | 1 5 4 4 99 | Check No. 879 | | 9 00 | 3 2 7 00 |
| Adjusted balance | | $2 6 3 0 99 | Adjusted balance | | | $2 6 3 0 99 |

**Entries must be made in the depositor's accounts for any items that affect the business's record of cash.**

No entries are necessary on the depositor's records as a result of the information included in the first section of the bank reconciliation. This section begins with the cash balance according to the bank statement. However, the bank should be notified of any errors that need to be corrected on its records.

Any items in the second section of the bank reconciliation must be recorded in the depositor's accounts. This section begins with the cash balance according to the depositor's records. For example, journal entries should be made for any unrecorded bank memorandums and any depositor's errors.

The journal entries for Power Networking, based on the preceding bank reconciliation, are as follows:

| | | | | | |
|---|---|---|---|---|---|
| July | 31 | Cash | | 4 0 8 00 | |
| | | Notes Receivable | | | 4 0 0 00 |
| | | Interest Revenue | | | 8 00 |
| | | Note collected by bank. | | | |

| | July | 31 | Accounts Receivable—Thomas Ivey | 3 0 0 00 | | |
|---|---|---|---|---|---|---|
| | | | Miscellaneous Administrative Expense | 1 8 00 | | |
| | | | Accounts Payable—Taylor Co. | 9 00 | | |
| | | | Cash | | | 3 2 7 00 |
| | | | NSF check, bank service charges, and error | | | |
| | | | in recording Check No. 879. | | | |

After these entries have been posted, the cash account will have a debit balance of $2,630.99. This balance agrees with the adjusted cash balance shown on the bank reconciliation. This is the amount of cash available as of July 31 and the amount that would be reported on Power Networking's July 31 balance sheet.

Although businesses may reconcile their bank accounts in a slightly different format from what we described above, the objective is the same: to control cash by reconciling the company's records to the records of an independent outside source, the bank. In doing so, any errors or misuse of cash may be detected.

For effective control, the bank reconciliation should be prepared by an employee who does not take part in or record cash transactions. When these duties are not properly separated, mistakes are likely to occur, and it is more likely that cash will be stolen or otherwise misapplied. For example, an employee who takes part in all of these duties could prepare and cash an unauthorized check, omit it from the accounts, and omit it from the reconciliation.

**POINT OF INTEREST**  If you reconcile your bank account each month, you first scan your bank statement for any bank entries that you have not yet recorded. Examples of such entries include service charges (a debit entry) and interest earned (a credit entry). You then enter these amounts in your checkbook (register) and determine the balance of your account. If you stop at this point, you are assuming that the bank hasn't made any errors.

If you fully reconcile your account, you should also scan your checkbook for items that the bank has not yet recorded: (1) deposits in transit and (2) outstanding checks. Deposits in transit should be added to the bank balance, and outstanding checks should be subtracted from the bank balance. The result is an adjusted bank balance, which should agree with the balance of your checkbook. If the two are not equal, either you or the bank has made an error.

# Petty Cash

As in your own day-to-day life, it is usually not practical for a business to write checks to pay small amounts, such as postage. Yet, these small payments may occur often enough to add up to a significant total amount. Thus, it is desirable to control such payments. For this purpose, a special cash fund, called a ***petty cash fund***, is used.

A petty cash fund is established by first estimating the amount of cash needed for payments from the fund during a period, such as a week or a month. After necessary approvals, a check is written and cashed for this amount. The money obtained from cashing the check is then given to an employee, called the petty cash custodian, who is authorized to disburse monies from the fund. For control purposes, the company may place restrictions on the maximum amount and the types of payments that can be made from the fund.

Each time monies are paid from petty cash, the custodian records the details of the payment on a petty cash receipt form. A typical petty cash receipt is illustrated in Exhibit 7.

The petty cash fund is normally replenished at periodic intervals, or when it is depleted or reaches a minimum amount. When a petty cash fund is replenished, the accounts debited are determined by summarizing the petty cash receipts. A check is then written for this amount, payable to the petty cash custodian.

## •Exhibit 7

**Petty Cash Receipt**

```
┌─────────────────────────────────────────────────────────────────┐
│                      PETTY CASH RECEIPT                            │
│                                                                   │
│   No. _____121_____            Date __August 1, 2006__        │
│                                                      ┌──────────┐ │
│   Paid to _____Metropolitan Times_____   Amount │          │ │
│                                                      │  3 │ 00  │ │
│   For _____Daily newspaper_____             └──────────┘ │
│                                                                   │
│   Charge to ___Miscellaneous Administrative Expense___            │
│                                                                   │
│   Payment received:                                               │
│                                                                   │
│   _____S.O. Hall_____   Approved by ____N.E.R.____      │
└─────────────────────────────────────────────────────────────────┘
```

To illustrate normal petty cash fund entries, assume that a petty cash fund of $100 is established on August 1. The entry to record this transaction is as follows:

| Aug. | 1 | Petty Cash | 1 0 0 00 | |
|---|---|---|---|---|
| | | Cash | | 1 0 0 00 |
| | | Established petty cash fund. | | |

At the end of August, the petty cash receipts indicate expenditures for the following items: office supplies, $28; postage (office supplies), $22; store supplies, $35; and daily newspapers (miscellaneous administrative expense), $3. The entry to replenish the petty cash fund on August 31 is as follows:

| Aug. | 31 | Office Supplies | 5 0 00 | |
|---|---|---|---|---|
| | | Store Supplies | 3 5 00 | |
| | | Miscellaneous Administrative Expense | 3 00 | |
| | | Cash | | 8 8 00 |
| | | Replenished petty cash fund. | | |

If the petty cash account has a balance of $200, the cash in the fund totals $20, and the petty cash receipts total $180 at the end of a period, what account is credited and what is the amount of the credit in the entry to replenish the fund?

------------------------------------

*Cash is credited for $180.*

> **Petty Cash is debited only when the fund is set up or the amount of the fund is increased.**

Replenishing the petty cash fund restores it to its original amount of $100. You should note that there is no entry in Petty Cash when the fund is replenished. Petty Cash is debited only when the fund is initially set up or when the amount of the fund is increased at a later time. Petty Cash is credited if it is being decreased.

# Presentation of Cash on the Balance Sheet

Summarize how cash is presented on the balance sheet.

Cash is the most liquid asset, and therefore it is listed as the first asset in the Current Assets section of the balance sheet. Most companies present only a single cash amount on the balance sheet by combining all their bank and cash fund accounts.

A company may have cash in excess of its operating needs. In such cases, the company normally invests in highly liquid investments in order to earn interest.

These investments are called ***cash equivalents***.[3] Examples of cash equivalents include U.S. Treasury Bills, notes issued by major corporations (referred to as commercial paper), and money market funds. Companies that have invested excess cash in cash equivalents usually report *Cash and cash equivalents* as one amount on the balance sheet.

Banks may require depositors to maintain minimum cash balances in their bank accounts. Such a balance is called a **compensating balance**. This requirement is often imposed by the bank as a part of a loan agreement or line of credit. A *line of credit* is a preapproved amount the bank is willing to lend to a customer upon request. Compensating balance requirements should be disclosed in notes to the financial statements.

**REAL WORLD** The following note discloses compensating balance requirements for **Kmart Corporation**: . . . *In support of lines of credit, it is expected that compensating balances will be maintained on deposit with the banks, which will average 10% of the line to the extent that it is not in use and an additional 10% on the portion in use.* . . .

---

## FINANCIAL REPORTING AND DISCLOSURE

### MICROSOFT CORPORATION

**M**icrosoft Corporation develops, manufactures, licenses, and supports software products for computing devices. Microsoft software products include computer operating systems, such as Windows, and application software, such as Microsoft Word™ and Excel.™ Microsoft is actively involved in the video game market through its Xbox and is also involved in online products and services.

Microsoft is known for its strong cash position. Microsoft's June 30, 2002 balance sheet reported over $38 billion of cash and short-term investments, as shown below.

**Balance Sheet**
**June 30, 2002**
**(In millions)**
**Assets**

| | |
|---|---:|
| Current assets: | |
| Cash and equivalents | $ 3,016 |
| Short-term investments | 35,636 |
| Total cash and short-term investments | $38,652 |

The cash and cash equivalents of $3 billion are further described in the notes to the financial statements, as shown below.

The short-term investments are invested in short-term securities so that they can easily be converted to cash for operating or strategic cash needs, such as possible mergers or acquisitions.

| | |
|---|---:|
| Cash and equivalents: | |
| Cash | $1,114 |
| Commercial paper | 260 |
| Certificates of deposit | 31 |
| Money market mutual funds | 714 |
| Corporate notes and bonds | 560 |
| Municipal securities | 337 |
| Total cash and equivalents | $3,016 |

---

[3]To be classified as a cash equivalent, according to *FASB Statement 95*, the investment is expected to be converted to cash within 90 days.

# Financial Analysis and Interpretation

objective 8

Compute and interpret the ratio of cash to current liabilities.

In an earlier chapter, we discussed the use of working capital and the current ratio in evaluating a company's ability to pay its current liabilities (short-term solvency). Both of these measures assume that the noncash current assets will be converted to cash in time to pay the current liabilities. For most companies, these measures are useful for assessing short-term solvency. However, a company that is in financial distress may have difficulty converting its receivables, inventory, and prepaid assets to cash on a timely basis. In these cases, the ratio of cash to current liabilities may be useful in assessing the ability of creditors to collect what they are owed. Because this ratio is most relevant for companies in financial distress, it is called the ***doomsday ratio***.[4] Its name comes from the worst case assumption that the business ceases to exist and only the cash on hand is available to meet creditor obligations.

In computing the ratio of cash to current liabilities, cash and cash equivalents are used in the numerator, as shown below.

$$\text{Doomsday ratio} = \frac{\text{Cash and cash equivalents}}{\text{Current liabilities}}$$

To illustrate, assume the following data for Laettner Co. and Oakley Co. for the current year:

|  | Laettner Co. | Oakley Co. |
| --- | --- | --- |
| Cash and cash equivalents | $100,000 | $ 120,000 |
| Current liabilities | 400,000 | 1,500,000 |

The doomsday ratio for each company is computed as follows. In this case, Oakley Co. is more risky to creditors than is Laettner.

|  | Doomsday Ratio |  |
| --- | --- | --- |
| Laettner Co. | 0.25 | ($100,000/$400,000) |
| Oakley Co. | 0.08 | ($120,000/$1,500,000) |

Because most businesses maintain cash and cash equivalents at amounts substantially less than their current liabilities, the doomsday ratio is almost always less than one. For example, the doomsday ratio for **Radio Shack Corporation** is 0.18. For **La-Z-Boy Chair Company**, it is 0.25.

Differences among companies will occur because of differences in management philosophy and operating styles. Nevertheless, a comparison over time that indicates a decreasing ratio generally indicates more risk for creditors.

---

[4]This ratio is discussed more fully in *101 Business Ratios* by Sheldon Gates, McLane Publications, Scottsdale, Arizona, 1993.

## SPOTLIGHT ON STRATEGY

### TURN OFF THE LIGHT?

**K**mart recently filed for bankruptcy. What happened? What went wrong?

Most analysts blame Kmart's problems on a strategy that relied heavily upon advertising circulars to get customers into its stores. Such circulars, which are expensive to produce, accounted for 10.6% of Kmart's operating expenses, as compared to 2.2% for **Target** and 0.4% for **Wal-Mart**. In addition, Kmart continued to use its "blue-light specials," in which merchandise prices would be reduced at periodic intervals for customers who were shopping within its stores. These specials created inventory shortages as merchandise sold out and suppliers could not accurately predict customer needs. As a result, suppliers increased Kmart's prices, which in turn were passed on to customers. In contrast, Wal-Mart employs an "always

low price" strategy for getting customers into its stores. Kmart reacted by promoting a "Blue-Light Always" program, developing a Bluelight.com Web site, and reducing its use of ad circulars. Unfortunately, Kmart's traditional customers who were used to the circulars stopped shopping at Kmart. In addition, Kmart couldn't compete with Wal-Mart's efficiency and low costs. Thus, Kmart filed for bankruptcy, eventually reorganizing and hoping once again to become competitive and profitable.

**Sources:** Amy Merrick, "Expensive Ad Circulars Precipitate Kmart President's Departure," *The Wall Street Journal*, January 18, 2002; Michael Levy and Dhruv Grewal, "So Long, Kmart Shoppers," *The Wall Street Journal*, January 28, 2002; and "Blue Light Blues," *The Economist*, January 18, 2002.

# ey Points

**1 Describe the nature of cash and the importance of internal control over cash.**

Cash includes coins, currency (paper money), checks, money orders, and money on deposit that is available for unrestricted withdrawal from banks and other financial institutions. Because of the ease with which money can be transferred, businesses should design and use controls that safeguard cash and authorize cash transactions.

**2 Summarize basic procedures for achieving internal control over cash receipts.**

One of the most important controls to protect cash received in over-the-counter sales is a cash register. A remittance advice is a preventive control for cash received through the mail. Separating the duties of handling cash and recording cash is also a preventive control.

**3 Summarize basic procedures for achieving internal control over cash payments, including the use of a voucher system.**

A voucher system is a set of procedures for authorizing and recording liabilities and cash payments. A voucher system uses vouchers, a file for unpaid vouchers, and a file for paid vouchers.

**4 Describe the nature of a bank account and its use in controlling cash.**

The forms used with bank accounts are a signature card, deposit ticket, check, and record of checks drawn. Each month, the bank usually sends a bank statement to the depositor, summarizing all of the transactions for the month. The bank statement allows a business to compare the cash transactions recorded in the accounting records to those recorded by the bank.

**5 Prepare a bank reconciliation and journalize any necessary entries.**

The first section of the bank reconciliation begins with the cash balance according to the bank statement. This balance is adjusted for the deposi-

tor's changes in cash that do not appear on the bank statement and for any bank errors. The second section begins with the cash balance according to the depositor's records. This balance is adjusted for the bank's changes in cash that do not appear on the depositor's records and for any depositor errors. The adjusted balances for the two sections must be equal.

No entries are necessary on the depositor's records as a result of the information included in the first section of the bank reconciliation. However, the items in the second section must be journalized on the depositor's records.

**6 Account for small cash transactions using a petty cash fund.**

A petty cash fund may be used by a business to make small payments that occur frequently. The money in a petty cash fund is placed in the custody of a specific employee, who authorizes payments from the fund. Periodically or when the amount of money in the fund is depleted or reduced to a minimum amount, the fund is replenished.

**7 Summarize how cash is presented on the balance sheet.**
Cash is listed as the first asset in the Current Assets section of the balance sheet. Companies that have invested

excess cash in highly liquid investments usually report *Cash and cash equivalents* on the balance sheet.

**8 Compute and interpret the ratio of cash to current liabilities.**
A company that is in financial distress may have difficulty converting

its receivables, inventory, and prepaid assets to cash on a timely basis. In these cases, the ratio of cash to current liabilities, called the doomsday ratio, may be useful in assessing the ability of creditors to collect what they are owed.

# ey Terms

bank reconciliation (293)
cash (284)
cash equivalents (297)

cash short and over account (286)
doomsday ratio (298)
electronic funds transfer (EFT) (289)

petty cash fund (295)
voucher (287)
voucher system (287)

# Illustrative Problem

The bank statement for Urethane Company for June 30, 2006, indicates a balance of $9,143.11. All cash receipts are deposited each evening in a night depository, after banking hours. The accounting records indicate the following summary data for cash receipts and payments for June:

| | |
|---|---|
| Cash balance as of June 1 | $ 3,943.50 |
| Total cash receipts for June | 28,971.60 |
| Total amount of checks issued in June | 28,388.85 |

Comparing the bank statement and the accompanying canceled checks and memorandums with the records reveals the following reconciling items:

a. The bank had collected for Urethane Company $1,030 on a note left for collection. The face of the note was $1,000.
b. A deposit of $1,852.21, representing receipts of June 30, had been made too late to appear on the bank statement.
c. Checks outstanding totaled $5,265.27.
d. A check drawn for $139 had been incorrectly charged by the bank as $157.
e. A check for $30 returned with the statement had been recorded in the depositor's records as $240. The check was for the payment of an obligation to Avery Equipment Company for the purchase of office supplies on account.
f. Bank service charges for June amounted to $18.20.

## Instructions
1. Prepare a bank reconciliation for June.
2. Journalize the entries that should be made by Urethane Company.

## Solution
**1.**

**Urethane Company**
**Bank Reconciliation**
**June 30, 2006**

| | | |
|---|---:|---:|
| Cash balance according to bank statement | | $ 9,143.11 |
| Add: Deposit of June 30 not recorded by bank | $1,852.21 | |
| Bank error in charging check as $157 instead of $139 | 18.00 | 1,870.21 |
| | | $11,013.32 |
| Deduct: Outstanding checks | | 5,265.27 |
| Adjusted balance | | $ 5,748.05 |

| | | |
|---|---:|---:|
| Cash balance according to depositor's records . . . . . . . . . . . . . . . . . | | $ 4,526.25* |
| Add: Proceeds of note collected by bank, including $30 interest . . . . . | $1,030.00 | |
| Error in recording check . . . . . . . . . . . . . . . . . . . . . . . . . . . . . | 210.00 | 1,240.00 |
| | | $ 5,766.25 |
| Deduct: Bank service charges . . . . . . . . . . . . . . . . . . . . . . . . . . . . . | | 18.20 |
| Adjusted balance . . . . . . . . . . . . . . . . . . . . . . . . . . . . . . . . . . . . . | | $ 5,748.05 |

*$3,943.50 + $28,971.60 − $28,388.85

| | | |
|---|---:|---:|
| **2.** Cash . . . . . . . . . . . . . . . . . . . . . . . . . . . . . . . . . . . . . . . . . . . . | 1,240.00 | |
| Notes Receivable . . . . . . . . . . . . . . . . . . . . . . . . . . . . . . . | | 1,000.00 |
| Interest Revenue . . . . . . . . . . . . . . . . . . . . . . . . . . . . . . . | | 30.00 |
| Accounts Payable—Avery Equipment . . . . . . . . . . . . . . . . . . . | | 210.00 |
| | | |
| Miscellaneous Administrative Expense . . . . . . . . . . . . . . . . . . . . | 18.20 | |
| Cash . . . . . . . . . . . . . . . . . . . . . . . . . . . . . . . . . . . . . . . | | 18.20 |

# Self-Examination Questions (Answers at End of Chapter)

1. The bank erroneously charged Tropical Services' account for $450.50 for a check that was correctly written and recorded by Tropical Services as $540.50. To reconcile the bank account of Tropical Services at the end of the month, you would:
   A. add $90 to the cash balance according to the bank statement.
   B. add $90 to the cash balance according to Tropical Services' records.
   C. deduct $90 from the cash balance according to the bank statement.
   D. deduct $90 from the cash balance according to Tropical Services' records.

2. In preparing a bank reconciliation, the amount of checks outstanding would be:
   A. added to the cash balance according to the bank statement.
   B. deducted from the cash balance according to the bank statement.
   C. added to the cash balance according to the depositor's records.
   D. deducted from the cash balance according to the depositor's records.

3. Journal entries based on the bank reconciliation are required for:
   A. additions to the cash balance according to the depositor's records.
   B. deductions from the cash balance according to the depositor's records.
   C. both A and B.
   D. neither A nor B.

4. A petty cash fund is:
   A. used to pay relatively small amounts.
   B. established by estimating the amount of cash needed for disbursements of relatively small amounts during a specified period.
   C. reimbursed when the amount of money in the fund is reduced to a predetermined minimum amount.
   D. all of the above.

5. Which of the following is the correct entry to replenish a petty cash fund?
   A. Debit Petty Cash; credit Cash
   B. Debit various expense accounts; credit Petty Cash
   C. Debit various expense accounts; credit Cash
   D. Debit Cash; credit Petty Cash

# Class Discussion Questions

1. Why is cash the asset that often warrants the most attention in the design of an effective internal control structure?
2. The combined cash count of all cash registers at the close of business is $110 less than the cash sales indicated by the cash register records. (a) In what account

is the cash shortage recorded? (b) Are cash shortages debited or credited to this account?

3. In which section of the income statement would a credit balance in Cash Short and Over be reported?

4. Before a voucher for the purchase of merchandise is approved for payment, supporting documents should be compared to verify the accuracy of the liability. Name an example of a supporting document for the purchase of merchandise.

5. When is a voucher recorded?

6. The accounting clerk pays all obligations by prenumbered checks. What are the strengths and weaknesses in the internal control over cash payments in this situation?

7. In what order are vouchers ordinarily filed (a) in the unpaid voucher file and (b) in the paid voucher file? Give reasons for the answers.

8. The balance of Cash is likely to differ from the bank statement balance. What two factors are likely to be responsible for the difference?

9. What is the purpose of preparing a bank reconciliation?

10. Do items reported on the bank statement as credits represent (a) additions made by the bank to the depositor's balance, or (b) deductions made by the bank from the depositor's balance?

11. What entry should be made if a check received from a customer and deposited is returned by the bank for lack of sufficient funds (an NSF check)?

12. Explain why some cash payments are made in coins and currency from a petty cash fund.

13. What account or accounts are debited when (a) establishing a petty cash fund and (b) replenishing a petty cash fund?

14. The petty cash account has a debit balance of $800. At the end of the accounting period, there is $110 in the petty cash fund, along with petty cash receipts totaling $690. Should the fund be replenished as of the last day of the period? Discuss.

15. How are cash equivalents reported in the financial statements?

16. How is a compensating balance reported in the financial statements?

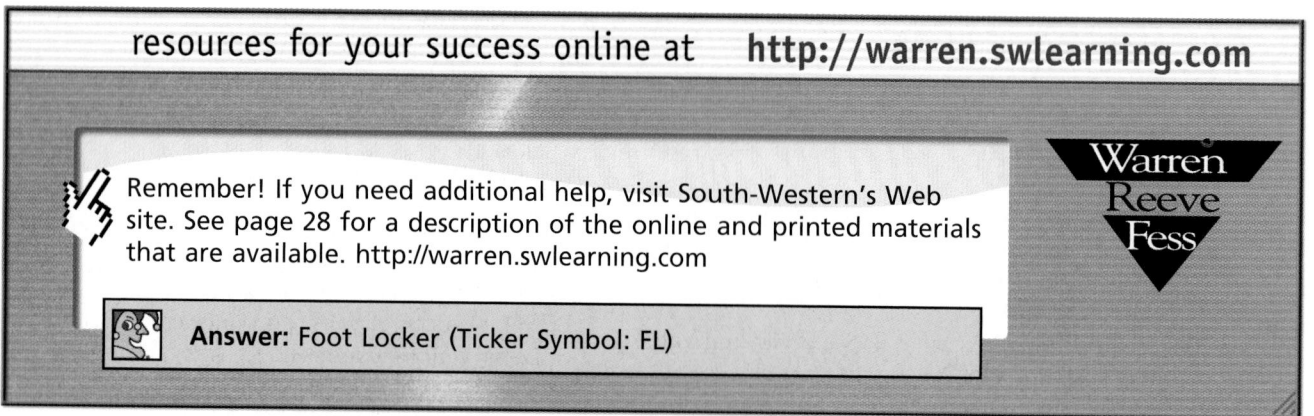

resources for your success online at    http://warren.swlearning.com

Remember! If you need additional help, visit South-Western's Web site. See page 28 for a description of the online and printed materials that are available. http://warren.swlearning.com

Answer: Foot Locker (Ticker Symbol: FL)

# Exercises

**EXERCISE 7-1**
*Internal control of cash receipts*

**Objective 2**

The procedures used for over-the-counter receipts are as follows. At the close of each day's business, the sales clerks count the cash in their respective cash drawers, after which they determine the amount recorded by the cash register and prepare the memorandum cash form, noting any discrepancies. An employee from the cashier's office counts the cash, compares the total with the memorandum, and takes the cash to the cashier's office.

    a. ▭▭▷ Indicate the weak link in internal control.
    b. ▭▭▷ How can the weakness be corrected?

**EXERCISE 7-2**
*Internal control of cash receipts*
**Objective 2**

Deana Crisman works at the drive-through window of Awesome Burgers. Occasionally, when a drive-through customer orders, Deana fills the order and pockets the customer's money. She does not ring up the order on the cash register.
▭▭▷ Identify the internal control weaknesses that exist at Awesome Burgers, and discuss what can be done to prevent this theft.

**EXERCISE 7-3**
*Internal control of cash receipts*
**Objective 2**

The mailroom employees send all remittances and remittance advices to the cashier. The cashier deposits the cash in the bank and forwards the remittance advices and duplicate deposit slips to the Accounting Department.

    a. ▭▭▷ Indicate the weak link in internal control in the handling of cash receipts.
    b. ▭▭▷ How can the weakness be corrected?

**EXERCISE 7-4**
*Entry for cash sales; cash short*
**Objective 2**

The actual cash received from cash sales was $17,572.40, and the amount indicated by the cash register total was $17,589.65. Journalize the entry to record the cash receipts and cash sales.

**EXERCISE 7-5**
*Entry for cash sales; cash over*
**Objective 2**

The actual cash received from cash sales was $6,973.60, and the amount indicated by the cash register total was $6,932.15. Journalize the entry to record the cash receipts and cash sales.

**EXERCISE 7-6**
*Internal control of cash payments*
**Objective 3**

Migraine Co. is a medium-size merchandising company. An investigation revealed that in spite of a sufficient bank balance, a significant amount of available cash discounts had been lost because of failure to make timely payments. In addition, it was discovered that several purchases invoices had been paid twice.
▭▭▷ Outline procedures for the payment of vendors' invoices, so that the possibilities of losing available cash discounts and of paying an invoice a second time will be minimized.

**EXERCISE 7-7**
*Internal control of cash payments*
**Objective 3**

Satchell Company, a communications equipment manufacturer, recently fell victim to an embezzlement scheme masterminded by one of its employees. To understand the scheme, it is necessary to review Satchell's procedures for the purchase of services.

The purchasing agent is responsible for ordering services (such as repairs to a photocopy machine or office cleaning) after receiving a service requisition from an authorized manager. However, since no tangible goods are delivered, a receiving report is not prepared. When the Accounting Department receives an invoice billing Satchell for a service call, the accounts payable clerk calls the manager who requested the service in order to verify that it was performed.

The embezzlement scheme involves Drew Brogan, the manager of plant and facilities. Drew arranged for his uncle's company, Brogan Industrial Supply and Service, to be placed on Satchell's approved vendor list. Drew did not disclose the family relationship.

On several occasions, Drew would submit a requisition for services to be provided by Brogan Industrial Supply and Service. However, the service requested was really not needed, and it was never performed. Brogan would bill Satchell for the service and then split the cash payment with Drew.
▭▭▷ Explain what changes should be made to Satchell's procedures for ordering and paying for services in order to prevent such occurrences in the future.

**EXERCISE 7-8**
*Bank reconciliation*
**Objective 5**

Identify each of the following reconciling items as: (a) an addition to the cash balance according to the bank statement, (b) a deduction from the cash balance according to the bank statement, (c) an addition to the cash balance according to the depositor's records, or (d) a deduction from the cash balance according to the depositor's records. (None of the transactions reported by bank debit and credit memorandums have been recorded by the depositor.)

1. Check drawn by depositor for $300 but incorrectly recorded as $3,000.
2. Check of a customer returned by bank to depositor because of insufficient funds, $775.
3. Bank service charges, $35.
4. Check for $129 incorrectly charged by bank as $219.
5. Outstanding checks, $6,137.68.
6. Deposit in transit, $7,500.
7. Note collected by bank, $12,000.

**EXERCISE 7-9**
*Entries based on bank reconciliation*
**Objective 5**

Which of the reconciling items listed in Exercise 7-8 require an entry in the depositor's accounts?

**EXERCISE 7-10**
*Bank reconciliation*
**Objective 5**

**SPREADSHEET**

✓ *Adjusted balance:*
*$7,961.45*

The following data were accumulated for use in reconciling the bank account of Kidstock Co. for March:

a. Cash balance according to the depositor's records at March 31, $7,671.45.
b. Cash balance according to the bank statement at March 31, $4,457.25.
c. Checks outstanding, $2,276.20.
d. Deposit in transit, not recorded by bank, $5,780.40.
e. A check for $145 in payment of an account was erroneously recorded in the check register as $451.
f. Bank debit memorandum for service charges, $16.00.

Prepare a bank reconciliation, using the format shown in Exhibit 6.

**EXERCISE 7-11**
*Entries for bank reconciliation*
**Objective 5**

Using the data presented in Exercise 7-10, journalize the entry or entries that should be made by the depositor.

**EXERCISE 7-12**
*Entries for note collected by bank*
**Objective 5**

Accompanying a bank statement for Covershot Company is a credit memorandum for $15,300, representing the principal ($15,000) and interest ($300) on a note that had been collected by the bank. The depositor had been notified by the bank at the time of the collection, but had made no entries. Journalize the entry that should be made by the depositor to bring the accounting records up to date.

**EXERCISE 7-13**
*Bank reconciliation*
**Objective 5**

**SPREADSHEET**

✓ *Adjusted balance:*
*$14,452.75*

An accounting clerk for Dubitzky Co. prepared the following bank reconciliation:

**Dubitzky Co.**
**Bank Reconciliation**
**July 31, 2006**

| | | |
|---|---:|---:|
| Cash balance according to depositor's records . . . . . . . . . . . . . . . . | | $8,100.75 |
| Add: Outstanding checks . . . . . . . . . . . . . . . . . . . . . . . . . . . . . . . . | $6,557.12 | |
|     Error by Dubitzky Co. in recording Check | | |
|       No. 4217 as $6,315 instead of $3,615 . . . . . . . . . . . . . . . . | 2,700.00 | |
|       Note for $3,600 collected by bank, including interest . . . . . . . | 3,672.00 | 12,929.12 |
| | | $21,029.87 |
| Deduct: Deposit in transit on July 31 . . . . . . . . . . . . . . . . . . . . . . | $7,150.00 | |
|       Bank service charges . . . . . . . . . . . . . . . . . . . . . . . . . . . . . | 20.00 | 7,170.00 |
| Cash balance according to bank statement . . . . . . . . . . . . . . . . . . | | $13,859.87 |

a. From the data in the above bank reconciliation, prepare a new bank reconciliation for Dubitzky Co., using the format shown in the illustrative problem.
b. If a balance sheet were prepared for Dubitzky Co. on July 31, 2006, what amount should be reported for cash?

**EXERCISE 7-14**
*Bank reconciliation*
Objective 5

**WHAT'S WRONG
WITH THIS?**

✓ *Corrected adjusted
balance: $8,898.02*

Identify the errors in the following bank reconciliation:

**Imaging Services Co.**
**Bank Reconciliation**
**For the Month Ended April 30, 2006**

| | | | |
|---|---|---:|---:|
| Cash balance according to bank statement . . . . . . . . | | | $ 9,767.76 |
| Add outstanding checks: | | | |
| No. 821 . . . . . . . . . . . . . . . . . . . . . . . . . . . . . . | | $ 345.95 | |
| 839 . . . . . . . . . . . . . . . . . . . . . . . . . . . . . . | | 272.75 | |
| 843 . . . . . . . . . . . . . . . . . . . . . . . . . . . . . . | | 759.60 | |
| 844 . . . . . . . . . . . . . . . . . . . . . . . . . . . . . . | | 501.50 | 1,879.80 |
| | | | $11,647.56 |
| Deduct deposit of April 30, not recorded by bank . . . . | | | 1,010.06 |
| Adjusted balance . . . . . . . . . . . . . . . . . . . . . . . . | | | $ 9,637.50 |
| | | | |
| Cash balance according to depositor's records . . . . . . . | | | $ 1,118.32 |
| Add: Proceeds of note collected by bank: | | | |
| Principal . . . . . . . . . . . . . . . . . . . . . . . . . . | $8,000.00 | | |
| Interest . . . . . . . . . . . . . . . . . . . . . . . . . . | 280.00 | $8,280.00 | |
| Service charges . . . . . . . . . . . . . . . . . . . . . . | | 18.00 | 8,298.00 |
| | | | $ 9,416.32 |
| Deduct: Check returned because of | | | |
| insufficient funds . . . . . . . . . . . . . . . . . . | | $ 752.30 | |
| Error in recording April 10 | | | |
| deposit of $4,850 as $4,580 . . . . . . . . . . . . | | 270.00 | 1,022.30 |
| Adjusted balance . . . . . . . . . . . . . . . . . . . . . . . . | | | $ 8,394.02 |

**EXERCISE 7-15**
*Using bank reconciliation to
determine cash receipts
stolen*
Objective 5

**SPREADSHEET**

Prometheus Co. records all cash receipts on the basis of its cash register tapes. Prometheus Co. discovered during April 2006 that one of its sales clerks had stolen an undetermined amount of cash receipts when she took the daily deposits to the bank. The following data have been gathered for April:

| | |
|---|---:|
| Cash in bank according to the general ledger | $12,573.22 |
| Cash according to the April 30, 2006 bank statement | 13,271.14 |
| Outstanding checks as of April 30, 2006 | 1,750.20 |
| Bank service charge for April | 45.10 |
| Note receivable, including interest collected by bank in April | 5,200.00 |

No deposits were in transit on April 30, which fell on a Sunday.

a. Determine the amount of cash receipts stolen by the sales clerk.
b. ▭▬➤ What accounting controls would have prevented or detected this theft?

**EXERCISE 7-16**
*Petty cash fund entries*
Objective 6

Journalize the entries to record the following:

a. Check No. 2715 is issued to establish a petty cash fund of $750.
b. The amount of cash in the petty cash fund is now $119.57. Check No. 3120 is issued to replenish the fund, based on the following summary of petty cash receipts: office supplies, $415.83; miscellaneous selling expense, $107.90; miscellaneous administrative expense, $88.10. (Since the amount of the check to replenish the fund plus the balance in the fund do not equal $750, record the discrepancy in the cash short and over account.)

**EXERCISE 7-17**
*Variation in cash balances*
Objective 7

For a recent fiscal year, **Circuit City**'s quarterly balances of cash and cash equivalents were as follows:

| | |
|---|---|
| End of February | $885 million |
| End of May | $1,176 million |
| End of August | $847 million |
| End of November | $438 million |

▭▬➤ What would you expect would be the cause of the variation in Circuit City's balances of cash and cash equivalents?

**EXERCISE 7-18**
*Doomsday ratio*

**Objective 8**

The financial statements for **Home Depot** are presented in Appendix E at the end of the text.

a. Compute the doomsday ratio for Home Depot for 2003 and 2002.
b.  What conclusions can be drawn from comparing the ratios for 2003 and 2002?

# Problems Series A

**PROBLEM 7-1A**
*Evaluate internal control of cash*

**Objectives 1, 2, 3**

The following procedures were recently installed by The Geodesic Company:

a. All sales are rung up on the cash register, and a receipt is given to the customer. All sales are recorded on a record locked inside the cash register.
b. Vouchers and all supporting documents are perforated with a PAID designation after being paid by the treasurer.
c. Checks received through the mail are given daily to the accounts receivable clerk for recording collections on account and for depositing in the bank.
d. At the end of a shift, each cashier counts the cash in his or her cash register, unlocks the cash register record, and compares the amount of cash with the amount on the record to determine cash shortages and overages.
e. Each cashier is assigned a separate cash register drawer to which no other cashier has access.
f. The bank reconciliation is prepared by the accountant.
g. Disbursements are made from the petty cash fund only after a petty cash receipt has been completed and signed by the payee.

**Instructions**

 Indicate whether each of the procedures of internal control over cash represents (1) a strength or (2) a weakness. For each weakness, indicate why it exists.

**PROBLEM 7-2A**
*Transactions for petty cash, cash short and over*

**Objectives 2, 6**

SPREADSHEET

The Orchid Company completed the following selected transactions during June 2006:

June 1. Established a petty cash fund of $600.
  6. The cash sales for the day, according to the cash register records, totaled $7,998.50. The actual cash received from cash sales was $8,008.15.
  30. Petty cash on hand was $50.75. Replenished the petty cash fund for the following disbursements, each evidenced by a petty cash receipt:
    June 3. Store supplies, $30.75.
      8. Express charges on merchandise purchased, $100.75 (Merchandise Inventory).
      12. Office supplies, $74.30.
      15. Office supplies, $35.20.
      19. Postage stamps, $52.00 (Office Supplies).
      20. Repair to fax, $110.00 (Miscellaneous Administrative Expense).
      21. Repair to printer, $51.50 (Miscellaneous Administrative Expense).
      22. Postage due on special delivery letter, $18.00 (Miscellaneous Administrative Expense).
      27. Express charges on merchandise purchased, $65.50 (Merchandise Inventory).
  30. The cash sales for the day, according to the cash register records, totaled $9,009.50. The actual cash received from cash sales was $8,988.35.
  30. Decreased the petty cash fund by $150.

**Instructions**
Journalize the transactions.

**PROBLEM 7-3A**
*Bank reconciliation and entries*

**Objective 5**

SPREADSHEET
P.A.S.S.

✓ 1. Adjusted balance: $26,315.40

The cash account for Showtime Systems at February 28, 2006, indicated a balance of $19,144.15. The bank statement indicated a balance of $31,391.40 on February 28, 2006. Comparing the bank statement and the accompanying canceled checks and memorandums with the records reveals the following reconciling items:

a. Checks outstanding totaled $11,021.50.
b. A deposit of $6,215.50, representing receipts of February 28, had been made too late to appear on the bank statement.
c. The bank had collected $6,300 on a note left for collection. The face of the note was $6,000.
d. A check for $1,275 returned with the statement had been incorrectly recorded by Showtime Systems as $2,175. The check was for the payment of an obligation to Wilson Co. for the purchase of office supplies on account.
e. A check drawn for $855 had been incorrectly charged by the bank as $585.
f. Bank service charges for February amounted to $28.75.

**Instructions**
1. Prepare a bank reconciliation.
2. Journalize the necessary entries. The accounts have not been closed.

**PROBLEM 7-4A**
*Bank reconciliation and entries*

**Objective 5**

SPREADSHEET
P.A.S.S.

✓ 1. Adjusted balance: $16,821.88

The cash account for Alpine Sports Co. on April 1, 2006, indicated a balance of $16,911.95. During April, the total cash deposited was $65,500.40, and checks written totaled $68,127.47. The bank statement indicated a balance of $18,880.45 on April 30, 2006. Comparing the bank statement, the canceled checks, and the accompanying memorandums with the records revealed the following reconciling items:

a. Checks outstanding totaled $5,180.27.
b. A deposit of $3,481.70, representing receipts of April 30, had been made too late to appear on the bank statement.
c. A check for $620 had been incorrectly charged by the bank as $260.
d. A check for $479.30 returned with the statement had been recorded by Alpine Sports Co. as $497.30. The check was for the payment of an obligation to Bray & Son on account.
e. The bank had collected for Alpine Sports Co. $3,424 on a note left for collection. The face of the note was $3,200.
f. Bank service charges for April amounted to $25.
g. A check for $880 from Shuler Co. was returned by the bank because of insufficient funds.

**Instructions**
1. Prepare a bank reconciliation as of April 30.
2. Journalize the necessary entries. The accounts have not been closed.

**PROBLEM 7-5A**
*Bank reconciliation and entries*

**Objective 5**

SPREADSHEET

✓ 1. Adjusted balance: $14,244.09

Rocky Mountain Interiors deposits all cash receipts each Wednesday and Friday in a night depository, after banking hours. The data required to reconcile the bank statement as of May 31 have been taken from various documents and records and are reproduced as follows. The sources of the data are printed in capital letters. All checks were written for payments on account.

BANK RECONCILIATION FOR PRECEDING MONTH (DATED APRIL 30):

| | | |
|---|---:|---:|
| Cash balance according to bank statement | | $10,422.80 |
| Add deposit of April 30, not recorded by bank | | 780.80 |
| | | $11,203.60 |
| Deduct outstanding checks: | | |
| No. 580 | $310.10 | |
| No. 602 | 85.50 | |
| No. 612 | 92.50 | |
| No. 613 | 137.50 | 625.60 |
| Adjusted balance | | $10,578.00 |
| Cash balance according to depositor's records | | $10,605.70 |
| Deduct service charges | | 27.70 |
| Adjusted balance | | $10,578.00 |

CASH ACCOUNT:
Balance as of May 1                                                        $10,578.00

CASH RECEIPTS FOR MONTH OF MAY                                             6,630.60

CHECKS WRITTEN:
Number and amount of each check issued in May:

| Check No. | Amount | Check No. | Amount | Check No. | Amount |
|-----------|--------|-----------|--------|-----------|--------|
| 614 | $243.50 | 621 | $309.50 | 628 | $ 837.70 |
| 615 | 350.10 | 622 | Void | 629 | 329.90 |
| 616 | 279.90 | 623 | Void | 630 | 882.80 |
| 617 | 395.50 | 624 | 707.01 | 631 | 1,081.56 |
| 618 | 435.40 | 625 | 158.63 | 632 | 624.00 |
| 619 | 320.10 | 626 | 550.03 | 633 | 310.08 |
| 620 | 238.87 | 627 | 318.73 | 634 | 303.30 |

Total amount of checks issued in May                                       $8,676.61

MAY BANK STATEMENT:

```
                                    MEMBER FDIC                         PAGE   1
 A
 N  AMERICAN NATIONAL BANK          ACCOUNT NUMBER
 B     OF DETROIT
                                    FROM   5/01/20–    TO   5/31/20–
DETROIT, MI 48201-2500  (313)933-8547
                                    BALANCE            10,422.80

                                  9 DEPOSITS           6,086.35

                                 20 WITHDRAWALS        7,514.11

       ROCKY MOUNTAIN INTERIORS    4 OTHER DEBITS
                                    AND CREDITS        5,150.50CR

                                    NEW BALANCE        14,145.54
```

| * – – – – CHECKS AND OTHER DEBITS – – – – – * – | | | | DEPOSITS – * – DATE – * – BALANCE– * | | |
|---|---|---|---|---|---|---|
| No.580 | 310.10 | No.612 | 92.50 | 780.80 | 05/01 | 10,801.00 |
| No.613 | 137.50 | No.614 | 243.50 | 569.50 | 05/03 | 10,989.50 |
| No.615 | 350.10 | No.616 | 279.90 | 701.80 | 05/06 | 11,061.30 |
| No.617 | 395.50 | No.618 | 435.40 | 819.24 | 05/11 | 11,049.64 |
| No.619 | 320.10 | No.620 | 238.87 | 580.70 | 05/13 | 11,071.37 |
| No.621 | 309.50 | No.624 | 707.01 | MS 5,000.00 | 05/14 | 15,054.86 |
| No.625 | 158.63 | No.626 | 550.03 | MS 400.00 | 05/14 | 14,746.20 |
| No.627 | 318.73 | No.629 | 329.90 | 600.10 | 05/17 | 14,697.67 |
| No.630 | 882.80 | No.631 | 1,081.56 NSF 225.40 | | 05/20 | 12,507.91 |
| No.632 | 62.40 | No.633 | 310.08 | 701.26 | 05/21 | 12,836.69 |
| | | | | 731.45 | 05/24 | 13,568.14 |
| | | | | 601.50 | 05/28 | 14,169.64 |
| | | SC | 24.10 | | 05/31 | 14,145.54 |

```
     EC — ERROR CORRECTION              OD — OVERDRAFT
     MS — MISCELLANEOUS                 PS — PAYMENT STOPPED
     NSF — NOT SUFFICIENT FUNDS         SC — SERVICE CHARGE
 * * *                         * * *                         * * *
       THE RECONCILEMENT OF THIS STATEMENT WITH YOUR RECORDS IS ESSENTIAL.
        ANY ERROR OR EXCEPTION SHOULD BE REPORTED IMMEDIATELY.
```

DUPLICATE DEPOSIT TICKETS:
Date and amount of each deposit in May:

| Date | Amount | Date | Amount | Date | Amount |
|---|---|---|---|---|---|
| May 2 | $569.50 | May 12 | $580.70 | May 23 | $ 731.45 |
| 5 | 701.80 | 16 | 600.10 | 26 | 601.50 |
| 9 | 819.24 | 19 | 701.26 | 31 | 1,325.05 |

## Instructions

1. Prepare a bank reconciliation as of May 31. If errors in recording deposits or checks are discovered, assume that the errors were made by the company. Assume that all deposits are from cash sales. All checks are written to satisfy accounts payable.
2. Journalize the necessary entries. The accounts have not been closed.
3. What is the amount of Cash that should appear on the balance sheet as of May 31?
4.  Assume that a canceled check for $1,375 has been incorrectly recorded by the bank as $1,735. Briefly explain how the error would be included in a bank reconciliation and how it should be corrected.

# Problems Series B

**PROBLEM 7-1B**
*Evaluating internal control of cash*

**Objectives 1, 2, 3**

The following procedures were recently installed by Pancreas Company:

a. At the end of each day, an accounting clerk compares the duplicate copy of the daily cash deposit slip with the deposit receipt obtained from the bank.
b. The bank reconciliation is prepared by the cashier, who works under the supervision of the treasurer.
c. At the end of the day, cash register clerks are required to use their own funds to make up any cash shortages in their registers.
d. Along with petty cash expense receipts for postage, office supplies, etc., several post-dated employee checks are in the petty cash fund.
e. The accounts payable clerk prepares a voucher for each disbursement. The voucher along with the supporting documentation is forwarded to the treasurer's office for approval.
f. All mail is opened by the mail clerk, who forwards all cash remittances to the cashier. The cashier prepares a listing of the cash receipts and forwards a copy of the list to the accounts receivable clerk for recording in the accounts.
g. After necessary approvals have been obtained for the payment of a voucher, the treasurer signs and mails the check. The treasurer then stamps the voucher and supporting documentation as paid and returns the voucher and supporting documentation to the accounts payable clerk for filing.
h. At the end of each day, any deposited cash receipts are placed in the bank's night depository.

## Instructions

Indicate whether each of the procedures of internal control over cash represents (1) a strength or (2) a weakness. For each weakness, indicate why it exists.

**PROBLEM 7-2B**
*Transactions for petty cash; cash short and over*

**Objectives 2, 6**

Kewpie Company completed the following selected transactions during March 2006:

Mar. 1. Established a petty cash fund of $850.
18. The cash sales for the day, according to the cash register records, totaled $11,970.60. The actual cash received from cash sales was $12,007.50.

*(continued)*

SPREADSHEET

Mar. 31. Petty cash on hand was $20.18. Replenished the petty cash fund for the following disbursements, each evidenced by a petty cash receipt:
Mar. 3. Store supplies, $198.10.
    6. Express charges on merchandise sold, $120 (Transportation Out).
    9. Office supplies, $13.75.
    18. Office supplies, $49.30.
    20. Postage stamps, $74 (Office Supplies).
    21. Repair to office printer, $150.00 (Miscellaneous Administrative Expense).
    22. Postage due on special delivery letter, $40.00 (Miscellaneous Administrative Expense).
    24. Express charges on merchandise sold, $125 (Transportation Out).
    27. Office supplies, $41.15.
  31. The cash sales for the day, according to the cash register records, totaled $9,055.50. The actual cash received from cash sales was $9,010.25.
  31. Increased the petty cash fund by $100.

**Instructions**
Journalize the transactions.

## PROBLEM 7-3B
*Bank reconciliation and entries*
**Objective 5**

SPREADSHEET
P.A.S.S.

✓ *1. Adjusted balance: $16,215.95*

The cash account for Pickron Co. at April 30, 2006, indicated a balance of $13,290.95. The bank statement indicated a balance of $18,016.30 on April 30, 2006. Comparing the bank statement and the accompanying canceled checks and memorandums with the records revealed the following reconciling items:

a. Checks outstanding totaled $7,169.75.
b. A deposit of $5,189.40, representing receipts of April 30, had been made too late to appear on the bank statement.
c. The bank had collected $3,240 on a note left for collection. The face of the note was $3,000.
d. A check for $1,960 returned with the statement had been incorrectly recorded by Pickron Co. as $1,690. The check was for the payment of an obligation to Jones Co. for the purchase of office equipment on account.
e. A check drawn for $1,680 had been erroneously charged by the bank as $1,860.
f. Bank service charges for April amounted to $45.00.

**Instructions**
1. Prepare a bank reconciliation.
2. Journalize the necessary entries. The accounts have not been closed.

## PROBLEM 7-4B
*Bank reconciliation and entries*
**Objective 5**

SPREADSHEET
P.A.S.S.

✓ *1. Adjusted balance: $5,689.87*

The cash account for Seal-Tek Co. at December 1, 2006, indicated a balance of $3,945.90. During December, the total cash deposited was $31,077.75, and checks written totaled $30,395.78. The bank statement indicated a balance of $5,465.50 on December 31. Comparing the bank statement, the canceled checks, and the accompanying memorandums with the records revealed the following reconciling items:

a. Checks outstanding totaled $3,003.84.
b. A deposit of $2,148.21, representing receipts of December 31, had been made too late to appear on the bank statement.
c. The bank had collected for Seal-Tek Co. $1,908 on a note left for collection. The face of the note was $1,800.
d. A check for $120 returned with the statement had been incorrectly charged by the bank as $1,200.
e. A check for $318 returned with the statement had been recorded by Seal-Tek Co. as $138. The check was for the payment of an obligation to Kenyon Co. on account.
f. Bank service charges for December amounted to $30.
g. A check for $636 from Fontana Co. was returned by the bank because of insufficient funds.

**Instructions**
1. Prepare a bank reconciliation as of December 31.
2. Journalize the necessary entries. The accounts have not been closed.

**PROBLEM 7-5B**
*Bank reconciliation and entries*
**Objective 5**

SPREADSHEET

✓ 1. Adjusted balance: $10,322.02

Heritage Furniture Company deposits all cash receipts each Wednesday and Friday in a night depository, after banking hours. The data required to reconcile the bank statement as of November 30 have been taken from various documents and records and are reproduced as follows. The sources of the data are printed in capital letters. All checks were written for payments on account.

NOVEMBER BANK STATEMENT:

MEMBER FDIC

**AMERICAN NATIONAL BANK OF DETROIT**

DETROIT, MI 48201-2500     (313)933-8547

PAGE  1

ACCOUNT NUMBER

FROM 11/01/20–  TO 11/30/20–

| | |
|---|---|
| BALANCE | 7,447.20 |
| 9 DEPOSITS | 8,691.77 |
| 20 WITHDRAWALS | 7,345.91 |
| 4 OTHER DEBITS AND CREDITS | 2,298.70CR |
| NEW BALANCE | 11,091.76 |

HERITAGE FURNITURE COMPANY

| \* – – CHECKS AND OTHER DEBITS – – – \* | | | | – – DEPOSITS – – \* | – DATE – \* | – – BALANCE– – \* |
|---|---|---|---|---|---|---|
| No.731 | 162.15 | No.738 | 251.40 | 690.25 | 11/01 | 7,723.90 |
| No.739 | 60.55 | No.740 | 237.50 | 1,080.50 | 11/02 | 8,506.35 |
| No.741 | 495.15 | No.742 | 501.90 | 854.17 | 11/04 | 8,363.47 |
| No.743 | 671.30 | No.744 | 506.88 | 840.50 | 11/09 | 8,025.79 |
| No.745 | 117.25 | No.746 | 298.66 | MS 2,500.00 | 11/09 | 10,109.88 |
| No.748 | 450.90 | No.749 | 640.13 | MS 125.00 | 11/09 | 9,143.85 |
| No.750 | 276.77 | No.751 | 299.37 | 896.61 | 11/11 | 9,464.32 |
| No.752 | 537.01 | No.753 | 380.95 | 882.95 | 11/16 | 9,429.31 |
| No.754 | 449.75 | No.756 | 113.95 | 1,606.74 | 11/18 | 10,472.35 |
| No.757 | 407.95 | No.760 | 486.39 | 897.34 | 11/23 | 10,475.35 |
| | | | | 942.71 | 11/25 | 11,418.06 |
| | | NSF | 291.90 | | 11/28 | 11,126.16 |
| | | SC | 34.40 | | 11/30 | 11,091.76 |

EC — ERROR CORRECTION     OD — OVERDRAFT
MS — MISCELLANEOUS        PS — PAYMENT STOPPED
NSF — NOT SUFFICIENT FUNDS  SC — SERVICE CHARGE

\* \* \*            \* \* \*            \* \* \*

THE RECONCILEMENT OF THIS STATEMENT WITH YOUR RECORDS IS ESSENTIAL.
ANY ERROR OR EXCEPTION SHOULD BE REPORTED IMMEDIATELY.

CASH ACCOUNT:
Balance as of November 1                                $7,317.40

CASH RECEIPTS FOR MONTH OF NOVEMBER                     $8,651.58

DUPLICATE DEPOSIT TICKETS:
Date and amount of each deposit in November:

| Date | Amount | Date | Amount | Date | Amount |
|---|---|---|---|---|---|
| Nov. 1 | $1,080.50 | Nov. 10 | $ 896.61 | Nov. 22 | $ 537.34 |
| 3 | 854.17 | 15 | 882.95 | 24 | 942.71 |
| 8 | 840.50 | 17 | 1,606.74 | 29 | 1,010.06 |

CHECKS WRITTEN:
Number and amount of each check issued in November:

| Check No. | Amount | Check No. | Amount | Check No. | Amount |
|-----------|--------|-----------|--------|-----------|--------|
| 740 | $237.50 | 747 | Void | 754 | $ 449.75 |
| 741 | 495.15 | 748 | $450.90 | 755 | 272.75 |
| 742 | 501.90 | 749 | 640.13 | 756 | 113.95 |
| 743 | 671.30 | 750 | 276.77 | 757 | 407.95 |
| 744 | 506.88 | 751 | 299.37 | 758 | 259.60 |
| 745 | 117.25 | 752 | 337.01 | 759 | 901.50 |
| 746 | 298.66 | 753 | 380.95 | 760 | 486.39 |

Total amount of checks issued in November       $8,105.66

BANK RECONCILIATION FOR PRECEDING MONTH:

**Heritage Furniture Company**
**Bank Reconciliation**
**October 31, 20—**

| | | |
|---|---|---|
| Cash balance according to bank statement . . . . . . . . . . . . . . . . . . . . | | $7,447.20 |
| Add deposit for October 31, not recorded by bank . . . . . . . . . . . . . | | 690.25 |
| | | $8,137.45 |
| Deduct outstanding checks: | | |
|    No. 731 . . . . . . . . . . . . . . . . . . . . . . . . . . . . . . . . . . . . . . . | $162.15 | |
|        736 . . . . . . . . . . . . . . . . . . . . . . . . . . . . . . . . . . . . . . . | 345.95 | |
|        738 . . . . . . . . . . . . . . . . . . . . . . . . . . . . . . . . . . . . . . . | 251.40 | |
|        739 . . . . . . . . . . . . . . . . . . . . . . . . . . . . . . . . . . . . . . . | 60.55 | 820.05 |
| Adjusted balance . . . . . . . . . . . . . . . . . . . . . . . . . . . . . . . . . . . . . | | $7,317.40 |
| Cash balance according to depositor's records . . . . . . . . . . . . . . . . | | $7,352.50 |
| Deduct service charges . . . . . . . . . . . . . . . . . . . . . . . . . . . . . . . . . | | 35.10 |
| Adjusted balance . . . . . . . . . . . . . . . . . . . . . . . . . . . . . . . . . . . . . | | $7,317.40 |

### Instructions

1. Prepare a bank reconciliation as of November 30. If errors in recording deposits or checks are discovered, assume that the errors were made by the company. Assume that all deposits are from cash sales. All checks are written to satisfy accounts payable.
2. Journalize the necessary entries. The accounts have not been closed.
3. What is the amount of Cash that should appear on the balance sheet as of November 30?
4. ⬛➤ Assume that a canceled check for $580 has been incorrectly recorded by the bank as $850. Briefly explain how the error would be included in a bank reconciliation and how it should be corrected.

# Special Activities

**ACTIVITY 7-1**
*Ethics and professional conduct in business*

ETHICS

During the preparation of the bank reconciliation for The Image Co., Chris Renees, the assistant controller, discovered that Empire National Bank incorrectly recorded a $936 check written by The Image Co. as $396. Chris has decided not to notify the bank but wait for the bank to detect the error. Chris plans to record the $540 error as Other Income if the bank fails to detect the error within the next three months. ⬛➤ Discuss whether Chris is behaving in a professional manner.

**ACTIVITY 7-2**
*Internal controls*

The following is an excerpt from a conversation between two sales clerks, Carol Dickson and Jill Kesner. Both Carol and Jill are employed by Reboot Electronics, a locally owned and operated computer retail store.

*Carol:* Did you hear the news?

*Jill:* What news?

*Carol:* Candis and Albert were both arrested this morning.

*Jill:* What? Arrested? You're putting me on!

*Carol:* No, really! The police arrested them first thing this morning. Put them in handcuffs, read them their rights—the whole works. It was unreal!

*Jill:* What did they do?

*Carol:* Well, apparently they were filling out merchandise refund forms for fictitious customers and then taking the cash.

*Jill:* I guess I never thought of that. How did they catch them?

*Carol:* The store manager noticed that returns were twice that of last year and seemed to be increasing. When he confronted Candis, she became flustered and admitted to taking the cash, apparently over $2,800 in just three months. They're going over the last six months' transactions to try to determine how much Albert stole. He apparently started stealing first.

Suggest appropriate control procedures that would have prevented or detected the theft of cash.

**ACTIVITY 7-3**
*Internal controls*

The following is an excerpt from a conversation between the store manager of Piper Grocery Stores, Bill Dowell, and Cary Wynne, president of Piper Grocery Stores.

*Cary:* Bill, I'm concerned about this new scanning system.

*Bill:* What's the problem?

*Cary:* Well, how do we know the clerks are ringing up all the merchandise?

*Bill:* That's one of the strong points about the system. The scanner automatically rings up each item, based on its bar code. We update the prices daily, so we're sure that the sale is rung up for the right price.

*Cary:* That's not my concern. What keeps a clerk from pretending to scan items and then simply not charging his friends? If his friends were buying 10–15 items, it would be easy for the clerk to pass through several items with his finger over the bar code or just pass the merchandise through the scanner with the wrong side showing. It would look normal for anyone observing. In the old days, we at least could hear the cash register ringing up each sale.

*Bill:* I see your point.

Suggest ways that Piper Grocery Stores could prevent or detect the theft of merchandise as described.

**ACTIVITY 7-4**
*Ethics and professional conduct in business*

Tim Jost and Kerri Stein are both cash register clerks for Frontier Markets. Kathy Rostad is the store manager for Frontier Markets. The following is an excerpt of a conversation between Tim and Kerri:

*Tim:* Kerri, how long have you been working for Frontier Markets?

*Kerri:* Almost five years this August. You just started two weeks ago . . . right?

*Tim:* Yes. Do you mind if I ask you a question?

*Kerri:* No, go ahead.

*Tim:* What I want to know is, have they always had this rule that if your cash register is short at the end of the day, you have to make up the shortage out of your own pocket?

*Kerri:* Yes, as long as I've been working here.

*Tim:* Well, it's the pits. Last week I had to pay in almost $30.

*Kerri:* It's not that big a deal. I just make sure that I'm not short at the end of the day.

*Tim:* How do you do that?

*Kerri:* I just short-change a few customers early in the day. There are a few jerks that deserve it anyway. Most of the time, their attention is elsewhere and they don't think to check their change.

*Tim:* What happens if you're over at the end of the day?

*Kerri:* Rostad lets me keep it as long as it doesn't get to be too large. I've not been short in over a year. I usually clear about $20 to $30 extra per day.

➤ Discuss this case from the viewpoint of proper controls and professional behavior.

**ACTIVITY 7-5**
*Bank reconciliation and internal control*

The records of Lumberjack Company indicate a July 31 cash balance of $9,806.05, which includes undeposited receipts for July 30 and 31. The cash balance on the bank statement as of July 31 is $6,004.95. This balance includes a note of $4,000 plus $240 interest collected by the bank but not recorded in the journal. Checks outstanding on July 31 were as follows: No. 670, $781.20; No. 679, $610; No. 690, $716.50; No. 1996, $127.40; No. 1997, $520; and No. 1999, $851.50.

On July 3, the cashier resigned, effective at the end of the month. Before leaving on July 31, the cashier prepared the following bank reconciliation:

| | | |
|---|---:|---:|
| Cash balance per books, July 31 . . . . . . . . . . . . . . | | $ 9,806.05 |
| Add outstanding checks: | | |
| No. 1996 . . . . . . . . . . . . . . . . . . . . . . . . . . . | $127.40 | |
| 1997 . . . . . . . . . . . . . . . . . . . . . . . . . . . | 520.00 | |
| 1999 . . . . . . . . . . . . . . . . . . . . . . . . . . . | 851.50 | 1,198.90 |
| | | $11,004.95 |
| Less undeposited receipts . . . . . . . . . . . . . . . . . | | 5,000.00 |
| Cash balance per bank, July 31 . . . . . . . . . . . . . . | | $ 6,004.95 |
| Deduct unrecorded note with interest . . . . . . . . . | | 4,240.00 |
| True cash, July 31 . . . . . . . . . . . . . . . . . . . . . . | | $ 1,764.95 |

> *Calculator Tape of Outstanding Checks:*
> 0.00 *
> 127.40 +
> 520.00 +
> 851.50 +
> 1,198.90 *

Subsequently, the owner of Lumberjack Company discovered that the cashier had stolen an unknown amount of undeposited receipts, leaving only $5,000 to be deposited on July 31. The owner, a close family friend, has asked your help in determining the amount that the former cashier has stolen.

1. Determine the amount the cashier stole from Lumberjack Company. Show your computations in good form.
2. How did the cashier attempt to conceal the theft?
3. a. Identify two major weaknesses in internal controls, which allowed the cashier to steal the undeposited cash receipts.
   b. ➤ Recommend improvements in internal controls, so that similar types of thefts of undeposited cash receipts can be prevented.

**ACTIVITY 7-6**
*Observe internal controls over cash*

GROUP ACTIVITY

Select a business in your community and observe its internal controls over cash receipts and cash payments. The business could be a bank or a bookstore, restaurant, department store, or other retailer. In groups of three or four, identify and discuss the similarities and differences in each business's cash internal controls.

**ACTIVITY 7-7**
*Invest excess cash*

INTERNET

Assume that you have just received a $100,000 check! Go to the Web site of (or visit) a local bank and collect information about the savings and checking options that are available. Identify the option that is best for you and why it is best.

# Answers to Self-Examination Questions

1. **C** The error was made by the bank, so the cash balance according to the bank statement needs to be adjusted. Since the bank deducted $90 ($540.50 − $450.50) too little, the error of $90 should be deducted from the cash balance according to the bank statement (answer C).

2. **B** On any specific date, the cash account in a depositor's ledger may not agree with the account in the bank's ledger because of delays and/or errors by either party in recording transactions. The purpose of a bank reconciliation, therefore, is to determine the reasons for any differences between the two account balances. All errors should then be corrected by the depositor or the bank, as appropriate. In arriving at the adjusted (correct) cash balance according to the bank statement, outstanding checks must be deducted (answer B) to adjust for checks that have been written by the depositor but that have not yet been presented to the bank for payment.

3. **C** All reconciling items that are added to and deducted from the cash balance according to the depositor's records on the bank reconciliation (answer C) require that journal entries be made by the depositor to correct errors made in recording transactions or to bring the cash account up to date for delays in recording transactions.

4. **D** To avoid the delay, annoyance, and expense that is associated with paying all obligations by check, relatively small amounts (answer A) are paid from a petty cash fund. The fund is established by estimating the amount of cash needed to pay these small amounts during a specified period (answer B), and it is then reimbursed when the amount of money in the fund is reduced to a predetermined minimum amount (answer C).

5. **C** The journal entry to replenish the petty cash account debits the various expense accounts for which funds were disbursed and credits Cash (answer C). A petty cash account is established or increased by debiting Petty Cash and crediting Cash (answer A). A petty cash account is decreased or done away with by debiting Cash and crediting Petty Cash (answer D). Entry B is not a normal entry involving petty cash.

# 8

# RECEIVABLES

## objectives

*After studying this chapter, you should be able to:*

1    List the common classifications of receivables.

2    Summarize and provide examples of internal control procedures that apply to receivables.

3    Describe the nature of and the accounting for uncollectible receivables.

4    Journalize the entries for the allowance method of accounting for uncollectibles, and estimate uncollectible receivables based on sales and on an analysis of receivables.

5    Journalize the entries for the direct write-off of uncollectible receivables.

6    Describe the nature and characteristics of promissory notes.

7    Journalize the entries for notes receivable transactions.

8    Prepare the Current Assets presentation of receivables on the balance sheet.

9    Compute and interpret the accounts receivable turnover and the number of days' sales in receivables.

**A**ssume that you have decided to sell your car to a neighbor for $7,500. Your neighbor agrees to pay you $1,500 immediately and the remaining $6,000 in a year. How much should you charge your neighbor for interest?

You could determine an appropriate interest rate by asking some financial institutions what they currently charge their customers. Using this information as a starting point, you could then negotiate with your neighbor and agree upon a rate. Assuming that the agreed-upon rate is 8%, you will receive interest totaling $480 for the one-year loan.

In this chapter, we will describe and illustrate how interest is computed. In addition, we will discuss the accounting for receivables, including uncollectible receivables. Most of these receivables result from a business providing services or selling merchandise on account.

# Classification of Receivables

**objective    1**

List the common classifications of receivables.

**REAL WORLD**

An annual report of **La-Z-Boy Chair Company** reported that receivables made up over 60% of La-Z-Boy's current assets.

**POINT OF INTEREST**

If you have purchased an automobile on credit, you probably signed a note. From your viewpoint, the note is a note payable. From the creditor's viewpoint, the note is a note receivable.

Many companies sell on credit in order to sell more services or products. The receivables that result from such sales are normally classified as accounts receivable or notes receivable. The term *receivables* includes all money claims against other entities, including people, business firms, and other organizations. These receivables are usually a significant portion of the total current assets.

## Accounts Receivable

The most common transaction creating a receivable is selling merchandise or services on credit. The receivable is recorded as a debit to the accounts receivable account. Such *accounts receivable* are normally expected to be collected within a relatively short period, such as 30 or 60 days. They are classified on the balance sheet as a current asset.

## Notes Receivable

*Notes receivable* are amounts that customers owe, for which a formal, written instrument of credit has been issued. As long as notes receivable are expected to be collected within a year, they are normally classified on the balance sheet as a current asset.

Notes are often used for credit periods of more than sixty days. For example, a dealer in automobiles or furniture may require a down payment at the time of sale and accept a note or a series of notes for the remainder. Such arrangements usually provide for monthly payments.

Notes may be used to settle a customer's account receivable. Notes and accounts receivable that result from sales transactions are sometimes called **trade receivables**. Unless we indicate otherwise, we will assume that all notes and accounts receivable in this chapter are from sales transactions.

## Other Receivables

Other receivables are normally listed separately on the balance sheet. If they are expected to be collected within one year, they are classified as current assets. If collection is expected beyond one year, they are classified as noncurrent assets and reported under the caption *Investments*. **Other receivables** include interest receivable, taxes receivable, and receivables from officers or employees.

# Internal Control of Receivables

**objective** **2**

Summarize and provide examples of internal control procedures that apply to receivables.

The principles of internal control that we discussed in prior chapters can be used to establish controls to safeguard receivables. For example, the four functions of credit approval, sales, accounting, and collections should be separated, as shown in Exhibit 1.

The individuals responsible for sales should be separate from the individuals accounting for the receivables and approving credit. By doing so, the accounting and credit approval functions serve as independent checks on sales. The employee who handles the accounting for receivables should not be involved with collecting receivables. Separating these functions reduces the possibility of errors and misuse of funds.

## •Exhibit 1

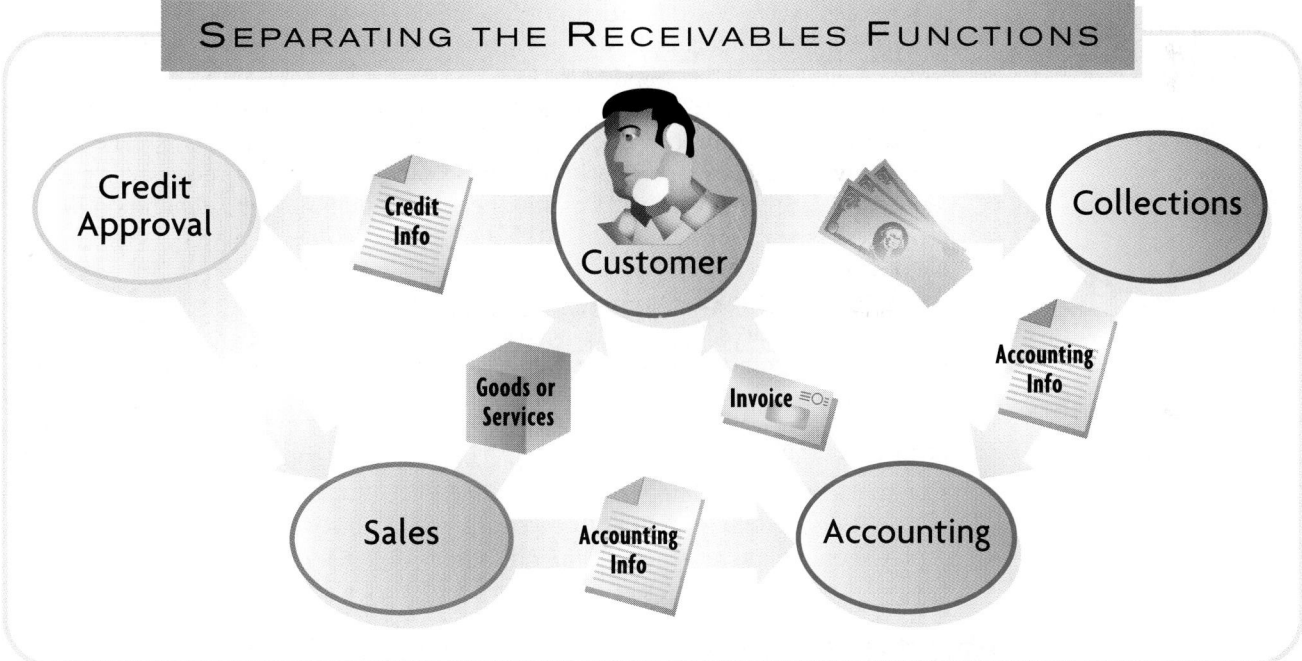

**SEPARATING THE RECEIVABLES FUNCTIONS**

 I was founded in 1886 when a railroad station agent began selling watches. I competed effectively against high-priced rural stores via railroads and mail delivery. By 1895 I had a 532-page catalog and my annual sales topped $750,000. Henry Ford reportedly studied my assembly-line process. I opened my first retail store in 1925 in Chicago, where I tower today. In 1931 retail sales topped mail-order sales, and I created Allstate Insurance Co. I launched the Discover Card in 1985 and bought Lands' End in 2002. Today I operate more than 2,000 retail locations and rake in more than $40 billion annually. Who am I? (Go to page 337 for answer.)

To illustrate the need to separate functions, assume that the accounts receivable billing clerk has access to cash receipts from customer collections. The clerk can steal a customer's cash payment and then alter the customer's monthly statement to indicate that the payment was received. The customer would not complain and the theft could go undetected.

To further illustrate the need for internal control of receivables, assume that salespersons have authority to approve credit. If the salespersons are paid commissions, say 10% of sales, they can increase their commissions by approving poor credit risks. Thus, the credit approval function is normally assigned to individuals outside the sales area.

# Uncollectible Receivables

objective **3**

Describe the nature of and the accounting for uncollectible receivables.

**REAL WORLD**

In addition to their own credit departments, many businesses use external credit agencies, such as **Dun and Bradstreet**, to evaluate credit customers.

In prior chapters, we described and illustrated the accounting for transactions involving sales of merchandise or services on credit. A major issue that we have not yet discussed is uncollectible receivables from these transactions.

Businesses attempt to limit the number and amount of uncollectible receivables by using various controls. The primary controls in this area involve the credit-granting function. These controls normally involve investigating customer creditworthiness, using references and background checks. For example, most of us have completed credit application forms requiring such information. Companies may also impose credit limits on new customers. For example, you may have been limited to a maximum of $500 or $1,000 when your credit card was first issued to you.

Once a receivable is past due, companies should use procedures to maximize the collection of an account. After repeated attempts at collection, such procedures may include turning an account over to a collection agency.

Retail businesses often attempt to shift the risk of uncollectible receivables to other companies. For example, some retailers do not accept sales on account but will only accept cash or credit cards. Such policies effectively shift the risk to the credit card companies. Other retailers, however, such as **Macy's**, **Sears**, and **J.C.Penney's**, have issued their own credit cards.

Companies often sell their receivables to other companies. This transaction is called **factoring** the receivables, and the buyer of the receivables is called a **factor**. An advantage of factoring is that the company selling its receivables receives immediate cash for operating and other needs. In addition, depending upon the factoring agreement, some of the risk of uncollectible accounts may be shifted to the factor.[1]

Regardless of the care used in granting credit and the collection procedures used, a part of the credit sales will not be collectible. The operating expense incurred because of the failure to collect receivables is called ***uncollectible accounts expense***, **bad debts expense**, or **doubtful accounts expense**.[2]

When does an account or a note become uncollectible? There is no general rule for determining when an account becomes uncollectible. The fact that a debtor fails to pay an account according to a sales contract or fails to pay a note on the due date does not necessarily mean that the account will be uncollectible. The debtor's bankruptcy is one of the most significant indications of partial or complete uncollectibility.

## INTEGRITY IN BUSINESS

### SELLER BEWARE

A company in financial distress will still try to purchase goods and services on account. In these cases, rather than "buyer beware," it is more like "seller beware." Sellers must be careful in advancing credit to such companies, because trade creditors have low priority for cash payments in the event of bankruptcy. To help suppliers, third-party services specialize in evaluating financially distressed customers. These services analyze credit risk for these firms by evaluating recent management payment decisions (who is getting paid and when), court actions (if in bankruptcy), and other supplier credit tightening or suspension actions. Such information helps a supplier monitor and tune trade credit amounts and terms with the financially distressed customer.

---

[1]The accounting for the factoring of accounts receivable is discussed in advanced accounting texts.
[2]If both notes and accounts are involved, both may be included in the expense account title, as in Uncollectible Notes and Accounts Expense, or Uncollectible Receivables Expense.

Other indications include the closing of the customer's business and the failure of repeated attempts to collect.

There are two methods of accounting for receivables that appear to be uncollectible. The ***allowance method*** provides an expense for uncollectible receivables in advance of their write-off.[3] The other procedure, called the ***direct write-off method***, recognizes the expense only when accounts are judged to be worthless. We will discuss each of these methods next.

# Allowance Method of Accounting for Uncollectibles

**objective   4**

Journalize the entries for the allowance method of accounting for uncollectibles, and estimate uncollectible receivables based on sales and on an analysis of receivables.

Most large businesses use the allowance method to estimate the uncollectible portion of their trade receivables. To illustrate this method, we will use assumed data for Richards Company. This new business began in August and chose to use the calendar year as its fiscal year. The accounts receivable account has a balance of $105,000 at the end of December.

The customer accounts making up the $105,000 balance in Accounts Receivable include some that are past due. However, Richards doesn't know which specific accounts will be uncollectible at this time. It is likely that some accounts will be collected only in part and that others will become worthless. Based on a careful study, Richards estimates that a total of $4,000 will eventually be uncollectible. The following adjusting entry at the end of the fiscal period records this estimate:

| | | *Adjusting Entry* | | |
|---|---|---|---|---|
| Dec. | 31 | Uncollectible Accounts Expense | 4 0 0 0 00 | |
| | | Allowance for Doubtful Accounts | | 4 0 0 0 00 |

Because the $4,000 reduction in accounts receivable is an estimate, it cannot be credited to specific customer accounts or to the accounts receivable controlling account. Instead, a ***contra asset*** account entitled *Allowance for Doubtful Accounts* is credited.

As with all periodic adjustments, the entry above serves two purposes. First, it reduces the value of the receivables to the amount of cash expected to be realized in the future. This amount, which is $101,000 ($105,000 − $4,000), is called the **net realizable value** of the receivables. Second, the adjusting entry matches the $4,000 expense of uncollectible accounts with the related revenues of the period.

> The adjusting entry reduces receivables to their net realizable value and matches the uncollectible expense with revenues.

After the adjusting entry has been posted, as shown in the following T accounts, Accounts Receivable still has a debit balance of $105,000. This balance is the amount of the total claims against customers on account. The credit balance of $4,000 in Allowance for Doubtful Accounts is the amount to be deducted from Accounts Receivable to determine the net realizable value. The balance of the Uncollectible Accounts Expense is reported in the current period income statement, normally as an administrative expense. This classification is used because the credit-granting and collection duties are the responsibilities of departments within the administrative area.

If the balance of accounts receivable is $380,000 and the balance of the allowance for doubtful accounts is $56,000, what is the net realizable value of the receivables?

----------------------------------------

*$324,000 ($380,000 − $56,000)*

---

[3]The allowance method is not acceptable for determining the federal income tax of most taxpayers.

| Accounts Receivable | | | | | Allowance for Doubtful Accounts | | |
|---|---|---|---|---|---|---|---|
| Aug. 31 | 20,000 | Sept. 30 | 15,000 | | | Dec. 31 Adj. | 4,000 |
| Sept. 30 | 25,000 | Oct. 31 | 25,000 | | | | |
| Oct. 31 | 40,000 | Nov. 30 | 23,000 | | | | |
| Nov. 30 | 38,000 | Dec. 31 | 30,000 | | | | |
| Dec. 31 | 75,000 | | | | | | |
| | | | 93,000 | | Uncollectible Accounts Expense | | |
| Bal. 105,000 | 198,000 | | | | Dec. 31 Adj. | 4,000 | |

# Write-Offs to the Allowance Account

When a customer's account is identified as uncollectible, it is written off against the allowance account as follows:

| | | | | | | | |
|---|---|---|---|---|---|---|---|
| Jan. | 21 | Allowance for Doubtful Accounts | | 6 1 0 00 | | | |
| | | Accounts Receivable—John Parker | | | | 6 1 0 00 | |
| | | To write off the uncollectible | | | | | |
| | | account. | | | | | |

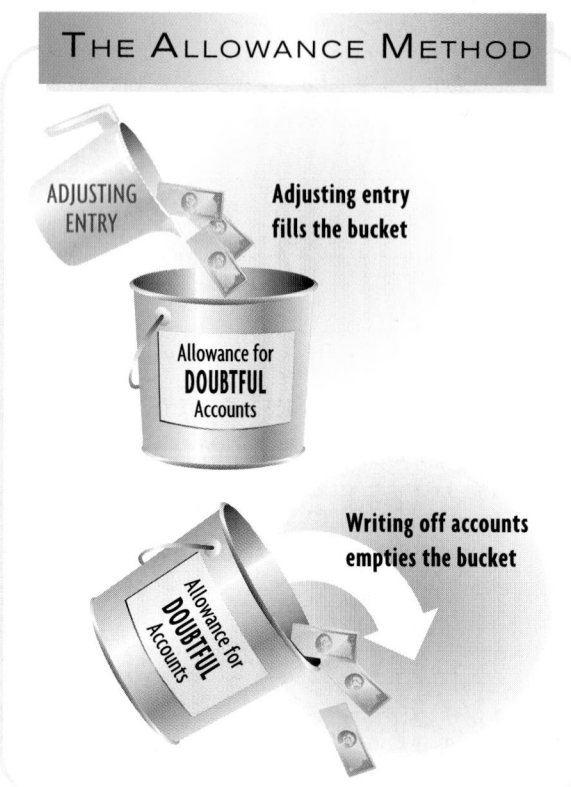

**THE ALLOWANCE METHOD**

ADJUSTING ENTRY

**Adjusting entry fills the bucket**

Allowance for **DOUBTFUL** Accounts

**Writing off accounts empties the bucket**

Allowance for DOUBTFUL Accounts

The authorization to support this entry should come from a designated manager. It should normally be in writing.

The total amount written off against the allowance account during a period will rarely be equal to the amount in the account at the beginning of the period. The allowance account will have a credit balance at the end of the period if the write-offs during the period are less than the beginning balance. It will have a debit balance if the write-offs exceed the beginning balance. However, after the year-end adjusting entry is recorded, the allowance account should have a credit balance. The flow into and out of the allowance account can be shown as in the illustration at the left.

An account receivable that has been written off against the allowance account may later be collected. In such cases, the account should be reinstated by an entry that reverses the write-off entry. The cash received in payment should then be recorded as a receipt on account. For example, assume that the account of $610 written off in the preceding entry is later collected on June 10. The entry to reinstate the account and the entry to record its collection are as follows:

| | | | | | | | |
|---|---|---|---|---|---|---|---|
| June | 10 | Accounts Receivable—John Parker | | 6 1 0 00 | | | |
| | | Allowance for Doubtful Accounts | | | | 6 1 0 00 | |
| | | To reinstate account written off | | | | | |
| | | earlier in the year. | | | | | |
| | 10 | Cash | | 6 1 0 00 | | | |
| | | Accounts Receivable—John Parker | | | | 6 1 0 00 | |
| | | To record collection on account. | | | | | |

The percentage of uncollectible accounts will vary across companies and industries. For example, in their annual reports, **J.C.Penney** reported 1.7% of its receivables as uncollectible, **Deere & Company** (manufacturer of John Deere tractors, etc.) reported only 1.0% of its dealer receivables as uncollectible, and **HCA Inc.**, a hospital management company, reported 42% of its receivables as uncollectible.

The two preceding entries can be combined. However, recording two separate entries in the customer's account, with proper notation of the write-off and reinstatement, provides useful credit information.

## Estimating Uncollectibles

How is the amount of uncollectible accounts estimated? The estimate of uncollectibles at the end of a fiscal period is based on past experience and forecasts of the future. When the general economy is doing well, the amount of uncollectible expense is normally less than it would be when the economy is doing poorly. The estimate of uncollectibles is usually based on either (1) the amount of sales, as shown on the income statement for the period, or (2) the amount of the receivables, as shown on the balance sheet at the end of the period, and the age of the receivable accounts.

### Estimate Based on Sales

Accounts receivable are created by credit sales. The amount of credit sales during the period may therefore be used to estimate the amount of uncollectible accounts expense. The amount of this estimate is added to whatever balance exists in Allowance for Doubtful Accounts. For example, assume that the allowance account has a credit balance of $700 before adjustment. It is estimated from past experience that 1% of credit sales will be uncollectible. If credit sales for the period are $300,000, the adjusting entry for uncollectible accounts at the end of the period is as follows:

> **The estimate based on sales is <u>added</u> to any balance in Allowance for Doubtful Accounts.**

|  |  | *Adjusting Entry* |  |  |
|---|---|---|---|---|
| Dec. | 31 | Uncollectible Accounts Expense | 3 0 0 0 00 |  |
|  |  | Allowance for Doubtful Accounts |  | 3 0 0 0 00 |

---

## FINANCIAL REPORTING AND DISCLOSURE

### DELTA AIR LINES

**D**elta Air Lines is a major air carrier that services over 200 cities in 45 states within the United States and 46 cities in 31 countries throughout the world. Delta is the second largest airline in terms of passengers carried and the third largest in operating revenues and revenue passenger miles flown. In its operations, Delta generates accounts receivable as reported in the following note to its financial statements:

*Our accounts receivable are generated largely from the sale of passenger airline tickets and cargo transportation services to customers. The majority of these sales are processed through major credit card companies, resulting in accounts receivable which are generally short-term in duration. We also have receivables from the sale of mileage credits to partners, such as credit card companies, hotels and car rental agencies, that participate in our SkyMiles program. We believe that the credit risk associated with these receivables is minimal and that the allowance for bad debts that we have provided is sufficient.*

In its December 31, 2002 balance sheet, Delta reported the following accounts receivable (in millions):

|  | 2002 | 2001 |
|---|---|---|
| *Current Assets:* |  |  |
| . . . |  |  |
| *Accounts receivable, net of an allowance for uncollectible accounts of $43 at 12/31/01 and $33 at 12/31/02* | 292 | 368 |

Finally, Delta also reported that it took a separate non-recurring charge of $9 million in accounts receivable write-offs due to the September 11 terrorist attacks, as follows:

*It (nonrecurring charge) also includes $9 million related to the write-off of certain receivables that we believe we will not be able to realize as a result of the September 11 terrorist attacks.*

Before the year-end adjustment, Allowance for Doubtful Accounts has a credit balance of $45,000. Uncollectible accounts are estimated as 2% of credit sales of $1,200,000. The accounts receivable balance before adjustment is $290,000. What are (1) the uncollectible expense for the period, (2) the balance of Allowance for Doubtful Accounts after adjustment, and (3) the net realizable value of the receivables after adjustment?

---

*(1) $24,000 (2% × $1,200,000); (2) $69,000 ($24,000 + $45,000); and (3) $221,000 ($290,000 − $69,000)*

The Commercial Collection Agency Section of the Commercial Law League of America reported the following collection rates by number of months past due:

**REAL WORLD**

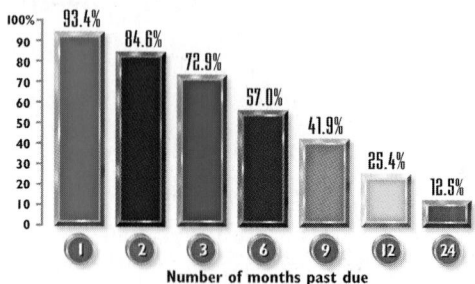

Number of months past due

After the adjusting entry has been posted, the balance of the allowance account is $3,700. If there had been a debit balance of $200 in the allowance account before the year-end adjustment, the amount of the adjustment would still have been $3,000. The balance in the allowance account would have been $2,800 ($3,000 − $200).

The estimate-based-on-sales method *emphasizes the matching of uncollectible accounts expense with the related sales of the period.* Thus, this method places more emphasis on the income statement than on the balance sheet.

## Estimate Based on Analysis of Receivables

The longer an account receivable remains outstanding, the less likely that it will be collected. Thus, we can base the estimate of uncollectible accounts on how long the accounts have been outstanding. For this purpose, we can use a process called ***aging the receivables***.

In aging the receivables, an aging schedule is prepared by classifying each receivable by its due date. The number of days an account is past due is determined from the due date of the account to the date the aging schedule is prepared. To illustrate, assume that Rodriguez Company is preparing an aging schedule as of August 31. Its account receivable for Saxon Woods Company was due on May 29. As of August 31, Saxon's account is 94 days past due, as shown below.

| | |
|---|---|
| Number of days past due in May | 2 days (31–29) |
| Number of days past due in June | 30 days |
| Number of days past due in July | 31 days |
| Number of days past due in August | 31 days |
| Total number of days past due | 94 days |

After the number of days past due has been determined for each account, an aging schedule is prepared similar to the one shown in Exhibit 2.

The aging schedule is completed by adding the columns to determine the total amount of receivables in each age class. A sliding scale of percentages, based on industry or company experience, is used to estimate the amount of uncollectibles in each age class, as shown in Exhibit 3.

> **The estimate based on receivables is compared to the balance in the allowance account to determine the amount of the adjusting entry.**

## •Exhibit 2   Aging of Accounts Receivable

| Customer | Balance | Not Past Due | Days Past Due | | | | | |
|---|---|---|---|---|---|---|---|---|
| | | | 1–30 | 31–60 | 61–90 | 91–180 | 181–365 | over 365 |
| Ashby & Co. | $ 150 | | | $ 150 | | | | |
| B.T. Barr | 610 | | | | | $ 350 | $260 | |
| Brock Co. | 470 | $ 470 | | | | | | |
| Saxon Woods Co. | 160 | | | | | 160 | | |
| Total | $86,300 | $75,000 | $4,000 | $3,100 | $1,900 | $1,200 | $800 | $300 |

## •Exhibit 3  Estimate of Uncollectible Accounts

| Age Interval | Balance | Estimated Uncollectible Accounts | |
|---|---|---|---|
| | | Percent | Amount |
| Not past due | $75,000 | 2% | $1,500 |
| 1–30 days past due | 4,000 | 5 | 200 |
| 31–60 days past due | 3,100 | 10 | 310 |
| 61–90 days past due | 1,900 | 20 | 380 |
| 91–180 days past due | 1,200 | 30 | 360 |
| 181–365 days past due | 800 | 50 | 400 |
| Over 365 days past due | 300 | 80 | 240 |
| Total | $86,300 | | $3,390 |

Before the year-end adjustment, Allowance for Doubtful Accounts has a debit balance of $3,000. Using the aging-of-receivables method, the desired balance of the allowance for doubtful accounts is estimated as $55,000. The accounts receivable balance before adjustment is $290,000. What are (1) the uncollectible expense for the period, (2) the balance of Allowance for Doubtful Accounts after adjustment, and (3) the net realizable value of the receivables after adjustment?

----------------------------------------

(1) $58,000 ($3,000 + $55,000); (2) $55,000; and (3) $235,000 ($290,000 − $55,000)

Based on Exhibit 3, the desired balance for the Allowance for Doubtful Accounts is estimated as $3,390. Comparing this estimate with the unadjusted balance of the allowance account determines the amount of the adjusting entry for Uncollectible Accounts Expense. For example, assume that the unadjusted balance of the allowance account is a credit balance of $510. The amount to be added to this balance is therefore $2,880 ($3,390 − $510). The adjusting entry is as follows:

| | | | | | |
|---|---|---|---|---|---|
| | | *Adjusting Entry* | | | |
| Aug. | 31 | Uncollectible Accounts Expense | 2 8 8 0 00 | | |
| | | Allowance for Doubtful Accounts | | | 2 8 8 0 00 |

After the adjusting entry has been posted, the credit balance in the allowance account is $3,390, the desired amount. The net realizable value of the receivables is $82,910 ($86,300 − $3,390). If the unadjusted balance of the allowance account had been a debit balance of $300, the amount of the adjustment would have been $3,690 ($3,390 + $300).

Estimates of the uncollectible accounts expense based on the analysis of receivables *emphasizes the current net realizable value of the receivables*. Thus, this method places more emphasis on the balance sheet than on the income statement.

# Direct Write-Off Method of Accounting for Uncollectibles

Journalize the entries for the direct write-off of uncollectible receivables.

The allowance method emphasizes reporting uncollectible accounts expense in the period in which the related sales occur. This emphasis on matching expenses with related revenue is the preferred method of accounting for uncollectible receivables.

There are situations, however, where it is impossible to estimate, with reasonable accuracy, the uncollectibles at the end of the period. Also, if a business sells most of its goods or services on a cash basis, the amount of its expense from uncollectible accounts is usually small. In such cases, the amount of receivables is also likely to represent a small part of the current assets. Examples of such a business are a restaurant, an attorney's office, and a small retail store such as a hardware store. In such cases, the direct write-off method of recording uncollectible expense may be used.

Under the direct write-off method, uncollectible accounts expense is not recorded until an account has been determined to be worthless. Thus, an allowance account and an adjusting entry are not needed at the end of the period. The entry to write off an account that has been determined to be uncollectible is as follows:

| | | | | | |
|---|---|---|---|---|---|
| May | 10 | Uncollectible Accounts Expense | | 4 2 0 00 | |
| | | Accounts Receivable—D. L. Ross | | | 4 2 0 00 |
| | | To write off uncollectible account. | | | |

What if a customer later pays on an account that has been written off? If this happens, the account should be reinstated. The account is reinstated by reversing the earlier write-off entry. For example, assume that the account written off in the May 10 entry is collected in November of the same fiscal year.[4] The entry to reinstate the account is as follows:

| | | | | | |
|---|---|---|---|---|---|
| Nov. | 21 | Accounts Receivable—D. L. Ross | | 4 2 0 00 | |
| | | Uncollectible Accounts Expense | | | 4 2 0 00 |
| | | To reinstate account written off | | | |
| | | earlier in the year. | | | |

Cash received in payment of the reinstated amount is recorded in the usual manner. That is, Cash is debited and Accounts Receivable is credited for $420.

## INTEGRITY IN BUSINESS

### SALES AND COLLECTION FRAUD

A sales transaction may involve "sales fraud" or "collection fraud." Sales fraud occurs when money is received in advance of the sale and the goods are either not delivered or are not what was promised. This type of fraud has occurred in **eBay** auctions where buyers must pay for the goods prior to receiving them. eBay's seller ratings help reduce the incidence of fraudulent sellers. In collection fraud, the goods are delivered to a customer that does not intend to pay for them. This type of fraud is common among customers of small businesses that fail to screen such customers by using credit reports and analyses.

# Characteristics of Notes Receivable

objective **6**

Describe the nature and characteristics of promissory notes.

A claim supported by a note has some advantages over a claim in the form of an account receivable. By signing a note, the debtor recognizes the debt and agrees to pay it according to the terms listed. A note is therefore a stronger legal claim if there is a court action.

A **promissory note** is a written promise to pay a sum of money on demand or at a definite time. It is payable to the order of a person or firm or to the bearer or holder of the note. It is signed by the person or firm that makes the promise. The

---

[4]As a practical matter, the entries to record the collection on an account previously written off are the same, regardless of whether the collection occurs in the current period or in a later fiscal period.

one to whose order the note is payable is called the **payee**, and the one making the promise is called the **maker**. In the example in Exhibit 4, Judson Company is the payee and Willard Company is the maker.

## •Exhibit 4   Promissory Note

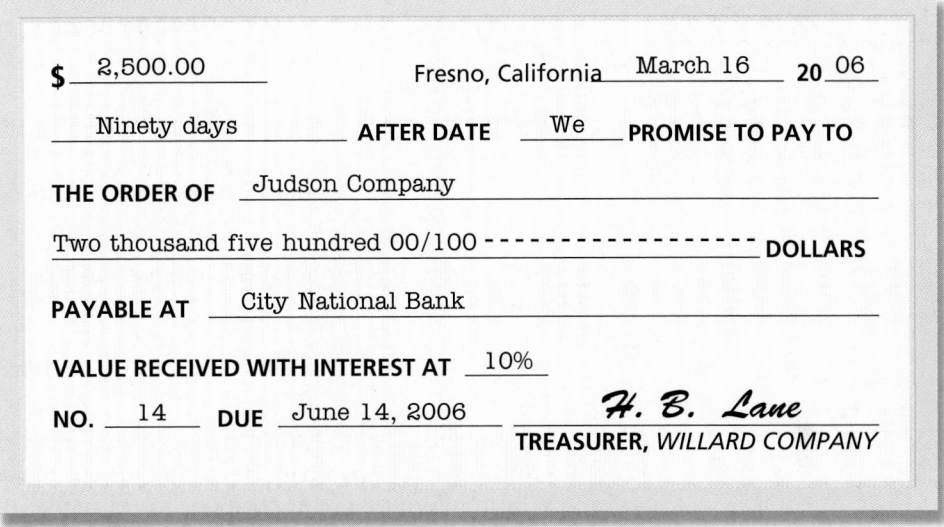

Notes have several characteristics that affect how they are recorded and reported in the financial statements. We describe these characteristics next.

## Due Date

The date a note is to be paid is called the **due date** or **maturity date**. The period of time between the issuance date and the due date of a short-term note may be stated in either days or months. When the term of a note is stated in days, the due date is the specified number of days after its issuance. To illustrate, the due date of the 90-day note in Exhibit 4 is determined as follows:

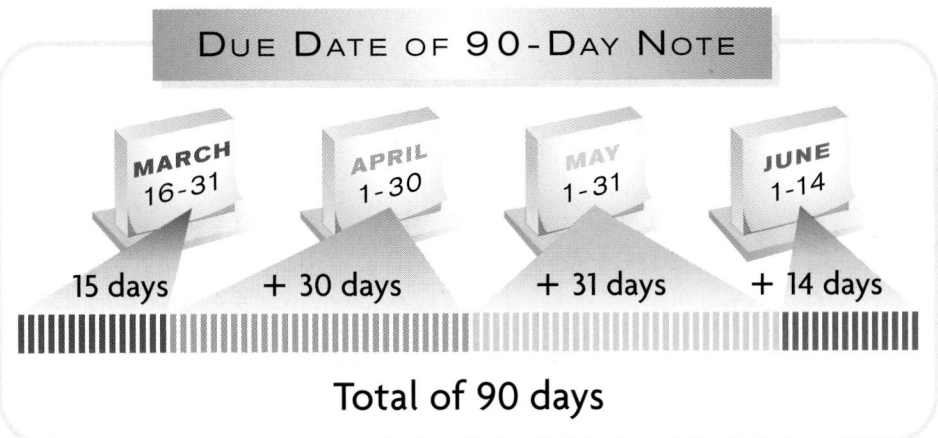

The term of a note may be stated as a certain number of months after the issuance date. In such cases, the due date is determined by counting the number of months from the issuance date. For example, a three-month note dated June 5 would be due on September 5. A two-month note dated July 31 would be due on September 30.

What is the due date of a 120-day note receivable dated September 9?

*January 7 [21 days in September (30 days − 9 days) + 31 days in October + 30 days in November + 31 days in December + 7 days in January = 120 days]*

What is the maturity value of a $15,000, 90-day, 12% note?

----------------------------------------

$15,450 [$15,000 + ($15,000 × 0.12 × 90/360)]

## Interest

A note normally specifies that interest be paid for the period between the issuance date and the due date.[5] Notes covering a period of time longer than one year normally provide that the interest be paid semiannually, quarterly, or at some other stated interval. When the term of the note is less than one year, the interest is usually payable on the due date of the note.

The interest rate on notes is normally stated in terms of a year, regardless of the actual period of time involved. Thus, the interest on $2,000 for one year at 12% is $240 (12% of $2,000). The interest on $2,000 for one-fourth of one year at 12% is $60 (1/4 of $240).

The basic formula for computing interest is as follows:

$$\text{Face Amount (or Principal)} \times \text{Rate} \times \text{Time} = \text{Interest}$$

To illustrate the formula, the interest on the note in Exhibit 4 is computed as follows:

$$\$2,500 \times 0.10 \times \frac{90}{360} = \$62.50 \text{ interest}$$

In computing interest for a period of less than one year, agencies of the federal government and many financial institutions use the actual number of days in the year, 365. In the preceding computation, for example, the time would have been stated as 90/365 of one year. To simplify computations, however, we will use 360 days.

## Maturity Value

The amount that is due at the maturity or due date is called the **maturity value**. The maturity value of a note is the sum of the face amount and the interest. In the note in Exhibit 4, the maturity value is $2,562.50 ($2,500 face amount plus $62.50 interest).

# Accounting for Notes Receivable

**objective 7**

Journalize the entries for notes receivable transactions.

As we mentioned earlier, a note may be received from a customer to replace an account receivable. To illustrate, assume that a 30-day, 12% note dated November 21, 2006, is accepted in settlement of the account of W. A. Bunn Co., which is past due and has a balance of $6,000. The entry to record the transaction is as follows:

| | | | | |
|---|---|---|---|---|
| Nov. | 21 | Notes Receivable | 6 0 0 0 00 | |
| | | Accounts Receivable—W. A. Bunn Co. | | 6 0 0 0 00 |
| | | Received 30-day, 12% note dated | | |
| | | November 21, 2006. | | |

When the note matures, the entry to record the receipt of $6,060 ($6,000 principal plus $60 interest) is as follows:

---

[5]You may occasionally see references to non-interest-bearing notes receivable. Such notes, which are not widely used, normally include an implicit interest rate.

| | | | | | | | |
|---|---|---|---|---|---|---|---|
| Dec. | 21 | Cash | | 6 0 6 0 00 | | | |
| | | Notes Receivable | | | 6 0 0 0 00 | | |
| | | Interest Revenue | | | 6 0 00 | | |
| | | Received principal and interest on | | | | | |
| | | matured note. | | | | | |

If the maker of a note fails to pay the debt on the due date, the note is a ***dishonored note receivable***. When a note is dishonored, the face value of the note plus any interest due is transferred to the accounts receivable account. For example, assume that the $6,000, 30-day, 12% note received from W. A. Bunn Co. and recorded on November 21 is dishonored at maturity. The entry to transfer the note and the interest back to the customer's account is as follows:

| | | | | | |
|---|---|---|---|---|---|
| Dec. | 21 | Accounts Receivable—W. A. Bunn Co. | 6 0 6 0 00 | | |
| | | Notes Receivable | | 6 0 0 0 00 | |
| | | Interest Revenue | | 6 0 00 | |
| | | To record dishonored note and | | | |
| | | interest. | | | |

The interest of $60 has been earned, even though the note has been dishonored. If the account receivable is uncollectible, the amount of $6,060 will be written off against the Allowance for Doubtful Accounts.

If a note matures in a later fiscal period, the interest accrued in the period in which the note is received must be recorded by an adjusting entry. For example, assume that a 90-day, 12% note dated December 1, 2006, is received from Crawford Company to settle its account, which has a balance of $4,000. Assuming that the accounting period ends on December 31, the entries to record the receipt of the note, accrued interest, and payment of the note at maturity are shown below.

| | | | | | |
|---|---|---|---|---|---|
| 2006 Dec. | 1 | Notes Receivable | 4 0 0 0 00 | | |
| | | Accounts Receivable—Crawford | | | |
| | | Company | | 4 0 0 0 00 | |
| | | Received note in settlement of | | | |
| | | account. | | | |
| Dec. | 31 | Interest Receivable | 4 0 00 | | |
| | | Interest Revenue | | 4 0 00 | |
| | | Adjusting entry for accrued | | | |
| | | interest, $4,000 × 0.12 × 30/360. | | | |

| | | | | | |
|---|---|---|---|---|---|
| 2007 Mar. | 1 | Cash | 4 1 2 0 00 | | |
| | | Notes Receivable | | 4 0 0 0 00 | |
| | | Interest Receivable | | 4 0 00 | |
| | | Interest Revenue | | 8 0 00 | |
| | | Received payment of note and | | | |
| | | interest; maturity value, $4,000 + | | | |
| | | ($4,000 × 0.12 × 90/360). | | | |

The interest revenue account is closed at the end of each accounting period. The amount of interest revenue is normally reported in the Other Income section of the income statement.

# Receivables on the Balance Sheet

**objective 8**

Prepare the Current Assets presentation of receivables on the balance sheet.

All receivables that are expected to be realized in cash within a year are presented in the Current Assets section of the balance sheet. It is normal to list the assets in the order of their liquidity. This is the order in which they are expected to be converted to cash during normal operations. An example of the presentation of receivables is shown in the partial balance sheet for Crabtree Co. in Exhibit 5.

## •Exhibit 5  Receivables on Balance Sheet

**Crabtree Co.**
**Balance Sheet**
**December 31, 2006**

| Assets | | |
|---|---:|---:|
| Current assets: | | |
| Cash | | $119 500 00 |
| Notes receivable | | 250 000 00 |
| Accounts receivable | $445 000 00 | |
| Less allowance for doubtful accounts | 15 000 00 | 430 000 00 |
| Interest receivable | | 14 500 00 |

**REAL WORLD**

The following credit risk disclosure appeared in the financial statements of **Deere & Company**:

*Credit receivables have significant concentrations of credit risk in the agricultural, industrial, lawn and grounds care, and recreational (non-Deere equipment) business sectors. . . . The portion of credit receivables related to the agricultural equipment business was 60%; that related to the industrial equipment business was 12%; that related to the lawn and grounds care equipment business was 7%; and that related to the recreational equipment business was 21%. On a geographic basis, there is not a disproportionate concentration of credit risk in any area. . . .*

The balance of Crabtree's notes receivable, accounts receivable, and interest receivable accounts are reported in Exhibit 5. The allowance for doubtful accounts is subtracted from the accounts receivable. Alternatively, the accounts receivable may be listed on the balance sheet at its net realizable value of $430,000, with a note showing the amount of the allowance. If the allowance account includes provisions for doubtful notes as well as accounts, it should be deducted from the total of Notes Receivable and Accounts Receivable.

Other disclosures related to receivables are presented either on the face of the financial statements or in the accompanying notes. Such disclosures include the market (fair) value of the receivables.[6] In addition, if unusual credit risks exist within the receivables, the nature of the risks should be disclosed. For example, if the majority of the receivables are due from one customer or are due from customers located in one area of the country or one industry, these facts should be disclosed.[7]

# Financial Analysis and Interpretation

**objective 9**

Compute and interpret the accounts receivable turnover and the number of days' sales in receivables.

Businesses that grant long credit terms tend to have relatively greater amounts tied up in accounts receivable than those granting short credit terms. In either case, it is

---

[6]*Statement of Financial Accounting Standards, No. 107*, "Disclosures about Fair Value of Financial Instruments," Financial Accounting Standards Board, Norwalk, 1991, pars. 10 and 19.

[7]*Statement of Financial Accounting Standards, No. 105*, "Disclosure of Information about Financial Instruments with Off-Balance-Sheet Risk and Financial Instruments with Concentrations of Credit Risk," Financial Accounting Standards Board, Norwalk, 1990, par. 20, and *Statement of Financial Accounting Standards, No. 107, op.cit.*, par. 13.

desirable to collect receivables as promptly as possible. The cash collected from receivables improves solvency and lessens the risk of loss from uncollectible accounts. Two financial measures that are especially useful in evaluating the efficiency in collecting receivables are (1) the accounts receivable turnover and (2) the number of days' sales in receivables.

The ***accounts receivable turnover*** measures how frequently during the year the accounts receivable are being converted to cash. For example, with credit terms of 2/10, n/30 days, the accounts receivable should turn over less than 36 times per year. The accounts receivable turnover is computed as follows:[8]

$$\text{Accounts receivable turnover} = \frac{\text{Net sales}}{\text{Average accounts receivable}}$$

The average accounts receivable can be determined by using monthly data or by simply adding the beginning and ending accounts receivable balances and dividing by two. For example, assume that Sidner Company offers credit terms of 2/10, n/30 and has net sales of $36,000,000 and beginning and ending accounts receivable balances of $1,080,000 and $1,220,000. The accounts receivable turnover is 31.3, as shown below.

$$\text{Accounts receivable turnover} = \frac{\text{Net sales}}{\text{Average accounts receivable}}$$

$$= \frac{\$36,000,000}{(\$1,080,000 + \$1,220,000)/2} = 31.3$$

The ***number of days' sales in receivables*** is an estimate of the length of time the accounts receivable have been outstanding. With credit terms of 2/10, n/30 days, the number of days' sales in receivables should be more than 10 days. It is computed as follows:

$$\text{Number of days' sales in receivables} = \frac{\text{Accounts receivable, end of year}}{\text{Average daily sales}}$$

Average daily sales is determined by dividing net sales by 365 days. For example, using the preceding data for Sidner Company, the number of days' sales in receivables is 12.4, as shown below.

$$\text{Number of days' sales in receivables} = \frac{\text{Accounts receivable, end of year}}{\text{Average daily sales}}$$

$$= \frac{\$1,220,000}{(\$36,000,000/365 \text{ days})} = 12.4$$

For these measures to be meaningful, a company should compare its current measures with those from prior periods and with industry figures. An improvement in the efficiency in collecting accounts receivable is indicated when the accounts receivable turnover increases and the number of days' sales in receivables decreases.

---

[8] If known, credit sales should be used in the numerator. Because credit sales are not normally known by external users, we use net sales in the numerator.

#  ppendix  Discounting Notes Receivable

Although it is not a common transaction, a company may endorse its notes receivable and transfer them to a bank. The bank transfers cash (the **proceeds**) to the company after deducting a **discount** (interest) that is computed on the maturity value of the note for the discount period. The discount period is the time that the bank must hold the note before it becomes due.

To illustrate, assume that a 90-day, 12%, $1,800 note receivable from Pryor & Co., dated April 8, is discounted at the payee's bank on May 3 at the rate of 14%. The data used in determining the effect of the transaction are as follows:

| | |
|---|---:|
| Face value of note dated April 8 | $1,800.00 |
| Interest on note (90 days at 12%) | 54.00 |
| Maturity value of note due July 7 | $1,854.00 |
| Discount on maturity value (65 days from May 3 to July 7, at 14%) | 46.87 |
| Proceeds | $1,807.13 |

The endorser records as interest revenue the excess of the proceeds from discounting the note, $1,807.13, over its face value, $1,800, as follows:

| | | | | | |
|---|---|---|---:|---:|---:|
| May | 3 | Cash | | 1 8 0 7 13 | |
| | | Notes Receivable | | | 1 8 0 0 00 |
| | | Interest Revenue | | | 7 13 |
| | | Discounted $1,800, 90-day, 12% note | | | |
| | | at 14%. | | | |

What if the proceeds from discounting a note receivable are less than the face value? When this situation occurs, the endorser records the excess of the face value over the proceeds as interest expense. The length of the discount period and the difference between the interest rate and the discount rate determine whether interest expense or interest revenue will result from discounting.

Without a statement limiting responsibility, the endorser of a note is committed to paying the note if the maker defaults. This potential liability is called a **contingent liability**. Thus, the endorser of a note that has been discounted has a contingent liability until the due date. If the maker pays the promised amount at maturity, the contingent liability is removed without any action on the part of the endorser. If, on the other hand, the maker dishonors the note and the endorser is notified according to legal requirements, the endorser's liability becomes an actual one.

When a discounted note receivable is dishonored, the bank notifies the endorser and asks for payment. In some cases, the bank may charge a **protest fee** for notifying the endorser that a note has been dishonored. The entire amount paid to the bank by the endorser, including the interest and protest fee, should be debited to the account receivable of the maker. For example, assume that the $1,800, 90-day, 12% note discounted on May 3 is dishonored at maturity by the maker, Pryor & Co. The bank charges a protest fee of $12. The endorser's entry to record the payment to the bank is as follows:

| | | | | | |
|---|---|---|---|---|---|
| July | 7 | Accounts Receivable—Pryor & Co. | | 1 8 6 6 00 | |
| | | Cash | | | 1 8 6 6 00 |
| | | Paid dishonored, discounted note | | | |
| | | (maturity value of $1,854 plus protest | | | |
| | | fee of $12). | | | |

# **K**ey Points

**1 List the common classifications of receivables.**

The term receivables includes all money claims against other entities, including people, business firms, and other organizations. They are normally classified as accounts receivable, notes receivable, or other receivables.

**2 Summarize and provide examples of internal control procedures that apply to receivables.**

The internal controls that apply to receivables include the separation of responsibilities for related functions. In this way, the work of one employee can serve as a check on the work of another employee.

**3 Describe the nature of and the accounting for uncollectible receivables.**

The two methods of accounting for uncollectible receivables are the al-

lowance method and the direct write-off method. The allowance method provides in advance for uncollectible receivables. The direct write-off method recognizes the expense only when the account is judged to be uncollectible.

**4 Journalize the entries for the allowance method of accounting for uncollectibles, and estimate uncollectible receivables based on sales and on an analysis of receivables.**

A year-end adjusting entry provides for (1) the reduction of the value of the receivables to the amount of cash expected to be realized from them in the future and (2) the allocation to the current period of the expected expense resulting from such reduction. The adjusting entry debits Uncollectible Accounts Expense and credits Allowance for Doubtful Accounts. When an ac-

count is believed to be uncollectible, it is written off against the allowance account.

When the estimate of uncollectibles is based on the amount of sales for the fiscal period, the adjusting entry is made without regard to the balance of the allowance account. When the estimate of uncollectibles is based on the amount and the age of the receivable accounts at the end of the period, the adjusting entry is recorded so that the balance of the allowance account will equal the estimated uncollectibles at the end of the period.

The allowance account, which will have a credit balance after the adjusting entry has been posted, is a contra asset account. The uncollectible accounts expense is generally reported on the income statement as an administrative expense.

**5 Journalize the entries for the direct write-off of uncollectible receivables.**

Under the direct write-off method, the entry to write off an account debits Uncollectible Accounts Expense and credits Accounts Receivable. Neither an allowance account nor an adjusting entry is needed at the end of the period.

**6 Describe the nature and characteristics of promissory notes.**

A note is a written promise to pay a sum of money on demand or at a definite time. Characteristics of notes that affect how they are recorded and reported include the due date, interest rate, and maturity value. The basic formula for computing interest on a note is: Principal × Rate × Time = Interest. The due date is the date a note is to be paid, and the period of time between the issuance date and the due date is normally stated in either days or months. The maturity value of a note is the sum of the face amount and the interest.

**7 Journalize the entries for notes receivable transactions.**

A note received in settlement of an account receivable is recorded as a debit to Notes Receivable and a credit to Accounts Receivable. When a note matures, Cash is debited, Notes Receivable is credited, and Interest Revenue is credited. If the maker of a note fails to pay the debt on the due date, the note is said to be dishonored. When a note is dishonored, the maturity value of the note is debited to an accounts receivable account, while the face value is credited to Notes Receivable and Interest Revenue is credited for the difference.

**8 Prepare the Current Assets presentation of receivables on the balance sheet.**

All receivables that are expected to be realized in cash within a year are presented in the Current Assets section of the balance sheet. It is normal to list the assets in the order of their liquidity, which is the order in which they can be converted to cash in normal operations.

**9 Compute and interpret the accounts receivable turnover and the number of days' sales in receivables.**

The accounts receivable turnover is net sales divided by average accounts receivable. It measures how frequently accounts receivable are being converted into cash. The number of days' sales in receivables is the end-of-year accounts receivable divided by the average daily sales. It measures the length of time the accounts receivable have been outstanding.

# Key Terms

accounts receivable (318)
accounts receivable turnover (331)
aging the receivables (324)
allowance method (321)
contra asset (321)
direct write-off method (321)

dishonored note receivable (329)
maturity value (328)
notes receivable (318)
number of days' sales in receivables (331)
promissory note (326)

receivables (318)
uncollectible accounts expense (320)

# Illustrative Problem

Ditzler Company, a construction supply company, uses the allowance method of accounting for uncollectible accounts receivable. Selected transactions completed by Ditzler Company are as follows:

Feb. 1. Sold merchandise on account to Ames Co., $8,000. The cost of the merchandise sold was $4,500.

Mar. 15. Accepted a 60-day, 12% note for $8,000 from Ames Co. on account.

Apr. 9. Wrote off a $2,500 account from Dorset Co. as uncollectible.

21. Loaned $7,500 cash to Jill Klein, receiving a 90-day, 14% note.

May 14. Received the interest due from Ames Co. and a new 90-day, 14% note as a renewal of the loan. (Record both the debit and the credit to the notes receivable account.)

June 13. Reinstated the account of Dorset Co., written off on April 9, and received $2,500 in full payment.

July 20. Jill Klein dishonored her note.

Aug. 12. Received from Ames Co. the amount due on its note of May 14.

19. Received from Jill Klein the amount owed on the dishonored note, plus interest for 30 days at 15%, computed on the maturity value of the note.

Dec. 16. Accepted a 60-day, 12% note for $12,000 from Global Company on account.

31. It is estimated that 3% of the credit sales of $1,375,000 for the year ended December 31 will be uncollectible.

### Instructions

1. Journalize the transactions. Omit explanations.
2. Journalize the adjusting entry to record the accrued interest on December 31 on the Global Company note.

### Solution

**1.**

| Date | | Account | Debit | Credit |
|---|---|---|---|---|
| Feb. | 1 | Accounts Receivable—Ames Co. | 8 000 00 | |
| | | Sales | | 8 000 00 |
| | 1 | Cost of Merchandise Sold | 4 500 00 | |
| | | Merchandise Inventory | | 4 500 00 |
| Mar. | 15 | Notes Receivable—Ames Co. | 8 000 00 | |
| | | Accounts Receivable—Ames Co. | | 8 000 00 |
| Apr. | 9 | Allowance for Doubtful Accounts | 2 500 00 | |
| | | Accounts Receivable—Dorset Co. | | 2 500 00 |
| | 21 | Notes Receivable—Jill Klein | 7 500 00 | |
| | | Cash | | 7 500 00 |
| May | 14 | Notes Receivable—Ames Co. | 8 000 00 | |
| | | Cash | 160 00 | |
| | | Notes Receivable—Ames Co. | | 8 000 00 |
| | | Interest Revenue | | 160 00 |
| June | 13 | Accounts Receivable—Dorset Co. | 2 500 00 | |
| | | Allowance for Doubtful Accounts | | 2 500 00 |
| | 13 | Cash | 2 500 00 | |
| | | Accounts Receivable—Dorset Co. | | 2 500 00 |
| July | 20 | Accounts Receivable—Jill Klein | 7 762 50 | |
| | | Notes Receivable—Jill Klein | | 7 500 00 |
| | | Interest Revenue | | 262 50 |
| Aug. | 12 | Cash | 8 280 00 | |
| | | Notes Receivable—Ames Co. | | 8 000 00 |
| | | Interest Revenue | | 280 00 |
| | 19 | Cash | 7 859 53 | |
| | | Accounts Receivable—Jill Klein | | 7 762 50 |
| | | Interest Revenue | | 97 03 |
| | | ($7,762.50 × 15% × 30/360) | | |

| Dec. | 16 | Notes Receivable—Global Company | | 12 0 0 0 00 | |
| | | Accounts Receivable—Global Company | | | 12 0 0 0 00 |
| | | | | | |
| | 31 | Uncollectible Accounts Expense | | 41 2 5 0 00 | |
| | | Allowance for Doubtful Accounts | | | 41 2 5 0 00 |

**2.**

| Dec. | 31 | Interest Receivable | | 6 0 00 | |
| | | Interest Revenue | | | 6 0 00 |
| | | ($12,000 × 12% × 15/360) | | | |

# Self-Examination Questions (Answers at End of Chapter)

1. At the end of the fiscal year, before the accounts are adjusted, Accounts Receivable has a balance of $200,000 and Allowance for Doubtful Accounts has a credit balance of $2,500. If the estimate of uncollectible accounts determined by aging the receivables is $8,500, the amount of uncollectible accounts expense is:
   A. $2,500
   B. $6,000
   C. $8,500
   D. $11,000

2. At the end of the fiscal year, Accounts Receivable has a balance of $100,000 and Allowance for Doubtful Accounts has a balance of $7,000. The expected net realizable value of the accounts receivable is:
   A. $7,000
   B. $93,000
   C. $100,000
   D. $107,000

3. What is the maturity value of a 90-day, 12% note for $10,000?

   A. $8,800
   B. $10,000
   C. $10,300
   D. $11,200

4. What is the due date of a $12,000, 90-day, 8% note receivable dated August 5?
   A. October 31
   B. November 2
   C. November 3
   D. November 4

5. When a note receivable is dishonored, Accounts Receivable is debited for what amount?
   A. The face value of the note
   B. The maturity value of the note
   C. The maturity value of the note less accrued interest
   D. The maturity value of the note plus accrued interest

# Class Discussion Questions

1. What are the three classifications of receivables?
2. What types of transactions give rise to accounts receivable?
3. In what section of the balance sheet should a note receivable be listed if its term is (a) 120 days, (b) 6 years?
4. Give two examples of other receivables.
5. The accounts receivable clerk is also responsible for handling cash receipts. Which principle of internal control is violated in this situation?
6. Which of the two methods of accounting for uncollectible accounts provides for the recognition of the expense in the period of sale?
7. What kind of an account (asset, liability, etc.) is Allowance for Doubtful Accounts, and is its normal balance a debit or a credit?

8. After the accounts are adjusted and closed at the end of the fiscal year, Accounts Receivable has a balance of $883,150 and Allowance for Doubtful Accounts has a balance of $123,250. Describe how the accounts receivable and the allowance for doubtful accounts are reported on the balance sheet.

9. A firm has consistently adjusted its allowance account at the end of the fiscal year by adding a fixed percent of the period's net sales on account. After five years, the balance in Allowance for Doubtful Accounts has become very large in relationship to the balance in Accounts Receivable. Give two possible explanations.

10. Which of the two methods of estimating uncollectibles provides for the most accurate estimate of the current net realizable value of the receivables?

11. For a business, what are the advantages of a note receivable in comparison to an account receivable?

12. Mobley Company issued a promissory note to Ellsworth Company. (a) Who is the payee? (b) What is the title of the account used by Ellsworth Company in recording the note?

13. If a note provides for payment of principal of $90,000 and interest at the rate of 7%, will the interest amount to $6,300? Explain.

14. The maker of a $20,000, 9%, 120-day note receivable failed to pay the note on the due date of July 30. What accounts should be debited and credited by the payee to record the dishonored note receivable?

15. The note receivable dishonored in Question 14 is paid on August 29 by the maker, plus interest for 30 days, 12%. What entry should be made to record the receipt of the payment?

16. Under what caption should accounts receivable be reported on the balance sheet?

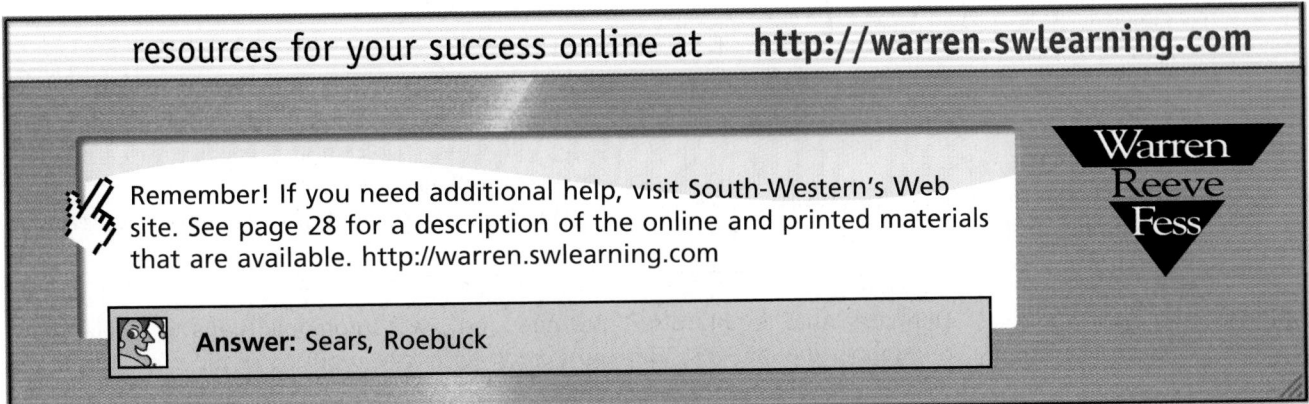

resources for your success online at   **http://warren.swlearning.com**

Remember! If you need additional help, visit South-Western's Web site. See page 28 for a description of the online and printed materials that are available. http://warren.swlearning.com

Warren Reeve Fess

**Answer: Sears, Roebuck**

# Exercises

**EXERCISE 8-1**
*Internal control procedures*

**Objective 2**

Fridley Company sells carpeting. Over 50% of all carpet sales are on credit. The following procedures are used by Fridley to process this large number of credit sales and the subsequent collections.

a. A formal ledger is not maintained for customers who sign promissory notes. Fridley simply keeps a copy of each signed note in a file cabinet. These unpaid notes are filed by due date.

b. Fridley employs an accounts receivable clerk. The clerk is responsible for recording customer credit sales (based on sales tickets), receiving cash from customers, giving customers credit for their payments, and handling all customer billing complaints.

c. The general ledger control account for Accounts Receivable is maintained by the General Accounting Department at Fridley. This department records total credit sales, based on credit sale information from the store's electronic cash register, and total customer receipts, based on the bank deposit slip.

d. All credit sales to a first-time customer must be approved by the Credit Department. Salespersons will assist the customer in filling out a credit application, but an employee in the Credit Department is responsible for verifying employment and checking the customer's credit history before granting credit.

e. Fridley's standard credit period is 45 days. The Credit Department may approve an extension of this repayment period of up to one year. Whenever an extension is granted, the customer signs a promissory note. Up to 15% of the credit sales in any one year are for repayment periods exceeding 45 days.

State whether each of these procedures is appropriate or inappropriate, considering the principles of internal control. If inappropriate, state which internal control procedure is violated.

**EXERCISE 8-2**
*Nature of uncollectible accounts*
**Objective 3**

**REAL WORLD**

✓ a. 4.3%

**Hilton Hotels Corporation** owns and operates casinos at several of its hotels, located primarily in Nevada. At the end of a fiscal year, the following accounts and notes receivable were reported (in thousands):

| | | |
|---|---|---|
| Hotel accounts and notes receivable | $75,796 | |
| Less: Allowance for doubtful accounts | 3,256 | |
| | | $72,540 |
| | | |
| Casino accounts receivable | $26,334 | |
| Less: Allowance for doubtful accounts | 6,654 | |
| | | 19,680 |

a. Compute the percentage of allowance for doubtful accounts to the gross hotel accounts and notes receivable for the end of the fiscal year.

b. Compute the percentage of the allowance for doubtful accounts to the gross casino accounts receivable for the end of the fiscal year.

c. Discuss possible reasons for the difference in the two ratios computed in (a) and (b).

**EXERCISE 8-3**
*Number of days past due*
**Objective 4**

✓ Bear Creek Body Shop, 53 days

Herman's Auto Supply distributes new and used automobile parts to local dealers throughout the Midwest. Herman's credit terms are n/30. As of the end of business on July 31, the following accounts receivable were past due.

| Account | Due Date | Amount |
|---|---|---|
| Bear Creek Body Shop | June 8 | $3,000 |
| First Auto | July 3 | 2,500 |
| Kaiser Repair | March 20 | 500 |
| Master's Auto Repair | May 15 | 1,000 |
| Richter Auto | June 18 | 750 |
| Sabol's | April 12 | 1,800 |
| Uptown Auto | May 8 | 500 |
| Westside Repair & Tow | May 31 | 1,100 |

Determine the number of days each account is past due.

**EXERCISE 8-4**
*Aging-of-receivables schedule*
**Objective 4**

The accounts receivable clerk for Intimacy Mattress Company prepared the following partially completed aging-of-receivables schedule as of the end of business on November 30.

| Customer | Balance | Not Past Due | Days Past Due | | | |
|---|---|---|---|---|---|---|
| | | | 1–30 | 31–60 | 61–90 | Over 90 |
| Aaker Brothers Inc. | 2,000 | 2,000 | | | | |
| Aitken Company | 1,500 | | 1,500 | | | |
| Zollo Company | 5,000 | | | | 5,000 | |
| Subtotals | 972,500 | 640,000 | 180,000 | 78,500 | 42,300 | 31,700 |

The following accounts were unintentionally omitted from the aging schedule.

| Customer | Balance | Due Date |
|---|---|---|
| Janzen Industries | $40,000 | August 29 |
| Kuehn Company | 8,500 | September 3 |
| Mauer Inc. | 18,000 | October 21 |
| Pollack Company | 6,500 | November 23 |
| Simrill Company | 7,500 | December 3 |

a. Determine the number of days past due for each of the preceding accounts.
b. Complete the aging-of-receivables schedule by including the omitted amounts.

**EXERCISE 8-5**
*Estimating allowance for doubtful accounts*
**Objective 4**

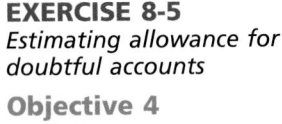

✓ *$60,495*

Intimacy Mattress Company has a past history of uncollectible accounts, as shown below. Estimate the allowance for doubtful accounts, based on the aging-of-receivables schedule you completed in Exercise 8-4.

| Age Class | Percentage Uncollectible |
|---|---|
| Not past due | 1% |
| 1–30 days past due | 4 |
| 31–60 days past due | 8 |
| 61–90 days past due | 20 |
| Over 90 days past due | 40 |

**EXERCISE 8-6**
*Adjustment for uncollectible accounts*
**Objective 4**

Using the data in Exercise 8-5, assume that the allowance for doubtful accounts for Intimacy Mattress Company has a credit balance of $7,180 before adjustment on November 30. Journalize the adjusting entry for uncollectible accounts as of November 30.

**EXERCISE 8-7**
*Estimating doubtful accounts*
**Objective 4**

Kubota Co. is a wholesaler of office supplies. An aging of the company's accounts receivable on December 31, 2006, and a historical analysis of the percentage of uncollectible accounts in each age category are as follows:

| Age Interval | Balance | Percent Uncollectible |
|---|---|---|
| Not past due | $450,000 | 2% |
| 1–30 days past due | 110,000 | 4 |
| 31–60 days past due | 51,000 | 6 |
| 61–90 days past due | 12,500 | 20 |
| 91–180 days past due | 7,500 | 60 |
| Over 180 days past due | 5,500 | 80 |
| | $636,500 | |

Estimate what the proper balance of the allowance for doubtful accounts should be as of December 31, 2006.

**EXERCISE 8-8**
*Entry for uncollectible accounts*
**Objective 4**

Using the data in Exercise 8-7, assume that the allowance for doubtful accounts for Kubota Co. had a debit balance of $1,575 as of December 31, 2006.

Journalize the adjusting entry for uncollectible accounts as of December 31, 2006.

**EXERCISE 8-9**
*Providing for doubtful accounts*
**Objective 4**

✓ a. $17,875
✓ b. $13,600

At the end of the current year, the accounts receivable account has a debit balance of $840,000, and net sales for the year total $7,150,000. Determine the amount of the adjusting entry to provide for doubtful accounts under each of the following assumptions:

a. The allowance account before adjustment has a credit balance of $1,780. Uncollectible accounts expense is estimated at 1/4 of 1% of net sales.
b. The allowance account before adjustment has a credit balance of $2,750. An aging of the accounts in the customer's ledger indicates estimated doubtful accounts of $16,350.
c. The allowance account before adjustment has a debit balance of $3,050. Uncollectible accounts expense is estimated at 1/2 of 1% of net sales.
d. The allowance account before adjustment has a debit balance of $3,050. An aging of the accounts in the customer's ledger indicates estimated doubtful accounts of $38,400.

**EXERCISE 8-10**
*Entries to write off accounts receivable*
**Objectives 4, 5**

Anchor.com, a computer consulting firm, has decided to write off the $7,130 balance of an account owed by a customer. Journalize the entry to record the write-off, (a) assuming that the allowance method is used, and (b) assuming that the direct write-off method is used.

**EXERCISE 8-11**
*Entries for uncollectible receivables, using allowance method*
**Objective 4**

Journalize the following transactions in the accounts of Linden Company, a restaurant supply company that uses the allowance method of accounting for uncollectible receivables:

Feb. 20. Sold merchandise on account to Darlene Brogan, $12,100. The cost of the merchandise sold was $7,260.
May 30. Received $6,000 from Darlene Brogan and wrote off the remainder owed on the sale of February 20 as uncollectible.
Aug. 3. Reinstated the account of Darlene Brogan that had been written off on May 30 and received $6,100 cash in full payment.

**EXERCISE 8-12**
*Entries for uncollectible accounts, using direct write-off method*
**Objective 5**

Journalize the following transactions in the accounts of Graybeal Co., a hospital supply company that uses the direct write-off method of accounting for uncollectible receivables:

July 6. Sold merchandise on account to Dr. Jerry Jagers, $18,500. The cost of the merchandise sold was $11,100.
Sept. 12. Received $9,000 from Dr. Jerry Jagers and wrote off the remainder owed on the sale of July 6 as uncollectible.
Dec. 20. Reinstated the account of Dr. Jerry Jagers that had been written off on September 12 and received $9,500 cash in full payment.

**EXERCISE 8-13**
*Effect of doubtful accounts on net income*
**Objectives 4, 5**

During its first year of operations, O'Hara Automotive Supply Co. had net sales of $4,050,000, wrote off $112,350 of accounts as uncollectible using the direct write-off method, and reported net income of $212,800. If the allowance method of accounting for uncollectibles had been used, 2½% of net sales would have been estimated as uncollectible. Determine what the net income would have been if the allowance method had been used.

**EXERCISE 8-14**
*Effect of doubtful accounts on net income*
**Objectives 4, 5**

Using the data in Exercise 8-13, assume that during the second year of operations O'Hara Automotive Supply Co. had net sales of $4,800,000, wrote off $114,800 of accounts as uncollectible using the direct write-off method, and reported net income of $262,300.

a. Determine what net income would have been in the second year if the allowance method (using 2½% of net sales) had been used in both the first and second years.
b. Determine what the balance of the allowance for doubtful accounts would have been at the end of the second year if the allowance method had been used in both the first and second years.

**EXERCISE 8-15**
*Determine due date and interest on notes*
**Objective 6**

SPREADSHEET

✓ a. August 31, $120

Determine the due date and the amount of interest due at maturity on the following notes:

| | Date of Note | Face Amount | Term of Note | Interest Rate |
|---|---|---|---|---|
| a. | June 2 | $ 8,000 | 90 days | 6% |
| b. | August 30 | 18,000 | 120 days | 8% |
| c. | October 1 | 12,500 | 60 days | 12% |
| d. | March 6 | 10,000 | 60 days | 9% |
| e. | May 20 | 6,000 | 60 days | 10% |

**EXERCISE 8-16**
*Entries for notes receivable*
**Objectives 6, 7**

✓ b. $24,480

Magpie Interior Decorators issued a 120-day, 6% note for $24,000, dated April 10, to Peel's Furniture Company on account.

a. Determine the due date of the note.
b. Determine the maturity value of the note.
c. Journalize the entries to record the following: (1) receipt of the note by the payee, and (2) receipt by the payee of payment of the note at maturity.

**EXERCISE 8-17**
*Entries for notes receivable*
**Objective 7**

The series of seven transactions recorded in the following T accounts were related to a sale to a customer on account and the receipt of the amount owed. Briefly describe each transaction.

| Cash | | | | Notes Receivable | | |
|---|---|---|---|---|---|---|
| (7) | 21,777 | | | (5) | 21,000 | (6) 21,000 |

| Accounts Receivable | | | | Merchandise Inventory | | |
|---|---|---|---|---|---|---|
| (1) | 24,000 | (3) | 3,000 | (4) 1,800 | (2) | 15,000 |
| (6) | 21,420 | (5) | 21,000 | | | |
| | | (7) | 21,420 | | | |

| Sales | | | Sales Returns and Allowances | |
|---|---|---|---|---|
| | (1) | 24,000 | (3) 3,000 | |

| Cost of Merchandise Sold | | | Interest Revenue | | |
|---|---|---|---|---|---|
| (2) | 15,000 | (4) 1,800 | | (6) | 420 |
| | | | | (7) | 357 |

**EXERCISE 8-18**
*Entries for notes receivable, including year-end entries*
**Objective 7**

The following selected transactions were completed by Cassidy Co., a supplier of elastic bands for clothing:

2005
Dec. 13. Received from Visage Co., on account, a $25,000, 120-day, 6% note dated December 13.

Dec. 31. Recorded an adjusting entry for accrued interest on the note of December 13.

31. Closed the interest revenue account. The only entry in this account originated from the December 31 adjustment.

2006

Apr. 12. Received payment of note and interest from Visage Co.

Journalize the transactions.

**EXERCISE 8-19**
*Entries for receipt and dishonor of note receivable*
**Objective 7**

Journalize the following transactions of Prairie Theater Productions:

July 8. Received a $30,000, 90-day, 8% note dated July 8 from Pennington Company on account.

Oct. 6. The note is dishonored by Pennington Company.

Nov. 5. Received the amount due on the dishonored note plus interest for 30 days at 10% on the total amount charged to Pennington Company on October 6.

**EXERCISE 8-20**
*Entries for receipt and dishonor of notes receivable*
**Objectives 4, 7**

Journalize the following transactions in the accounts of Blue Sky Co., which operates a riverboat casino:

Mar. 1. Received a $15,000, 60-day, 5% note dated March 1 from Absaroka Co. on account.

18. Received a $12,000, 90-day, 9% note dated March 18 from Sturgis Co. on account.

Apr. 30. The note dated March 1 from Absaroka Co. is dishonored, and the customer's account is charged for the note, including interest.

June 16. The note dated March 18 from Sturgis Co. is dishonored, and the customer's account is charged for the note, including interest.

July 11. Cash is received for the amount due on the dishonored note dated March 1 plus interest for 72 days at 8% on the total amount debited to Absaroka Co. on April 30.

Oct. 12. Wrote off against the allowance account the amount charged to Sturgis Co. on June 16 for the dishonored note dated March 18.

**EXERCISE 8-21**
*Receivables in the balance sheet*
**Objective 8**

**WHAT'S WRONG WITH THIS?**

List any errors you can find in the following partial balance sheet.

**Pembroke Company**
**Balance Sheet**
**July 31, 2006**

| Assets | | |
|---|---:|---:|
| Current assets: | | |
| Cash . . . . . . . . . . . . . . . . . . . . . . . . . . . . . . . . . . . . . . . . . . . . . | | $ 43,750 |
| Notes receivable . . . . . . . . . . . . . . . . . . . . . . . . . . . . . . . . . . . | $300,000 | |
| Less interest receivable . . . . . . . . . . . . . . . . . . . . . . . . . . . . . | 18,000 | 282,000 |
| Accounts receivable . . . . . . . . . . . . . . . . . . . . . . . . . . . . . . . . . . | $576,180 | |
| Plus allowance for doubtful accounts . . . . . . . . . . . . . . . . . . . . | 71,200 | 647,380 |

**EXERCISE 8-22**
*Accounts receivable turnover*
**Objective 9**

**REAL WORLD**

✓ a. 2002: 19.5

**Circuit City Stores, Inc.** is a national retailer of brand-name consumer electronics including televisions, DVD players, compact disc players, personal computers, printers, video games, DVD movies, and music. For the fiscal years 2003 and 2002, Circuit City reported the following (in thousands):

| | Year Ending February 28, | |
|---|---:|---:|
| | **2003** | **2002** |
| Net sales | $9,953,530 | $9,518,231 |
| Accounts Receivable | 216,200 | 159,477 |

Assume that the accounts receivable (in thousands) were $265,515 at March 1, 2001.

a. Compute the accounts receivable turnover for 2003 and 2002. Round to one decimal place.

b. What conclusions can be drawn from these analyses regarding Circuit City's efficiency in collecting receivables?

**EXERCISE 8-23**
*Days' sales in receivables*
**Objective 9**

REAL WORLD

✓ a. 2002: 20.7 days

Use the Circuit City data in Exercise 8-22 to analyze days' sales in receivables.

a. Compute the days' sales in receivables at the end of 2002 and 2001. Round to one decimal place.

b. What conclusions can be drawn from these analyses regarding Circuit City's efficiency in collecting receivables?

**EXERCISE 8-24**
*Accounts receivable turnover and days' sales in receivables*
**Objective 9**

REAL WORLD

✓ a. 2002: 108.2

The **Limited Inc.** sells women's and men's clothing through specialty retail stores, including **Structure, Limited, Express, Lane Bryant,** and **Lerner New York**. The Limited sells women's intimate apparel and personal care products through **Victoria Secret** and **Bath & Body Works** stores. For the fiscal years 2002 and 2001, The Limited reported the following (in thousands):

|  | Year Ending February 2, | |
|---|---|---|
|  | **2002** | **2001** |
| Net sales | $9,363,000 | $10,105,000 |
| Accounts Receivable | 79,000 | 94,000 |

Assume that the accounts receivable (in thousands) were $109,000 at the beginning of the 2001 fiscal year.

a. Compute the accounts receivable turnover for 2002 and 2001. Round to one decimal place.

b. Compute the days' sales in receivables at the end of 2002 and 2001. Round to one decimal place.

c. What conclusions can be drawn from these analyses regarding The Limited's efficiency in collecting receivables?

**APPENDIX EXERCISE 8-25**
*Discounting notes receivable*

✓ a. $20,300

Theisen Co., a building construction company, holds a 90-day, 6% note for $20,000, dated March 15, which was received from a customer on account. On April 14, the note is discounted at the bank at the rate of 8%.

a. Determine the maturity value of the note.

b. Determine the number of days in the discount period.

c. Determine the amount of the discount. Round to the nearest dollar.

d. Determine the amount of the proceeds.

e. Journalize the entry to record the discounting of the note on April 14.

**APPENDIX EXERCISE 8-26**
*Entries for receipt and discounting of note receivable and dishonored notes*

Journalize the following transactions in the accounts of Allied Theater Productions:

June  1. Received a $60,000, 60-day, 8% note dated June 1 from Rhodes Company on account.

July  1. Discounted the note at City Bank at 9%.

    31. The note is dishonored by Rhodes Company; paid the bank the amount due on the note, plus a protest fee of $200.

Aug. 30. Received the amount due on the dishonored note plus interest for 30 days at 12% on the total amount charged to Rhodes Company on July 31.

# Problems Series A

**PROBLEM 8-1A**
*Entries related to uncollectible accounts*

**Objective 4**

**P.A.S.S.**

✓ 3. $522,050

The following transactions, adjusting entries, and closing entries were completed by Elko Contractors Co. during the year ended December 31, 2006:

Mar. 15. Received 60% of the $18,500 balance owed by Bimba Co., a bankrupt business, and wrote off the remainder as uncollectible.
Apr. 16. Reinstated the account of Tom Miner, which had been written off in the preceding year as uncollectible. Journalized the receipt of $5,782 cash in full payment of Miner's account.
July 20. Wrote off the $5,500 balance owed by Martz Co., which has no assets.
Oct. 31. Reinstated the account of Two Bit Saloon Co., which had been written off in the preceding year as uncollectible. Journalized the receipt of $6,100 cash in full payment of the account.
Dec. 31. Wrote off the following accounts as uncollectible (compound entry): Asche Co., $950; Dorsch Co., $4,600; Krebs Distributors, $2,500; J. J. Levi, $1,200.
  31. Based on an analysis of the $535,750 of accounts receivable, it was estimated that $13,700 will be uncollectible. Journalized the adjusting entry.
  31. Journalized the entry to close the appropriate account to Income Summary.

## Instructions

1. Post the January 1 credit balance of $12,050 to Allowance for Doubtful Accounts.
2. Journalize the transactions and the adjusting and closing entries. Post each entry that affects the following three selected accounts and determine the new balances:

> 115    Allowance for Doubtful Accounts
> 313    Income Summary
> 718    Uncollectible Accounts Expense

3. Determine the expected net realizable value of the accounts receivable as of December 31.
4. Assuming that instead of basing the provision for uncollectible accounts on an analysis of receivables, the adjusting entry on December 31 had been based on an estimated expense of 1/2 of 1% of the net sales of $3,100,000 for the year, determine the following:
   a. Uncollectible accounts expense for the year.
   b. Balance in the allowance account after the adjustment of December 31.
   c. Expected net realizable value of the accounts receivable as of December 31.

**PROBLEM 8-2A**
*Aging of receivables; estimating allowance for doubtful accounts*

**Objective 4**

**SPREADSHEET**

✓ 3. $65,212

Blue Ribbon Flies Company supplies flies and fishing gear to sporting goods stores and outfitters throughout the western United States. The accounts receivable clerk for Blue Ribbon Flies prepared the partially completed aging-of-receivables schedule as of the end of business on December 31, 2006, shown at the top of the following page.
  The following accounts were unintentionally omitted from the aging schedule.

| Customer | Due Date | Balance |
|---|---|---|
| Able Sports & Flies | June 15, 2006 | 3,500 |
| Red Tag Sporting Goods | July 28, 2006 | 4,000 |
| Highlite Flies | Sept. 11, 2006 | 2,500 |
| Midge Co. | Sept. 30, 2006 | 3,100 |
| Snake River Outfitters | Oct. 7, 2006 | 4,500 |
| Pheasant Tail Sports | Oct. 27, 2006 | 1,600 |
| Big Sky Sports | Oct. 30, 2006 | 2,000 |
| Ross Sports | Nov. 18, 2006 | 500 |
| Sawyer's Pheasant Tail | Nov. 26, 2006 | 2,800 |
| Tent Caddis Outfitters | Nov. 29, 2006 | 3,500 |
| Wulff Company | Dec. 10, 2006 | 1,000 |
| Zug Bug Sports | Jan. 6, 2007 | 6,200 |

| Customer | Balance | Not Past Due | Days Past Due | | | | |
| | | | 1–30 | 31–60 | 61–90 | 91–120 | Over 120 |
|---|---|---|---|---|---|---|---|
| Alpha Fishery | 5,000 | 5,000 | | | | | |
| Brown Trout Sports | 6,400 | | | 6,400 | | | |
| Zinger Sports | 2,900 | | 2,900 | | | | |
| Subtotals | 580,000 | 248,600 | 147,250 | 98,750 | 33,300 | 29,950 | 22,150 |

Blue Ribbon Flies Company has a past history of uncollectible accounts by age category, as follows:

| Age Class | Percentage Uncollectible |
|---|---|
| Not past due | 1% |
| 1–30 days past due | 4 |
| 31–60 days past due | 8 |
| 61–90 days past due | 25 |
| 91–120 days past due | 40 |
| Over 120 days past due | 80 |

**Instructions**
1. Determine the number of days past due for each of the preceding accounts.
2. Complete the aging-of-receivables schedule.
3. Estimate the allowance for doubtful accounts, based on the aging-of-receivables schedule.
4. Assume that the allowance for doubtful accounts for Blue Ribbon Flies Company has a debit balance of $2,800 before adjustment on December 31, 2006. Journalize the adjusting entry for uncollectible accounts.

**PROBLEM 8-3A**
*Compare two methods of accounting for uncollectible receivables*

**Objectives 4, 5**

SPREADSHEET

✓ *1. Year 4: Balance of allowance account, end of year, $14,625.*

Kiohertz Company, a telephone service and supply company, has just completed its fourth year of operations. The direct write-off method of recording uncollectible accounts expense has been used during the entire period. Because of substantial increases in sales volume and amount of uncollectible accounts, the firm is considering changing to the allowance method. Information is requested as to the effect that an annual provision of 3/4% of sales would have had on the amount of uncollectible accounts expense reported for each of the past four years. It is also considered desirable to know what the balance of Allowance for Doubtful Accounts would have been at the end of each year. The following data have been obtained from the accounts:

| Year | Sales | Uncollectible Accounts Written Off | Year of Origin of Accounts Receivable Written Off as Uncollectible | | | |
| | | | 1st | 2nd | 3rd | 4th |
|---|---|---|---|---|---|---|
| 1st | $ 850,000 | $3,500 | $3,500 | | | |
| 2nd | 960,000 | 3,250 | 1,900 | $1,350 | | |
| 3rd | 1,200,000 | 6,300 | 800 | 4,500 | $1,000 | |
| 4th | 1,800,000 | 8,400 | | 1,800 | 2,550 | $4,050 |

## Instructions

1. Assemble the desired data, using the following column headings:

| | Uncollectible Accounts Expense | | | Balance of |
| --- | --- | --- | --- | --- |
| Year | Expense Actually Reported | Expense Based on Estimate | Increase (Decrease) in Amount of Expense | Allowance Account, End of Year |

2. ▬▬▶ Experience during the first four years of operations indicated that the receivables were either collected within two years or had to be written off as uncollectible. Does the estimate of 3/4% of sales appear to be reasonably close to the actual experience with uncollectible accounts originating during the first two years? Explain.

**PROBLEM 8-4A**
*Details of notes receivable and related entries*
**Objectives 6, 7**

**SPREADSHEET**

✓ 1. Note 2: Due date, July 18; Interest due at maturity, $126.

Matrix Co. wholesales bathroom fixtures. During the current fiscal year, Matrix Co. received the following notes.

| | Date | Face Amount | Term | Interest Rate |
| --- | --- | --- | --- | --- |
| 1. | March 7 | $24,000 | 60 days | 6% |
| 2. | June 18 | 16,800 | 30 days | 9% |
| 3. | Aug. 30 | 10,200 | 120 days | 6% |
| 4. | Oct. 31 | 27,000 | 60 days | 9% |
| 5. | Nov. 19 | 12,000 | 60 days | 6% |
| 6. | Dec. 23 | 16,000 | 30 days | 9% |

### Instructions

1. Determine for each note (a) the due date and (b) the amount of interest due at maturity, identifying each note by number.
2. Journalize the entry to record the dishonor of Note (3) on its due date.
3. Journalize the adjusting entry to record the accrued interest on Notes (5) and (6) on December 31.
4. Journalize the entries to record the receipt of the amounts due on Notes (5) and (6) in January.

**PROBLEM 8-5A**
*Notes receivable entries*
**Objective 7**

The following data relate to notes receivable and interest for Clyde Park Optic Co., a cable manufacturer and supplier. (All notes are dated as of the day they are received.)

June  4. Received an $18,800, 9%, 60-day note on account.
July 15. Received a $27,000, 10%, 120-day note on account.
Aug.  3. Received $19,082 on note of June 4.
Sept.  1. Received a $24,000, 9%, 60-day note on account.
Oct. 31. Received $24,360 on note of September 1.
Nov.  5. Received a $9,600, 7%, 30-day note on account.
    12. Received $27,900 on note of July 15.
    30. Received a $15,000, 10%, 30-day note on account.
Dec.  5. Received $9,656 on note of November 5.
    30. Received $15,125 on note of November 30.

### Instructions
Journalize entries to record the transactions.

**PROBLEM 8-6A**
*Sales and notes receivable transactions*
**Objective 7**

The following were selected from among the transactions completed by Rimrock Co. during the current year. Rimrock Co. sells and installs home and business security systems.

Jan.  10. Loaned $12,000 cash to Brenda Norby, receiving a 90-day, 8% note.
Feb.  4. Sold merchandise on account to Emerson and Son, $24,000. The cost of the merchandise sold was $14,400.

Feb. 12. Sold merchandise on account to Gwyn Co., $25,000. The cost of merchandise sold was $15,000.

Mar. 6. Accepted a 60-day, 6% note for $24,000 from Emerson and Son on account.

14. Accepted a 60-day, 12% note for $25,000 from Gwyn Co. on account.

Apr. 10. Received the interest due from Brenda Norby and a new 90-day, 9% note as a renewal of the loan of January 10. (Record both the debit and the credit to the notes receivable account.)

May 5. Received from Emerson and Son the amount due on the note of March 6.

13. Gwyn Co. dishonored its note dated March 14.

June 12. Received from Gwyn Co. the amount owed on the dishonored note, plus interest for 30 days at 12% computed on the maturity value of the note.

July 9. Received from Brenda Norby the amount due on her note of April 10.

Aug. 24. Sold merchandise on account to Haggerty Co., $10,200. The cost of the merchandise sold was $6,000.

Sept. 3. Received from Haggerty Co. the amount of the invoice of August 24, less 1% discount.

### Instructions

Journalize the transactions. Round to the nearest dollar.

# Problems Series B

**PROBLEM 8-1B**
*Entries related to uncollectible accounts*

**Objective 4**

✓ 3. $857,050

The following transactions, adjusting entries, and closing entries were completed by The Eagle Rock Gallery during the year ended December 31, 2006:

Feb. 24. Reinstated the account of Dina Ibis, which had been written off in the preceding year as uncollectible. Journalized the receipt of $1,025 cash in full payment of Ibis's account.

Mar. 29. Wrote off the $7,500 balance owed by Hoxsey Co., which is bankrupt.

July 10. Received 40% of the $12,000 balance owed by Foust Co., a bankrupt business, and wrote off the remainder as uncollectible.

Sept. 8. Reinstated the account of Louis Sabo, which had been written off two years earlier as uncollectible. Recorded the receipt of $1,200 cash in full payment.

Dec. 31. Wrote off the following accounts as uncollectible (compound entry): Emery Co., $8,050; Darigold Co., $6,260; Zheng Furniture, $3,775; Carey Wenzel, $2,820.

31. Based on an analysis of the $887,550 of accounts receivable, it was estimated that $30,500 will be uncollectible. Journalized the adjusting entry.

31. Journalized the entry to close the appropriate account to Income Summary.

### Instructions

1. Post the January 1 credit balance of $28,500 to Allowance for Doubtful Accounts.
2. Journalize the transactions and the adjusting and closing entries. Post each entry that affects the following three selected accounts and determine the new balances:

| | |
|---|---|
| 115 | Allowance for Doubtful Accounts |
| 313 | Income Summary |
| 718 | Uncollectible Accounts Expense |

3. Determine the expected net realizable value of the accounts receivable as of December 31.
4. Assuming that instead of basing the provision for uncollectible accounts on an analysis of receivables, the adjusting entry on December 31 had been based on

an estimated expense of 1/4 of 1% of the net sales of $12,750,000 for the year, determine the following:

a. Uncollectible accounts expense for the year.

b. Balance in the allowance account after the adjustment of December 31.

c. Expected net realizable value of the accounts receivable as of December 31.

**PROBLEM 8-2B**
*Aging of receivables; estimating allowance for doubtful accounts*

**Objective 4**

SPREADSHEET

✓ 3. $54,473

Vanity Wigs Company supplies wigs and hair care products to beauty salons throughout California and the Pacific Northwest. The accounts receivable clerk for Vanity Wigs prepared the following partially completed aging-of-receivables schedule as of the end of business on December 31, 2006:

| Customer | Balance | Not Past Due | Days Past Due | | | | |
|---|---|---|---|---|---|---|---|
| | | | 1–30 | 31–60 | 61–90 | 91–120 | Over 120 |
| Adams Beauty | 8,000 | 8,000 | | | | | |
| Barkell Wigs | 7,500 | | | 7,500 | | | |
| Zimmer's Beauty | 2,900 | | 2,900 | | | | |
| Subtotals | 880,000 | 498,600 | 197,250 | 88,750 | 43,300 | 29,950 | 22,150 |

The following accounts were unintentionally omitted from the aging schedule.

| Customer | Due Date | Balance |
|---|---|---|
| Allison's Uniquely Yours | July 6, 2006 | 1,000 |
| Western Designs | Aug. 10, 2006 | 2,500 |
| Treat's | Sept. 6, 2006 | 1,800 |
| Nicole's Beauty Store | Sept. 29, 2006 | 4,000 |
| Ginburg Supreme | Oct. 10, 2006 | 1,500 |
| Jeremy's Hair Products | Oct. 20, 2006 | 600 |
| Hairy's Hair Care | Oct. 31, 2006 | 2,000 |
| Southern Images | Nov. 18, 2006 | 1,200 |
| Lopez's Blond Bombs | Nov. 23, 2006 | 1,800 |
| Josset Ritz | Nov. 30, 2006 | 3,500 |
| Cool Designs | Dec. 4, 2006 | 1,000 |
| Buttram Images | Jan. 3, 2007 | 5,200 |

Vanity Wigs has a past history of uncollectible accounts by age category, as follows:

| Age Class | Percentage Uncollectible |
|---|---|
| Not past due | 1% |
| 1–30 days past due | 4 |
| 31–60 days past due | 6 |
| 61–90 days past due | 15 |
| 91–120 days past due | 30 |
| Over 120 days past due | 70 |

**Instructions**

1. Determine the number of days past due for each of the preceding accounts.

2. Complete the aging-of-receivables schedule.

3. Estimate the allowance for doubtful accounts, based on the aging-of-receivables schedule.

4. Assume that the allowance for doubtful accounts for Vanity Wigs has a credit balance of $8,350 before adjustment on December 31, 2006. Journalize the adjusting entry for uncollectible accounts.

## PROBLEM 8-3B
*Compare two methods of accounting for uncollectible receivables*

**Objectives 4, 5**

SPREADSHEET

✓ 1. Year 4: Balance of allowance account, end of year, $5,350

Blue Goose Company, which operates a chain of 50 electronics supply stores, has just completed its fourth year of operations. The direct write-off method of recording uncollectible accounts expense has been used during the entire period. Because of substantial increases in sales volume and amount of uncollectible accounts, the firm is considering changing to the allowance method. Information is requested as to the effect that an annual provision of 1/2% of sales would have had on the amount of uncollectible accounts expense reported for each of the past four years. It is also considered desirable to know what the balance of Allowance for Doubtful Accounts would have been at the end of each year. The following data have been obtained from the accounts:

| Year | Sales | Uncollectible Accounts Written Off | Year of Origin of Accounts Receivable Written Off as Uncollectible | | | |
| | | | 1st | 2nd | 3rd | 4th |
|---|---|---|---|---|---|---|
| 1st | $ 650,000 | $1,000 | $1,000 | | | |
| 2nd | 920,000 | 2,650 | 750 | $1,900 | | |
| 3rd | 1,050,000 | 6,200 | 1,800 | 1,400 | $3,000 | |
| 4th | 2,250,000 | 9,150 | | 1,900 | 2,950 | $4,300 |

### Instructions
1. Assemble the desired data, using the following column headings:

| | Uncollectible Accounts Expense | | | Balance of Allowance Account, End of Year |
| Year | Expense Actually Reported | Expense Based on Estimate | Increase (Decrease) in Amount of Expense | |
|---|---|---|---|---|

2. ▬▬➤ Experience during the first four years of operations indicated that the receivables were either collected within two years or had to be written off as uncollectible. Does the estimate of 1/2% of sales appear to be reasonably close to the actual experience with uncollectible accounts originating during the first two years? Explain.

## PROBLEM 8-4B
*Details of notes receivable and related entries*

**Objectives 6, 7**

SPREADSHEET

✓ 1. Note 2: Due date, Sept. 8; Interest due at maturity, $300

Incubate Co. produces advertising videos. During the last six months of the current fiscal year, Incubate Co. received the following notes.

| | Date | Face Amount | Term | Interest Rate |
|---|---|---|---|---|
| 1. | May 23 | $18,000 | 45 days | 8% |
| 2. | July 10 | 20,000 | 60 days | 9% |
| 3. | Aug. 8 | 36,000 | 90 days | 6% |
| 4. | Sept. 16 | 20,000 | 90 days | 7% |
| 5. | Nov. 23 | 18,000 | 60 days | 9% |
| 6. | Dec. 18 | 48,000 | 60 days | 12% |

### Instructions
1. Determine for each note (a) the due date and (b) the amount of interest due at maturity, identifying each note by number.
2. Journalize the entry to record the dishonor of Note (3) on its due date.
3. Journalize the adjusting entry to record the accrued interest on Notes (5) and (6) on December 31.
4. Journalize the entries to record the receipt of the amounts due on Notes (5) and (6) in January and February.

## PROBLEM 8-5B
*Notes receivable entries*

**Objective 7**

The following data relate to notes receivable and interest for Sciatic Co., a financial services company. (All notes are dated as of the day they are received.)

Mar. 3. Received a $14,000, 9%, 60-day note on account.
21. Received a $9,500, 8%, 90-day note on account.
May 2. Received $14,210 on note of March 3.
16. Received a $40,000, 7%, 90-day note on account.
31. Received a $6,000, 8%, 30-day note on account.
June 19. Received $9,690 on note of March 21.
30. Received $6,040 on note of May 31.
July 1. Received a $12,000, 12%, 30-day note on account.
31. Received $12,120 on note of July 1.
Aug. 14. Received $40,700 on note of May 16.

**Instructions**
Journalize the entries to record the transactions.

**PROBLEM 8-6B**
*Sales and notes receivable transactions*

**Objective 7**

P.A.S.S.

The following were selected from among the transactions completed during the current year by Westphal Co., an appliance wholesale company:

Jan. 6. Sold merchandise on account to Alta Co., $10,500. The cost of merchandise sold was $6,300.
Mar. 9. Accepted a 60-day, 8% note for $10,500 from Alta Co. on account.
May 8. Received from Alta Co. the amount due on the note of March 9.
June 1. Sold merchandise on account to Witmer's for $8,000. The cost of merchandise sold was $4,800.
5. Loaned $11,000 cash to Dru York, receiving a 30-day, 6% note.
11. Received from Witmer's the amount due on the invoice of June 1, less 2% discount.
July 5. Received the interest due from Dru York and a new 60-day, 9% note as a renewal of the loan of June 5. (Record both the debit and the credit to the notes receivable account.)
Sept. 3. Received from Dru York the amount due on her note of July 5.
8. Sold merchandise on account to Rochin Co., $10,000. The cost of merchandise sold was $6,000.
Oct. 8. Accepted a 60-day, 6% note for $10,000 from Rochin Co. on account.
Dec. 7. Rochin Co. dishonored the note dated October 8.
28. Received from Rochin Co. the amount owed on the dishonored note, plus interest for 21 days at 9% computed on the maturity value of the note.

**Instructions**
Journalize the transactions. Round to the nearest dollar.

# Special Activities

**ACTIVITY 8-1**
*Ethics and professional conduct in business*

ETHICS

Precilla Strauss, vice-president of operations for Sturgis National Bank, has instructed the bank's computer programmer to use a 365-day year to compute interest on depository accounts (payables). Precilla also instructed the programmer to use a 360-day year to compute interest on loans (receivables).
➤ Discuss whether Precilla is behaving in a professional manner.

**ACTIVITY 8-2**
*Collecting accounts receivable*

The following is an excerpt from a conversation between the office manager, Tamie Mauro, and the president of Stonecipher Construction Supplies Co., Bruce Vogel. Stonecipher sells building supplies to local contractors.

*Tamie:* Bruce, we're going to have to do something about these overdue accounts receivable. One-third of our accounts are over 60 days past due, and I've had accounts that have stayed open for almost a year!

*Bruce:* I didn't realize it was that bad. Any ideas?

*Tamie:* Well, we could stop giving credit. Make everyone pay with cash or a credit card. We accept MasterCard and Visa already, but only the walk-in customers use them. Almost all of the contractors put purchases on their bills.

*Bruce:* Yes, but we've been allowing credit for years. As far as I know, all of our competitors allow contractors credit. If we stopped giving credit, we'd lose many of our contractors. They'd just go elsewhere. You know, some of these guys run up bills as high as $50,000 or $60,000. There's no way they could put that kind of money on a credit card.

*Tamie:* That's a good point. But we've got to do something.

*Bruce:* How many of the contractor accounts do you actually end up writing off as uncollectible?

*Tamie:* Not many. Almost all eventually pay. It's just that they take so long!

➤ Suggest one or more solutions to Stonecipher Construction Supplies Co.'s problem concerning the collection of accounts receivable.

---

**ACTIVITY 8-3**
*Value of receivables*

The following is an excerpt from a conversation between Pam Cahill, the president and owner of Mullion Wholesale Co., and Eric Hogg, Mullion controller. The conversation took place on January 3, 2006, shortly after Eric began preparing the financial statements for the year ending December 31, 2005.

*Eric:* Pam, I've completed my analysis of the collectibility of our accounts receivable. My staff and I estimate that the allowance for doubtful accounts should be somewhere between $60,000 and $90,000. Right now, the balance of the allowance account is $18,000.

*Pam:* Oh, no! We are already below the estimated earnings projection I gave the bank last year. We used that as a basis for obtaining a $300,000 loan. They're going to be upset! Is there any way we can increase the allowance without the adjustment increasing expenses?

*Eric:* I'm afraid not. The allowance can only be increased by debiting the uncollectible accounts expense account.

*Pam:* Well, I guess we're stuck. The bank will just have to live with it. But let's increase the allowance by only $42,000. That gets us into our range of estimates with the minimum expense increase.

*Eric:* Pam, there is one more thing we need to discuss.

*Pam:* What now?

*Eric:* Ross, my staff accountant, noticed that you haven't made any payments on your receivable for over a year. Also, it has increased from $20,000 last year to $70,000. Ross thinks we ought to reclassify it as a noncurrent asset and report it as an "other receivable."

*Pam:* What's the problem? Didn't we just include it in accounts receivable last year?

*Eric:* Yes, but last year it was immaterial.

*Pam:* Look, I'll make a $50,000 payment next week. So let's report it as we did last year.

➤ If you were Eric, how would you address Pam's suggestions?

---

**ACTIVITY 8-4**
*Estimate uncollectible accounts*

For several years, sales have been on a "cash only" basis. On January 1, 2003, however, Filet Co. began offering credit on terms of n/30. The amount of the adjusting entry to record the estimated uncollectible receivables at the end of each year has been 1/4 of 1% of credit sales, which is the rate reported as the average for the industry. Credit sales and the year-end credit balances in Allowance for Doubtful Accounts for the past four years are as follows:

| Year | Credit Sales | Allowance for Doubtful Accounts |
|------|-------------|-------------------------------|
| 2003 | $6,800,000 | $ 7,100 |
| 2004 | 7,000,000 | 13,200 |
| 2005 | 7,100,000 | 18,900 |
| 2006 | 7,250,000 | 27,350 |

Lesley Quade, president of Filet Co., is concerned that the method used to account for and write off uncollectible receivables is unsatisfactory. She has asked for your advice in the analysis of past operations in this area and for recommendations for change.

1. Determine the amount of (a) the addition to Allowance for Doubtful Accounts and (b) the accounts written off for each of the four years.
2. a. ▸ Advise Lesley Quade as to whether the estimate of 1/4 of 1% of credit sales appears reasonable.
   b. ▸ Assume that after discussing (a) with Lesley Quade, she asked you what action might be taken to determine what the balance of Allowance for Doubtful Accounts should be at December 31, 2006, and what possible changes, if any, you might recommend in accounting for uncollectible receivables. How would you respond?

**ACTIVITY 8-5**
*Granting credit*

GROUP ACTIVITY

In groups of three or four, determine how credit is typically granted to customers. Interview an individual responsible for granting credit for a bank, a department store, an automobile dealer, or other business in your community. You should ask such questions as the following:

1. What procedures are used to decide whether to grant credit to a customer?
2. What procedures are used to try to collect from customers who are delinquent in their payments?
3. Approximately what percentage of customers' accounts are written off as uncollectible in a year?

▸ Summarize your findings in a report to the class.

**ACTIVITY 8-6**
*Collection of receivables*

REAL WORLD        INTERNET

Go to the Web page of two department store chains, **Federated Department Stores Inc.** and **Dillard's Inc.** The Internet sites for these companies are linked to the text's Web site at **http://warren.swlearning.com**.

Using the financial information provided at each site, calculate the most recent accounts receivable turnover for each company, and identify which company is collecting its receivables faster.

**ACTIVITY 8-7**
*Accounts receivable turnover and days' sales in receivables*

REAL WORLD

**Earthlink, Inc.,** is a nationwide Internet Service Provider (ISP). Earthlink provides a variety of services to its customers, including narrowband access, broadband or high-speed access, and Web hosting services. For the years ending December 31, 2002 and 2001, Earthlink reported the following (in thousands):

| | Year Ending December 31, | |
|---|---|---|
| | 2002 | 2001 |
| Net sales | $1,357,421 | $1,244,928 |
| Accounts receivable at end of year | 59,014 | 46,736 |

Assume that the accounts receivable (in thousands) were $59,211 at January 1, 2001.

1. Compute the accounts receivable turnover for 2002 and 2001. Round to one decimal place.

2. Compute the days' sales in receivables at the end of 2002 and 2001.
3. What conclusions can be drawn from (1) and (2) regarding Earthlink's efficiency in collecting receivables?
4. Given the nature of Earthlink's operations, do you believe Earthlink's accounts receivable turnover ratio would be higher or lower than a typical manufacturing company, such as **Boeing** or **Kellogg**? Explain.

**ACTIVITY 8-8**
*Accounts receivable turnover*

**REAL WORLD**     **INTERNET**

The accounts receivable turnover ratio will vary across companies, depending upon the nature of the company's operations. For example, an accounts receivable turnover of six for an Internet Services Provider is unacceptable, but might be excellent for a manufacturer of specialty milling equipment. A list of well-known companies is listed below.

| | | |
|---|---|---|
| Alcoa | Delta Air Lines | Kroger |
| AutoZone | Gillette | Maytag Corporation |
| Barnes & Noble | Home Depot | Wal-Mart |
| Coca-Cola | IBM | Whirlpool |

1. Using the **PriceWaterhouseCoopers** Web site, **http://edgarscan.pwcglobal .com**, look up each company by entering its name. Click on each company's name and then scroll down to the bottom of the page to "Set Preferences." Select "Receivables Turnover" in the Ratios list. Then click "Save Preferences."
2. Categorize each of the preceding companies as to whether its turnover ratio is above or below 15.
3. Based upon (2), identify a characteristic of companies with accounts receivable turnover ratios above 15.

# Answers to Self-Examination Questions

1. **B**  The estimate of uncollectible accounts, $8,500 (answer C), is the amount of the desired balance of Allowance for Doubtful Accounts after adjustment. The amount of the current provision to be made for uncollectible accounts expense is thus $6,000 (answer B), which is the amount that must be added to the Allowance for Doubtful Accounts credit balance of $2,500 (answer A) so that the account will have the desired balance of $8,500.

2. **B**  The amount expected to be realized from accounts receivable is the balance of Accounts Receivable, $100,000, less the balance of Allowance for Doubtful Accounts, $7,000, or $93,000 (answer B).

3. **C**  Maturity value is the amount that is due at the maturity or due date. The maturity value of $10,300 (answer C) is determined as follows:

| | |
|---|---|
| Face amount of note | $10,000 |
| Plus interest ($10,000 × 0.12 × 90/360) | 300 |
| Maturity value of note | $10,300 |

4. **C**  November 3 is the due date of a $12,000, 90-day, 8% note receivable dated August 5 [26 days in August (31 days − 5 days) + 30 days in September + 31 days in October + 3 days in November].

5. **B**  If a note is dishonored, Accounts Receivable is debited for the maturity value of the note (answer B). The maturity value of the note is its face value (answer A) plus the accrued interest. The maturity value of the note less accrued interest (answer C) is equal to the face value of the note. The maturity value of the note plus accrued interest (answer D) is incorrect, since the interest would be added twice.

# 9

# INVENTORIES

## objectives

*After studying this chapter, you should be able to:*

1 Summarize and provide examples of internal control procedures that apply to inventories.

2 Describe the effect of inventory errors on the financial statements.

3 Describe three inventory cost flow assumptions and how they impact the income statement and balance sheet.

4 Compute the cost of inventory under the perpetual inventory system, using the following costing methods: first-in, first-out; last-in, first-out; and average cost.

5 Compute the cost of inventory under the periodic inventory system, using the following costing methods: first-in, first-out; last-in, first-out; and average cost.

6 Compare and contrast the use of the three inventory costing methods.

7 Compute the proper valuation of inventory at other than cost, using the lower-of-cost-or-market and net realizable value concepts.

8 Prepare a balance sheet presentation of merchandise inventory.

9 Estimate the cost of inventory, using the retail method and the gross profit method.

10 Compute and interpret the inventory turnover ratio and the number of days' sales in inventory.

**A**ssume that you purchased a Compact Disc (CD)/Receiver in June. You planned on attaching two pairs of speakers to the system. Initially, however, you could afford only one pair of speakers, which cost $160. In October, you purchased the second pair of speakers at a cost of $180.

Over the holidays, someone broke into your home and stole one pair of speakers. Luckily, your renters/homeowners insurance policy will cover the theft, but the insurance company needs to know the cost of the speakers that were stolen.

All of the speakers are identical. To respond to the insurance company, however, you will need to identify which pair of speakers was stolen. Was it the first pair, which cost $160? Or was it the second pair, which cost $180? Whichever assumption you make may determine the amount that you receive from the insurance company.

Merchandising businesses make similar assumptions when identical merchandise is purchased at different costs. At the end of a period, some of the merchandise will be in inventory and some will have been sold. But which costs relate to the sold merchandise and which costs relate to the merchandise in inventory? The company's assumption can involve large dollar amounts and thus can have a significant impact on the financial statements. For example, **The Home Depot, Inc.**, has merchandise inventories that total almost $8.3 billion, while **Xerox Corporation**'s inventories total over $1.2 million.

In this chapter, we will discuss such issues as how to determine the cost of merchandise in inventory and the cost of merchandise sold. However, we begin this chapter by discussing internal controls over merchandise inventory.

# Internal Control of Inventories

**objective** **1**

Summarize and provide examples of internal control procedures that apply to inventories.

**REAL WORLD**

**Circuit City**'s inventory represents over 45% of its current assets and over 35% of its total assets. Circuit City's cost of merchandise sold represents over 75% of its net sales.

The cost of inventory is a significant item in many businesses' financial statements. What do we mean by the term inventory? **Inventory** is used to indicate (1) merchandise held for sale in the normal course of business and (2) materials in the process of production or held for production. In this chapter, we focus primarily on inventory of merchandise purchased for resale.

What costs should be included in inventory? As we have illustrated in earlier chapters, the cost of merchandise is its purchase price, less any purchases discounts. These costs are usually the largest portion of the inventory cost. Merchandise inventory also includes other costs, such as transportation, import duties, and insurance against losses in transit.

Not only must the cost inventory be determined, but good internal control over inventory must also be maintained. Two primary objectives of internal control over inventory are safeguarding the inventory and properly reporting it in the financial statements. These internal controls can be either preventive or detective in nature. A **preventive control** is designed to prevent errors or misstatements from occurring. A **detective control** is designed to detect an error or misstatement after it has occurred.

Control over inventory should begin as soon as the inventory is received. Prenumbered receiving reports should be completed by the company's receiving department in order to establish the initial accountability for the inventory. To make sure the inventory received is what was ordered, each receiving report should agree with the company's original purchase order for the merchandise. Likewise, the price at which the inventory was ordered, as shown on the purchase order, should be compared to the price at which the vendor billed the company, as shown on the vendor's invoice. After the receiving report, purchase order, and vendor's invoice have been reconciled, the company should record the inventory and related account payable in the accounting records.

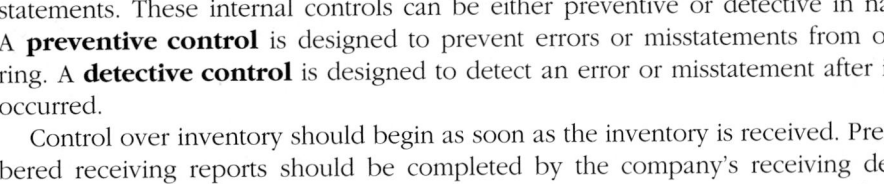

Jewelry stores normally keep diamond rings, bracelets, and other items in a locked glass case. Is this a preventive or a detective control?

-------------------------------------------------------------

*This is a preventive control to protect against theft (shoplifting).*

Controls for safeguarding inventory include developing and using security measures to prevent inventory damage or employee theft. For example, inventory should be stored in a warehouse or other area to which access is restricted to authorized employees. The removal of merchandise from the warehouse should be controlled by using requisition forms, which should be properly authorized. The storage area should also be climate controlled to prevent damage from heat or cold. Further, when the business is not operating or is not open, the storage area should be locked.

When shopping, you may have noticed how retail stores protect inventory from customer theft. Retail stores often use such devices as two-way mirrors, cameras, and security guards. High-priced items are often displayed in locked cabinets. Retail clothing stores often place plastic alarm tags on valuable items such as leather coats. Sensors at the exit doors set off alarms if the tags have not been removed by the clerk. These controls are designed to prevent customers from shoplifting.

Using a perpetual inventory system for merchandise also provides an effective means of control over inventory. The amount of each type of merchandise is always readily available in a subsidiary **inventory ledger**. In addition, the subsidiary ledger can be an aid in maintaining inventory quantities at proper levels. Frequently comparing balances with predetermined minimum and maximum levels allows for timely reordering and prevents ordering excess inventory.

To ensure the accuracy of the amount of inventory reported in the financial statements, a merchandising business should take a *physical inventory* (i.e., count the merchandise). In a perpetual inventory system, the physical inventory is compared to the recorded inventory in order to determine the amount of shrinkage or shortage. If the inventory shrinkage is unusually large, management can investigate further and take any necessary corrective action. Knowledge that a physical inventory will be taken also helps prevent employee thefts or misuses of inventory.

How does a business "take" a physical inventory? The first step in this process is to determine the quantity of each kind of merchandise owned by the business. A common practice is to use teams of two persons. One person determines the quantity, and the other lists the quantity and description on inventory count sheets. Quantities of high-cost items are usually verified by supervisors or a second count team.

What merchandise should be included in inventory? All the merchandise *owned* by the business on the inventory date should be included. For

> All merchandise <u>owned</u> by a business should be included in the business's inventory.

merchandise in transit, the party (the seller or the buyer) who has title to the merchandise on the inventory date is the owner. To determine who has title, it may be necessary to examine purchases and sales invoices of the last few days of the current period and the first few days of the following period.

As we discussed in an earlier chapter, shipping terms determine when title passes. When goods are purchased or sold **FOB shipping point**, title passes to the buyer when the goods are shipped. When the terms are **FOB destination**, title passes to the buyer when the goods are delivered.

To illustrate, assume that Roper Co. orders $25,000 of merchandise on December 28, 2006. The merchandise is shipped FOB shipping point by the seller on December 30 and arrives at Roper Co.'s warehouse on January 4, 2007. As a result, the merchandise is not counted by the inventory crew on December 31, the end of

**REAL WORLD**

Sam's Club and Wal-Mart stores use a greeter at the entry of each store to welcome customers. The greeter also serves as a preventive control by asking customers not to bring in packages or other bags, which could be used for shoplifting.

**REAL WORLD**

Most companies take their physical inventories when their inventory levels are the lowest. For example, most retailers take their physical inventory in late January or early February, which is after the holiday selling season but before restocking for spring.

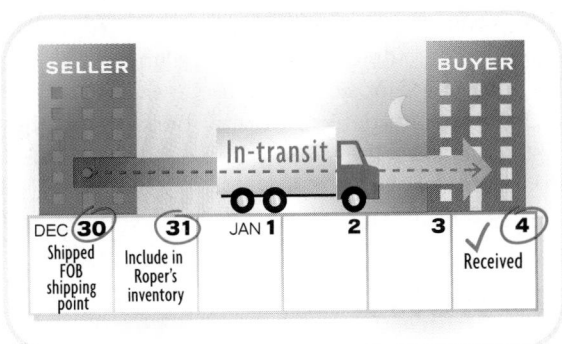

Roper Co.'s fiscal year. However, the $25,000 of merchandise should be included in Roper's inventory because title has passed. Roper Co. should record the merchandise in transit on December 31, debiting Merchandise Inventory and crediting Accounts Payable for $25,000.

Manufacturers sometimes ship merchandise to retailers who act as the manufacturer's agent when selling the merchandise. The manufacturer retains title until the goods are sold. Such merchandise is said to be shipped *on consignment* to the retailers. The unsold merchandise is a part of the manufacturer's (consignor's) inventory, even though the merchandise is in the hands of the retailers. The consigned merchandise should not be included in the retailer's (consignee's) inventory.

# Effect of Inventory Errors on Financial Statements

objective **2**

Describe the effect of inventory errors on the financial statements.

Any errors in the inventory count will affect both the balance sheet and the income statement. For example, an error in the physical inventory will misstate the ending inventory, current assets, and total assets on the balance sheet. This is because the physical inventory is the basis for recording the adjusting entry for inventory shrinkage. Also, an error in taking the physical inventory misstates the cost of goods sold, gross profit, and net income on the income statement. In addition, because net income is closed to the owner's equity at the end of the period, owner's equity will also be misstated on the balance sheet. This misstatement of owner's equity will equal the misstatement of the ending inventory, current assets, and total assets.

Inventory fraud reared its ugly head during the early 2000s. Officers of **HealthSouth**, one of the largest healthcare providers in the United States, have been indicted for falsifying financial information, including allegedly making false entries in the accounting records to artificially inflate the value of inventory. A former financial officer of **Network Associates**, a supplier of security software for e-businesses, plead guilty to a scheme involving secret fees paid to distributors to hold excess inventory and prevent returns of unsold products. Senior officers of **Rite Aid Corporation**, a drugstore chain, plead guilty to a variety of schemes, including fraudulently taking purchase discounts and allowances on good merchandise claimed as outdated or damaged.

To illustrate, assume that in taking the physical inventory on December 31, 2006, Sapra Company incorrectly recorded its physical inventory as $115,000 instead of the correct amount of $125,000. As a result, the merchandise inventory, current assets, and total assets reported on the December 31, 2006 balance sheet would be understated by $10,000 ($125,000 − $115,000). Because the ending physical inventory is understated, the inventory shrinkage and the cost of merchandise sold will be overstated by $10,000. Thus, the gross profit and the net income for the year will be understated by $10,000. Since the net income is closed to owner's equity at the end of the period, the owner's equity on the December 31, 2006 balance sheet will also be understated by $10,000. The effects on Sapra Company's financial statements are summarized as follows:

At the end of 2006, the physical ending inventory of Melchor Co. was overstated by $25,000. What is the effect of this error on the financial statements?

----------------------------------------

*On the 2006 balance sheet, the merchandise inventory, current assets, total assets, and owner's equity are overstated by $25,000. On the income statement, the cost of merchandise sold is understated by $25,000, and the gross profit and net income are overstated by $25,000.*

|  | Amount of Misstatement |
|---|---|
| **Balance Sheet:** |  |
| Merchandise inventory understated | $(10,000) |
| Current assets understated | (10,000) |
| Total assets understated | (10,000) |
| Owner's equity understated | (10,000) |
|  |  |
| **Income Statement:** |  |
| Cost of merchandise sold overstated | $ 10,000 |
| Gross profit understated | (10,000) |
| Net income understated | (10,000) |

Now assume that in the preceding example the physical inventory had been *overstated* on December 31, 2006, by $10,000. That is, Sapra Company erroneously recorded its inventory as $135,000. In this case, the effects on the balance sheet and income statement would be just the *opposite* of those indicated above.

Errors in the physical inventory are normally detected in the period after they occur. In such cases, the financial statements of the prior year must be corrected. We will discuss such corrections in a later chapter.

# Inventory Cost Flow Assumptions

**objective 3**

Describe three inventory cost flow assumptions and how they impact the income statement and balance sheet.

A major accounting issue arises when identical units of merchandise are acquired at different unit costs during a period. In such cases, when an item is sold, it is necessary to determine its unit cost so that the proper accounting entry can be recorded. To illustrate, assume that three identical units of Item X are purchased during May, as shown below.

| | Item X | Units | Cost |
|---|---|---|---|
| May 10 | Purchase | 1 | $ 9 |
| 18 | Purchase | 1 | 13 |
| 24 | Purchase | 1 | 14 |
| | Total | 3 | $36 |
| | Average cost per unit | | $12 |

**REAL WORLD**

The specific identification method is normally used by automobile dealerships, jewelry stores, and art galleries.

Assume that one unit is sold on May 30 for $20. If this unit can be identified with a specific purchase, the **specific identification method** can be used to determine the cost of the unit sold. For example, if the unit sold was purchased on May 18, the cost assigned to the unit is $13 and the gross profit is $7 ($20 − $13). If, however, the unit sold was purchased on May 10, the cost assigned to the unit is $9 and the gross profit is $11 ($20 − $9).

The specific identification method is not practical unless each unit can be identified accurately. An automobile dealer, for example, may be able to use this method, since each automobile has a unique serial number. For many businesses, however, identical units cannot be separately identified, and a cost flow must be assumed. That is, which units have been sold and which units are still in inventory must be assumed.

There are three common cost flow assumptions used in business. Each of these assumptions is identified with an inventory costing method, as shown below.

| Cost Flow Assumption | 1. Cost flow is in the order in which the costs were incurred. | 2. Cost flow is in the reverse order in which the costs were incurred. | 3. Cost flow is an average of the costs. |
|---|---|---|---|
| Inventory Costing Method | First-in, first-out (fifo) | Last-in, first-out (lifo) | Average cost |

When the *first-in, first-out (fifo) method* is used, the ending inventory is made up of the most recent costs. When the *last-in, first-out (lifo) method* is used, the ending inventory is made up of the earliest costs. When the *average cost method* is used, the cost of the units in inventory is an average of the purchase costs.

To illustrate, we use the preceding example to prepare the income statement for May and the balance sheet as of May 31 for each of the cost flow methods, again assuming that one unit is sold. These financial statements are shown in Exhibit 1.

## •Exhibit 1   Effect of Inventory Costing Methods on Financial Statements

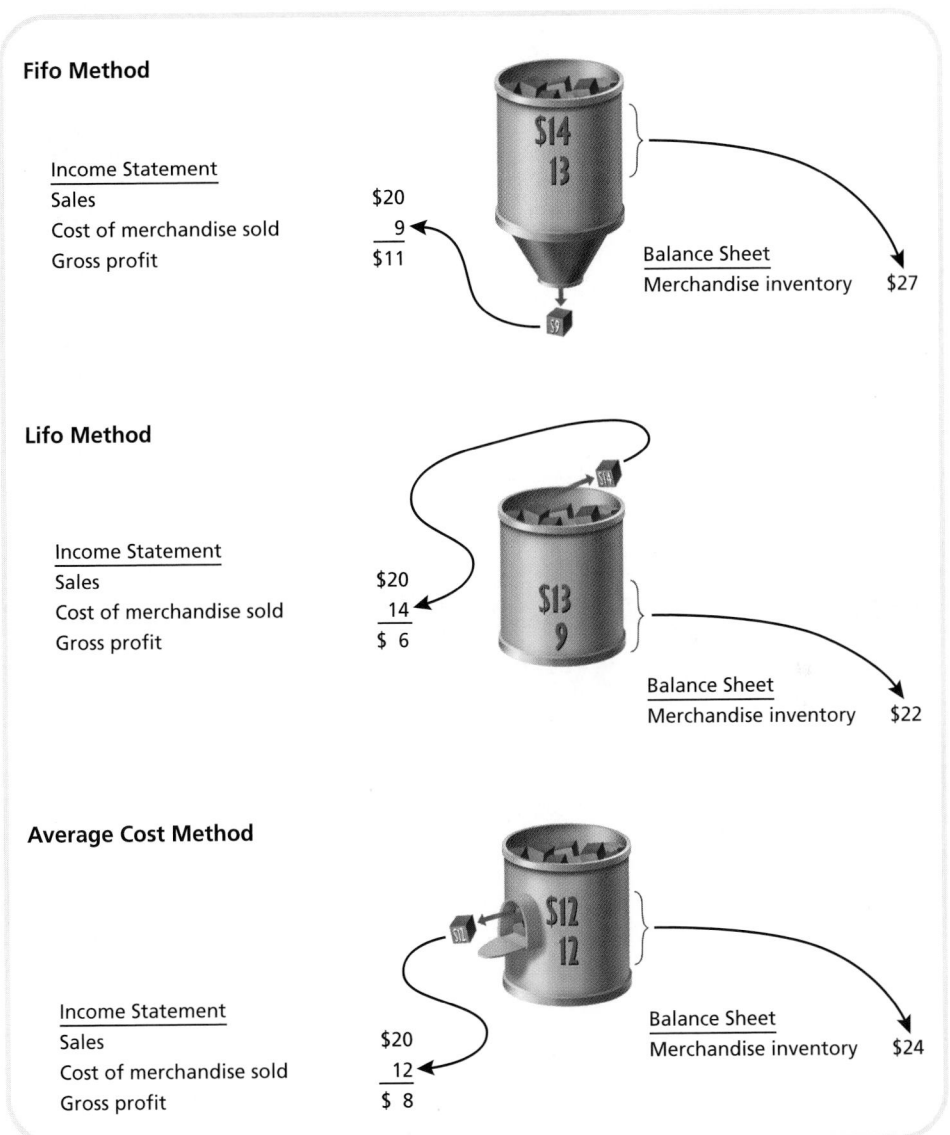

**Fifo Method**

Income Statement
| | |
|---|---|
| Sales | $20 |
| Cost of merchandise sold | 9 |
| Gross profit | $11 |

Balance Sheet
Merchandise inventory    $27

**Lifo Method**

Income Statement
| | |
|---|---|
| Sales | $20 |
| Cost of merchandise sold | 14 |
| Gross profit | $ 6 |

Balance Sheet
Merchandise inventory    $22

**Average Cost Method**

Income Statement
| | |
|---|---|
| Sales | $20 |
| Cost of merchandise sold | 12 |
| Gross profit | $ 8 |

Balance Sheet
Merchandise inventory    $24

My namesake, born in Bavaria in 1829, founded me as a dry-goods store in San Francisco in 1853. I was cranking out copper-riveted "waist overalls" in 1873. In 1912, I introduced "Koveralls," one-piece playsuits for tots. I entered the sportswear business in 1954, with my "denim family" line, and debuted bell-bottoms around 1969 and Dockers in 1986. I went public in 1971, only to become a private entity again later. Always progressive, I've been named one of America's most admired companies and employers. I have been supporting community charities for 148 years. Who am I? (Go to page 377 for answer.)

As you can see, the selection of an inventory costing method can have a significant impact on the financial statements. For this reason, the selection has important implications for managers and others in analyzing and interpreting the financial statements. The chart in Exhibit 2 shows the frequency with which fifo, lifo, and the average methods are used in practice.

•**Exhibit 2**   **Inventory Costing Methods***

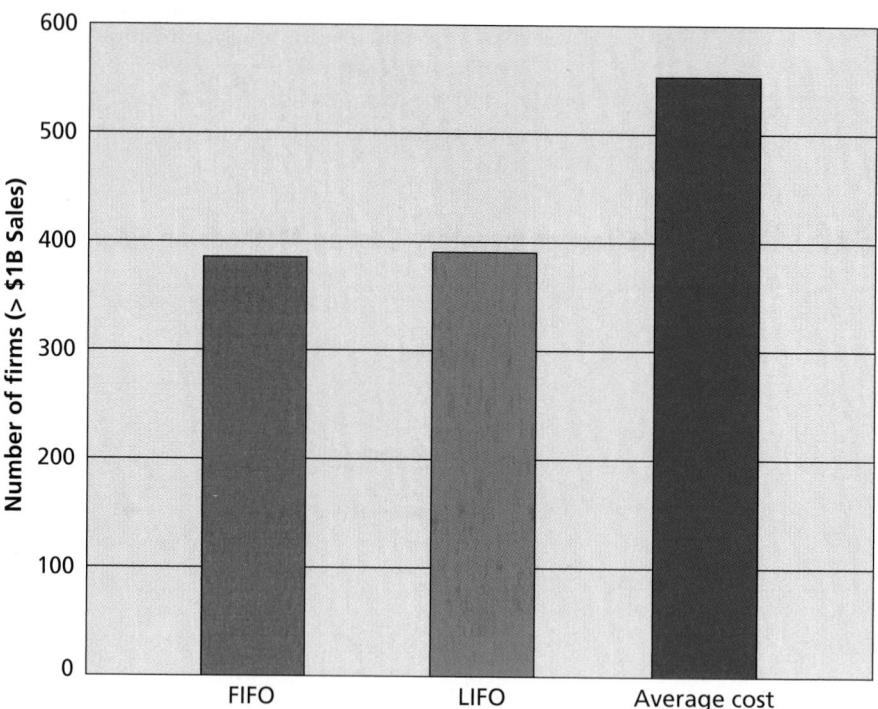

**Source:** Derived from Disclosure financial database.

*Firms may be counted more than once for using multiple methods.

# Inventory Costing Methods Under a Perpetual Inventory System

objective **4**

Compute the cost of inventory under the perpetual inventory system, using the following costing methods: first-in, first-out; last-in, first-out; and average cost.

In a perpetual inventory system, as we discussed in a previous chapter, all merchandise increases and decreases are recorded in a manner similar to recording increases and decreases in cash. The merchandise inventory account at the beginning of an accounting period indicates the merchandise in stock on that date. Purchases are recorded by debiting *Merchandise Inventory* and crediting *Cash* or *Accounts Payable*. On the date of each sale, the cost of the merchandise sold is recorded by debiting *Cost of Merchandise Sold* and crediting *Merchandise Inventory*.

As we illustrated in the preceding section, when identical units of an item are purchased at different unit costs during a period, a cost flow must be assumed. In such cases, the fifo, lifo, or average cost method is used. We illustrate each of these methods, using the data for Item 127B, shown below.

| | Item 127B | Units | Cost |
|---|---|---|---|
| Jan. 1 | Inventory | 10 | $20 |
| 4 | Sale | 7 | |
| 10 | Purchase | 8 | 21 |
| 22 | Sale | 4 | |
| 28 | Sale | 2 | |
| 30 | Purchase | 10 | 22 |

**REAL WORLD**

Although e-tailers, such as **eToys**, **Amazon.com**, and **Furniture .com**, don't have retail stores, they still take possession of inventory in warehouses. Thus, they must account for inventory as we are illustrating in this chapter.

## First-In, First-Out Method

Most businesses dispose of goods in the order in which the goods are purchased. This would be especially true of perishables and goods whose styles or models often change. For example, grocery stores shelve their milk products by expiration dates. Likewise, men's and women's clothing stores display clothes by season. At the end of a season, they often have sales to clear their stores of off-season or out-of-style clothing. Thus, the fifo method is often consistent with the *physical flow* or movement of merchandise. To the extent that this is the case, the fifo method provides results that are about the same as those obtained by identifying the specific costs of each item sold and in inventory.

**Using fifo, costs are included in the merchandise sold in the order in which they were incurred.**

When the fifo method of costing inventory is used, costs are included in the cost of merchandise sold in the order in which they were incurred. To illustrate, Exhibit 3 shows the journal entries for purchases and sales and the inventory subsidiary ledger account for Item 127B. The number of units in inventory after each transaction, together with total costs and unit costs, are shown in the account. We assume that the units are sold for $30 each on account.

**•Exhibit 3**   **Entries and Perpetual Inventory Account (Fifo)**

| Jan. 4 | Accounts Receivable | 210 | |
| | Sales | | 210 |
| 4 | Cost of Merchandise Sold | 140 | |
| | Merchandise Inventory | | 140 |
| 10 | Merchandise Inventory | 168 | |
| | Accounts Payable | | 168 |
| 22 | Accounts Receivable | 120 | |
| | Sales | | 120 |
| 22 | Cost of Merchandise Sold | 81 | |
| | Merchandise Inventory | | 81 |
| 28 | Accounts Receivable | 60 | |
| | Sales | | 60 |
| 28 | Cost of Merchandise Sold | 42 | |
| | Merchandise Inventory | | 42 |
| 30 | Merchandise Inventory | 220 | |
| | Accounts Payable | | 220 |

**Item 127B**

| | Purchases | | | Cost of Merchandise Sold | | | Inventory | | |
|---|---|---|---|---|---|---|---|---|---|
| Date | Quantity | Unit Cost | Total Cost | Quantity | Unit Cost | Total Cost | Quantity | Unit Cost | Total Cost |
| Jan. 1 | | | | | | | 10 | 20 | 200 |
| 4 | | | | 7 | 20 | 140 | 3 | 20 | 60 |
| 10 | 8 | 21 | 168 | | | | 3 | 20 | 60 |
| | | | | | | | 8 | 21 | 168 |
| 22 | | | | 3 | 20 | 60 | | | |
| | | | | 1 | 21 | 21 | 7 | 21 | 147 |
| 28 | | | | 2 | 21 | 42 | 5 | 21 | 105 |
| 30 | 10 | 22 | 220 | | | | 5 | 21 | 105 |
| | | | | | | | 10 | 22 | 220 |

You should note that after the 7 units were sold on January 4, there was an inventory of 3 units at $20 each. The 8 units purchased on January 10 were acquired at a unit cost of $21, instead of $20. Therefore, the inventory after the January 10 purchase is reported on two lines, 3 units at $20 each and 8 units at $21 each. Next, note that the $81 cost of the 4 units sold on January 22 is made up of the remaining 3 units at $20 each and 1 unit at $21. At this point, 7 units are in inventory at a cost of $21 per unit. The remainder of the illustration is explained in a similar manner.

## Last-In, First-Out Method

**Using lifo, the cost of units sold is the cost of the most recent purchases.**

When the lifo method is used in a perpetual inventory system, the cost of the units sold is the cost of the most recent purchases. To illustrate, Exhibit 4 shows the journal entries for purchases and sales and the subsidiary ledger account for Item 127B, prepared on a lifo basis.

## •Exhibit 4   Entries and Perpetual Inventory Account (Lifo)

| Jan. 4 | Accounts Receivable | 210 | |
|---|---|---|---|
| | Sales | | 210 |
| 4 | Cost of Merchandise Sold | 140 | |
| | Merchandise Inventory | | 140 |
| 10 | Merchandise Inventory | 168 | |
| | Accounts Payable | | 168 |
| 22 | Accounts Receivable | 120 | |
| | Sales | | 120 |
| 22 | Cost of Merchandise Sold | 84 | |
| | Merchandise Inventory | | 84 |
| 28 | Accounts Receivable | 60 | |
| | Sales | | 60 |
| 28 | Cost of Merchandise Sold | 42 | |
| | Merchandise Inventory | | 42 |
| 30 | Merchandise Inventory | 220 | |
| | Accounts Payable | | 220 |

**Item 127B**

| Date | Purchases Quantity | Purchases Unit Cost | Purchases Total Cost | Cost of Merchandise Sold Quantity | Cost of Merchandise Sold Unit Cost | Cost of Merchandise Sold Total Cost | Inventory Quantity | Inventory Unit Cost | Inventory Total Cost |
|---|---|---|---|---|---|---|---|---|---|
| Jan. 1 | | | | | | | 10 | 20 | 200 |
| 4 | | | | 7 | 20 | 140 | 3 | 20 | 60 |
| 10 | 8 | 21 | 168 | | | | 3 | 20 | 60 |
| | | | | | | | 8 | 21 | 168 |
| 22 | | | | 4 | 21 | 84 | 3 | 20 | 60 |
| | | | | | | | 4 | 21 | 84 |
| 28 | | | | 2 | 21 | 42 | 3 | 20 | 60 |
| | | | | | | | 2 | 21 | 42 |
| 30 | 10 | 22 | 220 | | | | 3 | 20 | 60 |
| | | | | | | | 2 | 21 | 42 |
| | | | | | | | 10 | 22 | 220 |

If you compare the ledger accounts for the fifo perpetual system and the lifo perpetual system, you should discover that the accounts are the same through the January 10 purchase. Using lifo, however, the cost of the 4 units sold on January 22 is the cost of the units from the January 10 purchase ($21 per unit). The cost of the 7 units in inventory after the sale on January 22 is the cost of the 3 units remaining from the beginning inventory and the cost of the 4 units remaining from the January 10 purchase. The remainder of the lifo illustration is explained in a similar manner.

When the lifo method is used, the inventory ledger is sometimes maintained in units only. The units are converted to dollars when the financial statements are prepared at the end of the period.

The use of the lifo method was originally limited to rare situations in which the units sold were taken from the most recently acquired goods. For tax reasons, which we will discuss later, its use has greatly increased during the past few decades. Lifo is now often used even when it does not represent the physical flow of goods.

## Average Cost Method

When the average cost method is used in a perpetual inventory system, an average unit cost for each type of item is computed each time a purchase is made. This unit cost is then used to determine the cost of each sale until another purchase is made and a new average is computed. This averaging technique is called a *moving average*. Since the average cost method is rarely used in a perpetual inventory system, we do not illustrate it in this chapter.

## Computerized Perpetual Inventory Systems

The records for a perpetual inventory system may be maintained manually. However, such a system is costly and time consuming for businesses with a large number of inventory items with many purchase and sales transactions. In most cases, the record keeping for perpetual inventory systems is computerized.

An example of using computers in maintaining perpetual inventory records for retail stores follows.

**REAL WORLD**

The fifo, lifo, and average cost flow assumptions also apply to other areas of business. For example, individuals and businesses often purchase marketable securities at different costs per share. When such investments are sold, the investor must either specifically identify which shares are sold or use the fifo cost flow assumption. To illustrate, assume that a business purchased 100 shares of **Microsoft Corporation** at $25 and 100 shares at $35. If the business later sells 100 shares for $30, which shares did it sell? The business must determine the cost of the shares sold so that it can report either a gain or loss on the sale for tax purposes. In addition, it must report the gain or loss on its income statement.

1. The relevant details for each inventory item, such as a description, quantity, and unit size, are stored in an inventory record. The individual inventory records make up the computerized inventory file, the total of which agrees with the balance of the inventory ledger account.
2. Each time an item is purchased or returned by a customer, the inventory data are entered into the computer's inventory records and files.
3. Each time an item is sold, a salesclerk scans the item's bar code with an optical scanner. The scanner reads the magnetic code and rings up the sale on the cash register. The inventory records and files are then updated for the cost of goods sold.
4. After a physical inventory is taken, the inventory count data are entered into the computer. These data are compared with the current balances, and a listing of the overages and shortages is printed. The inventory balances are then adjusted to the quantities determined by the physical count.

Such systems can be extended to aid managers in controlling and managing inventory quantities. For example, items that are selling fast can be reordered before the stock is depleted. Past sales patterns can be analyzed to determine when to mark down merchandise for sales and when to restock seasonal merchandise. In addition, such systems can provide managers with data for developing and fine-tuning their marketing strategies. For example, such data can be used to evaluate the effectiveness of advertising campaigns and sales promotions.

**REAL WORLD**

**Wal-Mart, Target, Sears,** and other retailers use bar code scanners as part of their perpetual inventory systems.

# Inventory Costing Methods Under a Periodic Inventory System

**objective 5**

Compute the cost of inventory under the periodic inventory system, using the following costing methods: first-in, first-out; last-in, first-out; and average cost.

When the periodic inventory system is used, only revenue is recorded each time a sale is made. No entry is made at the time of the sale to record the cost of the merchandise sold. At the end of the accounting period, a physical inventory is taken to determine the cost of the inventory and the cost of the merchandise sold.[1]

Like the perpetual inventory system, a cost flow assumption must be made when identical units are acquired at different unit costs during a period. In such cases, the fifo, lifo, or average cost method is used.

## First-In, First-Out Method

To illustrate the use of the fifo method in a periodic inventory system, we assume the following data:

| | | | | |
|---|---|---|---|---|
| Jan. 1 | Inventory: | 200 units at | $ 9 | $ 1,800 |
| Mar. 10 | Purchase: | 300 units at | 10 | 3,000 |
| Sept. 21 | Purchase: | 400 units at | 11 | 4,400 |
| Nov. 18 | Purchase: | 100 units at | 12 | 1,200 |
| Available for sale during year | | 1,000 | | $10,400 |

The physical count on December 31 shows that 300 units have not been sold. Using the fifo method, the cost of the 700 units sold is determined as follows:

| | | | |
|---|---|---|---|
| Earliest costs, Jan. 1: | 200 units at | $ 9 | $1,800 |
| Next earliest costs, Mar. 10: | 300 units at | 10 | 3,000 |
| Next earliest costs, Sept. 21: | 200 units at | 11 | 2,200 |
| Cost of merchandise sold: | 700 | | $7,000 |

---

[1] Computing the cost of merchandise sold using the periodic method was illustrated in Chapter 6.

Deducting the cost of merchandise sold of **$7,000** from the **$10,400** of merchandise available for sale yields **$3,400** as the cost of the inventory at December 31. The $3,400 inventory is made up of the most recent costs incurred for this item. Exhibit 5 shows the relationship of the cost of merchandise sold during the year and the inventory at December 31.

## •Exhibit 5    First-In, First-Out Flow of Costs

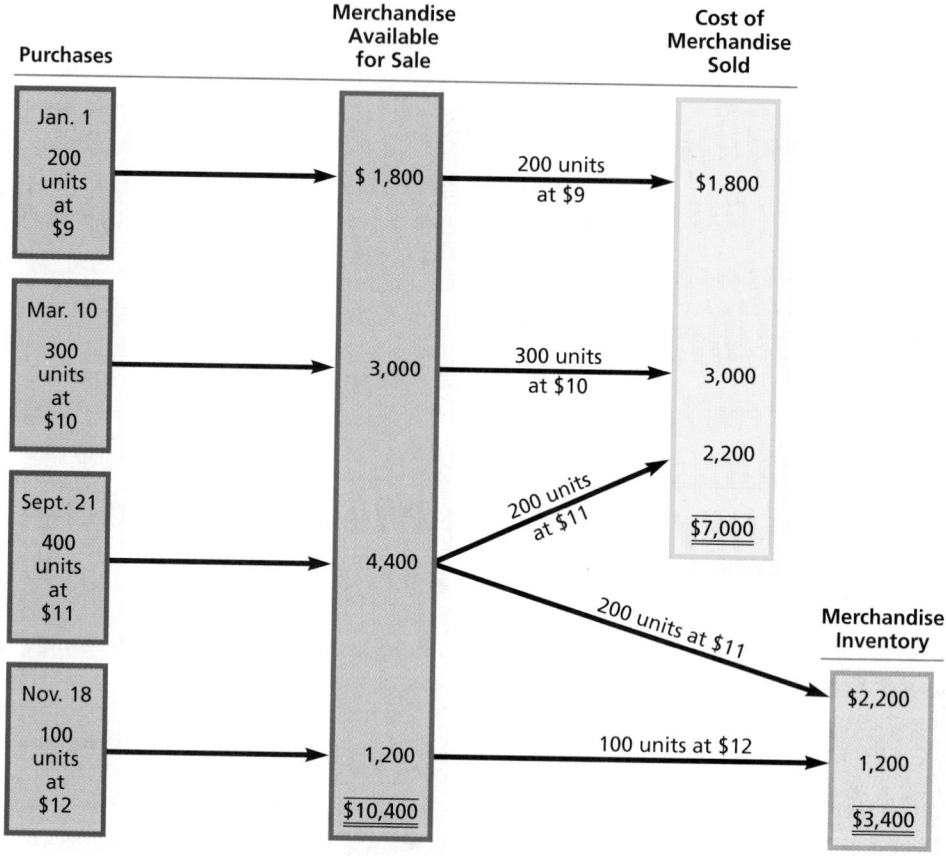

## Last-In, First-Out Method

When the lifo method is used, the cost of merchandise sold is made up of the most recent costs. Based on the data in the fifo example, the cost of the 700 units of inventory is determined as follows:

| | | |
|---|---|---|
| Most recent costs, Nov. 18: | 100 units at $12 | $1,200 |
| Next most recent costs, Sept. 21: | 400 units at  11 | 4,400 |
| Next most recent costs, Mar. 10: | 200 units at  10 | 2,000 |
| Cost of merchandise sold: | 700 | $7,600 |

Deducting the cost of merchandise sold of **$7,600** from the **$10,400** of merchandise available for sale yields **$2,800** as the cost of the inventory at December 31. The $2,800 inventory is made up of the earliest costs incurred for this item. Exhibit 6 shows the relationship of the cost of merchandise sold during the year and the inventory at December 31.

## Average Cost Method

The average cost method is sometimes called the **weighted average method**. When this method is used, costs are matched against revenue according to an average of

## •Exhibit 6   Last-In, First-Out Flow of Costs

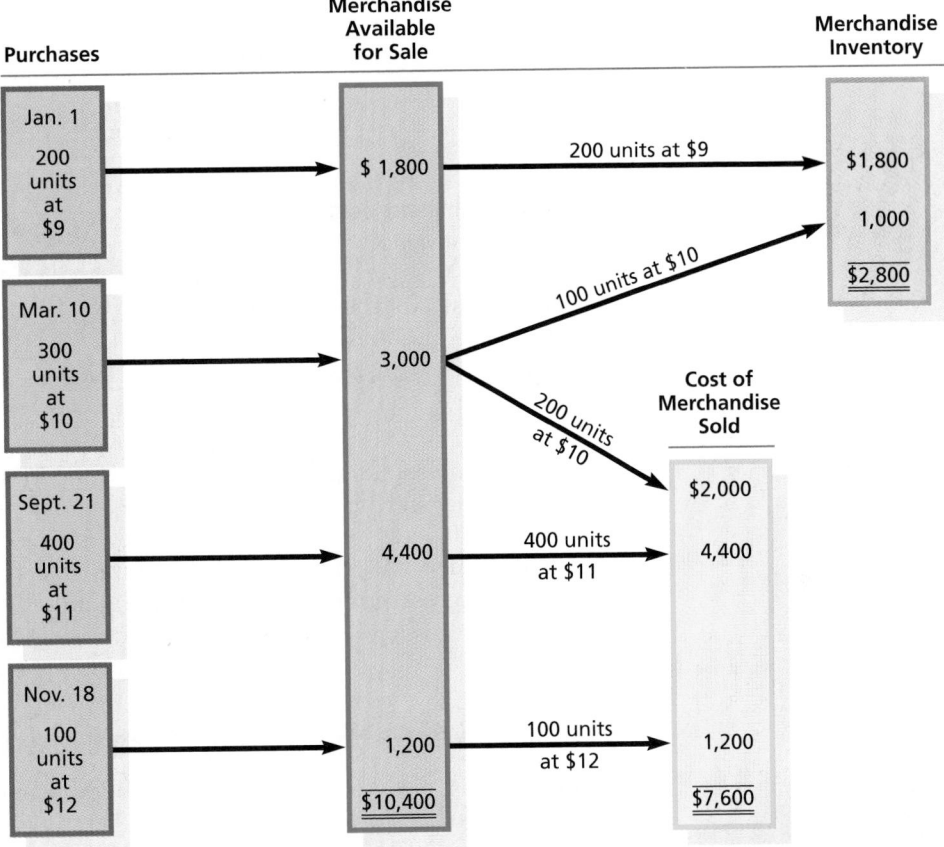

the unit costs of the goods sold. The same weighted average unit costs are used in determining the cost of the merchandise inventory at the end of the period. For businesses in which merchandise sales may be made up of various purchases of identical units, the average method approximates the physical flow of goods.

The weighted average unit cost is determined by dividing the total cost of the units of each item available for sale during the period by the related number of units of that item. Using the same cost data as in the fifo and lifo examples, the average cost of the 1,000 units, $10.40, and the cost of the 700 units, $7,280, are determined as follows:

Average unit cost: $10,400/1,000 units = $10.40
Cost of merchandise sold: 700 units at $10.40 = $7,280

Deducting the cost of merchandise sold of **$7,280** from the **$10,400** of merchandise available for sale yields **$3,120** as the cost of the inventory at December 31.

# Comparing Inventory Costing Methods

**objective  6**

Compare and contrast the use of the three inventory costing methods.

As we have illustrated, a different cost flow is assumed for each of the three alternative methods of costing inventories. You should note that if the cost of units had remained stable, all three methods would have yielded the same results. Since prices do change, however, the three methods will normally yield different amounts for (1) the cost of the merchandise sold for the period, (2) the gross profit (and net income) for the period, and (3) the ending inventory. Using the preceding examples for the periodic inventory system and assuming that net sales were $15,000, the following partial income statements indicate the effects of each method when prices are rising:[2]

**Partial Income Statements**

|  | First-In, First-Out | Average Cost | Last-In, First-Out |
|---|---|---|---|
| Net sales | $15,000 | $15,000 | $15,000 |
| Cost of merchandise sold: | | | |
| Beginning inventory | $ 1,800 | $ 1,800 | $ 1,800 |
| Purchases | 8,600 | 8,600 | 8,600 |
| Merchandise available for sale | $10,400 | $10,400 | $10,400 |
| Less ending inventory | 3,400 | 3,120 | 2,800 |
| Cost of merchandise sold | 7,000 | 7,280 | 7,600 |
| Gross profit | $ 8,000 | $ 7,720 | $ 7,400 |

As shown above, the fifo method yielded the lowest amount for the cost of merchandise sold and the highest amount for gross profit (and net income). It also yielded the highest amount for the ending inventory. On the other hand, the lifo method yielded the highest amount for the cost of merchandise sold, the lowest amount for gross profit (and net income), and the lowest amount for ending inventory. The average cost method yielded results that were between those of fifo and lifo.

# Use of the First-In, First-Out Method

When the fifo method is used during a period of inflation or rising prices, the earlier unit costs are lower than the more recent unit costs, as shown in the preceding fifo example. Thus, fifo will show a larger gross profit. However, the inventory must be replaced at prices higher than indicated by the cost of merchandise sold. In fact, the balance sheet will report the ending merchandise inventory at an amount that is about the same as its current replacement cost. When the rate of inflation reaches double digits, as it did during the 1970s, the larger gross profits that result from the fifo method are often called *inventory profits* or *illusory profits*. You should note that in a period of deflation or declining prices, the effect is just the opposite.

# Use of the Last-In, First-Out Method

When the lifo method is used during a period of inflation or rising prices, the results are opposite those of the other two methods. As shown in the preceding example, the lifo method will yield a higher amount of cost of merchandise sold, a lower amount of gross profit, and a lower amount of inventory at the end of the period than the other two methods. The reason for these effects is that the cost of the most recently acquired units is about the same as the cost of their replacement. In a period of inflation, the more recent unit costs are higher than the earlier unit costs. Thus, it can be argued that the lifo method more nearly matches current costs with current revenues.

During periods of rising prices, using lifo offers an income tax savings. The income tax savings results because lifo reports the lowest amount of net income of the three methods. During the double-digit inflationary period of the 1970s, many businesses changed from fifo to lifo for the tax savings. However, the ending inventory on the balance sheet may be quite different from its current replacement cost. In such cases, the financial statements normally include a note that states the estimated difference between the lifo inventory and the inventory if fifo had been

---

[2]Similar results would also occur when comparing inventory costing methods under a perpetual inventory system.

used. Again, you should note that in a period of deflation or falling price levels, the effects are just the opposite.

## Use of the Average Cost Method

As you might have already reasoned, the average cost method of inventory costing is, in a sense, a compromise between fifo and lifo. The effect of price trends is averaged in determining the cost of merchandise sold and the ending inventory. For a series of purchases, the average cost will be the same, regardless of the direction of price trends. For example, a complete reversal of the sequence of unit costs presented in the preceding illustration would not affect the reported cost of merchandise sold, gross profit, or ending inventory.

---

## INTEGRITY IN BUSINESS

### WHERE'S THE BONUS?

**M**anagers are often given bonuses based on reported earnings numbers. This can create a conflict. Lifo can improve the value of the company through lower taxes. However, lifo also produces a lower earnings number and, therefore, lower management bonuses. Ethically, managers should select accounting procedures that will maximize the value of the firm, rather than their own compensation. Compensation specialists can help avoid this ethical dilemma by adjusting the bonus plan for the accounting procedure differences.

---

# Valuation of Inventory at Other than Cost

objective **7**

Compute the proper valuation of inventory at other than cost, using the lower-of-cost-or-market and net realizable value concepts.

**REAL WORLD**

**Dell Computer Company** recorded over $39.3 million of charges (expenses) in writing down its inventory of notebook computers. The remaining inventories of computers were then sold at significantly reduced prices.

As we indicated earlier, cost is the primary basis for valuing inventories. In some cases, however, inventory is valued at other than cost. Two such cases arise when (1) the cost of replacing items in inventory is below the recorded cost and (2) the inventory is not salable at normal sales prices. This latter case may be due to imperfections, shop wear, style changes, or other causes.

## Valuation at Lower of Cost or Market

If the cost of replacing an item in inventory is lower than the original purchase cost, the **lower-of-cost-or-market (LCM) method** is used to value the inventory. *Market*, as used in *lower of cost or market*, is the cost to replace the merchandise on the inventory date. This market value is based on quantities normally purchased from the usual source of supply. In businesses where inflation is the norm, market prices rarely decline. In businesses where technology changes rapidly (e.g., microcomputers and televisions), market declines are common. The primary advantage of the lower-of-cost-or-market method is that gross profit (and net income) is reduced in the period in which the market decline occurred.

In applying the lower-of-cost-or-market method, the cost and replacement cost can be determined in one of three ways. Cost and replacement cost can be determined for (1) each item in the inventory, (2) major classes or categories of inventory, or (3) the inventory as a whole. In practice, the cost and replacement cost of each item are usually determined.

To illustrate, assume that there are 400 identical units of Item A in inventory, acquired at a unit cost of $10.25 each. If at the inventory date the item would cost $10.50 to replace, the cost price of $10.25 would be multiplied by 400 to determine

If the cost of an item is $410, its current replacement cost is $400, and its selling price is $525, at what amount should the item be included in the inventory according to the LCM method?

---

*$400*

the inventory value. On the other hand, if the item could be replaced at $9.50 a unit, the replacement cost of $9.50 would be used for valuation purposes.

Exhibit 7 illustrates a method of organizing inventory data and applying the lower-of-cost-or-market method to each inventory item. The amount of the market decline, $450 ($15,520 − $15,070), may be reported as a separate item on the income statement or included in the cost of merchandise sold. Regardless, net income will be reduced by the amount of the market decline.

## •Exhibit 7   Determining Inventory at Lower of Cost or Market

| Commodity | Inventory Quantity | Unit Cost Price | Unit Market Price | Total Cost | Total Market | Lower of C or M |
|-----------|-------------------|-----------------|-------------------|------------|--------------|-----------------|
| A | 400 | $10.25 | $ 9.50 | $ 4,100 | $ 3,800 | $ 3,800 |
| B | 120 | 22.50 | 24.10 | 2,700 | 2,892 | 2,700 |
| C | 600 | 8.00 | 7.75 | 4,800 | 4,650 | 4,650 |
| D | 280 | 14.00 | 14.75 | 3,920 | 4,130 | 3,920 |
| Total | | | | $15,520 | $15,472 | $15,070 |

## Valuation at Net Realizable Value

**REAL WORLD**

Out-of-date merchandise is a major problem for many types of retailers. For example, you may have noticed the shelf-life dates of grocery products, such as milk, eggs, canned goods, and meat. Grocery stores often mark down the prices of products nearing the end of their shelf life to avoid having to dispose of the products as waste.

As you would expect, merchandise that is out of date, spoiled, or damaged or that can be sold only at prices below cost should be written down. Such merchandise should be valued at net realizable value. **Net realizable value** is the estimated selling price less any direct cost of disposal, such as sales commissions. For example, assume that damaged merchandise costing $1,000 can be sold for only $800, and direct selling expenses are estimated to be $150. This inventory should be valued at $650 ($800 − $150), which is its net realizable value.

# Presenting Merchandise Inventory on the Balance Sheet

**objective 8**

Prepare a balance sheet presentation of merchandise inventory.

Merchandise inventory is usually presented in the Current Assets section of the balance sheet, following receivables. Both the method of determining the cost of the inventory (fifo, lifo, or average) and the method of valuing the inventory (cost or the lower of cost or market) should be shown. It is not unusual for large businesses with varied activities to use different costing methods for different segments of their inventories. The details may be disclosed in parentheses on the balance sheet or in a footnote to the financial statements. Exhibit 8 shows how parentheses may be used.

A company may change its inventory costing methods for a valid reason. In such cases, the effect of the change and the reason for the change should be disclosed in the financial statements for the period in which the change occurred.

**REAL WORLD**

**General Motors Corporation** uses the last-in, first-out (lifo) method to account for all U.S. inventories other than those of **Saturn Corporation**. The cost of non-U.S., Saturn inventories is determined by using either first-in, first-out (fifo) or average cost.

**•Exhibit 8**   Merchandise Inventory on the Balance Sheet

| Metro Arts Balance Sheet December 31, 2007 | | | |
|---|---|---|---|
| **Assets** | | | |
| Current assets: | | | |
| Cash | | | $ 19 4 0 0 00 |
| Accounts receivable | $80 0 0 0 00 | | |
| Less allowance for doubtful accounts | 3 0 0 0 00 | | 77 0 0 0 00 |
| Merchandise inventory—at lower of cost (first-in, | | | |
| first-out method) or market | | | 216 3 0 0 00 |

## FINANCIAL REPORTING AND DISCLOSURE

### COSTCO WHOLESALE CORPORATION

**C**ostco Wholesale Corporation operates over three hundred membership warehouses that offer members low prices on a limited selection of nationally branded and selected private label products. Costco's business strategy is to generate high sales volumes and rapid inventory turnover. This enables Costco to operate profitably at significantly lower gross margins than traditional wholesalers, discount retailers, and supermarkets. In addition, Costco's rapid turnover provides it the opportunity to conserve on its cash, as described below.

*Because of its high sales volume and rapid inventory turnover, Costco generally has the opportunity to receive cash from the sale of a substantial portion of its inventory at mature warehouse operations before it is required to pay all its merchandise vendors, even though Costco takes advantage of early payment terms to obtain payment discounts. As sales in a given warehouse increase and inventory turnover becomes more rapid, a greater percentage of the inventory is financed through payment terms provided by vendors rather than by working capital (cash).*

On its September 1, 2002 balance sheet, Costco reported over $3 billion of inventory, as follows. Costco uses the

FIFO method in its foreign operations because some countries do not permit the use of the LIFO method.

*Merchandise inventories (in thousands):*

| | |
|---|---|
| United States (LIFO) | $2,552,820 |
| Foreign (FIFO) | 574,401 |
| Total | $3,127,221 |

*Merchandise inventories are valued at the lower of cost or market . . . and are stated using the last-in, first-out (LIFO) method for . . . U.S. merchandise inventories. Merchandise inventories for all foreign operations are . . . stated using the first-in, first-out (FIFO) method. The Company believes the LIFO method more fairly presents the results of operations by more closely matching current costs with current revenues.*

As with all retailers, Costco experiences inventory shrinkage, as described below.

*The Company provides for estimated inventory losses between physical inventory counts on the basis of a standard percentage of sales. This provision is adjusted periodically to reflect the actual shrinkage results of the physical inventory counts . . . .*

# Estimating Inventory Cost

**objective 9**

Estimate the cost of inventory, using the retail method and the gross profit method.

It may be necessary for a business to know the amount of inventory when perpetual inventory records are not maintained and it is impractical to take a physical inventory. For example, a business that uses a periodic inventory system may need monthly income statements, but taking a physical inventory each month may be too costly. Moreover, when a disaster such as a fire has destroyed the inventory, the amount of the loss must be determined. In this case, taking a physical inventory is impossible, and even if perpetual inventory records have been kept, the accounting records may also have been destroyed. In such cases, the inventory cost can be estimated by using (1) the retail method or (2) the gross profit method.

# Retail Method of Inventory Costing

The *retail inventory method* of estimating inventory cost is based on the relationship of the cost of merchandise available for sale to the retail price of the same merchandise. To use this method, the retail prices of all merchandise are maintained and totaled. Next, the inventory at retail is determined by deducting sales for the period from the retail price of the goods that were available for sale during the period. The estimated inventory cost is then computed by multiplying the inventory at retail by the ratio of cost to selling (retail) price for the merchandise available for sale, as illustrated in Exhibit 9.

## •Exhibit 9   Determining Inventory by the Retail Method

|  | Cost | Retail |
|---|---|---|
| Merchandise inventory, January 1 | $19,400 | $ 36,000 |
| Purchases in January (net) | 42,600 | 64,000 |
| Merchandise available for sale | $62,000 | $100,000 |
| Ratio of cost to retail price: $\dfrac{\$62,000}{\$100,000} = 62\%$ | | |
| Sales for January (net) | | 70,000 |
| Merchandise inventory, January 31, at retail | | $ 30,000 |
| Merchandise inventory, January 31, at estimated cost ($30,000 × 62%) | | $ 18,600 |

When estimating the percent of cost to selling price, we assume that the mix of the items in the ending inventory is the same as the entire stock of merchandise available for sale. In Exhibit 9, for example, it is unlikely that the retail price of every item was made up of exactly 62% cost and 38% gross profit. We assume, however, that the weighted average of the cost percentages of the merchandise in the inventory ($30,000) is the same as in the merchandise available for sale ($100,000).

When the inventory is made up of different classes of merchandise with very different gross profit rates, the cost percentages and the inventory should be developed for each class of inventory.

One of the major advantages of the retail method is that it provides inventory figures for preparing monthly or quarterly statements when the periodic system is used. Department stores and similar merchandisers like to determine gross profit and operating income each month but may take a physical inventory only once or twice a year. In addition, comparing the estimated ending inventory with the physical ending inventory, both at retail prices, will help identify inventory shortages resulting from shoplifting and other causes. Management can then take appropriate actions.

The retail method may also be used as an aid in taking a physical inventory. In this case, the items counted are recorded on the inventory sheets at their retail (selling) prices instead of their cost prices. The physical inventory at selling price is then converted to cost by applying the ratio of cost to selling (retail) price for the merchandise available for sale.

If the ratio of cost to retail is 70% and the ending inventory at retail is $100,000, what is the estimated ending inventory at cost?

------------------------------------

*$70,000 (70% × $100,000)*

To illustrate, assume that the data in Exhibit 9 are for an entire fiscal year rather than for only January. If the physical inventory taken at the end of the year totaled $29,000, priced at retail, this amount rather than the $30,000 would be converted to cost. Thus, the inventory at cost would be $17,980 ($29,000 × 62%) instead of $18,600 ($30,000 × 62%). The $17,980 would be used for the year-end financial statements and for income tax purposes.

## Gross Profit Method of Estimating Inventories

The **gross profit method** uses the estimated gross profit for the period to estimate the inventory at the end of the period. The gross profit is usually estimated from the actual rate for the preceding year, adjusted for any changes made in the cost and sales prices during the current period. By using the gross profit rate, the dollar amount of sales for a period can be divided into its two components: (1) gross profit and (2) cost of merchandise sold. The latter amount may then be deducted from the cost of merchandise available for sale to yield the estimated cost of the inventory.

Exhibit 10 illustrates the gross profit method for estimating a company's inventory on January 31. In this example, the inventory on January 1 is assumed to be $57,000, the net purchases during the month are $180,000, and the net sales during the month are $250,000. In addition, the historical gross profit was 30% of net sales.

**•Exhibit 10** **Estimating Inventory by Gross Profit Method**

| | | |
|---|---:|---:|
| Merchandise inventory, January 1 . . . . . . . . . . . . . . . | | $ 57,000 |
| Purchases in January (net) . . . . . . . . . . . . . . . . . . . . | | 180,000 |
| Merchandise available for sale . . . . . . . . . . . . . . . . | | $237,000 |
| Sales in January (net) . . . . . . . . . . . . . . . . . . . . . . | $250,000 | |
| Less estimated gross profit ($250,000 × 30%) . . . . . . | 75,000 | |
| Estimated cost of merchandise sold . . . . . . . . . . . . . | | 175,000 |
| Estimated merchandise inventory, January 31 . . . . . . . | | $ 62,000 |

 What is the estimated cost of the ending inventory if the merchandise available for sale is $350,000, sales are $500,000, and the gross profit percentage is 40%?

The gross profit method is useful for estimating inventories for monthly or quarterly financial statements in a periodic inventory system. It is also useful in estimating the cost of merchandise destroyed by fire or other disasters.

$50,000 [$350,000 − (60% × $500,000)]

# Financial Analysis and Interpretation

**objective 10**

Compute and interpret the inventory turnover ratio and the number of days' sales in inventory.

A merchandising business should keep enough inventory on hand to meet the needs of its customers. A failure to do so may result in lost sales. At the same time, too much inventory reduces solvency by tying up funds that could be better used to expand or improve operations. In addition, excess inventory increases expenses such as storage, insurance, and property taxes. Finally, excess inventory increases the risk of losses due to price declines, damage, or changes in customers' buying patterns.

As with many types of financial analyses, it is possible to use more than one measure to analyze the efficiency and effectiveness by which a business manages its inventory. Two such measures are the inventory turnover and the number of days' sales in inventory.

***Inventory turnover*** measures the relationship between the volume of goods (merchandise) sold and the amount of inventory carried during the period. It is computed as follows:

$$\text{Inventory turnover} = \frac{\text{Cost of merchandise sold}}{\text{Average inventory}}$$

The average inventory can be computed using weekly, monthly, or yearly figures. To simplify, we determine the average inventory by dividing the sum of the inventories at the beginning and end of the year by 2. As long as the amount of inventory carried throughout the year remains stable, this average will be accurate enough for our analysis.

To illustrate, the following data have been taken from recent annual reports for **SUPERVALU INC.** and **Zale Corporation**:

|  | SUPERVALU | Zale |
|---|---|---|
| Cost of merchandise sold | $16,567,397,000 | $1,083,053,000 |
| Inventories: |  |  |
|   Beginning of year | $1,038,050,000 | $724,157,000 |
|   End of year | $1,049,283,000 | $782,316,000 |
|   Average | $1,043,666,000 | $753,236,000 |
| Inventory turnover | 15.9 | 1.4 |

The inventory turnover is 15.9 for SUPERVALU and 1.4 for Zale. Generally, the larger the inventory turnover, the more efficient and effective the management of inventory. However, differences in companies and industries are too great to allow specific statements as to what is a good inventory turnover. For example, SUPERVALU is a leading food distributor and the tenth largest food retailer in the United States. Because SUPERVALU's inventory is perishable, we would expect it to have a high inventory turnover. In contrast, Zale Corporation is the largest speciality retailer of fine jewelry in the United States. Thus, we would expect Zale to have a lower inventory turnover than SUPERVALU. As with other financial measures we have discussed, a comparison of a company's inventory turnover over time and with industry averages will provide useful insights into the management of its inventory.

The ***number of days' sales in inventory*** is a rough measure of the length of time it takes to acquire, sell, and replace the inventory. It is computed as follows:

$$\text{Number of days' sales in inventory} = \frac{\text{Inventory, end of year}}{\text{Average daily cost of merchandise sold}}$$

The average daily cost of merchandise sold is determined by dividing the cost of merchandise sold by 365. The number of days' sales in inventory for SUPERVALU and Zale is computed as shown below.

|  | SUPERVALU | Zale |
|---|---|---|
| Average daily cost of merchandise sold: |  |  |
|   $16,567,397,000/365 . . . . . . . . . . . . . . . . . . . . | $45,370,129 |  |
|   $1,083,053,000/365 . . . . . . . . . . . . . . . . . . . . |  | $2,967,268 |
| Ending inventory . . . . . . . . . . . . . . . . . . . . . . . . | $1,049,283,000 | $782,316,000 |
| Number of days' sales in inventory . . . . . . . . . . | 23.1 days | 263.6 days |

Generally, the lower the number of days' sales in inventory, the better. As with inventory turnover, we should expect differences among industries, such as those for SUPERVALU and Zale.

# Key Points

**1 Summarize and provide examples of internal control procedures that apply to inventories.**
Internal control procedures for inventories include those developed to protect the inventories from damage, employee theft, and customer theft. In addition, a physical inventory count should be taken periodically to detect shortages as well as to deter employee thefts.

**2 Describe the effect of inventory errors on the financial statements.**
Any errors in reporting inventory based upon the physical inventory will misstate the ending inventory, current assets, total assets, and owner's equity on the balance sheet. In addition, the cost of goods sold, gross profit, and net income will be misstated on the income statement.

**3 Describe three inventory cost flow assumptions and how they impact the income statement and balance sheet.**
The three common cost flow assumptions used in business are the (1) first-in, first-out method, (2) last-in, first-out method, and (3) average cost method. Each method normally yields different amounts for the cost of merchandise sold and the ending

merchandise inventory. Thus, the choice of a cost flow assumption directly affects the income statement and balance sheet.

**4 Compute the cost of inventory under the perpetual inventory system, using the following costing methods: first-in, first-out; last-in, first-out; and average cost.**
In a perpetual inventory system, the number of units and the cost of each type of merchandise are recorded in a subsidiary inventory ledger, with a separate account for each type of merchandise. Inventory costs and the amounts charged against revenue are illustrated using the fifo and lifo methods.

**5 Compute the cost of inventory under the periodic inventory system, using the following costing methods: first-in, first-out; last-in, first-out; and average cost.**
In a periodic inventory system, a physical inventory is taken to determine the cost of the inventory and the cost of merchandise sold. Inventory costs and the amounts charged against revenue are illustrated using fifo, lifo, and average cost methods.

**6 Compare and contrast the use of the three inventory costing methods.**
The three inventory costing methods will normally yield different amounts for (1) the ending inventory, (2) the cost of the merchandise sold for the period, and (3) the gross profit (and net income) for the period. During periods of inflation, the fifo method yields the lowest amount for the cost of merchandise sold, the highest amount for gross profit (and net income), and the highest amount for the ending inventory. The lifo method yields the opposite results. During periods of deflation, the preceding effects are reversed. The average cost method yields results that are between those of fifo and lifo.

**7 Compute the proper valuation of inventory at other than cost, using the lower-of-cost-or-market and net realizable value concepts.**
If the market price of an item of inventory is lower than its cost, the lower market price is used to compute the value of the item. Market price is the cost to replace the merchandise on the inventory date. It is possible to apply the lower of cost or market to each item in the inventory,

to major classes or categories, or to the inventory as a whole.

Merchandise that can be sold only at prices below cost should be valued at net realizable value, which is the estimated selling price less any direct cost of disposal.

## 8 Prepare a balance sheet presentation of merchandise inventory.

Merchandise inventory is usually presented in the Current Assets section of the balance sheet, following receivables. Both the method of determining the cost of the inventory (fifo, lifo, or average) and the method of valuing the inventory (cost or the lower of cost or market) should be shown.

## 9 Estimate the cost of inventory, using the retail method and the gross profit method.

In using the retail method to estimate inventory, the retail prices of all merchandise acquired are accumulated. The inventory at retail is determined by deducting sales for the period from the retail price of the goods that were available for sale during the period. The inventory at retail is then converted to cost on the basis of the ratio of cost to selling (retail) price for the merchandise available for sale.

In using the gross profit method to estimate inventory, the estimated gross profit is deducted from the sales to determine the estimated cost of merchandise sold. This amount is then deducted from the cost of mer-

chandise available for sale to determine the estimated ending inventory.

## 10 Compute and interpret the inventory turnover ratio and the number of days' sales in inventory.

The inventory turnover ratio, computed as the cost of merchandise sold divided by the average inventory, measures the relationship between the volume of goods (merchandise) sold and the amount of inventory carried during the period. The number of days' sales in inventory, computed as the ending inventory divided by the average daily cost of merchandise sold, measures the length of time it takes to acquire, sell, and replace the inventory.

# Key Terms

average cost method (359)
first-in, first-out (fifo) method (359)
gross profit method (371)
inventory turnover (372)

last-in, first-out (lifo) method (359)
lower-of-cost-or-market (LCM) method (367)
net realizable value (368)

number of days' sales in inventory (372)
physical inventory (356)
retail inventory method (370)

# Illustrative Problem

Stewart Co.'s beginning inventory and purchases during the year ended December 31, 2007, were as follows:

|  |  | Units | Unit Cost | Total Cost |
|---|---|---|---|---|
| January 1 | Inventory | 1,000 | $50.00 | $ 50,000 |
| March 10 | Purchase | 1,200 | 52.50 | 63,000 |
| June 25 | Sold 800 units |  |  |  |
| August 30 | Purchase | 800 | 55.00 | 44,000 |
| October 5 | Sold 1,500 units |  |  |  |
| November 26 | Purchase | 2,000 | 56.00 | 112,000 |
| December 31 | Sold 1,000 units |  |  |  |
| Total |  | 5,000 |  | $269,000 |

## Instructions

1. Determine the cost of inventory on December 31, 2007, using the perpetual inventory system and each of the following inventory costing methods:
   a. first-in, first-out
   b. last-in, first-out

2. Determine the cost of inventory on December 31, 2007, using the periodic inventory system and each of the following inventory costing methods:
   a. first-in, first-out
   b. last-in, first-out
   c. average cost
3. Assume that during the fiscal year ended December 31, 2007, sales were $290,000 and the estimated gross profit rate was 40%. Estimate the ending inventory at December 31, 2007, using the gross profit method.

### Solution

**1.** a. First-in, first-out method: $95,200

| Date | Purchases Quantity | Purchases Unit Cost | Purchases Total Cost | Cost of Merchandise Sold Quantity | Cost of Merchandise Sold Unit Cost | Cost of Merchandise Sold Total Cost | Inventory Quantity | Inventory Unit Cost | Inventory Total Cost |
|---|---|---|---|---|---|---|---|---|---|
| 2007 Jan. 1 | | | | | | | 1,000 | 50.00 | 50,000 |
| Mar. 10 | 1,200 | 52.50 | 63,000 | | | | 1,000 | 50.00 | 50,000 |
| | | | | | | | 1,200 | 52.50 | 63,000 |
| June 25 | | | | 800 | 50.00 | 40,000 | 200 | 50.00 | 10,000 |
| | | | | | | | 1,200 | 52.50 | 63,000 |
| Aug. 30 | 800 | 55.00 | 44,000 | | | | 200 | 50.00 | 10,000 |
| | | | | | | | 1,200 | 52.50 | 63,000 |
| | | | | | | | 800 | 55.00 | 44,000 |
| Oct. 5 | | | | 200 | 50.00 | 10,000 | 700 | 55.00 | 38,500 |
| | | | | 1,200 | 52.50 | 63,000 | | | |
| | | | | 100 | 55.00 | 5,500 | | | |
| Nov. 26 | 2,000 | 56.00 | 112,000 | | | | 700 | 55.00 | 38,500 |
| | | | | | | | 2,000 | 56.00 | 112,000 |
| Dec. 31 | | | | 700 | 55.00 | 38,500 | 1,700 | 56.00 | 95,200 |
| | | | | 300 | 56.00 | 16,800 | | | |

b. Last-in, first-out method: $91,000 ($35,000 + $56,000)

| Date | Purchases Quantity | Purchases Unit Cost | Purchases Total Cost | Cost of Merchandise Sold Quantity | Cost of Merchandise Sold Unit Cost | Cost of Merchandise Sold Total Cost | Inventory Quantity | Inventory Unit Cost | Inventory Total Cost |
|---|---|---|---|---|---|---|---|---|---|
| 2007 Jan. 1 | | | | | | | 1,000 | 50.00 | 50,000 |
| Mar. 10 | 1,200 | 52.50 | 63,000 | | | | 1,000 | 50.00 | 50,000 |
| | | | | | | | 1,200 | 52.50 | 63,000 |
| June 25 | | | | 800 | 52.50 | 42,000 | 1,000 | 50.00 | 50,000 |
| | | | | | | | 400 | 52.50 | 21,000 |
| Aug. 30 | 800 | 55.00 | 44,000 | | | | 1,000 | 50.00 | 50,000 |
| | | | | | | | 400 | 52.50 | 21,000 |
| | | | | | | | 800 | 55.00 | 44,000 |
| Oct. 5 | | | | 800 | 55.00 | 44,000 | 700 | 50.00 | 35,000 |
| | | | | 400 | 52.50 | 21,000 | | | |
| | | | | 300 | 50.00 | 15,000 | | | |
| Nov. 26 | 2,000 | 56.00 | 112,000 | | | | 700 | 50.00 | 35,000 |
| | | | | | | | 2,000 | 56.00 | 112,000 |
| Dec. 31 | | | | 1,000 | 56.00 | 56,000 | 700 | 50.00 | 35,000 |
| | | | | | | | 1,000 | 56.00 | 56,000 |

**2.** a. First-in, first-out method:
   1,700 units at $56 = $95,200

*(continued)*

b. Last-in, first-out method:

| | |
|---|---|
| 1,000 units at $50.00 | $50,000 |
| 700 units at $52.50 | 36,750 |
| 1,700 units | $86,750 |

c. Average cost method:

| | |
|---|---|
| Average cost per unit: | $269,000 ÷ 5,000 units = $53.80 |
| Inventory, December 31, 2007: | 1,700 units at $53.80 = $91,460 |

**3.** 
| | | |
|---|---|---|
| Merchandise inventory, January 1, 2007 . . . . . . . . . . . . . . . . . . | | $ 50,000 |
| Purchases (net) . . . . . . . . . . . . . . . . . . . . . . . . . . . . . . . . . . . | | 219,000 |
| Merchandise available for sale . . . . . . . . . . . . . . . . . . . . . . . . | | $269,000 |
| Sales (net) . . . . . . . . . . . . . . . . . . . . . . . . . . . . . . . . . . . . . . | $290,000 | |
| Less estimated gross profit ($290,000 × 40%) . . . . . . . . . . . . . . | 116,000 | |
| Estimated cost of merchandise sold . . . . . . . . . . . . . . . . . . . . . | | 174,000 |
| Estimated merchandise inventory, December 31, 2007 . . . . . . . . . | | $ 95,000 |

# Self-Examination Questions (Answers at End of Chapter)

1. If the inventory shrinkage at the end of the year is overstated by $7,500, the error will cause an:
   A. understatement of cost of merchandise sold for the year by $7,500.
   B. overstatement of gross profit for the year by $7,500.
   C. overstatement of merchandise inventory for the year by $7,500.
   D. understatement of net income for the year by $7,500.

2. The inventory costing method that is based on the assumption that costs should be charged against revenue in the order in which they were incurred is:
   A. fifo
   B. lifo
   C. average cost
   D. perpetual inventory

3. The following units of a particular item were purchased and sold during the period:

   | | |
   |---|---|
   | Beginning inventory | 40 units at $20 |
   | First purchase | 50 units at $21 |
   | Second purchase | 50 units at $22 |
   | First sale | 110 units |
   | Third purchase | 50 units at $23 |
   | Second sale | 45 units |

   What is the cost of the 35 units on hand at the end of the period as determined under the perpetual inventory system by the lifo costing method?
   A. $715
   B. $705
   C. $700
   D. $805

4. The following units of a particular item were available for sale during the period:

   | | |
   |---|---|
   | Beginning inventory | 40 units at $20 |
   | First purchase | 50 units at $21 |
   | Second purchase | 50 units at $22 |
   | Third purchase | 50 units at $23 |

   What is the unit cost of the 35 units on hand at the end of the period as determined under the periodic inventory system by the fifo costing method?
   A. $20
   B. $21
   C. $22
   D. $23

5. If merchandise inventory is being valued at cost and the price level is steadily rising, the method of costing that will yield the highest net income is:
   A. lifo
   B. fifo
   C. average
   D. periodic

# Class Discussion Questions

1. What security measures may be used by retailers to protect merchandise inventory from customer theft?

2. Which inventory system provides the more effective means of controlling inventories (perpetual or periodic)? Why?

3. Before inventory purchases are recorded, the receiving report should be reconciled to what documents?

4. What document should be presented by an employee requesting inventory items to be released from the company's warehouse?

5. Why is it important to periodically take a physical inventory if the perpetual system is used?

6. The inventory shrinkage at the end of the year was understated by $18,500. (a) Did the error cause an overstatement or an understatement of the gross profit for the year? (b) Which items on the balance sheet at the end of the year were overstated or understated as a result of the error?

7. Martin Co. sold merchandise to Fess Company on December 31, FOB shipping point. If the merchandise is in transit on December 31, the end of the fiscal year, which company would report it in its financial statements? Explain.

8. A manufacturer shipped merchandise to a retailer on a consignment basis. If the merchandise is unsold at the end of the period, in whose inventory should the merchandise be included?

9. Do the terms *fifo* and *lifo* refer to techniques used in determining quantities of the various classes of merchandise on hand? Explain.

10. Does the term *last-in* in the lifo method mean that the items in the inventory are assumed to be the most recent (last) acquisitions? Explain.

11. If merchandise inventory is being valued at cost and the price level is steadily rising, which of the three methods of costing—fifo, lifo, or average cost—will yield (a) the highest inventory cost, (b) the lowest inventory cost, (c) the highest gross profit, (d) the lowest gross profit?

12. Which of the three methods of inventory costing—fifo, lifo, or average cost—will in general yield an inventory cost most nearly approximating current replacement cost?

13. If inventory is being valued at cost and the price level is steadily rising, which of the three methods of costing—fifo, lifo, or average cost—will yield the lowest annual income tax expense? Explain.

14. Can a company change its method of costing inventory? Explain.

15. Because of imperfections, an item of merchandise cannot be sold at its normal selling price. How should this item be valued for financial statement purposes?

16. How is the method of determining the cost of the inventory and the method of valuing it disclosed in the financial statements?

17. What uses can be made of the estimate of the cost of inventory determined by the gross profit method?

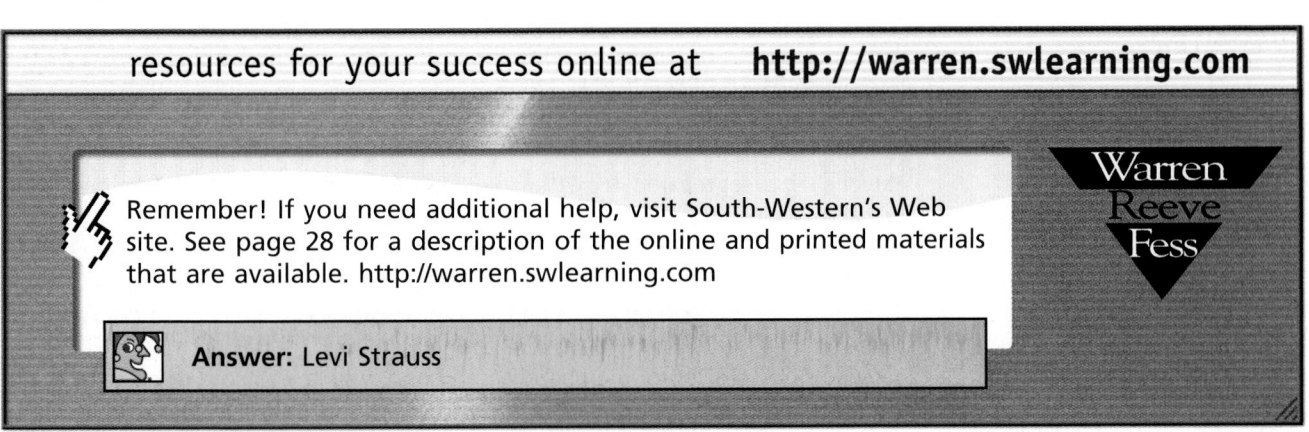

resources for your success online at    **http://warren.swlearning.com**

Remember! If you need additional help, visit South-Western's Web site. See page 28 for a description of the online and printed materials that are available. http://warren.swlearning.com

Warren Reeve Fess

**Answer:** Levi Strauss

# Exercises

**EXERCISE 9-1**
*Internal control of inventories*
**Objective 1**

Onsite Hardware Store currently uses a periodic inventory system. Dana Cogburn, the owner, is considering the purchase of a computer system that would make it feasible to switch to a perpetual inventory system.

Dana is unhappy with the periodic inventory system because it does not provide timely information on inventory levels. Dana has noticed on several occasions that the store runs out of good-selling items, while too many poor-selling items are on hand.

Dana is also concerned about lost sales while a physical inventory is being taken. Onsite Hardware currently takes a physical inventory twice a year. To minimize distractions, the store is closed on the day inventory is taken. Dana believes that closing the store is the only way to get an accurate inventory count.

➡ Will switching to a perpetual inventory system strengthen Onsite Hardware's control over inventory items? Will switching to a perpetual inventory system eliminate the need for a physical inventory count? Explain.

**EXERCISE 9-2**
*Internal control of inventories*
**Objective 1**

Pacific Luggage Shop is a small retail establishment located in a large shopping mall. This shop has implemented the following procedures regarding inventory items:

a. Whenever Pacific receives a shipment of new inventory, the items are taken directly to the stockroom. Pacific's accountant uses the vendor's invoice to record the amount of inventory received.
b. Since the shop carries mostly high-quality, designer luggage, all inventory items are tagged with a control device that activates an alarm if a tagged item is removed from the store.
c. Since the display area of the store is limited, only a sample of each piece of luggage is kept on the selling floor. Whenever a customer selects a piece of luggage, the salesclerk gets the appropriate piece from the store's stockroom. Since all salesclerks need access to the stockroom, it is not locked. The stockroom is adjacent to the break room used by all mall employees.

➡ State whether each of these procedures is appropriate or inappropriate, considering the principles of internal control. If it is inappropriate, state which internal control procedure is violated.

**EXERCISE 9-3**
*Identifying items to be included in inventory*
**Objective 1**

Marcelle's Boutiques, which is located in Iowa City, Iowa, has identified the following items for possible inclusion in its December 31, 2005 year-end inventory.

a. Merchandise Marcelle's shipped to a customer FOB shipping point was picked up by the freight company on December 26, 2005, but had still not arrived at its destination as of December 31, 2005.
b. Marcelle's has in its warehouse $30,500 of merchandise on consignment from Putnam Co.
c. Marcelle's has segregated $6,570 of merchandise ordered by one of its customers for shipment on January 3, 2006.
d. Merchandise Marcelle's shipped FOB shipping point on December 31, 2005, was picked up by the freight company at 11:52 p.m.
e. Marcelle's has sent $78,000 of merchandise to various retailers on a consignment basis.
f. Marcelle's has $18,750 of merchandise on hand, which was sold to customers earlier in the year, but which has been returned by customers to Marcelle's for various warranty repairs.
g. On December 31, 2005, Marcelle's received $17,050 of merchandise that had been returned by customers because the wrong merchandise had been shipped. The replacement order is to be shipped overnight on January 3, 2006.

h. On December 21, 2005, Marcelle's ordered $21,000 of merchandise, FOB Iowa City. The merchandise was shipped from the supplier on December 28, 2005, but had not been received by December 31, 2005.

i. On December 27, 2005, Marcelle's ordered $15,750 of merchandise from a supplier in Davenport. The merchandise was shipped FOB Davenport on December 30, 2005, but had not been received by December 31, 2005.

Indicate which items should be included (I) and which should be excluded (E) from the inventory.

**EXERCISE 9-4**
*Effect of errors in physical inventory*
**Objective 2**

Crazy Rapids Co. sells canoes, kayaks, whitewater rafts, and other boating supplies. During the taking of its physical inventory on December 31, 2006, Crazy Rapids incorrectly counted its inventory as $117,800 instead of the correct amount of $119,750.

a. State the effect of the error on the December 31, 2006 balance sheet of Crazy Rapids.

b. State the effect of the error on the income statement of Crazy Rapids for the year ended December 31, 2006.

**EXERCISE 9-5**
*Effect of errors in physical inventory*
**Objective 2**

Ray's Motorcycle Shop sells motorcycles, jet skis, and other related supplies and accessories. During the taking of its physical inventory on December 31, 2006, Ray's Motorcycle Shop incorrectly counted its inventory as $187,900 instead of the correct amount of $183,750.

a. State the effect of the error on the December 31, 2006 balance sheet of Ray's Motorcycle Shop.

b. State the effect of the error on the income statement of Ray's Motorcycle Shop for the year ended December 31, 2006.

**EXERCISE 9-6**
*Error in inventory shrinkage*
**Objective 2**

**WHAT'S WRONG WITH THIS?**

During 2006, the accountant discovered that the physical inventory at the end of 2005 had been understated by $12,800. Instead of correcting the error, however, the accountant assumed that a $12,800 overstatement of the physical inventory in 2006 would balance out the error.

➤ Are there any flaws in the accountant's assumption? Explain.

**EXERCISE 9-7**
*Perpetual inventory using fifo*
**Objectives 3, 4**

**SPREADSHEET**

✓*Inventory balance, April 30, $802*

Beginning inventory, purchases, and sales data for portable CD players are as follows:

| April | 1 | Inventory | 35 units at $50 |
|---|---|---|---|
| | 5 | Sale | 26 units |
| | 11 | Purchase | 15 units at $53 |
| | 21 | Sale | 12 units |
| | 28 | Sale | 4 units |
| | 30 | Purchase | 7 units at $54 |

The business maintains a perpetual inventory system, costing by the first-in, first-out method. Determine the cost of the merchandise sold for each sale and the inventory balance after each sale, presenting the data in the form illustrated in Exhibit 3.

**EXERCISE 9-8**
*Perpetual inventory using lifo*
**Objectives 3, 4**

**SPREADSHEET**

✓*Inventory balance, April 30, $778*

Assume that the business in Exercise 9-7 maintains a perpetual inventory system, costing by the last-in, first-out method. Determine the cost of merchandise sold for each sale and the inventory balance after each sale, presenting the data in the form illustrated in Exhibit 4.

**EXERCISE 9-9**
*Perpetual inventory using lifo*

**Objectives 3, 4**

**SPREADSHEET**

✓*Inventory balance, March 31, $1,295*

Beginning inventory, purchases, and sales data for cell phones for March are as follows:

| Inventory | | Purchases | | Sales | |
|---|---|---|---|---|---|
| Mar. 1 | 25 units at $90 | Mar. 5 | 20 units at $94 | Mar. 9 | 18 units |
| | | 21 | 15 units at $95 | 13 | 20 units |
| | | | | 31 | 8 units |

Assuming that the perpetual inventory system is used, costing by the lifo method, determine the cost of merchandise sold for each sale and the inventory balance after each sale, presenting the data in the form illustrated in Exhibit 4.

**EXERCISE 9-10**
*Perpetual inventory using fifo*

**Objectives 3, 4**

**SPREADSHEET**

✓*Inventory balance, March 31, $1,330*

Assume that the business in Exercise 9-9 maintains a perpetual inventory system, costing by the first-in, first-out method. Determine the cost of merchandise sold for each sale and the inventory balance after each sale, presenting the data in the form illustrated in Exhibit 3.

**EXERCISE 9-11**
*Fifo, lifo costs under perpetual inventory system*

**Objectives 3, 4**

✓*a. $700*

The following units of a particular item were available for sale during the year:

| | |
|---|---|
| Beginning inventory | 20 units at $45 |
| Sale | 15 units at $80 |
| First purchase | 31 units at $47 |
| Sale | 27 units at $80 |
| Second purchase | 40 units at $50 |
| Sale | 35 units at $80 |

The firm uses the perpetual inventory system, and there are 14 units of the item on hand at the end of the year. What is the total cost of the ending inventory according to (a) fifo, (b) lifo?

**EXERCISE 9-12**
*Periodic inventory by three methods*

**Objectives 3, 5**

✓*b. $318*

The units of an item available for sale during the year were as follows:

| | | |
|---|---|---|
| Jan. 1 | Inventory | 6 units at $28 |
| Feb. 4 | Purchase | 12 units at $30 |
| July 20 | Purchase | 14 units at $32 |
| Dec. 30 | Purchase | 8 units at $33 |

There are 11 units of the item in the physical inventory at December 31. The periodic inventory system is used. Determine the inventory cost by (a) the first-in, first-out method, (b) the last-in, first-out method, and (c) the average cost method.

**EXERCISE 9-13**
*Periodic inventory by three methods; cost of merchandise sold*

**Objectives 3, 5**

**SPREADSHEET**

✓*a. Inventory, $5,016*

The units of an item available for sale during the year were as follows:

| | | |
|---|---|---|
| Jan. 1 | Inventory | 42 units at $120 |
| Mar. 4 | Purchase | 58 units at $130 |
| Aug. 7 | Purchase | 20 units at $136 |
| Nov. 15 | Purchase | 30 units at $140 |

There are 36 units of the item in the physical inventory at December 31. The periodic inventory system is used. Determine the inventory cost and the cost of merchandise sold by three methods, presenting your answers in the following form:

| | Cost | |
|---|---|---|
| **Inventory Method** | **Merchandise Inventory** | **Merchandise Sold** |
| a. First-in, first-out | $ | $ |
| b. Last-in, first-out | | |
| c. Average cost | | |

**EXERCISE 9-14**
*Comparing inventory methods*
Objective 6

Assume that a firm separately determined inventory under fifo and lifo and then compared the results.

1. In each space below, place the correct sign [less than (<), greater than (>), or equal (=)] for each comparison, assuming periods of rising prices.

|  |  |  |
|---|---|---|
| a. Lifo inventory | _____ | Fifo inventory |
| b. Lifo cost of goods sold | _____ | Fifo cost of goods sold |
| c. Lifo net income | _____ | Fifo net income |
| d. Lifo income tax | _____ | Fifo income tax |

2. Why would management prefer to use lifo over fifo in periods of rising prices?

**EXERCISE 9-15**
*Lower-of-cost-or-market inventory*
Objective 7

SPREADSHEET

✓ *LCM: $8,325*

On the basis of the following data, determine the value of the inventory at the lower of cost or market. Assemble the data in the form illustrated in Exhibit 7.

| Commodity | Inventory Quantity | Unit Cost Price | Unit Market Price |
|---|---|---|---|
| M76 | 8 | $150 | $160 |
| T53 | 20 | 75 | 70 |
| A19 | 10 | 275 | 260 |
| J81 | 15 | 50 | 40 |
| K10 | 25 | 101 | 105 |

**EXERCISE 9-16**
*Merchandise inventory on the balance sheet*
Objective 8

Based on the data in Exercise 9-15 and assuming that cost was determined by the fifo method, show how the merchandise inventory would appear on the balance sheet.

**EXERCISE 9-17**
*Retail inventory method*
Objective 9

A business using the retail method of inventory costing determines that merchandise inventory at retail is $825,750. If the ratio of cost to retail price is 60%, what is the amount of inventory to be reported on the financial statements?

**EXERCISE 9-18**
*Retail inventory method*
Objective 9

SPREADSHEET

✓ *Inventory, June 30: $227,500*

On the basis of the following data, estimate the cost of the merchandise inventory at June 30 by the retail method:

|  |  | Cost | Retail |
|---|---|---|---|
| June 1 | Merchandise inventory | $160,000 | $ 180,000 |
| June 1–30 | Purchases (net) | 680,000 | 1,020,000 |
| June 1–30 | Sales (net) |  | 875,000 |

**EXERCISE 9-19**
*Gross profit inventory method*
Objective 9

The merchandise inventory was destroyed by fire on May 17. The following data were obtained from the accounting records:

|  |  |  |
|---|---|---|
| Jan. 1 | Merchandise inventory | $ 180,000 |
| Jan. 1–May 17 | Purchases (net) | 750,000 |
|  | Sales (net) | 1,250,000 |
|  | Estimated gross profit rate | 35% |

a. Estimate the cost of the merchandise destroyed.
b. Briefly describe the situations in which the gross profit method is useful.

**EXERCISE 9-20**
*Inventory turnover*
Objective 10

The following data were taken from recent annual reports of **Apple Computer, Inc.**, a manufacturer of personal computers and related products, and **American Greetings Corporation**, a manufacturer and distributor of greeting cards and related products:

| | Apple | American Greetings |
|---|---|---|
| Cost of goods sold | $4,139,000,000 | $881,771,000 |
| Inventory, end of year | 45,000,000 | 278,807,000 |
| Inventory, beginning of the year | 11,000,000 | 290,804,000 |

a. Determine the inventory turnover for Apple and American Greetings. Round to two decimal places.
b. Would you expect American Greetings' inventory turnover to be higher or lower than Apple's? Why?

**EXERCISE 9-21**
*Inventory turnover and number of days' sales in inventory*
**Objective 10**

✓a. Albertson's, 43 days' sales in inventory

Kroger Co., Albertson's Inc., and Safeway Inc. are the three largest grocery chains in the United States. Inventory management is an important aspect of the grocery retail business. Recent balance sheets for these three companies indicated the following merchandise inventory information:

| | Merchandise Inventory | |
|---|---|---|
| | End of Year (in millions) | Beginning of Year (in millions) |
| Albertson's | $2,973 | $3,196 |
| Kroger | 4,175 | 4,178 |
| Safeway | 2,558 | 2,437 |

The cost of goods sold for each company were:

| | Cost of Goods Sold (in millions) |
|---|---|
| Albertson's | $25,242 |
| Kroger | 37,810 |
| Safeway | 22,303 |

a. Determine the number of days' sales in inventory and inventory turnover for the three companies. Round to the nearest day and one decimal place.
b. Interpret your results in (a).
c. If Albertson's had Kroger's number of days' sales in inventory, how much additional cash flow would have been generated from the hypothetically smaller inventory relative to its actual ending inventory position?

# Problems Series A

**PROBLEM 9-1A**
*Fifo perpetual inventory*
**Objectives 3, 4**

✓3. $240,100

The beginning inventory of drift boats at Heritage Float Co. and data on purchases and sales for a three-month period are as follows:

| Date | | Transaction | Number of Units | Per Unit | Total |
|---|---|---|---|---|---|
| August | 1 | Inventory | 22 | $2,200 | $ 48,400 |
| | 8 | Purchase | 18 | 2,250 | 40,500 |
| | 11 | Sale | 12 | 4,800 | 57,600 |
| | 22 | Sale | 11 | 4,800 | 52,800 |
| September | 3 | Purchase | 16 | 2,300 | 36,800 |
| | 10 | Sale | 10 | 5,000 | 50,000 |
| | 21 | Sale | 5 | 5,000 | 25,000 |
| | 30 | Purchase | 20 | 2,350 | 47,000 |
| October | 5 | Sale | 20 | 5,250 | 105,000 |
| | 13 | Sale | 12 | 5,250 | 63,000 |
| | 21 | Purchase | 30 | 2,400 | 72,000 |
| | 28 | Sale | 15 | 5,400 | 81,000 |

## Instructions

1. Record the inventory, purchases, and cost of merchandise sold data in a perpetual inventory record similar to the one illustrated in Exhibit 3, using the first-in, first-out method.
2. Determine the total sales and the total cost of drift boats sold for the period. Journalize the entries in the sales and cost of merchandise sold accounts. Assume that all sales were on account.
3. Determine the gross profit from sales of drift boats for the period.
4. Determine the ending inventory cost.

**PROBLEM 9-2A**
*Lifo perpetual inventory*
**Objectives 3, 4**

SPREADSHEET

✓ *2. Gross profit, $238,900*

The beginning inventory of drift boats and data on purchases and sales for a three-month period are shown in Problem 9-1A.

## Instructions

1. Record the inventory, purchases, and cost of merchandise sold data in a perpetual inventory record similar to the one illustrated in Exhibit 4, using the last-in, first-out method.
2. Determine the total sales, the total cost of drift boats sold, and the gross profit from sales for the period.
3. Determine the ending inventory cost.

**PROBLEM 9-3A**
*Periodic inventory by three methods*
**Objectives 3, 5**

SPREADSHEET

✓ *1. $12,701*

Henning Appliances uses the periodic inventory system. Details regarding the inventory of appliances at January 1, 2006, purchases invoices during the year, and the inventory count at December 31, 2006, are summarized as follows:

| Model | Inventory, January 1 | Purchases Invoices 1st | Purchases Invoices 2nd | Purchases Invoices 3rd | Inventory Count, December 31 |
|---|---|---|---|---|---|
| 231T | 3 at $208 | 3 at $212 | 5 at $213 | 4 at $225 | 6 |
| 673W | 2 at 520 | 2 at 527 | 2 at 530 | 2 at 535 | 4 |
| 193Q | 6 at 520 | 8 at 531 | 4 at 549 | 6 at 542 | 7 |
| 144Z | 9 at 213 | 7 at 215 | 6 at 222 | 6 at 225 | 11 |
| 160M | 6 at 305 | 3 at 310 | 3 at 316 | 4 at 317 | 5 |
| 180X | — | 4 at 222 | 4 at 232 | — | 2 |
| 971K | 4 at 140 | 6 at 144 | 8 at 148 | 7 at 156 | 6 |

## Instructions

1. Determine the cost of the inventory on December 31, 2006, by the first-in, first-out method. Present data in columnar form, using the following headings:

| Model | Quantity | Unit Cost | Total Cost |
|---|---|---|---|

If the inventory of a particular model comprises one entire purchase plus a portion of another purchase acquired at a different unit cost, use a separate line for each purchase.

2. Determine the cost of the inventory on December 31, 2006, by the last-in, first-out method, following the procedures indicated in (1).
3. Determine the cost of the inventory on December 31, 2006, by the average cost method, using the columnar headings indicated in (1).
4. ▭▶ Discuss which method (fifo or lifo) would be preferred for income tax purposes in periods of (a) rising prices and (b) declining prices.

*If the working papers correlating with this textbook are not used, omit Problem 9-4A.*

**PROBLEM 9-4A**
*Lower-of-cost-or-market inventory*
**Objective 7**

✓ *Total LCM, $38,238*

Data on the physical inventory of Timberline Co. as of December 31, 2006, are presented in the working papers. The quantity of each commodity on hand has been determined and recorded on the inventory sheet. Unit market prices have also been determined as of December 31 and recorded on the sheet. The inventory is to be determined at cost and also at the lower of cost or market, using the first-in, first-out method. Quantity and cost data from the last purchases invoice of the year and the next-to-the-last purchases invoice are summarized as follows:

| Description | Last Purchases Invoice | | Next-to-the-Last Purchases Invoice | |
|---|---|---|---|---|
| | Quantity Purchased | Unit Cost | Quantity Purchased | Unit Cost |
| A90 | 25 | $ 59 | 40 | $ 58 |
| C18 | 25 | 188 | 15 | 191 |
| D41 | 16 | 145 | 15 | 142 |
| E34 | 150 | 25 | 100 | 27 |
| F17 | 6 | 550 | 15 | 540 |
| G68 | 75 | 14 | 100 | 13 |
| K41 | 8 | 400 | 4 | 398 |
| Q79 | 500 | 6 | 500 | 7 |
| R72 | 70 | 18 | 50 | 16 |
| S60 | 5 | 250 | 4 | 260 |
| W21 | 120 | 20 | 115 | 17 |
| Z35 | 8 | 701 | 7 | 699 |

### Instructions

Record the appropriate unit costs on the inventory sheet, and complete the pricing of the inventory. When there are two different unit costs applicable to an item:

1. Draw a line through the quantity, and insert the quantity and unit cost of the last purchase.
2. On the following line, insert the quantity and unit cost of the next-to-the-last purchase.
3. Total the cost and market columns and insert the lower of the two totals in the Lower of C or M column. The first item on the inventory sheet has been completed as an example.

**PROBLEM 9-5A**
*Retail method; gross profit method*
**Objective 9**
✓ 1. $131,100

Selected data on merchandise inventory, purchases, and sales for Bozeman Co. and Gallatin Co. are as follows:

| | Cost | Retail |
|---|---|---|
| **Bozeman Co.** | | |
| Merchandise inventory, February 1 | $ 210,000 | $ 300,000 |
| Transactions during February: | | |
| Purchases (net) | 1,135,500 | 1,650,000 |
| Sales | | 1,800,000 |
| Sales returns and allowances | | 40,000 |
| **Gallatin Co.** | | |
| Merchandise inventory, March 1 | $ 250,000 | |
| Transactions during March and April: | | |
| Purchases (net) | 1,385,000 | |
| Sales | 2,510,000 | |
| Sales returns and allowances | 110,000 | |
| Estimated gross profit rate | 36% | |

### Instructions

1. Determine the estimated cost of the merchandise inventory of Bozeman Co. on February 28 by the retail method, presenting details of the computations.
2. a. Estimate the cost of the merchandise inventory of Gallatin Co. on April 30 by the gross profit method, presenting details of the computations.
   b. Assume that Gallatin Co. took a physical inventory on April 30 and discovered that $88,125 of merchandise was on hand. What was the estimated loss of inventory due to theft or damage during March and April?

# roblems Series B

## PROBLEM 9-1B
*Fifo perpetual inventory*

**Objectives 3, 4**

SPREADSHEET

✓ 3. $4,895

The beginning inventory of floor mats at Intermountain Office Supplies and data on purchases and sales for a three-month period are as follows:

| Date | Transaction | Number of Units | Per Unit | Total |
|------|-------------|-----------------|----------|-------|
| Apr. 1 | Inventory | 200 | $2.10 | $ 420 |
| 8 | Purchase | 800 | 2.20 | 1,760 |
| 20 | Sale | 350 | 4.00 | 1,400 |
| 30 | Sale | 450 | 4.00 | 1,800 |
| May 8 | Sale | 50 | 4.10 | 205 |
| 10 | Purchase | 500 | 2.30 | 1,150 |
| 27 | Sale | 350 | 4.20 | 1,470 |
| 31 | Sale | 200 | 4.50 | 900 |
| June 5 | Purchase | 750 | 2.40 | 1,800 |
| 13 | Sale | 350 | 5.00 | 1,750 |
| 23 | Purchase | 400 | 2.60 | 1,040 |
| 30 | Sale | 500 | 5.00 | 2,500 |

### Instructions
1. Record the inventory, purchases, and cost of merchandise sold data in a perpetual inventory record similar to the one illustrated in Exhibit 3, using the first-in, first-out method.
2. Determine the total sales and the total cost of floor mats sold for the period. Journalize the entries in the sales and cost of merchandise sold accounts. Assume that all sales were on account.
3. Determine the gross profit from sales for the period.
4. Determine the ending inventory cost.

## PROBLEM 9-2B
*Lifo perpetual inventory*

**Objectives 3, 4**

SPREADSHEET

✓ 2. Gross profit, $4,785

The beginning inventory of floor mats at Intermountain Office Supplies and data on purchases and sales for a three-month period are shown in Problem 9-1B.

### Instructions
1. Record the inventory, purchases, and cost of merchandise sold data in a perpetual inventory record similar to the one illustrated in Exhibit 4, using the last-in, first-out method.
2. Determine the total sales, the total cost of floor mats sold, and the gross profit from sales for the period.
3. Determine the ending inventory cost.

## PROBLEM 9-3B
*Periodic inventory by three methods*

**Objectives 3, 5**

SPREADSHEET

✓ 1. $8,053

Three Forks Appliances uses the periodic inventory system. Details regarding the inventory of appliances at May 1, 2005, purchases invoices during the year, and the inventory count at April 30, 2006, are summarized as follows:

| Model | Inventory, May 1 | Purchases Invoices | | | Inventory Count, April 30 |
| | | 1st | 2nd | 3rd | |
|-------|------------------|-----|-----|-----|---------------------------|
| AC54 | 2 at $250 | 2 at $260 | 4 at $271 | 4 at $272 | 6 |
| BH43 | 6 at 80 | 5 at 82 | 8 at 89 | 8 at 90 | 6 |
| GI13 | 2 at 108 | 2 at 110 | 3 at 128 | 3 at 130 | 5 |
| K243 | 8 at 88 | 4 at 79 | 3 at 85 | 6 at 92 | 8 |
| PM18 | 7 at 242 | 6 at 250 | 5 at 260 | 10 at 259 | 8 |
| Q661 | 5 at 160 | 4 at 170 | 4 at 175 | 7 at 180 | 8 |
| W490 | — | 4 at 150 | 4 at 200 | 4 at 202 | 5 |

## Instructions

1. Determine the cost of the inventory on April 30, 2006, by the first-in, first-out method. Present data in columnar form, using the following headings:

| Model | Quantity | Unit Cost | Total Cost |
| --- | --- | --- | --- |

If the inventory of a particular model comprises one entire purchase plus a portion of another purchase acquired at a different unit cost, use a separate line for each purchase.
2. Determine the cost of the inventory on April 30, 2006, by the last-in, first-out method, following the procedures indicated in (1).
3. Determine the cost of the inventory on April 30, 2006, by the average cost method, using the columnar headings indicated in (1).
4. ▬▬▶ Discuss which method (fifo or lifo) would be preferred for income tax purposes in periods of (a) rising prices and (b) declining prices.

*If the working papers correlating with this textbook are not used, omit Problem 9-4B.*

**PROBLEM 9-4B**
*Lower-of-cost-or-market inventory*
**Objective 7**
✓ *Total LCM, $38,585*

Data on the physical inventory of Cinnabar Company as of December 31, 2006, are presented in the working papers. The quantity of each commodity on hand has been determined and recorded on the inventory sheet. Unit market prices have also been determined as of December 31 and recorded on the sheet. The inventory is to be determined at cost and also at the lower of cost or market, using the first-in, first-out method. Quantity and cost data from the last purchases invoice of the year and the next-to-the-last purchases invoice are summarized as follows:

| Description | Last Purchases Invoice Quantity Purchased | Last Purchases Invoice Unit Cost | Next-to-the-Last Purchases Invoice Quantity Purchased | Next-to-the-Last Purchases Invoice Unit Cost |
| --- | --- | --- | --- | --- |
| A90 | 25 | $ 59 | 30 | $ 58 |
| C18 | 35 | 206 | 20 | 205 |
| D41 | 10 | 144 | 25 | 142 |
| E34 | 150 | 25 | 100 | 24 |
| F17 | 10 | 565 | 10 | 560 |
| G68 | 100 | 15 | 100 | 14 |
| K41 | 10 | 385 | 5 | 384 |
| Q79 | 500 | 6 | 500 | 6 |
| R72 | 80 | 20 | 50 | 18 |
| S60 | 5 | 250 | 4 | 260 |
| W21 | 100 | 20 | 75 | 19 |
| Z35 | 7 | 701 | 6 | 699 |

## Instructions

Record the appropriate unit costs on the inventory sheet, and complete the pricing of the inventory. When there are two different unit costs applicable to an item, proceed as follows:

1. Draw a line through the quantity, and insert the quantity and unit cost of the last purchase.
2. On the following line, insert the quantity and unit cost of the next-to-the-last purchase.
3. Total the cost and market columns and insert the lower of the two totals in the Lower of C or M column. The first item on the inventory sheet has been completed as an example.

**PROBLEM 9-5B**
*Retail method; gross profit method*
**Objective 9**

Selected data on merchandise inventory, purchases, and sales for Avalanche Co. and Bridger Co. are as follows:

✓1. $204,000

|  | Cost | Retail |
|---|---|---|
| **Avalanche Co.** | | |
| Merchandise inventory, October 1 | $ 98,000 | $ 140,000 |
| Transactions during October: | | |
| Purchases (net) | 813,200 | 1,200,000 |
| Sales | | 1,080,000 |
| Sales returns and allowances | | 40,000 |
| | | |
| **Bridger Co.** | | |
| Merchandise inventory, August 1 | $ 150,000 | |
| Transactions during August and September: | | |
| Purchases (net) | 1,375,000 | |
| Sales | 1,800,000 | |
| Sales returns and allowances | 100,000 | |
| Estimated gross profit rate | 35% | |

### Instructions

1. Determine the estimated cost of the merchandise inventory of Avalanche Co. on October 31 by the retail method, presenting details of the computations.
2. a. Estimate the cost of the merchandise inventory of Bridger Co. on September 30 by the gross profit method, presenting details of the computations.
   b. Assume that Bridger Co. took a physical inventory on September 30 and discovered that $402,600 of merchandise was on hand. What was the estimated loss of inventory due to theft or damage during August and September?

# Special Activities

**ACTIVITY 9-1**
*Ethics and professional conduct in business*

Follicle Co. is experiencing a decrease in sales and operating income for the fiscal year ending December 31, 2006. Preston Shipley, controller of Follicle Co., has suggested that all orders received before the end of the fiscal year be shipped by midnight, December 31, 2006, even if the shipping department must work overtime. Since Follicle Co. ships all merchandise FOB shipping point, it would record all such shipments as sales for the year ending December 31, 2006, thereby offsetting some of the decreases in sales and operating income.

➤ Discuss whether Preston Shipley is behaving in a professional manner.

**ACTIVITY 9-2**
*Fifo vs. lifo*

The following note was taken from the 2002 financial statements of **Walgreen Co.**:

*Inventories are valued on a . . . last-in, first-out (LIFO) cost . . . basis. At August 31, 2002 and 2001, inventories would have been greater by $693,500,000 and $637,600,000 respectively, if they had been valued on a lower of first-in, first-out (FIFO) cost or market basis.*

Additional data are as follows:

| | |
|---|---|
| Earnings before income taxes, 2002 | $1,637,300,000 |
| Total lifo inventories, August 31, 2002 | 3,645,200,000 |

Based on the preceding data, determine (a) what the total inventories at August 31, 2002, would have been, using the fifo method, and (b) what the earnings before income taxes for the year ended August 31, 2002, would have been if fifo had been used instead of lifo.

**ACTIVITY 9-3**
*Lifo and inventory flow*

The following is an excerpt from a conversation between Jaime Noll, the warehouse manager for Baltic Wholesale Co., and its accountant, Tara Stroud. Baltic Wholesale operates a large regional warehouse that supplies produce and other grocery products to grocery stores in smaller communities.

*Jaime:* Tara, can you explain what's going on here with these monthly statements?

*Tara:* Sure, Jaime. How can I help you?

*Jaime:* I don't understand this last-in, first-out inventory procedure. It just doesn't make sense.

*Tara:* Well, what it means is that we assume that the last goods we receive are the first ones sold. So the inventory is made up of the items we purchased first.

*Jaime:* Yes, but that's my problem. It doesn't work that way! We always distribute the oldest produce first. Some of that produce is perishable! We can't keep any of it very long or it'll spoil.

*Tara:* Jaime, you don't understand. We only *assume* that the products we distribute are the last ones received. We don't actually have to distribute the goods in this way.

*Jaime:* I always thought that accounting was supposed to show what really happened. It all sounds like "make believe" to me! Why not report what really happens?

Respond to Jaime's concerns.

**ACTIVITY 9-4**
*Observe internal controls over inventory*

GROUP ACTIVITY

Select a business in your community and observe its internal controls over inventory. In groups of three or four, identify and discuss the similarities and differences in each business's inventory controls. Prepare a written summary of your findings.

**ACTIVITY 9-5**
*Costing inventory*

Feedbag Company began operations in 2005 by selling a single product. Data on purchases and sales for the year were as follows:

**Purchases:**

| Date | Units Purchased | Unit Cost | Total Cost |
|---|---|---|---|
| April 3 | 7,750 | $24.40 | $ 189,100 |
| May 15 | 8,250 | 26.00 | 214,500 |
| June 6 | 10,000 | 26.40 | 264,000 |
| July 10 | 10,000 | 28.00 | 280,000 |
| August 3 | 6,800 | 28.50 | 193,800 |
| October 5 | 3,200 | 29.00 | 92,800 |
| November 1 | 2,000 | 29.90 | 59,800 |
| December 10 | 2,000 | 32.00 | 64,000 |
| | 50,000 | | $1,358,000 |

**Sales:**

| | |
|---|---|
| April | 4,000 units |
| May | 4,000 |
| June | 5,000 |
| July | 6,000 |
| August | 7,000 |
| September | 7,000 |
| October | 4,500 |
| November | 2,500 |
| December | 2,000 |
| Total units | 42,000 |
| Total sales | $1,300,000 |

On January 3, 2006, the president of the company, Heather Ola, asked for your advice on costing the 8,000-unit physical inventory that was taken on December 31,

2005. Moreover, since the firm plans to expand its product line, she asked for your advice on the use of a perpetual inventory system in the future.

1. Determine the cost of the December 31, 2005 inventory under the periodic system, using the (a) first-in, first-out method, (b) last-in, first-out method, and (c) average cost method.
2. Determine the gross profit for the year under each of the three methods in (1).
3. a. ▣▶ Explain varying viewpoints why each of the three inventory costing methods may best reflect the results of operations for 2005.
   b. ▣▶ Which of the three inventory costing methods may best reflect the replacement cost of the inventory on the balance sheet as of December 31, 2005?
   c. ▣▶ Which inventory costing method would you choose to use for income tax purposes? Why?
   d. ▣▶ Discuss the advantages and disadvantages of using a perpetual inventory system. From the data presented in this case, is there any indication of the adequacy of inventory levels during the year?

---

**ACTIVITY 9-6**
*SAKS Incorporated inventory note*

REAL WORLD

**SAKS Incorporated** disclosed the following note regarding its merchandise inventories for its February 1, 2003 financial statements:

*Merchandise inventories are . . . stated at the lower of cost (last-in, first-out ["lifo"]), or market and include freight and certain buying and distribution costs. The company also takes markdowns related to slow moving inventory, ensuring an appropriate inventory valuation. At February 1, 2003 and February 2, 2002, the lifo value of inventories exceeded market value and, as a result, inventory was stated at the lower market amount.*

*Consignment merchandise on hand of $112,435 and $110,567 at February 1, 2003, and February 2, 2002, respectively, is not reflected in the consolidated balance sheets.*

a. Why were inventories recorded at market value?
b. What are consignment inventories and why were they excluded from the balance sheet valuation?

---

**ACTIVITY 9-7**
*Inventory ratios for Dell and HP*

REAL WORLD

**Dell Computer Corporation** and **Hewlett-Packard Company (HP)** are both manufacturers of computer equipment and peripherals. However, the two companies follow two different strategies. Dell follows a build-to-order strategy, where the consumer orders the computer from a Web page. The order is then manufactured and shipped to the customer within days of the order. In contrast, HP follows a build-to-stock strategy, where the computer is first built for inventory, then sold from inventory to retailers, such as **Best Buy**. The two strategies can be seen in the difference between the inventory turnover and number of days' sales in inventory ratios for the two companies. The following financial statement information is provided for Dell and HP for a recent fiscal year (in millions):

|  | Dell | HP |
|---|---|---|
| Inventory, beginning of period | $ 278 | $ 5,204 |
| Inventory, end of period | 306 | 5,797 |
| Cost of goods sold | 29,055 | 34,573 |

a. Determine the inventory turnover ratio and number of days' sales in inventory ratio for each company.
b. Interpret the difference between the ratios for the two companies.

---

**ACTIVITY 9-8**
*Compare inventory cost flow assumptions*

In groups of three or four, examine the financial statements of a well-known retailing business. You may obtain the financial statements you need from one of the following sources:

GROUP ACTIVITY    INTERNET

1. Your school or local library.
2. The investor relations department of the company.
3. The company's Web site on the Internet.
4. EDGAR (Electronic Data Gathering, Analysis, and Retrieval), the electronic archives of financial statements filed with the Securities and Exchange Commission. SEC documents can be retrieved using the EdgarScan service from **Pricewaterhouse-Coopers** at **http://edgarscan.pwcglobal.com**. To obtain annual report information, type in a company name in the appropriate space. EdgarScan will list the reports available to you for the company you've selected. Select the most recent annual report filing, identified as a 10-K or 10-K405. EdgarScan provides an outline of the report, including the separate financial statements. You can double-click the income statement and balance sheet for the selected company into an Excel spreadsheet for further analysis.

Determine the cost flow assumption(s) that the company is using for its inventory, and determine whether the company is using the lower-of-cost-or-market rule. Prepare a written summary of your findings.

# Answers to Self-Examination Questions

1. **D** The overstatement of inventory shrinkage by $7,500 at the end of the year will cause the cost of merchandise sold for the year to be overstated by $7,500, the gross profit for the year to be understated by $7,500, the merchandise inventory to be understated by $7,500, and the net income for the year to be understated by $7,500 (answer D).

2. **A** The fifo method (answer A) is based on the assumption that costs are charged against revenue in the order in which they were incurred. The lifo method (answer B) charges the most recent costs incurred against revenue, and the average cost method (answer C) charges a weighted average of unit costs of items sold against revenue. The perpetual inventory system (answer D) is a system and not a method of costing.

3. **A** The lifo method of costing is based on the assumption that costs should be charged against revenue in the reverse order in which costs were

incurred. Thus, the oldest costs are assigned to inventory. Thirty of the 35 units would be assigned a unit cost of $20 (since 110 of the beginning inventory units were sold on the first sale), and the remaining 5 units would be assigned a cost of $23, for a total of $715 (answer A).

4. **D** The fifo method of costing is based on the assumption that costs should be charged against revenue in the order in which they were incurred (first-in, first-out). Thus, the most recent costs are assigned to inventory. The 35 units would be assigned a unit cost of $23 (answer D).

5. **B** When the price level is steadily rising, the earlier unit costs are lower than recent unit costs. Under the fifo method (answer B), these earlier costs are matched against revenue to yield the highest possible net income. The periodic inventory system (answer D) is a system and not a method of costing.

# 10

# FIXED ASSETS AND INTANGIBLE ASSETS

## objectives

*After studying this chapter, you should be able to:*

**1** Define fixed assets and describe the accounting for their cost.

**2** Compute depreciation, using the following methods: straight-line method, units-of-production method, and declining-balance method.

**3** Classify fixed asset costs as either capital expenditures or revenue expenditures.

**4** Journalize entries for the disposal of fixed assets.

**5** Define a lease and summarize the accounting rules related to the leasing of fixed assets.

**6** Describe internal controls over fixed assets.

**7** Compute depletion and journalize the entry for depletion.

**8** Describe the accounting for intangible assets, such as patents, copyrights, and goodwill.

**9** Describe how depreciation expense is reported in an income statement, and prepare a balance sheet that includes fixed assets and intangible assets.

**10** Compute and interpret the ratio of fixed assets to long-term liabilities.

**A**ssume that you are a certified flight instructor and you would like to earn a little extra money by teaching people how to fly. Since you don't own an airplane, one of the pilots at the local airport is willing to let you use her airplane for a fixed fee per year. You will also have to pay your share of the annual operating costs, based on hours flown. In addition, the owner will consider your request for upgrading the plane's equipment. At the end of the year, the owner has the right to cancel the agreement.

One of your friends is an airplane mechanic. He is familiar with the plane and has indicated that it needs its annual inspection. There is some structural damage on the right aileron. In addition to this repair, you would like to equip the plane with another radio and a better navigation system.

Since you will not have any ownership in the airplane, it is important for you to distinguish between normal operating costs and costs that add future value or worth to the airplane. These latter costs should be the responsibility of the owner. In this case, you should be willing to pay for part of the cost of the annual inspection. The cost of repairing the structural damage and upgrading the navigation system should be the responsibility of the owner.

Businesses also distinguish between the cost of a fixed asset and the cost of operating the asset. In this chapter, we discuss how to determine the portion of a fixed asset's cost that becomes an expense over a period of time. We also discuss accounting for the disposal of fixed assets and accounting for intangible assets, such as patents and copyrights.

# **N**ature of Fixed Assets

<table>
<tr><td>

**objective** **1**

Define fixed assets and describe the accounting for their cost.

</td><td>

Businesses use a variety of fixed assets, such as equipment, furniture, tools, machinery, buildings, and land. *Fixed assets* are long-term or relatively permanent assets. They are **tangible assets** because they exist physically. They are owned and used by the business and are not offered for sale as part of normal operations. Other descriptive titles for these assets are **plant assets** or **property, plant, and equipment**.

The fixed assets of a business can be a significant part of the total assets. Exhibit 1 shows the percent of fixed assets to total assets for some select companies, divided between service, manufacturing, and merchandising firms. As you can see, the fixed

</td></tr>
</table>

**•Exhibit 1** Fixed Assets as a Percent of Total Assets—Selected Companies

|  | Fixed Assets as a Percentage of Total Assets |
|---|---|
| **Service Firms** |  |
| Pacific Gas and Electric Co. | 47% |
| Sprint Corporation | 59% |
| Computer Associates | 6% |
| **Manufacturing Firms** |  |
| Sun Microsystems Inc. | 15% |
| Boeing Co. | 21% |
| Dupont E I De Nemours & Co. | 36% |
| **Merchandising Firms** |  |
| Barnes & Noble Inc. | 49% |
| Kroger Company | 48% |
| Wal-Mart Stores Inc. | 52% |

assets for most firms comprise a significant proportion of their total assets. In contrast, **Computer Associates** is a consulting firm that relies less on fixed assets to deliver value to customers.

## Classifying Costs

Exhibit 2 displays questions that help classify costs. If the purchased item is long-lived, then it should be *capitalized*, which means it should appear on the balance sheet as an asset. Otherwise, the cost should be reported as an expense on the income statement. Capitalized costs are normally expected to last more than a year. If the asset is also used for a productive purpose, which involves a repeated use or benefit, then it should be classified as a fixed asset, such as land, buildings, or equipment. An asset need not actually be used on an ongoing basis or even often. For example, standby equipment for use in the event of a breakdown of regular equipment or for use only during peak periods is included in fixed assets. Fixed assets that have been abandoned or are no longer used should not be classified as a fixed asset.

**•Exhibit 2**   **Classifying Costs**

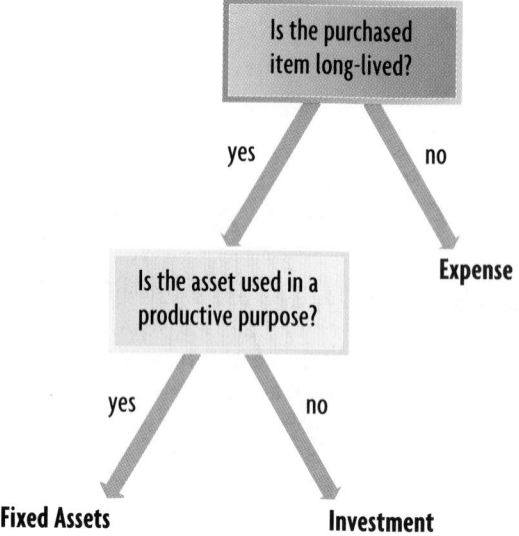

St. Mary's Hospital maintains an auxiliary generator for use in electrical outages. Such outages are rare, and the generator has not been used for the past two years. Should the generator be reported as a fixed asset on St. Mary's balance sheet?

--------------------------------------------

*Yes. Even though the generator has not been used recently, it should be reported as a fixed asset.*

Fixed assets are owned and used by the business and are not offered for resale. Long-lived assets held for resale are not classified as fixed assets, but should be listed on the balance sheet in a section entitled *investments*. For example, undeveloped land acquired as an investment for resale would be classified as an investment, not land.

## The Cost of Fixed Assets

The costs of acquiring fixed assets include all amounts spent to get the asset in place and ready for use. For example, freight costs and the costs of installing equipment are included as part of the asset's total cost. The direct costs associated with new construction, such as labor and materials, should be debited to a "construction in progress" asset account. When the construction is complete, the costs should be reclassified by crediting the construction in progress account and debiting the appropriate fixed asset account. For growing companies, construction in progress can be significant. For example, **Intel Corporation** disclosed $2.7 billion of construction in progress, which was over 15 percent of its total fixed assets.

The details of fixed assets are disclosed on the face of the balance sheet or the notes to the financial statements. For example, **Marriott International Inc.** had the following fixed asset disclosures on a recent balance sheet:

| | ($ in millions) |
|---|---|
| Land | $ 386 |
| Buildings | 547 |
| Furniture and equipment | 676 |
| Timeshare properties | 1,270 |
| Construction in progress | 180 |
| Total | $3,059 |

These categories are typical for a lodging company. Other types of companies would have categories to fit their particular business.

Exhibit 3 summarizes some of the common costs of acquiring fixed assets. These costs should be recorded by debiting the related fixed asset account, such as Land,[1] Building, Land Improvements, or Machinery and Equipment.

Only costs necessary for preparing a long-lived asset for use should be included as a cost of the asset. Unnecessary costs that do not increase the asset's usefulness are recorded as an expense. For example, the following costs are included as an expense:

- Vandalism
- Mistakes in installation
- Uninsured theft
- Damage during unpacking and installing
- Fines for not obtaining proper permits from governmental agencies

Founded in 1849 in Brooklyn, my first product was an anti-parasitic. By 1900, I mainly sold citric acid, camphor, cream of tartar, borax, and iodine. I began making penicillin during World War II and was soon the world's largest producer of it. My animal products division began in 1952. My portfolio, including Lipitor, Norvasc, Zithromax, Diflucan, Viracept, Zoloft, Aricept, Celebrex, and Zyrtec, features many of the world's top-selling medicines. Eight generate more than $1 billion in sales annually each. To help low-income Americans, I introduced my Share Card program in 2002. My annual sales top $30 billion and I'm buying Pharmacia Corp. Who am I? (Go to page 420 for answer.)

## Donated Assets

Civic groups and municipalities sometimes give land or buildings to a corporation as an incentive to locate or remain in a community. In such cases, the corporation debits the assets for their fair market value and credits a revenue account.[2] To illustrate, assume that on April 20 the city of Moraine donates land to Merrick Corporation as an incentive to relocate its headquarters to Moraine. The land was valued at $500,000. Merrick Corporation would record the land as follows:

| | | | | |
|---|---|---|---|---|
| Apr. | 20 | Land | 500 0 0 0 00 | |
| | | Revenue from Donated Land | | 500 0 0 0 00 |

## Nature of Depreciation

As we have discussed in earlier chapters, land has an unlimited life and therefore can provide unlimited services. On the other hand, other fixed assets such as equipment, buildings, and land improvements lose their ability, over time, to provide services. As a result, the costs of equipment, buildings, and land improvements should be transferred to expense accounts in a systematic manner during their expected useful lives. This periodic transfer of cost to expense is called *depreciation*.

> **The adjusting entry to record depreciation debits Depreciation Expense and credits Accumulated Depreciation.**

The adjusting entry to record depreciation is usually made at the end of each month or at the end of the year. This entry debits *Depreciation Expense* and credits a *contra asset* account entitled *Accumulated Depreciation* or *Allowance for Depreciation*. The use of a contra asset account allows the original cost to remain unchanged in the fixed asset account.

---

[1]As discussed here, land is assumed to be used only as a location or site and not for its mineral deposits or other natural resources.
[2]*Statement of Financial Accounting Standards No. 116*, "Accounting for Contributions Received and Contributions Made," Financial Accounting Standards Board (Norwalk, Connecticut: 1993).

## •Exhibit 3    Costs of Acquiring Fixed Assets

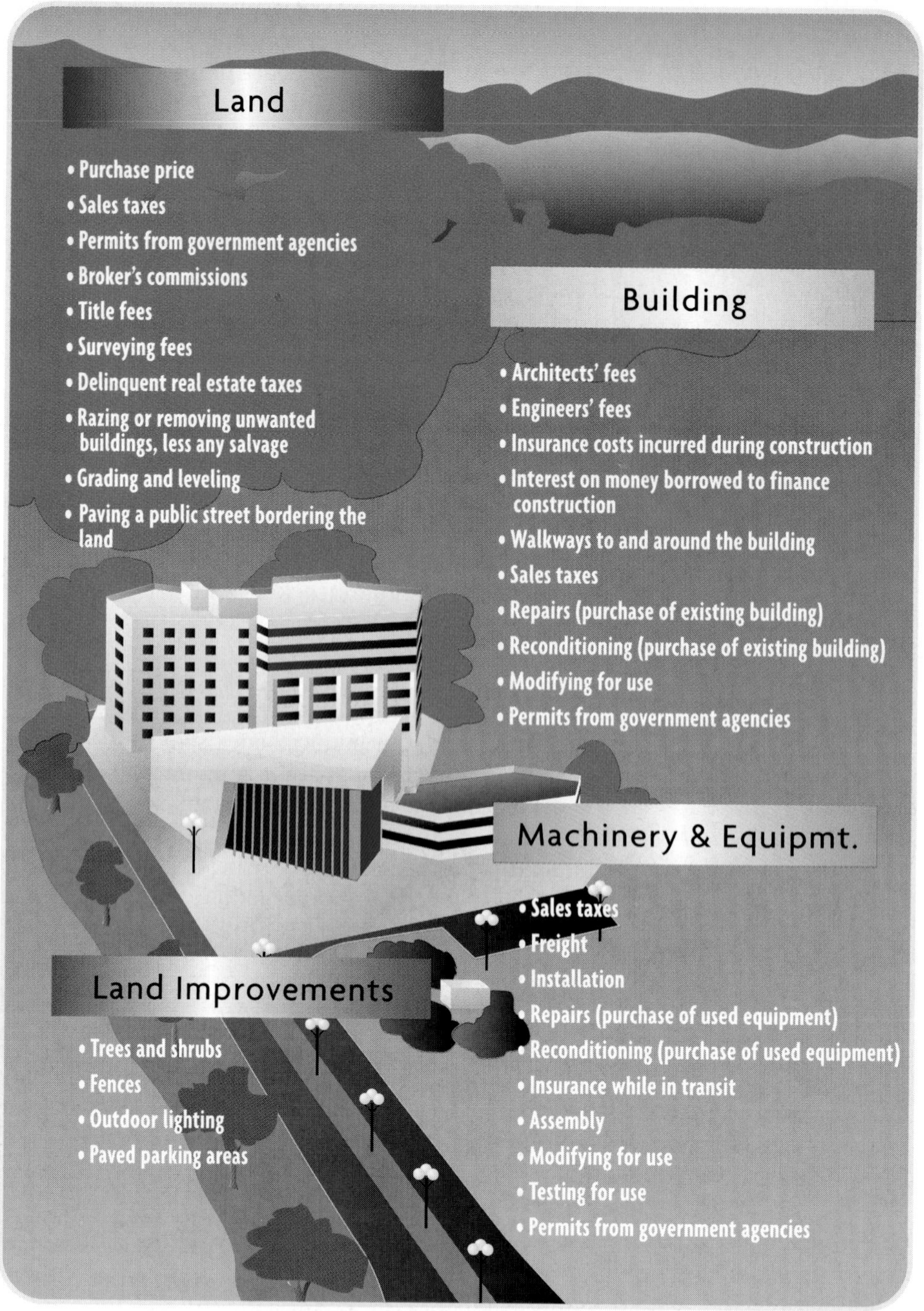

### Land

- Purchase price
- Sales taxes
- Permits from government agencies
- Broker's commissions
- Title fees
- Surveying fees
- Delinquent real estate taxes
- Razing or removing unwanted buildings, less any salvage
- Grading and leveling
- Paving a public street bordering the land

### Building

- Architects' fees
- Engineers' fees
- Insurance costs incurred during construction
- Interest on money borrowed to finance construction
- Walkways to and around the building
- Sales taxes
- Repairs (purchase of existing building)
- Reconditioning (purchase of existing building)
- Modifying for use
- Permits from government agencies

### Machinery & Equipmt.

- Sales taxes
- Freight
- Installation
- Repairs (purchase of used equipment)
- Reconditioning (purchase of used equipment)
- Insurance while in transit
- Assembly
- Modifying for use
- Testing for use
- Permits from government agencies

### Land Improvements

- Trees and shrubs
- Fences
- Outdoor lighting
- Paved parking areas

**REAL WORLD**

Companies often use different useful lives for similar assets. For example, the primary useful life for buildings is 50 years for **J.C.Penney Co.**, while the useful life for buildings for **Radio Shack** varies from 10 to 40 years.

Factors that cause a decline in the ability of a fixed asset to provide services may be identified as physical depreciation or functional depreciation. **Physical depreciation** occurs from wear and tear while in use and from the action of the weather. **Functional depreciation** occurs when a fixed asset is no longer able to provide services at the level for which it was intended. For example, a personal computer made in the 1980s would not be able to provide an Internet connection. Such advances in technology during this century have made functional depreciation an increasingly important cause of depreciation.

The term *depreciation* as used in accounting is often misunderstood because the same term is also used in business to mean a decline in the market value of an asset. However, the amount of a fixed asset's unexpired cost reported in the balance

**POINT OF INTEREST**

Would you have more cash if you depreciated your car? The answer is no. Depreciation does not affect your cash flows. Likewise, depreciation does not affect the cash flows of a business. However, depreciation is subtracted in determining net income.

sheet usually does not agree with the amount that could be realized from its sale. Fixed assets are held for use in a business rather than for sale. It is assumed that the business will continue as a going concern. Thus, a decision to dispose of a fixed asset is based mainly on the usefulness of the asset to the business and not on its market value.

Another common misunderstanding is that accounting for depreciation provides cash needed to replace fixed assets as they wear out. This misunderstanding probably occurs because depreciation, unlike most expenses, does not require an outlay of cash in the period in which it is recorded. The cash account is neither increased nor decreased by the periodic entries that transfer the cost of fixed assets to depreciation expense accounts.

# Accounting for Depreciation

### objective 2

Compute depreciation, using the following methods: straight-line method, units-of-production method, and declining-balance method.

Three factors are considered in determining the amount of depreciation expense to be recognized each period. These three factors are (a) the fixed asset's initial cost, (b) its expected useful life, and (c) its estimated value at the end of its useful life. This third factor is called the **residual value**, **scrap value**, **salvage value**, or **trade-in value**. Exhibit 4 shows the relationship among the three factors and the periodic depreciation expense.

A fixed asset's ***residual value*** at the end of its expected useful life must be estimated at the time the asset is placed in service. If a fixed asset is expected to have little or no residual value when it is taken out of service, then its initial cost should be spread over its expected useful life as depreciation expense. If, however, a fixed asset is expected to have a significant residual value, the difference between its initial cost and its residual value, called the asset's **depreciable cost**, is the amount that is spread over the asset's useful life as depreciation expense.

•**Exhibit 4**

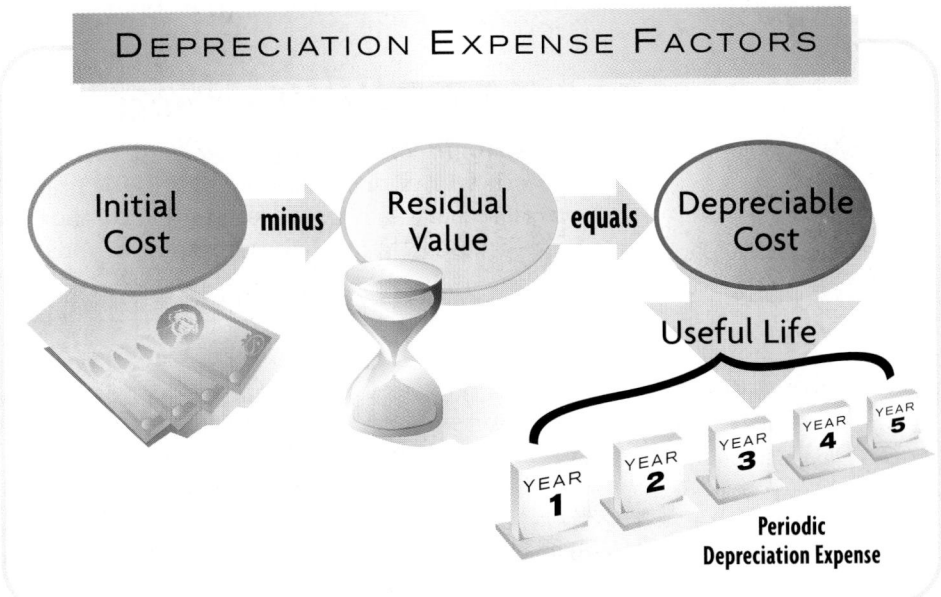

A fixed asset's **expected useful life** must also be estimated at the time the asset is placed in service. Estimates of expected useful lives are available from various trade associations and other publications. For federal income tax purposes, the Internal Revenue Service has established guidelines for useful lives. These guidelines may also be helpful in determining depreciation for financial reporting purposes.

The Internal Revenue Service guideline for the useful life of automobiles and light-duty trucks is 5 years, while the designated life for most machinery and equipment is 7 years.

In practice, many businesses use the guideline that all assets placed in or taken out of service during the first half of a month are treated as if the event occurred on the first day of *that* month. That is, these businesses compute depreciation on these assets for the entire month. Likewise, all fixed asset additions and deductions during the second half of a month are treated as if the event occurred on the first day of the *next* month. We will follow this practice in this chapter.

It is not necessary that a business use a single method of computing depreciation for all its depreciable assets. The methods used in the accounts and financial statements may also differ from the methods used in determining income taxes and property taxes. The three methods used most often are (1) straight-line, (2) units-of-production, and (3) declining-balance.[3] Exhibit 5 shows the extent of the use of these methods in financial statements.

## •Exhibit 5   Use of Depreciation Methods

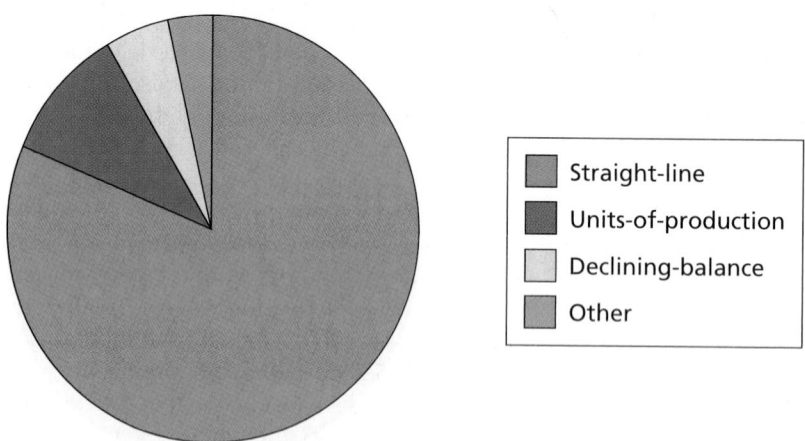

**Source:** *Accounting Trends & Techniques*, 56th ed., American Institute of Certified Public Accountants, New York, 2002.

## Straight-Line Method

A truck that cost $35,000 has a residual value of $5,000 and a useful life of 12 years. What are (a) the depreciable cost, (b) the straight-line rate, and (c) the annual straight-line depreciation?

--------------------------------------------

*(a) $30,000 ($35,000 − $5,000), (b) 8¹/₃% (¹/₁₂), (c) $2,500 ($30,000 × 8¹/₃%).*

The ***straight-line method*** provides for the same amount of depreciation expense for each year of the asset's useful life. For example, assume that the cost of a depreciable asset is $24,000, its estimated residual value is $2,000, and its estimated life is 5 years. The annual depreciation is computed as follows:

$$\frac{\$24{,}000 \text{ cost} - \$2{,}000 \text{ estimated residual value}}{5 \text{ years estimated life}} = \$4{,}400 \text{ annual depreciation}$$

When an asset is used for only part of a year, the annual depreciation is prorated. For example, assume that the fiscal year ends on December 31 and that the asset in the above example is placed in service on October 1. The depreciation for the first fiscal year of use would be $1,100 ($4,400 × 3/12).

For ease in applying the straight-line method, the annual depreciation may be converted to a percentage of the depreciable cost. This percentage is determined by dividing 100% by the number of years of useful life. For example, a useful life of 20 years converts to a 5% rate (100%/20), 8 years converts to a 12.5% rate (100%/8), and so on.[4] In the above example, the annual depreciation of $4,400 can be computed by multiplying the depreciable cost of $22,000 by 20% (100%/5).

---

[3]Another method not often used today, called the *sum-of-the-years-digits method*, is described and illustrated in the appendix at the end of this chapter.
[4]The depreciation rate may also be expressed as a fraction. For example, the annual straight-line rate for an asset with a 3-year useful life is 1/3.

The straight-line method is simple and is widely used. It provides a reasonable transfer of costs to periodic expense when the asset's use and the related revenues from its use are about the same from period to period.

## Units-of-Production Method

How would you depreciate a fixed asset when its service is related to use rather than time? When the amount of use of a fixed asset varies from year to year, the units-of-production method is more appropriate than the straight-line method. In such cases, the units-of-production method better matches the depreciation expense with the related revenue.

The **units-of-production method** provides for the same amount of depreciation expense for each unit produced or each unit of capacity used by the asset. To apply this method, the useful life of the asset is expressed in terms of units of productive capacity such as hours or miles. The total depreciation expense for each accounting period is then determined by multiplying the unit depreciation by the number of units produced or used during the period. For example, assume that a machine with a cost of $24,000 and an estimated residual value of $2,000 is expected to have an estimated life of 10,000 operating hours. The depreciation for a unit of one hour is computed as follows:

$$\frac{\$24,000 \text{ cost} - \$2,000 \text{ estimated residual value}}{10,000 \text{ estimated hours}} = \$2.20 \text{ hourly depreciation}$$

Assuming that the machine was in operation for 2,100 hours during a year, the depreciation for that year would be $4,620 ($2.20 × 2,100 hours).

## Declining-Balance Method

The **declining-balance method** provides for a declining periodic expense over the estimated useful life of the asset. To apply this method, the annual straight-line depreciation rate is doubled. For example, the declining-balance rate for an asset with an estimated life of 5 years is 40%, which is double the straight-line rate of 20% (100%/5).

For the first year of use, the cost of the asset is multiplied by the declining-balance rate. After the first year, the declining **book value** (cost minus accumulated depreciation) of the asset is multiplied by this rate. To illustrate, the annual declining-balance depreciation for an asset with an estimated 5-year life and a cost of $24,000 is shown below.

| Year | Cost | Accum. Depr. at Beginning of Year | Book Value at Beginning of Year | | Rate | Depreciation for Year | Book Value at End of Year |
|---|---|---|---|---|---|---|---|
| 1 | $24,000 | | $24,000.00 | × | 40% | $9,600.00 | $14,400.00 |
| 2 | 24,000 | $ 9,600.00 | 14,400.00 | × | 40% | 5,760.00 | 8,640.00 |
| 3 | 24,000 | 15,360.00 | 8,640.00 | × | 40% | 3,456.00 | 5,184.00 |
| 4 | 24,000 | 18,816.00 | 5,184.00 | × | 40% | 2,073.60 | 3,110.40 |
| 5 | 24,000 | 20,889.60 | 3,110.40 | | — | 1,110.40 | 2,000.00 |

You should note that when the declining-balance method is used, the estimated residual value is *not* considered in determining the depreciation rate. It is also ignored in computing the periodic depreciation. However, the asset should not be depreciated below its estimated residual value. In the above example, the estimated residual value was $2,000. Therefore, the depreciation for the fifth year is $1,110.40 ($3,110.40 − $2,000.00) instead of $1,244.16 (40% × $3,110.40).

In the example above, we assumed that the first use of the asset occurred at the beginning of the fiscal year. This is normally not the case in practice, however, and depreciation for the first partial year of use must be computed. For example, assume that the asset above was in service at the end of the *third* month of the fiscal

A truck that cost $35,000 has a residual value of $5,000 and a useful life of 125,000 miles. What are (a) the depreciation rate per mile and (b) the first year's depreciation if 18,000 miles were driven?

(a) $0.24 per mile [($35,000 − $5,000)/125,000 miles], (b) $4,320 (18,000 miles × $0.24 per mile)

A truck that cost $35,000 has a residual value of $5,000 and a useful life of 12 years. What is the double-declining balance depreciation for the second full year of use?

$4,861 {[$35,000 − ($35,000 × 16²/₃%)] × 16²/₃%}

year. In this case, only a portion (9/12) of the first full year's depreciation of $9,600 is allocated to the first fiscal year. Thus, depreciation of $7,200 (9/12 × $9,600) is allocated to the first partial year of use. The depreciation for the second fiscal year would then be $6,720 [40% × ($24,000 − $7,200)].

## Comparing Depreciation Methods

The straight-line method provides for the same periodic amounts of depreciation expense over the life of the asset. The units-of-production method provides for periodic amounts of depreciation expense that vary, depending upon the amount the asset is used.

The declining-balance method provides for a higher depreciation amount in the first year of the asset's use, followed by a gradually declining amount. For this reason, the declining-balance method is called an *accelerated depreciation method*. It is most appropriate when the decline in an asset's productivity or earning power is greater in the early years of its use than in later years. Further, using this method is often justified because repairs tend to increase with the age of an asset. The reduced amounts of depreciation in later years are thus offset to some extent by increased repair expenses.

The periodic depreciation amounts for the straight-line method and the declining-balance method are compared in Exhibit 6. This comparison is based on an asset cost of $24,000, an estimated life of 5 years, and an estimated residual value of $2,000.

•**Exhibit 6**    **Comparing Depreciation Methods**

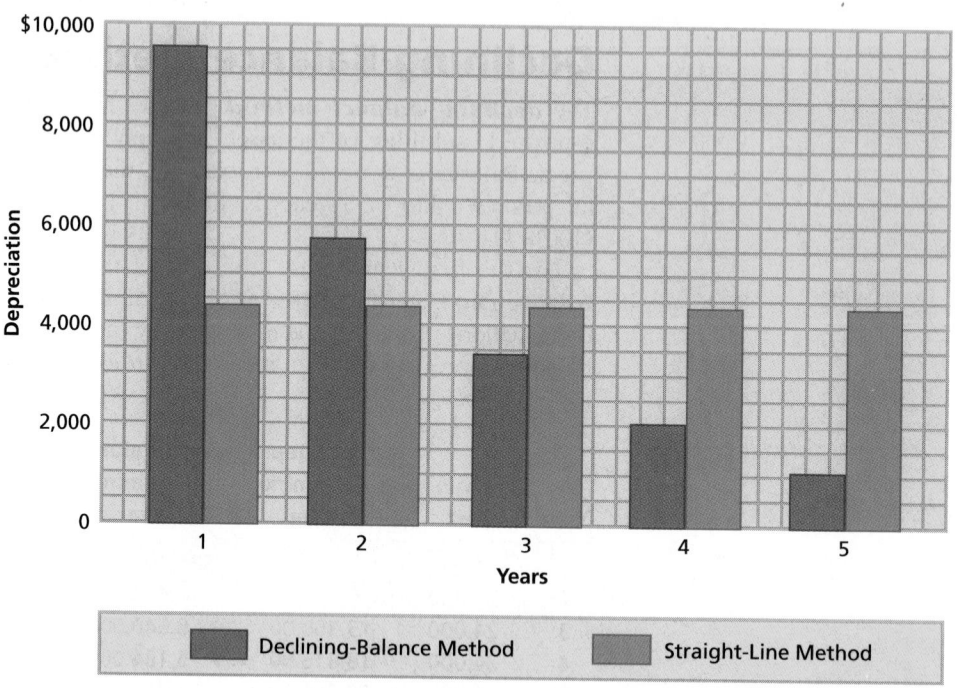

## Depreciation for Federal Income Tax

The Internal Revenue Code specifies the *Modified Accelerated Cost Recovery System (MACRS)* for use by businesses in computing depreciation for tax purposes. MACRS specifies eight classes of useful life and depreciation rates for each class. The two most common classes, other than real estate, are the 5-year class and the 7-year class.[5] The 5-year class includes automobiles and light-duty trucks, and the

---

[5] Real estate is in 27½-year classes and 31½-year classes and is depreciated by the straight-line method.

7-year class includes most machinery and equipment. The depreciation deduction for these two classes is similar to that computed using the declining-balance method.

In using the MACRS rates, residual value is ignored, and all fixed assets are assumed to be put in and taken out of service in the middle of the year. For the 5-year-class assets, depreciation is spread over six years, as shown in the following MACRS schedule of depreciation rates:

| Year | 5-Year-Class Depreciation Rates |
|---|---|
| 1 | 20.0% |
| 2 | 32.0 |
| 3 | 19.2 |
| 4 | 11.5 |
| 5 | 11.5 |
| 6 | 5.8 |
| | 100.0% |

To simplify its record keeping, a business will sometimes use the MACRS method for both financial statement and tax purposes. This is acceptable if MACRS does not result in significantly different amounts than would have been reported using one of the three depreciation methods discussed earlier in this chapter.

Using MACRS for both financial statement and tax purposes may, however, hurt a business. In one case, a business that had used MACRS depreciation for its financial statements lost a $1 million order because its fixed assets had low book values. The bank viewed these low book values as inadequate, so it would not loan the business the amount needed to produce the order.

## Revising Depreciation Estimates

Revising the estimates of the residual value and the useful life is normal. When these estimates are revised, they are used to determine the depreciation expense in future periods. They do not affect the amounts of depreciation expense recorded in earlier years.

To illustrate, assume that a fixed asset purchased for $130,000 was originally estimated to have a useful life of 30 years and a residual value of $10,000. The asset has been depreciated at $4,000 per year [($130,000 − $10,000) ÷ 30 years] for 10 years by the straight-line method. At the end of ten years, the asset's book value (undepreciated cost) is $90,000, determined as follows:

| | |
|---|---|
| Asset cost | $130,000 |
| Less accumulated depreciation ($4,000 per year × 10 years) | 40,000 |
| Book value (undepreciated cost), end of tenth year | $ 90,000 |

During the eleventh year, it is estimated that the remaining useful life is 25 years (instead of 20) and that the residual value is $5,000 (instead of $10,000). The depreciation expense for each of the remaining 25 years is $3,400, computed as follows:

| | |
|---|---|
| Book value (undepreciated cost), end of tenth year | $90,000 |
| Less revised estimated residual value | 5,000 |
| Revised remaining depreciable cost | $85,000 |
| Remaining years | ÷ 25 |
| Revised annual depreciation expense | $ 3,400 |

What is the third year's MACRS depreciation for an automobile that cost $26,000 and has a residual value of $6,500?

*$4,992 ($26,000 × 19.2%)*

For the $130,000 asset in the example on this page, assume that after 10 more years (20 years in total) its remaining useful life is estimated at 5 years with no residual value. What is the revised depreciation for the twenty-first year?

*$11,200 ($130,000 − $40,000 depreciation for years 1–10 = $90,000; $90,000 − $34,000 depreciation for years 11–20 = $56,000; $56,000 divided by 5 years = $11,200)*

## Composite-Rate Method

Assets may be grouped according to common traits, such as similar useful lives. For example, a group might include all delivery trucks with useful lives of less than 8 years. Likewise, a group might include all office equipment or all store fixtures. Depreciation may be determined for each group of assets, using a single *composite rate*, rather than a rate for each individual asset. The depreciation computations are similar for groups of assets as for individual assets.

# Capital and Revenue Expenditures

**objective 3**

Classify fixed asset costs as either capital expenditures or revenue expenditures.

The costs of acquiring fixed assets, adding to a fixed asset, improving a fixed asset, or extending a fixed asset's useful life are called **capital expenditures**. Such expenditures are recorded by either debiting the asset account or its related accumulated depreciation account. Costs that benefit only the current period or costs incurred for normal maintenance and repairs are called **revenue expenditures**. Such expenditures are debited to expense accounts. For example, the cost of replacing spark plugs in an automobile or the cost of repainting a building should be debited to an expense account.

To properly match revenues and expenses, it is important to distinguish between capital and revenue expenditures. Capital expenditures will affect the depreciation expense of more than one period, while revenue expenditures will affect the expenses of only the current period.

## Stages of Acquiring Fixed Assets

The costs incurred for fixed assets can be classified into four stages: preliminary, preacquisition, acquisition or construction, and in-service. These stages are illustrated in Exhibit 7.

**•Exhibit 7**   **Fixed Asset Project Stages**

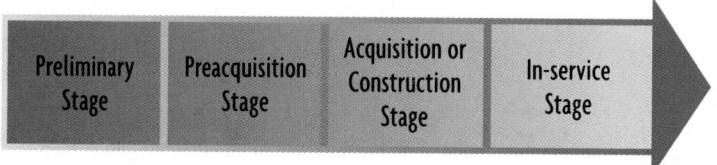

The *preliminary stage* occurs *before* management believes acquiring a fixed asset is probable. During this stage, a company may conduct feasibility studies, marketing studies, and financial analyses to determine the viability of a fixed asset acquisition. These costs are not associated with a particular fixed asset, so must be treated as revenue expenditures.[6]

At the *preacquisition stage*, acquiring the fixed asset has become probable, but has not yet occurred. Costs that are incurred during this stage, such as surveys, zoning, and engineering studies, can be associated with a specific fixed asset and should be treated as a capital expenditure. As we stated previously, capital expenditures are the costs of acquiring, constructing, adding, or replacing fixed assets.

During the *acquisition* or *construction stage*, the acquisition has occurred or construction has begun, but the fixed asset is not yet ready for use. Costs directly iden-

---

[6]Payments made to acquire options to purchase fixed assets should be capitalized.

tified with the fixed asset during this stage should be capitalized in the fixed asset account or in a construction in progress account. General and administrative costs should *not* be allocated to fixed asset acquisition or construction for capitalization. These costs are debited to the appropriate general and administrative expense account. When the fixed asset is ready for use, the capitalized costs should be transferred from construction in progress to the related fixed asset account.

During the *in-service stage*, the fixed asset is complete and ready for use. During this stage, the fixed asset should be depreciated as described in the previous section. In addition, normal, recurring, or periodic repairs and maintenance activities related to fixed assets during this stage should be charged to maintenance expense for the period. Costs incurred to either acquire additional components of fixed assets or replace existing components of fixed assets should be capitalized, as described in the next section.

Exhibit 8 summarizes the accounting for capital and revenue expenditures for the four stages of acquiring fixed assets.

### •Exhibit 8    Capital and Revenue Expenditures

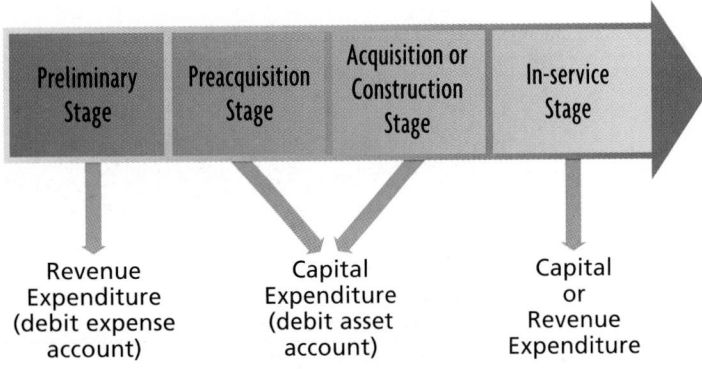

## INTEGRITY IN BUSINESS

### CAPITAL CRIME

**O**ne of the largest alleged accounting frauds in history involved the improper accounting for capital expenditures. **WorldCom, Inc.,** the second largest telecommunications company in the United States, improperly treated maintenance expenditures on its telecommunications network as capital expenditures. As a result, the company had to restate its prior years' earnings downward by nearly $4 billion to correct this error. The company declared bankruptcy within months of disclosing the error.

## Fixed Asset Components

An in-service stage fixed asset often includes one or more components. A **component** is a tangible portion of a fixed asset that can be separately identified as an asset and depreciated over its own separate expected useful life. For example, the roof or elevator of a building could be identified as components that are depreciated separately from the building itself. When a company *acquires* or *constructs a new component*, the costs should be capitalized as described for the previous project stages. Once installed, the component would be depreciated over its useful service life. For example, on April 1, Boxter Company purchased and installed a new crane within a warehouse for $150,000. This cost would be capitalized as a separate component as follows:

| | | | | | | |
|---|---|---|---|---|---|---|
| Apr. | 1 | Crane | | 150 0 0 0 00 | | |
| | | Cash | | | 150 0 0 0 00 | |

Identify each of the items related to a truck as capitalized or expensed: (a) a snowplow attachment that allows the truck to be used for snow removal, (b) a new transmission, (c) a hydraulic hitch to replace a manual hitch, (d) the cost of scheduled maintenance.

- - - - - - - - - - - - - - - - - - - - - - - - -

(a) capitalize (new component),
(b) capitalize (replaced component),
(c) capitalize (replaced component),
(d) expense (normal repair)

A company can also *replace a component.* Replacements are accounted for in two steps. First, the book value of the replaced component is debited to Depreciation Expense and credited to Accumulated Depreciation. This treatment is consistent with a change of estimate. That is, the fixed asset component is now recognized as being fully depreciated upon replacement. In addition, any costs to remove the old component should be charged to expense. Second, the identifiable direct costs associated with the new component are then capitalized. To illustrate, assume that Boxter removes a warehouse roof on August 1 at a cost of $1,000. As of August 1, the old roof has a remaining book value ($40,000 initial cost less $31,000 accumulated depreciation) of $9,000. On August 5, the new roof is completed at a cost of $60,000 and is estimated to have a 20-year life, which is the remaining life of the building. First, the cost of removing the old roof must be expensed, and the book value of the replaced roof must be completely depreciated, as follows:

| | | | | | | |
|---|---|---|---|---|---|---|
| Aug. | 1 | Removal Expenses | | 1 0 0 0 00 | | |
| | | Cash | | | 1 0 0 0 00 | |
| | | | | | | |
| | 1 | Depreciation Expense | | 9 0 0 0 00 | | |
| | | Accumulated Depreciation—Warehouse | | | 9 0 0 0 00 | |

After the preceding entry, the book value of the old roof is zero ($40,000 cost less $40,000 accumulated depreciation). Since the old roof is being replaced, its cost and related depreciation must now be removed from the accounting records, as shown in the following entry:

| | | | | | | |
|---|---|---|---|---|---|---|
| | | Accumulated Depreciation—Warehouse | | 40 0 0 0 00 | | |
| | | Warehouse | | | 40 0 0 0 00 | |

Next, the cost of the new roof must be capitalized as a separate component as follows:

| | | | | | | |
|---|---|---|---|---|---|---|
| Aug. | 5 | Warehouse | | 60 0 0 0 00 | | |
| | | Cash | | | 60 0 0 0 00 | |

Using the straight-line method, the new roof will be depreciated over 20 years at $3,000 per year ($60,000 ÷ 20 years).

# Disposal of Fixed Assets

objective **4**

Journalize entries for the disposal of fixed assets.

Fixed assets that are no longer useful may be discarded, sold, or traded for other fixed assets. The details of the entry to record a disposal will vary. In all cases, however, the book value of the asset must be removed from the accounts. The entry for this purpose debits the asset's accumulated depreciation account for its balance on the date of disposal and credits the asset account for the cost of the asset.

> **The entry to record the disposal of a fixed asset removes the cost of the asset and its accumulated depreciation from the accounts.**

A fixed asset should not be removed from the accounts only because it has been fully depreciated. If the asset is still used by the business, the cost and accumulated depreciation should remain in the ledger. This maintains accountability for the asset in the ledger. If the book value of the asset was removed from the ledger, the accounts would contain no evidence of the continued existence of the asset. In addition, the cost and the accumulated depreciation data on such assets are often needed for property tax and income tax reports.

## Discarding Fixed Assets

When fixed assets are no longer useful to the business and have no residual or market value, they are discarded. To illustrate, assume that an item of equipment acquired at a cost of $25,000 is fully depreciated at December 31, the end of the preceding fiscal year. On February 14, the equipment is discarded. The entry to record this is as follows:

| | | | | |
|---|---|---|---|---|
| Feb. | 14 | Accumulated Depreciation—Equipment | 25 0 0 0 00 | |
| | | Equipment | | 25 0 0 0 00 |
| | | To write off equipment discarded. | | |

If an asset has not been fully depreciated, depreciation should be recorded prior to removing it from service and from the accounting records. To illustrate, assume that equipment costing $6,000 is depreciated at an annual straight-line rate of 10%. In addition, assume that on December 31 of the preceding fiscal year, the accumulated depreciation balance, after adjusting entries, is $4,750. Finally, assume that the asset is removed from service on the following March 24. The entry to record the depreciation for the three months of the current period prior to the asset's removal from service is as follows:

| | | | | |
|---|---|---|---|---|
| Mar. | 24 | Depreciation Expense—Equipment | 1 5 0 00 | |
| | | Accumulated Depreciation—Equipment | | 1 5 0 00 |
| | | To record current depreciation on | | |
| | | equipment discarded ($600 × 3/12). | | |

The discarding of the equipment is then recorded by the following entry:

| | | | | |
|---|---|---|---|---|
| Mar. | 24 | Accumulated Depreciation—Equipment | 4 9 0 0 00 | |
| | | Loss on Disposal of Fixed Assets | 1 1 0 0 00 | |
| | | Equipment | | 6 0 0 0 00 |
| | | To write off equipment discarded. | | |

The loss of $1,100 is recorded because the balance of the accumulated depreciation account ($4,900) is less than the balance in the equipment account ($6,000). Losses on the discarding of fixed assets are nonoperating items and are normally reported in the Other Expense section of the income statement.

## Selling Fixed Assets

The entry to record the sale of a fixed asset is similar to the entries illustrated above, except that the cash or other asset received must also be recorded. If the selling price is more than the book value of the asset, the transaction results in a gain. If the selling price is less than the book value, there is a loss.

To illustrate, assume that equipment is acquired at a cost of $10,000 and is depreciated at an annual straight-line rate of 10%. The equipment is sold for cash on October 12 of the eighth year of its use. The balance of the accumulated depreciation account as of the preceding December 31 is $7,000. The entry to update the depreciation for the nine months of the current year is as follows:

| | | | | | |
|---|---|---|---|---|---|
| Oct. | 12 | Depreciation Expense—Equipment | | 750 00 | |
| | | Accumulated Depreciation—Equipment | | | 750 00 |
| | | To record current depreciation on | | | |
| | | equipment sold ($10,000 × ¾ × 10%). | | | |

After the current depreciation is recorded, the book value of the asset is $2,250 ($10,000 − $7,750). The entries to record the sale, assuming three different selling prices, are as follows:

Sold at book value, for $2,250. No gain or loss.

| | | | | | |
|---|---|---|---|---|---|
| Oct. | 12 | Cash | | 2 250 00 | |
| | | Accumulated Depreciation—Equipment | | 7 750 00 | |
| | | Equipment | | | 10 000 00 |

Sold below book value, for $1,000. Loss of $1,250.

| | | | | | |
|---|---|---|---|---|---|
| Oct. | 12 | Cash | | 1 000 00 | |
| | | Accumulated Depreciation—Equipment | | 7 750 00 | |
| | | Loss on Disposal of Fixed Assets | | 1 250 00 | |
| | | Equipment | | | 10 000 00 |

Sold above book value, for $2,800. Gain of $550.

| | | | | | |
|---|---|---|---|---|---|
| Oct. | 12 | Cash | | 2 800 00 | |
| | | Accumulated Depreciation—Equipment | | 7 750 00 | |
| | | Equipment | | | 10 000 00 |
| | | Gain on Disposal of Fixed Assets | | | 550 00 |

# Exchanging Similar Fixed Assets

Old equipment is often traded in for new equipment having a similar use. In such cases, the seller allows the buyer an amount for the old equipment traded in. This amount, called the **trade-in allowance**, may be either greater or less than the book value of the old equipment. The remaining balance—the amount owed—is either paid in cash or recorded as a liability. It is normally called **boot**, which is its tax name.

### Gains on Exchanges

Gains on exchanges of similar fixed assets are not recognized for financial reporting purposes.[7] This is based on the theory that revenue occurs from the production and sale of goods produced by fixed assets and not from the exchange of similar fixed assets.

When the trade-in allowance exceeds the book value of an asset traded in and no gain is recognized, the cost recorded for the new asset can be determined in either of two ways:

**REAL WORLD**

Gains on exchanges of similar fixed assets are also not recognized for federal income tax purposes.

---

[7]Gains on exchanges of similar fixed assets are recognized if cash (boot) is received. This topic is discussed in advanced accounting texts.

> 1. Cost of new asset = List price of new asset − Unrecognized gain
>
> *or*
>
> 2. Cost of new asset = Cash given (or liability assumed) + Book value of old asset

To illustrate, assume the following exchange:

*Similar equipment acquired (new):*

| | |
|---|---:|
| List price of new equipment | $5,000 |
| Trade-in allowance on old equipment | 1,100 |
| Cash paid at June 19, date of exchange | $3,900 |

*Equipment traded in (old):*

| | |
|---|---:|
| Cost of old equipment | $4,000 |
| Accumulated depreciation at date of exchange | 3,200 |
| Book value at June 19, date of exchange | $ 800 |

*Recorded cost of new equipment:*

**Method One:**

| | | |
|---|---:|---:|
| List price of new equipment | | $5,000 |
| Trade-in allowance | $1,100 | |
| Book value of old equipment | 800 | |
| Unrecognized gain on exchange | | (300) |
| Cost of new equipment | | $4,700 |

**Method Two:**

| | |
|---|---:|
| Book value of old equipment | $ 800 |
| Cash paid at date of exchange | 3,900 |
| Cost of new equipment | $4,700 |

The entry to record this exchange and the payment of cash is as follows:

| | | | | |
|---|---|---|---:|---:|
| June | 19 | Accumulated Depreciation—Equipment | 3 2 0 0 00 | |
| | | Equipment (new equipment) | 4 7 0 0 00 | |
| | | Equipment (old equipment) | | 4 0 0 0 00 |
| | | Cash | | 3 9 0 0 00 |
| | | To record exchange of equipment. | | |

Equipment with a book value of $14,000 is traded in for similar equipment with a list price of $50,000. A trade-in allowance of $15,000 was allowed on the old equipment. What is the cost of the new equipment to be recorded in the accounts?

--------------------------------------------

*$49,000 ($50,000 − $1,000 gain, or $14,000 + $35,000 boot)*

Not recognizing the $300 gain ($1,100 trade-in allowance minus $800 book value) at the time of the exchange reduces future depreciation expense. That is, the depreciation expense for the new asset is based on a cost of $4,700 rather than on the list price of $5,000. In effect, the unrecognized gain of $300 reduces the total amount of depreciation taken during the life of the equipment by $300.

## Losses on Exchanges

For financial reporting purposes, losses are recognized on exchanges of similar fixed assets if the trade-in allowance is less than the book value of the old equipment. When there is a loss, the cost recorded for the new asset should be the market (list) price. To illustrate, assume the following exchange:

**REAL WORLD**

Losses on exchanges of similar fixed assets are *not* recognized for federal income tax purposes.

*Similar equipment acquired (new):*

| | |
|---|---:|
| List price of new equipment | $10,000 |
| Trade-in allowance on old equipment | 2,000 |
| Cash paid at September 7, date of exchange | $ 8,000 |

*Equipment traded in (old):*

| | |
|---|---:|
| Cost of old equipment . . . . . . . . . . . . . . . . . . . . . . . . . . . | $ 7,000 |
| Accumulated depreciation at date of exchange . . . . . . . . | 4,600 |
| Book value at September 7, date of exchange . . . . . . . . . | $ 2,400 |
| Trade-in allowance on old equipment . . . . . . . . . . . . . . . | 2,000 |
| Loss on exchange . . . . . . . . . . . . . . . . . . . . . . . . . . . . . . | $ 400 |

The entry to record the exchange is as follows:

| | | | | | |
|---|---|---|---:|---:|---|
| Sept. | 7 | Accumulated Depreciation—Equipment | 4 6 0 0 00 | | |
| | | Equipment | 10 0 0 0 00 | | |
| | | Loss on Disposal of Fixed Assets | 4 0 0 00 | | |
| | | Equipment | | 7 0 0 0 00 | |
| | | Cash | | 8 0 0 0 00 | |
| | | To record exchange of equipment, | | | |
| | | with loss. | | | |

## Review of Accounting for Exchanges of Similar Fixed Assets

Exhibit 9 reviews the accounting for exchanges of similar fixed assets, using the following data:

| | |
|---|---:|
| List price of new equipment acquired . . . . . . . . . . . . . . . | $15,000 |
| Cost of old equipment traded in . . . . . . . . . . . . . . . . . . . | $12,500 |
| Accumulated depreciation at date of exchange . . . . . . . . | 10,100 |
| Book value at date of exchange . . . . . . . . . . . . . . . . . . . | $ 2,400 |

# Leasing Fixed Assets

**objective 5**

Define a lease and summarize the accounting rules related to the leasing of fixed assets.

You are probably familiar with leases. A *lease* is a contract for the use of an asset for a stated period of time. Leases are frequently used in business. For example, automobiles, computers, medical equipment, buildings, and airplanes are often leased.

The two parties to a lease contract are the lessor and the lessee. The *lessor* is the party who owns the asset. The *lessee* is the party to whom the rights to use the asset are granted by the lessor. The lessee is obligated to make periodic rent payments for the lease term. All leases are classified by the lessee as either capital leases or operating leases.

A **capital lease** is accounted for as if the lessee has, in fact, purchased the asset. The lessee debits an asset account for the fair market value of the asset and credits a long-term lease liability account. The asset is then written off as expense (amortized) over the life of the capital lease. The accounting for capital leases and the criteria that a capital lease must satisfy are discussed in more advanced accounting texts.

A lease that is not classified as a capital lease for accounting purposes is classified as an **operating lease**. The lessee records the payments under an operating lease by debiting *Rent Expense* and crediting *Cash*. Neither future lease obligations nor the future rights to use the leased asset are recognized in the accounts. However, the lessee must disclose future lease commitments in notes to the financial statements.

The asset rentals described in earlier chapters of this text were accounted for as operating leases. To simplify, we will continue to treat asset leases as operating leases.

**•Exhibit 9**    **Summary Illustration—Accounting for Exchanges of Similar Fixed Assets**

---

**CASE ONE (GAIN): Trade-in allowance is more than book value of asset traded in.**

*Trade-in allowance, $3,000; cash paid, $12,000 ($15,000 − $3,000)*

| Cost of new asset | List price of new asset acquired, less unrecognized gain: $14,400 ($15,000 − $3,000 − $2,400) |
|---|---|
| | **or** |
| | Cash paid plus book value of asset traded in: $14,400 ($12,000 + $2,400) |
| *Gain recognized* | None |
| *Entry* | Equipment                               14,400 |

```
Entry    Equipment                        14,400
         Accumulated Depreciation         10,100
              Equipment                              12,500
              Cash                                   12,000
```

**CASE TWO (LOSS): Trade-in allowance is less than book value of asset traded in.**

*Trade-in allowance, $2,000; cash paid, $13,000 ($15,000 − $2,000)*

| Cost of new asset | List price of new asset acquired: $15,000 |
|---|---|
| *Loss recognized* | $400 |

```
Entry    Equipment                        15,000
         Accumulated Depreciation         10,100
         Loss on Disposal of Fixed Assets    400
              Equipment                              12,500
              Cash                                   13,000
```

---

# Internal Control of Fixed Assets

**objective 6**

Describe internal controls over fixed assets.

Because of their dollar value and long-term nature, it is important to design and apply effective internal controls over fixed assets. Such controls should begin with authorization and approval procedures for the purchase of fixed assets. Controls should also exist to ensure that fixed assets are acquired at the lowest possible costs. One procedure to achieve this objective is to require competitive bids from preapproved vendors.

As soon as a fixed asset is received, it should be inspected and tagged for control purposes and recorded in a subsidiary ledger. This establishes the initial accountability for the asset. Subsidiary ledgers for fixed assets are also useful in determining depreciation expense and recording disposals. Operating data that may be recorded in the subsidiary ledger, such as number of breakdowns, length of time out of service, and cost of repairs, are useful in deciding

**Subsidiary ledger**

7 83134-6170570

whether to replace the asset. A company that maintains a computerized subsidiary ledger may use bar-coded tags, similar to the one on the back of this textbook, so that fixed asset data can be directly scanned into computer records.

Fixed assets should be insured against theft, fire, flooding, or other disasters. They should also be safeguarded from theft, misuse, or other damage. For example, fixed assets that are highly open to theft, such as computers, should be locked or otherwise protected when not in use. For computers, safeguarding also includes climate controls and special fire-extinguishing equipment. Procedures should also exist for training employees to properly operate fixed assets such as equipment and machinery.

A physical inventory of fixed assets should be taken periodically in order to verify the accuracy of the accounting records. Such an inventory would detect missing, obsolete, or idle fixed assets. In addition, fixed assets should be inspected periodically in order to determine their condition.

Careful control should also be exercised over the disposal of fixed assets. All disposals should be properly authorized and approved. Fully depreciated assets should be retained in the accounting records until disposal has been authorized and they are removed from service.

# Natural Resources

**objective 7**

Compute depletion and journalize the entry for depletion.

A business purchased mineral rights to 250,000 tons of ore for $1,500,000. If 35,000 tons of ore were mined in the first year, what are (a) the depletion rate per ton and (2) the depletion expense for the first year?

----

*(a) $6 per ton ($1,500,000/ 250,000 tons); (b) $210,000 (35,000 tons × $6)*

The fixed assets of some businesses include timber, metal ores, minerals, or other natural resources. As these businesses harvest or mine and then sell these resources, a portion of the cost of acquiring them must be debited to an expense account. This process of transferring the cost of natural resources to an expense account is called **depletion**. The amount of depletion is determined by multiplying the quantity extracted during the period by the depletion rate. This rate is computed by dividing the cost of the mineral deposit by its estimated size.

Computing depletion is similar to computing units-of-production depreciation. To illustrate, assume that a business paid $400,000 for the mining rights to a mineral deposit estimated at 1,000,000 tons of ore. The depletion rate is $0.40 per ton ($400,000/1,000,000 tons). If 90,000 tons are mined during the year, the periodic depletion is $36,000 (90,000 tons × $0.40). The entry to record the depletion is shown below.

| | | Adjusting Entry | | | |
|---|---|---|---|---|---|
| Dec. | 31 | Depletion Expense | 36 0 0 0 00 | |
| | | Accumulated Depletion | | 36 0 0 0 00 |

Like the accumulated depreciation account, Accumulated Depletion is a *contra asset* account. It is reported on the balance sheet as a deduction from the cost of the mineral deposit.

# Intangible Assets

**objective 8**

Describe the accounting for intangible assets, such as patents, copyrights, and goodwill.

Patents, copyrights, trademarks, and goodwill are long-lived assets that are useful in the operations of a business and are not held for sale. These assets are called **intangible assets** because they do not exist physically.

The basic principles of accounting for intangible assets are like those described earlier for fixed assets. The major concerns are determining (1) the initial cost and

(2) the **amortization**—the amount of cost to transfer to expense. Amortization results from the passage of time or a decline in the usefulness of the intangible asset.

# Patents

Manufacturers may acquire exclusive rights to produce and sell goods with one or more unique features. Such rights are granted by **patents**, which the federal government issues to inventors. These rights continue in effect for 20 years. A business may purchase patent rights from others, or it may obtain patents developed by its own research and development efforts.

The initial cost of a purchased patent, including any related legal fees, is debited to an asset account. This cost is written off, or amortized, over the years of the patent's expected usefulness. This period of time may be less than the remaining legal life of the patent. The estimated useful life of the patent may also change as technology or consumer tastes change.

The straight-line method is normally used to determine the periodic amortization. When the amortization is recorded, it is debited to an expense account and credited directly to the patents account. A separate contra asset account is usually *not* used for intangible assets.

To illustrate, assume that at the beginning of its fiscal year, a business acquires patent rights for $100,000. The patent had been granted 6 years earlier by the Federal Patent Office. Although the patent will not expire for 14 years, its remaining useful life is estimated as 5 years. The adjusting entry to amortize the patent at the end of the fiscal year is as follows:

| Dec. | 31 | Amortization Expense—Patents | 20 0 0 0 00 | |
|------|----|------------------------------|-------------|----------------|
|      |    | Patents                      |             | 20 0 0 0 00 |

Rather than purchase patent rights, a business may incur significant costs in developing patents through its own research and development efforts. Such *research and development costs* are usually accounted for as current operating expenses in the period in which they are incurred. Expensing research and development costs is justified because the future benefits from research and development efforts are highly uncertain.

# Copyrights and Trademarks

The exclusive right to publish and sell a literary, artistic, or musical composition is granted by a **copyright**. Copyrights are issued by the federal government and extend for 70 years beyond the author's death. The costs of a copyright include all costs of creating the work plus any administrative or legal costs of obtaining the copyright. A copyright that is purchased from another should be recorded at the price paid for it. Copyrights are amortized over their estimated useful lives. For example, **Sony Corporation** states the following amortization policy with respect to its artistic and music intangible assets:

*Intangibles, which mainly consist of artist contracts and music catalogs, are being amortized on a straight-line basis principally over 16 years and 21 years, respectively.*

A **trademark** is a name, term, or symbol used to identify a business and its products. For example, the distinctive red-and-white **Coca-Cola** logo is an example of a trademark. Most businesses identify their trademarks with ® in their advertisements and on their products. Under federal law, businesses can protect against others using

**REAL WORLD**

Coke® is one of the world's most recognizable trademarks. As stated in *LIFE*, "Two-thirds of the earth is covered by water; the rest is covered by Coke. If the French are known for wine and the Germans for beer, America achieved global beverage dominance with fizzy water and caramel color."

their trademarks by registering them for 10 years and renewing the registration for 10-year periods thereafter. Like a copyright, the legal costs of registering a trademark with the federal government are recorded as an asset. Thus, even though the Coca-Cola trademarks are extremely valuable, they are not shown on the balance sheet, because the legal costs for establishing these trademarks are immaterial. If, however, a trademark is purchased from another business, the cost of its purchase is recorded as an asset. The cost of a trademark is in most cases considered to have an indefinite useful life. Thus, trademarks are not amortized over a useful life, as are the previously discussed intangible assets. Rather, trademarks should be tested periodically for impaired value. When a trademark is impaired from competitive threats or other circumstances, the trademark should be written down and a loss recognized.

## INTEGRITY IN BUSINESS

### 21st CENTURY PIRATES

Pirated software is a major concern of software companies. For example, during a recent global sweep, **Microsoft** seized nearly five million units of counterfeit Microsoft software with an estimated retail value of $1.7 billion. U.S. copyright laws and practices are sometimes ignored or disputed in other parts of the world.

Businesses must honor the copyrights held by software companies by eliminating pirated software from corporate computers. The **Business Software Alliance (BSA)** represents the largest software companies in campaigns to investigate illegal use of unlicensed software by businesses. The BSA estimates software industry losses of nearly $12 billion annually from software piracy. Employees using pirated software on business assets risk bringing legal penalties to themselves and their employers.

## Goodwill

In business, *goodwill* refers to an intangible asset of a business that is created from such favorable factors as location, product quality, reputation, and managerial skill. Goodwill allows a business to earn a rate of return on its investment that is often in excess of the normal rate for other firms in the same business.

Generally accepted accounting principles permit goodwill to be recorded in the accounts only if it is objectively determined by a transaction. An example of such a transaction is the purchase of a business at a price in excess of the net assets (assets − liabilities) of the acquired business. The excess is recorded as goodwill and reported as an intangible asset. Unlike patents and copyrights, goodwill is not amortized. However, a loss should be recorded if the business prospects of the acquired firm become significantly impaired. This loss would normally be disclosed in the Other Expense section of the income statement. To illustrate, **Time Warner** recorded one of the largest losses in corporate history (nearly $54 billion) for the write-down of goodwill associated with the AOL and Time Warner merger. The entry is recorded as:

| | | | | | | | | | | | | | | | | | | | | | | | | | | | | |
|---|---|---|---|---|---|---|---|---|---|---|---|---|---|---|---|---|---|---|---|---|---|---|---|---|---|---|---|---|
| | Loss from Impaired Goodwill | 54 | 0 | 0 | 0 | 0 | 0 | 0 | 0 | 0 | 00 | | | | | | | | | | | | |
| | Goodwill | | | | | | | | | | | | 54 | 0 | 0 | 0 | 0 | 0 | 0 | 0 | 0 | 00 |

Exhibit 10 shows the frequency of intangible asset disclosures for a sample of 600 large firms. As you can see, goodwill is the most frequently reported intangible asset. This is because goodwill arises from merger transactions, which are very common.

## •Exhibit 10   Frequency of Intangible Asset Disclosures for 600 Firms

| Intangible Asset Category | Number of Firms |
|---|---|
| Goodwill | 490 |
| Trademarks, brand names, and copyrights | 120 |
| Patents | 73 |
| Customer lists | 52 |
| Technology | 51 |
| Franchises and licenses | 45 |
| Other | 102 |

**Source:** *Accounting Trends & Techniques*, 56th ed., American Institute of Certified Public Accountants, New York, 2002.
Note: Some firms have multiple disclosures.

# FINANCIAL REPORTING AND DISCLOSURE

## DELTA AIR LINES

**D**elta Air Lines, Inc., provides air transportation for passengers and freight throughout the United States and around the world. Delta is the second largest carrier in terms of passengers carried and third largest as measured by operating revenues and revenue passenger miles flown. Delta is the leading U.S. transatlantic airline, offering the most daily flight departures, serving the largest number of nonstop markets, and carrying more passengers than any other U.S. airline.

Delta reported the following financial information on its fixed assets in its financial statements for a recent year.

*ASSETS (in millions)*
*Property and Equipment:*

| | |
|---|---|
| Flight equipment | $19,427 |
| Less: Accumulated depreciation | 5,730 |
| Flight equipment, net | $13,697 |
| | |
| Flight equipment under capital leases | $ 382 |
| Less: Accumulated amortization | 262 |
| Flight equipment under capital leases, net | $ 120 |
| | |
| Ground property and equipment | $ 4,412 |
| Less: Accumulated depreciation | 2,355 |
| Ground property and equipment, net | $ 2,057 |
| | |
| Advance payments for equipment | $ 223 |
| Total property and equipment, net | $16,097 |

We record our property and equipment at cost and depreciate these assets on a straight-line basis to their estimated residual values over their respective estimated useful life. Residual values for flight equipment range from 5%-40% of cost. The estimated useful lives for major asset classifications are as follows:

| Asset Classification | Estimated Useful Life |
|---|---|
| Owned flight equipment | 15–25 years |
| Flight equipment under capital lease | Lease Term |
| Ground property and equipment | 3–30 years |
| Leasehold rights and landing slots | Lease Term |

. . . We capitalize interest on advance payments for the acquisition of new aircraft and on construction of ground facilities as an additional cost of the related assets. . . . Interest capitalization ends when the equipment or facility is ready for service or its intended use.

. . . We record impairment losses on long-lived assets used in operations, goodwill and other intangible assets when events and circumstances indicate the assets may be impaired . . . .

. . . We record maintenance costs in operating expense as they are incurred.

. . . Future expenditures for aircraft and engines on firm order as of January 31, 2002, are estimated to be $6.0 billion.

. . . [We recorded] a $363 million charge resulting from a decrease in value of certain aircraft. This charge includes . . . $191 million related to our 16 MD-90 and eight owned MD-11 aircraft . . . $83 million related to the accelerated retirement of 40 B-727 aircraft . . . $77 million writedown related to our decision to accelerate the retirement of nine B-737 aircraft in 2002 and a $12 million writedown . . . of 18 L-1011 aircraft which are held for disposal. We recorded $303 million of these charges as a result of the effects of the September 11 terrorist attacks. The remaining $60 million was recorded . . . when we initially decided to accelerate the retirement of the nine B-737 aircraft to more closely align capacity and demand, and to improve scheduling and operating efficiency.

# Financial Reporting for Fixed Assets and Intangible Assets

Describe how depreciation expense is reported in an income statement, and prepare a balance sheet that includes fixed assets and intangible assets.

How should fixed assets and intangible assets be reported in the financial statements? The amount of depreciation and amortization expense of a period should be reported separately in the income statement or disclosed in a note. A general description of the method or methods used in computing depreciation should also be reported.

The amount of each major class of fixed assets should be disclosed in the balance sheet or in notes. The related accumulated depreciation should also be disclosed, either by major class or in total. The fixed assets may be shown at their **book value** (cost less accumulated depreciation), which can also be described as their **net** amount. If there are too many classes of fixed assets, a single amount may be presented in the balance sheet, supported by a separate detailed listing. Fixed assets are normally presented under the more descriptive caption of **property, plant, and equipment**.

The cost of mineral rights or ore deposits is normally shown as part of the fixed assets section of the balance sheet. The related accumulated depletion should also be disclosed. In some cases, the mineral rights are shown net of depletion on the face of the balance sheet, accompanied by a note that discloses the amount of the accumulated depletion.

Intangible assets are usually reported in the balance sheet in a separate section immediately following fixed assets. The balance of each major class of intangible assets should be disclosed at an amount net of amortization taken to date. Exhibit 11 is a partial balance sheet that shows the reporting of fixed assets and intangible assets.

# Financial Analysis and Interpretation

Compute and interpret the ratio of fixed assets to long-term liabilities.

Long-term liabilities are often secured by fixed assets. The ratio of total fixed assets to long-term liabilities provides a solvency measure that indicates the margin of safety to creditors. It also gives an indication of the potential ability of the business to borrow additional funds on a long-term basis. The ***ratio of fixed assets to long-term liabilities*** is computed as follows:

$$\text{Ratio of fixed assets to long-term liabilities (debt)} = \frac{\text{Fixed assets (net)}}{\text{Long-term liabilities (debt)}}$$

To illustrate, the following data were taken from the 2002 and 2001 financial statements of **Procter & Gamble**:

|  | (in millions) | |
| --- | --- | --- |
|  | **2002** | **2001** |
| Property, plant, and equipment (net) | $13,349 | $13,095 |
| Long-term debt | 11,201 | 9,792 |

The ratio of fixed assets to long-term liabilities (debt) is 1.2 ($13,349/$11,201) for 2002 and 1.3 ($13,095/$9,792) for 2001. The decrease in the ratio from 2001 to 2002 indicates less of a margin of safety for creditors. As with other financial measures, the interpretation and analysis is enhanced by comparisons over time and with industry averages.

## •Exhibit 11    Fixed Assets and Intangible Assets in the Balance Sheet

**Discovery Mining Co.**
**Balance Sheet**
**December 31, 2006**

**Assets**

| | Cost | Accum. Depr. | Book Value | |
|---|---|---|---|---|
| Total current assets . . . . . . . . . . . . . . . . . . . . . . . . . . . . . . . . . . . . . . . . . | | | | $ 462,500 |
| Property, plant, and equipment: | Cost | Accum. Depr. | Book Value | |
| Land . . . . . . . . . . . . . . . . . . . | $ 30,000 | — | $ 30,000 | |
| Buildings . . . . . . . . . . . . . . . | 110,000 | $ 26,000 | 84,000 | |
| Factory equipment . . . . . . . . | 650,000 | 192,000 | 458,000 | |
| Office equipment . . . . . . . . . | 120,000 | 13,000 | 107,000 | |
| | $ 910,000 | $ 231,000 | | $679,000 |
| Mineral deposits: | Cost | Accum. Depl. | Book Value | |
| Alaska deposit . . . . . . . . . | $1,200,000 | $ 800,000 | $ 400,000 | |
| Wyoming deposit . . . . . . . | 750,000 | 200,000 | 550,000 | |
| | $1,950,000 | $1,000,000 | | 950,000 |
| Total property, plant, and equipment . . . . . . . . . . . . . . . . . . . . . . . . . . . . . . . . . . . . | | | | 1,629,000 |
| Intangible assets: | | | | |
| Patents . . . . . . . . . . . . . . . . . . . . . . . . . . . . . . . . . . . . . . . . . . . . . . . . | | | $ 75,000 | |
| Goodwill . . . . . . . . . . . . . . . . . . . . . . . . . . . . . . . . . . . . . . . . . . . . . . | | | 50,000 | |
| Total intangible assets . . . . . . . . . . . . . . . . . . . . . . . . . . . . . . . . . | | | | 125,000 |

## SPOTLIGHT ON STRATEGY

### HUB-AND-SPOKE OR POINT-TO-POINT?

**S**outhwest Airlines uses a simple fare structure, featuring low, unrestricted, unlimited, everyday coach fares. These fares are possible by Southwest's use of a point-to-point, rather than hub-and-spoke, business strategy. **United**, **Delta**, and **American** employ a hub-and-spoke strategy in which an airline establishes major hubs that serve as connecting links to other cities. For example, Delta has established major connecting hubs in Atlanta, Cincinnati, and Salt Lake City. In contrast, Southwest focuses on point-to-point service between selected cities with over 300 one-way, nonstop city pairs with an average length of 500 miles and average flying time of 1.5 hours. As a result, Southwest minimizes connections, delays, and total trip time. Southwest also focuses on serving conveniently located satellite or downtown airports, such as Dallas Love Field, Houston Hobby, and Chicago Midway. Because these airports are normally less congested than hub airports, Southwest is better able to maintain high employee productivity and reliable ontime performance. This operating strategy permits the company to achieve high asset utilization of its fixed assets, such as its 737 aircraft. For example, aircraft are scheduled to spend only 25 minutes at the gate, thereby reducing the number of aircraft and gate facilities that would otherwise be required.

# Appendix   Sum-of-the-Years-Digits Depreciation

**REAL WORLD**

A recent edition of *Accounting Trends & Techniques* reported that only 1%–2% of the surveyed companies now use this method for financial reporting purposes.

At one time, the sum-of-the-years-digits method of depreciation was used by many businesses. However, tax law changes limited its use for tax purposes.

Under the **sum-of-the-years-digits method**, depreciation expense is determined by multiplying the original cost of the asset less its estimated residual value by a smaller fraction each year. Thus, the sum-of-the-years-digits method is similar to the declining-balance method in that the depreciation expense declines each year.

The denominator of the fraction used in determining the depreciation expense is the sum of the digits of the years of the asset's useful life. For example, an asset with a useful life of 5 years would have a denominator of 15 (5 + 4 + 3 + 2 + 1).[8] The numerator of the fraction is the number of years of useful life remaining at the beginning of each year for which depreciation is being computed. Thus, the numerator decreases each year by 1. For a useful life of 5 years, the numerator is 5 the first year, 4 the second year, 3 the third year, and so on.

The following depreciation schedule illustrates the sum-of-the-years-digits method for an asset with a cost of $24,000, an estimated residual value of $2,000, and an estimated useful life of 5 years:

| Year | Cost Less Residual Value | Rate | Depreciation for Year | Accum. Depr. at End of Year | Book Value at End of Year |
|---|---|---|---|---|---|
| 1 | $22,000 | $5/15$ | $7,333.33 | $ 7,333.33 | $16,666.67 |
| 2 | 22,000 | $4/15$ | 5,866.67 | 13,200.00 | 10,800.00 |
| 3 | 22,000 | $3/15$ | 4,400.00 | 17,600.00 | 6,400.00 |
| 4 | 22,000 | $2/15$ | 2,933.33 | 20,533.33 | 3,466.67 |
| 5 | 22,000 | $1/15$ | 1,466.67 | 22,000.00 | 2,000.00 |

What if the fixed asset is not placed in service at the beginning of the year? When the date an asset is first put into service is not the beginning of a fiscal year, each full year's depreciation must be allocated between the two fiscal years benefited. To illustrate, assume that the asset in the above example was put into service at the beginning of the fourth month of the first fiscal year. The depreciation for that year would be $5,500 (9/12 × 5/15 × $22,000). The depreciation for the second year would be $6,233.33, computed as follows:

| | |
|---|---|
| $3/12 \times 5/15 \times$ **$22,000** | **$1,833.33** |
| $9/12 \times 4/15 \times$ **$22,000** | 4,400.00 |
| Total depreciation for second fiscal year | **$6,233.33** |

# Key Points

**1 Define fixed assets and describe the accounting for their cost.**
Fixed assets are long-term tangible assets that are owned by the business and are used in the normal operations of the business. Examples of fixed assets are equipment, buildings, and land. The initial cost of a fixed asset includes all amounts spent to get the asset in place and ready for use. For example, sales tax, freight, insurance in transit, and

---

[8]The denominator can also be determined from the following formula: $S = N[(N + 1)/2]$, where $S$ = sum of the digits and $N$ = number of years of estimated life.

installation costs are all included in the cost of a fixed asset. As time passes, all fixed assets except land lose their ability to provide services. As a result, the cost of a fixed asset should be transferred to an expense account, in a systematic manner, during the asset's expected useful life. This periodic transfer of cost to expense is called depreciation.

## 2 Compute depreciation, using the following methods: straight-line method, units-of-production method, and declining-balance method.

In computing depreciation, three factors need to be considered: (1) the fixed asset's initial cost, (2) the useful life of the asset, and (3) the residual value of the asset.

The straight-line method spreads the initial cost less the residual value equally over the useful life. The units-of-production method spreads the initial cost less the residual value equally over the units expected to be produced by the asset during its useful life. The declining-balance method is applied by multiplying the declining book value of the asset by twice the straight-line rate.

## 3 Classify fixed asset costs as either capital expenditures or revenue expenditures.

Fixed assets are acquired and used through the following four stages: preliminary, preacquistion, acquisition or construction, and in-service. The costs incurred during the preliminary stage are generally expensed, while the direct costs incurred during the preacquisition and acquisition stages are capitalized. During the in-service stage, ordinary and normal repairs are expensed, while new and replaced components are capitalized.

## 4 Journalize entries for the disposal of fixed assets.

The journal entries to record disposals of fixed assets will vary. In all cases, however, any depreciation for the current period should be recorded, and the book value of the asset is then removed from the accounts. The entry to remove the book value from the accounts is a debit to the asset's accumulated depreciation account and a credit to the asset account for the cost of the asset. For assets retired from service, a loss may be recorded for any remaining book value of the asset.

When a fixed asset is sold, the book value is removed and the cash or other asset received is also recorded. If the selling price is more than the book value of the asset, the transaction results in a gain. If the selling price is less than the book value, there is a loss.

When a fixed asset is exchanged for another of similar nature, no gain is recognized on the exchange. The acquired asset's cost is adjusted for any gains. A loss on an exchange of similar assets is recorded.

## 5 Define a lease and summarize the accounting rules related to the leasing of fixed assets.

A lease is a contract for the use of an asset for a period of time. A capital lease is accounted for as if the lessee has purchased the asset. The lease payments under an operating lease are accounted for as rent expense for the lessee.

## 6 Describe internal controls over fixed assets.

Internal controls over fixed assets should include procedures for authorizing the purchase of assets. Once acquired, fixed assets should be safeguarded from theft, misuse, or damage. A physical inventory of fixed assets should be taken periodically.

## 7 Compute depletion and journalize the entry for depletion.

The amount of periodic depletion is computed by multiplying the quantity of minerals extracted during the period by a depletion rate. The depletion rate is computed by dividing the cost of the mineral deposit by its estimated size. The entry to record depletion debits a depletion expense account and credits an accumulated depletion account.

## 8 Describe the accounting for intangible assets, such as patents, copyrights, and goodwill.

Long-term assets that are without physical attributes but are used in the business are classified as intangible assets. Examples of intangible assets are patents, copyrights, trademarks, and goodwill. The initial cost of an intangible asset should be debited to an asset account. For patents and copyrights, this cost should be written off, or amortized, over the years of the asset's expected usefulness by debiting an expense account and crediting the intangible asset account. Trademarks and goodwill are not amortized, but are written down only upon impairment.

## 9 Describe how depreciation expense is reported in an income statement, and prepare a balance sheet that includes fixed assets and intangible assets.

The amount of depreciation expense and the method or methods used in computing depreciation should be disclosed in the financial statements. In addition, each major class of fixed assets should be disclosed, along with the related accumulated depreciation. Intangible assets are usually presented in the balance sheet in a separate section immediately following fixed assets. Each major class of intangible assets should be disclosed at an amount net of the amortization recorded to date.

## 10 Compute and interpret the ratio of fixed assets to long-term liabilities.

The ratio of fixed assets to long-term liabilities is a solvency measure that indicates the margin of safety to creditors. It also provides an indication of the ability of a company to borrow additional funds on a long-term basis.

# Key Terms

accelerated depreciation method (400)

amortization (411)

book value (399)

boot (406)

capital expenditures (402)

capital lease (408)

component (403)

copyright (411)

declining-balance method (399)

depletion (410)

depreciation (395)

fixed assets (393)

goodwill (412)

intangible assets (410)

operating lease (408)

patents (411)

ratio of fixed assets to long-term liabilities (414)

residual value (397)

revenue expenditures (402)

straight-line method (398)

trade-in allowance (406)

trademark (411)

units-of-production method (399)

# Illustrative Problem

McCollum Company, a furniture wholesaler, acquired new equipment at a cost of $150,000 at the beginning of the fiscal year. The equipment has an estimated life of 5 years and an estimated residual value of $12,000. Ellen McCollum, the president, has requested information regarding alternative depreciation methods.

## Instructions

1. Determine the annual depreciation for each of the five years of estimated useful life of the equipment, the accumulated depreciation at the end of each year, and the book value of the equipment at the end of each year by (a) the straight-line method and (b) the declining-balance method (at twice the straight-line rate).

2. Assume that the equipment was depreciated under the declining-balance method. In the first week of the fifth year, the equipment was traded in for similar equipment priced at $175,000. The trade-in allowance on the old equipment was $10,000, and cash was paid for the balance. Journalize the entry to record the exchange.

## Solution

**1.**

| | Year | Depreciation Expense | Accumulated Depreciation, End of Year | Book Value, End of Year |
|---|---|---|---|---|
| a. | 1 | $27,600* | $ 27,600 | $122,400 |
| | 2 | 27,600 | 55,200 | 94,800 |
| | 3 | 27,600 | 82,800 | 67,200 |
| | 4 | 27,600 | 110,400 | 39,600 |
| | 5 | 27,600 | 138,000 | 12,000 |

*$27,600 = ($150,000 − $12,000) ÷ 5

| | Year | Depreciation Expense | Accumulated Depreciation, End of Year | Book Value, End of Year |
|---|---|---|---|---|
| b. | 1 | $60,000** | $ 60,000 | $ 90,000 |
| | 2 | 36,000 | 96,000 | 54,000 |
| | 3 | 21,600 | 117,600 | 32,400 |
| | 4 | 12,960 | 130,560 | 19,440 |
| | 5 | 7,440*** | 138,000 | 12,000 |

**$60,000 = $150,000 × 40%

***The asset is not depreciated below the estimated residual value of $12,000.

2.

| | | Accumulated Depreciation—Equipment | 130 5 6 0 00 | | |
|---|---|---|---|---|---|
| | | Equipment | 175 0 0 0 00 | | |
| | | Loss on Disposal of Fixed Assets | 9 4 4 0 00 | | |
| | |     Equipment | | 150 0 0 0 00 |
| | |     Cash | | 165 0 0 0 00 |

# Self-Examination Questions (Answers at End of Chapter)

1. Which of the following expenditures incurred in connection with acquiring machinery is a proper charge to the asset account?
   A. Freight
   B. Installation costs
   C. Both A and B
   D. Neither A nor B

2. What is the amount of depreciation, using the declining-balance method (twice the straight-line rate) for the second year of use for equipment costing $9,000, with an estimated residual value of $600 and an estimated life of 3 years?
   A. $6,000
   B. $3,000
   C. $2,000
   D. $400

3. An example of an accelerated depreciation method is:
   A. Straight-line
   B. Declining-balance
   C. Units-of-production
   D. Depletion

4. A fixed asset priced at $100,000 is acquired by trading in a similar asset that has a book value of $25,000. Assuming that the trade-in allowance is $30,000 and that $70,000 cash is paid for the new asset, what is the cost of the new asset for financial reporting purposes?
   A. $100,000
   B. $95,000
   C. $70,000
   D. $30,000

5. Which of the following is an example of an intangible asset?
   A. Patents
   B. Goodwill
   C. Copyrights
   D. All of the above

# Class Discussion Questions

1. Which of the following qualities are characteristic of fixed assets? (a) tangible, (b) capable of repeated use in the operations of the business, (c) held for sale in the normal course of business, (d) used rarely in the operations of the business, (e) long-lived.

2. Wang Office Equipment Co. has a fleet of automobiles and trucks for use by salespersons and for delivery of office supplies and equipment. Lake City Auto Sales Co. has automobiles and trucks for sale. Under what caption would the automobiles and trucks be reported on the balance sheet of (a) Wang Office Equipment Co., (b) Lake City Auto Sales Co.?

3. Muskegon Co. acquired an adjacent vacant lot with the hope of selling it in the future at a gain. The lot is not intended to be used in Muskegon's business operations. Where should such real estate be listed in the balance sheet?

4. Redding Company solicited bids from several contractors to construct an addition to its office building. The lowest bid received was for $420,000. Redding Company decided to construct the addition itself at a cost of $375,000. What amount should be recorded in the building account?

5. Are the amounts at which fixed assets are reported in the balance sheet their approximate market values as of the balance sheet date? Discuss.

6. a. Does the recognition of depreciation in the accounts provide a special cash fund for the replacement of fixed assets? Explain.

   b. Describe the nature of depreciation as the term is used in accounting.

7. Lowell Company purchased a machine that has a manufacturer's suggested life of 18 years. The company plans to use the machine on a special project that will last 12 years. At the completion of the project, the machine will be sold. Over how many years should the machine be depreciated?

8. Is it necessary for a business to use the same method of computing depreciation (a) for all classes of its depreciable assets, (b) in the financial statements and in determining income taxes?

9. a. Under what conditions is the use of an accelerated depreciation method most appropriate?

   b. Why is an accelerated depreciation method often used for income tax purposes?

   c. What is the Modified Accelerated Cost Recovery System (MACRS), and under what conditions is it used?

10. A company revised the estimated useful lives of its fixed assets, which resulted in an increase in the remaining lives of several assets. Do GAAP permit the company to include, as income of the current period, the cumulative effect of the changes, which reduces the depreciation expense of past periods? Discuss.

11. Differentiate between the accounting for capital expenditures and revenue expenditures.

12. Immediately after a used truck is acquired, a new motor is installed and the tires are replaced at a total cost of $5,750. Is this a capital expenditure or a revenue expenditure?

13. For some of the fixed assets of a business, the balance in Accumulated Depreciation is exactly equal to the cost of the asset. (a) Is it permissible to record additional depreciation on the assets if they are still useful to the business? Explain. (b) When should an entry be made to remove the cost and the accumulated depreciation from the accounts?

14. a. Describe the internal controls for acquiring fixed assets.

    b. Explain why a physical count of fixed assets is desirable.

15. a. Over what period of time should the cost of a patent acquired by purchase be amortized?

    b. In general, what is the required accounting treatment for research and development costs?

    c. How should goodwill be amortized?

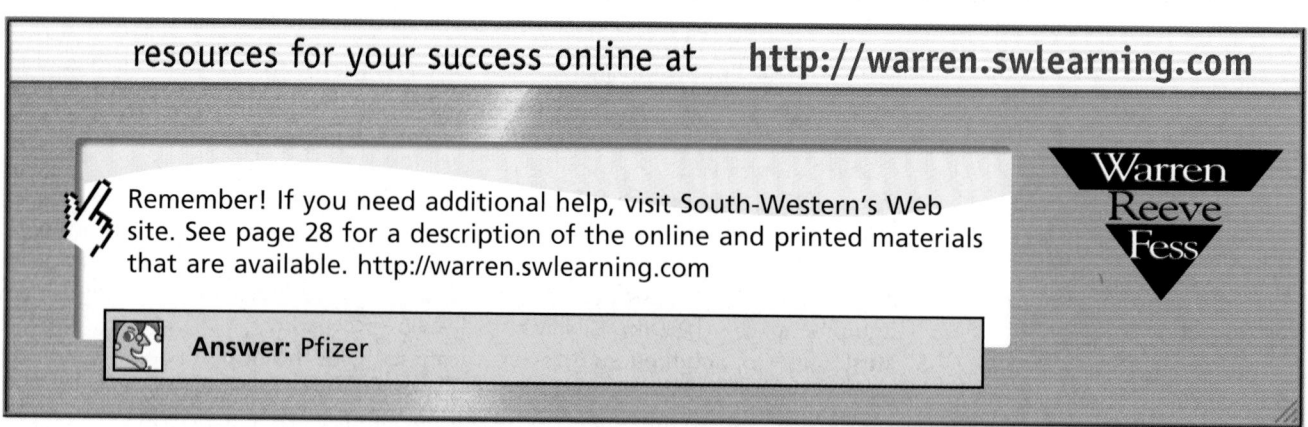

resources for your success online at     http://warren.swlearning.com

Remember! If you need additional help, visit South-Western's Web site. See page 28 for a description of the online and printed materials that are available. http://warren.swlearning.com

Warren Reeve Fess

Answer: Pfizer

# Exercises

**EXERCISE 10-1**
*Costs of acquiring fixed assets*
**Objective 1**

Cristy Fleming owns and operates Quesenberry Print Co. During February, Quesenberry Print Co. incurred the following costs in acquiring two printing presses. One printing press was new, and the other was used by a business that recently filed for bankruptcy.

Costs related to new printing press:

1. Freight
2. Special foundation
3. Sales tax on purchase price
4. Insurance while in transit
5. Fee paid to factory representative for installation
6. New parts to replace those damaged in unloading

Costs related to secondhand printing press:

7. Repair of vandalism during installation
8. Replacement of worn-out parts
9. Freight
10. Installation
11. Repair of damage incurred in reconditioning the press
12. Fees paid to attorney to review purchase agreement

a. Indicate which costs incurred in acquiring the new printing press should be debited to the asset account.
b. Indicate which costs incurred in acquiring the secondhand printing press should be debited to the asset account.

**EXERCISE 10-2**
*Determine cost of land*
**Objective 1**

A company has developed a tract of land into a ski resort. The company has cut the trees, cleared and graded the land and hills, and constructed ski lifts. (a) Should the tree cutting, land clearing, and grading costs of constructing the ski slopes be debited to the land account? (b) If such costs are debited to Land, should they be depreciated?

**EXERCISE 10-3**
*Determine cost of land*
**Objective 1**
✓ $188,000

Alligator Delivery Company acquired an adjacent lot to construct a new warehouse, paying $35,000 and giving a short-term note for $125,000. Legal fees paid were $1,100, delinquent taxes assumed were $12,500, and fees paid to remove an old building from the land were $18,000. Materials salvaged from the demolition of the building were sold for $3,600. A contractor was paid $512,500 to construct a new warehouse. Determine the cost of the land to be reported on the balance sheet.

**EXERCISE 10-4**
*Nature of depreciation*
**Objective 1**

Ball-Peen Metal Casting Co. reported $859,600 for equipment and $317,500 for accumulated depreciation—equipment on its balance sheet.
➤ Does this mean (a) that the replacement cost of the equipment is $859,600 and (b) that $317,500 is set aside in a special fund for the replacement of the equipment? Explain.

**EXERCISE 10-5**
*Straight-line depreciation rates*
**Objective 2**
✓ a. 5%

Convert each of the following estimates of useful life to a straight-line depreciation rate, stated as a percentage, assuming that the residual value of the fixed asset is to be ignored: (a) 20 years, (b) 25 years, (c) 40 years, (d) 4 years, (e) 5 years, (f) 10 years, (g) 50 years.

**EXERCISE 10-6**
*Straight-line depreciation*
**Objective 2**

✓ *$18,000*

A refrigerator used by a meat processor has a cost of $312,000, an estimated residual value of $42,000, and an estimated useful life of 15 years. What is the amount of the annual depreciation computed by the straight-line method?

**EXERCISE 10-7**
*Depreciation by units-of-production method*
**Objective 2**

✓ *$5,450*

A diesel-powered generator with a cost of $345,000 and estimated residual value of $18,000 is expected to have a useful operating life of 75,000 hours. During July, the generator was operated 1,250 hours. Determine the depreciation for the month.

**EXERCISE 10-8**
*Depreciation by units-of-production method*
**Objective 2**

✓ *a. Truck #1, credit Accumulated Depreciation, $8,000*

Prior to adjustment at the end of the year, the balance in Trucks is $182,600 and the balance in Accumulated Depreciation—Trucks is $75,500. Details of the subsidiary ledger are as follows:

| Truck No. | Cost | Estimated Residual Value | Estimated Useful Life | Accumulated Depreciation at Beginning of Year | Miles Operated During Year |
|---|---|---|---|---|---|
| 1 | $68,000 | $8,000 | 300,000 miles | $27,000 | 40,000 miles |
| 2 | 48,600 | 6,600 | 200,000 | 39,900 | 12,000 |
| 3 | 38,000 | 3,000 | 200,000 | 8,050 | 36,000 |
| 4 | 28,000 | 4,000 | 120,000 | — | 21,000 |

a. Determine the depreciation rates per mile and the amount to be credited to the accumulated depreciation section of each of the subsidiary accounts for the miles operated during the current year.
b. Journalize the entry to record depreciation for the year.

**EXERCISE 10-9**
*Depreciation by two methods*
**Objective 2**

✓ *a. $7,000*

A backhoe acquired on January 5 at a cost of $84,000 has an estimated useful life of 12 years. Assuming that it will have no residual value, determine the depreciation for each of the first two years (a) by the straight-line method and (b) by the declining-balance method, using twice the straight-line rate. Round to the nearest dollar.

**EXERCISE 10-10**
*Depreciation by two methods*
**Objective 2**

✓ *a. $9,100*

A dairy storage tank acquired at the beginning of the fiscal year at a cost of $98,500 has an estimated residual value of $7,500 and an estimated useful life of 10 years. Determine the following: (a) the amount of annual depreciation by the straight-line method and (b) the amount of depreciation for the first and second year computed by the declining-balance method (at twice the straight-line rate).

**EXERCISE 10-11**
*Partial-year depreciation*
**Objective 2**

✓ *a. First year, $2,700*

Sandblasting equipment acquired at a cost of $54,000 has an estimated residual value of $10,800 and an estimated useful life of 12 years. It was placed in service on April 1 of the current fiscal year, which ends on December 31. Determine the depreciation for the current fiscal year and for the following fiscal year by (a) the straight-line method and (b) the declining-balance method, at twice the straight-line rate.

**EXERCISE 10-12**
*Revision of depreciation*
**Objective 2**

✓ *a. $15,000*

A warehouse with a cost of $800,000 has an estimated residual value of $200,000, an estimated useful life of 40 years, and is depreciated by the straight-line method. (a) What is the amount of the annual depreciation? (b) What is the book value at the end of the twentieth year of use? (c) If at the start of the twenty-first year it is estimated that the remaining life is 25 years and that the residual value is $150,000, what is the depreciation expense for each of the remaining 25 years?

**EXERCISE 10-13**
*Book value of fixed assets*
**Objective 2**

The following data were taken from recent annual reports of **Interstate Bakeries Corporation (IBC)**. Interstate Bakeries produces, distributes, and sells fresh bakery products nationwide through supermarkets, convenience stores, and its 67 bakeries and 1,500 thrift stores.

|  | Current Year | Preceding Year |
|---|---|---|
| Land and buildings | $ 426,322,000 | $ 418,928,000 |
| Machinery and equipment | 1,051,861,000 | 1,038,323,000 |
| Accumulated depreciation | 633,178,000 | 582,941,000 |

a. Compute the book value of the fixed assets for the current year and the preceding year and explain the differences, if any.

b. Would you normally expect the book value of fixed assets to increase or decrease during the year?

**EXERCISE 10-14**
*Capital and revenue expenditures*
**Objective 3**

Hicks Co. incurred the following costs related to trucks and vans used in operating its delivery service:

1. Removed a two-way radio from one of the trucks and installed a new radio with a greater range of communication.
2. Overhauled the engine on one of the trucks that had been purchased three years ago.
3. Changed the oil and greased the joints of all the trucks and vans.
4. Installed security systems on four of the newer trucks.
5. Changed the radiator fluid on a truck that had been in service for the past 4 years.
6. Installed a hydraulic lift to a van.
7. Tinted the back and side windows of one of the vans to discourage theft of contents.
8. Repaired a flat tire on one of the vans.
9. Rebuilt the transmission on one of the vans that had been driven 40,000 miles. The van was no longer under warranty.
10. Replaced the trucks' suspension system with a new suspension system that allows for the delivery of heavier loads.

Classify each of the costs as a capital expenditure or a revenue expenditure. For those costs identified as capital expenditures, classify each as an additional or replacement component.

**EXERCISE 10-15**
*Capital and revenue expenditures*
**Objective 3**

Felix Little owns and operates Big Sky Transport Co. During the past year, Felix incurred the following costs related to his 18-wheel truck.

1. Replaced a headlight that had burned out.
2. Removed the old CB radio and replaced it with a newer model with a greater range.
3. Replaced a shock absorber that had worn out.
4. Installed a television in the sleeping compartment of the truck.
5. Replaced the old radar detector with a newer model that detects the KA frequencies now used by many of the state patrol radar guns. The detector is wired directly into the cab, so that it is partially hidden. In addition, Felix fastened the detector to the truck with a locking device that prevents its removal.
6. Installed fog and cab lights.
7. Installed a wind deflector on top of the cab to increase fuel mileage.
8. Modified the factory-installed turbo charger with a special-order kit designed to add 50 more horsepower to the engine performance.
9. Replaced the hydraulic brake system that had begun to fail during his latest trip through the Rocky Mountains.
10. Overhauled the engine.

Classify each of the costs as a capital expenditure or a revenue expenditure. For those costs identified as capital expenditures, classify each as an additional or replacement component.

**EXERCISE 10-16**
*Fixed asset component replacement*

Objectives 2, 3

✓ c. Depreciation Expense, $2,250

Jacobs Company replaced carpeting throughout its general offices. The old carpet was removed at a cost of $1,500 on March 15. The book value of the old carpet was $6,000 on March 15 ($18,000 original cost less $12,000 accumulated depreciation). New carpet was purchased and installed during the last two weeks of March for a total cost of $45,000. The carpet is estimated to have a 15-year useful life.

a. Record the cost of removing the old carpet.
b. Prepare the journal entries necessary for recording the replacement of the old carpet with the new carpet.
c. Record the December 31 adjusting entry for the partial-year depreciation expense for the carpet, assuming that Jacobs uses the straight-line method.

**EXERCISE 10-17**
*Fixed asset component replacement*

Objectives 2, 3

✓ b. $29,000

Dale's Edge, Inc., purchased and installed an alarm system for its retail store on January 1, 1999, at a cost of $50,000. The alarm system was estimated to have a ten-year life with no salvage value. On January 1, 2006, the alarm system was replaced with a system having more advanced technology. The removal of the old alarm system cost $2,000. The new system cost $120,000 and is estimated to have a ten-year life, with no residual value. Dale's Edge uses the straight-line depreciation method.

a. Determine the total depreciation expense for 2006 related to the alarm system.
b. Determine the total expense reported in the income statement in 2006 from these transactions.

**EXERCISE 10-18**
*Entries for sale of fixed asset*

Objective 4

Metal recycling equipment acquired on January 3, 2003, at a cost of $240,000, has an estimated useful life of 10 years, an estimated residual value of $15,000, and is depreciated by the straight-line method.

a. What was the book value of the equipment at December 31, 2006, the end of the fiscal year?
b. Assuming that the equipment was sold on July 1, 2007, for $135,000, journalize the entries to record (1) depreciation for the six months until the sale date, and (2) the sale of the equipment.

**EXERCISE 10-19**
*Disposal of fixed asset*

Objective 4

✓ b. $51,000

Equipment acquired on January 3, 2003, at a cost of $96,000, has an estimated useful life of 6 years and an estimated residual value of $6,000.

a. What was the annual amount of depreciation for the years 2003, 2004, and 2005, using the straight-line method of depreciation?
b. What was the book value of the equipment on January 1, 2006?
c. Assuming that the equipment was sold on January 2, 2006, for $38,000, journalize the entry to record the sale.
d. Assuming that the equipment had been sold on January 2, 2006, for $53,000 instead of $38,000, journalize the entry to record the sale.

**EXERCISE 10-20**
*Asset traded for similar asset*

Objective 4

✓ a. $205,000

A printing press priced at $315,000 is acquired by trading in a similar press and paying cash for the difference between the trade-in allowance and the price of the new press.

a. Assuming that the trade-in allowance is $110,000, what is the amount of cash given?
b. Assuming that the book value of the press traded in is $98,750, what is the cost of the new press for financial reporting purposes?

**EXERCISE 10-21**
*Asset traded for similar asset*

Objective 4

✓ a. $205,000

Assume the same facts as in Exercise 10-20, except that the book value of the press traded in is $128,500. (a) What is the amount of cash given? (b) What is the cost of the new press for financial reporting purposes?

**EXERCISE 10-22**
*Entries for trade of fixed asset*
Objective 4

On July 1, Jaguar Co., a water distiller, acquired new bottling equipment with a list price of $385,000. Jaguar received a trade-in allowance of $100,000 on the old equipment of a similar type, paid cash of $35,000, and gave a series of five notes payable for the remainder. The following information about the old equipment is obtained from the account in the equipment ledger: cost, $280,000; accumulated depreciation on December 31, the end of the preceding fiscal year, $144,000; annual depreciation, $16,000. Journalize the entries to record (a) the current depreciation of the old equipment to the date of trade-in and (b) the exchange transaction on July 1 for financial reporting purposes.

**EXERCISE 10-23**
*Entries for trade of fixed asset*
Objective 4

On April 1, O'Dell Co. acquired a new truck with a list price of $80,000. O'Dell received a trade-in allowance of $29,000 on an old truck of similar type, paid cash of $11,000, and gave a series of five notes payable for the remainder. The following information about the old truck is obtained from the account in the equipment ledger: cost, $62,500; accumulated depreciation on December 31, the end of the preceding fiscal year, $36,000; annual depreciation, $6,000. Journalize the entries to record (a) the current depreciation of the old truck to the date of trade-in and (b) the transaction on April 1 for financial reporting purposes.

**EXERCISE 10-24**
*Depreciable cost of asset acquired by exchange*
Objective 4

On the first day of the fiscal year, a delivery truck with a list price of $55,000 was acquired in exchange for an old delivery truck and $30,000 cash. The old truck had a book value of $28,250 at the date of the exchange.

a. Determine the depreciable cost for financial reporting purposes.
b. Assuming that the book value of the old delivery truck was $24,000, determine the depreciable cost for financial reporting purposes.

**EXERCISE 10-25**
*Internal control of fixed assets*
Objective 6

MarketNet Co. is a computer software company marketing products in the United States and Canada. While MarketNet Co. has over 90 sales offices, all accounting is handled at the company's headquarters in Phoenix, Arizona.

MarketNet Co. keeps all its fixed asset records on a computerized system. The computer maintains a subsidiary ledger of all fixed assets owned by the company and calculates depreciation automatically. Whenever a manager at one of the 90 sales offices wants to purchase a fixed asset, a purchase request is submitted to headquarters for approval. Upon approval, the fixed asset is purchased and the invoice is sent back to headquarters so that the asset can be entered into the fixed asset system.

A manager who wants to dispose of a fixed asset simply sells or disposes of the asset and notifies headquarters to remove the asset from the system. Company cars and personal computers are frequently purchased by employees when they are disposed of. Most pieces of office equipment are traded in when new assets are acquired.

What internal control weakness exists in the procedures used to acquire and dispose of fixed assets at MarketNet Co.?

**EXERCISE 10-26**
*Depletion entries*
Objective 7
✓ a. $12,400,000

Discovery Co. acquired mineral rights for $80,000,000. The mineral deposit is estimated at 100,000,000 tons. During the current year, 15,500,000 tons were mined and sold for $16,500,000.

a. Determine the amount of depletion expense for the current year.
b. Journalize the adjusting entry to recognize the depletion expense.

**EXERCISE 10-27**
*Amortization entries*
Objective 8
✓ a. $37,750

Colmey Company acquired patent rights on January 3, 2003, for $472,500. The patent has a useful life equal to its legal life of 15 years. On January 5, 2006, Colmey successfully defended the patent in a lawsuit at a cost of $75,000.

a. Determine the patent amortization expense for the current year ended December 31, 2006.
b. Journalize the adjusting entry to recognize the amortization.

**EXERCISE 10-28**
*Balance sheet presentation*

**Objective 9**

**WHAT'S WRONG WITH THIS?**

List the errors you find in the following partial balance sheet:

**Kraftmaid Company**
**Balance Sheet**
**December 31, 2006**

**Assets**

Total current assets . . . . . . . . . . . . . . . . . . . . . . . . . . . . . . . . . . . . . . . . . . . $597,500

| | Replacement Cost | Accumulated Depreciation | Book Value |
|---|---|---|---|
| Property, plant, and equipment: | | | |
| Land . . . . . . . . . . . . . . . . . . . . . | $ 100,000 | $ 20,000 | $ 80,000 |
| Buildings . . . . . . . . . . . . . . . . . . | 260,000 | 76,000 | 184,000 |
| Factory equipment . . . . . . . . . . . | 550,000 | 292,000 | 258,000 |
| Office equipment . . . . . . . . . . . . | 120,000 | 80,000 | 40,000 |
| Patents . . . . . . . . . . . . . . . . . . . . | 80,000 | — | 80,000 |
| Goodwill . . . . . . . . . . . . . . . . . . . | 45,000 | 5,000 | 40,000 |
| Total property, plant, and equipment . . . . . . . . . . | $1,155,000 | $473,000 | 682,000 |

**EXERCISE 10-29**
*Ratio of fixed assets to long-term liabilities*

**Objective 10**

**REAL WORLD**

The following data were taken from recent annual reports of **Intuit Inc.**, a developer and distributor of financial planning software:

| | Current Year | Preceding Year |
|---|---|---|
| Property and equipment (net) | $181,758,000 | $174,659,000 |
| Long-term liabilities | 14,610,000 | 12,150,000 |

a. Compute the ratio of fixed assets to long-term liabilities for the current and preceding year. Round to one decimal place.
b. What conclusions can you draw?

**EXERCISE 10-30**
*Ratio of fixed assets to long-term liabilities*

**Objective 10**

**REAL WORLD**

The financial statements of **Home Depot** are presented in Appendix E at the end of the text.

a. Compute the ratio of fixed assets to long-term liabilities for 2002 and 2001.
b. What conclusions can you draw?

**APPENDIX**
**EXERCISE 10-31**
*Sum-of-the-years-digits depreciation*

✓ *First year: $12,923*

Based on the data in Exercise 10-9, determine the depreciation for the backhoe for each of the first two years, using the sum-of-the-years-digits depreciation method. Round to the nearest dollar.

**APPENDIX**
**EXERCISE 10-32**
*Sum-of-the-years-digits depreciation*

✓ *First year: $16,545*

Based on the data in Exercise 10-10, determine the depreciation for the dairy storage tank for each of the first two years, using the sum-of-the-years-digits depreciation method. Round to the nearest dollar.

**APPENDIX
EXERCISE 10-33**
*Partial-year depreciation*

✓ *First year: $4,985*

Based on the data in Exercise 10-11, determine the depreciation for the sandblasting equipment for each of the first two years, using the sum-of-the-years-digits depreciation method. Round to the nearest dollar.

# Problems Series A

**PROBLEM 10-1A**
*Allocate payments and receipts to fixed asset accounts*

**Objective 1**

SPREADSHEET

The following payments and receipts are related to land, land improvements, and buildings acquired for use in a wholesale apparel business. The receipts are identified by an asterisk.

| | |
|---|---:|
| a. Finder's fee paid to real estate agency . . . . . . . . . . . . . . . . . . . | $ 5,000 |
| b. Cost of real estate acquired as a plant site:  Land . . . . . . . . . . . . | 100,000 |
| Building . . . . . . . . . . | 60,000 |
| c. Fee paid to attorney for title search . . . . . . . . . . . . . . . . . . . | 3,500 |
| d. Delinquent real estate taxes on property, assumed by purchaser . . . | 17,500 |
| e. Cost of razing and removing building . . . . . . . . . . . . . . . . . . | 16,250 |
| f. Cost of filling and grading land . . . . . . . . . . . . . . . . . . . . . | 12,500 |
| g. Proceeds from sale of salvage materials from old building . . . . . . . | 4,500* |
| h. Special assessment paid to city for extension of water main to the property . . . . . . . . . . . . . . . . . . . . . . . . . . . . . . . . . . . | 11,000 |
| i. Premium on 1-year insurance policy during construction . . . . . . . . | 7,200 |
| j. Architect's and engineer's fees for plans and supervision . . . . . . . | 50,000 |
| k. Cost of repairing windstorm damage during construction . . . . . . . | 2,500 |
| l. Cost of repairing vandalism damage during construction . . . . . . . | 1,800 |
| m. Cost of trees and shrubbery planted . . . . . . . . . . . . . . . . . . | 12,000 |
| n. Cost of paving parking lot to be used by customers . . . . . . . . . . | 18,500 |
| o. Proceeds from insurance company for windstorm and vandalism damage . . . . . . . . . . . . . . . . . . . . . . . . . . . . . . . . . . . | 4,000* |
| p. Interest incurred on building loan during construction . . . . . . . . . | 65,000 |
| q. Money borrowed to pay building contractor . . . . . . . . . . . . . . | 1,000,000* |
| r. Payment to building contractor for new building . . . . . . . . . . . . | 1,250,000 |
| s. Refund of premium on insurance policy (i) canceled after 10 months | 1,200* |

**Instructions**

1. Assign each payment and receipt to Land (unlimited life), Land Improvements (limited life), Building, or Other Accounts. Indicate receipts by an asterisk. Identify each item by letter and list the amounts in columnar form, as follows:

| Item | Land | Land Improvements | Building | Other Accounts |
|------|------|-------------------|----------|----------------|

2. Determine the amount debited to Land, Land Improvements, and Building.
3. ▭▭▭▶ The costs assigned to the land, which is used as a plant site, will not be depreciated, while the costs assigned to land improvements will be depreciated. Explain this seemingly contradictory application of the concept of depreciation.

**PROBLEM 10-2A**
*Compare three depreciation methods*

**Objective 2**

Cero Company purchased waterproofing equipment on January 2, 2005, for $214,000. The equipment was expected to have a useful life of 4 years, or 31,250 operating hours, and a residual value of $14,000. The equipment was used for 10,750 hours during 2005, 9,500 hours in 2006, 6,000 hours in 2007, and 5,000 hours in 2008.

**Instructions**

Determine the amount of depreciation expense for the years ended December 31, 2005, 2006, 2007, and 2008, by (a) the straight-line method, (b) the units-of-production

✓ a. 2005: straight-line depreciation, $50,000

method, and (c) the declining-balance method, using twice the straight-line rate. Also determine the total depreciation expense for the four years by each method. The following columnar headings are suggested for recording the depreciation expense amounts:

| | Depreciation Expense | | |
| | Straight-Line | Units-of-Production | Declining-Balance |
| Year | Method | Method | Method |
|---|---|---|---|

**PROBLEM 10-3A**
*Depreciation by three methods; partial years*

**Objective 2**

✓ a. 2005, $30,600

Caribou Company purchased tool sharpening equipment on July 1, 2005, for $194,400. The equipment was expected to have a useful life of 3 years, or 22,950 operating hours, and a residual value of $10,800. The equipment was used for 4,650 hours during 2005, 7,500 hours in 2006, 7,350 hours in 2007, and 3,450 hours in 2008.

**Instructions**
Determine the amount of depreciation expense for the years ended December 31, 2005, 2006, 2007, and 2008, by (a) the straight-line method, (b) the units-of-production method, and (c) the declining-balance method, using twice the straight-line rate.

**PROBLEM 10-4A**
*Depreciation by two methods; trade of fixed asset*

**Objectives 2, 4**

✓ 1. b. Year 1, $80,000 depreciation expense
✓ 2. $196,000

New tire retreading equipment, acquired at a cost of $160,000 at the beginning of a fiscal year, has an estimated useful life of 4 years and an estimated residual value of $16,000. The manager requested information regarding the effect of alternative methods on the amount of depreciation expense each year. On the basis of the data presented to the manager, the declining-balance method was selected.

In the first week of the fourth year, the equipment was traded in for similar equipment priced at $200,000. The trade-in allowance on the old equipment was $24,000, cash of $16,000 was paid, and a note payable was issued for the balance.

**Instructions**
1. Determine the annual depreciation expense for each of the estimated 4 years of use, the accumulated depreciation at the end of each year, and the book value of the equipment at the end of each year by (a) the straight-line method and (b) the declining-balance method (at twice the straight-line rate). The following columnar headings are suggested for each schedule:

| | | Accumulated | |
| Year | Depreciation Expense | Depreciation, End of Year | Book Value, End of Year |
|---|---|---|---|

2. For financial reporting purposes, determine the cost of the new equipment acquired in the exchange.
3. Journalize the entry to record the exchange.
4. Journalize the entry to record the exchange, assuming that the trade-in allowance was $12,800 instead of $24,000.

**PROBLEM 10-5A**
*Transactions for fixed assets, including trade*

**Objectives 1, 3, 4**

The following transactions, adjusting entries, and closing entries were completed by Yellowstone Furniture Co. during a 3-year period. All are related to the use of delivery equipment. The declining-balance method (at twice the straight-line rate) of depreciation is used.

2005
Jan.   2 Purchased a used delivery truck for $37,000, paying cash.
       5 Paid $5,000 to replace the engine. The old engine was estimated to have a value of $2,000. The new engine is expected to have a useful life equal to the remaining life of the truck.
Apr.   7 Paid garage $125 for changing the oil, replacing the oil filter, and tuning the engine on the delivery truck.

2005

Dec. 31 Recorded depreciation on the truck and engine component for the fiscal year. The estimated useful life of the truck and engine is 8 years, with a residual value of $3,000 for the truck.

2006

Jan.  1 Purchased a new truck for $80,000, paying cash.

Mar. 13 Paid garage $180 to tune the engine and make other minor repairs on the truck.

Apr. 30 Sold the used truck for $24,500. (Record depreciation to date in 2006 for the truck.)

Dec. 31 Recorded depreciation on the truck. It has an estimated trade-in value of $4,000 and an estimated life of 10 years.

2007

July  1 Purchased a new truck for $45,000, paying cash.

Oct.  2 Sold the truck purchased Jan. 1, 2006, for $63,075. (Record depreciation for the year.)

Dec. 31 Recorded depreciation on the remaining truck. It has an estimated residual value of $4,500 and an estimated useful life of 10 years.

**Instructions**

Journalize the transactions and the adjusting entries.

**PROBLEM 10-6A**
*Amortization and depletion entries*

**Objectives 7, 8**

✓*1. b. $14,100*

Data related to the acquisition of timber rights and intangible assets during the current year ended December 31 are as follows:

a. Goodwill in the amount of $29,500,000 was purchased on January 18.

b. Governmental and legal costs of $225,600 were incurred on July 5 in obtaining a patent with an estimated economic life of 8 years. Amortization is to be for one-half year.

c. Timber rights on a tract of land were purchased for $820,000 on April 10. The stand of timber is estimated at 4,000,000 board feet. During the current year, 550,000 board feet of timber were cut.

**Instructions**

1. Determine the amount of the amortization or depletion expense for the current year for each of the foregoing items.

2. Journalize the adjusting entries to record the amortization or depletion expense for each item.

# Problems Series B

**PROBLEM 10-1B**
*Allocate payments and receipts to fixed asset accounts*

**Objective 1**

SPREADSHEET

The following payments and receipts are related to land, land improvements, and buildings acquired for use in a wholesale ceramic business. The receipts are identified by an asterisk.

| | |
|---|---:|
| a. Fee paid to attorney for title search .................. | $  2,500 |
| b. Cost of real estate acquired as a plant site:   Land ............ | 150,000 |
|                                                               Building ........... | 40,000 |
| c. Delinquent real estate taxes on property, assumed by purchaser .... | 13,750 |
| d. Cost of razing and removing building ..................... | 4,800 |
| e. Special assessment paid to city for extension of water main to the property ......................................... | 10,200 |
| f. Proceeds from sale of salvage materials from old building ........ | 5,000* |
| g. Cost of filling and grading land ...................... | 29,700 |
| h. Premium on 1-year insurance policy during construction ......... | 6,600 |
| i. Cost of repairing windstorm damage during construction ......... | 3,500 |

*(continued)*

j. Cost of paving parking lot to be used by customers . . . . . . . . . . .     $ 12,500
k. Cost of trees and shrubbery planted . . . . . . . . . . . . . . . . . . . . . .     7,000
l. Architect's and engineer's fees for plans and supervision . . . . . . . . .     75,000
m. Cost of repairing vandalism damage during construction . . . . . . . . .     1,600
n. Interest incurred on building loan during construction . . . . . . . . . . .     30,000
o. Cost of floodlights installed on parking lot . . . . . . . . . . . . . . . . . .     8,500
p. Money borrowed to pay building contractor . . . . . . . . . . . . . . . .     500,000*
q. Payment to building contractor for new building . . . . . . . . . . . . .     750,000
r. Proceeds from insurance company for windstorm and vandalism
   damage . . . . . . . . . . . . . . . . . . . . . . . . . . . . . . . . . . . . . . . . .     4,000*
s. Refund of premium on insurance policy (h) canceled after 11 months     550*

**Instructions**

1. Assign each payment and receipt to Land (unlimited life), Land Improvements (limited life), Building, or Other Accounts. Indicate receipts by an asterisk. Identify each item by letter and list the amounts in columnar form, as follows:

| Item | Land | Land Improvements | Building | Other Accounts |
|------|------|-------------------|----------|----------------|

2. Determine the amount debited to Land, Land Improvements, and Building.
3. ▬▬▶ The costs assigned to the land, which is used as a plant site, will not be depreciated, while the costs assigned to land improvements will be depreciated. Explain this seemingly contradictory application of the concept of depreciation.

**PROBLEM 10-2B**
*Compare three depreciation methods*

**Objective 2**

**SPREADSHEET**

✓ a. 2005: straight-line depreciation, $55,800

Red Tiger Company purchased packaging equipment on January 3, 2005, for $180,000. The equipment was expected to have a useful life of 3 years, or 22,320 operating hours, and a residual value of $12,600. The equipment was used for 12,500 hours during 2005, 6,000 hours in 2006, and 3,820 hours in 2007.

**Instructions**

Determine the amount of depreciation expense for the years ended December 31, 2005, 2006, and 2007, by (a) the straight-line method, (b) the units-of-production method, and (c) the declining-balance method, using twice the straight-line rate. Also determine the total depreciation expense for the three years by each method. The following columnar headings are suggested for recording the depreciation expense amounts:

|  | Depreciation Expense | | |
|------|----------------------|-------------------------|--------------------|
| Year | Straight-Line Method | Units-of-Production Method | Declining-Balance Method |

**PROBLEM 10-3B**
*Depreciation by three methods; partial years*

**Objective 2**

**SPREADSHEET**

✓ a. 2005: $28,050

Rhymer Company purchased plastic laminating equipment on July 1, 2005, for $174,000. The equipment was expected to have a useful life of 3 years, or 14,025 operating hours, and a residual value of $5,700. The equipment was used for 2,500 hours during 2005, 5,500 hours in 2006, 4,025 hours in 2007, and 2,000 hours in 2008.

**Instructions**

Determine the amount of depreciation expense for the years ended December 31, 2005, 2006, 2007, and 2008, by (a) the straight-line method, (b) the units-of-production method, and (c) the declining-balance method, using twice the straight-line rate. Round to the nearest dollar.

**PROBLEM 10-4B**
*Depreciation by two methods; trade of fixed asset*

**Objectives 2, 4**

New lithographic equipment, acquired at a cost of $100,000 at the beginning of a fiscal year, has an estimated useful life of 5 years and an estimated residual value of $8,000. The manager requested information regarding the effect of alternative methods on the amount of depreciation expense each year. On the basis of the data presented to the manager, the declining-balance method was selected.

**SPREADSHEET**

**P.A.S.S.**

✓ 1. b. Year 1: $40,000
depreciation expense

✓ 2. $116,960

In the first week of the fifth year, the equipment was traded in for similar equipment priced at $120,000. The trade-in allowance on the old equipment was $16,000, cash of $24,000 was paid, and a note payable was issued for the balance.

**Instructions**

1. Determine the annual depreciation expense for each of the estimated 5 years of use, the accumulated depreciation at the end of each year, and the book value of the equipment at the end of each year by (a) the straight-line method and (b) the declining-balance method (at twice the straight-line rate). The following columnar headings are suggested for each schedule:

| Year | Depreciation Expense | Accumulated Depreciation, End of Year | Book Value, End of Year |
|------|------|------|------|

2. For financial reporting purposes, determine the cost of the new equipment acquired in the exchange.
3. Journalize the entry to record the exchange.
4. Journalize the entry to record the exchange, assuming that the trade-in allowance was $12,000 instead of $16,000.

**PROBLEM 10-5B**
*Transactions for fixed assets, including trade*

**Objectives 1, 3, 4**

**P.A.S.S.**

The following transactions, adjusting entries, and closing entries were completed by Lodge Pole Pine Furniture Co. during a 3-year period. All are related to the use of delivery equipment. The declining-balance method (at twice the straight-line rate) of depreciation is used.

2005
Jan.  3 Purchased a used delivery truck for $26,500, paying cash.
      5 Paid $4,000 for a new transmission for the truck. The old transmission was estimated to have a value of $500. The new transmission is expected to have a useful life equal to the remaining life of the truck.
Aug. 16 Paid garage $285 for miscellaneous repairs to the truck.
Dec. 31 Recorded depreciation on the truck and transmission component for the fiscal year. The estimated useful life of the truck and transmission is 4 years, with a residual value of $6,000 for the truck.

2006
Jan.  1 Purchased a new truck for $65,000, paying cash.
June 30 Sold the used truck for $12,000. (Record depreciation to date in 2006 for the truck.)
Aug. 10 Paid garage $175 for miscellaneous repairs to the truck.
Dec. 31 Recorded depreciation on the truck. It has an estimated residual value of $7,500 and an estimated life of 5 years.

2007
July  1 Purchased a new truck for $84,000, paying cash.
Oct.  1 Sold the truck purchased January 1, 2006, for $26,750. (Record depreciation for the year.)
Dec. 31 Recorded depreciation on the remaining truck. It has an estimated residual value of $5,000 and an estimated useful life of 8 years.

**Instructions**
Journalize the transactions and the adjusting entries.

**PROBLEM 10-6B**
*Amortization and depletion entries*

**Objectives 7, 8**

✓ 1. a. $192,000

Data related to the acquisition of timber rights and intangible assets during the current year ended December 31 are as follows:

a. Timber rights on a tract of land were purchased for $720,000 on July 11. The stand of timber is estimated at 2,250,000 board feet. During the current year, 600,000 board feet of timber were cut.
b. Goodwill in the amount of $10,000,000 was purchased on January 3.

c. Governmental and legal costs of $420,000 were incurred on October 2 in obtaining a patent with an estimated economic life of 10 years. Amortization is to be for one-fourth year.

**Instructions**

1. Determine the amount of the amortization or depletion expense for the current year for each of the foregoing items.
2. Journalize the adjusting entries required to record the amortization or depletion for each item.

# Special Activities

**ACTIVITY 10-1**
*Ethics and professional conduct in business*

ETHICS

Lizzie Paulk, CPA, is an assistant to the controller of Insignia Co. In her spare time, Lizzie also prepares tax returns and performs general accounting services for clients. Frequently, Lizzie performs these services after her normal working hours, using Insignia Co.'s computers and laser printers. Occasionally, Lizzie's clients will call her at the office during regular working hours.

Discuss whether Lizzie is performing in a professional manner.

**ACTIVITY 10-2**
*Financial vs. tax depreciation*

The following is an excerpt from a conversation between two employees of Ermine Co., Jody Terpin and Hal Graves. Jody is the accounts payable clerk, and Hal is the cashier.

*Jody:* Hal, could I get your opinion on something?
*Hal:* Sure, Jody.
*Jody:* Do you know Margaret, the fixed assets clerk?
*Hal:* I know who she is, but I don't know her real well. Why?
*Jody:* Well, I was talking to her at lunch last Monday about how she liked her job, etc. You know, the usual . . . and she mentioned something about having to keep two sets of books . . . one for taxes and one for the financial statements. That can't be good accounting, can it? What do you think?
*Hal:* Two sets of books? It doesn't sound right.
*Jody:* It doesn't seem right to me either. I was always taught that you had to use generally accepted accounting principles. How can there be two sets of books? What can be the difference between the two?

How would you respond to Hal and Jody if you were Margaret?

**ACTIVITY 10-3**
*Effect of depreciation on net income*

Five Points Construction Co. specializes in building replicas of historic houses. Sharon Higgs, president of Five Points, is considering the purchase of various items of equipment on July 1, 2004, for $120,000. The equipment would have a useful life of 5 years and no residual value. In the past, all equipment has been leased. For tax purposes, Sharon is considering depreciating the equipment by the straight-line method. She discussed the matter with her CPA and learned that, although the straight-line method could be elected, it was to her advantage to use the modified accelerated cost recovery system (MACRS) for tax purposes. She asked for your advice as to which method to use for tax purposes.

1. Compute depreciation for each of the years (2004, 2005, 2006, 2007, 2008, and 2009) of useful life by (a) the straight-line method and (b) MACRS. In using the straight-line method, one-half year's depreciation should be computed for 2004 and 2009. Use the MACRS rates presented in the chapter.
2. Assuming that income before depreciation and income tax is estimated to be $200,000 uniformly per year and that the income tax rate is 30%, compute the

net income for each of the years 2004, 2005, 2006, 2007, 2008, and 2009, if (a) the straight-line method is used and (b) MACRS is used.

3. ━━▶ What factors would you present for Sharon's consideration in the selection of a depreciation method?

**ACTIVITY 10-4**
*Shopping for a delivery truck*

GROUP ACTIVITY

You are planning to acquire a delivery truck for use in your business for three years. In groups of three or four, explore a local dealer's purchase and leasing options for the truck. Summarize the costs of purchasing versus leasing, and list other factors that might help you decide whether to buy or lease the truck.

**ACTIVITY 10-5**
*Applying for patents, copyrights, and trademarks*

INTERNET

Go to the Internet and review the procedures for applying for a patent, a copyright, and a trademark. One Internet site that is useful for this purpose is **idresearch.com**, which is linked to the text's Web site at **http://warren.swlearning.com**. Prepare a written summary of these procedures.

# Answers to Self-Examination Questions

1. **C**  All amounts spent to get a fixed asset (such as machinery) in place and ready for use are proper charges to the asset account. In the case of machinery acquired, the freight (answer A) and the installation costs (answer B) are both (answer C) proper charges to the machinery account.

2. **C**  The periodic charge for depreciation under the declining-balance method (twice the straight-line rate) for the second year is determined by first computing the depreciation charge for the first year. The depreciation for the first year of $6,000 (answer A) is computed by multiplying the cost of the equipment, $9,000, by 2/3 (the straight-line rate of 1/3 multiplied by 2). The depreciation for the second year of $2,000 (answer C) is then determined by multiplying the book value at the end of the first year, $3,000 (the cost of $9,000 minus the first-year depreciation of $6,000), by 2/3. The third year's depreciation is $400 (answer D). It is determined by multiplying the book value at the end of the second year, $1,000, by 2/3, thus yielding $667. However, the equipment cannot be depreciated

below its residual value of $600; thus, the third-year depreciation is $400 ($1,000 − $600).

3. **B**  A depreciation method that provides for a higher depreciation amount in the first year of the use of an asset and a gradually declining periodic amount thereafter is called an accelerated depreciation method. The declining-balance method (answer B) is an example of such a method.

4. **B**  The acceptable method of accounting for an exchange of similar assets in which the trade-in allowance ($30,000) exceeds the book value of the old asset ($25,000) requires that the cost of the new asset be determined by adding the amount of cash given ($70,000) to the book value of the old asset ($25,000), which totals $95,000. Alternatively, the unrecognized gain ($5,000) can be subtracted from the list price ($100,000).

5. **D**  Long-lived assets that are useful in operations, not held for sale, and without physical qualities are called intangible assets. Patents, goodwill, and copyrights are examples of intangible assets (answer D).

# 11

# CURRENT LIABILITIES

## objectives

*After studying this chapter, you should be able to:*

1   Define and give examples of current liabilities.

2   Prepare journal entries for short-term notes payable and the disclosure for the current portion of long-term debt.

3   Describe the accounting treatment for contingent liabilities and journalize entries for product warranties.

4   Determine employer liabilities for payroll, including liabilities arising from employee earnings and deductions from earnings.

5   Describe payroll accounting systems that use a payroll register, employee earnings records, and a general journal.

6   Journalize entries for employee fringe benefits, including vacation pay and pensions.

7   Use the quick ratio to analyze the ability of a business to pay its current liabilities.

If you are employed, you know that your paycheck is normally less than the total amount you earned because your employer deducted amounts for such items as federal income tax and social security tax. For example, if you worked 20 hours last week at $10 per hour and you are paid weekly, your payroll check could appear as follows:

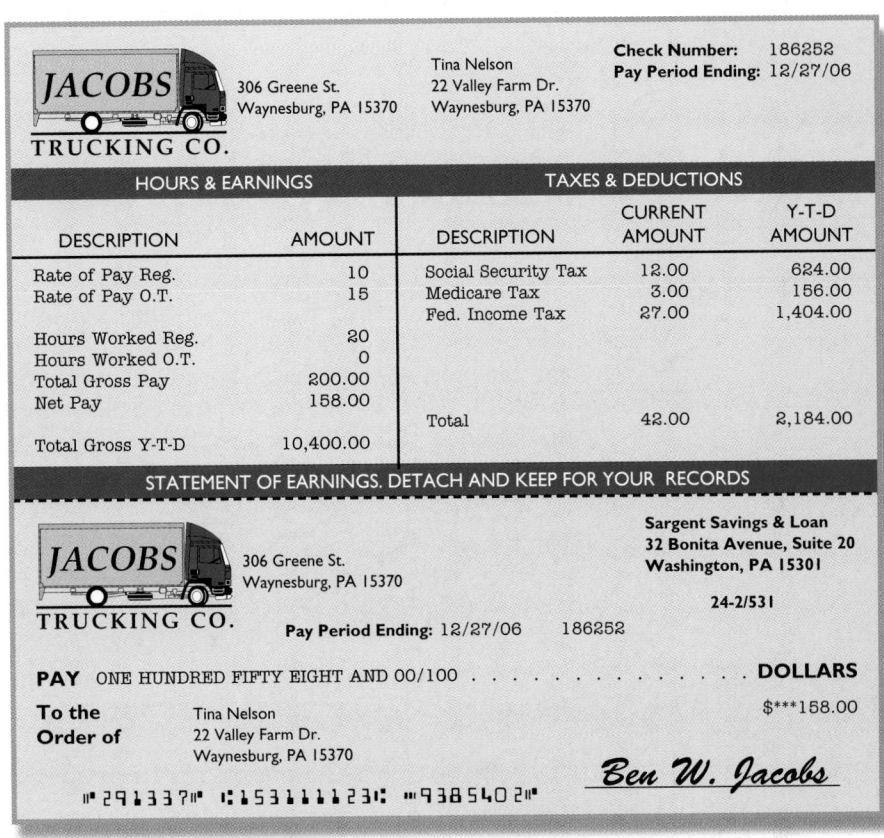

Your employer has a liability to you for your earnings until you are paid. Your employer also has a liability to deposit the taxes withheld. In this chapter, we will discuss liabilities for amounts that must be paid within a short period of time. In addition to liabilities related to payroll and payroll taxes, we will discuss liabilities from notes payable and product warranties.

# The Nature of Current Liabilities

objective  1

Define and give examples of current liabilities.

Your credit card balance is probably due within a short time, such as 30 days. Such liabilities that are to be paid out of current assets and are due within a short time, usually within one year, are called **current liabilities**. Most current liabilities arise from two basic transactions:

1. Receiving goods or services prior to making payment.
2. Receiving payment prior to delivering goods or services.

An example of the first type of transaction is **accounts payable** arising from purchases of merchandise for resale. An example of the second type of transaction is **unearned rent** arising from the receipt of rent in advance. Some additional examples of current liabilities that we discussed in previous chapters are:

- Taxes payable—the amount of taxes owed to governmental units
- Interest payable—the amount of interest owed on borrowed funds
- Wages payable—the amount owed to employees

In this chapter, we will introduce some other common current liabilities. These include short-term notes payable, contingencies, payroll liabilities, and employee fringe benefits.

# Short-Term Notes Payable and Current Portion of Long-Term Debt

**objective 2**

Prepare journal entries for short-term notes payable and the disclosure for the current portion of long-term debt.

The current liability section of the balance sheet can contain items that are used to finance business operations, such as short-term notes payable and the portion of long-term debt that is due within the coming period.

## Short-Term Notes Payable

Notes may be issued when merchandise or other assets are purchased. They may also be issued to creditors to temporarily satisfy an account payable created earlier. For example, assume that a business issues a 90-day, 12% note for $1,000, dated August 1, 2006, to Murray Co. for a $1,000 overdue account. The entry to record the issuance of the note is as follows:

| | | | | | |
|---|---|---|---|---|---|
| Aug. | 1 | Accounts Payable—Murray Co. | | 1 0 0 0 00 | |
| | | Notes Payable | | | 1 0 0 0 00 |
| | | Issued a 90-day, 12% note on account. | | | |

When the note matures, the entry to record the payment of $1,000 principal plus $30 interest ($1,000 × 12% × 90/360) is as follows:

| | | | | | |
|---|---|---|---|---|---|
| Oct. | 30 | Notes Payable | | 1 0 0 0 00 | |
| | | Interest Expense | | 3 0 00 | |
| | | Cash | | | 1 0 3 0 00 |
| | | Paid principal and interest due on note. | | | |

The interest expense is reported in the Other Expense section of the income statement for the year ended December 31, 2006. The interest expense account is closed at December 31.

The preceding entries for notes payable are similar to those we discussed in an earlier chapter for notes receivable. Notes payable entries are presented from the viewpoint of the borrower, while notes receivable entries are presented from the viewpoint of the creditor or lender. To illustrate, the following entries are journalized for a borrower (Bowden Co.), who issues a note payable to a creditor (Coker Co.):

| | Bowden Co. (Borrower) | | | Coker Co. (Creditor) | | |
|---|---|---|---|---|---|---|
| May 1. Bowden Co. purchased merchandise on account from Coker Co., $10,000, 2/10, n/30. The merchandise cost Coker Co. $7,500. | Merchandise Inventory<br>  Accounts Payable | 10,000 | 10,000 | Accounts Receivable<br>  Sales | 10,000 | 10,000 |
| | | | | Cost of Merchandise Sold<br>  Merchandise Inventory | 7,500 | 7,500 |
| May 31. Bowden Co. issued a 60-day, 12% note for $10,000 to Coker Co. on account. | Accounts Payable<br>  Notes Payable | 10,000 | 10,000 | Notes Receivable<br>  Accounts Receivable | 10,000 | 10,000 |
| July 30. Bowden Co. paid Coker Co. the amount due on the note of May 31. Interest: $10,000 × 12% × 60/360. | Notes Payable<br>Interest Expense<br>  Cash | 10,000<br>200 | 10,200 | Cash<br>  Interest Revenue<br>  Notes Receivable | 10,200 | 200<br>10,000 |

I began as a small store in 1943 in Cleveland, founded by immigrants from Nazi Germany. Today I'm America's premiere fabric and crafts chain, with nearly 1,000 locations and more than 20,000 employees. In 1976, I joined the New York Stock Exchange under the name "Fabri-Centers of America." In 1994, I acquired Clothworld and its 342 stores. I opened my first giant superstore in 1995. In 2002, my superstores generated more than four times the revenue of our traditional stores. The name I go by today reflects the names of two daughters of my founding families. Who am I? (Go to page 461 for answer.)

Notes may also be issued when money is borrowed from banks. Although the terms may vary, many banks would accept from the borrower an interest-bearing note for the amount of the loan. For example, assume that on September 19 a firm borrows $4,000 from First National Bank by giving the bank a 90-day, 15% note. The entry to record the receipt of cash and the issuance of the note is as follows:

| | | | | |
|---|---|---|---|---|
| Sep. | 19 | Cash | 4 0 0 0 00 | |
| | | Notes Payable | | 4 0 0 0 00 |
| | | Issued a 90-day, 15% note to the bank. | | |

On the due date of the note (December 18), the borrower owes $4,000, the principal of the note, plus interest of $150 ($4,000 × 15% × 90/360). The entry to record the payment of the note is as follows:

| | | | | |
|---|---|---|---|---|
| Dec. | 18 | Notes Payable | 4 0 0 0 00 | |
| | | Interest Expense | 1 5 0 00 | |
| | | Cash | | 4 1 5 0 00 |
| | | Paid principal and interest due on note. | | |

**REAL WORLD**

The U.S. Treasury issues short-term treasury bills to investors at a discount.

Sometimes a borrower will issue to a creditor a discounted note rather than an interest-bearing note. Although such a note does not specify an interest rate, the creditor sets a rate of interest and deducts the interest from the face amount of the note. This interest is called the ***discount***. The rate used in computing the discount is called the ***discount rate***. The borrower is given the remainder, called the ***proceeds***.

To illustrate, assume that on August 10, Cary Company issues a $20,000, 90-day note to Rock Company in exchange for inventory. Rock discounts the note at a rate of 15%. The amount of the discount, $750, is debited to *Interest Expense*. The proceeds, $19,250, are debited to *Merchandise Inventory*. *Notes Payable* is credited for the face amount of the note, which is also its maturity value. This entry is shown below.

In buying a used delivery truck, a business issues an $8,000, 60-day note dated July 15, which the truck's seller discounts at 12%. What is the cost of the truck (the proceeds)?

------------------------------------

*$7,840 [$8,000 − ($8,000 × 12% × 60/360)]*

| | | | | |
|---|---|---|---|---|
| Aug. | 10 | Merchandise Inventory | 19 2 5 0 00 | |
| | | Interest Expense | 7 5 0 00 | |
| | | Notes Payable | | 20 0 0 0 00 |
| | | Issued a 90-day note to Rock Co., | | |
| | | discounted at 15%. | | |

When the note is paid, the following entry is recorded:[1]

| | | | | |
|---|---|---|---|---|
| Nov. | 8 | Notes Payable | 20 0 0 0 00 | |
| | | Cash | | 20 0 0 0 00 |
| | | Paid note due. | | |

## Current Portion of Long-Term Debt

Long-term liabilities are often paid back in periodic payments, called **installments**, much like a car loan. Long-term liability installments that are due *within* the coming year must be classified as a current liability. The total amount of the installments due *after* the coming year is classified as a long-term liability. To illustrate, **Starbucks**

---

[1]If the accounting period ends before a discounted note is paid, an adjusting entry should record the prepaid (deferred) interest that is not yet an expense. This deferred interest would be deducted from Notes Payable in the Current Liabilities section of the balance sheet.

**Corp.** reported the following scheduled debt payments in the notes to its September 30, 2002 annual report to shareholders:

| Fiscal year ending | |
|---|---|
| 2003 | $ 710,000 |
| 2004 | 722,000 |
| 2005 | 735,000 |
| 2006 | 748,000 |
| 2007 | 762,000 |
| Thereafter | 2,109,000 |
| Total principal payments | $5,786,000 |

The debt of $710,000 due in 2003 would be reported as a current liability on the September 30, 2002 balance sheet. The remaining debt of $5,076,000 ($5,786,000 − $710,000) would be reported as a long-term liability on the balance sheet, which we will discuss in a later chapter.

# Contingent Liabilities

**objective  3**

Describe the accounting treatment for contingent liabilities and journalize entries for product warranties.

Some past transactions will result in liabilities if certain events occur in the future. These potential obligations are called **contingent liabilities**. For example, **Ford Motor Company** would have a contingent liability for the estimated costs associated with warranty work on new car sales. The obligation is contingent upon a *future event*, namely, a customer requiring warranty work on a vehicle. The obligation is the result of a *past transaction*, which is the original sale of the vehicle.

If a contingent liability is *probable* and the amount of the liability can be *reasonably estimated*, it should be recorded in the accounts. **Ford Motor Company**'s vehicle warranty costs are an example of a *recordable* contingent liability. The warranty costs are *probable* because it is known that warranty repairs will be required on some vehicles. In addition, the costs can be *estimated* from past warranty experience.

To illustrate, assume that during June a company sells a product for $60,000 on which there is a 36-month warranty for repairing defects. Past experience indicates that the average cost to repair defects is 5% of the sales price over the warranty period. The entry to record the estimated product warranty expense for June is as follows:

| | | | | | |
|---|---|---|---|---|---|
| June | 30 | Product Warranty Expense | 3 0 0 0 00 | |
| | | Product Warranty Payable | | 3 0 0 0 00 |
| | | Warranty expense for June, 5% × $60,000. | | |

A business sells to a customer $120,000 of commercial audio equipment with a one-year repair and replacement warranty. Historically, the average cost to repair or replace is 2% of sales. How is this contingent liability recorded?

Product Warranty Expense       2,400
    Product Warranty Payable                2,400

This transaction matches revenues and expenses properly by recording warranty costs in the same period in which the sale is recorded. When the defective product is repaired, the repair costs are recorded by debiting *Product Warranty Payable* and crediting *Cash*, *Supplies*, or other appropriate accounts. Thus, if a customer required a $200 part replacement on August 16, the entry would be:

| | | | | | |
|---|---|---|---|---|---|
| Aug. | 16 | Product Warranty Payable | 2 0 0 00 | |
| | | Supplies | | 2 0 0 00 |
| | | Replaced defective part under warranty. | | |

If a contingent liability is probable but cannot be *reasonably estimated* or is only *possible*, then the nature of the contingent liability should be disclosed in the footnotes to the financial statements. Professional judgment is required in distinguishing between contingent liabilities that are probable versus those that are only possible.

Common examples of contingent liabilities disclosed in notes to the financial statements are litigation, environmental matters, guarantees, and contingencies from the sale of receivables. The following example of a contingency disclosure, related to litigation, was taken from a recent annual report of **eBay Inc.**:

> . . . *eBay was served with a lawsuit . . . filed on behalf of a purported class of eBay users who purchased allegedly forged autographed sports memorabilia on eBay. The lawsuit claims eBay was negligent in permitting certain named (and other unnamed) defendants to sell allegedly forged autographed sports memorabilia on eBay. . . . Management believes that the ultimate resolution of these disputes will not have a material adverse impact on eBay's consolidated financial positions, results of operations, or cash flows.*

The accounting treatment of contingent liabilities is summarized in Exhibit 1.

## •Exhibit 1  Accounting Treatment of Contingent Liabilities

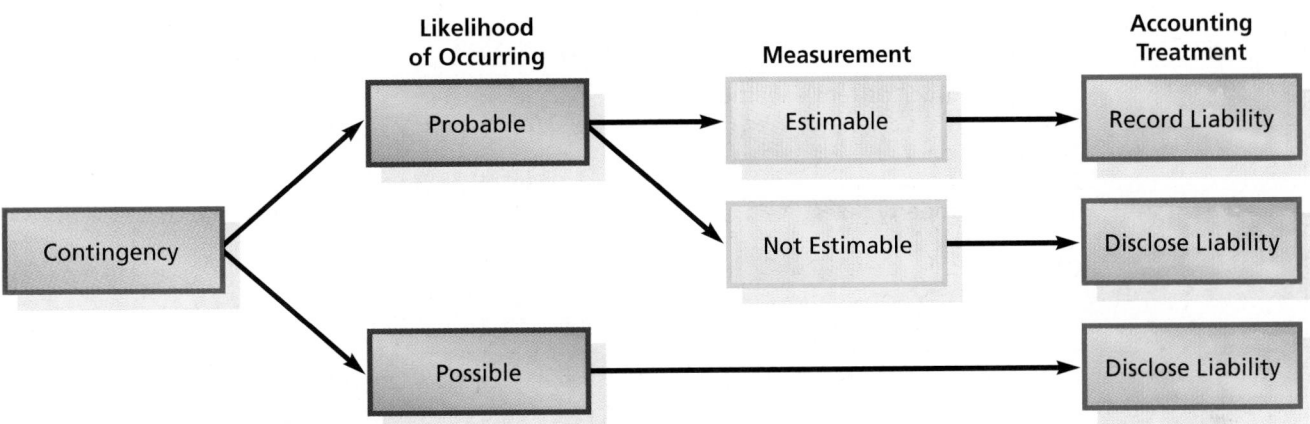

---

### INTEGRITY IN BUSINESS

#### TODAY'S MISTAKES CAN BE TOMORROW'S LIABILITY

Environmental and public health claims are quickly growing into some of the largest contingent liabilities facing companies. For example, tobacco, asbestos, and environmental cleanup claims have reached billions of dollars and have led to a number of corporate bankruptcies. Managers must be careful that today's decisions do not become tomorrow's nightmare.

---

# Payroll and Payroll Taxes

**objective   4**

Determine employer liabilities for payroll, including liabilities arising from employee earnings and deductions from earnings.

We are all familiar with the term payroll. In accounting, the term **payroll** refers to the amount paid to employees for the services they provide during a period. A business's payroll is usually significant for several reasons. First, employees are sensitive to payroll errors and irregularities. Maintaining good employee morale requires that the payroll be paid on a timely, accurate basis. Second, the payroll is subject to various federal and state regulations. Finally, the payroll and related payroll taxes have

## FINANCIAL REPORTING AND DISCLOSURE

### WARRANTY AND CURRENT LIABILITIES

**C**ompanies with significant warranty costs disclose the method of *estimating* warranty expense for the period. However, companies are not required to disclose the actual warranty expense or the product warranty payable. The warranty expense is rarely disclosed, while the product warranty payable is disclosed in the notes, if deemed material. The following is the warranty accounting policy for **Dell Computer Corp.**:

*Warranty—The Company provides for an estimate of costs that may be incurred under its basic limited warranty at the time product revenue is recognized. These costs primarily include parts and labor associated with service dispatches. Factors that affect the Company's warranty liability include the number of installed units, historical and anticipated rate of warranty claims on those units, and*

*cost per claim to satisfy the Company's warranty obligation. As these factors are impacted by actual experience and future expectations, the Company assesses the adequacy of its recorded warranty liabilities and adjusts the amounts as necessary. Costs associated with service and extended warranty contracts for which the Company is obligated to perform are recognized over the term of the contract.*

Dell accounts for warranties the way we described in the chapter. The warranty expense is recognized at the same time revenue from product sales is recognized. The amount of the expense is estimated from the number of installed units, historical and anticipated rate of claim, and the estimated cost per claim. Dell discloses the warranty liability in the notes to its financial statements as follows:

|  | January 31, 2003 | February 1, 2002 |
| --- | --- | --- |
| Accrued and other current liabilities: | | |
| Warranty | $ 674 | $ 444 |
| Compensation | 545 | 384 |
| Deferred income | 360 | 322 |
| Sales and property taxes | 239 | 259 |
| Income taxes | 54 | 5 |
| Other | 1,072 | 1,030 |
|  | $2,944 | $2,444 |

As can be seen, the warranty liability is included in the broad category of "accrued and other current liabilities" along with other current liabilities discussed in this chapter, such as salaries payable (compensation), taxes payable (sales, property, and income), and unearned revenue (deferred income).

a significant effect on the net income of most businesses. Although the amount of such expenses varies widely, it is not unusual for a business's payroll and payroll-related expenses to equal nearly one-third of its revenue.

## Liability for Employee Earnings

Salaries and wages paid to employees are an employer's labor expenses. The term **salary** usually refers to payment for managerial, administrative, or similar services. The rate of salary is normally expressed in terms of a month or a year. The term **wages** usually refers to payment for manual labor, both skilled and unskilled. The rate of wages is normally stated on an hourly or weekly basis. In practice, the terms salary and wages are often used interchangeably.

The basic salary or wage of an employee may be increased by commissions, profit sharing, or cost-of-living adjustments. Many businesses pay managers an annual bonus in addition to a basic salary. The amount of the bonus is often based on some measure of productivity, such as income or profit of the business. Although payment is usually made by check or in cash, it may be in the form of securities, notes, lodging, or other property or services. Generally, the form of payment has no effect on how salaries and wages are treated by either the employer or the employee.

**Employee salaries and wages are expenses to an employer.**

## INTEGRITY IN BUSINESS

### $15,000 UMBRELLA STAND

Dennis Kozlowski, ex-CEO of **Tyco International**, was indicted for enterprise corruption and grand larceny for allegedly stealing corporate funds through unauthorized executive compensation. He was accused of taking millions of dollars in excused loans and unauthorized expenses, including a $15,000 dog umbrella stand, $97,000 for flowers, and a $2,200 waste basket.

**Source:** Tyco Reveals Tens of Millions in Unauthorized Payments, Harry R. Weber, The Associated Press, 09/18/2002, St. Louis Post-Dispatch, C.12.

**POINT OF INTEREST**

Information on average salaries for a variety of professions can be found at the *Economic Research Institute's* Web site, which is linked to the text's Web site at **http://warren.swlearning.com**.

Salary and wage rates are determined by agreement between the employer and the employees. Businesses engaged in interstate commerce must follow the requirements of the Fair Labor Standards Act. Employers covered by this legislation, which is commonly called the Federal Wage and Hour Law, are required to pay a minimum rate of 1½ times the regular rate for all hours worked in excess of 40 hours per week. Exemptions are provided for executive, administrative, and certain supervisory positions. Premium rates for overtime or for working at night, holidays, or other less desirable times are fairly common, even when not required by law. In some cases, the premium rates may be as much as twice the base rate.

To illustrate computing an employee's earnings, assume that John T. McGrath is a salesperson employed by McDermott Supply Co. at the rate of $34 per hour. Any hours in excess of 40 hours per week are paid at a rate of 1½ times the normal rate, or $51 ($34 + $17) per hour. For the week ended December 27, McGrath's time card indicates that he worked 42 hours. His earnings for that week are computed as follows:

| | |
|---|---|
| Earnings at base rate (40 × $34) | $1,360 |
| Earnings at overtime rate (2 × $51) | 102 |
| Total earnings | $1,462 |

**REAL WORLD**

Professional athletes must pay local taxes in each location in which they play their sport.

# Deductions from Employee Earnings

The total earnings of an employee for a payroll period, including bonuses and overtime pay, are called **gross pay**. From this amount is subtracted one or more **deductions** to arrive at the net pay. **Net pay** is the amount the employer must pay the employee. The deductions for federal taxes are usually the largest deduction. Deductions may also be required for state or local income taxes. Other deductions may be made for medical insurance, contributions to pensions, and for items authorized by individual employees.

**REAL WORLD**

Federal income tax withholding tables are subject to frequent changes and are available from the Internal Revenue Service in Publication 15-A.

## Income Taxes

Except for certain types of employment, all employers must withhold a portion of employee earnings for payment of the employees' federal income tax. As a basis for determining the amount to be withheld, each employee completes and submits to the employer an "Employee's Withholding Allowance Certificate," often called a W-4. Exhibit 2 is an example of a completed W-4 form.

You may recall filling out a W-4 form. On the W-4, an employee indicates marital status, the number of withholding allowances, and whether any additional withholdings are authorized. A single employee may claim one withholding allowance. A married employee may claim an additional allowance for a spouse. An employee may also claim an allowance for each dependent other than a spouse. Each allowance claimed reduces the amount of federal income tax withheld from the employee's check.

# •Exhibit 2  Employee's Withholding Allowance Certificate (W-4 Form)

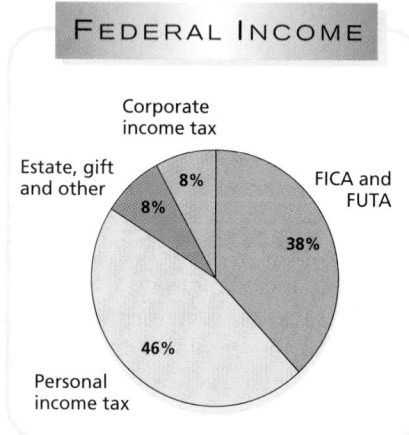

**Form W-4**
Department of the Treasury
Internal Revenue Service

**Employee's Withholding Allowance Certificate**
► For Privacy Act and Paperwork Reduction Act Notice, see page 2.

OMB No. 1545-0010
**2005**

1 Type or print your first name and middle initial: John T.    Last name: McGrath
2 Your social security number: 381 48 9120

Home address (number and street or rural route): 1830 4th Street
3 ☒ Single ☐ Married ☐ Married, but withhold at higher Single rate.
Note: If married, but legally separated, or spouse is a nonresident alien, check the "Single" box.

City or town, state, and ZIP code: Clinton, Iowa 52732-6142
4 If your last name differs from that shown on your social security card, check here. You must call 1-800-772-1213 for a new card. ► ☐

5 Total number of allowances you are claiming (from line H above or from the applicable worksheet on page 2)  **5** 1
6 Additional amount, if any, you want withheld from each paycheck  **6** $
7 I claim exemption from withholding for 2005, and I certify that I meet **both** of the following conditions for exemption:
• Last year I had a right to a refund of **all** Federal income tax withheld because I had **no** tax liability **and**
• This year I expect a refund of **all** Federal income tax withheld because I expect to have **no** tax liability.
If you meet both conditions, write "Exempt" here ► **7**

Under penalties of perjury, I certify that I am entitled to the number of withholding allowances claimed on this certificate, or I am entitled to claim exempt status.
Employee's signature (Form is not valid unless you sign it.) ► *John T. McGrath*    Date ► June 2, 2005

8 Employer's name and address (Employer: Complete lines 8 and 10 only if sending to the IRS.)
9 Office code (optional)
10 Employer identification number

Cat. No. 10220Q

**REAL WORLD**

The U.S. Government receives income from various taxes, which are spent on a variety of government services. The relative sizes of these incomes and outlays for a recent fiscal year, as reported by the Internal Revenue Service, are:

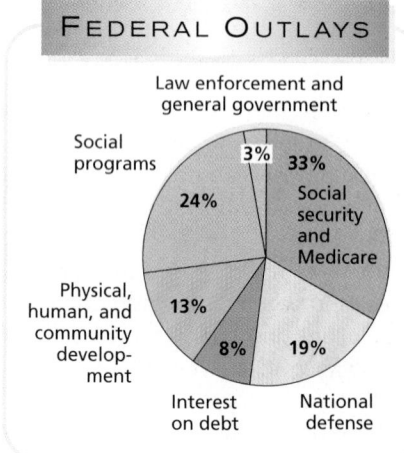

**FEDERAL INCOME**

Corporate income tax 8%
Estate, gift and other 8%
FICA and FUTA 38%
Personal income tax 46%

**FEDERAL OUTLAYS**

Law enforcement and general government 3%
Social programs 24%
Social security and Medicare 33%
Physical, human, and community development 13%
Interest on debt 8%
National defense 19%

The amount that must be withheld for income tax differs, depending upon each employee's gross pay and completed W-4. Most employers use wage bracket withholding tables furnished by the Internal Revenue Service to determine the amount to be withheld.

Exhibit 3 is an example of a wage bracket withholding table. This table is for a single employee who is paid weekly. Other tables are used for employees who are married or who are paid in time periods other than weekly. In using the withholding table, the amount of federal income tax withheld each pay period is determined by the following computational procedure:

1. Identify the appropriate subsection for the number of allowances claimed by the employee.
2. Read across the selected subsection and locate the applicable wage bracket in columns A and B.
3. Subtract the amount shown in column C from the employee's gross wages.[2]
4. Multiply the result by the withholding percentage rate shown in column D to obtain the tax to be withheld.

For example, assume that John T. McGrath, who is single and has declared one withholding allowance, made $1,462 for the week ended December 27. Using the computational procedure and information in Exhibit 3 would yield the following federal income tax withholding:

| | |
|---|---|
| Amount of wage | $1,462.00 |
| Less: Amount from column C | 463.76 |
| Wage, net of deduction | $ 998.24 |
| Multiplier from column D | × 28% |
| Federal income tax withholding | $ 279.51 |

[2]The amount subtracted represents the tax benefit of the allowances and lower tax rates applied at lower income thresholds.

## •Exhibit 3   Wage Bracket Withholding Table

### Wage Bracket Percentage Method Table for Computing Income Tax Withholding From Gross Wages

#### Weekly Payroll Period

| If the number of allowances is— | And gross wages are— | | from gross wages | | Multiply result by— |
|---|---|---|---|---|---|
| | Over | But not over | | | |
| | **A** | **B** | **C** | | **D** |
| **0** | $0.00 | $187.00 | subtract | $51.00 | 10% |
| | $187.00 | $592.00 | subtract | $96.33 | 15% |
| | $592.00 | $1,317.00 | subtract | $294.60 | 25% |
| | $1,317.00 | $2,860.00 | subtract | $404.14 | 28% |
| | $2,860.00 | $6,177.00 | subtract | $776.24 | 33% |
| | $6,177.00 | . . . . . . | subtract | $1,084.86 | 35% |
| **1** | $0.00 | $246.62 | subtract | $110.62 | 10% |
| | $246.62 | $651.62 | subtract | $155.95 | 15% |
| | $651.62 | $1,376.62 | subtract | $354.22 | 25% |
| | $1,376.62 | $2,919.62 | subtract | $463.76 | 28% |
| | $2,919.62 | $6,236.62 | subtract | $835.86 | 33% |
| | $6,236.62 | | subtract | $1,144.48 | 35% |
| **2** | $0.00 | $306.24 | subtract | $170.24 | 10% |
| | $306.24 | $711.24 | subtract | $215.57 | 15% |
| | $711.24 | $1,436.24 | subtract | $413.84 | 25% |
| | $1,436.24 | $2,979.24 | subtract | $523.38 | 28% |
| | $2,979.24 | $6,296.24 | subtract | $895.48 | 33% |
| | $6,296.24 | . . . . . . | subtract | $1,204.10 | 35% |
| **3** | $0.00 | $365.86 | subtract | $229.86 | 10% |
| | $365.86 | $770.86 | subtract | $275.19 | 15% |
| | $770.86 | $1,495.86 | subtract | $473.46 | 25% |
| | $1,495.86 | $3,038.86 | subtract | $583.00 | 28% |
| | $3,038.86 | $6,355.86 | subtract | $955.10 | 33% |
| | $6,355.86 | . . . . . . | subtract | $1,263.72 | 35% |

**POINT OF INTEREST**

In 1936, the Social Security Board described how the tax was expected to affect a worker's pay, as follows:

*The taxes called for in this law will be paid both by your employer and by you. For the next 3 years you will pay maybe 15 cents a week, maybe 25 cents a week, maybe 30 cents or more, according to what you earn. That is to say, during the next 3 years, beginning January 1, 1937, you will pay 1 cent for every dollar you earn, and at the same time your employer will pay 1 cent for every dollar you earn, up to $3,000 a year. . . .*

*. . . Beginning in 1940 you will pay, and your employer will pay, 1¹/₂ cents for each dollar you earn, up to $3,000 a year . . . and then beginning in 1943, you will pay 2 cents, and so will your employer, for every dollar you earn for the next three years. After that, you and your employer will each pay half a cent more for 3 years, and finally, beginning in 1949, . . . you and your employer will each pay 3 cents on each dollar you earn, up to $3,000 a year. That is the most you will ever pay.*

The rate on January 1, 2003, was 7.65 cents per dollar earned (7.65%). The social security portion was 6.20% on the first $87,000 of earnings. The Medicare portion was 1.45% on all earnings.

**Source:** Arthur Lodge, "That Is the Most You Will Ever Pay," *Journal of Accountancy*, October 1985, p. 44.

In addition to the federal income tax, employees may also be required to pay a state income tax and a city income tax. State and city taxes are withheld from employees' earnings and paid to state and city governments.

### FICA Tax

Most of us have FICA tax withheld from our payroll checks by our employers. Employers are required by the Federal Insurance Contributions Act (FICA) to withhold a portion of the earnings of each of the employees. The amount of **FICA tax** withheld is the employees' contribution to two federal programs. Tax is withheld separately under each program. The first program, called **social security**, is for old age, survivors, and disability insurance (OASDI). The second program, called **Medicare**, is health insurance for senior citizens.

The amount of tax that employers are required to withhold from each employee is normally based on the amount of earnings paid in the *calendar* year. Although both the schedule of future tax rates and the maximum amount subject to tax are revised often by Congress, such changes have little effect on the basic payroll system. In this text, we will use a social security rate of 6% on the first $100,000 of annual earnings and a Medicare rate of 1.5% on all annual earnings.

To illustrate, assume that John T. McGrath's annual earnings prior to the current payroll period total $99,038. Assume also that the current period earnings are $1,462. The total FICA tax of $79.65 is determined as follows:

If an employee earns $9,000 per month and has been employed since January 1 of the current year, what is the total FICA tax deducted from the employee's December paycheck?

*Social security tax*
  ($1,000* × 6%)    $ 60.00
*Medicare tax*
  ($9,000 × 1.5%)    135.00
  *Total FICA tax*    $195.00

*$100,000 − ($9,000 × 11)

| | | |
|---|---|---|
| Earnings subject to 6% social security tax ($100,000 − $99,038) | $ 962 | |
| Social security tax rate | × 6% | |
| Social security tax | | $57.72 |
| Earnings subject to 1.5% Medicare tax | $1,462 | |
| Medicare tax rate | × 1.5% | |
| Medicare tax | | 21.93 |
| Total FICA tax | | $79.65 |

## Other Deductions

Neither the employer nor the employee has any choice in deducting taxes from gross earnings. However, employees may choose to have additional amounts deducted for other purposes. For example, you as an employee may authorize deductions for retirement savings, for contributions to charitable organizations, or for premiums on employee insurance. A union contract may also require the deduction of union dues.

## Computing Employee Net Pay

Gross earnings less payroll deductions equals the amount to be paid to an employee for the payroll period. This amount is the *net pay*, which is often called the *take-home pay*. Assuming that John T. McGrath authorized deductions for retirement savings and for a United Way contribution, the amount to be paid McGrath for the week ended December 27 is $1,077.84, as shown below.

| | | |
|---|---|---|
| Gross earnings for the week | | $1,462.00 |
| Deductions: | | |
| Social security tax | $ 57.72 | |
| Medicare tax | 21.93 | |
| Federal income tax | 279.51 | |
| Retirement savings | 20.00 | |
| United Way | 5.00 | |
| Total deductions | | 384.16 |
| Net pay | | $1,077.84 |

## Liability for Employer's Payroll Taxes

So far, we have discussed the payroll taxes that are withheld from the employees' earnings. Most employers are also subject to federal and state payroll taxes based on the amount paid their employees. Such taxes are an operating expense of the business. Exhibit 4 summarizes the responsibility for employee and employer payroll taxes.

### FICA Tax

Employers are required to contribute to the social security and Medicare programs for each employee. The employer must match the employee's contribution to each program.

### Federal Unemployment Compensation Tax

The Federal Unemployment Tax Act (FUTA) provides for temporary payments to those who become unemployed as a result of layoffs due to economic causes beyond their control. Types of employment subject to this program are similar to those covered by FICA taxes. A tax of 6.2% is levied on employers only, rather than on both employers and employees.[3] It is applied to only the first $7,000 of the earn-

[3]This rate may be reduced to 0.8% for credits for state unemployment compensation tax.

## •Exhibit 4

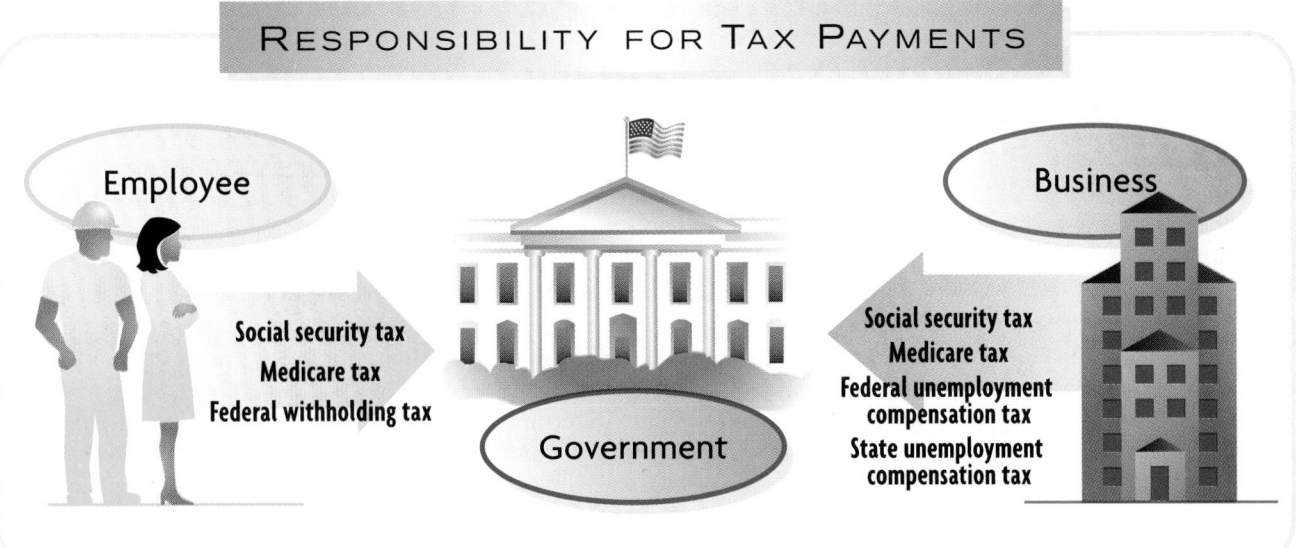

RESPONSIBILITY FOR TAX PAYMENTS

**Employee**

Social security tax
Medicare tax
Federal withholding tax

**Government**

**Business**

Social security tax
Medicare tax
Federal unemployment
compensation tax
State unemployment
compensation tax

ings of each covered employee during a calendar year. Congress often revises the rate and maximum earnings subject to federal unemployment compensation tax. The funds collected by the federal government are not paid directly to the unemployed but are allocated among the states for use in state programs.

### State Unemployment Compensation Tax

State Unemployment Tax Acts (SUTA) also provide for payments to unemployed workers. The amounts paid as benefits are obtained, for the most part, from a tax levied upon employers only. A few states require employee contributions also. The rates of tax and the tax bases vary. In most states, employers who provide stable employment for their employees are granted reduced rates. The employment experience and the status of each employer's tax account are reviewed annually, and the tax rates are adjusted accordingly.[4]

## INTEGRITY IN BUSINESS

### RESUMÉ PADDING

**M**isrepresenting your accomplishments on your resumé could come back to haunt you. In one case, the Chief Financial Officer (CFO) of **Veritas Software** was forced to resign his position when it was discovered that he had lied about earning an MBA from Stanford University, when in actuality he had earned only an undergraduate degree from Idaho State University.

**Source:** Reuters News Service, October 4, 2002

---

[4]As of January 1, 2004, the maximum state rate credited against the federal unemployment current rate was 5.4% of the first $7,000 of each employee's earnings during a calendar year.

# Accounting Systems for Payroll and Payroll Taxes

**objective 5**

Describe payroll accounting systems that use a payroll register, employee earnings records, and a general journal.

In designing payroll systems, the requirements of various federal, state, and local agencies for payroll data are considered. Payroll data must also be maintained accurately for each payroll period and for each employee. Periodic reports using payroll data must be submitted to government agencies. The payroll data itself must be retained for possible inspection by the various agencies.

Payroll systems must be designed to pay employees on a timely basis. Payroll systems should also be designed to provide useful data for management decision-making needs. Such needs might include settling employee grievances and negotiating retirement or other benefits with employees.

Although payroll systems differ among businesses, the major elements common to most payroll systems are the payroll register, employee's earnings record, and payroll checks. We discuss and illustrate each of these elements next. We have kept the illustrations relatively simple, and they may be modified in practice to meet the needs of each individual business.

## Payroll Register

The **payroll register** is a multicolumn report used for summarizing the data for each payroll period. Its design varies according to the number and classes of employees and the extent to which computers are used. Exhibit 5 shows a report suitable for a small number of employees.

The nature of the data appearing in the payroll register is evident from the column headings. The number of hours worked and the earnings and deduction data are inserted in their proper columns. The sum of the deductions for each employee is then subtracted from the total earnings to yield the amount to be paid. The check numbers are recorded in the payroll register as evidence of payment.

The last two columns of the payroll register are used to accumulate the total wages or salaries to be debited to the various expense accounts. This process is usually called **payroll distribution**.

**•Exhibit 5** Payroll Register

| | Employee Name | Total Hours | Earnings | | | |
| | | | Regular | Overtime | Total | |
|---|---|---|---|---|---|---|
| 1 | Abrams, Julie S. | 40 | 500.00 | | 500.00 | 1 |
| 2 | Elrod, Fred G. | 44 | 392.00 | 58.80 | 450.80 | 2 |
| 3 | Gomez, Jose C. | 40 | 840.00 | | 840.00 | 3 |
| 4 | McGrath, John T. | 42 | 1,360.00 | 102.00 | 1,462.00 | 4 |
| 25 | Wilkes, Glenn K. | 40 | 480.00 | | 480.00 | 25 |
| 26 | Zumpano, Michael W. | 40 | 600.00 | | 600.00 | 26 |
| 27 | Total | | 13,328.00 | 574.00 | 13,902.00 | 27 |
| 28 | | | | | | 28 |

## Recording Employees' Earnings

The column totals of the payroll register support the journal entry for payroll. The entry based on the payroll register in Exhibit 5 follows.

| | | | | | |
|---|---|---|---|---|---|
| Dec. | 27 | Sales Salaries Expense | 11 12 2 00 | | |
| | | Office Salaries Expense | 2 78 0 00 | | |
| | | Social Security Tax Payable | | 6 43 07 | |
| | | Medicare Tax Payable | | 2 08 53 | |
| | | Employees Federal Income Tax Payable | | 3 33 2 00 | |
| | | Retirement Savings Deductions Payable | | 6 80 00 | |
| | | United Way Deductions Payable | | 4 70 00 | |
| | | Accounts Receivable—Fred G. Elrod (emp.) | | 50 00 | |
| | | Salaries Payable | | 8 51 8 40 | |
| | | Payroll for week ended December 27. | | | |

## Recording and Paying Payroll Taxes

> **Payroll taxes become a liability to the employer when the payroll is paid.**

The employer's payroll taxes become liabilities when the related payroll is *paid* to employees. In addition, employers are required to compute and report payroll taxes on a *calendar-year* basis, even if a different fiscal year is used for financial reporting and income tax purposes.

To illustrate, assume that Everson Company's fiscal year ends on April 30. Also, assume that Everson Company owes its employees $26,000 of wages on December 31. The following portions of the $26,000 of wages are subject to payroll taxes on December 31:

| | Earnings Subject to Payroll Taxes |
|---|---|
| Social Security Tax (6.0%) | $18,000 |
| Medicare Tax (1.5%) | 26,000 |
| State and Federal Unemployment Compensation Tax | 1,000 |

If the payroll is paid on December 31, the payroll taxes will be based on the preceding amounts. If the payroll is paid on January 2, however, the *entire* $26,000 will be subject to *all* payroll taxes. This is because the maximum earnings limitation for determining social security and unemployment taxes will not be exceeded at the beginning of the calendar year.

## •Exhibit 5 (concluded)

| | Deductions | | | | | | Paid | | Accounts Debited | | |
|---|---|---|---|---|---|---|---|---|---|---|---|
| | Social Security Tax | Medicare Tax | Federal Income Tax | Retirement Savings | Misc. | Total | Net Amount | Check No. | Sales Salaries Expense | Office Salaries Expense | |
| 1 | 30.00 | 7.50 | 74.00 | 20.00 | UW 10.00 | 141.50 | 358.50 | 6857 | 500.00 | | 1 |
| 2 | 27.05 | 6.76 | 62.00 | | AR 50.00 | 145.81 | 304.99 | 6858 | | 450.80 | 2 |
| 3 | 50.40 | 12.60 | 131.00 | 25.00 | UW 10.00 | 229.00 | 611.00 | 6859 | 840.00 | | 3 |
| 4 | 57.72 | 21.93 | 279.51 | 20.00 | UW 5.00 | 384.16 | 1,077.84 | 6860 | 1,462.00 | | 4 |
| 25 | 28.80 | 7.20 | 69.00 | 10.00 | | 115.00 | 365.00 | 6880 | 480.00 | | 25 |
| 26 | 36.00 | 9.00 | 79.00 | 5.00 | UW 2.00 | 131.00 | 469.00 | 6881 | | 600.00 | 26 |
| 27 | 643.07 | 208.53 | 3,332.00 | 680.00 | UW 470.00 | 5,383.60 | 8,518.40 | | 11,122.00 | 2,780.00 | 27 |
| 28 | | | | | AR 50.00 | | | | | | 28 |

Miscellaneous Deductions: UW—United Way; AR—Accounts Receivable

The payroll register for McDermott Supply Co. in Exhibit 5 indicates that the amount of social security tax withheld is $643.07 and Medicare tax withheld is $208.53. Since the employer must match the employees' FICA contributions, the employer's social security payroll tax will also be $643.07, and the Medicare tax will be $208.53. Further, assume that the earnings subject to state and federal unemployment compensation taxes are $2,710. Multiplying this amount by the state (5.4%) and federal (0.8%) rates yields the unemployment compensation taxes shown in the following payroll tax computation:

| | |
|---|---:|
| Social security tax | $ 643.07 |
| Medicare tax | 208.53 |
| State unemployment compensation tax (5.4% × $2,710) | 146.34 |
| Federal unemployment compensation tax (0.8% × $2,710) | 21.68 |
| Total payroll tax expense | $1,019.62 |

The entry to journalize the payroll tax expense for the week and the liability for the taxes accrued is shown below.

| | | | | |
|---|---|---|---:|---:|
| Dec. | 27 | Payroll Tax Expense | 1 0 1 9 62 | |
| | | Social Security Tax Payable | | 6 4 3 07 |
| | | Medicare Tax Payable | | 2 0 8 53 |
| | | State Unemployment Tax Payable | | 1 4 6 34 |
| | | Federal Unemployment Tax Payable | | 2 1 68 |
| | | Payroll taxes for week ended | | |
| | | December 27. | | |

# Employee's Earnings Record

The amount of each employee's earnings to date must be available at the end of each payroll period. This cumulative amount is required in order to compute each employee's social security and Medicare tax withholding and the employer's payroll taxes. It is essential, therefore, that a detailed payroll record be maintained for each employee. This record is called an ***employee's earnings record***.

Exhibit 6, on pages 450–451, shows a portion of the employee's earnings record for John T. McGrath. The relationship between this record and the payroll register can be seen by tracing the amounts entered on McGrath's earnings record for December 27 back to its source—the fourth line of the payroll register in Exhibit 5.

In addition to spaces for recording data for each payroll period and the cumulative total of earnings, the employee's earnings record has spaces for quarterly totals and the yearly total. These totals are used in various reports for tax, insurance, and other purposes. One such report is the Wage and Tax Statement, commonly called a **Form W-2**. You may recall receiving a W-2 form for use in preparing your individual tax return. This form must be provided annually to each employee as well as to the Social Security Administration. The amounts reported in the Form W-2 shown at the top of the following page were taken from McGrath's employee's earnings record.

# Payroll Checks

At the end of each pay period, **payroll checks** are prepared. Each check includes a detachable statement showing the details of how the net pay was computed. Exhibit 7, on page 452, is a payroll check for John T. McGrath.

The amount paid to employees is normally recorded as a single amount, regardless of the number of employees. There is no need to record each payroll check separately in the journal, since all of the details are available in the payroll register.

For paying their payroll, most employers use payroll checks drawn on a special bank account. After the data for the payroll period have been recorded and summarized in the payroll register, a single check for the total amount to be paid is

| a Control number | 22222 | Void ☐ | For Official Use Only ► OMB No. 1545-0008 | | |
|---|---|---|---|---|---|

| b Employer identification number 61-8436524 | | 1 Wages, tips, other compensation $ 100,500.00 | 2 Federal income tax withheld $ 21,387.65 |
|---|---|---|---|
| c Employer's name, address, and ZIP code McDermott Supply Co. 415 5th Ave. So. Dubuque, IA 52736-0142 | | 3 Social security wages $ 100,000.00 | 4 Social security tax withheld $ 6,000.00 |
| | | 5 Medicare wages and tips $ 100,500.00 | 6 Medicare tax withheld $ 1,507.50 |
| | | 7 Social security tips $ | 8 Allocated tips $ |
| d Employee's social security number 381-48-9120 | | 9 Advance EIC payment $ | 10 Dependent care benefits $ |
| e Employee's first name and initial John T. | Last name McGrath | 11 Nonqualified plans $ | 12a See instructions for box 12 $ |
| | | 13 Statutory employee ☐ Retirement plan ☐ Third-party sick pay ☐ | 12b $ |
| 1830 4th St. Clinton, IA 52732-6142 | | 14 Other | 12c $ |
| | | | 12d $ |
| f Employee's address and ZIP code | | | |

| 15 State IA | Employer's state ID number | 16 State wages, tips, etc. $ $ | 17 State income tax $ $ | 18 Local wages, tips, etc. $ $ | 19 Local income tax $ $ | 20 Locality name Dubuque |
|---|---|---|---|---|---|---|

Form **W-2** Wage and Tax Statement (99)   **2005**   Department of the Treasury—Internal Revenue Service

Copy A For Social Security Administration—Send this entire page with Form W-3 to the Social Security Administration; photocopies are **not** acceptable.   Cat. No. 10134D   For Privacy Act and Paperwork Reduction Act Notice, see separate instructions.

**Do Not Cut, Fold, or Staple Forms on This Page — Do Not Cut, Fold, or Staple Forms on This Page**

written on the firm's regular bank account. This check is then deposited in the special payroll bank account. Individual payroll checks are written from the payroll account, and the numbers of the payroll checks are inserted in the payroll register.

An advantage of using a separate payroll bank account is that the task of reconciling the bank statements is simplified. In addition, a payroll bank account establishes control over payroll checks by preventing the theft or misuse of uncashed payroll checks.

Currency may be used to pay payroll. However, many employees have their net pay deposited directly in a bank. In these cases, funds are transferred electronically.

## Payroll System Diagram

You may find Exhibit 8, on page 452, useful in following the flow of data within the payroll segment of an accounting system. The diagram indicates the relationships among the primary components of the payroll system we described in this chapter.

Our focus in the preceding discussion has been on the outputs of a payroll system: the payroll register, payroll checks, the employees' earnings records, and tax and other reports. As shown in the diagram in Exhibit 8, the inputs into a payroll system may be classified as either constants or variables.

Constants are data that remain unchanged from payroll to payroll and thus do not need to be entered into the system each pay period. Examples of constants include such data as each employee's name and social security number, marital status, number of income tax withholding allowances, rate of pay, payroll category (office, sales, etc.), and department where employed. The FICA tax rates and various tax tables are also constants that apply to all employees. In a computerized accounting system, constants are stored within a payroll file.

Variables are data that change from payroll to payroll and thus must be entered into the system each pay period. Examples of variables include such data as the number of hours or days worked for each employee during the payroll period, days of sick leave with pay, vacation credits, and cumulative earnings and taxes withheld. If salespersons are paid commissions, the amount of their sales would also vary from period to period.

## Internal Controls for Payroll Systems

Payroll processing, as we discussed above, requires the input of a large amount of data, along with numerous and sometimes complex computations. These factors,

# •Exhibit 6    Employee's Earnings Record

**John T. McGrath**
**1830 4th Street**
**Clinton, IA 52732-6142**                                                 **PHONE: 555-3148**

| SINGLE | NUMBER OF WITHHOLDING ALLOWANCES: 1 | PAY RATE: | $1,360.00 Per Week |
| --- | --- | --- | --- |
| OCCUPATION:    Salesperson | | EQUIVALENT HOURLY RATE: $34 | |

| | | | Earnings | | | | |
| --- | --- | --- | --- | --- | --- | --- | --- |
| | Period Ending | Total Hours | Regular Earnings | Overtime Earnings | Total Earnings | Cumulative Total | |
| 42 | SEP. 27 | 53 | 1,360.00 | 663.00 | 2,023.00 | 75,565.00 | 42 |
| 43 | THIRD QUARTER | | 17,680.00 | 7,605.00 | 25,285.00 | | 43 |
| 44 | OCT. 4 | 51 | 1,360.00 | 561.00 | 1,921.00 | 77,486.00 | 44 |
| 50 | NOV. 15 | 50 | 1,360.00 | 510.00 | 1,870.00 | 89,382.00 | 50 |
| 51 | NOV. 22 | 53 | 1,360.00 | 663.00 | 2,023.00 | 91,405.00 | 51 |
| 52 | NOV. 29 | 47 | 1,360.00 | 357.00 | 1,717.00 | 93,122.00 | 52 |
| 53 | DEC. 6 | 53 | 1,360.00 | 663.00 | 2,023.00 | 95,145.00 | 53 |
| 54 | DEC.13 | 52 | 1,360.00 | 612.00 | 1,972.00 | 97,117.00 | 54 |
| 55 | DEC. 20 | 51 | 1,360.00 | 561.00 | 1,921.00 | 99,038.00 | 55 |
| 56 | DEC. 27 | 42 | 1,360.00 | 102.00 | 1,462.00 | 100,500.00 | 56 |
| 57 | FOURTH QUARTER | | 17,680.00 | 7,255.00 | 24,935.00 | | 57 |
| 58 | YEARLY TOTAL | | 70,720.00 | 29,780.00 | 100,500.00 | | 58 |

combined with the large dollar amounts involved, require controls to ensure that payroll payments are timely and accurate. In addition, the system must also provide adequate safeguards against theft or other misuse of funds.

The cash payment controls we discussed in the cash chapter also apply to payrolls. Thus, it is normally desirable to use a system that includes procedures for proper authorization and approval of payroll. When a check-signing machine is used, it is important that blank payroll checks and access to the machine be carefully controlled to prevent the theft or misuse of payroll funds.

It is especially important to authorize and approve in writing employee additions and deletions and changes in pay rates. For example, numerous payroll frauds have involved a supervisor adding fictitious employees to the payroll. The supervisor then cashes the fictitious employees' checks. Similar frauds have occurred where employees have been fired but the Payroll Department is not notified. As a result, payroll checks to the fired employees are prepared and cashed by a supervisor.

To prevent or detect frauds such as those we described above, employees' attendance records should be controlled. For example, you may have used an "In and Out" card on which your time of arrival to and departure from work was recorded when you inserted the card into a time clock. A Payroll Department employee may be stationed near the time clock during normal arrival and departure times in order to verify that employees "clock in" only once and only for themselves. Employee identification cards or badges may also be used to verify that only authorized employees are clocking in and are permitted to enter work areas. When payroll checks

**•Exhibit 6**   (concluded)

| SOC. SEC. NO.: 381-48-9120 | | | | | | | | EMPLOYEE NO.: 814 | |
|---|---|---|---|---|---|---|---|---|---|

**DATE OF BIRTH: February 15, 1980**

**DATE EMPLOYMENT TERMINATED:**

| | Deductions | | | | | | | Paid | | |
|---|---|---|---|---|---|---|---|---|---|---|
| | Social Security Tax | Medicare Tax | Federal Income Tax | Retirement Savings | Other | | Total | Net Amount | Check No. | |
| 42 | 121.38 | 30.35 | 436.59 | 20.00 | | | 608.32 | 1,416.68 | 6175 | 42 |
| 43 | 1,517.10 | 379.28 | 5,391.71 | 260.00 | UF | 40.00 | 7,588.09 | 17,696.91 | | 43 |
| 44 | 115.26 | 28.82 | 408.03 | 20.00 | | | 572.11 | 1,348.89 | 6225 | 44 |
| | | | | | | | | | | 49 |
| 50 | 112.20 | 28.05 | 393.75 | 20.00 | | | 554.00 | 1,316.00 | 6530 | 50 |
| 51 | 121.38 | 30.35 | 436.59 | 20.00 | | | 608.32 | 1,414.68 | 6582 | 51 |
| 52 | 103.02 | 25.76 | 350.91 | 20.00 | | | 499.69 | 1,217.31 | 6640 | 52 |
| 53 | 121.38 | 30.35 | 436.59 | 20.00 | UF | 5.00 | 613.32 | 1,409.68 | 6688 | 53 |
| 54 | 118.32 | 29.58 | 422.31 | 20.00 | | | 590.21 | 1,381.79 | 6743 | 54 |
| 55 | 115.26 | 28.82 | 408.03 | 20.00 | | | 572.11 | 1,348.89 | 6801 | 55 |
| 56 | 57.72 | 21.93 | 279.51 | 20.00 | UF | 5.00 | 384.16 | 1,077.84 | 6860 | 56 |
| 57 | 1,466.10 | 374.03 | 5,293.71 | 260.00 | UF | 15.00 | 7,408.84 | 17,526.16 | | 57 |
| 58 | 6,000.00 | 1,507.50 | 21,387.65 | 1,040.00 | UF | 100.00 | 30,035.15 | 70,464.85 | | 58 |

are distributed, employee identification cards may be used to deter one employee from picking up another's check.

Other controls include verifying and approving all payroll rate changes. In addition, in a computerized system, all program changes should be properly approved and tested by employees who are independent of the payroll system. The use of a special payroll bank account, as we discussed earlier in this chapter, also enhances control over payroll.

## INTEGRITY IN BUSINESS

### $8 MILLION FOR 18 MINUTES WORK

Computer system controls can be very important in issuing payroll checks. In one case, a Detroit schoolteacher was paid $4,015,625 after deducting $3,884,375 in payroll deductions for 18 minutes of overtime work. The error was caused by a computer glitch when the teacher's employee identification number was substituted incorrectly in the "hourly wage" field and wasn't caught by the payroll software. After six days, the error was discovered and the money was returned. "One of the things that came with (the software) is a fail-safe that prevents that. It doesn't work," a financial officer said. The district has since installed a program to flag any paycheck exceeding $10,000.

**Source:** Associated Press, September 27, 2002.

# •Exhibit 7

**Payroll Check**

**MS** McDermott Supply Co.
415 5th Ave. So.
Dubuque, IA 52736-0142

John T. McGrath
1830 4th St.
Clinton, IA 52732-6142

Check Number: 6860
Pay Period Ending: 12/27/05

| HOURS & EARNINGS | | TAXES & DEDUCTIONS | | |
| --- | --- | --- | --- | --- |
| DESCRIPTION | AMOUNT | DESCRIPTION | CURRENT AMOUNT | Y-T-D AMOUNT |
| Rate of Pay Reg. | 34 | Social Security Tax | 57.72 | 6,000.00 |
| Rate of Pay O.T. | 51 | Medicare Tax | 21.93 | 1,507.50 |
| Hours Worked Reg. | 40 | Fed. Income Tax | 279.51 | 21,387.65 |
| Hours Worked O.T. | 2 | U.S. Savings Bonds | 20.00 | 1,040.00 |
| | | United Fund | 5.00 | 100.00 |
| Net Pay | 1,077.84 | | | |
| Total Gross Pay | 1,462.00 | Total | 384.16 | 30,035.15 |
| Total Gross Y-T-D | 100,500.00 | | | |

STATEMENT OF EARNINGS. DETACH AND KEEP FOR YOUR RECORDS

**MS** McDermott Supply Co.
415 5th Ave. So.
Dubuque, IA 52736-0142

LaGesse Savings & Loan
33 Katie Avenue, Suite 33
Clinton, IA 52736-3581

24-2/531

Pay Period Ending: 12/27/05    6860

**PAY**  ONE THOUSAND SEVENTY-SEVEN AND 84/100 . . . . . . . . . . . . . **DOLLARS**

**To the Order of**   JOHN T. MCGRATH
1830 4TH ST.
CLINTON, IA 52732-6142

$1,077.84

*Franklin D. McDermott*

⑈6860⑈ ⑆153111123⑈ ⑈938540 2⑈

# •Exhibit 8

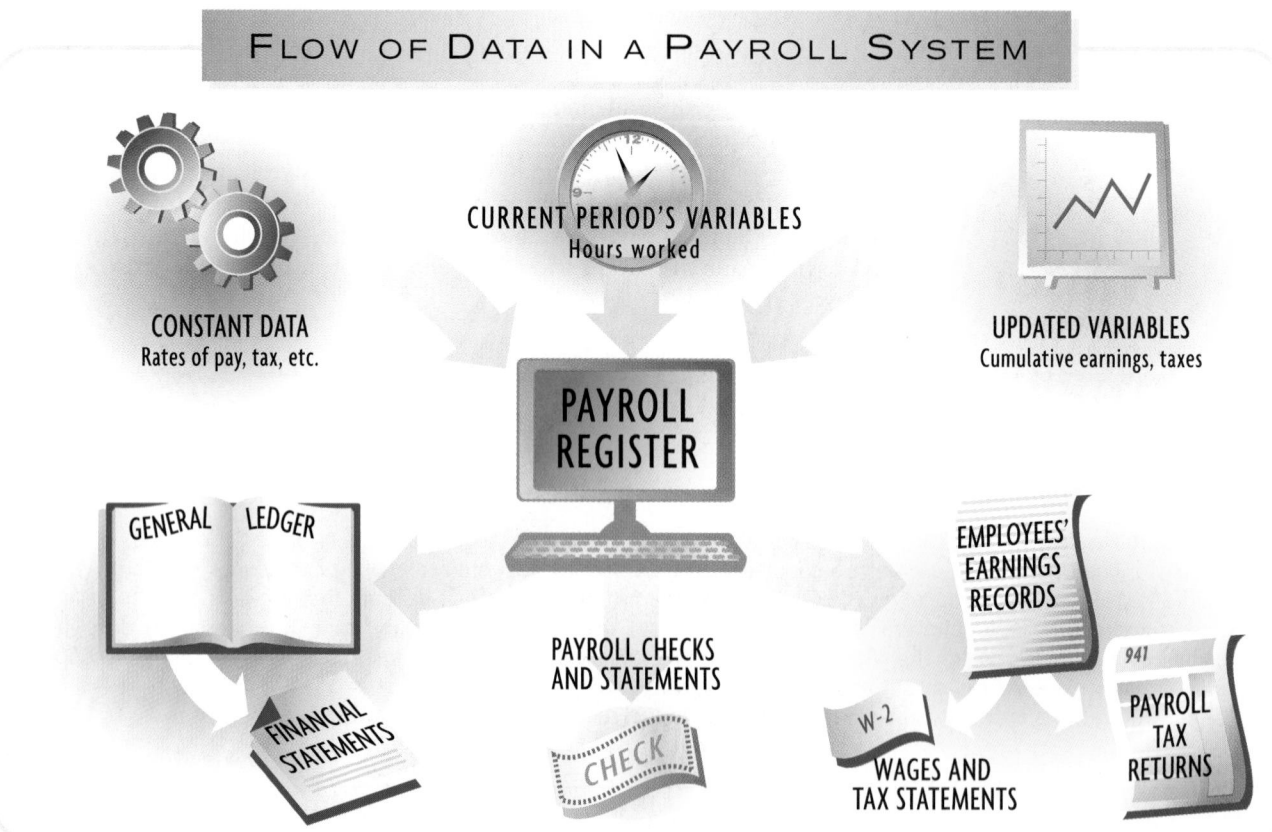

**FLOW OF DATA IN A PAYROLL SYSTEM**

# Employees' Fringe Benefits

objective | 6

Journalize entries for employee fringe benefits, including vacation pay and pensions.

Many companies provide their employees a variety of benefits in addition to salary and wages earned. Such **_fringe benefits_** may take many forms, including vacations, medical, and postretirement benefits, such as pension plans. The U.S. Chamber of Commerce has estimated that fringe benefits average approximately 37% of gross wages. Exhibit 9 shows benefit dollars as a percent of total benefits as reported from the same survey.[5]

**•Exhibit 9**

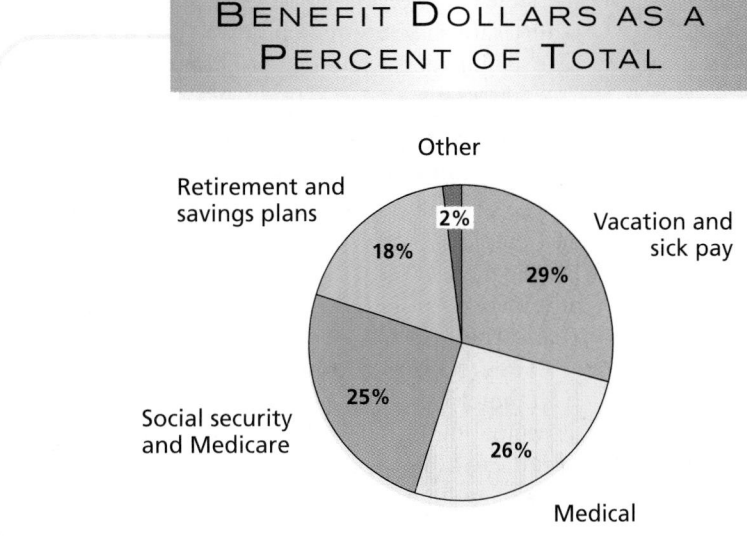

When the employer pays part or all of the cost of the fringe benefits, these costs must be recognized as expenses. To properly match revenues and expenses, the estimated cost of these benefits should be recorded as an expense during the period in which the employee earns the benefit, as we will illustrate in the next section for vacation pay.

## Vacation Pay

> **Vacation pay becomes the employer's liability as the employee earns vacation rights.**

Most employers grant vacation rights, sometimes called **compensated absences**, to their employees. Such rights give rise to a recordable contingent liability. The liability for employees' vacation pay should be accrued as a liability as the vacation rights are earned. The entry to accrue vacation pay may be recorded in total at the end of each fiscal year, or it may be recorded at the end of each pay period. To illustrate this latter case, assume that employees earn one day of vacation for each month worked during the year. Assume also that the estimated vacation pay for the payroll period ending May 5 is $2,000. The entry to record the accrued vacation pay for this pay period is shown as follows.

| | | | | |
|---|---|---|---|---|
| May | 5 | Vacation Pay Expense | 2 0 0 0 00 | |
| | | Vacation Pay Payable | | 2 0 0 0 00 |
| | | Vacation pay for week ended May 5. | | |

[5]*Employee Benefit Survey*, U.S. Chamber of Commerce, 2001.

If employees are required to take all their vacation time within one year, the vacation pay payable is reported on the balance sheet as a current liability. If employees are allowed to accumulate their vacation time, the estimated vacation pay liability that is applicable to time that will *not* be taken within one year is a long-term liability.

When payroll is prepared for the period in which employees have taken vacations, the vacation pay payable is reduced. The entry debits *Vacation Pay Payable* and credits *Salaries Payable* and the other related accounts for taxes and withholdings.

# Pensions

A **pension** represents a cash payment to retired employees. Rights to pension payments are earned by employees during their working years, based on the pension plan established by the employer. One of the fundamental characteristics of such a plan is whether it is a defined contribution plan or a defined benefit plan.

## Defined Contribution Plan

**REAL WORLD**

Investment professionals advise employees to diversify their 401K investments and avoid concentrating investments in their employer's common stock. Many WorldCom employees learned this lesson the hard way, as they watched their pension savings disappear in the aftermath of WorldCom's bankruptcy.

In a ***defined contribution plan***, a fixed amount of money is invested on the employee's behalf during the employee's working years. It is common for the employee and employer to make contributions. There is no promise of future pension benefits payments. The amount of the final pension depends on the total contributions and investment returns earned on those contributions over the employee's working years. The employee bears the investment risk under defined contribution plans.

One of the more popular defined contribution plans is the 401K plan. Under this plan, employees may contribute a limited part of their income to investments, such as mutual funds. A 401K plan offers employees two advantages: (1) the contribution is deducted, before taxes, from current period income, and (2) the contributions and future investment earnings are tax deferred until withdrawn at retirement. In addition, in 90% of the 401K plans, the employer matches some portion of the employee's contribution. These advantages are why nearly 70% of eligible employees elect to enroll in a 401K.

The employer's cost of a defined contribution plan is debited to *Pension Expense*. To illustrate, assume that the pension plan of Heaven Scent Perfumes, Inc., requires an employer contribution of 10% of employee monthly salaries, paid at the end of the month to the employee's plan administrator. The journal entry to record the transaction, assuming $500,000 of monthly salaries, is as follows:

| | | | | | |
|---|---|---|---|---|---|
| Dec | 31 | Pension Expense | | 50 0 0 0 00 | |
| | | Cash | | | 50 0 0 0 00 |
| | | Contributed 10% of monthly salaries to | | | |
| | | pension plan. | | | |

## Defined Benefit Plan

Employers may choose to promise employees a fixed annual pension benefit at retirement, based on years of service and compensation levels. An example would be a promise to pay an annual pension based on a formula, such as the following:

**1.5% × years of service × average salary for most recent 3 years prior to retirement**

Pension benefits based on a formula are termed a ***defined benefit plan***. Unlike a defined contribution plan, the employer bears the investment risk in funding a future retirement income benefit. As a result, many companies are replacing their defined benefit plans with defined contribution plans.

The accounting for defined benefit plans is usually very complex due to the uncertainties of projecting future pension obligations. These obligations depend upon such factors as employee life expectancies, employee turnover, expected employee compensation levels, and investment income on pension contributions.

The pension cost of a defined benefit plan is debited to *Pension Expense.* The amount funded is credited to *Cash.* Any unfunded amount is credited to *Unfunded Pension Liability.* For example, assume that the pension plan of Hinkle Co. requires an annual pension cost of $80,000, based on an estimate of the future benefit obligation. Further assume that Hinkle Co. pays $60,000 to the pension fund. The entry to record this transaction is as follows:

While nearly 40 million American workers are covered by defined benefit plans, the number of defined contribution plans has been increasing. Over 75% of all new plans are structured as defined contribution plans.

| | | | | | |
|---|---|---|---|---|---|
| Dec. | 31 | Pension Expense | 80 0 0 0 00 | | |
| | | Cash | | 60 0 0 0 00 | |
| | | Unfunded Pension Liability | | 20 0 0 0 00 | |
| | | To record annual pension cost and | | | |
| | | contribution to pension plan. | | | |

If the unfunded pension liability is to be paid within one year, it will be classified as a current liability. That portion of the liability to be paid beyond one year is a long-term liability.

## Postretirement Benefits Other Than Pensions

In addition to the pension benefits described above, employees may earn rights to other **postretirement benefits** from their employer. Such benefits may include dental care, eye care, medical care, life insurance, tuition assistance, tax services, and legal services for employees or their dependents. The amount of the annual benefits expense is based upon health statistics of the workforce. This amount is recorded by debiting *Postretirement Benefits Expense. Cash* is credited for the same amount if the benefits are fully funded. If the benefits are not fully funded, a postretirement benefits plan liability account is credited. Thus, the accounting for postretirement health benefits is very similar to that of defined benefit pension plans.

A business's financial statements should fully disclose the nature of its postretirement benefit obligations. These disclosures are usually included as notes to the financial statements. The complex nature of accounting for postretirement benefits is described in more advanced accounting courses.

# Financial Analysis and Interpretation

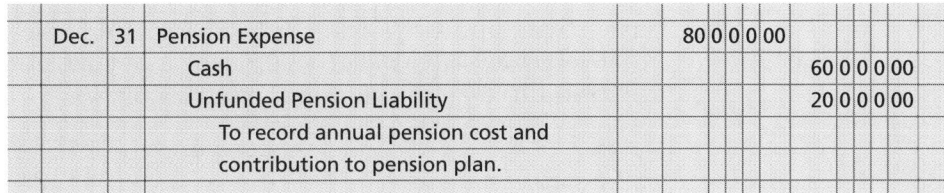

objective **7**

Use the quick ratio to analyze the ability of a business to pay its current liabilities.

Current liabilities are listed on the balance sheet usually on the basis of size and maturity date of the liability. Current maturities of long-term debt followed by accounts payable are frequently the first two listed items. The current asset and current liability sections of the balance sheet for Noble Co. and Hart Co. are illustrated as follows:

| | Noble Co. | Hart Co. |
|---|---|---|
| Current assets: | | |
| Cash | $100,000 | $ 55,000 |
| Cash equivalents | 47,000 | 65,000 |
| Accounts receivable (net) | 84,000 | 472,000 |
| Inventory | 150,000 | 200,000 |
| Total | $381,000 | $792,000 |

*(continued)*

| | Noble Co. | Hart Co. |
|---|---|---|
| Current liabilities: | | |
| Current portion of long-term debt | $ 50,000 | $200,000 |
| Accounts payable | 75,000 | 227,000 |
| Wages payable | 65,000 | 120,000 |
| Employees federal income tax payable | 18,000 | 36,000 |
| Social security tax payable | 3,025 | 7,200 |
| Medicare tax payable | 975 | 1,800 |
| Notes payable | 8,000 | 148,000 |
| Total | $220,000 | $740,000 |

We can use this information to evaluate Noble's and Hart's ability to pay their current liabilities within a short period of time, using the *quick ratio* or **acid-test ratio**. The quick ratio is computed as follows:

$$\text{Quick Ratio} = \frac{\text{Quick Assets}}{\text{Current Liabilities}}$$

The quick ratio measures the "instant" debt-paying ability of a company, using quick assets. **Quick assets** are cash, cash equivalents, and receivables that can quickly be converted into cash. It is often considered desirable to have a quick ratio exceeding 1.0. A ratio less than 1 would indicate that current liabilities cannot be covered by cash and "near cash" assets.

To illustrate, the quick ratios for both companies would be,

$$\text{Noble Co:} \quad \frac{\$100,000 + \$47,000 + \$84,000}{\$220,000} = 1.05$$

$$\text{Hart Co:} \quad \frac{\$55,000 + \$65,000 + \$472,000}{\$740,000} = 0.80$$

As you can see, Noble Co. has quick assets in excess of current liabilities, or a quick ratio of 1.05. The ratio exceeds 1, indicating that the quick assets should be sufficient to meet current liabilities. Hart Co., however, has a quick ratio of 0.8. Its quick assets will not be sufficient to cover the current liabilities. Hart could solve this problem by working with a bank to convert its short-term debt of $148,000 into a long-term obligation. This would remove the notes payable from current liabilities. If Hart did this, then its quick ratio would improve to 1 ($592,000 ÷ $592,000), which would be just sufficient for quick assets to cover current liabilities.

## DO YOU WANT TO BE A MILLIONAIRE?

A recent survey found that 66% of individuals believe that their standard of living at retirement will be the same or higher than during their current working years. Yet, a third of these respondents don't have a formal savings plan for retirement. One-fourth of these respondents believe that they will need to save only $100,000 in order to maintain their lifestyle in retirement. However, experts believe that today's 25-year-old will need savings of $750,000 to $1 million to support a basic retirement, given increased life expectancies and inflation. How do you save this much money? The two keys to savings success are (1) save regularly, such as monthly or quarterly, even if it's a small amount, and (2) start early. For example, to have the same retirement income as a 25-year-old saving $100

per month, a 30-year-old would need to save $200 per month. Waiting until you are 35 years old would require saving $400 per month. Every five years of delay requires doubling the necessary contribution. This is the power of compound interest. Therefore, the worst strategy is to begin retirement saving at middle age.

So how much would a 25-year-old need to save monthly to reach the $1 million mark? There are many assumptions that go into such a calculation. Let's assume that an individual begins saving $150 per month at the age of 25, earns 8% on these savings, increases the amount contributed by 5% per year (to match salary increases), and retires at the age of 65. Under these assumptions, the individual would accumulate $975,000 by age 65.

## SPOTLIGHT ON STRATEGY

### POWER TO THE PEOPLE

Many firms have discovered the strategic advantage of an engaged and empowered workforce. For example, Edward Jones, a stock brokerage firm, avoided layoffs during a recent business downturn by cutting back bonuses. According to CEO John Bachmann, "We want to build the kind of relationship with workers that makes them willing to go the extra mile. . . . You can't do that if you get rid of them whenever times are rocky."

Every year, *Fortune* magazine publishes the "100 Best Companies to Work For" based on employee surveys and corporate culture audit. In a recent list, familiar companies such as **Cisco Systems**, **Microsoft**, **AFLAC**, **Deloitte & Touche**, and **Intel** were included within the top 50 names on this list. According to **Great Place to Work®** **Institute**, the administrator of the surveys, a great place to work is one where "you trust people you work for, have pride in what you do, and enjoy the people you work with." It goes on to say that earning the trust of employees requires (1) establishing management *credibility* through open communication and integrity, (2) showing

employees *respect* by sharing decision-making authority and caring about employees as people, and (3) treating employees *fairly* on the basis of merit and equity.

Why is maintaining good employee relations good business? A Department of Labor study has showed a positive relationship between employee empowerment and financial performance. Improved financial performance comes in the form of lower employee turnover, lower absenteeism, higher levels of customer satisfaction, and greater innovation and risk taking. For example, mass layoffs can create anger, fear, anxiety, and decreased risk taking. According to David Noer, an employment consultant in Greensboro, North Carolina, "Just when you need employees to take risks to turn the organization around, they take to the trenches. You end up with a double loss."

**Sources:** Great Place to Work Web site and Robert Levering and Milton Moskowitz, "Best Companies to Work For The Best in the Worst of Times," *Fortune*, February 4, 2002.

# Key Points

**1 Define and give examples of current liabilities.**

Current liabilities are obligations that are to be paid out of current assets and are due within a short time, usually within one year. Current liabilities arise from either (1) receiving goods or services prior to making payment or (2) receiving payment prior to delivering goods or services.

**2 Prepare journal entries for short-term notes payable and the disclosure for the current portion of long-term debt.**

A note issued to a creditor to temporarily satisfy an account payable is recorded as a debit to *Accounts Payable* and a credit to *Notes Payable*. At the time the note is paid, *Notes Payable* and *Interest Expense* are debited and *Cash* is credited. Notes may also be issued to purchase merchandise or other assets or to borrow money from a bank.

When a discounted note is issued, *Interest Expense* is debited for the interest deduction at the time of issuance, an asset account is debited for the proceeds, and *Notes Payable* is credited for the face value of the note. The face value and the maturity value of a discounted note are equal. In addition, the current portion of an installment note payable should be disclosed as a current liability.

**3 Describe the accounting treatment for contingent liabilities and journalize entries for product warranties.**

A contingent liability is a potential obligation that results from a past transaction but depends on a future event. If the contingent liability is both probable and estimable, the liability should be recorded. If the contingent liability is reasonably possible or is not estimable, it should be

disclosed in the notes to the financial statements. An example of a recordable contingent liability is product warranties. If a company grants a warranty on a product, an estimated warranty expense and liability should be recorded in the period of the sale. The expense and the liability are recorded by debiting *Product Warranty Expense* and crediting *Product Warranty Payable*.

**4 Determine employer liabilities for payroll, including liabilities arising from employee earnings and deductions from earnings.**

An employer's liability for payroll is calculated by determining employees' total earnings for a payroll period, including overtime pay. From this amount, employee deductions are subtracted to arrive at the net pay to be paid each employee. The employer's liabilities for employee deductions are recognized at the time the payroll is recorded. Most employers also incur liabilities for payroll taxes, such as social security tax, Medicare tax, federal unemployment compensation tax, and state unemployment compensation tax.

## 5 Describe payroll accounting systems that use a payroll register, employee earnings records, and a general journal.

The payroll register is used in assembling and summarizing the data needed for each payroll period. The data recorded in the payroll register include the number of hours worked and the earnings and deduction data for each employee. The payroll register also includes columns for accumulating total wages or salaries to be debited to the various expense accounts. It is supported by a detailed payroll record for each employee, called an employee's earnings record.

## 6 Journalize entries for employee fringe benefits, including vacation pay and pensions.

Fringe benefits are expenses of the period in which the employees earn the benefits. Fringe benefits are recorded by debiting an expense account and crediting a liability account. For example, the entry to record accrued vacation pay debits *Vacation Pay Expense* and credits *Vacation Pay Payable*.

## 7 Use the quick ratio to analyze the ability of a business to pay its current liabilities.

The quick ratio or acid-test ratio is a measure of a business's ability to pay current liabilities within a short period of time. The quick ratio is quick assets divided by current liabilities. A quick ratio exceeding 1 is usually desirable.

# Key Terms

defined benefit plan (454)
defined contribution plan (454)
discount (437)
discount rate (437)
employee's earnings record (448)

FICA tax (443)
fringe benefits (453)
gross pay (441)
net pay (441)
payroll (439)

payroll register (446)
proceeds (437)
quick assets (456)
quick ratio (456)

# Illustrative Problem

Selected transactions of Taylor Company, completed during the fiscal year ended December 31, are as follows:

Mar. 1. Purchased merchandise on account from Kelvin Co., $20,000.
Apr. 10. Issued a 60-day, 12% note for $20,000 to Kelvin Co. on account.
June 9. Paid Kelvin Co. the amount owed on the note of April 10.
Aug. 1. Issued a $50,000, 90-day note to Harold Co. in exchange for a building. Harold Co. discounted the note at 15%.
Oct. 30. Paid Harold Co. the amount due on the note of August 1.
Dec. 27. Journalized the entry to record the biweekly payroll. A summary of the payroll record follows:

| Salary distribution: | | |
|---|---|---|
| Sales | $63,400 | |
| Officers | 36,600 | |
| Office | 10,000 | $110,000 |
| Deductions: | | |
| Social security tax | $ 5,050 | |
| Medicare tax | 1,650 | |
| Federal income tax withheld | 17,600 | |
| State income tax withheld | 4,950 | |
| Savings bond deductions | 850 | |
| Medical insurance deductions | 1,120 | 31,220 |
| Net amount | | $ 78,780 |

Dec. 30. Issued a check in payment of liabilities for employees' federal income tax of $17,600, social security tax of $10,100, and Medicare tax of $3,300.

31. Issued a check for $9,500 to the pension fund trustee to fully fund the pension cost for December.

31. Journalized an entry to record the employees' accrued vacation pay, $36,100.

31. Journalized an entry to record the estimated accrued product warranty liability, $37,240.

## Instructions
Journalize the preceding transactions.

## Solution

| Date | | Account | Debit | Credit |
|---|---|---|---|---|
| Mar. | 1 | Merchandise Inventory | 20 000 00 | |
| | | Accounts Payable—Kelvin Co. | | 20 000 00 |
| | | | | |
| Apr. | 10 | Accounts Payable—Kelvin Co. | 20 000 00 | |
| | | Notes Payable | | 20 000 00 |
| | | | | |
| June | 9 | Notes Payable | 20 000 00 | |
| | | Interest Expense | 400 00 | |
| | | Cash | | 20 400 00 |
| | | | | |
| Aug. | 1 | Building | 48 125 00 | |
| | | Interest Expense | 1 875 00 | |
| | | Notes Payable | | 50 000 00 |
| | | | | |
| Oct. | 30 | Notes Payable | 50 000 00 | |
| | | Cash | | 50 000 00 |
| | | | | |
| Dec. | 27 | Sales Salaries Expense | 63 400 00 | |
| | | Officers Salaries Expense | 36 600 00 | |
| | | Office Salaries Expense | 10 000 00 | |
| | | Social Security Tax Payable | | 5 050 00 |
| | | Medicare Tax Payable | | 1 650 00 |
| | | Employees Federal Income Tax Payable | | 17 600 00 |
| | | Employees State Income Tax Payable | | 4 950 00 |
| | | Bond Deductions Payable | | 850 00 |
| | | Medical Insurance Payable | | 1 120 00 |
| | | Salaries Payable | | 78 780 00 |
| | | | | |
| | 30 | Employees Federal Income Tax Payable | 17 600 00 | |
| | | Social Security Tax Payable | 10 100 00 | |
| | | Medicare Tax Payable | 3 300 00 | |
| | | Cash | | 31 000 00 |
| | | | | |
| | 31 | Pension Expense | 9 500 00 | |
| | | Cash | | 9 500 00 |
| | | | | |
| | 31 | Vacation Pay Expense | 36 100 00 | |
| | | Vacation Pay Payable | | 36 100 00 |
| | | | | |
| | 31 | Product Warranty Expense | 37 240 00 | |
| | | Product Warranty Payable | | 37 240 00 |

# Self-Examination Questions (Answers at End of Chapter)

1. A business issued a $5,000, 60-day, 12% note to the bank. The amount due at maturity is:
   A. $4,900
   B. $5,000
   C. $5,100
   D. $5,600

2. A business issued a $5,000, 60-day note to a supplier, which discounted the note at 12%. The proceeds are:
   A. $4,400
   B. $4,900
   C. $5,000
   D. $5,100

3. Which of the following taxes are employers usually not required to withhold from employees?
   A. Federal income tax
   B. Federal unemployment compensation tax
   C. Medicare tax
   D. State and local income tax

4. An employee's rate of pay is $40 per hour, with time and a half for all hours worked in excess of 40 during a week. The social security rate is 6.0% on the first $100,000 of annual earnings, and the Medicare rate is 1.5% on all earnings. The following additional data are available:

   | | |
   |---|---:|
   | Hours worked during current week | 45 |
   | Year's cumulative earnings prior to current week | $99,400 |
   | Federal income tax withheld | $450 |

   Based on these data, the amount of the employee's net pay for the current week is:
   A. $1,307.50
   B. $1,405.00
   C. $1,450.00
   D. $1,385.50

5. Within limitations on the maximum earnings subject to the tax, employers do not incur an expense for which of the following payroll taxes?
   A. Social security tax
   B. Federal unemployment compensation tax
   C. State unemployment compensation tax
   D. Employees' federal income tax

# Class Discussion Questions

1. When should the liability associated with a product warranty be recorded? Discuss.
2. **General Motors Corp.** reported $8.8 billion of product warranties in the current liabilities section of a recent balance sheet. How would costs of repairing a defective product be recorded?
3. The "Questions and Answers Technical Hotline" in the *Journal of Accountancy* included the following question:

   *Several years ago, Company B instituted legal action against Company A. Under a memorandum of settlement and agreement, Company A agreed to pay Company B a total of $17,500 in three installments—$5,000 on March 1, $7,500 on July 1, and the remaining $5,000 on December 31. Company A paid the first two installments during its fiscal year ended September 30. Should the unpaid amount of $5,000 be presented as a current liability at September 30?*

   How would you answer this question?
4. a. Identify the federal taxes that most employers are required to withhold from employees.
   b. Give the titles of the accounts to which the amounts withheld are credited.
5. For each of the following payroll-related taxes, indicate whether there is a ceiling on the annual earnings subject to the tax: (a) social security tax, (b) Medicare tax, (c) federal income tax, (d) federal unemployment compensation tax.
6. Why are deductions from employees' earnings classified as liabilities for the employer?
7. Taylor Company, with 20 employees, is expanding operations. It is trying to decide whether to hire one employee full-time for $25,000 or two employees part-time for a total of $25,000. Would any of the employer's payroll taxes discussed in this chapter have a bearing on this decision? Explain.

8. For each of the following payroll-related taxes, indicate whether they generally apply to (a) employees only, (b) employers only, (c) both employees and employers:
   1. Social security tax
   2. Medicare tax
   3. Federal income tax
   4. Federal unemployment compensation tax
   5. State unemployment compensation tax
9. What are the principal reasons for using a special payroll checking account?
10. In a payroll system, what type of input data are referred to as (a) constants, (b) variables?
11. Explain how a payroll system that is properly designed and operated tends to ensure that (a) wages paid are based on hours actually worked and (b) payroll checks are not issued to fictitious employees.
12. To match revenues and expenses properly, should the expense for employee vacation pay be recorded in the period during which the vacation privilege is earned or during the period in which the vacation is taken? Discuss.
13. Identify several factors that influence the future pension obligation of an employer under a defined benefit pension plan.

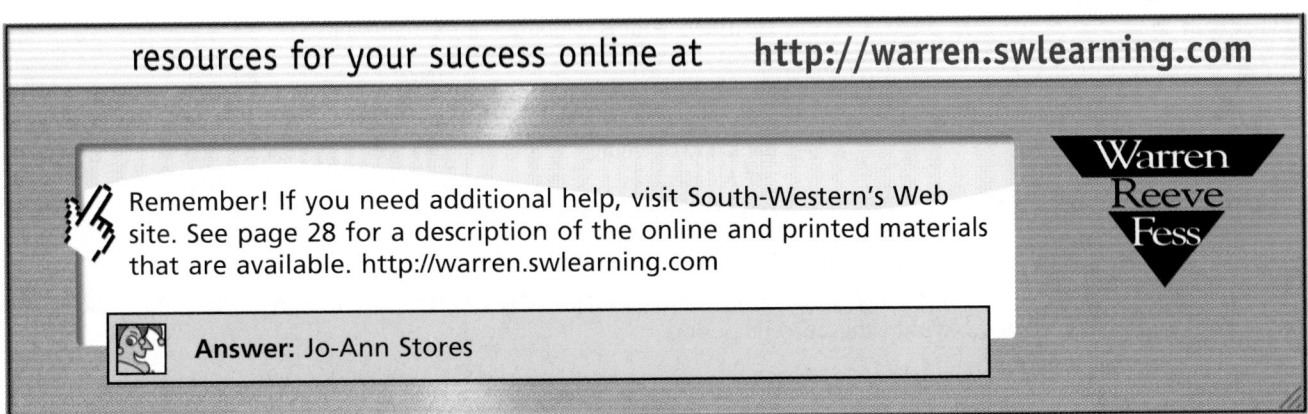

resources for your success online at **http://warren.swlearning.com**

Remember! If you need additional help, visit South-Western's Web site. See page 28 for a description of the online and printed materials that are available. http://warren.swlearning.com

Warren Reeve Fess

**Answer:** Jo-Ann Stores

# Exercises

**EXERCISE 11-1**
*Current liabilities*

**Objective 1**

✓*Total current liabilities, $197,250*

Web World Magazine Inc. sold 6,900 annual subscriptions of *Web World* for $30 during December 2006. These new subscribers will receive monthly issues, beginning in January 2007. In addition, the business had taxable income of $120,000 during the first calendar quarter of 2007. The federal tax rate is 35%. A quarterly tax payment will be made on April 7, 2007.

Prepare the current liabilities section of the balance sheet for Web World Magazine Inc. on March 31, 2007.

**EXERCISE 11-2**
*Entries for discounting notes payable*

**Objective 2**

Builder's Supply issues a 90-day note for $200,000 to Gem Lighting Co. for merchandise inventory. Gem Lighting Co. discounts the note at 8%.

a. Journalize Builder's Supply's entries to record:
   1. the issuance of the note.
   2. the payment of the note at maturity.
b. Journalize Gem Lighting Co.'s entries to record:
   1. the receipt of the note.
   2. the receipt of the payment of the note at maturity.

**EXERCISE 11-3**
*Evaluate alternative notes*
Objective 2

A borrower has two alternatives for a loan: (1) issue a $90,000, 90-day, 6% note or (2) issue a $90,000, 90-day note that the creditor discounts at 6%.

a. Calculate the amount of the interest expense for each option.
b. Determine the proceeds received by the borrower in each situation.
c. ▬▬► Which alternative is more favorable to the borrower? Explain.

**EXERCISE 11-4**
*Entries for notes payable*
Objective 2

A business issued a 60-day, 5% note for $9,000 to a creditor on account. Journalize the entries to record (a) the issuance of the note and (b) the payment of the note at maturity, including interest.

**EXERCISE 11-5**
*Fixed asset purchases with note*
Objective 2

On June 30, Mystic Mountain Game Company purchased land for $250,000 and a building for $730,000, paying $180,000 cash and issuing an 8% note for the balance, secured by a mortgage on the property. The terms of the note provide for 20 semi-annual payments of $40,000 on the principal plus the interest accrued from the date of the preceding payment. Journalize the entry to record (a) the transaction on June 30, (b) the payment of the first installment on December 31, and (c) the payment of the second installment the following June 30.

**EXERCISE 11-6**
*Current portion of long-term debt*
Objective 2

REAL WORLD

**WD-40 Co.**, the manufacturer and marketer of WD-40® lubricant, reported the following information about its long-term debt in the notes to a recent financial statement:

Long-term debt is comprised of the following:

|  | 2002 | 2001 |
|---|---|---|
| Term loans | $95,000,000 | $45,000,000 |
| Bank line of credit | 299,000 | 34,783,000 |
| Total debt | 95,299,000 | 79,783,000 |
| Less current portion | (299,000) | (4,650,000) |
| Long-term debt | $95,000,000 | $75,133,000 |

Term loans are long-term notes payable, while a bank line of credit is usually due within the current period.

a. How much was disclosed as a current liability on the 2001 balance sheet?
b. ▬▬► What appears to have happened to the 2001 bank credit line during 2002?
c. How much did the total current liabilities change between 2001 and 2002 as a result of the current portion of long-term debt?

**EXERCISE 11-7**
*Accrued product warranty*
Objective 3

Crystal Audio Company warrants its products for one year. The estimated product warranty is 2% of sales. Assume that sales were $750,000 for January. In February, a customer received warranty repairs requiring $390 of parts and $570 of labor.

a. Journalize the adjusting entry required at January 31, the end of the first month of the current year, to record the accrued product warranty.
b. Journalize the entry to record the warranty work provided in February.

**EXERCISE 11-8**
*Accrued product warranty*
Objective 3

REAL WORLD

**Ford Motor Company** disclosed estimated product warranty payable for comparative years as follows.

|  | (in millions) | |
|---|---|---|
|  | 12/31/02 | 12/31/01 |
| Current estimated product warranty payable | $14,166 | $13,605 |
| Noncurrent estimated product warranty payable | 9,125 | 6,805 |
| Total | $23,291 | $20,410 |

Ford's sales were $130,800 million in 2001 and increased to $134,400 million in 2002. Assume that the total cash paid on warranty claims during 2002 was $12,000 million.

a. ▬▬► Why are short- and long-term estimated warranty liabilities separately disclosed?

b. Provide the journal entry for the 2002 product warranty expense.

c. ▬▬▶ Assuming $12,000 million in warranty claims paid during 2002, explain the $2,881 million increase in the total warranty liability.

**EXERCISE 11-9**
*Contingent liabilities*

**Objective 3**

Several months ago, Satin Cover Paint Company experienced a hazardous materials spill at one of its plants. As a result, the Environmental Protection Agency (EPA) fined the company $390,000. The company is contesting the fine. In addition, an employee is seeking $600,000 damages related to the spill. Lastly, a homeowner has sued the company for $150,000. The homeowner lives 25 miles from the plant, but believes that the incident has reduced the home's resale value by $150,000.

Satin Cover's legal counsel believes that it is probable that the EPA fine will stand. In addition, counsel indicates that an out-of-court settlement of $280,000 has recently been reached with the employee. The final papers will be signed next week. Counsel believes that the homeowner's case is much weaker and will be decided in favor of Satin. Other litigation related to the spill is possible, but the damage amounts are uncertain.

a. Journalize the contingent liabilities associated with the hazardous materials spill.

b. ▬▬▶ Prepare a note disclosure relating to this incident.

**EXERCISE 11-10**
*Contingent liabilities*

**Objective 3**

REAL WORLD

The following note accompanied recent financial statements for **Goodyear Tire and Rubber Company**:

> *Goodyear is a defendant in numerous lawsuits involving at December 31, 2002, approximately 62,000 claimants alleging various asbestos related personal injuries purported to result from exposure to asbestos in certain rubber coated products manufactured by Goodyear in the past or in certain Goodyear facilities. . . . In the past, Goodyear has disposed of approximately 23,500 cases by defending and obtaining the dismissal thereof or by entering into a settlement.*
>
> *At December 31, 2002, Goodyear has recorded liabilities aggregating $229.1 million for potential product liability and other (asbestos) tort claims, including related legal fees expected to be incurred, presently asserted against Goodyear.*
>
> *The portion of the recorded liabilities for potential product liability and other tort claims relating to asbestos claims is based on pending claims. The amount recorded reflects an estimate of the cost of defending and resolving pending claims, based on available information and our experience in disposing of asbestos claims in the past.*

a. Provide a journal entry to record the contingent liability, assuming that all the liabilities for the 62,000 claimants were accrued on December 31, 2002.

b. Assume that $75 million was accrued on December 31, 2001, for the cases settled in 2002. Provide a summary journal entry for the settlements.

c. ▬▬▶ Why was the contingent liability accrued on December 31, 2002?

**EXERCISE 11-11**
*Calculate payroll*

**Objective 4**

✔ *b. Net pay, $730.75*

An employee earns $18 per hour and 1½ times that rate for all hours in excess of 40 hours per week. Assume that the employee worked 50 hours during the week, and that the gross pay prior to the current week totaled $38,540. Assume further that the social security tax rate was 6.0% (on earnings up to $100,000), the Medicare tax rate was 1.5%, and federal income tax to be withheld was $185.

a. Determine the gross pay for the week.

b. Determine the net pay for the week.

**EXERCISE 11-12**
*Calculate payroll*

**Objective 4**

Omega Business Consultants has three employees—a consultant, a computer programmer, and an administrator. The following payroll information is available for each employee:

✓ *Administrator net pay,*
*$739.36*

| | Consultant | Computer Programmer | Administrator |
|---|---|---|---|
| Regular earnings rate | $2,500 per week | $40 per hour | $20 per hour |
| Overtime earnings rate | Not applicable | 1½ times hourly rate | 1½ times hourly rate |
| Gross pay prior to current pay period | $120,000 | $98,900 | $38,800 |
| Number of withholding allowances | 1 | 0 | 3 |

For the current pay period, the computer programmer worked 46 hours and the administrator worked 44 hours. The federal income tax withheld for all three employees, who are single, can be determined from the wage bracket withholding table in Exhibit 3 in the chapter. Assume further that the social security tax rate was 6.0% on the first $100,000 of annual earnings, and the Medicare tax rate was 1.5%.

Determine the gross pay and the net pay for each of the three employees for the current pay period.

**EXERCISE 11-13**
*Summary payroll data*
**Objectives 4, 5**

✓ *a. (3) Total earnings,*
*$269,000*

In the following summary of data for a payroll period, some amounts have been intentionally omitted:

| Earnings: | |
|---|---|
| 1. At regular rate | ? |
| 2. At overtime rate | $ 44,200 |
| 3. Total earnings | ? |
| Deductions: | |
| 4. Social security tax | 15,730 |
| 5. Medicare tax | 4,035 |
| 6. Income tax withheld | 47,915 |
| 7. Medical insurance | 7,860 |
| 8. Union dues | ? |
| 9. Total deductions | 80,000 |
| 10. Net amount paid | 189,000 |
| Accounts debited: | |
| 11. Factory Wages | 135,400 |
| 12. Sales Salaries | ? |
| 13. Office Salaries | 57,800 |

a. Calculate the amounts omitted in lines (1), (3), (8), and (12).
b. Journalize the entry to record the payroll accrual.
c. Journalize the entry to record the payment of the payroll.
d. ▪▪▪▪▶ From the data given in this exercise and your answer to (a), would you conclude that this payroll was paid sometime during the first few weeks of the calendar year? Explain.

**EXERCISE 11-14**
*Payroll internal control procedures*
**Objective 5**

Opry Sounds is a retail store specializing in the sale of country music. The store employs 3 full-time and 10 part-time workers. The store's weekly payroll averages $2,200 for all 13 workers.

Opry Sounds uses a personal computer to assist in preparing paychecks. Each week, the store's accountant collects employee time cards and enters the hours worked into the payroll program. The payroll program calculates each employee's pay and prints a paycheck. The accountant uses a check-signing machine to sign the paychecks. Next, the store's owner authorizes the transfer of funds from the store's regular bank account to the payroll account.

For the week of May 10, the accountant accidentally recorded 400 hours worked instead of 40 hours for one of the full-time employees.

▪▪▪▪▶ Does Opry Sounds have internal controls in place to catch this error? If so, how will this error be detected?

**EXERCISE 11-15**
*Internal control procedures*
**Objective 5**

Shop-Aid Tools is a small manufacturer of home workshop power tools. The company employs 30 production workers and 10 administrative persons. The following procedures are used to process the company's weekly payroll:

a. Paychecks are signed by using a check-signing machine. This machine is located in the main office so that it can be easily accessed by anyone needing a check signed.

b. Shop-Aid maintains a separate checking account for payroll checks. Each week, the total net pay for all employees is transferred from the company's regular bank account to the payroll account.

c. Whenever an employee receives a pay raise, the supervisor must fill out a wage adjustment form, which is signed by the company president. This form is used to change the employee's wage rate in the payroll system.

d. Whenever a salaried employee is terminated, Personnel authorizes Payroll to remove the employee from the payroll system. However, this procedure is not required when an hourly worker is terminated. Hourly employees only receive a paycheck if their time cards show hours worked. The computer automatically drops an employee from the payroll system when that employee has six consecutive weeks with no hours worked.

e. All employees are required to record their hours worked by clocking in and out on a time clock. Employees must clock out for lunch break. Due to congestion around the time clock area at lunch time, management has not objected to having one employee clock in and out for an entire department.

State whether each of the procedures is appropriate or inappropriate after considering the principles of internal control. If a procedure is inappropriate, describe the appropriate procedure.

**EXERCISE 11-16**
*Payroll tax entries*
**Objective 5**

According to a summary of the payroll of Glamour Publishing Co., $480,000 was subject to the 6.0% social security tax and $540,000 was subject to the 1.5% Medicare tax. Also, $12,000 was subject to state and federal unemployment taxes.

a. Calculate the employer's payroll taxes, using the following rates: state unemployment, 4.3%; federal unemployment, 0.8%.

b. Journalize the entry to record the accrual of payroll taxes.

**EXERCISE 11-17**
*Payroll procedures*
**Objective 5**

**WHAT'S WRONG WITH THIS?**

The fiscal year for Tip Top Stores Inc. ends on June 30. In addition, the company computes and reports payroll taxes on a fiscal-year basis. Thus, it applies social security and FUTA maximum earnings limitations to the fiscal-year payroll.

What is wrong with these procedures for accounting for payroll taxes?

**EXERCISE 11-18**
*Accrued vacation pay*
**Objective 6**

A business provides its employees with varying amounts of vacation per year, depending on the length of employment. The estimated amount of the current year's vacation pay is $165,120. Journalize the adjusting entry required on January 31, the end of the first month of the current year, to record the accrued vacation pay.

**EXERCISE 11-19**
*Pension plan entries*
**Objective 6**

Keepsake Photos Inc. operates a chain of photography stores. The company maintains a defined contribution pension plan for its employees. The plan requires quarterly installments to be paid to the funding agent, Boston Funds, by the fifteenth of the month following the end of each quarter. Assuming that the pension cost is $315,000 for the quarter ended December 31, journalize entries to record (a) the accrued pension liability on December 31 and (b) the payment to the funding agent on January 15.

**EXERCISE 11-20**
*Defined benefit pension plan terms*

Objective 6

REAL WORLD

In a recent year's financial statements, **Procter & Gamble Co.** showed an unfunded pension liability of $1,032 million and a periodic pension cost of $151 million.

Explain the meaning of the $1,032 million unfunded pension liability and the $151 million periodic pension cost.

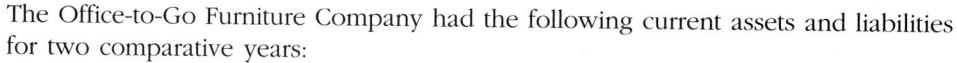

**EXERCISE 11-21**
*Quick ratio*

Objective 7

✓ a. 2005: 1.10

The Office-to-Go Furniture Company had the following current assets and liabilities for two comparative years:

|  | Dec. 31, 2006 | Dec. 31, 2005 |
|---|---|---|
| Current assets: |  |  |
| Cash | $ 356,000 | $ 530,000 |
| Accounts receivable | 400,000 | 350,000 |
| Inventory | 800,000 | 500,000 |
| Total current assets | $1,556,000 | $1,380,000 |
| Current liabilities: |  |  |
| Current portion of long-term debt | $ 150,000 | $ 150,000 |
| Accounts payable | 570,000 | 450,000 |
| Accrued expenses payable | 180,000 | 200,000 |
| Total current liabilities | $ 900,000 | $ 800,000 |

a. Determine the quick ratio for December 31, 2006 and 2005.
b. Interpret the change in the quick ratio between the two balance sheet dates.

**EXERCISE 11-22**
*Quick ratio*

Objective 7

REAL WORLD

The current assets and current liabilities for **Apple Computer Inc.** and **Dell Computer Corp.** are shown as follows at the end of a recent fiscal period:

|  | Apple Computer Inc. (In millions) Sept. 29, 2002 | Dell Computer Corp. (In millions) Jan. 31, 2003 |
|---|---|---|
| Current assets: |  |  |
| Cash and cash equivalents | $2,252 | $4,232 |
| Short-term investments | 2,085 | 406 |
| Accounts receivable | 565 | 2,586 |
| Inventories | 45 | 306 |
| Other current assets* | 441 | 1,394 |
| Total current assets | $5,388 | $8,924 |
| Current liabilities: |  |  |
| Accounts payable | $ 911 | $5,989 |
| Accrued and other current liabilities | 747 | 2,944 |
| Total current liabilities | $1,658 | $8,933 |

*These represent deferred tax assets, prepaid expenses, and other nonquick current assets

a. Determine the quick ratio for both companies.
b. Interpret the quick ratio difference between the two companies.

# Problems Series A

## PROBLEM 11-1A
*Liability transactions*

Objectives 2, 3

P.A.S.S.

The following items were selected from among the transactions completed by Made Rite Products Co. during the current year:

Feb. 15. Purchased merchandise on account from Ranier Co., $30,000, terms n/30.
Mar. 17. Issued a 30-day, 5% note for $30,000 to Ranier Co., on account.
Apr. 16. Paid Ranier Co. the amount owed on the note of March 17.
July 15. Borrowed $40,000 from Security Bank, issuing a 90-day, 6% note.
     25. Purchased tools by issuing a $45,000, 120-day note to Sun Supply Co., which discounted the note at the rate of 7%.
Oct. 13. Paid Security Bank the interest due on the note of July 15 and renewed the loan by issuing a new 30-day, 9% note for $40,000. (Journalize both the debit and credit to the notes payable account.)
Nov. 12. Paid Security Bank the amount due on the note of October 13.
     22. Paid Sun Supply Co. the amount due on the note of July 25.
Dec. 1. Purchased office equipment from Valley Equipment Co. for $80,000, paying $20,000 and issuing a series of ten 8% notes for $6,000 each, coming due at 30-day intervals.
     17. Settled a product liability lawsuit with a customer for $41,000, payable in January. Made Rite accrued the loss in a litigation claims payable account.
     31. Paid the amount due Valley Equipment Co. on the first note in the series issued on December 1.

### Instructions
1. Journalize the transactions.
2. Journalize the adjusting entry for each of the following accrued expenses at the end of the current year: (a) product warranty cost, $15,680; (b) interest on the nine remaining notes owed to Valley Equipment Co.

## PROBLEM 11-2A
*Entries for payroll and payroll taxes*

Objectives 4, 5

P.A.S.S.

✓ 1. (b) Dr. Payroll Taxes
*Expense, $22,722*

The following information about the payroll for the week ended December 30 was obtained from the records of Capstone Suppy Co.:

| Salaries: | | Deductions: | |
|---|---|---|---|
| Sales salaries | $185,300 | Income tax withheld | $55,440 |
| Warehouse salaries | 47,800 | Social security tax withheld | 17,402 |
| Office salaries | 74,900 | Medicare tax withheld | 4,620 |
| | $308,000 | U.S. savings bonds | 10,780 |
| | | Group insurance | 17,556 |

Tax rates assumed:
    Social security, 6% on first $100,000 of employee annual earnings
    Medicare, 1.5%
    State unemployment (employer only), 4.2%
    Federal unemployment (employer only), 0.8%

### Instructions
1. Assuming that the payroll for the last week of the year is to be paid on December 31, journalize the following entries:
   a. December 30, to record the payroll.
   b. December 30, to record the employer's payroll taxes on the payroll to be paid on December 31. Of the total payroll for the last week of the year, $14,000 is subject to unemployment compensation taxes.
2. Assuming that the payroll for the last week of the year is to be paid on January 5 of the following fiscal year, journalize the following entries:
   a. December 30, to record the payroll.
   b. January 5, to record the employer's payroll taxes on the payroll to be paid on January 5.

## PROBLEM 11-3A
*Wage and tax statement data on employer FICA tax*

**Objectives 4, 5**

SPREADSHEET

✓ 2. (e) $30,063

Wholesome Dairy Co. began business on January 2, 2005. Salaries were paid to employees on the last day of each month, and social security tax, Medicare tax, and federal income tax were withheld in the required amounts. An employee who is hired in the middle of the month receives half the monthly salary for that month. All required payroll tax reports were filed, and the correct amount of payroll taxes was remitted by the company for the calendar year. Early in 2006, before the Wage and Tax Statements (Form W-2) could be prepared for distribution to employees and for filing with the Social Security Administration, the employees' earnings records were inadvertently destroyed.

None of the employees resigned or were discharged during the year, and there were no changes in salary rates. The social security tax was withheld at the rate of 6.0% on the first $100,000 of salary and Medicare tax at the rate of 1.5% on salary. Data on dates of employment, salary rates, and employees' income taxes withheld, which are summarized as follows, were obtained from personnel records and payroll records.

| Employee | Date First Employed | Monthly Salary | Monthly Income Tax Withheld |
|---|---|---|---|
| Alvarez | Jan. 16 | $10,800 | $2,700 |
| Carver | Nov. 1 | 3,000 | 450 |
| Felix | Jan. 2 | 3,400 | 544 |
| Lydall | July 16 | 4,000 | 700 |
| Porter | Jan. 2 | 8,500 | 2,040 |
| Song | May 1 | 4,500 | 810 |
| Walker | Feb. 16 | 5,600 | 1,064 |

### Instructions

1. Calculate the amounts to be reported on each employee's Wage and Tax Statement (Form W-2) for 2005, arranging the data in the following form:

| Employee | Gross Earnings | Federal Income Tax Withheld | Social Security Tax Withheld | Medicare Tax Withheld |
|---|---|---|---|---|

2. Calculate the following employer payroll taxes for the year: (a) social security; (b) Medicare; (c) state unemployment compensation at 4.2% on the first $7,000 of each employee's earnings; (d) federal unemployment compensation at 0.8% on the first $7,000 of each employee's earnings; (e) total.

*If the working papers correlating with this textbook are not used, omit Problem 11-4A.*

## PROBLEM 11-4A
*Payroll register*

**Objectives 4, 5**

✓ 3. Dr. Payroll Taxes Expense, $671.91

The payroll register for Scottish Heritage Stores, Inc., for the week ended December 12, 2006, is presented in the working papers.

### Instructions
1. Journalize the entry to record the payroll for the week.
2. Journalize the entry to record the issuance of the checks to employees.
3. Journalize the entry to record the employer's payroll taxes for the week. Assume the following tax rates: state unemployment, 3.6%; federal unemployment, 0.8%. Of the earnings, $1,250 is subject to unemployment taxes.
4. Journalize the entry to record a check issued on December 15 to Second National Bank in payment of employees' income taxes, $1,402.06, social security taxes, $987.06, and Medicare taxes, $246.76.

## PROBLEM 11-5A
*Payroll register*

**Objectives 4, 5**

The following data for Southern Home Products Inc. relate to the payroll for the week ended December 7, 2006:

**SPREADSHEET**

✓ 1. Total net amount payable, $7,248.29

| Employee | Hours Worked | Hourly Rate | Weekly Salary | Federal Income Tax | U.S. Savings Bonds | Accumulated Earnings, Nov. 30 |
|---|---|---|---|---|---|---|
| M | 45.00 | $28.00 | | $292.60 | $35.00 | $ 64,200.00 |
| N | 25.00 | 22.00 | | 82.50 | | 12,600.00 |
| O | | | $2,350.00 | 564.00 | 50.00 | 112,800.00 |
| P | 40.00 | 18.00 | | 144.00 | 15.00 | 35,600.00 |
| Q | 40.00 | 20.00 | | 168.00 | 10.00 | 40,500.00 |
| R | 46.00 | 18.50 | | 190.37 | | 38,700.00 |
| S | 40.00 | 16.00 | | 121.60 | 15.00 | 30,720.00 |
| T | | | 1,000.00 | 215.00 | | 48,000.00 |
| U | 50.00 | 36.00 | | 455.40 | 40.00 | 82,600.00 |

Employees O and T are office staff, and all of the other employees are sales personnel. All sales personnel are paid 1½ times the regular rate for all hours in excess of 40 hours per week. The social security tax rate is 6.0% on the first $100,000 of each employee's annual earnings, and Medicare tax is 1.5% of each employee's annual earnings. The next payroll check to be used is No. 818.

**Instructions**
1. Prepare a payroll register for Southern Home Products Inc. for the week ended December 7, 2006.
2. Journalize the entry to record the payroll for the week.

**PROBLEM 11-6A**
*Payroll accounts and year-end entries*

**Objectives 4, 5, 6**

**P.A.S.S.**

The following accounts, with the balances indicated, appear in the ledger of Brownie Points Gifts Inc. on December 1 of the current year:

| | | | | | | |
|---|---|---|---|---|---|---|
| 211 | Salaries Payable | — | 218 | Bond Deductions Payable | $ 2,400 |
| 212 | Social Security Tax Payable | $ 8,276 | 219 | Medical Insurance Payable | 9,000 |
| 213 | Medicare Tax Payable | 2,178 | 611 | Operations Salaries Expense | 946,000 |
| 214 | Employees Federal Income Tax Payable | 13,431 | 711 | Officers Salaries Expense | 404,800 |
| 215 | Employees State Income Tax Payable | 13,068 | 712 | Office Salaries Expense | 246,400 |
| 216 | State Unemployment Tax Payable | 1,200 | 719 | Payroll Taxes Expense | 123,244 |
| 217 | Federal Unemployment Tax Payable | 300 | | | |

The following transactions relating to payroll, payroll deductions, and payroll taxes occurred during December:

Dec. 2. Issued Check No. 728 for $2,400 to First National Bank to purchase U.S. savings bonds for employees.
 3. Issued Check No. 729 to First National Bank for $23,885, in payment of $8,276 of social security tax, $2,178 of Medicare tax, and $13,431 of employees' federal income tax due.
 14. Journalized the entry to record the biweekly payroll. A summary of the payroll record follows:

| Salary distribution: | | |
|---|---|---|
| Operations | $42,500 | |
| Officers | 18,500 | |
| Office | 11,000 | $72,000 |
| Deductions: | | |
| Social security tax | $ 3,960 | |
| Medicare tax | 1,080 | |
| Federal income tax withheld | 12,816 | |
| State income tax withheld | 3,240 | |
| Savings bond deductions | 1,200 | |
| Medical insurance deductions | 1,500 | 23,796 |
| Net amount | | $48,204 |

 14. Issued Check No. 738 in payment of the net amount of the biweekly payroll.

*(continued)*

Dec. 14. Journalized the entry to record payroll taxes on employees' earnings of December 14: social security tax, $3,960; Medicare tax, $1,080; state unemployment tax, $285; federal unemployment tax, $71.

17. Issued Check No. 744 to First National Bank for $22,896, in payment of $7,920 of social security tax, $2,160 of Medicare tax, and $12,816 of employees' federal income tax due.

18. Issued Check No. 750 to Pico Insurance Company for $9,000, in payment of the semiannual premium on the group medical insurance policy.

28. Journalized the entry to record the biweekly payroll. A summary of the payroll record follows:

| Salary distribution: | | |
|---|---|---|
| Operations | $43,200 | |
| Officers | 18,200 | |
| Office | 11,400 | $72,800 |
| Deductions: | | |
| Social security tax | $ 3,931 | |
| Medicare tax | 1,092 | |
| Federal income tax withheld | 12,958 | |
| State income tax withheld | 3,276 | |
| Savings bond deductions | 1,200 | 22,457 |
| Net amount | | $50,343 |

28. Issued Check No. 782 in payment of the net amount of the biweekly payroll.

28. Journalized the entry to record payroll taxes on employees' earnings of December 28: social security tax, $3,931; Medicare tax, $1,092; state unemployment tax, $166; federal unemployment tax, $42.

30. Issued Check No. 791 to First National Bank for $2,400 to purchase U.S. savings bonds for employees.

30. Issued Check No. 792 for $19,584 to First National Bank in payment of employees' state income tax due on December 31.

31. Paid $46,000 to the employee pension plan. The annual pension cost is $50,000. (Record both the payment and unfunded pension liability.)

**Instructions**

1. Journalize the transactions.
2. Journalize the following adjusting entries on December 31:
   a. Salaries accrued: operations salaries, $4,320; officers salaries, $1,820; office salaries, $1,140. The payroll taxes are immaterial and are not accrued.
   b. Vacation pay, $13,200.

# Problems Series B

**PROBLEM 11-1B**
*Liability transactions*

Objectives 2, 3

P.A.S.S.

The following items were selected from among the transactions completed by Electronic Universe Stores during the current year:

Apr. 7. Borrowed $20,000 from First Financial Corporation, issuing a 60-day, 6% note for that amount.

May 10. Purchased equipment by issuing a $90,000, 120-day note to Milford Equipment Co., which discounted the note at the rate of 8%.

June 6. Paid First Financial Corporation the interest due on the note of April 7 and renewed the loan by issuing a new 30-day, 9% note for $20,000. (Record both the debit and credit to the notes payable account.)

July 6. Paid First Financial Corporation the amount due on the note of June 6.

Aug. 3. Purchased merchandise on account from Hamilton Co., $18,000, terms, n/30.

Sept. 2. Issued a 60-day, 7.5% note for $18,000 to Hamilton Co., on account.
   7. Paid Milford Equipment Co. the amount due on the note of May 10.
Nov. 1. Paid Hamilton Co. the amount owed on the note of September 2.
   15. Purchased store equipment from Merchandising Systems, Inc., for $100,000, paying $37,000 and issuing a series of seven 6% notes for $9,000 each, coming due at 30-day intervals.
Dec. 15. Paid the amount due Merchandising Systems, Inc., on the first note in the series issued on November 15.
   21. Settled a personal injury lawsuit with a customer for $45,000, to be paid in January. Electronic Universe Stores accrued the loss in a litigation claims payable account.

### Instructions

1. Journalize the transactions.
2. Journalize the adjusting entry for each of the following accrued expenses at the end of the current year:
   a. Product warranty cost, $13,900.
   b. Interest on the six remaining notes owed to Merchandising Systems, Inc.

**PROBLEM 11-2B**
*Entries for payroll and payroll taxes*

**Objectives 4, 5**

P.A.S.S.

✓ *1. (b) Dr. Payroll Taxes Expense, $51,450*

The following information about the payroll for the week ended December 30 was obtained from the records of Sparta Co.:

| Salaries: | | Deductions: | |
|---|---|---|---|
| Sales salaries | $436,000 | Income tax withheld | $127,440 |
| Warehouse salaries | 93,400 | Social security tax withheld | 40,002 |
| Office salaries | 178,600 | Medicare tax withheld | 10,620 |
| | $708,000 | U.S. savings bonds | 24,780 |
| | | Group insurance | 40,356 |

Tax rates assumed:
  Social security, 6% on first $100,000 of employee annual earnings
  Medicare, 1.5%
  State unemployment (employer only), 3.8%
  Federal unemployment (employer only), 0.8%

### Instructions

1. Assuming that the payroll for the last week of the year is to be paid on December 31, journalize the following entries:
   a. December 30, to record the payroll.
   b. December 30, to record the employer's payroll taxes on the payroll to be paid on December 31. Of the total payroll for the last week of the year, $18,000 is subject to unemployment compensation taxes.
2. Assuming that the payroll for the last week of the year is to be paid on January 4 of the following fiscal year, journalize the following entries:
   a. December 30, to record the payroll.
   b. January 4, to record the employer's payroll taxes on the payroll to be paid on January 4.

**PROBLEM 11-3B**
*Wage and tax statement data and employer FICA tax*

**Objectives 4, 5**

SPREADSHEET

✓ *2. (e) $30,633*

Diamond Distribution Company began business on January 2, 2005. Salaries were paid to employees on the last day of each month, and social security tax, Medicare tax, and federal income tax were withheld in the required amounts. An employee who is hired in the middle of the month receives half the monthly salary for that month. All required payroll tax reports were filed, and the correct amount of payroll taxes was remitted by the company for the calendar year. Early in 2006, before the Wage and Tax Statements (Form W-2) could be prepared for distribution to employees and for filing with the Social Security Administration, the employees' earnings records were inadvertently destroyed.

None of the employees resigned or were discharged during the year, and there were no changes in salary rates. The social security tax was withheld at the rate of

6.0% on the first $100,000 of salary and Medicare tax at the rate of 1.5% on salary. Data on dates of employment, salary rates, and employees' income taxes withheld, which are summarized as follows, were obtained from personnel records and payroll records.

| Employee | Date First Employed | Monthly Salary | Monthly Income Tax Withheld |
|---|---|---|---|
| Albright | June 2 | $ 6,600 | $1,452 |
| Charles | Jan. 2 | 8,500 | 2,074 |
| Given | Mar. 1 | 5,300 | 1,007 |
| Nelson | Jan. 2 | 3,600 | 648 |
| Quinn | Nov. 15 | 4,000 | 740 |
| Ramirez | Apr. 15 | 3,200 | 560 |
| Wu | Jan. 16 | 10,000 | 2,480 |

### Instructions

1. Calculate the amounts to be reported on each employee's Wage and Tax Statement (Form W-2) for 2005, arranging the data in the following form:

| Employee | Gross Earnings | Federal Income Tax Withheld | Social Security Tax Withheld | Medicare Tax Withheld |
|---|---|---|---|---|

2. Calculate the following employer payroll taxes for the year: (a) social security; (b) Medicare; (c) state unemployment compensation at 3.8% on the first $7,000 of each employee's earnings; (d) federal unemployment compensation at 0.8% on the first $7,000 of each employee's earnings; (e) total.

*If the working papers correlating with this textbook are not used, omit Problem 11-4B.*

**PROBLEM 11-4B**
*Payroll register*
**Objectives 4, 5**

✓ *3. Dr. Payroll Taxes Expense, $646.91*

The payroll register for Goyi Guitar Co. for the week ended December 12, 2006, is presented in the working papers.

### Instructions

1. Journalize the entry to record the payroll for the week.
2. Journalize the entry to record the issuance of the checks to employees.
3. Journalize the entry to record the employer's payroll taxes for the week. Assume the following tax rates: state unemployment, 3.2%; federal unemployment, 0.8%. Of the earnings, $750 is subject to unemployment taxes.
4. Journalize the entry to record a check issued on December 15 to Second National Bank in payment of employees' income taxes, $1,402.06, social security taxes, $987.06, and Medicare taxes, $246.76.

**PROBLEM 11-5B**
*Payroll register*
**Objectives 4, 5**

SPREADSHEET

✓ *1. Total net amount payable, $6,580.50*

The following data for College Publishing Co. relate to the payroll for the week ended December 7, 2006:

| Employee | Hours Worked | Hourly Rate | Weekly Salary | Federal Income Tax | U.S. Savings Bonds | Accumulated Earnings, Nov. 30 |
|---|---|---|---|---|---|---|
| A | 50.00 | $28.00 | | $354.20 | $15.00 | $ 70,800.00 |
| B | 42.00 | 22.00 | | 189.20 | | 41,500.00 |
| C | | | $2,150.00 | 537.50 | 70.00 | 103,200.00 |
| D | 46.00 | 18.00 | | 176.40 | 10.00 | 43,200.00 |
| E | 40.00 | 15.00 | | 108.00 | | 28,800.00 |
| F | 45.00 | 22.50 | | 224.44 | 20.00 | 47,400.00 |
| G | 40.00 | 16.00 | | 108.80 | 25.00 | 30,700.00 |
| H | | | 1,100.00 | 242.00 | | 4,400.00 |
| I | 30.00 | 12.00 | | 43.20 | 15.00 | 14,400.00 |

Employees C and H are office staff, and all of the other employees are sales personnel. All sales personnel are paid 1½ times the regular rate for all hours in excess of 40 hours per week. The social security tax rate is 6.0% on the first $100,000 of each employee's annual earnings, and Medicare tax is 1.5% of each employee's annual earnings. The next payroll check to be used is No. 981.

**Instructions**
1. Prepare a payroll register for College Publishing Co. for the week ended December 7, 2006.
2. Journalize the entry to record the payroll for the week.

**PROBLEM 11-6B**
*Payroll accounts and year-end entries*

**Objectives 4, 5, 6**

P.A.S.S.

The following accounts, with the balances indicated, appear in the ledger of Acadia Outdoor Equipment Company on December 1 of the current year:

| | | |
|---|---|---|
| 211 | Salaries Payable | — |
| 212 | Social Security Tax Payable | $ 6,236 |
| 213 | Medicare Tax Payable | 1,641 |
| 214 | Employees Federal Income Tax Payable | 10,120 |
| 215 | Employees State Income Tax Payable | 9,846 |
| 216 | State Unemployment Tax Payable | 1,100 |
| 217 | Federal Unemployment Tax Payable | 275 |
| 218 | Bond Deductions Payable | 1,500 |
| 219 | Medical Insurance Payable | 4,200 |
| 611 | Sales Salaries Expense | 745,800 |
| 711 | Officers Salaries Expense | 347,600 |
| 712 | Office Salaries Expense | 110,000 |
| 719 | Payroll Taxes Expense | 94,207 |

The following transactions relating to payroll, payroll deductions, and payroll taxes occurred during December:

Dec. 1. Issued Check No. 728 to Pico Insurance Company for $4,200, in payment of the semiannual premium on the group medical insurance policy.
  2. Issued Check No. 729 to First National Bank for $17,997, in payment for $6,236 of social security tax, $1,641 of Medicare tax, and $10,120 of employees' federal income tax due.
  3. Issued Check No. 730 for $1,500 to First National Bank to purchase U.S. savings bonds for employees.
  14. Journalized the entry to record the biweekly payroll. A summary of the payroll record follows:

| Salary distribution: | | |
|---|---|---|
| Sales | $33,000 | |
| Officers | 15,600 | |
| Office | 5,000 | $53,600 |
| Deductions: | | |
| Social security tax | $ 2,948 | |
| Medicare tax | 804 | |
| Federal income tax withheld | 9,541 | |
| State income tax withheld | 2,412 | |
| Savings bond deductions | 750 | |
| Medical insurance deductions | 700 | 17,155 |
| Net amount | | $36,445 |

  14. Issued Check No. 738 in payment of the net amount of the biweekly payroll.
  14. Journalized the entry to record payroll taxes on employees' earnings of December 14: social security tax, $2,948; Medicare tax, $804; state unemployment tax, $260; federal unemployment tax, $65.

*(continued)*

Dec. 17. Issued Check No. 744 to First National Bank for $17,045, in payment for $5,896 of social security tax, $1,608 of Medicare tax, and $9,541 of employees' federal income tax due.

28. Journalized the entry to record the biweekly payroll. A summary of the payroll record follows:

| Salary distribution: | | |
|---|---|---|
| Sales | $33,600 | |
| Officers | 16,000 | |
| Office | 5,200 | $54,800 |
| Deductions: | | |
| Social security tax | $ 2,959 | |
| Medicare tax | 822 | |
| Federal income tax withheld | 9,754 | |
| State income tax withheld | 2,466 | |
| Savings bond deductions | 750 | 16,751 |
| Net amount | | $38,049 |

28. Issued Check No. 782 for the net amount of the biweekly payroll.

28. Journalized the entry to record payroll taxes on employees' earnings of December 28: social security tax, $2,959; Medicare tax, $822; state unemployment tax, $160; federal unemployment tax, $40.

30. Issued Check No. 791 for $14,724 to First National Bank, in payment of employees' state income tax due on December 31.

30. Issued Check No. 792 to First National Bank for $1,500 to purchase U.S. savings bonds for employees.

31. Paid $59,500 to the employee pension plan. The annual pension cost is $65,000. (Record both the payment and the unfunded pension liability.)

### Instructions

1. Journalize the transactions.
2. Journalize the following adjusting entries on December 31:
   a. Salaries accrued: sales salaries, $3,360; officers salaries, $1,600; office salaries, $520. The payroll taxes are immaterial and are not accrued.
   b. Vacation pay, $13,600.

# Comprehensive Problem 3

P.A.S.S.

✓ 5. Total assets, $1,221,890

Selected transactions completed by Calico Interiors, Inc., during its first fiscal year ending December 31 were as follows:

Jan.   2. Issued a check to establish a petty cash fund of $800.

Mar.   1. Replenished the petty cash fund, based on the following summary of petty cash receipts: office supplies, $265; miscellaneous selling expense, $304; miscellaneous administrative expense, $158.

Apr.   5. Purchased $10,000 of merchandise on account, terms 1/10, n/30. The perpetual inventory system is used to account for inventory.

May   5. Paid the invoice of April 5 after the discount period had passed.

10. Received cash from daily cash sales for $8,480. The amount indicated by the cash register was $8,490.

June   2. Received a 60-day, 7.2% note for $50,000 on account.

Aug.   1. Received amount owed on June 2 note, plus interest at the maturity date.

3. Received $1,400 on account and wrote off the remainder owed on a $2,000 accounts receivable balance. (The allowance method is used in accounting for uncollectible receivables.)

28. Reinstated the account written off on August 3 and received $600 cash in full payment.

Sept.  2. Purchased land by issuing a $120,000, 90-day note to Ace Development Co., which discounted it at 6%.

Oct.   2. Traded office equipment for new similar equipment with a list price of $135,000. A trade-in allowance of $66,000 was received on the old equipment that had cost $96,000 and had accumulated depreciation of $35,000 as of October 1. A 120-day, 9% note was issued for the balance owed.

Nov. 30. Journalized the monthly payroll for November, based on the following data:

| Salaries | | Deductions | |
|---|---|---|---|
| Sales salaries | $42,500 | Income tax withheld | $13,650 |
| Office salaries | 22,500 | Social security tax | |
| | $65,000 | withheld | 3,770 |
| | | Medicare tax withheld | 975 |

| Unemployment tax rates: | |
|---|---|
| State unemployment | 3.8% |
| Federal unemployment | 0.8% |
| Amount subject to unemployment taxes: | |
| State unemployment | $1,000 |
| Federal unemployment | 1,000 |

      30. Journalized the employer's payroll taxes on the payroll.

Dec.   1. Journalized the payment of the September 2 note at maturity.

      30. The pension cost for the year was $65,000, of which $61,300 was paid to the pension plan trustee.

## Instructions

1. Journalize the selected transactions.
2. Based on the following data, prepare a bank reconciliation for December of the current year:
   a. Balance according to the bank statement at December 31, $105,700.
   b. Balance according to the ledger at December 31, $93,600.
   c. Checks outstanding at December 31, $22,680.
   d. Deposit in transit, not recorded by bank, $10,400.
   e. Bank debit memorandum for service charges, $80.
   f. A check for $110 in payment of an invoice was incorrectly recorded in the accounts as $10.
3. Based on the bank reconciliation prepared in (2), journalize the entry or entries to be made by Calico Interiors, Inc.
4. Based on the following selected data, journalize the adjusting entries as of December 31 of the current year:
   a. Estimated uncollectible accounts at December 31, $5,980, based on an aging of accounts receivable. The balance of Allowance for Doubtful Accounts at December 31 was $500 (debit).
   b. The physical inventory on December 31 indicated an inventory shrinkage of $1,260.
   c. Prepaid insurance expired during the year, $14,300.
   d. Office supplies used during the year, $5,680.
   e. Depreciation is computed as follows:

| Asset | Cost | Residual Value | Acquisition Date | Useful Life in Years | Depreciation Method Used |
|---|---|---|---|---|---|
| Buildings | $320,000 | $      0 | January 2 | 50 | Straight-line |
| Office Equip. | 130,000 | 14,000 | October 2 | 5 | Straight-line |
| Store Equip. | 42,000 | 10,000 | January 3 | 8 | Declining-balance (at twice the straight-line rate) |

   f. A patent costing $42,900 when acquired on January 2 has a remaining legal life of 9 years and is expected to have value for 6 years. *(continued)*

g. The cost of mineral rights was $105,000. Of the estimated deposit of 42,000 tons of ore, 6,000 tons were mined during the year.

h. Total vacation pay expense for the year, $11,400.

i. A product warranty was granted beginning December 1 and covering a one-year period. The estimated cost is 2.5% of sales, which totaled $568,000 in December.

j. Interest was accrued on the note payable issued on October 2.

5. Based on the following information and the post-closing trial balance shown below, prepare a balance sheet in report form at December 31 of the current year.

Notes receivable is a current asset.

The merchandise inventory is stated at cost by the LIFO method.

The product warranty payable is a current liability.

Vacation pay payable:
| | |
|---|---|
| Current liability | $10,000 |
| Long-term liability | 1,400 |

The unfunded pension liability is a long-term liability.

Notes payable:
| | |
|---|---|
| Current liability | $69,000 |
| Long-term liability | 26,000 |

**Calico Interiors, Inc.**
**Post-Closing Trial Balance**
**December 31, 2006**

| | | |
|---|---:|---:|
| Petty Cash | 800 | |
| Cash | 93,420 | |
| Notes Receivable | 40,000 | |
| Accounts Receivable | 202,300 | |
| Allowance for Doubtful Accounts | | 5,980 |
| Merchandise Inventory | 140,600 | |
| Prepaid Insurance | 28,600 | |
| Office Supplies | 7,100 | |
| Land | 118,200 | |
| Buildings | 320,000 | |
| Accumulated Depreciation—Buildings | | 6,400 |
| Office Equipment | 130,000 | |
| Accumulated Depreciation—Office Equipment | | 5,800 |
| Store Equipment | 42,000 | |
| Accumulated Depreciation—Store Equipment | | 10,500 |
| Mineral Rights | 105,000 | |
| Accumulated Depletion | | 15,000 |
| Patents | 35,750 | |
| Social Security Tax Payable | | 7,772 |
| Medicare Tax Payable | | 2,010 |
| Employees Federal Income Tax Payable | | 14,070 |
| State Unemployment Tax Payable | | 33 |
| Federal Unemployment Tax Payable | | 6 |
| Salaries Payable | | 67,000 |
| Accounts Payable | | 125,300 |
| Interest Payable | | 1,553 |
| Product Warranty Payable | | 14,200 |
| Vacation Pay Payable | | 11,400 |
| Unfunded Pension Liability | | 3,700 |
| Notes Payable | | 95,000 |
| B. Joiner, Capital | | 878,046 |
| | 1,263,770 | 1,263,770 |

6. On February 7 of the following year, the merchandise inventory was destroyed by fire. Based on the following data obtained from the accounting records, estimate the cost of the merchandise destroyed:

| | |
|---|---|
| Jan. 1 Merchandise inventory | $140,600 |
| Jan. 1–Feb. 7 Purchases (net) | 246,720 |
| Jan. 1–Feb. 7 Sales (net) | 430,000 |
| Estimated gross profit rate | 40% |

# Special Activities

**ACTIVITY 11-1**
*Ethics and professional conduct in business*

ETHICS

Sarah Lindsay is a certified public accountant (CPA) and staff assistant for Kim and Horkin, a local CPA firm. It had been the policy of the firm to provide a holiday bonus equal to two weeks' salary to all employees. The firm's new management team announced on November 25 that a bonus equal to only one week's salary would be made available to employees this year. Sarah thought that this policy was unfair because she and her co-workers planned on the full two-week bonus. The two-week bonus had been given for ten straight years, so it seemed as though the firm had breached an implied commitment. Thus, Sarah decided that she would make up the lost bonus week by working an extra six hours of overtime per week over the next five weeks until the end of the year. Kim and Horkin's policy is to pay overtime at 150% of straight time.

Sarah's supervisor was surprised to see overtime being reported, since there is generally very little additional or unusual client service demands at the end of the calendar year. However, the overtime was not questioned, since firm employees are on the "honor system" in reporting their overtime.

➤ Discuss whether the firm is acting in an ethical manner by changing the bonus. Is Sarah behaving in an ethical manner?

**ACTIVITY 11-2**
*Recognizing pension expense*

WHAT DO YOU THINK?

The annual examination of Horizon Company's financial statements by its external public accounting firm (auditors) is nearing completion. The following conversation took place between the controller of Horizon Company (Peter) and the audit manager from the public accounting firm (Connie).

*Connie:* You know, Peter, we are about to wrap up our audit for this fiscal year. Yet, there is one item still to be resolved.

*Peter:* What's that?

*Connie:* Well, as you know, at the beginning of the year, Horizon began a defined benefit pension plan. This plan promises your employees an annual payment when they retire, using a formula based on their salaries at retirement and their years of service. I believe that a pension expense should be recognized this year, equal to the amount of pension earned by your employees.

*Peter:* Wait a minute. I think you have it all wrong. The company doesn't have a pension expense until it actually pays the pension in cash when the employee retires. After all, some of these employees may not reach retirement, and if they don't, the company doesn't owe them anything.

*Connie:* You're not really seeing this the right way. The pension is earned by your employees during their working years. You actually make the payment much later—when they retire. It's like one long accrual—much like incurring wages in one period and paying them in the next. Thus, I think that you should recognize the expense in the period the pension is earned by the employees.

*Peter:* Let me see if I've got this straight. I should recognize an expense this period for something that may or may not be paid to the employees in 20 or 30 years, when they finally retire. How am I supposed to determine what the expense is for the current year? The amount of the final retirement depends on many uncertainties: salary levels, employee longevity, mortality rates, and interest earned on investments to fund the pension. I don't think that an amount can be determined, even if I accepted your arguments.

 ➤ Evaluate Connie's position. Is she right or is Peter correct?

**ACTIVITY 11-3**
*Executive bonuses and accounting methods*

Mark Cary, the owner of Cary Trucking Company, initiated an executive bonus plan for his chief executive officer (CEO). The new plan provides a bonus to the CEO equal to 3% of the income before taxes. Upon learning of the new bonus arrangement, the CEO issued instructions to change the company's accounting for trucks. The CEO has asked the controller to make the following two changes:

a. Change from the double-declining-balance method to the straight-line method of depreciation.
b. Add 50% to the useful lives of all trucks.

Why did the CEO ask for these changes? How would you respond to the CEO's request?

**ACTIVITY 11-4**
*Ethics and professional conduct in business*

Carl Mason was discussing summer employment with Kevin Cross, president of Juniper Landscaping Service:

*Kevin:* I'm glad that you're thinking about joining us for the summer. We could certainly use the help.
*Carl:* Sounds good. I enjoy outdoor work, and I could use the money to help with next year's school expenses.
*Kevin:* I've got a plan that can help you out on that. As you know, I'll pay you $10 per hour, but in addition, I'd like to pay you with cash. Since you're only working for the summer, it really doesn't make sense for me to go to the trouble of formally putting you on our payroll system. In fact, I do some jobs for my clients on a strictly cash basis, so it would be easy to just pay you that way.
*Carl:* Well, that's a bit unusual, but I guess money is money.
*Kevin:* Yeah, not only that, its tax-free!
*Carl:* What do you mean?
*Kevin:* Didn't you know? Any money that you receive in cash is not reported to the IRS on a W-2 form; therefore, the IRS doesn't know about the income—hence, it's the same as tax-free earnings.

a. Why does Kevin Cross want to conduct business transactions using cash (not check or credit card)?
b. How should Carl respond to Kevin's suggestion?

**ACTIVITY 11-5**
*Salary survey*

Several Internet services provide career guidance, classified employment ads, placement services, resumé posting, career questionnaires, and salary surveys. Select one of the following Internet sites, which are linked to the text's Web site at **http://warren.swlearning.com**, to determine current average salary levels for one of your career options:

| | |
|---|---|
| **Creative Financial Staffing** | Accounting salary information |
| **Spherion®** | Links to computer, engineering, finance, marketing, and accounting salary information |
| **Monster®** | Online Career Center, with links to salary information |
| **Institute of Management Accountants** | Salary survey information (see Career Center) |

**ACTIVITY 11-6**
*Payroll forms*

Payroll accounting involves the use of government-supplied forms to account for payroll taxes. Three common forms are the W-2, Form 940, and Form 941. Form a team with three of your classmates and retrieve copies of each of these forms. They may be obtained from a local IRS office, a library, or downloaded from the Internet at **http://www.irs.gov** (go to forms and publications).

Briefly describe the purpose of each of the three forms.

# Answers to Self-Examination Questions

1. **C**  The maturity value is $5,100, determined as follows:

   | | |
   |---|---:|
   | Face amount of note | $5,000 |
   | Plus interest ($5,000 × 12% × 60/360) | 100 |
   | Maturity value | $5,100 |

2. **B**  The net amount available to a borrower from discounting a note payable is called the proceeds. The proceeds of $4,900 (answer B) is determined as follows:

   | | |
   |---|---:|
   | Face amount of note | $5,000 |
   | Less discount ($5,000 × 12% × 60/360) | 100 |
   | Proceeds | $4,900 |

3. **B**  Employers are usually required to withhold a portion of their employees' earnings for payment of federal income taxes (answer A), Medicare tax (answer C), and state and local income taxes (answer D). Generally, federal unemployment compensation taxes (answer B) are levied against the employer only and thus are not deducted from employee earnings.

4. **D**  The amount of net pay of $1,385.50 (answer D) is determined as follows:

   | | | | |
   |---|---:|---:|---:|
   | Gross pay: | | | |
   | 40 hours at $40 . . . . . . . . . . . . . | $1,600.00 | | |
   | 5 hours at $60 . . . . . . . . . . . . . | 300.00 | $1,900.00 | |
   | Deductions: | | | |
   | Federal income | | | |
   | tax withheld . . . . . . . . . . . . . | | $ 450.00 | |
   | FICA: | | | |
   | Social security tax | | | |
   | ($600 × 0.06) . . . . . . | $36.00 | | |
   | Medicare tax | | | |
   | ($1,900 × 0.015) . . . | 28.50 | 64.50 | 514.50 |
   | | | | $1,385.50 |

5. **D**  The employer incurs an expense for social security tax (answer A), federal unemployment compensation tax (answer B), and state unemployment compensation tax (answer C). The employees' federal income tax (answer D) is not an expense of the employer. It is withheld from the employees' earnings.

# 12

# CORPORATIONS: ORGANIZATION, CAPITAL STOCK TRANSACTIONS, AND DIVIDENDS

## objectives

*After studying this chapter, you should be able to:*

**1** Describe the nature of the corporate form of organization.

**2** List the two main sources of stockholders' equity.

**3** List the major sources of paid-in capital, including the various classes of stock.

**4** Journalize the entries for issuing stock.

**5** Journalize the entries for treasury stock transactions.

**6** State the effect of stock splits on corporate financial statements.

**7** Journalize the entries for cash dividends and stock dividends.

**8** Describe and illustrate the reporting of stockholders' equity.

**9** Compute and interpret the dividend yield on common stock.

If you own stock in a corporation, you are interested in how the stock is doing in the market. If you are considering buying stocks, you are interested in your rights as a stockholder and returns that you can expect from the stock. In either case, you should be able to interpret stock market quotations, such as the following:

| Ytd % Chg | 52 Weeks | | Stock | Sym | Div | Yld % | PE | Vol 100s | Close | Net Chg |
|---|---|---|---|---|---|---|---|---|---|---|
| | Hi | Lo | | | | | | | | |
| 4.9 | 37.70 | 26.90 | Walgreen | WAG | .17f | .6 | 28 | 27361 | 30.63 | −0.24 |
| 12.2 | 58.03 | 43.72 | WalMart | WMT | .36 | .6 | 30 | 89617 | 56.65 | 0.12 |
| 23.8 | 43.99 | 27.80 | WashMut | WM | 1.20f | 2.8 | 10 | 37919 | 42.75 | 0.70 |
| −1.7 | 764 | 516 | WashPost B | WPO | 5.80 | .8 | 26 | 74 | 725.50 | −2.00 |
| −7.9 | 39.98 | 25.60 | WsteConn | WCN | | ... | 18 | 1260 | 35.56 | 0.18 |
| 6.8 | 26.39 | 19.39 | WasteMgt | WMI | .01 | ... | 19 | 10754 | 24.48 | 0.07 |
| 8.2 | 12.58 | 6.22 | WtrPikTch | PIK | | ... | 26 | 107 | 7.95 | −0.01 |

Although you may not own any stocks, you probably buy services or products from corporations, and you may work for a corporation. Understanding the corporate form of organization will help you in your role as a stockholder, a consumer, or an employee. In this chapter, we discuss the characteristics of corporations, as well as how corporations account for stocks.

# Nature of a Corporation

<table>
<tr>
<td>

**objective 1**

Describe the nature of the corporate form of organization.

</td>
<td>

In the preceding chapters, we used the proprietorship in illustrations. As we mentioned in a previous chapter, more than 70% of all businesses are proprietorships and 10% are partnerships. Most of these businesses are small businesses. The remaining 20% of businesses are corporations. Many corporations are large and, as a result, they generate more than 90% of the total business dollars in the United States.

</td>
</tr>
</table>

**REAL WORLD**

A corporation was defined in the Dartmouth College case of 1819, in which Chief Justice Marshall of the United States Supreme Court stated: "A corporation is an artificial being, invisible, intangible, and existing only in contemplation of the law."

**REAL WORLD**

The Coca-Cola Corporation is a well-known public corporation. The Mars Candy Company, which is owned by family members, is a well-known private corporation.

## Characteristics of a Corporation

A **corporation** is a legal entity, distinct and separate from the individuals who create and operate it. As a legal entity, a corporation may acquire, own, and dispose of property in its own name. It may also incur liabilities and enter into contracts. Most importantly, it can sell shares of ownership, called *stock*. This characteristic gives corporations the ability to raise large amounts of capital.

The *stockholders* or *shareholders* who own the stock own the corporation. They can buy and sell stock without affecting the corporation's operations or continued existence. Corporations whose shares of stock are traded in public markets are called **public corporations**. Corporations whose shares are not traded publicly are usually owned by a small group of investors and are called **nonpublic** or **private corporations**.

The stockholders of a corporation have **limited liability**. This means that a corporation's creditors usually may not go beyond the assets of the corporation to satisfy their claims. Thus, the financial loss that a stockholder may suffer is limited to the amount invested. This feature has contributed to the rapid growth of the corporate form of business.

The stockholders control a corporation by electing a **board of directors**. This board meets periodically to establish corporate policies. It also selects the chief executive officer (CEO) and other major officers to manage the corporation's day-to-day affairs. Exhibit 1 shows the organizational structure of a corporation.

As a separate entity, a corporation is subject to taxes. For example, corporations must pay federal income taxes on their income.[1] Thus, corporate income that is dis-

---

[1] A majority of states also require corporations to pay income taxes.

**•Exhibit 1** Organizational Structure of a Corporation

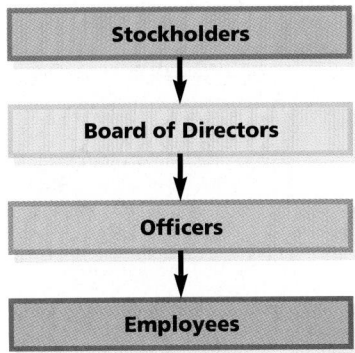

Corporations have a separate legal existence, transferable units of ownership, and limited stockholder liability.

tributed to stockholders in the form of **dividends** has already been taxed. In turn, stockholders must pay income taxes on the dividends they receive. This *double taxation* of corporate earnings is a major disadvantage of the corporate form.[2]

## INTEGRITY IN BUSINESS

### THE RESPONSIBLE BOARD

Recent corporate failures, such as **Enron**, **WorldCom**, and **Global Crossing**, have highlighted the roles of boards of directors in executing their responsibilities. New standards for corporate governance are being suggested, such as (1) independent directors to oversee management, (2) board member expertise and education, (3) separation of the Board Chairmanship from the CEO position, (4) transparent disclosure of all board activities and transactions with the corporation (insider trades), and (5) an independent audit committee. Indeed, one study found that "audit committees of companies where financial statement fraud has occurred generally were less independent, less expert, met less often and were less likely to have internal audit support."

**Sources:** R. Luke, "Inquisitive Directors: Tough Audit Questions Loom Large Since Enron," *Atlanta Journal—Constitution*, March 29, 2002; and *21st Century Governance Principles for U.S. Corporations* (Corporate Governance Center), 2002.

**REAL WORLD** Corporations may be organized for nonprofit reasons, such as recreational, educational, charitable, or humanitarian purposes. Such corporations are not required to pay federal taxes. Examples of nonprofit corporations include the **Sierra Club** and the **National Audubon Society**. However, most corporations are organized to earn a profit and a fair rate of return for their stockholders. Examples of for-profit corporations include **PepsiCo**, **General Motors**, and **Microsoft**.

## Forming a Corporation

The first step in forming a corporation is to file an **application of incorporation** with the state. State incorporation laws differ, and corporations often organize in those states with the more favorable laws. For this reason, more than half of the largest companies are incorporated in Delaware. Exhibit 2 lists some corporations that you may be familiar with, their states of incorporation, and the location of their headquarters.

After the application of incorporation has been approved, the state grants a **charter** or **articles of incorporation**. The articles

---

[2]Dividends presently receive a preferential individual tax rate of 15% to reduce the impact of double taxation.

## •Exhibit 2    Examples of Corporations and Their States of Incorporation

| Corporation | State of Incorporation | Headquarters |
|---|---|---|
| Borden, Inc. | New Jersey | New York, N.Y. |
| Caterpillar, Inc. | Delaware | Peoria, Ill. |
| Delta Air Lines, Inc. | Delaware | Atlanta, Ga. |
| Dow Chemical Company | Delaware | Midland, Mich. |
| General Electric Company | New York | Fairfield, Conn. |
| The Home Depot | Delaware | Atlanta, Ga. |
| Kellogg Company | Delaware | Battle Creek, Mich. |
| 3M | Delaware | St. Paul, Minn. |
| May Department Stores | New York | St. Louis, Mo. |
| RJR Nabisco | Delaware | New York, N.Y. |
| Radio Shack | Delaware | Ft. Worth, Tex. |
| The Washington Post Company | Delaware | Washington, D.C. |
| Whirlpool Corporation | Delaware | Benton Harbor, Mich. |

of incorporation formally create the corporation.[3] The corporate management and board of directors then prepare a set of **bylaws**, which are the rules and procedures for conducting the corporation's affairs.

Costs may be incurred in organizing a corporation. These costs include legal fees, taxes, state incorporation fees, license fees, and promotional costs. Such costs are debited to an expense account entitled *Organizational Expenses*. To illustrate, the recording of a corporation's organizing costs of $8,500 on January 5 is shown below.

| | | | | | |
|---|---|---|---|---|---|
| Jan. | 5 | Organizational Expenses | | 8 5 0 0 00 | |
| | | Cash | | | 8 5 0 0 00 |
| | | Paid costs of organizing the corporation. | | | |

# Stockholders' Equity

**objective 2**

List the two main sources of stockholders' equity.

The owners' equity in a corporation is commonly called ***stockholders' equity***, **shareholders' equity**, **shareholders' investment**, or **capital**. In a corporation balance sheet, the Stockholders' Equity section reports the amount of each of the two main sources of stockholders' equity. The first source is capital contributed to the corporation by the stockholders and others, called ***paid-in capital*** or **contributed capital**. The second source is net income retained in the business, called ***retained earnings***.

An example of a Stockholders' Equity section of a corporation balance sheet is shown below.[4]

**Stockholders' Equity**
Paid-in capital:
  Common stock                    $330,000
  Retained earnings                 80,000
      Total stockholders' equity              $410,000

---

[3]The articles of incorporation may also restrict a corporation's activities in certain areas, such as owning certain types of real estate, conducting certain types of business activities, or purchasing its own stock.
[4]The reporting of stockholders' equity is further discussed and illustrated later in this chapter.

# FINANCIAL REPORTING AND DISCLOSURE

## ADOLPH COORS COMPANY

**A**dolph Coors Company is a multinational brewer, marketer, and seller of beer and other malt-based beverages. For the year ending December 29, 2002, Coors reported sales of almost $5 billion and net income of $162 million.

Coors is incorporated in Colorado and has its headquarters in Golden, Colorado. Recently, Coors amended its articles of incorporation with the state of Colorado. Some excerpts from its articles of incorporation are shown below.

*Pursuant to the provisions of the Colorado Business Corporation Act (the "Act"), the . . . corporation adopts the following . . . Articles of Incorporation.*

### ARTICLE I
*The name of the Corporation is Adolph Coors Company.*

### ARTICLE II
*The Corporation shall have perpetual existence.*
*. . .*

### ARTICLE IV
*. . . Authorized Capital. The aggregate number of shares of Capital Stock which the Corporation shall have authority to issue is 226,260,000, said shares to consist of the following:*

*(1) 1,260,000 shares of Class A Common Stock (Voting), without par value ("Class A Stock");*

*(2) 200,000,000 shares of Class B Common Stock (Non-Voting), without par value ("Class B Stock");*

*(3) 25,000,000 shares of Preferred Stock, without par value ("Preferred Stock").*

*. . . Rights of Common Stock. The Class A Stock and Class B Stock shall be identical in all respects, share for share, except with respect to the right to vote. The right to vote for the election of directors and for all other purposes shall be vested exclusively in the holders of Class A Stock. . . . The holders of Class A Stock and the holders of Class B Stock shall*

*be entitled to receive such dividends as shall be declared from time to time by the Board of Directors (the "Board") out of funds legally available therefor, except that so long as any shares of Class B Stock are outstanding, no dividends shall be declared or paid on any Class A Stock unless at the same time there shall be declared or paid on Class B Stock in an amount per share equal to the amount per share of the dividend declared or paid on the Class A Stock. . . . The Board may declare and distribute dividends to the holders of Class A Stock and the holders of Class B Stock in the form of shares of Common Stock of the Corporation. . . .*

*. . . Rights of Preferred Stock. The Board is authorized . . .to establish . . . any dividend rights . . . whether such dividends are cumulative . . . whether any of the shares of such series shall be redeemable . . . whether such series shall have a . . . fund for the redemption or purchase of shares . . . the rights of the shares of such series upon the voluntary or involuntary liquidation, dissolution or winding up of the Corporation . . . voting rights of shares, and . . . conversion privileges.*

*. . .*

### ARTICLE VIII
*. . . Board of Directors. The affairs of the Corporation shall be governed by a Board of not less than three (3) directors. Subject to such limitation, the number of directors and the method by which the directors shall be elected shall be set forth in the Bylaws of the Corporation.*

*. . .*

### ARTICLE X
*. . . The Board shall be vested with the power to alter, amend, or repeal the Bylaws and to adopt new Bylaws.*

The paid-in capital contributed by the stockholders is recorded in separate accounts for each class of stock. If there is only one class of stock, the account is entitled *Common Stock* or *Capital Stock.*

Retained earnings are generated from operations. Net income increases retained earnings, while dividends decrease retained earnings. Thus, retained earnings represents a corporation's accumulated net income that has not been distributed to stockholders as dividends.

The balance of the retained earnings account at the end of the fiscal year is created by closing entries. First, the balance in the income summary account (the net income or net loss) is transferred to Retained Earnings. Second, the balance of the dividends account, which is similar to the drawing account for a proprietorship, is transferred to Retained Earnings.

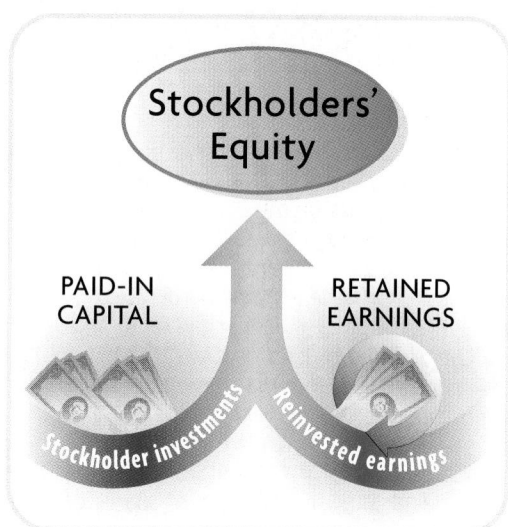

Other terms that may be used to identify retained earnings in the financial statements include *earnings retained for use in the business* and *earnings reinvested in the business*. A debit balance in Retained Earnings is called a **deficit**. Such a balance results from accumulated net losses. In the Stockholders' Equity section, a deficit is deducted from paid-in capital in determining total stockholders' equity.

The balance of retained earnings should not be interpreted as representing surplus cash or cash left over for dividends. The reason for this is that earnings retained in the business and the related cash generated from these earnings are normally used by management to improve or expand operations. As cash is used to expand or improve operations, its balance decreases. However, the balance of the retained earnings account is unaffected. As a result, over time the balance of the retained earnings account normally becomes less and less related to the balance of the cash account.

# Sources of Paid-In Capital

**objective** **3**

List the major sources of paid-in capital, including the various classes of stock.

As we mentioned in the preceding section, the two main sources of stockholders' equity are paid-in capital (or contributed capital) and retained earnings. The main source of paid-in capital is from issuing stock. In the following paragraphs, we discuss the characteristics of the various classes of stock.

## Stock

The number of shares of stock that a corporation is *authorized* to issue is stated in its charter. The term *issued* refers to the shares issued to the stockholders. A corporation may, under circumstances we discuss later in this chapter, reacquire some of the stock that it has issued. The stock remaining in the hands of stockholders is then called **outstanding stock**. The relationship between authorized, issued, and outstanding stock is shown in the graphic at the left.

Shares of stock are often assigned a monetary amount, called **par**. Corporations may issue **stock certificates** to stockholders to document their ownership. Printed on a stock certificate is the par value of the stock, the name of the stockholder, and the number of shares owned. Stock may also be issued without par, in which case it is called **no-par stock**. Some states require the board of directors to assign a **stated value** to no-par stock.

Some corporations have stopped issuing stock certificates except on special request. In these cases, the corporation maintains records of ownership by using electronic media.

**Number of shares authorized, issued, and outstanding**

Because corporations have limited liability, creditors have no claim against the personal assets of stockholders. However, some state laws require that corporations maintain a minimum stockholder contribution to protect creditors. This minimum amount is called **legal capital**. The amount of required legal capital varies among the states, but it usually includes the amount of par or stated value of the shares of stock issued.

The major rights that accompany ownership of a share of stock are as follows:

On its balance sheet, a corporation reports the following three numbers related to its common stock: 200,000 shares; 150,000 shares; and 138,000 shares. What is the number of shares authorized, issued, outstanding, and reacquired?

*200,000 shares authorized; 150,000 shares issued; 138,000 shares outstanding; 12,000 (150,000 − 138,000) shares reacquired.*

1. The right to vote in matters concerning the corporation.
2. The right to share in distributions of earnings.
3. The right to share in assets on liquidation.

When only one class of stock is issued, it is called ***common stock***. In this case, each share of common stock has equal rights. To appeal to a broader investment market, a corporation may issue one or more classes of stock with various preference rights. A common example of such a right is the preference to dividends. Such a stock is generally called a ***preferred stock***.

The dividend rights of preferred stock are usually stated in monetary terms or as a percent of par. For example, *$4 preferred stock* has a right to an annual $4 per share dividend. If the par value of the preferred stock were $50, the same right to dividends could be stated as *8% ($4/$50) preferred stock*.

The board of directors of a corporation has the sole authority to distribute dividends to the stockholders. When such action is taken, the directors are said to *declare* a dividend. Since dividends are normally based on earnings, a corporation cannot guarantee dividends even to preferred stockholders. However, because they have first rights to any dividends, the preferred stockholders have a greater chance of receiving regular dividends than do the common stockholders.

> The two primary classes of paid-in capital are common stock and preferred stock.

### Nonparticipating Preferred Stock

Preferred stockholders' dividend rights are usually limited to a certain amount. Such stock is said to be ***nonparticipating preferred stock***.[5] To continue our preceding example, assume that a corporation has 1,000 shares of $4 nonparticipating preferred stock and 4,000 shares of common stock outstanding. Also assume that the net income, amount of earnings retained, and the amount of earnings distributed by the board of directors for the first three years of operations are as follows:

|  | 2005 | 2006 | 2007 |
|---|---|---|---|
| Net income | $20,000 | $55,000 | $62,000 |
| Amount retained | 10,000 | 20,000 | 40,000 |
| Amount distributed | $10,000 | $35,000 | $22,000 |

Exhibit 3 shows the earnings distributed each year to the preferred stock and the common stock. In this example, the preferred stockholders received an annual dividend of $4 per share, compared to the common stockholders' dividends of $1.50, $7.75, and $4.50 per share. You should note that although preferred stockholders have a greater chance of receiving a regular dividend, common stockholders have a greater chance of receiving larger returns than do the preferred stockholders.

### •Exhibit 3   Dividends to Nonparticipating Preferred Stock

|  | 2005 | 2006 | 2007 |
|---|---|---|---|
| Amount distributed | $10,000 | $35,000 | $22,000 |
| Preferred dividend (1,000 shares) | 4,000 | 4,000 | 4,000 |
| Common dividend (4,000 shares) | $ 6,000 | $31,000 | $18,000 |
| Dividends per share: |  |  |  |
| Preferred | $   4.00 | $   4.00 | $   4.00 |
| Common | $   1.50 | $   7.75 | $   4.50 |

[5]In some cases, preferred stock may receive additional dividends if certain conditions are met. Such stock is called *participating preferred stock*. It is rarely used in today's financial markets.

## Cumulative Preferred Stock

***Cumulative preferred stock*** has a right to receive regular dividends that were not paid (not declared) in prior years before any common stock dividends are paid. Noncumulative preferred stock does not have this right.

Romer Corporation has 50,000 shares of $2, cumulative preferred stock outstanding. Preferred dividends are three years in arrears (not including the current year). What amount of preferred dividends must be paid before any dividends on common shares can be paid?

Dividends that have not been declared in prior years are said to be **in arrears**. Such dividends should be disclosed, normally in a note to the financial statements.

To illustrate how dividends on cumulative preferred stock are calculated, assume that the preferred stock in Exhibit 3 is cumulative, and that no dividends were paid in 2005 and 2006. In 2007, the board of directors declares dividends of $22,000. Exhibit 4 shows how the dividends paid in 2007 are distributed between the preferred and common stockholders.

*$400,000 [3 years in arrears (50,000 × $2 × 3) plus the current year's dividend of $100,000]*

## •Exhibit 4  Dividends to Cumulative Preferred Stock

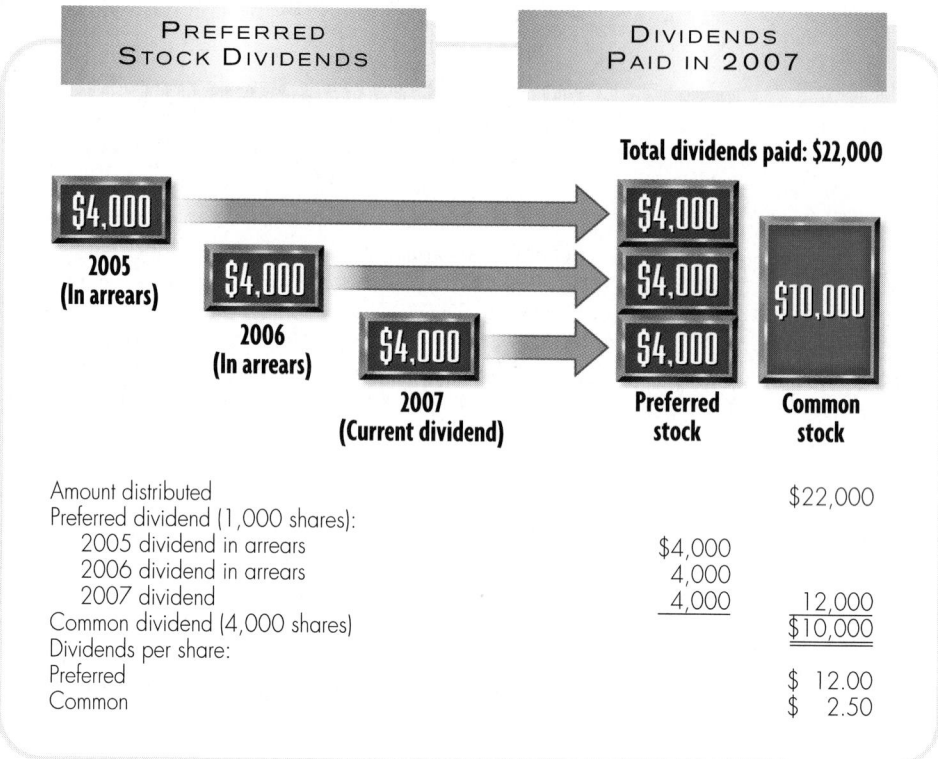

| | Preferred stock | Common stock |
|---|---|---|
| Amount distributed | | $22,000 |
| Preferred dividend (1,000 shares): | | |
| 2005 dividend in arrears | $4,000 | |
| 2006 dividend in arrears | 4,000 | |
| 2007 dividend | 4,000 | 12,000 |
| Common dividend (4,000 shares) | | $10,000 |
| Dividends per share: | | |
| Preferred | | $ 12.00 |
| Common | | $  2.50 |

## Other Preferential Rights

In addition to dividend preference, preferred stock may be given preferences to assets if the corporation goes out of business and is liquidated. However, claims of creditors must be satisfied first. Preferred stockholders are next in line to receive any remaining assets, followed by the common stockholders.

# Issuing Stock

**objective  4**

Journalize the entries for issuing stock.

A separate account is used for recording the amount of each class of stock issued to investors in a corporation. For example, assume that a corporation is authorized to issue 10,000 shares of preferred stock, $100 par, and 100,000 shares of common stock, $20 par. One-half of each class of authorized shares is issued at par for cash. The corporation's entry to record the stock issue is as follows:[6]

| | | | |
|---|---|---|---|
| Cash | 1,500 0 0 0 00 | | |
| Preferred Stock | | 500 0 0 0 00 | |
| Common Stock | | 1,000 0 0 0 00 | |
| Issued preferred stock and common | | | |
| stock at par for cash. | | | |

Stock is often issued by a corporation at a price other than its par. This is because the par value of a stock is simply its legal capital. The price at which stock can be sold by a corporation depends on a variety of factors, such as:

1. The financial condition, earnings record, and dividend record of the corporation.
2. Investor expectations of the corporation's potential earning power.
3. General business and economic conditions and prospects.

When stock is issued for a price that is more than its par, the stock has sold at a *premium*. When stock is issued for a price that is less than its par, the stock has sold at a *discount*. Thus, if stock with a par of $50 is issued for a price of $60, the stock has sold at a premium of $10. If the same stock is issued for a price of $45, the stock has sold at a discount of $5. Many states do not permit stock to be issued at a discount. In others, it may be done only under unusual conditions. Since issuing stock at a discount is rare, we will not illustrate it.

A corporation issuing stock must maintain records of the stockholders in order to issue dividend checks and distribute financial statements and other reports. Large public corporations normally use a financial institution, such as a bank, for this purpose.[7] In such cases, the financial institution is referred to as a *transfer agent* or *registrar*. For example, the transfer agent and registrar for **Coca-Cola Enterprises** is **First Chicago Trust Company of New York**.

**REAL WORLD**

## Premium on Stock

When stock is issued at a premium, Cash or other asset accounts are debited for the amount received. Common Stock or Preferred Stock is then credited for the par amount. The excess of the amount paid over par is a part of the total investment of the stockholders in the corporation. Therefore, such an amount in excess of par should be classified as a part of the paid-in capital. An account entitled *Paid-In Capital in Excess of Par* is usually credited for this amount.

To illustrate, assume that Caldwell Company issues 2,000 shares of $50 par preferred stock for cash at $55. The entry to record this transaction is as follows:

| | | | |
|---|---|---|---|
| Cash | 110 0 0 0 00 | | |
| Preferred Stock | | 100 0 0 0 00 | |
| Paid-In Capital in Excess of Par— | | | |
| Preferred Stock | | 10 0 0 0 00 | |
| Issued $50 par preferred stock at $55. | | | |

---

[6]The accounting for investments in stocks from the point of view of the investor is discussed in a later chapter.

[7]Small corporations may use a subsidiary ledger, called a *stockholders ledger*. In this case, the stock accounts (Preferred Stock and Common Stock) are controlling accounts for the subsidiary ledger.

When stock is issued in exchange for assets other than cash, such as land, buildings, and equipment, the assets acquired should be recorded at their fair market value. If this value cannot be objectively determined, the fair market price of the stock issued may be used.

To illustrate, assume that a corporation acquired land for which the fair market value cannot be determined. In exchange, the corporation issued 10,000 shares of its $10 par common. Assuming that the stock has a current market price of $12 per share, this transaction is recorded as follows:

| | | | | |
|---|---|---|---|---|
| Land | 120 0 0 0 00 | |
| Common Stock | | 100 0 0 0 00 |
| Paid-In Capital in Excess of Par | | 20 0 0 0 00 |
| Issued $10 par common stock, valued | | |
| at $12 per share, for land. | | |

## INTEGRITY IN BUSINESS

### WHAT'S THE REAL VALUE?

**S**tock fraud often involves illegal methods to sell stock or other investments at a price that is higher than its actual value. This can be done through illegally manipulating the stock price, selling stock in nonexistent companies, or using the proceeds of later investors to pay off earlier investors (pyramid scheme). You can avoid these kinds of fraud by following three rules:

1. Don't invest in small new companies that have market prices below $1, based on hot tips from callers in high-pressure "boiler rooms."
2. Don't invest on advice from acquaintances in social or religious groups, without checking the merits yourself.
3. Don't invest in unsolicited "risk-free" and "guaranteed" investments that promise quick profits if you act immediately.

I was born in 1913, when a banker, a bookkeeper, a lawyer, a miner, and a wood and coal purveyor invested $100 each to form the **Electro-Alkaline Co.**, to convert local brine into a liquid cleanser and germicide. My first customers were laundries, breweries, walnut processing sheds, and municipal water companies. I was briefly owned by **Procter & Gamble**. Today I'm a worldwide producer of household grocery, food, and insecticide products, with annual sales totaling $4 billion, and products sold in more than 110 countries. My brands include Glad, Pine-Sol, Hidden Valley, S.O.S., Kingsford, Fresh Step, Black Flag, and STP. Who am I? (Go to page 502 for answer.)

## No-Par Stock

In most states, both preferred and common stock may be issued without a par value. When no-par stock is issued, the entire proceeds are credited to the stock account. This is true even though the issue price varies from time to time. For example, assume that a corporation issues 10,000 shares of no-par common stock at $40 a share and at a later date issues 1,000 additional shares at $36. The entries to record the no-par stock are as follows:

| | | | | |
|---|---|---|---|---|
| Cash | 400 0 0 0 00 | |
| Common Stock | | 400 0 0 0 00 |
| Issued 10,000 shares of no-par | | |
| common at $40. | | |
| | | |
| Cash | 36 0 0 0 00 | |
| Common Stock | | 36 0 0 0 00 |
| Issued 1,000 shares of no-par | | |
| common at $36. | | |

Some states require that the entire proceeds from the issue of no-par stock be recorded as legal capital. In this case, the preceding entries would be proper. In other states, no-par stock may be assigned a *stated value per share*. The stated value is recorded like a par value, and the excess of the proceeds over the stated value is recorded as follows:

| | | | | |
|---|---|---|---|---|
| Cash | 400 0 0 0 00 | | | |
| Common Stock | | 250 0 0 0 00 | | |
| Paid-In Capital in Excess of Stated Value | | 150 0 0 0 00 | | |
| Issued 10,000 shares of no-par common | | | | |
| at $40; stated value, $25. | | | | |
| | | | | |
| Cash | 36 0 0 0 00 | | | |
| Common Stock | | 25 0 0 0 00 | | |
| Paid-In Capital in Excess of Stated Value | | 11 0 0 0 00 | | |
| Issued 1,000 shares of no-par common | | | | |
| at $36; stated value, $25. | | | | |

# Treasury Stock Transactions

A corporation may buy its own stock to provide shares for resale to employees, for reissuing as a bonus to employees, or for supporting the market price of the stock. For example, **General Motors** bought back its common stock and stated that two primary uses of this stock would be for incentive compensation plans and employee savings plans. Such stock that a corporation has once issued and then reacquires is called **treasury stock**.

A commonly used method of accounting for the purchase and resale of treasury stock is the **cost method**.[8] When the stock is purchased by the corporation, paid-in capital is reduced by debiting *Treasury Stock* for its cost (the price paid for it). The par value and the price at which the stock was originally issued are ignored. When the stock is resold, Treasury Stock is credited for its cost, and any difference between the cost and the selling price is normally debited or credited to *Paid-In Capital from Sale of Treasury Stock.*

To illustrate, assume that the paid-in capital of a corporation is as follows:

Common stock, $25 par (20,000 shares authorized
   and issued)                                        $500,000
Excess of issue price over par            150,000      $650,000

The purchase and sale of the treasury stock are recorded as follows:

| | | | | |
|---|---|---|---|---|
| Treasury Stock | 45 0 0 0 00 | | | |
| Cash | | 45 0 0 0 00 | | |
| Purchased 1,000 shares of treasury | | | | |
| stock at $45. | | | | |
| | | | | |
| Cash | 12 0 0 0 00 | | | |
| Treasury Stock | | 9 0 0 0 00 | | |
| Paid-In Capital from Sale of Treasury Stock | | 3 0 0 0 00 | | |
| Sold 200 shares of treasury stock at $60. | | | | |

*(continued)*

[8]Another method that is infrequently used, called the *par value method*, is discussed in advanced accounting texts.

| | Cash | | 8 0 0 0 00 | |
|---|---|---|---|---|
| | Paid-In Capital from Sale of Treasury Stock | | 1 0 0 0 00 | |
| | Treasury Stock | | | 9 0 0 0 00 |
| | Sold 200 shares of treasury stock at $40. | | | |

As shown above, a sale of treasury stock may result in a decrease in paid-in capital. To the extent that Paid-In Capital from Sale of Treasury Stock has a credit balance, it should be debited for any decrease. Any remaining decrease should then be debited to the retained earnings account.

# Stock Splits

**objective 6**

State the effect of stock splits on corporate financial statements.

**REAL WORLD**

When **Nature's Sunshine Products Inc.** declared a two-for-one stock split, the company president said:

*We believe the split will place our stock price in a range attractive to both individual and institutional investors, broadening the market for the stock.*

LTM Corporation announced a 4-for-1 stock split of its $50 par value common stock, which is currently trading for $120 per share. What is the new par value and the estimated market price of the stock after the split?

*$12.50 ($50/4) par value; $30 ($120/4) estimated market price.*

Corporations sometimes reduce the par or stated value of their common stock and issue a proportionate number of additional shares. When this is done, a corporation is said to have *split* its stock, and the process is called a **stock split**.

When stock is split, the reduction in par or stated value applies to all shares, including the unissued, issued, and treasury shares. A major objective of a stock split is to reduce the market price per share of the stock. This, in turn, should attract more investors to enter the market for the stock and broaden the types and numbers of stockholders.

To illustrate a stock split, assume that Rojek Corporation has 10,000 shares of $100 par common stock outstanding with a current market price of $150 per share. The board of directors declares a 5-for-1 stock split, reduces the par to $20, and increases the number of shares to 50,000. The amount of common stock outstanding is $1,000,000 both before and after the stock split. Only the number of shares and the par per share are changed. Each Rojek Corporation shareholder owns the same total par amount of stock before and after the stock split. For example, a stockholder who owned 4 shares of $100 par stock before the split (total par of $400) would own 20 shares of $20 par stock after the split (total par of $400).

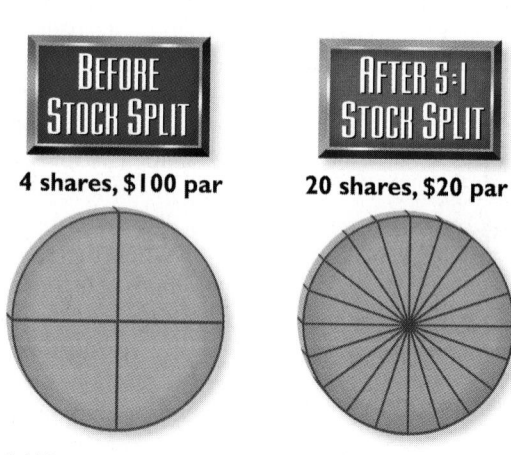

Since there are more shares outstanding after the stock split, we would expect that the market price of the stock would fall. For example, in the preceding example, there would be 5 times as many shares outstanding after the split. Thus, we would expect the market price of the stock to fall from $150 to approximately $30 ($150/5).

Since a stock split changes only the par or stated value and the number of shares outstanding, it is not recorded by a journal entry. Although the accounts are not affected, the details of stock splits are normally disclosed in the notes to the financial statements.

**A stock split does not change the balance of any corporation accounts.**

# Accounting for Dividends

When a board of directors declares a cash dividend, it authorizes the distribution of a portion of the corporation's cash to stockholders. When a board of directors declares a stock dividend, it authorizes the distribution of a portion of its stock. In both cases, the declaration of a dividend reduces the retained earnings of the corporation.[9]

## Cash Dividends

A cash distribution of earnings by a corporation to its shareholders is called a **cash dividend**. Although dividends may be paid in the form of other assets, cash dividends are the most common form.

There are usually three conditions that a corporation must meet to pay a cash dividend:

1. Sufficient retained earnings
2. Sufficient cash
3. Formal action by the board of directors

A large amount of retained earnings does not always mean that a corporation is able to pay dividends. As we indicated earlier in the chapter, the balances of the cash and retained earnings accounts are often unrelated. Thus, a large retained earnings account does not mean that there is cash available to pay dividends.

A corporation's board of directors is not required by law to declare dividends. This is true even if both retained earnings and cash are large enough to justify a dividend. However, many corporations try to maintain a stable dividend record in order to make their stock attractive to investors. Although dividends may be paid once a year or semiannually, most corporations pay dividends quarterly. In years of high profits, a corporation may declare a *special* or *extra* dividend.

You may have seen announcements of dividend declarations in financial newspapers or investor services. An example of such an announcement is shown below.

*On June 26, the board of directors of* **Campbell Soup Co.** *declared a quarterly cash dividend of $0.225 per common share to stockholders of record as of the close of business on July 8, payable on July 31.*

This announcement includes three important dates: the *date of declaration* (June 26), the *date of record* (July 8), and the *date of payment* (July 31). During the period of time between the record date and the payment date, the stock price is usually quoted as selling *ex-dividends*. This means that since the date of record has passed, a new investor will not receive the dividend.

To illustrate, assume that on *December 1* the board of directors of Hiber Corporation declares the following quarterly cash dividends. The date of record is *December 10*, and the date of payment is *January 2*.

| DATE OF DECLARATION | DATE OF RECORD | DATE OF PAYMENT |
|---|---|---|
| **JUNE 26** | **JULY 8** | **JULY 31** |
| Board of Directors takes action to declare dividends. **ENTRY:** Debit *Cash Dividends* Credit *Cash Dividends Payable* | Ownership of shares determines who receives dividend (no entry required). | Dividend is paid. **ENTRY:** Debit *Cash Dividends Payable* Credit *Cash* |

|  | Dividend per Share | Total Dividends |
|---|---|---|
| Preferred stock, $100 par, 5,000 shares outstanding . . . . . | $2.50 | $12,500 |
| Common stock, $10 par, 100,000 shares outstanding . . . . | $0.30 | 30,000 |
| Total . . . . . . . . . . . . . . . . . . . . . . . . . . . . . . . . . . . . . . . . |  | $42,500 |

---

[9]In rare cases, when a corporation is reducing its operations or going out of business, a dividend may be a distribution of paid-in capital. Such a dividend is called a *liquidating dividend*.

Hiber Corporation records the $42,500 liability for the dividends on December 1, the declaration date, as follows:

| | | | | |
|---|---|---|---|---|
| Dec. | 1 | Cash Dividends | 42 5 0 0 00 | |
| | | Cash Dividends Payable | | 42 5 0 0 00 |
| | | Declared cash dividend. | | |

No entry is required on the date of record, December 10, since this date merely determines which stockholders will receive the dividend. On the date of payment, January 2, the corporation records the $42,500 payment of the dividends as follows:

| | | | | |
|---|---|---|---|---|
| Jan. | 2 | Cash Dividends Payable | 42 5 0 0 00 | |
| | | Cash | | 42 5 0 0 00 |
| | | Paid cash dividend. | | |

If Hiber Corporation's fiscal year ends December 31, the balance in Cash Dividends will be transferred to Retained Earnings as a part of the closing process by debiting Retained Earnings and crediting Cash Dividends. Cash Dividends Payable will be listed on the December 31 balance sheet as a current liability.

If a corporation that holds treasury stock declares a cash dividend, the dividends are not paid on the treasury shares. To do so would place the corporation in the position of earning income through dealing with itself. For example, if Hiber Corporation in the preceding illustration had held 5,000 shares of its own common stock, the cash dividends on the common stock would have been $28,500 [(100,000 − 5,000) × $0.30] instead of $30,000.

## INTEGRITY IN BUSINESS

### THE PROFESSOR WHO KNEW TOO MUCH

A major Midwestern University released a quarterly "American Customer Satisfaction Index" based upon its research of customers of popular U.S. products and services. Before the release of the index to the public, the professor in charge of the research bought and sold stocks of some of the companies being reported upon. The professor was quoted as saying that he thought it was important to test his theories of customer satisfaction with "real" [his own] money.

Is this proper or ethical? Apparently, the Dean of the Business School didn't think so. In a statement to the press, the Dean stated: "I have instructed anyone affiliated with the (index) not to make personal use of information gathered in the course of producing the quarterly index, prior to the index's release to the general public, and they [the researchers] have agreed."

**Sources:** Jon E. Hilsenrath and Dan Morse, "Researcher Uses Index to Buy, Short Stocks," *The Wall Street Journal*, February 18, 2003; and Jon E. Hilsenrath, "Satisfaction Theory: Mixed Results," *The Wall Street Journal*, February 19, 2003.

## Stock Dividends

A distribution of shares of stock to stockholders is called a **stock dividend**. Usually, such distributions are in common stock and are issued to holders of common stock. Stock dividends are different from cash dividends in that there is no distribution of cash or other assets to stockholders.

The effect of a stock dividend on the stockholders' equity of the issuing corporation is to transfer retained earnings to paid-in capital. For public corporations, the amount transferred from retained earnings to paid-in capital is normally the *fair value* (market price) of the shares issued in the stock dividend.[10] To illustrate, assume that the stockholders' equity accounts of Hendrix Corporation as of December 15 are as follows:

| | |
|---|---|
| Common Stock, $20 par (2,000,000 shares issued) | $40,000,000 |
| Paid-In Capital in Excess of Par—Common Stock | 9,000,000 |
| Retained Earnings | 26,600,000 |

On December 15, the board of directors declares a stock dividend of 5% or 100,000 shares (2,000,000 shares × 5%) to be issued on January 10 to stockholders of record on December 31. The market price of the stock on the declaration date is $31 a share. The entry to record the declaration is as follows:

| | | | | |
|---|---|---|---|---|
| Dec. | 15 | Stock Dividends (100,000 × $31 market price) | 3,100 0 0 0 00 | |
| | | Stock Dividends Distributable | | |
| | | (100,000 × $20 Par) | | 2,000 0 0 0 00 |
| | | Paid-In Capital in Excess of | | |
| | | Par—Common Stock | | 1,100 0 0 0 00 |
| | | Declared stock dividend. | | |

The $3,100,000 balance in Stock Dividends is closed to Retained Earnings on December 31. The stock dividends distributable account is listed in the Paid-In Capital section of the balance sheet. Thus, the effect of the stock dividend is to transfer $3,100,000 of retained earnings to paid-in capital.

On January 10, the number of shares outstanding is increased by 100,000 by the following entry to record the issue of the stock:

| | | | | |
|---|---|---|---|---|
| Jan. | 10 | Stock Dividends Distributable | 2,000 0 0 0 00 | |
| | | Common Stock | | 2,000 0 0 0 00 |
| | | Issued stock for the stock dividend. | | |

A stock dividend does not change the assets, liabilities, or total stockholders' equity of the corporation. Likewise, it does not change a stockholder's proportionate interest (equity) in the corporation. For example, if a stockholder owned 1,000 of a corporation's 10,000 shares outstanding, the stockholder owns 10% (1,000/10,000) of the corporation. After declaring a 6% stock dividend, the corporation will issue 600 additional shares (10,000 shares × 6%), and the total shares outstanding will be 10,600. The stockholder of 1,000 shares will receive 60 additional shares and will now own 1,060 shares, which is still a 10% equity interest.

# Reporting Stockholders' Equity

**objective 8**

Describe and illustrate the reporting of stockholders' equity.

We illustrated the stockholders' equity section of the balance sheet earlier in this chapter. However, as with other sections of the balance sheet, alternative terms and formats may be used in reporting stockholders' equity. In addition, the significant changes in the sources of stockholders' equity—paid-in capital and retained earnings—may be reported in separate statements or notes that support the balance sheet presentation.

[10]The use of fair market value is justified as long as the number of shares issued for the stock dividend is small (less than 25% of the shares outstanding).

# Stockholders' Equity in the Balance Sheet

Two alternatives for reporting stockholders' equity in the balance sheet are shown in Exhibit 5. In the first example, each class of stock is listed first, followed by its related paid-in capital accounts. In the second example, the stock accounts are listed first. The other paid-in capital accounts are listed as a single item described as *Additional paid-in capital*. These combined accounts could also be described as *Capital in excess of par (or stated value) of shares* or a similar title.

**•Exhibit 5**  Stockholders' Equity Section of a Balance Sheet

**Stockholders' Equity**

| | | | |
|---|---|---|---|
| Paid-in capital: | | | |
| Preferred 10% stock, cumulative, $50 par (2,000 shares authorized and issued) | $100,000 | | |
| Excess of issue price over par | 10,000 | $ 110,000 | |
| Common stock, $20 par (50,000 shares authorized, 45,000 shares issued) | $900,000 | | |
| Excess of issue price over par | 190,000 | 1,090,000 | |
| From sale of treasury stock | | 2,000 | |
| Total paid-in capital | | | $1,202,000 |
| Retained earnings | | | 350,000 |
| Total | | | $1,552,000 |
| Deduct treasury stock (600 shares at cost) | | | 27,000 |
| Total stockholders' equity | | | $1,525,000 |

**Shareholders' Equity**

| | | |
|---|---|---|
| Contributed capital: | | |
| Preferred 10% stock, cumulative, $50 par (2,000 shares authorized and issued) | $100,000 | |
| Common stock, $20 par (50,000 shares authorized, 45,000 shares issued) | 900,000 | |
| Additional paid-in capital | 202,000 | |
| Total contributed capital | | $1,202,000 |
| Retained earnings | | 350,000 |
| Total | | $1,552,000 |
| Deduct treasury stock (600 shares at cost) | | 27,000 |
| Total stockholders' equity | | $1,525,000 |

Significant changes in stockholders' equity during a period may be presented either in a *statement of stockholders' equity* or in notes to the financial statements.[11] In addition, relevant rights and privileges of the various classes of stock outstanding

[11]We describe and illustrate the statement of stockholders' equity in the next chapter.

must be disclosed.[12] Examples of types of information that must be disclosed include dividend and liquidation preferences, rights to participate in earnings, conversion rights, and redemption rights. Such information may be disclosed on the face of the balance sheet or in the accompanying notes.

# Reporting Retained Earnings

A corporation may report changes in retained earnings by preparing a separate retained earnings statement, a combined income and retained earnings statement, or a statement of stockholders' equity.

When a separate *retained earnings statement* is prepared, the beginning balance of retained earnings is reported. The net income is then added (or net loss is subtracted) and any dividends are subtracted to arrive at the ending retained earnings for the period. An example of a such a statement for Adang Corporation is shown in Exhibit 6.

An alternative format for presenting the retained earnings statement is to combine it with the income statement. An advantage of the combined format is that it emphasizes net income as the connecting link between the income statement and the retained earnings portion of stockholders' equity. Since the combined form is not often used, we do not illustrate it.

**REAL WORLD**

The 2002 edition of *Accounting Trends & Techniques* indicated that 1.5% of the companies surveyed presented a separate statement of retained earnings, 1% presented a combined income and retained earnings statement, and 1% presented changes in retained earnings in the notes to the financial statements. The other 96% of the companies presented changes in retained earnings in a statement of stockholders' equity.

## •Exhibit 6   Retained Earnings Statement

| Adang Corporation Retained Earnings Statement For the Year Ended June 30, 2006 | | |
|---|---:|---:|
| Retained earnings, July 1, 2005 . . . . . . . . . . . . . . . . . . . . | | $350,000 |
| Net income . . . . . . . . . . . . . . . . . . . . . . . . . . . . . . . . . . . | $280,000 | |
| Less dividends declared . . . . . . . . . . . . . . . . . . . . . . . . . | 75,000 | |
| Increase in retained earnings . . . . . . . . . . . . . . . . . . . . . | | 205,000 |
| Retained earnings, June 30, 2006 . . . . . . . . . . . . . . . . . . | | $555,000 |

## Restrictions

The retained earnings available for use as dividends may be limited by action of a corporation's board of directors. These amounts, called *restrictions* or **appropriations**, remain part of the retained earnings. However, they must be disclosed, usually in the notes to the financial statements.

Restrictions may be classified as either legal, contractual, or discretionary. The board of directors may be legally required to restrict retained earnings because of state laws. For example, some state laws require that retained earnings be restricted by the amount of treasury stock purchased, so that legal capital will not be used for dividends. The board may also be required to restrict retained earnings because of contractual requirements. For example, the terms of a bank loan may require restrictions, so that money for repaying the loan will not be used for dividends. Finally, the board may restrict retained earnings voluntarily. For example, the board may limit dividend distributions so that more money is available for expanding the business.

## Prior Period Adjustments

Material errors in a prior period's net income may arise from mathematical mistakes and from mistakes in applying accounting principles. The effect of material errors

---

[12]*Statement of Financial Accounting Standards No. 129*, "Disclosure Information about Capital Structure," Financial Accounting Standards Board (Norwalk, Connecticut: 1997).

that are not discovered within the same fiscal period in which they occurred should not be included in determining net income for the current period. Instead, corrections of such errors, called ***prior period adjustments***, are reported in the retained earnings statement. These adjustments are reported as an adjustment to the retained earnings balance at the beginning of the period in which the error is discovered and corrected.[13]

# Financial Analysis and Interpretation

**objective 9**

Compute and interpret the dividend yield on common stock.

The ***dividend yield*** indicates the rate of return to stockholders in terms of cash dividend distributions. Although the dividend yield can be computed for both preferred and common stock, it is most often computed for common stock. This is because most preferred stock has a stated dividend rate or amount. In contrast, the amount of common stock dividends normally varies with the profitability of the corporation.

The dividend yield is computed by dividing the annual dividends paid per share of common stock by the market price per share at a specific date, as shown below.

$$\text{Dividend Yield} = \frac{\text{Dividends per Share of Common Stock}}{\text{Market Price per Share of Common Stock}}$$

To illustrate, the market price of **Coca-Cola**'s common stock was $44.28 as of the close of business, July 15, 2003. During the past year, Coca-Cola had paid dividends of $0.88 per share. Thus, the dividend yield of Coca-Cola's common stock is 2.0% ($0.88/$44.28). Because the market price of a corporation's stock will vary from day to day, its dividend yield will also vary from day to day.

The dividend yield on common stock is of special interest to investors whose main objective is to receive a current dividend return on their investment. This is in contrast to investors whose main objective is a rapid increase in the market price of their investments. For example, technology companies often do not pay dividends but reinvest their earnings in research and development. The main attraction of such stocks, such as **Cisco Systems, Inc.**'s common stock, is the expectation of the market price of the stock rising. Since many factors affect stock prices, an investment strategy relying solely on market price increases is more risky than a strategy based on dividend yields.

## SPOTLIGHT ON STRATEGY

### FASHION BLUES

During the 1990s, **The Gap** became the nation's largest specialty apparel retailer, with sales rising from $1.93 billion in 1990 to $11.64 billion in 1999. The Gap achieved this rapid growth by employing a strategy that emphasized simple, high-quality, casual clothing. Its strategy was aided by the shift in the 1990s to casual attire in the workplace. However, The Gap's same-store sales and profits have plummeted over the past year and a half. Perhaps never before have so many shoppers stopped patronizing a retail chain so quickly. So what happened?

Many former customers blame The Gap's changing fashion mix towards more far-fetched fashions, such as a denim trenchcoat with faux-fur collar, a bleached graphic T shirt, and fuschia-glittered disco jeans. In other words, The Gap became too trendy for its targeted customers, who are between the ages of 20 and 30. In addition, as The Gap expanded its trendy fashions, it curtailed customer choices within its basic apparel. For example, one former customer visited a Gap store in search of Capri pants but wasn't pleased with what she found. "You can't take pink and baby-blue to work, " she said.

**Source:** Adapted from "Gap's Image Is Wearing Out," by Amy Merrick, *The Wall Street Journal*, December 6, 2001.

---

[13]Prior period adjustments are illustrated in advanced texts.

# Key Points

### 1 Describe the nature of the corporate form of organization.

Corporations have a separate legal existence, transferable units of stock, and limited stockholders' liability. Corporations may be either public or private corporations, and they are subject to federal income taxes.

The documents included in forming a corporation include an application of incorporation, articles of incorporation, and bylaws. Costs often incurred in organizing a corporation include legal fees, taxes, state incorporation fees, and promotional costs. Such costs are debited to an expense account entitled Organizational Expenses.

### 2 List the two main sources of stockholders' equity.

The two main sources of stockholders' equity are (1) capital contributed by the stockholders and others, called paid-in capital, and (2) net income retained in the business, called retained earnings. Stockholders' equity is reported in a corporation balance sheet according to these two sources.

### 3 List the major sources of paid-in capital, including the various classes of stock.

The main source of paid-in capital is from issuing stock. The two primary classes of stock are common stock and preferred stock. Preferred stock is normally nonparticipating and may be cumulative or noncumulative. In addition to the issuance of stock, paid-in capital may arise from treasury stock transactions.

### 4 Journalize the entries for issuing stock.

When a corporation issues stock at par for cash, the cash account is debited and the class of stock issued is credited for its par amount. When a corporation issues stock at more than par, Paid-In Capital in Excess of Par is credited for the difference between the cash received and the par value of the stock. When stock is issued in exchange for assets other than cash, the assets acquired should be recorded at their fair market value.

When no-par stock is issued, the entire proceeds are credited to the stock account. No-par stock may be assigned a stated value per share, and the excess of the proceeds over the stated value may be credited to Paid-In Capital in Excess of Stated Value.

### 5 Journalize the entries for treasury stock transactions.

When a corporation buys its own stock, the cost method of accounting is normally used. Treasury Stock is debited for its cost, and Cash is credited. If the stock is resold, Treasury Stock is credited for its cost and any difference between the cost and the selling price is normally debited or credited to Paid-In Capital from Sale of Treasury Stock.

### 6 State the effect of stock splits on corporate financial statements.

When a corporation reduces the par or stated value of its common stock and issues a proportionate number of additional shares, a stock split has occurred. There are no changes in the balances of any corporation accounts, and no entry is required for a stock split.

### 7 Journalize the entries for cash dividends and stock dividends.

The entry to record a declaration of cash dividends debits Dividends and credits Dividends Payable for each class of stock. The payment of dividends is recorded in the normal manner. When a stock dividend is declared, Stock Dividends is debited for the fair value of the stock to be issued. Stock Dividends Distributable is credited for the par or stated value of the common stock to be issued. The difference between the fair value of the stock and its par or stated value is credited to Paid-In Capital in Excess of Par—Common Stock. When the stock is issued on the date of payment, Stock Dividends Distributable is debited and Common Stock is credited for the par or stated value of the stock issued.

### 8 Describe and illustrate the reporting of stockholders' equity.

Significant changes in the sources of stockholders' equity—paid-in capital and retained earnings—may be reported in separate statements or notes that support the balance sheet presentation. Changes in retained earnings may be reported by preparing a separate retained earnings statement, a combined income and retained earnings statement, or a statement of stockholders' equity. Restrictions to retained earnings must be disclosed, usually in the notes to the financial statements. Material errors in a prior period's net income, called prior-period adjustments, are reported in the retained earnings statement.

### 9 Compute and interpret the dividend yield on common stock.

The dividend yield indicates the rate of return to stockholders in terms of cash dividend distributions. It is computed by dividing the annual dividends paid per share of common stock by the market price per share at a specific date. This ratio is of special interest to investors whose main objective is to receive a current dividend return on their investment.

# Key Terms

| | | |
|---|---|---|
| cash dividend (493) | outstanding stock (486) | retained earnings statement (497) |
| common stock (487) | paid-in capital (484) | stated value (486) |
| cumulative preferred stock (488) | par (486) | stock (482) |
| deficit (486) | preferred stock (487) | stock dividend (494) |
| discount (489) | premium (489) | stock split (492) |
| dividend yield (498) | prior period adjustments (498) | stockholders (482) |
| nonparticipating preferred stock (487) | restrictions (497) | stockholders' equity (484) |
| | retained earnings (484) | treasury stock (491) |

# Illustrative Problem

Altenburg Inc. is a lighting fixture wholesaler located in Arizona. During its current fiscal year, ended December 31, 2006, Altenburg Inc. completed the following selected transactions:

Feb.    3. Purchased 2,500 shares of its own common stock at $26, recording the stock at cost. (Prior to the purchase, there were 40,000 shares of $20 par common stock outstanding.)

May    1. Declared a semiannual dividend of $1 on the 10,000 shares of preferred stock and a 30¢ dividend on the common stock to stockholders of record on May 31, payable on June 15.

June 15. Paid the cash dividends.

Sept. 23. Sold 1,000 shares of treasury stock at $28, receiving cash.

Nov.    1. Declared semiannual dividends of $1 on the preferred stock and 30¢ on the common stock. In addition, a 5% common stock dividend was declared on the common stock outstanding, to be capitalized at the fair market value of the common stock, which is estimated at $30.

Dec.    1. Paid the cash dividends and issued the certificates for the common stock dividend.

### Instructions
Journalize the entries to record the transactions for Altenburg Inc.

### Solution

| 2006 | | | | | |
|---|---|---|---|---|---|
| Feb. | 3 | Treasury Stock | | 65 0 0 0 00 | |
| | |     Cash | | | 65 0 0 0 00 |
| | | | | | |
| May | 1 | Cash Dividends | | 21 2 5 0 00 | |
| | |     Cash Dividends Payable | | | 21 2 5 0 00 * |
| | |        *(10,000 × $1) + [(40,000 − 2,500) | | | |
| | |        × $0.30] | | | |
| | | | | | |
| June | 15 | Cash Dividends Payable | | 21 2 5 0 00 | |
| | |     Cash | | | 21 2 5 0 00 |
| | | | | | |
| Sept. | 23 | Cash | | 28 0 0 0 00 | |
| | |     Treasury Stock | | | 26 0 0 0 00 |
| | |     Paid-In Capital from Sale of Treasury Stock | | | 2 0 0 0 00 |

| | | | | | |
|---|---|---|---|---|---|
| Nov. | 1 | Cash Dividends | 21 5 5 0 00 * | | |
| | | Cash Dividends Payable | | 21 5 5 0 00 | |
| | | *(10,000 × $1) + [(40,000 − 1,500) | | | |
| | | × $0.30] | | | |
| | | | | | |
| | 1 | Stock Dividends | 57 7 5 0 00 * | | |
| | | Stock Dividends Distributable | | 38 5 0 0 00 | |
| | | Paid-In Capital in Excess of | | | |
| | | Par—Common Stock | | 19 2 5 0 00 | |
| | | *(40,000 − 1,500) × 5% × $30 | | | |
| | | | | | |
| Dec. | 1 | Cash Dividends Payable | 21 5 5 0 00 | | |
| | | Stock Dividends Distributable | 38 5 0 0 00 | | |
| | | Cash | | 21 5 5 0 00 | |
| | | Common Stock | | 38 5 0 0 00 | |

# Self-Examination Questions (Answers at End of Chapter)

1. If a corporation has outstanding 1,000 shares of 9% cumulative preferred stock of $100 par and dividends have been passed for the preceding three years, what is the amount of preferred dividends that must be declared in the current year before a dividend can be declared on common stock?
   A. $ 9,000        C. $36,000
   B. $27,000        D. $45,000

2. Paid-in capital for a corporation may arise from which of the following sources?
   A. Issuing cumulative preferred stock
   B. Receiving donations of real estate
   C. Selling the corporation's treasury stock
   D. All of the above

3. The Stockholders' Equity section of the balance sheet may include:

   A. Common Stock
   B. Stock Divdiends Distributable
   C. Preferred Stock
   D. All of the above

4. If a corporation reacquires its own stock, the stock is listed on the balance sheet in the:
   A. Current Assets section.
   B. Long-Term Liabilities section.
   C. Stockholders' Equity section.
   D. Investments section.

5. A corporation has issued 25,000 shares of $100 par common stock and holds 3,000 of these shares as treasury stock. If the corporation declares a $2 per share cash dividend, what amount will be recorded as cash dividends?
   A. $22,000        C. $44,000
   B. $25,000        D. $50,000

# Class Discussion Questions

1. Describe the stockholders' liability to creditors of a corporation.
2. Why are most large businesses organized as corporations?
3. Of two corporations organized at approximately the same time and engaged in competing businesses, one issued $75 par common stock, and the other issued $1 par common stock. Do the par designations provide any indication as to which stock is preferable as an investment? Explain.
4. A stockbroker advises a client to "buy cumulative preferred stock. . . . With that type of stock, . . . [you] will never have to worry about losing the dividends." Is the broker right?

5. What are some of the factors that influence the market price of a corporation's stock?

6. When a corporation issues stock at a premium, is the premium income? Explain.

7. a. In what respect does treasury stock differ from unissued stock?

   b. How should treasury stock be presented on the balance sheet?

8. A corporation reacquires 10,000 shares of its own $25 par common stock for $420,000, recording it at cost. (a) What effect does this transaction have on revenue or expense of the period? (b) What effect does it have on stockholders' equity?

9. The treasury stock in Question 8 is resold for $500,000. (a) What is the effect on the corporation's revenue of the period? (b) What is the effect on stockholders' equity?

10. What is the primary purpose of a stock split?

11. (a) What are the three conditions for the declaration and the payment of a cash dividend? (b) The dates in connection with the declaration of a cash dividend are July 1, August 15, and September 1. Identify each date.

12. A corporation with both cumulative preferred stock and common stock outstanding has a substantial credit balance in its retained earnings account at the beginning of the current fiscal year. Although net income for the current year is sufficient to pay the preferred dividend of $250,000 each quarter and a common dividend of $610,000 each quarter, the board of directors declares dividends only on the preferred stock. Suggest possible reasons for passing the dividends on the common stock.

13. An owner of 150 shares of Morse Company common stock receives a stock dividend of 3 shares. (a) What is the effect of the stock dividend on the stockholder's proportionate interest (equity) in the corporation? (b) How does the total equity of 153 shares compare with the total equity of 150 shares before the stock dividend?

14. a. Where should a declared but unpaid cash dividend be reported on the balance sheet?

    b. Where should a declared but unissued stock dividend be reported on the balance sheet?

15. What is the primary advantage of combining the retained earnings statement with the income statement?

16. What are the three classifications of appropriations and how are appropriations normally reported in the financial statements?

17. Indicate how prior period adjustments would be reported on the financial statements presented only for the current period.

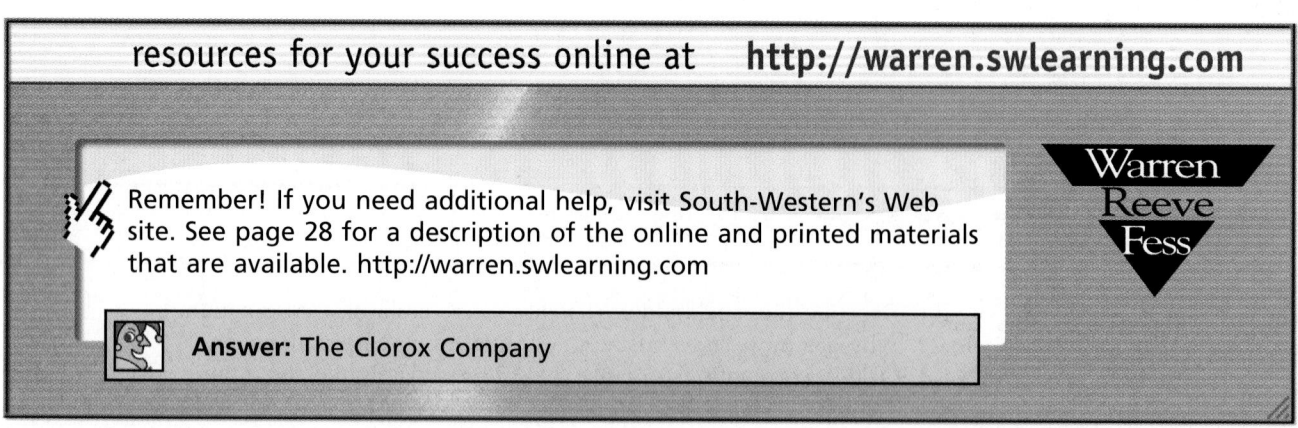

resources for your success online at **http://warren.swlearning.com**

Remember! If you need additional help, visit South-Western's Web site. See page 28 for a description of the online and printed materials that are available. http://warren.swlearning.com

Warren Reeve Fess

**Answer:** The Clorox Company

# Exercises

**EXERCISE 12-1**
*Dividends per share*
**Objective 3**

✓ *Preferred stock, 3rd year: $1.40*

Fiji Inc., a developer of radiology equipment, has stock outstanding as follows: 25,000 shares of 1% nonparticipating, cumulative preferred stock of $100 par, and 250,000 shares of $50 par common. During its first five years of operations, the following amounts were distributed as dividends: first year, none; second year, $40,000; third year, $80,000; fourth year, $120,000; fifth year, $140,000. Calculate the dividends per share on each class of stock for each of the five years.

**EXERCISE 12-2**
*Dividends per share*
**Objective 3**

✓ *Preferred stock, 3rd year: $0.75*

Infinity.com, a software development firm, has stock outstanding as follows: 100,000 shares of 2% cumulative, nonparticipating preferred stock of $20 par, and 50,000 shares of $100 par common. During its first five years of operations, the following amounts were distributed as dividends: first year, none; second year, $45,000; third year, $110,000; fourth year, $130,000; fifth year, $180,000. Calculate the dividends per share on each class of stock for each of the five years.

**EXERCISE 12-3**
*Entries for issuing par stock*
**Objective 4**

On July 7, Sloth Inc., a marble contractor, issued for cash 40,000 shares of $25 par common stock at $40, and on October 20, it issued for cash 15,000 shares of $100 par preferred stock at $120.

a. Journalize the entries for July 7 and October 20.
b. What is the total amount invested (total paid-in capital) by all stockholders as of October 20?

**EXERCISE 12-4**
*Entries for issuing no-par stock*
**Objective 4**

On February 20, Mudguard Corp., a carpet wholesaler, issued for cash 100,000 shares of no-par common stock (with a stated value of $10) at $15, and on April 30, it issued for cash 4,000 shares of $25 par preferred stock at $30.

a. Journalize the entries for February 20 and April 30, assuming that the common stock is to be credited with the stated value.
b. What is the total amount invested (total paid-in capital) by all stockholders as of April 30?

**EXERCISE 12-5**
*Issuing stock for assets other than cash*
**Objective 4**

On August 29, Welch Corporation, a wholesaler of hydraulic lifts, acquired land in exchange for 10,000 shares of $15 par common stock with a current market price of $28. Journalize the entry to record the transaction.

**EXERCISE 12-6**
*Selected stock transactions*
**Objective 4**

Megaton Corp., an electric guitar retailer, was organized by Bonita Eaves, Helen Brock, and Freida Sager. The charter authorized 400,000 shares of common stock with a par of $10. The following transactions affecting stockholders' equity were completed during the first year of operations:

a. Issued 5,000 shares of stock at par to Brock for cash.
b. Issued 200 shares of stock at par to Eaves for promotional services provided in connection with the organization of the corporation, and issued 1,200 shares of stock at par to Eaves for cash.
c. Purchased land and a building from Sager. The building is mortgaged for $180,000 for 20 years at 6%, and there is accrued interest of $900 on the mortgage note at the time of the purchase. It is agreed that the land is to be priced at $60,000 and the building at $200,000, and that Sagar's equity will be exchanged for stock at par. The corporation agreed to assume responsibility for paying the mortgage note and the accrued interest.

Journalize the entries to record the transactions.

**EXERCISE 12-7**
*Issuing stock*
**Objective 4**

Pearl.com, with an authorization of 50,000 shares of preferred stock and 200,000 shares of common stock, completed several transactions involving its stock on May 1, the first day of operations. The trial balance at the close of the day follows:

| | | |
|---|---:|---:|
| Cash | 475,000 | |
| Land | 45,000 | |
| Buildings | 80,000 | |
| Preferred 4% Stock, $50 par | | 100,000 |
| Paid-In Capital in Excess of Par—Preferred Stock | | 25,000 |
| Common Stock, $100 par | | 400,000 |
| Paid-In Capital in Excess of Par—Common Stock | | 75,000 |
| | 600,000 | 600,000 |

All shares within each class of stock were sold at the same price. The preferred stock was issued in exchange for the land and buildings.

Journalize the two entries to record the transactions summarized in the trial balance.

**EXERCISE 12-8**
*Issuing stock*
**Objective 4**

Calvert Products Inc., a wholesaler of office products, was organized on January 5 of the current year, with an authorization of 80,000 shares of 2% noncumulative preferred stock, $50 par and 250,000 shares of $100 par common stock. The following selected transactions were completed during the first year of operations:

Jan.  5. Issued 10,000 shares of common stock at par for cash.
  18. Issued 100 shares of common stock at par to an attorney in payment of legal fees for organizing the corporation.
Feb. 13. Issued 4,250 shares of common stock in exchange for land, buildings, and equipment with fair market prices of $50,000, $280,000, and $120,000, respectively.
April 1. Issued 3,500 shares of preferred stock at $52 for cash.

Journalize the transactions.

**EXERCISE 12-9**
*Treasury stock transactions*
**Objective 5**
✓b. $5,500 credit

Crystal Springs Inc. bottles and distributes spring water. On June 1 of the current year, Crystal reacquired 2,500 shares of its common stock at $60 per share. On July 8, Crystal sold 1,500 of the reacquired shares at $65 per share. The remaining 1,000 shares were sold at $58 per share on November 2.

a. Journalize the transactions of June 1, July 8, and November 2.
b. What is the balance in Paid-In Capital from Sale of Treasury Stock on December 31 of the current year?
c. ▬▬➤ For what reasons might Crystal Springs have purchased the treasury stock?

**EXERCISE 12-10**
*Treasury stock transactions*
**Objectives 5, 8**
✓b. $50,000 credit

Geyser Inc. develops and produces spraying equipment for lawn maintenance and industrial uses. On March 3 of the current year, Geyser Inc. reacquired 7,500 shares of its common stock at $120 per share. On August 11, 4,000 of the reacquired shares were sold at $130 per share, and on October 3, 2,500 of the reacquired shares were sold at $124.

a. Journalize the transactions of March 3, August 11, and October 3.
b. What is the balance in Paid-In Capital from Sale of Treasury Stock on December 31 of the current year?
c. What is the balance in Treasury Stock on December 31 of the current year?
d. How will the balance in Treasury Stock be reported on the balance sheet?

**EXERCISE 12-11**
*Treasury stock transactions*
**Objectives 5, 8**
✓b. $1,500 credit

Aspen Inc. bottles and distributes spring water. On August 1 of the current year, Aspen Inc. reacquired 12,000 shares of its common stock at $36 per share. On September 23, Aspen Inc. sold 7,500 of the reacquired shares at $38 per share. The remaining 4,500 shares were sold at $33 per share on December 29.

a. Journalize the transactions of August 1, September 23, and December 29.

b. What is the balance in Paid-In Capital from Sale of Treasury Stock on December 31 of the current year?

c. Where will the balance in Paid-In Capital from Sale of Treasury Stock be reported on the balance sheet?

d. ▭▭▶ For what reasons might Aspen Inc. have purchased the treasury stock?

**EXERCISE 12-12**
*Effect of stock split*
Objective 6

Paranormal Corporation wholesales ovens and ranges to restaurants throughout the Midwest. Paranormal Corporation, which had 25,000 shares of common stock outstanding, declared a 5-for-1 stock split (4 additional shares for each share issued).

a. What will be the number of shares outstanding after the split?

b. If the common stock had a market price of $165 per share before the stock split, what would be an approximate market price per share after the split?

**EXERCISE 12-13**
*Effect of cash dividend and stock split*
Objectives 6, 7

Indicate whether the following actions would (+) increase, (−) decrease, or (0) not affect Indigo Inc.'s total assets, liabilities, and stockholders' equity:

| | | Assets | Liabilities | Stockholders' Equity |
|---|---|---|---|---|
| (1) | Declaring a cash dividend | _____ | _____ | _____ |
| (2) | Paying the cash dividend declared in (1) | _____ | _____ | _____ |
| (3) | Authorizing and issuing stock certificates in a stock split | _____ | _____ | _____ |
| (4) | Declaring a stock dividend | _____ | _____ | _____ |
| (5) | Issuing stock certificates for the stock dividend declared in (4) | _____ | _____ | _____ |

**EXERCISE 12-14**
*Entries for cash dividends*
Objective 7

The dates of importance in connection with a cash dividend of $120,000 on a corporation's common stock are February 13, March 15, and April 10. Journalize the entries required on each date.

**EXERCISE 12-15**
*Entries for stock dividends*
Objective 7

✓ b. (1) $13,250,000
   (3) $43,828,000

Health Co. is an HMO for twelve businesses in the Chicago area. The following account balances appear on the balance sheet of Health Co.: Common stock (250,000 shares authorized), $100 par, $12,500,000; Paid-in capital in excess of par—common stock, $750,000; and Retained earnings, $30,578,000. The board of directors declared a 2% stock dividend when the market price of the stock was $110 a share. Health Co. reported no income or loss for the current year.

a. Journalize the entries to record (1) the declaration of the dividend, capitalizing an amount equal to market value, and (2) the issuance of the stock certificates.

b. Determine the following amounts before the stock dividend was declared: (1) total paid-in capital, (2) total retained earnings, and (3) total stockholders' equity.

c. Determine the following amounts after the stock dividend was declared and closing entries were recorded at the end of the year: (1) total paid-in capital, (2) total retained earnings, and (3) total stockholders' equity.

**EXERCISE 12-16**
*Selected stock and dividend transactions*
Objectives 6, 7

Selected transactions completed by Indy Boating Supply Corporation during the current fiscal year are as follows:

Feb. 9. Split the common stock 3 for 1 and reduced the par from $120 to $40 per share. After the split, there were 900,000 common shares outstanding.

Apr. 10. Declared semiannual dividends of $1 on 12,000 shares of preferred stock and $0.05 on the common stock to stockholders of record on April 20, payable on May 1.

May 1. Paid the cash dividends.

Oct. 12. Declared semiannual dividends of $1 on the preferred stock and $0.15 on the common stock (before the stock dividend). In addition, a 1% common stock dividend was declared on the common stock outstanding. The fair market value of the common stock is estimated at $48.

Nov. 14. Paid the cash dividends and issued the certificates for the common stock dividend.

Journalize the transactions.

**EXERCISE 12-17**
*Reporting paid-in capital*
**Objective 8**

✓ *Total paid-in capital, $1,541,250*

The following accounts and their balances were selected from the unadjusted trial balance of Sailors Inc., a freight forwarder, at August 31, the end of the current fiscal year:

| | |
|---|---:|
| Preferred 2% Stock, $100 par | $ 750,000 |
| Paid-In Capital in Excess of Par—Preferred Stock | 90,000 |
| Common Stock, no par, $5 stated value | 562,500 |
| Paid-In Capital in Excess of Stated Value—Common Stock | 75,000 |
| Paid-In Capital from Sale of Treasury Stock | 63,750 |
| Retained Earnings | 1,875,000 |

Prepare the Paid-In Capital portion of the Stockholders' Equity section of the balance sheet. There are 200,000 shares of common stock authorized and 80,000 shares of preferred stock authorized.

**EXERCISE 12-18**
*Stockholders' equity section of balance sheet*
**Objective 8**

SPREADSHEET

✓ *Total stockholders' equity, $2,165,000*

The following accounts and their balances appear in the ledger of Dimension Inc. on June 30 of the current year:

| | |
|---|---:|
| Common Stock, $25 par | $ 750,000 |
| Paid-In Capital in Excess of Par | 120,000 |
| Paid-In Capital from Sale of Treasury Stock | 25,000 |
| Retained Earnings | 1,350,000 |
| Treasury Stock | 80,000 |

Prepare the Stockholders' Equity section of the balance sheet as of June 30. Sixty thousand shares of common stock are authorized, and 2,000 shares have been reacquired.

**EXERCISE 12-19**
*Stockholders' equity section of balance sheet*
**Objective 8**

SPREADSHEET

✓ *Total stockholders' equity, $5,193,000*

Big Boy Toys Inc. retails racing products for BMWs, Porsches, and Ferraris. The following accounts and their balances appear in the ledger of Big Boy Toys Inc. on October 31, the end of the current year:

| | |
|---|---:|
| Common Stock, $4 par | $ 600,000 |
| Paid-In Capital in Excess of Par—Common Stock | 210,000 |
| Paid-In Capital in Excess of Par—Preferred Stock | 78,000 |
| Paid-In Capital from Sale of Treasury Stock—Common | 42,000 |
| Preferred 2% Stock, $100 par | 480,000 |
| Retained Earnings | 3,903,000 |
| Treasury Stock—Common | 120,000 |

Ten thousand shares of preferred and 250,000 shares of common stock are authorized. There are 12,000 shares of common stock held as treasury stock.

Prepare the Stockholders' Equity section of the balance sheet as of October 31, the end of the current year.

**EXERCISE 12-20**
*Retained earnings statement*
**Objective 8**

✓ *Retained earnings, July 31, $2,441,400*

Bravo Corporation, a manufacturer of industrial pumps, reports the following results for the year ending July 31, 2006:

| | |
|---|---:|
| Retained earnings, August 1, 2005 | $2,213,400 |
| Net income | 558,000 |
| Cash dividends declared | 180,000 |
| Stock dividends declared | 150,000 |

Prepare a retained earnings statement for the fiscal year ended July 31, 2006.

**EXERCISE 12-21**
*Stockholders' equity section of balance sheet*
Objective 8

WHAT'S WRONG WITH THIS?

✓ Corrected total stockholders' equity, $3,064,200

List the errors in the following Stockholders' Equity section of the balance sheet prepared as of the end of the current year.

**Stockholders' Equity**

| | | |
|---|---:|---:|
| Paid-in capital: | | |
| Preferred 2% stock, cumulative, $50 par | | |
| (9,800 shares authorized and issued) | $ 490,000 | |
| Excess of issue price over par | 84,000 | $ 574,000 |
| Retained earnings | | 906,000 |
| Treasury stock (5,000 shares at cost) | | 105,000 |
| Dividends payable | | 140,000 |
| Total paid-in capital | | $1,725,000 |
| Common stock, $20 par (100,000 shares | | |
| authorized, 75,000 shares issued) | | 1,789,200 |
| Organizing costs | | 100,000 |
| Total stockholders' equity | | $3,614,200 |

**EXERCISE 12-22**
*Dividend yield*
Objective 9

REAL WORLD

eBay developed a Web-based marketplace at **http://www.ebay.com**, in which individuals can buy and sell a variety of items. eBay also developed PayPal, an on-line payments system that allows businesses and individuals to send and receive online payments securely. In a recent annual report, eBay published the following dividend policy:

> *We have never paid cash dividends on our stock, and currently anticipate that we will continue to retain any future earnings to finance the growth of our business.*

Given eBay's dividend policy, why would an investor be attracted to its stock?

**EXERCISE 12-23**
*Dividend yield*
Objective 9

REAL WORLD

In 2002, **Hershey Foods Corporation** paid dividends of $1.26 per share to its common stockholders (excluding its Class B Common Stock). The market price of Hershey's common stock on December 31, 2002, was $67.44.

a. Determine Hershey's dividend yield on its common stock as of December 31, 2002.
b. What conclusions can you draw from an analysis of Hershey's dividend yield?

# Problems Series A

**PROBLEM 12-1A**
*Dividends on preferred and common stock*
Objective 3

SPREADSHEET

✓ 1. Common dividends in 2002: $10,000

Lemonds Corp. manufactures mountain bikes and distributes them through retail outlets in Oregon and Washington. Lemonds Corp. has declared the following annual dividends over a six-year period: 2002, $40,000; 2003, $18,000; 2004, $24,000; 2005, $27,000; 2006, $65,000; and 2007, $54,000. During the entire period, the outstanding stock of the company was composed of 25,000 shares of cumulative, non-participating, 6% preferred stock, $20 par, and 40,000 shares of common stock, $1 par.

**Instructions**

1. Calculate the total dividends and the per-share dividends declared on each class of stock for each of the six years. There were no dividends in arrears on January 1, 2002. Summarize the data in tabular form, using the following column headings:

| Year | Total Dividends | Preferred Dividends | | Common Dividends | |
|---|---|---|---|---|---|
| | | Total | Per Share | Total | Per Share |
| 2002 | $40,000 | | | | |
| 2003 | 18,000 | | | | |
| 2004 | 24,000 | | | | |
| 2005 | 27,000 | | | | |
| 2006 | 65,000 | | | | |
| 2007 | 54,000 | | | | |

2. Calculate the average annual dividend per share for each class of stock for the six-year period.

3. Assuming that the preferred stock was sold at par and common stock was sold at $8 at the beginning of the six-year period, calculate the average annual percentage return on initial shareholders' investment, based on the average annual dividend per share (a) for preferred stock and (b) for common stock.

**PROBLEM 12-2A**
*Stock transaction for corporate expansion*
Objective 4

P.A.S.S.

Diamond Optics produces medical lasers for use in hospitals. The following accounts and their balances appear in the ledger of Diamond Optics on September 30 of the current year:

| | |
|---|---|
| Preferred 5% Stock, $100 par (20,000 shares authorized, 12,000 shares issued) | $1,200,000 |
| Paid-In Capital in Excess of Par—Preferred Stock | 180,000 |
| Common Stock, $25 par (100,000 shares authorized, 72,000 shares issued) | 1,800,000 |
| Paid-In Capital in Excess of Par—Common Stock | 240,000 |
| Retained Earnings | 3,572,500 |

At the annual stockholders' meeting on October 19, the board of directors presented a plan for modernizing and expanding plant operations at a cost of approximately $2,500,000. The plan provided (a) that the corporation borrow $780,000, (b) that 6,000 shares of the unissued preferred stock be issued through an underwriter, and (c) that a building, valued at $900,000, and the land on which it is located, valued at $120,000, be acquired in accordance with preliminary negotiations by the issuance of 24,000 shares of common stock. The plan was approved by the stockholders and accomplished by the following transactions:

Nov. 5. Borrowed $780,000 from Bozeman National Bank, giving a 7% mortgage note.

20. Issued 6,000 shares of preferred stock, receiving $120 per share in cash from the underwriter.

23. Issued 24,000 shares of common stock in exchange for land and a building, according to the plan.

No other transactions occurred during November.

**Instructions**
Journalize the entries to record the foregoing transactions.

**PROBLEM 12-3A**
*Selected stock transactions*
Objectives 4, 5, 7

P.A.S.S.

Elk River Corporation sells and services pipe welding equipment in Wyoming. The following selected accounts appear in the ledger of Elk River Corporation on January 1, 2006, the beginning of the current fiscal year:

| | |
|---|---|
| Preferred 2% Stock, $100 par (80,000 shares authorized, 18,000 shares issued) | $1,800,000 |
| Paid-In Capital in Excess of Par—Preferred Stock | 172,500 |
| Common Stock, $10 par (800,000 shares authorized, 500,000 shares issued) | 5,000,000 |
| Paid-In Capital in Excess of Par—Common Stock | 1,236,000 |
| Retained Earnings | 6,450,000 |

During the year, the corporation completed a number of transactions affecting the stockholders' equity. They are summarized as follows:

a. Purchased 60,000 shares of treasury common for $1,080,000.
b. Sold 20,000 shares of treasury common for $420,000.
c. Sold 7,000 shares of preferred 2% stock at $108.
d. Issued 40,000 shares of common stock at $23, receiving cash.
e. Sold 35,000 shares of treasury common for $595,000.
f. Declared cash dividends of $2 per share on preferred stock and $0.16 per share on common stock.
g. Paid the cash dividends.

**Instructions**

Journalize the entries to record the transactions. Identify each entry by letter.

**PROBLEM 12-4A**
*Entries for selected corporate transactions*

**Objectives 4, 5, 7, 8**

SPREADSHEET

P.A.S.S.

✓ 4. Total stockholders' equity, $1,796,950

Areotronics Enterprises Inc. produces aeronautical navigation equipment. The stockholders' equity accounts of Areotronics Enterprises Inc., with balances on January 1, 2006, are as follows:

| | |
|---|---|
| Common Stock, $10 stated value (100,000 shares authorized, 60,000 shares issued) | $600,000 |
| Paid-In Capital in Excess of Stated Value | 150,000 |
| Retained Earnings | 497,750 |
| Treasury Stock (7,500 shares, at cost) | 120,000 |

The following selected transactions occurred during the year:

Jan. 19. Paid cash dividends of $0.60 per share on the common stock. The dividend had been properly recorded when declared on December 28 of the preceding fiscal year for $31,500.
Feb. 2. Sold all of the treasury stock for $150,000.
Mar. 15. Issued 20,000 shares of common stock for $480,000.
July 30. Declared a 2% stock dividend on common stock, to be capitalized at the market price of the stock, which is $25 a share.
Aug. 30. Issued the certificates for the dividend declared on July 30.
Oct. 10. Purchased 5,000 shares of treasury stock for $105,000.
Dec. 30. Declared a $0.50-per-share dividend on common stock.
      31. Closed the credit balance of the income summary account, $182,500.
      31. Closed the two dividends accounts to Retained Earnings.

**Instructions**

1. Enter the January 1 balances in T accounts for the stockholders' equity accounts listed. Also prepare T accounts for the following: Paid-In Capital from Sale of Treasury Stock; Stock Dividends Distributable; Stock Dividends; Cash Dividends.
2. Journalize the entries to record the transactions, and post to the eight selected accounts.
3. Prepare a retained earnings statement for the year ended December 31, 2006.
4. Prepare the stockholders' equity section of the December 31, 2006 balance sheet.

**PROBLEM 12-5A**
*Entries for selected corporate transactions*

**Objectives 4, 5, 6, 7**

SPREADSHEET

P.A.S.S.

Serra do Mar Corporation manufactures and distributes leisure clothing. Selected transactions completed by Serra do Mar during the current fiscal year are as follows:

Jan. 8. Split the common stock 3 for 1 and reduced the par from $18 to $6 per share. After the split, there were 600,000 common shares outstanding.
Mar. 20. Declared semiannual dividends of $1 on 20,000 shares of preferred stock and $0.14 on the 600,000 shares of $10 par common stock to stockholders of record on March 31, payable on April 20.
Apr. 20. Paid the cash dividends.
May 8. Purchased 50,000 shares of the corporation's own common stock at $48, recording the stock at cost.

Aug. 2. Sold 30,000 shares of treasury stock at $56, receiving cash.

Sept. 15. Declared semiannual dividends of $1 on the preferred stock and $0.07 on the common stock (before the stock dividend). In addition, a 1% common stock dividend was declared on the common stock outstanding, to be capitalized at the fair market value of the common stock, which is estimated at $52.

Oct. 15. Paid the cash dividends and issued the certificates for the common stock dividend.

**Instructions**

Journalize the transactions.

# Problems Series B

### PROBLEM 12-1B
*Dividends on preferred and common stock*

**Objective 3**

SPREADSHEET

✓ *1. Common dividends in 2004: $22,000*

Da Show Inc. owns and operates movie theaters throughout Texas and California. Da Show has declared the following annual dividends over a six-year period: 2002, $18,000; 2003, $54,000; 2004, $70,000; 2005, $75,000; 2006, $80,000; and 2007, $90,000. During the entire period, the outstanding stock of the company was composed of 20,000 shares of cumulative, nonparticipating, 2% preferred stock, $100 par, and 25,000 shares of common stock, $10 par.

**Instructions**

1. Calculate the total dividends and the per-share dividends declared on each class of stock for each of the six years. There were no dividends in arrears on January 1, 2002. Summarize the data in tabular form, using the following column headings:

| Year | Total Dividends | Preferred Dividends | | Common Dividends | |
|------|-----------------|---------------------|------------|------------------|------------|
| | | Total | Per Share | Total | Per Share |
| 2002 | $18,000 | | | | |
| 2003 | 54,000 | | | | |
| 2004 | 70,000 | | | | |
| 2005 | 75,000 | | | | |
| 2006 | 80,000 | | | | |
| 2007 | 90,000 | | | | |

2. Calculate the average annual dividend per share for each class of stock for the six-year period.

3. Assuming that the preferred stock was sold at par and common stock was sold at $39.20 at the beginning of the six-year period, calculate the average annual percentage return on initial shareholders' investment, based on the average annual dividend per share (a) for preferred stock and (b) for common stock.

### PROBLEM 12-2B
*Stock transactions for corporate expansion*

**Objective 4**

P.A.S.S.

On January 1 of the current year, the following accounts and their balances appear in the ledger of Dahof Corp., a meat processor:

| | |
|---|---|
| Preferred 4% Stock, $100 par (20,000 shares authorized, 6,000 shares issued) . . . . . . . . . . . . . . . . . . . . . . . . . . . . . | $ 600,000 |
| Paid-In Capital in Excess of Par—Preferred Stock . . . . . . . . . . | 120,000 |
| Common Stock, $50 par (100,000 shares authorized, 50,000 shares issued) . . . . . . . . . . . . . . . . . . . . . . . . . . . . . | 2,500,000 |
| Paid-In Capital in Excess of Par—Common Stock . . . . . . . . . . . | 320,000 |
| Retained Earnings . . . . . . . . . . . . . . . . . . . . . . . . . . . . . . . . . | 1,675,000 |

At the annual stockholders' meeting on March 6, the board of directors presented a plan for modernizing and expanding plant operations at a cost of approximately

$800,000. The plan provided (a) that a building, valued at $225,000, and the land on which it is located, valued at $45,000, be acquired in accordance with preliminary negotiations by the issuance of 4,800 shares of common stock, (b) that 3,000 shares of the unissued preferred stock be issued through an underwriter, and (c) that the corporation borrow $155,000. The plan was approved by the stockholders and accomplished by the following transactions:

April 3. Issued 4,800 shares of common stock in exchange for land and a building, according to the plan.
18. Issued 3,000 shares of preferred stock, receiving $125 per share in cash from the underwriter.
28. Borrowed $155,000 from Northeast National Bank, giving an 8% mortgage note.

No other transactions occurred during April.

**Instructions**
Journalize the entries to record the foregoing transactions.

**PROBLEM 12-3B**
*Selected stock transactions*
**Objectives 4, 5, 7**

P.A.S.S.

The following selected accounts appear in the ledger of Kingfisher Environmental Corporation on March 1, 2006, the beginning of the current fiscal year:

| | |
|---|---|
| Preferred 2% Stock, $75 par (10,000 shares authorized, 8,000 shares issued) | $ 600,000 |
| Paid-In Capital in Excess of Par—Preferred Stock | 100,000 |
| Common Stock, $10 par (50,000 shares authorized, 35,000 shares issued) | 350,000 |
| Paid-In Capital in Excess of Par—Common Stock | 85,000 |
| Retained Earnings | 1,050,000 |

During the year, the corporation completed a number of transactions affecting the stockholders' equity. They are summarized as follows:

a. Issued 7,500 shares of common stock at $24, receiving cash.
b. Sold 800 shares of preferred 2% stock at $81.
c. Purchased 3,000 shares of treasury common for $66,000.
d. Sold 1,800 shares of treasury common for $50,400.
e. Sold 750 shares of treasury common for $14,250.
f. Declared cash dividends of $1.50 per share on preferred stock and $0.40 per share on common stock.
g. Paid the cash dividends.

**Instructions**
Journalize the entries to record the transactions. Identify each entry by letter.

**PROBLEM 12-4B**
*Entries for selected corporate transactions*
**Objectives 4, 5, 7, 8**

SPREADSHEET
P.A.S.S.

✓ *4. Total stockholders' equity, $2,859,825*

Shoshone Enterprises Inc. manufactures bathroom fixtures. The stockholders' equity accounts of Shoshone Enterprises Inc., with balances on January 1, 2006, are as follows:

| | |
|---|---|
| Common Stock, $20 stated value (100,000 shares authorized, 75,000 shares issued) | $1,500,000 |
| Paid-In Capital in Excess of Stated Value | 180,000 |
| Retained Earnings | 725,000 |
| Treasury Stock (5,000 shares, at cost) | 140,000 |

The following selected transactions occurred during the year:

Jan. 28. Paid cash dividends of $0.80 per share on the common stock. The dividend had been properly recorded when declared on December 30 of the preceding fiscal year for $56,000.
Mar. 21. Issued 15,000 shares of common stock for $480,000.
May 10. Sold all of the treasury stock for $165,000.

July 1. Declared a 4% stock dividend on common stock, to be capitalized at the market price of the stock, which is $36 a share.

Aug. 11. Issued the certificates for the dividend declared on July 1.

Oct. 20. Purchased 7,500 shares of treasury stock for $255,000.

Dec. 27. Declared a $0.75-per-share dividend on common stock.

31. Closed the credit balance of the income summary account, $269,400.

31. Closed the two dividends accounts to Retained Earnings.

### Instructions

1. Enter the January 1 balances in T accounts for the stockholders' equity accounts listed. Also prepare T accounts for the following: Paid-In Capital from Sale of Treasury Stock; Stock Dividends Distributable; Stock Dividends; Cash Dividends.

2. Journalize the entries to record the transactions, and post to the eight selected accounts.

3. Prepare a retained earnings statement for the year ended December 31, 2006.

4. Prepare the stockholders' equity section of the December 31, 2006 balance sheet.

**PROBLEM 12-5B**
*Entries for selected corporate transactions*
**Objectives 4, 5, 6, 7**

SPREADSHEET
P.A.S.S.

Selected transactions completed by Mead Boating Supply Corporation during the current fiscal year are as follows:

Jan. 20. Split the common stock 5 for 1 and reduced the par from $50 to $10 per share. After the split, there were 500,000 common shares outstanding.

Apr. 1. Purchased 20,000 shares of the corporation's own common stock at $30, recording the stock at cost.

May 1. Declared semiannual dividends of $1.50 on 24,000 shares of preferred stock and $0.15 on the common stock to stockholders of record on May 20, payable on June 1.

June 1. Paid the cash dividends.

Aug. 7. Sold 12,000 shares of treasury stock at $38, receiving cash.

Nov. 15. Declared semiannual dividends of $1.50 on the preferred stock and $0.08 on the common stock (before the stock dividend). In addition, a 2% common stock dividend was declared on the common stock outstanding. The fair market value of the common stock is estimated at $35.

Dec. 15. Paid the cash dividends and issued the certificates for the common stock dividend.

### Instructions

Journalize the transactions.

# Special Activities

**ACTIVITY 12-1**
*Business strategy*

GROUP ACTIVITY

INTERNET

REAL WORLD

**7-Eleven** operates more than 22,000 convenience food stores worldwide. 7-Eleven stores are normally less than 3,000 square feet and carry a variety of items, including soft drinks, candy and snacks, cigarettes, milk, and t-shirts. Many stores also sell CITGO-brand gasoline. 7-Eleven faces increasing competition from other convenience store chains as well as from grocery and supermarket chains, grocery wholesalers and buying clubs, gasoline/miniconvenience stores, food stores, fast food chains, and variety, drug, and candy stores. In groups of three to four, answer the following questions:

1. Go to the 7-Eleven Web site, which is linked to the text's Web site at **http://warren.swlearning.com**. How did the name 7-Eleven orginate?

2. How many items do you think an average 7-Eleven carries?

3. Excluding gasoline, rank the following "seven" categories of merchandise in the order in which you believe they generate the most sales for 7-Eleven. Rank the merchandise category with the most sales 1, the second most sales 2, and so on.

<u>Merchandise Category</u>
- baked and fresh foods, such as bread and rolls
- beer and wine
- beverages, such as soft drinks and coffee
- candy and snacks
- dairy products
- nonfood products and services, such as automobile oil, toothpaste, coolers, money orders, and lottery tickets
- tobacco products

4. Describe some ways (strategies) that you think 7-Eleven can increase its same-store sales in the face of increasing competition.

## ACTIVITY 12-2
*Board of directors' actions*

**REAL WORLD**   **ETHICS**

In early 2002, Bernie Ebbers, the CEO of **WorldCom Group**, a major telecommunications company, was having personal financial troubles. Ebbers pledged a large stake of his Worldcom stock as security for some personal loans. As the price of Worldcom stock sank, Ebbers' bankers threatened to sell his stock in order to protect their loans. To avoid having his stock sold, Ebbers asked the board of directors of Worldcom to loan him nearly $400 million of corporate assets at 2.5% interest to pay off his bankers. The board agreed to lend him the money.

Comment on the decision of the board of directors in this situation.

## ACTIVITY 12-3
*Ethics and professional conduct in business*

**ETHICS**

Lois Heck and Keith Ryan are organizing Beaufort Unlimited Inc. to undertake a high-risk gold-mining venture in Canada. Lois and Keith tentatively plan to request authorization for 80,000,000 shares of common stock to be sold to the general public. Lois and Keith have decided to establish par of $1 per share in order to appeal to a wide variety of potential investors. Lois and Keith feel that investors would be more willing to invest in the company if they received a large quantity of shares for what might appear to be a "bargain" price.

Discuss whether Lois and Keith are behaving in a professional manner.

## ACTIVITY 12-4
*Issuing stock*

**WHAT DO YOU THINK?**

Kilimanjaro Inc. began operations on January 6, 2006, with the issuance of 400,000 shares of $50 par common stock. The sole stockholders of Kilimanjaro Inc. are Donna White and Dr. Larry Klein, who organized Kilimanjaro Inc. with the objective of developing a new flu vaccine. Dr. Klein claims that the flu vaccine, which is nearing the final development stage, will protect individuals against 98% of the flu types that have been medically identified. To complete the project, Kilimanjaro Inc. needs $20,000,000 of additional funds. The local banks have been unwilling to loan the funds because of the lack of sufficient collateral and the riskiness of the business.

The following is a conversation between Donna White, the chief executive officer of Kilimanjaro Inc., and Dr. Larry Klein, the leading researcher.

*White:* What are we going to do? The banks won't loan us any more money, and we've got to have $20 million to complete the project. We are so close! It would be a disaster to quit now. The only thing I can think of is to issue additional stock. Do you have any suggestions?

*Klein:* I guess you're right. But if the banks won't loan us any more money, how do you think we can find any investors to buy stock?

*White:* I've been thinking about that. What if we promise the investors that we will pay them 2% of net sales until they have received an amount equal to what they paid for the stock?

*Klein:* What happens when we pay back the $20 million? Do the investors get to keep the stock? If they do, it'll dilute our ownership.

*White:* How about, if after we pay back the $20 million, we make them turn in their stock for $100 per share? That's twice what they paid for it, plus they would have already gotten all their money back. That's a $100 profit per share for the investors.

*Klein:* It could work. We get our money, but don't have to pay any interest, dividends, or the $100 until we start generating net sales. At the same time, the investors could get their money back plus $100 per share.

*White:* We'll need current financial statements for the new investors. I'll get our accountant working on them and contact our attorney to draw up a legally binding contract for the new investors. Yes, this could work.

In late 2006, the attorney and the various regulatory authorities approved the new stock offering, and 400,000 shares of common stock were privately sold to new investors at the stock's par of $50.

In preparing financial statements for 2006, Donna White and Anita Sparks, the controller for Kilimanjaro Inc., have the following conversation.

*Sparks:* Donna, I've got a problem.

*White:* What's that, Anita?

*Sparks:* Issuing common stock to raise that additional $20 million was a great idea. But . . .

*White:* But what?

*Sparks:* I've got to prepare the 2006 annual financial statements, and I am not sure how to classify the common stock.

*White:* What do you mean? It's common stock.

*Sparks:* I'm not so sure. I called the auditor and explained how we are contractually obligated to pay the new stockholders 2% of net sales until $50 per share is paid. Then, we may be obligated to pay them $100 per share.

*White:* So . . .

*Sparks:* So the auditor thinks that we should classify the additional issuance of $20 million as debt, not stock! And, if we put the $20 million on the balance sheet as debt, we will violate our other loan agreements with the banks. And, if these agreements are violated, the banks may call in all our debt immediately. If they do that, we are in deep trouble. We'll probably have to file for bankruptcy. We just don't have the cash to pay off the banks.

1. Discuss the arguments for and against classifying the issuance of the $20 million of stock as debt.

2. What do you think might be a practical solution to this classification problem?

**ACTIVITY 12-5**
*Dividends*

Matterhorn Inc. has paid quarterly cash dividends since 1993. These dividends have steadily increased from $0.05 per share to the latest dividend declaration of $0.40 per share. The board of directors would like to continue this trend and is hesitant to suspend or decrease the amount of quarterly dividends. Unfortunately, sales dropped sharply in the fourth quarter of 2006 because of worsening economic conditions and increased competition. As a result, the board is uncertain as to whether it should declare a dividend for the last quarter of 2006.

On November 1, 2006, Matterhorn Inc. borrowed $400,000 from Cheyenne National Bank to use in modernizing its retail stores and to expand its product line in reaction to its competition. The terms of the 10-year, 12% loan require Matterhorn Inc. to:

a. Pay monthly interest on the last day of month.

b. Pay $40,000 of the principal each November 1, beginning in 2007.

c. Maintain a current ratio (current assets ÷ current liabilities) of 2.

d. Maintain a minimum balance (a compensating balance) of $20,000 in its Cheyenne National Bank account.

On December 31, 2006, $100,000 of the $400,000 loan had been disbursed in modernization of the retail stores and in expansion of the product line. Matterhorn Inc.'s balance sheet as of December 31, 2006, is as follows:

**Matterhorn Inc.**
**Balance Sheet**
**December 31, 2006**

### Assets

| | | | |
|---|---|---|---|
| Current assets: | | | |
| Cash | | $ 32,000 | |
| Marketable securities | | 300,000 | |
| Accounts receivable | $ 73,200 | | |
| Less allowance for doubtful accounts | 5,200 | 68,000 | |
| Merchandise inventory | | 100,000 | |
| Prepaid expenses | | 3,600 | |
| Total current assets | | | $ 503,600 |
| Property, plant, and equipment: | | | |
| Land | | $120,000 | |
| Buildings | $760,000 | | |
| Less accumulated depreciation | 172,000 | 588,000 | |
| Equipment | $368,000 | | |
| Less accumulated depreciation | 88,000 | 280,000 | |
| Total property, plant, and equipment | | | 988,000 |
| Total assets | | | $1,491,600 |

### Liabilities

| | | | |
|---|---|---|---|
| Current liabilities: | | | |
| Accounts payable | $ 57,440 | | |
| Notes payable (Cheyenne National Bank) | 40,000 | | |
| Salaries payable | 2,560 | | |
| Total current liabilities | | $100,000 | |
| Long-term liabilities: | | | |
| Notes payable (Cheyenne National Bank) | | 360,000 | |
| Total liabilities | | | $ 460,000 |

### Stockholders' Equity

| | | | |
|---|---|---|---|
| Paid-in capital: | | | |
| Common stock, $20 par (50,000 shares authorized, 20,000 shares issued) | $400,000 | | |
| Excess of issue price over par | 32,000 | | |
| Total paid-in capital | | $432,000 | |
| Retained earnings | | 599,600 | |
| Total stockholders' equity | | | 1,031,600 |
| Total liabilities and stockholders' equity | | | $1,491,600 |

The board of directors is scheduled to meet January 6, 2007, to discuss the results of operations for 2006 and to consider the declaration of dividends for the fourth quarter of 2006. The chairman of the board has asked for your advice on the declaration of dividends.

1.  What factors should the board consider in deciding whether to declare a cash dividend?
2.  The board is considering the declaration of a stock dividend instead of a cash dividend. Discuss the issuance of a stock dividend from the point of view of (a) a stockholder and (b) the board of directors.

**ACTIVITY 12-6**
*Profiling a corporation*

GROUP ACTIVITY    INTERNET

Select a public corporation you are familiar with or which interests you. Using the Internet, your school library, and other sources, develop a short (2 to 5 pages) profile of the corporation. Include in your profile the following information:

1. Name of the corporation.
2. State of incorporation.
3. Nature of its operations.
4. Total assets for the most recent balance sheet.
5. Total revenues for the most recent income statement.
6. Net income for the most recent income statement.

*(continued)*

7. Classes of stock outstanding.
8. Market price of the stock outstanding.
9. High and low price of the stock for the past year.
10. Dividends paid for each share of stock during the past year.

In groups of three or four, discuss each corporate profile. Select one of the corporations, assuming that your group has $100,000 to invest in its stock. Summarize why your group selected the corporation it did and how financial accounting information may have affected your decision. Keep track of the performance of your corporation's stock for the remainder of the term.

*Note:* Most major corporations maintain "home pages" on the Internet. This home page provides a variety of information on the corporation and often includes the corporation's financial statements. In addition, the New York Stock Exchange Web site (**http://www.nyse.com**) includes links to the home pages of many listed companies. Financial statements can also be accessed using EDGAR, the electronic archives of financial statements filed with the Securities and Exchange Commission (SEC).

SEC documents can also be retrieved using the EdgarScan™ service from **PricewaterhouseCoopers** at **http://edgarscan.pwcglobal.com**. To obtain annual report information, key in a company name in the appropriate space. EdgarScan will list the reports, available to you for the company you've selected. Select the most recent annual report filing, identified as a 10-K or 10-K405. EdgarScan provides an outline of the report, including the separate financial statements, which can also be selected in an Excel® spreadsheet.

 # nswers to Self-Examination Questions

1. **C**  If a corporation has cumulative preferred stock outstanding, dividends that have been passed for prior years plus the dividend for the current year must be paid before dividends may be declared on common stock. In this case, dividends of $27,000 ($9,000 × 3) have been passed for the preceding three years, and the current year's dividends are $9,000, making a total of $36,000 (answer C) that must be paid to preferred stockholders before dividends can be declared on common stock.

2. **D**  Paid-in capital is one of the two major subdivisions of the stockholders' equity of a corporation. It may result from many sources, including the issuance of cumulative preferred stock (answer A), the receipt of donated real estate (answer B), or the sale of a corporation's treasury stock (answer C).

3. **D**  The Stockholders' Equity section of corporate balance sheets is divided into two principal subsections: (1) investments contributed by the stock-

holders and others and (2) net income retained in the business. Included as part of the investments by stockholders and others is the par of common stock (answer A), stock dividends distributable (answer B), and the par of preferred stock (answer C).

4. **C**  Reacquired stock, known as treasury stock, should be listed in the Stockholders' Equity section (answer C) of the balance sheet. The price paid for the treasury stock is deducted from the total of all the stockholders' equity accounts.

5. **C**  If a corporation that holds treasury stock declares a cash dividend, the dividends are not paid on the treasury shares. To do so would place the corporation in the position of earning income through dealing with itself. Thus, the corporation will record $44,000 (answer C) as cash dividends [(25,000 shares issued less 3,000 shares held as treasury stock) × $2 per share dividend].

# 13

# ACCOUNTING FOR PARTNERSHIPS AND LIMITED LIABILITY CORPORATIONS

## objectives

*After studying this chapter, you should be able to:*

**1** Describe the basic characteristics of proprietorships, corporations, partnerships, and limited liability corporations.

**2** Describe and illustrate the equity reporting for proprietorships, corporations, partnerships, and limited liability corporations.

**3** Describe and illustrate the accounting for forming a partnership.

**4** Describe and illustrate the accounting for dividing the net income and net loss of a partnership.

**5** Describe and illustrate the accounting for the dissolution of a partnership.

**6** Describe and illustrate the accounting for liquidating a partnership.

**7** Describe the life cycle of a business, including the role of venture capitalists, initial public offerings, and underwriters.

**I**f you were to start up any type of business, you would want to separate the business's affairs from your personal affairs. Keeping business transactions separate from personal transactions aids business analysis and simplifies tax reporting. For example, if you provided freelance photography services, you would want to keep a business checking account for depositing receipts for services rendered and writing checks for expenses. At the end of the year, you would have a basis for determining the earnings from your business and the information necessary for completing your tax return. In this case, forming the business would be as simple as establishing a name and a separate checking account. As a business becomes more complex, the form of the business entity becomes an important consideration. The entity form has an impact on the owners' legal liability, taxation, and the ability to raise capital. The four major forms of business entities that we will discuss in this chapter are the proprietorship, corporation, partnership, and limited liability corporation.

# **A**lternate Forms of Business Entities

**objective** **1**

Describe the basic characteristics of proprietorships, corporations, partnerships, and limited liability corporations.

A variety of legal forms exist for forming and operating a business. The four most common legal forms are proprietorships, corporations, partnerships, and limited liability corporations. In this section, we describe the characteristics of each of these business entities.

## Proprietorships

As we discussed in Chapter 1, a proprietorship is a business enterprise owned by a single individual. Internal Revenue Service (IRS) data indicate that proprietorships comprise 70% of the business tax returns filed but only 5% of all business revenues. This statistic suggests that proprietorships, although numerous, consist mostly of small businesses. The most common type of proprietorships are professional service providers, such as lawyers, architects, realtors, and physicians.

A proprietorship is simple to form. Indeed, you may already be a proprietor. For example, a person providing child-care services for friends of the family is a proprietor. There are no legal restrictions or forms to file in forming a proprietorship. The ease of forming a proprietorship is one of its main advantages. In addition, the individual owner can usually make business decisions without consulting others. This ability to be one's own boss is a major reason why many individuals organize their businesses as proprietorships.

A proprietorship is a separate entity for accounting purposes, and when the owner dies or retires, the proprietorship ceases to exist. For federal income tax purposes, however, the proprietorship is not treated as a separate taxable entity. The income or loss is said to "pass through" to the owner's individual income tax return.[1] Thus, the income from a proprietorship is taxed only at the individual level.

A primary disadvantage of a proprietorship is the difficulty in raising large amounts of capital. Investment in the business is limited to the amounts that the owner can provide from personal resources, plus any additional amounts that can be raised through borrowing. In addition, the owner is personally liable for any debts or legal claims against the business. In other words, if the business fails, creditors have rights to the personal assets of the owner, regardless of the amount of the owner's actual investment in the enterprise.

## Corporations

As we discussed in Chapter 12, the major benefits of the corporate form are its ability to provide limited liability to its owners and its potential for raising large amounts

---

[1]The proprietor's statement of income is included on Schedule C of the individual 1040 tax return.

of capital through issuing stock. For these reasons, most large businesses use the corporate form of entity.

However, corporations also have disadvantages. Forming a corporation requires legal filings to and approvals by state regulatory agencies. In addition, corporations are more complex to manage and must be operated in accordance with the corporate bylaws. Corporations are taxed as a separate entity. Thus, when earnings are distributed to shareholders in the form of dividends, they are also taxed again at the individual level.

To avoid the double taxation of dividends, a business may organize an S Corporation. Under an **S corporation**, the IRS allows income to pass through the corporation to the individual stockholders without the corporation having to pay taxes on the income. However, the S corporation has a number of legal limitations, including a limitation on the number of stockholders.[2] In recent years, the S corporation has become less popular due to the emergence of the limited liability corporation and its many advantages, which we will discuss later in this chapter.

## INTEGRITY IN BUSINESS

### THE TEMPTATION OF COMPENSATION

An owner/manager of a corporation can be taxed on income at the corporate level and again at the individual level for dividends. In contrast, compensation is a tax-deductible expense for business purposes and therefore is taxed only at the individual level. An owner/manager might be tempted to pay himself or herself "compensation" rather than dividends. However, the IRS requires that compensation not exceed the fair value of the services delivered to the company. Using compensation to subvert the double taxation of dividends is considered fraudulent.

 I'm an agricultural cooperative founded in 1930 and owned by more than 900 growers in the United States and Canada. Most of my products are based on a fruit grown primarily in Wisconsin and Massachusetts that's commonly harvested in large beds of water. In 1995, I introduced dried Craisins. I'm the No. 1 brand of canned and bottled juice drinks in America and my offerings are sold in nearly 50 countries around the world. I'm popular around the holidays. My annual sales top $1 billion, and my competitors include Northland, Tropicana, and the National Grape Cooperative. Who am I? (Go to page 543 for answer.)

# Partnerships

A *partnership* is an association of two or more persons who own and manage a business for profit.[3] Partnerships have several characteristics with accounting implications.

A partnership has a **limited life**. A partnership dissolves whenever a partner ceases to be a member of the firm. For example, a partnership is dissolved if a partner withdraws due to bankruptcy, incapacity, or death. Likewise, admitting a new partner dissolves the old partnership. When a partnership is dissolved, the remaining partners must form a new partnership if operations of the business are to continue.

In most partnerships, the partners have **unlimited liability**. That is, each partner is individually liable to creditors for debts incurred by the partnership. Thus, if a partnership becomes insolvent, the partners must contribute sufficient personal assets to settle the debts of the partnership.

Partners have **co-ownership of partnership property**. The property invested in a partnership by a partner becomes the joint property of all the partners. When a partnership is dissolved, the partners' claims against the assets are measured by the amount of the balances in their capital accounts.

Another characteristic of a partnership is **mutual agency**. This means that each partner is an agent of the partnership. The acts of each partner bind the entire partnership and become the obligations of all partners. For example, any partner can enter into a contract on behalf of all the members of the partnership. This is why partnerships should be formed only with people you trust.

An important right of partners is **participation in income** of the partnership. Net income and net loss are distributed among the partners according to their agreement.

---

[2]Presently, the law limits S corporations to 75 stockholders, who must be natural persons (not other business entities).
[3]The definition of a partnership is included in the Uniform Partnership Act, which has been adopted by most states.

> A partnership is a nontaxable entity that has a limited life and unlimited liability, and it is bound by the actions of each partner.

A partnership, like a proprietorship, is a **nontaxable entity** and thus does not pay federal income taxes. However, revenue and expense and other results of partnership operations must be reported annually to the Internal Revenue Service. The partners must, in turn, report their share of partnership income on their personal tax returns.

A partnership is created by a contract, known as the ***partnership agreement*** or **articles of partnership**. It should include statements regarding such matters as amounts to be invested, limits on withdrawals, distributions of income and losses, and admission and withdrawal of partners.

A variant of the regular partnership is a limited partnership. A **limited partnership** is a unique legal form that allows partners who are not involved in the operations of the partnership to retain limited liability. In such a form, at least one general partner must operate the partnership and retain unlimited liability. The remaining partners are considered limited partners.

The partnership form is less widely used than the proprietorship and corporate forms. For many business purposes, however, the advantages of the partnership form are greater than its disadvantages.

A partnership is relatively easy and inexpensive to organize, requiring only an agreement between two or more persons. A partnership has the advantage of bringing together more capital, managerial skills, and experience than does a proprietorship. Since a partnership is a nontaxable entity, the combined income taxes paid by the individual partners may be lower than the income taxes that would be paid by a corporation, which is a taxable entity.

A major disadvantage of the partnership is the unlimited liability feature for partners. Other disadvantages of a partnership are that its life is limited, and one partner can bind the partnership to contracts. Also, raising large amounts of capital is more difficult for a partnership than for a corporation. To overcome these limitations, other hybrid forms of organization, such as limited liability corporations (LLCs), have been replacing partnerships as a means of organization.

## Limited Liability Corporations

A ***limited liability corporation (LLC)***[4] is a relatively new business entity form that combines the advantages of the corporate and partnership forms. Many features of a partnership are retained in an LLC. The owners of an LLC are termed "members" rather than "partners." The members must create an **operating agreement**, which is similar to a partnership agreement. For example, the operating agreement normally indicates how income is to be distributed to the members. Thus, unlike a corporation, income need not be distributed according to the number of shares owned by each member. Instead, income might be distributed according to the amount of time each member devotes to the business.

For tax purposes, an LLC may elect to be treated as a partnership. In this way, income passes through the LLC and is taxed on the individual members' tax returns.[5] Thus, the LLC may avoid the double taxation characterized by the corporate form.

Unless specified in the operating agreement, LLCs have a limited life and must dissolve when a member withdraws. In addition, the members may elect to operate the LLC as a "member-managed" entity, which allows individual members to legally bind the LLC, like partners bind a partnership.

LLCs also have some features of a corporation. One of the most important corporate features is that LLCs provide limited liability for the members, even if they are active participants in the business. Thus, members' personal assets are not subject to claims by creditors of the LLC.

**REAL WORLD**

Companies commonly use partnerships and LLCs in forming joint ventures. Joint ventures are used to diversify risk or expand expertise in operating identifiable businesses or projects. For example, Viacom Inc. uses regionally placed joint venture partners to broadcast MTV, VH1, Nickelodeon, and TV Land around the world. Viacom's joint venture partners bring local customs, language, and culture to the broadcast offerings.

---

[4]The term limited liability *company* is the correct legal term, while the term limited liability *corporation* is the common business term. We will use the common terminology in this text rather than the seldom used, although correct, legal term.

[5]LLCs may also elect to be treated as a corporation for tax purposes, although this election would remove any "pass-through" benefits. Thus, this is a less common election.

Like a corporation, LLCs must file "articles of organization" with state governmental authorities. In addition, the LLC may elect to be "manager-managed" rather than "member-managed." In a "manager-managed" structure, only authorized members may legally bind the LLC. This allows members to share in the income of the LLC without being concerned about managing the business, much like stockholders of a corporation.

## Comparison of Alternate Entity Characteristics

Exhibit 1 summarizes the four business entity forms discussed in this section. The columns of Exhibit 1 are the major characteristics of the organizational forms: ease of formation, legal liability, taxation, limitation on life of the entity, and access to capital. As one expert who has been involved in a number of start-up businesses replied when asked what structure makes the most sense: "It depends. Each situation I've been involved with has been different. You can't just make an assumption that one form is better than another."[6] Generally, the corporate form will be preferred if the business is risky and requires access to capital. Otherwise, the other three forms all have their advantages, depending on the need for simplicity, liability limitation, flexibility, and tax considerations.

**•Exhibit 1**   **Characteristics of Organizational Forms**

| Organizational Form | Ease of Formation | Legal Liability | Taxation | Limitation on Life of Entity | Access to Capital |
|---|---|---|---|---|---|
| Proprietorship | Simple | No limitation | Nontaxable (pass-through) entity | Yes | Limited |
| Corporation | Complex | Limited liability | Taxable entity | No | Extensive |
| Partnership | Simple | No limitation | Nontaxable (pass-through) entity | Yes | Average |
| Limited Liability Corporation | Moderate | Limited liability | Nontaxable (pass-through) entity by election | Yes | Average |

# Equity Reporting for Alternate Entity Forms

**objective 2**

Describe and illustrate the equity reporting for proprietorships, corporations, partnerships, and limited liability corporations.

The owners of any business are concerned with their proportional ownership and changes in their ownership. This is because the owners' proportional ownership often determines their share of earnings and the value of their ownership interest. As a result, a business reports the ownership equity balances and changes in those balances. In the following sections, such equity reports are illustrated for each entity form.

---

[6]Laura Tiffany, "Choose Your Business Structure," *Entrepreneur*, March 19, 2001.

# Equity Reporting for Proprietorships

Since the proprietorship is a separate entity for accounting purposes, the transactions of the proprietorship must be kept separate from the personal financial affairs of the owner. Only in this way can the financial condition and the results of operations of the proprietorship be accurately measured and reported.

The accounting for a proprietorship was illustrated earlier in this text. This accounting includes the use of a capital account to record investments by the owner in the business. At the end of the period, the net income or net loss is closed to the owner's capital account by using Income Summary. Withdrawals by the owners are recorded in the owner's drawing account. At the end of the period, the drawing account is closed to the owner's capital account, and a statement of owner's equity is prepared.

The **statement of owner's equity** summarizes changes in owner's capital for a period of time. To illustrate, the statement of owner's equity for a proprietorship, Greene Landscapes, owned by Duncan Greene, is shown below.

| Greene Landscapes Statement of Owner's Equity For the Year Ended December 31, 2006 | | |
|---|---|---|
| Duncan Greene, capital, January 1, 2006 | | $345 0 0 0 |
| Net income | $79 0 0 0 | |
| Less withdrawals | 35 0 0 0 | |
| Increase in owner's equity | | 44 0 0 0 |
| Duncan Greene, capital, December 31, 2006 | | $389 0 0 0 |

# Equity Reporting for Corporations

The accounting for a corporation was illustrated in Chapter 12. This accounting includes the use of capital stock accounts, such as Common Stock and Preferred Stock, to record investments by the stockholders. Through the closing process, dividends and the net income or net loss are recorded in the retained earnings account.

Significant changes in stockholders' equity should be reported for the period in which they occur. When the only change in stockholders' equity is due to net income or net loss and dividends, a retained earnings statement such as the one illustrated in the previous chapter is sufficient. However, when a corporation also has changes in stock and other paid-in capital accounts, a *statement of stockholders' equity* is normally prepared. This statement is often prepared in a columnar format, where each column represents a major stockholders' equity classification. Changes in each classification are then described in the left-hand column. Exhibit 2 illustrates a statement of stockholders' equity for Telex Inc.

# Equity Reporting for Partnerships and Limited Liability Corporations

Reporting changes in partnership capital accounts is similar to that for a proprietorship, except that there is an owner's capital account for each partner. The change in the owners' capital accounts for a period of time is reported in a *statement of partnership equity*. The statement of partnership equity discloses each partner's capital account in the columns and the reasons for the change in capital in the rows.

## •Exhibit 2   Statement of Stockholders' Equity

**Telex Inc.**
**Statement of Stockholders' Equity**
**For the Year Ended December 31, 2006**

| | Preferred Stock | Common Stock | Paid-In Capital in Excess of Par | Retained Earnings | Treasury Stock | Total |
|---|---|---|---|---|---|---|
| Balance, January 1, 2006 | $5,000 0 0 0 | $3,000 0 0 0 | $10,000 0 0 0 | $2,000 0 0 0 | $(500 0 0 0) | $19,500 0 0 0 |
| Net income | | | | 850 0 0 0 | | 850 0 0 0 |
| Dividends on preferred stock | | | | (250 0 0 0) | | (250 0 0 0) |
| Dividends on common stock | | | | (400 0 0 0) | | (400 0 0 0) |
| Issuance of additional common stock | | 50 0 0 0 | 500 0 0 0 | | | 550 0 0 0 |
| Purchase of treasury stock | | | | | (30 0 0 0) | (30 0 0 0) |
| Balance, December 31, 2006 | $5,000 0 0 0 | $3,050 0 0 0 | $10,500 0 0 0 | $2,200 0 0 0 | $(530 0 0 0) | $20,220 0 0 0 |

Exhibit 3 illustrates the disclosure for Investors Associates, a partnership of Dan Cross and Kelly Baker.

## •Exhibit 3   Statement of Partnership Equity

**Investors Associates**
**Statement of Partnership Equity**
**For the Year Ended December 31, 2006**

| | Dan Cross, Capital | Kelly Baker, Capital | Total Partnership Capital |
|---|---|---|---|
| Balance, January 1, 2006 | $245 0 0 0 | $365 0 0 0 | $610 0 0 0 |
| Capital additions | 50 0 0 0 | | 50 0 0 0 |
| Net income for the year | 40 0 0 0 | 80 0 0 0 | 120 0 0 0 |
| Less partner withdrawals | (5 0 0 0) | (45 0 0 0) | (50 0 0 0) |
| Balance, December 31, 2006 | $330 0 0 0 | $400 0 0 0 | $730 0 0 0 |

The equity reporting for an LLC is similar to that of a partnership. Instead of a statement of partnership capital, a statement of members' equity is prepared. The **statement of members' equity** discloses the changes in member equity for a period. The disclosure would be very similar to Exhibit 3, except that the columns would be the members of the LLC rather than partners. The statement of members' equity for HealthNet, LLC, is illustrated in Exhibit 4.

# Accounting for Partnerships and Limited Liability Corporations

Most of the day-to-day accounting for a partnership or an LLC is the same as the accounting for any other form of business organization. The accounting system described in previous chapters may, with minimal changes, be used by a partnership

## •Exhibit 4 Statement of Members' Equity

### HealthNet, LLC
### Statement of Members' Equity
### For the Year Ended December 31, 2006

| | Dr. Roland Campbell, Member Equity | Dr. Phyllis Lambert, Member Equity | Total Members' Equity |
|---|---|---|---|
| Balance, January 1, 2006 | $320 0 0 0 | $175 0 0 0 | $495 0 0 0 |
| Capital additions | | 25 0 0 0 | 25 0 0 0 |
| Net income for the year | 280 0 0 0 | 240 0 0 0 | 520 0 0 0 |
| Less member withdrawals | (200 0 0 0) | (180 0 0 0) | (380 0 0 0) |
| Balance, December 31, 2006 | $400 0 0 0 | $260 0 0 0 | $660 0 0 0 |

## FINANCIAL REPORTING AND DISCLOSURE

### FOX SPORTS NETWORKS

An example of the statement of members' equity for an LLC is provided below for the **Fox Sports Networks**. As can be seen, the columns are the three major members of the network. The members are not natural persons but, rather, another LLC and two other companies. Each member represents a class of investors that have similar rights according to the operating agreement. The Fox Regional Sports Holdings (FRSH) II, Inc., member has a negative capital account, while the Fox Sports Net Financing, LLC, has the largest positive capital account. This may be the result of different initial capital contributions or the timing of the capital contributions. Also, FRSH, Inc., and FRSH II, Inc., share the same proportional net earnings of the LLC, since they both have the same net income attributed to their member capital accounts. Fox Sports Net Financing, LLC, receives a slightly higher portion of the LLC's net income. None of the members withdrew money from the LLC during this period.

### FOX SPORTS NETWORKS, LLC
### CONSOLIDATED STATEMENTS OF MEMBERS' EQUITY
### For the Period Ended June 30, 2001
### (Dollars in thousands)

| | Fox Regional Sports Holdings II, Inc. | Fox Sports Net Financing, LLC | Fox Regional Sports Holdings, Inc. | Total Members' Equity |
|---|---|---|---|---|
| BALANCE, JUNE 30, 2000 . . . . . | $(91,680) | $119,753 | $ (3,380) | $24,693 |
| Net income . . . . . . . . . . . . . . | 10,466 | 13,000 | 10,466 | 33,932 |
| BALANCE, JUNE 30, 2001 . . . . . | $(81,214) | $132,753 | $ 7,086 | $58,625 |

Fill in the LLC term comparable to the given partnership term.

| Partnership Term | Equivalent LLC Term |
|---|---|
| Partner | _____ |
| Partnership agreement | _____ |
| Partner capital | _____ |

*Answer: Member, Operating agreement, Member equity*

or an LLC. However, the formation, division of net income or net loss, dissolution, and liquidation of partnerships and LLCs give rise to unique transactions.

In the following sections of this chapter, we will discuss and illustrate these unique transactions for a partnership and an LLC. Since an LLC is treated in the same manner as a partnership, except that the terms "member" and "members' equity" are used rather than "partner" or "owners' capital," we show the parallel journal entries for an LLC alongside the partnership entries.

# Forming a Partnership

objective **3**

Describe and illustrate the accounting for forming a partnership.

In forming a partnership, the investments of each partner are recorded in separate entries. The assets contributed by a partner are debited to the partnership asset accounts. If liabilities are assumed by the partnership, the partnership liability accounts are credited. The partner's capital account is credited for the net amount.

To illustrate, assume that Joseph Stevens and Earl Foster, owners of competing hardware stores, agree to combine their businesses in a partnership. Each is to contribute certain amounts of cash and other assets. Stevens and Foster also agree that the partnership is to assume the liabilities of the separate businesses. The entry to record the assets contributed and the liabilities transferred by Stevens is as follows:

| LLC Alternative | |
| --- | --- |
| Cash | 7,200 |
| Accounts Receivable | 16,300 |
| Merchandise Inventory | 28,700 |
| Store Equipment | 5,400 |
| Office Equipment | 1,500 |
| Allowance for Doubtful Accounts | 1,500 |
| Accounts Payable | 2,600 |
| Joseph Stevens, Member Equity | 55,000 |

| | | | | | | | |
| --- | --- | --- | --- | --- | --- | --- | --- |
| Apr. | 1 | Cash | 7 2 0 0 00 | | |
| | | Accounts Receivable | 16 3 0 0 00 | | |
| | | Merchandise Inventory | 28 7 0 0 00 | | |
| | | Store Equipment | 5 4 0 0 00 | | |
| | | Office Equipment | 1 5 0 0 00 | | |
| | | Allowance for Doubtful Accounts | | 1 5 0 0 00 |
| | | Accounts Payable | | 2 6 0 0 00 |
| | | Joseph Stevens, Capital | | 55 0 0 0 00 |

A similar entry would record the assets contributed and the liabilities transferred by Foster. In each entry, the noncash assets are recorded at values agreed upon by the partners. These values normally represent current market values and thus usually differ from the book values of the assets in the records of the separate businesses. For example, the store equipment recorded at $5,400 in the preceding entry may have had a book value of $3,500 in Stevens' ledger (cost of $10,000 less accumulated depreciation of $6,500). As a further example, receivables contributed to the partnership are recorded at their face amount. Only accounts that are likely to be collected are normally transferred to the partnership.

# Dividing Income

objective **4**

Describe and illustrate the accounting for dividing the net income and net loss of a partnership.

Many partnerships have been dissolved because partners could not agree on how to distribute income equitably. Therefore, the method of dividing partnership income should be stated in the partnership agreement. In the absence of any agreement or if the agreement is silent on dividing net income or net losses, all partners share equally. However, if one partner contributes a larger portion of capital than the others, then net income should be divided to reflect the unequal capital contributions. Likewise, if the services rendered by one partner are more important than those of the others, net income should be divided to reflect the unequal service contributions. In the following paragraphs, we illustrate partnership agreements that recognize these differences.

## Dividing Income—Services of Partners

One method of recognizing differences in partners' abilities and in amount of time devoted to the business provides for salary allowances to partners. Since partners are legally not employees of the partnership, such allowances are treated as divisions of the net income and are credited to the partners' capital accounts.

To illustrate, assume that the partnership agreement of Jennifer Stone and Crystal Mills provides for monthly salary allowances. Stone is to receive a monthly allowance of $2,500 ($30,000 annually), and Mills is to receive $2,000 a month ($24,000 annually). Any net income remaining after the salary allowances is to be divided equally. Assume also that the net income for the year is $75,000.

A report of the division of net income may be presented as a separate statement to accompany the balance sheet and the income statement or disclosed within the statement of partnership capital. Another format is to add the division to the bottom of the income statement. If the latter format is used, the lower part of the income statement would appear as follows:

Net income . . . . . . . . . . . . . . . . . . . . . . . . . . . . . . . . $75,000

Division of net income:

|  | J. Stone | C. Mills | Total |
|---|---|---|---|
| Annual salary allowance | $30,000 | $24,000 | $54,000 |
| Remaining income | 10,500 | 10,500 | 21,000 |
| Net income | $40,500 | $34,500 | $75,000 |

The net income division is recorded as a closing entry, even if the partners do not actually withdraw the amounts of their salary allowances. The entry for dividing net income is as follows:

**LLC Alternative**

| *Income Summary* | 75,000 | |
|---|---|---|
| *Jennifer Stone, Member Equity* | | 40,500 |
| *Crystal Mills, Member Equity* | | 34,500 |

| | | | | | |
|---|---|---|---|---|---|
| Dec. | 31 | Income Summary | 75 0 0 0 00 | |
| | | Jennifer Stone, Capital | | 40 5 0 0 00 |
| | | Crystal Mills, Capital | | 34 5 0 0 00 |

If Stone and Mills had withdrawn their salary allowances monthly, the withdrawals would have been debited to their drawing accounts during the year. At the end of the year, the debit balances of $30,000 and $24,000 in their drawing accounts would be transferred as reductions to their capital accounts.

Accountants should be careful to distinguish between salary allowances and partner withdrawals. The amount of net income distributed to each partner's capital account at the end of the year may differ from the amount the partner withdraws during the year. In some cases, the partnership agreement may limit the amount of withdrawals a partner may make during a period.

## Dividing Income—Services of Partners and Investments

Partners may agree that the most equitable plan of dividing income is to provide for (1) salary allowances and (2) interest on capital investments. Any remaining net income is then divided as agreed upon. For example, assume that the partnership agreement for Stone and Mills divides income as follows:

1. Monthly salary allowances of $2,500 for Stone and $2,000 for Mills.
2. Interest of 12% on each partner's capital balance on January 1.
3. Any remaining net income divided equally between the partners.

Stone had a credit balance of $80,000 in her capital account on January 1 of the current fiscal year, and Mills had a credit balance of $60,000 in her capital account. The $75,000 net income for the year is divided per the following schedule:

A partnership has net income of $120,000. One of the partners, Don Lowe, is the only partner with a salary allowance. Lowe's salary allowance is $32,000, of which $25,000 was withdrawn during the year. Lowe shares in 20% of the remaining income. How much income is allocated to Lowe?

Answer: $49,600 {$32,000 + [20% × ($120,000 − $32,000)]}

Net income . . . . . . . . . . . . . . . . . . . . . . . . . . . . . . . . . $75,000

Division of net income:

|  | J. Stone | C. Mills | Total |
|---|---|---|---|
| Annual salary allowance | $30,000 | $24,000 | $54,000 |
| Interest allowance | 9,600[1] | 7,200[2] | 16,800 |
| Remaining income | 2,100 | 2,100 | 4,200 |
| Net income | $41,700 | $33,300 | $75,000 |

[1]0.12 × $80,000
[2]0.12 × $60,000

For the above example, the entry to close the income summary account is shown below.

**LLC Alternative**

| Income Summary | 75,000 | |
|---|---|---|
| Jennifer Stone, Member Equity | | 41,700 |
| Crystal Mills, Member Equity | | 33,300 |

| Dec. | 31 | Income Summary | 75 0 0 0 00 | |
|---|---|---|---|---|
| | | Jennifer Stone, Capital | | 41 7 0 0 00 |
| | | Crystal Mills, Capital | | 33 3 0 0 00 |

# Dividing Income—Allowances Exceed Net Income

In the preceding example, the net income exceeded the total of the salary and interest allowances. If the net income is less than the total of the allowances, the remaining balance will be a negative amount. This amount must be divided among the partners as though it were a net loss.

To illustrate, assume the same salary and interest allowances as in the preceding example but that the net income is $50,000. The salary and interest allowances total $39,600 for Stone and $31,200 for Mills. The sum of these amounts, $70,800, exceeds the net income of $50,000 by $20,800. This $20,800 excess must be divided between Stone and Mills. Under the partnership agreement, any net income or net loss remaining after deducting the allowances is divided equally between Stone and Mills. Thus, each partner is allocated one-half of the $20,800, and $10,400 is deducted from each partner's share of the allowances. The final division of net income between Stone and Mills is shown below.

Net income . . . . . . . . . . . . . . . . . . . . . . . . . . . . . . . . . $50,000

Division of net income:

|  | J. Stone | C. Mills | Total |
|---|---|---|---|
| Annual salary allowance | $30,000 | $24,000 | $54,000 |
| Interest allowance | 9,600 | 7,200 | 16,800 |
| Total | $39,600 | $31,200 | $70,800 |
| Deduct excess of allowances over income | 10,400 | 10,400 | 20,800 |
| Net income | $29,200 | $20,800 | $50,000 |

In closing Income Summary at the end of the year, $29,200 would be credited to Jennifer Stone, Capital, and $20,800 would be credited to Crystal Mills, Capital.

# Partnership Dissolution

When a partnership dissolves, its affairs are not necessarily finished. For example, a partnership of two partners may admit a third partner. Or if one of the partners in a business withdraws, the remaining partners may continue to operate the business. In such cases, a new partnership is formed and a new partnership agreement should be prepared. Many partnerships provide for the admission of new partners and partner withdrawals in the partnership agreement so that the partnership may continue operations without having to execute a new agreement.

## Admitting a Partner

A person may be admitted to a partnership only with the consent of all the current partners by:

1. Purchasing an interest from one or more of the current partners.
2. Contributing assets to the partnership.

When the first method is used, the equity of the incoming partner is obtained from current partners, and *neither the total assets nor the total owner's equity of the business is affected.* When the second method is used, *both the total assets and the total owner's equity of the business are increased.* In the following paragraphs, we discuss each of these methods.

### Purchasing an Interest in a Partnership

The purchase and sale of a partnership interest occurs between the new partner and the existing partners acting as individuals. The only entry needed is to transfer owner's equity amounts from the capital accounts of the selling partners to the capital account established for the incoming partner.

As an example, assume that partners Tom Andrews and Nathan Bell have capital balances of $50,000 each. On June 1, each sells one-fifth of his equity to Joe Canter for $10,000 in cash. The exchange of cash is not a partnership transaction and thus is not recorded by the partnership. The only entry required in the partnership accounts is as follows:

**LLC Alternative**

| | |
|---|---|
| *Tom Andrews, Member Equity* | *10,000* |
| *Nathan Bell, Member Equity* | *10,000* |
| *Joe Canter, Member Equity* | *20,000* |

| | | | | |
|---|---|---|---|---|
| June | 1 | Tom Andrews, Capital | 10 0 0 0 00 | |
| | | Nathan Bell, Capital | 10 0 0 0 00 | |
| | | Joe Canter, Capital | | 20 0 0 0 00 |

The effect of the transaction on the partnership accounts is presented in the following diagram:

**Partnership Accounts**

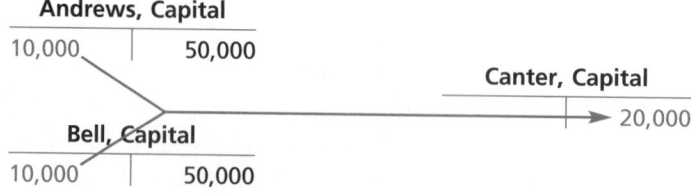

The preceding entry is not affected by the amount paid by Canter for the one-fifth interest. Any gain or loss on the sale of the partnership interest accrues to the selling partners as individuals, not to the partnership. Thus, in either case, the entry to transfer the capital interests is the same as shown above.

After Canter is admitted to the partnership, the total owners' equity of the firm is still $100,000. Canter now has a one-fifth interest, or a $20,000 capital balance. However, Canter may not be entitled to a one-fifth share of the partnership net income. The division of the net income or net loss will be made according to the new partnership agreement.

## Contributing Assets to a Partnership

When a new partner is admitted by contributing assets to the partnership, both the assets and the owners' equity of the firm increase. For example, assume that Donald Lewis and Gerald Morton are partners with capital accounts of $35,000 and $25,000. On June 1, Sharon Nelson invests $20,000 cash in the business for ownership equity of $20,000. The entry to record this transaction is as follows:

**LLC Alternative**

| | | |
|---|---|---|
| Cash | 20,000 | |
| Sharon Nelson, Member Equity | | 20,000 |

| | | | | | |
|---|---|---|---|---|---|
| June | 1 | Cash | 20 0 0 0 00 | | |
| | | Sharon Nelson, Capital | | 20 0 0 0 00 | |

The major difference between admitting Nelson and admitting Canter in the preceding example may be observed by comparing the following diagram with the preceding diagram.

**Partnership Accounts**

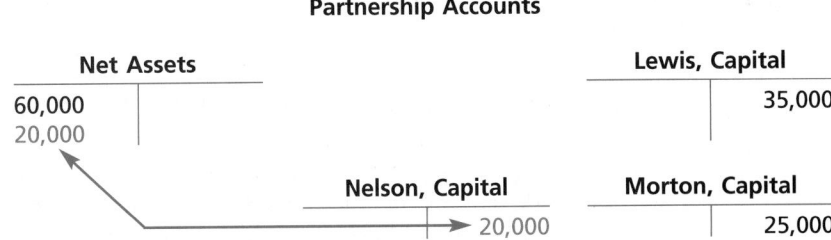

By admitting Nelson, the total owners' equity of the new partnership becomes $80,000, of which Nelson has a one-fourth interest, or $20,000. The extent of Nelson's share in partnership net income will be determined by the partnership agreement.

## Revaluation of Assets

A partnership's asset account balances should be stated at current values when a new partner is admitted. If the accounts do not approximate current market values, the accounts should be adjusted. The net adjustment (increase or decrease) in asset values is divided among the capital accounts of the existing partners according to their income-sharing ratio. Failure to adjust the accounts for current values may result in the new partner sharing in asset gains or losses that arose in prior periods.

To illustrate, assume that in the preceding example for the Lewis and Morton partnership, the balance of the merchandise inventory account is $14,000 and the current replacement value is $17,000. Assuming that Lewis and Morton share net income equally, the revaluation is recorded as follows:

**LLC Alternative**

| | | |
|---|---|---|
| Merchandise Inventory | 3,000 | |
| Donald Lewis, Member Equity | | 1,500 |
| Gerald Morton, Member Equity | | 1,500 |

| | | | | | |
|---|---|---|---|---|---|
| June | 1 | Merchandise Inventory | 3 0 0 0 00 | | |
| | | Donald Lewis, Capital | | 1 5 0 0 00 | |
| | | Gerald Morton, Capital | | 1 5 0 0 00 | |

## Partner Bonuses

When a new partner is admitted to a partnership, the incoming partner may pay a bonus to the existing partners for the privilege of joining the partnership. Such a bonus is usually paid expecting high partnership profits in the future due to the contributions of the existing partners. Alternatively, the existing partners may pay the incoming partner a bonus to join the partnership. In this case, the bonus is usually paid recognizing special qualities or skills that the incoming partner is bringing to the partnership. For example, celebrities such as actors, musicians, or sports figures often provide name recognition that is expected to increase partnership profits in the future.

The amount of any bonus paid to the partnership is distributed among the partner capital accounts.[7] To illustrate, assume that on March 1 the partnership of Marsha Jenkins and Helen Kramer is considering admitting a new partner, Alex Diaz. After the assets of the partnership have been adjusted to current market values, the capital balance of Jenkins is $20,000 and the capital balance of Kramer is $24,000. Jenkins and Kramer agree to admit Diaz to the partnership for $31,000. In return, Diaz will receive a one-third equity in the partnership and will share equally with Jenkins and Kramer in partnership income or losses.

In this case, Diaz is paying Jenkins and Kramer a $6,000 bonus to join the partnership. This bonus is computed as follows:

Lowman has a capital balance of $45,000 after adjusting assets to fair market value. Conrad contributes $24,000 to receive a 30% interest in a new partnership with Lowman. How much bonus does Conrad pay to Lowman?

Answer: $3,300 {24,000 − [($45,000 + $24,000) × 30%]}

| | |
|---|---:|
| Equity of Jenkins | $20,000 |
| Equity of Kramer | 24,000 |
| Diaz's contribution | 31,000 |
| Total equity after admitting Diaz | $75,000 |
| Diaz's equity interest after admission | × 1/3 |
| Diaz's equity after admission | $25,000 |
| Diaz's contribution | $31,000 |
| Diaz's equity after admission | 25,000 |
| Bonus paid to Jenkins and Kramer | $ 6,000 |

The bonus is distributed to Jenkins and Kramer according to their income-sharing ratio. Assuming that Jenkins and Kramer share profits and losses equally, the entry to record the admission of Diaz to the partnership is as follows:

**LLC Alternative**

| | | |
|---|---:|---:|
| *Cash* | 31,000 | |
| *Alex Diaz, Member Equity* | | 25,000 |
| *Marsha Jenkins, Member Equity* | | 3,000 |
| *Helen Kramer, Member Equity* | | 3,000 |

| | | | | |
|---|---|---|---:|---:|
| Mar. | 1 | Cash | 31 0 0 0 00 | |
| | | Alex Diaz, Capital | | 25 0 0 0 00 |
| | | Marsha Jenkins, Capital | | 3 0 0 0 00 |
| | | Helen Kramer, Capital | | 3 0 0 0 00 |

If a new partner possesses unique qualities or skills, the existing partners may agree to pay the new partner a bonus to join the partnership. To illustrate, assume that after adjusting assets to market values, the capital balance of Janice Cowen is $80,000 and the capital balance of Steve Dodd is $40,000. Cowen and Dodd agree to admit Ellen Chou to the partnership on June 1 for an investment of $30,000. In return, Chou will receive a one-fourth equity interest in the partnership and will share in one-fourth of the profits and losses. In this case, Cowen and Dodd are paying Chou a $7,500 bonus to join the partnership. This bonus is computed as follows:

| | |
|---|---:|
| Equity of Cowen | $ 80,000 |
| Equity of Dodd | 40,000 |
| Chou's contribution | 30,000 |
| Total equity after admitting Chou | $150,000 |
| Chou's equity interest after admission | × 25% |
| Chou's equity after admission | $ 37,500 |
| Chou's contribution | 30,000 |
| Bonus paid to Chou | $ 7,500 |

---

[7]Another method used to record the admission of partners attributes goodwill rather than a bonus to the partners. This method is discussed in advanced accounting textbooks.

Assuming that the income-sharing ratio of Cowen and Dodd was 2:1 before the admission of Chou, the entry to record the bonus and admission of Chou to the partnership is as follows:

**LLC Alternative**

| | | |
|---|---|---|
| Cash | 30,000 | |
| Janice Cowen, Member Equity | 5,000 | |
| Steve Dodd, Member Equity | 2,500 | |
| Ellen Chou, Member Equity | | 37,500 |

| | | | | | | | |
|---|---|---|---|---|---|---|---|
| June | 1 | Cash | 30 0 0 0 00 | | | |
| | | Janice Cowen, Capital | 5 0 0 0 00 | | | |
| | | Steve Dodd, Capital | 2 5 0 0 00 | | | |
| | | Ellen Chou, Capital | | | 37 5 0 0 00 | |

# Withdrawal of a Partner

When a partner retires or withdraws from a partnership, one or more of the remaining partners may buy the withdrawing partner's interest. The firm may then continue its operations uninterrupted. In such cases, the purchase and sale of the partnership interest is between the partners as individuals. The only entry on the partnership's records is to debit the capital account of the partner withdrawing and to credit the capital account of the partner or partners buying the additional interest.

If the withdrawing partner sells the interest directly to the partnership, both the assets and the owner's equity of the partnership are reduced. Before the sale, the asset accounts should be adjusted to current values, so that the withdrawing partner's equity may be accurately determined. The net amount of the adjustment should be divided among the capital accounts of the partners according to their income-sharing ratio. If not enough partnership cash or other assets are available to pay the withdrawing partner, a liability may be created (credited) for the amount owed the withdrawing partner.

# Death of a Partner

When a partner dies, the accounts should be closed as of the date of death. The net income for the current year should be determined and divided among the partners' capital accounts. The balance in the capital account of the deceased partner is then transferred to a liability account with the deceased's estate. The remaining partner or partners may continue the business or terminate it. If the partnership continues in business, the procedures for settling with the estate are the same as those discussed for the withdrawal of a partner.

# Liquidating Partnerships

**objective  6**

Describe and illustrate the accounting for liquidating a partnership.

> **In liquidation, cash is distributed to partners according to their capital balances.**

When a partnership goes out of business, it usually sells the assets, pays the creditors, and distributes the remaining cash or other assets to the partners. This winding-up process is called the *liquidation* of the partnership. Although *liquidating* refers to the payment of liabilities, it often includes the entire winding-up process.

When the partnership goes out of business and the normal operations are discontinued, the accounts should be adjusted and closed. The only accounts remaining open will be the asset, contra asset, liability, and owner's equity accounts.

The sale of the assets is called *realization*. As cash is realized, it is used to pay the claims of creditors. After all liabilities have been paid, the remaining cash is distributed to the partners based on the balances in their capital accounts.

The liquidating process may extend over a long period of time as individual assets are sold. This delays the distribution of cash to partners but does not affect the amount each partner will receive.

To illustrate, assume that Farley, Greene, and Hall share income and losses in a ratio of 5:3:2 (5/10, 3/10, 2/10). On April 9, after discontinuing business operations of the partnership and closing the accounts, the following trial balance in summary form was prepared:

| | | |
|---|---:|---:|
| Cash | 11,000 | |
| Noncash Assets | 64,000 | |
| Liabilities | | 9,000 |
| Jean Farley, Capital | | 22,000 |
| Brad Greene, Capital | | 22,000 |
| Alice Hall, Capital | | 22,000 |
| Total | 75,000 | 75,000 |

Based on these facts, we show the accounting for liquidating the partnership by using three different selling prices for the noncash assets. To simplify, we assume that all noncash assets are sold in a single transaction and that all liabilities are paid at one time. In addition, Noncash Assets and Liabilities will be used as account titles in place of the various asset, contra asset, and liability accounts.

# Gain on Realization

Between April 10 and April 30 of the current year, Farley, Greene, and Hall sell all noncash assets for $72,000. Thus, a gain of $8,000 ($72,000 − $64,000) is realized. The gain is divided among the capital accounts in the income-sharing ratio of 5:3:2. The liabilities are paid, and the remaining cash is distributed to the partners. *The cash is distributed to the partners based on the balances in their capital accounts.* A **statement of partnership liquidation**, which summarizes the liquidation process, is shown in Exhibit 5.

The entries to record the steps in the liquidating process are as follows:

Sale of assets:

**LLC Alternative**

| | | |
|---|---:|---:|
| Cash | 72,000 | |
| Noncash Assets | | 64,000 |
| Gain on Realization | | 8,000 |

| | | | |
|---|---|---:|---:|
| | Cash | 72 0 0 0 00 | |
| | Noncash Assets | | 64 0 0 0 00 |
| | Gain on Realization | | 8 0 0 0 00 |

Division of gain:

**LLC Alternative**

| | | |
|---|---:|---:|
| Gain on Realization | 8,000 | |
| Jean Farley, Member Equity | | 4,000 |
| Brad Greene, Member Equity | | 2,400 |
| Alice Hall, Member Equity | | 1,600 |

| | | | |
|---|---|---:|---:|
| | Gain on Realization | 8 0 0 0 00 | |
| | Jean Farley, Capital | | 4 0 0 0 00 |
| | Brad Greene, Capital | | 2 4 0 0 00 |
| | Alice Hall, Capital | | 1 6 0 0 00 |

Payment of liabilities:

**LLC Alternative**

| | | |
|---|---:|---:|
| Liabilities | 9,000 | |
| Cash | | 9,000 |

| | | | |
|---|---|---:|---:|
| | Liabilities | 9 0 0 0 00 | |
| | Cash | | 9 0 0 0 00 |

Distribution of cash to partners:

**LLC Alternative**

| | | |
|---|---:|---:|
| Jean Farley, Member Equity | 26,000 | |
| Brad Greene, Member Equity | 24,400 | |
| Alice Hall, Member Equity | 23,600 | |
| Cash | | 74,000 |

| | | | |
|---|---|---:|---:|
| | Jean Farley, Capital | 26 0 0 0 00 | |
| | Brad Greene, Capital | 24 4 0 0 00 | |
| | Alice Hall, Capital | 23 6 0 0 00 | |
| | Cash | | 74 0 0 0 00 |

## •Exhibit 5   Gain on Realization

**Farley, Greene, and Hall**
**Statement of Partnership Liquidation**
**For Period April 10–30, 2006**

| | Cash | + | Noncash Assets | = | Liabilities | + | Farley (50%) | + | Greene (30%) | + | Hall (20%) |
|---|---|---|---|---|---|---|---|---|---|---|---|
| | | | | | | | **Capital** | | | | |
| Balances before realization | $ 11,000 | | $ 64,000 | | $ 9,000 | | $ 22,000 | | $ 22,000 | | $ 22,000 |
| Sale of assets and division of gain | +72,000 | | −64,000 | | — | | + 4,000 | | + 2,400 | | + 1,600 |
| Balances after realization | $ 83,000 | | $ 0 | | $ 9,000 | | $ 26,000 | | $ 24,400 | | $ 23,600 |
| Payment of liabilities | − 9,000 | | — | | −9,000 | | — | | — | | — |
| Balances after payment of liabilities | $ 74,000 | | $ 0 | | $ 0 | | $ 26,000 | | $ 24,400 | | $ 23,600 |
| Cash distributed to partners | −74,000 | | — | | — | | −26,000 | | −24,400 | | −23,600 |
| Final balances | $ 0 | | $ 0 | | $ 0 | | $ 0 | | $ 0 | | $ 0 |

As shown in Exhibit 5, the cash is distributed to the partners based on the balances of their capital accounts. These balances are determined after the gain on realization has been divided among the partners. *The income-sharing ratio should not be used as a basis for distributing the cash to partners.*

## Loss on Realization

Assume that in the preceding example, Farley, Greene, and Hall dispose of all noncash assets for $44,000. A loss of $20,000 ($64,000 − $44,000) is realized. The steps in liquidating the partnership are summarized in Exhibit 6.

## •Exhibit 6   Loss on Realization

**Farley, Greene, and Hall**
**Statement of Partnership Liquidation**
**For Period April 10–30, 2006**

| | Cash | + | Noncash Assets | = | Liabilities | + | Farley (50%) | + | Greene (30%) | + | Hall (20%) |
|---|---|---|---|---|---|---|---|---|---|---|---|
| | | | | | | | **Capital** | | | | |
| Balances before realization | $ 11,000 | | $ 64,000 | | $ 9,000 | | $ 22,000 | | $ 22,000 | | $ 22,000 |
| Sale of assets and division of loss | +44,000 | | −64,000 | | — | | −10,000 | | − 6,000 | | − 4,000 |
| Balances after realization | $ 55,000 | | $ 0 | | $ 9,000 | | $ 12,000 | | $ 16,000 | | $ 18,000 |
| Payment of liabilities | − 9,000 | | — | | −9,000 | | — | | — | | — |
| Balances after payment of liabilities | $ 46,000 | | $ 0 | | $ 0 | | $ 12,000 | | $ 16,000 | | $ 18,000 |
| Cash distributed to partners | −46,000 | | — | | — | | −12,000 | | −16,000 | | −18,000 |
| Final balances | $ 0 | | $ 0 | | $ 0 | | $ 0 | | $ 0 | | $ 0 |

The entries to liquidate the partnership are as follows:

Sale of assets:

| LLC Alternative | | |
|---|---|---|
| Cash | 44,000 | |
| Loss on Realization | 20,000 | |
| Noncash Assets | | 34,000 |

| | | Cash | 44 0 0 0 00 | |
|---|---|---|---|---|
| | | Loss on Realization | 20 0 0 0 00 | |
| | | Noncash Assets | | 64 0 0 0 00 |

Division of loss:

| LLC Alternative | | |
|---|---|---|
| Jean Farley, Member Equity | 10,000 | |
| Brad Greene, Member Equity | 6,000 | |
| Alice Hall, Member Equity | 4,000 | |
| Loss on Realization | | 20,000 |

| | | Jean Farley, Capital | 10 0 0 0 00 | |
|---|---|---|---|---|
| | | Brad Greene, Capital | 6 0 0 0 00 | |
| | | Alice Hall, Capital | 4 0 0 0 00 | |
| | | Loss on Realization | | 20 0 0 0 00 |

Payment of liabilities:

| LLC Alternative | | |
|---|---|---|
| Liabilities | 9,000 | |
| Cash | | 9,000 |

| | | Liabilities | 9 0 0 0 00 | |
|---|---|---|---|---|
| | | Cash | | 9 0 0 0 00 |

Distribution of cash to partners:

| LLC Alternative | | |
|---|---|---|
| Jean Farley, Member Equity | 12,000 | |
| Brad Greene, Member Equity | 16,000 | |
| Alice Hall, Member Equity | 18,000 | |
| Cash | | 46,000 |

| | | Jean Farley, Capital | 12 0 0 0 00 | |
|---|---|---|---|---|
| | | Brad Greene, Capital | 16 0 0 0 00 | |
| | | Alice Hall, Capital | 18 0 0 0 00 | |
| | | Cash | | 46 0 0 0 00 |

# Loss on Realization—Capital Deficiency

In the preceding example, the capital account of each partner was large enough to absorb the partner's share of the loss from realization. The partners received cash to the extent of the remaining balances in their capital accounts. The share of loss on realization may exceed, however, the balance in the partner's capital account. The resulting debit balance in the capital account is called a **deficiency**. It represents a claim of the partnership against the partner.

To illustrate, assume that Farley, Greene, and Hall sell all of the noncash assets for $10,000. A loss of $54,000 ($64,000 − $10,000) is realized. The share of the loss allocated to Farley, $27,000 (50% of $54,000), exceeds the $22,000 balance in her capital account. This $5,000 deficiency represents an amount that Farley owes the partnership. Assuming that Farley pays the entire deficiency to the partnership, sufficient cash is available to distribute to the remaining partners according to their capital balances. The steps in liquidating the partnership in this case are summarized in Exhibit 7.

The entries to record the liquidation are as follows:

Sale of assets:

| LLC Alternative | | |
|---|---|---|
| Cash | 10,000 | |
| Loss on Realization | 54,000 | |
| Noncash Assets | | 64,000 |

| | | Cash | 10 0 0 0 00 | |
|---|---|---|---|---|
| | | Loss on Realization | 54 0 0 0 00 | |
| | | Noncash Assets | | 64 0 0 0 00 |

Division of loss:

| | | LLC Alternative | | |
|---|---|---|---|---|
| Jean Farley, Member Equity | 27,000 | | | |
| Brad Greene, Member Equity | 16,200 | | | |
| Alice Hall, Member Equity | 10,800 | | | |
| Loss on Realization | | 54,000 | | |

| | | | | |
|---|---|---|---|---|
| | Jean Farley, Capital | | 27 0 0 0 00 | |
| | Brad Greene, Capital | | 16 2 0 0 00 | |
| | Alice Hall, Capital | | 10 8 0 0 00 | |
| | Loss on Realization | | | 54 0 0 0 00 |

Payment of liabilities:

| | | LLC Alternative | | |
|---|---|---|---|---|
| Liabilities | 9,000 | | | |
| Cash | | 9,000 | | |

| | | | | |
|---|---|---|---|---|
| | Liabilities | | 9 0 0 0 00 | |
| | Cash | | | 9 0 0 0 00 |

Receipt of deficiency:

| | | LLC Alternative | | |
|---|---|---|---|---|
| Cash | 5,000 | | | |
| Jean Farley, Member Equity | | 5,000 | | |

| | | | | |
|---|---|---|---|---|
| | Cash | | 5 0 0 0 00 | |
| | Jean Farley, Capital | | | 5 0 0 0 00 |

Distribution of cash to partners:

| | | LLC Alternative | | |
|---|---|---|---|---|
| Brad Greene, Member Equity | 5,800 | | | |
| Alice Hall, Member Equity | 11,200 | | | |
| Cash | | 17,000 | | |

| | | | | |
|---|---|---|---|---|
| | Brad Greene, Capital | | 5 8 0 0 00 | |
| | Alice Hall, Capital | | 11 2 0 0 00 | |
| | Cash | | | 17 0 0 0 00 |

**•Exhibit 7**   **Loss on Realization—Capital Deficiency**

**Farley, Greene, and Hall**
**Statement of Partnership Liquidation**
**For Period April 10–30, 2006**

| | Cash | + | Noncash Assets | = | Liabilities | + | Farley (50%) | + | Greene (30%) | + | Hall (20%) |
|---|---|---|---|---|---|---|---|---|---|---|---|
| | | | | | | | **Capital** | | | | |
| Balances before realization | $ 11,000 | | $ 64,000 | | $ 9,000 | | $ 22,000 | | $ 22,000 | | $ 22,000 |
| Sale of assets and division of loss | +10,000 | | −64,000 | | — | | −27,000 | | −16,200 | | −10,800 |
| Balances after realization | $ 21,000 | | $      0 | | $ 9,000 | | $  5,000 (Dr.) | | $  5,800 | | $ 11,200 |
| Payment of liabilities | − 9,000 | | — | | −9,000 | | — | | — | | — |
| Balances after payment of liabilities | $ 12,000 | | $      0 | | $      0 | | $  5,000 (Dr.) | | $  5,800 | | $ 11,200 |
| Receipt of deficiency | + 5,000 | | — | | — | | + 5,000 | | — | | — |
| Balances | $ 17,000 | | $      0 | | $      0 | | $      0 | | $  5,800 | | $ 11,200 |
| Cash distributed to partners | −17,000 | | — | | — | | — | | − 5,800 | | −11,200 |
| Final balances | $      0 | | $      0 | | $      0 | | $      0 | | $      0 | | $      0 |

If cash is not collected from a deficient partner, the partnership cash will not be large enough to pay the other partners in full. Any uncollected deficiency becomes a loss to the partnership and is divided among the remaining partners' capital balances, based on their income-sharing ratio. The cash balance will then equal the sum of the capital account balances. Cash is then distributed to the remaining partners, based on the balances of their capital accounts.[8]

## Errors in Liquidation

The most common error that occurs in liquidating a partnership is making an improper distribution of cash to the partners. Such an error occurs because the distribution of cash to partners in liquidation is confused with the division of gains and losses on realization.

Gains and losses on realization result from the disposal of assets to outsiders. *Realized gains and losses should be divided among the partner capital accounts in the same manner as the net income or net loss from normal business operations—using the income-sharing ratio.* On the other hand, the distribution of cash (or other assets) to the partners in liquidation is not directly related to the income-sharing ratio. The distribution of assets to the partners in liquidation is the exact reverse of the contribution of assets by the partners at the time the partnership was established. *The distribution of assets to partners in liquidation is equal to the credit balances in their capital accounts after all gains and losses on realization have been divided and allowances have been made for any partner deficiencies.*

# Business Life Cycle

objective   7

Describe the life cycle of a business, including the role of venture capitalists, initial public offerings, and underwriters.

Just as a person experiences a life cycle, so, too, does a business—from its initial inception (birth) to its liquidation (death). During its life cycle, a business may change entity forms. A business entity's life cycle may begin as a proprietorship and end as a corporation. In addition, during its life cycle, a business often utilizes venture capitalists, initial public offerings, and underwriters to raise funds.

To illustrate, consider the life cycle of the business shown in Exhibit 8. Jeff Jacobi began the business as a proprietorship by obtaining a local business license and opening a bank account in the name of the proprietorship, Della's Delights (proprietorship). The business manufactured and sold ice cream made from a family recipe. Over several years, the business became successful locally and Jacobi decided to grow the business regionally. To grow regionally, Jacobi invited a family friend, Kim Lange, to join the business as the sales manager. To entice Lange, Jacobi offered to admit her as a partner in the business and form Della's Delights (partnership). Lange agreed and was admitted to the new partnership by purchasing an interest in Della's Delights for cash.

Within three years, Jacobi and Lange had expanded the business regionally and were considering going national. To go national, however, the business needed additional funds (capital) that the partners were not able to raise from their personal assets. A local banker suggested that they consider contacting a venture capitalist. A **venture capitalist (VC)** is an individual or firm that provides equity financing for new companies. The business strategy of most venture capitalists is to invest in successful businesses, intending to sell their equity interest at a profit. In this way, the venture capitalist earns income and obtains funds for investing in yet more businesses. Jacobi and Lange contacted a venture capitalist, who expressed interest in owning a part of Della's Delights. However, the venture capitalist was concerned about the unlimited liability risk of the partnership form of organization. As a result, after consulting with their attorney and certified public accountant, Jacobi and Lange changed Della's Delights from a partnership to a limited liability corporation (LLC). Having satisfied the venture capitalist's concerns, the venture capitalist invested in Della Delights, LLC, for an equity interest.

Why might owners choose to form a new business as an LLC rather than as a regular corporation?

----------------------------------

*Answer: An LLC is moderately easy to form and is not taxed as a separate entity. Thus, dividend distributions from an LLC to the members are taxed once only. Additionally, an LLC has the benefit of limited liability.*

---

[8]The accounting for uncollectible deficiencies is discussed and illustrated in advanced accounting texts.

## •Exhibit 8

## LIFE CYCLE OF A BUSINESS

| BUSINESS STAGE | PRINCIPAL ADVANTAGE |

**Formation as
Proprietorship**

**Is formed easily:**
Jacobi forms a business by obtaining a local business license and opening a bank account.

**Formation as
Partnership**

**Expands capital and expertise:**
Jacobi admits a new partner that contributes capital and expertise.

**Formation as
Limited Liability
Corporation**

**Has limited legal liability:**
The partnership is changed to an LLC to limit the legal liability of owners.

**Formation as
Corporation**

**Simplifies raising capital:**
The LLC is changed to a corporation to raise capital from the public.

**Exit by Sale
of Corporation**

**Provides exit:**
The company is sold for cash.

Over the next five years, Della's Delights candy became nationally known, and the venture capitalist expressed interest in selling its equity interest and thus exiting the business. One way to sell this interest would be to establish a public market for Della's Delights common stock. Thus, the venture capitalist suggested that Jacobi and Lange take Della's Delights public with a stock offering. In addition to allowing the venture capitalist to exit the business, a public offering of stock would bring more cash into the business to fund further expansion into international markets. As a result, Jacobi and Lange agreed to take Della's Delights public with an ***initial public offering (IPO)*** of common stock.

On the advice of their attorney and certified public accountant and with the approval of the venture capitalist, Jacobi and Lange decided to transfer the assets of Della Delights, LLC, to a regular corporation, Della's Delights, Inc. In return for the transfer of assets, Jacobi, Lange, and the venture capitalist received common stock in the new corporation in proportion to their LLC interests. Nine months later, Della's Delights retained an underwriter and filed the necessary forms with the Securities and Exchange Commission for an initial public offering of common stock. ***Underwriting firms***, or **investment banks**, such as **Merrill Lynch**, help a company determine the offering price for its stock. Underwriting firms also help market the stock to their clients and the public.

---

# INTEGRITY IN BUSINESS

## ANALYST INDEPENDENCE

**M**ajor investment banks such as **Salomon Smith Barney** and **Merrill Lynch** underwrite new common stock offerings. They also provide investors with analyses of public companies. These two roles should be independent. Recently, however, research analysts have been accused of compromising independence by acting as cheerleaders for recent common stock issues underwritten by their firm. Criticism has been leveled that such research may be unobjective, or even misleading. **Merrill Lynch** settled a $100 million lawsuit brought by the New York state attorney general over these questionable analyst behaviors.

---

**REAL WORLD**

Pleasant Roland began producing Amercian Girl® dolls in 1986 with a $1 million investment. Twelve years later, she sold Pleasant Company to **Mattel, Inc.,** for $700 million. Today, American Girl dolls are one of the most profitable items for Mattel.

Later that year, Della's Delights common stock was offered to the public and was completely sold out within the first day. Subsequently, Della's Delights stock was publicly traded on NASDAQ under the stock symbol DLITE. Within the next year, the venture capitalist gradually sold its shares of stock and exited the business. Also, Jacobi and Lange began implementing their international strategy by opening a manufacturing and distribution facility in Belgium.

As Della's Delights' success grew internationally, it attracted the attention of International Foods, Inc., a large diversified food company. As a result, International Foods offered to acquire the stock of Della's Delights at a premium price, 25% above the current selling price of Della's Delights' common stock. Since Jacobi and Lange controlled the majority of Della's Delights' common stock, they met to discuss what action to recommend to the Board of Directors of Della's Delights. Jacobi and Lange decided that it was time to slow down and enjoy life. As a result, Jacobi and Lange recommended that Della's Board of Directors accept the bid of International Foods.

The Board approved the acquisition, and Jacobi and Lange exited the business as multimillionaires. Subsequently, Jacobi retired to Montana to nurture his passions for fly fishing and skiing. Lange, on the other hand, was last seen sailing with her husband in the Caribbean on their 80-foot sailboat named DELIGHT.

In our illustration, Della's Delights was purchased by another corporation. However, the last stages of a company may differ greatly from that of Della's Delights. Some businesses simply cease to exist, such as the **Smith Corona Corporation** (a typewriter company), which ended in bankruptcy. Others may last a long time, such as **General Electric Company**, which is over 125 years old. More frequently, though, firms lose their separate identities through merger or acquisition, as we illustrated with Della's Delights.

Not all businesses move sequentially through the business forms as we've illustrated here. Some businesses will remain in their initial form, while still others may skip one or more of the forms. For example, a business may move directly from a proprietorship to a corporation or begin as a limited liability corporation. It would be rare, however, for a business to reverse the sequence we've illustrated in this section, such as moving from a corporation to a partnership.

## SPOTLIGHT ON STRATEGY

### ORGANIZATIONAL FORMS IN THE ACCOUNTING AND CONSULTING INDUSTRY

The four major accounting firms, **KPMG Peat Marwick**, **Ernst & Young**, **PricewaterhouseCoopers**, and **Deloitte & Touche**, all began as partnerships. This form was legally required due to the theory of mutual agency. That is, the partnership form was thought to create public trust by requiring all partners to be jointly liable and responsible for each other's judgments. Each partner's personal assets were backing up every partner's judgment. The partnership form also restricted investment to the professionals that actually provide the service in the public trust. Thus, the partnership prevented outside investors from influencing professional decisions from a purely profit motive.

As these firms grew and the risk increased, all of these firms were allowed to change, by law, to limited liability partnerships (LLPs). Thus, while remaining a partnership, the liability of the partners was limited to their investment in the firm. For example, the partners of **Arthur Andersen**, while losing most of their investment in the firm due to the **Enron** fiasco, were protected against most additional claims on their personal assets due to the LLP structure.

All of these firms also had significant consulting practices that were consolidated inside the LLP structure. The recently enacted Sarbanes-Oxley Act has prohibited accounting firms from providing auditing and consulting services to the same client. As a result, the consulting segments of these firms were spun out into separate corporations. These newly created consulting firms, such as **Bearing Point** (formally of **KPMG**), **Cap Gemini Ernst & Young** (formally of **Ernst & Young**), and **Accenture** (formally of **Arthur Andersen**) all trade on the stock market as independent companies. As independent companies, they are free to raise additional capital on the stock market, reward executives with stock options, and more readily focus on consulting. Very few of the large consulting firms have remained as partnerships, due to the limitations of this organizational form. One of the few exceptions is **McKinsey & Co.**, a strategy-consulting firm. In the future, we might expect to see new consulting firms try the emerging limited liability company (LLC) form of organization, since it retains attractive features of both partnerships and corporations.

# Key Points

**1 Describe the basic characteristics of proprietorships, corporations, partnerships, and limited liability corporations.**

The advantages and disadvantages of each of the four basic forms of business organization—proprietorships, corporations, partnerships, and limited liability corporations—were discussed. Proprietorships have the major advantage that they are easy to form. Corporations provide ease in raising capital and limited liability for stockholders. Corporations are taxed as a separate entity. Partnerships do not provide limited liability but have the advantage of providing additional expertise and capital from partners. Partnership income flows through to the individual tax return and thus is not taxed as a separate entity. Limited liability corporations provide limited liability for members while maintaining the tax advantages of a partnership.

**2 Describe and illustrate the equity reporting for proprietorships, corporations, partnerships, and limited liability corporations.**

The equity reporting for proprietorships shows the change in the owner's capital account from contributions, net income, and withdrawals. The statement of stockholders' equity of a corporation shows the changes in the major stockholder equity accounts, such as common stock, paid-in capital in excess of par value, retained earnings, and treasury stock, in tabular form. The statement of partnership capital for a partnership shows the changes in each partner's capital account for a year, including the partner's contributions, share of net income, and withdrawals. The statement of members' equity for a limited liability corporation shows the changes in each member's equity account for a year, including the member's contributions, share of net income, and withdrawals.

### 3 Describe and illustrate the accounting for forming a partnership.

When a partnership is formed, accounts are debited for the assets contributed, accounts are credited for the liabilities assumed, and the partners' capital accounts are credited for their respective net amounts. Noncash assets are recorded at amounts agreed upon by the partners.

### 4 Describe and illustrate the accounting for dividing the net income and net loss of a partnership.

The net income (net loss) of a partnership is divided among the partners by debiting (crediting) Income Summary and crediting (debiting) the partners' capital accounts. The net income or net loss may be divided on the basis of services rendered by individual partners and/or on the basis of the investments of the individual partners. In the absence of any agreement, net income is divided equally among the partners.

### 5 Describe and illustrate the accounting for the dissolution of a partnership.

Any change in the personnel or ownership dissolves the partnership. A partnership may be dissolved by admission of a new partner, withdrawal of a partner, or death of a partner. A partnership's asset account balances should be stated at current values at the time of dissolution of the partnership.

A new partner may be admitted to a partnership by buying an interest from one or more of the existing partners. When a new partner is admitted to a partnership, the incoming partner may pay a bonus to the existing partners. Alternatively, the existing partners may pay a bonus to the new partner to join the partnership. When a partner retires, dies, or withdraws from a partnership, one or more of the remaining partners may buy the withdrawing partner's interest.

### 6 Describe and illustrate the accounting for liquidating a partnership.

When a partnership liquidates, it sells its noncash assets, pays the creditors, and distributes the remaining cash or other assets to the partners. Any gain or loss on the sale of the noncash assets should be divided among the partners according to their income-sharing ratio. The final asset distribution to partners is based on the balance of the partners' capital accounts after all noncash assets have been sold and liabilities paid.

### 7 Describe the life cycle of a business, including the role of venture capitalists, initial public offerings, and underwriters.

A business often moves through different organizational forms over a life cycle. A business may begin as a proprietorship, then become a partnership and/or LLC, and finally end as a regular corporation. Each stage has advantages and disadvantages. Venture capitalists provide equity financing for young businesses. Underwriters assist a company in making an initial public offering of common stock to the investing public.

# Key Terms

# Illustrative Problem

Radcliffe, Sonders, and Towers, who share in income and losses in the ratio of 2:3:5, decided to discontinue operations as of April 30 and liquidate their partnership. After the accounts were closed on April 30, the following trial balance was prepared:

|  |  |  |
|---|---:|---:|
| Cash | 5,900 | |
| Noncash Assets | 109,900 | |
| Liabilities | | 26,800 |
| Radcliffe, Capital | | 14,600 |
| Sonders, Capital | | 27,900 |
| Towers, Capital | | 46,500 |
| Total | 115,800 | 115,800 |

Between May 1 and May 18, the noncash assets were sold for $27,400, and the liabilities were paid.

### Instructions

1. Assuming that the partner with the capital deficiency pays the entire amount owed to the partnership, prepare a statement of partnership liquidation.
2. Journalize the entries to record (a) the sale of the assets, (b) the division of loss on the sale of the assets, (c) the payment of the liabilities, (d) the receipt of the deficiency, and (e) the distribution of cash to the partners.

### Solution

1.

**Radcliff, Sonders, and Towers**
**Statement of Partnership Liquidation**
**For Period May 1–18, 2006**

|  | Cash | + | Noncash Assets | = | Liabilities | + | Capital Radcliffe (20%) | + | Capital Sonders (30%) | + | Capital Towers (50%) |
|---|---:|---|---:|---|---:|---|---:|---|---:|---|---:|
| Balances before realization | $ 5,900 | | $ 109,900 | | $ 26,800 | | $ 14,600 | | $ 27,900 | | $ 46,500 |
| Sale of assets and division of loss | +27,400 | | −109,900 | | — | | −16,500 | | −24,750 | | −41,250 |
| Balances after realization | $ 33,300 | | $ 0 | | $ 26,800 | | $ 1,900 (Dr.) | | $ 3,150 | | $ 5,250 |
| Payment of liabilities | −26,800 | | — | | −26,800 | | — | | — | | — |
| Balances after payment of liabilities | $ 6,500 | | $ 0 | | $ 0 | | $ 1,900 (Dr.) | | $ 3,150 | | $ 5,250 |
| Receipt of deficiency | + 1,900 | | — | | — | | + 1,900 | | — | | — |
| Balances | $ 8,400 | | $ 0 | | $ 0 | | $ 0 | | $ 3,150 | | $ 5,250 |
| Cash distributed to partners | − 8,400 | | — | | — | | — | | − 3,150 | | − 5,250 |
| Final balances | $ 0 | | $ 0 | | $ 0 | | $ 0 | | $ 0 | | $ 0 |

2. a.

| | | |
|---|---:|---:|
| Cash | 27 40 0 00 | |
| Loss and Gain on Realization | 82 50 0 00 | |
|    Noncash Assets | | 109 90 0 00 |

b.

| | | |
|---|---:|---:|
| Radcliffe, Capital | 16 50 0 00 | |
| Sonders, Capital | 24 75 0 00 | |
| Towers, Capital | 41 25 0 00 | |
|    Loss and Gain on Realization | | 82 50 0 00 |

c.

| | | |
|---|---:|---:|
| Liabilities | 26 80 0 00 | |
|    Cash | | 26 80 0 00 |

d.

| | | |
|---|---:|---:|
| Cash | 1 90 0 00 | |
|    Radcliffe, Capital | | 1 90 0 00 |

e.

| | | | | |
|---|---|---|---|---|
| Sonders, Capital | | 3 1 5 0 00 | | |
| Towers, Capital | | 5 2 5 0 00 | | |
| Cash | | | | 8 4 0 0 00 |

# Self-Examination Questions (Answers at End of Chapter)

1. As part of the initial investment, a partner contributes office equipment that had cost $20,000 and on which accumulated depreciation of $12,500 had been recorded. If the partners agree on a valuation of $9,000 for the equipment, what amount should be debited to the office equipment account?
   A. $7,500          C. $12,500
   B. $9,000          D. $20,000

2. Chip and Dale agree to form a partnership. Chip is to contribute $50,000 in assets and to devote one-half time to the partnership. Dale is to contribute $20,000 and to devote full time to the partnership. How will Chip and Dale share in the division of net income or net loss?
   A. 5:2          C. 1:1
   B. 1:2          D. 2.5:1

3. Tracey and Hepburn invest $100,000 and $50,000 respectively in a partnership and agree to a division of net income that provides for an allowance of interest at 10% on original investments, salary allowances of $12,000 and $24,000 respectively, with the remainder divided equally. What would be Tracey's share of a net income of $45,000?
   A. $22,500          C. $19,000
   B. $22,000          D. $10,000

4. Lee and Stills are partners who share income in the ratio of 2:1 and who have capital balances of $65,000 and $35,000 respectively. If Morr, with the consent of Stills, acquired one-half of Lee's interest for $40,000, for what amount would Morr's capital account be credited?
   A. $32,500          C. $50,000
   B. $40,000          D. $72,500

5. Pavin and Abdel share gains and losses in the ratio of 2:1. After selling all assets for cash, dividing the losses on realization, and paying liabilities, the balances in the capital accounts were as follows: Pavin, $10,000 Cr.; Abdel, $2,000 Cr. How much of the cash of $12,000 would be distributed to Pavin?
   A. $2,000          C. $10,000
   B. $8,000          D. $12,000

# Class Discussion Questions

1. What are the main advantages of (a) proprietorships, (b) corporations, (c) partnerships, and (d) limited liability corporations?
2. What are the disadvantages of a partnership over the corporate form of organization for a profit-making business?
3. Alan Biles and Joan Crandall joined together to form a partnership. Is it possible for them to lose a greater amount than the amount of their investment in the partnership? Explain.
4. What are the major features of a partnership agreement for a partnership or operating agreement for a limited liability corporation?
5. In the absence of an agreement, how will the net income be distributed between Michael Evans and Janice Farr, partners in the firm of E and F Environmental Consultants?
6. Paul Boyer, Fran Carrick, and Ed DiPano are contemplating the formation of a partnership. According to the partnership agreement, Boyer is to invest $60,000 and devote one-half time, Carrick is to invest $40,000 and devote three-fourths time, and DiPano is to make no investment and devote full time. Would DiPano be correct in assuming that, since he is not contributing any assets to the firm, he is risking nothing? Explain.

7. What are the required disclosures in the statement of stockholders' equity for a corporation?

8. How is the statement of members' equity similar to the statement of partners' equity?

9. As a part of the initial investment, a partner contributes delivery equipment that had originally cost $50,000 and on which accumulated depreciation of $37,500 had been recorded. The partners agree on a valuation of $15,000. How should the delivery equipment be recorded in the accounts of the partnership?

10. All partners agree that $200,000 of accounts receivable invested by a partner will be collectible to the extent of 90%. How should the accounts receivable be recorded in the general ledger of the partnership?

11. During the current year, Helen Bray withdrew $3,000 monthly from the partnership of Bray and Cox Water Management Consultants. Is it possible that her share of partnership net income for the current year might be more or less than $36,000? Explain.

12. a. What accounts are debited and credited to record a partner's cash withdrawal in lieu of salary?

    b. At the end of the fiscal year, what accounts are debited and credited to record the division of net income among partners?

    c. The articles of partnership provide for a salary allowance of $5,000 per month to partner C. If C withdrew only $4,000 per month, would this affect the division of the partnership net income?

13. Explain the difference between the admission of a new partner to a partnership (a) by purchase of an interest from another partner and (b) by contribution of assets to the partnership.

14. Why is it important to state all partnership assets in terms of current prices at the time of the admission of a new partner?

15. Why might a partnership pay a bonus to a newly admitted partner?

16. In the liquidation process, (a) how are losses and gains on realization divided among the partners, and (b) how is cash distributed among the partners?

17. Why might a business go through different organizational forms through its life cycle?

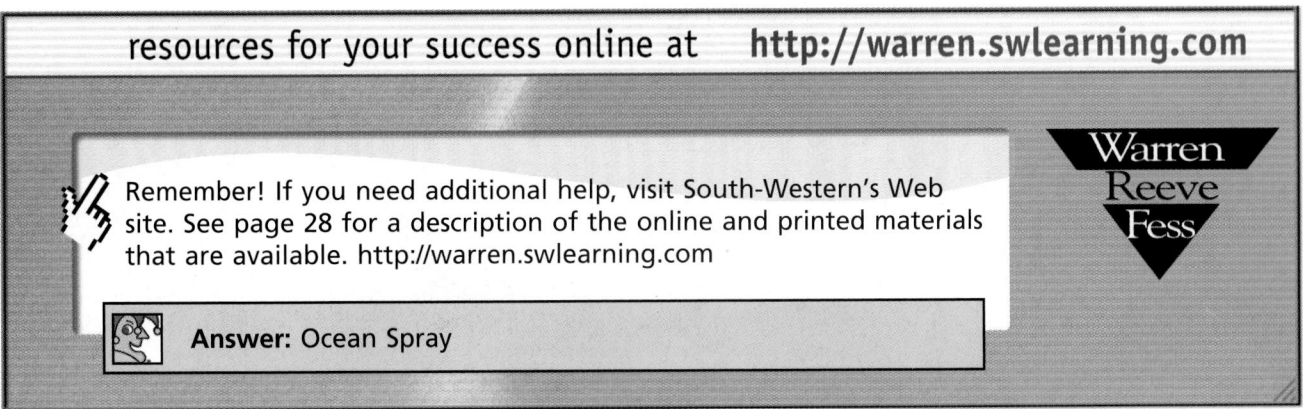

resources for your success online at   **http://warren.swlearning.com**

**W**arren **R**eeve **F**ess

Remember! If you need additional help, visit South-Western's Web site. See page 28 for a description of the online and printed materials that are available. http://warren.swlearning.com

**Answer:** Ocean Spray

# **E**xercises

**EXERCISE 13-1**
*Statement of stockholders' equity*

**Objective 2**

The stockholders' equity accounts of Tender Heart Greeting Cards Inc. for the current fiscal year ended December 31, 2006, are shown on the following page. Prepare a statement of stockholders' equity for the fiscal year ended December 31, 2006.

✓ *Total stockholders' equity, Dec. 31, $2,285,000*

**ACCOUNT** Common Stock, $2 Par

| Date | | Item | Debit | Credit | Balance Debit | Balance Credit |
|---|---|---|---|---|---|---|
| 2006 Jan. | 1 | Balance | | | | 500 0 0 0 00 |
| Mar. | 13 | Issued 50,000 shares | | 100 0 0 0 00 | | 600 0 0 0 00 |

**ACCOUNT** Paid-In Capital in Excess of Par

| Date | | Item | Debit | Credit | Balance Debit | Balance Credit |
|---|---|---|---|---|---|---|
| 2006 Jan. | 1 | Balance | | | | 400 0 0 0 00 |
| Mar. | 13 | Issued 50,000 shares | | 45 0 0 0 00 | | 445 0 0 0 00 |

**ACCOUNT** Treasury Stock

| Date | | Item | Debit | Credit | Balance Debit | Balance Credit |
|---|---|---|---|---|---|---|
| 2006 Apr. | 30 | Purchased 10,000 shares | 25 0 0 0 00 | | 25 0 0 0 00 | |

**ACCOUNT** Retained Earnings

| Date | | Item | Debit | Credit | Balance Debit | Balance Credit |
|---|---|---|---|---|---|---|
| 2006 Jan. | 1 | Balance | | | | 1,075 0 0 0 00 |
| Dec. | 31 | Income summary | | 240 0 0 0 00 | | 1,315 0 0 0 00 |
| | 31 | Cash dividends | 50 0 0 0 00 | | | 1,265 0 0 0 00 |

**ACCOUNT** Cash Dividends

| Date | | Item | Debit | Credit | Balance Debit | Balance Credit |
|---|---|---|---|---|---|---|
| 2006 June | 30 | | 25 0 0 0 00 | | 25 0 0 0 00 | |
| Dec. | 30 | | 25 0 0 0 00 | | 50 0 0 0 00 | |
| | 31 | Closing | | 50 0 0 0 00 | — | — |

**EXERCISE 13-2**
*Entry for partner's original investment*
**Objective 3**

Todd Jost and D. Caldwell decide to form a partnership by combining the assets of their separate businesses. Jost contributes the following assets to the partnership: cash, $6,000; accounts receivable with a face amount of $96,000 and an allowance for doubtful accounts of $6,600; merchandise inventory with a cost of $85,000; and equipment with a cost of $140,000 and accumulated depreciation of $90,000.

The partners agree that $5,000 of the accounts receivable are completely worthless and are not to be accepted by the partnership, that $8,000 is a reasonable allowance for the uncollectibility of the remaining accounts, that the merchandise inventory is to be recorded at the current market price of $76,500, and that the equipment is to be valued at $90,000.

Journalize the partnership's entry to record Jost's investment.

**EXERCISE 13-3**
*Dividing partnership income*

Objective 4

✓ b. Moore, $80,000

Dan Moore and T. J. Knell formed a partnership, investing $240,000 and $120,000 respectively. Determine their participation in the year's net income of $120,000 under each of the following independent assumptions: (a) no agreement concerning division of net income; (b) divided in the ratio of original capital investment; (c) interest at the rate of 10% allowed on original investments and the remainder divided in the ratio of 2:3; (d) salary allowances of $40,000 and $50,000 respectively, and the balance divided equally; (e) allowance of interest at the rate of 10% on original investments, salary allowances of $40,000 and $50,000 respectively, and the remainder divided equally.

**EXERCISE 13-4**
*Dividing partnership income*

Objective 4

✓ c. Moore, $81,600

Determine the participation of Moore and Knell in the year's net income of $180,000, according to each of the five assumptions as to income division listed in Exercise 13-3.

**EXERCISE 13-5**
*Dividing partnership net loss*

Objective 4

Jane Williams and Y. Osaka formed a partnership in which the partnership agreement provided for salary allowances of $40,000 and $60,000, respectively. Determine the division of a $20,000 net loss for the current year.

**EXERCISE 13-6**
*Negotiating income-sharing ratio*

Objective 4

WHAT'S WRONG
WITH THIS?

Sixty-year-old Jim Ebers retired from his computer consulting business in Boston and moved to Florida. There he met 27-year-old Ann Bowers, who had just graduated from Eldon Community College with an associate degree in computer science. Jim and Ann formed a partnership called E&B Computer Consultants. Jim contributed $15,000 for startup costs and devoted one-half time to the business. Ann devoted full time to the business. The monthly drawings were $1,500 for Jim and $3,000 for Ann.

At the end of the first year of operations, the two partners disagreed on the division of net income. Jim reasoned that the division should be equal. Although he devoted only one-half time to the business, he contributed all of the startup funds. Ann reasoned that the income-sharing ratio should be 2:1 in her favor because she devoted full time to the business and her monthly drawings were twice those of Jim. Can you identify any flaws in the partners' reasoning regarding the income-sharing ratio?

**EXERCISE 13-7**
*Dividing LLC income*

Objective 4

✓ a. Bennings, $44,600

LaToya Bennings and Lamar Hodges formed a limited liability corporation (LLC) with an operating agreement that provided a salary allowance of $32,000 and $53,000 to each member, respectively. In addition, the operating agreement specified an income-sharing ratio of 3:2. The two members withdrew amounts equal to their salary allowances.

a. Determine the division of $106,000 net income for the year.
b. Provide journal entries to close the (1) income summary and (2) drawing accounts for the two members.

**EXERCISE 13-8**
*Dividing LLC net income and statement of members' equity*

Objectives 2, 4

SPREADSHEET

✓ a. Higgins, $295,980

Media Properties, LLC, has three members: WXXY Radio Partners, John Higgins, and Daily Call Newspaper, LLC. On January 1, 2006, the three members had equity of $160,000, $95,000, and $250,000, respectively. WXXY Radio Partners contributed an additional $50,000 to Media Properties, LLC, on June 1, 2006. John Higgins received an annual salary allowance of $125,000 during 2006. The members' equity accounts are also credited with 8% interest on each member's January 1 capital balance. Any remaining income is to be shared in the ratio of 4:3:3 among the three members. The net income for Media Properties, LLC, for 2006 was $710,000. The salary and interest allowances were distributed to the members.

a. Determine the division of income among the three members.
b. Prepare the journal entry to close the net income and withdrawals to the individual member equity accounts.
c. Prepare a statement of members' equity for 2006.

**EXERCISE 13-9**
*Partnership entries and statement of partners' equity*

**Objectives 2, 4**

SPREADSHEET

✓ *b. Higgins, capital, Dec. 31, $98,000*

The capital accounts of Walt Bigney and Dan Harris have balances of $80,000 and $95,000, respectively, on January 1, 2006, the beginning of the current fiscal year. On April 10, Bigney invested an additional $10,000. During the year, Bigney and Harris withdrew $72,000 and $84,000, respectively, and net income for the year was $160,000. The articles of partnership make no reference to the division of net income.

a. Journalize the entries to close (1) the income summary account and (2) the drawing accounts.
b. Prepare a statement of partners' equity for the current year for the partnership of Bigney and Harris.

**EXERCISE 13-10**
*Partner income and withdrawal journal entries*

**Objective 4**

REAL WORLD

The notes to the annual report for **KPMG LLP** (U.K.) indicated the following policies regarding the partners' capital:

*The allocation of profits to those who were partners during the financial year occurs following the finalization of the annual financial statements. During the year, partners receive monthly drawings and, from time to time, additional profit distributions. Both the monthly drawings and profit distributions represent payments on account of current-year profits and are reclaimable from partners until profits have been allocated.*

Assume that the partners draw £20,000 million per month for 2006 and the net income for the year is £200 million.

a. Provide the journal entry for the monthly partner drawing for January.
b. Provide the journal entry to close the income summary account at the end of the year.
c. Provide the journal entry to close the drawing account at the end of the year.
d. Provide the journal entry required by the partners at the end of the year, due to the reclaimable portion according to the operating agreement.

**EXERCISE 13-11**
*Admitting new partners*

**Objective 5**

Jenny Kirk and Harold Spock are partners who share in the income equally and have capital balances of $90,000 and $62,500, respectively. Kirk, with the consent of Spock, sells one-third of her interest to Benjamin McCoy. What entry is required by the partnership if the sale price is (a) $20,000? (b) $40,000?

**EXERCISE 13-12**
*Admitting new partners*

**Objective 5**

REAL WORLD

The public accounting firm of **Grant Thornton** disclosed global revenues of $1.84 billion for a recent year. The revenues were attributable to 2,270 active partners.

a. What was the average revenue per partner? Round to the nearest $1,000.
b. Assuming that the total partners' capital is $300,000,000 and that it approximates the fair market value of the firm's net assets, what would be considered a minimum contribution for admitting a new partner to the firm, assuming no bonus is paid to the new partner? Round to the nearest $1,000.
c. Why might the amount to be contributed by a new partner for admission to the firm exceed the amount determined in (b)?

**EXERCISE 13-13**
*Admitting new partners who buy an interest and contribute assets*

**Objective 5**

✓ *b. Yu, $75,000*

The capital accounts of Susan Yu and Ben Hardy have balances of $100,000 and $90,000 respectively. Ken Mahl and Jeff Wood are to be admitted to the partnership. Mahl buys one-fourth of Yu's interest for $27,500 and one-fifth of Hardy's interest for $20,000. Wood contributes $35,000 cash to the partnership, for which he is to receive an ownership equity of $35,000.

a. Journalize the entries to record the admission of (1) Mahl and (2) Wood.
b. What are the capital balances of each partner after the admission of the new partners?

**EXERCISE 13-14**
*Admitting new partner who contributes assets*
**Objective 5**

✓ *b. Jacobs, $56,000*

After the tangible assets have been adjusted to current market prices, the capital accounts of Cecil Jacobs and Maria Estaban have balances of $61,000 and $59,000 respectively. Lee White is to be admitted to the partnership, contributing $45,000 cash to the partnership, for which she is to receive an ownership equity of $55,000. All partners share equally in income.

a. Journalize the entry to record the admission of White, who is to receive a bonus of $10,000.
b. What are the capital balances of each partner after the admission of the new partner?

**EXERCISE 13-15**
*Admitting a new LLC member*
**Objective 5**

Center City Medical, LLC, consists of two doctors, Conway and Patel, who share in all income and losses according to a 2:3 income-sharing ratio. Dr. Lindsey Truett has been asked to join the LLC. Prior to admitting Truett, the assets of Center City were revalued to reflect their current market values. The revaluation resulted in medical equipment being reduced by $14,000. Prior to the revaluation, the equity balances for Conway and Patel were $300,000 and $340,000, respectively.

a. Provide the journal entry for the asset revaluation.
b. Provide the journal entry for the bonus under the following independent situations:
    1. Truett purchased a 30% interest in Center City Medical, LLC, for $340,000.
    2. Truett purchased a 26% interest in Center City Medical, LLC, for $190,000.

**EXERCISE 13-16**
*Partner bonuses, statement of partners' equity*
**Objectives 2, 5**

**SPREADSHEET**

✓ *Strous capital, Dec. 31, 2006, $59,200*

The partnership of Angel Investor Associates began operations on January 1, 2005, with contributions from two partners as follows:

| | |
|---|---|
| Jan Strous | $31,500 |
| Cara Wright | 58,500 |

Strous and Wright agree to an income-sharing ratio equal to their capital contribution ratio.

The following additional partner transactions took place during the year:

1. In late March, Michael Black is admitted to the partnership by contributing $30,000 cash for a 20% interest. Assets were adjusted downwards by $10,000 prior to admitting Black.
2. Net income of $172,000 was earned in 2006. In addition, Jan Strous received a salary allowance of $12,000 for the year.
3. The partners withdrawals are equal to half of the increase in their capital balances resulting from net income.

Prepare a statement of partnership equity for the year ended December 31, 2006.

**EXERCISE 13-17**
*Withdrawal of partner*
**Objective 5**

Glenn Otis is to retire from the partnership of Otis and Associates as of March 31, the end of the current fiscal year. After closing the accounts, the capital balances of the partners are as follows: Glenn Otis, $200,000; Tammie Sawyer, $125,000; and Joe Parrott, $140,000. They have shared net income and net losses in the ratio of 3:2:2. The partners agree that the merchandise inventory should be increased by $15,000, and the allowance for doubtful accounts should be increased by $3,100. Otis agrees to accept a note for $150,000 in partial settlement of his ownership equity. The remainder of his claim is to be paid in cash. Sawyer and Parrott are to share equally in the net income or net loss of the new partnership.

Journalize the entries to record (a) the adjustment of the assets to bring them into agreement with current market prices and (b) the withdrawal of Otis from the partnership.

**EXERCISE 13-18
AZTEC MINES, LLC**
*Statement of members'
equity, admitting new
member*

**Objectives 2, 4, 5**

✓ a. 2:3

The statement of members' equity for Aztec Mines, LLC, is as follows:

**Aztec Mines, LLC
Statement of Members' Equity
For the Years Ended December 31, 2005 and 2006**

| | Golden Properties, LLC, Member Equity | Aztec Holdings, Ltd., Member Equity | Jason Fields, Member Equity | Total Members' Equity |
|---|---|---|---|---|
| Members' equity, January 1, 2005 | $290,000 | $420,000 | | $ 710,000 |
| Net income | 50,000 | 75,000 | | 125,000 |
| Members' equity, December 31, 2005 | $340,000 | $495,000 | | $ 835,000 |
| Member contribution (reduction) | (8,000) | (12,000) | $203,750 | 183,750 |
| Net income | 106,880 | 160,320 | 66,800 | 334,000 |
| Less member withdrawals | (32,000) | (48,000) | (50,000) | (130,000) |
| Members' equity, December 31, 2006 | $406,880 | $595,320 | $220,550 | $1,222,750 |

a. What was the income-sharing ratio in 2005?

b. What was the income-sharing ratio in 2006?

c. Do the member withdrawals in 2006 match the income-sharing ratios for the three members? Why or why not?

d. How much cash did Jason Fields contribute to Aztec Mines, LLC, for his interest?

e. Why do the member equity accounts of Golden Properties, LLC, and Aztec Holdings, Ltd., have negative entries for Jason Fields' contribution?

f. What percentage interest of Aztec Mines did Jason Fields acquire?

**EXERCISE 13-19**
*Distribution of cash upon
liquidation*

**Objective 6**

✓ a. $5,000 loss

Hires and Bellman are partners, sharing gains and losses equally. At the time they decide to terminate their partnership, their capital balances are $5,000 and $20,000, respectively. After all noncash assets are sold and all liabilities are paid, there is a cash balance of $20,000.

a. What is the amount of a gain or loss on realization?

b. How should the gain or loss be divided between Hires and Bellman?

c. How should the cash be divided between Hires and Bellman?

**EXERCISE 13-20**
*Distribution of cash upon
liquidation*

**Objective 6**

✓ Goldberg, $42,000

Jacob Goldburg and Harlan Luce, with capital balances of $57,000 and $40,000 respectively, decide to liquidate their partnership. After selling the noncash assets and paying the liabilities, there is $67,000 of cash remaining. If the partners share income and losses equally, how should the cash be distributed?

**EXERCISE 13-21**
*Liquidating partnerships—
capital deficiency*

**Objective 6**

✓ b. $60,000

Bakki, Towers, and Nell share equally in net income and net losses. After the partnership sells all assets for cash, divides the losses on realization, and pays the liabilities, the balances in the capital accounts are as follows: Bakki, $20,000 Cr.; Towers, $57,500 Cr.; Nell, $17,500 Dr.

a. What term is applied to the debit balance in Nell's capital account?

b. What is the amount of cash on hand?

c. Journalize the transaction that must take place for Bakki and Towers to receive cash in the liquidation process equal to their capital account balances.

**EXERCISE 13-22**
*Distribution of cash upon
liquidation*

**Objective 6**

✓ a. Meyer, $275

Allyn Meyer, Jim Ball, and Laura David arranged to import and sell orchid corsages for a university dance. They agreed to share equally the net income or net loss of the venture. Meyer and Ball advanced $175 and $125 of their own respective funds to pay for advertising and other expenses. After collecting for all sales and paying creditors, the partnership has $600 in cash.

a. How should the money be distributed?

b. Assuming that the partnership has only $120 instead of $600, do any of the three partners have a capital deficiency? If so, how much?

**EXERCISE 13-23**
*Liquidating partnerships—capital deficiency*
**Objective 6**

Duncan, Tribe, and Ho are partners sharing income 3:2:1. After the firm's loss from liquidation is distributed, the capital account balances were: Duncan, $15,000 Dr.; Tribe, $50,000 Cr.; and Ho, $40,000 Cr. If Duncan is personally bankrupt and unable to pay any of the $15,000, what will be the amount of cash received by Tribe and Ho upon liquidation?

**EXERCISE 13-24**
*Statement of partnership liquidation*
**Objective 6**

SPREADSHEET

After closing the accounts on July 1, prior to liquidating the partnership, the capital account balances of Gibbs, Hill, and Manson are $24,000, $28,000, and $14,000, respectively. Cash, noncash assets, and liabilities total $11,000, $85,000, and $30,000, respectively. Between July 1 and July 29, the noncash assets are sold for $61,000, the liabilities are paid, and the remaining cash is distributed to the partners. The partners share net income and loss in the ratio of 3:2:1. Prepare a statement of partnership liquidation for the period July 1–29.

**EXERCISE 13-25**
*Statement of LLC liquidation*
**Objective 6**

SPREADSHEET

Ellis, Roane, and Clausen are members of City Signs, LLC, sharing income and losses in the ratio of 2:2:1, respectively. The members decide to liquidate the limited liability corporation (LLC). The members' equity prior to liquidation and asset realization on March 1, 2006, are:

|  |  |
|---|---|
| Ellis | $28,000 |
| Roane | 45,000 |
| Clausen | 12,000 |
| Total | $85,000 |

In winding up operations during the month of March, noncash assets with a book value of $125,000 are sold for $96,000, and liabilities of $44,000 are satisfied. Prior to realization, City Signs has a cash balance of $4,000.

a. Prepare a statement of LLC liquidation.
b. Provide the journal entry for the final cash distribution to members.

# Problems Series A

**PROBLEM 13-1A**
*Entries and balance sheet for partnership*
**Objectives 3, 4**

SPREADSHEET
P.A.S.S.

✓ 3. Tsao net income, $40,000

On November 1, 2005, E. Tsao and Mark Ivens form a partnership. Tsao agrees to invest $15,000 cash and merchandise inventory valued at $55,000. Ivens invests certain business assets at valuations agreed upon, transfers business liabilities, and contributes sufficient cash to bring his total capital to $85,000. Details regarding the book values of the business assets and liabilities, and the agreed valuations, follow:

|  | Ivens' Ledger Balance | Agreed-Upon Valuation |
|---|---|---|
| Accounts Receivable | $33,250 | $31,500 |
| Allowance for Doubtful Accounts | 500 | 800 |
| Merchandise Inventory | 42,500 | 42,900 |
| Equipment | 50,000 | 25,000 |
| Accumulated Depreciation | 29,700 | |
| Accounts Payable | 9,700 | 9,700 |
| Notes Payable | 10,000 | 10,000 |

The partnership agreement includes the following provisions regarding the division of net income: interest of 10% on original investments, salary allowances of $24,000 and $18,000 respectively, and the remainder equally.

**Instructions**
1. Journalize the entries to record the investments of Tsao and Ivens in the partnership accounts.    *(continued)*

2. Prepare a balance sheet as of November 1, 2005, the date of formation of the partnership of Tsao and Ivens.

3. After adjustments and the closing of revenue and expense accounts at October 31, 2006, the end of the first full year of operations, the income summary account has a credit balance of $75,500, and the drawing accounts have debit balances of $26,000 (Tsao) and $17,500 (Ivens). Journalize the entries to close the income summary account and the drawing accounts at October 31.

**PROBLEM 13-2A**
*Dividing partnership income*

**Objective 4**

SPREADSHEET

✓ *1. f. Haddox net income, $93,000*

Phil Haddox and Russ French have decided to form a partnership. They have agreed that Haddox is to invest $120,000 and that French is to invest $180,000. Haddox is to devote full time to the business, and French is to devote one-half time. The following plans for the division of income are being considered:

a. Equal division.
b. In the ratio of original investments.
c. In the ratio of time devoted to the business.
d. Interest of 10% on original investments and the remainder in the ratio of 3:2.
e. Interest of 10% on original investments, salary allowances of $60,000 to Haddox and $30,000 to French, and the remainder equally.
f. Plan (e), except that Haddox is also to be allowed a bonus equal to 20% of the amount by which net income exceeds the salary allowances.

**Instructions**

For each plan, determine the division of the net income under each of the following assumptions: (1) net income of $150,000 and (2) net income of $90,000. Present the data in tabular form, using the following columnar headings:

| | $150,000 | | $90,000 | |
|---|---|---|---|---|
| Plan | Haddox | French | Haddox | French |

**PROBLEM 13-3A**
*Financial statements for partnerships*

**Objective 4**

SPREADSHEET

✓ *2. Dec. 31 capital—Strange, $91,000*

The ledger of Dan Reeves and Ron Strange, Attorneys-at-Law, contains the following accounts and balances after adjustments have been recorded on December 31, 2006:

| | |
|---|---|
| Cash | $ 24,500 |
| Accounts Receivable | 40,500 |
| Supplies | 2,400 |
| Land | 50,000 |
| Building | 150,000 |
| Accumulated Depreciation—Building | 77,500 |
| Office Equipment | 40,000 |
| Accumulated Depreciation—Office Equipment | 22,400 |
| Accounts Payable | 1,000 |
| Salaries Payable | 1,500 |
| Dan Reeves, Capital | 75,000 |
| Dan Reeves, Drawing | 50,000 |
| Ron Strange, Capital | 55,000 |
| Ron Strange, Drawing | 60,000 |
| Professional Fees | 316,750 |
| Salary Expense | 84,500 |
| Depreciation Expense—Building | 10,500 |
| Property Tax Expense | 10,000 |
| Heating and Lighting Expense | 9,900 |
| Supplies Expense | 5,750 |
| Depreciation Expense—Office Equipment | 5,000 |
| Miscellaneous Expense | 6,100 |

The balance in Strange's capital account includes an additional investment of $5,000 made on April 5, 2006.

**Instructions**

1. Prepare an income statement for the current fiscal year, indicating the division of net income. The articles of partnership provide for salary allowances of $25,000

to Reeves and $35,000 to Strange, allowances of 12% on each partner's capital balance at the beginning of the fiscal year, and equal division of the remaining net income or net loss.
2. Prepare a statement of partner's equity for 2006.
3. Prepare a balance sheet as of the end of 2006.

**PROBLEM 13-4A**
*Admitting new partner*

Objective 5

P.A.S.S.

✓ 3. Total assets, $232,600

Adrian Capps and Lisa Knight have operated a successful firm for many years, sharing net income and net losses equally. Todd Aguero is to be admitted to the partnership on June 1 of the current year, in accordance with the following agreement:

a. Assets and liabilities of the old partnership are to be valued at their book values as of May 31, except for the following:
  • Accounts receivable amounting to $3,250 are to be written off, and the allowance for doubtful accounts is to be increased to 5% of the remaining accounts.
  • Merchandise inventory is to be valued at $63,400.
  • Equipment is to be valued at $108,000.
b. Aguero is to purchase $25,000 of the ownership interest of Capps for $37,500 cash and to contribute $25,000 cash to the partnership for a total ownership equity of $50,000.
c. The income-sharing ratio of Capps, Knight, and Aguero is to be 2:1:1.

The post-closing trial balance of Capps and Knight as of May 31 is as follows:

**Capps and Knight**
**Post-Closing Trial Balance**
**May 31, 2006**

| | | |
|---|---:|---:|
| Cash | 9,500 | |
| Accounts Receivable | 29,250 | |
| Allowance for Doubtful Accounts | | 500 |
| Merchandise Inventory | 60,100 | |
| Prepaid Insurance | 2,000 | |
| Equipment | 162,000 | |
| Accumulated Depreciation—Equipment | | 72,500 |
| Accounts Payable | | 9,850 |
| Notes Payable | | 20,000 |
| Adrian Capps, Capital | | 120,000 |
| Lisa Knight, Capital | | 40,000 |
| | 262,850 | 262,850 |

**Instructions**
1. Journalize the entries as of May 31 to record the revaluations, using a temporary account entitled Asset Revaluations. The balance in the accumulated depreciation account is to be eliminated.
2. Journalize the additional entries to record the remaining transactions relating to the formation of the new partnership. Assume that all transactions occur on June 1.
3. Present a balance sheet for the new partnership as of June 1, 2006.

**PROBLEM 13-5A**
*Statement of partnership liquidation*

Objective 6

SPREADSHEET

After the accounts are closed on May 10, 2006, prior to liquidating the partnership, the capital accounts of Mark Wilson, Donna Crowder, and Janice Patel are $27,800, $8,300, and $13,900, respectively. Cash and noncash assets total $6,500 and $89,100, respectively. Amounts owed to creditors total $45,600. The partners share income and losses in the ratio of 2:1:1. Between May 10 and May 30, the noncash assets are sold for $37,500, the partner with the capital deficiency pays his or her deficiency to the partnership, and the liabilities are paid.

**Instructions**
1. Prepare a statement of partnership liquidation, indicating (a) the sale of assets and division of loss, (b) the receipt of the deficiency (from the appropriate partner), (c) the payment of liabilities, and (d) the distribution of cash.

*(continued)*

2. ▰▰▰▰▰ If the partner with the capital deficiency declares bankruptcy and is unable to pay the deficiency, explain how the deficiency would be divided between the partners.

**PROBLEM 13-6A**
*Statement of partnership liquidation*

**Objective 6**

SPREADSHEET

On May 3, 2006, the firm of Imhoff, Baxter, and Wise decided to liquidate their partnership. The partners have capital balances of $30,000, $90,000, and $120,000, respectively. The cash balance is $10,000, the book values of noncash assets total $285,000, and liabilities total $55,000. The partners share income and losses in the ratio of 1:2:2.

**Instructions**

Prepare a statement of partnership liquidation, covering the period May 3 through May 29 for each of the following independent assumptions:

1. All of the noncash assets are sold for $345,000 in cash, the creditors are paid, and the remaining cash is distributed to the partners.
2. All of the noncash assets are sold for $175,000 in cash, the creditors are paid, and the remaining cash is distributed to the partners.
3. All of the noncash assets are sold for $105,000 in cash, the creditors are paid, the partner with the debit capital balance pays the amount owed to the firm, and the remaining cash is distributed to the partners.

# roblems Series B

**PROBLEM 13-1B**
*Entries and balance sheet for partnership*

**Objectives 3, 4**

SPREADSHEET
P.A.S.S.

✔ *3. Hall net income, $35,200*

On May 1, 2005, Crystal Hall and Doug Tucker form a partnership. Hall agrees to invest $10,500 in cash and merchandise inventory valued at $36,500. Tucker invests certain business assets at valuations agreed upon, transfers business liabilities, and contributes sufficient cash to bring his total capital to $40,000. Details regarding the book values of the business assets and liabilities, and the agreed valuations, follow:

|  | Tucker's Ledger Balance | Agreed-Upon Valuation |
|---|---|---|
| Accounts Receivable | $20,750 | $18,000 |
| Allowance for Doubtful Accounts | 950 | 1,000 |
| Equipment | 79,100 ⎱ | 40,000 |
| Accumulated Depreciation | 35,200 ⎰ |  |
| Accounts Payable | 14,000 | 14,000 |
| Notes Payable | 15,000 | 15,000 |

The partnership agreement includes the following provisions regarding the division of net income: interest on original investments at 10%, salary allowances of $18,000 and $21,000 respectively, and the remainder equally.

**Instructions**

1. Journalize the entries to record the investments of Hall and Tucker in the partnership accounts.
2. Prepare a balance sheet as of May 1, 2005, the date of formation of the partnership of Hall and Tucker.
3. After adjustments and the closing of revenue and expense accounts at April 30, 2006, the end of the first full year of operations, the income summary account has a credit balance of $72,700, and the drawing accounts have debit balances of $20,000 (Hall) and $26,000 (Tucker). Journalize the entries to close the income summary account and the drawing accounts at April 30.

**PROBLEM 13-2B**
*Dividing partnership income*

**Objective 4**

SPREADSHEET

✓ 1. f. Garland net income, $36,000

Garland and Driscoe have decided to form a partnership. They have agreed that Garland is to invest $200,000 and that Driscoe is to invest $100,000. Garland is to devote one-half time to the business and Driscoe is to devote full time. The following plans for the division of income are being considered:

a. Equal division.
b. In the ratio of original investments.
c. In the ratio of time devoted to the business.
d. Interest of 12% on original investments and the remainder equally.
e. Interest of 12% on original investments, salary allowances of $30,000 to Garland and $60,000 to Driscoe, and the remainder equally.
f. Plan (e), except that Driscoe is also to be allowed a bonus equal to 20% of the amount by which net income exceeds the salary allowances.

**Instructions**

For each plan, determine the division of the net income under each of the following assumptions: (1) net income of $90,000 and (2) net income of $240,000. Present the data in tabular form, using the following columnar headings:

| | $90,000 | | $240,000 | |
|---|---|---|---|---|
| **Plan** | **Garland** | **Driscoe** | **Garland** | **Driscoe** |

**PROBLEM 13-3B**
*Financial statements for partnership*

**Objective 4**

SPREADSHEET

✓ 2. Dec. 31 capital— Fawler, $67,000

The ledger of Peter Dixon and May Fawler, attorneys-at-law, contains the following accounts and balances after adjustments have been recorded on December 31, 2006:

| | |
|---|---|
| Cash | $ 22,000 |
| Accounts Receivable | 38,900 |
| Supplies | 1,900 |
| Land | 25,000 |
| Building | 130,000 |
| Accumulated Depreciation—Building | 69,200 |
| Office Equipment | 39,000 |
| Accumulated Depreciation—Office Equipment | 21,500 |
| Accounts Payable | 2,100 |
| Salaries Payable | 2,000 |
| Peter Dixon, Capital | 75,000 |
| Peter Dixon, Drawing | 60,000 |
| May Fawler, Capital | 55,000 |
| May Fawler, Drawing | 75,000 |
| Professional Fees | 285,650 |
| Salary Expense | 80,500 |
| Depreciation Expense—Building | 10,500 |
| Property Tax Expense | 8,000 |
| Heating and Lighting Expense | 7,900 |
| Supplies Expense | 2,850 |
| Depreciation Expense—Office Equipment | 2,800 |
| Miscellaneous Expense | 6,100 |

The balance in Fawler's capital account includes an additional investment of $5,000 made on August 10, 2006.

**Instructions**

1. Prepare an income statement for 2006, indicating the division of net income. The articles of partnership provide for salary allowances of $30,000 to Dixon and $40,000 to Fawler, allowances of 12% on each partner's capital balance at the beginning of the fiscal year, and equal division of the remaining net income or net loss.
2. Prepare a statement of partner's equity for 2006.
3. Prepare a balance sheet as of the end of 2006.

**PROBLEM 13-4B**
*Admitting new partner*
Objective 5

P.A.S.S.

✓3. Total assets, $202,220

Tom Denney and Cheryl Burks have operated a successful firm for many years, sharing net income and net losses equally. Sara Wold is to be admitted to the partnership on May 1 of the current year, in accordance with the following agreement:

a. Assets and liabilities of the old partnership are to be valued at their book values as of April 30, except for the following:
  • Accounts receivable amounting to $1,900 are to be written off, and the allowance for doubtful accounts is to be increased to 5% of the remaining accounts.
  • Merchandise inventory is to be valued at $53,100.
  • Equipment is to be valued at $100,000.
b. Wold is to purchase $20,000 of the ownership interest of Burks for $25,000 cash and to contribute $20,000 cash to the partnership for a total ownership equity of $40,000.
c. The income-sharing ratio of Denney, Burks, and Wold is to be 2:1:1.

The post-closing trial balance of Denney and Burks as of April 30 is as follows:

**Denney and Burks**
**Post-Closing Trial Balance**
**April 30, 2006**

| | | |
|---|---|---|
| Cash | 7,900 | |
| Accounts Receivable | 22,500 | |
| Allowance for Doubtful Accounts | | 550 |
| Merchandise Inventory | 50,600 | |
| Prepaid Insurance | 1,650 | |
| Equipment | 145,000 | |
| Accumulated Depreciation—Equipment | | 65,000 |
| Accounts Payable | | 12,100 |
| Notes Payable | | 10,000 |
| Tom Denney, Capital | | 80,000 |
| Cheryl Burks, Capital | | 60,000 |
| | 227,650 | 227,650 |

**Instructions**
1. Journalize the entries as of April 30 to record the revaluations, using a temporary account entitled Asset Revaluations. The balance in the accumulated depreciation account is to be eliminated.
2. Journalize the additional entries to record the remaining transactions relating to the formation of the new partnership. Assume that all transactions occur on May 1.
3. Present a balance sheet for the new partnership as of May 1, 2006.

**PROBLEM 13-5B**
*Statement of partnership liquidation*
Objective 6

SPREADSHEET

After the accounts are closed on May 3, 2006, prior to liquidating the partnership, the capital accounts of Ann Booth, Harold Owen, and Carla Ramariz are $20,000, $3,900, and $10,000, respectively. Cash and noncash assets total $1,900 and $62,000, respectively. Amounts owed to creditors total $30,000. The partners share income and losses in the ratio of 2:1:1. Between May 3 and May 29, the noncash assets are sold for $26,000, the partner with the capital deficiency pays his deficiency to the partnership, and the liabilities are paid.

**Instructions**
1. Prepare a statement of partnership liquidation, indicating (a) the sale of assets and division of loss, (b) the receipt of the deficiency (from the appropriate partner), (c) the payment of liabilities, and (d) the distribution of cash.
2. ▅▅▅▶ If the partner with the capital deficiency declares bankruptcy and is unable to pay the deficiency, explain how the deficiency would be divided between the partners.

**PROBLEM 13-6B**
*Statement of partnership liquidation*

**Objective 6**

**SPREADSHEET**

On October 1, 2006, the firm of Ewing, Johnson, and Landry, decided to liquidate their partnership. The partners have capital balances of $100,000, $90,000, and $30,000, respectively. The cash balance is $20,000, the book values of noncash assets total $250,000, and liabilities total $50,000. The partners share income and losses in the ratio of 2:2:1.

**Instructions**
Prepare a statement of partnership liquidation, covering the period October 1 through October 30 for each of the following independent assumptions:

1. All of the noncash assets are sold for $330,000 in cash, the creditors are paid, and the remaining cash is distributed to the partners.
2. All of the noncash assets are sold for $120,000 in cash, the creditors are paid, and the remaining cash is distributed to the partners.
3. All of the noncash assets are sold for $50,000 in cash, the creditors are paid, the partner with the debit capital balance pays the amount owed to the firm, and the remaining cash is distributed to the partners.

# Special Activities

**ACTIVITY 13-1**
*Partnership agreement*

**ETHICS**

Ted Miller, M.D., and Glen Harrison, M.D., are sole owners of two medical practices that operate in the same medical building. The two doctors agree to combine assets and liabilities of the two businesses to form a partnership. The partnership agreement calls for dividing income equally between the two doctors. After several months, the following conversation takes place between the two doctors:

*Miller:* I've noticed that your patient load has dropped over the last couple of months. When we formed our partnership, we were seeing about the same number of patients per week. However, now our patient records show that you have been seeing about half as many patients as I have. Are there any issues that I should be aware of?

*Harrison:* There's nothing going on. When I was working on my own, I was really putting in the hours. One of the reasons I formed this partnership was to enjoy life a little more and scale back a little bit.

*Miller:* I see. Well, I find that I'm working as hard as I did when I was on my own, yet making less than I did previously. Essentially, you're sharing in half of my billings and I'm sharing in half of yours. Since you are working much less than I am, I end up on the short end of the bargain.

*Harrison:* Well, I don't know what to say. An agreement is an agreement. The partnership is based on a 50/50 split. That's what a partnership is all about.

*Miller:* If that's so, then it applies equally well on the effort end of the equation as on the income end.

➤ Discuss whether Harrison is acting in an ethical manner. How could Miller rewrite the partnership agreement to avoid this dispute?

**ACTIVITY 13-2**
*Dividing partnership income*

**WHAT DO YOU THINK?**

John Adair and Raul Fontana decide to form a partnership. Adair will contribute $300,000 to the partnership, while Fontana will contribute only $30,000. However, Fontana will be responsible for running the day-to-day operations of the partnership, which are anticipated to require about 50 hours per week. In contrast, Adair will only work 5 hours per week for the partnership. The two partners are attempting to determine a formula for dividing partnership net income. Adair believes the partners should divide income in the ratio of 7:3, favoring Adair, since Adair provides the majority of the capital. Fontana believes the income should be divided 7:3, favoring Fontana, since Fontana provides the majority of effort in running the partnership business.

How would you advise the partners in developing a method for dividing income?

**ACTIVITY 13-3**
*Four largest public accounting firms*

REAL WORLD

The following table shows key operating statistics for the four largest public accounting firms:

| | U.S. Net Revenues (in millions) | No of. Partners | No. of Professional Staff | Revenue Split | | |
|---|---|---|---|---|---|---|
| | | | | Accounting and Auditing | Tax | Management Consulting |
| PricewaterhouseCoopers | $8,056 | 2,784 | 33,454 | 35% | 19% | 46% |
| Deloitte & Touche | 6,130 | 2,283 | 20,472 | 33 | 21 | 35 |
| Ernst & Young | 4,485 | 1,934 | 13,871 | 58 | 39 | 0 |
| KPMG | 3,171 | 1,471 | 10,438 | 62 | 38 | 0 |

**Source:** "PAR Top 100 Report," *Public Accounting Report,* Aspen Publishers.

a. Determine the revenue per partner and revenue per professional staff for each firm. Round to the nearest dollar.
b. Interpret the differences between the firms in terms of your answer in (a) and the table information.

**ACTIVITY 13-4**
*Financial analysis*

The partnership of Felix and Diaz, CPAs, has 200 partners and 1,500 staff professionals. Each partner shares equally in partnership income. Assume that the average income for partners in CPA firms across the country is $230,000 per year, and the average income for staff professionals is $75,000 per year. The partnership income statement for the year is as follows:

| Revenues | | $174,000,000 |
|---|---|---|
| Staff professional salaries | $120,000,000 | |
| Nonprofessional salaries | 6,000,000 | |
| Supplies | 1,000,000 | |
| Travel | 2,000,000 | |
| Litigation losses | 10,000,000 | 139,000,000 |
| Net income | | $ 35,000,000 |

The total partnership capital balance is $20,000,000 for 200 partners or $100,000 per partner.

a. Evaluate the financial performance of the partnership from a partner's perspective. That is, if you were a partner in this firm, would you be satisfied or dissatisfied with partnership performance? Support your answer.
b. What are some explanations for the partnership's performance.

**ACTIVITY 13-5**
*Ethical role of the underwriter*

REAL WORLD          ETHICS

Henry Blodget was the famed Internet analyst for **Merrill Lynch**, a Wall Street underwriter, and stockbroker. The Attorney General of the state of New York released internal Merrill Lynch e-mails that gave a picture of the inside of the research arm of a major investment bank. The following article summarizes some of those insights:

*InfoSpace, an investment banking client from August 2000 to December 2000, was featured as a "Favored 15" Merrill Lynch stock. During that time Blodget wrote [internally] that he had "enormous skepticism" about the stock and called it a "piece of junk," about which large investors had made "bad smell comments."*

*However, InfoSpace wasn't downgraded until December 11, 2000, when it had fallen more than 90 percent from its high. And even then, it was only downgraded to "accumulate" for investors looking for gains within 12 months and "buy" for those with a longer-term horizon.*

*Then there's GoTo.com, now known as Overture Service. Blodget got an inquiry from an institutional investor asking "what's so interesting about GoTo except banking fees?" Blodget replied, "Nothin." But that didn't stop his team from rating GoTo as a long-term "buy."*

*In addition, in a move fraught with conflicts of interest, a junior analyst solicited input from GoTo management, which sometimes typed recommended changes right onto a draft report.*

*Frustrated with pressures to inflate the rating, the junior analyst wrote to Blodget in an expletive-filled e-mail. The rating, she said, would mean "John and Mary Smith are losing their retirement because we don't want [GoTo's CFO] to be mad at us."*

*She went on to say that "the whole idea that we are independent from banking is a big lie." Without the investment banking pressures, she said, she'd rate the stock "neutral" in the short term and "accumulate" in the longer term.*

*Yet another case involved Internet Capital Group, an investment banking client that Merrill rated starting in August 1999 at "accumulate" for the next 12 months and "buy" in the longer term. After reaching a high of $212 in the late 1990s, the stock was trading at $12.38 in October 2000.*

*Blodget confided in an e-mail to another analyst that he thought the stock was "going to 5," adding the next day that Internet Capital "has been a disaster . . . there really is no floor to the stock."*

*However, it wasn't until a month later that Merrill downgraded the stock, and then only to "accumulate" for both the short- and long-term.*

**Source:** Deborah Lohse, "Probe Finds Analysts Recommending Stocks They Privately Bad-Mouthed," *San Jose Mercury News*, Calif. 04/12/2002, KRTBN Knight-Ridder Tribune Business News: San Jose Mercury News.

1.  ➜ What is the nature of the problem identified in the article above?
2.  ➜ How could this problem be solved?

**ACTIVITY 13-6**
*Life cycle of a business*

REAL WORLD

INTERNET

**ebay, Inc.,** the Internet auction company, was founded in 1995 by Pierre Omidyar as a result of his interest in collecting and trading Pez dispensers. The company quickly became successful and on May 20, 1996, was incorporated, with 14,700,000 shares being sold to Omidyar for $14,262. Benchmark Capital, a venture capital firm, purchased approximately 3,000,000 shares in the middle of 1997 for approximately $3,000,000. In September 1998, the company had an initial public offering of common stock. The offering prospectus made the following disclosures:

| | |
|---|---|
| Common stock offered by the Company . . . . | *3,489,275 shares* |
| Common stock to be outstanding after this offering . . . . . . . . . . . . . . . . . . . . . . | *39,739,076 shares* |
| Use of proceeds . . . . . . . . . . . . . . . . . . . . | *For capital expenditures, to repay indebtedness, and for general corporate purposes, including working capital.* |
| *Proposed Nasdaq National Market* symbol . . . . . . . . . . . . . . . . . . . . . . . . . . | *"EBAY"* |

| | Initial Public Offering Price | Underwriting Discount | Proceeds to Company | Proceeds to Selling Stockholder |
|---|---|---|---|---|
| Per share . . . . . . | $18.00 | $1.26 | $16.74 | $16.74 |
| Total . . . . . . . . | $63,000,000 | $4,410,000 | $58,410,463 | $179,537 |

The stockholders' equity prior to the IPO showed a balance of approximately $9 million, including contributions from a variety of venture capital firms and individuals.

a. Why did Omidyar incorporate the business in 1996?
b. If Benchmark Capital sold its interest in eBay shortly after the IPO, how much was its gain?
c. How much was the underwriter paid for underwriting eBay's IPO?

*(continued)*

d. What percent of eBay's voting stock did public shareholders receive on the IPO date?

e. What percent of the shareholders' equity did the public shareholders supply to eBay as of the IPO date?

f. How much unrealized gain does Omidyar have in eBay stock today, assuming that no stock has been acquired or sold since the initial purchase at incorporation? Use the Internet to find eBay's current stock price to answer this question.

# nswers to Self-Examination Questions

1. **B**   Noncash assets contributed to a partnership should be recorded at the amounts agreed upon by the partners. The preferred practice is to record the office equipment at $9,000 (answer B).

2. **C**   Net income and net loss are divided among the partners in accordance with their agreement. In the absence of any agreement, all partners share equally (answer C).

3. **C**   Tracey's share of the $45,000 of net income is $19,000 (answer C), determined as follows:

| | Tracey | Hepburn | Total |
|---|---|---|---|
| Interest allowance | $10,000 | $ 5,000 | $15,000 |
| Salary allowance | 12,000 | 24,000 | 36,000 |
| Total | $22,000 | $29,000 | $51,000 |
| Excess of allowances over income | 3,000 | 3,000 | 6,000 |
| Net income distribution | $19,000 | $26,000 | $45,000 |

4. **A**   When an additional person is admitted to a partnership by purchasing an interest from one or more of the partners, the purchase price is paid directly to the selling partner(s). The amount of capital transferred from the capital account(s) of the selling partner(s) to the capital account of the incoming partner is the capital interest acquired from the selling partner(s). In the question, the amount is $32,500 (answer A), which is one-half of Lee's capital balance of $65,000.

5. **C**   Partnership cash would be distributed in accordance with the credit balances in the partners' capital accounts. Therefore, $10,000 (answer C) would be distributed to Pavin (Pavin's $10,000 capital balance).

# INCOME TAXES, UNUSUAL INCOME ITEMS, AND INVESTMENTS IN STOCKS

## objectives

*After studying this chapter, you should be able to:*

1   Journalize the entries for corporate income taxes, including deferred income taxes.

2   Prepare an income statement reporting the following unusual items: fixed asset impairments, restructuring charges, discontinued operations, extraordinary items, and cumulative changes in accounting principles.

3   Prepare an income statement reporting earnings per share data.

4   Describe the concept and the reporting of comprehensive income.

5   Describe the accounting for investments in stocks.

6   Describe alternative methods of combining businesses and how consolidated financial statements are prepared.

7   Compute and interpret the price-earnings ratio.

If you apply for a bank loan, you will be required to list your assets and liabilities on a loan application. In addition, you will be asked to indicate your monthly income. Assume that the day you were filling out the application, you won $4,000 in the state lottery. The $4,000 lottery winnings increase your assets by $4,000. Should you also show your lottery winnings as part of your monthly income?

The answer, of course, is no. Winning the lottery is an unusual event and, for most of us, a nonrecurring event. In determining whether to grant the loan, the bank is interested in your ability to make monthly loan payments. Such payments depend upon your recurring monthly income.

Businesses also experience unusual and nonrecurring events that affect their financial statements. Such events should be clearly disclosed in the financial statements so that stakeholders in the business will not misinterpret the financial effects of the events.

In this chapter, we discuss unusual items that affect income statements and illustrate how such items should be reported. In addition, we discuss other specialized accounting and reporting topics, including accounting for income taxes, investments, and business combinations.

# Corporate Income Taxes

objective 1

Journalize the entries for corporate income taxes, including deferred income taxes.

Under the United States tax code, corporations are taxable entities that must pay federal income taxes.[1] Depending upon where it is located, a corporation may also be required to pay state and local income taxes. Although we limit our discussion to federal income taxes, the basic concepts also apply to other income taxes.

## Payment of Income Taxes

Most corporations are required to pay estimated federal income taxes in four installments throughout the year. For example, assume that a corporation with a calendar-year accounting period estimates its income tax expense for the year as $84,000. The entry to record the first of the four estimated tax payments of $21,000 (1/4 of $84,000) is as follows:

| | | | | | |
|---|---|---|---|---|---|
| Apr. | 15 | Income Tax Expense | | 21 0 0 0 00 | |
| | | Cash | | | 21 0 0 0 00 |

**REAL WORLD**

Individuals pay quarterly estimated taxes if the amount of tax withholding is not sufficient to pay their taxes at the end of the year. This usually occurs when a significant portion of an individual's income is from rent, dividends, or interest.

At year-end, the actual taxable income and the related tax are determined.[2] If additional taxes are owed, the additional liability is recorded. If the total estimated tax payments are greater than the tax liability based on actual taxable income, the overpayment should be debited to a receivable account and credited to *Income Tax Expense.*[3]

Income taxes are normally disclosed as a deduction at the bottom of the income statement in determining net income, as shown at the top of the next page, in an excerpt from an income statement for the **Procter & Gamble Company.**

---

[1]Limited liability corporations (LLCs) are not separate taxable entities and thus are not subject to federal (and most state) income taxes. For this reason, the material in this section would not generally apply to an LLC.

[2]A corporation's income tax returns and supporting records are subject to audits by taxing authorities, who may assess additional taxes. Because of this possibility, the liability for income taxes is sometimes described in the balance sheet as *Estimated income tax payable.*

[3]Another common term used for income taxes on the income statement and note disclosures is "provision for income taxes."

| Year Ended June 30, 2002 | (Amounts in Millions) |
|---|---:|
| **Net Sales** . . . . . . . . . . . . . . . . . . . . . . . . . . . . . . . . . . . | **$40,238** |
| Cost of products sold . . . . . . . . . . . . . . . . . . . . . . . . . | 20,989 |
| Marketing, research, and administrative expenses . . . . . . | 12,571 |
| **Income from Operations** . . . . . . . . . . . . . . . . . . . . . | **$ 6,678** |
| Interest expense . . . . . . . . . . . . . . . . . . . . . . . . . . . . . | (603) |
| Other income, net . . . . . . . . . . . . . . . . . . . . . . . . . . . | 308 |
| **Earnings Before Income Taxes** . . . . . . . . . . . . . . . . . | **$ 6,383** |
| Income taxes . . . . . . . . . . . . . . . . . . . . . . . . . . . . . . . | 2,031 |
| **Net Earnings** . . . . . . . . . . . . . . . . . . . . . . . . . . . . . . | **$ 4,352** |

The ratio of reported income tax expense to earnings before taxes is shown for selected industries, as follows:

| Industry | Percent of Reported Income Tax Expense to Earnings before Taxes |
|---|:---:|
| Automobiles | 33% |
| Banking | 35 |
| Computers | 35 |
| Food | 35 |
| Integrated oil | 39 |
| Pharmaceuticals | 30 |
| Retail | 39 |
| Telecommunication | 37 |
| Transportation | 38 |

As you can see, the reported income tax expense is normally between 30%–40% of earnings before tax. Therefore, taxes are a significant expense for most companies and must be considered when analyzing a company. Differences in tax rates between industries can be due to tax regulations unique to certain industries.

# Allocating Income Taxes

The **taxable income** of a corporation is determined according to the tax laws and is reported to taxing authorities on the corporation's tax return.[4] It is often different from the income before income taxes reported in the income statement according to generally accepted accounting principles. As a result, the *income tax based on taxable income* usually differs from the *income tax based on income before taxes*. This difference may need to be allocated between various financial statement periods, depending on the nature of the items causing the differences.

Some differences between taxable income and income before income taxes are created because items are recognized in one period for tax purposes and in another period for income statement purposes. Such differences, called **temporary differences**, reverse or turn around in later years. Some examples of items that create temporary differences are listed below.

1. *Revenues or gains are taxed* ***after*** *they are reported in the income statement.*
   Example: In some cases, companies that make sales under an installment plan

---

[4]Accounting for deferred income taxes is a complex topic that is treated in greater detail in advanced accounting texts. The treatment here provides a general overview and conceptual understanding of the topic.

recognize revenue for financial reporting purposes when a sale is made but defer recognizing revenue for tax purposes until cash is collected.

2. *Expenses or losses are deducted in determining taxable income **after** they are reported in the income statement.* Example: Product warranty expense estimated and reported in the year of the sale for financial statement reporting is deducted for tax reporting when paid.

3. *Revenues or gains are taxed **before** they are reported in the income statement.* Example: Cash received in advance for magazine subscriptions is included in taxable income when received but included in the income statement only when earned in a future period.

4. *Expenses or losses are deducted in determining taxable income **before** they are reported in the income statement.* Example: MACRS depreciation is used for tax purposes, and the straight-line method is used for financial reporting purposes.

Since temporary differences reverse in later years, they do not change or reduce the total amount of taxable income over the life of a business. Exhibit 1 illustrates the reversing nature of temporary differences in which a business uses MACRS depreciation for tax purposes and straight-line depreciation for financial statement purposes. Exhibit 1 assumes that MACRS recognizes more depreciation in the early years and less depreciation in the later years. The total depreciation expense is the same for both methods over the life of the asset.

•**Exhibit 1**

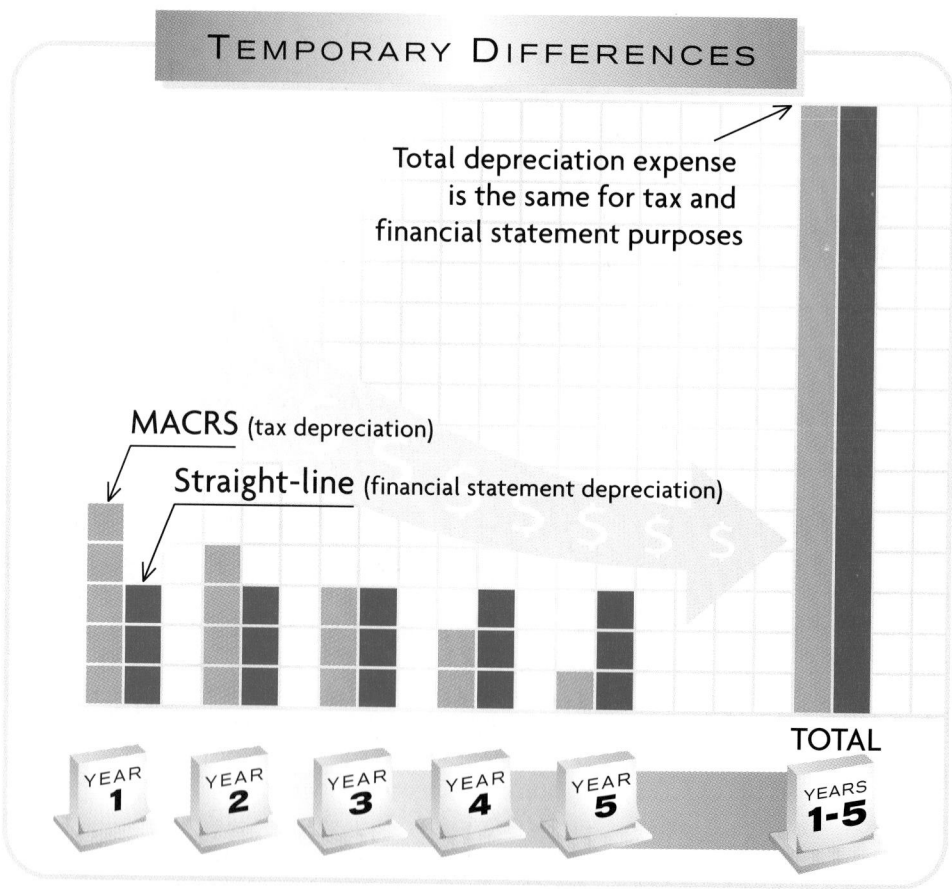

TEMPORARY DIFFERENCES

Total depreciation expense is the same for tax and financial statement purposes

MACRS (tax depreciation)

Straight-line (financial statement depreciation)

| YEAR 1 | YEAR 2 | YEAR 3 | YEAR 4 | YEAR 5 | TOTAL YEARS 1-5 |

As Exhibit 1 illustrates, temporary differences affect only the timing of when revenues and expenses are recognized for tax purposes. As a result, the total amount of taxes paid does not change. Only the timing of the payment of taxes is affected. In most cases, managers use tax-planning techniques so that temporary differences delay or defer the payment of taxes to later years. As a result, at the end of each year the amount of the current tax liability and the postponed (deferred) liability must be recorded.

To illustrate, assume that at the end of the first year of operations a corporation reports $300,000 income before income taxes on its income statement. If we assume an income tax rate of 40%, the income tax expense reported on the income statement is $120,000 ($300,000 × 40%).[5] However, to reduce the amount owed for current income taxes, the corporation uses tax planning to reduce the taxable income to $100,000. Thus, the income tax actually due for the year is only $40,000 ($100,000 × 40%). The $80,000 ($120,000 − $40,000) difference between the two tax amounts is created by timing differences in recognizing revenue. This amount is deferred to future years. The example is summarized below.

| | |
|---|---:|
| Income tax based on $300,000 reported income at 40% | $120,000 |
| Income tax based on $100,000 taxable income at 40% | 40,000 |
| Income tax deferred to future years | $ 80,000 |

To match the current year's expenses (including income tax) against the current year's revenue on the income statement, income tax is allocated between periods, using the following journal entry:

| | | | |
|---|---|---:|---:|
| Income Tax Expense | | 120 000 00 | |
|   Income Tax Payable | | | 40 000 00 |
|   Deferred Income Tax Payable | | | 80 000 00 |

The income tax expense reported on the income statement is the total tax, $120,000, expected to be paid on the income for the year. In future years, the $80,000 in *Deferred Income Tax Payable* will be transferred to *Income Tax Payable* as the timing differences reverse and the taxes become due. For example, if $48,000 of the deferred tax reverses and becomes due in the second year, the following journal entry would be made in the second year:

| | | | |
|---|---|---:|---:|
| Deferred Income Tax Payable | | 48 000 00 | |
|   Income Tax Payable | | | 48 000 00 |

# Reporting and Analyzing Taxes

The balance of *Deferred Income Tax Payable* at the end of a year is reported as a liability.[6] The amount due within one year is classified as a current liability. The remainder is classified as a long-term liability or reported in a Deferred Credits section following the Long-Term Liabilities section.[7]

Differences between taxable income and income (before taxes) reported on the income statement may also arise because certain revenues are exempt from tax and certain expenses are not deductible in determining taxable income. Such differences, which will not reverse with the passage of time, are sometimes called **permanent differences**. For example, interest income on municipal bonds may be exempt from taxation. Such differences create no special financial reporting problems, since the amount of income tax determined according to the tax laws is the *same* amount reported on the income statement.

**POINT OF INTEREST**

Interest from investments in municipal bonds is also tax exempt for individual taxpayers.

---

[5]For purposes of illustration, the 40% rate is assumed to include all federal, state, and local income taxes.
[6]In some cases, a deferred tax asset may arise for tax benefits to be received in the future. Such deferred tax assets are reported as either current or long-term assets, depending on when the benefits are expected to be realized.
[7]Additional note disclosures for deferred income taxes are also required. These are discussed in advanced accounting texts.

# Unusual Items Affecting the Income Statement

<table><tr><td>**objective** 2</td></tr></table>

Prepare an income statement reporting the following unusual items: fixed asset impairments, restructuring charges, discontinued operations, extraordinary items, and cumulative changes in accounting principles.

Generally accepted accounting principles require that certain unusual items be reported separately on the income statement. These items can be classified into the following two categories:

1. Those items that are reported in determining income from continuing operations, sometimes called **above-the-line** items.
2. Those items that are reported as deductions from income from continuing operations, sometimes called **below-the-line** items.

In the following paragraphs, we discuss each of these unusual items.

## Unusual Items Affecting Income from Continuing Operations

Some unusual items are deducted from gross profit in arriving at income from continuing operations. Unusual above-the-line items consist of fixed asset impairments and restructuring charges.

### Fixed Asset Impairments

A *fixed asset impairment* occurs when the fair value of a fixed asset falls below its book value and is not expected to recover.[8] Examples of events that might cause an asset impairment are (1) decreases in the market price of fixed assets, (2) significant changes in the business or regulations related to fixed assets, (3) adverse conditions affecting the use of fixed assets, or (4) expected cash flow losses from using fixed assets.[9] For example, on March 1, assume that Jones Company consolidates operations by closing a factory. As a result of the closing, plant and equipment is impaired by $750,000. The journal entry to record the impairment is as follows:

| | | | | |
|---|---|---|---|---|
| Mar. | 1 | Loss on Fixed Asset Impairment | 750 0 0 0 00 | |
| | | Fixed Assets—Plant and Equipment | | 750 0 0 0 00 |

The loss on fixed asset impairment is reported as a separate expense item deducted from gross profit in determining income from continuing operations, as illustrated for Jones Company in Exhibit 2. In addition, note disclosure should describe the nature of the asset impaired and the cause of the impairment, as shown in Note A of Exhibit 2.

The loss reduces the book value of the fixed asset and thus reduces the depreciation expense for future periods. If the asset could be salvaged for sale, the gain or loss on the sale would be based on the lower book value. Therefore, asset impairment accounting recognizes the loss when it is first identified, rather than at a later sale date.

[8]Fixed assets that are discontinued components, such as an operating segment, subsidiary, or asset group, should be treated as discontinued items as discussed in a later section.
[9]*Statement of Financial Accounting Standards, No. 144*, "Accounting for the Impairment or Disposal of Long-Lived Assets," Financial Accounting Standards Board (Norwalk, Connecticut: 2001).

## •Exhibit 2    Unusual Items in Income Statement

### Jones Corporation
### Income Statement
### For the Year Ended December 31, 2006

| | | |
|---|---:|---:|
| Net sales . . . . . . . . . . . . . . . . . . . . . . . . . . . . . . . . . . . . . . . . . . . . . . . . . . . . . . . . . . . . . . . . . . . | | $12,350,000 |
| Cost of merchandise sold. . . . . . . . . . . . . . . . . . . . . . . . . . . . . . . . . . . . . . . . . . . . . . . . . . . . . . . | | 5,800,000 |
| Gross profit. . . . . . . . . . . . . . . . . . . . . . . . . . . . . . . . . . . . . . . . . . . . . . . . . . . . . . . . . . . . . . . . . . | | $ 6,550,000 |
| Operating expenses . . . . . . . . . . . . . . . . . . . . . . . . . . . . . . . . . . . . . . . . . . . | $3,490,000 | |
| Restructuring charge (Note A) . . . . . . . . . . . . . . . . . . . . . . . . . . . . . . . . . . . . | 1,000,000 | |
| Loss from asset impairment (Note A) . . . . . . . . . . . . . . . . . . . . . . . . . . . . . . . | 750,000 | 5,240,000 |
| Income from continuing operations before income tax . . . . . . . . . . . . . . . . . . . . . . . . . . | | $ 1,310,000 |
| Income tax expense . . . . . . . . . . . . . . . . . . . . . . . . . . . . . . . . . . . . . . . . . . . . . . . . . . . . . . . . . | | 620,000 |
| Income from continuing operations . . . . . . . . . . . . . . . . . . . . . . . . . . . . . . . . . . . . . . . . . . . . . | | $ 690,000 |
| Loss on discontinued operations (Note B) . . . . . . . . . . . . . . . . . . . . . . . . . . . . . . . . . . . . . . . . | | 100,000 |
| Income before extraordinary items and cumulative effect of a change in . . . . . . . . . . . . . . . . | | |
|     accounting principle . . . . . . . . . . . . . . . . . . . . . . . . . . . . . . . . . . . . . . . . . . . . . . . . . . . . . . | | $ 590,000 |
| Extraordinary item: | | |
|     Gain on condemnation of land, net of applicable income tax of $65,000 . . . . . . . . . . . . . . | | 150,000 |
| Cumulative effect on prior years of changing to a different depreciation method (Note C). . . | | 92,000 |
| Net income . . . . . . . . . . . . . . . . . . . . . . . . . . . . . . . . . . . . . . . . . . . . . . . . . . . . . . . . . . . . . . . . | | $ 832,000 |

**Note A**

*As a result of a downturn in the economy, the company consolidated operations by closing its Dekalb, Illinois, factory on March 1 of the current year. The factory closing impaired the factory building and equipment. The building and equipment were written down by $400,000 and $350,000 to reflect their respective salvage values. In addition, 200 employees at the Dekalb facility were offered $1,000,000 in termination benefits. As of the end of the fiscal year, no obligation remains with regard to the termination benefit arrangement.*

**Note B**

*On July 1 of the current year, the electrical products division of the corporation was sold at a loss of $100,000, net of applicable income tax of $50,000. The net sales of the division for the current year were $2,900,000. The assets sold were composed of inventories, equipment, and plant totaling $2,100,000. The purchaser assumed liabilities of $600,000.*

**Note C**

*Depreciation of all property, plant, and equipment has been computed by the straight-line method in 2006. Prior to 2006, depreciation of equipment for one of the divisions had been computed on the declining-balance method. In 2006, the straight-line method was adopted for this division in order to achieve uniformity and to better match depreciation charges with the estimated economic utility of such assets. Consistent with APB Opinion No. 20, this change in depreciation has been applied to prior years. The effect of the change was to increase income by $30,000 before extraordinary items for 2006. The adjustment of $92,000 (after reduction for income tax of $88,000) to apply the new method to prior years is also included in net income for 2006.*

## INTEGRITY IN BUSINESS

### WHEN IS AN ASSET IMPAIRED?

The asset impairment rule is designed to reduce the subjectivity of timing asset write-downs. That is, write-downs should occur when the impairment is deemed permanent. In practice, however, there still remains judgment in determining when such impairment has occurred. Ethical managers will recognize asset write-downs when they occur, not when it is most convenient. For example, the SEC investigated **Avon Corporation** for delaying the write-off of a computer software project. In settling the formal investigation, Avon had to restate its earnings to reflect the earlier write-off date.

## Restructuring Charges

*Restructuring charges* are costs associated with involuntarily terminating employees, terminating contracts, consolidating facilities, or relocating employees. Often, these events incur initial one-time costs in order to capture long-term savings. For example, involuntarily terminated employees often receive a one-time termination or severance benefit at the time of their dismissal. Employee termination benefits are normally the most significant restructuring charges; thus, they will be the focus of this section.

Employee termination benefits arise when a plan specifying the number of terminated employees, the benefit, and the benefit timing has been authorized by senior management and communicated to the employees.[10] To illustrate, assume that the management of Jones Company communicates a plan to terminate 200 employees from the closed manufacturing plant on March 1. The plan calls for a termination benefit of $5,000 per employee. Once the plan is communicated to employees, they have the legal right to work for 60 days but may elect to leave the firm earlier. In other words, employees may be paid severance at the end of 60 days or at any time in between. The expense and liability to provide employee benefits should be recognized at its fair value on the plan communication date.[11] The fair value of this plan would be $1,000,000 (200 × $5,000), which is the aggregate expected cost of terminating the employees. Thus, the $1,000,000 restructuring charge would be recorded as follows:

| Mar. | 1 | Restructuring Charge | | 1,000 0 0 0 00 | |
|---|---|---|---|---|---|
| | | Employee Termination Obligation | | | 1,000 0 0 0 00 |

The restructuring charge is reported as a separate expense deducted from gross profit in determining income from continuing operations, as shown in Exhibit 2. The employee termination obligation would be shown as a current liability. If the plan called for expected severance payments beyond one year, then a long-term liability would be recognized. In addition, a note should disclose the nature and cause of the restructuring event and the costs associated with the type of restructuring event.

The actual benefits paid to terminated employees should be debited to the liability as employees leave the firm. For example, assume that 25 employees find other employment and leave the company on March 25. The journal entry to record the severance payment to these employees would be as follows:

| Mar. | 25 | Employee Termination Obligation | | 125 0 0 0 00 | |
|---|---|---|---|---|---|
| | | Cash | | | 125 0 0 0 00 |

# Unusual Items Not Affecting Income from Continuing Operations

Some unusual items are deducted from income from continuing operations in arriving at net income. Unusual items not affecting income from continuing operations consist of discontinued operations, extraordinary items, and changes in accounting principles.

---

[10]*Statement of Financial Accounting Standards, No. 146*, "Accounting for Costs Associated with Exit or Disposal Activities," Financial Accounting Standards Board (Norwalk, Connecticut: 2002).

[11]For longer-term severance agreements, present value concepts may be required to determine fair value. We will assume short-term agreements where the time value of money is assumed to be immaterial. Present value concepts are discussed in the bonds payable chapter.

## FINANCIAL REPORTING AND DISCLOSURE

### ROBERT MONDAVI CORPORATION

Restructuring charges and asset impairments can be disclosed using a variety of titles on the financial statements. Often, the charges are combined under a single title on the income statement. For example, **Robert Mondavi Corporation**, a leading producer of California table wines, disclosed $12,240,000 in "special charges" on its income statement above the operating income line. These charges were explained in the notes to the financial statements as follows:

*The Company changed from an operator to a sponsor role at Disney's California Adventure. With this change,* the Company eliminated any further operational risk associated with the project while it continues a business relationship with Disney and maintains a presence at the theme park. As a result of this change, the Company has recorded special charges through June 30, 2002, totaling $12,240,000 or $0.47 per diluted share, primarily reflecting fixed asset write-offs, employee separation expenses and lease cancellation fees.

As can be seen in this disclosure, Mondavi chose to combine restructuring charges and fixed asset impairments under a single expense line item called special charges.

## Discontinued Operations

A gain or loss from disposing of a business segment or component of an entity is reported on the income statement as a gain or loss from ***discontinued operations***. The term **business segment** refers to a major line of business for a company, such as a division or a department or a certain class of customer. A **component** of an entity is the lowest level at which the operations and cash flows can be clearly distinguished, operationally and for financial reporting purposes, from the rest of the entity.[12] Examples would be a store for a retailer, a territory for a sales organization, or a product category for a consumer products company. To illustrate the disclosure, assume that Jones Corporation has separate divisions that produce electrical products, hardware supplies, and lawn equipment. Jones sells its electrical products division at a loss. As shown in Exhibit 2, this loss is deducted from Jones' income from continuing operations (income from its hardware and lawn equipment divisions). In addition, Note B discloses the identity of the segment sold, the disposal date, a description of the segment's assets and liabilities, and the manner of disposal.

## Extraordinary Items

An ***extraordinary item*** results from events and transactions that (1) are significantly different (unusual) from the typical or the normal operating activities of the business **and** (2) occur infrequently. The gains and losses resulting from natural disasters that occur infrequently, such as floods, earthquakes, and fires, are extraordinary items. Gains or losses from condemning land or buildings for public use are also extraordinary. Such gains and losses, other than those from disposing of a business segment, should be reported in the income statement as extraordinary items, as shown in Exhibit 2.

Sometimes extraordinary items result in unusual financial results. For example, **Delta Air Lines** once reported an extraordinary gain of over $5.5 million as the result of the crash of one of its 727s. The plane that crashed was insured for $6.5 million, but its book value in Delta's accounting records was $962,000.

Gains and losses on the disposal of fixed assets are *not* extraordinary items. This is because (1) they are not unusual and (2) they recur from time to time in the normal operations of a business. Likewise, gains and losses from the sale of investments are usual and recurring for most businesses.

---

[12]*Statement of Financial Accounting Standards, No. 144*, op. cit., par. 41.

### Changes in Accounting Principles

Businesses are often required to change their accounting principles when the Financial Accounting Standards Board (FASB) issues a new accounting standard. In addition, a business may voluntarily change from one generally accepted accounting principle to another. For example, a corporation may change from the FIFO to the LIFO method of costing inventory to better match revenues and expenses. Changes in generally accepted accounting principles should be disclosed in the financial statements (or in notes to the statements) of the period in which they occur. This disclosure should include the following information:

1. The nature of the change.
2. The justification for the change.
3. The effect on the current year's net income.
4. The cumulative effect of the change on the net income of prior periods.

To illustrate, assume that one of Jones Corporation's divisions changes from the declining-balance method to the straight-line method of depreciation. As shown in Exhibit 2, the cumulative effect of this change is reported after the extraordinary items. The effect on the prior period is explained in Note C. If financial statements for prior periods are also presented, they should be restated as if the change had been made in the prior periods, and the effect of the restatement should be reported either on the face of the statements or in a note.

Reporting unusual items separately on the income statement allows investors to isolate the effects of these items on income and cash flows. By reporting such items, investors and other users of the financial statements can consider such factors in assessing a business's future income and cash flows.

## Reporting Unusual Below-the-Line Items

The three unusual items discussed in this section are reported separately in the income statement, below the income from continuing operations, as shown in Exhibit 2 on page 565. Many different terms and formats may be used. Unlike above-the-line unusual items, the related tax effects of below-the-line items are reported either with the item with which they are associated or in the notes to the statement. Approximately 29% of U.S. companies reported one of these unusual items on their income statement for a recent fiscal year.[13]

# Earnings per Common Share

**objective 3**

Prepare an income statement reporting earnings per share data.

The amount of net income is often used by investors and creditors in evaluating a company's profitability. However, net income by itself is difficult to use in comparing companies of different sizes. Also, trends in net income may be difficult to evaluate, using only net income, if there have been significant changes in a company's stockholders' equity. Thus, the profitability of companies is often expressed as earnings per share. **Earnings per common share (EPS)**, sometimes called **basic earnings per share**, is the net income per share of common stock outstanding during a period.

Because of its importance, earnings per share is reported in the financial press and by various investor services, such as **Moody's** and **Standard & Poor's**. Changes in earnings per share can lead to significant changes in the price of a corporation's stock in the marketplace. For example, the stock of **Texas Instruments Inc.** surged by over 12% to $16 per share after the company announced earnings per share of 6¢ as compared to Wall Street analysts' estimate of 3¢ per share.

---

[13]Determined from U.S. firms in excess of $5 billion sales on Disclosure® database.

Corporations whose stock is traded in a public market must report earnings per common share on their income statements.[14] If no preferred stock is outstanding, the earnings per common share is calculated as follows:

$$\text{Earnings per Common Share} = \frac{\text{Net Income}}{\text{Number of Common Shares Outstanding}}$$

When the number of common shares outstanding has changed during the period, a weighted average number of shares outstanding is used. If a company has preferred stock outstanding, the net income must be reduced by the amount of any preferred dividends, as shown below.

$$\text{Earnings per Common Share} = \frac{\text{Net Income} - \text{Preferred Stock Dividends}}{\text{Number of Common Shares Outstanding}}$$

Comparing the earnings per share of two or more years, based on only the net incomes of those years, could be misleading. For example, assume that Jones Corporation, whose partial income statement was presented in Exhibit 2, reported $700,000 net income for 2005. Also assume that no extraordinary or other unusual items were reported in 2005. Jones has no preferred stock outstanding and has 200,000 common shares outstanding in 2005 and 2006. The earnings per common share is $3.50 ($700,000/200,000 shares) for 2005 and $4.16 ($832,000/200,000 shares) for 2006. Comparing the two earnings per share amounts suggests that operations have improved. However, the 2006 earnings per share comparable to the $3.50 is $3.45, which is the income from continuing operations of $690,000 divided by 200,000 shares. The latter amount indicates a slight downturn in normal earnings.

When unusual below-the-line items exist, earnings per common share should be reported for those items. To illustrate, a partial income statement for Jones Corporation, showing earnings per common share, is shown in Exhibit 3. In this income statement, Jones reports all the earnings per common share amounts on the face of the income statement. However, only earnings per share amounts for income from continuing operations and net income are required to be presented on the face of

•**Exhibit 3**   **Income Statement with Earnings per Share**

**Jones Corporation**
**Income Statement**
**For the Year Ended December 31, 2006**

| | |
|---|---|
| Earnings per common share: | |
| Income from continuing operations | $ 3.45 |
| Loss on discontinued operations (Note B) | 0.50 |
| Income before extraordinary items and cumulative effect of a change in accounting principle | $ 2.95 |
| Extraordinary item: | |
| Gain on condemnation of land, net of applicable income tax of $65,000 | 0.75 |
| Cumulative effect on prior years of changing to a different depreciation method (Note C) | 0.46 |
| Net income | $ 4.16 |

[14]*Statement of Financial Accounting Standards, No. 128,* "Earnings per Share," Financial Accounting Standards Board (Norwalk, Connecticut: 1997).

the statement. The other per share amounts may be presented in the notes to the financial statements.[15]

In the preceding paragraphs, we have assumed a simple capital structure with only common stock or common stock and preferred stock outstanding. Often, however, corporations have complex capital structures with various types of securities outstanding, such as convertible preferred stock, options, warrants, and contingently issuable shares. In such cases, the possible effects of converting such securities to common stock must be calculated and reported as *earnings per common share assuming dilution or diluted earnings per share*.[16] This topic is discussed further in advanced accounting texts.

# Comprehensive Income

objective **4**

Describe the concept and the reporting of comprehensive income.

**REAL WORLD**

In the 2002 edition of *Accounting Trends & Techniques*, over 90% of the surveyed companies reported other comprehensive income, and the majority of these companies disclosed it in the statement of stockholders' equity.

***Comprehensive income*** is defined as all changes in stockholders' equity during a period, except those resulting from dividends and stockholders' investments. Companies must report traditional net income plus or minus other comprehensive income items to arrive at comprehensive income.

***Other comprehensive income items*** include foreign currency items, pension liability adjustments, and unrealized gains and losses on investments. These "other" comprehensive income transactions are reported in a middle ground that requires disclosure of these items but does not include them as part of reported earnings on the income statement. The FASB wanted these items disclosed separately from earnings in order to avoid potential confusion in interpreting the income statement. To the extent that other comprehensive income items give rise to tax effects, the taxes should be allocated to these items, which was illustrated for unusual below-the-line items. The cumulative effects of other comprehensive income items must be reported separately from retained earnings and paid-in capital, on the balance sheet, as ***accumulated other comprehensive income***. When other comprehensive income items are not present, the income statement and balance sheet formats are similar to those we have illustrated in this and preceding chapters.

Companies may report comprehensive income on the income statement, in a separate statement of comprehensive income, or in the statement of stockholders' equity. In addition, companies may use terms other than comprehensive income, such as "total nonowner changes in equity."

To illustrate reporting for comprehensive income, assume that Triple-A Enterprises, Inc., reported comprehensive income on a separate statement, called the *statement of comprehensive income*, as follows:

| **Triple-A Enterprises, Inc.** **Statement of Comprehensive Income** **For the Year Ended December 31, 2006** | |
|---|---:|
| Net income | $8 5 0 0 00 |
| Other comprehensive income, net of tax | 9 0 00 |
| Total comprehensive income | $8 5 9 0 00 |

The stockholders' equity section of the balance sheet for Triple-A Enterprises is as follows:

---

[15]Ibid., pars. 36 and 37.
[16]Ibid., pars. 11–39.

| Triple-A Enterprises, Inc. Stockholders' Equity December 31, 2005 and 2006 | | |
|---|---|---|
| | 2006 | 2005 |
| Stockholders' equity: | | |
| Common stock | $ 20 0 0 0 00 | $ 20 0 0 0 00 |
| Paid-in capital in excess of par | 36 0 0 0 00 | 36 0 0 0 00 |
| Retained earnings | 165 5 0 0 00 | 157 0 0 0 00 |
| Accumulated other comprehensive income | 1 2 9 0 00 | 1 2 0 0 00 |
| Total stockholders' equity | $222 7 9 0 00 | $214 2 0 0 00 |

Accumulated other comprehensive income is the cumulative effect of other comprehensive income items. Thus, the additional other comprehensive income of $90 for 2006 is added to the accumulated other comprehensive income beginning balance of $1,200 to yield the December 31, 2006 balance of $1,290.

You should note that comprehensive income does not affect net income or retained earnings, as we have discussed and illustrated. In the next section, we will illustrate the determination of other comprehensive income, using unrealized gains and losses on investments.

# Accounting for Investments in Stocks

**objective 5**

Describe the accounting for investments in stocks.

Corporations not only issue stock, but they also purchase stocks of other companies for investment purposes. Like individuals, businesses have a variety of reasons for investing in stocks, called **equity securities**. A business may purchase stocks as a means of earning a return (income) on excess cash that it does not need for its normal operations. Such investments are usually for a short period of time. In other cases, a business may purchase the stock of another company as a means of developing or maintaining business relationships with the other company. A business may also purchase common stock as a means of gaining control of another company's operations. In these two latter cases, the business usually intends to hold the investment for a long period of time.

The equity securities in which a business invests may be classified as trading securities or available-for-sale securities. **Trading securities** are securities that management intends to actively trade for profit. Businesses holding trading securities are those whose normal operations involve buying and selling securities. Examples of such businesses include banks and insurance companies. **Available-for-sale securities** are securities that management expects to sell in the future but which are not actively traded for profit. For example, Warren Buffett, one of the wealthiest men in the world, invests through a public company called **Berkshire Hathaway Inc.** In a recent annual report, Berkshire Hathaway reported over $28 billion of equity investment holdings listed on its balance sheet as available-for-sale securities. Some of these investments include **Coca-Cola Company**, **Gillette Company**, and **American Express**. In this section, we describe and illustrate the accounting for available-for-sale equity securities. The accounting for trading securities is described and illustrated in advanced accounting texts.

## Short-Term Investments in Stocks

Rather than allow excess cash to be idle until it is needed, a business may invest in available-for-sale securities. These investments are classified as **temporary investments** or **marketable securities**. Although such investments may be retained for several years, they continue to be classified as temporary, provided they meet two conditions. First, the securities are readily marketable and can be sold for cash at any time. Second, management intends to sell the securities when the business needs cash for operations.

Temporary investments in available-for-sale securities are recorded in a current asset account, *Marketable Securities*, at their cost. This cost includes all amounts spent to acquire the securities, such as broker's commissions. Any dividends received on the investment are recorded as a debit to *Cash* and a credit to *Dividend Revenue*.[17]

To illustrate, assume that on June 1 Crabtree Co. purchased 2,000 shares of Inis Corporation common stock at $89.75 per share plus a brokerage fee of $500. On October 1, Inis declared a $0.90 per share cash dividend payable on November 30. Crabtree's entries to record the stock purchase and the receipt of the dividend are as follows:

| | | | | |
|---|---|---|---|---|
| June | 1 | Marketable Securities | 180 000 00 | |
| | | Cash | | 180 000 00 |
| | | Purchased 2,000 shares of Inis Corporation | | |
| | | common stock [($89.75 × 2,000 shares) + $500]. | | |
| | | | | |
| Nov. | 30 | Cash | 1 800 00 | |
| | | Dividend Revenue | | 1 800 00 |
| | | Received dividend on Inis Corporation | | |
| | | common stock (2,000 shares × $0.90). | | |

On the balance sheet, temporary investments are reported at their fair market value. Market values are normally available from stock quotations in financial newspapers, such as *The Wall Street Journal*. Any difference between the fair market values of the securities and their cost is an **unrealized holding gain or loss**. This gain or loss is termed "unrealized" because a transaction (the sale of the securities) is necessary before a gain or loss becomes real (realized).

To illustrate, assume that Crabtree Co.'s portfolio of temporary investments was purchased during 2006 and has the following fair market values and unrealized gains and losses on December 31, 2006:

| Common Stock | Cost | Market | Unrealized Gain (Loss) |
|---|---|---|---|
| Edwards Inc. | $150,000 | $190,000 | $40,000 |
| SWS Corp. | 200,000 | 200,000 | — |
| Inis Corporation | 180,000 | 210,000 | 30,000 |
| Bass Co. | 160,000 | 150,000 | (10,000) |
| Total | $690,000 | $750,000 | $60,000 |

If income taxes of $18,000 are allocated to the unrealized gain, Crabtree's temporary investments should be reported at their total cost of $690,000, plus the unrealized gain (net of applicable income tax) of $42,000 ($60,000 − $18,000), as shown in Exhibit 4.

The unrealized gain (net of applicable taxes) of $42,000 should also be reported as an *other comprehensive income item*, as we mentioned in the preceding section. For example, assume that Crabtree Co. has net income of $720,000 for the year ended December 31, 2006. Crabtree elects to report comprehensive income in the *statement of comprehensive income*, as shown in Exhibit 5. In addition, the accumu-

---

[17]Stock dividends received on an investment are not journalized, since they have no effect on the investor's assets and revenues.

**•Exhibit 4**    **Temporary Investments on the Balance Sheet**

**Crabtree Co.**
**Balance Sheet (selected items)**
**December 31, 2006**

**Assets**

| | | |
|---|---|---|
| Current assets: | | |
| Cash........................................... | | $119,500 |
| Temporary investments in marketable | | |
| securities at cost......................... | $690,000 | |
| Unrealized gain (net of applicable | | |
| income tax of $18,000)................... | 42,000 | 732,000 |

**Stockholders' Equity**

| | |
|---|---|
| Accumulated other comprehensive income.............. | $ 42,000 |

**•Exhibit 5**    **Statement of Comprehensive Income**

**Crabtree Co.**
**Statement of Comprehensive Income**
**For the Year Ended December 31, 2006**

| | |
|---|---|
| Net income.............................................. | $720,000 |
| Other comprehensive income: | |
| Unrealized gain on temporary investments in marketable | |
| securities (net of applicable income tax of $18,000)............... | 42,000 |
| Comprehensive income...................................... | $762,000 |

lated other comprehensive income on the balance sheet would also be $42,000, representing the beginning balance of zero plus other comprehensive income of $42,000, as shown in Exhibit 4.

Unrealized losses are reported in a similar manner. Unrealized gains and losses are reported as other comprehensive income items until the related securities are sold. When temporary securities are sold, the unrealized gains or losses become realized and are included in determining net income.

## Long-Term Investments in Stocks

Long-term investments in stocks are not intended as a source of cash in the normal operations of the business. Rather, such investments are often held for their income, long-term gain potential, or influence over another business entity. They are reported in the balance sheet under the caption ***Investments***, which usually follows the Current Assets section.

Long-term investments in stock are treated as available-for-sale securities, as we illustrated previously for short-term available-for-sale securities. However, if the investor (the buyer of the stock) has significant influence over the operating and financing activities of the investee (company whose stock is owned), the ***equity method*** is used.

**Accounting for Long-Term
Stock Investments**

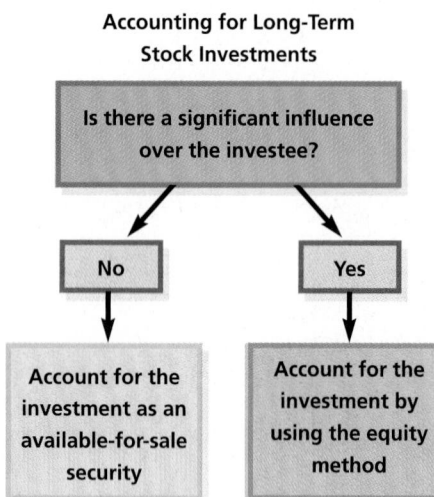

When the investor does not have a significant influence over the investee, the investment is recorded at cost and reported at fair market value net of any applicable income tax effects. In addition, any unrealized gains and losses are reported as part of the comprehensive income.[18] For example, **Delta Air Lines** disclosed investments in **Priceline.com** preferred stock as a noncurrent investment at the appraised fair market value.

When the investor has a significant influence and the equity method is used, a stock purchase is recorded at cost, as shown previously. Evidence of significant influence includes the percentage of ownership, the existence of intercompany transactions, and the interchange of managerial personnel. Generally, if the investor owns 20% or more of the voting stock of the investee, it is assumed that the investor has significant influence over the investee.

Under the equity method, the investment is *not* subsequently adjusted to fair value. Rather, the book value of the investment is adjusted as follows:

1. The investor's share of the periodic net income of the investee is recorded as an *increase in the investment account* and as *income for the period.* Likewise, the investor's share of an investee's net loss is recorded as a *decrease in the investment account* and as a *loss for the period.*
2. The investor's share of cash dividends from the investee is recorded as an *increase in the cash account* and a *decrease in the investment account.*

To illustrate, assume that on January 2, Hally Inc. pays cash of $350,000 for 40% of the common stock and net assets of Brock Corporation. Assume also that, for the year ending December 31, Brock Corporation reports net income of $105,000 and declares and pays $45,000 in dividends. Using the equity method, Hally Inc. (the investor) records these transactions as follows:

REAL WORLD

The 2002 edition of *Accounting Trends & Techniques* indicated that over 55% of the companies surveyed used the equity method to account for investments.

| Jan. | 2 | Investment in Brock Corp. Stock | 350 0 0 0 00 | |
|---|---|---|---|---|
| | | Cash | | 350 0 0 0 00 |
| | | Purchased 40% of Brock Corp. stock. | | |
| Dec. | 31 | Investment in Brock Corp. Stock | 42 0 0 0 00 | |
| | | Income of Brock Corp. | | 42 0 0 0 00 |
| | | Recorded 40% share of Brock Corp. net income of $105,000. | | |
| Dec. | 31 | Cash | 18 0 0 0 00 | |
| | | Investment in Brock Corp. Stock | | 18 0 0 0 00 |
| | | Recorded 40% share of Brock Corp. dividends. | | |

Assume that Hally Inc. increased its ownership in Brock Corporation to 45% at the beginning of the next year. If Brock Corporation reported net income of $80,000 and declared dividends of $50,000, by how much would Hally Inc. adjust the Investment in Brock Corp. Stock?

$13,500 [($80,000 × 45%) − ($50,000 × 45%)]

The combined effect of recording 40% of Brock Corporation's net income and dividends is to increase Hally's interest in the net assets of Brock by $24,000 ($42,000 − $18,000), as shown at the top of the following page.

The equity method causes the investment account to mirror the proportional changes in the book value of the investee. Thus, Brock Corporation's book value increased by $60,000 ($105,000 − $45,000), while the investment in Brock account increased by Hally's proportional share of that increase, or $24,000 ($60,000 × 40%). Both the book value of Brock Corporation and Hally's investment in Brock increased at the same rate from the original cost.

---
[18]An exception to reporting unrealized gains and losses as part of comprehensive income is made if the decrease in the market value for a stock is considered permanent. In this case, the cost of the individual stock is written down (decreased), and the amount of the write-down is included in net income.

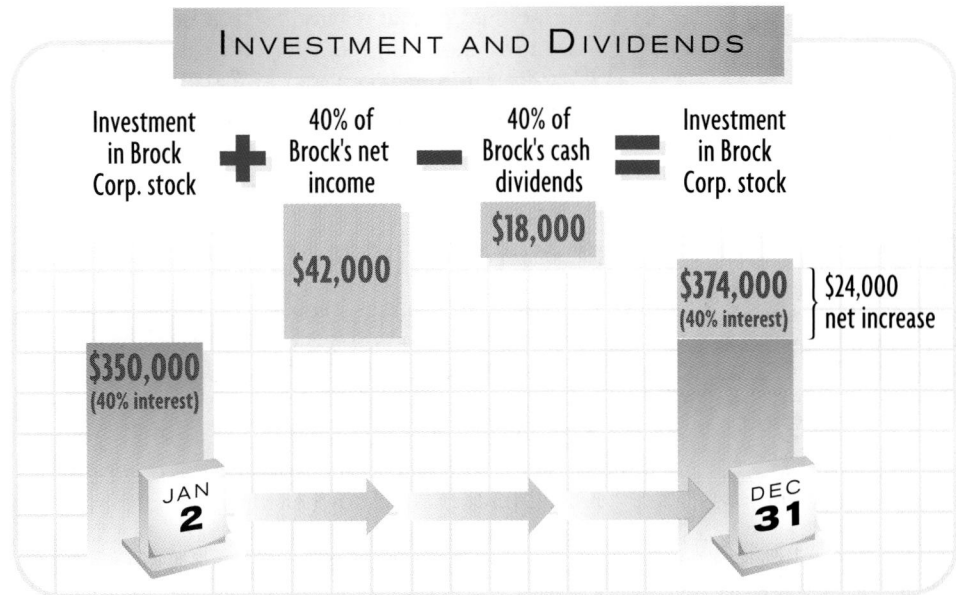

## Sale of Investments in Stocks

Accounting for the sale of stock is the same for both short-term and long-term investments. When shares of stock are sold, the investment account is credited for the carrying amount (book value) of the shares sold. The cash or receivables account is debited for the proceeds (sales price less commission and other selling costs). Any difference between the proceeds and the carrying amount is recorded as a gain or loss on the sale and is included in determining net income.

To illustrate, assume that an investment in Drey Inc. stock has a carrying amount of $15,700 when it is sold on March 1. If the proceeds from the sale of the stock are $17,500, the entry to record the transaction is as follows:

| | | | | |
|---|---|---|---:|---:|
| Mar. | 1 | Cash | 17 5 0 0 00 | |
| | | Investment in Drey Inc. Stock | | 15 7 0 0 00 |
| | | Gain on Sale of Investments | | 1 8 0 0 00 |

# Business Combinations

**objective** 6

Describe alternative methods of combining businesses and how consolidated financial statements are prepared.

Each year, many businesses combine in order to produce more efficiently or to diversify product lines. Business combinations often involve complex accounting principles and terminology. The objective of this section is to introduce some of the unique terminology and concepts related to business combinations. The use and preparation of consolidated financial statements are also briefly described.

## Mergers and Consolidations

One corporation may acquire all the assets and liabilities of a second corporation, which is then dissolved. This joining of two corporations is called a *merger*. The acquiring company may use cash, debt, or its own stock as the payment. Whatever the form of payment, the amount received by the dissolving corporation is distributed to its stockholders in final liquidation. For example, **Mattel Inc.** acquired **Mindscape Inc.** for $152 million in cash and stock. As a result of the merger, Mindscape no longer exists as a separate company.

A new corporation may be created, and the assets and liabilities of two or more existing corporations transferred to it. This type of combination is called a **consolidation**. The new corporation usually issues its own stock in exchange for the net assets acquired. The original corporations are then dissolved. For example, **Exxon-Mobil Corporation** became the new consolidated company that resulted from combining two individual corporations—Exxon and Mobil.

## Parent and Subsidiary Corporations

I'm the top supplier of first-run syndicated programming in America. Under my roof you'll find "Wheel of Fortune" and "Jeopardy!" (the two highest-rated series in syndication), and "The Oprah Winfrey Show" (the No. 1 daytime talk show), as well as "Hollywood Squares," "Inside Edition," "Martha Stewart Living," "Bob Vila's Home Again," and "CBS Marketwatch Weekend." I also distribute "Everybody Loves Raymond," "CSI: Crime Scene Investigation," among other shows you might have heard of. My biggest recent home run is the "Dr. Phil" show. CBS bought me for $2.5 billion in 1999. Who am I? (Go to page 584 for answer.)

Business combinations may also occur when one corporation buys a controlling share of the outstanding voting stock of one or more other corporations. In this case, none of the corporations dissolve. The corporations continue as separate legal entities in a parent-subsidiary relationship. The corporation owning all or a majority of the voting stock of the other corporation is called the **parent company**. The corporation that is controlled is called the **subsidiary company**. Two or more corporations closely related through stock ownership are sometimes called **affiliated** companies. An example of an affiliated company is **ESPN, Inc.**, a subsidiary of **Walt Disney Company**.

A corporation (the acquiring company) may acquire the controlling share of the voting common stock of another corporation (the target company) by paying cash, exchanging other assets, issuing debt, or using some combination of these methods. In addition, a parent-subsidiary relationship may be created by exchanging the voting common stock of the acquiring corporation (the parent) for the common stock of the acquired corporation (the subsidiary). Regardless if there is an outright purchase of assets or common stock or an exchange of common stock, the transaction is recorded like a normal purchase of assets, and the combination is accounted for by the **purchase method**.

Under the purchase method, the subsidiary's net assets are reported in the consolidated balance sheet at their fair market value at the time of the purchase. In some cases, a parent may pay more than the fair market value of a subsidiary's net assets because the subsidiary has prospects for high future earnings. The difference between the amount paid by the parent and the fair market value of the subsidiary's net assets is reported on the consolidated balance sheet as an intangible asset. This asset is identified as **Goodwill** or **Excess of cost of business acquired over related net assets**.

## Consolidated Financial Statements

Although parent and subsidiary corporations may operate as a single economic unit, they continue to maintain separate accounting records and prepare their own periodic financial statements. At the end of the year, the financial statements of the parent and subsidiary are combined and reported as a single company. These combined financial statements are called **consolidated financial statements**. Such statements are usually identified by adding "and subsidiary(ies)" to the name of the parent corporation or by adding "consolidated" to the statement title.

To the stockholders of the parent company, consolidated financial statements are more meaningful than separate statements for each corporation. This is because the parent company, in substance, controls the subsidiaries, even though the parent and its subsidiaries are separate entities.

When a consolidated balance sheet is prepared, the ownership interest of the parent in the subsidiary's stock, which is the balance in the parent's investment in subsidiary account, must be eliminated. This is done by eliminating the parent's investment in subsidiary account against the balances of the subsidiary's stockholders' equity accounts.

If the parent owns less than 100% of the subsidiary stock, the subsidiary stock owned by outsiders is *not* eliminated but is normally reported immediately following the consolidated total liabilities. This amount is described as the **minority interest**.

When the data on the financial statements of the parent and its subsidiaries are combined to form the consolidated statements, intercompany transactions are given special attention. An example of such a transaction is the parent purchasing goods

# INTEGRITY IN BUSINESS

## CONFLICTS OF INTEREST

**E**nron Corporation, once the seventh largest company in the United States, collaped into bankruptcy in a matter of months. Most of Enron's travails were related to undisclosed losses from complex financial transactions with certain partnerships that were run by its own officers, including the CFO (chief financial officer). Enron management came under severe criticism for (1) providing minimum disclosure about these partnership investments to the investing public and (2) allowing senior officers to hold significant individual investments in these partnerships. Regarding the potential conflict of interest, Wayne Shaw, a professor of accounting, stated, "If it was the CFO, why was he put in a position where no one knew what he was doing? If the blame's being placed on one party, you have to wonder about the internal controls of the company. There's got to be checks and balances, and they weren't there." The lessons from the Enron debacle are that unconsolidated investments may require significant additional disclosures in the notes, and senior officers should avoid a conflict of interest caused by holding individual interests in the investee while being an officer of the investor.

from the subsidiary or the subsidiary loaning money to the parent. These transactions affect the individual accounts of the parent and subsidiary and thus the financial statements of both companies.[19] To illustrate, assume that P Inc. (the parent) sold merchandise to S Inc. (the subsidiary) for $90,000. The merchandise cost P Inc. $50,000. In turn, S Inc. sold the merchandise to a customer for $120,000.

The individual income statements for P Inc. and S Inc. are shown in Exhibit 6. The consolidated (combined) income statement is shown in Exhibit 7. The consolidated income statement presents the income statements for P Inc. and S Inc. as if they were one operating entity. Thus, the $90,000 sale (P Inc.) and the $90,000 cost of merchandise sold (S Inc.) are eliminated. This is because the consolidated entity cannot sell to itself or buy from itself.

## •Exhibit 6    Income Statements for P Inc. and S Inc.

|  | P Inc. | | S Inc. | |
| --- | --- | --- | --- | --- |
| Sales | | $950,000 | | $400,000 |
| Cost of merchandise sold | | 625,000 | | 240,000 |
| Gross profit | | $325,000 | | $160,000 |
| Operating expenses: | | | | |
| Selling expenses | $155,000 | | $55,000 | |
| Administrative expenses | 85,000 | 240,000 | 35,000 | 90,000 |
| Net income | | $ 85,000 | | $ 70,000 |

Many U.S. corporations own subsidiaries in foreign countries. Such corporations are often called *multinational corporations*. The financial statements of the foreign subsidiary are usually prepared in the foreign currency. Before the financial statements of foreign subsidiaries are consolidated with their domestic parent's financial statements, the amounts shown on the statements for the foreign companies must be converted to U.S. dollars.[20] For example, **General Motors Corporation** is a multinational company that consolidates its foreign subsidiaries, such as the European **Opel** division, into U.S. dollars.

---

[19]Examples of accounts often affected by intercompany transactions include *Accounts Receivable* and *Accounts Payable*, *Interest Receivable* and *Interest Income*, and *Interest Expense* and *Interest Payable*.
[20]Appendix D at the end of the text discusses and illustrates the accounting for foreign currency transactions.

•**Exhibit 7**   Consolidated Income Statement for P Inc. and S Inc.

| | | |
|---|---:|---:|
| Sales . . . . . . . . . . . . . . . . . . . . . . . . . . . . . . . . . . . . . . . . . . . . . . . . | | $1,260,000* |
| Cost of merchandise sold . . . . . . . . . . . . . . . . . . . . . . . . . . . | | 775,000** |
| Gross profit . . . . . . . . . . . . . . . . . . . . . . . . . . . . . . . . . . . . . . . . . | | $ 485,000 |
| Operating expenses: | | |
|    Selling expenses . . . . . . . . . . . . . . . . . . . . . . . . . . . . . | $210,000 | |
|    Administrative expenses . . . . . . . . . . . . . . . . . . . . . . . | 120,000 | 330,000 |
| Net income . . . . . . . . . . . . . . . . . . . . . . . . . . . . . . . . . . . . . . . . | | $ 155,000 |

*$950,000 − $90,000 + $400,000
**$625,000 + $240,000 − $90,000

# Financial Analysis and Interpretation

**objective**  **7**

Compute and interpret the
price-earnings ratio.

A firm's growth potential and future earnings prospects are indicated by how much the market is willing to pay per dollar of a company's earnings. This ratio, called the ***price-earnings ratio***, or **P/E ratio**, is commonly included in stock market quotations reported by the financial press. A high P/E ratio indicates that the market expects high growth and earnings in the future. Likewise, a low P/E ratio indicates lower growth and earnings expectations.

The price-earnings ratio on common stock is computed by dividing the stock's market price per share at a specific date by the company's annual earnings per share, as shown below.

$$\text{Price-Earnings Ratio} = \frac{\text{Market Price per Share of Common Stock}}{\text{Earnings per Share of Common Stock}}$$

Investors that invest in high price-earnings ratio companies are often referred to as **growth** investors. Growth investors pay a high price for shares because they expect the company to grow and provide a superior return. That is, high price-earnings ratios can be related to investor optimism. Examples of growth companies are **Intel Corp.** (P/E 47), **eBay** (P/E 96), and **Genentech Inc.** (P/E 91). Growth companies are considered risky because high growth expectations are already reflected in the market price. Thus, if the company's high growth expectations are not realized, the stock price will likely fall.

In contrast, investors in low price-earnings ratio companies are often referred to as **value** investors. Value investors invest in companies with stable and predictable earnings. The value investor believes that the low price-earnings ratio investment is safer than a high price-earnings investment, since the stock is priced at a "bargain" level. Value investing is generally considered the "tortoise" strategy to the growth investor's "hare" strategy. Examples of value stocks are **Bank of America** (P/E 12), **Florida Power and Light** (P/E 12), and **DaimlerChrysler** (P/E 7).

To illustrate the calculation of the price-earnings ratio, assume that Harper Inc. reported earnings per share of $1.64 in 2006 and $1.35 in 2005. The market prices per common share are $20.50 at the end of 2006 and $13.50 at the end of 2005. The price-earnings ratio on this stock is computed as follows:

| | Price-Earnings Ratio |
|---|---|
| Year 2006 | 12.5 ($20.50/$1.64) |
| Year 2005 | 10.0 ($13.50/$1.35) |

The price-earnings ratio indicates that a share of Harper Inc.'s common stock was selling for 10 times the amount of earnings per share at the end of 2005. At the end of 2006, the common stock was selling for 12.5 times the amount of earnings per share. These results would indicate a generally improving expectation of growth and earnings for Harper Inc. However, a prospective investor should also consider the price-earnings ratios for competing firms in the same industry.

## SPOTLIGHT ON STRATEGY

### THE SYNERGY OF MERGERS

Companies merge in order to create synergy, which occurs when the sum is greater than the parts. How do mergers create synergy? The four basic strategies for creating value in a merger are explained below.

1. *Reduce costs:* When two companies combine, they may be able to eliminate duplicate administrative expenses. For example, the combined company does not need two CEOs or two CFOs, or the company can run on a single computer system or distribution network. Thus, the combined costs of the merged enterprises are less than the costs of the companies if run separately. **Hewlett Packard Corp.** identified cost savings such as these in justifying its acquisition of **Compaq Computer Corp.**

2. *Replace management:* If the target company has been suffering from mismanagement, the acquirer can purchase the target for a low price and replace the target company's management.

3. *Horizontal integration:* The acquirer may purchase the target company because it has a complementary prod-uct line, territory, or customer base to its own. The new combined entity is able to serve customers with a broader reach than were two separate entities. For example, **Starbucks Corp.** acquired **Seattle Coffee Holdings LTD** of the United Kingdom in order to expand its geographical reach. Similarly, **Microsoft Corp.** acquired **Great Plains Software Co.** to strengthen its presence in the business software application market.

4. *Vertical integration:* A vertical integration occurs when a business acquires another business within its value chain. One common type of vertical integration is to acquire a supplier. Acquiring a supplier may provide a more stable source of supply of a strategic resource and reduce coordination costs. For example, **Delta Air Lines** acquired **Comair Holdings**, a regional jet carrier, to supply passengers from smaller cities into its large city hub system. Vertical integration may also involve acquiring distribution or customer service capabilities. For example, the **AOL Time Warner** merger was designed to provide distribution access of **Time Warner** content via **AOL**.

# Key Points

**1 Journalize the entries for corporate income taxes, including deferred income taxes.**
Corporations are subject to federal income tax and are required to make estimated payments throughout the year. To record the payment of estimated tax, Income Tax is debited and Cash is credited. If additional taxes are owed at the end of the year, Income Tax is debited and Income Tax Payable is credited for the amount owed. If the estimated tax payments are greater than the actual tax liability, a receivable account is debited and Income Tax is credited.

The tax effects of temporary differences between taxable income and income before income taxes must be allocated between periods. The journal entry for such allocations normally debits Income Tax and credits Income Tax Payable and Deferred Income Tax Payable.

**2 Prepare an income statement reporting the following unusual items: fixed asset impairments, restructuring charges, discontinued operations, extraordinary items, and cumulative changes in accounting principles.**

Fixed asset impairments occur when the fair value of a fixed asset falls below its book value and is not expected to recover. The asset is written down and a loss is recognized. The loss is deducted from gross profit on the income statement.

Restructuring charges are costs associated with involuntarily terminating employees, terminating contracts, consolidating facilities, or relocating employees. The accrued expenses associated with such a plan are recognized in the period that senior executives approve and communicate the plan. The expense is deducted from gross profit on the income statement.

A gain or loss resulting from the disposal of a business segment, net of related tax, should be added to or deducted from income from continuing operations on the income statement.

Gains and losses may result from events and transactions that are unusual and occur infrequently. Such extraordinary items, net of related income tax, should be added to or deducted from income from continuing operations on the income statement.

A change in an accounting principle results from the adoption of a generally accepted accounting principle different from the one used previously for reporting purposes. The effect of the change in principle on net income in the current period, as well as the cumulative effect on income of prior periods, should be disclosed in the financial statements, net of tax, below income from continuing operations.

## 3 Prepare an income statement reporting earnings per share data.

Earnings per share is reported on the income statements of public corporations. If there are unusual items below income from continuing operations on the income statement, the per share amount should be presented for each of these items as well as net income.

## 4 Describe the concept and the reporting of comprehensive income.

Comprehensive income is all changes in stockholders' equity during a period except those resulting from dividends and stockholders' investments. Companies must report traditional net income plus or minus other comprehensive income items to arrive at comprehensive income. Other comprehensive income items include transactions and events that are excluded from net income, such as unrealized gains and losses on certain investments in debt and equity securities. Accumulated other comprehensive income is separately reported in the stockholders' equity section of the balance sheet.

## 5 Describe the accounting for investments in stocks.

A business may purchase stocks as a means of earning a return (income) on excess cash that it does not need for its normal operations. Such investments are recorded in a marketable securities account. Their cost includes all amounts spent to acquire the securities. Any dividends received on an investment are recorded as a debit to Cash and a credit to Dividend Revenue. On the balance sheet, temporary investments are reported as available-for-sale securities at their fair market values. Any difference between the fair market values of the securities and their cost is an unrealized holding gain or loss (net of applicable taxes) that is reported as an other comprehensive income item.

Long-term investments in stocks are not intended as a source of cash in the normal operations of the business. They are reported in the balance sheet either as available-for-sale securities, and disclosed at fair value, or reported under the equity method.

The accounting for the sale of stock is the same for both short-term and long-term investments. The investment account is credited for the carrying amount (book value) of the shares sold, the cash or receivables account is debited for the proceeds, and any difference between the proceeds and the carrying amount is recorded as a gain or loss on the sale.

## 6 Describe alternative methods of combining businesses and how consolidated financial statements are prepared.

Businesses may combine in a merger or a consolidation. Business combinations may also occur when one corporation acquires a controlling share of the outstanding voting stock of another corporation. In this case, a parent-subsidiary relationship exists, and the companies are called affiliated companies.

Although the corporations that make up a parent-subsidiary affiliation may operate as a single economic unit, they usually continue to maintain separate accounting records and prepare their own periodic financial statements. The financial statements prepared by combining the parent and subsidiary statements are called consolidated financial statements.

When a parent corporation purchases less than 100% of the subsidiary's stock, the remaining stockholders' equity is identified as minority interest. The minority interest is reported on the consolidated balance sheet, usually following the total liabilities.

In preparing consolidated income statements for a parent and its subsidiary, all amounts from intercompany transactions, such as intercompany sales of merchandise and cost of merchandise sold, are eliminated.

## 7 Compute and interpret the price-earnings ratio.

The assessment of a firm's growth potential and future earnings prospects is indicated by the price-earnings ratio, or P/E ratio. It is computed by dividing the stock's market price per share at a specific date by the company's annual earnings per share.

# Key Terms

accumulated other comprehensive income (570)
available-for-sale securities (571)
comprehensive income (570)
consolidated financial statements (576)
consolidation (576)
discontinued operations (567)
earnings per common share (EPS) (568)
equity method (573)

equity securities (571)
extraordinary items (567)
fixed asset impairment (564)
investments (573)
merger (575)
minority interest (576)
other comprehensive income items (570)
parent company (576)
permanent differences (563)
price-earnings ratio (578)

purchase method (576)
restructuring charge (566)
subsidiary company (576)
taxable income (561)
temporary differences (561)
temporary investments (571)
trading securities (571)
unrealized holding gain or loss (572)

# Illustrative Problem

The following data were selected from the records of Botanica Greenhouses Inc. for the current fiscal year ended August 31:

| | |
|---|---:|
| Administrative expenses | $   82,200 |
| Cost of merchandise sold | 750,000 |
| Fixed asset impairment | 115,000 |
| Gain on condemnation of land | 25,000 |
| Income tax: | |
|    Applicable to continuing operations | 27,200 |
|    Applicable to gain on condemnation of land | 10,000 |
|    Applicable to loss on discontinued operations (reduction) | 24,000 |
| Interest expense | 15,200 |
| Loss on discontinued operations | 60,200 |
| Restructuring charge | 40,000 |
| Sales | 1,252,500 |
| Selling expenses | 182,100 |

## Instructions

Prepare a multiple-step income statement, concluding with a section for earnings per share in the form illustrated in this chapter. There were 10,000 shares of common stock (no preferred) outstanding throughout the year. Assume that the gain on condemnation of land is an extraordinary item.

**Solution**

**Botanica Greenhouses Inc.**
**Income Statement**
**For the Year Ended August 31, 2006**

| | | |
|---|---:|---:|
| Sales | | $1,252,500 |
| Cost of merchandise sold | | 750,000 |
| Gross profit | | $ 502,500 |
| Operating expenses: | | |
| Selling expenses | $182,100 | |
| Administrative expenses | 82,200 | |
| Fixed asset impairment | 115,000 | |
| Restructuring charge | 40,000 | |
| Total operating expenses | | 419,300 |
| Income from operations | | $ 83,200 |
| Other expense: | | |
| Interest expense | | 15,200 |
| Income from continuing operations before | | |
| income tax | | $ 68,000 |
| Income tax expense | | 27,200 |
| Income from continuing operations | | $ 40,800 |
| Loss on discontinued operations | $ 60,200 | |
| Less applicable income tax | 24,000 | 36,200 |
| Income before extraordinary item | | $ 4,600 |
| Extraordinary item: | | |
| Gain on condemnation of land | $ 25,000 | |
| Less applicable income tax | 10,000 | 15,000 |
| Net income | | $ 19,600 |
| | | |
| Earnings per share: | | |
| Income from continuing operations | | $4.08 |
| Loss on discontinued operations | | 3.62 |
| Income before extraordinary item | | $0.46 |
| Extraordinary item | | 1.50 |
| Net income | | $1.96 |

# Self-Examination Questions (Answers at End of Chapter)

1. During its first year of operations, a corporation elected to use the straight-line method of depreciation for financial reporting purposes and MACRS in determining taxable income. If the income tax rate is 40% and the amount of depreciation expense is $60,000 under the straight-line method and $100,000 under MACRS, what is the amount of income tax deferred to future years?
A. $16,000
B. $24,000
C. $40,000
D. $60,000

2. A material gain resulting from condemning land for public use would be reported on the income statement as a(n):
A. extraordinary item.
B. other income item.
C. restructuring charge.
D. fixed asset impairment.

3. Gwinnett Corporation's temporary investments cost $100,000 and have a market value of $120,000 at

the end of the accounting period. Assuming a tax rate of 40%, the difference between the cost and market value would be reported as a:

A. $12,000 realized gain.
B. $12,000 unrealized gain.
C. $20,000 realized gain.
D. $20,000 unrealized gain.

4. Cisneros Corporation owns 75% of Harrell Inc. During the current year, Harrell Inc. reported net income of $150,000 and declared dividends of $40,000. How much would Cisneros Corporation increase Investment in Harrell Inc. Stock for the current year?

A. $0         C. $82,500
B. $30,000    D. $112,500

5. Harkin Company has a market price of $60 per share on December 31. The total stockholders' equity is $2,400,000, and the net income is $800,000. There are 200,000 shares outstanding. Preferred dividends are $50,000. The price-earnings ratio would be:

A. 3.
B. 15.
C. 16.
D. 20.

# Class Discussion Questions

1. How would the amount of deferred income tax payable be reported in the balance sheet if (a) it is payable within one year and (b) it is payable beyond one year?

2. Maxwell Company owns an equipped plant that has a book value of $150 million. Due to a permanent decline in consumer demand for the products produced by this plant, the market value of the plant and equipment is appraised at $20 million. Describe the accounting treatment for this impairment.

3. How should the severance costs of terminated employees be accounted for?

4. During the current year, 40 acres of land that cost $200,000 were condemned for construction of an interstate highway. Assuming that an award of $350,000 in cash was received and that the applicable income tax on this transaction is 40%, how would this information be presented in the income statement?

5. Corporation X realized a material gain when its facilities at a designated floodway were acquired by the urban renewal agency. How should the gain be reported in the income statement?

6. An annual report of **Ford Motor Company** disclosed the sale of its ownership interest in **Visteon Corporation**, a major automotive components manufacturer. The estimated after-tax loss on disposal of these operations was $2.3 billion. Indicate how the loss from discontinued operations should be reported by Ford on its income statement.

7. If significant changes are made in the accounting principles applied from one period to the next, why should the effect of these changes be disclosed in the financial statements?

8. A corporation reports earnings per share of $1.38 for the most recent year and $1.10 for the preceding year. The $1.38 includes a $0.45-per-share gain from insurance proceeds related to a fully depreciated asset that was destroyed by fire.
   a. Should the composition of the $1.38 be disclosed in the financial reports?
   b. On the basis of the limited information presented, would you conclude that operations had improved or declined?

9. a. List some examples of other comprehensive income items.
   b. Does the reporting of other comprehensive income affect the determination of net income and retained earnings?

10. Why might a business invest in another company's stock?

11. How are temporary investments in marketable securities reported on the balance sheet?

12. How are unrealized gains and losses on temporary investments in marketable securities reported on the statement of comprehensive income?

13. a. What method of accounting is used for long-term investments in stock in which there is significant influence over the investee?

    b. Under what caption are long-term investments in stock reported on the balance sheet?

14. Plaster Inc. received a $0.15-per-share cash dividend on 50,000 shares of Gestalt Corporation common stock, which Plaster Inc. carries as a long-term investment. Assuming that Plaster Inc. uses the equity method of accounting for its investment in Gestalt Corporation, what account would be credited for the receipt of the $7,500 dividend?

15. Parent Corporation owns 90% of the outstanding common stock of Subsidiary Corporation, which has no preferred stock. (a) What is the term applied to the remaining 10% interest? (b) On the consolidated balance sheet, where is the amount of Subsidiary's book equity allocable to outsiders reported?

16. An annual report of **The Campbell Soup Company** reported on its income statement $2.4 million as "equity in earnings of affiliates." Journalize the entry that Campbell would have made to record this equity in earnings of affiliates.

resources for your success online at **http://warren.swlearning.com**

Remember! If you need additional help, visit South-Western's Web site. See page 28 for a description of the online and printed materials that are available. http://warren.swlearning.com

Warren
Reeve
Fess

**Answer:** King World Productions

# Exercises

**EXERCISE 14-1**
*Income tax entries*
**Objective 1**

Journalize the entries to record the following selected transactions of Grove Monuments, Inc.:

Apr.  15. Paid the first installment of the estimated income tax for the current fiscal year ending December 31, $70,000. No entry had been made to record the liability.

June 15. Paid the second installment of $70,000.

Sept. 15. Paid the third installment of $70,000.

Dec. 31. Recorded the estimated income tax liability for the year just ended and the deferred income tax liability, based on the transactions above and the following data:

| | |
|---|---|
| Income tax rate | 40% |
| Income before income tax | $900,000 |
| Taxable income according to tax return | $800,000 |

Jan.  15. Paid the fourth installment of $110,000.

**EXERCISE 14-2**
*Deferred income taxes*
**Objective 1**

Integrated Systems, Inc. recognized service revenue of $300,000 on its financial statements in 2005. Assume, however, that the Tax Code requires this amount to be recognized for tax purposes in 2006. The taxable income for 2005 and 2006 is $2,000,000 and $2,500,000, respectively. Assume a tax rate of 40%.

Prepare the journal entries to record the tax expense, deferred taxes, and taxes payable for 2005 and 2006, respectively.

**EXERCISE 14-3**
*Fixed asset impairment*
**Objective 2**

✓ *a. $84,000,000*

LightWave Communications, Inc. spent $100 million expanding its fiber optic communication network between Chicago and Los Angeles during 2004. The fiber optic network was assumed to have a 10-year life, with a $20 million salvage value, when it was put into service on January 1, 2005. The network is depreciated using the straight-line method. At the end of 2006, the expected traffic volume on the fiber optic network was only 60% of what was originally expected. The reduced traffic volume caused the fair market value of the asset to be estimated at $45 million on December 31, 2006. The loss is not expected to be recoverable.

a. Determine the book value of the network on December 31, 2006, prior to the impairment adjustment.
b. Provide the journal entry to record the fixed asset impairment on December 31, 2006.
c. Provide the balance sheet disclosure for fixed assets on December 31, 2006.

**EXERCISE 14-4**
*Fixed asset impairment*
**Objective 2**

Sunset Resorts, Inc. owns and manages resort properties. On January 15, 2006, one of its properties was found to be adjacent to a toxic chemical disposal site. As a result of the negative publicity, this property's bookings dropped 40% during 2006. On December 31, 2006, the accounts of the company showed the following details regarding the impaired property:

| | |
|---|---|
| Land | $ 25,000,000 |
| Buildings and improvements (net) | 80,000,000 |
| Equipment (net) | 15,000,000 |
| Total | $120,000,000 |

Management decides that closing the resort is the only option. As a result, it is estimated that the buildings and improvements will be written off completely. The land can be sold for other uses for $17 million, while the equipment can be disposed of for $4 million, net of disposal costs.

a. Provide the journal entry to record the asset impairment on December 31, 2006.
b. Provide the note disclosure for the impairment.

**EXERCISE 14-5**
*Restructuring charge*
**Objective 2**

✓ *a. Restructuring charge,*
*$3,600,000*

Jen-King Company's board of directors approved and communicated an employee severance plan in response to a decline in demand for the company's products. The plan called for the elimination of 150 headquarters positions by providing a severance equal to 5% of the annual salary multiplied by the number of years of service. The average annual salary of the eliminated positions is $60,000. The average tenure of terminated employees is 8 years. The plan was communicated to employees on November 1, 2006. Actual termination notices will be distributed over the period between December 1, 2006, and April 1, 2007. On December 15, 2006, 40 employees received a lay-off notice and were terminated with severance.

a. Provide the appropriate journal entry for the restructuring charge.
b. Provide the journal entry to record the severance payment on December 15, 2006, assuming that the actual tenure and salary of terminated employees were consistent with the overall average.
c. Provide the balance sheet and note disclosures on December 31, 2006.

**EXERCISE 14-6**
*Restructuring charge*
**Objective 2**

✓ *a. Restructuring charge,*
*$3,039,200*

Mango Juice Company has been suffering a downturn in its juice business due to adverse publicity regarding the caffeine content of its drink products. As a result, the company has been required to restructure operations. The board of directors approved and communicated a plan on July 1, 2006, calling for the following actions:

1. Close a juice plant on October 15, 2006. Closing, equipment relocation, and employee relocation costs are expected to be $500,000 during October.

2. Eliminate 280 plant positions. A severance will be paid to the terminated employees equal to 400% of their estimated monthly earnings payable in four quarterly installments on October 15, 2006; January 15, 2007; April 15, 2007; and July 15, 2007.

3. Terminate a juice supply contract, activating a $120,000 cancellation penalty, payable upon notice of termination. The notice will be formally delivered to the supplier on August 15, 2006.

The 280 employees earn an average of $12 per hour. The average employee works 180 hours per month.

a. Determine the total restructuring charge.
b. Provide the journal entry for the restructuring charge on July 1, 2006. (*Note:* Use Restructuring Obligation as the liability account, since the charges involve more than just employee terminations.)
c. Provide the journal entry for the October 15, 2006 employee severance payment.
d. Provide the balance sheet disclosure for December 31, 2006.
e. Provide a note disclosure for December 31, 2006.

---

**EXERCISE 14-7**
*Restructuring charges and asset impairments*

**Objective 2**

✓ *a. Severance restructuring charge, $650,000*

Conway Transportation Company has suffered losses due to increased competition in its service market from low-cost independent truckers. As a result, on December 31, 2006, the board of directors of the company approved and communicated a restructuring plan that calls for selling 50 tractor-trailers out of a fleet of 400. In addition, the plan calls for the elimination of 50 driver positions and 15 staff support positions. The market price for used tractor-trailers is depressed due to general overcapacity in the transportation industry. As a result, the market value of tractor-trailers is estimated to be only 40% of the book value of these assets. It is not believed that the impairment in fixed assets is recoverable. The cost and accumulated depreciation of the total tractor-trailer fleet on December 31 are $34 million and $9 million, respectively. The restructuring plan will provide a severance to the drivers and staff totaling $10,000 per employee, payable on March 14, 2007, which is the expected employee termination date.

a. Provide the journal entries on December 31, 2006, for the fixed asset impairment and the employee severance costs.
b. Provide the balance sheet and note disclosure on December 31, 2006.
c. Provide the journal entry for March 14, 2007.

---

**EXERCISE 14-8**
*Restructuring charges and fixed asset impairment disclosure*

**Objective 2**

REAL WORLD

The notes to the financial statements for **Maytag Corporation** provided a table of special charges, as follows:

**Schedule of Special Charges**
**Maytag Corporation**
**For the Year Ended December 31, 2002 (in thousands)**

| Description of Reserve | Balance, Dec. 31, 2001 | Charged to Earnings | Cash Utilization | Noncash Utilization | Balance, Dec. 31, 2002 |
|---|---|---|---|---|---|
| Severance and related expense | $6,903 | $ 4,128 | $(4,629) | $ (2,292) | $4,110 |
| Asset write-downs | 0 | 28,627 | 0 | (28,627) | 0 |
| Total | $6,903 | $32,755 | $(4,629) | $(30,919) | $4,110 |

The special charges include both severance-related expenses and asset impairments. The columns of the table indicate the balances and change in balances of the balance sheet accounts affected by the special charges. The notes to the financial statements also indicated the following:

*The asset impairment charge was determined using estimated future cash flows through the closure date and directly reduced Property, plant and equipment on the Consolidated Balance Sheets. . . . The severance and related costs are reflected in Accrued liabilities on the Consolidated Balance Sheets.*

a. Provide the journal entry to record "Special Charges" for 2002.
b. Provide the journal entry to record the cash utilization of the special charges.
c. Provide the balance sheet disclosure on December 31, 2002.

**EXERCISE 14-9**
*Extraordinary item*
**Objective 2**

A company received life insurance proceeds on the death of its president before the end of its fiscal year. It intends to report the amount in its income statement as an extraordinary item.

⬛▶ Would this reporting be in conformity with generally accepted accounting principles? Discuss.

**EXERCISE 14-10**
*Extraordinary item*
**Objective 2**

**REAL WORLD**

For the year ended December 31, 2002, **Delta Air Lines, Inc.** provided the following note to its financial statements:

*On September 22, 2001, the Air Transportation Safety and System Stabilization Act (Stabilization Act) became effective. The Stabilization Act is intended to preserve the viability of the U.S. air transportation system following the terrorist attacks on September 11, 2001 by, among other things, (1) providing for payments from the U.S. Government totaling $5 billion to compensate U.S. air carriers for losses incurred from September 11, 2001, through December 31, 2001, as a result of the September 11 terrorist attacks and (2) permitting the Secretary of Transportation to sell insurance to U.S. air carriers.*

*Our allocated portion of compensation under the Stabilization Act was $668 million. Due to uncertainties regarding the U.S. government's calculation of compensation, we recognized $634 million of this amount in our 2001 Consolidated Statement of Operations. We recognized the remaining $34 million of compensation in our 2002 Consolidated Statement of Operations. We received $112 million and $556 million in cash for the years ended December 31, 2002 and 2001, respectively, under the Stabilization Act.*

⬛▶ Do you believe that the income related to the Stabilization Act should be reported as an extraordinary item on the income statement of Delta Air Lines?

**EXERCISE 14-11**
*Identifying extraordinary items*
**Objective 2**

Assume that the amount of each of the following items is material to the financial statements. Classify each item as either normally recurring (NR) or extraordinary (E).

a. Interest revenue on notes receivable.
b. Uninsured flood loss. (Flood insurance is unavailable because of periodic flooding in the area.)
c. Loss on sale of fixed assets.
d. Restructuring charge related to employee termination benefits.
e. Gain on sale of land condemned for public use.
f. Uncollectible accounts expense.
g. Uninsured loss on building due to hurricane damage. The firm was organized in 1920 and had not previously incurred hurricane damage.
h. Loss on disposal of equipment considered to be obsolete because of development of new technology.

**EXERCISE 14-12**
*Income statement*
**Objectives 2, 3**

Wave Runner, Inc. produces and distributes equipment for sailboats. On the basis of the following data for the current fiscal year ended June 30, 2006, prepare a multiple-step income statement for Wave Runner, including an analysis of earnings per share in the form illustrated in this chapter. There were 10,000 shares of $150 par common stock outstanding throughout the year.

SPREADSHEET

✓ Net income, $24,000

| | |
|---|---:|
| Administrative expenses | $ 92,400 |
| Cost of merchandise sold | 431,900 |
| Cumulative effect on prior years of changing to a different depreciation method (decrease in income) | 60,000 |
| Gain on condemnation of land (extraordinary item) | 43,000 |
| Income tax reduction applicable to change in depreciation method | 24,000 |
| Income tax applicable to gain on condemnation of land | 17,200 |
| Income tax reduction applicable to loss from discontinued operations | 36,000 |
| Income tax applicable to ordinary income | 58,800 |
| Loss on discontinued operations | 90,000 |
| Loss from fixed asset impairment | 100,000 |
| Restructuring charge | 80,000 |
| Sales | 976,400 |
| Selling expenses | 125,100 |

**EXERCISE 14-13**
*Income statement*

**Objectives 2, 3**

WHAT'S WRONG
WITH THIS?

✓ Correct EPS for net income, $8.25

Audio Affection, Inc. sells automotive and home stereo equipment. It has 50,000 shares of $100 par common stock outstanding and 10,000 shares of $2, $100 par cumulative preferred stock outstanding as of December 31, 2006. List the errors you find in the following income statement for the year ended December 31, 2006.

**Audio Affection, Inc.**
**Income Statement**
**For the Year Ended December 31, 2006**

| | | |
|---|---:|---:|
| Net sales | | $9,450,000 |
| Cost of merchandise sold | | 7,100,000 |
| Gross profit | | $2,350,000 |
| Operating expenses: | | |
| Selling expenses | $820,000 | |
| Administrative expenses | 320,000 | 1,140,000 |
| Income from continuing operations before income tax | | $1,210,000 |
| Income tax expense | | 420,000 |
| Income from continuing operations | | $ 790,000 |
| Cumulative effect on prior years' income (decrease) of changing to a different depreciation method (net of applicable income tax of $86,000) | | (204,000) |
| Fixed asset impairment | | (30,000) |
| Income before condemnation of land, restructuring charge, and discontinued operations | | $ 556,000 |
| Extraordinary items: | | |
| Gain on condemnation of land, net of applicable income tax of $80,000 | | 120,000 |
| Restructuring charge, net of applicable income tax of $25,500 | | (59,500) |
| Loss on discontinued operations (net of applicable income tax of $76,000) | | (184,000) |
| Net income | | $ 432,500 |
| Earnings per common share: | | |
| Income from continuing operations | | $    15.80 |
| Cumulative effect on prior years' income (decrease) of changing to a different depreciation method | | (4.08) |
| Fixed asset impairment | | (0.60) |
| Income before extraordinary item and discontinued operations | | $    11.12 |
| Extraordinary items: | | |
| Gain on condemnation of land | | 2.40 |
| Restructuring charge | | (1.19) |
| Loss on discontinued operations | | (3.68) |
| Net income | | $      8.65 |

**EXERCISE 14-14**
*Earnings per share with preferred stock*

**Objective 3**

Glow-Rite Lighting Company had earnings for 2006 of $740,000. The company had 125,000 shares of common stock outstanding during the year. In addition, the company issued 50,000 shares of $100 par value preferred stock on January 5, 2006. The preferred stock has a dividend of $6 per share. There were no transactions in either common or preferred stock during 2006.

Determine the basic earnings per share for Glow-Rite.

**EXERCISE 14-15**
*Comprehensive income*

**Objective 4**

REAL WORLD          SPREADSHEET

✓ a. Comprehensive loss,
$240

A recent statement of comprehensive income for the **Procter & Gamble Company** was disclosed as follows (all amounts in millions):

**Procter & Gamble Company**
**Statement of Comprehensive Income**
**For the Fiscal Year Ending June 30, 2002**

| | |
|---|---:|
| Net earnings | $4,352 |
| Other comprehensive income: | |
| Foreign currency translation | 263 |
| Net investment hedges, | |
| net of $238 tax benefit | (397) |
| Other, net of tax benefit | (106) |
| Total comprehensive income | $4,112 |

The balance sheet dated June 30, 2001, showed a retained earnings balance of $10,451 and an accumulated other comprehensive loss of $2,120. The company paid $2,823 in dividends during the fiscal year.

a. What is the total other comprehensive income or loss for Procter & Gamble for the fiscal year ended June 30, 2002?
b. What percentage decline did other comprehensive items have on net income in determining total comprehensive income?
c. What was the June 30, 2002 balance of (1) retained earnings and (2) accumulated other comprehensive income?

**EXERCISE 14-16**
*Comprehensive income and temporary investments*

**Objectives 4, 5**

✓ c. $37,000

The statement of comprehensive income for the years ended December 31, 2006 and 2007, plus selected items from comparative balance sheets of McClain Wholesalers, Inc. are as follows:

**McClain Wholesalers, Inc.**
**Statement of Comprehensive Income**
**For the Years Ended December 31, 2006 and 2007**

| | 2006 | 2007 |
|---|---|---:|
| Net income | a. | $36,000 |
| Other comprehensive income (loss), net of tax | b. | 2,000 |
| Total comprehensive income | c. | e. |

**McClain Wholesalers, Inc.**
**Selected Balance Sheet Items**
**December 31, 2005, 2006, and 2007**

| | Dec. 31, 2005 | Dec. 31, 2006 | Dec. 31, 2007 |
|---|---|---|---|
| Temporary investments in marketable securities at fair market value, net of taxes on unrealized gains or losses | $ 26,000 | d. | f. |
| Retained earnings | 140,000 | $180,000 | g. |
| Accumulated other comprehensive income or (loss) | (5,000) | (8,000) | h. |

There were no dividends or purchases or sales of temporary investments. Other comprehensive items included only after-tax unrealized gains and losses on investments.

Determine the missing lettered items.

**EXERCISE 14-17**
*Comprehensive income and temporary investments*

**Objectives 4, 5**

During 2006, Cosby Corporation held a portfolio of available-for-sale securities having a cost of $260,000. There were no purchases or sales of investments during the year. The market values after adjusting for the impact of taxes, at the beginning and end of the year, were $200,000 and $240,000, respectively. The net income for 2006 was $145,000, and no dividends were paid during the year. The stockholders' equity section of the balance sheet was as follows on December 31, 2005:

✓ a. Total comprehensive
income, $185,000

**Cosby Corporation**
**Stockholders' Equity**
**December 31, 2005**

| | |
|---|---:|
| Common stock | $ 35,000 |
| Paid-in capital in excess of par value | 350,000 |
| Retained earnings | 435,000 |
| Accumulated other comprehensive loss | (60,000) |
| Total | $760,000 |

a. Prepare a statement of comprehensive income for 2006.
b. Prepare the stockholders' equity section of the balance sheet for December 31, 2006.

**EXERCISE 14-18**
*Temporary investments and other comprehensive income*

**Objectives 4, 5**

✓ a. 2007 unrealized gain, $60,000

The temporary investments of Secure Connections, Inc. include only 10,000 shares of Lambert Acres Inc. common stock purchased on January 10, 2006, for $20 per share. As of the December 31, 2006 balance sheet date, assume that the share price declined to $17 per share. As of the December 31, 2007 balance sheet date, assume that the share price rose to $27 per share. The investment was held through December 31, 2007. Assume a tax rate of 40%.

a. Determine the net after-tax unrealized gain or loss from holding the Lambert Acres common stock for 2006 and 2007.
b. What is the balance of Other Accumulated Comprehensive Income or Loss for December 31, 2006, and December 31, 2007?
c. Where is Other Accumulated Comprehensive Income or Deficit disclosed on the financial statements?

**EXERCISE 14-19**
*Temporary investments in marketable securities*

**Objective 5**

During 2006, its first year of operations, Lyon Research Corporation purchased the following securities as a temporary investment:

| Security | Shares Purchased | Cost | Cash Dividends Received |
|---|---|---|---|
| M-Labs Inc. | 1,000 | $29,000 | $ 900 |
| Spectrum Corp. | 2,500 | 45,000 | 1,600 |

a. Record the purchase of the temporary investments for cash.
b. Record the receipt of the dividends.

**EXERCISE 14-20**
*Financial statement reporting of temporary investments*

**Objectives 4, 5**

✓ b. Comprehensive income, $73,400

Using the data for Lyon Research Corporation in Exercise 14-19, assume that as of December 31, 2006, the M-Labs Inc. stock had a market value of $28 per share and the Spectrum Corp. stock had a market value of $14 per share. For the year ending December 31, 2006, Lyon Research Corporation had net income of $80,000. Its tax rate is 40%.

a. Prepare the balance sheet presentation for the temporary investments.
b. Prepare a statement of comprehensive income presentation for the temporary investments.

**EXERCISE 14-21**
*Entries for investment in stock, receipt of dividends, and sale of shares*

**Objective 5**

On February 27, Ball Corporation acquired 3,000 shares of the 50,000 outstanding shares of Beach Co. common stock at 40.75 plus commission charges of $150. On July 8, a cash dividend of $1.50 per share and a 2% stock dividend were received. On December 7, 1,000 shares were sold at 49, less commission charges of $60. Record the entries to record (a) the purchase of the stock, (b) the receipt of dividends, and (c) the sale of the 1,000 shares.

**EXERCISE 14-22**
*Entries using equity method for stock investment*
**Objective 5**

At a total cost of $1,820,000, Joshua Corporation acquired 70,000 shares of Caleb Corp. common stock as a long-term investment. Joshua Corporation uses the equity method of accounting for this investment. Caleb Corp. has 280,000 shares of common stock outstanding, including the shares acquired by Joshua Corporation. Journalize the entries by Joshua Corporation to record the following information:

a. Caleb Corp. reports net income of $2,500,000 for the current period.
b. A cash dividend of $3.40 per common share is paid by Caleb Corp. during the current period.

**EXERCISE 14-23**
*Equity method for stock investment—Toys "R" Us*
**Objective 5**

REAL WORLD

Toys "R" Us Inc. is a major retailer of toys in the United States. A recent balance sheet disclosed a long-term investment in Toys-Japan, a public company trading on the Tokyo over-the-counter market. The balance sheet disclosure for two recent comparative years was as follows:

|  | Feb. 2, 2002 | Feb. 3, 2001 |
|---|---|---|
| Investment in Toys-Japan (in millions) | $123 | $108 |

In addition, the Toys "R" Us income statement disclosed equity earnings in the Toys-Japan investment as follows (in millions):

|  | Feb. 2, 2002 | Feb. 3, 2001 |
|---|---|---|
| Equity in net earnings of Toys-Japan | $29 | $31 |

The notes to the financial statements provided the following additional information about this investment:

*The company accounts for its investment in the common stock of Toys-Japan under the "equity method" of accounting since the initial public offering on April 24, 2000. The quoted market value of the company's investment in Toys-Japan was $283 at February 2, 2002.*

a. Explain the change in the investment in Toys-Japan account for fiscal year ended February 2, 2002.
b. Why is the Investment in Toys-Japan not recognized at market value?

**EXERCISE 14-24**
*Consolidated financial statements*
**Objectives 6**
✓ b. $219,000

For the current year ended September 30, the results of operations of Tennessee Corporation, and its wholly owned subsidiary, Volunteer Enterprises, are as follows:

|  | Tennessee Corporation | | Volunteer Enterprises | |
|---|---|---|---|---|
| Sales |  | $845,000 |  | $166,000 |
| Cost of merchandise sold | $390,000 |  | $68,000 |  |
| Selling expenses | 125,000 |  | 34,000 |  |
| Administrative expenses | 87,000 |  | 16,000 |  |
| Interest expenses (revenue) | (10,000) | 592,000 | 10,000 | 128,000 |
| Net income |  | $253,000 |  | $ 38,000 |

During the year, Tennessee sold merchandise to Volunteer for $45,000. The merchandise was sold by Volunteer to nonaffiliated companies for $60,000. Tennessee's interest revenue was realized from a long-term loan to Volunteer.

a. Determine the amounts to be eliminated from the following items in preparing a consolidated income statement for the current year: (1) sales and (2) cost of merchandise sold.
b. Determine the consolidated net income.

**EXERCISE 14-25**
*Price-earnings ratio calculation*
**Objectives 3, 7**

The following comparative net income and earnings per share data are provided for Krispy Kreme Doughnuts, Inc., for three recent fiscal years:

✓ a. 2001: 55.83

| Year Ended | Jan. 28, 2001 | Feb. 3, 2002 | Feb. 2, 2003 |
| --- | --- | --- | --- |
| Net income | $14,725 | $26,378 | $33,478 |
| Basic earnings per share | 0.30 | 0.49 | 0.61 |
| Diluted earnings per share | 0.27 | 0.45 | 0.56 |

The stock market prices at the end of each of the three fiscal years were as follows:

| | |
| --- | --- |
| Feb. 2, 2003 | $30.41 |
| Feb. 3, 2002 | 37.40 |
| Jan. 28, 2001 | 16.75 |

a. Determine the price-earnings ratio for Krispy Kreme Doughnuts, Inc. for each of the three fiscal years, using basic earnings per share and the ending stock market price.

b. 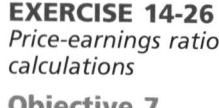 What conclusions can you reach by considering the price-earnings ratio?

c. 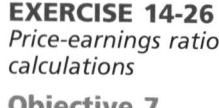 Why is the diluted earnings per share less than the basic earnings per share?

**EXERCISE 14-26**
*Price-earnings ratio calculations*
**Objective 7**

✓ a. 2001: 16.47

**ExxonMobil Corp.** is one of the largest companies in the world. The company explores, develops, refines, and markets petroleum products. The basic earnings per share for three comparative years were as follows:

| | Years Ended Dec. 31, | | |
| --- | --- | --- | --- |
| | **2002** | **2001** | **2000** |
| Basic earnings per share | $1.69 | $2.23 | $2.55 |

The market prices at the end of each year were $42, $39, and $35 for December 31, 2000, 2001, and 2002, respectively.

a. Determine the price-earnings ratio for 2000, 2001, and 2002, using end-of-year prices.

b. 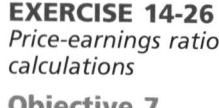 Interpret your results over the three years.

# Problems Series A

**PROBLEM 14-1A**
*Income tax allocation*
**Objective 1**

✓ 1. Year-end balance, 3rd year, $16,000

Differences between the accounting methods applied to accounts and financial reports and those used in determining taxable income yielded the following amounts for the first four years of a corporation's operations:

| | First Year | Second Year | Third Year | Fourth Year |
| --- | --- | --- | --- | --- |
| Income before income taxes | $200,000 | $240,000 | $300,000 | $400,000 |
| Taxable income | 150,000 | 230,000 | 320,000 | 425,000 |

The income tax rate for each of the four years was 40% of taxable income, and each year's taxes were promptly paid.

**Instructions**

1. Determine for each year the amounts described by the following captions, presenting the information in the form indicated:

| Year | Income Tax Deducted on Income Statement | Income Tax Payments for the Year | Deferred Income Tax Payable | |
| --- | --- | --- | --- | --- |
| | | | Year's Addition (Deduction) | Year-End Balance |

2. Total the first three amount columns.

**PROBLEM 14-2A**
*Income tax; income statement*

**Objectives 2, 3, 4**

SPREADSHEET

✓ *Net income, $180,100*

MotoSport Inc. produces and sells off-road motorcycles and jeeps. The following data were selected from the records of MotoSport Inc. for the current fiscal year ended October 31, 2006:

| | |
|---|---:|
| Advertising expense | $ 64,000 |
| Cost of merchandise sold | 612,400 |
| Depreciation expense—office equipment | 7,000 |
| Depreciation expense—store equipment | 23,000 |
| Gain on condemnation of land | 36,400 |
| Income tax: | |
|   Applicable to continuing operations | 92,500 |
|   Applicable to loss from discontinued operations (reduction) | 12,000 |
|   Applicable to gain on condemnation of land | 13,400 |
| Interest revenue | 12,000 |
| Loss from discontinued operations | 31,000 |
| Loss from fixed asset impairment | 110,000 |
| Miscellaneous administrative expense | 12,000 |
| Miscellaneous selling expense | 5,500 |
| Office salaries expense | 75,000 |
| Rent expense | 24,000 |
| Restructuring charge | 14,000 |
| Sales | 1,350,000 |
| Sales salaries expense | 140,000 |
| Store supplies expense | 6,500 |
| Unrealized loss on temporary investments | 7,000 |

**Instructions**

Prepare a multiple-step income statement, concluding with a section for earnings per share (rounded to the nearest cent) in the form illustrated in this chapter. There were 25,000 shares of common stock (no preferred) outstanding throughout the year. Assume that the gain on the condemnation of land is an extraordinary item.

**PROBLEM 14-3A**
*Income statement; retained earnings statement; balance sheet*

**Objectives 1, 2, 3, 4**

SPREADSHEET

✓ *Net income, $340,000*

The following data were taken from the records of Surf's Up Corporation for the year ended July 31, 2006.

**Retained earnings and balance sheet data:**

| | |
|---|---:|
| Accounts payable | $ 99,500 |
| Accounts receivable | 276,050 |
| Accumulated depreciation | 3,050,000 |
| Accumulated other comprehensive income | 15,000 |
| Allowance for doubtful accounts | 11,500 |
| Cash | 115,500 |
| Common stock, $10 par (500,000 shares authorized; 251,000 shares issued) | 2,510,000 |
| Deferred income taxes payable (current portion, $4,700) | 65,700 |
| Dividends: | |
|   Cash dividends for common stock | 80,000 |
|   Cash dividends for preferred stock | 100,000 |
|   Stock dividends for common stock | 40,000 |
| Dividends payable | 25,000 |
| Employee termination benefit obligation (current) | 90,000 |
| Equipment | 11,819,050 |
| Income tax payable | 55,900 |
| Interest receivable | 2,500 |
| Merchandise inventory (July 31, 2006), at lower of cost (FIFO) or market | 551,500 |
| Paid-in capital from sale of treasury stock | 5,000 |
| Paid-in capital in excess of par—common stock | 996,300 |
| Paid-in capital in excess of par—preferred stock | 240,000 |
| Patents | 85,000 |
| Preferred 6 2/3% stock, $100 par (30,000 shares authorized; 15,000 shares issued) | 1,500,000 |
| Prepaid expenses | 15,900 |
| Retained earnings, August 1, 2005 | 4,231,600 |
| Temporary investments in marketable equity securities (at cost) | 95,000 |
| Treasury stock (1,000 shares of common stock at cost of $40 per share) | 40,000 |
| Unrealized gain on marketable equity securities | 15,000 |

*(continued)*

**Income statement data:**

| | |
|---|---:|
| Administrative expenses | $ 140,000 |
| Cost of merchandise sold | 984,000 |
| Gain on condemnation of land | 30,000 |
| Income tax: | |
|   Applicable to continuing operations | 170,000 |
|   Applicable to loss from discontinued operations | 24,000 |
|   Applicable to gain on condemnation of land | 10,000 |
| Interest expense | 7,500 |
| Interest revenue | 1,500 |
| Loss from disposal of discontinued operations | 104,000 |
| Loss from fixed asset impairment | 60,000 |
| Restructuring charge | 300,000 |
| Sales | 2,600,000 |
| Selling expenses | 540,000 |

**Instructions**

1. Prepare a multiple-step income statement for the year ended July 31, 2006, concluding with earnings per share. In computing earnings per share, assume that the average number of common shares outstanding was 250,000 and preferred dividends were $100,000. Assume that the gain on the condemnation of land is an extraordinary item.
2. Prepare a retained earnings statement for the year ended July 31, 2006.
3. Prepare a balance sheet in report form as of July 31, 2006.

**PROBLEM 14-4A**
*Entries for investments in stock*

**Objective 5**

**P.A.S.S.**

Theater Arts Company produces and sells theater costumes. The following transactions relate to certain securities acquired by Theater Arts Company, which has a fiscal year ending on December 31:

2004

Feb. 10. Purchased 4,000 shares of the 150,000 outstanding common shares of Haslam Corporation at 48 plus commission and other costs of $168.

June 15. Received the regular cash dividend of $0.70 a share on Haslam Corporation stock.

Dec. 15. Received the regular cash dividend of $0.70 a share plus an extra dividend of $0.05 a share on Haslam Corporation stock.

    (Assume that all intervening transactions have been recorded properly and that the number of shares of stock owned have not changed from December 31, 2004, to December 31, 2006.)

2007

Jan. 3. Purchased controlling interest in Jacob Inc. for $1,250,000 by purchasing 40,000 shares directly from the estate of the founder of Jacob. There are 100,000 shares of Jacob Inc. stock outstanding.

Apr. 1. Received the regular cash dividend of $0.70 a share and a 2% stock dividend on the Haslam Corporation stock.

July 20. Sold 1,000 shares of Haslam Corporation stock at 41. The broker deducted commission and other costs of $50, remitting the balance.

Dec. 15. Received a cash dividend at the new rate of $0.80 a share on the Haslam Corporation stock.

31. Received $40,000 of cash dividends on Jacob Inc. stock. Jacob Inc. reported net income of $295,000 in 2007. Theater Arts uses the equity method of accounting for its investment in Jacob Inc.

**Instructions**

Journalize the entries for the preceding transactions.

# Problems Series B

**PROBLEM 14-1B**
*Income tax allocation*
Objective 1

SPREADSHEET

✓ *1. Year-end balance, 3rd year, $52,000*

Differences between the accounting methods applied to accounts and financial reports and those used in determining taxable income yielded the following amounts for the first four years of a corporation's operations:

| | First Year | Second Year | Third Year | Fourth Year |
|---|---|---|---|---|
| Income before income taxes | $400,000 | $480,000 | $600,000 | $520,000 |
| Taxable income | 300,000 | 420,000 | 630,000 | 600,000 |

The income tax rate for each of the four years was 40% of taxable income, and each year's taxes were promptly paid.

**Instructions**

1. Determine for each year the amounts described by the following captions, presenting the information in the form indicated:

| | | | Deferred Income Tax Payable | |
|---|---|---|---|---|
| Year | Income Tax Deducted on Income Statement | Income Tax Payments for the Year | Year's Addition (Deduction) | Year-End Balance |

2. Total the first three amount columns.

**PROBLEM 14-2B**
*Income tax; income statement*
Objectives 2, 3, 4

SPREADSHEET

✓ *Net income, $82,000*

The following data were selected from the records of Healthy Pantry Inc. for the current fiscal year ended June 30, 2006:

| | |
|---|---|
| Advertising expense | $ 46,000 |
| Cost of merchandise sold | 279,000 |
| Depreciation expense—office equipment | 6,000 |
| Depreciation expense—store equipment | 31,000 |
| Gain on discontinued operations | 42,500 |
| Income tax: | |
|   Applicable to continuing operations | 32,000 |
|   Applicable to gain on discontinued operations | 16,000 |
|   Applicable to loss on condemnation of land (reduction) | 8,000 |
| Insurance expense | 9,000 |
| Interest expense | 18,000 |
| Loss from condemnation of land | 24,500 |
| Loss from fixed asset impairment | 90,000 |
| Miscellaneous administrative expense | 7,500 |
| Miscellaneous selling expense | 5,500 |
| Office salaries expense | 60,000 |
| Rent expense | 29,000 |
| Restructuring charge | 150,000 |
| Sales | 980,000 |
| Sales commissions expense | 145,000 |
| Unrealized gain on temporary investments | 25,000 |

**Instructions**

Prepare a multiple-step income statement, concluding with a section for earnings per share in the form illustrated in this chapter. There were 75,000 shares of common stock (no preferred) outstanding throughout the year. Assume that the loss on the condemnation of land is an extraordinary item.

**PROBLEM 14-3B**
*Income statement; retained earnings statement; balance sheet*

**Objectives 1, 2, 3, 4, 5**

SPREADSHEET

✓ *Net income, $277,000*

The following data were taken from the records of Skate N' Ski Corporation for the year ended October 31, 2006.

**Income statement data:**

| | |
|---|---|
| Administrative expenses | $ 100,000 |
| Cost of merchandise sold | 732,000 |
| Gain on condemnation of land | 60,000 |
| Income tax: | |
|   Applicable to continuing operations | 206,000 |
|   Applicable to loss from discontinued operations | 28,800 |
|   Applicable to gain on condemnation of land | 24,000 |
| Interest expense | 8,000 |
| Interest revenue | 5,000 |
| Loss from discontinued operations | 76,800 |
| Loss from fixed asset impairment | 200,000 |
| Restructuring charge | 90,000 |
| Sales | 2,020,000 |
| Selling expenses | 400,000 |

**Retained earnings and balance sheet data:**

| | |
|---|---|
| Accounts payable | $ 89,500 |
| Accounts receivable | 309,050 |
| Accumulated depreciation | 3,050,000 |
| Accumulated other comprehensive loss | 24,000 |
| Allowance for doubtful accounts | 21,500 |
| Cash | 145,500 |
| Common stock, $15 par (400,000 shares authorized; 152,000 shares issued) | 2,280,000 |
| Deferred income taxes payable (current portion, $4,700) | 25,700 |
| Dividends: | |
|   Cash dividends for common stock | 40,000 |
|   Cash dividends for preferred stock | 100,000 |
|   Stock dividends for common stock | 60,000 |
| Dividends payable | 30,000 |
| Employee termination benefit obligation (current) | 60,000 |
| Equipment | 9,541,050 |
| Income tax payable | 55,900 |
| Interest receivable | 2,500 |
| Merchandise inventory (October 31, 2006), at lower of cost (FIFO) or market | 425,000 |
| Notes receivable | 77,500 |
| Paid-in capital from sale of treasury stock | 16,000 |
| Paid-in capital in excess of par—common stock | 894,750 |
| Paid-in capital in excess of par—preferred stock | 240,000 |
| Patents | 55,000 |
| Preferred 6 2/3% stock, $100 par (30,000 shares authorized; 15,000 shares issued) | 1,500,000 |
| Prepaid expenses | 15,900 |
| Retained earnings, November 1, 2005 | 2,446,150 |
| Temporary investment in marketable equity securities | 145,000 |
| Treasury stock (2,000 shares of common stock at cost of $35 per share) | 70,000 |
| Unrealized loss on temporary equity securities | 24,000 |

**Instructions**

1. Prepare a multiple-step income statement for the year ended October 31, 2006, concluding with earnings per share. In computing earnings per share, assume that the average number of common shares outstanding was 150,000 and preferred dividends were $100,000. Assume that the gain on condemnation of land is an extraordinary item.
2. Prepare a retained earnings statement for the year ended October 31, 2006.
3. Prepare a balance sheet in report form as of October 31, 2006.

**PROBLEM 14-4B**
*Entries for investments in stock*

**Objective 5**

P.A.S.S.

Samson Company is a wholesaler of men's hair products. The following transactions relate to certain securities acquired by Samson Company, which has a fiscal year ending on December 31:

2004
Jan. 3. Purchased 3,000 shares of the 40,000 outstanding common shares of Davidson Corporation at 67 plus commission and other costs of $468.
July 2. Received the regular cash dividend of $1.30 a share on Davidson Corporation stock.
Dec. 5. Received the regular cash dividend of $1.30 a share plus an extra dividend of $0.10 a share on Davidson Corporation stock.

(Assume that all intervening transactions have been recorded properly and that the number of shares of stock owned have not changed from December 31, 2004, to December 31, 2006.)

2007
Jan. 2. Purchased controlling interest in Comstock Inc. for $760,000 by purchasing 24,000 shares directly from the estate of the founder of Comstock. There are 80,000 shares of Comstock Inc. stock outstanding.
July 6. Received the regular cash dividend of $1.30 a share and a 3% stock dividend on the Davidson Corporation stock.
Oct. 23. Sold 750 shares of Davidson Corporation stock at 78. The broker deducted commission and other costs of $140, remitting the balance.
Dec. 10. Received a cash dividend at the new rate of $1.50 a share on the Davidson Corporation stock.
31. Received $32,000 of cash dividends on Comstock Inc. stock. Comstock Inc. reported net income of $350,000 in 2007. Samson uses the equity method of accounting for its investment in Comstock Inc.

**Instructions**
Record the entries for the preceding transactions.

# Special Activities

**ACTIVITY 14-1**
*Equity method disclosure*

REAL WORLD

The following note to the consolidated financial statements for **The Goodyear Tire and Rubber Co.** relates to the principles of consolidation used in preparing the financial statements:

*The Company's investments in 20% to 50% owned companies in which it has the ability to exercise significant influence over operating and financial policies are accounted for by the equity method. Accordingly, the Company's share of the earnings of these companies is included in consolidated net income.*

Is it a requirement that Goodyear use the equity method in this situation? Explain.

**ACTIVITY 14-2**
*Special charges analysis*

The two-year comparative income statements and a note disclosure for Fleet Shoes, Inc. were as follows:

**Income Statement**
**Fleet Shoes, Inc.**
**For the Years Ended December 31, 2005 and 2006**

|  | 2005 | 2006 |
|---|---|---|
| Sales | $ 430,000 | $ 510,000 |
| Cost of merchandise sold | 193,500 | 224,400 |
| Gross profit | $ 236,500 | $ 285,600 |
| Selling and administrative expenses | (107,500) | (122,400) |
| Loss on fixed asset impairment |  | (102,000) |
| Income from operations | $ 129,000 | $ 61,200 |
| Income tax expense | 51,600 | 24,480 |
| Net income | $ 77,400 | $ 36,720 |

*Note:* A fixed asset impairment of $102,000 was recognized in 2006 as the result of abandoning an order management software system. The system project was started in early 2005 and ran into significant delays and performance problems throughout 2006. It was determined that there was no incremental benefit from completing the system. Thus, the accumulated costs associated with the system were written off.

1. Construct a vertical analysis for 2005 and 2006 by determining for each line item its ratio as a percent of sales.
2. ▬▬▶ Interpret the performance of the company in 2006.

**ACTIVITY 14-3**
*Extraordinary items*

REAL WORLD

The following news item was published on October 7, 2001, less than one month after the September 11 terrorist incident at the World Trade Center:

*Many companies already are blaming the Sept. 11 terrorist attacks for a slow-down in profits. But accounting rule-makers aren't letting them off the hook so easily. A task force of the Financial Accounting Standards Board recently decided against allowing companies to treat costs related to the disaster as an "extraordinary item" in their financial statements. That means the costs must be considered part of normal business operations and deducted from the company's operating profit.*

*The FASB was worried that companies would blame the attack for a variety of unrelated costs—essentially hiding bad business decisions or other problems and making profits seems better than they were.*

*There also was concern that it was too difficult to tell what costs were related to terrorism and what weren't. The impact of Sept. 11 has been so pervasive, affecting virtually every company, that "it almost made it ordinary," says task-force member Dick Stock.*

*"The task force understood this was an extraordinary event in the English-language sense of the word," says FASB Chairman Tim Lucas. "But in the final analysis, we decided it wasn't going to improve the financial-reporting system to show it as an extraordinary item."* (Steve Liesman, "In Translation: What's Extraordinary—and What's Not," *The Wall Street Journal*, Sunday, October 7, 2001)

▬▬▶ Why would the FASB say that the September 11 terrorist incident was not "extraordinary"?

**ACTIVITY 14-4**
*Comprehensive income*

REAL WORLD

The stockholders' equity section of **YUM! Brands, Inc.**, the operator of Pizza Hut, KFC, and Taco Bell restaurants, for two recent comparative dates was as follows:

**YUM! Brands, Inc.**
**Stockholders' Equity**
**December 28, 2002 and December 29, 2001**
**(In millions)**

|  | 2002 | 2001 |
|---|---|---|
| Common stock, no par value | $1,046 | $1,097 |
| Accumulated deficit | (203) | (786) |
| Accumulated other comprehensive income (loss) | (249) | (207) |
| Total stockholders' equity | $ 594 | $ 104 |

1. What is the "other" comprehensive income or loss for the year ended December 28, 2002?
2. ▬▬▶ Explain the concept of other comprehensive income.

**ACTIVITY 14-5**
*Ethics and professional conduct in business*

ETHICS

At a recent dinner party, you met Steph Melick, the controller for Mojave Inc. Steph has worked for Mojave for the past seven years. During your conversation, you complained about having to pay your third-quarter estimated taxes on Monday, September 15. In response, Steph indicated that she always *underpays* her estimated taxes. That way, she can use her money as long as possible.

▬▬▶ Is it appropriate to deliberately underpay your estimated taxes?

**ACTIVITY 14-6**
*Ethics and professional conduct in business*

ETHICS

Reed Osborn is the president and chief operating officer of MoneyScope Corporation, a developer of personal financial planning software. During the past year, MoneyScope Corporation was forced to sell 10 acres of land to the city of Houston for expansion of a freeway exit. The corporation fought the sale; but after condemnation hearings, a judge ordered it to sell the land. Because of the land's location and the fact that MoneyScope Corporation had purchased the land over 15 years ago, the corporation recorded a $0.20-per-share gain on the sale. Always looking to turn a negative into a positive, Reed has decided to announce the corporation's earnings per share of $1.05, without identifying the $0.20 impact of selling the land. Although he will retain majority ownership, Reed plans on selling 20,000 of his shares in the corporation sometime within the next month.

▬▬▶ Are Reed's plans to announce earnings per share of $1.05 without mentioning the $0.20 impact of selling the land ethical and professional?

**ACTIVITY 14-7**
*Reporting extraordinary item*

Orlando Fruit Co. is in the process of preparing its annual financial statements. Orlando Fruit is a large citrus grower located in central Florida. The following is a discussion between Kevin Kirk, the controller, and Shirley Gwinn, the chief executive officer and president of Orlando Fruit Co.

*Shirley:* Kevin, I've got a question about your rough draft of this year's income statement.

*Kevin:* Sure, Shirley. What's your question?

*Shirley:* Well, your draft shows a net loss of $750,000.

*Kevin:* That's right. We'd have had a profit, except for this year's frost damage. I figured that the frost destroyed over 30% of our crop. We had a good year otherwise.

*Shirley:* That's my concern. I estimated that if we eliminate the frost damage, we'd show a profit of . . . let's see . . . about $250,000.

*Kevin:* That sounds about right.

*Shirley:* This income statement seems misleading. Why can't we show the loss on the frost damage separately? That way the bank and our outside investors will be able to see that this year's loss is just temporary. I'd hate to get them upset over nothing.

*Kevin:* Maybe we can do something. I recall from my accounting courses something about showing unusual items separately. Let's see . . . yes, I remember. They're called extraordinary items.

*Shirley:* Well, we haven't had any frost damage in over five years. This year's damage is certainly extraordinary. Let's do it!

▬▬▶ Discuss the appropriateness of revising Orlando Fruit's income statement to report the frost damage separately as an extraordinary item.

**ACTIVITY 14-8**
*Extraordinary items and discontinued operations*

GROUP ACTIVITY     INTERNET

In groups of three or four, search company annual reports, news releases, or the Internet for extraordinary items and announcements of discontinued operations. Identify the most unusual extraordinary item in your group. Also, select a discontinued operation of a well-known company that might be familiar to other students or might interest them.

Prepare a brief analysis of the earnings per share impact of both the extraordinary item and the discontinued operation. Estimate the *potential* impact on the company's market price by multiplying the current price-earnings ratio by the earnings per share amount of each item.

One Internet site that has annual reports is EDGAR (Electronic Data Gathering, Analysis, and Retrieval), the electronic archives of financial statements filed with the Securities and Exchange Commission. SEC documents can be retrieved using the EdgarScan service from **PricewaterhouseCoopers** at **http://edgarscan.pwcglobal .com**.

To obtain annual report information, type in a company name in the appropriate space. EdgarScan will list the reports available to you for the company you've selected. Select the most recent annual report filing, identified as a 10-K or 10-K405. EdgarScan provides an outline of the report, including the separate financial statements. You can double click the income statement and balance sheet for the selected company into an Excel™ spreadsheet for further analysis.

# Answers to Self-Examination Questions

1. **A**  The amount of income tax deferred to future years is $16,000 (answer A), determined as follows:

| | |
|---|---|
| Depreciation expense, MACRS | $100,000 |
| Depreciation expense, straight-line method | 60,000 |
| Excess expense in determining taxable income | $ 40,000 |
| Income tax rate | × 40% |
| Income tax deferred to future years | $ 16,000 |

2. **A**  Events and transactions that are distinguished by their unusual nature and by the infrequency of their occurrence, such as a gain on condemning land for public use, are reported in the income statement as extraordinary items (answer A). A restructuring charge (answer C) and fixed asset impairment (answer D) are unusual items that are related to different accounting events than land condemnation.

3. **B**  The difference between the cost of temporary investments held as available-for-sale securities and their market value is reported as an unrealized gain, net of applicable income taxes, as shown below.

| | |
|---|---|
| Market value of investments | $120,000 |
| Cost of investments | 100,000 |
| | $ 20,000 |
| Applicable taxes (40%) | 8,000 |
| Unrealized gain, net of taxes | $ 12,000 |

The unrealized gain of $12,000 (answer B) is reported on the balance sheet as an addition to the cost of the investments and as part of other comprehensive income.

4. **C**  Under the equity method of accounting for investments in stocks, Cisneros Corporation records its share of both net income and dividends of Harrell Inc. in Investment in Harrell Inc. Stock. Thus, Investment in Harrell Inc. Stock would increase by $82,500 [($150,000 × 75%) − ($40,000 × 75%)] for the current year. $30,000 (answer B) is only Cisneros Corporation's share of Harrell's dividends for the current year. $112,500 (answer D) is only Cisneros Corporation's share of Harrell's net income for the year.

5. **C**  Price-Earnings Ratio =

$$\frac{\text{Market Price per Common Share}}{\text{Earnings per Share}}, \text{ or}$$

$$\frac{\$60}{(\$800,000 - \$50,000)/200,000} = 16$$

# 15

# BONDS PAYABLE AND INVESTMENTS IN BONDS

## objectives

*After studying this chapter, you should be able to:*

**1** Compute the potential impact of long-term borrowing on the earnings per share of a corporation.

**2** Describe the characteristics of bonds.

**3** Compute the present value of bonds payable.

**4** Journalize entries for bonds payable.

**5** Describe bond sinking funds.

**6** Journalize entries for bond redemptions.

**7** Journalize entries for the purchase, interest, discount and premium amortization, and sale of bond investments.

**8** Prepare a corporation balance sheet.

**9** Compute and interpret the number of times interest charges are earned.

**A**ssume that you have just inherited $50,000 from a distant relative, and you are considering some options for investing the money. Some of your friends have suggested that you invest it in long-term bonds. As a result, you have searched the Internet for corporate bond listings. You've identified the following listings as possible bond investments, both of which mature in the year 2028:

- **Minnesota Mining & Manufacturing Co. (3M)** 6.4% Bonds
- **Merrill Lynch & Co.** zero

The 3M bonds are selling for 114.187, while the Merrill Lynch bonds are selling for only 19.82. The 3M bonds are selling for over five and one-half times the price of the Merrill Lynch bonds. Does this mean that the Merrill Lynch bonds are a better buy? Does the 6.4% mean that if you buy the 3M bonds you can actually earn 6.4% interest? What does the "zero" mean? Does it have anything to do with the fact that the Merrill Lynch bonds are only selling for 19.82?

In this chapter, we will answer each of these questions. We first discuss the advantages and disadvantages of financing a corporation's operations by issuing debt rather than equity. We then discuss the accounting principles related to issuing long-term debt. Finally, we discuss the accounting for investments in bonds.

# **F**inancing Corporations

| objective | 1 |
|---|---|

Compute the potential impact of long-term borrowing on the earnings per share of a corporation.

**POINT OF INTEREST**

Bonds of major corporations are actively traded on bond exchanges. You can purchase bonds through a financial services firm, such as **Merrill Lynch** or **A. G. Edwards & Sons**.

Most of you have financed (purchased on credit) an automobile, a home, or a computer. Similarly, corporations often finance their operations by purchasing on credit and issuing notes or bonds. We have discussed accounts payable and notes payable in earlier chapters. A **bond** is simply a form of an interest-bearing note. Like a note, a bond requires periodic interest payments, and the face amount must be repaid at the maturity date. Bondholders are creditors of the issuing corporation, and their claims on the assets of the corporation rank ahead of stockholders.

One of the many factors that influence the decision to issue debt or equity is the effect of each alternative on earnings per share. To illustrate the possible effects, assume that a corporation's board of directors is considering the following alternative plans for financing a $4,000,000 company:

Plan 1:  100% financing from issuing common stock, $10 par
Plan 2:  50% financing from issuing preferred 9% stock, $50 par
              50% financing from issuing common stock, $10 par
Plan 3:  50% financing from issuing 12% bonds
              25% financing from issuing preferred 9% stock, $50 par
              25% financing from issuing common stock, $10 par

In each case, we assume that the stocks or bonds are issued at their par or face amount. The corporation is expecting to earn $800,000 annually, before deducting interest on the bonds and income taxes estimated at 40% of income. Exhibit 1 shows the effect of the three plans on the income of the corporation and the earnings per share on common stock.

Exhibit 1 indicates that Plan 3 yields the highest earnings per share on common stock and is thus the most attractive for common stockholders. If the estimated earnings are more than $800,000, the difference between the earnings per share to common stockholders under Plan 1 and Plan 3 is even greater.[1] However, if smaller earnings occur, Plans 2 and 3 become less attractive to common stockholders. To illustrate, the effect of earnings of $440,000 rather than $800,000 is shown in Exhibit 2.

---

[1]The higher earnings per share under Plan 3 is due to a finance concept known as **leverage**. This concept is discussed further in a later chapter.

## •Exhibit 1

**Effect of Alternative
Financing Plans—
$800,000 Earnings**

|  | Plan 1 | Plan 2 | Plan 3 |
|---|---|---|---|
| 12% bonds | — | — | $2,000,000 |
| Preferred 9% stock, $50 par | — | $2,000,000 | 1,000,000 |
| Common stock, $10 par | $4,000,000 | 2,000,000 | 1,000,000 |
| Total | $4,000,000 | $4,000,000 | $4,000,000 |
| Earnings before interest and income tax | $ 800,000 | $ 800,000 | $ 800,000 |
| Deduct interest on bonds | — | — | 240,000 |
| Income before income tax | $ 800,000 | $ 800,000 | $ 560,000 |
| Deduct income tax | 320,000 | 320,000 | 224,000 |
| Net income | $ 480,000 | $ 480,000 | $ 336,000 |
| Dividends on preferred stock | — | 180,000 | 90,000 |
| Available for dividends on common stock | $ 480,000 | $ 300,000 | $ 246,000 |
| Shares of common stock outstanding | ÷ 400,000 | ÷ 200,000 | ÷ 100,000 |
| Earnings per share on common stock | $ 1.20 | $ 1.50 | $ 2.46 |

## •Exhibit 2

**Effect of Alternative
Financing Plans—
$440,000 Earnings**

|  | Plan 1 | Plan 2 | Plan 3 |
|---|---|---|---|
| 12% bonds | — | — | $2,000,000 |
| Preferred 9% stock, $50 par | — | $2,000,000 | 1,000,000 |
| Common stock, $10 par | $4,000,000 | 2,000,000 | 1,000,000 |
| Total | $4,000,000 | $4,000,000 | $4,000,000 |
| Earnings before interest and income tax | $ 440,000 | $ 440,000 | $ 440,000 |
| Deduct interest on bonds | — | — | 240,000 |
| Income before income tax | $ 440,000 | $ 440,000 | $ 200,000 |
| Deduct income tax | 176,000 | 176,000 | 80,000 |
| Net income | $ 264,000 | $ 264,000 | $ 120,000 |
| Dividends on preferred stock | — | 180,000 | 90,000 |
| Available for dividends on common stock | $ 264,000 | $ 84,000 | $ 30,000 |
| Shares of common stock outstanding | ÷ 400,000 | ÷ 200,000 | ÷ 100,000 |
| Earnings per share on common stock | $ 0.66 | $ 0.42 | $ 0.30 |

When interest rates are low, corporations usually finance their operations with debt. For example, as interest rates fell in the early 1990s, corporations rushed to issue new debt. In one day alone, more than $4.5 billion of debt was issued.

In addition to the effect on earnings per share, the board of directors should consider other factors in deciding whether to issue debt or equity. For example, once bonds are issued, periodic interest payments and repayment of the face value of the bonds are beyond the control of the corporation. That is, if these payments are not made, the bondholders could seek court action and could force the company into bankruptcy. In contrast, a corporation is not legally obligated to pay dividends.

# Characteristics of Bonds Payable

**objective 2**

Describe the characteristics of bonds.

A corporation that issues bonds enters into a contract, called a **bond indenture** or **trust indenture**, with the bondholders. A bond issue is normally divided into a number of individual bonds. Usually the face value of each bond, called the **principal**, is $1,000 or a multiple of $1,000. The interest on bonds may be payable annually, semiannually, or quarterly. Most bonds pay interest semiannually.

Time Warner 7.625% bonds maturing in 2031 were listed as selling for 112.698 on July 22, 2003.

The prices of bonds are quoted as a percentage of the bonds' face value. Thus, investors could purchase or sell **Wal-Mart** bonds quoted at 116.992 for $1,169.92. Likewise, bonds quoted at 109 could be purchased or sold for $1,090.

When all bonds of an issue mature at the same time, they are called **term bonds**. If the maturities are spread over several dates, they are called **serial bonds**. For example, one-tenth of an issue of $1,000,000 bonds, or $100,000, may mature 16 years from the issue date, another $100,000 in the 17th year, and so on until the final $100,000 matures in the 25th year.

Bonds that may be exchanged for other securities, such as common stock, are called **convertible bonds**. Bonds that a corporation reserves the right to redeem before their maturity are called **callable bonds**. Bonds issued on the basis of the general credit of the corporation are called **debenture bonds**.

# The Present-Value Concept and Bonds Payable

**objective   3**

Compute the present value of bonds payable.

When a corporation issues bonds, the price that buyers are willing to pay for the bonds depends upon the following three factors:

1. The face amount of the bonds, which is the amount due at the maturity date.
2. The periodic interest to be paid on the bonds.
3. The market rate of interest.

The face amount and the periodic interest to be paid on the bonds are identified in the bond indenture. The periodic interest is expressed as a percentage of the face amount of the bond. This percentage or rate of interest is called the **contract rate** or **coupon rate**.

The **market** or **effective rate of interest** is determined by transactions between buyers and sellers of similar bonds. The market rate of interest is affected by a variety of factors, including investors' assessment of current economic conditions as well as future expectations.

If the contract rate of interest equals the market rate of interest, the bonds will sell at their face amount. If the market rate is higher than the contract rate, the bonds will sell at a **discount**, or less than their face amount. Why is this the case? Buyers are not willing to pay the face amount for bonds whose contract rate is lower than the market rate. The discount, in effect, represents the amount necessary to make up for the difference in the market and the contract interest rates. In contrast, if the market rate is lower than the contract rate, the bonds will sell at a **premium**, or more than their face amount. In this case, buyers are willing to pay more than the face amount for bonds whose contract rate is higher than the market rate.

The face amount of the bonds and the periodic interest on the bonds represent cash to be received by the buyer in the future. The buyer determines how much to pay for the bonds by computing the present value of these future cash receipts, using the market rate of interest. The concept of present value is based on the time value of money.

The time value of money concept recognizes that an amount of cash to be received today is worth more than the same amount of cash to be received in the future. For example, what would you rather have: $100 today or $100 one year from now? You would rather have the $100 today because it could be invested to earn income. For example, if the $100 could be invested to earn 10% per year, the $100 will

MARKET RATE = CONTRACT RATE

Selling price of bond = $1,000

$1,000 BOND

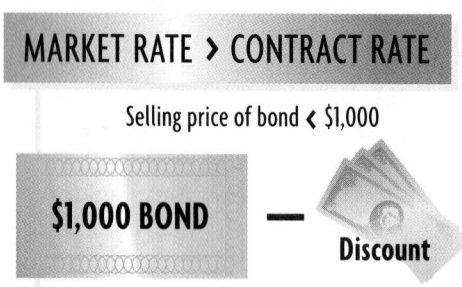

MARKET RATE > CONTRACT RATE

Selling price of bond < $1,000

$1,000 BOND   —   **Discount**

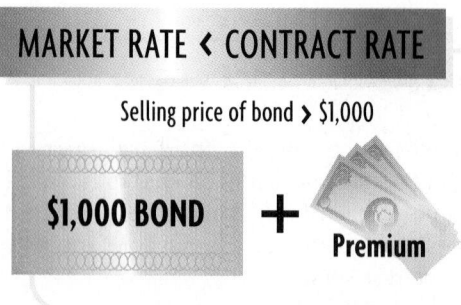

MARKET RATE < CONTRACT RATE

Selling price of bond > $1,000

$1,000 BOND   +   **Premium**

accumulate to $110 ($100 plus $10 earnings) in one year. In this sense, you can think of the $100 in hand today as the ***present value*** of $110 to be received a year from today. This present value is illustrated in the following time line:

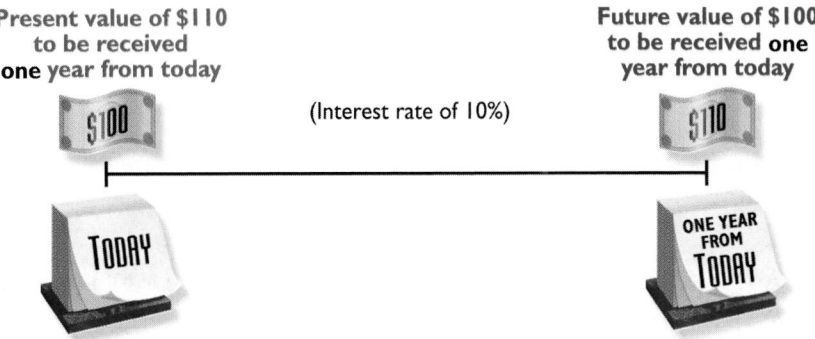

A related concept to present value is ***future value***. In the preceding illustration, the $110 to be received a year from today is the future value of $100 today, assuming an interest rate of 10%.

## Present Value of the Face Amount of Bonds

The present value of the face amount of bonds is the value today of the amount to be received at a future maturity date. For example, assume that you are to receive the face value of a $1,000 bond in one year. If the market rate of interest is 10%, the present value of the face value of the $1,000 bond is $909.09 ($1,000/1.10). This present value is illustrated in the following time line:

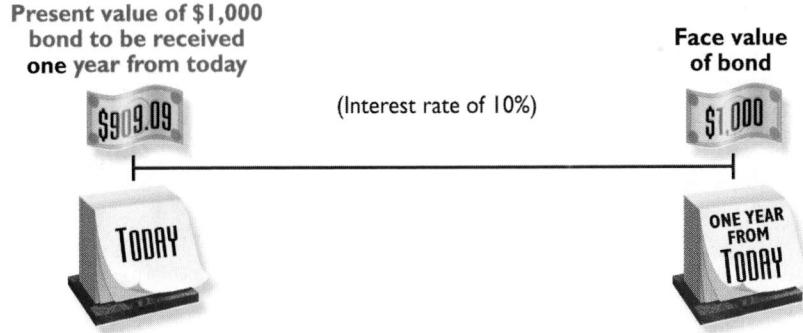

If you are to receive the face value of a $1,000 bond in two years, with interest of 10% compounded at the end of the first year, the present value is $826.45 ($909.09/1.10).[2] We illustrate this present value in the following time line:

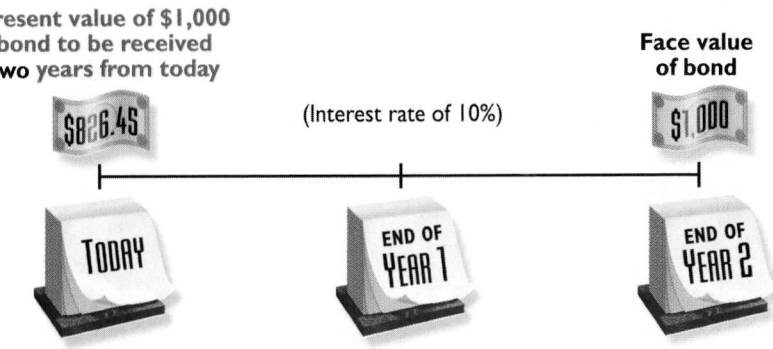

---

[2]Note that the future value of $826.45 in two years, at an interest rate of 10% compounded annually, is $1,000.

You can determine the present value of the face amount of bonds to be received in the future by a time line and a series of divisions. In practice, however, it is easier to use a table of present values. The *present value of $1 table* can be used to find the present-value factor for $1 to be received after a number of periods in the future. The face amount of the bonds is then multiplied by this factor to determine its present value. Exhibit 3 is a partial table of the present value of $1.[3]

## •Exhibit 3 Present Value of $1 at Compound Interest

| Periods | 5% | 5½% | 6% | 6½% | 7% | 10% | 11% | 12% | 13% | 14% |
|---|---|---|---|---|---|---|---|---|---|---|
| 1 | 0.95238 | 0.94787 | 0.94340 | 0.93897 | 0.93458 | 0.90909 | 0.90090 | 0.89286 | 0.88496 | 0.87719 |
| 2 | 0.90703 | 0.89845 | 0.89000 | 0.88166 | 0.87344 | 0.82645 | 0.81162 | 0.79719 | 0.78315 | 0.76947 |
| 3 | 0.86384 | 0.85161 | 0.83962 | 0.82785 | 0.81630 | 0.75132 | 0.73119 | 0.71178 | 0.69305 | 0.67497 |
| 4 | 0.82270 | 0.80722 | 0.79209 | 0.77732 | 0.76290 | 0.68301 | 0.65873 | 0.63552 | 0.61332 | 0.59208 |
| 5 | 0.78353 | 0.76513 | 0.74726 | 0.72988 | 0.71299 | 0.62092 | 0.59345 | 0.56743 | 0.54276 | 0.51937 |
| 6 | 0.74622 | 0.72525 | 0.70496 | 0.68533 | 0.66634 | 0.56447 | 0.53464 | 0.50663 | 0.48032 | 0.45559 |
| 7 | 0.71068 | 0.68744 | 0.66506 | 0.64351 | 0.62275 | 0.51316 | 0.48166 | 0.45235 | 0.42506 | 0.39964 |
| 8 | 0.67684 | 0.65160 | 0.62741 | 0.60423 | 0.58201 | 0.46651 | 0.43393 | 0.40388 | 0.37616 | 0.35056 |
| 9 | 0.64461 | 0.61763 | 0.59190 | 0.56735 | 0.54393 | 0.42410 | 0.39092 | 0.36061 | 0.33288 | 0.30751 |
| 10 | 0.61391 | 0.58543 | 0.55840 | 0.53273 | 0.50835 | 0.38554 | 0.35218 | 0.32197 | 0.29459 | 0.26974 |

What is the present value of $3,000 to be received in 5 years at a market rate of interest of 14% compounded annually?

-------------------------------------

*$1,558.11 ($3,000 × 0.51937)*

Exhibit 3 indicates that the present value of $1 to be received in two years with a market rate of interest of 10% a year is 0.82645. Multiplying the $1,000 face amount of the bond in the preceding example by 0.82645 yields $826.45.

In Exhibit 3, the Periods column represents the number of compounding periods, and the percentage columns represent the compound interest rate per period. For example, 10% for two years compounded *annually*, as in the preceding example, is 10% for two periods. Likewise, 10% for two years compounded *semiannually* would be 5% (10% per year/2 semiannual periods) for four periods (2 years × 2 semiannual periods). Similarly, 10% for three years compounded semiannually would be 5% (10%/2) for six periods (3 years × 2 semiannual periods).

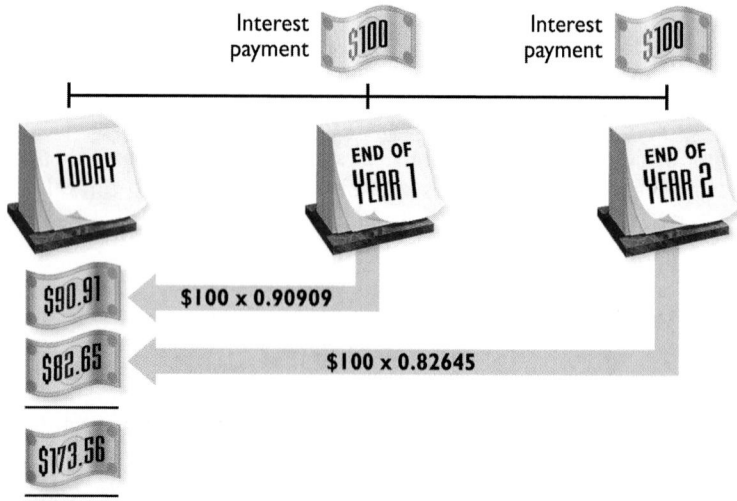

Present value of $100 interest payments to be received each year for 2 years (rounded to the nearest cent)

## Present Value of the Periodic Bond Interest Payments

The present value of the periodic bond interest payments is the value today of the amount of interest to be received at the end of each interest period. Such a series of equal cash payments at fixed intervals is called an *annuity*.

The *present value of an annuity* is the sum of the present values of each cash flow. To illustrate, assume that the $1,000 bond in the preceding example pays interest of 10% annually

---

[3]To simplify the illustrations and homework assignments, the tables presented in this chapter are limited to 10 periods for a small number of interest rates, and the amounts are carried to only five decimal places. Computer programs are available for determining present value factors for any number of interest rates, decimal places, or periods. More complete interest tables, including future value tables, are presented in Appendix A.

and that the market rate of interest is also 10%. In addition, assume that the bond matures at the end of two years. The present value of the two interest payments of $100 ($1,000 × 10%) is $173.56, as shown in the time line at the bottom of page 606. It can be determined by using the present value table shown in Exhibit 3.

## FINANCIAL REPORTING AND DISCLOSURE

### SAFEWAY INC.

**S**afeway is one of the largest food and drug retailers in North America, with over 1,600 stores located in California, Oregon, Washington, Alaska, Colorado, Arizona, Texas, the Chicago metropolitan area, the Mid-Atlantic region, and Canada. During 2002, Safeway reported over $32.4 billion in revenue, income from continuing operations of $569 million, and total assets of $16 billion.

Safeway's operations are financed by notes and debentures of $7.8 billion. Of these notes and debentures, $780 million mature within the current year, and the remainder of $7 billion are long-term debt. Safeway describes its debt financing in the following notes taken from its annual report:

*Notes and debentures were composed of the following at year-end (December 31)*

|  | (in millions) | |
| --- | ---: | ---: |
|  | **2002** | **2001** |
| Commercial paper | $1,744.1 | $1,723.8 |
| Bank credit agreement, unsecured | 25.3 | — |
| 9.30% Senior Secured Debentures due 2007 | 24.3 | 24.3 |
| 6.85% Senior Notes due 2004, unsecured | 200.0 | 200.0 |
| 7.00% Senior Notes due 2007, unsecured | 250.0 | 250.0 |
| 7.45% Senior Debentures due 2027, unsecured | 150.0 | 150.0 |
| 3.80% Senior Notes due 2005, unsecured | 225.0 | — |
| 4.80% Senior Notes due 2007, unsecured | 480.0 | — |
| 5.80% Senior Notes due 2012, unsecured | 800.0 | — |
| 6.05% Senior Notes due 2003, unsecured | 350.0 | 350.0 |
| 6.50% Senior Notes due 2008, unsecured | 250.0 | 250.0 |
| 7.00% Senior Notes due 2002, unsecured | — | 600.0 |
| 7.25% Senior Notes due 2004, unsecured | 400.0 | 400.0 |
| 7.50% Senior Notes due 2009, unsecured | 500.0 | 500.0 |
| 6.15% Senior Notes due 2006, unsecured | 700.0 | 700.0 |
| 6.50% Senior Notes due 2011, unsecured | 500.0 | 500.0 |
| 7.25% Senior Debentures due 2031, unsecured | 600.0 | 600.0 |
| 3.625% Senior Notes due 2003, unsecured | 400.0 | 400.0 |
| 9.65% Senior Subordinated Debentures due 2004, unsecured | 81.2 | 81.2 |
| 9.875% Senior Subordinated Debentures due 2007, unsecured | 24.2 | 24.2 |
| 10% Senior Notes due 2002, unsecured | — | 6.1 |
| Mortgage notes payable, secured | 39.7 | 60.5 |
| Other notes payable, unsecured | 21.6 | 31.7 |
| Medium-term notes, unsecured | 16.5 | 16.5 |
| Short-term bank borrowings, unsecured | 7.6 | 7.6 |
|  | $7,789.5 | $6,875.9 |
| Less current maturities | (780.3) | (639.1) |
| Long term portion | $7,009.2 | $6,236.8 |

The 9.30% Senior Secured Debentures due in 2007 traded on July 23, 2003, at 120.58 and yielded a rate of return of 3.068%.

Instead of using present value of amount tables, such as Exhibit 3, separate present value tables are normally used for annuities. Exhibit 4 is a partial table of the *present value of an annuity of $1* at compound interest. It shows the present value of $1 to be received at the end of each period for various compound rates of interest. For example, the present value of $100 to be received at the end of each of the next two years at 10% compound interest per period is $173.55 ($100 × 1.73554). This amount is the same amount that we computed previously, except for rounding.

 **Exhibit 4**  Present Value of Annuity of $1 at Compound Interest

| Periods | 5% | 5½% | 6% | 6½% | 7% | 10% | 11% | 12% | 13% | 14% |
|---|---|---|---|---|---|---|---|---|---|---|
| 1 | 0.95238 | 0.94787 | 0.94340 | 0.93897 | 0.93458 | 0.90909 | 0.90090 | 0.89286 | 0.88496 | 0.87719 |
| 2 | 1.85941 | 1.84632 | 1.83339 | 1.82063 | 1.80802 | 1.73554 | 1.71252 | 1.69005 | 1.66810 | 1.64666 |
| 3 | 2.72325 | 2.69793 | 2.67301 | 2.64848 | 2.62432 | 2.48685 | 2.44371 | 2.40183 | 2.36115 | 2.32163 |
| 4 | 3.54595 | 3.50515 | 3.46511 | 3.42580 | 3.38721 | 3.16987 | 3.10245 | 3.03735 | 2.97447 | 2.91371 |
| 5 | 4.32948 | 4.27028 | 4.21236 | 4.15568 | 4.10020 | 3.79079 | 3.69590 | 3.60478 | 3.51723 | 3.43308 |
| 6 | 5.07569 | 4.99553 | 4.91732 | 4.84101 | 4.76654 | 4.35526 | 4.23054 | 4.11141 | 3.99755 | 3.88867 |
| 7 | 5.78637 | 5.68297 | 5.58238 | 5.48452 | 5.38929 | 4.86842 | 4.71220 | 4.56376 | 4.42261 | 4.28830 |
| 8 | 6.46321 | 6.33457 | 6.20979 | 6.08875 | 5.97130 | 5.33493 | 5.14612 | 4.96764 | 4.79677 | 4.63886 |
| 9 | 7.10782 | 6.95220 | 6.80169 | 6.65610 | 6.51523 | 5.75902 | 5.53705 | 5.32825 | 5.13166 | 4.94637 |
| 10 | 7.72174 | 7.53763 | 7.36009 | 7.18883 | 7.02358 | 6.14457 | 5.88923 | 5.65022 | 5.42624 | 5.21612 |

As we stated earlier, the amount buyers are willing to pay for a bond is the sum of the present value of the face value and the periodic interest payments, calculated by using the market rate of interest. In our example, this calculation is as follows:

*What is the present value of a $10,000, 7%, 5-year bond that pays interest annually, assuming a market rate of interest of 7%?*

---

*$10,000 [($10,000 × 0.71299) + ($700 × 4.10020)]*

Present value of face value of $1,000 due in 2 years
at 10% compounded annually: $1,000 × 0.82645
(present value factor of $1 for 2 periods at 10%) . . . . . . . . .    $ 826.45
Present value of 2 annual interest payments of $100
at 10% compounded annually: $100 × 1.73554
(present value of annuity of $1 for 2 periods at 10%) . . . . . .    173.55
Total present value of bonds . . . . . . . . . . . . . . . . . . . . . . . .    $1,000.00

In this example, the market rate and the contract rate of interest are the same. Thus, the present value is the same as the face value.

# Accounting for Bonds Payable

**objective 4**

Journalize entries for bonds payable.

In the preceding section, we described and illustrated how present value concepts are used in determining how much buyers are willing to pay for bonds. In this section, we describe and illustrate how corporations record the issuance of bonds and the payment of bond interest.

## Bonds Issued at Face Amount

To illustrate the journal entries for issuing bonds, assume that on January 1, 2005, a corporation issues for cash $100,000 of 12%, five-year bonds, with interest of $6,000 payable *semiannually*. The market rate of interest at the time the bonds are issued is 12%. Since the contract rate and the market rate of interest are the same, the bonds will sell at their face amount. This amount is the sum of (1) the present value of the face amount of $100,000 to be repaid in five years and (2) the present value of ten *semiannual* interest payments of $6,000 each. This computation and a time line are shown below.

Present value of face amount of $100,000 due in 5 years,
    at 12% compounded semiannually: $100,000 × 0.55840
    (present value of $1 for 10 periods at 6%) . . . . . . . . . . . . . . . . . . . . .    $ 55,840
Present value of 10 semiannual interest payments of $6,000,
    at 12% compounded semiannually: $6,000 × 7.36009
    (present value of annuity of $1 for 10 periods at 6%) . . . . . . . . . . . .    44,160*
Total present value of bonds . . . . . . . . . . . . . . . . . . . . . . . . . . . . . .    $100,000

*Because the present-value tables are rounded to five decimal places, minor rounding differences may appear in the illustrations.

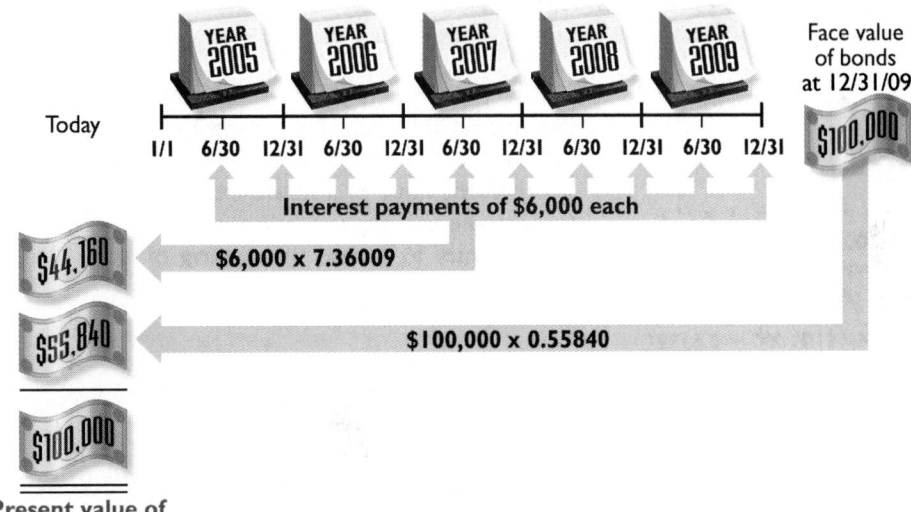

Present value of
12% bonds at
12% market rate

The following entry records the issuing of the $100,000 bonds at their face amount:

| | | | | | | |
|---|---|---|---|---|---|---|
| 2005 Jan. | 1 | Cash | | 100 0 0 0 00 | | |
| | | Bonds Payable | | | 100 0 0 0 00 | |
| | | Issued $100,000 bonds payable at | | | | |
| | | face amount. | | | | |

Every six months after the bonds have been issued, interest payments of $6,000 are made. The first interest payment is recorded as shown below.

| | | | | | | |
|---|---|---|---|---|---|---|
| June | 30 | Interest Expense | | 6 0 0 0 00 | | |
| | | Cash | | | 6 0 0 0 00 | |
| | | Paid six months' interest on bonds. | | | | |

At the maturity date, the payment of the principal of $100,000 is recorded as follows:

| | | | | | | |
|---|---|---|---|---|---|---|
| 2009 Dec. | 31 | Bonds Payable | | 100 0 0 0 00 | | |
| | | Cash | | | 100 0 0 0 00 | |
| | | Paid bond principal at maturity date. | | | | |

# Bonds Issued at a Discount

What if the market rate of interest is higher than the contract rate of interest? If the market rate of interest is 13% and the contract rate is 12% on the five-year, $100,000 bonds, the bonds will sell at a discount. The present value of these bonds is calculated as follows:

> **Bonds will sell at a discount when the market rate of interest is higher than the contract rate.**

Present value of face amount of $100,000 due in 5 years,
    at 13% compounded semiannually: $100,000 × 0.53273
    (present value of $1 for 10 periods at 6½%) . . . . . . . . . . . . . .   $53,273
Present value of 10 semiannual interest payments of $6,000,
    at 13% compounded semiannually: $6,000 × 7.18883
    (present value of an annuity of $1 for 10 periods at 6½%)  . . . .    43,133
Total present value of bonds  . . . . . . . . . . . . . . . . . . . . . . . . . . .   $96,406

*What is the present value of a $100,000, 6%, 5-year bond paying semiannual interest if the market rate of interest is 10%?*

- - - - - - - - - - - - - - - - - - - - - - - - - -

*$84,556 [($100,000 × 0.61391) + ($3,000 × 7.72174)]*

The two present values that make up the total are both less than the related amounts in the preceding example. This is because the market rate of interest was 12% in the first example, while the market rate of interest is 13% in this example. The present value of a future amount becomes less and less as the interest rate used to compute the present value increases.

The entry to record the issuing of the $100,000 bonds at a discount is shown below.

| | | | | | | |
|---|---|---|---|---|---|---|
| 2005<br>Jan. | 1 | Cash | | 96 4 0 6 00 | | |
| | | Discount on Bonds Payable | | 3 5 9 4 00 | | |
| | |     Bonds Payable | | | 100 0 0 0 00 | |
| | |         Issued $100,000 bonds at discount. | | | | |

The $3,594 discount may be viewed as the amount that is needed to entice investors to accept a contract rate of interest that is below the market rate. You may think of the discount as the market's way of adjusting a bond's contract rate of interest to the higher market rate of interest. Using this logic, generally accepted accounting principles require that bond discounts be amortized as interest expense over the life of the bond.

# Amortizing a Bond Discount

There are two methods of amortizing a bond discount: (1) the **straight-line method** and (2) the ***effective interest rate method***, often called the **interest method**. Both methods amortize the same total amount of discount over the life of the bonds. The interest method is required by generally accepted accounting principles. However, the straight-line method is acceptable if the results obtained do not materially differ from the results that would be obtained by using the interest method. Because the straight-line method illustrates the basic concept of amortizing discounts and is simpler, we will use it in this chapter. We illustrate the interest method in an appendix to this chapter.

*If the amount of a bond discount on a newly issued 6%, 5-year, $100,000 bond is $28,092, what are (a) the semiannual straight-line amortization of the discount and (b) the annual interest expense?*

- - - - - - - - - - - - - - - - - - - - - - - - - -

*(a) $2,809.20, (b) $11,618.40 ($2,809.20 + $2,809.20 + $6,000)*

The straight-line method of amortizing a bond discount provides for amortization in equal periodic amounts. Applying this method to the preceding example yields amortization of ¹⁄₁₀ of $3,594, or $359.40, each half year. The amount of the interest expense on the bonds is the same, $6,359.40 ($6,000 + $359.40) for each half year. The entry to record the first interest payment and the amortization of the related discount follows.

| | 2005<br>June | 30 | Interest Expense | | 6 3 5 9 40 | |
|---|---|---|---|---|---|---|
| | | | Discount on Bonds Payable | | | 3 5 9 40 |
| | | | Cash | | | 6 0 0 0 00 |
| | | | Paid semiannual interest and | | | |
| | | | amortized $^1/_{10}$ of bond discount. | | | |

> **Bonds will sell at a premium when the market rate of interest is less than the contract rate.**

## Bonds Issued at a Premium

If the market rate of interest is 11% and the contract rate is 12% on the five-year, $100,000 bonds, the bonds will sell at a premium. The present value of these bonds is computed as follows:

Present value of face amount of $100,000 due in 5 years,
   at 11% compounded semiannually: $100,000 × 0.58543
   (present value of $1 for 10 periods at 5½%) . . . . . . . . . . . . . . . . . . .    $ 58,543
Present value of 10 semiannual interest payments of $6,000,
   at 11% compounded semiannually: $6,000 × 7.53763
   (present value of an annuity of $1 for 10 periods at 5½%) . . . . . . . . . .    45,226
Total present value of bonds . . . . . . . . . . . . . . . . . . . . . . . . . . . . . . . . $103,769

The entry to record the issuing of the bonds is as follows:

| | 2005<br>Jan. | 1 | Cash | | 103 7 6 9 00 | |
|---|---|---|---|---|---|---|
| | | | Bonds Payable | | | 100 0 0 0 00 |
| | | | Premium on Bonds Payable | | | 3 7 6 9 00 |
| | | | Issued $100,000 bonds at a premium. | | | |

## Amortizing a Bond Premium

The amortization of bond premiums is basically the same as that for bond discounts, except that interest expense is decreased. In the above example, the straight-line method yields amortization of $^1/_{10}$ of $3,769, or $376.90, each half year. The entry to record the first interest payment and the amortization of the related premium is as follows:

If the amount of a bond premium on a newly issued 13%, 5-year, $100,000 bond is $11,581, what are (a) the semiannual straight-line amortization of the premium and (b) the annual interest expense?

- - - - - - - - - - - - - - - - - - - - - - - - - - - -

*(a) $1,158.10, (b) $10,683.80 ($13,000 − $1,158.10 − $1,158.10)*

| | 2005<br>June | 30 | Interest Expense | | 5 6 2 3 10 | |
|---|---|---|---|---|---|---|
| | | | Premium on Bonds Payable | | 3 7 6 90 | |
| | | | Cash | | | 6 0 0 0 00 |
| | | | Paid semiannual interest and | | | |
| | | | amortized $^1/_{10}$ of bond premium. | | | |

## Zero-Coupon Bonds

Some corporations issue bonds that provide for only the payment of the face amount at the maturity date. Such bonds are called **zero-coupon bonds**. Because they do not provide for interest payments, these bonds sell at a large discount. For example, **Merrill Lynch**'s zero-coupon bonds maturing in 2028 were selling for 19.82.

**REAL WORLD**

Some bonds with high contract rates, as well as some zero-coupon bonds, are issued by weak companies. Because such bonds are high-risk bonds, they are called **junk bonds**.

The issuing price of zero-coupon bonds is the present value of their face amount. To illustrate, if the market rate of interest is 13%, the present value of $100,000 zero-coupon, five-year bonds is calculated as follows:

> Present value of $100,000 due in 5 years, at 13%
> compounded semiannually: $100,000 × 0.53273
> (present value of $1 for 10 periods at 6½%) . . . . . . . . .   $53,273

The accounting for zero-coupon bonds is similar to that for interest-bearing bonds that have been sold at a discount. The discount is amortized as interest expense over the life of the bonds. The entry to record the issuing of the bonds is as follows:

| 2005<br>Jan. | 1 | Cash | | 53 2 7 3 00 | |
|---|---|---|---|---|---|
| | | Discount on Bonds Payable | | 46 7 2 7 00 | |
| | |     Bonds Payable | | | 100 0 0 0 00 |
| | |      Issued $100,000 zero-coupon | | | |
| | |      bonds | | | |

---

## LET'S DANCE—A BOND WITH A TUNE

How would you like to tune into some of the royalties from David Bowie's hit song, *Let's Dance*? The British rock star has offered bonds backed by future royalties from his hit songs and albums recorded prior to 1990. In addition to *Let's Dance*, other songs include *Jean Genie*, *A Space Oddity*, *Changes*, *Diamond Dogs*, and *Rebel*.

Bowie's bonds, which have an average maturity of 10 years, pay 7.9% annual interest. Such asset-backed bonds have grown in popularity. However, this is the first time that a popular artist has made use of future royalties as asset backing. The Bowie Bonds, which are officially called Class-A royalty-backed securities, were rated AAA—the highest rating—by **Moody's Investors Service**.

Bowie is one of the most financially savvy rock stars in the world, with a well-chosen art collection and an appreciation for market trends. Bowie's principal residence is a $3.4 million, 640-acre estate in County Wicklow, Ireland, a noted tax haven. He lives there with his second wife, the supermodel and actress Iman. Still, Bowie's business man-

ager said that when he approached him with the bond idea, "he [Bowie] kind of looked at me cross-eyed and said, 'What?' "

Potential investors were reassured by the fact that Bowie never sells fewer than a million albums a year. At the time of the offering, Bowie's album, "Earthling," was near the top of the European charts. In addition, the month before the offering, he performed for a sold-out concert at New York's Madison Square Garden.

**Prudential Insurance Co.** isn't kidding when it says you can own a piece of the *rock*. In a private placement, Prudential purchased all of David Bowie's $55 million bonds for its general investment fund, where the money of life insurance policyholders is invested.

In addition to Bowie, other musicians who have issued royalty-backed bonds include James Brown and the heavy-metal band Iron Maiden. The Iron Maiden bonds were successfully sold for $30 million.

---

# Bond Sinking Funds

**objective 5**

Describe bond sinking funds.

A bond indenture may restrict dividend payments to stockholders as a means of increasing the likelihood that the bonds will be paid at maturity. In addition to or instead of this restriction, the bond indenture may require that funds for the payment of the face value of the bonds at maturity be set aside over the life of the bond issue. The amounts set aside are kept separate from other assets in a special fund called a **sinking fund**.

When cash is transferred to the sinking fund, it is recorded in an account called *Sinking Fund Cash*. When investments are purchased with the sinking fund cash, they are recorded in an account called *Sinking Fund Investments*. As income (interest or dividends) is received, it is recorded in an account called *Sinking Fund Revenue*.

Sinking fund revenue represents earnings of the corporation and is reported in the income statement as Other Income. The cash and the securities making up the sinking fund are reported in the balance sheet as Investments, immediately below the Current Assets section.

# Bond Redemption

**objective 6**

Journalize entries for bond redemptions.

**REAL WORLD**

**Pacific Bell** issued 7.5% bonds, maturing in 2033 but callable in 2023.

A corporation may call or redeem bonds before they mature. This is often done if the market rate of interest declines significantly after the bonds have been issued. In this situation, the corporation may sell new bonds at a lower interest rate and use the funds to redeem the original bond issue. The corporation can thus save on future interest expenses.

A corporation often issues callable bonds to protect itself against significant declines in future interest rates. However, callable bonds are more risky for investors, who may not be able to replace the called bonds with investments paying an equal amount of interest.

**Callable bonds** can be redeemed by the issuing corporation within the period of time and at the price stated in the bond indenture. Normally, the call price is above the face value. A corporation may also redeem its bonds by purchasing them on the open market.

A corporation usually redeems its bonds at a price different from that of the carrying amount (or book value) of the bonds. The ***carrying amount*** of bonds payable is the balance of the bonds payable account (face amount of the bonds) less any unamortized discount or plus any unamortized premium. If the price paid for redemption is below the bond carrying amount, the difference in these two amounts is recorded as a gain. If the price paid for the redemption is above the carrying amount, a loss is recorded. Gains and losses on the redemption of bonds are reported in the Other Income and Expense section of the income statement.

To illustrate, assume that on June 30 a corporation has a bond issue of $100,000 outstanding, on which there is an unamortized premium of $4,000. Assuming that the corporation purchases one-fourth ($25,000) of the bonds for $24,000 on June 30, the entry to record the redemption is as follows:

| 2005 June | 30 | Bonds Payable | 25 0 0 0 00 | |
|---|---|---|---|---|
| | | Premium on Bonds Payable | 1 0 0 0 00 | |
| | | Cash | | 24 0 0 0 00 |
| | | Gain on Redemption of Bonds | | 2 0 0 0 00 |
| | | Redeemed $25,000 bonds for $24,000. | | |

In the preceding entry, only a portion of the premium relating to the redeemed bonds is written off. The difference between the carrying amount of the bonds purchased, $26,000 ($25,000 + $1,000), and the price paid for the redemption, $24,000, is recorded as a gain.

If the corporation calls the entire bond issue for $105,000 on June 30, the entry to record the redemption is as follows:

A $250,000 bond issue on which there is an unamortized discount of $20,000 is redeemed for $235,000. What is the gain or loss on the redemption of the bonds?

*$5,000 loss ($250,000 − $20,000 − $235,000)*

| 2005 June | 30 | Bonds Payable | 100 0 0 0 00 | |
|---|---|---|---|---|
| | | Premium on Bonds Payable | 4 0 0 0 00 | |
| | | Loss on Redemption of Bonds | 1 0 0 0 00 | |
| | | Cash | | 105 0 0 0 00 |
| | | Redeemed $100,000 bonds for $105,000. | | |

---

## INTEGRITY IN BUSINESS

### WHAT DOES IT TAKE TO SUCCEED IN LIFE?

The answer to this question, according to Warren Buffett, the noted investment authority, is three magic ingredients: intelligence, energy, and integrity. According to Buffett, "If you lack the third ingredient, the other two will kill you."

In other words, without integrity, your intelligence and energy may very well misguide you.

**Source:** Clifford, Eric, *University of Tennessee Torchbearer,* Summer 2002.

---

# Investments in Bonds

**objective** 7

Journalize entries for the purchase, interest, discount and premium amortization, and sale of bond investments.

**REAL WORLD**

**Walt Disney**'s 6.375% bonds maturing in 2012 were listed as selling for 107.365 on August 1, 2003.

Throughout this chapter, we have discussed bonds and the related transactions of the issuing corporation (the debtor). However, these transactions also affect investors. In this section, we discuss the accounting for bonds from the point of view of investors.

## Accounting for Bond Investments— Purchase, Interest, and Amortization

Bonds may be purchased either directly from the issuing corporation or through an organized bond exchange. Bond exchanges publish daily bond quotations. These quotations normally include the bond interest rate, maturity date, volume of sales, and the high, low, and closing prices for each corporation's bonds traded during the day. Prices for bonds are quoted as a percentage of the face amount. Thus, the price of a $1,000 bond quoted at 99.5 would be $995, while the price of a bond quoted at 104.25 would be $1,042.50.

As with other assets, the cost of a bond investment includes all costs related to the purchase. For example, for bonds purchased through an exchange, the amount paid as a broker's commission should be included as part of the cost of the investment.

When bonds are purchased between interest dates, the buyer normally pays the seller the interest accrued from the last interest payment date to the date of purchase. The amount of the interest paid is normally debited to *Interest Revenue*, since it is an offset against the amount that will be received at the next interest date.

To illustrate, assume that an investor purchases a $1,000 bond at 102 plus a brokerage fee of $5.30 and accrued interest of $10.20. The investor records the transaction as follows:

| 2005 | | | | | |
|------|---|------------------------------|--------|--------|--------|
| Apr. | 2 | Investment in Lewis Co. Bonds | 1 0 2 5 30 | | |
| | | Interest Revenue | | 1 0 20 | |
| | | Cash | | | 1 0 3 5 50 |

> **A premium or discount on a bond investment is recorded in the investment account and is amortized over the remaining life of the bonds.**

The cost of the bond is recorded in a single investment account. The face amount of the bond and the premium (or discount) are normally not recorded in separate accounts. This is different from the accounting for bonds payable. Separate premium and discount accounts are usually not used by investors, because they usually do not hold bond investments until the bonds mature.

When bonds held as long-term investments are purchased at a price other than the face amount, the premium or discount should be amortized over the remaining life of the bonds. The amortization of premiums and discounts affects the investment and interest accounts as shown below.

| *Premium Amortization:* | | | *Discount Amortization:* | | |
|---|---|---|---|---|---|
| Interest Revenue | XXX | | Investment in Bonds | XXX | |
| Investment in Bonds | | XXX | Interest Revenue | | XXX |

The amount of the amortization can be determined by using either the straight-line or interest methods. Unlike bonds payable, the amortization of premiums and discounts on bond investments is usually recorded at the end of the period, rather than when interest is received.

To illustrate the accounting for bond investments, assume that on July 1, 2005, Crenshaw Inc. purchases $50,000 of 8% bonds of Deitz Corporation, due in 8¾ years. Crenshaw Inc. purchases the bonds directly from Deitz Corporation to yield an effective interest rate of 11%. The purchase price is $41,706 plus interest of $1,000 ($50,000 × 8% × ³⁄₁₂) accrued from April 1, 2005, the date of the last semiannual interest payment. Entries in the accounts of Crenshaw Inc. at the time of purchase and for the remainder of the fiscal period ending December 31, 2005, are as follows:

*Calculations:*

Cost of $50,000 of Deitz
   Corp. bonds    $41,706
Interest accrued
   ($50,000 × 8% × ³⁄₁₂)   1,000
Total    $42,706

$50,000 × 8% × ⁶⁄₁₂ = $2,000

$50,000 × 8% × ³⁄₁₂ = $1,000

Face value of bonds   $50,000
Cost of bond invest.   41,706
Discount on bond
   investment   $ 8,294

Number of months
   to maturity
   (8¾ years × 12)   105 months
Monthly amortization
   ($8,294/105 months,
   rounded to nearest
   dollar)   $79 per mo.
Amortization for
6 months ($79 × 6)   $474

| 2005 | | | | | | | | | |
|---|---|---|---|---|---|---|---|---|---|
| July | 1 | Investment in Deitz Corp. Bonds | 41 7 0 6 00 | | |
| | | Interest Revenue | 1 0 0 0 00 | | |
| | | Cash | | 42 7 0 6 00 |
| | | Purchased investment in bonds, plus | | |
| | | accrued interest. | | |
| Oct. | 1 | Cash | 2 0 0 0 00 | | |
| | | Interest Revenue | | 2 0 0 0 00 |
| | | Received semiannual interest for | | |
| | | April 1 to October 1. | | |
| Dec. | 31 | Interest Receivable | 1 0 0 0 00 | | |
| | | Interest Revenue | | 1 0 0 0 00 |
| | | Adjusting entry for interest accrued | | |
| | | from October 1 to December 31. | | |
| | 31 | Investment in Deitz Corp. Bonds | 4 7 4 00 | | |
| | | Interest Revenue | | 4 7 4 00 |
| | | Adjusting entry for amortization of | | |
| | | discount for July 1 to December 31. | | |

The effect of these entries on the interest revenue account is shown below.

**Interest Revenue**

| | | | | |
|---|---|---|---|---|
| July 1 | 1,000 | Oct. 1 | 2,000 |
| | | Dec. 31 | 1,000 |
| | | 31 | 474 |
| | | *Bal. 2,474* | *3,474* |

# Accounting for Bond Investments—Sale

Many long-term investments in bonds are sold before their maturity date. When this occurs, the seller receives the sales price (less commissions and other selling costs) plus any accrued interest since the last interest payment date. Before recording the

If the Deitz Corporation bonds had been sold on September 30 instead of June 30, what would have been the amount of the loss?

----------------------------------------

$1,229 {$47,350 − [$48,342 + ($79 × 3 months)]}

*Calculations:*

$79 × 6 months

| | |
|---|---|
| Carrying amount of bonds on Jan. 1, 2009 | $47,868 |
| Discount amortized, Jan. 1 to June 30, 2009 | 474 |
| Carrying amount of bonds on June 30, 2009 | $48,342 |
| Proceeds of sale | 47,350 |
| Loss on sale | $ 992 |

cash proceeds, the seller should amortize any discount or premium for the current period up to the date of sale. Any gain or loss on the sale is then recorded when the cash proceeds are recorded. Such gains and losses are normally reported in the Other Income section of the income statement.

To illustrate, assume that the Deitz Corporation bonds in the preceding example are sold for $47,350 plus accrued interest on June 30, 2012. The *carrying amount* of the bonds (cost plus amortized discount) as of January 1, 2012 (78 months after their purchase) is $47,868 [$41,706 + ($79 per month × 78 months)]. The entries to amortize the discount for the current year and to record the sale of the bonds are as follows:

| | | | | | |
|---|---|---|---|---|---|
| 2012 June | 30 | Investment in Deitz Corp. Bonds | | 474 00 | |
| | | Interest Revenue | | | 474 00 |
| | | Amortized discount for current year. | | | |
| | | | | | |
| | 30 | Cash | | 48 350 00 | |
| | | Loss on Sale of Investments | | 992 00 | |
| | | Interest Revenue | | | 1 000 00 |
| | | Investment in Deitz Corp. Bonds | | | 48 342 00 |
| | | Received interest and proceeds from sale of bonds. | | | |
| | | Interest for April 1 to June 30 = | | | |
| | | $50,000 × 8% × 3/12 = $1,000 | | | |

# Corporation Balance Sheet

**objective** 8

Prepare a corporation balance sheet.

In previous chapters, we illustrated the income statement and retained earnings statement for a corporation. The consolidated balance sheet in Exhibit 5 illustrates the presentation of many of the items discussed in this and preceding chapters. These items include bond sinking funds, investments in bonds, goodwill, deferred income taxes, bonds payable and unamortized discount, and minority interest in subsidiaries.

## Balance Sheet Presentation of Bonds Payable

In Exhibit 5, Escoe Corporation's bonds payable are reported as long-term liabilities. If there were two or more bond issues, the details of each would be reported on the balance sheet or in a supporting schedule or note. Separate accounts are normally maintained for each bond issue.

When the balance sheet date is within one year of the maturity date of the bonds, the bonds may be classified as a current liability. This would be the case if the bonds are to be paid out of current assets. If the bonds are to be paid from a sinking fund or if they are to be refinanced with another bond issue, they should remain in the noncurrent category. In this case, the details of the retirement of the bonds are normally disclosed in a note to the financial statements.

## •Exhibit 5  Balance Sheet of a Corporation

### Escoe Corporation and Subsidiaries
### Consolidated Balance Sheet
### December 31, 2006

#### Assets

Current assets:

| | | | |
|---|---|---|---|
| Cash and cash equivalents | | | $ 407,500 |
| Accounts and notes receivable | | $ 722,000 | |
| Less allowance for doubtful receivables | | 37,000 | 685,000 |
| Inventories, at lower of cost (first-in, first-out) or market | | | 917,500 |
| Prepaid expenses | | | 70,000 |
| Total current assets | | | $2,080,000 |

Investments:

| | | | |
|---|---|---|---|
| Bond sinking fund (market value, $473,000) | | | $ 422,500 |
| Investment in bonds of Dalton Company | | | |
| (market value, $231,000) | | | 240,000 |
| Total investments | | | 662,500 |

| | Cost | Accumulated Depreciation | Book Value | |
|---|---|---|---|---|
| Property, plant, and equipment | | | | |
| (depreciated by the straight-line method): | | | | |
| Land | $ 250,000 | — | $ 250,000 | |
| Buildings | 920,000 | $ 379,955 | 540,045 | |
| Machinery and equipment | 2,764,400 | 766,200 | 1,998,200 | |
| Total property, plant, and equipment | $3,934,400 | $1,146,155 | | 2,788,245 |

Intangible assets:

| | | |
|---|---|---|
| Goodwill | | 350,000 |
| Total assets | | $5,880,745 |

#### Liabilities

Current liabilities:

| | | | |
|---|---|---|---|
| Accounts payable | | $ 508,810 | |
| Income tax payable | | 120,500 | |
| Dividends payable | | 94,000 | |
| Accrued liabilities | | 81,400 | |
| Deferred income tax payable | | 10,000 | |
| Total current liabilities | | | $ 814,710 |

Long-term liabilities:

| | | | |
|---|---|---|---|
| Debenture 8% bonds payable, due December 31, 2024 | | | |
| (market value, $950,000) | $1,000,000 | | |
| Less unamortized discount | 60,000 | $ 940,000 | |
| Minority interest in subsidiaries | | 115,000 | |
| Total long-term liabilities | | | 1,055,000 |

Deferred credits:

| | | |
|---|---|---|
| Deferred income tax payable | | 85,500 |
| Total liabilities | | $1,955,210 |

#### Stockholders' Equity

Paid-in capital:

| | | | |
|---|---|---|---|
| Common stock, $20 par (250,000 shares authorized, | | | |
| 100,000 shares issued) | $2,000,000 | | |
| Excess of issue price over par | 320,000 | | |
| Total paid-in capital | | $2,320,000 | |
| Retained earnings | | 1,605,535 | |
| Total stockholders' equity | | | 3,925,535 |
| Total liabilities and stockholders' equity | | | $5,880,745 |

The balance in Escoe's discount on bonds payable account is reported as a *deduction* from the bonds payable. Conversely, the balance in a bond premium account would be reported as an *addition* to the related bonds payable. Either on the face of the financial statements or in accompanying notes, a description of the bonds (terms, due date, and effective interest rate) and other relevant information such as sinking fund requirements should be disclosed.[4] Finally, the market (fair) value of the bonds payable should also be disclosed.

## Balance Sheet Presentation of Bond Investments

Investments in bonds or other debt securities that management intends to hold to their maturity are called **held-to-maturity securities**. Such securities are classified as long-term investments under the caption Investments. These investments are reported at their cost less any amortized premium or plus any amortized discount. In addition, the market (fair) value of the bond investments should be disclosed, either on the face of the balance sheet or in an accompanying note.

# Financial Analysis and Interpretation

objective **9**

Compute and interpret the number of times interest charges are earned.

Some corporations, such as railroads and public utilities, have a high ratio of debt to stockholders' equity. For such corporations, analysts often assess the relative risk of the debtholders in terms of the **number of times the interest charges are earned** during the year. The higher the ratio, the greater the chance that interest payments will continue to be made if earnings decrease.[5]

The amount available to make interest payments is not affected by taxes on income. This is because interest is deductible in determining taxable income. To illustrate, the following data were taken from the 2002 annual report of **Briggs & Stratton Corporation**:

| | |
|---|---|
| Interest expense | $44,433,000 |
| Income before income tax | $80,510,000 |

The number of times interest charges are earned, 2.81, is calculated below.

$$\text{Number of times interest charges earned} = \frac{\text{Income before income tax} + \text{Interest expense}}{\text{Interest expense}}$$

$$\text{Number of times interest charges earned} = \frac{\$80,510,000 + \$44,433,000}{\$44,433,000} = 2.81$$

The number of times interest charges are earned indicates that the debtholders of Briggs & Stratton have adequate protection against a potential drop in earnings jeopardizing their receipt of interest payments. However, a final assessment should include a review of trends of past years and a comparison with industry averages.

---

[4]*Statement of Financial Accounting Standards No. 129*, "Disclosure Information About Capital Structure," Financial Accounting Standards Board (Norwalk, Connecticut: 1997).

[5]A similar analysis can also be applied to dividends on preferred stock. In such cases, net income would be divided by the amount of preferred dividends to yield the number of times preferred dividends were earned. This measure gives an indication of the relative assurance of continued dividend payments to preferred stockholders.

# Appendix    Effective Interest Rate Method of Amortization

The effective interest rate method of amortizing discounts and premiums provides for a constant rate of interest on the carrying amount of the bonds at the beginning of each period. This is in contrast to the straight-line method, which provides for a constant amount of interest expense.

The interest rate used in the interest method of amortization is the market rate on the date the bonds are issued. The carrying amount of the bonds to which the interest rate is applied is the face amount of the bonds minus any unamortized discount or plus any unamortized premium. Under the interest method, the interest expense to be reported on the income statement is computed by multiplying the effective interest rate by the carrying amount of the bonds. The difference between the interest expense computed in this way and the periodic interest payment is the amount of discount or premium to be amortized for the period.

## Amortization of Discount by the Interest Method

To illustrate the interest method for amortizing bond discounts, we assume the following data from the chapter illustration of issuing $100,000 bonds at a discount:

| | |
|---|---|
| Face value of 12%, 5-year bonds, interest compounded semiannually | $100,000 |
| Present value of bonds at effective (market) rate of interest of 13% | 96,406 |
| Discount on bonds payable | $   3,594 |

Applying the interest method to these data yields the amortization table in Exhibit 6. You should note the following items in this table:

1. The interest paid (Column A) remains constant at 6% of $100,000, the face amount of the bonds.
2. The interest expense (Column B) is computed at 6½% of the bond carrying amount at the beginning of each period. This results in an increasing interest expense each period.
3. The excess of the interest expense over the interest payment of $6,000 is the amount of discount to be amortized (Column C).

## •Exhibit 6 Amortization of Discount on Bonds Payable

| Interest Payment | A Interest Paid (6% of Face Amount) | B Interest Expense (6½% of Bond Carrying Amount) | C Discount Amortization (B − A) | D Unamortized Discount (D − C) | E Bond Carrying Amount ($100,000 − D) |
|---|---|---|---|---|---|
| | | | | $3,594 | $ 96,406 |
| 1 | $6,000 | $6,266 (6½% of $96,406) | $266 | 3,328 | 96,672 |
| 2 | 6,000 | 6,284 (6½% of $96,672) | 284 | 3,044 | 96,956 |
| 3 | 6,000 | 6,302 (6½% of $96,956) | 302 | 2,742 | 97,258 |
| 4 | 6,000 | 6,322 (6½% of $97,258) | 322 | 2,420 | 97,580 |
| 5 | 6,000 | 6,343 (6½% of $97,580) | 343 | 2,077 | 97,923 |
| 6 | 6,000 | 6,365 (6½% of $97,923) | 365 | 1,712 | 98,288 |
| 7 | 6,000 | 6,389 (6½% of $98,288) | 389 | 1,323 | 98,677 |
| 8 | 6,000 | 6,414 (6½% of $98,677) | 414 | 909 | 99,091 |
| 9 | 6,000 | 6,441 (6½% of $99,091) | 441 | 468 | 99,532 |
| 10 | 6,000 | 6,470 (6½% of $99,532) | 468* | — | 100,000 |

*Cannot exceed unamortized discount.

4. The unamortized discount (Column D) decreases from the initial balance, $3,594, to a zero balance at the maturity date of the bonds.
5. The carrying amount (Column E) increases from $96,406, the amount received for the bonds, to $100,000 at maturity.

The entry to record the first interest payment on June 30, 2005, and the related discount amortization is as follows:

| | | | | | |
|---|---|---|---|---|---|
| 2005 June | 30 | Interest Expense | | 6 2 6 6 00 | |
| | | Discount on Bonds Payable | | | 2 6 6 00 |
| | | Cash | | | 6 0 0 0 00 |
| | | Paid semiannual interest and amortized | | | |
| | | bond discount for ½ year. | | | |

If the amortization is recorded only at the end of the year, the amount of the discount amortized on December 31 would be $550. This is the sum of the first two semiannual amortization amounts ($266 and $284) from Exhibit 6.

## Amortization of Premium by the Interest Method

To illustrate the interest method for amortizing bond premiums, we assume the following data from the chapter illustration of issuing $100,000 bonds at a premium:

| | |
|---|---|
| Present value of bonds at effective (market) rate of interest of 11% | $103,769 |
| Face value of 12%, 5-year bonds, interest compounded semiannually | 100,000 |
| Premium on bonds payable | $ 3,769 |

Using the interest method to amortize the above premium yields the amortization table in Exhibit 7. You should note the following items in this table:

1. The investers paid (Column A) remains constant at 6% of $100,000, the face amount of the bonds.

## •Exhibit 7    Amortization of Premium on Bonds Payable

| Interest Payment | A<br>Interest Paid<br>(6% of<br>Face Amount) | B<br>Interest Expense<br>(5½% of Bond<br>Carrying Amount) | C<br>Premium<br>Amortization<br>(A − B) | D<br>Unamortized<br>Premium<br>(D − C) | E<br>Bond Carrying<br>Amount<br>($100,000 + D) |
|---|---|---|---|---|---|
|  |  |  |  | $3,769 | $103,769 |
| 1 | $6,000 | $5,707 (5½% of $103,769) | $293 | 3,476 | 103,476 |
| 2 | 6,000 | 5,691 (5½% of $103,476) | 309 | 3,167 | 103,167 |
| 3 | 6,000 | 5,674 (5½% of $103,167) | 326 | 2,841 | 102,841 |
| 4 | 6,000 | 5,656 (5½% of $102,841) | 344 | 2,497 | 102,497 |
| 5 | 6,000 | 5,637 (5½% of $102,497) | 363 | 2,134 | 102,134 |
| 6 | 6,000 | 5,617 (5½% of $102,134) | 383 | 1,751 | 101,751 |
| 7 | 6,000 | 5,596 (5½% of $101,751) | 404 | 1,347 | 101,347 |
| 8 | 6,000 | 5,574 (5½% of $101,347) | 426 | 921 | 100,921 |
| 9 | 6,000 | 5,551 (5½% of $100,921) | 449 | 472 | 100,472 |
| 10 | 6,000 | 5,526 (5½% of $100,472) | 472* | — | 100,000 |

*Cannot exceed unamortized premium.

2. The interest expense (Column B) is computed at 5½% of the bond carrying amount at the beginning of each period. This results in a decreasing interest expense each period.
3. The excess of the periodic interest payment of $6,000 over the interest expense is the amount of premium to be amortized (Column C).
4. The unamortized premium (Column D) decreases from the initial balance, $3,769, to a zero balance at the maturity date of the bonds.
5. The carrying amount (Column E) decreases from $103,769, the amount received for the bonds, to $100,000 at maturity.

The entry to record the first interest payment on June 30, 2005, and the related premium amortization is as follows:

| | | | | | |
|---|---|---|---|---|---|
| 2005<br>June | 30 | Interest Expense | | 5 7 0 7 00 | |
| | | Premium on Bonds Payable | | 2 9 3 00 | |
| | | Cash | | | 6 0 0 0 00 |
| | | Paid semiannual interest and amortized | | | |
| | | bond premium for ½ year. | | | |

If the amortization is recorded only at the end of the year, the amount of the premium amortized on December 31, 2005, would be $602. This is the sum of the first two semiannual amortization amounts ($293 and $309) from Exhibit 7.

# Key Points

## 1 Compute the potential impact of long-term borrowing on the earnings per share of a corporation.

Three alternative plans for financing a corporation by issuing common stock, preferred stock, or bonds are illustrated in Exhibits 1 and 2. The effects of alternative financing on the earnings per share vary significantly, depending upon the level of earnings.

## 2 Describe the characteristics of bonds.

The characteristics of bonds depend upon the type of bonds issued by a corporation. Bonds that may be issued include term bonds, serial bonds, convertible bonds, callable bonds, and debenture bonds.

## 3 Compute the present value of bonds payable.

The concept of present value is based on the time value of money. That is, an amount of cash to be received at some date in the future is worth less than the same amount of cash held today. For example, if $100 cash today can be invested to earn 10% per year, the $100 today is referred to as the present value amount that is equal to $110 to be received a year from today.

A price that a buyer is willing to pay for a bond is the sum of (1) the present value of the face amount of the bonds at the maturity date and (2) the present value of the periodic interest payments.

## 4 Journalize entries for bonds payable.

The journal entry for issuing bonds payable debits Cash for the proceeds received and credits Bonds Payable for the face amount of the bonds. Any difference between the face amount of the bonds and the proceeds is debited to Discount on Bonds Payable or credited to Premium on Bonds Payable.

A discount or premium on bonds payable is amortized to interest expense over the life of the bonds. The entry to amortize a discount debits Interest Expense and credits Discount on Bonds Payable. The entry to amortize a premium debits Premium on Bonds Payable and credits Interest Expense.

## 5 Describe bond sinking funds.

A bond indenture may require that funds for the payment of the bonds at maturity be set aside over the life of the bonds. The amounts set aside are kept separate from other assets in a special fund called a sinking fund. A sinking fund is reported as an Investment on the balance sheet. Income from a sinking fund is reported as Other Income on the income statement.

## 6 Journalize entries for bond redemptions.

When a corporation redeems bonds, Bonds Payable is debited for the face amount of the bonds, the premium (discount) on bonds account is debited (credited) for its balance, Cash is credited, and any gain or loss on the redemption is recorded.

## 7 Journalize entries for the purchase, interest, discount and premium amortization, and sale of bond investments.

A long-term investment in bonds is recorded by debiting Investment in Bonds. When bonds are purchased between interest dates, the amount of the interest paid should be debited to Interest Revenue. Any discount or premium on bond investments should be amortized, using the straight-line or effective in-

terest rate methods. The amortization of a discount is recorded by debiting Investment in Bonds and crediting Interest Revenue. The amortization of a premium is recorded by debiting Interest Revenue and crediting Investment in Bonds.

When bonds held as long-term investments are sold, any discount or premium for the current period should first be amortized. Cash is then debited for the proceeds of the sale, Investment in Bonds is credited for its balance, and any gain or loss is recorded.

## 8 Prepare a corporation balance sheet.

The corporation balance sheet may include bond sinking funds, investments in bonds, goodwill, deferred income taxes, bonds payable and unamortized premium or discount, and minority interest in subsidiaries.

Bonds payable are usually reported as long-term liabilities. A discount on bonds should be reported as a deduction from the related bonds payable. A premium on bonds should be reported as an addition to the related bonds payable. Investments in bonds that are held-to-maturity securities are reported as Investments at cost less any amortized premium or plus any amortized discount.

## 9 Compute and interpret the number of times interest charges are earned.

The number of times interest charges are earned during the year is a measure of the risk that interest payments to debtholders will continue to be made if earnings decrease. It is computed by dividing income before income tax plus interest expense by interest expense.

# Key Terms

annuity (606)
bond (602)
bond indenture (603)
carrying amount (613)
contract rate (604)
discount (604)

effective interest rate method (610)
effective rate of interest (604)
future value (605)
held-to-maturity securities (618)
number of times interest charges
    are earned (618)

premium (604)
present value (605)
present value of an annuity (606)
sinking fund (612)

# Illustrative Problem

The fiscal year of Russell Inc., a manufacturer of acoustical supplies, ends December 31. Selected transactions for the period 2005 through 2012, involving bonds payable issued by Russell Inc., are as follows:

2005
June 30. Issued $2,000,000 of 25-year, 7% callable bonds dated June 30, 2005, for cash of $1,920,000. Interest is payable semiannually on June 30 and December 31.
Dec. 31. Paid the semiannual interest on the bonds.
    31. Recorded straight-line amortization of $1,600 of discount on the bonds.
    31. Closed the interest expense account.

2006
June 30. Paid the semiannual interest on the bonds.
Dec. 31. Paid the semiannual interest on the bonds.
    31. Recorded straight-line amortization of $3,200 of discount on the bonds.
    31. Closed the interest expense account.

2012
June 30. Recorded the redemption of the bonds, which were called at 101.5. The balance in the bond discount account is $57,600 after the payment of interest and amortization of discount have been recorded. (Record the redemption only.)

## Instructions

1. Journalize entries to record the preceding transactions.
2. Determine the amount of interest expense for 2005 and 2006.
3. Estimate the effective annual interest rate by dividing the interest expense for 2005 by the bond carrying amount at the time of issuance and multiplying by 2.
4. Determine the carrying amount of the bonds as of December 31, 2006.

## Solution

**1.**

| | | | | | |
|---|---|---|---|---|---|
| 2005 June | 30 | Cash | | 1,920 0 0 0 00 | |
| | | Discount on Bonds Payable | | 80 0 0 0 00 | |
| | | Bonds Payable | | | 2,000 0 0 0 00 |
| Dec. | 31 | Interest Expense | | 70 0 0 0 00 | |
| | | Cash | | | 70 0 0 0 00 |

*(continued)*

| | | | | | |
|---|---|---|---|---|---|
| 2005 Dec. | 31 | Interest Expense | | 1 6 0 0 00 | |
| | | Discount on Bonds Payable | | | 1 6 0 0 00 |
| | 31 | Income Summary | | 71 6 0 0 00 | |
| | | Interest Expense | | | 71 6 0 0 00 |
| 2006 June | 30 | Interest Expense | | 70 0 0 0 00 | |
| | | Cash | | | 70 0 0 0 00 |
| Dec. | 31 | Interest Expense | | 70 0 0 0 00 | |
| | | Cash | | | 70 0 0 0 00 |
| | 31 | Interest Expense | | 3 2 0 0 00 | |
| | | Discount on Bonds Payable | | | 3 2 0 0 00 |
| | 31 | Income Summary | | 143 2 0 0 00 | |
| | | Interest Expense | | | 143 2 0 0 00 |
| 2012 June | 30 | Bonds Payable | | 2,000 0 0 0 00 | |
| | | Loss on Redemption of Bonds Payable | | 87 6 0 0 00 | |
| | | Discount on Bonds Payable | | | 57 6 0 0 00 |
| | | Cash | | | 2,030 0 0 0 00 |

**2.** a. 2005—$71,600
   b. 2006—$143,200

**3.** $71,600 ÷ $1,920,000 = 3.73% rate for six months of a year
   3.73% × 2 = 7.46% annual rate

**4.**
| | |
|---|---|
| Initial carrying amount of bonds | $1,920,000 |
| Discount amortized on December 31, 2005 | 1,600 |
| Discount amortized on December 31, 2006 | 3,200 |
| Carrying amount of bonds, December 31, 2006 | $1,924,800 |

# Self-Examination Questions (Answers at End of Chapter)

1. If a corporation plans to issue $1,000,000 of 12% bonds at a time when the market rate for similar bonds is 10%, the bonds can be expected to sell at:
   A. their face amount
   B. a premium
   C. a discount
   D. a price below their face amount

2. If the bonds payable account has a balance of $500,000 and the discount on bonds payable account has a balance of $40,000, what is the carrying amount of the bonds?
   A. $460,000
   B. $500,000
   C. $540,000
   D. $580,000

3. The cash and securities that make up the sinking fund established for the payment of bonds at maturity are classified on the balance sheet as:

   A. current assets
   B. investments
   C. long-term liabilities
   D. current liabilities

4. If a firm purchases $100,000 of bonds of X Company at 101 plus accrued interest of $2,000 and pays broker's commissions of $50, the amount debited to Investment in X Company Bonds would be:
   A. $100,000
   B. $101,050
   C. $103,000
   D. $103,050

5. The balance in the discount on bonds payable account would usually be reported in the balance sheet in the:
   A. Current Assets section
   B. Current Liabilities section
   C. Long-Term Liabilities section
   D. Investments section

# Class Discussion Questions

1. Describe the two distinct obligations incurred by a corporation when issuing bonds.
2. Explain the meaning of each of the following terms as they relate to a bond issue: (a) convertible, (b) callable, and (c) debenture.
3. What is meant by the "time value of money"?
4. What has the higher present value: (a) $10,000 to be received at the end of two years, or (b) $5,000 to be received at the end of each of the next two years?
5. If you asked your broker to purchase for you a 7% bond when the market interest rate for such bonds was 8%, would you expect to pay more or less than the face amount for the bond? Explain.
6. A corporation issues $7,500,000 of 8% bonds to yield interest at the rate of 7%. (a) Was the amount of cash received from the sale of the bonds greater or less than $7,500,000? (b) Identify the following terms related to the bond issue: (1) face amount, (2) market or effective rate of interest, (3) contract rate of interest, and (4) maturity amount.
7. If bonds issued by a corporation are sold at a premium, is the market rate of interest greater or less than the contract rate?
8. The following data relate to a $1,800,000, 6% bond issue for a selected semi-annual interest period:

   | | |
   |---|---|
   | Bond carrying amount at beginning of period | $1,850,000 |
   | Interest paid during period | 108,000 |
   | Interest expense allocable to the period | 104,400 |

   (a) Were the bonds issued at a discount or at a premium? (b) What is the unamortized amount of the discount or premium account at the beginning of the period? (c) What account was debited to amortize the discount or premium?
9. Assume that Mixon Co. amortizes premiums and discounts on bonds payable at the end of the year rather than when interest is paid. What accounts would be debited and credited to record (a) the amortization of a discount on bonds payable and (b) the amortization of a premium on bonds payable?
10. Would a zero-coupon bond ever sell for its face amount?
11. What is the purpose of a bond sinking fund?
12. Assume that two 25-year, 6% bond issues are identical, except that one bond issue is callable at its face amount at the end of 5 years. Which of the two bond issues do you think will sell for a lower value?
13. Bonds Payable has a balance of $800,000, and Discount on Bonds Payable has a balance of $32,500. If the issuing corporation redeems the bonds at 97, is there a gain or loss on the bond redemption?
14. Where are investments in bonds that are classified as held-to-maturity securities reported on the balance sheet?
15. At what amount are held-to-maturity investments in bonds reported on the balance sheet?

# Exercises

**EXERCISE 15-1**
*Effect of financing on earnings per share*

**Objective 1**

✓ a. $0.48

Bridger Co., which produces and sells skiing equipment, is financed as follows:

| | |
|---|---|
| Bonds payable, 8% (issued at face amount) | $8,000,000 |
| Preferred $3 stock (nonparticipating), $50 par | 8,000,000 |
| Common stock, $40 par | 8,000,000 |

Income tax is estimated at 40% of income.

Determine the earnings per share of common stock, assuming that the income before bond interest and income tax is (a) $1,600,000, (b) $2,400,000, and (c) $4,000,000.

**EXERCISE 15-2**
*Evaluate alternative financing plans*

**Objective 1**

 Based upon the data in Exercise 15-1, discuss factors other than earnings per share that should be considered in evaluating such financing plans.

**EXERCISE 15-3**
*Corporate financing*

**Objective 1**

REAL WORLD

The financial statements for **Home Depot** are presented in Appendix E at the end of the text. What is the major source of financing for Home Depot?

**EXERCISE 15-4**
*Present value of amounts due*

**Objective 3**

Determine the present value of $100,000 to be received in three years, using an interest rate of 5%, compounded annually, as follows:

a. By successive divisions. (Round to the nearest dollar.)
b. By using the present value table in Exhibit 3.

**EXERCISE 15-5**
*Present value of annuity*

**Objective 3**

Determine the present value of $50,000 to be received at the end of each of four years, using an interest rate of 6%, compounded annually, as follows:

a. By successive computations, using the present value table in Exhibit 3.
b. By using the present value table in Exhibit 4.

**EXERCISE 15-6**
*Present value of an annuity*
Objective 3

On January 1, 2006, you win $25,000,000 in the state lottery. The $25,000,000 prize will be paid in equal installments of $1,000,000 over 25 years. The payments will be made on December 31 of each year, beginning on December 31, 2006. If the current interest rate is 6%, determine the present value of your winnings. Use the present value tables in Appendix A.

**EXERCISE 15-7**
*Present value of an annuity*
Objective 3

Assume the same data as in Exercise 15-6, except that the current interest rate is 12%.

➡ Will the present value of your winnings using an interest rate of 12% be one-half the present value of your winnings using an interest rate of 6%? Why or why not?

**EXERCISE 15-8**
*Present value of bonds payable; discount*
Objectives 3, 4

Fowler Co. produces and sells bottle capping equipment for soft drink and spring water bottlers. To finance its operations, Fowler Co. issued $12,000,000 of five-year, 8% bonds with interest payable semiannually at an effective interest rate of 12%. Determine the present value of the bonds payable, using the present value tables in Exhibits 3 and 4. Round to the nearest dollar.

**EXERCISE 15-9**
*Present value of bonds payable; premium*
Objectives 3, 4

Hallelujah Alarms Co. issued $40,000,000 of five-year, 11% bonds with interest payable semiannually, at an effective interest rate of 10%. Determine the present value of the bonds payable, using the present value tables in Exhibits 3 and 4. Round to the nearest dollar.

**EXERCISE 15-10**
*Bond price*
Objectives 3, 4

REAL WORLD

**Walt Disney** 2.125% bonds due in 2023 were reported in *The Wall Street Journal* as selling for 103.536.

➡ Were the bonds selling at a premium or at a discount? Explain.

**EXERCISE 15-11**
*Entries for issuing bonds*
Objective 4

Darigold Co. produces and distributes fiber optic cable for use by telecommunications companies. Darigold Co. issued $18,000,000 of 15-year, 7% bonds on April 1 of the current year, with interest payable on May 1 and November 1. The fiscal year of the company is the calendar year. Journalize the entries to record the following selected transactions for the current year:

May   1. Issued the bonds for cash at their face amount.
Nov.  1. Paid the interest on the bonds.
Dec. 31. Recorded accrued interest for two months.

**EXERCISE 15-12**
*Entries for issuing bonds and amortizing discount by straight-line method*
Objective 4

✓ b. $820,904

On the first day of its fiscal year, Monarch Company issued $8,000,000 of five-year, 8% bonds to finance its operations of producing and selling home electronics equipment. Interest is payable semiannually. The bonds were issued at an effective interest rate of 11%, resulting in Monarch Company receiving cash of $7,095,482.

a. Journalize the entries to record the following:
   1. Sale of the bonds.
   2. First semiannual interest payment. (Amortization of discount is to be recorded annually.)
   3. Second semiannual interest payment.
   4. Amortization of discount at the end of the first year, using the straight-line method. (Round to the nearest dollar.)
b. Determine the amount of the bond interest expense for the first year.

**EXERCISE 15-13**
*Computing bond proceeds, entries for bond issuing, and amortizing premium by straight-line method*
**Objectives 3, 4**

Snodgrass Corporation wholesales oil and grease products to equipment manufacturers. On March 1, 2006, Snodgrass Corporation issued $7,500,000 of five-year, 11% bonds at an effective interest rate of 10%. Interest is payable semiannually on March 1 and September 1. Journalize the entries to record the following:

a. Sale of bonds on March 1, 2006. (Use the tables of present values in Exhibits 3 and 4 to determine the bond proceeds. Round to the nearest dollar.)
b. First interest payment on September 1, 2006, and amortization of bond premium for six months, using the straight-line method. (Round to the nearest dollar.)

**EXERCISE 15-14**
*Entries for issuing and calling bonds; loss*
**Objectives 4, 6**

Buffalo Corp., a wholesaler of office furniture, issued $12,000,000 of 30-year, 8% callable bonds on April 1, 2006, with interest payable on April 1 and October 1. The fiscal year of the company is the calendar year. Journalize the entries to record the following selected transactions:

2006
Apr. 1.  Issued the bonds for cash at their face amount.
Oct. 1.  Paid the interest on the bonds.
2010
Oct. 1.  Called the bond issue at 102, the rate provided in the bond indenture. (Omit entry for payment of interest.)

**EXERCISE 15-15**
*Entries for issuing and calling bonds; gain*
**Objectives 4, 6**

Safeguard Corp. produces and sells automotive and aircraft safety belts. To finance its operations, Safeguard Corp. issued $18,000,000 of 25-year, 9% callable bonds on January 1, 2006, with interest payable on January 1 and July 1. The fiscal year of the company is the calendar year. Journalize the entries to record the following selected transactions:

2006
Jan. 1.  Issued the bonds for cash at their face amount.
July 1.  Paid the interest on the bonds.
2012
July 1.  Called the bond issue at 97, the rate provided in the bond indenture. (Omit entry for payment of interest.)

**EXERCISE 15-16**
*Reporting bonds*
**Objectives 5, 6, 8**

**WHAT'S WRONG WITH THIS?**

At the beginning of the current year, two bond issues (X and Y) were outstanding. During the year, bond issue X was redeemed and a significant loss on the redemption of bonds was reported as an extraordinary item on the income statement. At the end of the year, bond issue Y was reported as a current liability because its maturity date was early in the following year. A sinking fund of cash and securities sufficient to pay the series Y bonds was reported in the balance sheet as *Investments*. Identify the flaws in the reporting practices related to the two bond issues.

**EXERCISE 15-17**
*Amortizing discount on bond investment*
**Objective 7**

A company purchased a $1,000, 20-year zero-coupon bond for $189 to yield 8.5% to maturity. How is the interest revenue computed?

**EXERCISE 15-18**
*Entries for purchase and sale of investment in bonds; loss*
**Objective 7**

Laser Vision Co. sells optical supplies to opticians and ophthalmologists. Journalize the entries to record the following selected transactions of Laser Vision Co.:

a. Purchased for cash $450,000 of Pierce Co. 8% bonds at 101½ plus accrued interest of $9,000.
b. Received first semiannual interest.
c. At the end of the first year, amortized $540 of the bond premium.
d. Sold the bonds at 99 plus accrued interest of $3,000. The bonds were carried at $453,750 at the time of the sale.

**EXERCISE 15-19**
*Entries for purchase and sale of investment in bonds; gain*

**Objective 7**

Inez Company develops and sells graphics software for use by architects. Journalize the entries to record the following selected transactions of Inez Company:

a. Purchased for cash $270,000 of Theisen Co. 5% bonds at 98 plus accrued interest of $2,250.
b. Received first semiannual interest.
c. Amortized $450 on the bond investment at the end of the first year.
d. Sold the bonds at 100 plus accrued interest of $4,500. The bonds were carried at $267,250 at the time of the sale.

**EXERCISE 15-20**
*Number of times interest charges earned*

**Objective 9**

REAL WORLD

The following data were taken from recent annual reports of **Southwest Airlines**, which operates a low-fare airline service to over 50 cities in the U.S.

|  | Current Year | Preceding Year |
|---|---|---|
| Interest expense | $106,023,000 | $ 69,827,000 |
| Income before income tax | 392,682,000 | 827,659,000 |

a. Determine the number of times interest charges were earned for the current and preceding years. Round to one decimal place.
b. What conclusions can you draw?

**APPENDIX EXERCISE 15-21**
*Amortize discount by interest method*

✓ b. $784,367

On the first day of its fiscal year, Monarch Company issued $8,000,000 of five-year, 8% bonds to finance its operations of producing and selling home electronics equipment. Interest is payable semiannually. The bonds were issued at an effective interest rate of 11%, resulting in Monarch Company receiving cash of $7,095,482.

a. Journalize the entries to record the following:
  1. Sale of the bonds.
  2. First semiannual interest payment. (Amortization of discount is to be recorded annually.)
  3. Second semiannual interest payment.
  4. Amortization of discount at the end of the first year, using the interest method. (Round to the nearest dollar.)
b. Compute the amount of the bond interest expense for the first year.

**APPENDIX EXERCISE 15-22**
*Amortize premium by interest method*

✓ b. $777,803

Snodgrass Corporation wholesales oil and grease products to equipment manufacturers. On March 1, 2006, Snodgrass Corporation issued $7,500,000 of five-year, 11% bonds at an effective interest rate of 10%, receiving cash of $7,789,543. Interest is payable semiannually on March 1 and September 1. Snodgrass Corporation's fiscal year begins on March 1.

a. Journalize the entries to record the following:
  1. First interest payment on September 1, 2006. (Amortization of premium is to be recorded annually.)
  2. Second interest payment on March 1, 2007.
  3. Amortization of premium at the end of the first year, using the interest method. (Round to the nearest dollar.)
b. Determine the bond interest expense for the first year.

**APPENDIX EXERCISE 15-23**
*Compute bond proceeds, amortizing premium by interest method, and interest expense*

✓ a. $33,724,853
✓ b. $95,133

Federated Paint Co. produces and sells spray painting equipment for construction contractors. On the first day of its fiscal year, Federated Paint Co. issued $32,500,000 of five-year, 12% bonds at an effective interest rate of 11%, with interest payable semiannually. Compute the following, presenting figures used in your computations.

a. The amount of cash proceeds from the sale of the bonds. (Use the tables of present values in Exhibits 3 and 4. Round to the nearest dollar.)
b. The amount of premium to be amortized for the first semiannual interest payment period, using the interest method. (Round to the nearest dollar.)

*(continued)*

c. The amount of premium to be amortized for the second semiannual interest payment period, using the interest method. (Round to the nearest dollar.)

d. The amount of the bond interest expense for the first year.

**APPENDIX
EXERCISE 15-24**
*Compute bond proceeds,
amortizing discount by
interest method, and
interest expense*

✓ a. $16,212,079
✓ b. $97,725

La Porte Co. produces and sells concrete mixing equipment. On the first day of its fiscal year, La Porte Co. issued $17,500,000 of five-year, 10% bonds at an effective interest rate of 12%, with interest payable semiannually. Compute the following, presenting figures used in your computations.

a. The amount of cash proceeds from the sale of the bonds. (Use the tables of present values in Exhibits 3 and 4.)

b. The amount of discount to be amortized for the first semiannual interest payment period, using the interest method. (Round to the nearest dollar.)

c. The amount of discount to be amortized for the second semiannual interest payment period, using the interest method. (Round to the nearest dollar.)

d. The amount of the bond interest expense for the first year.

# Problems Series A

**PROBLEM 15-1A**
*Effect of financing on
earnings per share*
**Objective 1**

SPREADSHEET

✓ 1. Plan 3: $8.10

Three different plans for financing a $20,000,000 corporation are under consideration by its organizers. Under each of the following plans, the securities will be issued at their par or face amount, and the income tax rate is estimated at 40% of income.

|  | Plan 1 | Plan 2 | Plan 3 |
|---|---|---|---|
| 10% bonds |  |  | $10,000,000 |
| Preferred 6% stock, $100 par |  | $10,000,000 | 5,000,000 |
| Common stock, $5 par | $20,000,000 | 10,000,000 | 5,000,000 |
| Total | $20,000,000 | $20,000,000 | $20,000,000 |

**Instructions**

1. Determine for each plan the earnings per share of common stock, assuming that the income before bond interest and income tax is $15,000,000.

2. Determine for each plan the earnings per share of common stock, assuming that the income before bond interest and income tax is $1,600,000.

3. ▱▱▱▱▷ Discuss the advantages and disadvantages of each plan.

**PROBLEM 15-2A**
*Present value; bond
premium; entries for bonds
payable transactions*
**Objectives 3, 4**

P.A.S.S.

✓ 3. $483,920

Rest-In-Peace Corporation produces and sells burial vaults. On July 1, 2006, Rest-In-Peace Corporation issued $9,000,000 of ten-year, 12% bonds at an effective interest rate of 10%. Interest on the bonds is payable semiannually on December 31 and June 30. The fiscal year of the company is the calendar year.

**Instructions**

1. Journalize the entry to record the amount of the cash proceeds from the sale of the bonds. Use the tables of present values in Appendix A to compute the cash proceeds, rounding to the nearest dollar.

2. Journalize the entries to record the following:

a. The first semiannual interest payment on December 31, 2006, and the amortization of the bond premium, using the straight-line method. (Round to the nearest dollar.)

b. The interest payment on June 30, 2007, and the amortization of the bond premium, using the straight-line method.

3. Determine the total interest expense for 2006.

4. ▱▱▱▱▷ Will the bond proceeds always be greater than the face amount of the bonds when the contract rate is greater than the market rate of interest? Explain.

**PROBLEM 15-3A**
*Present value; bond discount; entries for bonds payable transactions*

**Objectives 3, 4**

P.A.S.S.

✓ 3. $668,822

On July 1, 2005, Westwind Corporation, a wholesaler of used robotic equipment, issued $12,000,000 of ten-year, 10% bonds at an effective interest rate of 12%. Interest on the bonds is payable semiannually on December 31 and June 30. The fiscal year of the company is the calendar year.

**Instructions**

1. Journalize the entry to record the amount of the cash proceeds from the sale of the bonds. Use the tables of present values in Appendix A to compute the cash proceeds, rounding to the nearest dollar.
2. Journalize the entries to record the following:
   a. The first semiannual interest payment on December 31, 2005, and the amortization of the bond discount, using the straight-line method. (Round to the nearest dollar.)
   b. The interest payment on June 30, 2006, and the amortization of the bond discount, using the straight-line method.
3. Determine the total interest expense for 2005.
4. ▭▶ Will the bond proceeds always be less than the face amount of the bonds when the contract rate is less than the market rate of interest? Explain.

**PROBLEM 15-4A**
*Entries for bonds payable transactions*

**Objectives 4, 6**

SPREADSHEET
P.A.S.S.

✓ 2. a. $381,776

The following transactions were completed by Prairie Renaissance Inc., whose fiscal year is the calendar year:

2005
July    1. Issued $8,000,000 of 5-year, 8% callable bonds dated July 1, 2005, at an effective rate of 10%, receiving cash of $7,382,236. Interest is payable semiannually on December 31 and June 30.
Dec. 31. Paid the semiannual interest on the bonds.
     31. Recorded bond discount amortization of $61,776, which was determined by using the straight-line method.
     31. Closed the interest expense account.

2006
June 30. Paid the semiannual interest on the bonds.
Dec. 31. Paid the semiannual interest on the bonds.
     31. Recorded bond discount amortization of $123,552, which was determined by using the straight-line method.
     31. Closed the interest expense account.

2007
June 30. Recorded the redemption of the bonds, which were called at 99. The balance in the bond discount account is $370,660 after payment of interest and amortization of discount have been recorded. (Record the redemption only.)

**Instructions**

1. Journalize the entries to record the foregoing transactions.
2. Indicate the amount of the interest expense in (a) 2005 and (b) 2006.
3. Determine the carrying amount of the bonds as of December 31, 2006.

**PROBLEM 15-5A**
*Entries for bond investments*

**Objective 7**

SPREADSHEET
P.A.S.S.

Danka Inc. develops and leases databases of publicly available information. The following selected transactions relate to certain securities acquired as a long-term investment by Danka Inc., whose fiscal year ends on December 31:

2005
Sept.  1. Purchased $480,000 of Sheehan Company 10-year, 8% bonds dated July 1, 2005, directly from the issuing company, for $494,750 plus accrued interest of $6,400.
Dec. 31. Received the semiannual interest on the Sheehan Company bonds.
     31. Recorded bond premium amortization of $500 on the Sheehan Company bonds. The amortization amount was determined by using the straight-line method.

(Assume that all intervening transactions and adjustments have been properly recorded and that the number of bonds owned has not changed from December 31, 2005, to December 31, 2010.)

2011
June 30. Received the semiannual interest on the Sheehan Company bonds.
Aug. 31. Sold one-half of the Sheehan Company bonds at 102 plus accrued interest. The broker deducted $400 for commission, etc., remitting the balance. Prior to the sale, $500 of premium on one-half of the bonds is to be amortized, reducing the carrying amount of those bonds to $242,875.
Dec. 31. Received the semiannual interest on the Sheehan Company bonds.
   31. Recorded bond premium amortization of $750 on the Sheehan Company bonds.

**Instructions**
Journalize the entries to record the foregoing transactions.

**APPENDIX PROBLEM 15-6A**
*Entries for bonds payable transactions; interest method of amortizing bond premium*

✓ 2. $506,080

Rest-In-Peace Corporation produces and sells burial vaults. On July 1, 2006, Rest-In-Peace Corporation issued $9,000,000 of ten-year, 12% bonds at an effective interest rate of 10%, receiving proceeds of $10,121,603. Interest on the bonds is payable semiannually on December 31 and June 30. The fiscal year of the company is the calendar year.

**Instructions**
1. Journalize the entries to record the following:
   a. The first semiannual interest payment on December 31, 2006, and the amortization of the bond premium, using the interest method. (Round to nearest dollar.)
   b. The interest payment on June 30, 2007, and the amortization of the bond premium, using the interest method. (Round to nearest dollar.)
2. Determine the total interest expense for 2006.

**APPENDIX PROBLEM 15-7A**
*Entries for bonds payable transactions; interest method of amortizing bond discount*

✓ 2. $637,413

On July 1, 2005, Westwind Corporation, a wholesaler of used robotic equipment, issued $12,000,000 of ten-year, 10% bonds at an effective interest rate of 12%, receiving proceeds of $10,623,552. Interest on the bonds is payable semiannually on December 31 and June 30. The fiscal year of the company is the calendar year.

**Instructions**
1. Journalize the entries to record the following:
   a. The first semiannual interest payment on December 31, 2005, and the amortization of the bond discount, using the interest method. (Round to nearest dollar.)
   b. The interest payment on June 30, 2006, and the amortization of the bond discount, using the interest method. (Round to nearest dollar.)
2. Determine the total interest expense for 2005.

# Problems Series

**PROBLEM 15-1B**
*Effect of financing on earnings per share*
**Objective 1**

SPREADSHEET

✓ 1. Plan 3: $2.60

Three different plans for financing a $27,000,000 corporation are under consideration by its organizers. Under each of the following plans, the securities will be issued at their par or face amount, and the income tax rate is estimated at 40% of income.

|  | Plan 1 | Plan 2 | Plan 3 |
|---|---|---|---|
| 12% bonds |  |  | $11,250,000 |
| Preferred $4 stock, $50 par |  | $13,500,000 | 9,000,000 |
| Common stock, $15 par | $27,000,000 | 13,500,000 | 6,750,000 |
| Total | $27,000,000 | $27,000,000 | $27,000,000 |

## Instructions

1. Determine for each plan the earnings per share of common stock, assuming that the income before bond interest and income tax is $4,500,000.
2. Determine for each plan the earnings per share of common stock, assuming that the income before bond interest and income tax is $2,700,000.
3.  Discuss the advantages and disadvantages of each plan.

---

**PROBLEM 15-2B**

*Present value; bond premium; entries for bonds payable transactions*

**Objectives 3, 4**

P.A.S.S.

✓ 3. $1,037,688

Frontier Inc. produces and sells voltage regulators. On July 1, 2005, Frontier Inc. issued $20,000,000 of ten-year, 11% bonds at an effective interest rate of 10%. Interest on the bonds is payable semiannually on December 31 and June 30. The fiscal year of the company is the calendar year.

### Instructions

1. Journalize the entry to record the amount of the cash proceeds from the sale of the bonds. Use the tables of present values in Appendix A to compute the cash proceeds, rounding to the nearest dollar.
2. Journalize the entries to record the following:
   a. The first semiannual interest payment on December 31, 2005, including the amortization of the bond premium, using the straight-line method.
   b. The interest payment on June 30, 2006, and the amortization of the bond premium, using the straight-line method.
3. Determine the total interest expense for 2005.
4.  Will the bond proceeds always be greater than the face amount of the bonds when the contract rate is greater than the market rate of interest? Explain.

---

**PROBLEM 15-3B**

*Present value; bond discount; entries for bonds payable transactions*

**Objectives 3, 4**

P.A.S.S.

✓ 3. $866,080

On July 1, 2005, Lamar Communications Equipment Inc. issued $18,000,000 of ten-year, 9% bonds at an effective interest rate of 10%. Interest on the bonds is payable semiannually on December 31 and June 30. The fiscal year of the company is the calendar year.

### Instructions

1. Journalize the entry to record the amount of the cash proceeds from the sale of the bonds. Use the tables of present values in Appendix A to compute the cash proceeds, rounding to the nearest dollar.
2. Journalize the entries to record the following:
   a. The first semiannual interest payment on December 31, 2005, and the amortization of the bond discount, using the straight-line method. (Round to the nearest dollar.)
   b. The interest payment on June 30, 2006, and the amortization of the bond discount, using the straight-line method.
3. Determine the total interest expense for 2005.
4.  Will the bond proceeds always be less than the face amount of the bonds when the contract rate is less than the market rate of interest? Explain.

---

**PROBLEM 15-4B**

*Entries for bonds payable transactions*

**Objectives 4, 6**

SPREADSHEET
P.A.S.S.

✓ 2. a. $939,591

Absaroka Co. produces and sells synthetic string for tennis rackets. The following transactions were completed by Absaroka Co., whose fiscal year is the calendar year:

2005
July   1. Issued $15,000,000 of 5-year, 14% callable bonds dated July 1, 2005, at an effective rate of 12%, receiving cash of $16,104,095. Interest is payable semiannually on December 31 and June 30.
Dec. 31. Paid the semiannual interest on the bonds.
      31. Recorded bond premium amortization of $110,409, which was determined by using the straight-line method.
      31. Closed the interest expense account.
2006
June 30. Paid the semiannual interest on the bonds.
Dec. 31. Paid the semiannual interest on the bonds.

Dec. 31. Recorded bond premium amortization of $220,818, which was determined by using the straight-line method.

31. Closed the interest expense account.

2007

July 1. Recorded the redemption of the bonds, which were called at 101. The balance in the bond premium account is $662,459 after the payment of interest and amortization of premium have been recorded. (Record the redemption only.)

**Instructions**

1. Journalize the entries to record the foregoing transactions.
2. Indicate the amount of the interest expense in (a) 2005 and (b) 2006.
3. Determine the carrying amount of the bonds as of December 31, 2006.

**PROBLEM 15-5B**
*Entries for bond investments*

**Objective 7**

SPREADSHEET
P.A.S.S.

The following selected transactions relate to certain securities acquired by Wildflower Blueprints Inc., whose fiscal year ends on December 31:

2005

Sept. 1. Purchased $400,000 of Churchill Company 20-year, 9% bonds dated July 1, 2005, directly from the issuing company, for $385,720 plus accrued interest of $6,000.

Dec. 31. Received the semiannual interest on the Churchill Company bonds.

31. Recorded bond discount amortization of $240 on the Churchill Company bonds. The amortization amount was determined by using the straight-line method.

(Assume that all intervening transactions and adjustments have been properly recorded and that the number of bonds owned has not changed from December 31, 2005, to December 31, 2009.)

2010

June 30. Received the semiannual interest on the Churchill Company bonds.

Oct. 31. Sold one-half of the Churchill Company bonds at 96½ plus accrued interest. The broker deducted $400 for commission, etc., remitting the balance. Prior to the sale, $300 of discount on one-half of the bonds was amortized, reducing the carrying amount of those bonds to $194,720.

Dec. 31. Received the semiannual interest on the Churchill Company bonds.

31. Recorded bond discount amortization of $360 on the Churchill Company bonds.

**Instructions**

Journalize the entries to record the foregoing transactions.

**APPENDIX PROBLEM 15-6B**
*Entries for bonds payable transactions; interest method of amortizing bond premium*

✓ 2. $1,062,312

Frontier Inc. produces and sells voltage regulators. On July 1, 2005, Frontier Inc. issued $20,000,000 of ten-year, 11% bonds at an effective interest rate of 10%, receiving proceeds of $21,246,231. Interest on the bonds is payable semiannually on December 31 and June 30. The fiscal year of the company is the calendar year.

**Instructions**

1. Journalize the entries to record the following:
   a. The first semiannual interest payment on December 31, 2005, and the amortization of the bond premium, using the interest method. (Round to nearest dollar.)
   b. The interest payment on June 30, 2006, and the amortization of the bond premium, using the interest method. (Round to nearest dollar.)
2. Determine the total interest expense for 2005.

**APPENDIX PROBLEM 15-7B**
*Entries for bonds payable transactions; interest method of amortizing bond discount*

On July 1, 2005, Lamar Communications Equipment Inc. issued $18,000,000 of ten-year, 9% bonds at an effective interest rate of 10%, receiving proceeds of $16,878,410. Interest on the bonds is payable semiannually on December 31 and June 30. The fiscal year of the company is the calendar year.

√2. $843,921

**Instructions**
1. Journalize the entries to record the following:
   a. The first semiannual interest payment on December 31, 2005, and the amortization of the bond discount, using the interest method.
   b. The interest payment on June 30, 2006, and the amortization of the bond discount, using the interest method.
2. Determine the total interest expense for 2005.

# Comprehensive Problem 4

√2.a. Net income, $177,800

Selected transactions completed by Hubcap Products Inc. during the fiscal year ending July 31, 2006, were as follows:

a. Issued 10,000 shares of $25 par common stock at $52, receiving cash.
b. Issued 8,000 shares of $100 par preferred 8% stock at $125, receiving cash.
c. Issued $12,000,000 of 10-year, 11% bonds at an effective interest rate of 10%, with interest payable semiannually. Use the present value tables in Appendix A to determine the bond proceeds. Round to the nearest dollar.
d. Declared a dividend of $0.25 per share on common stock and $2 per share on preferred stock. On the date of record, 100,000 shares of common stock were outstanding, no treasury shares were held, and 15,000 shares of preferred stock were outstanding.
e. Paid the cash dividends declared in (d).
f. Redeemed $400,000 of 8-year, 12% bonds at 101. The balance in the bond premium account is $4,920 after the payment of interest and amortization of premium have been recorded. (Record only the redemption of the bonds payable.)
g. Purchased 5,000 shares of treasury common stock at $50 per share.
h. Declared a 2% stock dividend on common stock and a $2 cash dividend per share on preferred stock. On the date of declaration, the market value of the common stock was $51 per share. On the date of record, 100,000 shares of common stock had been issued, 5,000 shares of treasury common stock were held, and 15,000 shares of preferred stock had been issued.
i. Issued the stock certificates for the stock dividends declared in (h) and paid the cash dividends to the preferred stockholders.
j. Purchased $120,000 of Athens Sports Inc. 10-year, 15% bonds, directly from the issuing company, for $116,400 plus accrued interest of $4,500.
k. Sold, at $58 per share, 3,000 shares of treasury common stock purchased in (g).
l. Recorded the payment of semiannual interest on the bonds issued in (c) and the amortization of the premium for six months. The amortization was determined using the straight-line method. (Round the amortization to the nearest dollar.)
m. Accrued interest for four months on the Athens Sports Inc. bonds purchased in (j). Also recorded amortization of $120.

**Instructions**
1. Journalize the selected transactions.
2. After all of the transactions for the year ended July 31, 2006, had been posted (including the transactions recorded in (1) and all adjusting entries), the data on the following page were taken from the records of Hubcap Products Inc.
   a. Prepare a multiple-step income statement for the year ended July 31, 2006, concluding with earnings per share. In computing earnings per share, assume that the average number of common shares outstanding was 100,000 and preferred dividends were $105,000. Round earnings per share to the nearest cent.
   b. Prepare a retained earnings statement for the year ended July 31, 2006.
   c. Prepare a balance sheet in report form as of July 31, 2006.

**Income statement data:**

| | |
|---|---:|
| Advertising expense | $ 120,000 |
| Cost of merchandise sold | 2,799,000 |
| Delivery expense | 27,000 |
| Depreciation expense—office buildings and equipment | 20,000 |
| Depreciation expense—store buildings and equipment | 72,000 |
| Gain on redemption of bonds | 920 |
| Income tax: | |
|   Applicable to continuing operations | 198,007 |
|     Applicable to loss from discontinued operations | 80,000 |
|     Applicable to gain from redemption of bonds | 120 |
| Interest expense | 622,613 |
| Interest revenue | 1,620 |
| Loss from discontinued operations | 200,000 |
| Loss from fixed asset impairment | 150,000 |
| Miscellaneous administrative expenses | 6,000 |
| Miscellaneous selling expenses | 11,000 |
| Office rent expense | 40,000 |
| Office salaries expense | 136,000 |
| Office supplies expense | 8,000 |
| Restructuring charges | 75,000 |
| Sales | 5,040,000 |
| Sales commissions | 156,000 |
| Sales salaries expense | 288,000 |
| Store supplies expense | 16,000 |

**Retained earnings and balance sheet data:**

| | |
|---|---:|
| Accounts payable | $ 175,000 |
| Accounts receivable | 450,000 |
| Accumulated depreciation—office buildings and equipment | 1,336,520 |
| Accumulated depreciation—store buildings and equipment | 3,543,000 |
| Allowance for doubtful accounts | 35,000 |
| Bonds payable, 11%, due 2016 | 12,000,000 |
| Cash | 200,000 |
| Common stock, $25 par (400,000 shares authorized; | |
|   101,900 shares outstanding) | 2,547,500 |
| Deferred income tax payable (current portion, $7,500) | 41,100 |
| Dividends: | |
|   Cash dividends for common stock | 55,000 |
|   Cash dividends for preferred stock | 105,000 |
|   Stock dividends for common stock | 96,900 |
| Dividends payable | 30,000 |
| Employee termination obligation (current) | 65,000 |
| Goodwill | 432,000 |
| Income tax payable | 32,000 |
| Interest receivable | 6,000 |
| Investment in Athens Sports Inc. bonds (long-term) | 116,520 |
| Merchandise inventory (July 31, 2006), at lower of | |
|   cost (fifo) or market | 680,000 |
| Notes receivable | 125,000 |
| Office buildings and equipment | 5,930,000 |
| Paid-in capital from sale of treasury stock | 24,000 |
| Paid-in capital in excess of par—common stock | 560,000 |
| Paid-in capital in excess of par—preferred stock | 240,000 |
| Preferred 8% stock, $100 par (30,000 shares authorized; | |
|   15,000 shares issued) | 1,500,000 |
| Premium on bonds payable | 710,352 |
| Prepaid expenses | 25,000 |
| Retained earnings, August 1, 2005 | 1,754,148 |
| Store buildings and equipment | 16,450,000 |
| Treasury stock (2,000 shares of common stock at cost | |
|   of $50 per share) | 100,000 |

# Special Activities

**ACTIVITY 15-1**
*Business strategy*

GROUP ACTIVITY    INTERNET

One reason that **PepsiCo**® purchased **Quaker Oats** in 2001 was to acquire rights to its sports drink, Gatorade. However, Gatorade is under increasing pressure from its competitors, including **Coca-Cola**'s Powerade®. As a result, PepsiCo is initiating an aggressive advertising campaign to promote and grow sales of Gatorade.

In groups of three or four, answer the following questions:

1. Go to the Gatorade Web site, which is linked to the text's Web site at **http://warren.swlearning.com**. (a) How and why was Gatorade developed? (b) What is Gatorade's share of the sports-drink market?
2. Drinks can be labeled as sports, lifestyle, or active thirst drinks. (a) How would you describe each of these drink labels? (b) Give an example of what you would label a sports, lifestyle, and active thirst drink.
3. Do you think PepsiCo's advertising campaign will focus on Gatorade as a sports, lifestyle, or active thirst drink? Explain.

**ACTIVITY 15-2**
*General Electric bond issuance*

ETHICS

**General Electric Capital**, a division of **General Electric**, uses long-term debt extensively. In early 2002, GE Capital issued $11 billion in long-term debt to investors, then within days filed legal documents to prepare for another $50 billion long-term debt issue. As a result of the $50 billion filing, the price of the initial $11 billion offering declined (due to higher risk of more debt).

*Bill Gross, a manager of a bond investment fund, "denounced a 'lack in candor' related to GE's recent debt deal. 'It was the most recent and most egregious example of how bondholders are mistreated.' Gross argued that GE was not forthright when GE Capital recently issued $11 billion in bonds, one of the largest issues ever from a U.S. corporation. What bothered Gross is that three days after the issue the company announced its intention to sell as much as $50 billion in additional debt, warrants, preferred stock, guarantees, letters of credit and promissory notes at some future date."*

In your opinion, did GE Capital act unethically by selling $11 billion of long-term debt without telling those investors that a few days later it would be filing documents to prepare for another $50 billion debt offering?

**Source:** Jennifer Ablan, "Gross Shakes the Bond Market; GE Calms It, a Bit," *Barron's*, March 25, 2002.

**ACTIVITY 15-3**
*Ethics and professional conduct in business*

ETHICS

Whoosh Inc. produces and sells water slides for theme parks. Whoosh Inc. has outstanding a $40,000,000, 25-year, 10% debenture bond issue dated July 1, 2001. The bond issue is due June 30, 2026. The bond indenture requires a sinking fund, which has a balance of $5,000,000 as of July 1, 2006. Whoosh Inc. is currently experiencing a shortage of funds due to a recent plant expansion. Terry Holter, treasurer of Whoosh Inc., has suggested using the sinking fund cash to temporarily relieve the shortage of funds. Terry's brother-in-law, who is trustee of the sinking fund, is willing to loan Whoosh Inc. the necessary funds from the sinking fund.

Discuss whether Terry Holter is behaving in a professional manner.

**ACTIVITY 15-4**
*Present values*

Nevin's Distributors Inc. is a wholesaler of oriental rugs. The following is a luncheon conversation between Pat Cameron, the assistant controller, and Cindy Bakke, an assistant financial analyst for Nevin's.

*Cindy:* Pat, do you mind if I spoil your lunch and ask you an accounting question?
*Pat:* No, go ahead. This chicken salad sandwich is pretty bad. It smells like it's three days old, and I've already picked three bones out of it.

*Cindy:* Well, as you know, in finance we use present values for capital budgeting analysis, assessing financing alternatives, etc. It's probably the most important concept that I learned in school that I actually use.

*Pat:* So . . . ?

*Cindy:* I was just wondering why accountants don't use present values more.

*Pat:* What do you mean?

*Cindy:* Well, it seems to me that you ought to value all the balance sheet liabilities at their present values.

How would you respond if you were Pat?

**ACTIVITY 15-5**
*Preferred stock vs. bonds*

Beacon Inc. has decided to expand its operations to owning and operating theme parks. The following is an excerpt from a conversation between the chief executive officer, Tracy Gaddis, and the vice-president of finance, Jeff Poulsen.

*Tracy:* Jeff, have you given any thought to how we're going to finance the acquisition of Extreme Fun Corporation?

*Jeff:* Well, the two basic options, as I see it, are to issue either preferred stock or bonds. The equity market is a little depressed right now. The rumor is that the Federal Reserve Bank's going to increase the interest rates either this month or next.

*Tracy:* Yes, I've heard the rumor. The problem is that we can't wait around to see what's going to happen. We'll have to move on this next week if we want any chance to complete the acquisition of Extreme Fun.

*Jeff:* Well, the bond market is strong right now. Maybe we should issue debt this time around.

*Tracy:* That's what I would have guessed as well. Extreme Fun's financial statements look pretty good, except for the volatility of its income and cash flows. But that's characteristic of the industry.

Discuss the advantages and disadvantages of issuing preferred stock versus bonds.

**ACTIVITY 15-6**
*Investing in bonds*

**GROUP ACTIVITY**

Select a bond from listings that appear daily in *The Wall Street Journal*, and summarize the information related to the bond you select. Include the following information in your summary:

1. Contract rate of interest
2. Year when the bond matures
3. Current yield (effective rate of interest)
4. Closing price of bond (indicate date)
5. Other information noted about the bond, such as whether it is a zero-coupon bond (see the Explanatory Notes to the listings)

In groups of three or four, share the information you developed about the bond you selected. As a group, select one bond to invest $100,000 in and prepare a justification for your choice for presentation to the class. For example, your justification should include a consideration of risk and return.

**ACTIVITY 15-7**
*Financing business expansion*

You hold a 25% common stock interest in the family-owned business, a soft drink bottling distributorship. Your sister, who is the manager, has proposed an expansion of plant facilities at an expected cost of $10,000,000. Two alternative plans have been suggested as methods of financing the expansion. Each plan is briefly described as follows:

Plan 1. Issue $10,000,000 of 20-year, 8% notes at face amount.
Plan 2. Issue an additional 140,000 shares of $10 par common stock at $25 per share, and $6,500,000 of 20-year, 8% notes at face amount.

The balance sheet as of the end of the previous fiscal year is as follows:

**North Star Bottling Co.**
**Balance Sheet**
**December 31, 2006**

### Assets

| | |
|---|---:|
| Current assets . . . . . . . . . . . . . . . . . . . . . . . . . . . . . . . . . . . . . . . . . . . . . . . | $ 4,700,000 |
| Property, plant, and equipment . . . . . . . . . . . . . . . . . . . . . . . . . . . . . . . . . . . | 10,300,000 |
| Total assets . . . . . . . . . . . . . . . . . . . . . . . . . . . . . . . . . . . . . . . . . . . . . | $15,000,000 |

### Liabilities and Stockholders' Equity

| | |
|---|---:|
| Liabilities . . . . . . . . . . . . . . . . . . . . . . . . . . . . . . . . . . . . . . . . . . . . . . . . . | $ 4,000,000 |
| Common stock, $10 . . . . . . . . . . . . . . . . . . . . . . . . . . . . . . . . . . . . . . . . . . . | 1,600,000 |
| Paid-in capital in excess of par . . . . . . . . . . . . . . . . . . . . . . . . . . . . . . . . . . | 160,000 |
| Retained earnings . . . . . . . . . . . . . . . . . . . . . . . . . . . . . . . . . . . . . . . . . . . . | 9,240,000 |
| Total liabilities and stockholders' equity . . . . . . . . . . . . . . . . . . . . . . . . . | $15,000,000 |

Net income has remained relatively constant over the past several years. The expansion program is expected to increase yearly income before bond interest and income tax from $1,000,000 in the previous year to $1,400,000 for this year. Your sister has asked you, as the company treasurer, to prepare an analysis of each financing plan.

1. Prepare a table indicating the expected earnings per share on the common stock under each plan. Assume an income tax rate of 40%.
2. a.  Discuss the factors that should be considered in evaluating the two plans.
   b.  Which plan offers the greater benefit to the present stockholders? Give reasons for your opinion.

**ACTIVITY 15-8**
*Bond ratings*

**REAL WORLD**    **INTERNET**

**Moody's Investors Service** maintains a Web site at **http://www.Moodys.com**. One of the services offered at this site is a listing of announcements of recent bond rating changes. Visit this site and read over some of these announcements. Write down several of the reasons provided for rating downgrades and upgrades. If you were a bond investor or bond issuer, would you care if Moody's changed the rating on your bonds? Why or why not?

# nswers to Self-Examination Questions

1. **B**  Since the contract rate on the bonds is higher than the prevailing market rate, a rational investor would be willing to pay more than the face amount, or a premium (answer B), for the bonds. If the contract rate and the market rate were equal, the bonds could be expected to sell at their face amount (answer A). Likewise, if the market rate is higher than the contract rate, the bonds would sell at a price below their face amount (answer D) or at a discount (answer C).

2. **A**  The bond carrying amount is the face amount plus unamortized premium or less unamortized discount. For this question, the carrying amount is $500,000 less $40,000, or $460,000 (answer A).

3. **B**  Although the sinking fund may consist of cash as well as securities, the fund is listed on the balance sheet as an investment (answer B) because it is to be used to pay the long-term liability at maturity.

4. **B**  The amount debited to the investment account is the cost of the bonds, which includes the amount paid to the seller for the bonds (101% × $100,000) plus broker's commissions ($50), or $101,050 (answer B). The $2,000 of accrued interest that is paid to the seller should be debited to Interest Revenue, since it is an offset against the amount that will be received as interest at the next interest date.

5. **C**  The balance of Discount on Bonds Payable is usually reported as a deduction from Bonds Payable in the Long-Term Liabilities section (answer C) of the balance sheet. Likewise, a balance in a premium on bonds payable account would usually be reported as an addition to Bonds Payable in the Long-Term Liabilities section of the balance sheet.

# 16

# STATEMENT OF CASH FLOWS

## objectives

*After studying this chapter, you should be able to:*

**1** Summarize the types of cash flow activities reported in the statement of cash flows.

**2** Prepare a statement of cash flows, using the indirect method.

**3** Prepare a statement of cash flows, using the direct method.

**4** Calculate and interpret the free cash flow.

How much cash do you have in the bank or in your wallet or purse? How much cash did you have at the beginning of the month? The difference between these two amounts is the net change in your cash during the month. Knowing the reasons for the change in cash may be useful in evaluating whether your financial position has improved and whether you will be able to pay your bills in the future.

For example, assume that you had $200 at the beginning of the month and $550 at the end of the month. The net change in cash is $350. Based on this net change, it appears that your financial position has improved. However, this conclusion may or may not be valid, depending upon how the change of $350 was created. If you borrowed $1,000 during the month and spent $650 on living expenses, your cash would have increased by $350 by living off borrowed funds. On the other hand, if you earned $1,000 and spent $650 on living expenses, your cash would have also increased by $350, but your financial position is improved compared to the first scenario.

In previous chapters, we have used the income statement, balance sheet, and retained earnings statement and other information to analyze the effects of management decisions on a business's financial position and operating performance. In this chapter, we present how to prepare and use the statement of cash flows.

# Reporting Cash Flows

objective 1

Summarize the types of cash flow activities reported in the statement of cash flows.

The **statement of cash flows** reports a firm's major cash inflows and outflows for a period.[1] It provides useful information about a firm's ability to generate cash from operations, maintain and expand its operating capacity, meet its financial obligations, and pay dividends.

The statement of cash flows is one of the basic financial statements. It is useful to managers in evaluating past operations and in planning future investing and financing activities. It is useful to investors, creditors, and others in assessing a firm's profit potential. In addition, it is a basis for assessing the firm's ability to pay its maturing debt.

The statement of cash flows reports cash flows by three types of activities:

1. **Cash flows from operating activities** are cash flows from transactions that affect net income. Examples of such transactions include the purchase and sale of merchandise by a retailer.
2. **Cash flows from investing activities** are cash flows from transactions that affect the investments in noncurrent assets. Examples of such transactions include the sale and purchase of fixed assets, such as equipment and buildings.
3. **Cash flows from financing activities** are cash flows from transactions that affect the equity and debt of the business. Examples of such transactions include issuing or retiring equity and debt securities.

> **The statement of cash flows reports cash flows from operating, investing, and financing activities.**

The cash flows from operating activities are normally presented first, followed by the cash flows from investing activities and financing activities. The total of the net cash flow from these activities is the net increase or decrease in cash for the period. The cash balance at the beginning of the period is added to the net increase or decrease in cash, resulting in the cash balance at the end of the period. The ending cash balance on the statement of cash flows equals the cash reported on the balance sheet.

Exhibit 1 shows common cash flow transactions reported in each of the three sections of the statement of cash flows. By reporting cash flows by operating, investing, and financing activities, significant relationships within and among the activities can be evaluated. For example, the cash receipts from issuing

---

[1]As used in this chapter, cash refers to cash and cash equivalents. Examples of cash equivalents include short-term, highly liquid investments, such as money market funds, commercial paper, and treasury bills.

## •Exhibit 1 Cash Flows

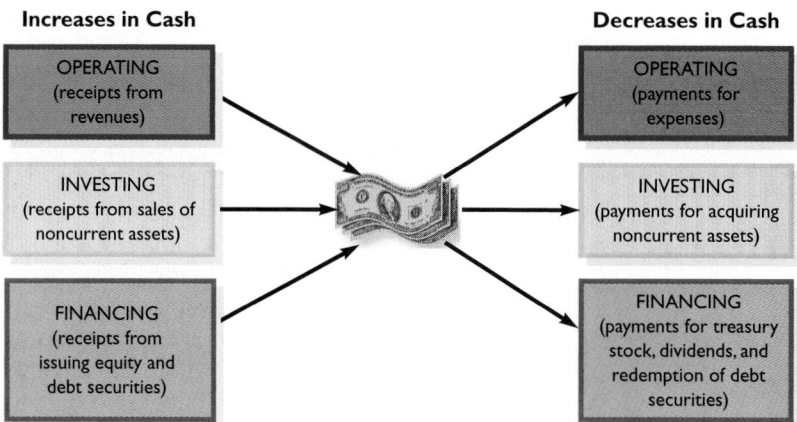

bonds can be related to repayments of borrowings when both are reported as financing activities. Also, the impact of each of the three activities (operating, investing, and financing) on cash flows can be identified. This allows investors and creditors to evaluate the effects of a firm's profits on cash flows, and the ability to generate cash flows for dividends and to pay debts.

## Cash Flows from Operating Activities

The most important cash flows of a business often relate to operating activities. There are two alternative methods for reporting cash flows from operating activities in the statement of cash flows. These methods are (1) the direct method and (2) the indirect method.

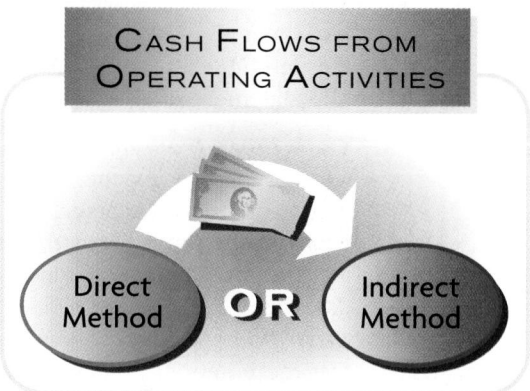

The ***direct method*** reports the sources of operating cash and the uses of operating cash. The major source of operating cash is cash received from customers. The major uses of operating cash include cash paid to suppliers for merchandise and services and cash paid to employees for wages. The difference between these operating cash receipts and cash payments is the net cash flow from operating activities.

The primary advantage of the direct method is that it reports the sources and uses of cash in the statement of cash flows. Its primary disadvantage is that the necessary data may not be readily available and may be costly to gather.

The ***indirect method*** reports the operating cash flows by beginning with net income and adjusting it for revenues and expenses that do not involve the receipt or payment of cash. In other words, accrual net income is adjusted to determine the net amount of cash flows from operating activities.

A major advantage of the indirect method is that it focuses on the differences between net income and cash flows from operations. In this sense, it shows the rela-

tionship between the income statement, the balance sheet, and the statement of cash flows. Because the data are readily available, the indirect method is normally less costly to use than the direct method. Because of these advantages, most firms use the indirect method to report cash flows from operations.

Exhibit 2 illustrates the cash flow from operating activities section of the statement of cash flows under the direct and indirect methods. Both statements are for NetSolutions for the month ended November 2005. Both methods show the same amount of net cash flow from operating activities, regardless of the method. We will illustrate both methods in detail later in this chapter.

## •Exhibit 2   Cash Flow from Operations: Direct and Indirect Methods

| Direct Method | |
|---|---|
| Cash flows from operating activities: | |
| Cash received from customers | $7,500 |
| Deduct cash payments for expenses and payments to creditors | 4,600 |
| Net cash flow from operating activities | $2,900 |

| Indirect Method | |
|---|---|
| Cash flows from operating activities: | |
| Net income, per income statement | $3,050 |
| Add increase in accounts payable | 400 |
| | $3,450 |
| Deduct increase in supplies | 550 |
| Net cash flow from operating activities | $2,900 |

**REAL WORLD**

The **Walt Disney Company** recently invested $1.8 billion in parks, resorts, and other properties, including expansion of Disney's California Adventure and Walt Disney World Resort.

# Cash Flows from Investing Activities

Cash inflows from investing activities normally arise from selling fixed assets, investments, and intangible assets. Cash outflows normally include payments to acquire fixed assets, investments, and intangible assets.

Cash flows from investing activities are reported on the statement of cash flows by first listing the cash inflows. The cash outflows are then presented. If the inflows are greater than the outflows, **net cash flow provided by investing activities** is reported. If the inflows are less than the outflows, **net cash flow used for investing activities** is reported.

The cash flows from investing activities section in the statement of cash flows for NetSolutions is shown below.

Cash flows from investing activities:
Cash payments for acquiring land  . . . . . . . . $(20,000)

# Cash Flows from Financing Activities

Cash inflows from financing activities normally arise from issuing debt or equity securities. Examples of such inflows include issuing bonds, notes payable, and preferred and common stocks. Cash outflows from financing activities include paying cash dividends, repaying debt, and acquiring treasury stock.

Cash flows from financing activities are reported on the statement of cash flows by first listing the cash inflows. The cash outflows are then presented. If the inflows are greater than the outflows, **net cash flow provided by financing activities** is reported. If the inflows are less than the outflows, **net cash flow used for financing activities** is reported.

The cash flows from financing activities section in the statement of cash flows for NetSolutions is shown below.

Cash flows from financing activities:
Cash received as owner's investment  . . . . . . . $25,000
Deduct cash withdrawal by owner . . . . . . . . . 2,000
Net cash flow from financing activities . . . . . . $23,000

# Noncash Investing and Financing Activities

A business may enter into investing and financing activities that do not directly involve cash. For example, it may issue common stock to retire long-term debt. Such a transaction does not have a direct effect on cash. However, the transaction does eliminate the need for future cash payments to pay interest and retire the bonds. Thus, because of their future effect on cash flows, such transactions should be reported to readers of the financial statements.

When noncash investing and financing transactions occur during a period, their effect is reported in a separate schedule. This schedule usually appears at the bottom of the statement of cash flows. For example, in such a schedule, **Amazon.com** recently disclosed the issuance of $112 million in common stock for business acquisitions. Other examples of noncash investing and financing transactions include acquiring fixed assets by issuing bonds or capital stock and issuing common stock in exchange for convertible preferred stock.

## SEASONAL CASH MANAGEMENT

A business must manage its cash position so that there is enough cash on hand to pay bills and other liabilities. Cash management is particularly important for seasonal businesses, which use cash in one part of the year and generate it in another. For example, consider this assumed cash position from operations for Smart Toys, Inc., a toy retailer:

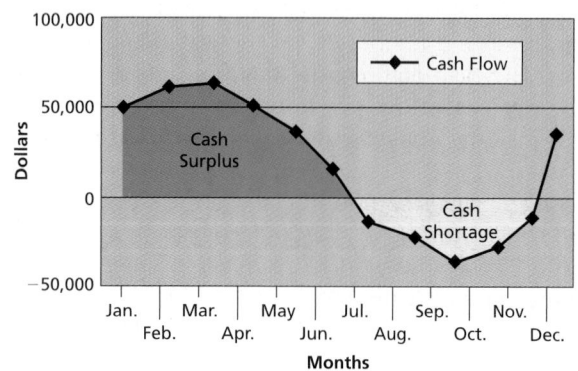

Smart Toys uses cash to purchase inventory prior to the winter holiday season. It is able to generate surplus cash by selling its inventory throughout the holiday season and into the early part of the calendar year.

If the cash required to purchase inventory exceeds Smart Toys' ability to generate operating cash flow, it may experience a cash shortage. In such a case, it must obtain short-term credit, which may be structured as a line of credit from a bank. A line of credit is an agreement that allows the business to borrow an unsecured amount of money up to some stated limit. For example, Smart Toys has a line of credit of $60,000, of which $40,000 was used during the year. Amounts drawn on a line of credit must usually be paid back within a year.

Seasonal businesses must be careful to avoid overextending their cash position during the "down cycle." For example, if Smart Toys purchases items that do not sell, a cash surplus will not be generated during the selling season.

# No Cash Flow per Share

The term *cash flow per share* is sometimes reported in the financial press. Often, the term is used to mean "cash flow from operations per share." Such reporting may be misleading to users of the financial statements. For example, users might interpret cash flow per share as the amount available for dividends. This would not be the case if most of the cash generated by operations is required for repaying loans or for reinvesting in the business. Users might also think that cash flow per share is equivalent or perhaps superior to earnings per share. For these reasons, the financial statements, including the statement of cash flows, should not report cash flow per share.

# Statement of Cash Flows—The Indirect Method

objective 2

Prepare a statement of cash flows, using the indirect method.

The indirect method of reporting cash flows from operating activities is normally less costly and more efficient than the direct method. In addition, when the direct method is used, the indirect method must also be used in preparing a supplemental reconciliation of net income with cash flows from operations. The 2002 edition of *Accounting Trends & Techniques* reported that 99% of the companies surveyed used the indirect method. For these reasons, we will discuss first the indirect method of preparing the statement of cash flows.

To collect the data for the statement of cash flows, all the cash receipts and cash payments for a period could be analyzed. However, this procedure is expensive and time-consuming. A more efficient approach is to analyze the changes in the noncash balance sheet accounts. The logic of this approach is that a change in any balance sheet account (including cash) can be analyzed in terms of changes in the other balance sheet accounts. To illustrate, the accounting equation is rewritten below to focus on the cash account:

$$\text{Assets} = \text{Liabilities} + \text{Stockholders' Equity}$$
$$\text{Cash} + \text{Noncash Assets} = \text{Liabilities} + \text{Stockholders' Equity}$$
$$\text{Cash} = \text{Liabilities} + \text{Stockholders' Equity} - \text{Noncash Assets}$$

Any change in the cash account results in a change in one or more noncash balance sheet accounts. That is, if the cash account changes, then a liability, stockholders' equity, or noncash asset account must also change.

Additional data are also obtained by analyzing the income statement accounts and supporting records. For example, since the net income or net loss for the period is closed to *Retained Earnings*, a change in the retained earnings account can be partially explained by the net income or net loss reported on the income statement.

There is no order in which the noncash balance sheet accounts must be analyzed. However, it is usually more efficient to analyze the accounts in the reverse order in which they appear on the balance sheet. Thus, the analysis of retained earnings provides the starting point for determining the cash flows from operating activities, which is the first section of the statement of cash flows.

The comparative balance sheet for Rundell Inc. on December 31, 2006 and 2005, is used to illustrate the indirect method. This balance sheet is shown in Exhibit 3. Selected ledger accounts and other data are presented as needed.[2]

## Retained Earnings

The comparative balance sheet for Rundell Inc. shows that retained earnings increased $80,000 during the year. Analyzing the entries posted to the retained earnings account indicates how this change occurred. The retained earnings account for Rundell Inc. is shown below.

| ACCOUNT Retained Earnings | | | | | ACCOUNT NO. | |
|---|---|---|---|---|---|---|
| | | | | | **Balance** | |
| Date | Item | Debit | Credit | Debit | Credit |
| 2006 Jan. 1 | Balance | | | | 202 3 0 0 00 |
| Dec. 31 | Net income | | 108 0 0 0 00 | | 310 3 0 0 00 |
| 31 | Cash dividends | 28 0 0 0 00 | | | 282 3 0 0 00 |

---

[2]An appendix that discusses using a work sheet as an aid in assembling data for the statement of cash flows is presented at the end of this chapter. This appendix illustrates a work sheet that can be used with the indirect method and a work sheet that can be used with the direct method of reporting cash flows from operating activities.

# •Exhibit 3  Comparative Balance Sheet

**Rundell Inc.**
**Comparative Balance Sheet**
**December 31, 2006 and 2005**

| Assets | 2006 | 2005 | Increase Decrease* |
|---|---|---|---|
| Cash.................................... | $ 97,500 | $ 26,000 | $ 71,500 |
| Accounts receivable (net)............... | 74,000 | 65,000 | 9,000 |
| Inventories........................... | 172,000 | 180,000 | 8,000* |
| Land................................. | 80,000 | 125,000 | 45,000* |
| Building.............................. | 260,000 | 200,000 | 60,000 |
| Accumulated depreciation—building...... | (65,300) | (58,300) | (7,000) |
| Total assets.......................... | $618,200 | $537,700 | $ 80,500 |
| **Liabilities** | | | |
| Accounts payable (merchandise creditors)........................... | $ 43,500 | $ 46,700 | $ 3,200* |
| Accrued expenses payable (operating expenses)................. | 26,500 | 24,300 | 2,200 |
| Income taxes payable.................... | 7,900 | 8,400 | 500* |
| Dividends payable....................... | 14,000 | 10,000 | 4,000 |
| Bonds payable.......................... | 100,000 | 150,000 | 50,000* |
| Total liabilities....................... | $191,900 | $239,400 | $ 47,500* |
| **Stockholders' Equity** | | | |
| Common stock ($2 par)................... | $ 24,000 | $ 16,000 | $ 8,000 |
| Paid-in capital in excess of par........... | 120,000 | 80,000 | 40,000 |
| Retained earnings...................... | 282,300 | 202,300 | 80,000 |
| Total stockholders' equity............... | $426,300 | $298,300 | $128,000 |
| Total liabilities and stockholders' equity.... | $618,200 | $537,700 | $ 80,500 |

The retained earnings account must be carefully analyzed because some of the entries to retained earnings may not affect cash. For example, a decrease in retained earnings resulting from issuing a stock dividend does not affect cash. Such transactions are not reported on the statement of cash flows.

For Rundell Inc., the retained earnings account indicates that the $80,000 change resulted from net income of $108,000 and cash dividends declared of $28,000. The effect of each of these items on cash flows is discussed in the following sections.

## Cash Flows from Operating Activities

The net income of $108,000 reported by Rundell Inc. normally is not equal to the amount of cash generated from operations during the period. This is because net income is determined using the accrual method of accounting.

Under the accrual method of accounting, revenues and expenses are recorded at different times from when cash is received or paid. For example, merchandise may be sold on account and the cash received at a later date.

Likewise, insurance expense represents the amount of insurance expired during the period. The premiums for the insurance may have been paid in a prior period. Thus, the net income reported on the income statement must be adjusted in determining cash flows from operating activities. The typical adjustments to net income are summarized in Exhibit 4.[3]

## •Exhibit 4 Adjustments to Net Income—Indirect Method

| | | |
|---|---|---|
| Net income, per income statement . . . . . . . . . . . . . . . . . . . . . . . . . . . . . . . . | | $XX |
| Add: Depreciation of fixed assets and amortization of intangible assets . . | $XX | |
|     Decreases in current assets (receivables, inventories, | | |
|         prepaid expenses) . . . . . . . . . . . . . . . . . . . . . . . . . . . . . . . . . . . . . . . | XX | |
|     Increases in current liabilities (accounts and notes payable, | | |
|         accrued liabilities) . . . . . . . . . . . . . . . . . . . . . . . . . . . . . . . . . . . . . . | XX | |
|     Losses on disposal of assets . . . . . . . . . . . . . . . . . . . . . . . . . . . . . . . . | XX | XX |
| Deduct: Increases in current assets (receivables, inventories, | | |
|         prepaid expenses) . . . . . . . . . . . . . . . . . . . . . . . . . . . . . . . . . . . . . . | $XX | |
|     Decreases in current liabilities (accounts and notes payable, | | |
|         accrued liabilities) . . . . . . . . . . . . . . . . . . . . . . . . . . . . . . . . . . . . . . | XX | |
|     Gains on disposal of assets . . . . . . . . . . . . . . . . . . . . . . . . . . . . . . . . . | XX | XX |
| Net cash flow from operating activities . . . . . . . . . . . . . . . . . . . . . . . . . . | | $XX |

I was started in an Iowa farmhouse in 1985 by a ponytail-wearing guy who'd borrowed $10,000 from his grandmother. Today I'm a billion dollar company, employing more than 10,000 people and raking in some $6 billion annually. In 1995, I was the first manufacturer to offer online ordering for my kind of product. I'm a "personal technology company," offering consumers, businesses, and government agencies digital music, photography, and video services, as well as high-speed Internet connections and networking for the home and office, among other things. I'm known for my bovine design, too. Who am I? (Go to page 672 for answer.)

Some of the adjustment items in Exhibit 4 are for expenses that affect noncurrent accounts but not cash. For example, depreciation of fixed assets and amortization of intangible assets are deducted from revenue but do not affect cash.

Some of the adjustment items in Exhibit 4 are for revenues and expenses that affect current assets and current liabilities but not cash flows. For example, a sale of $10,000 on account increases accounts receivable by $10,000. However, cash is not affected. Thus, the increase in accounts receivable of $10,000 between two balance sheet dates is deducted from net income in arriving at cash flows from operating activities.

Cash flows from operating activities should not include investing or financing transactions. For example, assume that land costing $50,000 was sold for $90,000 (a gain of $40,000). The sale should be reported as an investing activity: "Cash receipts from the sale of land, $90,000." However, the $40,000 gain on the sale of the land is included in net income on the income statement. Thus, the $40,000 gain is deducted from net income in determining cash flows from operations in order to avoid "double counting" the cash flow from the gain. Likewise, losses from the sale of fixed assets are added to net income in determining cash flows from operations.

The effect of dividends payable on cash flows from operating activities is omitted from Exhibit 4. Dividends payable is omitted because dividends do not affect net income. Later in the chapter, we will discuss how dividends are reported in the statement of cash flows. In the following paragraphs, we will discuss each of the adjustments that change Rundell Inc.'s net income to "Cash flows from operating activities."

## Depreciation

The comparative balance sheet in Exhibit 3 indicates that Accumulated Depreciation—Building increased by $7,000. As shown at the top of the following page, this account indicates that depreciation for the year was $7,000 for the building.

---

[3]Other items that also require adjustments to net income to obtain cash flow from operating activities include amortization of bonds payable discounts (add), losses on debt retirement (add), amortization of bonds payable premium (deduct), and gains on retirement of debt (deduct).

| ACCOUNT *Accumulated Depreciation—Building* | | | | ACCOUNT NO. | | |
| | | | | | Balance | |
| Date | Item | Debit | Credit | | Debit | Credit |
| 2006 Jan. 1 | Balance | | | | | 58 3 0 0 00 |
| Dec. 31 | Depreciation for year | | 7 0 0 0 00 | | | 65 3 0 0 00 |

Net income was $45,000 for the year. The accumulated depreciation balance increased by $15,000 over the year. There were no sales of fixed assets or changes in non-cash current assets or liabilities. What is the cash flow from operations?

-----------------------------------------

$60,000 ($45,000 + $15,000)

The $7,000 of depreciation expense reduced net income but did not require an outflow of cash. Thus, the $7,000 is added to net income in determining cash flows from operating activities, as follows:

| Cash flows from operating activities: | | |
| Net income | $108,000 | |
| Add depreciation | 7,000 | $115,000 |

## Current Assets and Current Liabilities

As shown in Exhibit 4, decreases in noncash current assets and increases in current liabilities are added to net income. In contrast, increases in noncash current assets and decreases in current liabilities are deducted from net income. The current asset and current liability accounts of Rundell Inc. are as follows:

| | December 31 | | Increase |
| Accounts | 2006 | 2005 | Decrease* |
| --- | --- | --- | --- |
| Accounts receivable (net) .................. | $ 74,000 | $ 65,000 | $9,000 |
| Inventories ............................. | 172,000 | 180,000 | 8,000* |
| Accounts payable (merchandise creditors) ....... | 43,500 | 46,700 | 3,200* |
| Accrued expenses payable (operating expenses) .. | 26,500 | 24,300 | 2,200 |
| Income taxes payable ..................... | 7,900 | 8,400 | 500* |

**REAL WORLD**

**Ford Motor Company**'s automotive business had a net loss of $6.6 billion but a positive cash flow from operating activities of $7.8 billion. This difference was mostly due to $5 billion of depreciation and amortization expenses and a $5 billion increase in accounts payable.

The $9,000 increase in **accounts receivable** indicates that the sales on account during the year are $9,000 more than collections from customers on account. The amount reported as sales on the income statement therefore includes $9,000 that did not result in a cash inflow during the year. Thus, $9,000 is deducted from net income.

The $8,000 decrease in **inventories** indicates that the merchandise sold exceeds the cost of the merchandise purchased by $8,000. The amount deducted as cost of merchandise sold on the income statement therefore includes $8,000 that did not require a cash outflow during the year. Thus, $8,000 is added to net income.

The $3,200 decrease in **accounts payable** indicates that the amount of cash payments for merchandise exceeds the merchandise purchased on account by $3,200. The amount reported on the income statement for cost of merchandise sold therefore excludes $3,200 that required a cash outflow during the year. Thus, $3,200 is deducted from net income.

The $2,200 increase in **accrued expenses payable** indicates that the amount incurred during the year for operating expenses exceeds the cash payments by $2,200. The amount reported on the income statement for operating expenses therefore includes $2,200 that did not require a cash outflow during the year. Thus, $2,200 is added to net income.

The $500 decrease in **income taxes payable** indicates that the amount paid for taxes exceeds the amount incurred during the year by $500. The amount reported on the income statement for income tax therefore is less than the amount paid by $500. Thus, $500 is deducted from net income.

## Gain on Sale of Land

The ledger or income statement of Rundell Inc. indicates that the sale of land resulted in a gain of $12,000. As we discussed previously, the sale proceeds, which include the gain and the carrying value of the land, are included in cash flows from investing activities.[4] The gain is also included in net income. Thus, to avoid double reporting, the gain of $12,000 is deducted from net income in determining cash flows from operating activities, as shown below.

Cash flows from operating activities:
Net income . . . . . . . . . . . . . . . . . . . . . . . . . . . . . . . . . . . . . . . . . $108,000
Deduct gain on sale of land . . . . . . . . . . . . . . . . . . . . . . . 12,000

---

## INTEGRITY IN BUSINESS

### CREDIT POLICY AND CASH FLOW

**M**anagement will sometimes feel pressured to boost earnings by relaxing credit policies. Thus, they are able to create more sales on account but at a higher collection risk. The result is a temporary positive impact on the income statement. However, cash flow may be negatively impacted if high credit risk customers delay payment or are unable to pay. For example, **Lucent Technologies, Inc.,** extended billions of dollars in credit to upstart telecom companies to support Lucent's equipment sales. Loans to companies like **Winstar** and **One.Tel Ltd.** were eventually written off to the tune of $1 billion. This has prompted shareholder lawsuits accusing Lucent's directors of "mismanaging the top U.S. maker of phone equipment by lending the company's money to financially shaky customers to promote sales."

**Source:** *Omaha World-Herald*, "Lucent to Cut Almost Half Its Work Force; Troubled Phone Equipment Maker to Eliminate 20,000 Jobs, Take a Charge of as Much as $9 Billion," July 24, 2001.

---

## Reporting Cash Flows from Operating Activities

We have now presented all the necessary adjustments to convert the net income to cash flows from operating activities for Rundell Inc. These adjustments are summarized in Exhibit 5 in a format suitable for the statement of cash flows.

**•Exhibit 5**   Cash Flows from Operating Activities—Indirect Method

| Cash flows from operating activities: | | | |
|---|---|---|---|
| Net income . . . . . . . . . . . . . . . . . . . . . . . . . . . . . | | | $108,000 |
| Add: Depreciation . . . . . . . . . . . . . . . . . . . . . . . . . | $ 7,000 | | |
| Decrease in inventories . . . . . . . . . . . . . . . . | 8,000 | | |
| Increase in accrued expenses . . . . . . . . . . . | 2,200 | 17,200 | |
| | | | $125,200 |
| Deduct: Increase in accounts receivable . . . . . . . . | $ 9,000 | | |
| Decrease in accounts payable . . . . . . . . . . | 3,200 | | |
| Decrease in income taxes payable . . . . . . | 500 | | |
| Gain on sale of land . . . . . . . . . . . . . . . . . | 12,000 | 24,700 | |
| Net cash flow from operating activities . . . . . . . . | | | $100,500 |

---

[4]The reporting of the proceeds (cash flows) from the sale of land as part of investing activities is discussed later in this chapter.

## FINANCIAL REPORTING AND DISCLOSURE

### SIX FLAGS, INC.

The cash flows from operating activities under the indirect method often have more adjustments than illustrated in this chapter. To illustrate, the cash flows from operating activities for **Six Flags, Inc.**, an amusement park operator, is as follows:

**Six Flags, Inc.**
**Cash Flows from Operating Activities**
**(Selected from the Statement of Cash Flows)**
**For Year Ended December 31, 2002**

| | 2002 |
|---|---|
| Cash flows from operating activities: | |
| Net loss | $(105,698,000) |
| Adjustments to reconcile net loss to net cash provided by operating activities: | |
| Depreciation and amortization | $ 151,849,000 |
| Equity in operations of theme parks | (15,664,000) |
| Cash received from theme parks | 26,679,000 |
| Noncash compensation | 9,256,000 |
| Interest accretion on notes payable | 37,818,000 |
| Extraordinary loss on early extinguishment of debt | 29,895,000 |
| Cumulative change in accounting principle | 61,054,000 |
| Amortization of debt issuance costs | 8,952,000 |
| Loss on disposal of fixed assets | 4,375,000 |
| (Increase) decrease in accounts receivable | (3,567,000) |
| Increase (decrease) in inventories and prepaid expenses | 2,050,000 |
| Decrease in deposits and other assets | 3,824,000 |
| Increase (decrease) in accounts payable, deferred revenue, accrued expenses, and other liabilities | 4,080,000 |
| Increase in accrued interest payable | 7,671,000 |
| Deferred income tax benefit | (18,091,000) |
| Total adjustments | $ 310,181,000 |
| Net cash provided by operating activities | $ 204,483,000 |

As can be seen, Six Flags had a loss of over $105 million but had positive cash flows from operating activities of over $204 million. The difference between the accrual earnings number and the cash flow from operating activities is explained by a long list of adjusting items, of which the largest is depreciation expense. Other noncash adjustments include the noncash compensation (deferred bonuses), interest revenue on non-interest-bearing notes, equity earnings (net of cash received) from partnerships, and debt issuance cost amortization (similar to discount amortizations). The cash flow impact of the extraordinary and ordinary losses are reflected in the financing and investing sections, respectively, and thus are added back in the operating activities section to avoid double-counting. The cumulative effect of the change in accounting principle was a noncash deduction in determining net income. The remaining items are the adjustments due to changes in the noncash current assets and liabilities, as described in the chapter.

## Cash Flows Used for Payment of Dividends

According to the retained earnings account of Rundell Inc., shown earlier in the chapter, cash dividends of $28,000 were declared during the year. However, the dividends payable account, shown at the top of the next page, indicates that dividends of only $24,000 were paid during the year.

**ACCOUNT** Dividends Payable — **ACCOUNT NO.**

| Date | | Item | Debit | Credit | Balance Debit | Balance Credit |
|---|---|---|---|---|---|---|
| 2006 Jan. | 1 | Balance | | | | 10 0 0 0 00 |
| | 10 | Cash paid | 10 0 0 0 00 | | — | — |
| June | 20 | Dividends declared | | 14 0 0 0 00 | | 14 0 0 0 00 |
| July | 10 | Cash paid | 14 0 0 0 00 | | — | — |
| Dec. | 20 | Dividends declared | | 14 0 0 0 00 | | 14 0 0 0 00 |

The $24,000 of dividend payments represents a cash outflow that is reported in the financing activities section as follows:

Cash flows from financing activities:
Cash paid for dividends . . . . . . . . . . . . . . . . . . . . . . . . . . . . $24,000

## Common Stock

The common stock account increased by $8,000, and the paid-in capital in excess of par—common stock account increased by $40,000, as shown below. These increases result from issuing 4,000 shares of common stock for $12 per share.

**ACCOUNT** Common Stock — **ACCOUNT NO.**

| Date | | Item | Debit | Credit | Balance Debit | Balance Credit |
|---|---|---|---|---|---|---|
| 2006 Jan. | 1 | Balance | | | | 16 0 0 0 00 |
| Nov. | 1 | 4,000 shares issued for cash | | 8 0 0 0 00 | | 24 0 0 0 00 |

**ACCOUNT** Paid-In Capital in Excess of Par—Common Stock — **ACCOUNT NO.**

| Date | | Item | Debit | Credit | Balance Debit | Balance Credit |
|---|---|---|---|---|---|---|
| 2006 Jan. | 1 | Balance | | | | 80 0 0 0 00 |
| Nov. | 1 | 4,000 shares issued for cash | | 40 0 0 0 00 | | 120 0 0 0 00 |

This cash inflow is reported in the financing activities section as follows:

Cash flows from financing activities:
Cash received from sale of common stock . . . . . . . . . . . . . . $48,000

## Bonds Payable

The bonds payable account decreased by $50,000, as shown below. This decrease results from retiring the bonds by a cash payment for their face amount.

**ACCOUNT** Bonds Payable — **ACCOUNT NO.**

| Date | | Item | Debit | Credit | Balance Debit | Balance Credit |
|---|---|---|---|---|---|---|
| 2006 Jan. | 1 | Balance | | | | 150 0 0 0 00 |
| June | 30 | Retired by payment of cash at face amount | 50 0 0 0 00 | | | 100 0 0 0 00 |

**REAL WORLD**

Amazon.com, Inc. has had negative cash flows from operations for most of its corporate life. However, it has been able to grow by obtaining cash from the sale of common stock. Investors are willing to purchase the common stock on the belief that Amazon.com, Inc. will have a very profitable future as e-commerce matures.

This cash outflow is reported in the financing activities section as follows:

Cash flows from financing activities:
Cash paid to retire bonds payable . . . . . . . . . . . . . . . . . . . . $50,000

# Building

The building account increased by $60,000, and the accumulated depreciation—building account increased by $7,000, as shown below.

| ACCOUNT Building | | | | | | ACCOUNT NO. | |
|---|---|---|---|---|---|---|---|
| Date | Item | Debit | Credit | Balance | | | |
| | | | | Debit | Credit | | |
| 2006 Jan. 1 | Balance | | | 200 0 0 0 00 | | | |
| Dec. 27 | Purchased for cash | 60 0 0 0 00 | | 260 0 0 0 00 | | | |

| ACCOUNT Accumulated Depreciation—Building | | | | | | ACCOUNT NO. | |
|---|---|---|---|---|---|---|---|
| Date | Item | Debit | Credit | Balance | | | |
| | | | | Debit | Credit | | |
| 2006 Jan. 1 | Balance | | | | 58 3 0 0 00 | | |
| Dec. 31 | Depreciation for the year | | 7 0 0 0 00 | | 65 3 0 0 00 | | |

The purchase of a building for cash of $60,000 is reported as an outflow of cash in the investing activities section, as follows:

Cash flows from investing activities:
Cash paid for purchase of building . . . . . . . . . . . . . . . . . . . $60,000

The credit in the accumulated depreciation—building account, shown earlier, represents depreciation expense for the year. This depreciation expense of $7,000 on the building has already been considered as an addition to net income in determining cash flows from operating activities, as reported in Exhibit 5.

A building with a cost of $145,000 and accumulated depreciation of $35,000 was sold for a $10,000 gain. How much cash was generated from this investing activity?

--------------------------------------------

$120,000 ($145,000 − $35,000 + $10,000)

# Land

The $45,000 decline in the land account resulted from two separate transactions, as shown below.

| ACCOUNT Land | | | | | | ACCOUNT NO. | |
|---|---|---|---|---|---|---|---|
| Date | Item | Debit | Credit | Balance | | | |
| | | | | Debit | Credit | | |
| 2006 Jan. 1 | Balance | | | 125 0 0 0 00 | | | |
| June 8 | Sold for $72,000 cash | | 60 0 0 0 00 | 65 0 0 0 00 | | | |
| Oct. 12 | Purchased for $15,000 cash | 15 0 0 0 00 | | 80 0 0 0 00 | | | |

The first transaction is the sale of land with a cost of $60,000 for $72,000 in cash. The $72,000 proceeds from the sale are reported in the investing activities section, as follows:

Cash flows from investing activities:
Cash received from sale of land (includes $12,000 gain
reported in net income) . . . . . . . . . . . . . . . . . . . . . . . . . .    $72,000

The proceeds of $72,000 include the $12,000 gain on the sale of land and the $60,000 cost (book value) of the land. As shown in Exhibit 5, the $12,000 gain is also deducted from net income in the cash flows from operating activities section. This is necessary so that the $12,000 cash inflow related to the gain is not included twice as a cash inflow.

The second transaction is the purchase of land for cash of $15,000. This transaction is reported as an outflow of cash in the investing activities section, as follows:

Cash flows from investing activities:
Cash paid for purchase of land . . . . . . . . . . . . . . . . . . . . . .    $15,000

# Preparing the Statement of Cash Flows

The statement of cash flows for Rundell Inc. is prepared from the data assembled and analyzed above, using the indirect method. Exhibit 6 shows the statement of cash flows prepared by Rundell Inc. The statement indicates that the cash position increased by $71,500 during the year. The most significant increase in net cash flows, $100,500, was from operating activities. The most significant use of cash, $26,000, was for financing activities.

**•Exhibit 6**   **Statement of Cash Flows—Indirect Method**

| Rundell Inc. Statement of Cash Flows For the Year Ended December 31, 2006 | | | |
|---|---:|---:|---:|
| Cash flows from operating activities: | | | |
| Net income . . . . . . . . . . . . . . . . . . . . . . . . . . . . . . | | $108,000 | |
| Add: Depreciation . . . . . . . . . . . . . . . . . . . . . . | $ 7,000 | | |
| Decrease in inventories . . . . . . . . . . . . . . | 8,000 | | |
| Increase in accrued expenses . . . . . . . . . . | 2,200 | 17,200 | |
| | | $125,200 | |
| Deduct: Increase in accounts receivable . . . . . . | $ 9,000 | | |
| Decrease in accounts payable . . . . . . . | 3,200 | | |
| Decrease in income taxes payable . . . | 500 | | |
| Gain on sale of land . . . . . . . . . . . . . | 12,000 | 24,700 | |
| Net cash flow from operating activities . . . . . . | | | $100,500 |
| Cash flows from investing activities: | | | |
| Cash from sale of land . . . . . . . . . . . . . . . . . . . . | | $ 72,000 | |
| Less: Cash paid to purchase land . . . . . . . . . . | $15,000 | | |
| Cash paid for purchase of building . . . . . | 60,000 | 75,000 | |
| Net cash flow used for investing activities . . . . | | | (3,000) |
| Cash flows from financing activities: | | | |
| Cash received from sale of common stock . . . . | | $ 48,000 | |
| Less: Cash paid to retire bonds payable . . . . . . | $50,000 | | |
| Cash paid for dividends . . . . . . . . . . . . . . | 24,000 | 74,000 | |
| Net cash flow used for financing activities . . . . | | | (26,000) |
| Increase in cash . . . . . . . . . . . . . . . . . . . . . . . . . . . . | | | $ 71,500 |
| Cash at the beginning of the year . . . . . . . . . . . . | | | 26,000 |
| Cash at the end of the year . . . . . . . . . . . . . . . . . | | | $ 97,500 |

---

## INTEGRITY IN BUSINESS

### MISLEADING CASH FLOWS

The Securities and Exchange Commission disagreed with a cash flow disclosure from a complex natural gas trading arrangement of **Dynegy Inc.**, a major energy provider and trader. As a result, the company was required to remove $300 million from cash flow from operations (a drop of 37%) and put it into the financing section. Although this change did not impact net cash flow from all sources, it did change the interpretation of cash flows. As quoted by one source, "the restatement is a big blow to the many investors who held onto the cash-flow statement as a beacon of truth even as their faith in earnings figure was shattered in recent months . . ." Dynegy's share price dropped 67% within two months of this announcement.

**Source:** Henny Sender, " 'Reliable' Cash Flow Has Shortcomings—Sums Aren't Always What They Seem," *The Wall Street Journal*, May 9, 2002.

---

# Statement of Cash Flows—The Direct Method

objective   **3**

Prepare a statement of cash flows, using the direct method.

As we discussed previously, the manner of reporting cash flows from investing and financing activities is the same under the direct and indirect methods. In addition, the direct method and the indirect method will report the same amount of cash flows from operating activities. However, the methods differ in how the cash flows from operating activities data are obtained, analyzed, and reported.

To illustrate the direct method, we will use the comparative balance sheet and the income statement for Rundell Inc. In this way, we can compare the statement of cash flows under the direct method and the indirect method.

Exhibit 7 shows the changes in the current asset and liability account balances for Rundell Inc. The income statement in Exhibit 7 shows additional data for Rundell Inc.

The direct method reports cash flows from operating activities by major classes of operating cash receipts and operating cash payments. The difference between the major classes of total operating cash receipts and total operating cash payments is the net cash flow from operating activities.

## Cash Received from Customers

The $1,180,000 of sales for Rundell Inc. is reported by using the accrual method. To determine the cash received from sales to customers, the $1,180,000 must be adjusted. The adjustment necessary to convert the sales reported on the income statement to the cash received from customers is summarized below.

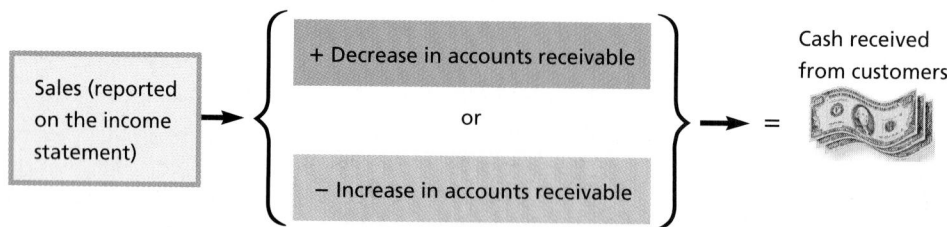

For Rundell Inc., the cash received from customers is $1,171,000, as shown below.

| | |
|---|---:|
| Sales | $1,180,000 |
| Less increase in accounts receivable | 9,000 |
| Cash received from customers | $1,171,000 |

**•Exhibit 7**    Balance Sheet and Income Statement Data for Direct Method

### Rundell Inc.
### Schedule of Changes in Current Accounts

| Accounts | December 31 2006 | December 31 2005 | Increase Decrease* |
|---|---|---|---|
| Cash ........................................... | $ 97,500 | $ 26,000 | $71,500 |
| Accounts receivable (net) ................. | 74,000 | 65,000 | 9,000 |
| Inventories ................................ | 172,000 | 180,000 | 8,000* |
| Accounts payable (merchandise creditors) ...... | 43,500 | 46,700 | 3,200* |
| Accrued expenses payable (operating expenses) .. | 26,500 | 24,300 | 2,200 |
| Income taxes payable .................... | 7,900 | 8,400 | 500* |
| Dividends payable ...................... | 14,000 | 10,000 | 4,000 |

### Rundell Inc.
### Income Statement
### For the Year Ended December 31, 2006

| | | |
|---|---|---|
| Sales ........................................... | | $1,180,000 |
| Cost of merchandise sold ........................ | | 790,000 |
| Gross profit ..................................... | | $ 390,000 |
| Operating expenses: | | |
|    Depreciation expense ......................... | $ 7,000 | |
|    Other operating expenses ..................... | 196,000 | |
|       Total operating expenses ................ | | 203,000 |
| Income from operations .......................... | | $ 187,000 |
| Other income: | | |
|    Gain on sale of land ......................... | $ 12,000 | |
| Other expense: | | |
|    Interest expense ............................. | 8,000 | 4,000 |
| Income before income tax ....................... | | $ 191,000 |
| Income tax expense ............................. | | 83,000 |
| Net income ..................................... | | $ 108,000 |

Sales reported on the income statement were $350,000. The accounts receivable balance declined $8,000 over the year. What was the amount of cash received from customers?

---------------------------------------

*$358,000 ($350,000 + $8,000)*

The additions to **accounts receivable** for sales on account during the year were $9,000 more than the amounts collected from customers on account. Sales reported on the income statement therefore included $9,000 that did not result in a cash inflow during the year. In other words, the increase of $9,000 in accounts receivable during 2006 indicates that sales on account exceeded cash received from customers by $9,000. Thus, $9,000 is deducted from sales to determine the cash received from customers. The $1,171,000 of cash received from customers is reported in the cash flows from operating activities section of the cash flow statement.

## Cash Payments for Merchandise

The $790,000 of cost of merchandise sold is reported on the income statement for Rundell Inc., using the accrual method. The adjustments necessary to convert the cost of merchandise sold to cash payments for merchandise during 2006 are summarized at the top of the following page.

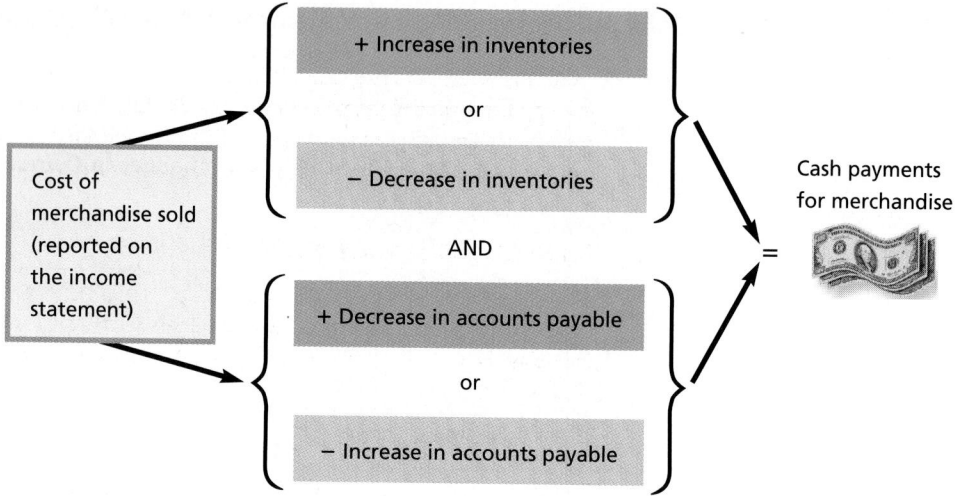

For Rundell Inc., the amount of cash payments for merchandise is $785,200, as determined below.

| | |
|---|---:|
| Cost of merchandise sold | $790,000 |
| Deduct decrease in inventories | (8,000) |
| Add decrease in accounts payable | 3,200 |
| Cash payments for merchandise | $785,200 |

The $8,000 decrease in **inventories** indicates that the merchandise sold exceeded the cost of the merchandise purchased by $8,000. The amount reported on the income statement for cost of merchandise sold therefore includes $8,000 that did not require a cash outflow during the year. Thus, $8,000 is deducted from the cost of merchandise sold in determining the cash payments for merchandise.

The $3,200 decrease in **accounts payable** (merchandise creditors) indicates a cash outflow that is excluded from cost of merchandise sold. In other words, the decrease in accounts payable indicates that cash payments for merchandise were $3,200 more than the purchases on account during 2006. Thus, $3,200 is added to the cost of merchandise sold in determining the cash payments for merchandise.

## Cash Payments for Operating Expenses

The $7,000 of depreciation expense reported on the income statement did not require a cash outflow. Thus, under the direct method, it is not reported on the statement of cash flows. The $196,000 reported for other operating expenses is adjusted to reflect the cash payments for operating expenses, as summarized below.

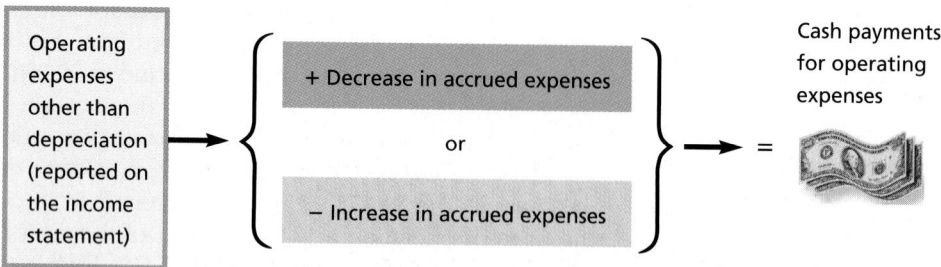

For Rundell Inc., the amount of cash payments for operating expenses is $193,800, determined as follows:

| | |
|---|---:|
| Operating expenses other than depreciation | $196,000 |
| Deduct increase in accrued expenses | 2,200 |
| Cash payments for operating expenses | $193,800 |

The increase in **accrued expenses** (operating expenses) indicates that operating expenses include $2,200 for which there was no cash outflow (payment) during the year. In other words, the increase in accrued expenses indicates that the cash payments for operating expenses were $2,200 less than the amount reported as an expense during the year. Thus, $2,200 is deducted from the operating expenses on the income statement in determining the cash payments for operating expenses.

## Gain on Sale of Land

The income statement for Rundell Inc. in Exhibit 7 reports a gain of $12,000 on the sale of land. As we discussed previously, the gain is included in the proceeds from the sale of land, which is reported as part of the cash flows from investing activities.

## Interest Expense

The income statement for Rundell Inc. in Exhibit 7 reports interest expense of $8,000. The interest expense is related to the bonds payable that were outstanding during the year. We assume that interest on the bonds is paid on June 30 and December 31. Thus, $8,000 cash outflow for interest expense is reported on the statement of cash flows as an operating activity.

If interest payable had existed at the end of the year, the interest expense would be adjusted for any increase or decrease in interest payable from the beginning to the end of the year. That is, a decrease in interest payable would be added to interest expense and an increase in interest payable would be subtracted from interest expense. This is similar to the adjustment for changes in income taxes payable, which we will illustrate in the following paragraphs.

## Cash Payments for Income Taxes

The adjustment to convert the income tax reported on the income statement to the cash basis is summarized below.

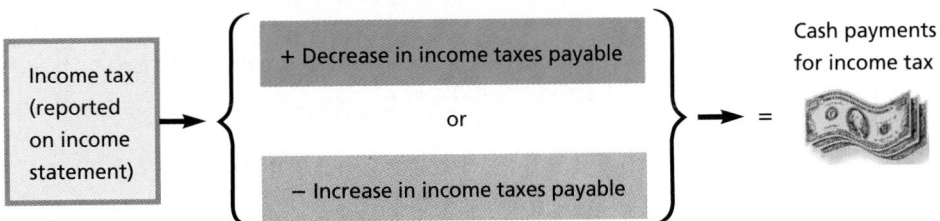

For Rundell Inc., cash payments for income tax are $83,500, determined as follows:

| | |
|---|---|
| Income tax | $83,000 |
| Add decrease in income taxes payable | 500 |
| Cash payments for income tax | $83,500 |

The cash outflow for income taxes exceeded the income tax deducted as an expense during the period by $500. Thus, $500 is added to the amount of income tax reported on the income statement in determining the cash payments for income tax.

## Reporting Cash Flows from Operating Activities—Direct Method

Exhibit 8 is a complete statement of cash flows for Rundell Inc., using the direct method for reporting cash flows from operating activities. The portions of this statement that differ from the indirect method are highlighted in color. Exhibit 8 also includes the separate schedule reconciling net income and net cash flow from operating

**REAL WORLD**

**Dell Computer Corporation** is one of the few companies that has a *negative cash conversion cycle*. This means that Dell receives payment for a computer before it pays for the parts that went into that computer. This can only be done by collecting the sale with a credit card, maintaining very little inventory, and holding accounts payable open for 30 days.

## •Exhibit 8   Statement of Cash Flows—Direct Method

**Rundell Inc.**
**Statement of Cash Flows**
**For the Year Ended December 31, 2006**

| | | | |
|---|---|---:|---:|
| Cash flows from operating activities: | | | |
| Cash received from customers . . . . . . . . . . . . . . . . . | | $1,171,000 | |
| Deduct: Cash payments for merchandise. . . . . . . . . | $785,200 | | |
| Cash payments for operating expenses. . . . | 193,800 | | |
| Cash payments for interest . . . . . . . . . . . . . | 8,000 | | |
| Cash payments for income taxes . . . . . . . . . | 83,500 | 1,070,500 | |
| Net cash flow from operating activities . . . . . . . . . . | | | $100,500 |
| Cash flows from investing activities: | | | |
| Cash from sale of land . . . . . . . . . . . . . . . . . . . . . . | | $  72,000 | |
| Less: Cash paid to purchase land . . . . . . . . . . . . . . | $ 15,000 | | |
| Cash paid for purchase of building . . . . . . . . . | 60,000 | 75,000 | |
| Net cash flow used for investing activities . . . . . . . . | | | (3,000) |
| Cash flows from financing activities: | | | |
| Cash received from sale of common stock . . . . . . . . | | $  48,000 | |
| Less: Cash paid to retire bonds payable . . . . . . . . . . | $ 50,000 | | |
| Cash paid for dividends . . . . . . . . . . . . . . . . . . . | 24,000 | 74,000 | |
| Net cash flow used for financing activities . . . . . . . . | | | (26,000) |
| Increase in cash . . . . . . . . . . . . . . . . . . . . . . . . . . . . . | | | $ 71,500 |
| Cash at the beginning of the year . . . . . . . . . . . . . . . . | | | 26,000 |
| Cash at the end of the year . . . . . . . . . . . . . . . . . . . . . | | | $ 97,500 |
| | | | |
| **Schedule Reconciling Net Income with Cash** | | | |
| **Flows from Operating Activities:** | | | |
| Net income, per income statement. . . . . . . . . . . . . | | $  108,000 | |
| Add: Depreciation. . . . . . . . . . . . . . . . . . . . . . . . . . | $  7,000 | | |
| Decrease in inventories . . . . . . . . . . . . . . . . . | 8,000 | | |
| Increase in accrued expenses. . . . . . . . . . . . . | 2,200 | 17,200 | |
| | | $  125,200 | |
| Deduct: Increase in accounts receivable . . . . . . . . . . | $  9,000 | | |
| Decrease in accounts payable . . . . . . . . . . . | 3,200 | | |
| Decrease in income taxes payable . . . . . . . . | 500 | | |
| Gain on sale of land . . . . . . . . . . . . . . . . . . | 12,000 | 24,700 | |
| Net cash flow from operating activities . . . . . . . . . . | | $  100,500 | |

activities. This schedule must accompany the statement of cash flows when the direct method is used. This schedule is similar to the cash flows from operating activities section of the statement of cash flows prepared using the indirect method.

# Financial Analysis and Interpretation

| objective 4 |
|---|

Calculate and interpret the free cash flow.

A valuable tool for evaluating the cash flows of a business is free cash flow. **Free cash flow** is a measure of operating cash flow available for corporate purposes after providing sufficient fixed asset additions to maintain current productive capacity and dividends. Thus, free cash flow can be calculated as follows:

Cash flow from operating activities
Less: Cash used to purchase fixed assets to maintain productive
      capacity used up in producing income during the period
Less: Cash used for dividends
      Free cash flow

The top five nonfinancial companies out of the Standard & Poor's 100 Index with the largest free cash flows for a recent year were as follows:

| | Free Cash Flow (in millions) |
|---|---|
| Ford Motor Co. | $14,705 |
| ExxonMobil | 12,900 |
| General Electric | 10,317 |
| Microsoft | 9,967 |
| IBM | 8,595 |

Each of these companies are large and successful organizations. In contrast, the three organizations with the largest *negative* free cash flows were:

| | |
|---|---|
| Lucent | $(4,839) |
| Delta Air Lines | (2,571) |
| Nextel Communications | (2,359) |

Both the telecommunications equipment and airline industries were suffering significantly during this timeframe.

**Source:** Ronald Fink, "Adjusting the Flow," *CFO Magazine*, December 1, 2002.

Analysts often use free cash flow, rather than cash flows from operating activities, to measure the financial strength of a business. Many high-technology firms must aggressively reinvest in new technology to remain competitive. This can reduce free cash flow. For example, **Motorola**'s free cash flow is less than 10% of the cash flow from operating activities. In contrast, **Coca-Cola**'s free cash flow is approximately 75% of the cash flow from operating activities.

To illustrate, the cash flow from operating activities for **Hewlett-Packard Co.** was $5,444 million in a recent fiscal year. The statement of cash flows indicated that the cash invested in property, plant, and equipment was $1,710 million and $801 million was paid for dividends. Assuming that the amount invested in property, plant, and equipment maintained existing operations, free cash flow would be calculated as follows (in millions):

| | | |
|---|---|---|
| Cash flow from operating activities | | $5,444 |
| Less: Cash invested in fixed assets to maintain productive capacity | $1,710 | |
| Cash for dividends | 801 | 2,511 |
| Free cash flow | | $2,933 |

During this period, Hewlett-Packard generated free cash flow in excess of $2.9 billion, which was 54% of cash flows from operations and over 5% of sales. The free cash flows for the other companies in the computer industry are shown for comparison purposes below (in thousands).

| | Dell Computer | Gateway Inc. | Apple Computer |
|---|---|---|---|
| Sales | $35,404,000 | $4,171,325 | $5,742,000 |
| Cash flow from operating activities | $3,538,000 | $ (24,667) | $ 89,000 |
| Cash used to purchase property, plant, and equipment (assumed to maintain productive capacity) | (305,000) | (78,497) | (174,000) |
| Cash used to pay dividends | — | — | — |
| Free cash flow | $3,233,000 | $(103,164) | $ (85,000) |
| Free cash flow as a percent of cash flow from operations | 91% | NA | −96.0% |
| Free cash flow as a percent of sales | 9% | −2.5% | −1.5% |

Positive free cash flow is considered favorable. A company that has free cash flow is able to fund internal growth, retire debt, and enjoy financial flexibility. A company with no free cash flow is unable to maintain current productive capacity or dividend payouts to stockholders. Lack of free cash flow can be an early indicator of liquidity problems. Indeed, as stated by one analyst, "Free cash flow gives the company firepower to reduce debt and ultimately generate consistent, actual income."[5]

[5]Jill Krutick, *Fortune*, March 30, 1998, p. 106.

### CORPORATE LIFE-CYCLE STAGES AND CASH FLOW MANAGEMENT

**M**any companies can expect to move through four corporate life-cycle stages, as illustrated below.

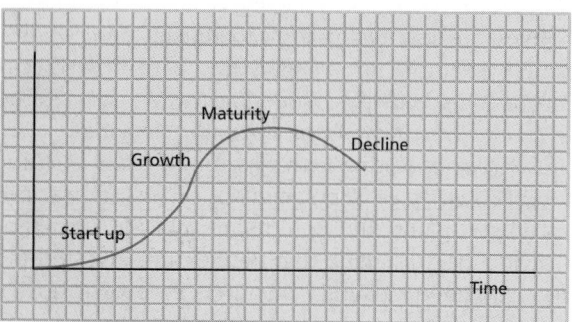

The **start-up phase** is the most risky. It has been reported that nine out of ten businesses fail during the start-up phase. During start-up, the business often generates negative cash flows from operations and thus must obtain cash from financing activities to survive. Banks usually will not lend money to start-up businesses unless there are assets to secure the loan. Thus, the start-up business must often obtain "F&F" (friends and family) financing, or equity investments by wealthy individuals, termed "angel investors."

As the start-up business begins to achieve success, it may move to the growth phase. During the **growth**

**phase**, the business may expand operations, product offerings, channels of distribution, and facilities. A growth business may be able to generate sufficient cash flows from operations to fund the growth, such as was the case with **Microsoft**. Sometimes, however, the cash flows from operations, while positive, are not sufficient to fund future growth. In these circumstances, the growth company will seek additional sources of financing from venture capitalists, public offerings of common stock, and debt. Examples of growth companies are **Krispy Kreme Doughnuts** and **Panera Bread Company**.

Eventually, a business becomes mature. **Mature** businesses have fewer opportunities to grow and are usually under competitive pressure from other large businesses. Mature businesses generate large cash flows from operations but do not need excess cash to grow the business. As such, mature businesses will use excess cash to pay dividends or purchase treasury stock as ways to provide returns to shareholders. Examples of mature businesses are **Procter & Gamble** and **International Paper**.

Not all businesses move into the fourth stage of decline. During **decline**, business opportunities are failing, operating budgets are reduced, advertising is scaled back, facilities are sold, and dividends are cut. Businesses in decline attempt to conserve cash in order to satisfy debtors, while reducing size in an orderly manner. **Kmart** is an example of a business that has suffered a decline.

 **ppendix   Work Sheet for Statement of Cash Flows**

A work sheet may be useful in assembling data for the statement of cash flows. Whether or not a work sheet is used, the concepts of cash flow and the statements of cash flows presented in this chapter are not affected. In this appendix, we will describe and illustrate the use of work sheets for the indirect method and the direct method.

## Work Sheet—Indirect Method

We will use the data for Rundell Inc., presented in Exhibit 3, as a basis for illustrating the work sheet for the indirect method. The procedures used in preparing this work sheet, shown in Exhibit 9, are outlined below.

1. List the title of each balance sheet account in the Accounts column. For each account, enter its balance as of December 31, 2005, in the first column and its balance as of December 31, 2006, in the last column. Place the credit balances in parentheses. The column totals should equal zero, since the total of the debits in a column should equal the total of the credits in a column.
2. Analyze the change during the year in each account to determine the net increase (decrease) in cash and the cash flows from operating activities, investing activities, financing activities, and the noncash investing and financing activities. Show the effect of the change on cash flows by making entries in the Transactions columns.

# •Exhibit 9   Work Sheet for Statement of Cash Flows—Indirect Method

**Rundell Inc.**
**Work Sheet for Statement of Cash Flows**
**For the Year Ended December 31, 2006**

| | Accounts | Balance Dec. 31, 2005 | Transactions Debit | Transactions Credit | Balance Dec. 31, 2006 | |
|---|---|---|---|---|---|---|
| 1 | Cash | 26 000 00 | (o) 71 500 00 | | 97 500 00 | 1 |
| 2 | Accounts receivable (net) | 65 000 00 | (n) 9 000 00 | | 74 000 00 | 2 |
| 3 | Inventories | 180 000 00 | | (m) 8 000 00 | 172 000 00 | 3 |
| 4 | Land | 125 000 00 | (k) 15 000 00 | (l) 60 000 00 | 80 000 00 | 4 |
| 5 | Building | 200 000 00 | (j) 60 000 00 | | 260 000 00 | 5 |
| 6 | Accumulated depreciation—building | (58 300 00) | | (i) 7 000 00 | (65 300 00) | 6 |
| 7 | Accounts payable (merchandise creditors) | (46 700 00) | (h) 3 200 00 | | (43 500 00) | 7 |
| 8 | Accrued expenses payable (operating expenses) | (24 300 00) | | (g) 2 200 00 | (26 500 00) | 8 |
| 9 | Income taxes payable | (8 400 00) | (f) 500 00 | | (7 900 00) | 9 |
| 10 | Dividends payable | (10 000 00) | | (e) 4 000 00 | (14 000 00) | 10 |
| 11 | Bonds payable | (150 000 00) | (d) 50 000 00 | | (100 000 00) | 11 |
| 12 | Common stock | (16 000 00) | | (c) 8 000 00 | (24 000 00) | 12 |
| 13 | Paid-in capital in excess of par | (80 000 00) | | (c) 40 000 00 | (120 000 00) | 13 |
| 14 | Retained earnings | (202 300 00) | (b) 28 000 00 | (a) 108 000 00 | (282 300 00) | 14 |
| 15 | Totals | 0 00 | 237 200 00 | 237 200 00 | 0 00 | 15 |
| 16 | Operating activities: | | | | | 16 |
| 17 | Net income | | (a) 108 000 00 | | | 17 |
| 18 | Depreciation of building | | (i) 7 000 00 | | | 18 |
| 19 | Decrease in inventories | | (m) 8 000 00 | | | 19 |
| 20 | Increase in accrued expenses | | (g) 2 200 00 | | | 20 |
| 21 | Increase in accounts receivable | | | (n) 9 000 00 | | 21 |
| 22 | Decrease in accounts payable | | | (h) 3 200 00 | | 22 |
| 23 | Decrease in income taxes payable | | | (f) 500 00 | | 23 |
| 24 | Gain on sale of land | | | (l) 12 000 00 | | 24 |
| 25 | Investing activities: | | | | | 25 |
| 26 | Sale of land | | (l) 72 000 00 | | | 26 |
| 27 | Purchase of land | | | (k) 15 000 00 | | 27 |
| 28 | Purchase of building | | | (j) 60 000 00 | | 28 |
| 29 | Financing activities: | | | | | 29 |
| 30 | Issued common stock | | (c) 48 000 00 | | | 30 |
| 31 | Retired bonds payable | | | (d) 50 000 00 | | 31 |
| 32 | Declared cash dividends | | | (b) 28 000 00 | | 32 |
| 33 | Increase in dividends payable | | (e) 4 000 00 | | | 33 |
| 34 | Net increase in cash | | | (o) 71 500 00 | | 34 |
| 35 | Totals | | 249 200 00 | 249 200 00 | | 35 |

## Analyzing Accounts

An efficient method of analyzing cash flows is to determine the type of cash flow activity that led to changes in balance sheet accounts during the period. As we analyze each noncash account, we will make entries on the work sheet for specific types of cash flow activities related to the noncash accounts. After we have analyzed all the noncash accounts, we will make an entry for the increase (decrease) in cash during the period. These entries, however, are not posted to the ledger. They only aid in assembling the data on the work sheet.

The order in which the accounts are analyzed is unimportant. However, it is more efficient to begin with the retained earnings account and proceed upward in the account listing.

**Retained Earnings**  The work sheet shows a Retained Earnings balance of $202,300 at December 31, 2005, and $282,300 at December 31, 2006. Thus, Retained Earnings increased $80,000 during the year. This increase resulted from two factors: (1) net income of $108,000 and (2) declaring cash dividends of $28,000. To identify the cash flows by activity, we will make two entries on the work sheet. These entries also serve to account for or explain, in terms of cash flows, the increase of $80,000.

In closing the accounts at the end of the year, the retained earnings account was credited for the net income of $108,000. The $108,000 is reported on the statement of cash flows as "cash flows from operating activities." The following entry is made in the Transactions columns on the work sheet. This entry (1) accounts for the credit portion of the closing entry (to Retained Earnings) and (2) identifies the cash flow in the bottom portion of the work sheet.

| | | | |
|---|---|---|---|
| (a) | Operating Activities—Net Income | 108,000 | |
| | Retained Earnings | | 108,000 |

In closing the accounts at the end of the year, the retained earnings account was debited for dividends declared of $28,000. The $28,000 is reported as a financing activity on the statement of cash flows. The following entry on the work sheet (1) accounts for the debit portion of the closing entry (to Retained Earnings) and (2) identifies the cash flow in the bottom portion of the work sheet.

| | | | |
|---|---|---|---|
| (b) | Retained Earnings | 28,000 | |
| | Financing Activities—Declared Cash Dividends | | 28,000 |

The $28,000 of declared dividends will be adjusted later for the actual amount of cash dividends paid during the year.

**Other Accounts**  The entries for the other accounts are made in the work sheet in a manner similar to entries (a) and (b). A summary of these entries is as follows:

| | | | |
|---|---|---|---|
| (c) | Financing Activities—Issued Common Stock | 48,000 | |
| | Common Stock | | 8,000 |
| | Paid-In Capital in Excess of Par—Common Stock | | 40,000 |
| (d) | Bonds Payable | 50,000 | |
| | Financing Activities—Retired Bonds Payable | | 50,000 |
| (e) | Financing Activities—Increase in Dividends Payable | 4,000 | |
| | Dividends Payable | | 4,000 |
| (f) | Income Taxes Payable | 500 | |
| | Operating Activities—Decrease in Income Taxes Payable | | 500 |
| (g) | Operating Activities—Increase in Accrued Expenses | 2,200 | |
| | Accrued Expenses Payable | | 2,200 |
| (h) | Accounts Payable | 3,200 | |
| | Operating Activities—Decrease in Accounts Payable | | 3,200 |
| (i) | Operating Activities—Depreciation of Building | 7,000 | |
| | Accumulated Depreciation—Building | | 7,000 |
| (j) | Building | 60,000 | |
| | Investing Activities—Purchase of Building | | 60,000 |

| | | | |
|---|---|---|---|
| (k) | Land | 15,000 | |
| | Investing Activities—Purchase of Land | | 15,000 |
| | | | |
| (l) | Investing Activities—Sale of Land | 72,000 | |
| | Operating Activities—Gain on Sale of Land | | 12,000 |
| | Land | | 60,000 |
| | | | |
| (m) | Operating Activities—Decrease in Inventories | 8,000 | |
| | Inventories | | 8,000 |
| | | | |
| (n) | Accounts Receivable | 9,000 | |
| | Operating Activities—Increase in Accounts Receivable | | 9,000 |
| | | | |
| (o) | Cash | 71,500 | |
| | Net Increase in Cash | | 71,500 |

## Completing the Work Sheet

After we have analyzed all the balance sheet accounts and made the entries on the work sheet, all the operating, investing, and financing activities are identified in the bottom portion of the work sheet. The accuracy of the work sheet entries is verified by the equality of each pair of the totals of the debit and credit Transactions columns.

## Preparing the Statement of Cash Flows

The statement of cash flows prepared from the work sheet is identical to the statement in Exhibit 6. The data for the three sections of the statement are obtained from the bottom portion of the work sheet.

In the cash flows from operating activities section, the effect of depreciation is normally presented first. The effects of increases and decreases in current assets and current liabilities are then presented. The effects of any gains and losses on operating activities are normally reported last. The cash paid for dividends is reported as $24,000 instead of the amount of dividends declared ($28,000) less the increase in dividends payable ($4,000). Any noncash investing and financing activities are usually reported in a separate schedule at the bottom of the statement.

# Work Sheet—Direct Method

As a basis for illustrating the direct method work sheet, we will use the balance sheet data for Rundell Inc. in Exhibit 3 and the income statement data in Exhibit 7. The procedures used in preparing the work sheet in Exhibit 10 are outlined below.

1. List the title of each balance sheet account in the Accounts column. For each account, enter its balance as of December 31, 2005, in the first column and its balance as of December 31, 2006, in the last column. Place the credit balances in parentheses. The column totals should equal zero, since the total of the debits in a column should equal the total of the credits in a column.
2. List the title of each income statement account and "Net income" on the work sheet.
3. Analyze the effect of each income statement item on cash flows from operating activities. Beginning with sales, enter the balance of each item in the proper Transactions column. Complete the entry in the Transactions columns to show the effect on cash flows.
4. Analyze the change during the year in each balance sheet account to determine the net increase (decrease) in cash and the cash flows from operating activities, investing activities, financing activities, and the noncash investing and financing activities. Show the effect of the change on cash flows by making entries in the Transactions columns.

# •Exhibit 10    Work Sheet for Statement of Cash Flows—Direct Method

**Rundell Inc.**
**Work Sheet for Statement of Cash Flows**
**For the Year Ended December 31, 2006**

| | Accounts | Balance Dec. 31, 2005 | Transactions Debit | Transactions Credit | Balance Dec. 31, 2006 | |
|---|---|---|---|---|---|---|
| 1 | **Balance Sheet** | | | | | 1 |
| 2 | Cash | 26 000 00 | (t) 71 500 00 | | 97 500 00 | 2 |
| 3 | Accounts receivable (net) | 65 000 00 | (s) 9 000 00 | | 74 000 00 | 3 |
| 4 | Inventories | 180 000 00 | | (r) 8 000 00 | 172 000 00 | 4 |
| 5 | Land | 125 000 00 | (q) 15 000 00 | (e) 60 000 00 | 80 000 00 | 5 |
| 6 | Building | 200 000 00 | (p) 60 000 00 | | 260 000 00 | 6 |
| 7 | Accumulated depreciation—building | (58 300 00) | | (c) 7 000 00 | (65 300 00) | 7 |
| 8 | Accounts payable (merchandise creditors) | (46 700 00) | (o) 3 200 00 | | (43 500 00) | 8 |
| 9 | Accrued expenses payable (operating expenses) | (24 300 00) | | (n) 2 200 00 | (26 500 00) | 9 |
| 10 | Income taxes payable | (8 400 00) | (m) 500 00 | | (7 900 00) | 10 |
| 11 | Dividends payable | (10 000 00) | | (l) 4 000 00 | (14 000 00) | 11 |
| 12 | Bonds payable | (150 000 00) | (k) 50 000 00 | | (100 000 00) | 12 |
| 13 | Common stock | (16 000 00) | | (j) 8 000 00 | (24 000 00) | 13 |
| 14 | Paid-in capital in excess of par | (80 000 00) | | (j) 40 000 00 | (120 000 00) | 14 |
| 15 | Retained earnings | (202 300 00) | (i) 28 000 00 | (h) 108 000 00 | (282 300 00) | 15 |
| 16 | Totals | 0 00 | 237 200 00 | 237 200 00 | 0 00 | 16 |
| 17 | **Income Statement** | | | | | 17 |
| 18 | Sales | | | (a) 1,180 000 00 | | 18 |
| 19 | Cost of merchandise sold | | (b) 790 000 00 | | | 19 |
| 20 | Depreciation expense | | (c) 7 000 00 | | | 20 |
| 21 | Other operating expenses | | (d) 196 000 00 | | | 21 |
| 22 | Gain on sale of land | | | (e) 12 000 00 | | 22 |
| 23 | Interest expense | | (f) 8 000 00 | | | 23 |
| 24 | Income taxes | | (g) 83 000 00 | | | 24 |
| 25 | Net income | | (h) 108 000 00 | | | 25 |
| 26 | **Cash Flows** | | | | | 26 |
| 27 | Operating activities: | | | | | 27 |
| 28 |   Cash received from customers | | (a) 1,180 000 00 | (s) 9 000 00 | | 28 |
| 29 |   Cash payments: | | | | | 29 |
| 30 |     Merchandise | | (r) 8 000 00 | (b) 790 000 00 | | 30 |
| 31 | | | | (o) 3 200 00 | | 31 |
| 32 |     Operating expenses | | (n) 2 200 00 | (d) 196 000 00 | | 32 |
| 33 |     Interest | | | (f) 8 000 00 | | 33 |
| 34 |     Income taxes | | | (g) 83 000 00 | | 34 |
| 35 | | | | (m) 500 00 | | 35 |
| 36 | Investing activities: | | | | | 36 |
| 37 |   Sale of land | | (e) 72 000 00 | | | 37 |
| 38 |   Purchase of land | | | (q) 15 000 00 | | 38 |
| 39 |   Purchase of building | | | (p) 60 000 00 | | 39 |
| 40 | Financing activities: | | | | | 40 |
| 41 |   Issued common stock | | (j) 48 000 00 | | | 41 |
| 42 |   Retired bonds payable | | | (k) 50 000 00 | | 42 |
| 43 |   Declared cash dividends | | | (i) 28 000 00 | | 43 |
| 44 |   Increase in dividends payable | | (l) 4 000 00 | | | 44 |
| 45 | Net increase in cash | | | (t) 71 500 00 | | 45 |
| 46 | Totals | | 2,506 200 00 | 2,506 200 00 | | 46 |

# Analyzing Accounts

Under the direct method of reporting cash flows from operating activities, analyzing accounts begins with the income statement. As we analyze each income statement account, we will make entries on the work sheet that show the effect on cash flows from operating activities. After we have analyzed the income statement accounts, we will analyze changes in the balance sheet accounts.

The order in which the balance sheet accounts are analyzed is unimportant. However, it is more efficient to begin with the retained earnings account and proceed upward in the account listing. As each noncash balance sheet account is analyzed, we will make entries on the work sheet for the related cash flow activities. After we have analyzed all the noncash accounts, we will make an entry for the increase (decrease) in cash during the period.

**Sales**   The income statement for Rundell Inc. shows sales of $1,180,000 for the year. Sales for cash provide cash when the sale is made. Sales on account provide cash when customers pay their bills. The entry on the work sheet is as follows:

| | | | |
|---|---|---|---|
| (a) | Operating Activities—Receipts from Customers | 1,180,000 | |
| | Sales | | 1,180,000 |

**Cost of Merchandise Sold**   The income statement for Rundell Inc. shows cost of merchandise sold of $790,000 for the year. The cost of merchandise sold requires cash payments for cash purchases of merchandise. For purchases on account, cash payments are made when the invoices are due. The entry on the work sheet is as follows:

| | | | |
|---|---|---|---|
| (b) | Cost of Merchandise Sold | 790,000 | |
| | Operating Activities—Payments for Merchandise | | 790,000 |

**Depreciation Expense**   The income statement for Rundell Inc. shows depreciation expense of $7,000. Depreciation expense does not require a cash outflow and thus is not reported on the statement of cash flows. The entry on the work sheet to fully account for the depreciation expense is as follows:

| | | | |
|---|---|---|---|
| (c) | Depreciation Expense | 7,000 | |
| | Accumulated Depreciation—Building | | 7,000 |

**Other Accounts**   The entries for the other accounts are made on the work sheet in a manner similar to entries (a), (b), and (c). A summary of these entries is as follows:

| | | | |
|---|---|---|---|
| (d) | Other Operating Expenses | 196,000 | |
| | Operating Activities—Paid Operating Expenses | | 196,000 |
| (e) | Investing Activities—Sale of Land | 72,000 | |
| | Land | | 60,000 |
| | Gain on Sale of Land | | 12,000 |
| (f) | Interest Expense | 8,000 | |
| | Operating Activities—Paid Interest | | 8,000 |
| (g) | Income Taxes | 83,000 | |
| | Operating Activities—Paid Income Taxes | | 83,000 |
| (h) | Net Income | 108,000 | |
| | Retained Earnings | | 108,000 |
| (i) | Retained Earnings | 28,000 | |
| | Financing Activities—Declared Cash Dividends | | 28,000 |

| (j) | Financing Activities—Issued Common Stock | 48,000 | |
| | Common Stock | | 8,000 |
| | Paid-In Capital in Excess of Par—Common Stock | | 40,000 |
| (k) | Bonds Payable | 50,000 | |
| | Financing Activities—Retired Bonds Payable | | 50,000 |
| (l) | Financing Activities—Increase in Dividends Payable | 4,000 | |
| | Dividends Payable | | 4,000 |
| (m) | Income Taxes Payable | 500 | |
| | Operating Activities—Cash Paid for Income Taxes | | 500 |
| (n) | Operating Activities—Cash Paid for Operating Expenses | 2,200 | |
| | Accrued Expenses Payable | | 2,200 |
| (o) | Accounts Payable | 3,200 | |
| | Operating Activities—Cash Paid for Merchandise | | 3,200 |
| (p) | Building | 60,000 | |
| | Investing Activities—Purchase of Building | | 60,000 |
| (q) | Land | 15,000 | |
| | Investing Activities—Purchase of Land | | 15,000 |
| (r) | Operating Activities—Cash Paid for Merchandise | 8,000 | |
| | Inventories | | 8,000 |
| (s) | Accounts Receivable | 9,000 | |
| | Operating Activities—Cash Received from Customers | | 9,000 |
| (t) | Cash | 71,500 | |
| | Net Increase in Cash | | 71,500 |

## Completing the Work Sheet

After we have analyzed all the income statement and balance sheet accounts and have made the entries on the work sheet, all the operating, investing, and financing activities are identified in the bottom portion of the work sheet. The mathematical accuracy of the work sheet entries is verified by the equality of each pair of the totals of the debit and credit Transactions columns.

## Preparing the Statement of Cash Flows

The statement of cash flows prepared from the work sheet is identical to the statement in Exhibit 8. The data for the three sections of the statement are obtained from the bottom portion of the work sheet. Some of these data may not be reported exactly as they appear on the work sheet. The cash paid for dividends is reported as $24,000 instead of the amount of dividends declared ($28,000) less the increase in the dividends payable ($4,000).

# Key Points

**1  Summarize the types of cash flow activities reported in the statement of cash flows.**

The statement of cash flows reports useful information about a firm's ability to generate cash from operations, maintain and expand its operating capacity, meet its financial obligations, and pay dividends.

The statement of cash flows reports cash receipts and cash payments by three types of activities: operating activities, investing activities, and financing activities.

Cash flows from operating activities are cash flows from transactions that affect net income. There are two methods of reporting cash flows from operating activities: (1) the direct method and (2) the indirect method.

Cash inflows from investing activities are cash flows from the sale of investments, fixed assets, and intangible assets. Cash outflows generally include payments to acquire investments, fixed assets, and intangible assets.

Cash inflows from financing activities include proceeds from issuing equity securities, such as preferred and common stock. Cash inflows also arise from issuing bonds, mortgage notes payable, and other long-term debt. Cash outflows from financing activities arise from paying cash dividends, purchasing treasury stock, and repaying amounts borrowed.

Investing and financing for a business may be affected by transactions that do not involve cash. The effect of such transactions should be reported in a separate schedule accompanying the statement of cash flows.

Because it may be misleading, cash flow per share is not reported in the statement of cash flows.

**2  Prepare a statement of cash flows, using the indirect method.**

To prepare the statement of cash flows, changes in the noncash balance sheet accounts are analyzed. This logic relies on the fact that a change in any balance sheet account can be analyzed in terms of changes in the other balance sheet accounts. Thus, by analyzing the noncash balance sheet accounts, those activities that resulted in cash flows can be identified. Although the noncash balance sheet accounts may be analyzed in any order, it is usually more efficient to begin with retained earnings. Additional data are obtained by analyzing the income statement accounts and supporting records.

**3  Prepare a statement of cash flows, using the direct method.**

The direct method and the indirect method will report the same amount of cash flows from operating activities. Also, the manner of reporting cash flows from investing and financing activities is the same under both methods. The methods differ in how the cash flows from operating activities data are obtained, an-

alyzed, and reported. The direct method reports cash flows from operating activities by major classes of operating cash receipts and cash payments. The difference between the major classes of total operating cash receipts and total operating cash payments is the net cash flow from operating activities.

The data for reporting cash flows from operating activities by the direct method can be obtained by analyzing the cash flows related to the revenues and expenses reported on the income statement. The revenues and expenses are adjusted from the accrual basis of accounting to the cash basis for purposes of preparing the statement of cash flows.

When the direct method is used, a reconciliation of net income and net cash flow from operating activities is reported in a separate schedule. This schedule is similar to the cash flows from operating activities section of the statement of cash flows prepared using the indirect method.

**4  Calculate and interpret the free cash flow.**

Free cash flow is the amount of operating cash flow remaining after replacing current productive capacity and maintaining current dividends. Free cash flow is the amount of cash available to reduce debt, expand the business, or return to shareholders through increased dividends or treasury stock purchases.

# Key Terms

cash flows from financing activities (641)

cash flows from investing activities (641)

cash flows from operating activities (641)

direct method (642)

free cash flow (658)

indirect method (642)

statement of cash flows (641)

# Illustrative Problem

The comparative balance sheet of Dowling Company for December 31, 2007 and 2006, is as follows:

**Dowling Company**
**Comparative Balance Sheet**
**December 31, 2007 and 2006**

| | 2007 | 2006 |
|---|---|---|
| **Assets** | | |
| Cash .......................................... | $ 140,350 | $ 95,900 |
| Accounts receivable (net) ........................ | 95,300 | 102,300 |
| Inventories .................................... | 165,200 | 157,900 |
| Prepaid expenses .............................. | 6,240 | 5,860 |
| Investments (long-term) ........................ | 35,700 | 84,700 |
| Land ......................................... | 75,000 | 90,000 |
| Buildings ..................................... | 375,000 | 260,000 |
| Accumulated depreciation—buildings ............. | (71,300) | (58,300) |
| Machinery and equipment ....................... | 428,300 | 428,300 |
| Accumulated depreciation—machinery and equipment ....... | (148,500) | (138,000) |
| Patents ....................................... | 58,000 | 65,000 |
| Total assets ................................... | $1,159,290 | $1,093,660 |
| | | |
| **Liabilities and Stockholders' Equity** | | |
| Accounts payable (merchandise creditors) ................ | $ 43,500 | $ 46,700 |
| Accrued expenses (operating expenses) ................. | 14,000 | 12,500 |
| Income taxes payable ........................... | 7,900 | 8,400 |
| Dividends payable ............................. | 14,000 | 10,000 |
| Mortgage note payable, due 2017 ................. | 40,000 | 0 |
| Bonds payable ................................ | 150,000 | 250,000 |
| Common stock, $30 par ......................... | 450,000 | 375,000 |
| Excess of issue price over par—common stock ............. | 66,250 | 41,250 |
| Retained earnings ............................. | 373,640 | 349,810 |
| Total liabilities and stockholders' equity ................. | $1,159,290 | $1,093,660 |

The income statement for Dowling Company is shown below.

**Dowling Company**
**Income Statement**
**For the Year Ended December 31, 2007**

| | | |
|---|---|---|
| Sales ......................................... | | $1,100,000 |
| Cost of merchandise sold ....................... | | 710,000 |
| Gross profit ................................... | | $ 390,000 |
| Operating expenses: | | |
|   Depreciation expense ........................ | $ 23,500 | |
|   Patent amortization .......................... | 7,000 | |
|   Other operating expenses ..................... | 196,000 | |
|     Total operating expenses ................. | | 226,500 |
| Income from operations ......................... | | $ 163,500 |
| Other income: | | |
|   Gain on sale of investments ................... | $ 11,000 | |
| Other expense: | | |
|   Interest expense ............................ | 26,000 | (15,000) |
| Income before income tax ....................... | | $ 148,500 |
| Income tax expense ............................ | | 50,000 |
| Net income ................................... | | $ 98,500 |

An examination of the accounting records revealed the following additional information applicable to 2007:

a. Land costing $15,000 was sold for $15,000.
b. A mortgage note was issued for $40,000.
c. A building costing $115,000 was constructed.
d. 2,500 shares of common stock were issued at 40 in exchange for the bonds payable.
e. Cash dividends declared were $74,670.

## Instructions

1. Prepare a statement of cash flows, using the indirect method of reporting cash flows from operating activities.
2. Prepare a statement of cash flows, using the direct method of reporting cash flows from operating activities.

## Solution

**1.**

**Dowling Company**
**Statement of Cash Flows—Indirect Method**
**For the Year Ended December 31, 2007**

| | | | |
|---|---:|---:|---:|
| Cash flows from operating activities: | | | |
| Net income, per income statement . . . . . . . . . . . . . . . | | $ 98,500 | |
| Add: Depreciation . . . . . . . . . . . . . . . . . . . . . . . . . . | $23,500 | | |
| Amortization of patents . . . . . . . . . . . . . . . . . . | 7,000 | | |
| Decrease in accounts receivable . . . . . . . . . . . . . | 7,000 | | |
| Increase in accrued expenses . . . . . . . . . . . . . . . . | 1,500 | 39,000 | |
| | | $137,500 | |
| Deduct: Increase in inventories . . . . . . . . . . . . . . . . . . | $ 7,300 | | |
| Increase in prepaid expenses . . . . . . . . . . . . . . | 380 | | |
| Decrease in accounts payable . . . . . . . . . . . . . . | 3,200 | | |
| Decrease in income taxes payable . . . . . . . . . . . | 500 | | |
| Gain on sale of investments . . . . . . . . . . . . . . | 11,000 | 22,380 | |
| Net cash flow from operating activities . . . . . . . . . . . . | | | $115,120 |
| Cash flows from investing activities: | | | |
| Cash received from sale of: | | | |
| Investments . . . . . . . . . . . . . . . . . . . . . . . . . . . . . . . . | $60,000 | | |
| Land . . . . . . . . . . . . . . . . . . . . . . . . . . . . . . . . . . . . | 15,000 | $ 75,000 | |
| Less: Cash paid for construction of building . . . . . . . . . | | 115,000 | |
| Net cash flow used for investing activities . . . . . . . . . . | | | (40,000) |
| Cash flows from financing activities: | | | |
| Cash received from issuing mortgage note payable . . . . | | $ 40,000 | |
| Less: Cash paid for dividends . . . . . . . . . . . . . . . . . . . . | | 70,670 | |
| Net cash flow used for financing activities . . . . . . . . . . | | | (30,670) |
| Increase in cash . . . . . . . . . . . . . . . . . . . . . . . . . . . . . . | | | $ 44,450 |
| Cash at the beginning of the year . . . . . . . . . . . . . . . . . | | | 95,900 |
| Cash at the end of the year . . . . . . . . . . . . . . . . . . . . . . | | | $140,350 |
| | | | |
| **Schedule of Noncash Investing and** | | | |
| **Financing Activities:** | | | |
| Issued common stock to retire bonds payable . . . . . . . . | | | $100,000 |

2.

**Dowling Company**
**Statement of Cash Flows—Direct Method**
**For the Year Ended December 31, 2007**

| | | | |
|---|---|---|---|
| Cash flows from operating activities: | | | |
| Cash received from customers[1] . . . . . . . . . . . . . . . . . | | $1,107,000 | |
| Deduct: Cash paid for merchandise[2] . . . . . . . . . . . . . | $720,500 | | |
| Cash paid for operating expenses[3] . . . . . . . . | 194,880 | | |
| Cash paid for interest expense . . . . . . . . . . . . | 26,000 | | |
| Cash paid for income tax[4] . . . . . . . . . . . . . . | 50,500 | 991,880 | |
| Net cash flow from operating activities . . . . . . . . . . . | | | $115,120 |
| Cash flows from investing activities: | | | |
| Cash received from sale of: | | | |
| Investments . . . . . . . . . . . . . . . . . . . . . . . . . . . . . | $ 60,000 | | |
| Land . . . . . . . . . . . . . . . . . . . . . . . . . . . . . . . . . . | 15,000 | $ 75,000 | |
| Less: Cash paid for construction of building . . . . . . . . | | 115,000 | |
| Net cash flow used for investing activities . . . . . . . . . | | | (40,000) |
| Cash flows from financing activities: | | | |
| Cash received from issuing mortgage note payable . . . | | $ 40,000 | |
| Less: Cash paid for dividends[5] . . . . . . . . . . . . . . . . . . | | 70,670 | |
| Net cash flow used for financing activities . . . . . . . . | | | (30,670) |
| Increase in cash . . . . . . . . . . . . . . . . . . . . . . . . . . . . | | | $ 44,450 |
| Cash at the beginning of the year . . . . . . . . . . . . . . . . | | | 95,900 |
| Cash at the end of the year . . . . . . . . . . . . . . . . . . . . | | | $140,350 |

**Schedule of Noncash Investing and**
**Financing Activities:**

| | |
|---|---|
| Issued common stock to retire bonds payable . . . . . . . | $100,000 |

*Computations:*
   [1]$1,100,000 + $7,000 = $1,107,000
   [2]$710,000 + $3,200 + $7,300 = $720,500
   [3]$196,000 + $380 − $1,500 = $194,880
   [4]$50,000 + $500 = $50,500
   [5]$74,670 + $10,000 − $14,000 = $70,670

# Self-Examination Questions (Answers at End of Chapter)

1. An example of a cash flow from an operating activity is:
   A. receipt of cash from the sale of stock
   B. receipt of cash from the sale of bonds
   C. payment of cash for dividends
   D. receipt of cash from customers on account

2. An example of a cash flow from an investing activity is:
   A. receipt of cash from the sale of equipment
   B. receipt of cash from the sale of stock
   C. payment of cash for dividends
   D. payment of cash to acquire treasury stock

3. An example of a cash flow from a financing activity is:
   A. receipt of cash from customers on account

   B. receipt of cash from the sale of equipment
   C. payment of cash for dividends
   D. payment of cash to acquire land

4. Which of the following methods of reporting cash flows from operating activities adjusts net income for revenues and expenses not involving the receipt or payment of cash?
   A. Direct method     C. Reciprocal method
   B. Purchase method     D. Indirect method

5. The net income reported on the income statement for the year was $55,000, and depreciation of fixed assets for the year was $22,000. The balances of the current asset and current liability accounts at the beginning and end of the year are as follows:

|  | End | Beginning |
|---|---|---|
| Cash | $ 65,000 | $ 70,000 |
| Accounts receivable | 100,000 | 90,000 |
| Inventories | 145,000 | 150,000 |
| Prepaid expenses | 7,500 | 8,000 |
| Accounts payable (merchandise creditors) | 51,000 | 58,000 |

The total amount reported for cash flows from operating activities in the statement of cash flows, using the indirect method, is:

A. $33,000            C. $65,500
B. $55,000            D. $77,000

# Class Discussion Questions

1. What is the principal disadvantage of the direct method of reporting cash flows from operating activities?
2. What are the major advantages of the indirect method of reporting cash flows from operating activities?
3. A corporation issued $200,000 of common stock in exchange for $200,000 of fixed assets. Where would this transaction be reported on the statement of cash flows?
4. a. What is the effect on cash flows of declaring and issuing a stock dividend?
   b. Is the stock dividend reported on the statement of cash flows?
5. A retail business, using the accrual method of accounting, owed merchandise creditors (accounts payable) $290,000 at the beginning of the year and $315,000 at the end of the year. How would the $25,000 increase be used to adjust net income in determining the amount of cash flows from operating activities by the indirect method? Explain.
6. If salaries payable was $75,000 at the beginning of the year and $65,000 at the end of the year, should $10,000 be added to or deducted from income to determine the amount of cash flows from operating activities by the indirect method? Explain.
7. A long-term investment in bonds with a cost of $75,000 was sold for $80,000 cash. (a) What was the gain or loss on the sale? (b) What was the effect of the transaction on cash flows? (c) How should the transaction be reported in the statement of cash flows if cash flows from operating activities are reported by the indirect method?
8. A corporation issued $5,000,000 of 20-year bonds for cash at 105. How would the transaction be reported on the statement of cash flows?
9. Fully depreciated equipment costing $55,000 was discarded. What was the effect of the transaction on cash flows if (a) $5,000 cash is received, (b) no cash is received?
10. For the current year, Accord Company decided to switch from the indirect method to the direct method for reporting cash flows from operating activities on the statement of cash flows. Will the change cause the amount of net cash flow from operating activities to be (a) larger, (b) smaller, or (c) the same as if the indirect method had been used? Explain.
11. Name five common major classes of operating cash receipts or operating cash payments presented on the statement of cash flows when the cash flows from operating activities are reported by the direct method.
12. In a recent annual report, **eBay Inc.** reported that during the year it issued stock of $128 million for acquisitions. How would this be reported on the statement of cash flows?

REAL WORLD

# Exercises

**EXERCISE 16-1**
*Cash flows from operating activities—net loss*
**Objective 1**

REAL WORLD

On its income statement for a recent year, **TimeWarner Inc.**, reported a net *loss* of $4.9 billion from operations. On its statement of cash flows, it reported $5.3 billion of cash flows from operating activities.

➤ Explain this apparent contradiction between the loss and the positive cash flows.

**EXERCISE 16-2**
*Effect of transactions on cash flows*
**Objective 1**

✓ *b. Cash receipt, $41,000*

State the effect (cash receipt or payment and amount) of each of the following transactions, considered individually, on cash flows:

a. Sold 5,000 shares of $30 par common stock for $45 per share.
b. Sold equipment with a book value of $42,500 for $41,000.
c. Purchased land for $120,000 cash.
d. Purchased 5,000 shares of $30 par common stock as treasury stock at $50 per share.
e. Sold a new issue of $100,000 of bonds at 101.
f. Paid dividends of $1.50 per share. There were 30,000 shares issued and 5,000 shares of treasury stock.
g. Retired $500,000 of bonds, on which there was $2,500 of unamortized discount, for $501,000.
h. Purchased a building by paying $30,000 cash and issuing a $90,000 mortgage note payable.

**EXERCISE 16-3**
*Classifying cash flows*
**Objective 1**

Identify the type of cash flow activity for each of the following events (operating, investing, or financing):

a. Purchased patents.
b. Purchased buildings.
c. Purchased treasury stock.
d. Sold equipment.
e. Net income.
f. Issued preferred stock.
g. Redeemed bonds.
h. Paid cash dividends.
i. Sold long-term investments.
j. Issued common stock.
k. Issued bonds.

**EXERCISE 16-4**
*Cash flows from operating activities—indirect method*
**Objective 2**

Indicate whether each of the following would be added to or deducted from net income in determining net cash flow from operating activities by the indirect method:

a. Increase in notes payable due in 90 days to vendors
b. Loss on disposal of fixed assets
c. Decrease in accounts payable
d. Increase in notes receivable due in 90 days from customers
e. Decrease in salaries payable
f. Decrease in prepaid expenses
g. Depreciation of fixed assets
h. Decrease in accounts receivable
i. Amortization of patent
j. Increase in merchandise inventory
k. Gain on retirement of long-term debt

**EXERCISE 16-5**
*Cash flows from operating activities—indirect method*
**Objectives 1, 2**

SPREADSHEET

✓ a. Cash flows from operating activities, $292,100

The net income reported on the income statement for the current year was $255,800. Depreciation recorded on equipment and a building amounted to $53,500 for the year. Balances of the current asset and current liability accounts at the beginning and end of the year are as follows:

|  | End of Year | Beginning of Year |
| --- | --- | --- |
| Cash | $ 42,000 | $ 44,200 |
| Accounts receivable (net) | 65,400 | 67,000 |
| Inventories | 125,900 | 112,600 |
| Prepaid expenses | 5,800 | 6,000 |
| Accounts payable (merchandise creditors) | 61,400 | 67,500 |
| Salaries payable | 8,300 | 7,900 |

a. Prepare the cash flows from operating activities section of the statement of cash flows, using the indirect method.
b. ▭▬▶ If the direct method had been used, would the net cash flow from operating activities have been the same? Explain.

**EXERCISE 16-6**
*Cash flows from operating activities—indirect method*
**Objective 2**

SPREADSHEET

✓ Cash flows from operating activities, $96,400

The net income reported on the income statement for the current year was $75,000. Depreciation recorded on store equipment for the year amounted to $22,500. Balances of the current asset and current liability accounts at the beginning and end of the year are as follows:

|  | End of Year | Beginning of Year |
| --- | --- | --- |
| Cash | $46,700 | $43,000 |
| Accounts receivable (net) | 28,800 | 32,500 |
| Merchandise inventory | 54,800 | 49,300 |
| Prepaid expenses | 4,000 | 3,600 |
| Accounts payable (merchandise creditors) | 40,500 | 42,400 |
| Wages payable | 25,500 | 22,500 |

Prepare the cash flows from operating activities section of the statement of cash flows, using the indirect method.

**EXERCISE 16-7**
*Determining cash payments to stockholders*
**Objective 2**

The board of directors declared cash dividends totaling $80,000 during the current year. The comparative balance sheet indicates dividends payable of $25,000 at the beginning of the year and $20,000 at the end of the year. What was the amount of cash payments to stockholders during the year?

**EXERCISE 16-8**
*Reporting changes in equipment on statement of cash flows*
**Objective 2**

An analysis of the general ledger accounts indicates that office equipment, which cost $30,000 and on which accumulated depreciation totaled $10,000 on the date of sale, was sold for $25,000 during the year. Using this information, indicate the items to be reported on the statement of cash flows.

**EXERCISE 16-9**
*Reporting changes in equipment on statement of cash flows*
**Objective 2**

An analysis of the general ledger accounts indicates that delivery equipment, which cost $120,000 and on which accumulated depreciation totaled $40,000 on the date of sale, was sold for $75,000 during the year. Using this information, indicate the items to be reported on the statement of cash flows.

**EXERCISE 16-10**
*Reporting land transactions on statement of cash flows*
**Objective 2**

On the basis of the details of the following fixed asset account, indicate the items to be reported on the statement of cash flows:

ACCOUNT **Land** ACCOUNT NO.

| Date | | Item | Debit | Credit | Balance Debit | Balance Credit |
|---|---|---|---|---|---|---|
| 2006 | | | | | | |
| Jan. | 1 | Balance | | | 900,000 | |
| Feb. | 5 | Purchased for cash | 300,000 | | 1,200,000 | |
| Oct. | 30 | Sold for $310,000 | | 250,000 | 950,000 | |

**EXERCISE 16-11**
*Reporting stockholders' equity items on statement of cash flows*
**Objective 2**

On the basis of the following stockholders' equity accounts, indicate the items, exclusive of net income, to be reported on the statement of cash flows. There were no unpaid dividends at either the beginning or the end of the year.

ACCOUNT **Common Stock, $10 Par** ACCOUNT NO.

| Date | | Item | Debit | Credit | Balance Debit | Balance Credit |
|---|---|---|---|---|---|---|
| 2006 | | | | | | |
| Jan. | 1 | Balance, 70,000 shares | | | | 700,000 |
| Feb. | 11 | 12,000 shares issued for cash | | 120,000 | | 820,000 |
| June | 30 | 4,100-share stock dividend | | 41,000 | | 861,000 |

ACCOUNT **Paid-In Capital in Excess of Par—Common Stock** ACCOUNT NO.

| Date | | Item | Debit | Credit | Balance Debit | Balance Credit |
|---|---|---|---|---|---|---|
| 2006 | | | | | | |
| Jan. | 1 | Balance | | | | 140,000 |
| Feb. | 11 | 12,000 shares issued for cash | | 360,000 | | 500,000 |
| June | 30 | Stock dividend | | 102,500 | | 602,500 |

ACCOUNT **Retained Earnings** ACCOUNT NO.

| Date | | Item | Debit | Credit | Balance Debit | Balance Credit |
|---|---|---|---|---|---|---|
| 2006 | | | | | | |
| Jan. | 1 | Balance | | | | 1,000,000 |
| June | 30 | Stock dividend | 143,500 | | | 856,500 |
| Dec. | 30 | Cash dividend | 240,000 | | | 616,500 |
| | 31 | Net income | | 800,000 | | 1,416,500 |

**EXERCISE 16-12**
*Reporting land acquisition for cash and mortgage note on statement of cash flows*
**Objective 2**

On the basis of the details of the following fixed asset account, indicate the items to be reported on the statement of cash flows:

ACCOUNT **Land** ACCOUNT NO.

| Date | | Item | Debit | Credit | Balance Debit | Balance Credit |
|---|---|---|---|---|---|---|
| 2006 | | | | | | |
| Jan. | 1 | Balance | | | 160,000 | |
| Feb. | 10 | Purchased for cash | 290,000 | | 450,000 | |
| Nov. | 20 | Purchased with long-term mortgage note | 200,000 | | 650,000 | |

**EXERCISE 16-13**
*Reporting issuance and retirement of long-term debt*
Objective 2

On the basis of the details of the following bonds payable and related discount accounts, indicate the items to be reported in the financing section of the statement of cash flows, assuming no gain or loss on retiring the bonds:

ACCOUNT *Bonds Payable*      ACCOUNT NO.

| Date | | Item | Debit | Credit | Balance Debit | Balance Credit |
|------|---|------|-------|--------|-------|--------|
| 2006 | | | | | | |
| Jan. | 1 | Balance | | | | 150,000 |
| Jan. | 3 | Retire bonds | 48,000 | | | 102,000 |
| July | 30 | Issue bonds | | 200,000 | | 302,000 |

ACCOUNT *Discount on Bonds Payable*      ACCOUNT NO.

| Date | | Item | Debit | Credit | Balance Debit | Balance Credit |
|------|---|------|-------|--------|-------|--------|
| 2006 | | | | | | |
| Jan. | 1 | Balance | | | 12,000 | |
| Jan. | 3 | Retire bonds | | 4,000 | 8,000 | |
| July | 30 | Issue bonds | 15,000 | | 23,000 | |
| Dec. | 31 | Amortize discount | | 1,200 | 21,800 | |

**EXERCISE 16-14**
*Determining net income from net cash flow from operating activities*
Objective 2

Tiger Golf Inc. reported a net cash flow from operating activities of $105,700 on its statement of cash flows for the year ended December 31, 2006. The following information was reported in the cash flows from operating activities section of the statement of cash flows, using the indirect method:

| | |
|---|---|
| Decrease in income taxes payable | $ 2,100 |
| Decrease in inventories | 6,400 |
| Depreciation | 11,000 |
| Gain on sale of investments | 3,600 |
| Increase in accounts payable | 4,700 |
| Increase in prepaid expenses | 2,000 |
| Increase in accounts receivable | 6,500 |

Determine the net income reported by Tiger Golf Inc. for the year ended December 31, 2006.

**EXERCISE 16-15**
*Cash flows from operating activities*
Objective 2

REAL WORLD    SPREADSHEET

✓ *Cash flows from operating activities, $205,006*

Selected data derived from the income statement and balance sheet of **Williams Sonoma, Inc.**, a specialty retailer of kitchen products, for a recent year are as follows:

| Income Statement Data (dollars in thousands) | |
|---|---|
| Net earnings | $75,096 |
| Depreciation | 81,594 |
| Loss on sale of fixed assets | 3,950 |
| Other noncash income | 7,242 |

| Balance Sheet Data (dollars in thousands) | |
|---|---|
| Decrease in accounts receivable | $ 6,025 |
| Decrease in merchandise inventories | 33,793 |
| Increase in prepaid assets | 4,511 |
| Increase in accounts payable and other accrued expenses | 4,156 |
| Increase in income tax payable | 12,145 |

Prepare the cash flows from operating activities section of the statement of cash flows (using the indirect method) for Williams Sonoma for the year.

**EXERCISE 16-16**
*Cash flows from operating
activities—direct method*
**Objective 3**
✓ a. $537,000

The cash flows from operating activities are reported by the direct method on the statement of cash flows. Determine the following:

a. If sales for the current year were $510,000 and accounts receivable decreased by $27,000 during the year, what was the amount of cash received from customers?

b. If income tax expense for the current year was $29,000 and income tax payable decreased by $3,900 during the year, what was the amount of cash payments for income tax?

**EXERCISE 16-17**
*Cash paid for merchandise
purchases*
**Objective 3**

**REAL WORLD**

The cost of merchandise sold for **Toys "R" Us, Inc.,** for a recent year was $7,604 million. The balance sheet showed the following current account balances (in millions):

|  | Balance, End of Year | Balance, Beginning of Year |
|---|---|---|
| Merchandise inventories | $2,041 | $2,307 |
| Accounts payable | 878 | 1,152 |

Determine the amount of cash payments for merchandise.

**EXERCISE 16-18**
*Determining selected
amounts for cash flows
from operating activities—
direct method*
**Objective 3**
✓ b. $79,600

Selected data taken from the accounting records of Floral Escape, Inc. for the current year ended December 31 are as follows:

|  | Balance, December 31 | Balance, January 1 |
|---|---|---|
| Accrued expenses (operating expenses) | $ 4,300 | $ 4,900 |
| Accounts payable (merchandise creditors) | 32,100 | 36,800 |
| Inventories | 59,500 | 71,200 |
| Prepaid expenses | 2,500 | 3,500 |

During the current year, the cost of merchandise sold was $450,000 and the operating expenses other than depreciation were $80,000. The direct method is used for presenting the cash flows from operating activities on the statement of cash flows.

Determine the amount reported on the statement of cash flows for (a) cash payments for merchandise and (b) cash payments for operating expenses.

**EXERCISE 16-19**
*Cash flows from operating
activities—direct method*
**Objective 3**

**SPREADSHEET**

✓ Cash flows from
operating activities, $97,000

The income statement of Heart Grain Bakeries, Inc. for the current year ended June 30 is as follows:

| | | |
|---|---|---|
| Sales | | $645,000 |
| Cost of merchandise sold | | 367,800 |
| Gross profit | | $277,200 |
| Operating expenses: | | |
| Depreciation expense | $ 45,000 | |
| Other operating expenses | 155,400 | |
| Total operating expenses | | 200,400 |
| Income before income tax | | $ 76,800 |
| Income tax expense | | 25,400 |
| Net income | | $ 51,400 |

Changes in the balances of selected accounts from the beginning to the end of the current year are as follows:

|  | Increase Decrease* |
|---|---|
| Accounts receivable (net) | $12,000* |
| Inventories | 4,200 |
| Prepaid expenses | 2,500* |
| Accounts payable (merchandise creditors) | 8,400* |
| Accrued expenses (operating expenses) | 2,300 |
| Income tax payable | 3,600* |

Prepare the cash flows from operating activities section of the statement of cash flows, using the direct method.

**EXERCISE 16-20**
*Cash flows from operating activities—direct method*
**Objective 3**

**SPREADSHEET**

✓ *Cash flows from operating activities, $27,100*

The income statement for Wholly Bagel Company for the current year ended June 30 and balances of selected accounts at the beginning and the end of the year are as follows:

| | | |
|---|---:|---:|
| Sales | | $265,000 |
| Cost of merchandise sold | | 95,800 |
| Gross profit | | $169,200 |
| Operating expenses: | | |
| Depreciation expense | $ 12,500 | |
| Other operating expenses | 125,700 | |
| Total operating expenses | | 138,200 |
| Income before income tax | | $ 31,000 |
| Income tax expense | | 12,300 |
| Net income | | $ 18,700 |

| | End of Year | Beginning of Year |
|---|---:|---:|
| Accounts receivable (net) | $14,800 | $12,500 |
| Inventories | 38,100 | 32,800 |
| Prepaid expenses | 6,000 | 6,400 |
| Accounts payable (merchandise creditors) | 27,900 | 24,300 |
| Accrued expenses (operating expenses) | 7,900 | 8,400 |
| Income tax payable | 1,500 | 1,500 |

Prepare the cash flows from operating activities section of the statement of cash flows, using the direct method.

**EXERCISE 16-21**
*Statement of cash flows*
**Objective 2**

**SPREADSHEET**

✓ *Net cash flow from operating activities, $29*

The comparative balance sheet of Contemporary Millworks, Inc. for December 31, 2006 and 2005, is as follows:

| | Dec. 31, 2006 | Dec. 31, 2005 |
|---|---:|---:|
| **Assets** | | |
| Cash ................................. | $ 50 | $ 16 |
| Accounts receivable (net) ............... | 30 | 32 |
| Inventories ........................... | 24 | 19 |
| Land ................................ | 35 | 50 |
| Equipment .......................... | 32 | 15 |
| Accumulated depreciation—equipment ... | (9) | (6) |
| Total ............................ | $162 | $126 |
| | | |
| **Liabilities and Stockholders' Equity** | | |
| Accounts payable (merchandise creditors) ... | $ 17 | $ 20 |
| Dividends payable ...................... | 1 | — |
| Common stock, $1 par .................. | 4 | 2 |
| Paid-in capital in excess of par—common stock ... | 20 | 10 |
| Retained earnings ..................... | 120 | 94 |
| Total ............................ | $162 | $126 |

The following additional information is taken from the records:

a. Land was sold for $13.
b. Equipment was acquired for cash.
c. There were no disposals of equipment during the year.
d. The common stock was issued for cash.
e. There was a $30 credit to Retained Earnings for net income.
f. There was a $4 debit to Retained Earnings for cash dividends declared.

Prepare a statement of cash flows, using the indirect method of presenting cash flows from operating activities.

**EXERCISE 16-22**
*Statement of cash flows*
**Objective 2**

WHAT'S WRONG
WITH THIS?

List the errors you find in the following statement of cash flows. The cash balance at the beginning of the year was $70,700. All other figures are correct, except the cash balance at the end of the year.

**Healthy Choice Nutrition Products, Inc.**
**Statement of Cash Flows**
**For the Year Ended December 31, 2006**

| | | | |
|---|---:|---:|---:|
| Cash flows from operating activities: | | | |
| Net income, per income statement . . . . . . . . . . . . . | | $100,500 | |
| Add: Depreciation . . . . . . . . . . . . . . . . . . . . . . . . | $ 49,000 | | |
| Increase in accounts receivable . . . . . . . . . . . . | 10,500 | | |
| Gain on sale of investments . . . . . . . . . . . . . | 5,000 | 64,500 | |
| | | $165,000 | |
| Deduct: Increase in accounts payable . . . . . . . . . . . | $ 4,400 | | |
| Increase in inventories . . . . . . . . . . . . . . . . | 18,300 | | |
| Decrease in accrued expenses . . . . . . . . . . | 1,600 | 24,300 | |
| Net cash flow from operating activities . . . . . . . . . . | | | $140,700 |
| Cash flows from investing activities: | | | |
| Cash received from sale of investments . . . . . . . . . . | | $ 85,000 | |
| Less: Cash paid for purchase of land . . . . . . . . . . . . | $ 90,000 | | |
| Cash paid for purchase of equipment . . . . . . . | 150,100 | 240,100 | |
| Net cash flow used for investing activities . . . . . . . . | | | (155,100) |
| Cash flows from financing activities: | | | |
| Cash received from sale of common stock . . . . . . . . | | $107,000 | |
| Cash paid for dividends . . . . . . . . . . . . . . . . . . . . . . | | 45,000 | |
| Net cash flow provided by financing activities . . . . . | | | 152,000 |
| Increase in cash . . . . . . . . . . . . . . . . . . . . . . . . . . . | | | $137,600 |
| Cash at the end of the year . . . . . . . . . . . . . . . . . . . | | | 105,300 |
| Cash at the beginning of the year . . . . . . . . . . . . . . | | | $242,900 |

**EXERCISE 16-23**
*Free cash flow*
**Objectives 2, 4**

Hacienda Tile Company has 100,000 shares of common stock issued and outstanding and 1,000 shares of 8%, $100 par value preferred stock issued and outstanding. Hacienda had cash flows from operating activities of $120,000. Cash flows used for investments in property, plant, and equipment totaled $45,000, of which 60% of this investment was used to replace existing capacity. A cash dividend of $0.20 per share was declared and paid on common stock.

Determine the free cash flow for Hacienda Tile Company.

**EXERCISE 16-24**
*Free cash flow*
**Objectives 2, 4**

REAL WORLD

The financial statements for **Home Depot** are provided in Appendix E at the end of the text.

a. Determine the free cash flow for the years ended February 2, 2003 and February 3, 2002. Assume that 80% of capital expenditures were for new store openings, and the remaining was for remodeling and updating existing stores.
b. Determine the percent of free cash flow to operating activities and net sales.
c. ➤ Interpret your results in (a) and (b).

# Problems Series A

**PROBLEM 16-1A**
*Statement of cash flows—*
*indirect method*
**Objective 2**

The comparative balance sheet of Winner's Edge Sporting Goods, Inc. for December 31, 2006 and 2005, is as follows:

| | Dec. 31, 2006 | Dec. 31, 2005 |
|---|---|---|
| **Assets** | | |
| Cash | $ 464,100 | $ 395,800 |
| Accounts receivable (net) | 163,200 | 145,700 |
| Inventories | 395,000 | 367,900 |
| Investments | 0 | 120,000 |
| Land | 160,000 | 0 |
| Equipment | 695,500 | 575,500 |
| Accumulated depreciation—equipment | (194,000) | (168,000) |
| | $1,683,800 | $1,436,900 |
| **Liabilities and Stockholders' Equity** | | |
| Accounts payable (merchandise creditors) | $ 228,700 | $ 210,500 |
| Accrued expenses (operating expenses) | 16,500 | 21,400 |
| Dividends payable | 14,000 | 10,000 |
| Common stock, $10 par | 75,000 | 60,000 |
| Paid-in capital in excess of par—common stock | 265,000 | 175,000 |
| Retained earnings | 1,084,600 | 960,000 |
| | $1,683,800 | $1,436,900 |

✓ Net cash flow from operating activities, $163,300

The following additional information was taken from the records:

a. The investments were sold for $132,000 cash.
b. Equipment and land were acquired for cash.
c. There were no disposals of equipment during the year.
d. The common stock was issued for cash.
e. There was a $180,600 credit to Retained Earnings for net income.
f. There was a $56,000 debit to Retained Earnings for cash dividends declared.

**Instructions**
Prepare a statement of cash flows, using the indirect method of presenting cash flows from operating activities.

**PROBLEM 16-2A**
*Statement of cash flows—indirect method*
**Objective 2**

✓ Net cash flow from operating activities, $78,400

The comparative balance sheet of Medalist Athletic Apparel Co. at December 31, 2006 and 2005, is as follows:

| | Dec. 31, 2006 | Dec. 31, 2005 |
|---|---|---|
| **Assets** | | |
| Cash | $ 37,200 | $ 45,300 |
| Accounts receivable (net) | 61,200 | 65,400 |
| Merchandise inventory | 91,000 | 85,600 |
| Prepaid expenses | 5,500 | 4,000 |
| Equipment | 190,500 | 155,500 |
| Accumulated depreciation—equipment | (41,200) | (35,800) |
| | $344,200 | $320,000 |
| **Liabilities and Stockholders' Equity** | | |
| Accounts payable (merchandise creditors) | $ 67,100 | $ 65,400 |
| Mortgage note payable | 0 | 95,000 |
| Common stock, $1 par | 14,000 | 10,000 |
| Paid-in capital in excess of par—common stock | 200,000 | 100,000 |
| Retained earnings | 63,100 | 49,600 |
| | $344,200 | $320,000 |

Additional data obtained from the income statement and from an examination of the accounts in the ledger for 2006 are as follows:

a. Net income, $61,500.
b. Depreciation reported on the income statement, $17,900.
c. Equipment was purchased at a cost of $47,500, and fully depreciated equipment costing $12,500 was discarded, with no salvage realized.

d. The mortgage note payable was not due until 2009, but the terms permitted earlier payment without penalty.

e. 4,000 shares of common stock were issued at $26 for cash.

f. Cash dividends declared and paid, $48,000.

**Instructions**

Prepare a statement of cash flows, using the indirect method of presenting cash flows from operating activities.

**PROBLEM 16-3A**
*Statement of cash flows—indirect method*

**Objective 2**

SPREADSHEET

✓ *Net cash flow from operating activities, ($53,000)*

The comparative balance sheet of Sunrise Juice Co. at December 31, 2006 and 2005, is as follows:

| | Dec. 31, 2006 | Dec. 31, 2005 |
|---|---|---|
| **Assets** | | |
| Cash | $ 405,200 | $ 432,100 |
| Accounts receivable (net) | 324,100 | 305,700 |
| Inventories | 602,300 | 576,900 |
| Prepaid expenses | 10,000 | 12,000 |
| Land | 100,000 | 190,000 |
| Buildings | 650,000 | 400,000 |
| Accumulated depreciation—buildings | (172,500) | (155,000) |
| Equipment | 225,600 | 210,700 |
| Accumulated depreciation—equipment | (48,100) | (56,500) |
| | $2,096,600 | $1,915,900 |
| **Liabilities and Stockholders' Equity** | | |
| Accounts payable (merchandise creditors) | $ 399,100 | $ 402,600 |
| Bonds payable | 80,000 | 0 |
| Common stock, $1 par | 60,000 | 50,000 |
| Paid-in capital in excess of par—common stock | 350,000 | 200,000 |
| Retained earnings | 1,207,500 | 1,263,300 |
| | $2,096,600 | $1,915,900 |

The noncurrent asset, the noncurrent liability, and the stockholders' equity accounts for 2006 are as follows:

**ACCOUNT** *Land*                                                      **ACCOUNT NO.**

| Date | | Item | Debit | Credit | Balance Debit | Balance Credit |
|---|---|---|---|---|---|---|
| 2006 Jan. | 1 | Balance | | | 190,000 | |
| April | 20 | Realized $81,000 cash from sale | | 90,000 | 100,000 | |

**ACCOUNT** *Buildings*                                                  **ACCOUNT NO.**

| Date | | Item | Debit | Credit | Balance Debit | Balance Credit |
|---|---|---|---|---|---|---|
| 2006 Jan. | 1 | Balance | | | 400,000 | |
| April | 20 | Acquired for cash | 250,000 | | 650,000 | |

**ACCOUNT** *Accumulated Depreciation—Buildings*                         **ACCOUNT NO.**

| Date | | Item | Debit | Credit | Balance Debit | Balance Credit |
|---|---|---|---|---|---|---|
| 2006 Jan. | 1 | Balance | | | | 155,000 |
| Dec. | 31 | Depreciation for year | | 17,500 | | 172,500 |

**ACCOUNT** *Equipment*                                                  **ACCOUNT NO.**

| Date | | Item | Debit | Credit | Balance Debit | Balance Credit |
|---|---|---|---|---|---|---|
| 2006 Jan. | 1 | Balance | | | 210,700 | |
| | 26 | Discarded, no salvage | | 18,000 | 192,700 | |
| Aug. | 11 | Purchased for cash | 32,900 | | 225,600 | |

**ACCOUNT** *Accumulated Depreciation—Equipment*                 **ACCOUNT NO.**

| Date | | Item | Debit | Credit | Balance Debit | Balance Credit |
|---|---|---|---|---|---|---|
| 2006 | | | | | | |
| Jan. | 1 | Balance | | | | 56,500 |
| | 26 | Equipment discarded | 18,000 | | | 38,500 |
| Dec. | 31 | Depreciation for year | | 9,600 | | 48,100 |

**ACCOUNT** *Bonds Payable*                 **ACCOUNT NO.**

| Date | | Item | Debit | Credit | Balance Debit | Balance Credit |
|---|---|---|---|---|---|---|
| 2006 | | | | | | |
| May | 1 | Issued 20-year bonds | | 80,000 | | 80,000 |

**ACCOUNT** *Common Stock, $1 Par*                 **ACCOUNT NO.**

| Date | | Item | Debit | Credit | Balance Debit | Balance Credit |
|---|---|---|---|---|---|---|
| 2006 | | | | | | |
| Jan. | 1 | Balance | | | | 50,000 |
| Dec. | 7 | Issued 10,000 shares of common stock for $16 per share | | 10,000 | | 60,000 |

**ACCOUNT** *Paid-In Capital in Excess of Par—Common Stock*                 **ACCOUNT NO.**

| Date | | Item | Debit | Credit | Balance Debit | Balance Credit |
|---|---|---|---|---|---|---|
| 2006 | | | | | | |
| Jan. | 1 | Balance | | | | 200,000 |
| Dec. | 7 | Issued 10,000 shares of common stock for $16 per share | | 150,000 | | 350,000 |

**ACCOUNT** *Retained Earnings*                 **ACCOUNT NO.**

| Date | | Item | Debit | Credit | Balance Debit | Balance Credit |
|---|---|---|---|---|---|---|
| 2006 | | | | | | |
| Jan. | 1 | Balance | | | | 1,263,300 |
| Dec. | 31 | Net loss | 43,800 | | | 1,219,500 |
| | 31 | Cash dividends | 12,000 | | | 1,207,500 |

## Instructions

Prepare a statement of cash flows, using the indirect method of presenting cash flows from operating activities.

**PROBLEM 16-4A**
*Statement of cash flows—direct method*

**Objective 3**

**SPREADSHEET**
**P.A.S.S.**

✓ *Net cash flow from operating activities, $345,200*

The comparative balance sheet of Village Markets, Inc., for December 31, 2007 and 2006, is as follows:

| | Dec. 31, 2007 | Dec. 31, 2006 |
|---|---|---|
| **Assets** | | |
| Cash | $ 421,900 | $ 456,700 |
| Accounts receivable (net) | 397,200 | 365,700 |
| Inventories | 658,900 | 623,100 |
| Investments | — | 175,000 |
| Land | 230,000 | — |
| Equipment | 590,000 | 450,000 |
| Accumulated depreciation | (282,100) | (234,500) |
| | $2,015,900 | $1,836,000 |
| | | |
| **Liabilities and Stockholders' Equity** | | |
| Accounts payable (merchandise creditors) | $ 471,200 | $ 456,300 |
| Accrued expenses (operating expenses) | 40,000 | 45,300 |
| Dividends payable | 61,000 | 58,000 |
| Common stock, $1 par | 23,000 | 20,000 |
| Paid-in capital in excess of par—common stock | 195,000 | 120,000 |
| Retained earnings | 1,225,700 | 1,136,400 |
| | $2,015,900 | $1,836,000 |

The income statement for the year ended December 31, 2007, is as follows:

| | |
|---|---|
| Sales | $4,367,800 |
| Cost of merchandise sold | 2,532,000 |
| Gross profit | $1,835,800 |
| Operating expenses: | |
| Depreciation expense $ 47,600 | |
| Other operating expenses 1,257,900 | |
| Total operating expenses | 1,305,500 |
| Operating income | $ 530,300 |
| Other expense: | |
| Loss on sale of investments | 25,000 |
| Income before income tax | $ 505,300 |
| Income tax expense | 175,000 |
| Net income | $ 330,300 |

The following additional information was taken from the records:

a. Equipment and land were acquired for cash.
b. There were no disposals of equipment during the year.
c. The investments were sold for $150,000 cash.
d. The common stock was issued for cash.
e. There was a $241,000 debit to Retained Earnings for cash dividends declared.

**Instructions**

Prepare a statement of cash flows, using the direct method of presenting cash flows from operating activities.

**PROBLEM 16-5A**
*Statement of cash flows—
direct method applied to
Problem 16–1A*

**Objective 3**

SPREADSHEET

✓ *Net cash flow from
operating activities,
$163,300*

The comparative balance sheet of Winner's Edge Sporting Goods, Inc. for December 31, 2006 and 2005, is as follows:

| | Dec. 31, 2006 | Dec. 31, 2005 |
|---|---|---|
| **Assets** | | |
| Cash ......................................... | $ 464,100 | $ 395,800 |
| Accounts receivable (net) ........................... | 163,200 | 145,700 |
| Inventories ...................................... | 395,000 | 367,900 |
| Investments ..................................... | 0 | 120,000 |
| Land ........................................... | 160,000 | 0 |
| Equipment ...................................... | 695,500 | 575,500 |
| Accumulated depreciation—equipment .............. | (194,000) | (168,000) |
| | $1,683,800 | $1,436,900 |
| | | |
| **Liabilities and Stockholders' Equity** | | |
| Accounts payable (merchandise creditors) ............. | $ 228,700 | $ 210,500 |
| Accrued expenses (operating expenses) ............... | 16,500 | 21,400 |
| Dividends payable ................................ | 14,000 | 10,000 |
| Common stock, $10 par ........................... | 75,000 | 60,000 |
| Paid-in capital in excess of par—common stock ......... | 265,000 | 175,000 |
| Retained earnings ................................ | 1,084,600 | 960,000 |
| | $1,683,800 | $1,436,900 |

The income statement for the year ended December 31, 2006, is as follows:

| | |
|---|---|
| Sales | $1,580,500 |
| Cost of merchandise sold | 957,300 |
| Gross profit | $ 623,200 |
| Operating expenses: | |
| Depreciation expense $ 26,000 | |
| Other operating expenses 329,400 | |
| Total operating expenses | 355,400 |
| Operating income | $ 267,800 |
| Other income: | |
| Gain on sale of investments | 12,000 |
| Income before income tax | $ 279,800 |
| Income tax expense | 99,200 |
| Net income | $ 180,600 |

The following additional information was taken from the records:

a. The investments were sold for $132,000 cash.
b. Equipment and land were acquired for cash.
c. There were no disposals of equipment during the year.
d. The common stock was issued for cash.
e. There was a $56,000 debit to Retained Earnings for cash dividends declared.

**Instructions**
Prepare a statement of cash flows, using the direct method of presenting cash flows from operating activities.

# roblem Series B

**PROBLEM 16-1B**
*Statement of cash flows—
indirect method*
Objective 2

SPREADSHEET

✓ *Net cash flow from
operating activities, $45,900*

The comparative balance sheet of True-Tread Flooring Co. for June 30, 2006 and 2005, is as follows:

|  | June 30, 2006 | June 30, 2005 |
|---|---|---|
| **Assets** | | |
| Cash | $ 68,900 | $ 53,700 |
| Accounts receivable (net) | 89,200 | 85,400 |
| Inventories | 145,800 | 132,700 |
| Investments | 0 | 45,000 |
| Land | 105,500 | 0 |
| Equipment | 210,800 | 185,600 |
| Accumulated depreciation | (52,800) | (45,100) |
|  | $567,400 | $457,300 |
| | | |
| **Liabilities and Stockholders' Equity** | | |
| Accounts payable (merchandise creditors) | $104,300 | $100,200 |
| Accrued expenses (operating expenses) | 15,200 | 14,300 |
| Dividends payable | 12,000 | 10,000 |
| Common stock, $11 par | 55,000 | 50,000 |
| Paid-in capital in excess of par—common stock | 200,000 | 100,000 |
| Retained earnings | 180,900 | 182,800 |
|  | $567,400 | $457,300 |

The following additional information was taken from the records of True-Tread Flooring Co.:

a. Equipment and land were acquired for cash.
b. There were no disposals of equipment during the year.
c. The investments were sold for $41,000 cash.
d. The common stock was issued for cash.
e. There was a $46,100 credit to Retained Earnings for net income.
f. There was a $48,000 debit to Retained Earnings for cash dividends declared.

**Instructions**
Prepare a statement of cash flows, using the indirect method of presenting cash flows from operating activities.

**PROBLEM 16-2B**
*Statement of cash flows—
indirect method*
Objective 2

The comparative balance sheet of Sky-Mate Luggage Company at December 31, 2006 and 2005, is as follows:

SPREADSHEET

✓ *Net cash flow from operating activities, $178,800*

|  | Dec. 31, 2006 | Dec. 31, 2005 |
|---|---|---|
| **Assets** | | |
| Cash | $ 184,200 | $ 165,400 |
| Accounts receivable (net) | 252,100 | 224,300 |
| Inventories | 300,200 | 348,700 |
| Prepaid expenses | 9,500 | 8,000 |
| Land | 120,000 | 120,000 |
| Buildings | 600,000 | 425,000 |
| Accumulated depreciation—buildings | (215,000) | (194,000) |
| Machinery and equipment | 310,000 | 310,000 |
| Accumulated depreciation—machinery & equipment | (83,500) | (75,000) |
| Patents | 50,000 | 54,000 |
| | $1,527,500 | $1,386,400 |
| | | |
| **Liabilities and Stockholders' Equity** | | |
| Accounts payable (merchandise creditors) | $ 284,300 | $ 295,700 |
| Dividends payable | 15,000 | 10,000 |
| Salaries payable | 19,500 | 22,500 |
| Mortgage note payable, due 2007 | 70,000 | — |
| Bonds payable | — | 102,000 |
| Common stock, $1 par | 22,000 | 20,000 |
| Paid-in capital in excess of par—common stock | 150,000 | 50,000 |
| Retained earnings | 966,700 | 886,200 |
| | $1,527,500 | $1,386,400 |

An examination of the income statement and the accounting records revealed the following additional information applicable to 2006:

a. Net income, $140,500.
b. Depreciation expense reported on the income statement: buildings, $21,000; machinery and equipment, $8,500.
c. Patent amortization reported on the income statement, $4,000.
d. A building was constructed for $175,000.
e. A mortgage note for $70,000 was issued for cash.
f. 2,000 shares of common stock were issued at $51 in exchange for the bonds payable.
g. Cash dividends declared, $60,000.

### Instructions

Prepare a statement of cash flows, using the indirect method of presenting cash flows from operating activities.

**PROBLEM 16-3B**
*Statement of cash flows—indirect method*

**Objective 2**

SPREADSHEET

✓ *Net cash flow from operating activities, $71,400*

The comparative balance sheet of Builder's Supply Co. at December 31, 2006 and 2005, is as follows:

|  | Dec. 31, 2006 | Dec. 31, 2005 |
|---|---|---|
| **Assets** | | |
| Cash | $ 40,400 | $ 45,200 |
| Accounts receivable (net) | 95,100 | 87,900 |
| Inventories | 140,700 | 122,800 |
| Prepaid expenses | 3,900 | 5,000 |
| Land | 75,000 | 100,000 |
| Buildings | 315,000 | 140,000 |
| Accumulated depreciation—buildings | (70,200) | (58,300) |
| Equipment | 225,600 | 210,400 |
| Accumulated depreciation—equipment | (81,400) | (85,900) |
| | $744,100 | $567,100 |

|  | Dec. 31, 2006 | Dec. 31, 2005 |
|---|---|---|
| **Liabilities and Stockholders' Equity** | | |
| Accounts payable (merchandise creditors) . . . . . . . . . . . . | $ 97,000 | $100,500 |
| Income tax payable . . . . . . . . . . . . . . . . . . . . . . . . . . . . . | 7,100 | 6,400 |
| Bonds payable . . . . . . . . . . . . . . . . . . . . . . . . . . . . . . . . | 40,000 | — |
| Common stock, $1 par . . . . . . . . . . . . . . . . . . . . . . . . . | 32,000 | 30,000 |
| Paid-in capital in excess of par—common stock . . . . . . . . | 200,000 | 120,000 |
| Retained earnings . . . . . . . . . . . . . . . . . . . . . . . . . . . . . | 368,000 | 310,200 |
| | $744,100 | $567,100 |

The noncurrent asset, the noncurrent liability, and the stockholders' equity accounts for 2006 are as follows:

**ACCOUNT** *Land*                         **ACCOUNT NO.**

| | | | | | Balance | |
|---|---|---|---|---|---|---|
| Date | | Item | Debit | Credit | Debit | Credit |
| 2006 | | | | | | |
| Jan. | 1 | Balance | | | 100,000 | |
| April | 20 | Realized $31,000 cash from sale | | 25,000 | 75,000 | |

**ACCOUNT** *Buildings*                         **ACCOUNT NO.**

| 2006 | | | | | | |
|---|---|---|---|---|---|---|
| Jan. | 1 | Balance | | | 140,000 | |
| April | 20 | Acquired for cash | 175,000 | | 315,000 | |

**ACCOUNT** *Accumulated Depreciation—Buildings*       **ACCOUNT NO.**

| 2006 | | | | | | |
|---|---|---|---|---|---|---|
| Jan. | 1 | Balance | | | | 58,300 |
| Dec. | 31 | Depreciation for year | | 11,900 | | 70,200 |

**ACCOUNT** *Equipment*                        **ACCOUNT NO.**

| 2006 | | | | | | |
|---|---|---|---|---|---|---|
| Jan. | 1 | Balance | | | 210,400 | |
| | 26 | Discarded, no salvage | | 24,000 | 186,400 | |
| Aug. | 11 | Purchased for cash | 39,200 | | 225,600 | |

**ACCOUNT** *Accumulated Depreciation—Equipment*       **ACCOUNT NO.**

| 2006 | | | | | | |
|---|---|---|---|---|---|---|
| Jan. | 1 | Balance | | | | 85,900 |
| | 26 | Equipment discarded | 24,000 | | | 61,900 |
| Dec. | 31 | Depreciation for year | | 19,500 | | 81,400 |

**ACCOUNT** *Bonds Payable*                      **ACCOUNT NO.**

| 2006 | | | | | | |
|---|---|---|---|---|---|---|
| May | 1 | Issued 20-year bonds | | 40,000 | | 40,000 |

**ACCOUNT** *Common Stock, $1 Par*               **ACCOUNT NO.**

| 2006 | | | | | | |
|---|---|---|---|---|---|---|
| Jan. | 1 | Balance | | | | 30,000 |
| Dec. | 7 | Issued 2,000 shares of common stock for $41 per share | | 2,000 | | 32,000 |

**ACCOUNT** *Paid-In Capital in Excess of Par—Common Stock*     **ACCOUNT NO.**

| 2006 | | | | | | |
|---|---|---|---|---|---|---|
| Jan. | 1 | Balance | | | | 120,000 |
| Dec. | 7 | Issued 2,000 shares of common stock for $41 per share | | 80,000 | | 200,000 |

**ACCOUNT** Retained Earnings

**ACCOUNT NO.**

| Date | | Item | Debit | Credit | Balance Debit | Balance Credit |
|------|---|------|-------|--------|-------|--------|
| 2006 | | | | | | |
| Jan. | 1 | Balance | | | | 310,200 |
| Dec. | 31 | Net income | | 72,800 | | 383,000 |
| | 31 | Cash dividends | 15,000 | | | 368,000 |

## Instructions

Prepare a statement of cash flows, using the indirect method of presenting cash flows from operating activities.

**PROBLEM 16-4B**
*Statement of cash flows—direct method*

**Objective 3**

SPREADSHEET
P.A.S.S.

✓ Net cash flow from operating activities, $110,900

The comparative balance sheet of Heaven's Bounty Nursery Inc. for December 31, 2006 and 2007, is as follows:

| | Dec. 31, 2007 | Dec. 31, 2006 |
|---|---|---|
| **Assets** | | |
| Cash . . . . . . . . . . . . . . . . . . . . . . . . . . . . . . . . . . | $ 134,200 | $154,300 |
| Accounts receivable (net) . . . . . . . . . . . . . . . . . . . . . . . | 203,200 | 189,700 |
| Inventories . . . . . . . . . . . . . . . . . . . . . . . . . . . . | 267,900 | 243,700 |
| Investments . . . . . . . . . . . . . . . . . . . . . . . . . . . . . | — | 110,000 |
| Land . . . . . . . . . . . . . . . . . . . . . . . . . . . . . . . . . | 140,000 | — |
| Equipment . . . . . . . . . . . . . . . . . . . . . . . . . . . . . | 290,000 | 210,000 |
| Accumulated depreciation . . . . . . . . . . . . . . . . . . . . . | (112,300) | (93,400) |
| | $ 923,000 | $814,300 |
| **Liabilities and Stockholders' Equity** | | |
| Accounts payable (merchandise creditors) . . . . . . . . . . . . . | $ 192,100 | $175,400 |
| Accrued expenses (operating expenses) . . . . . . . . . . . . . . | 12,400 | 14,600 |
| Dividends payable . . . . . . . . . . . . . . . . . . . . . . . . . | 32,100 | 30,400 |
| Common stock, $1 par . . . . . . . . . . . . . . . . . . . . . . . . | 10,000 | 8,000 |
| Paid-in capital in excess of par—common stock . . . . . . . . . | 180,000 | 100,000 |
| Retained earnings . . . . . . . . . . . . . . . . . . . . . . . . . | 496,400 | 485,900 |
| | $ 923,000 | $814,300 |

The income statement for the year ended December 31, 2007, is as follows:

| Sales | | $965,000 |
|---|---|---|
| Cost of merchandise sold | | 503,200 |
| Gross profit | | $461,800 |
| Operating expenses: | | |
| Depreciation expense | $ 18,900 | |
| Other operating expenses | 258,300 | |
| Total operating expenses | | 277,200 |
| Operating income | | $184,600 |
| Other income: | | |
| Gain on sale of investments | | 22,000 |
| Income before income tax | | $206,600 |
| Income tax expense | | 69,400 |
| Net income | | $137,200 |

The following additional information was taken from the records:

a. Equipment and land were acquired for cash.
b. There were no disposals of equipment during the year.
c. The investments were sold for $132,000 cash.
d. The common stock was issued for cash.
e. There was a $126,700 debit to Retained Earnings for cash dividends declared.

## Instructions

Prepare a statement of cash flows, using the direct method of presenting cash flows from operating activities.

**PROBLEM 16-5B**
*Statement of cash flows—
direct method applied to
Problem 16–1B*

**Objective 3**

**SPREADSHEET**

✓ *Net cash flow from
operating activities, $45,900*

The comparative balance sheet of True-Tread Flooring Co. for June 30, 2006 and 2005, is as follows:

|  | June 30, 2006 | June 30, 2005 |
|---|---|---|
| **Assets** | | |
| Cash ............................................ | $ 68,900 | $ 53,700 |
| Accounts receivable (net) ...................... | 89,200 | 85,400 |
| Inventories ................................... | 145,800 | 132,700 |
| Investments .................................. | 0 | 45,000 |
| Land ......................................... | 105,500 | 0 |
| Equipment ................................... | 210,800 | 185,600 |
| Accumulated depreciation ..................... | (52,800) | (45,100) |
| | $567,400 | $457,300 |
| | | |
| **Liabilities and Stockholders' Equity** | | |
| Accounts payable (merchandise creditors) ............. | $104,300 | $100,200 |
| Accrued expenses (operating expenses) ............... | 15,200 | 14,300 |
| Dividends payable ............................ | 12,000 | 10,000 |
| Common stock, $11 par ....................... | 55,000 | 50,000 |
| Paid-in capital in excess of par—common stock ........ | 200,000 | 100,000 |
| Retained earnings ............................ | 180,900 | 182,800 |
| | $567,400 | $457,300 |

The income statement for the year ended June 30, 2006, is as follows:

| | | |
|---|---|---|
| Sales | | $945,200 |
| Cost of merchandise sold | | 665,900 |
| Gross profit | | $279,300 |
| Operating expenses: | | |
|   Depreciation expense | $ 7,700 | |
|   Other operating expenses | 193,400 | |
|     Total operating expenses | | 201,100 |
| Operating income | | $ 78,200 |
| Other expenses: | | |
|   Loss on sale of investments | | 4,000 |
| Income before income tax | | $ 74,200 |
| Income tax expense | | 28,100 |
| Net income | | $ 46,100 |

The following additional information was taken from the records:

a. Equipment and land were acquired for cash.
b. There were no disposals of equipment during the year.
c. The investments were sold for $41,000 cash.
d. The common stock was issued for cash.
e. There was a $48,000 debit to Retained Earnings for cash dividends declared.

**Instructions**
Prepare a statement of cash flows, using the direct method of presenting cash flows from operating activities.

# Special Activities

**ACTIVITY 16-1**
*Ethics and professional
conduct in business*

Karen Holmes, president of Parisian Fashions Inc., believes that reporting operating cash flow per share on the income statement would be a useful addition to the company's just completed financial statements. The following discussion took place between Karen Holmes and Parisian Fashions' controller, Jeff May, in January, after the close of the fiscal year.

ETHICS

*Karen:* I have been reviewing our financial statements for the last year. I am disappointed that our net income per share has dropped by 10% from last year. This is not going to look good to our shareholders. Isn't there anything we can do about this?

*Jeff:* What do you mean? The past is the past, and the numbers are in. There isn't much that can be done about it. Our financial statements were prepared according to generally accepted accounting principles, and I don't see much leeway for significant change at this point.

*Karen:* No, no. I'm not suggesting that we "cook the books." But look at the cash flow from operating activities on the statement of cash flows. The cash flow from operating activities has increased by 20%. This is very good news—and, I might add, useful information. The higher cash flow from operating activities will give our creditors comfort.

*Jeff:* Well, the cash flow from operating activities is on the statement of cash flows, so I guess users will be able to see the improved cash flow figures there.

*Karen:* This is true, but somehow I feel that this information should be given a much higher profile. I don't like this information being "buried" in the statement of cash flows. You know as well as I do that many users will focus on the income statement. Therefore, I think we ought to include an operating cash flow per share number on the face of the income statement—someplace under the earnings per share number. In this way users will get the complete picture of our operating performance. Yes, our earnings per share dropped this year, but our cash flow from operating activities improved! And all the information is in one place where users can see and compare the figures. What do you think?

*Jeff:* I've never really thought about it like that before. I guess we could put the operating cash flow per share on the income statement, under the earnings per share. Users would really benefit from this disclosure. Thanks for the idea—I'll start working on it.

*Karen:* Glad to be of service.

How would you interpret this situation? Is Jeff behaving in an ethical and professional manner?

**ACTIVITY 16-2**
*Using the statement of cash flows*

WHAT DO YOU THINK?

You are considering an investment in a new start-up company, OmniTech Inc., an Internet service provider. A review of the company's financial statements reveals a negative retained earnings. In addition, it appears as though the company has been running a negative cash flow from operating activities since the company's inception. How is the company staying in business under these circumstances? Could this be a good investment?

**ACTIVITY 16-3**
*Analysis of cash flow from operations*

The Retailing Division of Buyer's Mart, Inc. provided the following information on its cash flow from operations:

| | |
|---|---:|
| Net income | $ 450,000 |
| Increase in accounts receivable | (540,000) |
| Increase in inventory | (600,000) |
| Decrease in accounts payable | (90,000) |
| Depreciation | 100,000 |
| Cash flow from operating activities | $(680,000) |

The manager of the Retailing Division provided the accompanying memo with this report:

From: Senior Vice President, Retailing Division

*I am pleased to report that we had earnings of $450,000 over the last period. This resulted in a return on invested capital of 10%, which is near our targets for this* *division. I have been aggressive in building the revenue volume in the division. As a result, I am happy to report that we have increased the number of new credit card customers as a result of an aggressive marketing campaign. In addition, we have found some excellent merchandise opportunities. Some of our suppliers have made some of their apparel merchandise available at a deep discount. We have purchased as much of these goods as possible in order to improve profitability. I'm also happy to report that our vendor payment problems have improved. We are nearly caught up on our overdue payables balances.*

➤ Comment on the senior vice president's memo in light of the cash flow information.

**ACTIVITY 16-4**
*Analysis of statement of cash flows*

Jabari Franklin is the president and majority shareholder of Kitchens By Design, Inc., a small retail store chain. Recently, Franklin submitted a loan application for Kitchens By Design, Inc., to Montvale National Bank. It called for a $200,000, 9%, ten-year loan to help finance the construction of a building and the purchase of store equipment, costing a total of $250,000, to enable Kitchens By Design, Inc., to open a store in Montvale. Land for this purpose was acquired last year. The bank's loan officer requested a statement of cash flows in addition to the most recent income statement, balance sheet, and retained earnings statement that Franklin had submitted with the loan application.

As a close family friend, Franklin asked you to prepare a statement of cash flows. From the records provided, you prepared the following statement.

**Kitchens By Design, Inc.**
**Statement of Cash Flows**
**For the Year Ended December 31, 2006**

| | | | |
|---|---|---|---|
| Cash flows from operating activities: | | | |
| Net income, per income statement | | $ 86,400 | |
| Add: Depreciation | $31,000 | | |
| Decrease in accounts receivable | 11,500 | 42,500 | |
| | | $128,900 | |
| Deduct: Increase in inventory | $12,000 | | |
| Increase in prepaid expenses | 1,500 | | |
| Decrease in accounts payable | 3,000 | | |
| Gain on sale of investments | 7,500 | 24,000 | |
| Net cash flow from operating activities | | | $104,900 |
| Cash flows from investing activities: | | | |
| Cash received from investments sold | | $ 42,500 | |
| Less: Cash paid for purchase of store equipment | | 31,000 | |
| Net cash flow from investing activities | | | 11,500 |
| Cash flows from financing activities: | | | |
| Cash paid for dividends | | $ 40,000 | |
| Net cash flow used for financing activities | | | (40,000) |
| Increase in cash | | | $ 76,400 |
| Cash at the beginning of the year | | | 27,500 |
| Cash at the end of the year | | | $103,900 |
| | | | |
| **Schedule of Noncash Financing and** | | | |
| **Investing Activities:** | | | |
| Issued common stock at par for land | | | $ 60,000 |

After reviewing the statement, Franklin telephoned you and commented, "Are you sure this statement is right?" Franklin then raised the following questions:

1. "How can depreciation be a cash flow?"
2. "Issuing common stock for the land is listed in a separate schedule. This transaction has nothing to do with cash! Shouldn't this transaction be eliminated from the statement?"
3. "How can the gain on sale of investments be a deduction from net income in determining the cash flow from operating activities?"

4. "Why does the bank need this statement anyway? They can compute the increase in cash from the balance sheets for the last two years."

After jotting down Franklin's questions, you assured him that this statement was "right." However, to alleviate Franklin's concern, you arranged a meeting for the following day.

a.  How would you respond to each of Franklin's questions?
b.  Do you think that the statement of cash flows enhances the chances of Kitchens By Design, Inc., receiving the loan? Discuss.

**ACTIVITY 16-5**
*Statement of cash flows*

**REAL WORLD**        **GROUP ACTIVITY**

**INTERNET**

This activity will require two teams to retrieve cash flow statement information from the Internet. One team is to obtain the most recent year's statement of cash flows for **Johnson & Johnson**, and the other team the most recent year's statement of cash flows for **AMR Corp.**

The statement of cash flows is included as part of the annual report information that is a required disclosure to the Securities and Exchange Commission (SEC). The SEC, in turn, provides this information online through its EDGAR service. EDGAR (Electronic Data Gathering, Analysis, and Retrieval) is the electronic archive of financial statements filed with the Securities and Exchange Commission (SEC). SEC documents can be retrieved using the EdgarScan service from **PricewaterhouseCoopers** at **http://edgarscan.pwcglobal.com**.

To obtain annual report information, type in a company name in the appropriate space. EdgarScan will list the reports available to you for the company you've selected. Select the most recent annual report filing, identified as a 10-K or 10-K405. EdgarScan provides an outline of the report, including the separate financial statements. You can double-click the income statement and balance sheet for the selected company into an Excel™ spreadsheet for further analysis.

As a group, compare the two statements of cash flows. How are Johnson & Johnson and United Airlines similar or different regarding cash flows?

# Answers to Self-Examination Questions

1. **D**   Cash flows from operating activities affect transactions that enter into the determination of net income, such as the receipt of cash from customers on account (answer D). Receipts of cash from the sale of stock (answer A) and the sale of bonds (answer B) and payments of cash for dividends (answer C) are cash flows from financing activities.

2. **A**   Cash flows from investing activities include receipts from the sale of noncurrent assets, such as equipment (answer A), and payments to acquire noncurrent assets. Receipts of cash from the sale of stock (answer B) and payments of cash for dividends (answer C) and to acquire treasury stock (answer D) are cash flows from financing activities.

3. **C**   Payment of cash dividends (answer C) is an example of a financing activity. The receipt of cash from customers on account (answer A) is an operating activity. The receipt of cash from the sale of equipment (answer B) is an investing activity. The

payment of cash to acquire land (answer D) is an example of an investing activity.

4. **D**   The indirect method (answer D) reports cash flows from operating activities by beginning with net income and adjusting it for revenues and expenses not involving the receipt or payment of cash.

5. **C**   The cash flows from operating activities section of the statement of cash flows would report net cash flow from operating activities of $65,500, determined as follows:

| | | |
|---|---:|---:|
| Net income | | $55,000 |
| Add: Depreciation | $22,000 | |
| Decrease in inventories | 5,000 | |
| Decrease in prepaid expenses | 500 | 27,500 |
| | | $82,500 |
| Deduct: Increase in accounts receivable | $10,000 | |
| Decrease in accounts payable | 7,000 | 17,000 |
| Net cash flow from operating activities | | $65,500 |

# 17

# FINANCIAL STATEMENT ANALYSIS

## objectives

*After studying this chapter, you should be able to:*

1 List basic financial statement analytical procedures.

2 Apply financial statement analysis to assess the solvency of a business.

3 Apply financial statement analysis to assess the profitability of a business.

4 Summarize the uses and limitations of analytical measures.

5 Describe the contents of corporate annual reports.

*T*he Wall Street Journal reported that the common stock of **Microsoft Corporation** was selling for $26.15 per share. If you had funds to invest, would you invest in Microsoft common stock?

Microsoft is a well-known, international company. However, **United Airlines**, **WorldCom**, **Kmart**, **Polaroid**, and **Planet Hollywood** were also well-known companies. These latter companies share the common characteristic of having declared bankruptcy!

Obviously, being well-known is not necessarily a good basis for investing. Knowledge that a company has a good product, by itself, may also be an inadequate basis for investing in the company. Even with a good product, a company may go bankrupt for a variety of reasons, such as inadequate financing. For example, Planet Hollywood sought bankruptcy protection, even though it was owned and promoted by such prominent Hollywood stars as Bruce Willis, Whoopi Goldberg, and Arnold Schwarzenegger.

How, then, does one decide on the companies in which to invest? This chapter describes and illustrates common financial data that can be analyzed to assist you in making investment decisions. In addition, the contents of corporate annual reports are also discussed.

# Basic Analytical Procedures

### objective    1

List basic financial statement analytical procedures.

The basic financial statements provide much of the information users need to make economic decisions about businesses. In this chapter, we illustrate how to perform a complete analysis of these statements by integrating individual analytical measures.

Analytical procedures may be used to compare items on a current statement with related items on earlier statements. For example, cash of $150,000 on the current balance sheet may be compared with cash of $100,000 on the balance sheet of a year earlier. The current year's cash may be expressed as 1.5 or 150% of the earlier amount, or as an increase of 50% or $50,000.

Analytical procedures are also widely used to examine relationships within a financial statement. To illustrate, assume that cash of $50,000 and inventories of $250,000 are included in the total assets of $1,000,000 on a balance sheet. In relative terms, the cash balance is 5% of the total assets, and the inventories are 25% of the total assets.

In this chapter, we will illustrate a number of common analytical measures. The measures are not ends in themselves. They are only guides in evaluating financial and operating data. Many other factors, such as trends in the industry and general economic conditions, should also be considered.

## Horizontal Analysis

The percentage analysis of increases and decreases in related items in comparative financial statements is called ***horizontal analysis***. The amount of each item on the most recent statement is compared with the related item on one or more earlier statements. The amount of increase or decrease in the item is listed, along with the percent of increase or decrease.

Horizontal analysis may compare two statements. In this case, the earlier statement is used as the base. Horizontal analysis may also compare three or more statements. In this case, the earliest date or period may be used as the base for comparing all later dates or periods. Alternatively, each statement may be compared to the immediately preceding statement. Exhibit 1 is a condensed comparative balance sheet for two years for Lincoln Company, with horizontal analysis.

We cannot fully evaluate the significance of the various increases and decreases in the items shown in Exhibit 1 without additional information. Although total as-

**•Exhibit 1**   Comparative Balance Sheet—Horizontal Analysis

## Lincoln Company
### Comparative Balance Sheet
### December 31, 2006 and 2005

| | 2006 | 2005 | Increase (Decrease) Amount | Percent |
|---|---|---|---|---|
| **Assets** | | | | |
| Current assets . . . . . . . . . . . . . . | $ 550,000 | $ 533,000 | $ 17,000 | 3.2% |
| Long-term investments . . . . . . . . | 95,000 | 177,500 | (82,500) | (46.5%) |
| Property, plant, and | | | | |
| equipment (net) . . . . . . . . . . | 444,500 | 470,000 | (25,500) | (5.4%) |
| Intangible assets . . . . . . . . . . . . | 50,000 | 50,000 | | |
| Total assets . . . . . . . . . . . . . . . . | $1,139,500 | $1,230,500 | $ (91,000) | (7.4%) |
| | | | | |
| **Liabilities** | | | | |
| Current liabilities . . . . . . . . . . . . | $ 210,000 | $ 243,000 | $ (33,000) | (13.6%) |
| Long-term liabilities . . . . . . . . . | 100,000 | 200,000 | (100,000) | (50.0%) |
| Total liabilities . . . . . . . . . . . . . . | $ 310,000 | $ 443,000 | $(133,000) | (30.0%) |
| | | | | |
| **Stockholders' Equity** | | | | |
| Preferred 6% stock, $100 par . . . | $ 150,000 | $ 150,000 | — | — |
| Common stock, $10 par . . . . . . . . | 500,000 | 500,000 | — | — |
| Retained earnings . . . . . . . . . . . | 179,500 | 137,500 | $ 42,000 | 30.5% |
| Total stockholders' equity . . . . . . | $ 829,500 | $ 787,500 | $ 42,000 | 5.3% |
| Total liabilities and | | | | |
| stockholders' equity . . . . . . . . | $1,139,500 | $1,230,500 | $ (91,000) | (7.4%) |

sets at the end of 2006 were $91,000 (7.4%) less than at the beginning of the year, liabilities were reduced by $133,000 (30%), and stockholders' equity increased $42,000 (5.3%). It appears that the reduction of $100,000 in long-term liabilities was achieved mostly through the sale of long-term investments.

The balance sheet in Exhibit 1 may be expanded to include the details of the various categories of assets and liabilities. An alternative is to present the details in separate schedules. Exhibit 2 is a supporting schedule with horizontal analysis.

**•Exhibit 2**   Comparative Schedule of Current Assets—Horizontal Analysis

## Lincoln Company
### Comparative Schedule of Current Assets
### December 31, 2006 and 2005

| | 2006 | 2005 | Increase (Decrease) Amount | Percent |
|---|---|---|---|---|
| Cash . . . . . . . . . . . . . . . . . . . . . . . . | $ 90,500 | $ 64,700 | $ 25,800 | 39.9% |
| Marketable securities . . . . . . . . . . | 75,000 | 60,000 | 15,000 | 25.0% |
| Accounts receivable (net) . . . . . . . . | 115,000 | 120,000 | (5,000) | (4.2%) |
| Inventories . . . . . . . . . . . . . . . . . . . | 264,000 | 283,000 | (19,000) | (6.7%) |
| Prepaid expenses . . . . . . . . . . . . . . | 5,500 | 5,300 | 200 | 3.8% |
| Total current assets . . . . . . . . . . . . | $550,000 | $533,000 | $ 17,000 | 3.2% |

Accounts Payable was $600,000 in the current year and $500,000 in the preceding year. What is the amount and the percentage of increase or decrease that would be shown in a balance sheet with horizontal analysis?

------------------------------------------

*$100,000 or 20% ($100,000/ $500,000) increase*

The decrease in accounts receivable may be due to changes in credit terms or improved collection policies. Likewise, a decrease in inventories during a period of increased sales may indicate an improvement in the management of inventories.

The changes in the current assets in Exhibit 2 appear favorable. This assessment is supported by the 24.8% increase in net sales shown in Exhibit 3.

An increase in net sales may not have a favorable effect on operating performance. The percentage increase in Lincoln Company's net sales is accompanied by a greater percentage increase in the cost of goods (merchandise) sold.[1] This has the effect of reducing gross profit. Selling expenses increased significantly, and administrative expenses increased slightly. Overall, operating expenses increased by 20.7%, whereas gross profit increased by only 19.7%.

The increase in income from operations and in net income is favorable. However, a study of the expenses and additional analyses and comparisons should be made before reaching a conclusion as to the cause.

## •Exhibit 3  Comparative Income Statement—Horizontal Analysis

| Lincoln Company Comparative Income Statement For the Years Ended December 31, 2006 and 2005 | | | | |
|---|---|---|---|---|
| | | | Increase (Decrease) | |
| | 2006 | 2005 | Amount | Percent |
| Sales | $1,530,500 | $1,234,000 | $296,500 | 24.0% |
| Sales returns and allowances | 32,500 | 34,000 | (1,500) | (4.4%) |
| Net sales | $1,498,000 | $1,200,000 | $298,000 | 24.8% |
| Cost of goods sold | 1,043,000 | 820,000 | 223,000 | 27.2% |
| Gross profit | $ 455,000 | $ 380,000 | $ 75,000 | 19.7% |
| Selling expenses | $ 191,000 | $ 147,000 | $ 44,000 | 29.9% |
| Administrative expenses | 104,000 | 97,400 | 6,600 | 6.8% |
| Total operating expenses | $ 295,000 | $ 244,400 | $ 50,600 | 20.7% |
| Income from operations | $ 160,000 | $ 135,600 | $ 24,400 | 18.0% |
| Other income | 8,500 | 11,000 | (2,500) | (22.7%) |
| | $ 168,500 | $ 146,600 | $ 21,900 | 14.9% |
| Other expense | 6,000 | 12,000 | (6,000) | (50.0%) |
| Income before income tax | $ 162,500 | $ 134,600 | $ 27,900 | 20.7% |
| Income tax expense | 71,500 | 58,100 | 13,400 | 23.1% |
| Net income | $ 91,000 | $ 76,500 | $ 14,500 | 19.0% |

Exhibit 4 illustrates a comparative retained earnings statement with horizontal analysis. It reveals that retained earnings increased 30.5% for the year. The increase is due to net income of $91,000 for the year, less dividends of $49,000.

## Vertical Analysis

A percentage analysis may also be used to show the relationship of each component to the total within a single statement. This type of analysis is called *vertical analysis*. Like horizontal analysis, the statements may be prepared in either detailed or condensed form. In the latter case, additional details of the changes in individual items may be presented in supporting schedules. In such schedules, the per-

------------

[1]The term *cost of goods sold* is often used in practice in place of *cost of merchandise sold*. Such usage is followed in this chapter.

## •Exhibit 4

Comparative Retained
Earnings Statement—
Horizontal Analysis

**Lincoln Company**
**Comparative Retained Earnings Statement**
**December 31, 2006 and 2005**

| | 2006 | 2005 | Increase (Decrease) Amount | Percent |
|---|---|---|---|---|
| Retained earnings, January 1 . . . . . | $137,500 | $100,000 | $37,500 | 37.5% |
| Net income for the year . . . . . . . . | 91,000 | 76,500 | 14,500 | 19.0% |
| Total . . . . . . . . . . . . . . . . . . . . . . . | $228,500 | $176,500 | $52,000 | 29.5% |
| Dividends: | | | | |
| On preferred stock . . . . . . . . . . | $  9,000 | $  9,000 | — | — |
| On common stock . . . . . . . . . . . | 40,000 | 30,000 | $10,000 | 33.3% |
| Total . . . . . . . . . . . . . . . . . . . . . . . | $ 49,000 | $ 39,000 | $10,000 | 25.6% |
| Retained earnings, December 31 . . . | $179,500 | $137,500 | $42,000 | 30.5% |

At the end of the current year,
Accounts Payable was $600,000
and total liabilities and stockholders' equity was $1,200,000. What
percent would be shown for Accounts Payable in a balance sheet
with vertical analysis?

--------------------------------------------

*50% ($600,000/$1,200,000)*

centage analysis may be based on either the total of the schedule or the statement total. Although vertical analysis is limited to an individual statement, its significance may be improved by preparing comparative statements.

In vertical analysis of the balance sheet, each asset item is stated as a percent of the total assets. Each liability and stockholders' equity item is stated as a percent of the total liabilities and stockholders' equity. Exhibit 5 is a condensed comparative balance sheet with vertical analysis for Lincoln Company.

## •Exhibit 5

Comparative Balance
Sheet—Vertical Analysis

**Lincoln Company**
**Comparative Balance Sheet**
**December 31, 2006 and 2005**

| | 2006 Amount | Percent | 2005 Amount | Percent |
|---|---|---|---|---|
| **Assets** | | | | |
| Current assets . . . . . . . . . . . . . . . . . . . | $  550,000 | 48.3% | $  533,000 | 43.3% |
| Long-term investments . . . . . . . . . . . . | 95,000 | 8.3 | 177,500 | 14.4 |
| Property, plant, and | | | | |
| equipment (net) . . . . . . . . . . . . . . . | 444,500 | 39.0 | 470,000 | 38.2 |
| Intangible assets . . . . . . . . . . . . . . . . . | 50,000 | 4.4 | 50,000 | 4.1 |
| Total assets . . . . . . . . . . . . . . . . . . . . | $1,139,500 | 100.0% | $1,230,500 | 100.0% |
| | | | | |
| **Liabilities** | | | | |
| Current liabilities . . . . . . . . . . . . . . . . | $  210,000 | 18.4% | $  243,000 | 19.7% |
| Long-term liabilities . . . . . . . . . . . . . . | 100,000 | 8.8 | 200,000 | 16.3 |
| Total liabilities . . . . . . . . . . . . . . . . . . | $  310,000 | 27.2% | $  443,000 | 36.0% |
| | | | | |
| **Stockholders' Equity** | | | | |
| Preferred 6% stock, $100 par . . . . . . . . | $  150,000 | 13.2% | $  150,000 | 12.2% |
| Common stock, $10 par . . . . . . . . . . . . | 500,000 | 43.9 | 500,000 | 40.6 |
| Retained earnings . . . . . . . . . . . . . . . . | 179,500 | 15.7 | 137,500 | 11.2 |
| Total stockholders' equity . . . . . . . . . . | $  829,500 | 72.8% | $  787,500 | 64.0% |
| Total liabilities and | | | | |
| stockholders' equity . . . . . . . . . . . | $1,139,500 | 100.0% | $1,230,500 | 100.0% |

The major percentage changes in Lincoln Company's assets are in the current asset and long-term investment categories. In the Liabilities and Stockholders' Equity sections of the balance sheet, the greatest percentage changes are in long-term liabilities and retained earnings. Stockholders' equity increased from 64% to 72.8% of total liabilities and stockholders' equity in 2006. There is a comparable decrease in liabilities.

In a vertical analysis of the income statement, each item is stated as a percent of net sales. Exhibit 6 is a condensed comparative income statement with vertical analysis for Lincoln Company.

## •Exhibit 6   Comparative Income Statement—Vertical Analysis

**Lincoln Company**
**Comparative Income Statement**
**For the Years Ended December 31, 2006 and 2005**

| | 2006 | | 2005 | |
|---|---|---|---|---|
| | Amount | Percent | Amount | Percent |
| Sales . . . . . . . . . . . . . . . . . . . . . . . . . . | $1,530,500 | 102.2% | $1,234,000 | 102.8% |
| Sales returns and allowances . . . . . . . | 32,500 | 2.2 | 34,000 | 2.8 |
| Net sales . . . . . . . . . . . . . . . . . . . . . . . | $1,498,000 | 100.0% | $1,200,000 | 100.0% |
| Cost of goods sold . . . . . . . . . . . . . . . | 1,043,000 | 69.6 | 820,000 | 68.3 |
| Gross profit . . . . . . . . . . . . . . . . . . . . | $ 455,000 | 30.4% | $ 380,000 | 31.7% |
| Selling expenses . . . . . . . . . . . . . . . . . | $ 191,000 | 12.8% | $ 147,000 | 12.3% |
| Administrative expenses . . . . . . . . . . . | 104,000 | 6.9 | 97,400 | 8.1 |
| Total operating expenses . . . . . . . . . | $ 295,000 | 19.7% | $ 244,400 | 20.4% |
| Income from operations . . . . . . . . . . . | $ 160,000 | 10.7% | $ 135,600 | 11.3% |
| Other income . . . . . . . . . . . . . . . . . . . | 8,500 | 0.6 | 11,000 | 0.9 |
| | $ 168,500 | 11.3% | $ 146,600 | 12.2% |
| Other expense . . . . . . . . . . . . . . . . . . . | 6,000 | 0.4 | 12,000 | 1.0 |
| Income before income tax . . . . . . . . . | $ 162,500 | 10.9% | $ 134,600 | 11.2% |
| Income tax expense . . . . . . . . . . . . . . . | 71,500 | 4.8 | 58,100 | 4.8 |
| Net income . . . . . . . . . . . . . . . . . . . . . | $ 91,000 | 6.1% | $ 76,500 | 6.4% |

We must be careful when judging the significance of differences between percentages for the two years. For example, the decline of the gross profit rate from 31.7% in 2005 to 30.4% in 2006 is only 1.3 percentage points. In terms of dollars of potential gross profit, however, it represents a decline of approximately $19,500 (1.3% × $1,498,000).

## Common-Size Statements

Horizontal and vertical analyses with both dollar and percentage amounts are useful in assessing relationships and trends in financial conditions and operations of a business. Vertical analysis with both dollar and percentage amounts is also useful in comparing one company with another or with industry averages. Such comparisons are easier to make with the use of common-size statements. In a ***common-size statement***, all items are expressed in percentages.

Common-size statements are useful in comparing the current period with prior periods, individual businesses, or one business with industry percentages. Industry data are often available from trade associations and financial information services. Exhibit 7 is a comparative common-size income statement for two businesses.

**REAL WORLD** The percentages of gross profit and net income to sales for a recent fiscal year for **Target Corp.** and **Wal-Mart Stores Inc.** are shown below.

| | Target Corp. | Wal-Mart Stores Inc. |
|---|---|---|
| Gross profit to sales | 31.7% | 22.1% |
| Net income to sales | 3.4% | 1.8% |

Wal-Mart has a significantly lower gross profit margin percentage than does Target, which is likely due to Wal-Mart's aggressive pricing strategy. However, Target's gross profit margin advantage shrinks when comparing the net income to sales ratio. Target must have larger selling and administrative expenses to sales than does Wal-Mart. Even so, Target's net income to sales is still 1.6 percentage points better than Wal-Mart.

## •Exhibit 7    Common-Size Income Statement

### Lincoln Company and Madison Corporation
### Condensed Common-Size Income Statement
### For the Year Ended December 31, 2006

|  | Lincoln Company | Madison Corporation |
|---|---|---|
| Sales ........................................ | 102.2% | 102.3% |
| Sales returns and allowances ......................... | 2.2 | 2.3 |
| Net sales ................................... | 100.0% | 100.0% |
| Cost of goods sold ............................. | 69.6 | 70.0 |
| Gross profit ................................. | 30.4% | 30.0% |
| Selling expenses .............................. | 12.8% | 11.5% |
| Administrative expenses ......................... | 6.9 | 4.1 |
| Total operating expenses ........................ | 19.7% | 15.6% |
| Income from operations ......................... | 10.7% | 14.4% |
| Other income ................................ | 0.6 | 0.6 |
|  | 11.3% | 15.0% |
| Other expense ............................... | 0.4 | 0.5 |
| Income before income tax ........................ | 10.9% | 14.5% |
| Income tax expense ............................ | 4.8 | 5.5 |
| Net income ................................. | 6.1% | 9.0% |

Exhibit 7 indicates that Lincoln Company has a slightly higher rate of gross profit than Madison Corporation. However, this advantage is more than offset by Lincoln Company's higher percentage of selling and administrative expenses. As a result, the income from operations of Lincoln Company is 10.7% of net sales, compared with 14.4% for Madison Corporation—an unfavorable difference of 3.7 percentage points.

## Other Analytical Measures

In addition to the preceding analyses, other relationships may be expressed in ratios and percentages. Often, these items are taken from the financial statements and thus are a type of vertical analysis. Comparing these items with items from earlier periods is a type of horizontal analysis.

# Solvency Analysis

### objective  2

Apply financial statement analysis to assess the solvency of a business.

Some aspects of a business's financial condition and operations are of greater importance to some users than others. However, all users are interested in the ability of a business to pay its debts as they are due and to earn income. The ability of a business to meet its financial obligations (debts) is called **solvency**. The ability of a business to earn income is called **profitability**.

The factors of solvency and profitability are interrelated. A business that cannot pay its debts on a timely basis may experience difficulty in obtaining credit. A lack of available credit may, in turn, lead to a decline in the business's profitability. Eventually, the business may be forced into bankruptcy. Likewise, a business that is less profitable than its competitors is likely to be at a disadvantage in obtaining credit or new capital from stockholders.

In the following paragraphs, we discuss various types of financial analyses that are useful in evaluating the solvency of a business. In the next section, we discuss various types of profitability analyses. The examples in both sections are based on

Two popular printed sources for industry ratios are available in *Annual Statement Studies* from **Robert Morris Associates** and *Industry Norms & Key Business Ratios* from **Dun's Analytical Services**. Online analysis is available from **Zacks Investment Research** site or **Market Guide's** site, both of which are linked to the text's Web site at **http://warren.swlearning.com**.

Lincoln Company's financial statements presented earlier. In some cases, data from Lincoln Company's financial statements of the preceding year and from other sources are also used. These historical data are useful in assessing the past performance of a business and in forecasting its future performance. The results of financial analyses may be even more useful when they are compared with those of competing businesses and with industry averages.

Solvency analysis focuses on the ability of a business to pay or otherwise satisfy its current and noncurrent liabilities. It is normally assessed by examining balance sheet relationships, using the following major analyses:

1. Current position analysis
2. Accounts receivable analysis
3. Inventory analysis
4. The ratio of fixed assets to long-term liabilities
5. The ratio of liabilities to stockholders' equity
6. The number of times interest charges are earned

> **Solvency analysis focuses on the ability of a business to pay or otherwise satisfy its current and noncurrent liabilities.**

## Current Position Analysis

To be useful in assessing solvency, a ratio or other financial measure must relate to a business's ability to pay or otherwise satisfy its liabilities. Using measures to assess a business's ability to pay its current liabilities is called **current position analysis**. Such analysis is of special interest to short-term creditors.

An analysis of a firm's current position normally includes determining the working capital, the current ratio, and the quick ratio. The current and quick ratios are most useful when analyzed together and compared to previous periods and other firms in the industry.

### Working Capital

The excess of the current assets of a business over its current liabilities is called working capital. The working capital is often used in evaluating a company's ability to meet currently maturing debts. It is especially useful in making monthly or other period-to-period comparisons for a company. However, amounts of working capital are difficult to assess when comparing companies of different sizes or in comparing such amounts with industry figures. For example, working capital of $250,000 may be adequate for a small local hardware store, but it would be inadequate for all of **Home Depot**.

### Current Ratio

Another means of expressing the relationship between current assets and current liabilities is the **current ratio**. This ratio is sometimes called the **working capital ratio** or **bankers' ratio**. The ratio is computed by dividing the total current assets by the total current liabilities. For Lincoln Company, working capital and the current ratio for 2006 and 2005 are as follows:

**Microsoft Corp.** maintains a high current ratio—4.2 for a recent year. Microsoft's stable and profitable software business has allowed it to develop a strong cash position coupled with no short-term notes payable.

|  | 2006 | 2005 |
|---|---|---|
| Current assets | $550,000 | $533,000 |
| Current liabilities | 210,000 | 243,000 |
| Working capital | $340,000 | $290,000 |
| Current ratio | 2.6 | 2.2 |

The current ratio is a more reliable indicator of solvency than is working capital. To illustrate, assume that as of December 31, 2006, the working capital of a competitor is much greater than $340,000, but its current ratio is only 1.3. Considering these facts alone, Lincoln Company, with its current ratio of 2.6, is in a more favorable position to obtain short-term credit than the competitor, which has the greater amount of working capital.

## Quick Ratio

The working capital and the current ratio do not consider the makeup of the current assets. To illustrate the importance of this consideration, the current position data for Lincoln Company and Jefferson Corporation as of December 31, 2006, are as follows:

|  | Lincoln Company | Jefferson Corporation |
| --- | --- | --- |
| Current assets: | | |
| Cash | $ 90,500 | $ 45,500 |
| Marketable securities | 75,000 | 25,000 |
| Accounts receivable (net) | 115,000 | 90,000 |
| Inventories | 264,000 | 380,000 |
| Prepaid expenses | 5,500 | 9,500 |
| Total current assets | $550,000 | $550,000 |
| Current liabilities | 210,000 | 210,000 |
| Working capital | $340,000 | $340,000 |
| Current ratio | 2.6 | 2.6 |

Both companies have a working capital of $340,000 and a current ratio of 2.6. But the ability of each company to pay its current debts is significantly different. Jefferson Corporation has more of its current assets in inventories. Some of these inventories must be sold and the receivables collected before the current liabilities can be paid in full. Thus, a large amount of time may be necessary to convert these inventories into cash. Declines in market prices and a reduction in demand could also impair its ability to pay current liabilities. In contrast, Lincoln Company has cash and current assets (marketable securities and accounts receivable) that can generally be converted to cash rather quickly to meet its current liabilities.

A ratio that measures the "instant" debt-paying ability of a company is called the **quick ratio** or **acid-test ratio**. It is the ratio of the total quick assets to the total current liabilities. **Quick assets** are cash and other current assets that can be quickly converted to cash. Quick assets normally include cash, marketable securities, and receivables. The quick ratio data for Lincoln Company are as follows:

A balance sheet shows $300,000 of cash, marketable securities, and receivables, and $250,000 of inventories. Current liabilities are $200,000. What are (a) the current ratio and (b) the quick ratio?

(a) 2.75 ($550,000/$200,000);
(b) 1.5 ($300,000/$200,000)

|  | 2006 | 2005 |
| --- | --- | --- |
| Quick assets: | | |
| Cash | $ 90,500 | $ 64,700 |
| Marketable equity securities | 75,000 | 60,000 |
| Accounts receivable (net) | 115,000 | 120,000 |
| Total quick assets | $280,500 | $244,700 |
| Current liabilities | $210,000 | $243,000 |
| Quick ratio | 1.3 | 1.0 |

# Accounts Receivable Analysis

The size and makeup of accounts receivable change constantly during business operations. Sales on account increase accounts receivable, whereas collections from customers decrease accounts receivable. Firms that grant long credit terms usually have larger accounts receivable balances than those granting short credit terms. Increases or decreases in the volume of sales also affect the balance of accounts receivable.

It is desirable to collect receivables as promptly as possible. The cash collected from receivables improves solvency. In addition, the cash generated by prompt collections from customers may be used in operations for such purposes as purchasing merchandise in large quantities at lower prices. The cash may also be used for payment of dividends to stockholders or for other investing or financing purposes. Prompt collection also lessens the risk of loss from uncollectible accounts.

## Accounts Receivable Turnover

The relationship between sales and accounts receivable may be stated as the ***accounts receivable turnover***. This ratio is computed by dividing net sales by the average net accounts receivable.[2] It is desirable to base the average on monthly balances, which allows for seasonal changes in sales. When such data are not available, it may be necessary to use the average of the accounts receivable balance at the beginning and the end of the year. If there are trade notes receivable as well as accounts, the two may be combined. The accounts receivable turnover data for Lincoln Company are as follows.

|  | 2006 | 2005 |
|---|---|---|
| Net sales | $1,498,000 | $1,200,000 |
| Accounts receivable (net): |  |  |
| Beginning of year | $ 120,000 | $ 140,000 |
| End of year | 115,000 | 120,000 |
| Total | $ 235,000 | $ 260,000 |
| Average (Total ÷ 2) | $ 117,500 | $ 130,000 |
| Accounts receivable turnover | 12.7 | 9.2 |

The increase in the accounts receivable turnover for 2006 indicates that there has been an improvement in the collection of receivables. This may be due to a change in the granting of credit or in collection practices or both.

## Number of Days' Sales in Receivables

Another measure of the relationship between sales and accounts receivable is the ***number of days' sales in receivables***. This ratio is computed by dividing the net accounts receivable at the end of the year by the average daily sales. Average daily sales is determined by dividing net sales by 365 days. The number of days' sales in receivables is computed for Lincoln Company as follows:

|  | 2006 | 2005 |
|---|---|---|
| Accounts receivable (net), end of year | $115,000 | $120,000 |
| Net sales | $1,498,000 | $1,200,000 |
| Average daily sales (sales ÷ 365) | $4,104 | $3,288 |
| Number of days' sales in receivables | 28.0* | 36.5* |

*Accounts receivable ÷ Average daily sales

Net sales were $960,000. The accounts receivable balance at the beginning of the year was $56,000, and at the end of the year it was $40,000. What are (a) the accounts receivable turnover and (b) the number of days' sales in receivables?

(a) 20 [$960,000/($56,000 + $40,000)/2]; (b) 15.2 days [$40,000/($960,000/365)]

The number of days' sales in receivables is an estimate of the length of time (in days) the accounts receivable have been outstanding. Comparing this measure with the credit terms provides information on the efficiency in collecting receivables. For example, assume that the number of days' sales in receivables for Grant Inc. is 40. If Grant Inc.'s credit terms are n/45, then its collection process appears to be efficient. On the other hand, if Grant Inc.'s credit terms are n/30, its collection process does not appear to be efficient. A comparison with other firms in the same industry and with prior years also provides useful information. Such comparisons may indicate efficiency of collection procedures and trends in credit management.

## Inventory Analysis

A business should keep enough inventory on hand to meet the needs of its customers and its operations. At the same time, however, an excessive amount of inventory reduces solvency by tying up funds. Excess inventories also increase insurance expense, property taxes, storage costs, and other related expenses. These expenses further reduce funds that could be used elsewhere to improve operations. Finally, excess inventory also increases the risk of losses because of price declines or obsolescence of

[2]If known, **credit** sales should be used in the numerator. Because credit sales are not normally known by external users, we use net sales in the numerator.

the inventory. Two measures that are useful for evaluating the management of inventory are the inventory turnover and the number of days' sales in inventory.

## Inventory Turnover

The relationship between the volume of goods (merchandise) sold and inventory may be stated as the ***inventory turnover***. It is computed by dividing the cost of goods sold by the average inventory. If monthly data are not available, the average of the inventories at the beginning and the end of the year may be used. The inventory turnover for Lincoln Company is computed as follows:

| | 2006 | 2005 |
|---|---|---|
| Cost of goods sold | $1,043,000 | $820,000 |
| Inventories: | | |
| Beginning of year | $ 283,000 | $311,000 |
| End of year | 264,000 | 283,000 |
| Total | $ 547,000 | $594,000 |
| Average (Total ÷ 2) | $ 273,500 | $297,000 |
| Inventory turnover | 3.8 | 2.8 |

The inventory turnover of **McDonald's Corporation** for a recent year was 36, while for **Toys "R" Us Inc.**, it was 3.7. McDonald's inventory turnover is higher because it sells perishable food products, while toys can sit on the shelf longer without "spoiling."

The inventory turnover improved for Lincoln Company because of an increase in the cost of goods sold and a decrease in the average inventories. Differences across inventories, companies, and industries are too great to allow a general statement on what is a good inventory turnover. For example, a firm selling food should have a higher turnover than a firm selling furniture or jewelry. Likewise, the perishable foods department of a supermarket should have a higher turnover than the soaps and cleansers department. However, for each business or each department within a business, there is a reasonable turnover rate. A turnover lower than this rate could mean that inventory is not being managed properly.

## Number of Days' Sales in Inventory

Another measure of the relationship between the cost of goods sold and inventory is the ***number of days' sales in inventory***. This measure is computed by dividing the inventory at the end of the year by the average daily cost of goods sold (cost of goods sold divided by 365). The number of days' sales in inventory for Lincoln Company is computed as follows:

| | 2006 | 2005 |
|---|---|---|
| Inventories, end of year | $264,000 | $283,000 |
| Cost of goods sold | $1,043,000 | $820,000 |
| Average daily cost of goods sold (COGS ÷ 365 days) | $2,858 | $2,247 |
| Number of days' sales in inventory | 92.4 | 125.9 |

The number of days' sales in inventory is a rough measure of the length of time it takes to acquire, sell, and replace the inventory. For Lincoln Company, there is a major improvement in the number of days' sales in inventory during 2006. However, a comparison with earlier years and similar firms would be useful in assessing Lincoln Company's overall inventory management.

# Ratio of Fixed Assets to Long-Term Liabilities

Long-term notes and bonds are often secured by mortgages on fixed assets. The ***ratio of fixed assets to long-term liabilities*** is a solvency measure that indicates the margin of safety of the noteholders or bondholders. It also indicates the ability of the business to borrow additional funds on a long-term basis. The ratio of fixed assets to long-term liabilities for Lincoln Company is as follows:

|  | 2006 | 2005 |
|---|---|---|
| Fixed assets (net) | $444,500 | $470,000 |
| Long-term liabilities | $100,000 | $200,000 |
| Ratio of fixed assets to long-term liabilities | 4.4 | 2.4 |

The major increase in this ratio at the end of 2006 is mainly due to liquidating one-half of Lincoln Company's long-term liabilities. If the company needs to borrow additional funds on a long-term basis in the future, it is in a strong position to do so.

## Ratio of Liabilities to Stockholders' Equity

Claims against the total assets of a business are divided into two groups: (1) claims of creditors and (2) claims of owners. The relationship between the total claims of the creditors and owners—the ***ratio of liabilities to stockholders' equity***—is a solvency measure that indicates the margin of safety for creditors. It also indicates the ability of the business to withstand adverse business conditions. When the claims of creditors are large in relation to the equity of the stockholders, there are usually significant interest payments. If earnings decline to the point where the company is unable to meet its interest payments, the business may be taken over by the creditors.

The relationship between creditor and stockholder equity is shown in the vertical analysis of the balance sheet. For example, the balance sheet of Lincoln Company in Exhibit 5 indicates that on December 31, 2006, liabilities represented 27.2% and stockholders' equity represented 72.8% of the total liabilities and stockholders' equity (100.0%). Instead of expressing each item as a percent of the total, this relationship may be expressed as a ratio of one to the other, as follows:

|  | 2006 | 2005 |
|---|---|---|
| Total liabilities | $310,000 | $443,000 |
| Total stockholders' equity | $829,500 | $787,500 |
| Ratio of liabilities to stockholders' equity | 0.37 | 0.56 |

The balance sheet of Lincoln Company shows that the major factor affecting the change in the ratio was the $100,000 decrease in long-term liabilities during 2006. The ratio at the end of both years shows a large margin of safety for the creditors.

## Number of Times Interest Charges Earned

Corporations in some industries, such as airlines, normally have high ratios of debt to stockholders' equity. For such corporations, the relative risk of the debtholders is normally measured as the ***number of times interest charges are earned***, sometimes called the **fixed charge coverage ratio**, during the year. The higher the ratio, the lower the risk that interest payments will not be made if earnings decrease. In other words, the higher the ratio, the greater the assurance that interest payments will be made on a continuing basis. This measure also indicates the general financial strength of the business, which is of interest to stockholders and employees as well as creditors.

The amount available to meet interest charges is not affected by taxes on income. This is because interest is deductible in determining taxable income. Thus, the number of times interest charges are earned is computed as shown below.

|  | 2006 | 2005 |
|---|---|---|
| Income before income tax | $ 900,000 | $ 800,000 |
| Add interest expense | 300,000 | 250,000 |
| Amount available to meet interest charges | $1,200,000 | $1,050,000 |
| Number of times interest charges earned | 4 | 4.2 |

**REAL WORLD**

The ratio of liabilities to stockholders' equity varies across industries. For example, recent annual reports of some selected companies showed the following ratio of liabilities to stockholders' equity:

| Continental Airlines | 7.43 |
|---|---|
| Procter & Gamble | 1.98 |
| Circuit City Stores | 0.66 |

The airline industry generally uses more debt financing than the consumer product or retail industries. Thus, the airline industry is generally considered more risky.

What would be the number of times interest charges are earned for a company with $1,500,000, 10% debt; net income of $120,000; and a corporate tax rate of 40%?

-------------------------------------------------

$$\frac{[\$120,000/(1.0 - 0.4)] + \$150,000}{\$150,000} = 2.33$$

Analysis such as this can also be applied to dividends on preferred stock. In such a case, net income is divided by the amount of preferred dividends to yield the **number of times preferred dividends are earned**. This measure indicates the risk that dividends to preferred stockholders may not be paid.

# FINANCIAL REPORTING AND DISCLOSURE

## SARBANES-OXLEY ACT

The Sarbanes-Oxley Act became law on June 30, 2002, in response to widespread concerns about conflicts of interest between auditors and their clients, perceived weaknesses in corporate governance, and inadequate financial disclosure. Thus, Sarbanes-Oxley provided reforms in three main areas: the accounting profession, corporate governance, and financial disclosure.

Accounting Profession: A new provision in Sarbanes-Oxley prevents the independent auditor from providing other non-aligned services to a client, such as bookkeeping or internal auditing services. Providing tax services to an audit client is still acceptable. In addition, the act established a new Public Accounting Oversight Board (PAOB), consisting of five members responsible for establishing and overseeing auditing, quality control, ethics, and independence standards related to preparing audit reports.

Corporate Governance: Corporate governance refers to methods for aligning the behavior of corporate managers with the interests of shareholders. Sarbanes-Oxley added important requirements to the audit committee of the Board of Directors. The audit committee must be members of the Board of Directors and independent of management. In addition, the audit committee is required to be responsible for appointment, compensation, and oversight of the independent auditors. In addition, Sarbanes-Oxley also requires the CEO and CFO to certify the fairness of financial statements and the effectiveness of the internal controls. For example, an excerpt from the certification of a recent quarterly report of **Bank of America** by its CEO, Kenneth D. Lewis, is shown as follows:

*I, Kenneth D. Lewis, certify that:*

*I have reviewed this quarterly report of Bank of America Corporation;*

*Based on my knowledge, the financial statements, and other financial information included in this quarterly report, fairly present in all material respects the financial condition, results of operations and cash flows of the (company) as of, and for, the periods presented in this quarterly report;*

*The . . . officers and I have disclosed, based on our most recent evaluation, to the (the company's) auditors and the audit committee . . .:*

- *all significant deficiencies in the design or operation of internal controls which could adversely affect (the company's) ability to record, process, summarize and report financial data and have identified for the (company's) auditors any material weaknesses in internal controls; and*
- *any fraud, whether or not material, that involves management or other employees who have a significant role in the (company's) internal controls;*

   *. . .*

*/s/ Kenneth D. Lewis*

Financial Disclosure: Sarbanes-Oxley also requires new or enhanced financial disclosures of transactions between related parties. These disclosures are prompted by a concern that such transactions are subject to a higher risk of self-dealing. In addition, the act requires material off-balance-sheet arrangements to be disclosed, such as the complex partnership transactions that led to the **Enron** failure.

# Profitability Analysis

The ability of a business to earn profits depends on the effectiveness and efficiency of its operations as well as the resources available to it. Profitability analysis, therefore, focuses primarily on the relationship between operating results as reported in the income statement and resources available to the business as reported in the balance sheet. Major analyses used in assessing profitability include the following:

1. Ratio of net sales to assets
2. Rate earned on total assets
3. Rate earned on stockholders' equity
4. Rate earned on common stockholders' equity
5. Earnings per share on common stock
6. Price-earnings ratio
7. Dividends per share
8. Dividend yield

> **Profitability analysis focuses on the relationship between operating results and the resources available to a business.**

## Ratio of Net Sales to Assets

The ratio of net sales to assets is a profitability measure that shows how effectively a firm utilizes its assets. For example, two competing businesses have equal amounts of assets. If the sales of one are twice the sales of the other, the business with the higher sales is making better use of its assets.

In computing the ratio of net sales to assets, any long-term investments are excluded from total assets, because such investments are unrelated to normal operations involving the sale of goods or services. Assets may be measured as the total at the end of the year, the average at the beginning and end of the year, or the average of monthly totals. The basic data and the computation of this ratio for Lincoln Company are as follows:

|  | 2006 | 2005 |
|---|---|---|
| Net sales | $1,498,000 | $1,200,000 |
| Total assets (excluding long-term investments): |  |  |
|     Beginning of year | $1,053,000 | $1,010,000 |
|     End of year | 1,044,500 | 1,053,000 |
|     Total | $2,097,500 | $2,063,000 |
|     Average (Total ÷ 2) | $1,048,750 | $1,031,500 |
| Ratio of net sales to assets | 1.4 | 1.2 |

This ratio improved during 2006, primarily due to an increase in sales volume. A comparison with similar companies or industry averages would be helpful in assessing the effectiveness of Lincoln Company's use of its assets.

## Rate Earned on Total Assets

The ***rate earned on total assets*** measures the profitability of total assets, without considering how the assets are financed. This rate is therefore not affected by whether the assets are financed primarily by creditors or stockholders.

The rate earned on total assets is computed by adding interest expense to net income and dividing this sum by the average total assets. Adding interest expense to net income eliminates the effect of whether the assets are financed by debt or equity. The rate earned by Lincoln Company on total assets is computed as follows:

|  | 2006 | 2005 |
|---|---|---|
| Net income | $ 91,000 | $ 76,500 |
| Plus interest expense | 6,000 | 12,000 |
| Total | $ 97,000 | $ 88,500 |
| Total assets: |  |  |
| Beginning of year | $1,230,500 | $1,187,500 |
| End of year | 1,139,500 | 1,230,500 |
| Total | $2,370,000 | $2,418,000 |
| Average (Total ÷ 2) | $1,185,000 | $1,209,000 |
| Rate earned on total assets | 8.2% | 7.3% |

The rate earned on total assets of Lincoln Company during 2006 improved over that of 2005. A comparison with similar companies and industry averages would be useful in evaluating Lincoln Company's profitability on total assets.

Sometimes it may be desirable to compute the **rate of income from operations to total assets**. This is especially true if significant amounts of nonoperating income and expense are reported on the income statement. In this case, any assets related to the nonoperating income and expense items should be excluded from total assets in computing the rate. In addition, using income from operations (which is before tax) has the advantage of eliminating the effects of any changes in the tax structure on the rate of earnings. When evaluating published data on rates earned on assets, you should be careful to determine the exact nature of the measure that is reported.

# Rate Earned on Stockholders' Equity

Another measure of profitability is the *rate earned on stockholders' equity*. It is computed by dividing net income by average total stockholders' equity. In contrast to the rate earned on total assets, this measure emphasizes the rate of income earned on the amount invested by the stockholders.

The total stockholders' equity may vary throughout a period. For example, a business may issue or retire stock, pay dividends, and earn net income. If monthly amounts are not available, the average of the stockholders' equity at the beginning and the end of the year is normally used to compute this rate. For Lincoln Company, the rate earned on stockholders' equity is computed as follows:

|  | 2006 | 2005 |
|---|---|---|
| Net income | $ 91,000 | $ 76,500 |
| Stockholders' equity: |  |  |
| Beginning of year | $ 787,500 | $ 750,000 |
| End of year | 829,500 | 787,500 |
| Total | $1,617,000 | $1,537,500 |
| Average (Total ÷ 2) | $ 808,500 | $ 768,750 |
| Rate earned on stockholders' equity | 11.3% | 10.0% |

The rate earned by a business on the equity of its stockholders is usually higher than the rate earned on total assets. This occurs when the amount earned on assets acquired with creditors' funds is more than the interest paid to creditors. This difference in the rate on stockholders' equity and the rate on total assets is called *leverage*.

Lincoln Company's rate earned on stockholders' equity for 2006, 11.3%, is greater than the rate of 8.2% earned on total assets. The leverage of 3.1% (11.3% − 8.2%) for 2006 compares favorably with the 2.7% (10.0% − 7.3%) leverage for 2005. Exhibit 8 shows the 2006 and 2005 leverages for Lincoln Company.

 Nobody doesn't like me. Based in Chicago, I employ more than 140,000 people and my wares are sold in almost every country on earth. My food and drinks, underwear, and household products sport more than 100 brands, such as Champion, Hanes, L'eggs, Bali, Just My Size, Playtex, Wonderbra, Jimmy Dean, Ball Park, Hillshire Farms, and the Kiwi shoe care brand. My 32 "megabrands" each generate more than $100 million in annual sales. I aim to hold the No. 1 or No. 2 brand position in every category in which I compete. One of my biggest brands is my own name. Who am I? (Go to page 717 for answer.)

## •Exhibit 8

**Leverage**

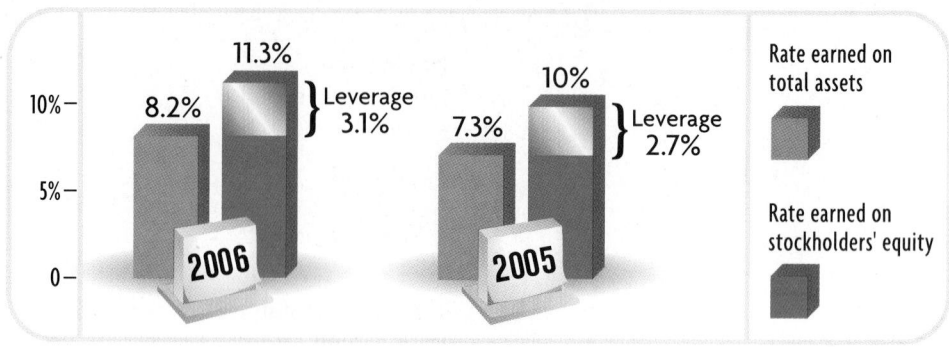

## Rate Earned on Common Stockholders' Equity

A corporation may have both preferred and common stock outstanding. In this case, the common stockholders have the residual claim on earnings. The **rate earned on common stockholders' equity** focuses only on the rate of profits earned on the amount invested by the common stockholders. It is computed by subtracting preferred dividend requirements from the net income and dividing by the average common stockholders' equity.

Lincoln Company has $150,000 of 6% nonparticipating preferred stock outstanding on December 31, 2006 and 2005. Thus, the annual preferred dividend requirement is $9,000 ($150,000 × 6%). The common stockholders' equity equals the total stockholders' equity, including retained earnings, less the par of the preferred stock ($150,000). The basic data and the rate earned on common stockholders' equity for Lincoln Company are as follows:

The approximate rates earned on assets and stockholders' equity for **Adolph Coors Company** and **Anheuser-Busch Companies** for a recent fiscal year are shown below.

| | Adolph Coors | Anheuser-Busch |
|---|---|---|
| Rate earned on assets | 7% | 15% |
| Rate earned on stockholders' equity | 13% | 42% |

Anheuser-Busch has been more profitable and has benefited from a greater use of leverage than has Adolph Coors.

| | 2006 | 2005 |
|---|---|---|
| Net income | $ 91,000 | $ 76,500 |
| Preferred dividends | 9,000 | 9,000 |
| Remainder—identified with common stock | $ 82,000 | $ 67,500 |
| Common stockholders' equity: | | |
| Beginning of year | $ 637,500 | $ 600,000 |
| End of year | 679,500 | 637,500 |
| Total | $1,317,000 | $1,237,500 |
| Average (Total ÷ 2) | $ 658,500 | $ 618,750 |
| Rate earned on common stockholders' equity | 12.5% | 10.9% |

The rate earned on common stockholders' equity differs from the rates earned by Lincoln Company on total assets and total stockholders' equity. This occurs if there are borrowed funds and also preferred stock outstanding, which rank ahead of the common shares in their claim on earnings. Thus, the concept of leverage, as we discussed in the preceding section, can also be applied to the use of funds from the sale of preferred stock as well as borrowing. Funds from both sources can be used in an attempt to increase the return on common stockholders' equity.

## Earnings per Share on Common Stock

One of the profitability measures often quoted by the financial press is **earnings per share (EPS) on common stock**. It is also normally reported in the income statement in corporate annual reports. If a company has issued only one class of stock, the earnings per share is computed by dividing net income by the number of shares of stock outstanding. If preferred and common stock are outstanding, the net income is first reduced by the amount of preferred dividend requirements.[3]

---

[3]Additional details related to earnings per share were discussed in a previous chapter.

The data on the earnings per share of common stock for Lincoln Company are as follows:

| | 2006 | 2005 |
|---|---|---|
| Net income | $91,000 | $76,500 |
| Preferred dividends | 9,000 | 9,000 |
| Remainder—identified with common stock | $82,000 | $67,500 |
| Shares of common stock outstanding | 50,000 | 50,000 |
| Earnings per share on common stock | $1.64 | $1.35 |

## Price-Earnings Ratio

Another profitability measure quoted by the financial press is the ***price-earnings (P/E) ratio*** on common stock. The price-earnings ratio is an indicator of a firm's future earnings prospects. It is computed by dividing the market price per share of common stock at a specific date by the annual earnings per share. To illustrate, assume that the market prices per common share are 41 at the end of 2006 and 27 at the end of 2005. The price-earnings ratio on common stock of Lincoln Company is computed as follows:

| | 2006 | 2005 |
|---|---|---|
| Market price per share of common stock | $41.00 | $27.00 |
| Earnings per share on common stock | ÷ 1.64 | ÷ 1.35 |
| Price-earnings ratio on common stock | 25 | 20 |

The price-earnings ratio indicates that a share of common stock of Lincoln Company was selling for 20 times the amount of earnings per share at the end of 2005. At the end of 2006, the common stock was selling for 25 times the amount of earnings per share.

## Dividends per Share and Dividend Yield

Since the primary basis for dividends is earnings, dividends per share and earnings per share on common stock are commonly used by investors in assessing alternative stock investments. The dividends per share for Lincoln Company were $0.80 ($40,000 ÷ 50,000 shares) for 2006 and $0.60 ($30,000 ÷ 50,000 shares) for 2005.

Dividends per share can be reported with earnings per share to indicate the relationship between dividends and earnings. Comparing these two per share amounts indicates the extent to which the corporation is retaining its earnings for use in operations. Exhibit 9 shows these relationships for Lincoln Company.

## •Exhibit 9   Dividends and Earnings per Share of Common Stock

The ***dividend yield*** on common stock is a profitability measure that shows the rate of return to common stockholders in terms of cash dividends. It is of special interest to investors whose main investment objective is to receive current returns (dividends) on an investment rather than an increase in the market price of the investment. The dividend yield is computed by dividing the annual dividends paid per share of common stock by the market price per share on a specific date. To illustrate, assume that the market price was 41 at the end of 2006 and 27 at the end of 2005. The dividend yield on common stock of Lincoln Company is as follows:

|  | 2006 | 2005 |
|---|---|---|
| Dividends per share of common stock | $ 0.80 | $ 0.60 |
| Market price per share of common stock | ÷ 41.00 | ÷ 27.00 |
| Dividend yield on common stock | 1.95% | 2.22% |

# Summary of Analytical Measures

**objective 4**

Summarize the uses and limitations of analytical measures.

Exhibit 10 presents a summary of the analytical measures that we have discussed. These measures can be computed for most medium-size businesses. Depending on the specific business being analyzed, some measures might be omitted or additional measures could be developed. The type of industry, the capital structure, and the diversity of the business's operations usually affect the measures used. For example, analysis for an airline might include revenue per passenger mile and cost per available seat as measures. Likewise, analysis for a hotel might focus on occupancy rates.

Percentage analyses, ratios, turnovers, and other measures of financial position and operating results are useful analytical measures. They are helpful in assessing a business's past performance and predicting its future. They are not, however, a substitute for sound judgment. In selecting and interpreting analytical measures, conditions peculiar to a business or its industry should be considered. In addition, the influence of the general economic and business environment should be considered.

In determining trends, the interrelationship of the measures used in assessing a business should be carefully studied. Comparable indexes of earlier periods should also be studied. Data from competing businesses may be useful in assessing the efficiency of operations for the firm under analysis. In making such comparisons, however, the effects of differences in the accounting methods used by the businesses should be considered.

# Corporate Annual Reports

**objective 5**

Describe the contents of corporate annual reports.

Corporations normally issue annual reports to their stockholders and other interested parties. Such reports summarize the corporation's operating activities for the past year and plans for the future. There are many variations in the order and form for presenting the major sections of annual reports. However, one section of the annual report is devoted to the financial statements, including the accompanying notes. In addition, annual reports usually include a management discussion and analysis (MDA) and an independent auditors' report. The footnotes, MDA, and independent auditors' report are illustrated in the 2002 annual report for **Home Depot, Inc.,** in Appendix E.

## •Exhibit 10    Summary of Analytical Measures

| | Method of Computation | Use |
|---|---|---|
| *Solvency measures:* | | |
| Working capital | Current assets − Current liabilities | To indicate the ability to meet currently maturing obligations |
| Current ratio | $\dfrac{\text{Current assets}}{\text{Current liabilities}}$ | |
| Quick ratio | $\dfrac{\text{Quick assets}}{\text{Current liabilities}}$ | To indicate instant debt-paying ability |
| Accounts receivable turnover | $\dfrac{\text{Net sales}}{\text{Average accounts receivable}}$ | To assess the efficiency in collecting receivables and in the management of credit |
| Numbers of days' sales in receivables | $\dfrac{\text{Accounts receivable, end of year}}{\text{Average daily sales}}$ | |
| Inventory turnover | $\dfrac{\text{Cost of goods sold}}{\text{Average inventory}}$ | To assess the efficiency in the management of inventory |
| Number of days' sales in inventory | $\dfrac{\text{Inventory, end of year}}{\text{Average daily cost of goods sold}}$ | |
| Ratio of fixed assets to long-term liabilities | $\dfrac{\text{Fixed assets (net)}}{\text{Long-term liabilities}}$ | To indicate the margin of safety to long-term creditors |
| Ratio of liabilities to stockholders' equity | $\dfrac{\text{Total liabilities}}{\text{Total stockholders' equity}}$ | To indicate the margin of safety to creditors |
| Number of times interest charges earned | $\dfrac{\text{Income before income tax + Interest expense}}{\text{Interest expense}}$ | To assess the risk to debtholders in terms of number of times interest charges were earned |
| *Profitability measures:* | | |
| Ratio of net sales to assets | $\dfrac{\text{Net sales}}{\text{Average total assets (excluding long-term investments)}}$ | To assess the effectiveness in the use of assets |
| Rate earned on total assets | $\dfrac{\text{Net income + Interest expense}}{\text{Average total assets}}$ | To assess the profitability of the assets |
| Rate earned on stockholders' equity | $\dfrac{\text{Net income}}{\text{Average total stockholders' equity}}$ | To assess the profitability of the investment by stockholders |
| Rate earned on common stockholders' equity | $\dfrac{\text{Net income − Preferred dividends}}{\text{Average common stockholders' equity}}$ | To assess the profitability of the investment by common stockholders |
| Earnings per share on common stock | $\dfrac{\text{Net income − Preferred dividends}}{\text{Shares of common stock outstanding}}$ | |
| Price-earnings ratio | $\dfrac{\text{Market price per share of common stock}}{\text{Earnings per share of common stock}}$ | To indicate future earnings prospects, based on the relationship between market value of common stock and earnings |
| Dividends per share of common stock | $\dfrac{\text{Dividends}}{\text{Shares of common stock outstanding}}$ | To indicate the extent to which earnings are being distributed to common stockholders |
| Dividend yield | $\dfrac{\text{Dividends per share of common stock}}{\text{Market price per share of common stock}}$ | To indicate the rate of return to common stockholders in terms of dividends |

## INTEGRITY IN BUSINESS

### DO YOU SWEAR. . .

The Sarbanes-Oxley Act of 2002 was enacted in response to the perceived abuses in accounting, corporate responsibility, and public disclosure in the early part of this decade. One of the provisions of this act is to require the principal executive and financial officers to certify under oath and penalty of law that the financial statements have been personally reviewed, contain no material omissions, and present fairly the financial condition and results of operations.

## Management Discussion and Analysis

A required disclosure in the annual report filed with the Securities and Exchange Commission is the ***Management Discussion and Analysis (MDA)***. The MDA provides critical information in interpreting the financial statements and assessing the future of the company.

The MDA includes an analysis of the results of operations and discusses management's opinion about future performance. It compares the prior year's income statement with the current year's to explain changes in sales, significant expenses, gross profit, and income from operations. For example, an increase in sales may be explained by referring to higher shipment volume or stronger prices.

The MDA also includes an analysis of the company's financial condition. It compares significant balance sheet items between successive years to explain changes in liquidity and capital resources. In addition, the MDA discusses significant risk exposure. For example, **Home Depot** has identified fluctuations in interest rates as its primary risk factor, since home building and improvement activities are sensitive to interest rates.

## INTEGRITY IN BUSINESS

### ONE BAD APPLE

A recent survey by *CFO* magazine reported that 17% of the chief financial officers were pressured by their chief executive officer to misrepresent financial results, while only 5% admitted to knowingly violating generally accepted accounting principles.

## Independent Auditors' Report

Before issuing annual statements, all publicly held corporations are required to have an independent audit (examination) of their financial statements. For the financial statements of most companies, the CPAs who conduct the audit render an opinion on the fairness of the statements.

In addition, beginning in 2004, the Sarbanes-Oxley Act will require the independent auditor to provide an additional report attesting to management's assessment of internal control. This report will express the auditor's opinion on the accuracy of management's internal control assertion.[4]

---

[4]Final reporting guidelines are being formulated by appropriate professional and regulatory bodies, including the SEC, AICPA, and PAOB.

# SPOTLIGHT ON STRATEGY

## INVESTING STRATEGIES

How does one decide in which companies to invest? Like any other significant purchase, you would need to do some research to guide your investment decision, and that research should stem from your overall investment philosophy. If you were buying a car for performance, you would research performance characteristics, but if you were purchasing for economy, then you would research economy characteristics. You should research investment alternatives in the same way. There are four different investment philosophies that match different investment preferences: value, growth, income, and technical investing.

### Value Investing
The value investor attempts to determine the intrinsic value of a business and then compare this value to the stock price. The investor is normally searching for undervalued stocks. That is, the investor attempts to discover stocks with an intrinsic value that is greater than the stock price. Value investors often look for quiet, out-of-favor, "boring" companies that have excellent financial performance. Investing in such stocks assumes that the stock price will eventually rise to match the intrinsic value. This method of investing was popularized by Benjamin Graham and is used by one of the most successful investors in the world, Warren Buffett. As stated by one author, "Graham's conviction rested on certain assumptions. First, he believed that the market frequently mispriced stocks. This mispricing was most often caused by human emotions of fear and greed. At the height of optimism, greed moved stocks beyond their intrinsic value, creating an overpriced market. At other times, fear moved prices below intrinsic value, creating an undervalued market."* Naturally, the key to successful value investing is to accurately determine a stock's intrinsic value. This will often include analyzing company financial ratios, as discussed in this chapter, relative to target ratios and industry norms.

### Growth Investing
The growth investor tries to identify companies that are growing sales and earnings through new products, mar-

kets, or opportunities. Growth companies are often young companies that are still unproven but that possess unique technologies or capabilities. Investors hope to "ride the wave" of growth by purchasing these companies before their potential becomes obvious. Unlike value investors, growth investors will often purchase companies that are the "Ferraris" of the stock market. Growth investing carries the risk that the growth may not occur. Any moderation in growth can lead to severe price declines. Growth investors use many of the ratios discussed in this chapter to identify high-potential growth companies.

### Income Investing
Income investors purchase common stocks for their dividend stream. High-dividend-paying companies are often in low-growth and stable industries. The stock price of such companies is usually not very volatile. Thus, the majority of the investment return comes from dividends. Many of the ratios discussed in this chapter can help identify companies with financial strength and high dividends.

### Technical Investing
Investors that use technical analysis do not concern themselves with the fundamental financial strength and performance of the business but, instead, attempt to find clues of future performance from past performance. Technical investors often use charts of the historical prices in order to discover recurring price patterns that will help them determine if the stock price is near a top (signal to sell) or near a bottom (signal to buy). Technical analysts believe that the recurring patterns provide clues into market psychology and can be used to develop buy-and-sell rules. These rules are as varied as the number of investors developing them. Naturally, if everyone agreed upon a technical rule that actually predicted the future, then everyone would use the rule and it would eventually cease to work.

*Robert G. Hagstrom, *The Warren Buffett Way*.

# Key Points

## 1 List basic financial statement analytical procedures.
The analysis of percentage increases and decreases in related items in comparative financial statements is

called horizontal analysis. The analysis of percentages of component parts to the total in a single statement is called vertical analysis.

Financial statements in which all amounts are expressed in percentages for purposes of analysis are called common-size statements.

## 2 Apply financial statement analysis to assess the solvency of a business.

The primary focus of financial statement analysis is the assessment of solvency and profitability. All users are interested in the ability of a business to pay its debts as they come due (solvency) and to earn income (profitability). Solvency analysis is normally assessed by examining the following balance sheet relationships: (1) current position analysis, (2) accounts receivable analysis, (3) inventory analysis, (4) the ratio of fixed assets to long-term liabilities, (5) the ratio of liabilities to stockholders' equity, and (6) the number of times interest charges are earned.

## 3 Apply financial statement analysis to assess the profitability of a business.

Profitability analysis focuses mainly on the relationship between operating results (income statement) and resources available (balance sheet). Major analyses used in assessing profitability include (1) the ratio of net sales to assets, (2) the rate earned on total assets, (3) the rate earned on stockholders' equity, (4) the rate earned on common stockholders' equity, (5) earnings per share on common stock, (6) the price-earnings ratio, (7) dividends per share, and (8) dividend yield.

## 4 Summarize the uses and limitations of analytical measures.

In selecting and interpreting analytical measures, conditions peculiar to a business or its industry should be considered. For example, the type of industry, capital structure, and diversity of the business's operations affect the measures used. In addition, the influence of the general economic and business environment should be considered.

## 5 Describe the contents of corporate annual reports.

Corporate annual reports normally include financial statements and the accompanying notes, the Management Discussion and Analysis, and the Independent Auditors' Report.

# Key Terms

accounts receivable turnover (700)
common-size statement (696)
current ratio (698)
dividend yield (708)
earnings per share (EPS) on
   common stock (706)
horizontal analysis (692)
inventory turnover (701)
leverage (705)
Management Discussion and
   Analysis (MDA) (710)
number of days' sales in inventory
   (701)

number of days' sales in
   receivables (700)
number of times interest charges
   are earned (702)
price-earnings (P/E) ratio (707)
profitability (697)
quick assets (699)
quick ratio (699)
rate earned on common
   stockholders' equity (706)
rate earned on stockholders' equity
   (705)
rate earned on total assets (704)

ratio of fixed assets to long-term
   liabilities (701)
ratio of liabilities to stockholders'
   equity (702)
solvency (697)
vertical analysis (694)

# Illustrative Problem

Rainbow Paint Co.'s comparative financial statements for the years ending December 31, 2006 and 2005, are as follows. The market price of Rainbow Paint Co.'s common stock was $30 on December 31, 2005, and $25 on December 31, 2006.

### Rainbow Paint Co.
### Comparative Income Statement
### For the Years Ended December 31, 2006 and 2005

|  | 2006 | 2005 |
|---|---|---|
| Sales | $5,125,000 | $3,257,600 |
| Sales returns and allowances | 125,000 | 57,600 |
| Net sales | $5,000,000 | $3,200,000 |
| Cost of goods sold | 3,400,000 | 2,080,000 |
| Gross profit | $1,600,000 | $1,120,000 |
| Selling expenses | $ 650,000 | $ 464,000 |
| Administrative expenses | 325,000 | 224,000 |
| Total operating expenses | $ 975,000 | $ 688,000 |
| Income from operations | $ 625,000 | $ 432,000 |
| Other income | 25,000 | 19,200 |
|  | $ 650,000 | $ 451,200 |
| Other expense (interest) | 105,000 | 64,000 |
| Income before income tax | $ 545,000 | $ 387,200 |
| Income tax expense | 300,000 | 176,000 |
| Net income | $ 245,000 | $ 211,200 |

### Rainbow Paint Co.
### Comparative Retained Earnings Statement
### For the Years Ended December 31, 2006 and 2005

|  | 2006 | 2005 |
|---|---|---|
| Retained earnings, January 1 | $723,000 | $581,800 |
| Add net income for year | 245,000 | 211,200 |
| Total | $968,000 | $793,000 |
| Deduct dividends: |  |  |
| On preferred stock | $ 40,000 | $ 40,000 |
| On common stock | 45,000 | 30,000 |
| Total | $ 85,000 | $ 70,000 |
| Retained earnings, December 31 | $883,000 | $723,000 |

### Rainbow Paint Co.
### Comparative Balance Sheet
### December 31, 2006 and 2005

|  | 2006 | 2005 |
|---|---|---|
| **Assets** |  |  |
| Current assets: |  |  |
| Cash | $ 175,000 | $ 125,000 |
| Marketable securities | 150,000 | 50,000 |
| Accounts receivable (net) | 425,000 | 325,000 |
| Inventories | 720,000 | 480,000 |
| Prepaid expenses | 30,000 | 20,000 |
| Total current assets | $1,500,000 | $1,000,000 |
| Long-term investments | 250,000 | 225,000 |
| Property, plant, and equipment (net) | 2,093,000 | 1,948,000 |
| Total assets | $3,843,000 | $3,173,000 |
| **Liabilities** |  |  |
| Current liabilities | $ 750,000 | $ 650,000 |
| Long-term liabilities: |  |  |
| Mortgage note payable, 10%, due 2009 | $ 410,000 | — |
| Bonds payable, 8%, due 2012 | 800,000 | $ 800,000 |
| Total long-term liabilities | $1,210,000 | $ 800,000 |
| Total liabilities | $1,960,000 | $1,450,000 |
| **Stockholders' Equity** |  |  |
| Preferred 8% stock, $100 par | $ 500,000 | $ 500,000 |
| Common stock, $10 par | 500,000 | 500,000 |
| Retained earnings | 883,000 | 723,000 |
| Total stockholders' equity | $1,883,000 | $1,723,000 |
| Total liabilities and stockholders' equity | $3,843,000 | $3,173,000 |

**Instructions**

Determine the following measures for 2006:

1. Working capital
2. Current ratio
3. Quick ratio
4. Accounts receivable turnover
5. Number of days' sales in receivables
6. Inventory turnover
7. Number of days' sales in inventory
8. Ratio of fixed assets to long-term liabilities
9. Ratio of liabilities to stockholders' equity
10. Number of times interest charges earned
11. Number of times preferred dividends earned
12. Ratio of net sales to assets
13. Rate earned on total assets
14. Rate earned on stockholders' equity
15. Rate earned on common stockholders' equity
16. Earnings per share on common stock
17. Price-earnings ratio
18. Dividends per share of common stock
19. Dividend yield

**Solution**

(Ratios are rounded to the nearest single digit after the decimal point.)

1. Working capital: $750,000
   $1,500,000 − $750,000

2. Current ratio: 2.0
   $1,500,000 ÷ $750,000

3. Quick ratio: 1.0
   $750,000 ÷ $750,000

4. Accounts receivable turnover: 13.3
   $5,000,000 ÷ [($425,000 + $325,000) ÷ 2]

5. Number of days' sales in receivables: 31 days
   $5,000,000 ÷ 365 = $13,699
   $425,000 ÷ $13,699

6. Inventory turnover: 5.7
   $3,400,000 ÷ [($720,000 + $480,000) ÷ 2]

7. Number of days' sales in inventory: 77.3 days
   $3,400,000 ÷ 365 = $9,315
   $720,000 ÷ $9,315

8. Ratio of fixed assets to long-term liabilities: 1.7
   $2,093,000 ÷ $1,210,000

9. Ratio of liabilities to stockholders' equity: 1.0
   $1,960,000 ÷ $1,883,000

10. Number of times interest charges earned: 6.2
    ($545,000 + $105,000) ÷ $105,000

11. Number of times preferred dividends earned: 6.1
    $245,000 ÷ $40,000

12. Ratio of net sales to assets: 1.5
    $5,000,000 ÷ [($3,593,000 + $2,948,000) ÷ 2]

13. Rate earned on total assets: 10.0%
    ($245,000 + $105,000) ÷ [($3,843,000 + $3,173,000) ÷ 2]

14. Rate earned on stockholders' equity: 13.6%
    $245,000 ÷ [($1,883,000 + $1,723,000) ÷ 2]

15. Rate earned on common stockholders' equity: 15.7%
    ($245,000 − $40,000) ÷ [($1,383,000 + $1,223,000) ÷ 2]

16. Earnings per share on common stock: $4.10
    ($245,000 − $40,000) ÷ 50,000

17. Price-earnings ratio: 6.1
    $25 ÷ $4.10

18. Dividends per share of common stock: $0.90
    $45,000 ÷ 50,000 shares

19. Dividend yield: 3.6%
    $0.90 ÷ $25

# Self-Examination Questions (Answers at End of Chapter)

1. What type of analysis is indicated by the following?

| | Amount | Percent |
|---|---|---|
| Current assets | $100,000 | 20% |
| Property, plant, and equipment | 400,000 | 80 |
| Total assets | $500,000 | 100% |

   A. Vertical analysis
   B. Horizontal analysis
   C. Profitability analysis
   D. Contribution margin analysis

2. Which of the following measures indicates the ability of a firm to pay its current liabilities?
   A. Working capital
   B. Current ratio
   C. Quick ratio
   D. All of the above

3. The ratio determined by dividing total current assets by total current liabilities is:
   A. current ratio
   B. working capital ratio
   C. bankers' ratio
   D. all of the above

4. The ratio of the quick assets to current liabilities, which indicates the "instant" debt-paying ability of a firm, is:
   A. current ratio
   B. working capital ratio
   C. quick ratio
   D. bankers' ratio

5. A measure useful in evaluating the efficiency in the management of inventories is:
   A. working capital ratio
   B. quick ratio
   C. number of days' sales in inventory
   D. ratio of fixed assets to long-term liabilities

# Class Discussion Questions

1. What is the difference between horizontal and vertical analysis of financial statements?
2. What is the advantage of using comparative statements for financial analysis rather than statements for a single date or period?
3. The current year's amount of net income (after income tax) is 15% larger than that of the preceding year. Does this indicate an improved operating performance? Discuss.
4. How would you respond to a horizontal analysis that showed an expense increasing by over 100%?
5. How would the current and quick ratios of a service business compare?

6. For Lindsay Corporation, the working capital at the end of the current year is $5,000 greater than the working capital at the end of the preceding year, reported as follows:

|  | Current Year | Preceding Year |
|---|---|---|
| Current assets: | | |
| Cash, marketable securities, and receivables . . . . . . . | $34,000 | $30,000 |
| Inventories . . . . . . . . . . . . . . . . . . . . . . . . . . . . . . . | 51,000 | 32,500 |
| Total current assets . . . . . . . . . . . . . . . . . . . . . . | $85,000 | $62,500 |
| Current liabilities . . . . . . . . . . . . . . . . . . . . . . . . . . | 42,500 | 25,000 |
| Working capital . . . . . . . . . . . . . . . . . . . . . . . . . . . | $42,500 | $37,500 |

Has the current position improved? Explain.

7. Why would the accounts receivable turnover ratio be different between **Wal-Mart Stores, Inc.** and **Procter & Gamble Company**?

8. A company that grants terms of n/30 on all sales has a yearly accounts receivable turnover, based on monthly averages, of 6. Is this a satisfactory turnover? Discuss.

9. a. Why is it advantageous to have a high inventory turnover?
   b. Is it possible for the inventory turnover to be too high? Discuss.
   c. Is it possible to have a high inventory turnover and a high number of days' sales in inventory? Discuss.

10. What do the following data taken from a comparative balance sheet indicate about the company's ability to borrow additional funds on a long-term basis in the current year as compared to the preceding year?

|  | Current Year | Preceding Year |
|---|---|---|
| Fixed assets (net) | $175,000 | $170,000 |
| Total long-term liabilities | 70,000 | 85,000 |

11. a. Why is the rate earned on stockholders' equity by a thriving business ordinarily higher than the rate earned on total assets?
    b. Should the rate earned on common stockholders' equity normally be higher or lower than the rate earned on total stockholders' equity? Explain.

12. The net income (after income tax) of A. L. Gibson Inc. was $25 per common share in the latest year and $40 per common share for the preceding year. At the beginning of the latest year, the number of shares outstanding was doubled by a stock split. There were no other changes in the amount of stock outstanding. What were the earnings per share in the preceding year, adjusted for comparison with the latest year?

13. The price-earnings ratio for the common stock of Essian Company was 10 at December 31, the end of the current fiscal year. What does the ratio indicate about the selling price of the common stock in relation to current earnings?

14. Why would the dividend yield differ significantly from the rate earned on common stockholders' equity?

15. Favorable business conditions may bring about certain seemingly unfavorable ratios, and unfavorable business operations may result in apparently favorable ratios. For example, Sanchez Company increased its sales and net income substantially for the current year, yet the current ratio at the end of the year is lower than at the beginning of the year. Discuss some possible causes of the apparent weakening of the current position, while sales and net income have increased substantially.

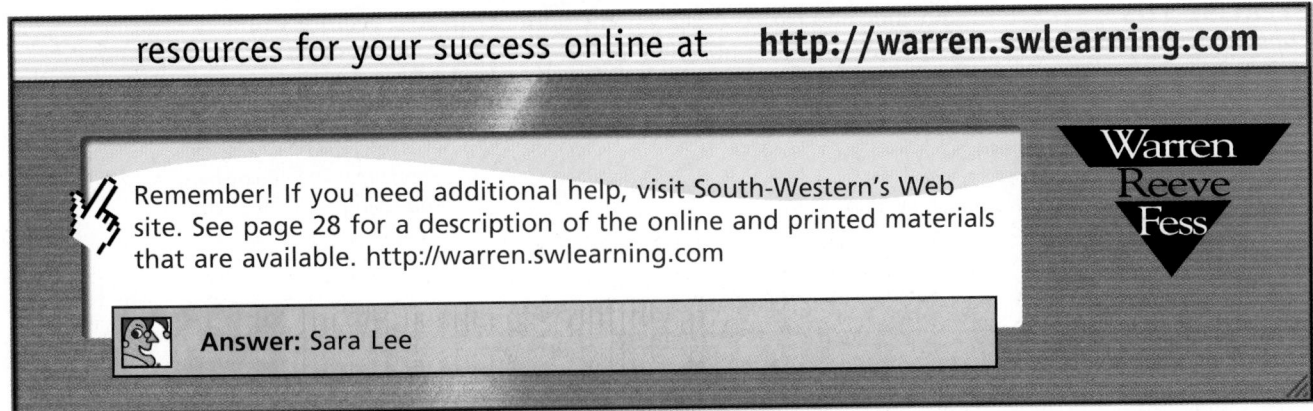

# Exercises

**EXERCISE 17-1**
*Vertical analysis of income statement*

**Objective 1**

SPREADSHEET

✓ *2006 net income: $50,000; 10% of sales*

Revenue and expense data for Home-Mate Appliance Co. are as follows:

| | 2006 | 2005 |
|---|---|---|
| Sales | $500,000 | $450,000 |
| Cost of goods sold | 275,000 | 234,000 |
| Selling expenses | 90,000 | 94,500 |
| Administrative expenses | 60,000 | 63,000 |
| Income tax expense | 25,000 | 22,500 |

a. Prepare an income statement in comparative form, stating each item for both 2006 and 2005 as a percent of sales.
b. Comment on the significant changes disclosed by the comparative income statement.

**EXERCISE 17-2**
*Vertical analysis of income statement*

**Objective 1**

REAL WORLD    SPREADSHEET

✓ *a. Fiscal year 2002 income from continuing operations, 26.8% of revenues*

The following comparative income statement (in thousands of dollars) for the fiscal years 2001 and 2002 was adapted from the annual report of **Speedway Motorsports, Inc.**, owner and operator of several major motor speedways, such as the Atlanta, Texas, and Las Vegas Motor Speedways.

| | Fiscal Year 2002 | Fiscal Year 2001 |
|---|---|---|
| Revenues: | | |
| Admissions | $141,315 | $136,362 |
| Event-related revenue | 122,172 | 133,289 |
| NASCAR broadcasting revenue | 77,936 | 67,488 |
| Other operating revenue | 34,537 | 38,111 |
| Total revenue | $375,960 | $375,250 |
| Expenses and other: | | |
| Direct expense of events | $ 69,297 | $ 76,579 |
| NASCAR purse and sanction fees | 61,217 | 54,479 |
| Other direct expenses | 87,427 | 88,582 |
| General and administrative | 57,235 | 59,331 |
| Total expenses and other | $275,176 | $278,971 |
| Income from continuing operations | $100,784 | $ 96,279 |

a. Prepare a comparative income statement for fiscal years 2001 and 2002 in vertical form, stating each item as a percent of revenues. Round to one digit after the decimal place.
b. Comment on the significant changes.

**EXERCISE 17-3**
*Common-size income statement*
**Objective 1**

SPREADSHEET

✔ *a. Horizon net income: $105,000; 7.5% of sales*

Revenue and expense data for the current calendar year for Horizon Publishing Company and for the publishing industry are as follows. The Horizon Publishing Company data are expressed in dollars. The publishing industry averages are expressed in percentages.

| | Horizon Publishing Company | Publishing Industry Average |
|---|---|---|
| Sales | $1,414,000 | 101.0% |
| Sales returns and allowances | 14,000 | 1.0 |
| Cost of goods sold | 504,000 | 40.0 |
| Selling expenses | 574,000 | 39.0 |
| Administrative expenses | 154,000 | 10.5 |
| Other income | 16,800 | 1.2 |
| Other expense | 23,800 | 1.7 |
| Income tax expense | 56,000 | 4.0 |

a. Prepare a common-size income statement comparing the results of operations for Horizon Publishing Company with the industry average. Round to one digit after the decimal place.

b. As far as the data permit, comment on significant relationships revealed by the comparisons.

**EXERCISE 17-4**
*Vertical analysis of balance sheet*
**Objective 1**

SPREADSHEET

✔ *Retained earnings, Dec. 31, 2006, 46.25%*

Balance sheet data for Santa Fe Tile Company on December 31, the end of the fiscal year, are as follows:

| | 2006 | 2005 |
|---|---|---|
| Current assets | $260,000 | $200,000 |
| Property, plant, and equipment | 500,000 | 450,000 |
| Intangible assets | 40,000 | 50,000 |
| Current liabilities | 170,000 | 150,000 |
| Long-term liabilities | 210,000 | 200,000 |
| Common stock | 50,000 | 50,000 |
| Retained earnings | 370,000 | 300,000 |

Prepare a comparative balance sheet for 2006 and 2005, stating each asset as a percent of total assets and each liability and stockholders' equity item as a percent of the total liabilities and stockholders' equity. Round to two digits after the decimal place.

**EXERCISE 17-5**
*Horizontal analysis of the income statement*
**Objective 1**

SPREADSHEET

✔ *a. Net income decrease, 77.5%*

Income statement data for Scribe Paper Company for the year ended December 31, 2006 and 2005, are as follows:

| | 2006 | 2005 |
|---|---|---|
| Sales | $66,300 | $85,000 |
| Cost of goods sold | 32,000 | 40,000 |
| Gross profit | $34,300 | $45,000 |
| Selling expenses | $24,000 | $25,000 |
| Administrative expenses | 7,500 | 6,000 |
| Total operating expenses | $31,500 | $31,000 |
| Income before income tax | $ 2,800 | $14,000 |
| Income tax expense | 1,000 | 6,000 |
| Net income | $ 1,800 | $ 8,000 |

a. Prepare a comparative income statement with horizontal analysis, indicating the increase (decrease) for 2006 when compared with 2005. Round to two digits after the decimal place.

b. What conclusions can be drawn from the horizontal analysis?

**EXERCISE 17-6**
*Current position analysis*
**Objective 2**

✓ *2006 working capital,*
*$625,000*

The following data were taken from the balance sheet of Marine Equipment Company:

|  | Dec. 31, 2006 | Dec. 31, 2005 |
|---|---|---|
| Cash | $118,000 | $ 95,000 |
| Marketable securities | 152,000 | 131,000 |
| Accounts and notes receivable (net) | 210,000 | 198,000 |
| Inventories | 345,000 | 326,000 |
| Prepaid expenses | 50,000 | 45,000 |
| Accounts and notes payable (short-term) | 190,000 | 208,000 |
| Accrued liabilities | 60,000 | 57,000 |

a. Determine for each year (1) the working capital, (2) the current ratio, and (3) the quick ratio.
b. What conclusions can be drawn from these data as to the company's ability to meet its currently maturing debts?

**EXERCISE 17-7**
*Current position analysis*
**Objective 2**

REAL WORLD

✓ *a. (1) Dec. 28, 2002*
*current ratio, 1.06*

**PepsiCo, Inc.**, the parent company of Frito-Lay snack foods and Pepsi beverages, had the following current assets and current liabilities at the end of two recent years:

|  | Dec. 28, 2002 (in millions) | Dec. 28, 2001 (in millions) |
|---|---|---|
| Cash and cash equivalents | $1,638 | $ 683 |
| Short-term investments, at cost | 207 | 966 |
| Accounts and notes receivable, net | 2,531 | 2,142 |
| Inventories | 1,342 | 1,310 |
| Prepaid expenses and other current assets | 695 | 752 |
| Short-term obligations | 562 | 354 |
| Accounts payable and other current liabilities | 4,998 | 4,461 |
| Income taxes payable | 492 | 183 |

a. Determine the (1) current ratio and (2) quick ratio for both years. Round to two digits after the decimal place.
b. What conclusions can you draw from these data?

**EXERCISE 17-8**
*Current position analysis*
**Objective 2**

WHAT'S WRONG
WITH THIS?

The bond indenture for the 10-year, 9½% debenture bonds dated January 2, 2005, required working capital of $350,000, a current ratio of 1.5, and a quick ratio of 1 at the end of each calendar year until the bonds mature. At December 31, 2006, the three measures were computed as follows:

1. Current assets:
   | | | |
   |---|---|---|
   | Cash | $275,000 | |
   | Marketable securities | 123,000 | |
   | Accounts and notes receivable (net) | 172,000 | |
   | Inventories | 295,000 | |
   | Prepaid expenses | 35,000 | |
   | Goodwill | 150,000 | |
   | Total current assets | | $1,050,000 |
   | Current liabilities: | | |
   | Accounts and short-term notes payable | $375,000 | |
   | Accrued liabilities | 250,000 | |
   | Total current liabilities | | 625,000 |
   | Working capital | | $ 425,000 |

2. Current ratio = 1.68 ($1,050,000 ÷ $625,000)
3. Quick ratio = 1.52 ($570,000 ÷ $375,000)

a. List the errors in the determination of the three measures of current position analysis.
b. Is the company satisfying the terms of the bond indenture?

**EXERCISE 17-9**
*Accounts receivable analysis*
**Objective 2**

✓ *a. Accounts receivable turnover, current year, 7.1*

The following data are taken from the financial statements of Ovation Industries Inc. Terms of all sales are 1/10, n/60.

| | Current Year | Preceding Year |
|---|---|---|
| Accounts receivable, end of year | $ 48,219 | $ 52,603 |
| Monthly average accounts receivable (net) | 45,070 | 46,154 |
| Net sales | 320,000 | 300,000 |

a. Determine for each year (1) the accounts receivable turnover and (2) the number of days' sales in receivables. Round to nearest dollar and one digit after the decimal place.
b. What conclusions can be drawn from these data concerning accounts receivable and credit policies?

**EXERCISE 17-10**
*Accounts receivable analysis*
**Objective 2**

REAL WORLD

✓ *a. (1) Sears' accounts receivable turnover, 1.2*

**Sears, Roebuck & Company** and **Federated Department Stores, Inc.** (Macy's, Rich's, Bloomingdale's) are two of the largest department store chains in the United States. Both companies offer credit to their customers through their own credit card operations. In addition, Sears offers credit to non-Sears customers through a Sears MasterCard®. Information from the financial statements for both companies for two recent years is as follows (all numbers are in millions):

| | Sears | Federated |
|---|---|---|
| Merchandise sales (fiscal 2002) | $35,698 | $15,434 |
| Credit card receivables—beginning | 28,155 | 2,379 |
| Credit card receivables—ending | 30,759 | 2,945 |

a. Determine the (1) accounts receivable turnover and (2) the number of days' sales in receivables for both companies. Round to one digit after the decimal place.
b. Compare the two companies with regard to their credit card policies.

**EXERCISE 17-11**
*Inventory analysis*
**Objective 2**

✓ *a. Inventory turnover, 2006, 8.0*

The following data were extracted from the income statement of Mountain Sports Inc.:

| | 2006 | 2005 |
|---|---|---|
| Sales | $656,000 | $774,000 |
| Beginning inventories | 42,000 | 44,000 |
| Cost of goods sold | 328,000 | 430,000 |
| Ending inventories | 40,000 | 42,000 |

a. Determine for each year (1) the inventory turnover and (2) the number of days' sales in inventory. Round to nearest dollar and two digits after the decimal place.
b. What conclusions can be drawn from these data concerning the inventories?

**EXERCISE 17-12**
*Inventory analysis*
**Objective 2**

REAL WORLD

✓ *a. (1) Dell inventory turnover, 99.5*

**Dell Computer Corporation** and **Hewlett-Packard Corporation (HP)** compete with each other in the personal computer market. Dell's strategy is to assemble computers to customer orders, rather than for inventory. Thus, for example, Dell will build and deliver a computer within four days of a customer entering an order on a Web page. Hewlett-Packard, on the other hand, builds some computers prior to receiving an order, then sells from this inventory once an order is received. Below is selected financial information for both companies from a recent year's financial statements (in millions):

| | Dell Computer Corporation | Hewlett-Packard Corporation |
|---|---|---|
| Sales | $35,404 | $45,955 |
| Cost of goods sold | 29,055 | 34,573 |
| Inventory, beginning of period | 278 | 5,204 |
| Inventory, end of period | 306 | 5,797 |

a. Determine for both companies (1) the inventory turnover and (2) the number of days' sales in inventory. Round to one digit after the decimal place.
b. Interpret the inventory ratios by considering Dell's and Hewlett-Packard's operating strategies.

**EXERCISE 17-13**
*Ratio of liabilities to stockholders' equity and number of times interest charges earned*

**Objective 2**

✓ *a. Ratio of liabilities to stockholders' equity, Dec. 31, 2006, 0.54*

The following data were taken from the financial statements of Durable Structures, Inc. for December 31, 2006 and 2005:

|  | December 31, 2006 | December 31, 2005 |
|---|---|---|
| Accounts payable | $ 150,000 | $ 140,000 |
| Current maturities of serial bonds payable | 200,000 | 200,000 |
| Serial bonds payable, 8%, issued 2001, due 2011 | 1,000,000 | 1,200,000 |
| Common stock, $1 par value | 100,000 | 100,000 |
| Paid-in capital in excess of par | 500,000 | 500,000 |
| Retained earnings | 1,900,000 | 1,600,000 |

The income before income tax was $528,000 and $336,000 for the years 2006 and 2005, respectively.

a. Determine the ratio of liabilities to stockholders' equity at the end of each year. Round to two digits after the decimal place.
b. Determine the number of times the bond interest charges are earned during the year for both years.
c. What conclusions can be drawn from these data as to the company's ability to meet its currently maturing debts?

**EXERCISE 17-14**
*Ratio of liabilities to stockholders' equity and number of times interest charges earned*

**Objective 2**

REAL WORLD

✓ *a. Hasbro, 1.49*

Hasbro Inc. and Mattel Inc. are the two largest toy companies in North America. Condensed liabilities and stockholders' equity from a recent balance sheet are shown for each company as follows:

|  | Hasbro Inc. | Mattel Inc. |
|---|---|---|
| Current liabilities | $ 758,591,000 | $1,596,981,000 |
| Long-term debt | 1,165,649,000 | 1,020,919,000 |
| Deferred liabilities | 91,875,000 | 184,203,000 |
| Total liabilities | $2,016,115,000 | $2,802,103,000 |
| Shareholders' equity: |  |  |
| Common stock, $0.50 par value | $ 104,847,000 | $ 436,307,000 |
| Additional paid-in capital | 457,544,000 | 1,638,993,000 |
| Retained earnings | 1,622,402,000 | 132,900,000 |
| Accumulated other comprehensive loss and other equity items | (71,394,000) | (307,798,000) |
| Treasury stock, at cost | (760,535,000) | (161,944,000) |
| Total stockholders' equity | $1,352,864,000 | $1,738,458,000 |
| Total liabilities and stockholders' equity | $3,368,979,000 | $4,540,561,000 |

The income from operations and interest expense from the income statement for both companies were as follows:

|  | Hasbro Inc. | Mattel Inc. |
|---|---|---|
| Income from operations | $ 96,199,000 | $430,010,000 |
| Interest expense | 103,688,000 | 155,132,000 |

a. Determine the ratio of liabilities to stockholders' equity for both companies. Round to two digits after the decimal place.
b. Determine the number of times interest charges are earned for both companies. Round to two digits after the decimal place.
c. ➤ Interpret the ratio differences between the two companies.

**EXERCISE 17-15**
*Ratio of liabilities to stockholders' equity and ratio of fixed assets to long-term liabilities*

**Objective 2**

REAL WORLD

Recent balance sheet information for two companies in the food industry, **H.J. Heinz Co.** and **Hershey Foods Corp.**, are as follows (in thousands of dollars):

|  | H.J. Heinz | Hershey Foods |
|---|---|---|
| Net property, plant, and equipment | $2,250,074 | $1,534,901 |
| Current liabilities | 2,509,169 | 606,444 |
| Long-term debt | 4,642,968 | 876,972 |
| Other liabilities (pensions, deferred taxes) | 1,407,607 | 1,223,254 |
| Stockholders' equity | 1,718,616 | 1,147,204 |

*✓a. Heinz, 4.98*

a. Determine the ratio of liabilities to stockholders' equity for both companies. Round to two digits after the decimal place.
b. Determine the ratio of fixed assets to long-term liabilities for both companies. Round to two digits after the decimal place.
c. ▭▭▭▭➤ Interpret the ratio differences between the two companies.

**EXERCISE 17-16**
*Ratio of net sales to total assets*
**Objective 3**

REAL WORLD

*✓a. Yellow, 2.55*

Three major segments of the transportation industry are motor carriers, such as **Yellow Corp.**; railroads, such as **Union Pacific Corp.**; and transportation arrangement services, such as **C.H. Robinson Worldwide**. Recent financial statement information for these three companies is shown as follows (in thousands of dollars):

|  | Yellow | Union Pacific | C.H. Robinson Worldwide |
|---|---|---|---|
| Net sales | $3,276,651 | $11,973,000 | $3,090,072 |
| Average total assets | 1,285,777 | 31,551,000 | 683,490 |

a. Determine the ratio of net sales to assets for all three companies. Round to two digits after the decimal place.
b. ▭▭▭▭➤ Assume that the ratio of net sales to assets for each company represents their respective industry segment. Interpret the differences in the ratio of net sales to assets in terms of the operating characteristics of each of the respective segments.

**EXERCISE 17-17**
*Profitability ratios*
**Objective 3**

*✓a. Rate earned on total assets, 2007, 12.0%*

The following selected data were taken from the financial statements of Yellowstone Group, Inc. for December 31, 2007, 2006, and 2005:

|  | December 31, 2007 | December 31, 2006 | December 31, 2005 |
|---|---|---|---|
| Total assets ......................... | $1,450,000 | $1,300,000 | $1,100,000 |
| Notes payable (8% interest) ............. | 187,500 | 187,500 | 187,500 |
| Common stock ....................... | 450,000 | 450,000 | 450,000 |
| Preferred $10 stock, $100 par, cumulative, nonparticipating (no change during year) .. | 200,000 | 200,000 | 200,000 |
| Retained earnings .................... | 495,000 | 365,000 | 205,000 |

The 2007 net income was $150,000, and the 2006 net income was $180,000. No dividends on common stock were declared between 2005 and 2007.

a. Determine the rate earned on total assets, the rate earned on stockholders' equity, and the rate earned on common stockholders' equity for the years 2006 and 2007. Round to two digits after the decimal place.
b. What conclusions can be drawn from these data as to the company's profitability?

**EXERCISE 17-18**
*Profitability ratios*
**Objective 3**

REAL WORLD

*✓a. 2002 rate earned on total assets, 9.2%*

**AnnTaylor Inc.** sells professional women's apparel through company-owned retail stores. Recent financial information for Ann Taylor is provided below (all numbers in thousands):

|  | Fiscal Year Ended | |
|---|---|---|
|  | Feb. 1, 2003 | Feb. 2, 2002 |
| Net income | $80,158 | $29,105 |
| Interest expense | 6,886 | 6,869 |

|  | Feb. 1, 2003 | Feb. 2, 2002 | Feb. 3, 2001 |
|---|---|---|---|
| Total assets | $1,010,826 | $883,166 | $848,115 |
| Total stockholders' equity | 714,418 | 612,129 | 574,029 |

An analysis of 70 apparel retail companies indicates an industry average rate earned on total assets of 6% and an average rate earned on stockholders' equity of 7.8% for fiscal 2002.

a. Determine the rate earned on total assets for Ann Taylor for the fiscal years ended February 1, 2003 and February 2, 2002. Round to two digits after the decimal place.

b. Determine the rate earned on stockholders' equity for Ann Taylor for the fiscal years ended February 1, 2003 and February 2, 2002. Round to two digits after the decimal place.

c. Evaluate the two-year trend for the profitability ratios determined in (a) and (b).

d. Evaluate Ann Taylor's profit performance relative to the industry.

**EXERCISE 17-19**
*Six measures of solvency or profitability*

**Objectives 2, 3**

✓ *c. Ratio of net sales to assets, 1.58*

The following data were taken from the financial statements of Orion Systems Inc. for the current fiscal year:

| | | | |
|---|---|---:|---:|
| Property, plant, and equipment (net) | | | $ 950,000 |
| Liabilities: | | | |
| Current liabilities | | $ 45,000 | |
| Mortgage note payable, 7.5%, issued 1996, due 2011 | | 680,000 | |
| Total liabilities | | | $ 725,000 |
| Stockholders' equity: | | | |
| Preferred $8 stock, $100 par, cumulative, nonparticipating (no change during year) | | | $ 200,000 |
| Common stock, $10 par (no change during year) | | | 650,000 |
| Retained earnings: | | | |
| Balance, beginning of year | $500,000 | | |
| Net income | 180,000 | $680,000 | |
| Preferred dividends | $ 16,000 | | |
| Common dividends | 48,000 | 64,000 | |
| Balance, end of year | | | 616,000 |
| Total stockholders' equity | | | $1,466,000 |
| Net sales | | | $3,000,000 |
| Interest expense | | | $ 51,000 |

Assuming that long-term investments totaled $200,000 throughout the year and that total assets were $2,009,000 at the beginning of the year, determine the following: (a) ratio of fixed assets to long-term liabilities, (b) ratio of liabilities to stockholders' equity, (c) ratio of net sales to assets, (d) rate earned on total assets, (e) rate earned on stockholders' equity, and (f) rate earned on common stockholders' equity. Round to two digits after the decimal place.

**EXERCISE 17-20**
*Six measures of solvency or profitability*

**Objectives 2, 3**

✓ *d. Price-earnings ratio, 20.83*

The balance sheet for Collier Medical, Inc. at the end of the current fiscal year indicated the following:

| | |
|---|---:|
| Bonds payable, 12% (issued in 1996, due in 2016) | $1,500,000 |
| Preferred $10 stock, $100 par | 250,000 |
| Common stock, $20 par | 2,500,000 |

Income before income tax was $450,000, and income taxes were $125,000 for the current year. Cash dividends paid on common stock during the current year totaled $100,000. The common stock was selling for $50 per share at the end of the year. Determine each of the following: (a) number of times bond interest charges were earned, (b) number of times preferred dividends were earned, (c) earnings per share on common stock, (d) price-earnings ratio, (e) dividends per share of common stock, and (f) dividend yield. Round to two digits after the decimal place.

**EXERCISE 17-21**
*Earnings per share, price-earnings ratio, dividend yield*

**Objective 3**

✓ *b. Price-earnings ratio, 20*

The following information was taken from the financial statements of Fashion Cosmetics, Inc. for December 31 of the current fiscal year:

| | |
|---|---:|
| Common stock, $12 par value (no change during the year) | $2,400,000 |
| Preferred $9 stock, $100 par, cumulative, nonparticipating (no change during year) | 600,000 |

The net income was $444,000 and the declared dividends on the common stock were $156,000 for the current year. The market price of the common stock is $39 per share.

For the common stock, determine the (a) earnings per share, (b) price-earnings ratio, (c) dividends per share, and (d) dividend yield. Round to two digits after the decimal place.

**EXERCISE 17-22**
*Earnings per share*
**Objective 3**

✓ b. Earnings per share on common stock, $1.14

The net income reported on the income statement of Cincinnati Soap Co. was $890,000. There were 500,000 shares of $20 par common stock and 40,000 shares of $8 cumulative preferred stock outstanding throughout the current year. The income statement included two extraordinary items: a $256,000 gain from condemnation of land and a $166,000 loss arising from flood damage, both after applicable income tax. Determine the per share figures for common stock for (a) income before extraordinary items and (b) net income.

**EXERCISE 17-23**
*Price-earnings ratio; dividend yield*
**Objective 3**

REAL WORLD

The table below shows the stock price, earnings per share, and dividends per share for three companies as of February 10, 2003:

| | Price | Earnings per Share | Dividends per Share |
|---|---|---|---|
| Bank of America Corp. | $68.20 | $5.91 | $2.56 |
| eBay, Inc. | 73.56 | 0.85 | 0.00 |
| Coca-Cola Company | 40.06 | 1.68 | 0.80 |

a. Determine the price-earnings ratio and dividend yield for the three companies. Round to two digits after the decimal place.
b.  Explain the differences in these ratios across the three companies.

# Problems Series A

**PROBLEM 17-1A**
*Horizontal analysis for income statement*
**Objective 1**

SPREADSHEET
P.A.S.S.

✓ 1. Net sales, 12% increase

For 2006, Turnberry Company reported its most significant decline in net income in years. At the end of the year, Hai Chow, the president, is presented with the following condensed comparative income statement:

**Turnberry Company**
**Comparative Income Statement**
**For the Years Ended December 31, 2006 and 2005**

| | 2006 | 2005 |
|---|---|---|
| Sales . . . . . . . . . . . . . . . . . . . . . . . . . . . . . . . . . . . . . . . . | $482,000 | $429,000 |
| Sales returns and allowances . . . . . . . . . . . . . . . . . . . . . . | 6,000 | 4,000 |
| Net sales . . . . . . . . . . . . . . . . . . . . . . . . . . . . . . . . . . . . . | $476,000 | $425,000 |
| Cost of goods sold . . . . . . . . . . . . . . . . . . . . . . . . . . . . . . | 216,000 | 180,000 |
| Gross profit . . . . . . . . . . . . . . . . . . . . . . . . . . . . . . . . . . . | $260,000 | $245,000 |
| Selling expenses . . . . . . . . . . . . . . . . . . . . . . . . . . . . . . | $109,250 | $ 95,000 |
| Administrative expenses . . . . . . . . . . . . . . . . . . . . . . . . . . | 52,500 | 30,000 |
| Total operating expenses . . . . . . . . . . . . . . . . . . . . . . . . . | $161,750 | $125,000 |
| Income from operations . . . . . . . . . . . . . . . . . . . . . . . . . . | $ 98,250 | $120,000 |
| Other income . . . . . . . . . . . . . . . . . . . . . . . . . . . . . . . . | 2,000 | 2,000 |
| Income before income tax . . . . . . . . . . . . . . . . . . . . . . . . | $100,250 | $122,000 |
| Income tax expense . . . . . . . . . . . . . . . . . . . . . . . . . . . . | 30,000 | 40,000 |
| Net income . . . . . . . . . . . . . . . . . . . . . . . . . . . . . . . . . . | $ 70,250 | $ 82,000 |

## Instructions

1. Prepare a comparative income statement with horizontal analysis for the two-year period, using 2005 as the base year. Round to two digits after the decimal place.
2. To the extent the data permit, comment on the significant relationships revealed by the horizontal analysis prepared in (1).

**PROBLEM 17-2A**
*Vertical analysis for income statement*
**Objective 1**

SPREADSHEET
P.A.S.S.

✓1. *Net income, 2006, 21.2%*

For 2006, Audio Tone Company initiated a sales promotion campaign that included the expenditure of an additional $13,800 for advertising. At the end of the year, Gordon Kincaid, the president, is presented with the following condensed comparative income statement:

**Audio Tone Company**
**Comparative Income Statement**
**For the Years Ended December 31, 2006 and 2005**

|  | 2006 | 2005 |
|---|---|---|
| Sales | $664,000 | $526,000 |
| Sales returns and allowances | 4,000 | 6,000 |
| Net sales | $660,000 | $520,000 |
| Cost of goods sold | 257,400 | 213,200 |
| Gross profit | $402,600 | $306,800 |
| Selling expenses | $138,600 | $124,800 |
| Administrative expenses | 72,600 | 67,600 |
| Total operating expenses | $211,200 | $192,400 |
| Income from operations | $191,400 | $114,400 |
| Other income | 2,500 | 2,000 |
| Income before income tax | $193,900 | $116,400 |
| Income tax expense | 54,000 | 30,000 |
| Net income | $139,900 | $ 86,400 |

**Instructions**

1. Prepare a comparative income statement for the two-year period, presenting an analysis of each item in relationship to net sales for each of the years. Round to two digits after the decimal place.
2. To the extent the data permit, comment on the significant relationships revealed by the vertical analysis prepared in (1).

**PROBLEM 17-3A**
*Effect of transactions on current position analysis*
**Objective 2**

SPREADSHEET

✓1. *Current ratio, 2.13*

Data pertaining to the current position of Anderson Lumber Company are as follows:

| | |
|---|---|
| Cash | $240,000 |
| Marketable securities | 110,000 |
| Accounts and notes receivable (net) | 380,000 |
| Inventories | 495,000 |
| Prepaid expenses | 30,000 |
| Accounts payable | 390,000 |
| Notes payable (short-term) | 150,000 |
| Accrued expenses | 50,000 |

**Instructions**

1. Compute (a) the working capital, (b) the current ratio, and (c) the quick ratio. Round to two digits after the decimal place.
2. List the following captions on a sheet of paper:

| Transaction | Working Capital | Current Ratio | Quick Ratio |
|---|---|---|---|

Compute the working capital, the current ratio, and the quick ratio after each of the following transactions, and record the results in the appropriate columns. Consider each transaction separately and assume that only that transaction affects the data given above. Round to two digits after the decimal point.

a. Sold marketable securities at no gain or loss, $56,000.
b. Paid accounts payable, $60,000.
c. Purchased goods on account, $80,000.
d. Paid notes payable, $40,000.
e. Declared a cash dividend, $25,000.
f. Declared a common stock dividend on common stock, $28,500.

*(continued)*

g. Borrowed cash from bank on a long-term note, $120,000.

h. Received cash on account, $164,000.

i. Issued additional shares of stock for cash, $250,000.

j. Paid cash for prepaid expenses, $10,000.

**PROBLEM 17-4A**
*Nineteen measures of solvency and profitability*
**Objectives 2, 3**

SPREADSHEET

✓ 5. Number of days' sales in receivables, 69.2

The comparative financial statements of Vision International, Inc. are as follows. The market price of Vision International, Inc. common stock was $20 on December 31, 2006.

**Vision International, Inc.**
**Comparative Retained Earnings Statement**
**For the Years Ended December 31, 2006 and 2005**

| | Dec. 31, 2006 | Dec. 31, 2005 |
|---|---|---|
| Retained earnings, January 1 | $375,000 | $327,000 |
| Add net income for year | 68,000 | 67,000 |
| Total | $443,000 | $394,000 |
| Deduct dividends: | | |
| On preferred stock | $ 15,000 | $ 12,000 |
| On common stock | 7,000 | 7,000 |
| Total | $ 22,000 | $ 19,000 |
| Retained earnings, December 31 | $421,000 | $375,000 |

**Vision International, Inc.**
**Comparative Income Statement**
**For the Years Ended December 31, 2006 and 2005**

| | 2006 | 2005 |
|---|---|---|
| Sales | $1,055,000 | $966,000 |
| Sales returns and allowances | 5,000 | 6,000 |
| Net sales | $1,050,000 | $960,000 |
| Cost of goods sold | 400,000 | 390,000 |
| Gross profit | $ 650,000 | $570,000 |
| Selling expenses | $ 270,000 | $275,000 |
| Administrative expenses | 195,000 | 165,000 |
| Total operating expenses | $ 465,000 | $440,000 |
| Income from operations | $ 185,000 | $130,000 |
| Other income | 20,000 | 15,000 |
| | $ 205,000 | $145,000 |
| Other expense (interest) | 96,000 | 48,000 |
| Income before income tax | $ 109,000 | $ 97,000 |
| Income tax expense | 41,000 | 30,000 |
| Net income | $ 68,000 | $ 67,000 |

**Vision International, Inc.**
**Comparative Balance Sheet**
**December 31, 2006 and 2005**

| | Dec. 31, 2006 | Dec. 31, 2005 |
|---|---|---|
| **Assets** | | |
| Current assets: | | |
| Cash | $ 165,000 | $ 126,000 |
| Marketable securities | 398,000 | 254,000 |
| Accounts receivable (net) | 199,000 | 165,000 |
| Inventories | 84,000 | 52,000 |
| Prepaid expenses | 25,000 | 18,000 |
| Total current assets | $ 871,000 | $ 615,000 |
| Long-term investments | 300,000 | 200,000 |
| Property, plant, and equipment (net) | 1,040,000 | 760,000 |
| Total assets | $2,211,000 | $1,575,000 |

*(continued)*

| | Dec. 31, 2006 | Dec. 31, 2005 |
|---|---|---|
| **Liabilities** | | |
| Current liabilities . . . . . . . . . . . . . . . . . . . . . . . . . . . . . . . . . . | $ 290,000 | $ 250,000 |
| Long-term liabilities: | | |
|    Mortgage note payable, 8%, due 2011 . . . . . . . . . . . . . . | $ 300,000 | — |
|    Bonds payable, 12%, due 2015 . . . . . . . . . . . . . . . . . . . | 600,000 | $ 400,000 |
|       Total long-term liabilities . . . . . . . . . . . . . . . . . . . | $ 900,000 | $ 400,000 |
| Total liabilities . . . . . . . . . . . . . . . . . . . . . . . . . . . . . . . . . . | $1,190,000 | $ 650,000 |
| **Stockholders' Equity** | | |
| Preferred $6 stock, $100 par . . . . . . . . . . . . . . . . . . . . . . | $ 250,000 | $ 200,000 |
| Common stock, $10 par . . . . . . . . . . . . . . . . . . . . . . . . . | 350,000 | 350,000 |
| Retained earnings . . . . . . . . . . . . . . . . . . . . . . . . . . . . . . | 421,000 | 375,000 |
|    Total stockholders' equity . . . . . . . . . . . . . . . . . . . . | $1,021,000 | $ 925,000 |
| Total liabilities and stockholders' equity . . . . . . . . . . . . . | $2,211,000 | $1,575,000 |

## Instructions

Determine the following measures for 2006, rounding to the nearest single digit after the decimal point:

1. Working capital
2. Current ratio
3. Quick ratio
4. Accounts receivable turnover
5. Number of days' sales in receivables
6. Inventory turnover
7. Number of days' sales in inventory
8. Ratio of fixed assets to long-term liabilities
9. Ratio of liabilities to stockholders' equity
10. Number of times interest charges earned
11. Number of times preferred dividends earned
12. Ratio of net sales to assets
13. Rate earned on total assets
14. Rate earned on stockholders' equity
15. Rate earned on common stockholders' equity
16. Earnings per share on common stock
17. Price-earnings ratio
18. Dividends per share of common stock
19. Dividend yield

**PROBLEM 17-5A**
*Solvency and profitability trend analysis*

**Objectives 2, 3**

Sage Software Company has provided the following comparative information:

| | 2006 | 2005 | 2004 | 2003 | 2002 |
|---|---|---|---|---|---|
| Net income | $1,200,000 | $ 800,000 | $ 600,000 | $ 400,000 | $ 300,000 |
| Interest expense | 200,000 | 170,000 | 150,000 | 120,000 | 100,000 |
| Income tax expense | 360,000 | 240,000 | 180,000 | 120,000 | 90,000 |
| Total assets (ending balance) | 6,000,000 | 4,500,000 | 3,500,000 | 2,600,000 | 2,000,000 |
| Total stockholders' equity (ending balance) | 4,000,000 | 2,800,000 | 2,000,000 | 1,400,000 | 1,000,000 |
| Average total assets | 5,250,000 | 4,000,000 | 3,050,000 | 2,300,000 | 1,800,000 |
| Average stockholders' equity | 3,400,000 | 2,400,000 | 1,700,000 | 1,200,000 | 900,000 |

You have been asked to evaluate the historical performance of the company over the last five years.

Selected industry ratios have remained relatively steady at the following levels for the last five years:

| | 2002–2006 |
|---|---|
| Rate earned on total assets | 15% |
| Rate earned on stockholders' equity | 25% |
| Number of times interest charges earned | 3.0 |
| Ratio of liabilities to stockholders' equity | 1.5 |

**Instructions**

1. Prepare four line graphs with the ratio on the vertical axis and the years on the horizontal axis for the following four ratios (rounded to two digits after the decimal place):
   a. Rate earned on total assets
   b. Rate earned on stockholders' equity
   c. Number of times interest charges earned
   d. Ratio of liabilities to stockholders' equity
   Display both the company ratio and the industry benchmark on each graph. That is, each graph should have two lines.
2. ▭▬▶ Prepare an analysis of the graphs in (1).

# **P**roblems Series B

**PROBLEM 17-1B**
*Horizontal analysis for income statement*
**Objective 1**

SPREADSHEET
P.A.S.S.

✓ *1. Net sales, 25% increase*

For 2006, Pet Care, Inc. reported its most significant increase in net income in years. At the end of the year, Jeff Newton, the president, is presented with the following condensed comparative income statement:

**Pet Care, Inc.**
**Comparative Income Statement**
**For the Years Ended December 31, 2006 and 2005**

|  | 2006 | 2005 |
|---|---|---|
| Sales | $76,200 | $61,000 |
| Sales returns and allowances | 1,200 | 1,000 |
| Net sales | $75,000 | $60,000 |
| Cost of goods sold | 42,000 | 35,000 |
| Gross profit | $33,000 | $25,000 |
| Selling expenses | $13,800 | $12,000 |
| Administrative expenses | 9,000 | 8,000 |
| Total operating expenses | $22,800 | $20,000 |
| Income from operations | $10,200 | $ 5,000 |
| Other income | 500 | 500 |
| Income before income tax | $10,700 | $ 5,500 |
| Income tax expense | 2,400 | 1,200 |
| Net income | $ 8,300 | $ 4,300 |

**Instructions**

1. Prepare a comparative income statement with horizontal analysis for the two-year period, using 2005 as the base year. Round to two digits after the decimal place.
2. To the extent the data permit, comment on the significant relationships revealed by the horizontal analysis prepared in (1).

**PROBLEM 17-2B**
*Vertical analysis for income statement*
**Objective 1**

SPREADSHEET
P.A.S.S.

✓ *1. Net loss, 2006, 4.28%*

For 2006, Industrial Sanitation Systems, Inc. initiated a sales promotion campaign that included the expenditure of an additional $26,000 for advertising. At the end of the year, Alex Gonzalez, the president, is presented with the condensed comparative income statement on the following page.

**Instructions**

1. Prepare a comparative income statement for the two-year period, presenting an analysis of each item in relationship to net sales for each of the years. Round to two digits after the decimal place.
2. To the extent the data permit, comment on the significant relationships revealed by the vertical analysis prepared in (1).

**Industrial Sanitation Systems, Inc.**
**Comparative Income Statement**
**For the Years Ended December 31, 2006 and 2005**

|  | 2006 | 2005 |
|---|---|---|
| Sales | $144,000 | $128,000 |
| Sales returns and allowances | 4,000 | 3,000 |
| Net sales | $140,000 | $125,000 |
| Cost of goods sold | 80,000 | 72,000 |
| Gross profit | $ 60,000 | $ 53,000 |
| Selling expenses | $ 56,000 | $ 30,000 |
| Administrative expenses | 14,000 | 12,000 |
| Total operating expenses | $ 70,000 | $ 42,000 |
| Income from operations | $ (10,000) | $ 11,000 |
| Other income | 2,000 | 1,800 |
| Income before income tax | $ (8,000) | $ 12,800 |
| Income tax expense (benefit) | (2,000) | 3,000 |
| Net income (loss) | $ (6,000) | $ 9,800 |

**PROBLEM 17-3B**
*Effect of transactions on current position analysis*

**Objective 2**

SPREADSHEET

✓ *1. Quick ratio, 1.34*

Data pertaining to the current position of Around Town Clothing Co. are as follows:

| | |
|---|---|
| Cash | $120,000 |
| Marketable securities | 56,000 |
| Accounts and notes receivable (net) | 185,000 |
| Inventories | 224,000 |
| Prepaid expenses | 9,000 |
| Accounts payable | 188,000 |
| Notes payable (short-term) | 55,000 |
| Accrued expenses | 26,000 |

**Instructions**
1. Compute (a) the working capital, (b) the current ratio, and (c) the quick ratio. Round to two digits after the decimal place.
2. List the following captions on a sheet of paper:

| Transaction | Working Capital | Current Ratio | Quick Ratio |
|---|---|---|---|

Compute the working capital, the current ratio, and the quick ratio after each of the following transactions, and record the results in the appropriate columns. Consider each transaction separately and assume that only that transaction affects the data given above. Round to two digits after the decimal point.
a. Sold marketable securities at no gain or loss, $34,000.
b. Paid accounts payable, $60,000.
c. Purchased goods on account, $40,000.
d. Paid notes payable, $20,000.
e. Declared a cash dividend, $25,000.
f. Declared a common stock dividend on common stock, $16,500.
g. Borrowed cash from bank on a long-term note, $120,000.
h. Received cash on account, $86,000.
i. Issued additional shares of stock for cash, $100,000.
j. Paid cash for prepaid expenses, $9,000.

**PROBLEM 17-4B**
*Nineteen measures of solvency and profitability*

**Objectives 2, 3**

The comparative financial statements of Quest Polymers, Inc. are as follows. The market price of Quest Polymers, Inc. common stock was $64 on December 31, 2006.

✓9. *Ratio of liabilities to stockholders' equity, 0.6*

## Quest Polymers, Inc.
### Comparative Retained Earnings Statement
#### For the Years Ended December 31, 2006 and 2005

| | Dec. 31, 2006 | Dec. 31, 2005 |
|---|---|---|
| Retained earnings, January 1 | $ 645,000 | $512,000 |
| Add net income for year | 361,000 | 221,000 |
| Total | $1,006,000 | $733,000 |
| Deduct dividends: | | |
| On preferred stock | $ 32,000 | $ 24,000 |
| On common stock | 64,000 | 64,000 |
| Total | $ 96,000 | $ 88,000 |
| Retained earnings, December 31 | $ 910,000 | $645,000 |

## Quest Polymers, Inc.
### Comparative Income Statement
#### For the Years Ended December 31, 2006 and 2005

| | 2006 | 2005 |
|---|---|---|
| Sales | $2,830,000 | $2,450,000 |
| Sales returns and allowances | 30,000 | 25,000 |
| Net sales | $2,800,000 | $2,425,000 |
| Cost of goods sold | 1,250,000 | 1,150,000 |
| Gross profit | $1,550,000 | $1,275,000 |
| Selling expenses | $ 605,000 | $ 575,000 |
| Administrative expenses | 405,000 | 380,000 |
| Total operating expenses | $1,010,000 | $ 955,000 |
| Income from operations | $ 540,000 | $ 320,000 |
| Other income | 40,000 | 30,000 |
| | $ 580,000 | $ 350,000 |
| Other expense (interest) | 79,000 | 34,000 |
| Income before income tax | $ 501,000 | $ 316,000 |
| Income tax expense | 140,000 | 95,000 |
| Net income | $ 361,000 | $ 221,000 |

## Quest Polymers, Inc.
### Comparative Balance Sheet
#### December 31, 2006 and 2005

| | Dec. 31, 2006 | Dec. 31, 2005 |
|---|---|---|
| **Assets** | | |
| Current assets: | | |
| Cash | $ 108,000 | $ 96,000 |
| Marketable securities | 320,000 | 126,000 |
| Accounts receivable (net) | 172,000 | 158,000 |
| Inventories | 325,000 | 265,000 |
| Prepaid expenses | 20,000 | 25,000 |
| Total current assets | $ 945,000 | $ 670,000 |
| Long-term investments | 250,000 | 200,000 |
| Property, plant, and equipment (net) | 2,100,000 | 1,500,000 |
| Total assets | $3,295,000 | $2,370,000 |
| **Liabilities** | | |
| Current liabilities | $ 285,000 | $ 225,000 |
| Long-term liabilities: | | |
| Mortgage note payable, 9%, due 2011 | $ 500,000 | — |
| Bonds payable, 8.5%, due 2015 | 400,000 | $ 400,000 |
| Total long-term liabilities | $ 900,000 | $ 400,000 |
| Total liabilities | $1,185,000 | $ 625,000 |
| **Stockholders' Equity** | | |
| Preferred $8 stock, $100 par | $ 400,000 | $ 300,000 |
| Common stock, $10 par | 800,000 | 800,000 |
| Retained earnings | 910,000 | 645,000 |
| Total stockholders' equity | $2,110,000 | $1,745,000 |
| Total liabilities and stockholders' equity | $3,295,000 | $2,370,000 |

## Instructions

Determine the following measures for 2006, rounding to nearest single digit after the decimal point:

1. Working capital
2. Current ratio
3. Quick ratio
4. Accounts receivable turnover
5. Number of days' sales in receivables
6. Inventory turnover
7. Number of days' sales in inventory
8. Ratio of fixed assets to long-term liabilities
9. Ratio of liabilities to stockholders' equity
10. Number of times interest charges earned
11. Number of times preferred dividends earned
12. Ratio of net sales to assets
13. Rate earned on total assets
14. Rate earned on stockholders' equity
15. Rate earned on common stockholders' equity
16. Earnings per share on common stock
17. Price-earnings ratio
18. Dividends per share of common stock
19. Dividend yield

**PROBLEM 17-5B**
*Solvency and profitability
trend analysis*

**Objectives 2, 3**

Crane Plastics Company has provided the following comparative information:

|  | 2006 | 2005 | 2004 | 2003 | 2002 |
|---|---|---|---|---|---|
| Net income | $ 30,000 | $ 50,000 | $ 100,000 | $ 150,000 | $ 150,000 |
| Interest expense | 102,000 | 95,000 | 85,000 | 80,000 | 75,000 |
| Income tax expense | 9,000 | 15,000 | 30,000 | 45,000 | 45,000 |
| Total assets (ending balance) | 1,600,000 | 1,500,000 | 1,350,000 | 1,200,000 | 1,000,000 |
| Total stockholders' equity (ending balance) | 580,000 | 550,000 | 500,000 | 400,000 | 250,000 |
| Average total assets | 1,550,000 | 1,425,000 | 1,275,000 | 1,100,000 | 900,000 |
| Average stockholders' equity | 565,000 | 525,000 | 450,000 | 325,000 | 225,000 |

You have been asked to evaluate the historical performance of the company over the last five years.

Selected industry ratios have remained relatively steady at the following levels for the last five years:

|  | 2002–2006 |
|---|---|
| Rate earned on total assets | 14% |
| Rate earned on stockholders' equity | 20% |
| Number of times interest charges earned | 3.0 |
| Ratio of liabilities to stockholders' equity | 2.0 |

## Instructions

1. Prepare four line graphs with the ratio on the vertical axis and the years on the horizontal axis for the following four ratios (rounded to two digits after the decimal place):
   a. Rate earned on total assets
   b. Rate earned on stockholders' equity
   c. Number of times interest charges earned
   d. Ratio of liabilities to stockholders' equity
   Display both the company ratio and the industry benchmark on each graph. That is, each graph should have two lines.
2. ▭▬▶ Prepare an analysis of the graphs in (1).

# Home Depot, Inc. Problem

**FINANCIAL STATEMENT ANALYSIS**

The financial statements for **Home Depot, Inc.**, are presented in Appendix E at the end of the text. The following additional information (in millions) is available:

| | |
|---|---|
| Accounts receivable at January 28, 2001 | $ 835 |
| Inventories at January 28, 2001 | 6,556 |
| Total assets at January 28, 2001 | 21,385 |
| Stockholders' equity at January 28, 2001 | 15,005 |

**Instructions**

1. Determine the following measures for years ending February 2, 2003 and February 3, 2002, rounding to two digits after the decimal place.
   a. Working capital
   b. Current ratio
   c. Quick ratio
   d. Accounts receivable turnover
   e. Number of days' sales in receivables
   f. Inventory turnover
   g. Number of days' sales in inventory
   h. Ratio of liabilities to stockholders' equity
   i. Ratio of net sales to average total assets
   j. Rate earned on average total assets
   k. Rate earned on average common stockholders' equity
   l. Price-earnings ratio, assuming that the market price was $21.31 per share on February 2, 2003 and $49.70 on February 3, 2002.
   m. Percentage relationship of net income to net sales
2. What conclusions can be drawn from these analyses?

# Special Activities

**ACTIVITY 17-1**
*Analysis of financing corporate growth*

**WHAT DO YOU THINK?**

Assume that the president of Ice Mountain Brewery made the following statement in the Annual Report to Shareholders:

"The founding family and majority shareholders of the company do not believe in using debt to finance future growth. The founding family learned from hard experience during Prohibition and the Great Depression that debt can cause loss of flexibility and eventual loss of corporate control. The company will not place itself at such risk. As such, all future growth will be financed either by stock sales to the public or by internally generated resources."

As a public shareholder of this company, how would you respond to this policy?

**ACTIVITY 17-2**
*Receivables and inventory turnover*

Peach Computer Company has completed its fiscal year on December 31, 2006. The auditor, Sandra Blake, has approached the CFO, Travis Williams, regarding the year-end receivables and inventory levels of Peach Computer. The following conversation takes place:

*Sandra:* We are beginning our audit of Peach Computer and have prepared ratio analyses to determine if there have been significant changes in operations or financial position. This helps us guide the audit process. This analysis indicates that the inventory turnover has decreased from 5 to 2.8, while the accounts receivable turnover has decreased from 12 to 8. I was wondering if you could explain this change in operations.

*Travis:* There is little need for concern. The inventory represents computers that we were unable to sell during the holiday buying season. We are confident, however, that we will be able to sell these computers as we move into the next fiscal year.

*Sandra:* What gives you this confidence?

*Travis:* We will increase our advertising and provide some very attractive price concessions to move these machines. We have no choice. Newer technology is already out there, and we have to unload this inventory.

*Sandra:* . . . and the receivables?

*Travis:* As you may be aware, the company is under tremendous pressure to expand sales and profits. As a result, we lowered our credit standards to our commercial customers so that we would be able to sell products to a broader customer base. As a result of this policy change, we have been able to expand sales by 35%.

*Sandra:* Your responses have not been reassuring to me.

*Travis:* I'm a little confused. Assets are good, right? Why don't you look at our current ratio? It has improved, hasn't it? I would think that you would view that very favorably.

➤ Why is Sandra concerned about the inventory and accounts receivable turnover ratios and Travis's responses to them? What action may Sandra need to take? How would you respond to Travis's last comment?

**ACTIVITY 17-3**
*Vertical analysis*

The condensed income statements through income from operations for **Dell Computer Corporation** and **Apple Computer Co.** are reproduced below for recent fiscal years (numbers in millions of dollars).

|  | Dell Computer Corporation | Apple Computer Co. |
|---|---|---|
| Sales (net) | $31,168 | $5,363 |
| Cost of sales | 25,661 | 4,128 |
| Gross profit | $ 5,507 | $1,235 |
| Selling, general, and administrative expenses | $ 2,784 | $1,138 |
| Research and development | 452 | 430 |
| Special charges | 482 | 11 |
| Operating expenses | $ 3,718 | $1,579 |
| Income from operations | $ 1,789 | $ (344) |

➤ Prepare comparative common-size statements, rounding to two digits after the whole percent. Interpret the analyses.

**ACTIVITY 17-4**
*Profitability ratios*

**Ford Motor Company** is the second largest automobile and truck manufacturer in the United States. In addition to manufacturing motor vehicles, Ford also provides vehicle-related financing, insurance, and leasing services. Historically, people have purchased automobiles when the economy was strong and delayed automobile purchases when the economy was faltering. For this reason, Ford is considered a cyclical company. This means that when the economy does well, Ford usually prospers, while when the economy is down, Ford usually suffers.

The following information is available for three recent years (in millions of dollars except per-share amounts):

|  | 2002 | 2001 | 2000 |
|---|---|---|---|
| Net income (loss) | $ (980) | $ (5,453) | $ 3,467 |
| Preferred dividends | 15 | 15 | 15 |
| Cash dividend per share | 0.40 | 1.05 | 1.8 |
| Average total assets | 285,882 | 279,967 | 277,305 |
| Average stockholders' equity | 6,668 | 13,198 | 23,107 |
| Average stock price | 13.57 | 21.32 | 24.10 |
| Shares outstanding for computing earnings per share | 1,819 | 1,820 | 1,483 |

1. Calculate the following ratios for each year:
   a. Rate earned on total assets
   b. Rate earned on stockholders' equity
   c. Earnings per share
   d. Dividend yield
   e. Price-earnings ratio
2. What is the ratio of average liabilities to average stockholders' equity for 2001?
3. ▸ Why does Ford have so much leverage?
4. ▸ Explain the direction of the dividend yield and price-earnings ratio in light of Ford's profitability trend.

**ACTIVITY 17-5**
*Projecting financial statements*

INTERNET

Go to **Microsoft**'s Web site at **http://www.microsoft.com** and click on the "Investor Relations" area of Microsoft's Web environment. Select the menu item "stock info and analysis." Select the "what if" tool. With this tool, use horizontal and vertical information to create a full-year projection of the Microsoft income statement. Make the following assumptions:

| | |
|---|---|
| Revenue growth | 16% |
| Cost of goods sold as a percent of revenue | 18% |
| Research and development growth | 12% |
| Sales and marketing as a percent of sales | 20% |
| General and administrative as a percent of sales | 4% |
| Tax rate | 35% |
| Diluted shares outstanding | 11,000 |

**ACTIVITY 17-6**
*Comprehensive profitability and solvency analysis*

**Marriott International Inc.** and **Hilton Hotels Corp.** are two major owners and managers of lodging and resort properties in the United States. Abstracted income statement information for the two companies is as follows for a recent year:

| | Marriott (in millions) | Hilton (in millions) |
|---|---|---|
| Operating profit before other expenses and interest | $ 590 | $ 495 |
| Other income (expenses) | (111) | 48 |
| Interest expense | (109) | (237) |
| Income before income taxes | $ 370 | $ 306 |
| Income tax expense | 134 | 130 |
| Net income | $ 236 | $ 176 |

Balance sheet information is as follows:

| | Marriott (in millions) | Hilton (in millions) |
|---|---|---|
| Total liabilities | $5,629 | $7,498 |
| Total stockholders' equity | 3,478 | 1,642 |
| Total liabilties and stockholders' equity | $9,107 | $9,140 |

The average liabilities, stockholders' equity, and total assets were as follows:

| | Marriott | Hilton |
|---|---|---|
| Average total liabilities | $5,300 | $7,250 |
| Average total stockholders' equity | 3,373 | 1,713 |
| Average total assets | 8,673 | 8,963 |

1. Determine the following ratios for both companies (round to the nearest two digits after the whole percent):
   a. Rate earned on total assets
   b. Rate earned on total stockholders' equity
   c. Number of times interest charges are earned
   d. Ratio of liabilities to stockholders' equity
2. ▸ Analyze and compare the two companies, using the information in (1).

# Answers to Self-Examination Questions

1. **A**  Percentage analysis indicating the relationship of the component parts to the total in a financial statement, such as the relationship of current assets to total assets (20% to 100%) in the question, is called vertical analysis (answer A). Percentage analysis of increases and decreases in corresponding items in comparative financial statements is called horizontal analysis (answer B). An example of horizontal analysis would be the presentation of the amount of current assets in the preceding balance sheet, along with the amount of current assets at the end of the current year, with the increase or decrease in current assets between the periods expressed as a percentage. Profitability analysis (answer C) is the analysis of a firm's ability to earn income. Contribution margin analysis (answer D) is discussed in a later managerial accounting chapter.

2. **D**  Various solvency measures, categorized as current position analysis, indicate a firm's ability to meet currently maturing obligations. Each measure contributes in the analysis of a firm's current position and is most useful when viewed with other measures and when compared with similar measures for other periods and for other firms. Working capital (answer A) is the excess of current assets over current liabilities; the current ratio (answer B) is the ratio of current assets to current liabilities; and the quick ratio (answer C) is the ratio of the sum of cash, receivables, and marketable securities to current liabilities.

3. **D**  The ratio of current assets to current liabilities is usually called the current ratio (answer A). It is sometimes called the working capital ratio (answer B) or bankers' ratio (answer C).

4. **C**  The ratio of the sum of cash, receivables, and marketable securities (sometimes called quick assets) to current liabilities is called the quick ratio (answer C) or acid-test ratio. The current ratio (answer A), working capital ratio (answer B), and bankers' ratio (answer D) are terms that describe the ratio of current assets to current liabilities.

5. **C**  The number of days' sales in inventory (answer C), which is determined by dividing the inventories at the end of the year by the average daily cost of goods sold, expresses the relationship between the cost of goods sold and inventory. It indicates the efficiency in the management of inventory. The working capital ratio (answer A) indicates the ability of the business to meet currently maturing obligations (debt). The quick ratio (answer B) indicates the "instant" debt-paying ability of the business. The ratio of fixed assets to long-term liabilities (answer D) indicates the margin of safety for long-term creditors.

# Appendices

# appendix A

# Interest Tables

| $n \backslash i$ | 5% | 5.5% | 6% | 6.5% | 7% | 8% |
|---|---|---|---|---|---|---|
| 1 | 0.95238 | 0.94787 | 0.94334 | 0.93897 | 0.93458 | 0.92593 |
| 2 | 0.90703 | 0.89845 | 0.89000 | 0.88166 | 0.87344 | 0.85734 |
| 3 | 0.86384 | 0.85161 | 0.83962 | 0.82785 | 0.81630 | 0.79383 |
| 4 | 0.82270 | 0.80722 | 0.79209 | 0.77732 | 0.76290 | 0.73503 |
| 5 | 0.78353 | 0.76513 | 0.74726 | 0.72988 | 0.71290 | 0.68058 |
| 6 | 0.74622 | 0.72525 | 0.70496 | 0.68533 | 0.66634 | 0.63017 |
| 7 | 0.71068 | 0.68744 | 0.66506 | 0.64351 | 0.62275 | 0.58349 |
| 8 | 0.67684 | 0.65160 | 0.62741 | 0.60423 | 0.58201 | 0.54027 |
| 9 | 0.64461 | 0.61763 | 0.59190 | 0.56735 | 0.54393 | 0.50025 |
| 10 | 0.61391 | 0.58543 | 0.55840 | 0.53273 | 0.50835 | 0.46319 |
| 11 | 0.58468 | 0.55491 | 0.52679 | 0.50021 | 0.47509 | 0.42888 |
| 12 | 0.55684 | 0.52598 | 0.49697 | 0.46968 | 0.44401 | 0.39711 |
| 13 | 0.53032 | 0.49856 | 0.46884 | 0.44102 | 0.41496 | 0.36770 |
| 14 | 0.50507 | 0.47257 | 0.44230 | 0.41410 | 0.38782 | 0.34046 |
| 15 | 0.48102 | 0.44793 | 0.41726 | 0.38883 | 0.36245 | 0.31524 |
| 16 | 0.45811 | 0.42458 | 0.39365 | 0.36510 | 0.33874 | 0.29189 |
| 17 | 0.43630 | 0.40245 | 0.37136 | 0.34281 | 0.31657 | 0.27027 |
| 18 | 0.41552 | 0.38147 | 0.35034 | 0.32189 | 0.29586 | 0.25025 |
| 19 | 0.39573 | 0.36158 | 0.33051 | 0.30224 | 0.27651 | 0.23171 |
| 20 | 0.37689 | 0.34273 | 0.31180 | 0.28380 | 0.25842 | 0.21455 |
| 21 | 0.35894 | 0.32486 | 0.29416 | 0.26648 | 0.24151 | 0.19866 |
| 22 | 0.34185 | 0.30793 | 0.27750 | 0.25021 | 0.22571 | 0.18394 |
| 23 | 0.32557 | 0.29187 | 0.26180 | 0.23494 | 0.21095 | 0.17032 |
| 24 | 0.31007 | 0.27666 | 0.24698 | 0.22060 | 0.19715 | 0.15770 |
| 25 | 0.29530 | 0.26223 | 0.23300 | 0.20714 | 0.18425 | 0.14602 |
| 26 | 0.28124 | 0.24856 | 0.21981 | 0.19450 | 0.17211 | 0.13520 |
| 27 | 0.26785 | 0.23560 | 0.20737 | 0.18263 | 0.16093 | 0.12519 |
| 28 | 0.25509 | 0.22332 | 0.19563 | 0.17148 | 0.15040 | 0.11591 |
| 29 | 0.24295 | 0.21168 | 0.18456 | 0.16101 | 0.14056 | 0.10733 |
| 30 | 0.23138 | 0.20064 | 0.17411 | 0.15119 | 0.13137 | 0.09938 |
| 31 | 0.22036 | 0.19018 | 0.16426 | 0.14196 | 0.12277 | 0.09202 |
| 32 | 0.20987 | 0.18027 | 0.15496 | 0.13329 | 0.11474 | 0.08520 |
| 33 | 0.19987 | 0.17087 | 0.14619 | 0.12516 | 0.10724 | 0.07889 |
| 34 | 0.19036 | 0.16196 | 0.13791 | 0.11752 | 0.10022 | 0.07304 |
| 35 | 0.18129 | 0.15352 | 0.13010 | 0.11035 | 0.09366 | 0.06764 |
| 40 | 0.14205 | 0.11746 | 0.09722 | 0.08054 | 0.06678 | 0.04603 |
| 45 | 0.11130 | 0.08988 | 0.07265 | 0.05879 | 0.04761 | 0.03133 |
| 50 | 0.08720 | 0.06877 | 0.05429 | 0.04291 | 0.03395 | 0.02132 |

Present Value of $1 at Compound Interest Due in $n$ Periods: $p_{\bar{n}\backslash i} = \dfrac{1}{(1 + i)^n}$

**Present Value of $1 at Compound Interest Due in $n$ Periods: $p_{\overline{n}\backslash i} = \dfrac{1}{(1 + i)^n}$**

| $n \backslash i$ | 9% | 10% | 11% | 12% | 13% | 14% |
|---|---|---|---|---|---|---|
| 1 | 0.91743 | 0.90909 | 0.90090 | 0.89286 | 0.88496 | 0.87719 |
| 2 | 0.84168 | 0.82645 | 0.81162 | 0.79719 | 0.78315 | 0.76947 |
| 3 | 0.77218 | 0.75132 | 0.73119 | 0.71178 | 0.69305 | 0.67497 |
| 4 | 0.70842 | 0.68301 | 0.65873 | 0.63552 | 0.61332 | 0.59208 |
| 5 | 0.64993 | 0.62092 | 0.59345 | 0.56743 | 0.54276 | 0.51937 |
| 6 | 0.59627 | 0.56447 | 0.53464 | 0.50663 | 0.48032 | 0.45559 |
| 7 | 0.54703 | 0.51316 | 0.48166 | 0.45235 | 0.42506 | 0.39964 |
| 8 | 0.50187 | 0.46651 | 0.43393 | 0.40388 | 0.37616 | 0.35056 |
| 9 | 0.46043 | 0.42410 | 0.39092 | 0.36061 | 0.33288 | 0.30751 |
| 10 | 0.42241 | 0.38554 | 0.35218 | 0.32197 | 0.29459 | 0.26974 |
| 11 | 0.38753 | 0.35049 | 0.31728 | 0.28748 | 0.26070 | 0.23662 |
| 12 | 0.35554 | 0.31863 | 0.28584 | 0.25668 | 0.23071 | 0.20756 |
| 13 | 0.32618 | 0.28966 | 0.25751 | 0.22917 | 0.20416 | 0.18207 |
| 14 | 0.29925 | 0.26333 | 0.23199 | 0.20462 | 0.18068 | 0.15971 |
| 15 | 0.27454 | 0.23939 | 0.20900 | 0.18270 | 0.15989 | 0.14010 |
| 16 | 0.25187 | 0.21763 | 0.18829 | 0.16312 | 0.14150 | 0.12289 |
| 17 | 0.23107 | 0.19784 | 0.16963 | 0.14564 | 0.12522 | 0.10780 |
| 18 | 0.21199 | 0.17986 | 0.15282 | 0.13004 | 0.11081 | 0.09456 |
| 19 | 0.19449 | 0.16351 | 0.13768 | 0.11611 | 0.09806 | 0.08295 |
| 20 | 0.17843 | 0.14864 | 0.12403 | 0.10367 | 0.08678 | 0.07276 |
| 21 | 0.16370 | 0.13513 | 0.11174 | 0.09256 | 0.07680 | 0.06383 |
| 22 | 0.15018 | 0.12285 | 0.10067 | 0.08264 | 0.06796 | 0.05599 |
| 23 | 0.13778 | 0.11168 | 0.09069 | 0.07379 | 0.06014 | 0.04911 |
| 24 | 0.12640 | 0.10153 | 0.08170 | 0.06588 | 0.05323 | 0.04308 |
| 25 | 0.11597 | 0.09230 | 0.07361 | 0.05882 | 0.04710 | 0.03779 |
| 26 | 0.10639 | 0.08390 | 0.06631 | 0.05252 | 0.04168 | 0.03315 |
| 27 | 0.09761 | 0.07628 | 0.05974 | 0.04689 | 0.03689 | 0.02908 |
| 28 | 0.08955 | 0.06934 | 0.05382 | 0.04187 | 0.03264 | 0.02551 |
| 29 | 0.08216 | 0.06304 | 0.04849 | 0.03738 | 0.02889 | 0.02237 |
| 30 | 0.07537 | 0.05731 | 0.04368 | 0.03338 | 0.02557 | 0.01963 |
| 31 | 0.06915 | 0.05210 | 0.03935 | 0.02980 | 0.02262 | 0.01722 |
| 32 | 0.06344 | 0.04736 | 0.03545 | 0.02661 | 0.02002 | 0.01510 |
| 33 | 0.05820 | 0.04306 | 0.03194 | 0.02376 | 0.01772 | 0.01325 |
| 34 | 0.05331 | 0.03914 | 0.02878 | 0.02121 | 0.01568 | 0.01162 |
| 35 | 0.04899 | 0.03558 | 0.02592 | 0.01894 | 0.01388 | 0.01019 |
| 40 | 0.03184 | 0.02210 | 0.01538 | 0.01075 | 0.00753 | 0.00529 |
| 45 | 0.02069 | 0.01372 | 0.00913 | 0.00610 | 0.00409 | 0.00275 |
| 50 | 0.01345 | 0.00852 | 0.00542 | 0.00346 | 0.00222 | 0.00143 |

Present Value of Ordinary Annuity of $1 per Period: $p_{\overline{n}|i} = \dfrac{1 - \dfrac{1}{(1 + i)^n}}{i}$

| $n \backslash i$ | 5% | 5.5% | 6% | 6.5% | 7% | 8% |
|---|---|---|---|---|---|---|
| 1 | 0.95238 | 0.94787 | 0.94340 | 0.93897 | 0.93458 | 0.92593 |
| 2 | 1.85941 | 1.84632 | 1.83339 | 1.82063 | 1.80802 | 1.78326 |
| 3 | 2.72325 | 2.69793 | 2.67301 | 2.64848 | 2.62432 | 2.57710 |
| 4 | 3.54595 | 3.50515 | 3.46511 | 3.42580 | 3.38721 | 3.31213 |
| 5 | 4.32948 | 4.27028 | 4.21236 | 4.15568 | 4.10020 | 3.99271 |
| 6 | 5.07569 | 4.99553 | 4.91732 | 4.84101 | 4.76654 | 4.62288 |
| 7 | 5.78637 | 5.68297 | 5.58238 | 5.48452 | 5.38923 | 5.20637 |
| 8 | 6.46321 | 6.33457 | 6.20979 | 6.08875 | 5.97130 | 5.74664 |
| 9 | 7.10782 | 6.95220 | 6.80169 | 6.65610 | 6.51523 | 6.24689 |
| 10 | 7.72174 | 7.53763 | 7.36009 | 7.18883 | 7.02358 | 6.71008 |
| 11 | 8.30641 | 8.09254 | 7.88688 | 7.68904 | 7.49867 | 7.13896 |
| 12 | 8.86325 | 8.61852 | 8.38384 | 8.15873 | 7.94269 | 7.53608 |
| 13 | 9.39357 | 9.11708 | 8.85268 | 8.59974 | 8.35765 | 7.90378 |
| 14 | 9.89864 | 9.58965 | 9.29498 | 9.01384 | 8.74547 | 8.22424 |
| 15 | 10.37966 | 10.03758 | 9.71225 | 9.40267 | 9.10791 | 8.55948 |
| 16 | 10.83777 | 10.46216 | 10.10590 | 9.76776 | 9.44665 | 8.85137 |
| 17 | 11.27407 | 10.86461 | 10.47726 | 10.11058 | 9.76322 | 9.12164 |
| 18 | 11.68959 | 11.24607 | 10.82760 | 10.43247 | 10.05909 | 9.37189 |
| 19 | 12.08532 | 11.60765 | 11.15812 | 10.73471 | 10.33560 | 9.60360 |
| 20 | 12.46221 | 11.95038 | 11.46992 | 11.01851 | 10.59401 | 9.81815 |
| 21 | 12.82115 | 12.27524 | 11.76408 | 11.28498 | 10.83553 | 10.01680 |
| 22 | 13.16300 | 12.58317 | 12.04158 | 11.53520 | 11.06124 | 10.20074 |
| 23 | 13.48857 | 12.87504 | 12.30338 | 11.77014 | 11.27219 | 10.37106 |
| 24 | 13.79864 | 13.15170 | 12.55036 | 11.99074 | 11.46933 | 10.52876 |
| 25 | 14.09394 | 13.41393 | 12.78336 | 12.19788 | 11.65358 | 10.67478 |
| 26 | 14.37518 | 13.66250 | 13.00317 | 12.39237 | 11.82578 | 10.80998 |
| 27 | 14.64303 | 13.89810 | 13.21053 | 12.57500 | 11.98671 | 10.93516 |
| 28 | 14.89813 | 14.12142 | 13.40616 | 12.74648 | 12.13711 | 11.05108 |
| 29 | 15.14107 | 14.33310 | 13.59072 | 12.90749 | 12.27767 | 11.15841 |
| 30 | 15.37245 | 14.53375 | 13.76483 | 13.05868 | 12.40904 | 11.25778 |
| 31 | 15.59281 | 14.72393 | 13.92909 | 13.20063 | 12.53181 | 11.34980 |
| 32 | 15.80268 | 14.90420 | 14.08404 | 13.33393 | 12.64656 | 11.43500 |
| 33 | 16.00255 | 15.07507 | 14.23023 | 13.45909 | 12.75379 | 11.51389 |
| 34 | 16.19290 | 15.23703 | 14.36814 | 13.57661 | 12.85401 | 11.58693 |
| 35 | 16.37420 | 15.39055 | 14.49825 | 13.68696 | 12.94767 | 11.65457 |
| 40 | 17.15909 | 16.04612 | 15.04630 | 14.14553 | 13.33171 | 11.92461 |
| 45 | 17.77407 | 16.54773 | 15.45583 | 14.48023 | 13.60552 | 12.10840 |
| 50 | 18.25592 | 16.93152 | 15.76186 | 14.72452 | 13.80075 | 12.23348 |

Present Value of Ordinary Annuity of $1 per Period: $p_{\overline{n}\backslash i} = \dfrac{1 - \dfrac{1}{(1 + i)^n}}{i}$

| $n \backslash i$ | 9% | 10% | 11% | 12% | 13% | 14% |
|---|---|---|---|---|---|---|
| 1 | 0.91743 | 0.90909 | 0.90090 | 0.89286 | 0.88496 | 0.87719 |
| 2 | 1.75911 | 1.73554 | 1.71252 | 1.69005 | 1.66810 | 1.64666 |
| 3 | 2.53130 | 2.48685 | 2.44371 | 2.40183 | 2.36115 | 2.32163 |
| 4 | 3.23972 | 3.16986 | 3.10245 | 3.03735 | 2.97447 | 2.91371 |
| 5 | 3.88965 | 3.79079 | 3.69590 | 3.60478 | 3.51723 | 3.43308 |
| 6 | 4.48592 | 4.35526 | 4.23054 | 4.11141 | 3.99755 | 3.88867 |
| 7 | 5.03295 | 4.86842 | 4.71220 | 4.56376 | 4.42261 | 4.28830 |
| 8 | 5.53482 | 5.33493 | 5.14612 | 4.96764 | 4.79677 | 4.63886 |
| 9 | 5.99525 | 5.75902 | 5.53705 | 5.32825 | 5.13166 | 4.94637 |
| 10 | 6.41766 | 6.14457 | 5.88923 | 5.65022 | 5.42624 | 5.21612 |
| 11 | 6.80519 | 6.49506 | 6.20652 | 5.93770 | 5.68694 | 5.45273 |
| 12 | 7.16072 | 6.81369 | 6.49236 | 6.19437 | 5.91765 | 5.66029 |
| 13 | 7.48690 | 7.10336 | 6.74987 | 6.42355 | 6.12181 | 5.84236 |
| 14 | 7.78615 | 7.36669 | 6.96187 | 6.62817 | 6.30249 | 6.00207 |
| 15 | 8.06069 | 7.60608 | 7.19087 | 6.81086 | 6.46238 | 6.14217 |
| 16 | 8.31256 | 7.82371 | 7.37916 | 6.97399 | 6.60388 | 6.26506 |
| 17 | 8.54363 | 8.02155 | 7.54879 | 7.11963 | 6.72909 | 6.37286 |
| 18 | 8.75562 | 8.20141 | 7.70162 | 7.24967 | 6.83991 | 6.46742 |
| 19 | 8.95012 | 8.36492 | 7.83929 | 7.36578 | 6.93797 | 6.55037 |
| 20 | 9.12855 | 8.51356 | 7.96333 | 7.46944 | 7.02475 | 6.62313 |
| 21 | 9.29224 | 8.64869 | 8.07507 | 7.56200 | 7.10155 | 6.68696 |
| 22 | 9.44242 | 8.77154 | 8.17574 | 7.64465 | 7.16951 | 6.74294 |
| 23 | 9.58021 | 8.88322 | 8.26643 | 7.71843 | 7.22966 | 6.79206 |
| 24 | 9.70661 | 8.98474 | 8.34814 | 7.78432 | 7.28288 | 6.83514 |
| 25 | 9.82258 | 9.07704 | 8.42174 | 7.84314 | 7.32998 | 6.87293 |
| 26 | 9.92897 | 9.16094 | 8.48806 | 7.89566 | 7.37167 | 6.90608 |
| 27 | 10.02658 | 9.23722 | 8.54780 | 7.94255 | 7.40856 | 6.93515 |
| 28 | 10.11613 | 9.30657 | 8.60162 | 7.98442 | 7.44120 | 6.96066 |
| 29 | 10.19828 | 9.36961 | 8.65011 | 8.02181 | 7.47009 | 6.98304 |
| 30 | 10.27365 | 9.42691 | 8.69379 | 8.05518 | 7.49565 | 7.00266 |
| 31 | 10.34280 | 9.47901 | 8.73315 | 8.08499 | 7.51828 | 7.01988 |
| 32 | 10.40624 | 9.52638 | 8.76860 | 8.11159 | 7.53830 | 7.03498 |
| 33 | 10.46444 | 9.56943 | 8.80054 | 8.13535 | 7.55602 | 7.04823 |
| 34 | 10.51784 | 9.60858 | 8.82932 | 8.15656 | 7.57170 | 7.05985 |
| 35 | 10.56682 | 9.64416 | 8.85524 | 8.17550 | 7.58557 | 7.07005 |
| 40 | 10.75736 | 9.77905 | 8.95105 | 8.24378 | 7.63438 | 7.10504 |
| 45 | 10.88118 | 9.86281 | 9.00791 | 8.28252 | 7.66086 | 7.12322 |
| 50 | 10.96168 | 9.91481 | 9.04165 | 8.30450 | 7.67524 | 7.13266 |

## Future Amount of $1 at Compound Interest Due in n Periods: $A_{\overline{n}|i} = (1 + i)^n$

| $n \backslash i$ | 5% | 5.5% | 6% | 6.5% | 7% | 8% |
|---|---|---|---|---|---|---|
| 1 | 1.05000 | 1.05500 | 1.06000 | 1.06500 | 1.07000 | 1.08000 |
| 2 | 1.10250 | 1.11303 | 1.12360 | 1.13423 | 1.14490 | 1.16640 |
| 3 | 1.15762 | 1.17424 | 1.19102 | 1.20795 | 1.22504 | 1.25971 |
| 4 | 1.21551 | 1.23882 | 1.26248 | 1.28647 | 1.31080 | 1.36049 |
| 5 | 1.27628 | 1.30696 | 1.33823 | 1.37009 | 1.40255 | 1.46933 |
| 6 | 1.34100 | 1.37884 | 1.41852 | 1.45914 | 1.50073 | 1.58687 |
| 7 | 1.40710 | 1.45468 | 1.50363 | 1.55399 | 1.60578 | 1.71382 |
| 8 | 1.54347 | 1.53469 | 1.59385 | 1.65500 | 1.71819 | 1.85093 |
| 9 | 1.55133 | 1.61909 | 1.68948 | 1.76257 | 1.83846 | 1.99900 |
| 10 | 1.62890 | 1.70814 | 1.79085 | 1.87714 | 1.96715 | 2.15892 |
| 11 | 1.71034 | 1.80209 | 1.89830 | 1.99915 | 2.10485 | 2.33164 |
| 12 | 1.79586 | 1.90121 | 2.01220 | 2.12910 | 2.25219 | 2.51817 |
| 13 | 1.88565 | 2.00577 | 2.13293 | 2.26749 | 2.40984 | 2.71962 |
| 14 | 1.97993 | 2.11609 | 2.26091 | 2.41487 | 2.57853 | 2.93719 |
| 15 | 2.07893 | 2.23248 | 2.39656 | 2.57184 | 2.75903 | 3.17217 |
| 16 | 2.18288 | 2.35526 | 2.54035 | 2.73901 | 2.95216 | 3.42594 |
| 17 | 2.29202 | 2.48480 | 2.69277 | 2.91705 | 3.15882 | 3.70002 |
| 18 | 2.40662 | 2.62147 | 2.85434 | 3.10665 | 3.37993 | 3.99602 |
| 19 | 2.52695 | 2.76565 | 3.02560 | 3.30859 | 3.61653 | 4.31570 |
| 20 | 2.65330 | 2.91776 | 3.20714 | 3.52365 | 3.86968 | 4.66096 |
| 21 | 2.78596 | 3.07823 | 3.39956 | 3.75268 | 4.14056 | 5.03383 |
| 22 | 2.92526 | 3.24754 | 3.60354 | 3.99661 | 4.43040 | 5.43654 |
| 23 | 3.07152 | 3.42615 | 3.81975 | 4.25639 | 4.74053 | 5.87146 |
| 24 | 3.22510 | 3.61459 | 4.04894 | 4.53305 | 5.07237 | 6.34118 |
| 25 | 3.38636 | 3.81339 | 4.29187 | 4.82770 | 5.42743 | 6.84848 |
| 26 | 3.55567 | 4.02313 | 4.54938 | 5.14150 | 5.80735 | 7.39635 |
| 27 | 3.73346 | 4.24440 | 4.82235 | 5.47570 | 6.21387 | 7.98806 |
| 28 | 3.92013 | 4.47784 | 5.11169 | 5.83162 | 6.64884 | 8.62711 |
| 29 | 4.11614 | 4.72412 | 5.41839 | 6.21067 | 7.11426 | 9.31728 |
| 30 | 4.32194 | 4.98395 | 5.74349 | 6.61437 | 7.61226 | 10.06266 |
| 31 | 4.53804 | 5.25807 | 6.08810 | 7.04430 | 8.14511 | 10.86767 |
| 32 | 4.76494 | 5.54726 | 6.45339 | 7.50218 | 8.71527 | 11.73708 |
| 33 | 5.00319 | 5.85236 | 6.84059 | 7.98982 | 9.32534 | 12.67605 |
| 34 | 5.25335 | 6.17424 | 7.25102 | 8.50916 | 9.97811 | 13.69013 |
| 35 | 5.51602 | 6.51383 | 7.68609 | 9.06225 | 10.67658 | 14.78534 |
| 40 | 7.03999 | 8.51331 | 10.28572 | 12.41607 | 14.97446 | 21.72452 |
| 45 | 8.98501 | 11.12655 | 13.76461 | 17.01110 | 21.00245 | 31.92045 |
| 50 | 11.46740 | 14.54196 | 18.42015 | 23.30668 | 29.45702 | 46.90161 |

## Future Amount of $1 at Compound Interest Due in n Periods: $A_{\bar{n}|i} = (1 + i)^n$

| n \ i | 9% | 10% | 11% | 12% | 13% | 14% |
|---|---|---|---|---|---|---|
| 1 | 1.09000 | 1.10000 | 1.11000 | 1.12000 | 1.13000 | 1.14000 |
| 2 | 1.18810 | 1.21000 | 1.23210 | 1.25440 | 1.27690 | 1.29960 |
| 3 | 1.29503 | 1.33100 | 1.36763 | 1.40493 | 1.44290 | 1.48154 |
| 4 | 1.41158 | 1.46410 | 1.51807 | 1.57352 | 1.63047 | 1.68896 |
| 5 | 1.53862 | 1.61051 | 1.68506 | 1.76234 | 1.84244 | 1.92541 |
| 6 | 1.67710 | 1.77156 | 1.87041 | 1.97382 | 2.08195 | 2.19497 |
| 7 | 1.82804 | 1.94872 | 2.07616 | 2.21068 | 2.35261 | 2.50227 |
| 8 | 1.99256 | 2.14359 | 2.30454 | 2.47596 | 2.65844 | 2.85259 |
| 9 | 2.17189 | 2.35795 | 2.55804 | 2.77308 | 3.00404 | 3.25195 |
| 10 | 2.36736 | 2.59374 | 2.83942 | 3.10585 | 3.39457 | 3.70722 |
| 11 | 2.58043 | 2.85312 | 3.15176 | 3.47855 | 3.83586 | 4.22623 |
| 12 | 2.81266 | 3.13843 | 3.49845 | 3.89598 | 4.33452 | 4.81790 |
| 13 | 3.06580 | 3.45227 | 3.88328 | 4.36349 | 4.89801 | 5.49241 |
| 14 | 3.34173 | 3.79750 | 4.31044 | 4.88711 | 5.53475 | 6.26135 |
| 15 | 3.64248 | 4.17725 | 4.78459 | 5.47357 | 6.25427 | 7.13794 |
| 16 | 3.97031 | 4.59497 | 5.31089 | 6.13039 | 7.06733 | 8.13725 |
| 17 | 4.32763 | 5.05447 | 5.89509 | 6.86604 | 7.98608 | 9.27646 |
| 18 | 4.71712 | 5.55992 | 6.54355 | 7.68997 | 9.02427 | 10.57517 |
| 19 | 5.14166 | 6.11591 | 7.26334 | 8.61276 | 10.19742 | 12.05569 |
| 20 | 5.60441 | 6.72750 | 8.06231 | 9.64629 | 11.52309 | 13.74349 |
| 21 | 6.10881 | 7.40025 | 8.94917 | 10.80385 | 13.02109 | 15.66758 |
| 22 | 6.65860 | 8.14028 | 9.93357 | 12.10031 | 14.71383 | 17.86104 |
| 23 | 7.25787 | 8.95430 | 11.02627 | 13.55235 | 16.62663 | 20.36158 |
| 24 | 7.91108 | 9.84973 | 12.23916 | 15.17863 | 18.78809 | 23.21221 |
| 25 | 8.62308 | 10.83471 | 13.58546 | 17.00006 | 21.23054 | 26.46192 |
| 26 | 9.39916 | 11.91818 | 15.07986 | 19.04007 | 23.99051 | 30.16658 |
| 27 | 10.24508 | 13.10999 | 16.73865 | 21.32488 | 27.10928 | 34.38991 |
| 28 | 11.16714 | 14.42099 | 18.57990 | 23.88387 | 30.63349 | 39.20449 |
| 29 | 12.17218 | 15.86309 | 20.62369 | 26.74993 | 34.61584 | 44.69312 |
| 30 | 13.26768 | 17.44940 | 22.89230 | 29.95992 | 39.11590 | 50.95016 |
| 31 | 14.46177 | 19.19434 | 25.41045 | 33.55511 | 44.20096 | 58.08318 |
| 32 | 15.76333 | 21.11378 | 28.20560 | 37.58173 | 49.94709 | 66.21483 |
| 33 | 17.18203 | 23.22515 | 31.30821 | 42.09153 | 56.44021 | 75.48490 |
| 34 | 18.72841 | 25.54767 | 34.75212 | 47.14252 | 63.77744 | 86.05279 |
| 35 | 20.41397 | 28.10244 | 38.57485 | 52.79962 | 72.06851 | 98.10018 |
| 40 | 31.40942 | 45.25926 | 65.00087 | 93.05097 | 132.78155 | 188.88351 |
| 45 | 48.32729 | 72.89048 | 109.53024 | 163.98760 | 244.64140 | 363.67907 |
| 50 | 74.35752 | 117.39085 | 184.56483 | 289.00219 | 450.73593 | 700.23299 |

## Future Amount of Ordinary Annuity of $1 per Period: $A_{\overline{n}|i} = \dfrac{(1 + i)^n - 1}{i}$

| n \ i | 5% | 5.5% | 6% | 6.5% | 7% | 8% |
|---|---|---|---|---|---|---|
| 1 | 1.00000 | 1.00000 | 1.00000 | 1.00000 | 1.00000 | 1.00000 |
| 2 | 2.05000 | 2.05500 | 2.06000 | 2.06500 | 2.07000 | 2.08000 |
| 3 | 3.15250 | 3.16802 | 3.18360 | 3.19922 | 3.21490 | 3.24640 |
| 4 | 4.31012 | 4.34227 | 4.37462 | 4.40717 | 4.43994 | 4.50611 |
| 5 | 5.52563 | 5.58109 | 5.63709 | 5.69364 | 5.75074 | 5.86660 |
| 6 | 6.80191 | 6.88805 | 6.97532 | 7.06373 | 7.15329 | 7.33593 |
| 7 | 8.14201 | 8.26689 | 8.39384 | 8.52287 | 8.65402 | 8.92280 |
| 8 | 9.54911 | 9.72157 | 9.89747 | 10.07688 | 10.25980 | 10.63663 |
| 9 | 11.02656 | 11.25626 | 11.49132 | 11.73185 | 11.97799 | 12.48756 |
| 10 | 12.57789 | 12.87535 | 13.18080 | 13.49442 | 13.81645 | 14.48656 |
| 11 | 14.20679 | 14.58350 | 14.97184 | 15.37156 | 15.78360 | 16.64549 |
| 12 | 15.91713 | 16.38559 | 16.86994 | 17.37071 | 17.88845 | 18.97713 |
| 13 | 17.71298 | 18.28680 | 18.88214 | 19.49981 | 20.14064 | 21.49530 |
| 14 | 19.59863 | 20.29257 | 21.01505 | 21.76730 | 22.55049 | 24.21492 |
| 15 | 21.57856 | 22.40866 | 23.27597 | 24.18217 | 25.12902 | 27.15211 |
| 16 | 23.65749 | 24.64114 | 25.67253 | 26.75401 | 27.88805 | 30.32428 |
| 17 | 25.84037 | 28.99640 | 28.21288 | 29.49302 | 30.84022 | 33.75023 |
| 18 | 28.13238 | 29.48120 | 30.90565 | 32.41007 | 33.99903 | 37.45024 |
| 19 | 30.53900 | 32.10267 | 33.75999 | 35.51672 | 37.37896 | 41.44626 |
| 20 | 33.06595 | 34.86832 | 36.78559 | 38.82531 | 40.99549 | 45.76196 |
| 21 | 35.71925 | 37.78608 | 39.99273 | 42.34895 | 44.86518 | 50.42292 |
| 22 | 38.50521 | 40.86431 | 43.39229 | 46.10164 | 49.00574 | 55.45676 |
| 23 | 41.43048 | 44.11185 | 46.99583 | 50.09824 | 53.43614 | 60.89330 |
| 24 | 44.50200 | 47.53800 | 50.81558 | 54.35463 | 58.17667 | 66.76476 |
| 25 | 47.72710 | 51.15259 | 54.86451 | 58.88768 | 63.24904 | 73.10594 |
| 26 | 51.11345 | 54.96598 | 59.15638 | 63.71538 | 68.67647 | 79.95442 |
| 27 | 54.66913 | 58.98911 | 63.70577 | 68.85688 | 74.48382 | 87.35077 |
| 28 | 58.40258 | 63.23351 | 68.52811 | 74.33257 | 80.69769 | 95.33883 |
| 29 | 62.32271 | 67.71135 | 73.62980 | 80.16419 | 87.34653 | 103.96594 |
| 30 | 66.43885 | 72.43548 | 79.05819 | 86.37486 | 94.46079 | 113.28321 |
| 31 | 70.76079 | 77.41943 | 84.80168 | 92.98923 | 102.07304 | 123.34587 |
| 32 | 75.29883 | 82.67750 | 90.88978 | 100.03353 | 110.21815 | 134.21354 |
| 33 | 80.06377 | 88.22476 | 97.34316 | 107.53571 | 118.93342 | 145.95062 |
| 34 | 85.06696 | 94.07712 | 104.18376 | 115.52553 | 128.25876 | 158.62667 |
| 35 | 90.32031 | 100.25136 | 111.43478 | 124.03469 | 138.23688 | 172.31680 |
| 40 | 120.79977 | 136.60561 | 154.76197 | 175.63192 | 199.63511 | 259.05652 |
| 45 | 159.70016 | 184.11917 | 212.74351 | 246.32459 | 285.74931 | 386.50562 |
| 50 | 209.34800 | 246.21748 | 290.33591 | 343.17967 | 406.52893 | 573.77016 |

## Future Amount of Ordinary Annuity of $1 per Period: $A_{\overline{n}|i} = (1 + i)^n - 1/i$

| $n \backslash i$ | 9% | 10% | 11% | 12% | 13% | 14% |
|---|---|---|---|---|---|---|
| 1 | 1.00000 | 1.00000 | 1.00000 | 1.00000 | 1.00000 | 1.00000 |
| 2 | 2.09000 | 2.10000 | 2.11000 | 2.12000 | 2.13000 | 2.14000 |
| 3 | 3.27810 | 3.31000 | 3.34210 | 3.37440 | 3.40690 | 3.43960 |
| 4 | 4.57313 | 4.64100 | 4.70973 | 4.77933 | 4.84980 | 4.92114 |
| 5 | 5.98471 | 6.10510 | 6.22780 | 6.35285 | 6.48027 | 6.61010 |
| 6 | 7.52334 | 7.71561 | 7.91286 | 8.11519 | 8.32271 | 8.53552 |
| 7 | 9.20044 | 9.48717 | 9.78327 | 10.08901 | 10.40466 | 10.73049 |
| 8 | 11.02847 | 11.43589 | 11.85943 | 12.29969 | 12.75726 | 13.23276 |
| 9 | 13.02104 | 13.57948 | 14.16397 | 14.77566 | 15.41571 | 16.08535 |
| 10 | 15.19293 | 15.93742 | 16.72201 | 17.54874 | 18.41975 | 19.33730 |
| 11 | 17.56029 | 18.53117 | 19.56143 | 20.65458 | 21.81432 | 23.04452 |
| 12 | 20.14072 | 21.38428 | 22.71319 | 24.13313 | 25.65018 | 27.27075 |
| 13 | 22.95338 | 24.52271 | 26.21164 | 28.02911 | 29.98470 | 32.08865 |
| 14 | 26.01919 | 27.97498 | 30.09492 | 32.39260 | 34.88271 | 37.58107 |
| 15 | 29.36092 | 31.77248 | 34.40536 | 37.27972 | 40.41746 | 43.84241 |
| 16 | 33.00340 | 35.94973 | 39.18995 | 42.75328 | 46.67173 | 50.98035 |
| 17 | 36.97370 | 40.54470 | 44.50084 | 48.88367 | 53.73906 | 59.11760 |
| 18 | 41.30134 | 45.59917 | 50.39594 | 55.74972 | 61.72514 | 68.39407 |
| 19 | 46.01846 | 51.15909 | 56.93949 | 63.43968 | 70.74941 | 78.96923 |
| 20 | 51.16012 | 57.27500 | 64.20283 | 72.05244 | 80.94683 | 91.02493 |
| 21 | 56.76453 | 64.00250 | 72.26514 | 81.69874 | 92.46992 | 104.76842 |
| 22 | 62.87334 | 71.40275 | 81.21431 | 92.50258 | 105.49101 | 120.43600 |
| 23 | 69.53194 | 79.54302 | 91.14788 | 104.60289 | 120.20484 | 138.29704 |
| 24 | 76.78981 | 88.49733 | 102.17415 | 118.15524 | 136.83147 | 158.65862 |
| 25 | 84.70090 | 98.34706 | 114.41331 | 133.33387 | 155.61956 | 181.87083 |
| 26 | 93.32398 | 109.18176 | 127.99877 | 150.33393 | 176.85010 | 208.33274 |
| 27 | 102.72314 | 121.09994 | 143.07864 | 169.37401 | 200.84061 | 238.49933 |
| 28 | 112.96822 | 134.20994 | 159.81729 | 190.69889 | 227.94989 | 272.88923 |
| 29 | 124.13536 | 148.63093 | 178.39719 | 214.58275 | 258.58338 | 312.09373 |
| 30 | 136.30754 | 164.49402 | 199.02088 | 241.33268 | 293.19922 | 356.78685 |
| 31 | 149.57522 | 181.94342 | 221.91317 | 271.29261 | 332.31511 | 407.73701 |
| 32 | 164.03699 | 201.13777 | 247.32362 | 304.84772 | 376.51608 | 465.82019 |
| 33 | 179.80032 | 222.25154 | 275.52922 | 342.42945 | 426.46317 | 532.03501 |
| 34 | 196.98234 | 245.47670 | 306.83744 | 384.52098 | 482.90338 | 607.51991 |
| 35 | 215.71076 | 271.02437 | 341.58955 | 431.66350 | 546.68082 | 693.57270 |
| 40 | 337.88244 | 442.59256 | 581.82607 | 767.09142 | 1013.70424 | 1342.02510 |
| 45 | 525.85873 | 718.90484 | 986.63856 | 1358.23003 | 1874.16463 | 2590.56480 |
| 50 | 815.08356 | 1163.90853 | 1668.77115 | 2400.01825 | 3459.50712 | 4994.52135 |

# appendix B

# Alternative Methods of Recording Deferrals

As discussed in Chapter 3, deferrals are created by recording a transaction in a way that delays or defers the recognition of an expense or a revenue. Deferrals may be either deferred expenses (prepaid expenses) or deferred revenues (unearned revenues).

In Chapter 2, deferred expenses (prepaid expenses) were debited to an *asset* account at the time of payment. As an alternative, deferred expenses may be debited to an *expense* account at the time of payment. In Chapter 2, deferred revenues (unearned revenues) were credited to a *liability* account at the time of receipt. As an alternative, deferred revenues may be credited to a *revenue* account at the time of receipt. This appendix describes and illustrates these alternative methods of recording deferred expenses and deferred revenues.

## Deferred Expenses (Prepaid Expenses)

As a basis for illustrating the alternative methods of recording deferred expenses, the insurance premium paid by NetSolutions in Chapter 2 is used. The amounts related to this insurance are as follows:

| | |
|---|---:|
| Prepayment of insurance for 24 months, starting December 1 | $2,400 |
| Insurance premium expired during December | 100 |
| Unexpired insurance premium at the end of December | $2,300 |

Based on the above data, the entries to account for the deferred expense (prepaid insurance) recorded initially as an *asset* are shown in the journal and T accounts in Exhibit 1. The adjusting entry in Exhibit 1 was shown in Chapter 3. The entries to account for the prepaid insurance recorded initially as an *expense* are shown in the journal and T accounts in Exhibit 2.

## •Exhibit 1

**Prepaid Expense Recorded Initially as Asset**

Initial entry (to record initial payment):

| Dec. 1 | Prepaid Insurance | 2,400 | |
| | Cash | | 2,400 |

Adjusting entry (to transfer amount *used* to the proper *expense* account):

| Dec. 31 | Insurance Expense | 100 | |
| | Prepaid Insurance | | 100 |

Closing entry (to close income statement accounts with debit balances):

| Income Summary | XXXX | |
| Supplies Expense | | XXXX |
| ～～～～～～ | | |
| Insurance Expense | | 100 |

**Prepaid Insurance**

| Dec. 1 | | 2,400 | Dec. 31 | Adjusting | 100 |

**Insurance Expense**

| Dec. 31 | Adjusting | 100 | Dec. 31 | Closing | 100 |

## •Exhibit 2

**Prepaid Expense Recorded Initially as Expense**

Initial entry (to record initial payment):

| Dec. 1 | Insurance Expense | 2,400 | |
| | Cash | | 2,400 |

Adjusting entry (to transfer amount *unused* to the proper *asset* account):

| Dec. 31 | Prepaid Insurance | 2,300 | |
| | Insurance Expense | | 2,300 |

Closing entry (to close income statement accounts with debit balances):

| Income Summary | XXXX | |
| Supplies Expense | | XXXX |
| ～～～～～～ | | |
| Insurance Expense | | 100 |

**Prepaid Insurance**

| Dec. 31 | Adjusting | 2,300 | | |

**Insurance Expense**

| Dec. 1 | | 2,400 | Dec. 31 | Adjusting | 2,300 |
| | | | 31 | Closing | 100 |

Either of the two methods of recording deferred expenses (prepaid expenses) may be used. As illustrated in Exhibits 1 and 2, both methods result in the same account balances after the adjusting entries have been recorded. Therefore, the amounts reported as expenses in the income statement and as assets on the balance sheet will not be affected by the method used. To avoid confusion, the method used by a business for each kind of prepaid expense should be followed consistently from year to year.

Some businesses record all deferred expenses using one method. Other businesses use one method to record the prepayment of some expenses and the other method for other expenses. Initial debits to the asset account are logical for prepayments of insurance, which are usually for periods of one to three years. On the other hand, rent on a building may be prepaid on the first of each month. The prepaid rent will expire by the end of the month. In this case, it is logical to record the payment of rent by initially debiting an expense account rather than an asset account.

## Deferred Revenues (Unearned Revenues)

To illustrate the alternative methods of recording deferred revenues, we will use the rent received by NetSolutions in Chapter 2. NetSolutions rented land on December 1 to a local retailer for use as a parking lot for three months and received $360 for the entire three months. On December 31, $120 (1/3 × $360) of the rent has been earned, and $240 (2/3 × $360) of the rent is still unearned.

Based on the above data, the entries to account for the deferred revenue (unearned rent) recorded initially as a liability are shown in the journal and ledger in Exhibit 3. The adjusting entry in Exhibit 3 was shown in Chapter 3. The entries to account for the unearned rent recorded initially as revenue are shown in the journal and ledger in Exhibit 4.

As illustrated in Exhibits 3 and 4, both methods result in the same account balances after the adjusting entries have been recorded. Therefore, the amounts reported as revenues in the income statement and as liabilities on the balance sheet will not be affected by the method used. Either of the methods may be used for all

---

## •Exhibit 3

**Unearned Revenue Recorded Initially as Liability**

Initial entry (to record initial receipt):

| Dec. | 1 | Cash | 360 | |
|---|---|---|---|---|
| | | Unearned Rent | | 360 |

Adjusting entry (to transfer amount *earned* to proper *revenue* account):

| Dec. | 31 | Unearned Rent | 120 | |
|---|---|---|---|---|
| | | Rent Revenue | | 120 |

Closing entry (to close income statement accounts with credit balances):

| Dec. | 31 | Fees Earned | XXXX | |
|---|---|---|---|---|
| | | Rent Revenue | 120 | |
| | | Income Summary | | XXXX |

**Unearned Rent**

| Dec. 31 | Adjusting | 120 | Dec. 1 | | 360 |
|---|---|---|---|---|---|

**Rent Revenue**

| Dec. 31 | Closing | 120 | Dec. 31 | Adjusting | 120 |
|---|---|---|---|---|---|

## •Exhibit 4

**Unearned Revenue Recorded Initially as Revenue**

Initial entry (to record initial receipt):

| Dec. | 1 | Cash | 360 | |
|---|---|---|---|---|
| | | Rent Revenue | | 360 |

Adjusting entry (to transfer amount *unearned* to proper *liability* account):

| Dec. | 31 | Rent Revenue | 240 | |
|---|---|---|---|---|
| | | Unearned Rent | | 240 |

Closing entry (to close income statement accounts with credit balances):

| Dec. | 31 | Fees Earned | XXXX | |
|---|---|---|---|---|
| | | Rent Revenue | 120 | |
| | | Income Summary | | XXXX |

**Unearned Rent**

| | | | Dec. 31 | Adjusting | 240 |
|---|---|---|---|---|---|

**Rent Revenue**

| Dec. 31 | Adjusting | 240 | Dec. 1 | | 360 |
|---|---|---|---|---|---|
| 31 | Closing | 120 | | | |

revenues received in advance. Alternatively, the first method may be used for advance receipts of some kinds of revenue and the second method for other kinds. To avoid confusion, the method used by a business for each kind of unearned revenue should be followed consistently from year to year.

## Reversing Entries for Deferrals

As discussed in the appendix at the end of Chapter 4, the use of reversing entries is optional. However, the use of reversing entries generally simplifies the analysis of transactions and reduces the likelihood of errors in the subsequent recording of transactions. Normally, reversing entries are prepared for deferrals in the following two cases:

1. When a deferred expense (prepaid expense) is initially recorded as an expense.
2. When a deferred revenue (unearned revenue) is initially recorded as a revenue.

The entry to reverse the adjustment to record the prepaid insurance in Exhibit 2 is as follows:

| | | | | |
|---|---|---|---|---|
| Jan. 1 | Insurance Expense | 2,300 | |
| | Prepaid Insurance | | 2,300 |

The entry to reverse the adjustment to record the unearned rent in Exhibit 4 is as follows:

| | | | | |
|---|---|---|---|---|
| Jan. 1 | Unearned Rent | 240 | |
| | Rent Revenue | | 240 |

# Exercises

**EXERCISE B-1**
*Adjusting entries for office supplies*

The office supplies purchased during the year total $4,570, and the amount of office supplies on hand at the end of the year is $460.

a. Record the following transactions directly in T accounts for Office Supplies and Office Supplies Expense, using the system of initially recording supplies as an asset: (1) purchases for the period; (2) adjusting entry at the end of the period. Identify each entry by number.
b. Record the following transactions directly in T accounts for Office Supplies and Office Supplies Expense, using the system of initially recording supplies as an expense: (1) purchases for the period; (2) adjusting entry at the end of the period. Identify each entry by number.

**EXERCISE B-2**
*Adjusting entries for prepaid insurance*

During the first year of operations, insurance premiums of $11,400 were paid. At the end of the year, unexpired premiums totaled $4,175. Journalize the adjusting entry at the end of the year, assuming that (a) prepaid expenses were initially recorded as assets and (b) prepaid expenses were initially recorded as expenses.

**EXERCISE B-3**
*Adjusting entries for advertising revenue*

The unearned advertising revenues collected in advance during the year total $482,800, and the unearned advertising revenue at the end of the year is $112,500.

a. Record the following transactions directly in T accounts for Unearned Advertising Revenue and Advertising Revenue, using the system of initially recording advertising fees as a liability: (1) revenues received during the period; (2) adjusting entry at the end of the period. Identify each entry by number.
b. Record the following transactions directly in T accounts for Unearned Advertising Revenue and Advertising Revenue, using the system of initially recording advertising fees as revenue: (1) revenues received during the period; (2) adjusting entry at the end of the period. Identify each entry by number.

**EXERCISE B-4**
*Year-end entries for deferred revenues*

In its first year of operation, Martin Publishing Co. received $3,275,000 in advance from advertising contracts and $9,195,000 in advance from magazine subscriptions, crediting the two amounts to Unearned Advertising Revenue and Circulation Revenue, respectively. At the end of the year, the unearned advertising revenue amounts to $396,000, and the circulation revenue amounts to $3,150,000. Journalize the adjusting entries that should be made at the end of the year.

# appendix C

# Periodic Inventory Systems for Merchandising Businesses

In this text, we emphasize the perpetual inventory system of accounting for purchases and sales of merchandise. Not all merchandise businesses, however, use perpetual inventory systems. For example, some managers/owners of small merchandise businesses, such as locally owned hardware stores, may feel more comfortable using manually kept records. Because a manual perpetual inventory system is time-consuming and costly to maintain, the periodic inventory system is often used in these cases.

## Merchandise Transactions in a Periodic Inventory System

In a periodic inventory system, the revenues from sales are recorded when sales are made in the same manner as in a perpetual inventory system. However, no attempt is made on the date of sale to record the cost of the merchandise sold. Instead, the merchandise inventory on hand at the end of the period is counted. This physical inventory is then used to determine (1) the cost of merchandise sold during the period and (2) the cost of merchandise on hand at the end of the period.

In a periodic inventory system, purchases of inventory are recorded in a purchases account rather than in a merchandise inventory account. No attempt is made to keep a detailed record of the amount of inventory on hand at any given time.

The purchases account is normally debited for the amount of the invoice before considering any purchases discounts. Purchases discounts are normally recorded in a separate purchases discounts account.[1] The balance of this account is reported as a deduction from the amount initially recorded in Purchases for the period. Thus, the purchases discounts account is viewed as a contra (or offsetting) account to Purchases.

Purchases returns and allowances are recorded in a similar manner as purchases discounts. A separate account is used to keep a record of the amount of purchases returns and allowances during a period. Purchases returns and allowances are reported as a deduction from the amount initially recorded as Purchases. Like Purchases Discounts, the purchases returns and allowances account is a contra (or offsetting) account to Purchases.

When merchandise is purchased FOB shipping point, the buyer is responsible for paying the freight charges. In a periodic inventory system, freight charges paid when purchasing merchandise FOB shipping point are debited to Transportation In, Freight In, or a similarly titled account.

To illustrate the recording of merchandise transactions in a periodic system, we will use the following selected transactions for Taylor Co. We will also explain how the transaction would have been recorded under a perpetual system.

June 5.   Purchased $30,000 of merchandise on account from Owen Clothing, terms 2/10, n/30.

| | | |
|---|---|---|
| Purchases | 30,000 | |
| Accounts Payable—Owen Clothing | | 30,000 |

*Under the perpetual inventory system, such purchases would be recorded in the merchandise inventory account at their cost, $30,000.*

---

[1]Some businesses prefer to credit the purchases account. If this alternative is used, the balance of the purchases account will be a net amount—the total purchases less the total purchases discounts for the period.

June 8.   Returned merchandise purchased on account from Owen Clothing on
June 5, $500.

| Accounts Payable—Owen Clothing | 500 | |
|---|---|---|
| Purchases Returns and Allowances | | 500 |

*Under the perpetual inventory system, returns would be recorded as a credit to the merchandise inventory account at their cost of $500.*

June 15.   Paid Owen Clothing for purchase of June 5, less return of $500 and
discount of $590 [($30,000 − $500) × 2%].

| Accounts Payable—Owen Clothing | 29,500 | |
|---|---|---|
| Cash | | 28,910 |
| Purchases Discounts | | 590 |

*Under a perpetual inventory system, a purchases discount account is not used. Instead the merchandise inventory account is credited for the amount of the discount, $590.*

June 18.   Sold merchandise on account to Jones Co., $12,500, 1/10, n/30. The cost of
the merchandise sold was $9,000.

| Accounts Receivable—Jones Co. | 12,500 | |
|---|---|---|
| Sales | | 12,500 |

*The entry to record the sale is the same under both systems. Under the perpetual inventory system, the cost of merchandise sold and the reduction in merchandise inventory would also be recorded on the date of sale.*

June 21.   Received merchandise returned on account from Jones Co., $4,000.
The cost of the merchandise returned was $2,800.

| Sales Returns and Allowances | 4,000 | |
|---|---|---|
| Accounts Receivable—Jones Co. | | 4,000 |

*The entry to record the sales return is the same under both systems. In addition, the cost of the merchandise returned would be debited to the merchandise inventory account and credited to the cost of merchandise sold account under the perpetual inventory system.*

June 22.   Purchased merchandise from Norcross Clothiers, $15,000, terms FOB
shipping point, 2/15, n/30, with prepaid transportation charges of
$750 added to the invoice.

| Purchases | 15,000 | |
|---|---|---|
| Transportation In | 750 | |
| Accounts Payable—Norcross Clothiers | | 15,750 |

*This entry is similar to the June 5 entry for the purchase of merchandise. Since the transportation terms were FOB shipping point, the prepaid freight charges of $750 must be added to the invoice cost of $15,000. Under the perpetual inventory system, the purchase is recorded in the merchandise inventory account at the cost of $15,750 (invoice price plus transportation).*

June 28.   Received $8,415 as payment on account from Jones Co., less return of
June 21 and less discount of $85 [($12,500 − $4,000) × 1%].

| Cash | 8,415 | |
|---|---|---|
| Sales Discounts | 85 | |
| Accounts Receivable—Jones Co. | | 8,500 |

*This entry is the same under the perpetual inventory system.*

June 29.   Received $19,600 from cash sales. The cost of the merchandise sold was $13,800.

| | | |
|---|---:|---:|
| Cash | 19,600 | |
| Sales | | 19,600 |

*The entry to record the sale is the same under both systems. Under the perpetual inventory system, the cost of merchandise sold and the reduction in merchandise inventory would also be recorded on the date of sale.*

The multiple-step income statement under the periodic inventory system is illustrated in Exhibit 1. The multiple-step income statement under a perpetual inventory system is similar, except that the cost of merchandise sold is reported as a single amount.

# Chart of Accounts for a Periodic Inventory System

Exhibit 2 is the chart of accounts for NetSolutions when a periodic inventory system is used. The periodic inventory accounts related to merchandising transactions are shown in color.

# End-of-Period Procedures in a Periodic Inventory System

The end-of-period procedures are generally the same for the periodic and perpetual inventory systems. In the remainder of this appendix, we will discuss the differences in procedures for the two systems that affect the work sheet, the adjusting entries, and the closing entries. As the basis for illustrations, we will use the data for NetSolutions, presented in Chapter 6.

# Work Sheet

The differences in the work sheet for a merchandising business that uses the periodic inventory system are highlighted in the work sheet for NetSolutions in Exhibit 3. As we illustrated earlier, accounts for purchases, purchases returns and allowances, purchases discounts, and transportation in are used in a periodic inventory system.

Under the periodic inventory system, the merchandise inventory account, throughout the accounting period, shows the inventory at the beginning of the period. The merchandise inventory on January 1, 2007, $59,700, is a part of the merchandise available for sale. At the end of the period, the beginning inventory amount in the ledger is replaced with the ending inventory amount. To update the inventory account, two adjusting entries are used.[2] The first adjusting entry transfers the beginning inventory balance to Income Summary. This entry, shown below, has the effect of increasing the cost of merchandise sold and decreasing net income.

| | | | |
|---|---|---:|---:|
| Dec. 31 | Income Summary | 59,700 | |
| | Merchandise Inventory | | 59,700 |

---

[2]Another method of updating the merchandise inventory account at the end of the period is called the *closing method*. This method adjusts the merchandise inventory through the use of closing entries. This method may not be appropriate for use in computerized accounting systems. Since the financial statements are the same under both methods and since computerized accounting systems are used by most businesses, the closing method is not illustrated.

•**Exhibit 1**    Multiple-Step Income Statement—Periodic Inventory System

---

**NetSolutions**
**Income Statement**
**For the Year Ended December 31, 2007**

| | | | |
|---|---|---|---|
| Revenue from sales: | | | |
|   Sales | | $720,185 | |
|   Less: Sales returns and allowances | $ 6,140 | | |
|       Sales discounts | 5,790 | 11,930 | |
|   Net sales | | | $708,255 |
| Cost of merchandise sold: | | | |
|   Merchandise inventory, January 1, 2007 | | $ 59,700 | |
|   Purchases | $521,980 | | |
|   Less: Purchases returns and allowances …… $9,100 | | | |
|       Purchases discounts …………… 2,525 | 11,625 | | |
|   Net purchases | $510,355 | | |
|   Add transportation in | 17,400 | | |
|     Cost of merchandise purchased | | $527,755 | |
|   Merchandise available for sale | | $587,455 | |
|   Less merchandise inventory, | | | |
|     December 31, 2007 | | 62,150 | |
|     Cost of merchandise sold | | | 525,305 |
| Gross profit | | | $182,950 |
| Operating expenses: | | | |
|   Selling expenses: | | | |
|     Sales salaries expense | $ 56,230 | | |
|     Advertising expense | 10,860 | | |
|     Depreciation expense—store equipment | 3,100 | | |
|     Miscellaneous selling expense | 630 | | |
|       Total selling expenses | | $ 70,820 | |
|   Administrative expenses: | | | |
|     Office salaries expense | $ 21,020 | | |
|     Rent expense | 8,100 | | |
|     Depreciation expense—office equipment | 2,490 | | |
|     Insurance expense | 1,910 | | |
|     Office supplies expense | 610 | | |
|     Miscellaneous administrative expense | 760 | | |
|       Total administrative expenses | | 34,890 | |
|     Total operating expenses | | | 105,710 |
| Income from operations | | | $ 77,240 |
| Other income and expense: | | | |
|   Rent revenue | | $   600 | |
|   Interest expense | | 2,440 | 1,840 |
| Net income | | | $ 75,400 |

---

After the first adjusting entry has been recorded and posted, the balance of the merchandise inventory account is zero. The second adjusting entry records the cost of the merchandise on hand at the end of the period by debiting Merchandise Inventory. Since the merchandise inventory at December 31, 2007, $62,150, is subtracted from the cost of merchandise available for sale in determining the cost of

## •Exhibit 2   Chart of Accounts—Periodic Inventory System

| Balance Sheet Accounts | Income Statement Accounts |
|---|---|
| **100 Assets** | **400 Revenues** |
| 110 Cash | 410 Sales |
| 111 Notes Receivable | 411 Sales Returns and Allowances |
| 112 Accounts Receivable | 412 Sales Discounts |
| 115 Merchandise Inventory | |
| 116 Office Supplies | **500 Costs and Expenses** |
| 117 Prepaid Insurance | 510 Purchases |
| 120 Land | 511 Purchases Returns and Allowances |
| 123 Store Equipment | 512 Purchases Discounts |
| 124 Accumulated Depreciation—Store Equipment | 513 Transportation In |
| 125 Office Equipment | 520 Sales Salaries Expense |
| 126 Accumulated Depreciation—Office Equipment | 521 Advertising Expense |
| | 522 Depreciation Expense—Store Equipment |
| **200 Liabilities** | 523 Transportation Out |
| 210 Accounts Payable | 529 Miscellaneous Selling Expense |
| 211 Salaries Payable | 530 Office Salaries Expense |
| 212 Unearned Rent | 531 Rent Expense |
| 215 Notes Payable | 532 Depreciation Expense—Office Equipment |
| | 533 Insurance Expense |
| **300 Owner's Equity** | 534 Office Supplies Expense |
| 310 Chris Clark, Capital | 539 Misc. Administrative Expense |
| 311 Chris Clark, Drawing | |
| 312 Income Summary | **600 Other Income** |
| | 610 Rent Revenue |
| | |
| | **700 Other Expense** |
| | 710 Interest Expense |

merchandise sold, Income Summary is credited. This credit has the effect of decreasing the cost of merchandise available for sale during the period, $587,455, by the cost of the unsold merchandise. The second adjusting entry is shown below.

Dec. 31   Merchandise Inventory        62,150
                Income Summary                         62,150

After the second adjusting entry has been recorded and posted, the balance of the merchandise inventory account is the amount of the ending inventory. The accounts for Merchandise Inventory and Income Summary after both entries have been posted would appear in T account form as follows:

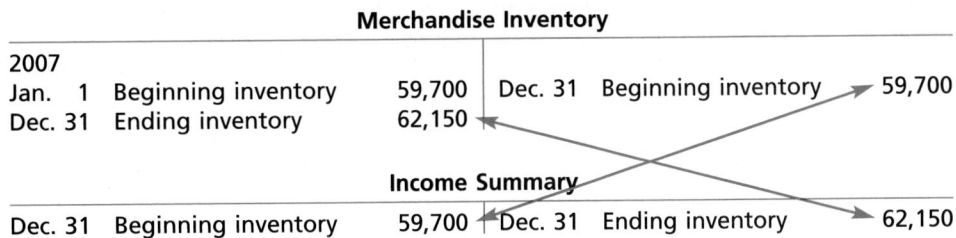

No separate adjusting entry can be made for merchandise inventory shrinkage in a periodic inventory system. This is because no perpetual inventory records are available to show what inventory should be on hand at the end of the period.

# •Exhibit 3   Work Sheet—Periodic Inventory System

**NetSolutions**
**Work Sheet**
**For the Year Ended December 31, 2007**

| Account Title | Trial Balance Dr. | Trial Balance Cr. | Adjustments Dr. | Adjustments Cr. | Adjusted Trial Balance Dr. | Adjusted Trial Balance Cr. | Income Statement Dr. | Income Statement Cr. | Balance Sheet Dr. | Balance Sheet Cr. |
|---|---|---|---|---|---|---|---|---|---|---|
| Cash | 52,950 | | | | 52,950 | | | | 52,950 | |
| Accounts Receivable | 91,080 | | | | 91,080 | | | | 91,080 | |
| Merchandise Inventory | 59,700 | | (b)62,150 | (a)59,700 | 62,150 | | | | 62,150 | |
| Office Supplies | 1,090 | | | (c) 610 | 480 | | | | 480 | |
| Prepaid Insurance | 4,560 | | | (d) 1,910 | 2,650 | | | | 2,650 | |
| Land | 20,000 | | | | 20,000 | | | | 20,000 | |
| Store Equipment | 27,100 | | | | 27,100 | | | | 27,100 | |
| Accum. Depr.—Store Equipment | | 2,600 | | (e) 3,100 | | 5,700 | | | | 5,700 |
| Office Equipment | 15,570 | | | | 15,570 | | | | 15,570 | |
| Accum. Depr.—Office Equipment | | 2,230 | | (f) 2,490 | | 4,720 | | | | 4,720 |
| Accounts Payable | | 22,420 | | | | 22,420 | | | | 22,420 |
| Salaries Payable | | | | (g) 1,140 | | 1,140 | | | | 1,140 |
| Unearned Rent | | 2,400 | (h) 600 | | | 1,800 | | | | 1,800 |
| Notes Payable (final payment, 2017) | | 25,000 | | | | 25,000 | | | | 25,000 |
| Chris Clark, Capital | | 153,800 | | | | 153,800 | | | | 153,800 |
| Chris Clark, Drawing | 18,000 | | | | 18,000 | | | | 18,000 | |
| Income Summary | | | (a)59,700 | (b)62,150 | 59,700 | 62,150 | 59,700 | 62,150 | | |
| Sales | | 720,185 | | | | 720,185 | | 720,185 | | |
| Sales Returns and Allowances | 6,140 | | | | 6,140 | | 6,140 | | | |
| Sales Discounts | 5,790 | | | | 5,790 | | 5,790 | | | |
| Purchases | 521,980 | | | | 521,980 | | 521,980 | | | |
| Purchases Returns & Allowances | | 9,100 | | | | 9,100 | | 9,100 | | |
| Purchases Discounts | | 2,525 | | | | 2,525 | | 2,525 | | |
| Transportation In | 17,400 | | | | 17,400 | | 17,400 | | | |
| Sales Salaries Expense | 55,450 | | (g) 780 | | 60,030 | | 60,030 | | | |
| Advertising Expense | 10,860 | | | | 10,860 | | 10,860 | | | |
| Depr. Expense—Store Equipment | | | (e) 3,100 | | 3,100 | | 3,100 | | | |
| Miscellaneous Selling Expense | 630 | | | | 630 | | 630 | | | |
| Office Salaries Expense | 20,660 | | (g) 360 | | 21,020 | | 21,020 | | | |
| Rent Expense | 8,100 | | | | 8,100 | | 8,100 | | | |
| Depr. Expense—Office Equipment | | | (f) 2,490 | | 2,490 | | 2,490 | | | |
| Insurance Expense | | | (d) 1,910 | | 1,910 | | 1,910 | | | |
| Office Supplies Expense | | | (c) 610 | | 610 | | 610 | | | |
| Misc. Administrative Expense | 760 | | | | 760 | | 760 | | | |
| Rent Revenue | | | | (h) 600 | | 600 | | 600 | | |
| Interest Expense | 2,440 | | | | 2,440 | | 2,440 | | | |
| | 940,260 | 940,260 | 131,700 | 131,700 | 1,009,140 | 1,009,140 | 719,160 | 794,560 | 289,980 | 214,580 |
| Net Income | | | | | | | 75,400 | | | 75,400 |
| | | | | | | | 794,560 | 794,560 | 289,980 | 289,980 |

(a) Beginning merchandise inventory, $59,700.
(b) Ending merchandise inventory, $62,150.
(c) Office supplies used, $610 ($1,090 − $480).
(d) Insurance expired, $1,910.
(e) Depreciation of store equipment, $3,100.

(f) Depreciation of office equipment, $2,490.
(g) Salaries accrued but not paid (sales salaries, $780; office salaries, $360), $1,140.
(h) Rent earned from amount received in advance, $600.

One disadvantage of the periodic inventory system is that inventory shrinkage cannot be measured.[3]

## Completing the Work Sheet

After all of the necessary adjustments have been entered on the work sheet, the work sheet is completed in the normal manner. An exception to the usual practice of extending only account balances is Income Summary. Both the debit and credit amounts for Income Summary are extended to the Adjusted Trial Balance columns. Extending both amounts aids in the preparation of the income statement because the debit adjustment (the beginning inventory of $59,700) and the credit adjustment (the ending inventory of $62,150) are reported as part of the cost of merchandise sold.

The purchases, purchases discounts, purchases returns and allowances, and transportation in accounts are extended to the Income Statement Columns of the work sheet, since they are used in computing the cost of merchandise sold. You should note that the two merchandise inventory amounts in Income Summary are extended to the Income Statement columns. After all of the items have been extended to the statement columns, the four columns are totaled and the net income or net loss is determined.

## Financial Statements

The financial statements for NetSolutions are essentially the same under both the perpetual and periodic inventory systems. The main difference is that the cost of goods is reported as a single amount under the perpetual system. Exhibit 1 illustrates the manner in which cost of merchandise sold is reported in a multiple-step income statement when the periodic inventory system is used.[4]

## Adjusting and Closing Entries

The adjusting entries are the same under both inventory systems, except for merchandise inventory. As indicated previously, two adjusting entries for beginning and ending merchandise inventory are necessary in a periodic inventory system.

The closing entries differ in the periodic inventory system in that there is no cost of merchandise sold account to be closed to Income Summary. Instead, the purchases, purchases discounts, purchases returns and allowances, and transportation in accounts are closed to Income Summary.[5] To illustrate, the adjusting and closing entries under a periodic inventory system for NetSolutions are shown at the top of the following pages.

---

[3]Any inventory shrinkage that does exist is part of the cost of merchandise sold and is reported on the income statement, since a smaller ending inventory is deducted from other merchandise available for sale.

[4]The single-step income statement would be the same for both the perpetual and the periodic inventory systems.

[5]The balance of Income Summary, after the merchandise inventory adjustments and the first two closing entries have been posted, is the net income or net loss for the period.

| | Date | | Description | Post. Ref. | Debit | Credit | |
|---|---|---|---|---|---|---|---|
| 1 | | | Adjusting Entries | | | | 1 |
| 2 | 2007 Dec. | 31 | Income Summary | 312 | 59 7 0 0 00 | | 2 |
| 3 | | | Merchandise Inventory | 115 | | 59 7 0 0 00 | 3 |
| 4 | | | | | | | 4 |
| 5 | | 31 | Merchandise Inventory | 115 | 62 1 5 0 00 | | 5 |
| 6 | | | Income Summary | 312 | | 62 1 5 0 00 | 6 |
| 7 | | | | | | | 7 |
| 8 | | 31 | Office Supplies Expense | 534 | 6 1 0 00 | | 8 |
| 9 | | | Office Supplies | 116 | | 6 1 0 00 | 9 |
| 10 | | | | | | | 10 |
| 11 | | 31 | Insurance Expense | 533 | 1 9 1 0 00 | | 11 |
| 12 | | | Prepaid Insurance | 117 | | 1 9 1 0 00 | 12 |
| 13 | | | | | | | 13 |
| 14 | | 31 | Depreciation Expense—Store Equip. | 522 | 3 1 0 0 00 | | 14 |
| 15 | | | Accumulated Depr.—Store Equip. | 124 | | 3 1 0 0 00 | 15 |
| 16 | | | | | | | 16 |
| 17 | | 31 | Depreciation Expense—Office Equip. | 532 | 2 4 9 0 00 | | 17 |
| 18 | | | Accumulated Depr.—Office Equip. | 126 | | 2 4 9 0 00 | 18 |
| 19 | | | | | | | 19 |
| 20 | | 31 | Sales Salaries Expense | 520 | 7 8 0 00 | | 20 |
| 21 | | | Office Salaries Expense | 530 | 3 6 0 00 | | 21 |
| 22 | | | Salaries Payable | 211 | | 1 1 4 0 00 | 22 |
| 23 | | | | | | | 23 |
| 24 | | 31 | Unearned Rent | 212 | 6 0 0 00 | | 24 |
| 25 | | | Rent Revenue | 610 | | 6 0 0 00 | 25 |

**JOURNAL**    Page 16

| | Date | | Description | Post. Ref. | Debit | Credit | |
|---|---|---|---|---|---|---|---|
| 1 | | | Closing Entries | | | | 1 |
| 2 | 2007 Dec. | 31 | Sales | 410 | 720 1 8 5 00 | | 2 |
| 3 | | | Purchases Returns and Allowances | 511 | 9 1 0 0 00 | | 3 |
| 4 | | | Purchases Discounts | 512 | 2 5 2 5 00 | | 4 |
| 5 | | | Rent Revenue | 610 | 6 0 0 00 | | 5 |
| 6 | | | Income Summary | 312 | | 732 4 1 0 00 | 6 |
| 7 | | | | | | | 7 |
| 8 | | 31 | Income Summary | 312 | 659 4 6 0 00 | | 8 |
| 9 | | | Sales Returns and Allowances | 411 | | 6 1 4 0 00 | 9 |
| 10 | | | Sales Discounts | 412 | | 5 7 9 0 00 | 10 |
| 11 | | | Purchases | 510 | | 521 9 8 0 00 | 11 |
| 12 | | | Transportation In | 513 | | 17 4 0 0 00 | 12 |
| 13 | | | Sales Salaries Expense | 520 | | 56 2 3 0 00 | 13 |
| 14 | | | Advertising Expense | 521 | | 10 8 6 0 00 | 14 |
| 15 | | | Depreciation Exp.—Store Equip. | 522 | | 3 1 0 0 00 | 15 |
| 16 | | | Miscellaneous Selling Expense | 529 | | 6 3 0 00 | 16 |
| 17 | | | Office Salaries Expense | 530 | | 21 0 2 0 00 | 17 |
| 18 | | | Rent Expense | 531 | | 8 1 0 0 00 | 18 |
| 19 | | | Depreciation Exp.—Office Equip. | 532 | | 2 4 9 0 00 | 19 |
| 20 | | | Insurance Expense | 533 | | 1 9 1 0 00 | 20 |
| 21 | | | Office Supplies Expense | 534 | | 6 1 0 00 | 21 |
| 22 | | | Miscellaneous Administrative Exp. | 539 | | 7 6 0 00 | 22 |
| 23 | | | Interest Expense | 710 | | 2 4 4 0 00 | 23 |
| 24 | | | | | | | 24 |
| 25 | | 31 | Income Summary | 312 | 75 4 0 0 00 | | 25 |
| 26 | | | Chris Clark, Capital | 310 | | 75 4 0 0 00 | 26 |
| 27 | | | | | | | 27 |
| 28 | | 31 | Chris Clark, Capital | 310 | 18 0 0 0 00 | | 28 |
| 29 | | | Chris Clark, Drawing | 311 | | 18 0 0 0 00 | 29 |

**JOURNAL** — Page 17

# Exercises

**EXERCISE C-1**
*Purchases-related transactions—periodic inventory system*

Journalize entries for the following related transactions, assuming that Mountain Gallery, Inc. uses the periodic inventory system.

a. Purchased $12,000 of merchandise from Yellowstone Co. on account, terms 2/10, n/30.
b. Discovered that some of the merchandise was defective and returned items with an invoice price of $2,500, receiving credit.
c. Paid the amount owed on the invoice within the discount period.
d. Purchased $9,000 of merchandise from Glacier, Inc. on account, terms 1/10, n/30.
e. Paid the amount owed on the invoice within the discount period.

**EXERCISE C-2**
*Sales-related transactions—periodic inventory system*

Journalize entries for the following related transactions, assuming that Aveda Company uses the periodic inventory system.

July 6 Sold merchandise to a customer for $18,500, terms FOB shipping point, 2/10, n/30.

6 Paid the transportation charges of $420, debiting the amount to Accounts Receivable.

9 Issued a credit memorandum for $4,700 to the customer for merchandise returned.

16 Received a check for the amount due from the sale.

**EXERCISE C-3**
*Adjusting entries for merchandise inventory—periodic inventory system*

Data assembled for preparing the work sheet for Meridian Co. for the fiscal year ended December 31, 2006, included the following:

| | |
|---|---|
| Merchandise inventory as of January 1, 2006 | $475,000 |
| Merchandise inventory as of December 31, 2006 | $528,300 |

Journalize the two adjusting entries for merchandise inventory that would appear on the work sheet, assuming that the periodic inventory system is used.

**EXERCISE C-4**
*Identification of missing items from income statement—periodic inventory system*

For (a) through (i), identify the items designated by "X" and "Y."

a. Sales $-$ (X + Y) = Net sales
b. Purchases $-$ (X + Y) = Net purchases
c. Net purchases + X = Cost of merchandise purchased
d. Merchandise inventory (beginning) + Cost of merchandise purchased = X
e. Merchandise available for sale $-$ X = Cost of merchandise sold
f. Net sales $-$ Cost of merchandise sold = X
g. Gross profit $-$ Operating expenses = X
h. X + Y = Operating expenses
i. Income from operations + X $-$ Y = Net income

**EXERCISE C-5**
*Multiple-step income statement—periodic inventory system*

✓ *Gross profit: $230,560*

Selected data for Canyon Ferry Stores Company for the year ended December 31, 2006, are as follows:

| | | | |
|---|---|---|---|
| Merchandise inventory, January 1 | $ 85,760 | Sales | $1,288,000 |
| Merchandise inventory, December 31 | 102,240 | Sales discounts | 10,400 |
| Purchases | 1,051,200 | Sales returns and allowances | 13,920 |
| Purchases discounts | 12,800 | Transportation in | 36,000 |
| Purchases returns and allowances | 24,800 | | |

Prepare a multiple-step income statement through gross profit for Canyon Ferry Stores Company for the current year ended December 31.

**EXERCISE C-6**
*Adjusting and closing entries—periodic inventory system*

Selected account titles and related amounts appearing in the Income Statement and Balance Sheet columns of the work sheet of Southern Bell Company for the year ended December 31 are listed in alphabetical order as follows:

| | | | |
|---|---|---|---|
| Administrative Expenses | $ 72,000 | Purchases | $ 820,000 |
| Building | 312,500 | Purchases Discounts | 14,000 |
| Cash | 58,500 | Purchases Returns and Allowances | 9,000 |
| Connie Sorum, Capital | 433,080 | Salaries Payable | 4,220 |
| Connie Sorum, Drawing | 40,000 | Sales | 1,450,000 |
| Interest Expense | 2,500 | Sales Discounts | 18,000 |
| Merchandise Inventory (1/1) | 300,000 | Sales Returns and Allowances | 32,000 |
| Merchandise Inventory (12/31) | 275,000 | Selling Expenses | 240,200 |
| Notes Payable | 25,000 | Store Supplies | 7,700 |
| Office Supplies | 10,600 | Transportation In | 21,300 |

All selling expenses have been recorded in the account entitled Selling Expenses, and all administrative expenses have been recorded in the account entitled Administrative Expenses. Assuming that Southern Bell Company uses the periodic inventory system, journalize (a) the adjusting entries for merchandise inventory and (b) the closing entries.

# Problems

**PROBLEM C-1**
*Sales-related and purchase-related transactions— periodic inventory system*

The following were selected from among the transactions completed by Infinet Shops, Inc., during November of the current year:

Nov. 2. Purchased merchandise on account from Loftin Co., list price $24,000, trade discount 25%, terms FOB destination, 2/10, n/30.

    8. Sold merchandise for cash, $8,100.

    9. Purchased merchandise on account from Chestnut Co., $12,000, terms FOB shipping point, 2/10, n/30, with prepaid transportation costs of $180 added to the invoice.

    10. Returned $3,000 of merchandise purchased on November 2 from Loftin Co.

    11. Sold merchandise on account to Fawcett Co., list price $2,500, trade discount 20%, terms 1/10, n/30.

    12. Paid Loftin Co. on account for purchase of November 2, less return of November 10 and discount.

    15. Sold merchandise on nonbank credit cards and reported accounts to the card company, American Express, $9,850.

    19. Paid Chestnut Co. on account for purchase of November 9, less discount.

    21. Received cash on account from sale of November 11 to Fawcett Co., less discount.

    25. Sold merchandise on account to Clemons Co., $3,000, terms 1/10, n/30.

    28. Received cash from American Express for nonbank credit card sales of November 15, less $380 service fee.

    30. Received merchandise returned by Clemons Co. from sale on November 25, $1,700.

### Instructions

Journalize the transactions for Infinet Shops, Inc., in a two-column general journal.

**PROBLEM C-2**
*Sales-related and purchase-related transactions— periodic inventory system*

The following were selected from among the transactions completed by Copra Sentry Company during July of the current year:

July 3. Purchased merchandise on account from Swanson Co., list price $60,000, trade discount 30%, terms FOB shipping point, 2/10, n/30, with prepaid transportation costs of $1,200 added to the invoice.

    4. Purchased merchandise on account from Lambert Co., $8,000, terms FOB destination, 1/10, n/30.

    7. Sold merchandise on account to Walsh Co., list price $12,000, trade discount 20%, terms 2/10, n/30.

    9. Returned merchandise purchased on July 4 from Lambert Co., $1,300.

    13. Paid Swanson Co. on account for purchase of July 3, less discount.

    14. Paid Lambert Co. on account for purchase of July 4, less return of July 9 and discount.

    17. Received cash on account from sale of July 7 to Walsh Co., less discount.

    19. Sold merchandise on nonbank credit cards and reported accounts to the card company, American Express, $7,450.

    22. Sold merchandise on account to Wu Co., $4,420, terms 2/10, n/30.

    24. Sold merchandise for cash, $4,350.

    25. Received merchandise returned by Wu Co. from sale on July 22, $1,610.

    31. Received cash from American Express for nonbank credit card sales of July 19, less $290 service fee.

### Instructions

Journalize the transactions for Copra Sentry Co. in a two-column general journal.

**PROBLEM C-3**
*Sales-related and purchase-related transactions for seller and buyer—periodic inventory system*

P.A.S.S.

The following selected transactions were completed during May between Simkins Company and Burk Co.:

May 6. Simkins Company sold merchandise on account to Burk Co., $18,500, terms FOB destination, 2/15, n/eom.

6. Simkins Company paid transportation costs of $600 for delivery of merchandise sold to Burk Co. on May 6.

10. Simkins Company sold merchandise on account to Burk Co., $15,750, terms FOB shipping point, n/eom.

11. Burk Co. returned merchandise purchased on account on May 6 from Simkins Company, $5,500.

14. Burk Co. paid transportation charges of $300 on May 10 purchase from Simkins Company.

17. Simkins Company sold merchandise on account to Burk Co., $30,000, terms FOB shipping point, 1/10, n/30. Simkins prepaid transportation costs of $1,750, which were added to the invoice.

21. Burk Co. paid Simkins Company for purchase of May 6, less discount and less return of May 11.

27. Burk Co. paid Simkins Company on account for purchase of May 17, less discount.

31. Burk Co. paid Simkins Company on account for purchase of May 10.

**Instructions**
Journalize the May transactions for (1) Simkins Company and for (2) Burk Co.

**PROBLEM C-4**
*Preparation of work sheet, financial statements, and adjusting and closing entries—periodic inventory system*

P.A.S.S.

✓ 1. Net income: $222,950

The accounts and their balances in the ledger of Sunshine Sports Co. on December 31, 2006, are as follows:

| | | | |
|---|---:|---|---:|
| Cash | $ 28,000 | Sales Discounts | $ 7,100 |
| Accounts Receivable | 142,500 | Purchases | 500,000 |
| Merchandise Inventory | 200,000 | Purchases Returns and Allowances | 10,100 |
| Prepaid Insurance | 9,700 | Purchases Discounts | 4,900 |
| Store Supplies | 4,250 | Transportation In | 11,200 |
| Office Supplies | 2,100 | Sales Salaries Expense | 81,400 |
| Store Equipment | 132,000 | Advertising Expense | 45,000 |
| Accumulated Depreciation— | | Depreciation Expense— | |
| Store Equipment | 40,300 | Store Equipment | — |
| Office Equipment | 50,000 | Store Supplies Expense | — |
| Accumulated Depreciation— | | Miscellaneous Selling Expense | 1,600 |
| Office Equipment | 17,200 | Office Salaries Expense | 44,000 |
| Accounts Payable | 56,700 | Rent Expense | 26,000 |
| Salaries Payable | — | Insurance Expense | — |
| Unearned Rent | 1,200 | Depreciation Expense— | |
| Note Payable (final payment, 2013) | 100,000 | Office Equipment | — |
| Sherri Vogel, Capital | 159,600 | Office Supplies Expense | — |
| Sherri Vogel, Drawing | 40,000 | Miscellaneous Administrative | |
| Income Summary | — | Expense | 1,650 |
| Sales | 960,000 | Rent Revenue | — |
| Sales Returns and Allowances | 11,900 | Interest Expense | 11,600 |

The data needed for year-end adjustments on December 31 are as follows:

| | | |
|---|---:|---:|
| Merchandise inventory on December 31 | | $215,000 |
| Insurance expired during the year | | 4,800 |
| Supplies on hand on December 31: | | |
| Store supplies | | 1,300 |
| Office supplies | | 750 |
| Depreciation for the year: | | |
| Store equipment | | 7,500 |
| Office equipment | | 3,800 |
| Salaries payable on December 31: | | |
| Sales salaries | $4,000 | |
| Office salaries | 2,000 | 6,000 |
| Unearned rent on December 31 | | 400 |

**Instructions**

1. Prepare a work sheet for the fiscal year ended December 31, listing all accounts in the order given.
2. Prepare a multiple-step income statement.
3. Prepare a statement of owner's equity.
4. Prepare a report form of balance sheet, assuming that the current portion of the note payable is $10,000.
5. Journalize the adjusting entries.
6. Journalize the closing entries.

# appendix D

# Foreign Currency Transactions

In this appendix, we describe and illustrate the accounting for transactions in which a U.S. company sells products or services to foreign companies or buys foreign products or services. If transactions with foreign companies require payment or receipt in U.S. dollars, no special accounting problems arise.[1] Such transactions are recorded as we described and illustrated earlier in this text. For example, the sale of merchandise to a Japanese company that is billed in and paid for in dollars would be recorded by the U.S. company in the normal manner. However, if the transaction is billed and payment is to be received in Japanese yen, the U.S. company may incur an exchange gain or loss. Some foreign manufacturers have begun building manufacturing plants in the United States, which avoids such gains and losses for denominated sales. For example, **BMW** has constructed its first U.S. plant.

## Realized Currency Exchange Gains and Losses

When a U.S. company receives foreign currency, the amount must be converted to its equivalent in U.S. dollars for recording in the accounts. When payment is to be made in a foreign currency, U.S. dollars must be exchanged for the foreign currency for payment. To illustrate, assume that a U.S. company purchases merchandise from a British company that requires payment in British pounds. In this case, U.S. dollars ($) must be exchanged for British pounds (£) to pay for the merchandise. This exchange of one currency for another involves using an exchange rate. The **exchange rate** is the rate at which one unit of currency (the dollar, for example) can be converted into another currency (the British pound, for example).

To continue the example, assume that the U.S. company had purchased merchandise for £1,000 from a British company on June 1, when the exchange rate was $1.40 per British pound. Thus, $1,400 must be exchanged for £1,000 to make the purchase.[2] The U.S. company records the transaction in dollars, as follows:

| | | | | | |
|---|---|---|---|---|---|
| June | 1 | Merchandise Inventory | 1 4 0 0 00 | | |
| | | Cash | | 1 4 0 0 00 | |
| | | Payment of Invoice No. 1725 from | | | |
| | | W. A. Sterling Co., £1,000; exchange | | | |
| | | rate, $1.40 per British pound. | | | |

Instead of a cash purchase, the purchase may be made on account. In this case, the exchange rate may change between the date of purchase and the date of payment of the account payable in the foreign currency. In practice, exchange rates vary daily.

To illustrate, assume that the preceding purchase was made on account. The entry to record it is as follows:

---

[1]This discussion is from the point of view of a U.S. company. Unless otherwise indicated, the reference to the dollar refers to the U.S. dollar rather than a dollar of another country, such as Canada.
[2]Foreign exchange rates are quoted in major financial reporting services. Because the exchange rates are quite volatile, those used in this chapter are assumed rates.

| | | | | | |
|---|---|---|---|---|---|
| June | 1 | Merchandise Inventory | 1 4 0 0 00 | | |
| | | Accounts Payable—W. A. Sterling Co. | | 1 4 0 0 00 | |
| | | Purchase on account; Invoice | | | |
| | | No. 1725 from W. A. Sterling Co., | | | |
| | | £1,000; exchange rate, $1.40 per | | | |
| | | British pound. | | | |

Assume that on the date of payment, June 15, the exchange rate was $1.45 per pound. The £1,000 account payable must be settled by exchanging $1,450 (£1,000 × $1.45) for £1,000. In this case, the U.S. company incurs an exchange loss of $50 because $1,450 was needed to settle a $1,400 account payable. The cash payment is recorded as follows:

| | | | | | |
|---|---|---|---|---|---|
| June | 15 | Accounts Payable—W. A. Sterling Co. | 1 4 0 0 00 | | |
| | | Exchange Loss | 5 0 00 | | |
| | | Cash | | 1 4 5 0 00 | |
| | | Cash paid on Invoice No. 1725, for | | | |
| | | £1,000, or $1,400, when exchange | | | |
| | | rate was $1.45 per pound. | | | |

We can analyze all transactions with foreign companies in the manner described. For example, assume that a sale on account for $1,000 to a Swiss company on May 1 was billed in Swiss francs. The cost of the merchandise sold was $600, and the selling company uses a perpetual inventory system. If the exchange rate was $0.25 per Swiss franc (F) on May 1, the transaction is recorded as follows:

| | | | | | |
|---|---|---|---|---|---|
| May | 1 | Accounts Receivable—D. W. Robinson Co. | 1 0 0 0 00 | | |
| | | Sales | | 1 0 0 0 00 | |
| | | Invoice No. 9772, F4,000; exchange | | | |
| | | rate, $0.25 per Swiss franc. | | | |
| | | | | | |
| | 1 | Cost of Merchandise Sold | 6 0 0 00 | | |
| | | Merchandise Inventory | | 6 0 0 00 | |

Assume that the exchange rate increases to $0.30 per Swiss franc on May 31 when cash is received. In this case, the U.S. company realizes an exchange gain of $200. This gain is realized because the F4,000, which had a value of $1,000 on the date of sale, has increased in value to $1,200 (F4,000 × $0.30) on May 31 when the payment is received. The receipt of the cash is recorded as follows:

| | | | | | |
|---|---|---|---|---|---|
| May | 31 | Cash | 1 2 0 0 00 | | |
| | | Accounts Receivable—D. W. Robinson Co. | | 1 0 0 0 00 | |
| | | Exchange Gain | | 2 0 0 00 | |
| | | Cash received on Invoice No. 9772, | | | |
| | | for F4,000, $1,000, when exchange | | | |
| | | rate was $0.30 per Swiss franc. | | | |

# Unrealized Currency Exchange Gains and Losses

In the previous examples, the transactions were completed by either the receipt or the payment of cash. On the date the cash was received or paid, any related exchange gain or loss was realized and was recorded in the accounts. However, financial statements may be prepared between the date of the sale or purchase on account and the date the cash is received or paid. In this case, any exchange gain or loss created by a change in exchange rates between the date of the original transaction and the balance sheet date must be recorded. Such an exchange gain or loss is reported in the financial statements as an unrealized exchange gain or loss.

To illustrate, assume that a sale on account for $1,000 had been made to a German company on December 20 and had been billed in euros. The cost of merchandise sold was $700. On this date, the exchange rate was $1.25 per euro. The transaction is recorded as follows:

| | | | | |
|---|---|---|---|---|
| Dec. | 20 | Accounts Receivable—T. A. Mueller Inc. | 1000 00 | |
| | | Sales | | 1000 00 |
| | | Invoice No. 1793, 800 euros; exchange | | |
| | | rate, $1.25 per euro. | | |
| | | | | |
| | 20 | Cost of Merchandise Sold | 700 00 | |
| | | Merchandise Inventory | | 700 00 |

Assume that the exchange rate decreases to $1.20 per euro on December 31, the date of the balance sheet. Thus, the $1,000 account receivable on December 31 has a value of only $960 (800 euros × $1.20). This unrealized loss of $40 ($1,000 − $960) is recorded as follows:

| | | | | |
|---|---|---|---|---|
| Dec. | 31 | Exchange Loss | 40 00 | |
| | | Accounts Receivable—T. A. Mueller Inc. | | 40 00 |
| | | Invoice No. 1793, 800 euros × $0.05 | | |
| | | decrease in exchange rate. | | |

Any additional change in the exchange rate during the following period is recorded when the cash is received. To continue the illustration, assume that the exchange rate declines from $1.20 to $1.18 per euro by January 19, when the 800 euros are received. The receipt of the cash on January 19 is recorded as follows:

| | | | | |
|---|---|---|---|---|
| Jan. | 19 | Cash (800 euros × $1.18) | 944 00 | |
| | | Exchange Loss (800 euros × $0.02) | 16 00 | |
| | | Accounts Receivable—T. A. Mueller Inc. | | 960 00 |
| | | Cash received on Invoice No. 1793, | | |
| | | for 800 euros, or $44, when exchange | | |
| | | rate was $1.18 per euro. | | |

In contrast, assume that in the preceding example the exchange rate increases between December 31 and January 19. In this case, an exchange gain would be recorded on January 19. For example, if the exchange rate increases from $1.20 to $1.24 per euro during this period, Exchange Gain would be credited for $32 (800 euros × $0.04).

A balance in the exchange loss account at the end of the fiscal period is reported in the Other Expense section of the income statement. A balance in the exchange gain account is reported in the Other Income section.

# Exercises

**EXERCISE D-1**
*Entries for sales made in foreign currency*

The E-Cube Toy Company makes sales on account to several Swedish companies that it bills in kronas. Journalize the entries for the following selected transactions completed during the current year, assuming that E-Cube uses the perpetual inventory system:

Mar. 9. Sold merchandise on account, 30,000 kronas; exchange rate, $0.12 per krona. The cost of merchandise sold was $2,100.

Apr. 8. Received cash from sale of March 9, 30,000 kronas; exchange rate, $0.13 per krona.

July 13. Sold merchandise on account, 27,000 kronas; exchange rate, $0.14 per krona. The cost of merchandise sold was $2,400.

Aug. 17. Received cash from sale of July 13, 27,000 kronas; exchange rate, $0.13 per krona.

**EXERCISE D-2**
*Entries for purchases made in foreign currency*

Crossroads Care Inc. sells artificial arms and legs to hospitals and physicians. It purchases merchandise from a German company that requires payment in Euros. Journalize the entries for the following selected transactions completed during the current year, assuming that Crossroads Care Inc. uses the perpetual inventory system:

Oct. 3. Purchased merchandise on account, net 30, 20,000 Euros; exchange rate, $0.99 per Euro.

Nov. 2. Paid invoice of October 3; exchange rate, $1.01 per Euro.

29. Purchased merchandise on account, net 30, 15,000 Euros; exchange rate, $1.00 per Euro.

Dec. 19. Paid invoice of Nov. 2; exchange rate, $0.98 per Euro.

# Problems

**PROBLEM D-1**
*Foreign currency transactions*

P.A.S.S.

Outdoor Sports is a wholesaler of sports equipment, including golf clubs and gym sets. It sells to and purchases from companies in Canada and the Philippines. These transactions are settled in the foreign currency. The following selected transactions were completed during the current fiscal year:

Feb. 10. Sold merchandise on account to Manco Company, net 30, 600,000 pesos; exchange rate, $0.018 per Philippines peso. The cost of merchandise sold was $6,000.

Mar. 12. Received cash from Manco Company; exchange rate, $0.017 per Philippines peso.

20. Purchased merchandise on account from Fossum Inc., net 30, $20,000 Canadian; exchange rate, $0.65 per Canadian dollar.

Apr. 11. Issued check for amount owed to Fossum Inc.; exchange rate, $0.63 per Canadian dollar.

June 27. Sold merchandise on account to Hu Company, net 30, 400,000 pesos; exchange rate, $0.016 per Philippines peso. The cost of merchandise sold was $3,800.

July 27. Received cash from Hu Company; exchange rate, $0.017 per Phillipines peso.

Oct. 8. Purchased merchandise on account from Chevalier Company, net 30, $50,000 Canadian; exchange rate, $0.64 per Canadian dollar.

Nov. 7. Issued check for amount owed to Chevalier Company; exchange rate, $0.65 per Canadian dollar.

Dec. 15. Sold merchandise on account to Cassandra Company, net 30, $120,000 Canadian; exchange rate, $0.65 per Canadian dollar. The cost of merchandise sold was $50,000.

16. Purchased merchandise on account from Juan Company, net 30, 500,000 pesos; exchange rate, $0.017 per Philippines peso.

31. Recorded unrealized currency exchange gain and/or loss on transactions of December 15 and 16. Exchange rates on December 31: $0.66 per Canadian dollar; $0.018 per Philippines peso.

**Instructions**

1. Journalize the entries to record the transactions and adjusting entries for the year, assuming that Outdoor Sports uses the perpetual inventory system.

2. Journalize the entries to record the payment of the December 16 purchase, on January 15, when the exchange rate was $0.016 per Philippines peso, and the receipt of cash from the December 15 sale, on January 17, when the exchange rate was $0.67 per Canadian dollar.

# appendix E

## The Home Depot Annual Report

2002 ANNUAL REPORT

MANAGEMENT'S DISCUSSION AND ANALYSIS
OF RESULTS OF OPERATIONS AND FINANCIAL CONDITION
THE HOME DEPOT, INC. AND SUBSIDIARIES

SELECTED CONSOLIDATED STATEMENTS OF EARNINGS DATA

The data below reflect selected sales data, the percentage relationship between sales and major categories in the Consolidated Statements of Earnings and the percentage change in the dollar amounts of each of the items.

| | Fiscal Year[1] | | | Percentage Increase (Decrease) In Dollar Amounts | |
| --- | --- | --- | --- | --- | --- |
| | 2002 | 2001 | 2000 | 2002 vs. 2001 | 2001 vs. 2000 |
| NET SALES | 100.0% | 100.0% | 100.0% | 8.8% | 17.1% |
| GROSS PROFIT | 31.1 | 30.2 | 29.9 | 12.1 | 18.0 |
| Operating Expenses: | | | | | |
| Selling and Store Operating | 19.2 | 19.0 | 18.6 | 10.0 | 19.4 |
| Pre-Opening | 0.2 | 0.2 | 0.3 | (17.9) | (17.6) |
| General and Administrative | 1.7 | 1.7 | 1.8 | 7.2 | 12.0 |
| Total Operating Expenses | 21.1 | 20.9 | 20.7 | 9.5 | 18.2 |
| OPERATING INCOME | 10.0 | 9.3 | 9.2 | 18.2 | 17.7 |
| Interest Income (Expense): | | | | | |
| Interest and Investment Income | 0.1 | 0.1 | 0.1 | 49.1 | 12.8 |
| Interest Expense | (0.0) | (0.1) | (0.1) | 32.1 | 33.3 |
| Interest, net | 0.1 | – | – | 68.0 | (3.8) |
| EARNINGS BEFORE PROVISION FOR INCOME TAXES | 10.1 | 9.3 | 9.2 | 18.5 | 17.5 |
| Provision for Income Taxes | 3.8 | 3.6 | 3.6 | 15.4 | 16.9 |
| NET EARNINGS | 6.3% | 5.7% | 5.6% | 20.4% | 17.9% |
| SELECTED SALES DATA [2] | | | | | |
| Number of Transactions (000s) | 1,160,994 | 1,090,975 | 936,519 | 6.4% | 16.5% |
| Average Sale per Transaction | $ 49.43 | $ 48.64 | $ 48.65 | 1.6 | – |
| Weighted Average Weekly Sales per Operating Store | $772,000 | $812,000 | $864,000 | (4.9) | (6.0) |
| Weighted Average Sales per Square Foot [3] | $ 370.21 | $ 387.93 | $ 414.68 | (4.6) | (6.5) |

[1] Fiscal years 2002, 2001 and 2000 refer to the fiscal years ended February 2, 2003, February 3, 2002 and January 28, 2001, respectively. Fiscal years 2002 and 2000 include 52 weeks, while fiscal year 2001 includes 53 weeks.

[2] Includes all retail locations in excess of 50,000 square feet and, therefore, excludes Apex Supply Company, Georgia Lighting, Maintenance Warehouse, Your "other" Warehouse, Designplace Direct (formerly National Blinds and Wallpaper) and HD Builder Solutions Group locations.

[3] Adjusted to reflect the first 52 weeks of the 53-week fiscal year in 2001.

FORWARD-LOOKING STATEMENTS

Certain statements made herein regarding implementation of store initiatives, store openings, capital expenditures and the effect of adopting certain accounting standards constitute "forward-looking statements" as defined in the Private Securities Litigation Reform Act of 1995. These statements are subject to various risks and uncertainties that could cause actual results to differ materially from our historical experience and our present expectations. These risks and uncertainties include, but are not limited to, fluctuations in and the overall condition of the U.S. economy, stability of costs and availability of sourcing channels, conditions affecting new store development, our ability to implement new technologies and processes, our ability to attract, train and retain highly-qualified associates, unanticipated weather conditions, the impact of competition and the effects of regulatory and litigation matters. You should not place undue reliance on such forward-looking statements as such statements speak only as of the date on which they are made. Additional information concerning these and other risks and uncertainties is contained in our periodic filings with the Securities and Exchange Commission.

RESULTS OF OPERATIONS

For an understanding of the significant factors that influenced our performance during the past three fiscal years, the following discussion should be read in conjunction with the consolidated financial statements and the notes to consolidated financial statements presented in this annual report.

## MANAGEMENT'S DISCUSSION AND ANALYSIS
## OF RESULTS OF OPERATIONS AND FINANCIAL CONDITION (CONTINUED)
THE HOME DEPOT, INC. AND SUBSIDIARIES

Fiscal year ended February 2, 2003 ("fiscal 2002") compared
to fiscal year ended February 3, 2002 ("fiscal 2001")

Fiscal 2002 included 52 weeks as compared to 53 weeks in fiscal
2001. Net sales for fiscal 2002 increased 8.8% to $58.2 billion
from $53.6 billion in fiscal 2001. This increase was attributable
to the 203 new stores opened during fiscal 2002 and full year
sales from the 204 new stores opened during fiscal 2001. The
increase was partially offset by the net sales attributable to the
additional week in fiscal 2001 of $880 million.

Comparable store-for-store sales were flat in fiscal 2002,
reflecting a number of internal and external factors. In the spring
and early summer, we experienced some inventory out-of-stock
positions as we transitioned through our new in-store Service
Performance Improvement ("SPI") initiative, in which our stores
handle and receive inventory at night. In addition, comparable
store-for-store sales were negatively impacted by the level of
merchandise resets implemented throughout the year, which
disrupted in-store service and had a negative impact on our
customers' experience in our stores. Kitchen and bath, plumbing
and paint categories experienced strong comparable store-
for-store sales growth for the year, which offset price deflation
and the resulting comparable store-for-store sales decline in
commodity categories such as lumber.

In order to meet our customer service objectives, we strate-
gically open stores near market areas served by existing strong
performing stores ("cannibalize") to enhance service levels, gain
incremental sales and increase market penetration. As of the
end of fiscal 2002, certain new stores cannibalized 21% of
our existing stores and we estimate that store cannibalization
reduced total comparable store-for-store sales by approximately
4%, or about the same percentage as in the prior year. As we
heavily cannibalized our most productive divisions, the weighted
average weekly sales per store decreased during fiscal 2002 to
$772,000 from $812,000 in the prior year. Additionally, we
believe that our sales performance has been, and could continue to be, negatively impacted by the level of competition that
we encounter in various markets. However, due to the highly-
fragmented U.S. home improvement industry, in which we estimate our market share is approximately 10%, measuring the
impact on our sales by our competitors is extremely difficult.

During fiscal 2002, we continued the implementation or
expansion of a number of in-store initiatives. We believe these
initiatives will increase customer loyalty and operating efficien-
cies as they are fully implemented in the stores. The professional
business customer ("Pro") initiative adds programs to our stores
to enhance service levels to the Pro customer base. As of the end
of fiscal 2002, the Pro initiative was in 1,135 stores or 74% of
total stores, compared to 535 stores or 40% of total stores as of
the end of fiscal 2001. This initiative is still in its early stages as
approximately half of our stores implemented the Pro initiative in

fiscal 2002. We expect to add the Pro initiative to an additional
204 stores by the end of fiscal 2003. As the Pro initiative matures
within the stores in which it has been implemented, we expect to
generate improvements in operating performance.

We continued to implement the Appliance initiative which
was started in the third quarter of fiscal 2001. The Appliance
initiative offers customers an assortment of in-stock name brand
appliances, including General Electric® and Maytag®, and offers
the ability to special order over 2,300 additional related products
through computer kiosks located in the stores. In the stores which
have implemented the Appliance initiative, we have enhanced
the offering of appliances through 1,500 to 2,000 square feet
of dedicated appliance selling space. Comparable store-for-store
sales in the appliance category increased by approximately 23%
in fiscal 2002. The Appliance initiative was in 743 or 48% of our
stores as of the end of fiscal 2002, compared to 73 or 5% of our
stores as of the end of fiscal 2001. We expect to add the Appliance
initiative to an additional 671 stores by the end of fiscal 2003.

We also continued to implement our Designplace initiative.
This initiative offers an enhanced shopping experience to our
design and décor customers by providing personalized service
from specially-trained associates and an enhanced merchandise
selection in an attractive setting. Although the Designplace
initiative is in its early stages, stores generally show a positive sales
trend after implementation. The Designplace initiative was in 873 or
57% of our stores as of the end of fiscal 2002, compared to
205 or 15% of our stores as of the end of fiscal 2001. We expect
to add the Designplace initiative to an additional 556 stores by
the end of fiscal 2003.

In addition, we continued to drive our services programs,
which focus primarily on providing products and services to our
do-it-for-me customers. These programs are offered through
Home Depot and EXPO Design Center stores. We also arrange
for the provision of flooring installation services to homebuilders
through HD Builder Solutions Group, Inc. Net service revenues
for fiscal 2002 increased 25% to $2.0 billion from $1.6 billion
for fiscal 2001.

Gross profit as a percent of sales was 31.1% for fiscal 2002
compared to 30.2% for fiscal 2001. The rate increase was
attributable to a reduction in the cost of merchandise sold which
resulted from centralized purchasing, as we continued rational-
izing vendor and sku assortments. Enhanced inventory control,
resulting in lower shrink levels, and an increase in direct import
penetration to 8% in fiscal 2002 from 6% in fiscal 2001 also
positively impacted the gross profit rate.

Operating expenses as a percent of sales were 21.1% for
fiscal 2002 compared to 20.9% for fiscal 2001. Included in
operating expenses are selling and store operating expenses
which, as a percent of sales, increased to 19.2% in fiscal 2002
from 19.0% in fiscal 2001. The increase in selling and store

operating expenses was primarily attributable to higher costs associated with merchandise resets and store renovations as we invested in new signage, fixtures and general maintenance of our stores, a continued investment in store leadership positions in our stores and rising workers' compensation expense due in part to medical cost inflation. These increases were partially offset by a decrease in store payroll expense which resulted from improvement in labor productivity and effective wage rate management.

Pre-opening expenses as a percent of sales were 0.2% for both fiscal 2002 and fiscal 2001. We opened 203 new stores in fiscal 2002 as compared to 204 new stores in fiscal 2001.

General and administrative expenses as a percent of sales were 1.7% for both fiscal 2002 and fiscal 2001.

Interest and investment income as a percent of sales was 0.1% for both fiscal 2002 and 2001. Interest expense as a percent of sales was 0.0% for fiscal 2002 and 0.1% for fiscal 2001.

Our combined federal and state effective income tax rate decreased to 37.6% for fiscal 2002 from 38.6% for fiscal 2001. The decrease in fiscal 2002 was attributable to higher tax credits and a lower effective state income tax rate compared to fiscal 2001.

### Fiscal 2001 compared to fiscal year ended January 28, 2001 ("fiscal 2000")

Fiscal 2001 included 53 weeks as compared to 52 weeks in fiscal 2000. Net sales for fiscal 2001 increased 17.1% to $53.6 billion from $45.7 billion in fiscal 2000. This increase was attributable to, among other things, the 204 new stores opened during fiscal 2001 and full year sales from the 204 new stores opened during fiscal 2000. Approximately $880 million of the increase in sales was attributable to the additional week in fiscal 2001. Comparable store-for-store sales were flat in fiscal 2001 due to the weak economic environment resulting from certain factors including, but not limited to, low consumer confidence and high unemployment.

Gross profit as a percent of sales was 30.2% for fiscal 2001 compared to 29.9% for fiscal 2000. The rate increase was primarily attributable to a lower cost of merchandise resulting from product line reviews, purchasing synergies created by our newly centralized merchandising structure and an increase in the number of tool rental centers from 342 at the end of fiscal 2000 to 466 at the end of fiscal 2001.

Operating expenses as a percent of sales were 20.9% for fiscal 2001 compared to 20.7% for fiscal 2000. Included in operating expenses are selling and store operating expenses which, as a percent of sales, increased to 19.0% in fiscal 2001 from 18.6% in fiscal 2000. The increase was primarily attributable to growth in store occupancy costs resulting from higher

depreciation and property taxes due to our investment in new stores, combined with increased energy costs. Also, credit card transaction fees were higher than the prior year due to increased penetration of total credit sales. These increases were partially offset by a decrease in store payroll expense due to an improvement in labor productivity which resulted from initiatives inside the store and new systems enhancements.

Store initiatives included our SPI initiative which was introduced to every Home Depot store in fiscal 2001. Under SPI our stores receive and handle inventory at night, allowing our associates to spend more time with customers during peak selling hours. In addition, our Pro program was in 535 of our Home Depot stores at the end of fiscal 2001, providing dedicated store resources to serve the specific needs of professional customers.

Pre-opening expenses as a percent of sales were 0.2% for fiscal 2001 and 0.3% for fiscal 2000. We opened 204 new stores in both fiscal 2001 and 2000. The decrease was primarily due to shorter pre-opening periods as we re-engineered our store opening process.

General and administrative expenses as a percent of sales were 1.7% for fiscal 2001 compared to 1.8% for fiscal 2000. This decrease was primarily due to cost savings associated with the reorganization of certain components of our organizational structure, such as the centralization of our merchandising organization and our focus on expense control in areas such as travel.

Interest and investment income as a percent of sales was 0.1% for both fiscal 2001 and 2000. Interest expense as a percent of sales was 0.1% for both fiscal 2001 and 2000.

Our combined federal and state effective income tax rate decreased to 38.6% for fiscal 2001 from 38.8% for fiscal 2000. The decrease in fiscal 2001 was attributable to higher tax credits and a lower effective state income tax rate compared to fiscal 2000.

### LIQUIDITY AND CAPITAL RESOURCES

Cash flow generated from operations provides us with a significant source of liquidity. For fiscal 2002, cash provided by operations decreased to $4.8 billion from $6.0 billion in fiscal 2001. The decrease was primarily due to a 7.9% increase in average inventory per store resulting from our focus on improving our in-stock position in fiscal 2002.

During fiscal 2002, we experienced a significant growth in days payable outstanding to 42 days at the end of fiscal 2002 from 34 days at the end of fiscal 2001. The growth in days payable is the result of our efforts to move our payment terms to industry averages. We have realized the majority of the benefit from our renegotiated payment terms.

MANAGEMENT'S DISCUSSION AND ANALYSIS
OF RESULTS OF OPERATIONS AND FINANCIAL CONDITION (CONTINUED)
THE HOME DEPOT, INC. AND SUBSIDIARIES

Cash used in investing activities decreased to $2.9 billion in fiscal 2002 from $3.5 billion in fiscal 2001. Capital expenditures decreased to $2.7 billion in fiscal 2002 from $3.4 billion in fiscal 2001. This decrease was due primarily to a shift in the timing of spending for future store openings. We opened 203 new stores in fiscal 2002 compared to 204 new stores in fiscal 2001. We own 195 and 188 of the stores opened in fiscal 2002 and fiscal 2001, respectively, and lease the remainder.

We plan to open 206 stores in fiscal 2003, including 6 Home Depot Landscape Supply stores, and expect total capital expenditures to be approximately $4.0 billion, which includes a higher level of investment in store remodeling, technology and other initiatives as compared to fiscal 2002.

Cash used in financing activities in fiscal 2002 was $2.2 billion compared with $173 million in fiscal 2001. This change is primarily due to the repurchase of approximately 68.6 million shares of our common stock for $2 billion, pursuant to the Share Repurchase Program approved by our Board of Directors in July 2002.

We have a commercial paper program that allows borrowings for up to a maximum of $1 billion. As of February 2, 2003, there were no borrowings outstanding under the program. In connection with the program, we have a back-up credit facility with a consortium of banks for up to $800 million. The credit facility, which expires in September 2004, contains various restrictive covenants, none of which are expected to impact our liquidity or capital resources.

We use capital and operating leases, as well as three off-balance sheet leases created under structured financing arrangements, to finance about 22% of our real estate. The net present value of capital lease obligations is reflected in our Consolidated Balance Sheets in Long-Term Debt. The three off-balance sheet leases were created to purchase land and fund the construction of certain stores, office buildings and distribution centers. Two of these lease agreements involve a special purpose entity ("SPE") which meets the criteria for non-consolidation established by generally accepted accounting principles and is not owned by or affiliated with our Company, management or officers. Operating and off-balance sheet leases are not reflected in our Consolidated Balance Sheets in accordance with generally accepted accounting principles.

As of the end of fiscal 2002, our long-term debt-to-equity ratio was 6.7%. If the estimated net present value of future payments under the operating and off-balance sheet leases were capitalized, our long-term debt-to-equity ratio would increase to 28.5%.

The following table summarizes our significant contractual obligations and commercial commitments as of February 2, 2003 (amounts in millions):

| Contractual Obligations[1] | Total | Payments Due By Fiscal Year | | | |
| | | 2003 | 2004-2005 | 2006-2007 | Thereafter |
|---|---|---|---|---|---|
| Long-Term Debt | $1,051 | $ 2 | $502 | $502 | $ 45 |
| Capital Lease Obligations | 834 | 44 | 89 | 93 | 608 |
| Operating Leases | 7,308 | 541 | 988 | 864 | 4,915 |

| Commercial Commitments[2] | Total | Amount of Commitment Expiration Per Fiscal Year | | | |
| | | 2003 | 2004-2005 | 2006-2007 | Thereafter |
|---|---|---|---|---|---|
| Letters of Credit | $ 930 | $921 | $ 9 | $ – | $ – |
| Guarantees | 799 | – | 72 | 504 | 223 |

[1] Contractual obligations include long-term debt comprised primarily of $1 billion of Senior Notes further discussed in "Quantitative and Qualitative Disclosures about Market Risk" and future minimum lease payments under capital and operating leases, which include off-balance sheet leases, used in the normal course of business.

[2] Commercial commitments include letters of credit for certain business transactions and guarantees provided under the off-balance sheet leases. We issue letters of credit for insurance programs, import purchases and construction contracts. Under the three off-balance sheet leases for certain stores, office buildings and distribution centers, we have provided residual value guarantees. The estimated maximum amount of the residual value guarantees at the end of the leases is $799 million. The leases expire at various dates during fiscal 2005 through 2008 with two of the leases having an option to renew through 2025. Events or circumstances that would require us to perform under the guarantees include 1) our default on the leases with the assets being sold for less than the initial book value, or 2) we decide not to purchase the assets at the end of the leases and the sale of the assets results in proceeds less than the initial book value of the assets. Our guarantees are limited to 82% of the initial book value of the assets. The expiration dates of the residual value guarantees as disclosed in the table above are based on the expiration of the leases; however, the expiration dates will change if the leases are renewed.

As of February 2, 2003, we had approximately $2.3 billion in cash and short-term investments. We believe that our current cash position, cash flow generated from operations, funds available from the $1 billion commercial paper program and the ability to obtain alternate sources of financing should be sufficient to enable us to complete our capital expenditure programs through the next several fiscal years.

### QUANTITATIVE AND QUALITATIVE DISCLOSURES ABOUT MARKET RISK

Our exposure to market risk results primarily from fluctuations in interest rates. Although we have international operating entities, our exposure to foreign currency rate fluctuations is not significant to our financial condition and results of operations. Our objective for holding derivative instruments is primarily to decrease the volatility of earnings and cash flow associated with fluctuations in interest rates.

We have financial instruments that are sensitive to changes in interest rates. These instruments include primarily fixed rate debt. As of February 2, 2003, we had $500 million of $5^3/_8$% Senior Notes and $500 million of $6^1/_2$% Senior Notes outstanding. The market values of the publicly traded $5^3/_8$% and $6^1/_2$% Senior Notes as of February 2, 2003, were approximately $538 million and $537 million, respectively. We have an interest rate swap agreement, with the notional amount of $300 million, that swaps fixed rate interest on $300 million of our $500 million $5^3/_8$% Senior Notes for a variable interest rate equal to LIBOR plus 30 basis points and expires on April 1, 2006.

### IMPACT OF INFLATION AND CHANGING PRICES

Although we cannot accurately determine the precise effect of inflation on operations, we do not believe inflation has had a material effect on sales or results of operations.

### CRITICAL ACCOUNTING POLICIES

Our significant accounting policies are disclosed in Note 1 to our consolidated financial statements. The following discussion addresses our most critical accounting policies, which are those that are both important to the portrayal of our financial condition and results of operations and that require significant judgment or use of complex estimates.

### REVENUE RECOGNITION

We recognize revenue, net of estimated returns, at the time the customer takes possession of the merchandise or receives services. We estimate the liability for sales returns based on our historical return levels. The methodology used is consistent with other retailers. We believe that our estimate for sales returns is an accurate reflection of future returns. When we receive payment from customers before the customer has taken possession of the merchandise or the service has been performed, the amount received is recorded in Deferred Revenue in the accompanying Consolidated Balance Sheets.

### INVENTORY

Our inventory is stated at the lower of cost (first-in, first-out) or market, with approximately 93% valued under the retail method and the remainder under the cost method. Retailers with many different types of merchandise at low unit cost with a large number of transactions frequently use the retail method. Under the retail method, inventory is stated at cost which is determined by applying a cost-to-retail ratio to the ending retail value of inventory. As our inventory retail value is adjusted regularly to reflect market conditions, our inventory methodology approximates the lower of cost or market. Accordingly, there were no significant valuation reserves related to our inventory as of February 2, 2003 and February 3, 2002. In addition, we reduce our ending inventory value for estimated losses related to shrink. This estimate is determined based upon analysis of historical shrink losses and recent shrink trends.

### SELF INSURANCE

We are self-insured for certain losses related to general liability, product liability, workers' compensation and medical claims. Our liability represents an estimate of the ultimate cost of claims incurred as of the balance sheet date. The estimated liability is not discounted and is established based upon analysis of historical data and actuarial estimates, and is reviewed by management and third party actuaries on a quarterly basis to ensure that the liability is appropriate. While we believe these estimates are reasonable based on the information currently available, if actual trends, including the severity or frequency of claims, medical cost inflation, or fluctuations in premiums, differ from our estimates, our results of operations could be impacted.

### CHANGE IN ACCOUNTING FOR STOCK-BASED COMPENSATION

During fiscal 2002 and all fiscal years prior, we elected to account for our stock-based compensation plans under Accounting Principles Board Opinion No. 25 ("APB 25"), "Accounting for Stock Issued to Employees," which requires the recording of compensation expense for some, but not all, stock-based compensation, rather than the alternative accounting permitted by Statement of Financial Accounting Standards ("SFAS") No. 123, "Accounting for Stock-Based Compensation."

In December 2002, SFAS No. 148, "Accounting for Stock-Based Compensation – Transition and Disclosure," was issued, which provides three alternative methods of transition for a voluntary change to the fair value method of accounting for stock-based compensation in accordance with SFAS No. 123.

MANAGEMENT'S DISCUSSION AND ANALYSIS
OF RESULTS OF OPERATIONS AND FINANCIAL CONDITION (CONTINUED)
THE HOME DEPOT, INC. AND SUBSIDIARIES

Effective February 3, 2003, we adopted the fair value method of recording compensation expense related to all stock options granted after February 2, 2003, in accordance with SFAS Nos. 123 and 148. Accordingly, the fair value of stock options as determined on the date of grant using the Black-Scholes option-pricing model will be expensed over the vesting period of the related stock options. The estimated negative impact on diluted earnings per share is approximately $.02 for fiscal 2003. The actual impact may differ from this estimate as the estimate is based upon a number of factors including, but not limited to, the number of stock options granted and the fair value of the stock options on the date of grant.

RECENT ACCOUNTING PRONOUNCEMENTS
In January 2003, the Financial Accounting Standards Board ("FASB") issued Interpretation No. 46, "Consolidation of Variable Interest Entities." Interpretation No. 46 requires consolidation of a variable interest entity if a company's variable interest absorbs a majority of the entity's losses or receives a majority of the entity's expected residual returns, or both. We do not have a variable interest in the SPE created as part of our off-balance sheet structured financing arrangements and, therefore, we are not required to consolidate the SPE. We do not expect Interpretation No. 46 to have any impact on our consolidated financial statements.

In January 2003, the Emerging Issues Task Force issued EITF 02-16, "Accounting by a Customer (Including a Reseller) for Certain Consideration Received from a Vendor," which states that cash consideration received from a vendor is presumed to be a reduction of the prices of the vendor's products or services and

should, therefore, be characterized as a reduction of Cost of Merchandise Sold when recognized in our Consolidated Statements of Earnings. That presumption is overcome when the consideration is either a reimbursement of specific, incremental, identifiable costs incurred to sell the vendor's products, or a payment for assets or services delivered to the vendor. EITF 02-16 is effective for arrangements entered into after December 31, 2002. We are currently assessing the impact of the adoption of EITF 02-16 and do not expect the adoption to materially impact net earnings in fiscal 2003. We do, however, expect that certain payments received from our vendors that are currently reflected as a reduction in advertising expense, which is classified as Selling and Store Operating Expense, will be reclassified as a reduction of Cost of Merchandise Sold.

In December 2002, the FASB issued Interpretation No. 45, "Guarantor's Accounting and Disclosure Requirements for Guarantees, Including Indirect Guarantees of Indebtedness of Others," which provides for additional disclosures to be made by a guarantor in its interim and annual financial statements about its obligations and requires, under certain circumstances, a guarantor to recognize, at the inception of a guarantee, a liability for the fair value of the obligation undertaken in issuing the guarantee. We have adopted the disclosure requirements for the fiscal year ended February 2, 2003. We do not expect the recognition and measurement provisions of Interpretation No. 45 for guarantees issued or modified after December 31, 2002, to have a material impact on our consolidated financial statements.

## CONSOLIDATED STATEMENTS OF EARNINGS

THE HOME DEPOT, INC. AND SUBSIDIARIES

| | Fiscal Year Ended[1] | | |
|---|---|---|---|
| amounts in millions, except per share data | February 2, 2003 | February 3, 2002 | January 28, 2001 |
| NET SALES | $58,247 | $53,553 | $45,738 |
| Cost of Merchandise Sold | 40,139 | 37,406 | 32,057 |
| GROSS PROFIT | 18,108 | 16,147 | 13,681 |
| | | | |
| Operating Expenses: | | | |
| Selling and Store Operating | 11,180 | 10,163 | 8,513 |
| Pre-Opening | 96 | 117 | 142 |
| General and Administrative | 1,002 | 935 | 835 |
| Total Operating Expenses | 12,278 | 11,215 | 9,490 |
| OPERATING INCOME | 5,830 | 4,932 | 4,191 |
| Interest Income (Expense): | | | |
| Interest and Investment Income | 79 | 53 | 47 |
| Interest Expense | (37) | (28) | (21) |
| Interest, net | 42 | 25 | 26 |
| EARNINGS BEFORE PROVISION FOR INCOME TAXES | 5,872 | 4,957 | 4,217 |
| | | | |
| Provision for Income Taxes | 2,208 | 1,913 | 1,636 |
| NET EARNINGS | $ 3,664 | $ 3,044 | $ 2,581 |
| | | | |
| Weighted Average Common Shares | 2,336 | 2,335 | 2,315 |
| BASIC EARNINGS PER SHARE | $ 1.57 | $ 1.30 | $ 1.11 |
| | | | |
| Diluted Weighted Average Common Shares | 2,344 | 2,353 | 2,352 |
| DILUTED EARNINGS PER SHARE | $ 1.56 | $ 1.29 | $ 1.10 |

[1] Fiscal years ended February 2, 2003 and January 28, 2001 include 52 weeks. Fiscal year ended February 3, 2002 includes 53 weeks.

See accompanying notes to consolidated financial statements.

## CONSOLIDATED BALANCE SHEETS

THE HOME DEPOT, INC. AND SUBSIDIARIES

| amounts in millions, except per share data | February 2, 2003 | February 3, 2002 |
|---|---|---|
| ASSETS | | |
| Current Assets: | | |
| Cash and Cash Equivalents | $ 2,188 | $ 2,477 |
| Short-Term Investments, including current maturities of long-term investments | 65 | 69 |
| Receivables, net | 1,072 | 920 |
| Merchandise Inventories | 8,338 | 6,725 |
| Other Current Assets | 254 | 170 |
| Total Current Assets | 11,917 | 10,361 |
| Property and Equipment, at cost: | | |
| Land | 5,560 | 4,972 |
| Buildings | 9,197 | 7,698 |
| Furniture, Fixtures and Equipment | 4,074 | 3,403 |
| Leasehold Improvements | 872 | 750 |
| Construction in Progress | 724 | 1,049 |
| Capital Leases | 306 | 257 |
| | 20,733 | 18,129 |
| Less Accumulated Depreciation and Amortization | 3,565 | 2,754 |
| Net Property and Equipment | 17,168 | 15,375 |
| Notes Receivable | 107 | 83 |
| Cost in Excess of the Fair Value of Net Assets Acquired, net of accumulated amortization of $50 at February 2, 2003 and $49 at February 3, 2002 | 575 | 419 |
| Other Assets | 244 | 156 |
| | $30,011 | $26,394 |
| LIABILITIES AND STOCKHOLDERS' EQUITY | | |
| Current Liabilities: | | |
| Accounts Payable | $ 4,560 | $ 3,436 |
| Accrued Salaries and Related Expenses | 809 | 717 |
| Sales Taxes Payable | 307 | 348 |
| Deferred Revenue | 998 | 851 |
| Income Taxes Payable | 227 | 211 |
| Other Accrued Expenses | 1,134 | 938 |
| Total Current Liabilities | 8,035 | 6,501 |
| Long-Term Debt, excluding current installments | 1,321 | 1,250 |
| Other Long-Term Liabilities | 491 | 372 |
| Deferred Income Taxes | 362 | 189 |
| STOCKHOLDERS' EQUITY | | |
| Common Stock, par value $0.05; authorized: 10,000 shares, issued and outstanding 2,362 shares at February 2, 2003 and 2,346 shares at February 3, 2002 | 118 | 117 |
| Paid-In Capital | 5,858 | 5,412 |
| Retained Earnings | 15,971 | 12,799 |
| Accumulated Other Comprehensive Loss | (82) | (220) |
| Unearned Compensation | (63) | (26) |
| Treasury Stock, at cost, 69 shares at February 2, 2003 | (2,000) | – |
| Total Stockholders' Equity | 19,802 | 18,082 |
| | $30,011 | $26,394 |

*See accompanying notes to consolidated financial statements.*

## CONSOLIDATED STATEMENTS OF STOCKHOLDERS' EQUITY AND COMPREHENSIVE INCOME

THE HOME DEPOT, INC. AND SUBSIDIARIES

| amounts in millions, except per share data | Common Stock Shares | Common Stock Amount | Paid-In Capital | Retained Earnings | Accumulated Other Comprehensive Income (Loss) | Treasury Stock Shares | Treasury Stock Amount | Unearned Compensation | Total Stockholders' Equity | Comprehensive Income[1] |
|---|---|---|---|---|---|---|---|---|---|---|
| BALANCE, JANUARY 30, 2000 | 2,304 | $115 | $4,319 | $ 7,941 | $ (27) | – | $ – | $ (7) | $12,341 | |
| Net Earnings | – | – | – | 2,581 | – | – | – | – | 2,581 | $2,581 |
| Shares Issued Under Employee Stock Purchase and Option Plans | 20 | 1 | 348 | – | – | – | – | 1 | 350 | |
| Tax Effect of Sale of Option Shares by Employees | – | – | 137 | – | – | – | – | – | 137 | |
| Translation Adjustments | – | – | – | – | (40) | – | – | – | (40) | (40) |
| Stock Compensation Expense | – | – | 6 | – | – | – | – | – | 6 | |
| Cash Dividends ($0.16 per share) | – | – | – | (371) | – | – | – | – | (371) | |
| Comprehensive Income | | | | | | | | | | $2,541 |
| BALANCE, JANUARY 28, 2001 | 2,324 | $116 | $4,810 | $10,151 | $ (67) | – | $ – | $ (6) | $15,004 | |
| Net Earnings | – | – | – | 3,044 | – | – | – | – | 3,044 | $3,044 |
| Shares Issued Under Employee Stock Purchase and Option Plans | 22 | 1 | 448 | – | – | – | – | (20) | 429 | |
| Tax Effect of Sale of Option Shares by Employees | – | – | 138 | – | – | – | – | – | 138 | |
| Translation Adjustments | – | – | – | – | (124) | – | – | – | (124) | (124) |
| Unrealized Loss on Derivative | – | – | – | – | (29) | – | – | – | (29) | (18) |
| Stock Compensation Expense | – | – | 16 | – | – | – | – | – | 16 | |
| Cash Dividends ($0.17 per share) | – | – | – | (396) | – | – | – | – | (396) | |
| Comprehensive Income | | | | | | | | | | $2,902 |
| BALANCE, FEBRUARY 3, 2002 | 2,346 | $117 | $5,412 | $12,799 | $(220) | – | $ – | $(26) | $18,082 | |
| Net Earnings | – | – | – | 3,664 | – | – | – | – | 3,664 | $3,664 |
| Shares Issued Under Employee Stock Purchase and Option Plans | 16 | 1 | 366 | – | – | – | – | (37) | 330 | |
| Tax Effect of Sale of Option Shares by Employees | – | – | 68 | – | – | – | – | – | 68 | |
| Translation Adjustments | – | – | – | – | 109 | – | – | – | 109 | 109 |
| Realized Loss on Derivative | – | – | – | – | 29 | – | – | – | 29 | 18 |
| Stock Compensation Expense | – | – | 12 | – | – | – | – | – | 12 | |
| Repurchase of Common Stock | – | – | – | – | – | (69) | (2,000) | – | (2,000) | |
| Cash Dividends ($0.21 per share) | – | – | – | (492) | – | – | – | – | (492) | |
| Comprehensive Income | | | | | | | | | | $3,791 |
| BALANCE, FEBRUARY 2, 2003 | 2,362 | $118 | $5,858 | $15,971 | $ (82) | (69) | $(2,000) | $(63) | $19,802 | |

[1] Components of comprehensive income are reported net of related income taxes.

See accompanying notes to consolidated financial statements.

## CONSOLIDATED STATEMENTS OF CASH FLOWS

THE HOME DEPOT, INC. AND SUBSIDIARIES

| | Fiscal Year Ended[1] | | |
|---|---|---|---|
| *amounts in millions* | February 2, 2003 | February 3, 2002 | January 28, 2001 |
| CASH FLOWS FROM OPERATIONS: | | | |
| Net Earnings | $3,664 | $3,044 | $2,581 |
| Reconciliation of Net Earnings to Net Cash Provided by Operations: | | | |
| Depreciation and Amortization | 903 | 764 | 601 |
| Increase in Receivables, net | (38) | (119) | (246) |
| Increase in Merchandise Inventories | (1,592) | (166) | (1,075) |
| Increase in Accounts Payable and Accrued Liabilities | 1,394 | 1,878 | 268 |
| Increase in Deferred Revenue | 147 | 200 | 486 |
| Increase in Income Taxes Payable | 83 | 272 | 151 |
| Increase (Decrease) in Deferred Income Taxes | 173 | (6) | 108 |
| Other | 68 | 96 | (78) |
| Net Cash Provided by Operations | 4,802 | 5,963 | 2,796 |
| CASH FLOWS FROM INVESTING ACTIVITIES: | | | |
| Capital Expenditures, net of $49, $5 and $16 of non-cash capital expenditures in fiscal 2002, 2001 and 2000, respectively | (2,749) | (3,393) | (3,558) |
| Payments for Businesses Acquired, net | (235) | (190) | (26) |
| Proceeds from Sales of Businesses, net | 22 | 64 | – |
| Proceeds from Sales of Property and Equipment | 105 | 126 | 95 |
| Purchases of Investments | (583) | (85) | (39) |
| Proceeds from Maturities of Investments | 506 | 25 | 30 |
| Other | – | (13) | (32) |
| Net Cash Used in Investing Activities | (2,934) | (3,466) | (3,530) |
| CASH FLOWS FROM FINANCING ACTIVITIES: | | | |
| (Repayments) Issuances of Commercial Paper Obligations, net | – | (754) | 754 |
| Proceeds from Long-Term Debt | 1 | 532 | 32 |
| Repayments of Long-Term Debt | – | – | (29) |
| Repurchase of Common Stock | (2,000) | – | – |
| Proceeds from Sale of Common Stock, net | 326 | 445 | 351 |
| Cash Dividends Paid to Stockholders | (492) | (396) | (371) |
| Net Cash (Used in) Provided by Financing Activities | (2,165) | (173) | 737 |
| Effect of Exchange Rate Changes on Cash and Cash Equivalents | 8 | (14) | (4) |
| (Decrease) Increase in Cash and Cash Equivalents | (289) | 2,310 | (1) |
| Cash and Cash Equivalents at Beginning of Year | 2,477 | 167 | 168 |
| Cash and Cash Equivalents at End of Year | $2,188 | $2,477 | $ 167 |
| SUPPLEMENTAL DISCLOSURE OF CASH PAYMENTS MADE FOR: | | | |
| Interest, net of interest capitalized | $   50 | $   18 | $   16 |
| Income Taxes | $1,951 | $ 1,685 | $ 1,386 |

[1] *Fiscal years ended February 2, 2003, and January 28, 2001, include 52 weeks. Fiscal year ended February 3, 2002, includes 53 weeks.*

*See accompanying notes to consolidated financial statements.*

## NOTES TO CONSOLIDATED FINANCIAL STATEMENTS
THE HOME DEPOT, INC. AND SUBSIDIARIES

### 1  SUMMARY OF SIGNIFICANT ACCOUNTING POLICIES

**BUSINESS, CONSOLIDATION AND PRESENTATION**

The Home Depot, Inc. and subsidiaries (the "Company") operate Home Depot stores, which are full-service, warehouse-style stores averaging approximately 108,000 square feet in size. The stores stock approximately 40,000 to 50,000 different kinds of building materials, home improvement supplies and lawn and garden products that are sold primarily to do-it-your-selfers, but also to home improvement contractors, trades-people and building maintenance professionals. In addition, the Company operates EXPO Design Center stores, which offer products and services primarily related to design and renovation projects, Home Depot Landscape Supply stores which service landscape professionals and garden enthusiasts with lawn, landscape and garden products and Home Depot Supply stores serving primarily professional customers. The Company also operates one Home Depot Floor Store, a test store that offers only flooring products and installation services. At the end of fiscal 2002, the Company was operating 1,532 stores in total, which included 1,370 Home Depot stores, 52 EXPO Design Center stores, 5 Home Depot Supply stores, 3 Home Depot Landscape Supply stores and 1 Home Depot Floor Store in the United States ("U.S."); 89 Home Depot stores in Canada and 12 Home Depot stores in Mexico. Included in the Company's Consolidated Balance Sheet at February 2, 2003, were $1.2 billion of net assets of the Canada and Mexico operations.

The consolidated results include several wholly-owned sub-sidiaries. The Company offers facilities maintenance and repair products as well as wallpaper and custom window treatments via direct shipment through its subsidiaries, Maintenance Warehouse America Corp. and National Blinds and Wallpaper, Inc. (doing business as Designplace Direct). Georgia Lighting, Inc. is a specialty lighting designer, distributor and retailer to both commer-cial and retail customers. The Company offers plumbing, HVAC and other professional plumbing products through wholesale plumbing distributors Apex Supply Company, Inc. and Home Depot Your "other" Warehouse, LLC. The Company also arranges for the provision of flooring installation services to homebuilders through HD Builder Solutions Group, Inc. The consolidated financial statements include the accounts of the Company and its wholly-owned subsidiaries. All significant intercompany transactions have been eliminated in consolidation.

**FISCAL YEAR**

The Company's fiscal year is a 52 or 53-week period ending on the Sunday nearest to January 31. Fiscal years 2002 and 2000, which ended February 2, 2003, and January 28, 2001, respec-tively, include 52 weeks. Fiscal year 2001, which ended February 3, 2002, includes 53 weeks.

**CASH EQUIVALENTS**

The Company considers all highly liquid investments purchased with a maturity of three months or less to be cash equivalents. The Company's cash and cash equivalents are carried at fair market value and consist primarily of high-grade commercial paper, money market funds, U.S. government agency securi-ties and tax-exempt notes and bonds.

**ACCOUNTS RECEIVABLE**

The Company has an agreement with a third-party service provider who manages the Company's private label credit card program and directly extends credit to customers. The Company's valuation reserve related to accounts receivable was not material as of February 2, 2003 and February 3, 2002.

**MERCHANDISE INVENTORIES**

The majority of the Company's inventory is stated at the lower of cost (first-in, first-out) or market, as determined by the retail inventory method.

Certain subsidiaries and distribution centers record inven-tories at lower of cost (first-in, first-out) or market, as determined by the cost method. These inventories represent approximately 7% of total inventory.

**INVESTMENTS**

The Company's investments, consisting primarily of high-grade debt securities, are recorded at fair value and are classified as available-for-sale.

**INCOME TAXES**

The Company provides for federal, state and foreign income taxes currently payable, as well as for those deferred due to timing differences between reporting income and expenses for financial statement purposes versus tax purposes. Federal, state and foreign incentive tax credits are recorded as a reduction of income taxes. Deferred tax assets and liabilities are recognized for the future tax consequences attributable to differences between the financial statement carrying amounts of existing assets and liabilities and their respective tax bases. Deferred tax assets and liabilities are measured using enacted income tax rates expected to apply to taxable income in the years in which those temporary differences are expected to be recovered or settled. The effect of a change in tax rates is recognized as income or expense in the period that includes the enactment date.

NOTES TO CONSOLIDATED FINANCIAL STATEMENTS (CONTINUED)
THE HOME DEPOT, INC. AND SUBSIDIARIES

The Company and its eligible subsidiaries file a consolidated U.S. federal income tax return. Non-U.S. subsidiaries, which are consolidated for financial reporting purposes, are not eligible to be included in consolidated U.S. federal income tax returns. Separate provisions for income taxes have been determined for these entities. The Company intends to reinvest the unremitted earnings of its non-U.S. subsidiaries and postpone their remittance indefinitely. Accordingly, no provision for U.S. income taxes for non-U.S. subsidiaries was recorded in the accompanying Consolidated Statements of Earnings.

### DEPRECIATION AND AMORTIZATION

The Company's buildings, furniture, fixtures and equipment are depreciated using the straight-line method over the estimated useful lives of the assets. Improvements to leased assets are amortized using the straight-line method over the life of the lease or the useful life of the improvement, whichever is shorter. The Company's property and equipment is depreciated using the following estimated useful lives:

|  | Life |
| --- | --- |
| Buildings | 10-45 years |
| Furniture, fixtures and equipment | 5-20 years |
| Leasehold improvements | 5-30 years |
| Computer equipment and software | 3-5 years |

### REVENUES

The Company recognizes revenue, net of estimated returns, at the time the customer takes possession of merchandise or receives services. When the Company receives payment from customers before the customer has taken possession of the merchandise or the service has been performed, the amount received is recorded in Deferred Revenue in the accompanying Consolidated Balance Sheets.

### SERVICE REVENUES

Total revenues include service revenues generated through a variety of installation and home maintenance programs in Home Depot and EXPO stores as well as through the Company's subsidiary, HD Builder Solutions Group, Inc. In these programs, the customer selects and purchases materials for a project and the Company provides or arranges professional installation. When the Company subcontracts the installation of a project and the subcontractor provides material as part of the installation, both the material and labor are included in service revenues. The Company recognizes this revenue when the service for the customer is completed. All payments received prior to the completion of services are recorded in Deferred Revenue in the accompanying Consolidated Balance Sheets. Net service revenues, including the impact of deferred revenue, were $2.0 billion, $1.6 billion and $1.3 billion for the fiscal years 2002, 2001 and 2000, respectively.

### SELF INSURANCE

The Company is self-insured for certain losses related to general liability, product liability, workers' compensation and medical claims. The expected ultimate cost for claims incurred as of the balance sheet date is not discounted and is recognized as a liability. The expected ultimate cost of claims is estimated based upon analysis of historical data and actuarial estimates.

### ADVERTISING

Television and radio advertising production costs along with media placement costs are expensed when the advertisement first appears. Included in Current Assets in the accompanying Consolidated Balance Sheets are $20 million and $15 million at the end of fiscal years 2002 and 2001, respectively, relating to prepayments of production costs for print and broadcast advertising.

Gross advertising expense is classified as Selling and Store Operating Expenses and was $895 million, $817 million and $722 million, in fiscal years 2002, 2001 and 2000, respectively. Advertising allowances earned from vendors fully offset gross advertising expenses. In fiscal 2002, 2001 and 2000, advertising allowances exceeded gross advertising expense by $30 million, $31 million and $62 million, respectively. These excess amounts were recorded as a reduction in Cost of Merchandise Sold in the accompanying Consolidated Statements of Earnings.

### SHIPPING AND HANDLING COSTS

The Company accounts for certain shipping and handling costs related to the shipment of product to customers from vendors as Cost of Merchandise Sold. However, cost of shipping and handling to customers by the Company is classified as Selling and Store Operating Expenses. The cost of shipping and handling, including internal costs and payments to third parties, classified as Selling and Store Operating Expenses was $341 million, $278 million and $226 million in fiscal years 2002, 2001 and 2000, respectively.

### COST IN EXCESS OF THE FAIR VALUE OF NET ASSETS ACQUIRED

Goodwill represents the excess of purchase price over fair value of net assets acquired. In accordance with Statement of Financial Accounting Standards ("SFAS") No. 142, "Goodwill and Other Intangible Assets," the Company stopped amortizing goodwill effective February 4, 2002. Amortization expense was $8 million in both fiscal 2001 and fiscal 2000. The Company assesses the recoverability of goodwill at least annually by determining whether the fair value of each reporting entity supports its carrying value. The Company completed its assessment of goodwill for fiscal 2002 and recorded an impairment charge of $1.3 million.

NOTES TO CONSOLIDATED FINANCIAL STATEMENTS (CONTINUED)
THE HOME DEPOT, INC. AND SUBSIDIARIES

### IMPAIRMENT OF LONG-LIVED ASSETS

The Company reviews long-lived assets for impairment when circumstances indicate the carrying amount of an asset may not be recoverable. Impairment is recognized to the extent the sum of undiscounted estimated future cash flows expected to result from the use of the asset is less than the carrying value. When the Company commits to relocate or close a location, a charge is recorded to Selling and Store Operating Expenses to write down the related assets to the estimated net recoverable value.

In August 2002, the Company adopted SFAS No. 146, "Accounting for Costs Associated with Exit or Disposal Activities." In accordance with SFAS No. 146, the Company recognizes Selling and Store Operating Expense for the net present value of future lease obligations, less estimated sublease income when the location closes. Prior to the adoption of SFAS No. 146, the Company recognized this Selling and Store Operating Expense when the Company committed to a plan to relocate or close a location.

### STOCK-BASED COMPENSATION

During fiscal 2002 and all fiscal years prior, the Company elected to account for its stock-based compensation plans under Accounting Principles Board Opinion No. 25 ("APB 25"), "Accounting for Stock Issued to Employees," which requires the recording of compensation expense for some, but not all, stock-based compensation rather than the alternative accounting permitted by SFAS No. 123, "Accounting for Stock-Based Compensation."

The following table illustrates the effect on net earnings and earnings per share if the Company had applied the fair value recognition provisions of SFAS No. 123 to stock-based compensation (amounts in millions, except per share data):

| | Fiscal Year Ended | | |
| | February 2, 2003 | February 3, 2002 | January 28, 2001 |
|---|---|---|---|
| Net Earnings | | | |
| As reported | $3,664 | $3,044 | $2,581 |
| Pro forma | $3,414 | $2,800 | $2,364 |
| Basic Earnings per Share | | | |
| As reported | $ 1.57 | $ 1.30 | $ 1.11 |
| Pro forma | $ 1.46 | $ 1.20 | $ 1.02 |
| Diluted Earnings per Share | | | |
| As reported | $ 1.56 | $ 1.29 | $ 1.10 |
| Pro forma | $ 1.46 | $ 1.19 | $ 1.01 |

In December 2002, SFAS No. 148, "Accounting for Stock-Based Compensation – Transition and Disclosure," was issued, which provides three alternative methods of transition for a voluntary change to the fair value method of accounting for stock-based compensation in accordance with SFAS No. 123.

Effective February 3, 2003, the Company adopted the fair value method of recording compensation expense related to all stock options granted after February 2, 2003, in accordance with SFAS Nos. 123 and 148. Accordingly, the fair value of stock options as determined on the date of grant using the Black-Scholes option-pricing model will be expensed over the vesting period of the related stock options. The estimated negative impact on diluted earnings per share is approximately $.02 for fiscal 2003. The actual impact may differ from this estimate as the estimate is based upon a number of factors including, but not limited to, the number of stock options granted and the fair value of the stock options on the date of grant.

### DERIVATIVES

The Company measures derivatives at fair value and recognizes these assets or liabilities on the Consolidated Balance Sheets. Recognition of changes in the fair value of a derivative in the Consolidated Statements of Earnings or Consolidated Statements of Stockholders' Equity and Comprehensive Income depends on the intended use of the derivative and its designation. The Company designates derivatives based upon criteria established by SFAS Nos. 133 and 138, "Accounting for Derivative Instruments and Hedging Activities." The Company's primary objective for holding derivative instruments is to decrease the volatility of earnings and cash flow associated with fluctuations in interest rates.

### COMPREHENSIVE INCOME

Comprehensive income includes net earnings adjusted for certain revenues, expenses, gains and losses that are excluded from net earnings under generally accepted accounting principles. Examples include foreign currency translation adjustments and unrealized gains and losses on certain hedge transactions.

### FOREIGN CURRENCY TRANSLATION

The assets and liabilities denominated in a foreign currency are translated into U.S. dollars at the current rate of exchange on the last day of the reporting period. Revenues and expenses are translated at the average monthly exchange rates, and equity transactions are translated using the actual rate on the day of the transaction.

### USE OF ESTIMATES

Management of the Company has made a number of estimates and assumptions relating to the reporting of assets and liabilities, the disclosure of contingent assets and liabilities, and reported amounts of revenues and expenses in preparing these financial statements in conformity with generally accepted accounting principles. Actual results could differ from these estimates.

## NOTES TO CONSOLIDATED FINANCIAL STATEMENTS (CONTINUED)
THE HOME DEPOT, INC. AND SUBSIDIARIES

**RECLASSIFICATIONS**

Certain amounts in prior fiscal years have been reclassified to conform with the presentation adopted in the current fiscal year.

## 2 LONG-TERM DEBT

The Company's long-term debt at the end of fiscal 2002 and fiscal 2001 consisted of the following (amounts in millions):

|  | February 2, 2003 | February 3, 2002 |
|---|---|---|
| 6$^1/_2$% Senior Notes; due September 15, 2004; interest payable semi-annually on March 15 and September 15 | $ 500 | $ 500 |
| 5$^3/_8$% Senior Notes; due April 1, 2006; interest payable semi-annually on April 1 and October 1 | 500 | 500 |
| Capital Lease Obligations; payable in varying installments through May 31, 2027 | 277 | 232 |
| Other | 51 | 23 |
| Total long-term debt | 1,328 | 1,255 |
| Less current installments | 7 | 5 |
| Long-term debt, excluding current installments | $1,321 | $1,250 |

The Company has a commercial paper program with maximum available borrowings for up to $1 billion. In connection with the program, the Company has a back-up credit facility with a consortium of banks for up to $800 million. The credit facility, which expires in September 2004, contains various restrictive covenants, none of which are expected to materially impact the Company's liquidity or capital resources.

The Company had $500 million of 6$^1/_2$% Senior Notes and $500 million of 5$^3/_8$% Senior Notes outstanding as of February 2, 2003, collectively referred to as "Senior Notes." The Senior Notes may be redeemed by the Company at any time, in whole or in part, at a redemption price plus accrued interest up to the redemption date. The redemption price is equal to the greater of (1) 100% of the principal amount of the Senior Notes to be redeemed, or (2) the sum of the present values of the remaining scheduled payments of principal and interest to maturity. The Senior Notes are not subject to sinking fund requirements.

Interest Expense in the accompanying Consolidated Statements of Earnings is net of interest capitalized of $59 million, $84 million and $73 million in fiscal years 2002, 2001 and 2000, respectively. Maturities of long-term debt are $7 million for fiscal 2003, $507 million for fiscal 2004, $8 million for fiscal 2005, $509 million for fiscal 2006 and $11 million for fiscal 2007.

As of February 2, 2003, the market values of the publicly traded 6$^1/_2$% and 5$^3/_8$% Senior Notes were approximately $537 million and $538 million, respectively. The estimated fair value of all other long-term borrowings, excluding capital lease obligations, approximated the carrying value of $51 million. These fair values were estimated using a discounted cash flow analysis based on the Company's incremental borrowing rate for similar liabilities.

## 3 INCOME TAXES

The provision for income taxes consisted of the following (in millions):

|  | Fiscal Year Ended | | |
|---|---|---|---|
|  | February 2, 2003 | February 3, 2002 | January 28, 2001 |
| Current: | | | |
| Federal | $1,679 | $1,594 | $1,267 |
| State | 239 | 265 | 216 |
| Foreign | 117 | 60 | 45 |
|  | 2,035 | 1,919 | 1,528 |
| Deferred: | | | |
| Federal | 174 | (12) | 98 |
| State | 1 | (1) | 9 |
| Foreign | (2) | 7 | 1 |
|  | 173 | (6) | 108 |
| Total | $2,208 | $1,913 | $1,636 |

The Company's combined federal, state and foreign effective tax rates for fiscal years 2002, 2001 and 2000, net of offsets generated by federal, state and foreign tax incentive credits, were approximately 37.6%, 38.6% and 38.8%, respectively.

A reconciliation of income tax expense at the federal statutory rate of 35% to actual tax expense for the applicable fiscal years is as follows (in millions):

| | Fiscal Year Ended | | |
| | February 2, 2003 | February 3, 2002 | January 28, 2001 |
|---|---|---|---|
| Income taxes at federal statutory rate | $2,055 | $1,735 | $1,476 |
| State income taxes, net of federal income tax benefit | 156 | 172 | 146 |
| Foreign rate differences | (1) | 4 | 5 |
| Other, net | (2) | 2 | 9 |
| Total | $2,208 | $1,913 | $1,636 |

The tax effects of temporary differences that give rise to significant portions of the deferred tax assets and deferred tax liabilities as of February 2, 2003, and February 3, 2002, were as follows (in millions):

| | February 2, 2003 | February 3, 2002 |
|---|---|---|
| Deferred Tax Assets: | | |
| Accrued self-insurance liabilities | $ 305 | $ 220 |
| Other accrued liabilities | 92 | 138 |
| Net loss on disposition of business | 31 | 31 |
| Total gross deferred tax assets | 428 | 389 |
| Valuation allowance | (31) | (31) |
| Deferred tax assets, net of valuation allowance | 397 | 358 |
| Deferred Tax Liabilities: | | |
| Accelerated depreciation | (571) | (492) |
| Accelerated inventory deduction | (149) | – |
| Other | (39) | (55) |
| Total gross deferred tax liabilities | (759) | (547) |
| Net deferred tax liability | $(362) | $(189) |

A valuation allowance existed as of February 2, 2003, and February 3, 2002, due to the uncertainty of capital loss utilization. Management believes the existing net deductible temporary differences comprising the deferred tax assets will reverse during periods in which the Company generates net taxable income.

## 4 EMPLOYEE STOCK PLANS

The 1997 Omnibus Stock Incentive Plan ("1997 Plan") provides that incentive stock options, non-qualified stock options, stock appreciation rights, restricted shares, performance shares, performance units and deferred shares may be issued to selected associates, officers and directors of the Company. The maximum number of shares of the Company's common stock authorized for issuance under the 1997 Plan includes the number of shares carried over from prior plans and the number of shares authorized but unissued in the prior year, plus one-half percent of the total number of outstanding shares as of the first day of each fiscal year. As of February 2, 2003, there were 108 million shares available for future grants under the 1997 Plan.

Under the 1997 Plan, as of February 2, 2003, the Company had granted incentive and non-qualified stock options for 167 million shares, net of cancellations (of which 86 million had been exercised). Incentive stock options and non-qualified options typically vest at the rate of 25% per year commencing on the first anniversary date of the grant and expire on the tenth anniversary date of the grant.

Under the 1997 Plan, as of February 2, 2003, 2 million shares of restricted stock had been issued net of cancellations (the restrictions on 4,600 shares have lapsed). Generally, the restrictions on 25% of the restricted shares lapse upon the third and sixth year anniversaries of the date of issuance with the remaining 50% of the restricted shares lapsing upon the associate's attainment of age 62. The fair value of the restricted shares is expensed over the period during which the restrictions lapse. The Company recorded compensation expense related to restricted stock of $3 million in both fiscal 2002 and 2001 and $455,000 in fiscal 2000.

As of February 2, 2003, there were 2.5 million non-qualified stock options and 1.4 million deferred stock units outstanding under non-qualified stock option and deferred stock unit plans that are not part of the 1997 Plan. The 2.5 million non-qualified stock options have an exercise price of $40.75 per share and were granted in fiscal 2000. During fiscal years 2002, 2001 and 2000, the Company granted 0, 629,000 and 750,000 deferred stock units, respectively, to several key officers vesting at various dates. Each deferred stock unit entitles the officer to one share of common stock to be received up to five years after the vesting date of the deferred stock unit, subject to certain deferral rights of the officer. The fair value of the deferred stock units on the grant dates was $27 million and $31 million for deferred units granted in fiscal 2001 and 2000, respectively. These amounts are being amortized over the vesting periods.

## NOTES TO CONSOLIDATED FINANCIAL STATEMENTS (CONTINUED)
THE HOME DEPOT, INC. AND SUBSIDIARIES

The Company recorded stock compensation expense related to deferred stock units of $12 million, $16 million and $6 million in fiscal 2002, 2001 and 2000, respectively.

The per share weighted average fair value of stock options granted during fiscal years 2002, 2001 and 2000 was $17.34, $20.51 and $31.96, respectively. The fair value of these options was determined at the date of grant using the Black-Scholes option-pricing model with the following assumptions:

| | Fiscal Year Ended | | |
| | February 2, 2003 | February 3, 2002 | January 28, 2001 |
| --- | --- | --- | --- |
| Risk-free interest rate | 4.0% | 5.1% | 6.4% |
| Assumed volatility | 44.3% | 48.1% | 54.6% |
| Assumed dividend yield | 0.5% | 0.4% | 0.3% |
| Assumed lives of options | 5 years | 6 years | 7 years |

The Company applies APB 25 in accounting for its stock-based compensation plans and, accordingly, no compensation expense has been recognized in the Company's financial statements for incentive or non-qualified stock options granted. If, under SFAS No. 123, the Company determined compensation expense based on the fair value at the grant date for its stock options, as computed and disclosed above, net earnings and earnings per share would have been reduced to the pro forma amounts below (in millions, except per share data):

| | Fiscal Year Ended | | |
| | February 2, 2003 | February 3, 2002 | January 28, 2001 |
| --- | --- | --- | --- |
| Net earnings, as reported | $3,664 | $3,044 | $2,581 |
| Add: Stock-based compensation expense included in reported net earnings, net of related tax effects | 10 | 13 | 4 |
| Deduct: Total stock-based compensation expense determined under fair value based method for all awards, net of related tax effects | (260) | (257) | (221) |
| Pro forma net earnings | $3,414 | $2,800 | $2,364 |
| Earnings per share: | | | |
| Basic – as reported | $ 1.57 | $ 1.30 | $ 1.11 |
| Basic – pro forma | $ 1.46 | $ 1.20 | $ 1.02 |
| Diluted – as reported | $ 1.56 | $ 1.29 | $ 1.10 |
| Diluted – pro forma | $ 1.46 | $ 1.19 | $ 1.01 |

The following table summarizes stock options outstanding at February 2, 2003, February 3, 2002 and January 28, 2001, and changes during the fiscal years ended on these dates (shares in thousands):

| | Number of Shares | Weighted Average Option Price |
| --- | --- | --- |
| Outstanding at January 30, 2000 | 68,419 | $18.79 |
| Granted | 14,869 | 49.78 |
| Exercised | (14,689) | 13.15 |
| Canceled | (2,798) | 30.51 |
| Outstanding at January 28, 2001 | 65,801 | $26.46 |
| Granted | 25,330 | 40.33 |
| Exercised | (16,614) | 15.03 |
| Canceled | (5,069) | 39.20 |
| Outstanding at February 3, 2002 | 69,448 | $33.33 |
| Granted | 31,656 | 40.86 |
| Exercised | (9,908) | 18.27 |
| Canceled | (8,030) | 42.74 |
| Outstanding at February 2, 2003 | 83,166 | $37.09 |
| Exercisable | 29,431 | $29.48 |

The following table summarizes information regarding stock options outstanding at February 2, 2003 (shares in thousands):

| Range of Exercise Prices | Options Outstanding | Weighted Average Remaining Life (Yrs) | Weighted Average Outstanding Option Price | Options Exercisable | Weighted Average Exercisable Option Price |
| --- | --- | --- | --- | --- | --- |
| $ 6.00 to 12.00 | 7,090 | 3.5 | $10.24 | 7,090 | $10.24 |
| 12.01 to 20.00 | 1,191 | 4.7 | 17.21 | 1,191 | 17.21 |
| 20.01 to 30.00 | 7,438 | 5.6 | 22.19 | 6,090 | 21.78 |
| 30.01 to 42.00 | 41,745 | 8.4 | 37.67 | 11,161 | 39.12 |
| 42.01 to 54.00 | 25,702 | 8.5 | 48.80 | 3,899 | 52.48 |
| | 83,166 | 7.7 | $37.09 | 29,431 | $29.48 |

The Company maintains two employee stock purchase plans (U.S. and non-U.S. plans). The plan for U.S. associates is a tax-qualified plan under Section 423 of the Internal Revenue Code. The non-U.S. plan is not a Section 423 plan. The Company had 43 million shares available for issuance under the Employee Stock Purchase Plans ("ESPPs") at February 2, 2003. The ESPPs allow associates to purchase up to 152 million shares of common stock, of which 109 million shares have been purchased from inception of the plan, at a price equal to the lower of 85% of the stock's fair market value on the first day or the last day of the purchase period. These shares were included in the pro forma calculation of stock-based compensation expense.

During fiscal 2002, 5.2 million shares were purchased under the ESPPs at an average price of $30.89 per share. At February 2, 2003, there were 2.3 million shares outstanding, net of cancellations, at an average price of $34.09 per share.

NOTES TO CONSOLIDATED FINANCIAL STATEMENTS (CONTINUED)
THE HOME DEPOT, INC. AND SUBSIDIARIES

# 5 LEASES

The Company leases certain retail locations, office space, warehouse and distribution space, equipment and vehicles. While the majority of the leases are operating leases, certain retail locations are leased under capital leases. As leases expire, it can be expected that, in the normal course of business, certain leases will be renewed or replaced.

The Company has two off-balance sheet lease agreements under which the Company leases assets totaling $882 million comprised of an initial lease agreement of $600 million and a subsequent agreement of $282 million. These two leases were created under structured financing arrangements and involve a special purpose entity which meets the criteria for non-consolidation established by generally accepted accounting principles and is not owned by or affiliated with the Company, its management or officers. The Company financed a portion of its new stores opened in fiscal years 1997 through 2002, as well as a distribution center and office buildings, under these lease agreements. Under both agreements, the lessor purchases the properties, pays for the construction costs and subsequently leases the facilities to the Company. The lease term for the $600 million agreement expires in fiscal 2006 and has three two-year renewal options. The lease term for the $282 million agreement expires in 2008 with no renewal option. Both lease agreements provide for substantial residual value guarantees and include purchase options at original cost of each property. Events or circumstances that would require the Company to perform under the guarantees include 1) initial default on the leases with the assets sold for less than book value, or 2) the Company's decision not to purchase the assets at the end of the leases and the sale of the assets results in proceeds less than the initial book value of the assets. The Company's guarantees are limited to 82% of the initial book value of the assets.

The Company also leases an import distribution facility, including its related equipment, under an off-balance sheet lease created as part of a structured financing arrangement totaling $85 million. The lease for the import distribution facility expires in fiscal 2005 and has four 5-year renewal options. The lease agreement provides for substantial residual value guarantees and includes purchase options at the higher of the cost or fair market value of the assets.

The maximum amount of the residual value guarantees relative to the assets under the three off-balance sheet lease agreements described above is estimated to be $799 million. As the leased assets are placed into service, the Company estimates its liability under the residual value guarantees and records additional rent expense on a straight-line basis over the remaining lease terms.

Total rent expense, net of minor sublease income for the fiscal years ended February 2, 2003, February 3, 2002 and January 28, 2001, was $533 million, $522 million and $479 million, respectively. Real estate taxes, insurance, maintenance and operating expenses applicable to the leased property are obligations of the Company under the lease agreements. Certain store leases provide for contingent rent payments based on percentages of sales in excess of specified minimums. Contingent rent expense for the fiscal years ended February 2, 2003, February 3, 2002 and January 28, 2001, was approximately $8 million, $10 million and $9 million, respectively.

The approximate future minimum lease payments under capital and all other leases, including off-balance sheet leases, at February 2, 2003, were as follows (in millions):

| Fiscal Year | Capital Leases | Operating Leases |
|---|---|---|
| 2003 | $ 44 | $ 541 |
| 2004 | 45 | 512 |
| 2005 | 44 | 476 |
| 2006 | 46 | 440 |
| 2007 | 47 | 424 |
| Thereafter through 2033 | 608 | 4,915 |
| | 834 | $7,308 |
| Less imputed interest | 557 | |
| Net present value of capital lease obligations | 277 | |
| Less current installments | 5 | |
| Long-term capital lease obligations, excluding current installments | $272 | |

Short-term and long-term obligations for capital leases are included in the accompanying Consolidated Balance Sheets in Other Accrued Expenses and Long-Term Debt, respectively. The assets under capital leases recorded in Property and Equipment, net of amortization, totaled $235 million and $199 million at February 2, 2003 and February 3, 2002, respectively.

## NOTES TO CONSOLIDATED FINANCIAL STATEMENTS (CONTINUED)
THE HOME DEPOT, INC. AND SUBSIDIARIES

### 6 EMPLOYEE BENEFIT PLANS

The Company maintains three active defined contribution retirement plans (the "Plans"). All associates satisfying certain service requirements are eligible to participate in the Plans. The Company makes cash contributions each payroll period to purchase shares of the Company's common stock, up to specified percentages of associates' contributions as approved by the Board of Directors.

The Company's contributions to the Plans were $99 million, $97 million and $84 million for fiscal years 2002, 2001 and 2000, respectively. At February 2, 2003, the Plans held a total of 33 million shares of the Company's common stock in trust for plan participants.

The Company also maintains a restoration plan to provide certain associates deferred compensation that they would have received under the Plans as a matching contribution if not for the maximum compensation limits under the Internal Revenue Code. The Company funds the restoration plan through contributions made to a grantor trust, which are then used to purchase shares of the Company's common stock in the open market. Compensation expense related to this plan for fiscal years 2002, 2001 and 2000 was not material.

### 7 BASIC AND DILUTED WEIGHTED AVERAGE COMMON SHARES

The reconciliation of basic to diluted weighted average common shares for fiscal years 2002, 2001 and 2000 was as follows (amounts in millions):

| | Fiscal Year Ended | | |
| | February 2, 2003 | February 3, 2002 | January 28, 2001 |
|---|---|---|---|
| Weighted average common shares | 2,336 | 2,335 | 2,315 |
| Effect of potentially dilutive securities: | | | |
| Stock Plans | 8 | 18 | 37 |
| Diluted weighted average common shares | 2,344 | 2,353 | 2,352 |

Stock plans include shares granted under the Company's employee stock purchase plans and stock incentive plans, as well as shares issued for deferred compensation stock plans. Options to purchase 72.1 million, 11.2 million and 10.9 million shares of common stock at February 2, 2003, February 3, 2002 and January 28, 2001, respectively, were excluded from the computation of diluted earnings per share because their effect would have been anti-dilutive.

### 8 COMMITMENTS AND CONTINGENCIES

At February 2, 2003, the Company was contingently liable for approximately $930 million under outstanding letters of credit issued for certain business transactions, including insurance programs, import inventory purchases and construction contracts. The Company's letters of credit are primarily performance-based and are not based on changes in variable components, a liability or an equity security of the other party.

The Company is involved in litigation arising from the normal course of business. In management's opinion, this litigation is not expected to materially impact the Company's consolidated results of operations or financial condition.

### 9 ACQUISITIONS AND DISPOSITIONS

In October 2002, the Company acquired substantially all of the assets of FloorWorks, Inc. and Arvada Hardwood Floor Company, and common stock of Floors, Inc., three flooring installation companies primarily servicing the new home builder industry. These acquisitions were accounted for under the purchase method of accounting.

In June 2002, the Company acquired the assets of Maderería Del Norte, S.A. de C.V., a four-store chain of home improvement stores in Juarez, Mexico. The acquisition was accounted for under the purchase method of accounting.

In fiscal 2001, the Company acquired Your "other" Warehouse and Soluciones Para Las Casas de Mexico, S. de R.L. de C.V. These acquisitions were accounted for under the purchase method of accounting.

Pro forma results of operations for fiscal years 2002, 2001 and 2000 would not be materially different as a result of the acquisitions discussed above and therefore are not presented.

In February 2002, the Company sold all of the assets of The Home Depot Argentina S.R.L. In connection with the sale, the Company received proceeds comprised of cash and notes. An impairment charge of $45 million was recorded in Selling and Store Operating Expenses in the accompanying Consolidated Statements of Earnings in fiscal 2001 to write down the net assets of The Home Depot Argentina S.R.L. to fair value.

In October 2001, the Company sold all of the assets of The Home Depot Chile S.A., resulting in a gain of $31 million included in Selling and Store Operating Expenses in the accompanying Consolidated Statements of Earnings.

NOTES TO CONSOLIDATED FINANCIAL STATEMENTS (CONTINUED)
THE HOME DEPOT, INC. AND SUBSIDIARIES

# 10 QUARTERLY FINANCIAL DATA (UNAUDITED)

The following is a summary of the quarterly consolidated results of operations for the fiscal years ended February 2, 2003 and February 3, 2002 (dollars in millions, except per share data):

| | Net Sales | Increase (Decrease) In Comparable Store Sales | Gross Profit | Net Earnings | Basic Earnings Per Share | Diluted Earnings Per Share |
|---|---|---|---|---|---|---|
| Fiscal year ended February 2, 2003:[1] | | | | | | |
| First quarter | $14,282 | 5% | $ 4,360 | $ 856 | $0.36 | $0.36 |
| Second quarter | 16,277 | 1% | 4,946 | 1,182 | 0.50 | 0.50 |
| Third quarter | 14,475 | (2%) | 4,580 | 940 | 0.40 | 0.40 |
| Fourth quarter | 13,213 | (6%) | 4,222 | 686 | 0.30 | 0.30 |
| Fiscal year | $58,247 | 0% | $18,108 | $3,664 | $ 1.57 | $ 1.56 |
| Fiscal year ended February 3, 2002:[1] | | | | | | |
| First quarter | $12,200 | (3%) | $ 3,655 | $ 632 | $0.27 | $0.27 |
| Second quarter | 14,576 | 1% | 4,326 | 924 | 0.40 | 0.39 |
| Third quarter | 13,289 | 0% | 4,010 | 778 | 0.33 | 0.33 |
| Fourth quarter | 13,488 | 5% | 4,156 | 710 | 0.30 | 0.30 |
| Fiscal year | $53,553 | 0% | $16,147 | $3,044 | $ 1.30 | $ 1.29 |

[1]Fiscal year ended February 2, 2003 includes 52 weeks and fiscal year ended February 3, 2002 includes 53 weeks.

Note: The quarterly data may not sum to fiscal year totals due to rounding.

## MANAGEMENT'S RESPONSIBILITY FOR FINANCIAL STATEMENTS

The financial statements presented in this Annual Report have been prepared with integrity and objectivity and are the responsibility of the management of The Home Depot, Inc. These financial statements have been prepared in conformity with accounting principles generally accepted in the United States of America and properly reflect certain estimates and judgments based upon the best available information.

The Company maintains a system of internal accounting controls, which is supported by an internal audit program and is designed to provide reasonable assurance, at an appropriate cost, that the Company's assets are safeguarded and transactions are properly recorded. This system is continually reviewed and modified in response to changing business conditions and operations and as a result of recommendations by the external and internal auditors. In addition, the Company has distributed to associates its policies for conducting business affairs in a lawful and ethical manner.

The financial statements of the Company have been audited by KPMG LLP, independent auditors. Their accompanying report is based upon an audit conducted in accordance with auditing standards generally accepted in the United States of America, including the related review of internal accounting controls and financial reporting matters.

The Audit Committee of the Board of Directors, consisting solely of outside directors, meets five times a year with the independent auditors, the internal auditors and representatives of management to discuss auditing and financial reporting matters. In addition, a telephonic meeting is held prior to each quarterly earnings release. The Audit Committee retains the independent auditors and regularly reviews the internal accounting controls, the activities of the outside auditors and internal auditors and the financial condition of the Company. Both the Company's independent auditors and the internal auditors have free access to the Audit Committee.

Carol B. Tomé
Executive Vice President and
Chief Financial Officer

## INDEPENDENT AUDITORS' REPORT

The Board of Directors and Stockholders
The Home Depot, Inc.:

We have audited the accompanying consolidated balance sheets of The Home Depot, Inc. and subsidiaries as of February 2, 2003 and February 3, 2002 and the related consolidated statements of earnings, stockholders' equity and comprehensive income, and cash flows for each of the years in the three-year period ended February 2, 2003. These consolidated financial statements are the responsibility of the Company's management. Our responsibility is to express an opinion on these consolidated financial statements based on our audits.

We conducted our audits in accordance with auditing standards generally accepted in the United States of America. Those standards require that we plan and perform the audit to obtain reasonable assurance about whether the financial statements are free of material misstatement. An audit includes examining, on a test basis, evidence supporting the amounts and disclosures in the financial statements. An audit also includes assessing the accounting principles used and significant estimates made by management, as well as evaluating the overall financial statement presentation. We believe that our audits provide a reasonable basis for our opinion.

In our opinion, the consolidated financial statements referred to above present fairly, in all material respects, the financial position of The Home Depot, Inc. and subsidiaries as of February 2, 2003 and February 3, 2002, and the results of their operations and their cash flows for each of the years in the three-year period ended February 2, 2003, in conformity with accounting principles generally accepted in the United States of America.

KPMG LLP

Atlanta, Georgia
February 24, 2003

# glossary

**accelerated depreciation method** A depreciation method that provides for a higher depreciation amount in the first year of the asset's use, followed by a gradually declining amount of depreciation. (400)

**account** An accounting form that is used to record the increases and decreases in each financial statement item. (48)

**account form** The form of balance sheet that resembles the basic format of the accounting equation, with assets on the left side and the liabilities and owner's equity sections on the right side. (21, 236)

**account payable** The liability created by a purchase on account. (15)

**account receivable** A claim against the customer created by selling merchandise or services on credit. (16, 318)

**accounting** An information system that provides reports to stakeholders about the economic activities and condition of a business. (8)

**accounting cycle** The process that begins with analyzing and journalizing transactions and ends with the post-closing trial balance. (140)

**accounting equation** Assets = Liabilities + Owner's Equity (13)

**accounting period concept** The accounting concept that assumes that the economic life of the business can be divided into time periods. (102)

**accounting system** The methods and procedures used by a business to collect, classify, summarize, and report financial data for use by management and external users. (183)

**accounts payable subsidiary ledger** The subsidiary ledger containing the individual accounts with suppliers (creditors). (190)

**accounts receivable subsidiary ledger** The subsidiary ledger containing the individual accounts with customers. (190)

**accounts receivable turnover** The relationship between net sales and accounts receivable, computed by dividing the net sales by the average net accounts receivable; measures how frequently during the year the accounts receivable are being converted to cash. (331, 700)

**accrual basis** Under this basis of accounting, revenues and expenses are reported in the income statement in the period in which they are earned or incurred. (102)

**accruals** A revenue or expense that has not been recorded. (103)

**accrued assets** *See* **accrued revenues**. (104)

**accrued expenses** Expenses that have been incurred *but not recorded* in the accounts. (103)

**accrued liabilities** *See* **accrued expenses**. (103)

**accrued revenues** Revenues that have been earned *but not recorded* in the accounts. (104)

**accumulated depreciation** The contra asset account credited when recording the depreciation of a fixed asset. (112)

**accumulated other comprehensive income** The cumulative effects of other comprehensive income items reported separately in the stockholders' equity section of the balance sheet. (570)

**adjusted trial balance** The trial balance prepared after all the adjusting entries have been posted. (113)

**adjusting entries** The journal entries that bring the accounts up to date at the end of the accounting period. (103)

**adjusting process** An analysis and updating of the accounts when financial statements are prepared. (103)

**administrative expenses (general expenses)** Expenses incurred in the administration or general operations of the business. (235)

**aging the receivables** The process of analyzing the accounts receivable and classifying them according to various age groupings, with the due date being the base point for determining age. (324)

**allowance method** The method of accounting for uncollectible accounts that provides an expense for uncollectible receivables in advance of their write-off. (321)

**amortization** The periodic transfer of the cost of an intangible asset to expense. (411)

**annuity** A series of equal cash flows at fixed intervals. (606)

**assets** The resources owned by a business. (13, 48)

**available-for-sale securities** Securities that management expects to sell in the future but which are not actively traded for profit. (571)

**average cost method** The method of inventory costing that is based upon the assumption that costs should be charged against revenue by using the weighted average unit cost of the items sold. (359)

**balance of the account** The amount of the difference between the debits and the credits that have been entered into an account. (50)

**balance sheet** A list of the assets, liabilities, and owner's equity *as of a specific date*, usually at the close of the last day of a month or a year. (19)

**bank reconciliation** The analysis that details the items responsible for the difference between the cash balance reported in the bank statement and the balance of the cash account in the ledger. (293)

**bond** A form of an interest-bearing note used by corporations to borrow on a long-term basis. (602)

**bond indenture** The contract between a corporation issuing bonds and the bondholders. (603)

**book value**  The cost of a fixed asset minus accumulated depreciation on the asset. (399)

**book value of the asset**  The difference between the cost of a fixed asset and its accumulated depreciation. (112)

**boot**  The amount a buyer owes a seller when a fixed asset is traded in on a similar asset. (406)

**business**  An organization in which basic resources (inputs), such as materials and labor, are assembled and processed to provide goods or services (outputs) to customers. (2)

**business entity concept**  A concept of accounting that limits the economic data in the accounting system to data related directly to the activities of the business. (13)

**business stakeholder**  A person or entity who has an interest in the economic performance of a business. (6)

**business strategy**  An integrated set of plans and actions designed to enable the business to gain an advantage over its competitors and, in so doing, to maximize its profits. (4)

**business transaction**  An economic event or condition that directly changes an entity's financial condition or directly affects its results of operations. (14)

**capital expenditures**  The costs of acquiring fixed assets, adding to a fixed asset, improving a fixed asset, or extending a fixed asset's useful life. (402)

**capital leases**  Leases that include one or more provisions that result in treating the leased assets as purchased assets in the accounts. (408)

**carrying amount**  The balance of the bonds payable account (face amount of the bonds) less any unamortized discount or plus any unamortized premium. (613)

**cash**  Coins, currency (paper money), checks, money orders, and money on deposit that is available for unrestricted withdrawal from banks and other financial institutions. (284)

**cash basis**  Under this basis of accounting, revenues and expenses are reported in the income statement in the period in which cash is received or paid. (102)

**cash dividend**  A cash distribution of earnings by a corporation to its shareholders. (493)

**cash equivalents**  Highly liquid investments that are usually reported with cash on the balance sheet. (297)

**cash flows from financing activities**  The section of the statement of cash flows that reports cash flows from transactions affecting the equity and debt of the business. (641)

**cash flows from investing activities**  The section of the statement of cash flows that reports cash flows from transactions affecting investments in noncurrent assets. (641)

**cash flows from operating activities**  The section of the statement of cash flows that reports the cash transactions affecting the determination of net income. (641)

**cash payments journal**  The special journal in which all cash payments are recorded. (197)

**cash receipts journal**  The special journal in which all cash receipts are recorded. (195)

**cash short and over account**  An account which has recorded errors in cash sales or errors in making change causing the amount of actual cash on hand to differ from the beginning amount of cash plus the cash sales for the day. (286)

**Certified Public Accountant (CPA)**  Public accountants who have met a state's education, experience, and examination requirements. (11)

**chart of accounts**  A list of the accounts in the ledger. (48)

**clearing account**  Another name for the Income Summary account because it has the effect of clearing the revenue and expense accounts of their balances. (145)

**closing entries**  The entries that transfer the balances of the revenue, expense, and drawing accounts to the owner's capital account. (144D)

**closing process**  The transfer process of converting temporary account balances to zero by transferring the revenue and expense account balances to Income Summary, transferring the Income Summary account balance to the owner's capital account, and transferring the owner's drawing account to the owner's capital account. (144D)

**combination strategy**  A business strategy that includes elements of both the low-cost and differentiation strategies. (5)

**common stock**  The stock outstanding when a corporation has issued only one class of stock. (487)

**common-size statement**  A financial statement in which all items are expressed only in relative terms. (696)

**component**  A tangible portion of a fixed asset that can be separately identified as an asset and depreciated over its own separate expected useful life. (403)

**comprehensive income**  All changes in stockholders' equity during a period, except those resulting from dividends and stockholders' investments. (570)

**consolidated financial statements**  Financial statements resulting from combining parent and subsidiary statements. (576)

**consolidation**  The creation of a new corporation by the transfer of assets and liabilities of two or more existing corporations, which are then dissolved. (576)

**contra account**  An account offset against another account. (112)

**contract rate**  The periodic interest to be paid on the bonds that is identified in the bond indenture; expressed as a percentage of the face amount of the bond. (604)

**controlling account**  The account in the general ledger that summarizes the balances of the accounts in a subsidiary ledger. (190)

**copyright**  An exclusive right to publish and sell a literary, artistic, or musical composition. (411)

**corporation** A business organized under state or federal statutes as a separate legal entity. (3)

**cost of merchandise sold** The cost that is reported as an expense when merchandise is sold. (231)

**credit memorandum** A form used by a seller to inform the buyer of the amount the seller proposes to credit to the account receivable due from the buyer. (241)

**credits** Amounts entered on the right side of an account. (50)

**cumulative preferred stock** A class of preferred stock that has a right to receive regular dividends that have been passed (not declared) before any common stock dividends are paid. (488)

**current assets** Cash and other assets that are expected to be converted to cash or sold or used up, usually within one year or less, through the normal operations of the business. (144A)

**current liabilities** Liabilities that will be due within a short time (usually one year or less) and that are to be paid out of current assets. (144A)

**current ratio** A financial ratio that is computed by dividing current assets by current liabilities. (154, 698)

**debit memorandum** A form used by a buyer to inform the seller of the amount the buyer proposes to debit to the account payable due the seller. (243)

**debits** Amounts entered on the left side of an account. (49)

**declining-balance method** A method of depreciation that provides periodic depreciation expense based on the declining book value of a fixed asset over its estimated life. (399)

**deferred expenses** Items that have been initially recorded as assets but are expected to become expenses over time or through the normal operations of the business. (103)

**deferred revenues** Items that have been initially recorded as liabilities but are expected to become revenues over time or through the normal operations of the business. (103)

**deficiency** The debit balance in the owner's equity account of a partner. (534)

**deficit** A debit balance in the retained earnings account. (486)

**defined benefit plan** A pension plan that promises employees a fixed annual pension benefit at retirement, based on years of service and compensation levels. (454)

**defined contribution plan** A pension plan that requires a fixed amount of money to be invested for the employee's behalf during the employee's working years. (454)

**depletion** The process of transferring the cost of natural resources to an expense account. (410)

**depreciation** The systematic periodic transfer of the cost of a fixed asset to an expense account during its expected useful life. (112, 395)

**depreciation expense** The portion of the cost of a fixed asset that is recorded as an expense each year of its useful life. (112)

**differentiation strategy** A business strategy in which a business designs and produces products or services that possess unique attributes or characteristics for which customers are willing to pay a premium price. (4)

**direct method** A method of reporting the cash flows from operating activities as the difference between the operating cash receipts and the operating cash payments. (642)

**direct write-off method** The method of accounting for uncollectible accounts that recognizes the expense only when accounts are judged to be worthless. (321)

**discontinued operations** Operations of a major line of business or component for a company, such as a division, a department, or a certain class of customer, that have been disposed of. (567)

**discount** The interest deducted from the maturity value of a note or the excess of the face amount of bonds over their issue price. (437, 489, 604)

**discount rate** The rate used in computing the interest to be deducted from the maturity value of a note. (437)

**dishonored note receivable** A note that the maker fails to pay on the due date. (329)

**dividend yield** A ratio, computed by dividing the annual dividends paid per share of common stock by the market price per share at a specific date, that indicates the rate of return to stockholders in terms of cash dividend distributions. (498, 708)

**doomsday ratio** The ratio of cash and cash equivalents to current liabilities. (298)

**double-entry accounting** A system of accounting for recording transactions, based on recording increases and decreases in accounts so that debits equal credits. (53)

**drawing** The account used to record amounts withdrawn by an owner of a proprietorship. (49)

**earnings per common share (EPS)** Net income per share of common stock outstanding during a period. (568)

**earnings per share (EPS) on common stock** The profitability ratio of net income available to common shareholders to the number of common shares outstanding. (706)

**e-commerce** The use of the Internet for performing business transactions. (204)

**effective interest rate method** The method of amortizing discounts and premiums that provides for a constant rate of interest on the carrying amount of the bonds at the beginning of each period; often called simply the "interest method." (610)

**effective rate of interest** The market rate of interest at the time bonds are issued. (604)

**electronic funds transfer (EFT)** A system in which computers rather than paper (money, checks, etc.) are used to effect cash transactions. (289)

**elements of internal control** The control environment, risk assessment, control activities, information and communication, and monitoring. (185)

**employee fraud** The intentional act of deceiving an employer for personal gain. (184)

**employee's earnings record** A detailed record of each employee's earnings. (448)

**equity method** A method of accounting for an investment in common stock by which the investment account is adjusted for the investor's share of periodic net income and cash dividends of the investee. (573)

**equity securities** The common and preferred stock of a firm. (571)

**ethics** Moral principles that guide the conduct of individuals. (9)

**expenses** Assets used up or services consumed in the process of generating revenues. (16, 49)

**extraordinary items** Events and transactions that (1) are significantly different (unusual) from the typical or the normal operating activities of a business and (2) occur infrequently. (567)

**FICA tax** Federal Insurance Contributions Act tax used to finance federal programs for old-age and disability benefits (social security) and health insurance for the aged (Medicare). (443)

**financial accounting** The branch of accounting that is concerned with recording transactions using generally accepted accounting principles (GAAP) for a business or other economic unit and with a periodic preparation of various statements from such records. (12)

**Financial Accounting Standards Board (FASB)** The authoritative body that has the primary responsibility for developing accounting principles. (12)

**financial statements** Financial reports that summarize the effects of events on a business. (19)

**first-in, first-out (fifo) method** The method of inventory costing based on the assumption that the costs of merchandise sold should be charged against revenue in the order in which the costs were incurred. (359)

**fiscal year** The annual accounting period adopted by a business. (153)

**fixed (plant) assets** Assets that depreciate over time, such as equipment, machinery, and buildings. (144A)

**fixed asset impairment** A condition when the fair value of a fixed asset falls below its book value and is not expected to recover. (564)

**fixed assets** Long-term or relatively permanent tangible assets that are used in the normal business operations. (112, 393)

**FOB (free on board) destination** Freight terms in which the seller pays the transportation costs from the shipping point to the final destination. (245)

**FOB (free on board) shipping point** Freight terms in which the buyer pays the transportation costs from the shipping point to the final destination. (245)

**free cash flow** The amount of operating cash flow remaining after replacing current productive capacity and maintaining current dividends. (658)

**fringe benefits** Benefits provided to employees in addition to wages and salaries. (453)

**future value** The estimated worth in the future of an amount of cash on hand today invested at a fixed rate of interest. (605)

**general journal** The two-column form used for entries that do not "fit" in any of the special journals. (192)

**general ledger** The primary ledger, when used in conjunction with subsidiary ledgers, that contains all of the balance sheet and income statement accounts. (190)

**generally accepted accounting principles (GAAP)** Generally accepted guidelines for the preparation of financial statements. (12)

**goodwill** An intangible asset that is created from such favorable factors as location, product quality, reputation, and managerial skill. (412)

**gross pay** The total earnings of an employee for an employee for a payroll period. (441)

**gross profit** Sales minus the cost of merchandise sold. (231)

**gross profit method** A method of estimating inventory cost that is based on the relationship of gross profit to sales. (371)

**held-to-maturity securities** Investments in bonds or other debt securities that management intends to hold to their maturity. (618)

**horizontal analysis** Financial analysis that compares an item in a current statement with the same item in prior statements. (71, 692)

**income from operations (operating income)** Revenues less operating expenses and service department charges for a profit or investment center. (235)

**income statement** A summary of the revenue and expenses *for a specific period of time*, such as a month or a year. (19)

**Income Summary** An account to which the revenue and expense account balances are transferred at the end of a period. (144D)

**indirect method** A method of reporting the cash flows from operating activities as the net income from operations adjusted for all deferrals of past cash receipts and payments and all accruals of expected future cash receipts and payments. (642)

**initial public offering (IPO)** A company's first offering of common stock to the investing public. (538)

**intangible assets** Long-term assets that are useful in the operations of a business, are not held for sale, and are without physical qualities. (410)

**internal controls** The policies and procedures used to safeguard assets, ensure accurate business information, and ensure compliance with laws and regulations. (183)

**inventory shrinkage** The amount by which the merchandise for sale, as indicated by the balance of the merchandise inventory account, is larger than the total amount of merchandise counted during the physical inventory. (250)

**inventory turnover** The relationship between the volume of goods sold and inventory, computed by dividing the cost of goods sold by the average inventory. (372, 701)

**investments** The balance sheet caption used to report long-term investments in stocks not intended as a source of cash in the normal operations of the business. (573)

**invoice** The bill that the seller sends to the buyer. (239)

**journal** The initial record in which the effects of a transaction are recorded. (51)

**journal entry** The form of recording a transaction in a journal. (51)

**journalizing** The process of recording a transaction in the journal. (51)

**last-in, first-out (lifo) method** A method of inventory costing based on the assumption that the most recent merchandise inventory costs should be charged against revenue. (359)

**ledger** A group of accounts for a business. (48)

**leverage** The amount of debt used by a firm to finance its assets; causes the rate earned on stockholders' equity to vary from the rate earned on total assets because the amount earned on assets acquired through the use of funds provided by creditors varies from the interest paid to these creditors. (705)

**liabilities** The rights of creditors that represent debts of the business. (13, 48)

**limited liability corporation (LLC)** A business form consisting of one or more persons or entities filing an operating agreement with a state to conduct business with limited liability to the owners, yet treated as a partnership for tax purposes. (4, 520)

**liquidation** The winding-up process when a partnership goes out of business. (531)

**long-term liabilities** Liabilities that usually will not be due for more than one year. (144A)

**low-cost strategy** A strategy wherein a business designs and produces products or services of acceptable quality at a cost lower than that of its competitors. (4)

**lower-of-cost-or-market (LCM) method** A method of valuing inventory that reports the inventory at the lower of its cost or current market value (replacement cost). (367)

**Management Discussion and Analysis (MDA)** An annual report disclosure that provides management's analysis of the results of operations and financial condition. (710)

**managerial accounting** The branch of accounting that uses both historical and estimated data in providing information that management uses in conducting daily operations, in planning future operations, and in developing overall business strategies. (12)

**manufacturing business** A type of business that changes basic inputs into products that are sold to individual customers. (2)

**matching concept** A concept of accounting in which expenses are matched with the revenue generated during a period by those expenses. (19, 102)

**materiality concept** A concept of accounting that implies that an error may be treated in the easiest possible way. (69)

**maturity value** The amount that is due at the maturity or due date of a note. (328)

**merchandise inventory** Merchandise on hand (not sold) at the end of an accounting period. (231)

**merchandising business** A type of business that purchases products from other businesses and sells them to customers. (3)

**merger** The joining of two corporations in which one company acquires all the assets and liabilities of another corporation, which is then dissolved. (575)

**minority interest** The portion of a subsidiary corporation's stock owned by outsiders. (576)

**multiple-step income statement** A form of income statement that contains several sections, subsections, and subtotals. (232)

**natural business year** A fiscal year that ends when business activities have reached the lowest point in an annual operating cycle. (153)

**net income** The amount by which revenues exceed expenses. (19)

**net loss** The amount by which expenses exceed revenues. (19)

**net pay** Gross pay less payroll deductions; the amount the employer is obligated to pay the employee. (441)

**net realizable value** The estimated selling price of an item of inventory less any direct costs of disposal, such as sales commissions. (368)

**nonparticipating preferred stock** A class of preferred stock whose dividend rights are usually limited to a certain amount. (487)

**note receivable** A customer's written promise to pay an amount and possibly interest at an agreed-upon rate. (144A, 318)

**number of days' sales in inventory** The relationship between the volume of sales and inventory, computed by dividing the inventory at the end of the year by the average daily cost of goods sold. (372, 701)

**number of days' sales in receivables** The relationship between sales and accounts receivable, computed by dividing the net accounts receivable at the end of the year by the average daily sales. (331, 700)

**number of times interest charges are earned** A ratio that measures creditor margin of safety for interest payments, calculated as income before interest and taxes divided by interest expense. (618, 702)

**operating leases** Leases that do not meet the criteria for capital leases and thus are accounted for as operating expenses. (408)

**other comprehensive income** Specified items that are reported separately from net income, including foreign currency items, pension liability adjustments, and unrealized gains and losses on investments. (570)

**other expense** Expenses that cannot be traced directly to operations. (236)

**other income** Revenue from sources other than the primary operating activity of a business. (236)

**outstanding stock** The stock in the hands of stockholders. (486)

**owner's equity** The owner's right to the assets of the business. (13, 48)

**paid-in capital** Capital contributed to a corporation by the stockholders and others. (484)

**par** The monetary amount printed on a stock certificate. (486)

**parent company** The corporation owning all or a majority of the voting stock of the other corporation. (576)

**partnership** An unincorporated business form consisting of two or more persons conducting business as co-owners for profit. (3, 519)

**partnership agreement** The formal written contract creating a partnership. (520)

**patents** Exclusive rights to produce and sell goods with one or more unique features. (411)

**payroll** The total amount paid to employees for a certain period. (439)

**payroll register** A multicolumn report used to assemble and summarize payroll data at the end of each payroll period. (446)

**periodic method** The inventory system in which the inventory records do not show the amount available for sale or sold during the period. (234)

**permanent differences** Differences between taxable and income (before taxes) reported on the income statement that may arise because certain revenues are exempt from tax and certain expenses are not deductible in determining taxable income. (563)

**perpetual method** The inventory system in which each purchase and sale of merchandise is recorded in an inventory account. (235)

**petty cash fund** A special cash fund to pay relatively small amounts. (295)

**physical inventory** A detailed listing of merchandise on hand. (356)

**post-closing trial balance** The trial balance prepared after the closing entries have been posted. (152)

**posting** The process of transferring the debits and credits from the journal entries to the accounts. (55)

**preferred stock** A class of stock with preferential rights over common stock. (487)

**premium** The excess of the issue price of a stock over its par value or the excess of the issue price of bonds over their face amount. (489, 604)

**prepaid expenses** Items such as supplies that will be used in the business in the future. *Also see* **deferred expenses**. (15, 103)

**present value** The estimated worth today of an amount of cash to be received (or paid) in the future. (605)

**present value of an annuity** The sum of the present values of a series of equal cash flows to be received at fixed intervals. (606)

**price-earnings (P/E) ratio** The ratio of the market price per share of common stock, at a specific date, to the annual earnings per share. (707)

**price-earnings ratio** The ratio computed by dividing a corporation's stock market price per share at a specific date by the company's annual earnings per share. (578)

**prior period adjustments** Corrections of material errors related to a prior period or periods, excluded from the determination of net income. (498)

**private accounting** The field of accounting where accountants and their staff provide services on a fee basis. (10)

**proceeds** The net amount available from discounting a note payable. (437)

**profitability** The ability of a firm to earn income. (697)

**promissory note** A written promise to pay a sum of money on demand or at a definite time. (326)

**property, plant, and equipment** The section of the balance sheet that includes equipment, machinery, buildings, and land. (144A)

**proprietorship** A business owned by one individual. (3)

**public accounting** The field of accounting whereby accountants are employed by a business firm or a not-for-profit organization. (10)

**purchase method** The accounting method used when a corporation acquires the controlling share of the voting common stock of another corporation by paying cash, exchanging other assets, issuing debt, or some combination of these methods. (576)

**purchase return or allowance** From the buyer's perspective, returned merchandise or an adjustment for defective merchandise. (234)

**purchases discounts** Discounts taken by the buyer for early payment of an invoice. (234)

**purchases journal** The journal in which all items purchased on account are recorded. (197)

**quick assets** Cash and other current assets that can be quickly converted to cash, such as marketable securities and receivables. (456, 699)

**quick ratio** A financial ratio that measures the ability to pay current liabilities with quick assets (cash, marketable securities, accounts receivable). (456, 699)

**rate earned on common stockholders' equity** A measure of profitability computed by dividing net income, reduced by preferred dividend requirements, by common stockholders' equity. (706)

**rate earned on stockholders' equity** A measure of profitability computed by dividing net income by total stockholders' equity. (705)

**rate earned on total assets** A measure of the profitability of assets, without regard to the equity of creditors and stockholders in the assets. (704)

**ratio of fixed assets to long-term liabilities** A leverage ratio that measures the margin of safety of long-term creditors, calculated as the net fixed assets divided by the long-term liabilities. (414, 701)

**ratio of liabilities to stockholders' equity** A comprehensive leverage ratio that measures the relationship of the claims of creditors to that stockholders' equity. (702)

**real accounts** Term for balance sheet accounts because they are relatively permanent and carried forward from year to year. (144D)

**realization** The sale of assets when a partnership is being liquidated. (531)

**receivables** All money claims against other entities, including people, business firms, and other organizations. (318)

**report form** The form of balance sheet with the liabilities and owner's equity sections presented below the assets section. (21)

**residual value** The estimated value of a fixed asset at the end of its useful life. (397)

**restrictions** Amounts of retained earnings that have been limited for use as dividends. (497)

**restructuring charge** The costs associated with involuntarily terminating employees, terminating contracts, consolidating facilities, or relocating employees. (566)

**retail inventory method** A method of estimating inventory cost that is based on the relationship of gross profit to sales. (370)

**retained earnings** Net income retained in a corporation. (484)

**retained earnings statement** A summary of the changes in the retained earnings in a corporation for a specific period of time, such as a month or a year. (497)

**revenue expenditures** Costs that benefit only the current period or costs incurred for normal maintenance and repairs of fixed assets. (402)

**revenue journal** The journal in which all sales and services on account are recorded. (193)

**revenue recognition concept** The accounting concept that supports reporting revenues when the services are provided to customers. (102)

**revenues** Increases in owner's equity as a result of selling services or products to customers. (16, 49)

**reversing entry** An entry, exactly opposite of the adjusting entry to which it relates, that may be used to simplify the analysis and recording of the first payroll entry in a period. (155)

**sales** The total amount charged customers for merchandise sold, including cash sales and sales on account. (232)

**sales discounts** From the seller's perspective, discounts that a seller may offer the buyer for early payment. (233)

**sales returns and allowances** From the seller's perspective, returned merchandise or an adjustment for defective merchandise. (233)

**selling expenses** Expenses that are incurred directly in the selling of merchandise. (235)

**service business** A business providing services rather than products to customers. (3)

**single-step income statement** A form of income statement in which the total of all expenses is deducted from the total of all revenues. (236)

**sinking fund** A fund in which cash or assets are set aside for the purpose of paying the face amount of the bonds at maturity. (612)

**slide** An error in which the entire number is moved one or more spaces to the right or the left, such as writing $542.00 as $54.20 or $5,420.00. (70)

**solvency** The ability of a firm to pay its debts as they come due. (154, 697)

**special journals** Journals designed to be used for recording a single type of transaction. (191)

**stated value** A value, similar to par value, approved by the board of directors of a corporation for no-par stock. (486)

**statement of cash flows** A summary of the cash receipts and cash payments *for a specific period of time,* such as a month or a year. (19, 641)

**statement of members' equity** A summary of the changes in each member's equity in a limited liability corporation that have occurred during a specific period of time. (523)

**statement of owner's equity** A summary of the changes in owner's equity that have occurred *during a specific period of time,* such as a month or a year. (19)

**statement of partnership equity** A summary of the changes in each partner's capital in a partnership that have occurred during a specific period of time. (522)

**statement of partnership liquidation** A summary of the liquidation process whereby cash is distributed to the partners based on the balances in their capital accounts. (532)

**statement of stockholders' equity** A summary of the changes in the stockholders' equity in a corporation that have occurred during a specific period of time. (522)

**stock** Shares of ownership of a corporation. (482)

**stock dividend** A distribution of shares of stock to its stockholders. (494)

**stock split** A reduction in the par or stated value of a common stock and the issuance of a proportionate number of additional shares. (492)

**stockholders** The owners of a corporation. (482)

**stockholders' equity** The owners' equity in a corporation. (484)

**straight-line method** A method of depreciation that provides for equal periodic depreciation expense over the estimated life of a fixed asset. (398)

**subsidiary company** The corporation that is controlled by a parent company. (576)

**subsidiary ledger** A ledger containing individual accounts with a common characteristic. (190)

**T account** The simplest form of an account. (49)

**taxable income** The income according to the tax laws that is used as a base for determining the amount of taxes owed. (561)

**temporary (nominal) accounts** Accounts that report amounts for only one period. (144D)

**temporary differences** Differences between taxable income and income before income taxes, created because items are recognized in one period for tax purposes and in another period for income statement purposes. Such differences reverse or turn around in later years. (561)

**temporary investments** The balances sheet caption used to report investments in income-yielding securities that can be quickly sold and converted to cash as needed. (571)

**trade discounts** Discounts from the list prices in published catalogs or special discounts offered to certain classes of buyers. (247)

**trade-in allowance** The amount a seller allows a buyer for a fixed asset that is traded in for a similar asset. (406)

**trademark** A name, term, or symbol used to identify a business and its products. (411)

**trading securities** Securities that management intends to actively trade for profit. (571)

**transposition** An error in which the order of the digits is changed, such as writing $542 as $452 or $524. (70)

**treasury stock** Stock that a corporation has once issued and then reacquires. (491)

**trial balance** A summary listing of the titles and balances of accounts in the ledger. (68)

**two-column journal** An all-purpose journal. (55)

**uncollectible accounts expense** The operating expense incurred because of the failure to collect receivables. (320)

**underwriting firms** Firms that assist companies in initial public offerings (IPO) by establishing offering prices and marketing IPOs to the public. (538)

**unearned revenue** The liability created by receiving revenue in advance. (58)

**unearned revenues** *See* **deferred revenues**. (103)

**unit of measure concept** A concept of accounting requiring that economic data be recorded in dollars. (13)

**units-of-production method** A method of depreciation that provides for depreciation expense based on the expected productive capacity of a fixed asset. (399)

**unrealized holding gain or loss** The difference between the fair market value of the securities and their cost. (572)

**value chain** The way a business adds value for its customers by processing inputs into a product or service. (6)

**venture capitalist (VC)** An individual or firm that provides equity financing to new firms, with the intent of selling its interest for a profit after the firm has matured. (536)

**vertical analysis** An analysis that compares each item in a current statement with a total amount within the same statement. (116, 694)

**voucher** A special form for recording relevant data about a liability and the details of its payment. (287)

**voucher system** A set of procedures for authorizing and recording liabilities and cash payments. (287)

**work sheet** A working paper that accountants may use to summarize adjusting entries and the account balances for the financial statements. (140)

**working capital** The excess of the current assets of a business over its current liabilities. (154)

# subject index